EP 2.1.5 Advance human rights and social and economic justice:
   a. Understand the forms and mechanisms of oppression and discrimination   **2, 10, 14, 18**
   b. Advocate for human rights and social and economic justice   **1, 2, 14**
   c. Engage in practices that advance social and economic justice   **1, 2, 14**

EP 2.1.6 Engage in research-informed practice and practice-informed research:
   a. Use practice experience to inform scientific inquiry   **2**
   b. Use research evidence to inform practice   **2, 11, 13, 14, 16, 18**

EP 2.1.7 Apply knowledge of human behavior and the social environment:
   a. Utilize conceptual frameworks to guide the processes of assessment, intervention, and evaluation   **3, 8, 9, 10, 11, 13, 15, 16**
   b. Critique and apply knowledge to understand person and environment   **3, 8, 9, 10, 12, 13, 15, 18**

EP 2.1.8 Engage in policy practice to advance social and economic well-being and to deliver effective social work services:
   a. Analyze, formulate, and advocate for policies that advance social well-being   **2, 14**
   b. Collaborate with colleagues and clients for effective policy action   **2**

EP 2.1.9 Respond to contexts that shape practice:
   a. Continuously discover, appraise, and attend to changing locales, populations, scientific and technological developments, and emerging societal trends to provide relevant services   **2, 13, 14, 16**
   b. Provide leadership in promoting sustainable changes in service delivery and practice to improve the quality of social services   **2, 14**

EP 2.1.10 Engage, assess, intervene, and evaluate with individuals, families, groups, organizations and communities:
   a. Substantively and affectively prepare for action with individuals, families, groups, organizations, and communities   **1, 3, 4, 5, 8, 9, 10, 11, 12, 13, 14, 15, 16, 18**
   b. Use empathy and other interpersonal skills   **1, 3, 5, 7, 13, 14, 15, 17, 18, 19**
   c. Develop a mutually agreed-on focus of work and desired outcomes   **1, 3, 12, 14, 15, 18**
   d. Collect, organize, and interpret client data   **1, 3, 6, 8, 9, 10, 11, 12, 13, 14, 15**
   e. Assess client strengths and limitations   **1, 3, 5, 8, 9, 10, 11, 12, 14, 15**
   f. Develop mutually agreed-on intervention goals and objectives   **3, 13, 15**
   g. Select appropriate intervention strategies   **3, 12, 13, 14, 16**
   h. Initiate actions to achieve organizational goals   **14**
   i. Implement prevention interventions that enhance client capacities   **5, 12, 13, 16, 18**
   j. Help clients resolve problems   **3, 11, 12, 13, 15, 16, 18**
   k. Negotiate, mediate, and advocate for clients   **2, 3**
   l. Facilitate transitions and endings   **3, 16, 19**
   m. Critically analyze, monitor, and evaluate interventions   **3, 6, 12, 13, 18, 19**

For more information about the standards themselves, and for a complete policy statement, visit the Council on Social Work Education website at www.cswe.org.

Adapted with permission from the Council on Social Work Education

Direct Social Work Practice

Direct Social Work Practice
Theory and Skills

Ninth Edition

DEAN H. HEPWORTH
Professor Emeritus, University of Utah and Arizona State University

RONALD H. ROONEY
University of Minnesota

GLENDA DEWBERRY ROONEY
Augsburg College

KIMBERLY STROM-GOTTFRIED
University of North Carolina at Chapel Hill

BROOKS/COLE
CENGAGE Learning

Australia • Brazil • Japan • Korea • Mexico • Singapore • Spain • United Kingdom • United States

Direct Social Work Practice: Theory and Skills, Ninth Edition, International Edition
Dean H. Hepworth, Ronald H. Rooney, Glenda Dewberry Rooney, and Kimberly Strom-Gottfried

Senior Publisher: Linda Ganster

Acquiring Sponsoring Editor: Seth Dobrin

Associate Development Editor: Nicolas Albert

Assistant Editor: Alicia McLaughlin

Associate Media Editor: Elizabeth Momb

Program Manager: Tami Strang

Art Direction, Production Services and Composition: PreMediaGlobal

Manufacturing Planner: Judy Inouye

Rights Acquisition Specialist: Thomas McDonough

Cover Direction: Caryl Gorska

Cover Designer: Carole Lawson

Cover Image: Tony Sweet

© 2013, 2010 Brooks/Cole, Cengage Learning

ALL RIGHTS RESERVED. No part of this work covered by the copyright herein may be reproduced, transmitted, stored or used in any form or by any means graphic, electronic, or mechanical, including but not limited to photocopying, recording, scanning, digitizing, taping, Web distribution, information networks, or information storage and retrieval systems, except as permitted under Section 107 or 108 of the 1976 United States Copyright Act, or applicable copyright law of another jurisdiction, without the prior written permission of the publisher.

> For permission to use material from this text or product, submit all requests online at **www.cengage.com/permissions**
> Further permissions questions can be e-mailed to
> **permissionrequest@cengage.com**

International Edition:

ISBN-13: 978-1-133-35493-2

ISBN-10: 1-133-35493-9

Cengage Learning International Offices

Asia
www.cengageasia.com
tel: (65) 6410 1200

Australia/New Zealand
www.cengage.com.au
tel: (61) 3 9685 4111

Brazil
www.cengage.com.br
tel: (55) 11 3665 9900

India
www.cengage.co.in
tel: (91) 11 4364 1111

Latin America
www.cengage.com.mx
tel: (52) 55 1500 6000

UK/Europe/Middle East/Africa
www.cengage.co.uk
tel: (44) 0 1264 332 424

Represented in Canada by Nelson Education, Ltd.
www.nelson.com
tel: (416) 752 9100 / (800) 668 0671

Cengage Learning is a leading provider of customized learning solutions with office locations around the globe, including Singapore, the United Kingdom, Australia, Mexico, Brazil, and Japan. Locate your local office at: www.cengage.com/global

For product information and free companion resources:
www.cengage.com/international

Visit your local office: **www.cengage.com/global**

Visit our corporate website: **www.cengage.com**

Printed in Canada
1 2 3 4 5 6 7 16 15 14 13 12

Brief Contents

Preface xv
About the Authors xxi

PART 1
INTRODUCTION TO DIRECT SOCIAL WORK PRACTICE 1

1 Social Work Challenges 3
2 The Domain, Philosophy, and Roles of Direct Practice 25
3 Helping Process Overview 35
4 The Cardinal Social Work Values 55

PART 2
PLANNING, EXPLORING, AND ASSESSING 81

5 Empathy and Authenticity: The Building Blocks of Communication 83
6 The Skills of Verbal Following, Exploring, and Focusing 123
7 Avoiding Counterproductive Communication Patterns 153
8 Assessment: Problems and Strengths 173
9 Intrapersonal, Interpersonal, and Environmental Factors in Assessment 201
10 Assessment: Family Functioning in Diverse Family and Cultural Contexts 235
11 Social Work Groups: Formation and Assessment 279
12 Goal Development and Contract Formulation 309

PART 3
THE CHANGE-ORIENTED PHASE ... 357

13 Change-Oriented Strategies: Planning and Implementation 359

14 Intervention Strategies: Developing Resources, Organizing, Planning, and Advocacy 417

15 Improving Relationships and Family Functioning 449

16 Social Work Group Interventions 485

17 Confrontation, Interpretation, and Additive Empathy 511

18 The Management of Barriers to Change 527

PART 4
THE FINAL PHASE ... 555

19 Evaluation and Termination 557

Competency Notes 573
Modeled Responses and Other Exercises 589
Notes 607
Bibliography 611
Author Index 659
Subject Index 669

Contents

Preface xv
About the Authors xxi

PART 1
INTRODUCTION TO DIRECT SOCIAL WORK PRACTICE 1

CHAPTER 1
Social Work Challenges 3
The Mission of Social Work   5
Purposes of Social Work   5
Social Work Values   7
  Values and Ethics   9
  Social Work's Code of Ethics   10
EPAS Competencies   10
  EPAS Competency 2.1.1   10
  EPAS Competency 2.1.2   11
  EPAS Competency 2.1.3   11
  EPAS Competency 2.1.4   11
  EPAS Competency 2.1.5   12
  EPAS Competency 2.1.6   13
  EPAS Competency 2.1.7   13
  EPAS Competency 2.1.8   13
  EPAS Competency 2.1.9   13
  EPAS 2.1.10   14
  EPAS Competency 2.1.10a   14
  EPAS Competency 2.1.10b   14
  EPAS Competency 2.1.10c   14
  EPAS Competency 2.1.10d   14
  EPAS Competency B 2.2   14
  EPAS Competency M 2.2   14
  EPAS Competency 2.1   15
  Orienting Frameworks to Achieve Competencies   16
  Limitations of Systems Theories   20

Deciding on and Carrying Out Interventions   20
  Guidelines Influencing Intervention Selection   22
Summary   23
CourseMate   23

CHAPTER 2
The Domain, Philosophy, and Roles of Direct Practice 25
Domain   25
  Generalist Practice   26
  Direct Practice   26
A Philosophy of Direct Practice   29
Roles of Direct Practitioners   30
  Direct Provision of Services   30
  System Linkage Roles   30
  System Maintenance and Enhancement   31
  Researcher/Research Consumer   33
  System Development   33
Summary   34
CourseMate   34

CHAPTER 3
Helping Process Overview 35
Common Elements among Diverse Theorists and Social Workers   35
The Helping Process   37
  Phase I: Exploration, Engagement, Assessment, and Planning   37
  Phase II: Implementation and Goal Attainment   42
  Phase III: Termination   44
The Interviewing Process: Structure and Skills   45
  Physical Conditions   46
  Structure of Interviews   47

Establishing Rapport 47
The Exploration Process 50
Focusing in Depth 52
Employing Outlines 52
Assessing Emotional Functioning 52
Exploring Cognitive Functioning 53
Exploring Substance Abuse, Violence, and Sexual Abuse 53
Negotiating Goals and a Contract 53
Ending Interviews 53
Goal Attainment 54

Summary 54

CourseMate 54

CHAPTER 4
The Cardinal Social Work Values 55

The Interaction Between Personal and Professional Values 55

The Cardinal Values of Social Work 56

Challenges in Embracing the Profession's Values 63

Ethics 64
The Intersection of Laws and Ethics 64
Key Ethical Principles 66
What Are the Limits on Confidentiality? 72
The Ethics of Practice with Minors 76

Understanding and Resolving Ethical Dilemmas 77

Summary 80

CourseMate 80

PART 2
PLANNING, EXPLORING, AND ASSESSING 81

CHAPTER 5
Empathy and Authenticity: The Building Blocks of Communication 83

Roles of the Participants 84

Communicating about Informed Consent, Confidentiality, and Agency Policies 87

Facilitative Conditions 88

Empathic Communication 89

Developing Perceptiveness to Feelings 90

Affective Words and Phrases 91
Use of the Lists of Affective Words and Phrases 92
Exercises in Identifying Surface and Underlying Feelings 94

Accurately Conveying Empathy 95
Empathic Communication Scale 95
Exercises in Discriminating Levels of Empathic Responding 98

Client Statements 98

Responding with Reciprocal Empathy 100
Constructing Reciprocal Responses 100
Leads for Empathic Responses 101
Employing Empathic Responding 101
Multiple Uses of Empathic Communication 102
Teaching Clients to Respond Empathically 106

Authenticity 107
Types of Self-Disclosure 108
Timing and Intensity of Self-Disclosure 108
A Paradigm for Responding Authentically 109
Guidelines for Responding Authentically 109
Cues for Authentic Responding 113
Positive Feedback: A Form of Authentic Responding 117

Relating Assertively to Clients 118
Making Requests and Giving Directives 118
Maintaining Focus and Managing Interruptions 119
Interrupting Problematic Processes 119
"Leaning Into" Clients' Anger 120
Saying No and Setting Limits 121

Summary 122

CourseMate 122

CHAPTER 6
The Skills of Verbal Following, Exploring, and Focusing 123

Maintaining Psychological Contact with Clients and Exploring Their Problems 123

Verbal Following Skills 124

Furthering Responses 125
Minimal Prompts 125
Accent Responses 125

Paraphrasing Responses 125
Exercises in Paraphrasing 126

Reflection 126
Exercises with Reflections 128

Closed- and Open-Ended Responses 128
Exercises in Identifying Closed- and Open-Ended Responses 129
Discriminant Use of Closed- and Open-Ended Responses 130

Seeking Concreteness 132
Types of Responses That Facilitate Specificity of Expression by Clients 133
Specificity of Expression by Social Workers 137
Exercises in Seeking Concreteness 138

Focusing: A Complex Skill 139
Selecting Topics for Exploration 139

Exploring Topics in Depth 141
Blending Open-Ended, Empathic, and Concrete
Responses to Maintain Focus 142
Managing Obstacles to Focusing 145
Summarizing Responses 146
Highlighting Key Aspects of Problems 146
Summarizing Lengthy Messages 147
Reviewing Focal Points of a Session 148
Providing Focus and Continuity 149
Analyzing Your Verbal Following Skills 149
Summary 151
CourseMate 151

CHAPTER 7
Avoiding Counterproductive Communication Patterns 153

Impacts of Counterproductive Communication Patterns 153

Eliminating Nonverbal Barriers to Effective Communication 154
Physical Attending 154
Cultural Nuances of Nonverbal Cues 154
Other Nonverbal Behaviors 155
Taking Inventory of Nonverbal Patterns of Responding 155

Eliminating Verbal Barriers to Communication 157
Reassuring, Sympathizing, Consoling, or Excusing 157
Advising and Giving Suggestions or Solutions Prematurely 158
Using Sarcasm or Employing Humor Inappropriately 160
Judging, Criticizing, or Placing Blame 160
Trying to Convince Clients about the Right Point of View through Logic, Lecturing, Instructing, or Arguing 161
Analyzing, Diagnosing, or Making Glib or Dramatic Interpretations 162
Threatening, Warning, or Counterattacking 162
Stacking Questions 163
Asking Leading Questions 163
Interrupting Inappropriately or Excessively 164
Dominating the Interaction 164
Fostering Safe Social Interaction 165
Responding Infrequently 165
Parroting or Overusing Certain Phrases or Clichés 166
Dwelling on the Remote Past 166
Going on Fishing Expeditions 167

Gauging the Effectiveness of Your Responses 167

The Challenge of Learning New Skills 168

Summary 171

CourseMate 171

CHAPTER 8
Assessment: Problems and Strengths 173

The Multidimensionality of Assessment 174

Defining Assessment: Process and Product 174

Assessment and Diagnosis 176
The Diagnostic and Statistical Manual (DSM-IV-TR) 177

Culturally Competent Assessment 178

Emphasizing Strengths in Assessments 180

The Role of Knowledge and Theory in Assessments 181

Sources of Information 183

Questions to Answer in Problem Assessment 187
Getting Started 188
Identifying the Problem, Its Expressions, and Other Critical Concerns 188
The Interaction of Other People or Systems 189
Assessing Needs and Wants 190
Typical Wants Involved in Presenting Problems 190
Stresses Associated with Life Transitions 191
Cultural, Societal, and Social Class Factors 192
Severity of the Problem 192
Meanings That Clients Ascribe to Problems 192
Sites of Problematic Behaviors 193
Temporal Context of Problematic Behaviors 193
Frequency of Problematic Behaviors 193
Duration of the Problem 194
Other Issues Affecting Client Functioning 194
Clients' Emotional Reactions to Problems 195
Coping Efforts and Needed Skills 195
Support Systems 196
Resources Needed 196

Assessing Children and Older Adults 197
Maltreatment 197

Summary 199

CourseMate 200

CHAPTER 9
Intrapersonal, Interpersonal, and Environmental Factors in Assessment 201

The Interaction of Multiple Systems in Human Problems 201

Intrapersonal Systems 202

Assessing Biophysical Functioning 202
Physical Characteristics and Presentation 203
Physical Health 203

Assessing Use and Abuse of Medications, Alcohol, and Drugs 204
Alcohol Use and Abuse 205
Use and Abuse of Other Substances 205
Dual Diagnosis: Addictive and Mental Disorders 205
Using Interviewing Skills to Assess Substance Use 206

Assessing Cognitive/Perceptual Functioning 208
  Intellectual Functioning 209
  Judgment 209
  Reality Testing 209
  Coherence 210
  Cognitive Flexibility 210
  Values 211
  Beliefs 211
  Self-Concept 211
Assessing Affective Functioning 212
  Emotional Control 213
  Range of Emotions 213
  Appropriateness of Affect 214
  Suicidal Risk 214
  Depression and Suicidal Risk with Children and Adolescents 216
  Depression and Suicidal Risk with Older Adults 217
Assessing Behavioral Functioning 218
  Risk of Aggression 221
Assessing Motivation 221
Assessing Environmental Systems 222
  Physical Environment 223
  Social Support Systems 224
  Spirituality and Affiliation with a Faith Community 226
Written Assessments 227
  Case Notes 232
Summary 233
CourseMate 233

CHAPTER 10
Assessment: Family Functioning in Diverse Family and Cultural Contexts 235

Social Work Practice with Families 236
Defining Family 236
Family Functions 236
Family Stressors 239
  Public Policy 240
  Poverty 240
  Extraordinary Life Transitions and Separations 241
  Work and Family 242
  Resilience in Families 243
A Systems Framework for Assessing Family Functioning 243
  Tools for Understanding Families 244
  Strengths-Based and Risk Assessments 244
Systems Concepts 245
  Application of Systems Concepts 245
  Family Homeostasis 245
Family Rules 246
  Functional and Rigid Rules 247
  Violation of Rules 248
  Flexibility of Rules 249
Content and Process Levels of Family Interactions 250
  Sequences of Interaction 251
  Employing "Circular" Explanations of Behavior 253
Assessing Problems Using the Systems Framework 254
Dimensions of Family Assessment 255
  Family Context 256
  Family Strengths 258
  Boundaries and Boundary Maintenance in Family Systems 259
  Disengaged Families 262
  Family Power Structure 263
  Family Decision-Making Processes 266
  Family Goals 268
  Family Myths and Cognitive Patterns 269
  Family Roles 270
  Communication Styles of Family Members 272
  Family Life Cycle 275
Summary 276
CourseMate 277

CHAPTER 11
Social Work Groups: Formation and Assessment 279

Classification of Groups 280
The Evidence Base for Groups 282
Formation of Treatment Groups 282
  Determining the Need for the Group 282
  Establishing the Group Purpose 283
  Deciding on Leadership 284
  Deciding on Group Composition 284
  Open versus Closed Groups 286
  Determining Group Size and Location 286
  Setting the Frequency and Duration of Meetings 287
  Conducting a Preliminary Interview 287
  Determine the Group Format 288
  Formulating Preliminary Group Guidelines 289
Assessing Group Processes 292
  A Systems Framework for Assessing Groups 293
  Assessing Individuals' Patterned Behaviors 293
  Assessing Individuals' Cognitive Patterns 296
  Assessing Groups' Patterned Behaviors 297
  Assessing Group Alliances 298
  Assessing Power and Decision-Making Styles 299
  Assessing Group Norms, Values, and Cohesion 300
Formation of Task Groups 302
  Planning for Task Groups 302
  Beginning the Task Group 303
Cultural Considerations in Forming and Assessing Groups 304

Ethics in Practice with Groups   306
    First Session   306
Summary   308
CourseMate   308

CHAPTER 12
Goal Development and Contract Formulation ... 309

Goals   309
    The Purpose and Function of Goals   310
    Linking Goals to Target Concerns   310
    Distinguishing Program Objectives and Client Goals   311
    Factors That Influence the Development of Goals   312
    Types of Goals   315
    Guidelines for Selecting and Defining Goals   315
    Motivational Congruence   318
    Agreeable Mandate   319
    Let's Make a Deal   319
    Getting Rid of the Mandate   319
    Partializing Goals   321
    Involuntary Clients' Mandated Case Plans   323

Applying Goal Selection and Development Guidelines with Minors   328
    Eliciting Minors' Understanding of the Goal and Point of View of the Problem, and Using this Information to Assist Them to Develop Goals   328

Process of Negotiating Goals   332
    Determine Clients' Readiness for Goal Negotiation   332
    Jointly Select Appropriate Goals   334
    Define Goals Explicitly and Specify Level of Change   334
    Risks and Benefits   335
    Rank Goals According to Client Priorities   337

Monitoring Progress and Evaluation   337
    Methods of Monitoring and Evaluating Progress   338
    Quantitative Measurements   339
    Monitoring Progress Using Qualitative Measures   343
    Evaluating Your Practice   346

Contracts   346
    The Rationale for Contracts   347
    Formal and Informal Contracts   347
    Developing Contracts   347
    Sample Contracts   350

Summary   353
CourseMate   355

PART 3
THE CHANGE-ORIENTED PHASE 357

CHAPTER 13
Change-Oriented Strategies: Planning and Implementation 359

Change-Oriented Approaches   360

Planning Goal Attainment Strategies   360
    Is the Approach Appropriate for Addressing the Problem for Work and the Service Goals?   360
    Is the Approach Appropriate to the Person, Family, or Group?   361
    Diverse Individuals, Families, and Groups   361
    What Empirical or Conceptual Evidence Supports the Effectiveness of the Approach?   362
    Is the Approach Compatible with Basic Values and Ethics of Social Work?   362
    Am I Sufficiently Knowledgeable and Skilled Enough in this Approach to Use with Others?   364

Models & Techniques of Practice   365
    The Task-Centered System   365
    Tenets of the Task-Centered Approach   365
    Theoretical Framework   366
    Empirical Evidence and Uses of the Task-Centered Model   366
    Utilization with Minors   366
    Application with Diverse Groups   366

Procedures of the Task-Centered Model   367
    Developing General Tasks   367
    General Tasks for the Social Worker   368
    Developing Specific Tasks   368
    Brainstorming Task Alternatives   368
    Task Implementation Sequence   369
    Failure to Complete Tasks   376
    Monitoring Progress   378

Crisis Intervention   379
    Tenets of the Crisis Intervention Equilibrium Model   379
    Definition and Stages of Crisis   379
    Duration of Contact   381
    Intervening with Minors   381
    Theoretical Framework   383
    Application with Diverse Groups   383
    Process and Procedures of Crisis Intervention   384
    Strengths and Limitations   388

Cognitive Restructuring   388
    Theoretical Framework   389
    Tenets of Cognitive Behavioral Therapy-Cognitive Restructuring   389
    What Are Cognitive Distortions?   390
    Empirical Evidence and Uses of Cognitive Restructuring   392
    Application of Cognitive Restructuring with Diverse Groups   393
    Procedures of Cognitive Restructuring   394
    Strengths, Limitations, and Cautions   401

Solution-Focused Brief Treatment   401
    Tenets of Solution-Focused   401
    Theoretical Framework   402

Empirical Evidence and Uses of Solution-Focused
   Strategies   402
Application with Diverse Groups   403
Solution-Focused Procedures and Techniques   403
Strengths & Limitations   407

Case Management   408
Tenets of Case Management   409
Standards of Case Management Practice   409
Empirical Evidence of Case Management   410
Case Management Functions   410
Case Managers   411
Strengths and Limitations   413

Summary   414

CourseMate   415

CHAPTER 14
Intervention Strategies: Developing Resources, Organizing, Planning, and Advocacy 417

Social Work's Commitment   418
Defining Macro Practice   418

Linking Micro and Macro Practice   419

Macro Practice Intervention Strategies   419
Empowerment and Strengths   420
Analyzing Social Problems and Conditions   420
Social Justice Issues   421

Developing and Mobilizing Resources   425
Developing Resources with Diverse Groups   427
Mobilizing Community Resources   427

Advocacy and Social Action   429
Case and Cause Advocacy   429
Indications for Advocacy or Social Action   430
Competence and Skills for Macro Practice and Social
   Action   430
Techniques and Steps of Advocacy and Social Action   431

Community Organization   432
Models and Strategies of Community Intervention   432

Steps and Skills of Community Intervention   434
Organizing Skills   434
Organizing and Planning with Diverse Groups   434

Ethical Issues in Community Organizing   435
Social Media as a Resource of Social Advocacy and
   Community Organizing   435

Improving Institutional Environments   435

Improving Organizational Environments   436
Staff   436
Organizational Policies and Practices   437
Institutional programs   437
Influence of Public Policy   439
Staff   439
Institutional Programs   442

Organizational Change   443
Risks, Benefits, and Opposition   444

Macro Practice Evaluation   445

Summary   446

CourseMate   447

CHAPTER 15
Improving Relationships and Family Functioning 449

Intervention Approaches with Families   449

Initial Contacts   450
Managing Initial Contact with Couples and
   Families   450
Safety Concerns   452
Managing Initial Contacts with Parents   452

Orchestrating the Initial Family or Couple Session   453
The Dynamics of Minority Status and Culture in
   Exploring Reservations   456

Intervening with Families: Cultural and Ecological Perspectives   461
Differences in Communication Styles   461
Hierarchical Considerations   462
Authority of the Social Worker   462
Engaging Diverse Families   463
Understanding Families Using an Ecological
   Perspective   463

Examples of Family Intervention   464
Twanna, the Adolescent Mother   464
Anna and Jackie, a Lesbian Couple   465

Intervening with Families: Focusing on the Future   466

Communication Patterns and Styles   467
Giving and Receiving Feedback   467
Educating Clients about the Vital Role of Positive
   Feedback   467
Cultivating Positive Cognitive Sets   468
Enabling Clients to Give and Receive Positive
   Feedback   469

Intervening with Families: Strategies to Modify Interactions   471
Metacommunication   471
Modifying Family Rules   472
To Father   474
To Other Family Members   474
On-the-Spot Interventions   474
Assisting Families to Disengage from Conflict   476
Modifying Complementary Interactions   477
Negotiating Agreements for Reciprocal Changes   478

Intervening with Families: Modifying Misconceptions and Distorted Cognitions   479

Intervening with Families: Modifying Family
   Alignments   480
Summary   483
CourseMate   483

CHAPTER 16
Social Work Group Interventions 485

Stages of Group Development   485
   Stage 1. Preaffiliation: Approach and Avoidance
      Behavior   486
   Stage 2. Power and Control: A Time of Transition   487
   Stage 3. Intimacy: Developing a Familial Frame of
      Reference   488
   Stage 4. Differentiation: Developing Group Identity and
      an Internal Frame of Reference   489
   Stage 5. Separation: Breaking Away   490
The Leader's Role in the Stages of Group Development   491
Interventions throughout the Life of the Group   491
   Fostering Cohesion   491
   Addressing Group Norms   492
   Intervening with Members' Roles   493
   Attending to Subgroup Structure   494
   Purposefully Using the Leadership Role   494
   Attending to Group and Individual Processes   495
Stage-Specific Interventions   495
   Interventions in the Preaffiliation Stage   496
   Interventions in the Power and Control Stage   499
   Interventions in the Intimacy and Differentiation
      Stages   502
   Interventions in the Termination Stage   504
   Errors in Group Interventions   506
Variations in Social Work with Groups   507
   Single Session Groups   507
   Technology-Mediated Groups   507
Work with Task Groups   508
   Problem Identification   508
   Getting Members Involved   509
   Enhancing Awareness of Stages of Development   509
Summary   510
CourseMate   510

CHAPTER 17
Confrontation, Interpretation, and Additive
Empathy 511

The Meaning and Significance of Client
   Self-Awareness   511
Additive Empathy and Interpretation   511
   Deeper Feelings   513
   Underlying Meanings of Feelings, Thoughts, and
      Behavior   514
   Wants and Goals   515

   Hidden Purposes of Behavior   516
   Unrealized Strengths and Potentialities   517
   Guidelines for Employing Interpretation and Additive
      Empathy   517
Confrontation   518
   Guidelines for Employing Confrontation   523
   Indications for Assertive Confrontation   525
Summary   526
CourseMate   526

CHAPTER 18
The Management of Barriers to Change 527

Barriers to Change   528
Relational Dynamics   528
   Under- and Over-Involvement of Social Workers
      with Clients   530
   Burnout, Compassion Fatigue, and Vicarious
      Trauma   533
Reactions of Clients: Assessing Potential Barriers
   and Intervening   534
   Pathological or Inept Social Workers   536
   Cross-Racial and Cross-Cultural Barriers   537
   Difficulties in Establishing Trust   540
   Transference Reactions   541
   Managing Countertransference Reactions   545
   Realistic Practitioner Reactions   546
   Sexual Attraction Toward Clients   547
Motivating Change   548
   Change Strategies   549
   Motivational Interviewing   550
   Guiding Principles of Motivational Interviewing   550
   Positive Connotation   552
   Redefining Problems as Opportunities for Growth   552
   Relabeling   553
   Reframing   553
   Therapeutic Binds   553
Summary   554
CourseMate   554

PART 4
THE FINAL PHASE 555

CHAPTER 19
Evaluation and Termination 557

Evaluation   557
   Outcomes   558
   Process   559
   Satisfaction   560
Termination   561
   Types of Termination   561

Understanding and Responding to Clients' Termination Reactions 566
Social Workers' Reactions to Termination 569

Consolidating Gains and Planning Maintenance Strategies 569
Follow-Up Sessions 570
Ending Rituals 570

Summary 572

CourseMate 572

Competency Notes 573
Modeled Responses and Other Exercises 589
Notes 607
Bibliography 611
Author Index 659
Subject Index 669

Preface

In our work teaching BSW and MSW students, we, your authors, are often confronted with the question, "What should I do if....?" The easy (and usually correct) answer is "It depends." How a social worker responds in any given situation *depends* on a variety of factors: the setting in which he or she is working, the client, the nature of the helping relationship that has developed, the advantages and disadvantages of any give action or choice, and so on.

We wrote this book to help answer the "it depends," to help equip you with the knowledge and critical thinking to weigh the factors involved in decisions throughout the helping process. It will educate you about the factors to consider when you address the questions that will arise throughout your work as a student social worker and as a professional. At first that process can seem cumbersome. It can be difficult to digest all this new information and recall it as needed in client interactions. We acknowledge that this learning *is* a process of becoming acquainted with the concepts in this book, of understanding the pros and cons of various choices, of becoming familiar with the different variables that affect practice and in using this knowledge and skills in supervision, in work with colleagues and classmates, and in practice with clients.

As social workers ourselves, we have the utmost respect for the complexity of the work, the power that professionals hold, and the grave situations in which we are entrusted to help others. In this text, we have tried to provide you with a foundation to practice with excellence and integrity in this vital profession.

The Structure of the Text

The book has four parts. Part 1 introduces the reader to the social work profession and direct practice and provides an overview of the helping process, including core competencies, the role of evidence-based practice, the domains and roles of social work, and the elements of ethical practice.

Part 2 presents the beginning phase of the helping process and each chapter includes examples from the videotapes developed for the text. It addresses relationship-building skills, strategies for providing direction and focus in interviews, and avoiding common communication errors. Subsequent chapters in this section address problem- and strengths- exploration; theories and techniques for individual, family, and group assessment; and the processes for goal setting.

Part 3 presents the middle, or goal attainment, phase of the helping process. It describes change-oriented strategies, including updated material on task-centered, crisis intervention, cognitive restructuring, solution-focused approaches to practice and case management, large-systems change, advocacy, family practice, and groupwork. Readers learn advanced communication and intervention techniques and common worker and client barriers to change.

Part 4 deals with the final phase of the helping process incorporating material on evaluating and terminating social work relationships in an array of circumstances.

Alternative Chapter Order

This book has been structured around phases of practice at systems levels ranging from individual, to family, to group, to macro. Some instructors prefer to teach all content about a particular mode of practice in one block. In particular, those instructors whose courses emphasize individual contacts may choose to present chapters in a different order than we have organized them (see Table 1). They may teach content in Chapters 5–9, skip ahead to Chapters 12 and 13, and then delve into chapters 17 and 18. Similarly, family content can be grouped by using Chapters 10 and 15 together, and groups by using 11 and 16 together. We have presented the chapters in the book in the current order because we think that presentation of intervention by phases fits a systems perspective better than beginning with a choice of intervention mode.

TABLE 1 ORGANIZATION OF CHAPTERS BY MODE OF PRACTICE

MODE OF PRACTICE	
Across levels	Chapters 1–4, 19
Individual	Chapters 5–8, 12, 13, 17, 18
Family	Chapters 10, 15
Group	Chapters 11, 16
Macro	Chapter 14

The Empowerment Series: Relationship with the Educational Policy Statement and Accreditation Standards (EPAS), and Professional Competencies

This book is part of the Brooks/Cole, Cengage Learning Empowerment Series and addresses accreditation standards established by the Council on Social Work Education (CSWE).[1] Our intent is to facilitate programs' ability to link content provided in this textbook with expectations for student learning and accomplishment. As is true in almost all learning, students must acquire knowledge before they are expected to apply it to practice situations.

CSWE has identified 41 practice behaviors that operationalize ten core competencies, which are critical for professional practice (CSWE, 2008). For clarity, we have alphabetized in lower case the practice behaviors under each competency. **"Helping Hands"** located within paragraphs clearly show the linkage between content in the textbook and specific practice behaviors and competencies. Each icon is labeled with the specific practice behavior or competency that relates directly to the content conveyed in the paragraph. For example, an icon might be labeled EP [Educational Policy] 2.1.2, which is the competency, "apply social work ethical principles to guide professional practice" (CSWE, 2008). Accredited social work programs are required to prove that students have mastered all practice behaviors for competence as specified in the EPAS. (Please refer to www.cswe.org for the EPAS document.)

For all icons, **"Competency Notes"** are provided at the end of the book. These "Competency Notes" explain the relationship between chapter content and CSWE's competencies and practice behaviors. They also list page numbers where icons are located and this content is discussed. A summary chart of the icons' locations in all chapters and their respective competency or practice behavior is placed in the front matter of the book.

New Features and Resources for the 9th Edition

- The 9th edition fully integrates many videos, including *new* videos demonstrating cross-cultural practice, engagement with an adolescent, sessions from the middle of the helping process, and motivational interviewing.
- The new edition addresses features of contemporary social work practice: case management, work with the emerging issue of hoarding, the challenges of Facebook and other online communication mechanisms, attention to ethics in all aspects of practice, discussion of the upcoming DSM-V, identification of evidence-based practices, attention to unique populations, such as minors, older adults, immigrants and refugees, assessing and addressing client aggression, integration of Motivational Interviewing concepts in interviewing chapters, and chapters on empathy and managing barriers to change.
- Cultural competence is conveyed in this edition though the approach of cultural humility, in which professionals are equipped with the ability to seek out and understand information about their clients as individuals and as members of diverse groups. This edition deemphasizes discussion of group characteristics, which can encourage overgeneralizations and

---

[1] Please note that this content addresses standards posed in EPAS. In no way does it claim to verify compliance with standards. Only the Council on social Work Education Commission on Accreditation can make those determinations.

- stereotypes that are harmful to the helping process.
- Structural features draw readers' attention to relevant practice behaviors identified by the Council on Social Work Education.
- New tables, layout, and editing offer readers increased clarity.
- Concepts in the book and classroom activities are enhanced by videos that depict segments or entire sessions with clients from a variety of backgrounds representing an array of circumstances. Many of these are called out in Video Case Example boxes.
- The book offers abundant examples to illustrate points and allow application to an array of social work settings and clientele. Many of these are called out in Case Example boxes.
- Skill development exercises at the end of the book allow opportunities for readers to apply concepts to practice.
- The glossary, online quiz questions, and other resources help clarify and deepen readers' understanding of core concepts.

Chapter-By-Chapter Changes
Chapter 1
- Includes a new figure and introduces ecomaps as a way of presenting systems theory.
- References and EPAS connections updated
- Content connected to new videos

Chapter 2
- Updated case examples
- EPAS competencies inserted
- New references

Chapter 3
- Updated references
- Added connections to new video "Hanging with **Hailey**"
- Added EPAS linkages

Chapter 4
- Added coverage of Facebook/social networking and a case vignette about it
- Updated "Ali's" Ideas in Action to include strengths, consultation, and growth
- Added coverage on resolving common boundary dilemmas
- Added new material on HIPAA and records
- Addressed self-disclosure as a boundary issue and referred readers to Chapter 5
- Added new examples including sleuthing clients online/on Facebook, military social work, reference to international case and the intergenerational clash of values

Chapter 5
- Updated references
- Added connections to videos
- Added EPAS linkages

Chapter 6
- Updated references
- Added connections to videos, especially "How Can I Help" with Peter Dimock
- Incorporated motivational interviewing concepts in elaboration of verbal following and empathy development skills
- Added EPAS linkages

Chapter 7
- References and linkages to a new video created for this edition in this chapter (Working with Yanping)
- Revised video examples from the previous edition
- Some sections rewritten for better readability
- Added EPAS linkages

Chapter 8
- Added material on the anticipated DSM-V.
- Condensed, revised and reorganized questions for problem exploration to balance strengths- and needs-focus
- Added section on support systems
- Added examples of items from Beck Depression inventory
- Added information on spirituality/end-of-life explorations regarding elder assessments
- Added new/updated references
- Added EPAS linkages

Chapter 9
- Added new /updated references throughout
- Fixed Fig 9.1 to clarify intrapersonal elements of assessment

- Added new figure to display environmental and spiritual elements
- Reinstated example of mental status exam
- Added guidance on assessing for violence and resources
- Added example of suicide assessment for adolescent (Hailey) case
- Added information on hoarding
- Added example of social history and applied it to video case
- Added EPAS linkages

Chapter 10
- Streamlined content, removing excessive and extraneous content
- Removed content that was related to intervening in families because it distracted from the dimensions and concepts for assessing families
- Emphasized the ways in which culturally competent practice with families is an ongoing process, including self-reflection
- Deleted old references
- Added EPAS linkages

Chapter 11
- Added EPAS linkages
- Added tables to clarify "outline" of major segments of chapter
- Reorganized content in planning to indicate usual flow of decisions (determining kind of group before preliminary meetings)
- Added a section on the evidence base for group work

Chapter 12
- Updated references.
- Added connections to videos, especially "Problem Solving with the Corning Family"
- Expanded the content related to the utilization of standardized instruments and evidence-based procedures for measuring progress
- Added questions that may be used to evaluate practice
- Added EPAS linkages

Chapter 13
- Updated references
- Added connections to videos, especially "Problem Solving with the Corning Family" and "Working with Yanping"
- Added a case example that illustrates solution-focused interviewing as suggested by reviewers
- Added case management, utilizing the Corning family to illustrate the practice method
- Added EPAS linkages

Chapter 14
- Removed a number of case examples that shortened the chapter
- Added new references and related content
- Added EPAS linkages
- Added content related to social justice and social media as a resource for advocacy and organizing
- Improved content related to the the linkage between micro-macro practice skills

Chapter 15
- Updated references
- Added EPAS linkages
- Reworked and reduced content to improve flow
- Added content on safety concerns related to home visits
- Improved video connections, especially "Home for the Holidays" and "Adolescent Teen Mother and Foster Parent"

Chapter 16
- Updated references
- Added EPAS connections
- Significant reorganization to increase clarity and reduce redundancy
- Changed section on "New Developments …" to "Variations …"
- Moved evaluation to interventions in final phase and added single session groups to that section along with technology section
- Added recent research

Chapter 17
- Updated references,
- Added EPAS connections
- Literature is updated on interpretation, additive empathy, and confrontation
- Extensive integration of new video by Peter Dimock "How Can I Help?" demonstrating motivational interviewing skills

Chapter 18
- Updated and added new references
- Elaborated upon the principles and techniques of motivational interviewing as a means to engage the

client and motivate change, which is demonstrated in the Video "How Can I Help?"
- Added EPAS connections

Chapter 19
- Added EPAS linkages
- Addressed role of past losses in reactions to termination
- Updated citations
- Addressed reviewer recommendation about clients assigned to a series of interns

Instructors Ancillaries

A suite of instructor's resources makes teaching with this edition easier. An online **Instructor's Manual** provides useful information for faculty, and an electronic **Test Bank** includes chapter-specific test questions that can be used immediately or adapted as needed. Featuring automatic grading, **ExamView®** allows you to create, deliver, and customize tests and study guides (both print and online) in minutes. A complete set of **PowerPoint lecture slides** is also available for download. Many videos, including *new videos* demonstrating **cross-cultural practice**, sessions from the middle of the helping process, and motivational interviewing are available via CourseMate at www.cengagebrain.com. Visit CourseMate at www.cengagebrain.com or work with your local Brooks/Cole Cengage Learning representative to have sample copies sent to you.

Student Ancillaries

A robust CourseMate includes study quizzes, videos, and other materials to help students better master content and skills. Please work with your local Brooks/Cole, Cengage Learning representative to receive a sample copy or to request a bundle ISBN so that the text and workbook come packaged together at the bookstore.

Acknowledgments

We dedicate this book to Lisa Gebo (1958–2010) our first editor, whose enthusiasm, innovations and encouragement continue to nourish us and influence this edition. We also wish to especially thank Dean Hepworth, a social work educator and the first author of this text, for his inspiration and example in developing a text that would help students become more effective practitioners.

We would like to thank the following colleagues for their help in providing useful comments and suggestions. We have been supported by members of our writers' groups including Mike Chovanec, Annete Gerten, Elena Izaksonas, Nancy Rodenborg and Catherine Marrs Fuchsel. A special thanks to colleagues Melissa Hensley and Sarah Johansen for their feedback and contributions. We also want to thank research assistants David DeVito, Hilary Anderson, Alison Prevost, Sheila Hanschen, Kathryn Cochrane, and Jenn Pike for their extensive research, reviews, and bibliographic assistance. We owe a special debt of gratitude to our video and simulation participants: Sarah Gottfried, Shannon Van Osdel, Emily Williams, Heather Parnell, Kristen Lukasiewicz, Erika Johnson, Angela Brandt, Irwin Thompson, Ali Vogel, Mrs. Janic Mays, Dorothy Flaherty, Val Velazquez, Kathy Ringham, Mary Pattridge, Cali Carpenter, Wu Yanping, Li Jilan, Emily Kruger, Hailey Lee, and Peter Dimock. We also wish to thank our students—the users of this text—and social workers in the field for their suggestions, case examples, and encouragement. In particular, we wish to acknowledge Samati Niyomchai of The George Warren Brown School of Social Work for his thoughtful and incisive feedback on fostering cultural competence. We are also grateful to the reviewers of this edition for their timely and constructive comments. They are:

Cynthia Bishop, Meredith College
Jean Hall, University of Tennessee
Tina Johnson, University of Louisville
Larry Livingston, University of Illinois, Springfield
Elizabeth Rompf, University of Kentucky
Craig Schwalbe, Columbia University
Patricia Sherman, Kean University
Jeff Skinner, University of Georgia

This edition could not have been completed without the support, inspiration and challenge of our colleagues, friends, and families including George Gottfried, Lola Dewberry, and Chris Rooney. And finally we want to express special appreciation to Seth Dobrin, Nicolas Albert, and the rest of the team from Cengage for their responsiveness, support, expertise, and patience.

About the Authors

Dean H. Hepworth is Professor Emeritus at the School of Social Work, Arizona State University, Tempe Arizona, and the University of Utah. Dean has extensive practice experience in individual psychotherapy and marriage and family therapy. Dean was the lead author and active in the production of the first four editions, and he is the co-author of *Improving Therapeutic Communication*. He is now retired and lives in Phoenix, Arizona.

Ronald H. Rooney is Professor, School of Social Work, University of Minnesota, Twin Cities. Ron's practice background is primarily in public and private child welfare, including work with involuntary clients, about which he does training and consultation. Ron is the editor of the second edition of *Strategies for Work with Involuntary Clients*.

Glenda Dewberry Rooney is a Professor at Augsburg College, Department of Social Work, Minneapolis, Minnesota. She teaches undergraduate and graduate direct practice courses, ethics, and research. Her practice experience includes child welfare, mental health and work with families. In addition to her practice experience, she has been involved with agencies concerned with children, youth, and families as a trainer, clinical and management consultant, and in community-based research projects. She continues to be an advocate for child welfare policies and practices that strengthen and support families. Dr. Rooney is a contributing author to *Strategies for Work with Involuntary Clients (2nd ed.)*.

Kim Strom-Gottfried is the Smith B. Theimann Distinguished Professor of Ethics and Professional Practice at the UNC Chapel Hill School of Social Work. She teaches in the areas of direct practice, communities and organizations, and human resource management, and her scholarly interests involve ethics, moral courage, and professional education. Kim's practice experience has been in the nonprofit and public sectors, focusing on mental health and suicide prevention, intervention, and bereavement. She has written numerous articles, monographs, and chapters on the ethics of practice and is the author of *Straight Talk about Professional Ethics* and *The Ethics of Practice with Minors: High Stakes and Hard Choices*. Dr. Strom-Gottfried is also the co-author of *Teaching Social Work Values and Ethics: A Curriculum Resource*.

PART 1

Introduction to Direct Social Work Practice

1 Social Work Challenges
2 The Domain, Philosophy, and Roles of Direct Practice
3 Helping Process Overview
4 The Cardinal Social Work Values

Part 1 of this book provides you with a background of concepts, values, historical perspectives, and information about systems. This information will, in turn, prepare you to learn the specific direct practice skills described in Part 2.

Chapter 1 introduces you to the social work profession; explains its mission, purposes, and values; and describes how systems perspectives can guide you in conceptualizing your work.

Chapter 2 elaborates on the roles played by social workers, including the distinctions made between clinical and direct social work practice, and presents a philosophy of direct practice.

Chapter 3 offers an overview of the helping process, including exploration, implementation, and termination.

Finally, Chapter 4 introduces the cardinal values and ethical concerns underlying social work.

CHAPTER 1
Social Work Challenges

CHAPTER OVERVIEW

This chapter presents a context and philosophy for direct practice, definitions of direct and clinical practice and descriptions of the varied roles played by direct social work practitioners. After completing this chapter, you will be able to:

- introduces the mission of social work and the purposes of social work services
- illustrates the roles played by social workers within the organizational context for such services
- identifies the value perspectives that guide social workers
- introduces systems and ecological concepts for understanding the interaction of individuals and families with their environments
- introduces competencies that you will be expected to achieve in your academic career
- introduces our perspective on diversity that will guide how we present issues related to diversity

EPAS COMPETENCIES IN THE 1ST CHAPTER

This chapter will give you the information needed to meet the following practice competencies:

2.1.1 Social workers Identify as professionals and conduct themselves accordingly

2.1.2 Social workers apply social work ethical principles to guide professional practice.

2.1.2a Social workers recognize and manage personal values in a way that allows professional values to guide practice

2.1.2b Social workers make ethical decisions by applying standards of the National Association of Social Workers Code of Ethics and, as applicable, of the International Federation of Social Workers/International Association of Schools of Social Work Ethics in Social Work, Statement of Principles

2.1.3 Social workers apply critical thinking to inform and communicate professional judgments.

2.1.3b Social workers analyze models of assessment, prevention, intervention, and evaluation

2.1.4 Social workers engage diversity and difference in practice

2.1.5b Social workers advocate for human rights and social and economic justice.

2.1.5c Social workers engage in practices that engage in social and economic justice.

2.1.6 Social workers engage in research-informed practice and practice-informed research.

2.1.7 Social workers apply knowledge of human behavior and the social environment.

2.1.8 Social workers engage in policy practice to advance social and economic well-being and to deliver effective social work services

2.1.9 Social workers respond to contexts that shape practice.

2.1.10 Social workers engage, assess, intervene, and evaluate with individuals, families, groups, organizations and communities.

2.1.10a Social workers substantively and affectively prepare for action with individuals, families, groups, organizations, and communities

2.1.10b Social workers use empathy and other interpersonal skills.

2.1.10c Social workers develop a mutually agreed-on focus of work and desired outcomes with clients.

2.1.10d Social workers collect, organize, and interpret client data to inform practice

2.1.10e Social workers assess client strengths and limitations.

B 2.2 Social workers carry out generalist practice.

M 2.2 Social workers carry out advanced practice.

This chapter begins with a case example that will provide the context for concepts to be introduced in the chapter.

This case example highlights several aspects of social work practice. As a profession, we are committed to the pursuit of social justice for poor, disadvantaged, disenfranchised, and oppressed people (Marsh, 2005; Finn & Jacobson, 2003a; Pelton, 2003; Van Wormer, 2002; Carniol, 1992). In this case, in addition to seeing Mrs. Ramirez as a parent struggling with school attendance issues, Tobias also saw her as a client experiencing challenges possibly related to the ambivalence and unresolved issues in the United States surrounding immigrants without documentation (Cleaveland, 2010; Padilla et al., 2008). A law passed by the U.S. House of Representatives in 2005, but not in the Senate, would have made it a crime for service providers to assist undocumented immigrants. However, according to the National Association of Social Workers' (NASW) Immigration

EP 2.1.5b & c

IDEAS IN ACTION

Marta Ramirez was referred to child welfare services because her two elementary school-aged children had more than seven days of unexcused absences from school during the semester, the standard for educational neglect in her state. When Tobias, a child welfare social worker, met with Mrs. Ramirez, he found that the children had missed similar amounts of time when they had previously lived in another state, as well as earlier, before they had emigrated without documents from Mexico. There had not been earlier investigations, however, as legal standards for educational neglect were different in the previous state. Mrs. Ramirez noted that her children had been frequently ill with "flu and asthma." She said that the children did not feel comfortable at the school. They felt that the teachers were mean to them because they were Hispanic. In addition, Mrs. Ramirez had sustained a back injury on her job that limited her ability to get out of bed some mornings. As an immigrant without documents, Mrs. Ramirez was ineligible for the surgery she needed. Finally, she acknowledged experiencing depression and anxiety.

Tobias shared with Mrs. Ramirez the reason for the referral under statute and asked for her perspective on school attendance. He explained that child welfare workers are called on to assist families in having their children educated. He also asked about how things were going for Mrs. Ramirez and her family in their community. In so doing, Tobias explained his dual roles of responding to the law violation by statute and helping families address issues of concern to them.

Many social workers practice in settings, such as schools, where they perform dual roles, protecting both the community at large and vulnerable individuals, in addition to playing other supportive roles (Trotter, 2006). No matter where they are employed, social workers are influenced by the social work value of self-determination for their clients. For this reason, in addition to exploring school attendance issues with Mrs. Ramirez and her children, Tobias addressed Mrs. Ramirez's other concerns.

Mrs. Ramirez acknowledged that her children's school attendance had been sporadic. She attributed this to their illnesses, their feeling uncomfortable and unwelcome in the school, and her own health difficulties that inhibited her in getting the children ready for school.

Tobias asked Mrs. Ramirez if she would like to receive assistance in problem solving, both about how to get the children to school and how to help them to have a better educational experience there. In addition, while health issues were not served directly by his child welfare agency, Tobias offered to explore linkages with the medical field to address Mrs. Ramirez's health and depression concerns.

Toolkit (NASW, 2006, p. 4), "the plight of refugees and immigrants must be considered on the basis of human values and needs rather than on the basis of an ideological struggle related to foreign policy." The contrast between these two positions suggests that social workers grapple with issues of social justice in their everyday practice. As a social worker, Tobias could not personally resolve the uncertain situation of undocumented immigrants. However, he could work with Mrs. Ramirez and local health institutions to explore possible solutions. Social workers are not the only helping professionals who provide direct services to clients in need. We have a special interest, however, in helping empower members of oppressed groups (Parsons, 2002).

Social workers work in quite diverse settings—governmental agencies, schools, health care centers, family and child welfare agencies, mental health centers, business and industry, correctional settings, and private practices. Social workers work with people of all ages, races, ethnic groups, socioeconomic levels, religions, sexual orientations, and abilities. Social workers themselves variously describe their work as rewarding, frustrating, satisfying, discouraging, stressful, and, most of all, challenging.

In the case example, Mrs. Ramirez did not seek assistance. Instead, she was *referred* by school staff because of her children's poor class attendance, although she acknowledged problems in getting the children to school, as well as her health and depression concerns. Those who *apply* for services are most clearly *voluntary clients*. Many potential clients, including Mrs. Ramirez become more voluntary if their own concerns are explicitly addressed. Social workers practice with clients whose level of voluntarism ranges from *applicants* who seek a service to *legally mandated clients* who receive services under the threat of a court order. Many potential clients fall between these two extremes, as they are neither legally coerced nor seeking a service (Trotter, 2006). These potential clients who experience non legal pressures from family members, teachers, and referral sources are known as *nonvoluntary clients* (Rooney, R.H. 2009).

With each type of client (voluntary, legally mandated, and nonvoluntary), social work assessments include three facets:

EP 2.1.7 & 2.1.10e

1. Exploration of multiple concerns expressed by potential clients
2. Circumstances that might involve legally mandated intervention or concerns about health or safety
3. Other potential problems that emerge from the assessment

Such assessments also include strengths and potential resources. For example, Mrs. Ramirez's potential strengths and resources include her determination that her children have a better life than their parents and other community and spiritual support systems, both locally and in Mexico. Those potential resources must be assessed in the context of challenges, both internal and external, such as the lack of a health care safety net of undocumented immigrants and Mrs. Ramirez's own medical and psychological concerns.

The Mission of Social Work

The perspectives taken by social workers in their professional roles will influence how Mrs. Ramirez's concerns are conceptualized and addressed. According to the NASW, "the primary mission of the social work profession is to enhance human well-being and help meet the basic human needs of all people with particular attention to the needs and empowerment of people who are vulnerable, oppressed, and living in poverty" (NASW, 2008a). The International Federation of Social Workers defines the purpose of social work as including the promotion of social change and the empowerment and liberation of people to enhance well-being (IFSW, 2000, p. 1). Comparisons of the mission of social work in the United States to the international definition note the shared focus on marginalized peoples and empowerment, but add an emphasis on global and cultural sensitivity (Bidgood, Holosko, & Taylor, 2003).

In this book, we will delineate the core elements that lie at the heart of social work wherever it is practiced. These core elements can be classified into two dimensions: purposes of the profession and core competencies, where core competencies include characteristic knowledge, values, and practice behaviors (CSWE, 2008, p. 1). Chapter 1 presents the purposes of social work and the first nine core competencies. The tenth competency, which is to "engage, assess, intervene, and evaluate with individuals, families, groups, organizations, and communities" (EPAS, 2.1.10) will be reviewed in Chapter 3 and will become the foundation of the remaining chapters.

Purposes of Social Work

Social work practitioners help clients move toward specific objectives. The means of accomplishing those objectives, however, varies based on the unique circumstances of each client. Even so, all social workers share common goals that constitute the purpose and objectives of the profession. These goals unify the profession and help members avoid developing narrow perspectives that are limited to particular practice settings. To best serve their clients, social workers must be willing to assume responsibilities and engage in actions that expand upon the functions of specific social agencies and their designated individual roles as staff members. For example, the child welfare social worker who met with Mrs. Ramirez assessed her issues and concerns and went beyond the child protection mission of the child welfare setting.

EP 2.1.5

According to CSWE, the purpose of the social work profession is to "promote human and community well-being." Furthermore, that purpose "is actualized through its quest for social and economic justice, the prevention of conditions that limit human rights, the elimination of poverty, and the enhancement of the quality of life for all persons" (CSWE, 2008, p. 1). The pursuit of social and economic justice is central to social work's purpose. Social justice refers to the creation of social institutions that support the welfare of individuals and groups (Center for Economic and Social Justice, www.cesj.org/thirdway/economicjustice-defined.htm). Economic justice, then, refers to those aspects of social justice that relate to economic well-being, such as a livable wage, pay equity, job discrimination, and social security.

In 2007, the columnist George Will and a group of conservative scholars charged that the social work Code of Ethics, as well as the authors of the previous edition of this book, prescribed political orthodoxy in violation of freedom of speech and in opposition to critical thinking (Will, 2007; NAS, 2007). While support for social and economic justice as national priorities ebbs and flows in the political landscape of the United States, the social work profession supports those goals at all times as part of our core mission. It is not relevant to the profession whether the political majority in such times label themselves as liberal, conservative, green, independent, or otherwise. Social workers ally with those political groups that benefit the oppressed groups who form their core constituencies. Following this purpose, social workers seek to promote social and economic justice for both Americans and immigrants with or without documentation. The prevention of conditions that limit human rights and quality of life principle guides Tobias to take seriously the allegation that Mrs. Ramirez and her family have not been made to feel welcome at the school. Indeed, with national priorities of raising testing scores for reading and writing, attention to the needs of those who speak English as a second language may be in conflict with the goal of increasing test scores.

The purposes outlined also suggest that Tobias might assist Mrs. Ramirez and her family in a variety of ways to meet their needs. Those ways include the creation of policies to find solutions to the health needs of immigrants without documents. Social workers perform preventive, restorative, and remedial functions in pursuit of this purpose.

- *Prevention* involves the timely provision of services to vulnerable persons, promoting social functioning before problems develop. It includes programs and activities such as family planning, well-baby clinics, parent education, premarital and pre-retirement counseling, and marital enrichment programs.
- *Restoration* seeks to restore functioning that has been impaired by physical or mental difficulties. Included in this group of clients are persons with varying degrees of paralysis caused by severe spinal injury, individuals afflicted with chronic mental illness, persons with developmental disabilities, persons with deficient educational backgrounds, and individuals with many other types of disability.
- *Remediation* entails the elimination or amelioration of existing social problems. Many potential clients in this category are similar to Mrs. Ramirez in that they are referred by others such as the school system, family members, neighbors, and doctors who have perceived a need.

The Educational Policy and Accreditation Standards (EPAS) affirms the commitment of social programs to the core values of the profession: service, social justice, dignity and worth of the person, importance of human relationships, integrity, competence, human rights, and scientific inquiry (NASW, 2008A; CSWE, 2008). The purpose of promoting human and community well-being is "guided by a person and environment construct, a global perspective, respect for human diversity, and knowledge based on scientific inquiry" (CSWE, 2008, p. 1). "Guided by a person and environment construct" suggests that social workers always examine individual behavior in its context, reflecting on how that behavior is both a response to and, in turn, influences the individual's environment. Adopting a global perspective suggests that the profession look beyond national borders in assessing needs. A "global perspective" also suggests that Tobias and his agency be aware of the significance of Mrs. Ramirez's migration from Mexico as part of the context of her current circumstances related to school attendance and health care.

Social Work Values

EP 2.1.2b

All professions have value preferences that give purpose and direction to their practitioners. Indeed, the purpose and objectives of social work and other professions come from their respective value systems. Professional values, however, are not separate from societal values. Rather, professions espouse selected societal values. Society, in turn, sanctions the activities of professions through supportive legislation, funding, delegation of responsibility for certain societal functions, and mechanisms for ensuring that those functions are adequately discharged. Because a profession is linked to certain societal values, it tends to serve as society's conscience with respect to those particular values.

Values represent strongly held beliefs about how the world should be, about how people should normally behave, and about what the preferred conditions of life are. Broad societal values in the United States are reflected in the Declaration of Independence, the Constitution, and the laws of the land, which declare and ensure certain rights of the people. In addition, societal values are reflected in governmental entities and programs designed to safeguard the rights of people and to promote the common good. Interpretations of values and rights, however, are not always uniform. Consider, for example, the heated national debates over the right of women to have abortions; the controversy over the rights of gays, lesbians, and bisexuals to enjoy the benefits of marriage; and conflicts between advocates of gun control and those espousing individual rights.

The values of the social work profession also reflect strongly held beliefs about the rights of people to free choice and opportunity. They recognize the preferred conditions of life that enhance people's welfare, ways that members of the profession should view and treat people, preferred goals for people, and ways in which those goals should be reached. We next consider five values and purposes that guide social work education. These five values are italicized, and the content that follows each is our commentary.

1. *Social workers' professional relationships are built on regard for individual worth and dignity, and are advanced by mutual participation, acceptance, confidentiality, honesty, and responsible handling of conflict* (CSWE, 2008). This value is also reflected in several parts of the Code of Ethics. The first value of the code is simple: "Social workers' primary goal is to serve" (NASW, 2008a). That is, service to others is elevated above self-interest and social workers should use their knowledge, values, and skills to help people in need and to address social problems. The second value states that they serve others in a fashion such that "social workers respect the inherent dignity and worth of the person." Every person is unique and has inherent worth; therefore, social workers' interactions with people as they pursue and utilize resources should enhance their dignity and individuality, enlarge their competence, and increase their problem-solving and coping abilities.

    People who receive social work services are often overwhelmed by their difficult circumstances and have exhausted their coping resources. Many feel stressed by a multitude of problems. In addition to helping clients reduce their stress level, practitioners aid clients in many other ways: They help them view their difficulties from a fresh perspective, consider various remedial alternatives, foster awareness of strengths, mobilize both active and latent coping resources, enhance self-awareness, and teach problem-solving strategies and interpersonal skills.

    Social workers perform these functions while recognizing "the central importance of human relationships" (NASW, 2008a). This principle suggests that social workers engage clients as partners in purposeful efforts to promote, restore, maintain, and enhance the clients' well-being. This value is reflected in yet another Code of Ethics principle: "Social workers behave in a trustworthy manner" (p. 6). This principle suggests that social workers practice consistently with the profession's mission, values, and ethical standards, and that they promote ethical practices in the organizations with which they are affiliated (p. 6).

2. *Social workers respect the individual's right to make independent decisions and to participate actively in the helping process.* People have a right to freedom as long as they do not infringe on the rights of others. Therefore, transactions with people who are seeking and utilizing resources should enhance their independence and self-determination. Too often in the past, social workers and other helping professionals have focused on "deficit, disease, and dysfunction" (Cowger, 1992). The attention currently devoted to empowerment and strengths behooves social workers to assist clients in increasing their personal potential and political power such that clients can improve their life situation (Finn & Jacobson, 2003; Parsons, 2002; Saleebey, 1997). Consistent with this value, this book incorporates an empowerment and strength-oriented perspective for working with clients. Chapter 13

focuses on skills designed to enhance empowerments and enhance their capacity for independent action.

3. *Social workers are committed to assisting client systems to obtain needed resources.* People should have access to the resources they need to meet life's challenges and difficulties as well as access to opportunities to realize their potential throughout their lives. Our commitment to client self-determination and empowerment is hollow if clients lack access to the resources necessary to achieve their goals (Hartman, 1993). Because people such as Mrs. Ramirez from the case example often know little about available resources, social workers must act as brokers by referring people to resource systems such as public legal services, health care agencies, child welfare divisions, mental health centers, centers for elderly persons, and family counseling agencies. Some individual clients or families may require goods and services from many different providers and may lack the language facility, physical or mental capacity, experience, or skills needed to avail themselves of essential goods and services. Practitioners then may assume the role of case manager; that is, they may not only provide direct services but also assume responsibility for linking the client to diverse resources and ensuring that the client receives needed services in a timely fashion.

Clients sometimes need resource systems that are not available. In these cases, practitioners must act as program developers by creating and organizing new resource systems. Examples of such efforts include the following: working with citizens and public officials to arrange transportation to health care agencies for the elderly, persons with disabilities, and indigent people; developing neighborhood organizations to campaign for better educational and recreational programs; organizing tenants to assert their rights to landlords and housing authorities for improved housing and sanitation; and organizing support groups, skill development groups, and self-help groups to assist people in coping with difficult problems of living.

Social workers also frequently pursue this goal by facilitating access to resources. They perform the role of facilitator or enabler in carrying out the following functions: enhancing communication among family members; coordinating efforts of teachers, school counselors, and social workers in assisting troubled students; helping groups provide maximal support to their members; opening channels of communication between coworkers; including patients or inmates in the governance of institutions; facilitating teamwork among members of different disciplines in hospitals and mental health centers; and providing for consumer input into agency policy-making boards.

4. *Social workers strive to make social institutions more humane and responsive to human needs.* Although direct practitioners work primarily in providing direct service, they also have a responsibility to work toward improving clients' quality of life by promoting policies and legislation that enhance physical and social environments. The problems of individuals, families, groups, and neighborhoods can often be prevented (or at least ameliorated) by implementing laws and policies that prohibit contamination of the physical environment and enrich both physical and social environments. Therefore, direct social workers should not limit themselves to remedial activities, but rather should seek out environmental causes of problems and sponsor or support efforts aimed at improving their clients' environments.

Social workers also demonstrate this value when they assume the role of expediter or troubleshooter by scrutinizing the policies and procedures of their own and other organizations to determine whether their clients have ready access to resources and whether services are delivered in ways that enhance their clients' dignity. Complex application procedures, needless delays in providing resources and services, discriminatory policies, inaccessible agency sites, inconvenient service delivery hours, dehumanizing procedures or staff behaviors, and other factors may deter clients from utilizing resources or subject them to demeaning experiences.

Systematically obtaining input from consumers is one method of monitoring an organization's responsiveness to clients. Advocacy actions in conjunction with and on behalf of clients are sometimes required to secure the services and resources to which clients are entitled. Social workers may support this value by performing the roles of coordinator, mediator, or disseminator of information. For example, as a case manager, a social worker may coordinate the medical, educational, mental health, and rehabilitative services provided to a given family by multiple resource systems. A mediator may be required to resolve conflicts between agencies, minority and majority groups, and neighborhood groups. The social worker may disseminate information regarding legislation or new funding sources that could potentially affect the relationships between public and private agencies by strengthening interactions between these resource systems.

Social workers must also collaborate with key organizations to facilitate mutual awareness of changes in policies and procedures that affect ongoing relationships and the availability of resources.

EP 2.1.4

5. *Social workers demonstrate respect for and acceptance of the unique characteristics of diverse populations.* Social workers perform their services with populations that are characterized by great diversity, including the intersection of dimensions such as "age, class, culture, disability, ethnicity, gender, gender identity and expression, immigration status, political ideology, race, religion, sex and sexual orientation, religion, physical or mental ability, age, and national origin" (CSWE, 2008, p. 5). Similarly, NASW's Code of Ethics requires social workers to understand cultures, recognize strengths in cultures, have a knowledge base of their clients' cultures, and deliver services that are sensitive to those cultures (NASW, 2008a). This value suggests that social workers must be informed about and respectful of differences. They must educate themselves over time as a part of lifelong learning—unfortunately, there is no "how-to" manual that will guide the practitioner in understanding all aspects of diversity. To demonstrate this value, the practitioner must continually update his or her knowledge about the strengths and resources associated with individuals from diverse groups to increase the sensitivity and effectiveness of the services provided to those clients.

An increasing number of social workers are themselves members of these diverse populations. They face the challenge of working effectively with both clients and agency staff from the majority culture as well as persons from their own groups.

Values and Ethics

EP 2.1.2a

Turning the five values just described into reality should be the mutual responsibility of individual citizens and of society. Society should foster conditions and provide opportunities for citizens to participate in policy-making processes. Citizens, in turn, should fulfill their responsibilities to society by actively participating in those processes.

Considered individually, these five values and the profession's mission are not unique to social work. Their unique combination, however, differentiates social work from other professions. Considered in their entirety, these ingredients make it clear that social work's identity derives from its connection with the institution of social welfare. According to Gilbert (1977), social welfare represents a special helping mechanism devised to aid those who suffer from the variety of ills found in industrial society: "Whenever other major institutions, be they familial, religious, economic, or educational in nature, fall short in their helping and resource providing functions, social welfare spans the gap" (p. 402).

These five values represent the prized ideals of the profession and, as such, are stated at high levels of abstraction. As Siporin (1975) and Levy (1973) have noted, however, different levels of professional values exist. At an intermediate level, values pertain to various segments of society—for example, characteristics of a strong community. At a third level, values are more operational, referring to preferred behaviors.

For example, the ideal social work practitioner is a warm, caring, open, and responsible person who safeguards the confidentiality of information disclosed by clients. Because you, the reader, have chosen to enter the field of social work, most of your personal values probably coincide with the cardinal values espoused by the majority of social work practitioners. By contrast, at the intermediate and third levels of values, your views may not always be in harmony with the specific value positions taken by the majority of social workers.

Self-determination refers to the right of people to exercise freedom of choice when making decisions. Issues such as those described may pose value dilemmas for individual practitioners because of conflicts between personal and professional values. In addition, conflicts between two professional values or principles are common. Public positions taken by the profession that emanate from its values also sometimes stand in opposition to the attitudes of a large segment of society. Recently, professional support for universal health coverage coincided with efforts to achieve some measure of this during the Obama administration.

We suggest that social workers should be sufficiently flexible to listen to many differing value positions on most moral and political issues. Different value positions do not necessarily reflect divergence among social workers on the five core values of the social work profession. Rather, they reflect the existence of many means of achieving given ends. Indeed, rigid assumptions about preferred means to ends often crumble when put to the test of hard experience. Consistent with our preference for flexibility, we reaffirm our commitment to the value that social workers, whatever their beliefs, should assert them in a forum of professional organizations such as NASW. We maintain further that social workers should accord colleagues who differ on certain value positions the same respect, dignity, and right to self-determination that would be accorded clients. Differences on issues may be frankly expressed. Those issues can be clarified and cohesiveness among professionals can be fostered by debate conducted in a climate of openness and mutual respect.

Conflicts between personal and/or professional values and the personal values of a client or group sometimes arise. Not infrequently, students (and even seasoned social workers) experience conflicts over value laden, problematic situations such as incest, infidelity, rape, child neglect or abuse, spousal abuse, and criminal behavior. Because direct practitioners encounter these and other problems typically viewed by the public as appalling, and because personal values inevitably shape the social worker's attitudes, perceptions, feelings, and responses to clients, it is vital that you remain flexible and nonjudgmental in your work. It is equally vital that you be aware of your own values, recognize how they fit with the profession's values, and assess how they may affect clients whose values differ from your own or whose behavior offends you.

Social Work's Code of Ethics

EP 2.1.2b

An essential attribute of legitimate professions is a code of ethics consisting of principles that define expectations of each profession's members. A code of ethics specifies rules of conduct to which members must adhere so as to remain in good standing within a professional organization. It thus defines expected responsibilities and behaviors as well as prescribed behaviors. Central to the purpose of a code of ethics is its function as a formalized expression of accountability of (1) the profession to the society that gives it sanction, (2) constituent practitioners to consumers who utilize their services, and (3) practitioners to their profession. By promoting accountability, a code of ethics serves additional vital purposes, including the following:

1. It safeguards the reputation of a professional by providing explicit criteria that can be employed to regulate the behavior of members.
2. It furthers competent and responsible practice by its members.
3. It protects the public from exploitation by unscrupulous or incompetent practitioners.

Most states now have licensing boards that certify social workers for practice and review allegations of unethical conduct (Bibus & Boutte Queen, 2011; Land, 1988; DeAngelis, 2000). Similarly, local and state chapters of the NASW establish professional review committees to investigate alleged violations of the profession's Code of Ethics, and national committees provide consultation to local committees and consider appeals of decisions made by local chapters. We have blended the values in the code of ethics in our presentation of the five values stated by CSWE. These values are prescribed to underlie the social work curriculum and support the profession's commitment to respect for all people and quest for social and economic justice (CSWE, 2008, p. 2).

EPAS Competencies

The Education Policy and Accreditation standards of CSWE are based on a competency-based education format that prescribes attention to outcome performance (CSWE, 2008, p. 2). These competencies are based on knowledge, values, and skills with emphasis on integrating into practice with individuals, families, groups, and communities. We will state these competencies in terms of what a competent social work graduate should be able to do when they have completed their courses of study. We hope that you do not feel apprehensive about whether you are capable of performing these competencies now. It will be your task and that of your educational program to prepare you to reach these competencies by the time that you graduate. While each of these competencies will be covered in greater detail in later chapters, the main points of each competency are summarized in the following.

EPAS Competency 2.1.1

specifies that students identify themselves as professional social workers and conduct themselves accordingly. In order to meet this competency, social workers should be knowledgeable about the profession's history and commit to the enhancement of the profession and their own professional conduct and growth. A social worker meeting this competency will ensure client access to services; engage in self-reflection, self-monitoring, and correction; attend to professional roles and boundaries; demonstrate professional demeanor in behavior, appearance, and communication; engage in career-long learning; and use supervision and consultation (CSWE, 2008, p. 3).

EPAS Competency 2.1.2

This competency requires you to apply social work ethical principles to guide your professional practice. You should be knowledgeable about the profession's value base, ethical standards, and relevant laws. In meeting this competency, social workers recognize and manage their personal values such that professional values guide practice. For example, if Tobias had any personal values that might impede his work with Mrs. Ramirez and her children, he would take care that his professional values supersede those personal values. Social workers also make ethical decisions in applying standards such as the NASW Code of Ethics, tolerate ambiguity in resolving ethical conflicts, and apply strategies of ethical reasoning to arrive at principled decisions (CSWE, 2008, p. 4).

EPAS Competency 2.1.3

This competency requires you to apply critical thinking to inform and communicate professional judgments. Despite George Will and the National Association of Scholars' (2007) allegation that the social work profession emphasizes political orthodoxy over critical thinking, in fact this competency specifically requires us to use critical thinking in the professional setting. In carrying out this competency, you demonstrate that you are knowledgeable about the principles of logic, scientific inquiry, and discernment. Critical thinking requires the synthesis of relevant information augmented by creativity and curiosity. Applying this competency, social workers distinguish, appraise, and integrate multiple sources of information, including the use of research-based knowledge and empirical wisdom, analysis of assessment models, and creativity to synthesize meanings (CSWE, 2008, p. 4). Following this competency, Tobias would consult research-based knowledge and integrate it with empirical wisdom to guide his practice. Pursuit of this competency requires the social worker to consult multiple sources of information in making decisions.

EPAS Competency 2.1.4

Social workers are guided in this competency to recognize and engage diversity in social work practice. Specifically, this means recognizing the relation between cultural structures and values in alienating, creating, or enhancing privilege and power (EPAS, 2.1.4a). This suggests that social work practitioners are responsible for assessing the role of privilege in how they perform their roles. They are expected to gain self-awareness to eliminate the influence of personal biases and values in work with diverse groups (EPAS 2.1.4b). While an admirable aspiration, we take the position that eliminating personal biases and values is probably not a feasible goal. Rather, social workers might better be expected to be aware of personal biases and reduce their negative impact on work with clients. For example, early on in working with Mrs. Ramirez, Tobias wrote in his case notes that he suspected that, in part, her children were not attending school because she and other undocumented immigrants did not value education as much as their fellow students and families in their new community in the United States. In fact, there is evidence to suggest that Mexican immigrants value education highly (Valencia and Black, 2002). This statement by Tobias might be seen as a belief, a hypothesis, or a possible bias that could have profound implications for his work with Mrs. Ramirez. If he acted on his belief that her children were not attending primarily because she and other Mexican immigrants were not motivated about education, he might not explore other community- or school-based barriers to their attendance, such as their perception that the children were not welcome. Holding members of oppressed groups personally responsible for all aspects of their condition is an unfortunate value predicated on the Horatio Alger myth that all successful people lifted themselves up by their own bootstraps. This competency requires sensitivity to structures that may act to oppress (p. 5).

Social workers are expected to "recognize and communicate their understanding of the importance of difference in shaping life experience" (EPAS 2.1.4c). Finally, social workers are expected to "view themselves as learners and engage those with whom they work as informants" (EPAS 2.1.4d.).

We also consider the importance of our commitment to diversity as we consider the Eurocentric assumptions that undergird many of our practice models (Sue & Sue, 2003). We take the position that some factors are universal. For example, pathology occurs across cultures although the forms may vary (Sue & Sue, 2003). On the other hand, much of social work practice relates to specific cultural manifestations of both difficulties and solutions.

We do not believe that cultural competence is attained as a satisfactory level of knowledge and skill that does not require continual upgrading over the course of your career. Just as your clinical or direct practice skills should continue to grow, so should your level of cultural competence. To do this, you will need to engage in continual education about the culture and experiences of client groups with whom you work. That also means that you must approach each client as a person whose experience is in many ways unique. That is, clients bear unique combinations of personality characteristics, family dynamics, experiences with acculturation and assimilation. You need to learn as much as you can about the cultural frames that are significant for the person before you can be open to learning the uniqueness of that person (Dean, 2001; Johnson and Munch, 2009). Hence, when we report some cultural characteristics as commonly represented in some groups, it is shared in the sense of background information that must be assessed with the person before you. For example, while some Asian American clients may expect the social worker to take an expert role and advise them, many will not according to their own individual experiences and personalities (Fong, 2007). Further, Asian American as a category can subsume great variation including Pacific Islanders and mainland Asians whose cultural heritages are very distinct from each other.

> **VIDEO CASE EXAMPLE**
>
> In the interview "Working with Yanping," Kim Strom-Gottfried interviews an exchange student from the Republic of China. She cannot assume that there are shared assumptions about help seeking, so Kim carefully explores expectations and explains what she can offer. In this way, she guards against applying stereotypic assumptions about how the client views her concerns and what is possible in seeking help. They explore possibilities including goals and ways of working as well as whether a referral to a social worker more familiar with Yan Ping's culture could be helpful.

EPAS Competency 2.1.5

This competency requires you to advance human rights and social justice and asserts that each person in society has basic human rights such as freedom, safety, privacy, an adequate standard of living, health care, and education (CSWE, 2008, p. 5). This competency is also reflected in the second value in the social work Code of Ethics: "Social workers challenge social injustice" (NASW, 2008a). This value encourages social workers to pursue social change on behalf of vulnerable or oppressed people who are subject to poverty, discrimination, and other forms of injustice. The focus of efforts geared toward populations at risk should increase the power of these individuals to influence their own lives. While the profession supports critical thinking about the means to achieve these goals, social work education is fully committed to human rights and social justice. If resources and opportunities are to be available to all members of society, then laws, governmental policies, and social programs must assure equal access of citizens to those resources and opportunities. Social workers promote social justice by advocating for clients who have been denied services, resources, or goods to which they are entitled. They also work to develop new resources to meet emerging needs.

To meet this competency, you should be aware of the global implications of oppression; be knowledgeable about theories of justice and strategies to promote human and civil rights; and strive to incorporate social justice practices into organizations, institutions, and society. You should also understand the mechanisms of oppression and discrimination in society and advocate for and engage in practices that advance human rights and social and economic justice. George Will and the National Association of Scholars reported that there were instances in which social work students were required by instructors to advocate for groups in conflict with their own religious beliefs (Will, 2007; NAS, 2007). For example, some students were required to advocate for gay and lesbian people to be able to adopt children. In many states, competency to adopt is not based on sexual orientation. There is room for debate whether it is ethical to require students to advocate for specific oppressed groups; however, this competency clearly specifies that advocating for human rights and social and economic justice is a professional expectation.

Following this competency, Tobias would attempt to understand the issue of children's school attendance in a broader framework of understanding why Mrs. Ramirez and her children had moved to his locality. Awareness of the economic incentive of seeking a better income as an influence on immigration would be appropriate. For example, in addition to working with Mrs. Ramirez alone, Tobias or other social workers might approach the circumstance of undocumented immigrants in their community from the standpoint of community organization and advocacy, working on the interests of the group rather than solely on those of the individual. While this book focuses primarily on direct social work intervention, other courses in your program and other texts will provide additional sources of information for pursuit of this goal.

EPAS Competency 2.1.6

This competency requires you to engage in research-informed practice and practice-informed research. To fulfill this competency, you use your practice experience to inform research, employ evidence-based interventions, evaluate your own practice, and use research findings to improve practice, policy, and social service delivery (p. 5). You will be knowledgeable about quantitative and qualitative research and understand scientific and ethical approaches to building knowledge. As a social worker, you will use your practice experience to inform scientific inquiry and use research evidence to inform practice (p. 5).

Some proponents suggest that employing evidence-based intervention entails being able to explain an evidence-based approach to clients, creating a useful, realistic evaluation format, refining such intervention and evaluation formats based on knowledge of the client, understanding the relevant elements of evidence-based techniques, incorporating evidence from use of the intervention, and being critical consumers of evidence in practice situations (Pollio, 2006, p. 224). Others suggest that knowledge of the context must also be employed in formulating such interventions, as well as considering the theoretical base in selecting interventions (Walsh, 2006; Payne, 2005; Adams, Matto & Le Croy, 2009). Given the range of evidence available in different fields of practice, we agree that evidence-based practice should be a highly valued source of information in the context of planning an intervention. Following this principle, Tobias and his agency would be advised to be mindful of evidence-based interventions that assist families with the problem of low school attendance. He and his agency would become familiar with programs that promote personal relationships between school personnel and families around attendance issues (Anderson et al, 2004). They would also need to integrate that knowledge with information about the environmental context and relevant interventions. For example, assisting Mrs. Ramirez in getting the children ready for transportation to school might be one part of the intervention, as well as working with the school to construct a more welcoming environment for the children. Part of this context is Mrs. Ramirez's physical and emotional health. She may be more likely to have her children ready for school if she is linked to health care providers who can assist her with her need for surgery and her depression.

EPAS Competency 2.1.7

This competency requires that you apply knowledge of human behavior and the social environment. To meet this competency, you should be knowledgeable about human behavior across the lifespan. You should also be knowledgeable about the social systems in which people live and how those systems promote or hinder people in maintaining or achieving health and well-being. You will apply theories and knowledge from the liberal arts to understand biological, social, cultural, psychological, and spiritual development (CSWE, 2008, p. 6). You will use those conceptual frameworks to guide the processes of assessment intervention and you will critique and apply that knowledge to understand the person and their environment (p. 6). In your academic program, you are likely to encounter other course work related to human behavior and the social environment to augment the knowledge available from this book.

EPAS Competency 2.1.8

This competency requires that you engage in policy practice to advance social and economic well-being and to deliver effective social work services (CSWE, 2008, p. 6). One of the distinguishing features of social work as a helping profession is the understanding that all direct practice occurs in a policy context. Hence, social workers need to know about the history of and current structures for policies and services. In pursuit of this competency, social workers analyze, formulate, and advocate for policies that advance the social well-being of clients (p. 6). They also collaborate with colleagues and clients for effective policy action. While some social workers provide direct services to clients, others act indirectly to influence the environments supporting clients, thereby developing and maintaining the social infrastructure that assists clients in meeting their needs. Many social work programs will contain one or more required courses in policy and practice as well as an advanced practice curriculum in this area. Tobias' interaction with Mrs. Ramirez must be considered in the context of policies related to school attendance and policies related to health care access.

EPAS Competency 2.1.9

This competency requires that you respond to and shape an ever-changing professional context. As described previously, social work as a helping profession is characterized by its sensitivity not only to the policy context of practice but also a broader professional context related to organizations, communities, and society. In pursuit of this competency, you should be informed, resourceful, and proactive in responding to the evolving organizations, community, and societal context at all levels of practice. You will discover, appraise, and attend to changing locales, populations, scientific and technological developments, and emerging societal trends in order to provide relevant services. Social workers also participate in providing leadership to promote sustainable changes in service delivery and practice to improve the quality of social services (CSWE, 2008, p. 6). Tobias would be acting in fulfillment of this competency if he had or gained knowledge of the circumstances of Hispanic speaking children in the elementary school that Mrs. Ramirez's children attended. As noted, pressures to increase reading scores for children may indirectly create pressure on children for whom English is a second language.

EPAS 2.1.10

This competency focuses on engaging with, assessing, intervening with, and evaluating individuals, families, groups, organizations, and communities (CSWE, 2008, p. 7). These competencies get at the heart of social work intervention and reflect the knowledge and skills that this book is designed to address.

EPAS Competency 2.1.10a

This competency focuses on engagement. In order to meet this competency, social workers prepare for action with individuals, families, groups, organizations and communities both substantively and emotionally (CSWE, 2008, p. 7). They do this by using empathy and other interpersonal skills and developing a mutually agreed-upon focus of work and identifying desired outcomes (p. 7). Utilizing these skills, Tobias would attempt to personally engage Mrs. Ramirez and her family. We recognize that the success of such engagement efforts depends in part on sensitivity to cultural norms and hence also include attention to Competency 2.1.3 on diversity.

EPAS Competency 2.1.10b

This competency focuses on assessment and refers to knowledge and skills required to collect, organize, and interpret client data. In this context, social workers must have skills in assessing both a client system's strengths and limitations. They must be able to develop mutually agreed-upon intervention goals and objectives and be able to select appropriate intervention strategies (CSWE, 2008, p. 7).

EPAS Competency 2.1.10c

This competency refers to knowledge and skills associated with intervention. Included here are knowledge and skills associated with prevention strategies designed to enhance client capacities; assist clients in resolving problems; negotiate, mediate, and advocate for client systems; and facilitate transitions and endings.

EPAS Competency 2.1.10d

This competency requires knowledge and skills in evaluation. To meet this competency, social workers must be able to critically analyze, monitor, and evaluate interventions (CSWE, 2008, p. 7). Following this competency, Tobias would establish goals with Mrs. Ramirez and regularly assess progress with her.

EPAS Competency B 2.2

This competency refers to knowledge and skills related to generalist practice. A generalist practitioner is grounded in the liberal arts and the personal and environmental constructs required to promote human and social well-being (CSWE, 2008, p. 8). The generalist practitioner uses a range of prevention and intervention methods to work with individuals, families, groups, organizations, and communities. This competency refers to the fact that many social work practitioners operate in agencies that provide varied services at many levels. Generalist practitioners identify with the social work profession and apply ethical principles and critical thinking in practice (p. 8). They incorporate diversity into their practice and are expected to advocate for human rights and social justice. They do so while building upon the strengths and resiliency of human beings. Finally, they engage in research-informed practice and are proactive in responding to an ever-changing professional context. Social work educations incorporate two practice degrees, BSW and MSW. This competency refers to what is expected of BSW practitioners and incorporates the first year of an MSW curriculum. As Tobias was a BSW practitioner, he was expected to use the range of skills and knowledge required of generalist practice.

EPAS Competency M 2.2

This competency refers to knowledge and skills required for advanced practice. Advanced practitioners are expected to be able to assess, intervene, and evaluate in order to promote human and social well-being in ways that are differentiated, discriminating, and self-critical (CSWE, 2008, p. 8). Advanced practitioners are expected to synthesize and apply a broad range of interdisciplinary and multi-disciplinary knowledge and skills. Such practitioners are expected to refine and advance the quality of social work practice and the larger social work profession. They incorporate the core competencies augmented by knowledge and skills specific to a specialized concentration. (CSWE, 2008, p. 8). Advanced practice in social work means completion of a concentration as defined by their program. Such concentrations are often divided into those that specialize in some forms of micro, mezzo, and macro practice.

- *Micro-level practice.* At this level, the population served by practitioners includes a variety of client systems, including individuals, couples, and families. Practice at the micro-level is designated as direct practice because practitioners deliver services directly to clients in face-to-face contact. Direct practice, however, is by no means limited to such face-to-face contact.
- *Mezzo-level practice.* The second level is defined as "interpersonal relations that are less intimate than those associated with family life; more meaningful than among organizational and institutional representatives; [including] relationships between individuals in a self-help or therapy group, among peers at school or work or among neighbors" (Sheafor, Horejsi, & Horejsi, 1994, pp. 9–10). Mezzo events are "the interface where the individual and those most immediate and important to him/her meet" (Zastrow & Kirst-Ashman, 1990, p. 11). Mezzo intervention is hence designed to change the systems that directly affect clients, such as the family, peer group, or classroom.
- *Macro-level practice.* Still further removed from face-to-face delivery of services, macro practice involves the processes of social planning and community organization. On this level, social workers serve as professional change agents who assist community action systems composed of individuals, groups, or organizations in dealing with social problems. For example, social workers may work with citizen groups or with private, public, or governmental organizations. Activities of practitioners at this level include the following: (1) development of and work with community groups and organizations; (2) program planning and development; and (3) implementation, administration, and evaluation of programs (Meenaghan, 1987).

Effective practice requires knowledge related to all three levels of practice. Nevertheless, schools of social work often offer "concentrations" in either micro or macro practice and require less preparation in the other methods. Concentrations are often designated around an area of direct practice in particular populations or settings such as adult mental health, child welfare, family practice, group work, school social work, aging, and work with children and adolescents. Such concentrations may emphasize micro practice or incorporate mezzo and macro practice. Some schools have generalist practice curricula, which require students to achieve balanced preparation in all three levels of practice. Undergraduate programs and the first year of graduate programs typically feature generalist practice curricula, which aim to prepare students for working with all levels of client systems.

Macro concentrations often refer to practice in community organization, planning, management, and advocacy. Administration entails playing a leadership role in human service organizations that seek to effectively deliver services in accordance with the values and laws of society. It includes the processes involved in policy formulation and subsequent translation of that policy into operational goals, program design and implementation, funding and resource allocation, management of internal and interorganizational operation, personnel direction and supervision, organizational representation and public relations, community education, monitoring, evaluation, and innovation to improve organizational productivity (Sarri, 1987, pp. 29–30). Direct practitioners are necessarily involved to some degree in administrative activities. In addition, many direct practitioners who hold master's degrees become supervisors or administrators later in their professional careers. Knowledge of administration, therefore, is vital to direct practitioners at the master's degree level, and courses in administration are frequently part of the required master's degree curriculum in social work. Although many direct practitioners engage in little or no macro-level practice, those who work in rural areas where practitioners are few and specialists in social planning are not available may work in concert with concerned citizens and community leaders in planning and developing resources to prevent or combat social problems.

EPAS Competency 2.1

This competency refers to the signature pedagogy of social work: field education. Signature pedagogy refers to the forms of instruction and learning by which the social work profession socializes students to perform the role of practitioner. Different professions have varied ways by which they train professionals to connect and integrate theory and practice. That is done in social work through field education. Field education is designed to connect the theoretical and conceptual contributions of classrooms with the practice setting (CSWE, 2008, p. 8). In social work, classroom and field are considered equally important in developing competent social work practice. It is designed, supervised, coordinated and evaluated in such a way that students can demonstrate achievement of program competencies. This text and practice workbook includes many exercises that are designed to be completed in field placements.

Orienting Frameworks to Achieve Competencies

Practitioners and beginning students need orienting frameworks to ground their work in achieving the competencies just described. There is ever increasing information from the social sciences, social work, and allied disciplines that point to specific interventions for specific problem situations. Successful use of such interventions represents formidable challenges because available knowledge is often fragmented. Further, since social work often takes place in agency settings with clients whose concerns cut across psychological and environmental needs, an orienting perspective is needed to address these levels of concerns and activities. The ecological systems model is useful in providing an orienting perspective (Germain, 1979, 1981; Meyer, 1983; Pincus & Minahan, 1973; Siporin, 1980). A system is a set of orderly elements that are related to make a whole. Systems theory emphasizes the interactions between these elements (Kirst-Ashman & Hull, 2012)

Ecological Systems Model

EP 2.1.3b

Adaptations of this model, originating in biology, make a close conceptual fit with the "person-in-environment" perspective that dominated social work until the mid-1970s. Although that perspective recognized the influence of environmental factors on human functioning, internal factors had received an inordinate emphasis in assessing human problems. In addition, a perception of the environment as constraining the individual did not sufficiently acknowledge the individual's ability to affect the environment.

This heavy emphasis, which resulted from the prominence and wide acceptance of Freud's theories in the 1920s and 1930s, reached its zenith in the 1940s and 1950s. With the emergence of ego psychology, systems theory, theories of family therapy, expanded awareness of the importance of ethnocultural factors, and emphasis on ecological factors in the 1960s and 1970s, increasing importance was accorded to environmental factors and to understanding the ways in which people interact with their environments. While systems models were first created in the natural sciences and ecological theory developed from the environmental movement in biology, ecological systems theory in social work adapted concepts from both systems and ecological theories.

Two concepts of ecological theory that are especially relevant to social workers are habitat and niche. ***Habitat*** refers to the places where organisms live and, in the case of humans, consists of the physical and social settings within particular cultural contexts. When habitats are rich in the resources required for growth and development, people tend to thrive. When habitats are deficient in vital resources, physical, social, and emotional development and ongoing functioning may be adversely affected. For example, a substantial body of research indicates that supportive social networks of friends, relatives, neighbors, work and church associates, and pets mitigate the damaging effects of painful life stresses. By contrast, people with deficient social networks may respond to life stresses by becoming severely depressed, resorting to abuse of drugs or alcohol, engaging in violent behavior, or coping in other dysfunctional ways.

Niche refers to the statuses or roles occupied by members of the community. One of the tasks in the course of human maturation is to find one's niche in society, which is essential to achieving self-respect and a stable sense of identity. Being able to locate one's niche, however, presumes that opportunities congruent with human needs exist in society. That presumption may not be valid for members of society who lack equal opportunities because of race, ethnicity, gender, poverty, age, disability, sexual identity, or other factors.

An objective of social work, as noted earlier, is to promote social justice so as to expand opportunities for people to create appropriate niches for themselves. Ecological systems theory posits that individuals constantly engage in transactions with other humans and with other systems in the environment, and that these individuals and systems reciprocally influence each other.

Each system is unique, varying in its characteristics and ways of interacting (e.g., no two individuals, families, groups, or neighborhoods are the same). As a consequence, people do not merely react to environmental forces. Rather, they act on their environments, thereby shaping the responses of other people, groups, institutions, and even the physical environment. For example, people make choices about where to live, whether to upgrade or to neglect their living arrangements, and whether to initiate or support policies that combat urban decay, safeguard the quality of air and water, and provide adequate housing for the elderly who are poor.

Adequate assessments of human problems and plans of interventions, therefore, must consider how people and environmental systems influence one another. The importance of considering this reciprocal interaction when formulating assessments has been reflected in changing views of certain human problems over the past decade. Disability, for example, is now defined in psychosocial terms rather than in medical or economic terms. As Roth (1987) has clarified, "What is significant can be revealed only by the ecological framework in which the disabled person exists, by the interactions through which society engages a disability, by the attitudes others hold, and by the architecture, means of transportation, and social organization constructed by the able bodied" (p. 434). Disability is thus minimized by maximizing the goodness of fit between the needs of people with physical or mental limitations and the environmental resources that correspond to their special needs (e.g., rehabilitation programs, special physical accommodations, education, and social support systems).

It is clear from the ecological systems perspective that the satisfaction of human needs and mastery of developmental tasks require adequate resources in the environment and positive transactions between people and their environments. For example, effective learning by a student requires adequate schools, competent teachers, parental support, adequate perception and intellectual ability, motivation to learn, and positive relationships between teachers and students. Any gaps in the environmental resources, limitations of individuals who need or utilize these resources, or dysfunctional transactions between individuals and environmental systems threaten to block the fulfillment of human needs and lead to stress or impaired functioning. To reduce or remove this stress requires coping efforts aimed at gratifying the needs—that is, achieving adaptive fit between person and environment. People, however, often do not have access to adequate resources or may lack effective coping methods. Social work involves helping such people meet their needs by linking them with or developing essential resources. It could also include enhancing clients' capacities to utilize resources or cope with environmental forces.

Assessment from an ecological systems perspective obviously requires knowledge of the diverse systems involved in interactions between people and their environments:

- *Subsystems of the individual (biophysical, cognitive, emotional, behavioral, motivational).*
- *Interpersonal systems (parent–child, marital, family, kin, friends, neighbors, cultural reference groups, spiritual belief systems, and other members of social networks).*
- *Organizations, institutions, and communities.*
- *The physical environment (housing, neighborhood environment, buildings, other artificial creations, water, and weather and climate).*

A major advantage of the ecological systems model is its broad scope. Typical human problems involving health care, family relations, inadequate income, mental health difficulties, conflicts with law enforcement agencies, unemployment, educational difficulties, and so on can all be subsumed under this model, enabling the practitioner to analyze the complex variables involved in such problems.

Assessing the sources of problems and determining the foci of interventions are the first steps in applying the ecological systems model. Assessment tools have been developed which can engage clients in gathering information to assist in discovering the strengths, resources, and challenges of the systems surrounding individuals and families. For example, ecomaps can depict a family context (Hartman, 1994). A solid line connecting systems to individuals and families can depict a strong relationship, a dotted line can depict a tenuous relationship, and hatch marks can depict a stressful relationship (Cournoyer, 2011; Mattaini, 1995). The ecomap depicted in Figure 1-1 follows suggests that Marta experiences her relationship with her spiritual community as sustaining while her relationships with the school system, health care system, and work are stressful. Those relationships are influenced by her work related injury and lack of access to health care as an undocumented person, and contribute to her symptoms of depression and oversleeping. Creation of an ecomap can then form the basis of a plan for utilizing available resources such as seeking assistance from her spiritual community and others.

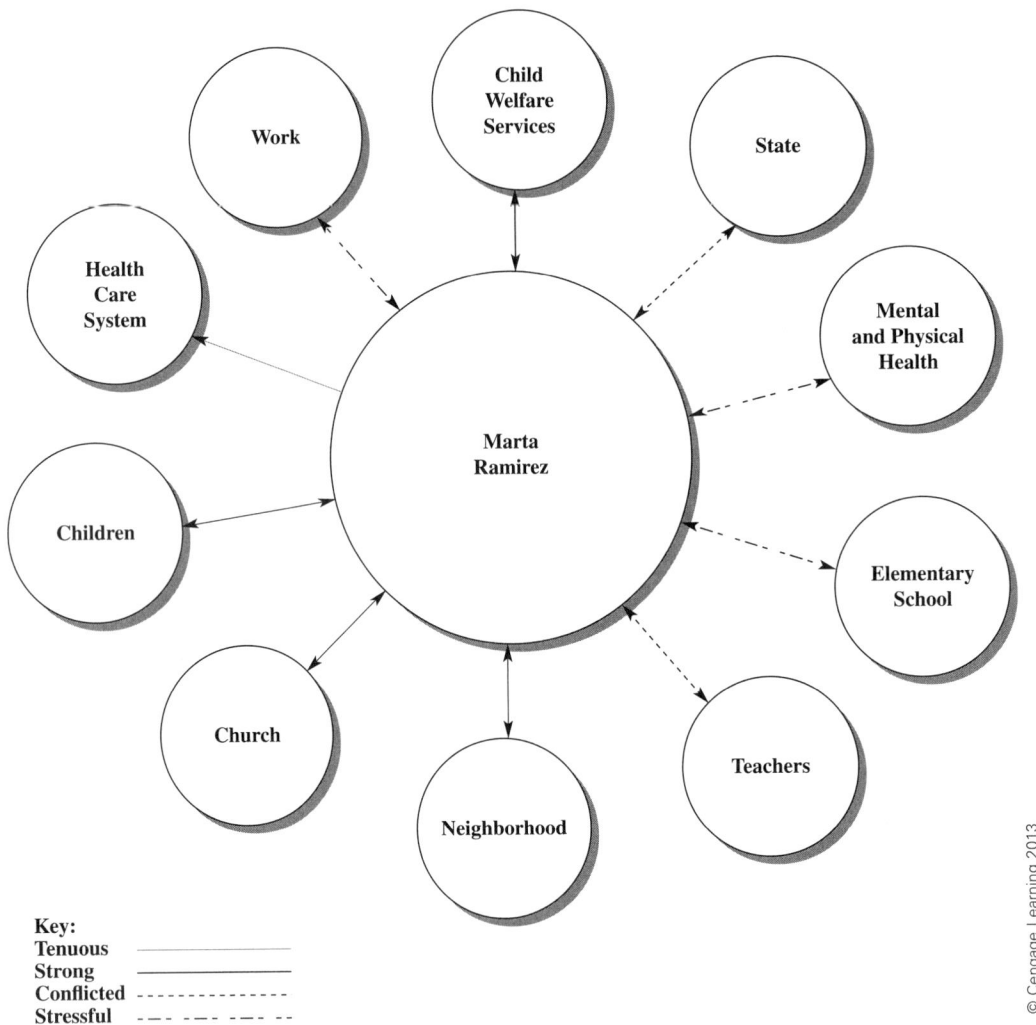

FIG-1-1 Ecomap

Pincus and Minahan adapted systems models to social work practice, suggesting that a *client system* includes those persons who are requesting a change, sanction it, are expected to benefit from it, and contract to receive it (Pincus & Minahan, 1973; Compton, Galaway, & Cournoyer, 2005). Potential clients who request a change are described as *applicants*. Many clients reach social workers not through their own choice but rather through referral from others. *Referrals* are persons who do not seek services on their own, but do so at the behest of other professionals and family members. Meanwhile, *contacted persons* are approached through an outreach effort (Compton & Galaway, 2005). Some referred and contacted individuals may not experience pressure from that contact. As noted earlier, some individuals do experience pressure and social workers should consider them to be "potential clients"

and to be aware of the route that brought them to the social worker and their response to that contact. For example, Mrs. Ramirez could be considered a potential client as she was approached by child welfare services as part of a possible educational neglect assessment.

The next step is to determine what should be done related to the pertinent systems involved in the problem situation. In this step, the practitioner surveys the broad spectrum of available practice theories and interventions. To be maximally effective, interventions must be directed to all systems that are critical in a given problem system.

The *target system* refers to the focus of change efforts. With a voluntary client, it will typically encompass the concerns that brought the individual to seek services. With nonvoluntary clients, it may include illegal or dangerous behaviors that the person does

Social Work Challenges   19

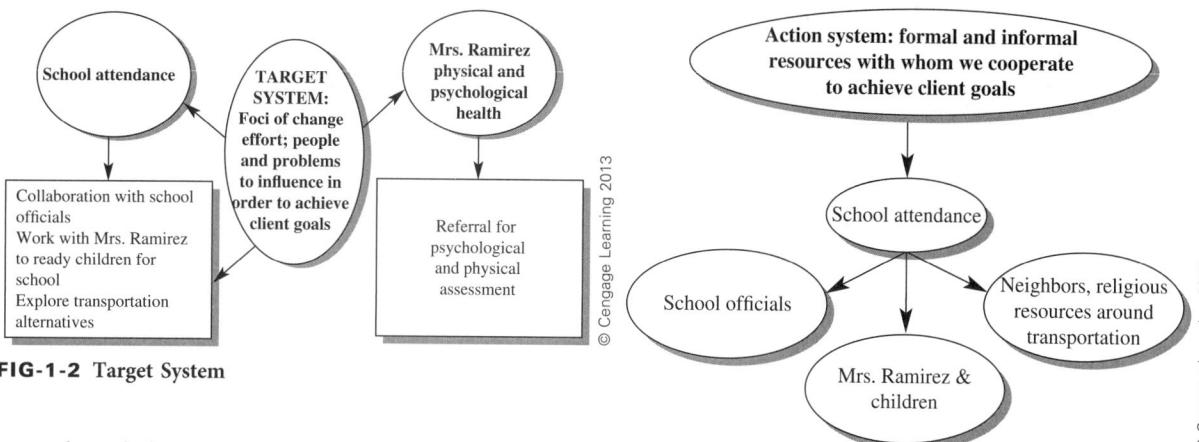

FIG-1-2 Target System

FIG-1-4 Action System

not acknowledge (see Figure 1-2). The *client system* consists of those persons who request or are expected to benefit from services. Note that this definition includes both voluntary clients (applicants) and nonvoluntary clients (see Figure 1-3).

When a client desires assistance on a personal problem, the target and client systems overlap. Frequently, however, clients request assistance with a problem outside themselves. In such instances, that problem could become the center of a target system. For example, Mrs. Ramirez acknowledges psychological and physical health concerns as well as concerns about how welcome her children feel in school. Meanwhile, Tobias must carry out a legally defined educational neglect assessment. These problem areas may merge as a contract is developed to address several concerns. It is important that target problems focus on a target concern rather than on the entire person as the target. Focusing on a person as the target system objectifies that individual and diminishes the respect for individuality to which each person is entitled. Hence, concerns with school attendance can be the target system rather than Mrs. Ramirez and her children.

The *action system* refers to those formal and informal resources and persons that the social worker needs to cooperate with to accomplish a purpose. It often includes family, friends, and other resources as well as more formal resources. For example, an action system for school attendance might include school attendance officers, teachers, relatives, neighbors, spiritual resources or transportation providers, according to the plan agreed upon by Mrs. Ramirez and Tobias (see Figure 1-4).

The *agency system* is a special subset of an action system that includes the practitioners and formal service systems involved in work on the target problems (Compton & Galaway, 2005). In this case, the agency system primarily includes the elementary school and the child welfare agency (see Figure 1-5).

Social systems also vary in the degree to which they are open and closed to new information or feedback. Closed systems have relatively rigid boundaries that prevent the input or export of information. Open systems have relatively permeable boundaries permitting a more free exchange. Families may vary from being predominantly closed to new information to being excessively open. In fact, all families and human systems exhibit a tension between trying to maintain stability

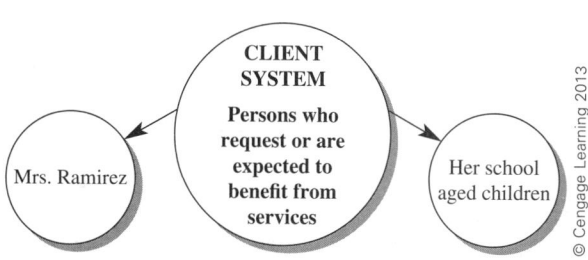

FIG-1-3 Client System

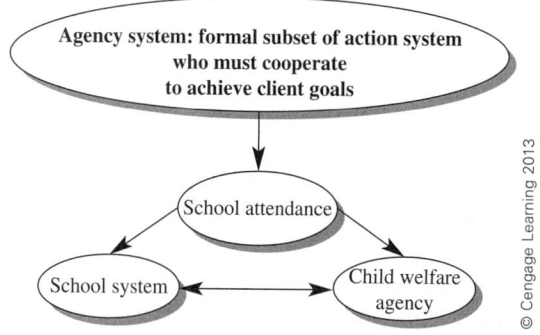

FIG-1-5 Agency System

and boundaries in some areas while seeking and responding to change in others. Systems theorists also suggest that change in one part of a system often affects other parts of the system. For example, Mrs. Ramirez's emotional and physical health may greatly influence her capacity to prepare her children for school. Hence, facilitating a referral for her may have a significant impact on the school attendance issue.

The principle of *equifinality* suggests that the same outcome can be achieved even with different starting points. For example, your classmates have come from different places both geographically and in terms of life experience. Despite their different origins, they have all ended up in the same program of study. The principle of *multifinality* suggests that beginning from the same starting points may end in different outcomes. Just as you and your classmates are engaged in the same course of study, you are likely to end in diverse settings and locales for your own practice experience.

Nonlinear Applications of Systems Theory

Traditional systems theory suggests that systems or organizations are characterized by order, rationality, and stability (Warren, Franklin, & Streeter, 1998). Hence, the emphasis in such stable systems is on concepts such as boundaries, homeostasis, and equilibrium. In addition to ordered circumstances, systems theory can be useful for consideration of nonlinear systems. Systems in the process of change can be very sensitive to initial events and feedback to those events. For example, a nonlinear change would be the circumstance in which an adolescent's voice changes by 1 decibel of loudness resulting in a change of 10 decibels in an adult (Warren et al., 1998). Minor incidents in the past can reverberate throughout a system. Some have suggested that this proliferation supports the notion that family systems can make significant changes as a result of a key intervention that reverberates and is reinforced in a system.

Such nonlinear circumstances emphasize the concept of multifinality—that is, the same initial conditions can lead to quite varied outcomes. Among the implications of multifinality are the possibility of considering chaos not as a lack of order but rather as an opportunity for flexibility and change.

Limitations of Systems Theories

While systems models often provide useful concepts for describing person–situation interactions, they may have limitations in suggesting specific intervention prescriptions (Whittaker & Tracy, 1989). Similarly, Wakefield (1996a, 1996b) has argued that systems concepts do not add much to domain-specific knowledge. Others claim that, however faulty or inadequate, systems theory provides useful metaphors for conceptualizing the relations between complex organizations.

Perhaps we should not place such high expectations on the theory (Gitterman, 1996). We take the view that systems theory provides useful metaphors for conceptualizing the varied levels of phenomena social workers must recognize. By themselves, those metaphors are insufficient to guide practice. Concepts such as equifinality and multifinality cannot be rigidly applied in all human and social systems.

Deciding on and Carrying Out Interventions

How do social workers decide on what interventions they will carry out to assist client systems in reaching their goals? Throughout our professional history, social workers have drawn selectively on theories to help understand circumstances  and guide intervention. Psychodynamic theory was an important early source of explanations to guide social work interventions through adaptations such as the functional approach, the psychosocial approach, and the problem-solving approach (Hollis and Woods, 1981; Perlman, 1957; Taft, 1937). In each of these approaches, ego psychology was a particularly valuable source in explaining how individuals coped with their environments. While psychodynamic theory provided a broad-ranging explanatory framework, it was less useful as a source for specific interventions, and the level of abstraction required in the approach did not lend itself well to the evaluation of its effectiveness.

EP 2.1.6

Concerns about the effectiveness of social work services led to an emphasis on employing methods that could be expected to be successful based on proven effectiveness (Fischer, 1973). Rather than seeking single approaches to direct practice in all circumstances, social workers were guided to find the approach that made the best fit for the particular client circumstance and problem (Fischer, 1978). Eclectic practice is designed to meet this goal, but carries its own concerns. For example, selecting techniques employed in particular approaches is best done based on knowledge of the approach the techniques come from and an assessment of the strengths and weaknesses of that approach (Coady and Lehmann, 2008; Marsh, 2004).

Berlin and Marsh suggest that there are legitimate roles for many influences on practice decision making. Those include clear conceptual frameworks to guide the social worker in what to look for, commitments and values, intuitive hunches, spontaneous improvisation, empathic understanding, and empirically derived data (Berlin and Marsh, 1993, p. 230) (see Figure 1-6).

Empirically derived data as a source has a prominent role in determining, together with clients, how to proceed. Empirically based practice refers to promoting models of practice based on scientific evidence (Barker, 2003). In such an approach, problems and outcomes are conceived in measurable terms, and data is gathered to monitor interventions and evaluate effectiveness. Interventions are selected based on their scientific support and effectiveness as systematically measured and evaluated (Cournoyer, 2004; Petr & Walter, 2005). The term "evidence-based practice" has been suggested as broader than "empirically based practice," since external research findings are considered in the context of fit to particular situations, which in turn are considered within the context of informed consent and client values and expectations (Gambrill, 2004; Petr & Walter, 2005, p. 252).

Evidence-based practice began in medicine as an attempt to make conscientiously identify best practices for client care, assess the quality of evidence available, and present that evidence to clients and patients so that they could share in decision making (Adams & Drake, 2006; Scheyett, 2006). More recently, two forms of evidence-based practice have become prominent.

The first form, the *process model,* is consistent with the medical definition of evidence-based practice cited previously and focuses on the practices of the individual practitioner. Specifically, the individual practitioner learns how to formulate a question that is answerable with data about his or her work with a client (Rubin, 2007). Based on that question, the practitioner gains access to appropriate empirical literature. The practitioner must have access to appropriate literature through computerized access to online journals and studies. The practitioner does not need to review all the relevant literature from all of the available studies but may seek secondary reviews and meta-analyses of an intervention that summarize the state of knowledge about that intervention. For example, the evidence about stages of change in a child welfare context has been summarized by Littell and Girvin (2004). In assessing studies of interventions, a hierarchy of levels has been developed to assess the reliability of an intervention measure. For example, multiple randomized studies are considered to provide potentially strong support for an intervention. With some social problems and settings such as child welfare, such studies are rare; however, studies with other adequate controls may be available (Thomlison, 2005; Whiting Blome, & Steib, 2004; Kessler, Gira, & Poertner, 2005). Whatever the range of studies available, the practitioner needs to have the skills to assess the level of support for the intervention. Based on this assessment of data, the social worker can share that evidence with his or her client in order to better make an informed decision together about what to do. After making this joint decision, the practitioner and client can implement the intervention with fidelity and assess how well it works. This has been characterized as a bottom-up model because the questions raised and interventions selected are assumed to be defined by the people closest to the intervention: the practitioner and client (Rubin, 2007).

There are several assumptions about the process model as presented in this form that must be assessed. It assumes that the practitioner is free to select an intervention and the client is free to accept or reject it. In fact, agency-level practice has many influences that determine which interventions can be utilized (Payne, 2005). Some interventions are supported by the agency and supervisor based on policies, laws, prior training, and accepted practices. Practitioners utilizing the process model hope that such interventions are supported by a review of the research evidence. Recognizing this issue and that the choice of intervention may not be fully in the control of the practitioner, some proponents have suggested that one solution is for teams to study

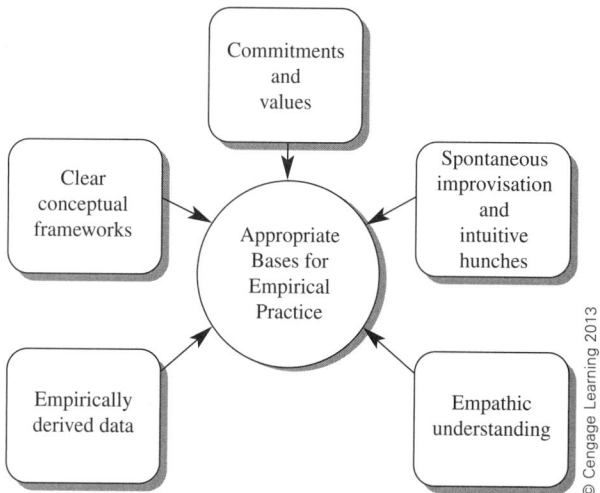

FIG-1-6 Appropriate Bases for Empirical Practice
Source: Adapted from Berlin and Marsh, 1993, p. 230.

evidence about particular problems and interventions and make recommendations about practices to be used by the team (Proctor, 2007). In partnership with schools of social work, agency teams can identify problems and secure administrative support while the schools provide training in evidence-based practices. Secondly, when clients are not entirely voluntary, practitioners and agencies may and should make evidence-based decisions; but involuntary clients may not feel empowered to reject them (Scheyett, 2006; Kessler et al, 2005). In such cases, however, clients are entitled through informed consent to know the rationale for the intervention and its evidence of effectiveness. This model also assumes that the practitioner has sufficient time to access the appropriate literature and appropriate resources. Finally, it assumes that the practitioner has the skill, training, and supervision to carry out the evidence-based intervention effectively (Rubin, 2007).

Partly in response to the difficulties associated with the process model, another version of evidence-based practice refers to training in these practices. In this approach, the emphasis is on identifying models of practice that have demonstrated efficacy for particular problems and populations, learning about them, and learning how to implement them. An advantage of this approach, according to proponents, is the fact that it focuses on not just knowing about the intervention but acquiring the skills necessary to carry it out effectively (Rubin, 2007). Critics suggest that this approach carries its own dangers. For one, students often experience anxiety in learning how to become effective practitioners and, having learned one evidence-based practice, might be inclined to generalize it beyond its original effectiveness, thus replicating in part the problem mentioned earlier of students trained in a theory or model and carrying it out without evidence of effectiveness and without having an alternative: If your only tool is a hammer, all problems may appear to be nails (Scheyett, 2006). Secondly, evidence-based practices have their own limited shelf life, with new studies supporting some methods and qualifying the support for others. Hence, the fact that you learn one evidence-based approach does not preclude and should not preclude learning others. In fact, we believe that becoming effective practitioners is a career-long proposition, not limited by the completion of your academic program. Finally, behavioral and cognitive-behavioral approaches are well-represented among evidence-based practices. Some have suggested that such approaches have some advantage because practice of the approach fits research protocols, and therefore that other approaches have been under-represented

(Coady & Lehmann, 2008; Walsh, 2006). It becomes a challenge to other approaches to enhance their effectiveness base rather than question the value of research protocols or representativeness of the model. There is growing evidence that some emerging approaches, such as the solution-focused approach are in fact increasing their effectiveness base (Kim, 2008).

Advocates suggest that there is room for both such approaches in social work education; that all students should learn how to carry out the process model of evidence-based practice and that all students should become proficient in at least one evidence-based practice modality (Rubin, 2007). These proponents also suggest that this kind of practice may require specialization in certain methods and may not be consistent with those programs that include an advanced generalist curriculum (Howard, Allen-Meares, & Ruffolo, 2007). We do not take sides on this issue, recognizing that programs that have developed advanced generalist curricula have done so mindful of the context and expectations for practitioners in their area, and that generalist practice remains the standard for BSW programs and the first year of MSW programs.

Guidelines Influencing Intervention Selection

We recommend the following guidelines to assist you in deciding when and how to intervene with clients in social work practice.

1. *Social workers value maximum feasible self-determination, empowerment, and enhancing strengths to increase the client's voice in decision making.* Thus, manualized approaches that imply that all major decisions are in the hands of and controlled by the social work practitioner are alien to these values. Following these values, we seek to include clients to the extent possible in access to information that would assist them in making decisions (Coady & Lehmann, 2008).

2. *Social workers assess circumstances from a systems perspective, mindful of the person in the situation, the setting, the community, and the organization.* We assess for the level of the problem and the appropriate level of interventions (Allen-Meares & Garvin, 2000). We recognize that resources are often needed at multiple levels and attempt to avoid a narrow clinical focus on the practitioner and client. Hence our use of data and perspectives to guide us must be governed in part by the multiple roles we play, including systems linkage as well as

direct practice or clinical interventions (Richey & Roffman, 1999).
3. *Social workers are sensitive to diversity in considering interventions.* We avoid assumptions that interventions tested with one population will necessarily generalize to another. In so doing, we are particularly sensitive to the clients' own perspectives about what is appropriate for them (Allen-Meares & Garvin, 2000).
4. *Social workers draw on evidence-based practices at both process and intervention levels as sources in determining, together with the client, how to proceed.* We expect social work practitioners to have access to evidence about efficacious interventions for the problem at hand. Such evidence may occur through individual study, through organizational priorities, or through collaboration with university teams to construct guidelines for practice in critical areas. Because our code of ethics requires us to act within our level of competence and supervision, knowledge of what interventions are efficacious does not mean that we can carry out those interventions. It may be a useful goal to learn how to carry out two or more evidence-based approaches as part of your education program. The goal of this book is, however, to equip you with the basic skills to carry out practice at the beginning level. We are influenced by the process model of evidence-based practice, and we seek to give you useful tools by modeling ways that questions can be asked and that data can be consulted in making decisions with clients. Further, in our chapters on intervention models we will be influenced by evidence-based practice models. It is not realistic at this level to attempt to teach evidence-based practice approaches such that you would be able to implement them right away. We can introduce you to them, but further training and supervision are required.
5. *Social workers think critically about practice, checking out assumptions and examining alternatives.* We try to avoid early social work patterns of applying theories more widely than data suggests by being open to examining alternatives (Briggs & Rzepnicki, 2004; Gambrill, 2004). One danger of following a single approach is that data that does not fit the preferences of the approach is discounted (Maguire, 2002). Conversely, this danger can also apply to selecting an approach based on its label as evidence-based, for example, without assessing fit with client and circumstances (Scheyett, 2006).

Summary

This chapter introduced social work as a profession marked by a specific mission and well-established values. As social workers and their clients operate in many different kinds and levels of environments, ecological and systems concepts are useful metaphors for conceptualizing what social workers and clients must deal with. Chapter 2 will delve deeper into specifying direct practice and the roles that social workers play.

CourseMate

Access an integrated eBook and chapter-specific learning tools including glossary terms, chapter outlines, relevant web links, videos, and practice quizzes. Go to **www.cengagebrain.com**.

CHAPTER 2

The Domain, Philosophy, and Roles of Direct Practice

CHAPTER OVERVIEW

This chapter presents a context and philosophy for direct practice, definitions of direct and clinical practice and descriptions of the varied roles played by direct social work practitioners. After completing this chapter, you will be able to:

- Define direct and clinical practice
- Delineate roles performed by direct practice social workers

EPAS COMPETENCIES IN THE 2ND CHAPTER

This chapter will give you the information needed to meet the following practice competencies:

2.1.1 Identify as a Professional Social Worker and Conduct One's Self Accordingly:
   a. Advocate for client access to services
   c. Attend to professional roles and boundaries

2.1.5 Advance Human Rights and Social and Economic Justice
   a. Understand forms and mechanisms of oppression and discrimination
   b. Advocate for human rights and social and economic justice
   c. Engage in practices that engage in social and economic justice

2.1.6 Engage in research-informed practice and practice-informed research
   a. Use practice experience to inform scientific inquiry
   b. Use research evidence to inform practice

2.1.8 Engage in policy practice to advance social and economic well-being and to deliver effective social work services
   a. Analyze, formulate, and advocate for policies that advance social well-being
   b. Collaborate with colleagues and clients for effective policy action

2.1.9 Respond to contexts that shape practice:
   a. Continuously discover, appraise, and attend to changing locales, populations, scientific and technological developments, and emerging societal trends to provide relevant services
   b. Provide leadership in promoting sustainable changes in service delivery and practice to improve the quality of social services

2.1.10 Engage, assess, intervene, and evaluate with individuals, families, groups, organizations and communities. Social workers engage in advocacy.
   k. Negotiate, mediate, and advocate for clients

Domain

Prior to 1970, social work practice was defined by methodologies or by fields of practice. Social workers were thus variously identified as caseworkers, group workers, community organizers, child welfare workers, psychiatric social workers, school social workers, medical social workers, and so on. The terms *direct practice* and *clinical practice* are relatively new in social work nomenclature.

The profession was unified in 1955 by the creation of the National Association of Social Workers (NASW) and, with the inauguration of the journal *Social Work*, the gradual transformation from more narrow views of practice to the current broader view was under way. This transformation accelerated during the 1960s and 1970s, when social unrest in the United States prompted challenges and criticisms of all institutions, including social work. Persons of color, organized groups of poor people, and other oppressed groups accused the profession of being irrelevant given their pressing needs. These accusations were often justified, because many social workers were engaged in narrowly focused and therapeutically oriented activities that did not address the social problems of concern to oppressed groups (Specht & Courtney, 1994).[1]

Casework had been the predominant social work method during this period. Casework comprised activities in widely varying settings, aimed at assisting individuals, couples, or families to cope more effectively with problems that impaired social functioning. At the same time group work had evolved as a practice method, and group workers were practicing in settlement houses and neighborhoods, on the streets with youth gangs, in hospitals and correctional institutions, and in other settings. Although the units targeted by group workers were larger, their objectives still did not address broad social problems. It was clear that urgent needs for broadly defined social services could not be met through the narrowly defined remedial (therapeutic) efforts of the casework and group work methods.

The efforts of Gordon (1965) and Bartlett (1970) to formulate a framework (i.e., common base) for social work practice composed of purpose, values, sanction, knowledge, and common skills resulted in a broadened perspective of social work. Because this new perspective was not oriented to methods of practice, a new generic term was created to describe it: *social work practice*.

Generalist Practice

EP 2.1.1

The Council on Social Work Education (CSWE) responded to the evolution of the social work practice framework by adopting a curriculum policy statement stipulating that to meet accreditation standards, social work educational programs must have a curriculum containing foundation courses that embody the common knowledge base of social work practice. Both undergraduate (BSW) and graduate (MSW) programs embody such foundation courses and thus prepare students for generalist practice. BSW curricula, however, are designed primarily to prepare generalist social workers and avoid specialization in practice methods. The rationale for generalist programs, is that practitioners should view problems holistically and be prepared to plan interventions aimed at multiple levels of systems related to client concerns. Similarly, client goals and needs should suggest appropriate interventions, rather than interventions inspiring the selection of compatible goals. Client systems range from micro systems (individuals, couples, families, and groups) to mezzo (communities) and macro systems (organizations, institutions, regions, and nations).

Connecting client systems to resource systems that can provide needed goods and services is a paramount function of BSW social workers. Many BSW programs, in fact, prepare students to assume the role of case manager, a role that focuses on linking clients to resources.

The foundation component of MSW programs also prepares graduate students for generalist practice. Although a few MSW programs prepare students for "advanced generalist practice," most second-year curricula in the MSW programs permit students to select specializations or "concentrations" within methods of practice or within fields of practice (e.g., substance abuse, aging, child welfare, work with families, health care, or mental health) (Raymond, Teare, & Atherton, 1996). MSW students thus are prepared for both generalist and specialized practice.

Similarities in orientation and differences in function between BSW and MSW social workers and the importance of having practitioners at both levels are highlighted in the following case example. Note that similarities and differences exist on a continuum such that some MSW social workers perform some of the tasks otherwise ascribed to the BSW practitioner, and vice versa. Similarly, differences in their tasks may arise based on geographic region, field of practice, and availability of MSW-trained practitioners.

Direct Practice

Direct practice includes work with individuals, couples, families, and groups. Direct social work practitioners perform many roles besides delivering face-to-face service; they work in collaboration with other professionals, organizations, and institutions, and they act as advocates with landlords, agency administrators, policy-making boards, and legislatures, among others. Direct social work practice is conducted in a variety of settings and problem areas. For example, direct practice includes services to clients organized by life-cycle stage (children, adolescents and young adults, aging), problem area (child welfare, domestic violence, health and mental health, substance abuse, antipoverty issues such as homelessness and housing programs, work programs), mode of intervention (work with families, work with groups), and agency setting (school social work, disability services) (see Figure 2-1).

The term *clinical practice* is used by some as synonymous with *direct practice*. Clinical social work practice has been defined as "the provision of mental health

IDEAS IN ACTION

Arthur Harrison and Marlene Fisher are unmarried adults, each of whom has developmental disabilities. They have two sons. Mr. Harrison and Ms. Fisher came to the attention of child protection services because Roger, the older of their sons, who also has a developmental disability, told his teacher that his younger brother, Roy, 13, who does not have a developmental disability, and Roy's friends had sexually molested Roger. Roy admitted to the offense when interviewed, as did his friends. Roy stated that he learned the behavior from a neighbor who had been sexually abusing him since age 7.

The family participated in an assessment conducted by Christine Summers, a BSW social worker employed by the county's child protection agency. Roger was placed in residential care, and Roy was charged with sexual assault. Meanwhile, the neighbor boy was charged with three counts of first-degree sexual assault and was incarcerated pending a hearing. Christine then met with the parents to conduct a strengths-based and risk assessment. This assessment revealed that Mr. Harrison and Ms. Fisher had coped well with parenting on many fronts, including maintaining their children in good school performance, and supporting their hobbies and avocations. Some concern was raised about their capacities to protect their children from danger in this instance. As a result of the collaborative assessment conducted by Ms. Summers, a plan was developed with the goal of Mr. Harrison and Ms. Fisher's resumption of care for their children.

Christine acted as the case manager, coordinating the efforts of several persons who were assisting Mr. Harrison and Ms. Fisher and their children in pursuit of their goal of restoration of custody. Christine played dual roles (Trotter, 2006) in this case: (1) ensuring social control designed to protect the public and vulnerable persons and (2) providing assistance to the family (i.e., a helping role). Sometimes those roles can be played simultaneously, sometimes they can be played in sequence, and sometimes only one of the two roles can be filled by the caseworker. In this instance, Ms. Summers initially carried out her assessment with her actions largely being guided by her role of protecting the public and vulnerable persons. After she came to agreement with the parents about the plan for regaining custody of their sons, Ms. Summers became more able to play a helping role. This plan included a referral to Debra Sontag, an MSW practitioner with special expertise in work with children with sexual behavior difficulties. Ms. Sontag was able to work with Roy, Roger, and their parents and make a recommendation to the child welfare agency and court about when and under what conditions living together as a family would again be safe.

As this example indicates, frequently MSW direct practitioners provide more in-depth individual and family services than fits the case-loads, responsibilities, and training of BSW practitioners. They can coordinate their services to better serve families.

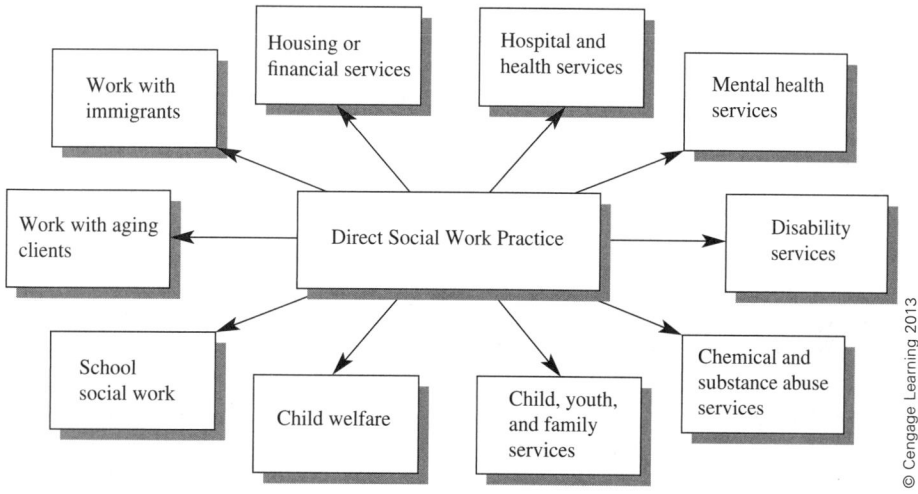

FIG-2-1 Direct Social Work Practice and Components

services for the diagnosis, treatment and prevention of mental, behavioral and emotional disorders in individuals, families and groups" (Clinical Social Work Federation, 1997). The focus of clinical work is said to be "to provide mental health treatment in agencies, clinics, hospitals and as private practitioners" (Clinical Social Work Association, 2008). Walsh defines clinical social work practice broadly to include "the application of social work theory and methods to the resolution and prevention of psychosocial problems experienced by individuals, families, and groups. These problems may include challenges, disabilities and impairments including mental, emotional, and behavioral disorders" (Walsh, 2006, p. 18). He further emphasizes the grounding of clinical practice in social work values such as promoting social and economic justice and focusing on diversity and multiculturalism. Clinical interventions include therapeutic, supportive, educational and advocacy functions (Walsh, 2006, p. 18). Clinical case management includes developing comprehensive assessments, monitoring client progress including mental status among other activities (Sherrer & O'Hare, 2008). Meanwhile, empirical clinical practice emphasizes the use of empirical information in the design and delivery of clinical services (Thyer, 2001). While this range of activities covers much of direct practice, pressures exist to emphasize the intensive individual end of the continuum through presenting billable hours (Frey & Dupper, 2005). Clinical social work practice might be considered to include the function of providing mental health services among its other roles. While mental health treatment may be provided to clients in many settings, such treatment is not the primary function in those settings. For example, while mental health services may be of use to some clients in a homeless shelter, environmental interventions to assist with housing are the primary function.

The *clinical social worker* title has special significance in some states, because an advanced license is labeled as clinical. Licensing provisions are such that diagnosis and treatment of mental health difficulties requires that the provider have a clinical license or be under the supervision of a person with such a license. Achievement of such a license is based on completion of specified hours in training and supervision as well as completion of an exam. Holding such a license then becomes a required credential for social workers to be eligible for third-party reimbursement for delivering psychotherapy or counseling.

While recognizing the significance of these licensing and reimbursement issues, as well as the attached status and prestige of the term "clinical social worker," we do not think it necessary to subsume all direct social work practice under the term *clinical practice*. Crucial interventions are performed to assist children and families in child welfare, for example, whether or not they are related to mental health services. Some seem to use the term *clinical practice* to connote "quality social work practice." We prefer to describe clinical services as a particular form of direct service that can be delivered in many fields of practice but which include the assessment and treatment of mental health issues as one function. In this book, we will use both of the terms *direct practice* and *clinical practice*, guided by the primary functions of the settings in which micro level services are delivered.

Direct practice encompasses a full range of roles, including acting as a caseworker or counselor. Central to assisting people with difficulties is knowledge of and skill in assisting people in deciding how best to work on their concerns. That assistance requires knowledge and skills in assessing human problems and in locating, developing, or utilizing appropriate resource systems. Skills in engaging clients, mutually planning relevant goals, and defining the roles of the participants are also integral parts of the helping process. Likewise, the practitioner must possess knowledge of interventions and skills in implementing them. A more extensive review of the helping process is contained in Chapter 3, and this entire book is devoted to explicating the theory and skills related to direct practice with clients.

Direct practitioners of social work must be knowledgeable and skilled in interviewing and in assessing and intervening in problematic interactions involving individuals, couples, families, and groups. Knowledge of group processes and skills in leading groups are also essential, as are skills in forming natural helping networks, functioning as a member of an interdisciplinary team, and negotiating within and between systems. The negotiating function requires skills in mediating conflicts, advocating for services, and obtaining resources, all of which embody high levels of interpersonal skills.

Some have questioned whether engaging in psychotherapy is appropriate for a profession whose mission focuses on social justice (Specht & Courtney, 1994). Others have countered that a social justice mission is not necessarily inconsistent with use of psychotherapy as one tool in pursuit of this goal (Wakefield, 1996a, 1996b). According to Swenson (1998), clinical work that draws on client strengths, that is mindful of social positions and power relationships, and that attempts to counter oppression is consistent with a social justice perspective. In our opinion, these debates are moot. Many of today's practitioners in social work and other helping professions practice psychotherapy that draws on additional theory bases such as behavioral and family systems models. Clinical practice in a managed care environment focuses on specific problems, strengths, and resources; is highly structured and goal oriented; and develops tangible objectives for each session intended to achieve overall treatment goals (Franklin, 2002).

A Philosophy of Direct Practice

As a profession evolves, its knowledge base expands and practitioners gain experience in applying abstract values and knowledge to specific practice situations. Instrumental values gradually evolve as part of this transformation; as they are adopted, they become principles or guidelines to practice. Such principles express preferred beliefs about the nature and causes of human problems. They also describe perspectives about people's capacity to deal with problems, desirable goals, and valued qualities in helping relationships. Finally, those principles include beliefs about vital elements of the helping process, the roles of the practitioner and the client, characteristics of effective group leaders, and the nature of the human growth process.

Over many years, we have evolved a philosophy of practice from a synthesis of principles gained from sources too diverse to acknowledge, including our own value preferences. We thus offer as our philosophy of direct practice the principles outlined in Figure 2-2.

PHILOSOPHY OF DIRECT PRACTICE

1. The problems experienced by social work clients stem from lack of resources, knowledge, and skills (societal, systemic, and personal sources), either alone or in combination.

2. Because social work clients are often subject to poverty, racism, sexism, heterosexism, discrimination, and lack of resources, social workers negotiate systems and advocate for change to ensure that their clients obtain access to their rights, resources, and treatment with dignity. They also attempt to modify or develop resource systems to make them more responsive to client needs.

3. People are capable of making their own choices and decisions. Although controlled to some extent by their environment, they are able to direct their environment more than they realize. Social workers aim to assist in the empowerment of their clients by helping them gain (1) the ability to make decisions and (2) access to critical resources that affect their lives and increase their ability to change those environmental influences that adversely affect them individually and as members of groups.

4. Because social service systems are often funded on the basis of individual dysfunctions, social workers play an educational function in sensitizing service delivery systems to more systemic problem-solving approaches that emphasize health, strengths, and natural support systems.

5. Frequently, social workers deal with persons who are reluctant to receive services through referrals pressured by others or under the threat of legal sanctions. While people have a right to their own values and beliefs, sometimes their behaviors violate the rights of others, and the social worker assists these clients in facing these aspects of their difficulties. Because reluctant or involuntary clients are often not seeking a helping relationship but rather wishing to escape one, negotiation is frequently required.

6. Some clients apply for services because they wish to experience change through a social worker's assistance. Such clients are often helped by having an accepting relationship, with appropriate self-disclosure, which will allow them to seek greater self-awareness and to live more fully in the reality of the moment.

7. All clients, whether voluntary or involuntary, are entitled to be treated with respect and dignity, and to have their choices facilitated.

8. Client behavior is goal directed, although these goals are often not readily discernible. Clients are, however, capable of learning new skills, knowledge, and approaches to resolving their difficulties. Social workers are responsible for helping clients discover their strengths and affirming their capacity for growth and change.

9. While clients' current problems are often influenced by past relationships and concerns, and although limited focus on the past is sometimes beneficial, most difficulties can be alleviated by focusing on present choices and by mobilizing strengths and coping patterns.

FIG-2-2 Principles of a Philosophy of Direct Practice

Roles of Direct Practitioners

EP 2.1.1

During recent years, increasing attention has been devoted to the various roles that direct practitioners perform in discharging their responsibilities. In Chapter 1, we referred to a number of these roles. In this section, we summarize these and other roles and refer to sections of the book where we discuss certain roles at greater length. We have categorized the roles based in part on a schema presented by Lister (1987) (see Figure 2-3).

Direct Provision of Services

Roles subsumed under this category include those in which social workers meet face to face with clients or consumer groups in providing services:

- *Individual casework or counseling.*
- *Couples and family therapy* (may include sessions with individuals, conjoint sessions, and group sessions).
- *Group work services* (may include support groups, therapy groups, self-help groups, task groups, and skill development groups).
- *Educator/disseminator of information.* The social worker may provide essential information in individual, conjoint, or group sessions or may make educational presentations to consumer groups or to the public. For example, practitioners may conduct educational sessions dealing with parenting skills, marital enrichment, stress management, or various aspects of mental health or health care (Dore, 1993)

These roles are primary in the work of most direct service social workers. Because this book is aimed at preparing social workers to provide such direct services, we will not elaborate further on these roles in this section.

System Linkage Roles

Because clients may need resources not provided by a given social agency and lack knowledge of or the ability to utilize other available resources, social workers often perform roles in linking people to other resources.

Broker

To perform the role of broker (i.e., an intermediary who assists in connecting people with resources), social workers must have a thorough knowledge of community resources so that they can make appropriate referrals. Familiarity with the policies of resource systems and working relationships with key contact persons are essential to making successful referrals. In the earlier case example, Christine Summers, the BSW-trained social worker, brokered services for Mr. Harrison, Ms. Fisher, and their children, including the referral to Debra Sontag, the MSW-trained sexual behaviors counselor. Before some people are able to avail themselves of resources, they may require the social worker's assistance in overcoming fears and misconceptions about those services.

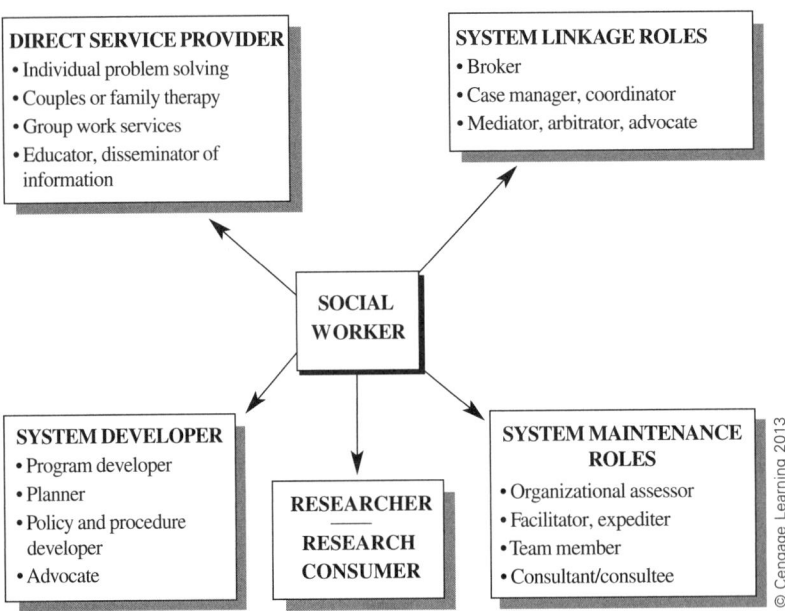

FIG-2-3 Roles Social Workers Play

Social workers also have responsibilities in developing simple and effective referral mechanisms and ways of monitoring whether clients actually follow through on referrals.

Case Manager/Coordinator

Some clients lack the ability, skills, knowledge, or resources to follow through on referrals to other systems. In such instances, the social worker may serve as case manager, a person who assumes primary responsibility for assessing the needs of a client and arranging and coordinating the delivery of essential goods and services provided by other resources. Case managers also work directly with clients to ensure that the needed goods and services are provided in a timely manner.

Case managers must maintain close contact with clients (sometimes even providing direct casework services) and with other service providers to ensure that plans for service delivery are in place and are delivered as planned. It is noteworthy that in the case manager role, social workers function at the interface between the client and the environment more so than in any other role. Because of recent dramatic increases in the numbers of people needing case management services (e.g., homeless individuals, elderly clients, and persons with serious and persistent mental illness), numerous articles have appeared in the literature focusing on the clients who need such services, issues related to case management, and various functions of case managers.

Mediator/Arbitrator

EP 2.1.10k

Occasionally breakdowns occur between clients and service providers so that clients do not receive the needed services to which they are entitled. For example, clients may be seeking a resource to which they believe they are entitled by their health insurance. In other cases, participants in workfare programs may find themselves sanctioned for failure to meet program expectations (Hage, 2004).

Service may be denied for several reasons. Perhaps clients did not adequately represent their eligibility for services, or strains that sometimes develop between clients and service providers may precipitate withdrawals of requests for services by clients or withholding of services by providers.

In such instances, practitioners may serve as mediators with the goal of eliminating obstacles to service delivery. *Mediation* is a process that "provides a neutral forum in which disputants are encouraged to find a mutually satisfactory resolution to their problems" (Chandler, 1985, p. 346). When serving as a mediator, you must carefully listen to and draw out facts and feelings from both parties to determine the cause of the breakdown. It is important not to take sides with either party until you are confident that you have accurate and complete information. When you have determined the nature of the breakdown, you can plan appropriate remedial action aimed at removing barriers, clarifying possible misunderstandings, and working through negative feelings that have impeded service delivery. The communication skills used in this process are delineated in subsequent chapters of this book.

In recent years, knowledge of mediation skills has evolved to a high level of sophistication. Today, a growing number of social workers are working independently or in tandem with attorneys to mediate conflicts between divorcing partners regarding child custody, visitation rights, and property settlements. These same skills can be used to mediate personnel disputes, labor management conflicts, and victim–offender situations (Nugent et al., 2001).

Client Advocate

EP 2.1.1a

Social workers have assumed the role of advocate for a client or group of clients since the inception of the profession. The obligation to assume this role has been reaffirmed most recently in the NASW Code of Ethics, which includes advocacy among the activities performed by social workers in pursuit of the professional mission (NASW, 2008).

With respect to linking clients with resources, advocacy is the process of working with and/or on behalf of clients to obtain services and resources that would not otherwise be provided.

System Maintenance and Enhancement

As staff members of social agencies, social workers bear responsibility for evaluating structures, policies, and functional relationships within agencies that impair effectiveness in service delivery.

Organizational Analyst

EP 2.1.5

Discharging the role of organizational analyst entails pinpointing factors in agency structure, policy, and procedures that have a negative impact on service delivery. Knowledge of organizational and administrative theory is essential to performing this role effectively. For example, it is well documented that African American children are overrepresented in the child welfare system of the United States (Race Matters, 2005; Johnson, Clark, Donald, Pederson & Piehotta, 2007; Curtis & Denby, 2004; Kossak, 2005). This means that a greater proportion of Caucasian children are returned to their parents after child welfare assessments. The reasons for this disproportion are complex and not tied to any one factor. Engaging in the organizational assessor role, social workers in child welfare would examine the decisions made in the system. They would then try to make sure that resources such as family group decision are especially available to families of color as that resource is promising as a way to safely preserve families.

Facilitator/Expediter

After pinpointing factors that impede service delivery, social workers have a responsibility to plan and implement ways of enhancing service delivery. This may involve providing relevant input to agency boards and administrators, recommending staff meetings to address problems, working collaboratively with other staff members to bring pressure to bear on resistant administrators, encouraging and participating in essential inservice training sessions, and other similar activities.

Team Member

In many agency and institutional settings (e.g., mental health, health care, rehabilitation, and education settings), practitioners function as members of clinical teams that collaborate in assessing clients' problems and delivering services (Sands, 1989; Sands, Stafford, & McClelland, 1990). Such teams commonly consist of a psychiatrist or physician, psychologist, a social worker, a nurse, and perhaps a rehabilitation counselor, occupational therapist, educator, or recreational therapist, depending on the setting. Members of the team have varying types of expertise that are tapped in formulating assessments and planning and implementing therapeutic interventions. As team members, social workers often contribute knowledge related to family dynamics and engage in therapeutic work with family members.

Sometimes such teams are dominated by members from more powerful professions (Bell, 2001). Dane and Simon (1991) note that social workers in such host settings, in which the mission and decision making may be dominated by non-social workers, often experience a discrepancy between their professional mission and the values of the employing institution. They can act, however, to sensitize team members to strengths and advocate for a more holistic approach while exercising their knowledge of resources and expertise in linking clients with resources. Social workers also are expected to apply their knowledge of community resources in planning for the discharge of patients and facilitating their reentry into the community following periods of hospitalization. In so doing, social workers bring their systems and strengths perspectives to teams that are sometimes more deficit-focused.

Social workers are also involved in interdisciplinary work across systems such as schools and child welfare, which require the ability to work within several systems simultaneously (Bailey-Dempsey & Reid, 1996). As team members, social workers also often serve as case managers in coordinating discharge planning for patients (Dane & Simon, 1991; Kadushin & Kulys, 1993).

Consultant/Consultee

Consultation is a process whereby an expert enables a consultee to deliver services more effectively to a client by increasing, developing, modifying, or freeing the consultee's knowledge, skills, attitudes, or behavior with respect to the problem at hand (Kadushin, 1977). Although social workers both provide and receive consultation, there has been a trend for MSW social workers to serve less as consumers of consultation and more as providers. BSW social workers may provide consultation regarding the availability of specific community resources. More often, however, they are consumers of consultation when they need information about how to work effectively in problem solving that encompasses complex situations and behaviors. Social workers assume the consultee role when they need expert knowledge from doctors and nurses, psychiatrists, psychologists, and other social workers who possess high levels of expertise related to certain types of problems (e.g., substance abuse, child maltreatment, sexual problems).

Social workers serve as consultants to members of other professions and to other social workers in need of their special expertise, including when they fill the role of supervisor. For example, they may provide consultation to school personnel who need assistance in understanding and coping with problem students; to health care providers who seek assistance in understanding a patient's family or ethnic and cultural factors; to court staff regarding matters that bear on child custody decisions and decisions about parole and probation; and in many other similar situations.

Supervisor

Relations between consultants and consultees in social work frequently occur within the supervisory relationship.

Supervisors play a critical role in the support of quality direct practice work performed by social work practitioners. Supervisors are responsible for orienting staff to how they can learn through supervision, lines of authority, requirements, and policies of the setting (Munson, 2002). Social work supervisors frequently utilize case presentations made by staff social workers as a key mechanism in learning. Such presentations should be organized around questions to be answered. Supervisors assist staff in linking assessment with intervention plans and evaluation. Special responsibilities include helping supervisees identify when client advocacy is needed, identifying and resolving ethical conflicts, and monitoring issues of race, ethnicity, lifestyle, and vulnerability as they affect the client–social worker interaction. In addition, supervisors often take the lead in securing resources for staff and facilitating linkages with other organizations.

Researcher/Research Consumer

EP 2.1.6a & b

Practitioners face responsibilities in both public and private settings to select interventions that can be evaluated, to evaluate the effectiveness of their interventions, and to systematically monitor the progress of their clients. Implementing these processes requires practitioners to conduct and make use of research.

As described in Chapter 1, social workers are expected to incorporate research skills into their practice. Such incorporation occurs at several levels. For example, being able to define questions in ways that help in consulting the research literature about effectiveness is one such competency. Conducting ongoing evaluation of the effectiveness of practice is another such competency. Some practitioners utilize single-subject (i.e., single-system) designs. This type of research design enables practitioners to obtain measures of the extent (frequency and severity) of problem behaviors before they implement interventions aimed at eliminating or reducing the problem behaviors or increasing the frequency of currently insufficient behaviors (e.g., doing homework, engaging in prosocial behaviors, setting realistic and consistent limits with children, sending positive messages, abstaining from drinking). These measures provide a baseline against which the results of the interventions can be assessed by applying the same measures periodically during the course of the interventions, at termination, and at follow-up (Reid, 1994). Perhaps more frequently, practitioners use some form of Goal Attainment Scaling that calls for rating goal achievement on a scale with points designated in advance (Corcoran & Vandiver, 1996).

System Development

EP 2.1.9

Direct practitioners sometimes have opportunities to improve or to expand agency services based on assessment of unmet client needs, gaps in service, needs for preventive services, or research indicating that more promising results might be achieved by interventions other than those currently employed.

Program Developer

As noted earlier, practitioners often have opportunities to develop services in response to emerging needs of clients. Such services may include educational programs (e.g., for immigrants or unwed pregnant teenagers), support groups (e.g., for rape victims, adult children of alcoholics, and victims of incest), and skill development programs (e.g., stress management, parenting, and assertiveness training groups).

Planner

In small communities and rural areas that lack access to community planners, direct practitioners may need to assume a planning role, usually in concert with community leaders. In this role, the practitioner works both formally and informally with influential people to plan programs that respond to unmet and emerging needs. Such needs could include child care programs, transportation for elderly and disabled persons, and recreational and health care programs, to name just a few.

Policy and Procedure Developer

EP 2.1.8

Participation of direct practitioners in formulating policies and procedures typically is limited to the agencies in which they provide direct services to clients. Their degree of participation in such activities is largely determined by the style of administration with a given agency. Able administrators generally solicit and invite input from professional staff about how the agency can more effectively respond to the consumers of its services. Because social workers serve on the "front lines," they are strategically positioned to evaluate clients' needs and to assess how policies and procedures serve—or fail to serve—the best interests of clients. For these reasons, social workers should become actively involved in decision-making processes related to policies and procedure.

In rural areas and small communities, direct practitioners often participate in policy development concerned with the needs of a broad community rather than the needs of a circumscribed target group. In such instances, social workers must draw from knowledge and skills gained in courses in social welfare policy and services and community planning.

Advocate

EP 2.1.1a

Just as social workers may advocate for an individual client, so they may also join client groups, other social workers, and allied professionals in advocating for legislation and social policies aimed at providing needed resources and enhancing social justice.

Summary

Direct social work practice is characterized by performance of multiple roles. Those roles are carried out at several system levels, depending on the level of the concerns addressed. Knowledge and skills related to some of these roles are taught in segments of the curriculum that lie outside direct practice courses. To do justice in one volume to the knowledge and skills entailed in all these roles is impossible; consequently, we have limited our focus primarily to the roles involved in providing direct service.

CourseMate

Access an integrated eBook and chapter-specific learning tools including glossary terms, chapter outlines, relevant web links, videos, and practice quizzes. Go to www.cengagebrain.com.

CHAPTER 3
Helping Process Overview

CHAPTER OVERVIEW

This chapter provides an overview of the three phases of the helping process: exploration, implementation, and termination. The helping process focuses on problem solving with social work clients in a variety of settings, including those found along a continuum of voluntarism. Hence, the process is presented with the larger systems context in mind. In addition, we present the structure and ingredients of interviews that will be examined in more detail in Chapters 5 and 6.

At the completion of your work on this chapter, you will be able to:

- Identify steps in the helping process from exploration through implementation and termination
- Plan the structure and environment for interviews

EPAS COMPETENCIES IN THE 3RD CHAPTER

This chapter will give you the information needed to meet the following practice competencies:

2.1.1 Identify as a professional social worker and conduct ones self accordingly:
   f. Use supervision and consultation

2.1.3 Apply critical thinking to inform and communicate professional judgments:
   b. Analyze models of assessment, prevention, intervention, and evaluation

2.1.4 Engage Diversity and Difference in Practice:
   b. Gain sufficient self-awareness to eliminate the influence of personal biases and values in working with diverse groups

2.1.7 Apply knowledge of human behavior and the social environment:
   a. Utilize conceptual frameworks to guide the process of assessment, intervention, and evaluation
   b. Critique and apply knowledge to understand person and environment

2.1.10 Engage, assess, intervene, and evaluate with individuals, families, groups, organizations and communities:
   a. Substantively and affectively prepare for action with individuals, families, groups, organizations, and communities
   b. Use empathy and other interpersonal skills
   c. Develop a mutually agreed-on focus of work and desired outcomes.
   d. Collect, organize, and interpret client data
   e. Assess client strengths and limitations
   f. Develop mutually agreed-on intervention goals and objectives
   g. Select appropriate intervention strategies
   j. Help clients resolve problems
   k. Negotiate, mediate, and advocate for clients
   l. Facilitate transitions and endings
   m. Critically analyze, monitor, and evaluate interventions

Common Elements among Diverse Theorists and Social Workers

Direct social workers working with individuals, couples, families, groups, and other systems draw on contrasting theories of human behavior, use different models of practice, implement diverse interventions, and serve widely varying clients (Cameron & Keenan, 2010). Despite these varied factors, such social workers share a common goal: to assist clients in coping more effectively with problems of living and improving the quality of their lives. People are impelled by either internal or external sources to secure social work services because current solutions are not succeeding in their lives. Helping approaches differ in the extent to which they are problem versus goal focused. We take the position that it is important for direct social workers to take seriously the problems compelling clients to seek services as well as to work creatively with them toward achieving solutions that *improve* upon the initial problematic situation (McMillen, Morris & Sherraden, 2004).

Whether a potential client perceives a need or seeks help is a critical issue in planning how services may be offered. Their reaction to those internal or external sources plays a part in their motivation for and reaction to the prospects for contact with a social worker. Often a need for help has been identified by external sources such as teachers, doctors, employers, or family members. Such persons might be best considered referrals because they did not apply for service (Compton, Galaway, & Cournoyer, 2005). Persons who are referred vary in the extent to which they perceive that referral as a source of pressure or simply as a source of potential assistance.). Individuals who initiate their contact as applicants, referrals, or involuntary clients are all potential clients if they can negotiate a contract addressing some of their concerns. Children are a special case of potential client as they are rarely applicants and usually referred by teachers or family members for concerns others have about their behavior.

However potential clients begin their contact, they face a situation of disequilibrium in which they can potentially enhance their problem-solving ability by developing new resources or employing untapped resources in ways that reduce tension and achieve mastery over problems. Whatever their approach to assisting clients, most direct social workers employ a process aimed at reducing client concerns. That is, social workers try to assist clients in assessing the concerns that they perceive or that their environment presses upon them, making decisions about fruitful ways to identify and prioritize those concerns. Next, the social worker and client jointly identify potential approaches to reduce those concerns and make decisions about which courses of action to pursue. Emily and Hailey jointly identify concerns related to Hailey's feeling lonely and isolated at the school, feeling disconnected to her mother, as well as concerns about her declining grades. In order to arrive at these joint concerns, Emily has to assess Hailey's depressed affect in their second session and conduct a danger assessment to determine whether she is at risk of self-harm. Intervention approaches are selected in part by available evidence about how effective they are at reducing client concerns. Involuntary clients face situations in which some of the concerns are not their own and some of the approaches to reduce those concerns may be mandated by other parties.

Even in these circumstances, clients have the power to make at least constrained choices regarding how they address these concerns or additional concerns beyond those that they have been mandated to address. After these strategic approaches have been identified and selected, they are implemented.

IDEAS IN ACTION

In the video, "Hanging with Hailey" (HWH), a school social worker, Emily, meets with Hailey, an adolescent referred by teachers because of their concern with her declining academic performance. Hailey is not legally required to meet with Emily, and yet she amply demonstrates that she is not a voluntary client, seeking service. She emphasizes that she has done nothing wrong and should not have to see the social worker. It is not unusual in these circumstances for adolescents to view a referral to the social worker as a stigma or punishment for bad behavior. The challenge for social workers such as Emily is to empathically respond to Hailey's concerns at the same time as she conducts an assessment to determine whether there might be a dangerous concern that might account for the change in behavior.

Working together, the client and the social worker then assess the success of their efforts and revise their plans as necessary. Social workers use a variety of communication skills to implement the problem-solving process given the many different systems involved in clients' concerns.

The first portion of this chapter gives an overview of the helping process and its three distinct phases; subsequent parts of the book are organized to correspond to these phases. The latter part of this chapter focuses on the structure and processes involved in interviewing—a critical aspect of dealing with clients. Later chapters deal with the structure, processes, and skills involved in modifying the processes of families and groups.

The Helping Process

The helping process consists of three major phases (see figure on inside cover of text):

Phase I: Exploration, engagement, assessment, and planning
Phase II: Implementation and goal attainment
Phase III: Termination

Each of these phases has distinct objectives, and the helping process generally proceeds successively through them. The three phases, however, are not sharply demarcated by the activities and skills employed. Indeed, the activities and skills employed in the three phases differ more in terms of their frequency and intensity than in the kind used. The processes of exploration and assessment, for example, are central during Phase I, but these processes continue in somewhat diminished significance during subsequent phases of the helping process.

Phase I: Exploration, Engagement, Assessment, and Planning

EP 2.1.10a

The first phase lays the groundwork for subsequent implementation of interventions and strategies aimed at resolving clients' problems and promoting problem-solving skills. It represents a key step in helping relationships of any duration and setting—from crisis intervention and discharge planning to long-term and institutional care. Processes involved and tasks to be accomplished during Phase I include the following:

1. Exploring clients' problems by eliciting comprehensive data about the person(s), the problem, and environmental factors, including forces influencing the referral for contact
2. Establishing rapport and enhancing motivation
3. Formulating a multidimensional assessment of the problem, identifying systems that play a significant role in the difficulties, and identifying relevant resources that can be tapped or must be developed
4. Mutually negotiating goals to be accomplished in remedying or alleviating problems and formulating a contract
5. Making referrals

We briefly discuss each of these five processes in the following sections and refer to portions of the book that include extensive discussions of these processes.

EP 2.1.7a

Exploring clients' problems by eliciting comprehensive data about the person(s), the problem, and environmental factors, including forces influencing the referral for contact. Contact begins with an initial exploration of the circumstances that have led the potential client to meet with the social worker. Social workers should not assume that potential clients are applicants at this point, because self-referred persons are the minority of clients served in many settings; even those who self-refer often do so at the suggestion or pressure of others (Cingolani, 1984).

Potential clients may be anxious about the prospect of seeking help and lack knowledge about what to expect. For many, the social worker will have information from an intake form or referral source about the circumstances that have brought them into contact. These many possibilities can be explored by asking questions such as the following:

- "I have read your intake form. Can you tell me what brings you here, in your own words?"
- "How can we help you?"

These questions should elicit a beginning elaboration of the concern or pressures that the potential client sees as relating to his or her contact. The social worker can begin to determine to what extent the motivation for contact was initiated by the potential client and to what extent the motivation represents a response to external forces. For example, adolescents such as Hailey in the video are often referred by teachers who are concerned about their classroom behavior or ability to learn in the classroom. The social worker should begin in such circumstances with a matter-of-fact, nonthreatening description of the circumstances that led to the referral, such as:

- In the HWH video, the social worker, Emily might have said "You were referred by a teacher who was concerned about some changes in your behavior. Be assured that you have not done anything wrong. I would like to check with you to see how things are going with you and whether I might be of service to you."

The social worker should also give a clear, brief description of his or her own view of the purpose of this first contact and encourage an exploration of how the social worker can be helpful:

- "We are meeting to both explore the teacher's concerns and also to hear from you about how things are going at school as you see it. My job is to find out what things you would like to see go better and to figure out with you ways that we might work together so that you get more out of school."

EP 2.1.10b

Establishing rapport and enhancing motivation. Effective communication in the helping relationship is crucial. Unless the social worker succeeds in engaging the potential client, the client may be reluctant to reveal vital information and feelings and, even worse, may not return after the initial session.

Engaging clients successfully means establishing rapport, which reduces the level of threat and gains the trust of clients, who recognize that the social worker intends to be helpful. One condition of rapport is that clients perceive a social worker as understanding and genuinely interested in their well-being. To create such a positive perception among clients who may differ in significant ways from the social worker (including race or ethnicity, gender, sexual orientation, age, for example), the social worker must attend to relevant cultural factors and vary interviewing techniques accordingly (interviewing is discussed later in this chapter and throughout the book). Potential clients may draw conclusions about the openness of the agency to their concerns through the intake forms that they must complete. For example, forms asking for marital status that do not allow for enduring relationships that cannot include legal marriage may communicate insensitivity to gay, lesbian, bisexual, and transgendered people (Charnley & Langley, 2007). Further, when potential clients have been referred by others, these individuals will need to be reassured that their wishes are important and that they do not have to necessarily work on the concerns seen by the referral source.

Potential clients who are not applicants or genuinely self-referred frequently have misgivings about the helping process. They do not perceive themselves as having a problem and often attribute the source of difficulties to another person or to untoward circumstances.

Such clients face social workers with several challenging tasks:

- *Neutralizing negative feelings*
- *Attempting to help potential clients understand problems identified by others and assessing the advantages and disadvantages of dealing with those concerns*
- *Creating an incentive to work on acknowledged problems*

Skillful social workers often succeed in tapping into the motivation of such involuntary clients, thus affirming the principle from systems theory that motivation is substantially influenced by the interaction between clients and social workers.

In other instances, clients may freely acknowledge problems and may have incentive for change but assume a passive role, expecting social workers to magically work out their difficulties for them. Social workers must avoid taking on the impossible role that some clients would ascribe to them. Instead, they should voice a belief in clients' abilities to work as partners in searching for remedial courses of action and mobilize clients' energies in implementing the tasks essential to successful problem resolution. In addition to concerns, it is helpful to identify what things are going well in the client's life and identify ways the client is now coping with difficult situations.

One very useful strategy is to acknowledge the client's problem and explicitly recognize the client's motivation to actively work toward its solution. Potential clients do not lack motivation; rather, they sometimes lack motivation to work on the problems and goals perceived by others. In addition, motivation relates to a person's past experience, which leads him or her to expect that behaviors will be successful or will fail in attempting to reach goals. Hence, individuals with limited expectations for success often appear to lack motivation. As a consequence, social workers must often attempt to increase motivation by assisting clients to discover that their actions can be effective in reaching their goals (Gold, 1990). Motivation can also be seen in terms of stages of change. In some cases, clients can be said to be in precontemplation and have not yet considered a problem that has been perceived by others (Di Clemente & Prochaska, 1998). For example, the student referred for lateness and perceived tiredness may not have thought about this as an issue of personal responsibility, perhaps feeling powerless over whether adults and siblings help him or her to get to school or to bed on time. Frequently, clients can be in the contemplation stage, in that they are aware of the issue but are not fully aware of the options, benefits for changing, and consequences for not changing (Di Clemente & Prochaska, 1998). Such clients can be helped to explore those possibilities. For example, the social worker can gather information from the child about sleeping patterns and rituals involved in getting ready for school. They can explore together what might happen if the child continues to arrive late and be tired in school and how things might be different if behavior patterns were modified to arrive at school on time and rested.

Social workers, therefore, must be able to tap into client motivation and assist those individuals who readily acknowledge a problem but are reluctant to expend the required effort or bear the discomfort involved in effecting essential change. A major task in this process is to provide information to the potential client about what to expect from the helping process. This socialization effort includes identifying the kinds of concerns with which the social worker and agency can help, client rights including confidentiality and circumstances in which it might be abridged, and information about what behavior to expect from the social worker and client (Trotter, 2006).

The task for clients in groups is twofold: They must develop trust in the social worker, and they must develop trust in the other group members. If group members vary in race, ethnicity, or social class, the group leader must be sensitive to such potential cultural influences on behavior. He or she must assume a facilitative role in breaking down related barriers to rapport not only between the social worker and individual group members, but also among group members.

Developing group norms and mutual expectations together assists in the creation of a group cohesiveness that helps groups become successful. Establishing rapport requires that social workers demonstrate a nonjudgmental attitude, acceptance, respect for clients' right of self-determination, and respect for clients' worth and dignity, uniqueness and individuality, and problem-solving capacities. Finally, social workers foster rapport when they relate to clients with empathy and authenticity. Both skills are considered in later chapters of this book.

Formulating a multidimensional assessment of the problem, identifying systems that play a significant role in the difficulties, and identifying relevant resources that can be tapped or must be developed. Social workers must simultaneously establish rapport with their clients and explore their problems. These activities reinforce each other, as astute exploration yields both information and a sense of trust and confidence in the social worker.

EP 2.1.10d & e

A social worker who demonstrates empathy is able to foster rapport and show the client that the social worker understands what he or she is expressing. This, in turn, encourages more openness on the client's part and expands his or her expression of feelings. The greater willingness to share deepens the social worker's understanding of the client's situation and the role that emotions play in both their difficulties and their capabilities. Thus the social worker's communication skills serve multiple functions: They facilitate relationship building, they encourage information sharing, and they establish rapport.

Problem exploration is a critical process, because comprehensive information must be gathered before all of the dimensions of a problem and their interaction can be understood. Exploration begins by attending to the emotional states and immediate concerns manifested by the client. Gradually, the social worker broadens the exploration to encompass relevant systems (individual, interpersonal, and environmental) and explores the most critical aspects of the problem in depth. During this discovery process, the social worker is also alert to and highlights client strengths, realizing that these strengths represent a vital resource to be tapped later during the goal attainment phase. Social workers can assist clients in identifying ways in which they are currently coping and exceptions when problems do not occur (Greene et al., 2005). For example, the social worker working with the child client can help the child identify days on which he or she is on time for school and rested and to trace back the environmental conditions at home that facilitated such an outcome.

Skills that are employed in the exploratory process with individuals, couples, families, and groups are delineated later in this chapter and at length in subsequent chapters. To explore problematic situations thoroughly, social workers must also be knowledgeable about the various systems commonly involved in human difficulties.

Problem exploration skills are used during the assessment process that begins with the first contact with clients and continues throughout the helping relationship. During interviews, social workers weigh the significance of clients' behavior, thoughts, beliefs, emotions, and, of course, information revealed. These moment-by-moment assessments guide social workers in deciding which aspects of problems to explore in depth, when to explore emotions more deeply, and so on. In addition to this ongoing process of assessment, social workers must formulate a working assessment from which flow the goals and contract upon which Phase II of the problem-solving process is based. An adequate assessment includes analysis of the problem, the person(s), and the ecological context.

Because there are many possible areas that can be explored but limited time available to explore them, focus in assessment is critical. Retaining such a focus is promoted by conducting the assessment in layers. At the first layer, you must focus your attention on issues of client safety, legal mandates, and the client's wishes for service. The rationale for this threefold set of priorities is that client wishes should take precedence in circumstances in which legal mandates do not impinge on choices or in which no dangers to self or others exist.

When you analyze the problem, you can identify which factors are contributing to difficulties—for example, inadequate resources; decisions about a crucial aspect of one's life; difficulties in individual, interpersonal, or societal systems; or interactions between any of the preceding factors. Analysis of the problem also involves making judgments about the duration and severity of a problem as well as the extent to which the problem is susceptible to change, given the client's potential coping capacity. In considering the nature and severity of problems, social workers must weigh these factors against their own competencies and the types of services provided by the agency. If the problems call for services that are beyond the agency's function, such as prescribing medication or rendering speech therapy, referral to another professional or agency may be indicated.

Analysis of the individual system includes assessment of the client's wants and needs, coping capacity, strengths and limitations, and motivation to work on the problem(s). In evaluating the first two dimensions, the social worker must assess such factors as flexibility, judgment, emotional characteristics, degree of responsibility, capacity to tolerate stress, ability to reason critically, and interpersonal skills. These factors, which are critical in selecting appropriate and attainable goals, are discussed at length in Chapter 9.

Assessment of ecological factors entails consideration of the adequacy or deficiency, success or failure, and strengths or weaknesses of salient systems in the environment that bear on the client's problem. Ecological assessment aims to identify systems that must be strengthened, mobilized, or developed to satisfy the client's unmet needs. Systems that often affect clients' needs include couple, family, and social support systems (e.g., kin, friends, neighbors, coworkers, peer groups, and ethnic reference groups); spiritual belief systems; child care, health care, and employment systems; various institutions; and the physical environment. For example, the social worker would work with the child and parent in our example to identify those persons and conditions in terms of availability of transportation, responsibilities for child care, and availability of others in the evening and in the morning to help the child get ready for school that could be pertinent support systems.

Cultural factors are also vital in ecological assessment, because personal and social needs and the means of satisfying them vary widely from culture to culture. Moreover, the resources that can be tapped to meet clients' needs vary according to cultural contexts. Some cultures include indigenous helping persons, such as folk healers, religious leaders, and relatives from extended family units who have been invested with authority to assist members of that culture in times of crisis. These persons can often provide valuable assistance to social workers and their clients.

Assessment of the client's situational context also requires analyzing the circumstances as well as the actions and reactions of participants in the problematic interaction. Knowledge of the circumstances and specific behaviors of participants before, during, and after troubling events is crucial to understanding the forces that shape and maintain problematic behavior. Assessment, therefore, requires that social workers elicit detailed information about actual transactions between people.

Whether making assessments of individuals per se or assessments of individuals as subsets of couples, families, or groups, it is important to assess the functioning of these larger systems. These systems have unique properties, including power distribution, role definitions, rules, norms, channels of communication, and repetitive interactional patterns. Such systems also boast both strengths and problems that strongly shape the behavior of constituent members. It follows that individual difficulties tend to be related to systemic difficulties, so interventions must therefore be directed to both the system and the individual.

Assessments of systems are based on a variety of data-gathering procedures. With couples and families, social workers may or may not conduct individual interviews, depending on the evidence available about the effectiveness of family intervention with particular concerns, agency practices, and impressions gained during preliminary contacts with family members. If exploration and assessment are implemented exclusively in conjoint sessions, these processes are similar to those employed in individual interviews except that the interaction between the participants assumes major significance. Whereas information gleaned through individual interviews is limited to reports and descriptions by clients, requiring the social worker to make inferences about the actual interaction within the relevant systems, social workers can view interactions directly in conjoint interviews and group sessions. In such cases, the social worker should be alert to strengths and difficulties in communication and interaction and to the properties of the system. As a consequence, assessment focuses heavily on the styles of communication employed by individual participants, interactional patterns among members, and the impact of individual members on processes that occur in the system. These factors are weighed when selecting interventions intended to enhance functioning at these different levels of the larger systems.

Finally, a working assessment involves synthesizing all relevant information gathered as part of the exploration process. To enhance the validity of such assessments, social workers should involve clients in the process by soliciting their perceptions and assisting them in gathering data about their perceived difficulties and hopes. Social workers can share their impressions with their clients, for example, and then invite affirmation or disconfirmation of those impressions. It is also beneficial to highlight their strengths and to identify other relevant resource systems that can be tapped or need to be developed to resolve the difficulties. When social workers and their clients reach agreement about the nature of the problems involved, they are ready to enter the process of negotiating goals.

EP 2.1.10f

Mutually negotiating goals to be accomplished in remedying or alleviating the problem and formulating a contract. If the social worker and the individual client, couple, family, or group have reached agreement concerning the nature of the difficulties and the systems that are involved, the participants are ready to negotiate individual and/or group goals. This mutual process aims to identify what needs to be changed and what related actions need to be taken to resolve or ameliorate the problematic situation. We briefly discuss the process of goal selection in this chapter and at length in Chapter 13. If agreement is not reached about the appropriateness of services or clients choose not to continue, then services may be terminated. In some situations, then, services are finished when the assessment is completed.

In the case of involuntary clients, some may continue the social work contact under pressure even if agreement is not reached about the appropriateness of services or if problems are not acknowledged. After goals have been negotiated, participants undertake the final task of Phase I: formulating a contract. The contract, which is also mutually negotiated, consists of a formal agreement or understanding between the social worker and the client that specifies the goals to be accomplished, relevant strategies to be implemented, roles and responsibilities of participants, practical arrangements, and other factors. When the client system is a couple, family, or group, the contract also specifies group goals that tend to accelerate group movement and to facilitate accomplishment of group goals.

Mutually formulating a contract is a vital process because it demystifies the helping process and clarifies for clients what they may realistically expect from the social worker and what is expected of them; what they will mutually be seeking to accomplish and in what ways; and what the problem-solving process entails. Contracting with voluntary clients is relatively straightforward; it specifies what the client desires to accomplish through social work contact. Contracting with involuntary clients contains another layer of legally mandated problems or concerns in addition to the clients' expressed wishes.

The solution-focused approach takes the position that goals are central when working with clients (De Jong & Berg, 2002). Those goals, however, may not be directly related to rectifying or eliminating the concern that initially prompted the contact. Utilizing a solution-focused approach, clients and practitioners can sometimes create or co-construct a solution that will meet the concerns of clients as well as legal requirements (De Jong & Berg, 2001). The solution may be reached without working from a problem viewpoint. For example, a child referred for setting fires might work toward a goal of becoming safe, trustworthy, and reliable in striking matches under adult supervision. By focusing on goals as perceived by clients, an empowering momentum may be created that draws out hidden strengths and resources. We also take the position that empowering clients to discover and make best use of available resources is desirable. Sometimes, focusing on problems can be counterproductive. However, in funding and agency environments that are problem focused both in terms of philosophy and funding streams, ignoring problem conceptions carries risk (McMillen et al., 2004).

In summary, we are influenced by solution-focused methods to support client ownership of goals and methods for seeking them (De Jong, 2001). We differ from the solution-focused method, however, in that we do not assume that all clients have within them the solutions to all of their concerns. Expert information about solutions that have worked for clients in similar situations can often prove valuable (Reid, 2000). Rather than assuming that "the client always knows" or "the social worker always knows," we take the position that the social worker's task is to facilitate a situation in which both client and worker share their information while constructing plans for problem resolution (Reid, 2000). We explore the solution-focused approach more in Chapter 13.

Making referrals. Exploration of clients' problems often reveals that resources or services beyond those provided by the agency are needed to remedy or ameliorate presenting difficulties. This is especially true of clients who have multiple unmet needs. In such instances, referrals to other resources and service providers may be necessary. Unfortunately, clients may lack the knowledge or skills needed to avail themselves of these badly needed resources. Social workers may assume the role of case manager in such instances (e.g., for persons with severe and persistent mental illness, individuals with developmental and physical disabilities, foster children, and infirm elderly clients). Linking clients to other resource systems requires careful handling if clients are to follow through in seeking and obtaining essential resources.

Phase II: Implementation and Goal Attainment

EP 2.1.10j

After mutually formulating a contract, the social worker and client(s) enter the heart of the problem-solving process—the implementation and goal attainment phase, also known as the action-oriented or change-oriented phase. Phase II involves translating the plans formulated jointly by the social worker and individual clients, couples, families, or groups into actions. In short, the participants combine their efforts in working toward the goal assigned the highest priority. This process begins by dissecting the goal into general tasks that identify general strategies to be employed in pursuit of the goal. These general tasks are then subdivided into specific tasks that designate what the client and social worker plan to do between one session and the next (Fortune, McCallion & Briar-Lawson, 2010; Epstein & Brown, 2002; Reid, 1992; Robinson, 1930; Taft, 1937).[1] Tasks may relate to the individual's personal functioning or to his or her interaction with others, or they may involve interaction with other resource systems, such as schools, hospitals, or law enforcement agencies. The processes of negotiating goals and tasks are discussed in detail in Chapter 12.

After formulating goals with clients, social workers select and implement interventions designed to assist clients in accomplishing those goals and subsidiary tasks. Interventions should directly relate to the problems that were identified and the goals that were mutually negotiated with clients and derived from accurate assessment. Helping efforts often fail when social workers employ global interventions without considering clients' views of their problems and ignore the uniqueness of each client's problems.

Enhancing Self-Efficacy

Research findings (Dolan et al., 2008, Bandura & Locke, 2003; Washington & Moxley, 2003; Lane, Daugherty, & Nyman, 1998) have strongly indicated that the helping process is greatly enhanced when clients experience an increased sense of self-efficacy as part of this process. Self-efficacy refers to an expectation or belief that one can successfully accomplish tasks or perform behaviors associated with specified goals. Note that the concept overlaps with notions of individual empowerment.

The most powerful means for enhancing self-efficacy is to assist clients in actually performing certain behaviors prerequisite to accomplishing their goals. Another potent technique is to make clients aware of their strengths and to recognize incremental progress of clients toward goal attainment.

Family and group members also represent potent resources for enhancing self-efficacy. Social workers can develop and tap these resources by assisting families and groups to accomplish tasks that involve perceiving and accrediting the strengths and progress of group and family members. We consider other sources of self-efficacy and relevant techniques in Chapter 13.

Monitoring Progress

EP 2.1.10m

As work toward goal attainment proceeds, it is important to monitor progress on a regular basis.

The reasons for this are fourfold:

1. *To evaluate the effectiveness of change strategies and interventions.* Social workers are increasingly required to document the efficacy of services to satisfy third-party payers with a managed care system. In addition, social workers owe it to their clients to select interventions based on the best available evidence (Thyer, 2002). If an approach or intervention is not producing desired effects, social workers should determine the reasons for this failure or consider negotiating a different approach.
2. *To guide clients' efforts toward goal attainment.* Evaluating progress toward goals enhances continuity of focus and efforts and promotes efficient use of time (Corcoran & Vandiver, 1996).
3. *To keep abreast of clients' reactions to progress or lack of progress.* When they believe they are not progressing, clients tend to become discouraged and may lose confidence in the helping process. By evaluating progress periodically, social workers will be alerted to negative client reactions that might otherwise undermine the helping process.
4. *To concentrate on goal attainment and evaluate progress.* These efforts will tend to sustain clients' motivation to work on their problems.

Methods of evaluating progress range from eliciting subjective opinions to using various types of measurement instruments. Chapters 12 and 19 include both quantitative and qualitative methods for monitoring progress and measuring change.

Barriers to Goal Accomplishment

As clients strive to accomplish goals and related tasks, their progress is rarely smooth and uneventful. Instead, clients typically encounter obstacles and experience anxiety, uncertainties, fears, and other undesirable reactions as they struggle to solve problems. Furthermore, family or group members or other significant persons may undermine the client's efforts to change by opposing such changes, by ridiculing the client for seeing a social worker, by making derisive comments about the social worker, or by otherwise making change even more difficult for the client. (For this reason, it is vital to involve significant others in the problem-solving process whenever feasible.) Because of the challenges posed by these barriers to change, social workers must be mindful of their clients' struggles and skillful in assisting them to surmount these obstacles.

Barriers to goal accomplishment are frequently encountered in work with families and groups. Such barriers include personality factors that limit participation of certain group members, problematic behaviors of group members, or processes within the group that impede progress. They also encompass impediments in the family's environment.

Still other barriers may involve organizational opposition to change within systems whose resources are essential to goal accomplishment. Denial of resources or services (e.g., health care, rehabilitation, or public assistance) by organizations, or policies and procedures that unduly restrict clients' access to resources, may require the social worker to assume the role of mediator or advocate.

Relational Reactions

As social workers and clients work together in solving problems, emotional reactions on the part of either party toward the other may impair the effectiveness of the working partnership and pose an obstacle to goal accomplishment.

EP 2.1.10b

Clients, for example, may have unrealistic expectations or may misperceive the intent of the social worker. Consequently, clients may experience disappointment, discouragement, hurt, anger, rejection, longing for closeness, or many other emotional reactions that may seriously impede progress toward goals.

Couple partners, parents, and group members may also experience relational reactions to other members of these larger client systems, resulting in problematic interactional patterns within these systems. Not uncommonly, these reactions reflect attitudes and beliefs learned from relationships with parents or significant others. In many other instances, however, the social worker or members of clients' systems may unknowingly behave in ways that trigger unfavorable relational reactions by individuals or family or group members. In either event, it is critical to explore and resolve these harmful relational reactions. Otherwise, clients' efforts may be diverted from working toward goal accomplishment or—even worse—clients may prematurely withdraw from the helping process.

Social workers are susceptible to relational reactions as well. Social workers who relate in an authentic manner provide clients with experience that is transferable to the real world of the client's social environment. They communicate

EP 2.1.1f

that they are human beings who are not immune to making blunders and experiencing emotions and desires as part of their relationships with clients. It is vital that social workers be aware of their reactions to clients and understand how to manage them. Otherwise, they may be working on their own problems rather than the client's issues, placing the helping process in severe jeopardy. For example, a student practitioner became aware that she was relating to a client who had difficulty in making and carrying out plans as if the client were a family member, with whom the student had similar difficulties. Becoming aware of those associations through supervision made it possible to separate out the client before her from the family member. Chapter 18 offers advice to assist social workers in coping with potential relational reactions residing with the client(s), the social worker, or both.

Enhancing Clients' Self-Awareness

As clients interact in a novel relationship with a social worker and risk trying out new interpersonal behaviors in their couple, family, or group contacts, they commonly experience emotions that may be pleasing, frightening, confusing, and even overwhelming. Although managing such emotional reactions may require a temporary detour from goal attainment activities, these efforts frequently represent rich opportunities for growth in self-awareness. Self-awareness is the first step to self-realization. Many voluntary clients wish to understand themselves more fully, and they can benefit from becoming more aware of feelings that have previously been buried or denied expression.

Social workers can facilitate the process of self-discovery by employing additive empathic responses during the goal attainment phase. Additive empathic responses focus on deeper feelings than do reciprocal empathic responses (referred to earlier in the discussion of Phase I). This technique can be appropriately applied in both individual and conjoint interviews as well as in group sessions. Additive empathy is particularly beneficial in assisting clients to get in touch with their emotions and express those feelings clearly to their significant others.

Another technique used to foster self-awareness is confrontation. This technique helps clients become aware of growth-defeating discrepancies in perceptions, feelings, communications, behavior, values, and attitudes, and then examine these discrepancies in relation to stated goals. Confrontation is also used in circumstances when clients act to violate laws or threaten their own safety or the safety of others. Confrontation must be offered in the context of goodwill, and it requires high skill.

Use of Self

EP 2.1.1b

As helping relationships grow stronger during the implementation and goal attainment phase, social workers increasingly use themselves as tools to facilitate growth and accomplishment. Relating spontaneously and appropriately disclosing one's feelings, views, and experiences ensure that clients have an encounter with an open and authentic human being. Modeling authentic behavior encourages clients to reciprocate by risking authentic behavior themselves, thereby achieving significant growth in self-realization and in interpersonal relations. Indeed there is research that demonstrates that those social workers who are perceived as acting in prosocial ways by their clients through actions such as returning telephone calls promptly, have better outcomes than clients who perceive their social workers as less responsive (Trotter, 2006).

Indeed, *when group leaders* model authentic behavior in groups, members may follow suit by exhibiting similar behavior. Social workers who relate in an authentic manner provide their clients with experience that is transferable to the clients' real-world social relationships. A contrived, detached, and sterile "professional" relationship, by contrast, lacks transferability to other relationships. Obviously, these issues should be covered in the training process for social workers.

Assertiveness involves dealing tactfully but firmly with problematic behaviors that impinge on the helping relationship or impede progress toward goal attainment. For example, when clients' actions conflict with their goals or are potentially harmful to themselves or others, the social worker must deal with these situations. Further, social workers must sometimes relate assertively to larger client systems—for example, to focus on behavior of group members that hinders the accomplishment of goals. Using oneself to relate authentically and assertively is a major focus of Chapter 5.

Phase III: Termination

The terminal phase of the helping process involves three major aspects:

EP 2.1.10l

1. Assessing when client goals have been satisfactorily attained

2. Helping the client develop strategies that maintain change and continue growth following the termination
3. Successfully terminating the helping relationship

Deciding when to terminate is relatively straightforward when time limits are specified in advance as part of the initial contact, as is done with the task-centered approach and other brief treatment strategies. Decisions about when to terminate are also simple when individual or group goals are clear-cut (e.g., to get a job, obtain a prosthetic device, arrange for nursing care, secure tutoring for a child, implement a specific group activity, or hold a public meeting).

In other instances, goals involve growth or changes that have no limits; thus judgments must be made by the social worker and client in tandem about when a satisfactory degree of change has been achieved. Examples of such goals include increasing self-esteem, communicating more effectively, becoming more outgoing in social situations, and resolving conflicts more effectively. In these cases, the ambiguity of termination can be reduced by developing specific, operational indicators of goal achievement. Today, however, many decisions about termination and extension involve third parties, as contracts for service and payers such as managed care may regulate the length and conditions of service (Corcoran & Vandiver, 1996).

Successfully Terminating Helping Relationships

Social workers and clients often respond positively to termination, reflecting pride and accomplishment on the part of both parties (Fortune, Pearlingi, & Rochelle, 1992). Clients who were required or otherwise pressured to see the social worker may experience a sense of relief at getting rid of the pressure or freeing themselves from the strictures of outside scrutiny. In contrast, because voluntary clients share personal problems and are accompanied through rough emotional terrain by a caring social worker, they often feel close to the social worker. Consequently, termination tends to produce mixed feelings for these types of clients. They are likely to feel strong gratitude to the social worker, but are also likely to experience a sense of relief over no longer having to go through the discomfort associated with exploring problems and making changes (not to mention the relief from paying fees).

Although clients are usually optimistic about the prospects of confronting future challenges independently, they sometimes experience a sense of loss over terminating the working relationship. Moreover, uncertainty about their ability to cope independently may be mixed with their optimism.

When they have been engaged in the helping process for a lengthy period of time, clients may develop a strong attachment to a social worker, especially if the social worker has fostered dependency in their relationship. For such individuals, termination involves a painful process of letting go of a relationship that has satisfied significant emotional needs. Moreover, these clients often experience apprehension about facing the future without the reassuring strength represented by the social worker. Group members may experience similar painful reactions as they face the loss of supportive relationships with the social worker and group members as well as a valued resource that has assisted them to cope with their problems.

To effect termination with individuals or groups and minimize psychological stress requires both perceptiveness to emotional reactions and skills in helping clients to work through such reactions.

Planning Change Maintenance Strategies

Social workers have voiced concern over the need to develop strategies that maintain clients' changes and continue their growth after formal social work service is terminated (Rzepnicki, 1991). These concerns have been prompted by findings that after termination many clients relapse or regress to their previous level of functioning. Consequently, more attention is now being paid to strategies for maintaining change. Planning for follow-up sessions not only makes it possible to evaluate the durability of results, but also facilitates the termination process by indicating the social worker's continuing interest in clients, a matter we discuss in Chapter 19.

The Interviewing Process: Structure and Skills

Direct social workers employ interviewing as the primary vehicle of influence, although administrators and social planners also rely heavily on interviewing skills to accomplish their objectives. With the increasing emphasis on evidence-based practice, it becomes yet more important to develop core skills in interviewing that can be applied and revised according to varied situations. Skills in interviewing, active listening, discerning and confronting discrepancies, reframing, and reciprocal empathy skills are key ingredients in the generalist practice model (Adams, Matto, & Le Croy, 2009). These nonspecific factors have a considerable impact on outcomes (Cameron & Kieran, 2010; Drisko, 2004). That is, the relationship or therapeutic alliance has been shown to have considerable influence across studies (Norcross & Lambert, 2006). In fact, such relationship factors have been shown to account for up to 30 percent of variation in social work outcomes, while particular model and technique factors have accounted for only about 15 percent (Duncan & Miller, 2000; Hubble, Duncan & Miller, 1999).

Interviews vary according to purpose, types of setting, client characteristics, and number of participants. For example, they may involve interaction between a social worker and individuals, couples, and family units. Interviews are conducted in offices, homes, hospitals, prisons, automobiles, and other diverse settings. Interviews conducted with children are different than interviews with adults or seniors. Despite the numerous variables that affect interviews, certain factors are common to all effective interviews. This section identifies and discusses these essential factors and highlights relevant skills.

Physical Conditions

EP 2.1.10a

Interviews sometimes occur in offices or other settings over which the social worker has some control. Interviews that take place in a client's home, of course, are more subject to the client's preferences. The physical climate in which an interview is conducted partly determines the attitudes, feelings, and degree of cooperation and responsiveness of people during interviews. That environment should be constructed to feel supportive and not intimidating to potential clients. Indeed, some of the first conclusions clients are likely to draw about the values and competency of a setting are likely to be reflected in their first encounters with staff over the telephone or in person. If these potential clients are responded to promptly, courteously and respectfully, this treatment may go a long way toward preparing for a successful interaction with the social worker. The following conditions are conducive to productive interviews:

1. Adequate ventilation and light
2. Comfortable room temperature
3. Ample space (to avoid a sense of being confined or crowded)
4. Attractive and clean furnishings and décor
5. Chairs that adequately support the back
6. Privacy appropriate to the cultural beliefs of the client
7. Freedom from distraction
8. Open space between participants

The first five items obviously are concerned with providing a pleasant and comfortable environment and need no elaboration.

Privacy is vital, of course, because people are likely to be guarded in revealing personal information and expressing feelings if other people can see or hear them. Likewise, interviewers sometimes have difficulty in concentrating or expressing themselves when others can hear them. Settings vary in the extent to which social workers can control these conditions. For example, in some circumstances families may prefer to have trusted family members, friends, or spiritual leaders present to consider resolution of some issues (Burford & Hudson, 2009). In some settings, it may be impossible to ensure complete privacy. Even when interviewing a patient in a hospital bed, however, privacy can be maximized by closing doors, drawing curtains that separate beds, and requesting that nursing staff avoid nonessential interruptions. Privacy during home interviews may be even more difficult to arrange, but people will often take measures to reduce unnecessary intrusions or distractions if interviewers stress that privacy enhances the productivity of sessions (Allen and Tracy, 2009). Social workers in public social service settings often work in cubicle offices. To ensure privacy, they can conduct client interviews in special interview rooms.

Because interviews sometimes involve intense emotions by participants, freedom from distraction is a critical requirement. Telephone calls, knocks on the door, and external noises can impair concentration and disrupt important dialogue. Moreover, clients are unlikely to feel important and valued if social workers permit avoidable intrusions. Other sources of distraction include crying, attention seeking, and restless behavior of clients' infants or children. Small children, of course, cannot be expected to sit quietly for more than short periods of time. For this reason, the social worker should encourage parents to make arrangements for the care of children during interviews (except when it is important to observe interaction between parents and their children). Because requiring such arrangements can create a barrier to service utilization, many social workers and agencies maintain a supply of toys for such occasions.

Having a desk between an interviewer and interviewee(s) emphasizes the authority of the social worker. For clients from some cultural groups, emphasizing the authority or position of the social worker may be a useful way to indicate that he or she occupies a formal, appropriate position. With many others, a desk between social worker and client creates a barrier that is not conducive to open communication. If safety of the social worker is an issue, then a desk barrier can be useful, unless it prevents the social worker from leaving if necessary. In some instances, an interviewer may believe that maximizing the social worker's authority through a desk barrier will promote his or her service objectives.

In most circumstances, however, social workers strive to foster a sense of equality. Hence, they arrange their desks so that they can rotate their chairs to a position where there is open space between them and their clients. Others prefer to leave their desks entirely and use other chairs in the room when interviewing.

Practitioners who interview children often find it useful to have available a small number of toys or items that the child can manipulate with their hands as well as materials for drawing pictures. Such practitioners have found that such tools or devices seem to reduce tension for children in communicating with unfamiliar adults and assist them in telling their story (Krähenbühl & Blades, 2006; Lamb & Brown, 2006; Lukas, 1993).

Structure of Interviews

Interviews in social work have a purpose, structure, direction, and focus. The purpose is to exchange information systematically with a view toward illuminating and solving problems, promoting growth, or planning strategies or actions aimed at improving the quality of life for people. The structure of interviews varies somewhat from setting to setting, from client to client, and from one phase of the helping process to another. Indeed, skillful interviewers adapt flexibly both to different contexts and to the ebb and flow of each individual session.

Each interview is unique. Nevertheless, effective interviews conform to a general structure, share certain properties, and reflect use of certain basic skills by interviewers. In considering these basic factors, we begin by focusing on the structure and processes involved in initial interviews.

Establishing Rapport

EP 2.1.10b

Before starting to explore clients' difficulties, it is important to establish rapport. Rapport with clients fosters open and free communication, which is the hallmark of effective interviews. Achieving rapport enables clients to gain trust in the helpful intent and goodwill of the social worker, such that they will be willing to risk revealing personal and sometimes painful feelings and information. Some clients readily achieve trust and confidence in a social worker, particularly when they have the capacity to form relationships easily. Voluntary clients often ask, "Who am I and why am I in this situation?"; involuntary clients have less reason to be initially trusting and ask, "Who are you and when will you leave?" (R. H. Rooney, 2009).

Establishing rapport begins by greeting the client(s) warmly and introducing yourself. If the client system is a family, you should introduce yourself to each family member. In making introductions and addressing clients, it is important to extend the courtesy of asking clients how they prefer to be addressed; doing so conveys your respect and desire to use the title they prefer. Although some clients prefer the informality involved in using first names, social workers should be discreet in using first-name introductions with all clients because of their diverse ethnic and social backgrounds. For example, some adult African Americans and members of other groups may interpret being addressed by their first names as indicative of a lack of respect (Edwards, 1982; McNeely & Badami, 1984).

With many clients, social workers must surmount formidable barriers before establishing rapport. Bear in mind that the majority of clients have had little or no experience with social work agencies and enter initial interviews or group sessions with uncertainty and apprehension. Many did not seek help initially; they may view having to seek assistance with their problems as evidence of failure, weakness, or inadequacy. Moreover, revealing personal problems is embarrassing and even humiliating for some people, especially those who have difficulty confiding in others.

Cultural factors and language differences compound potential barriers to rapport even further. For example, some Asian Americans and persons of other ethnic groups who retain strong ties to cultural traditions have been conditioned not to discuss personal or family problems with outsiders. Revealing problems to others may be perceived as a reflection of personal inadequacy and as a stigma upon the entire family. The resultant fear of shame may impede the development of rapport with clients from this ethnic group (Kumabe, Nishida, & Hepworth, 1985; Lum, 1996; Tsui & Schultz, 1985). Some African Americans, Native Americans, and Latinos may also experience difficulty in developing rapport because of distrust that derives from a history

EP 2.1.4b

of being exploited or discriminated against by other ethnic groups (Longres, 1991; Proctor & Davis, 1994).

Children may be unfamiliar with having conversational exchanges with unfamiliar adults (Lamb & Brown, 2006). For example, their exchanges with teachers may be primarily directive or a test of their knowledge. Asking them to describe events or family situations may be a new experience for them, and they may look for cues from the accompanying adult about how to proceed. Open-ended questions are advised to avoid providing leading questions.

Clients' difficulties in communicating openly tend to be exacerbated when their problems involve allegations of socially unacceptable behavior, such as child abuse, moral infractions, or criminal behavior. In groups, the pain is further compounded by having to expose one's difficulties to other group members, especially in early sessions when the reactions of other members represent the threat of the unknown.

EP 2.1.10b

One means of fostering rapport with clients is to employ a "warm-up" period. This is particularly important with some ethnic minority clients for whom such openings are the cultural norm, including Native Americans, persons with strong roots in the cultures of Asia and the Pacific Basin, and Latinos. Aguilar (1972), for example, has stressed the importance of warm-up periods in work with Mexican Americans. Many Native Hawaiians and Samoans also expect to begin new contacts with outside persons by engaging in "talk story," which involves warm, informal, and light personal conversation similar to that described by Aguilar. To plunge into discussion of serious problems without a period of talk story would be regarded by members of these cultural groups as rude and intrusive. Social workers who neglect to engage in a warm-up period are likely to encounter passive-resistant behavior from members of these cultural groups. A warm-up period and a generally slower tempo are also critically important with many Native American clients (Hull, 1982). Palmer and Pablo (1978) suggest that social workers who are most successful with Native Americans are low-key, nondirective individuals. Similarly, increased self-disclosure is reported by Hispanic practitioners as a useful part of developing rapport with Hispanic clients (Rosenthal-Gelman, 2004).

Warm-up periods are also important in establishing rapport with adolescents, many of whom are in a stage of emancipating themselves from adults. Consequently, they may be wary of social workers. This is especially true of individuals who are delinquent or are otherwise openly rebelling against authority. Moreover, adolescents who have had little or no experience with social workers have an extremely limited grasp of their roles. Many adolescents, at least initially, are involuntary clients and perceive social workers as adversaries, fearing that their role is to punish or to exercise power over them. The judgment of how much warm-up is necessary and how much is too much is a matter of art and experience with initially reluctant potential clients. This is seen in the HWH video in which Emily attempts to reduce Hailey's sense of strangeness and stigma about being referred for services.

With the majority of clients, a brief warm-up period is usually sufficient. When the preceding barriers do not apply, introductions and a brief discussion of a timely topic (unusual weather, a widely discussed local or national event, or a topic of known interest to the client) will adequately foster a climate conducive to exploring clients' concerns.

Most clients, in fact, expect to immediately plunge into discussion of their problems, and their anxiety level may grow if social workers delay getting to the business at hand (Ivanoff, Blythe, & Tripodi, 1994). This is particularly true with involuntary clients who did not seek the contact. With these clients, rapport often develops rapidly if social workers respond sensitively to their feelings and skillfully give direction to the process of exploration by sharing the circumstances of the referral, thereby defusing the threat sensed by such clients. Tuning in to their feelings and explaining what they can expect in terms of their role and that of the social worker goes a long way toward reducing these tensions (see Chapter 5).

Respect for clients is critical to establishing rapport, and we stress the importance of respecting clients' dignity and worth, uniqueness, capacities to solve problems, and other factors. An additional aspect of showing respect is demonstrating common courtesy. Being punctual, attending to the client's comfort, listening attentively, remembering the client's name, and assisting a client who has limited mobility convey the message that the social worker values the client and esteems his or her dignity and worth. Courtesy should never be taken lightly.

Verbal and nonverbal messages from social workers that convey understanding and acceptance of clients' feelings and views also facilitate the development of rapport. This does not mean agreeing with or condoning clients' views or problems, but rather apprehending and affirming clients' rights to have their own views, attitudes, and feelings.

Attentiveness to feelings and empathic responses to these feelings convey understanding that clients readily discern. Empathic responses clearly convey the message, "I am with you. I understand what you are saying and experiencing." The "workhorse" of successful helping persons, empathic responding, is important not only in Phase I of the helping process but in subsequent phases as well. Mastery of this vital skill (discussed extensively in Chapter 5) requires consistent and sustained practice.

Authenticity, or genuineness, is yet another social worker quality that facilitates rapport. Being authentic during Phase I of the helping process means relating as a genuine person rather than assuming a contrived and sterile professional role. Authentic behavior by social workers also models openness, which encourages clients to reciprocate by lowering their defenses and relating more openly (Doster & Nesbitt, 1979).

Encounters with authentic social workers also provide clients with a relationship experience that more closely approximates relationships in the real world than do relationships with people who conceal their real selves behind a professional facade. A moderate level of authenticity or genuineness during early interviews often fosters openness. At this level, the social worker is spontaneous and relates openly by being nondefensive and congruent. In other words, the social worker's behavior and responses match her or his inner experiencing.

Being authentic also permits the constructive use of humor, as elaborated in Chapter 6. Relating with a moderate level of authenticity, however, precludes a high level of self-disclosure. Rather, the focus is on the client, and the social worker reveals personal information or shares personal experiences judiciously. During the change-oriented phase of the helping process, however, social workers sometimes engage in self-disclosure when they believe that doing so may facilitate the growth of clients.

Rapport is also enhanced by avoiding certain types of responses that block communication. To avoid hindering communication, social workers must be knowledgeable about such types of responses and must eliminate them from their communication repertoires. Toward this end, Chapter 7 identifies various types of responses and interviewing patterns that inhibit communication and describes strategies for eliminating them. Video segments are also presented in the CourseMate for *Direct Social Work Practice* at www.cengagebrain.com that will allow you to consider alternative responses to challenging situations.

Beginning social workers often fear that they will forget something, freeze up or become tongue-tied, talk endlessly to reduce their anxiety, or fail to observe something crucial in the interview that will lead to dire consequences (Epstein and Brown, 2002). Practice interviews such as those presented in subsequent chapters will assist in reducing this fear. It also helps to be aware that referred clients need to know the circumstances of the referral and clarify choices, rights, and expectations before they are likely to establish rapport with the social worker.

Starting Where the Client Is

Social work researchers have suggested that *motivational congruence*—that is, the fit between client motivation and what the social worker attempts to provide—is a major factor in explaining more successful findings in studies of social work effectiveness (Reid & Hanrahan, 1982). Starting with client motivation aids social workers in establishing and sustaining rapport and in maintaining psychological contact with clients.

If, for example, a client appears to be in emotional distress at the beginning of the initial interview, the social worker might focus attention on the client's distress before proceeding to explore the client's problematic situation. An example of an appropriate focusing response would be, "I can sense that you are going through a difficult time. Could you tell me what this is like for you right now?" Discussion of the client's emotions and related factors tends to reduce the distress, which might otherwise impede the process of exploration. Moreover, responding sensitively to clients' emotions fosters rapport—clients begin to regard social workers as concerned, perceptive, and understanding persons.

Novice social workers sometimes have difficulty in starting where the client is because they worry that they will not present quickly and clearly the services of the agency, thus neglecting or delaying exploration of client concerns. Practice will allow them to relax and recognize that they can meet the expectations of their supervisors and others by focusing on client concerns while sharing content about the circumstances of referrals and their agency's services.

Starting where the client is has critical significance when you are working with involuntary clients. Because these clients are often compelled by external sources to see social workers, they frequently enter initial interviews with negative, hostile feelings. Social workers, therefore, should begin by eliciting these feelings and focusing on them until they have subsided. By responding empathically to negative feelings and conveying understanding and acceptance of them, skillful social workers often succeed in neutralizing these feelings, which enhances clients' receptivity to exploring their problem situations. For example, social workers can often reduce negative feelings by clarifying the choices available to the involuntary client. If social workers fail to deal with their clients' negativism, they are likely to encounter persistent oppositional responses. These responses are frequently labeled as resistance, opposition to change, and lack of motivation. It is useful to reframe these responses by choosing not to interpret them with deficit labels, but rather replacing them with expectations that these attitudes and behaviors are normal when something an individual values is threatened (Rooney, 2009). As children and adolescents are often referred because adults are concerned about their behavior, and they may therefore be particularly resistant, the practitioner can clarify that he or she wants to hear how things are going from the child's or adolescent's viewpoint.

Language also poses a barrier with many ethnic minority and immigrant clients who may have a limited grasp of the English language, which could cause difficulty in understanding even commonplace expressions. Where there are language differences, social workers must slow down the pace of communication and be especially sensitive to nonverbal indications that clients are confused. To avoid embarrassment, some clients who speak English as a second language sometimes indicate that they understand messages when, in fact, they are perplexed.

Using Interpreters

When ethnic minority and immigrant clients have virtually no command of the English language, effective communication requires the use of an interpreter of the same ethnicity as the client, so that the social worker and client bridge both cultural value differences and language differences. To work effectively together, however, both the social worker and the interpreter must possess special skills. For their part, interpreters must be carefully selected and trained to understand the importance of the interview and their role in the process, as well as to interpret cultural nuances to the social worker. In this way, skilled interpreters assist social workers by translating far more than verbal content—they also convey nonverbal communication, cultural attitudes and beliefs, subtle expressions, emotional reactions, and expectations of clients.

To achieve rapport, of course, the social worker must also convey empathy and establish an emotional connection with the ethnic minority client. The interpreter thus "must have the capacity to act exactly as the interviewer acts—express the same feelings, use the same intonations to the extent possible in another language, and through verbal and nonverbal means convey what the interviewer expresses on several levels" (Freed, 1988, p. 316).

The social worker should explain the interpreter's role to the client and ensure the client of neutrality and confidentiality on the part of both the social worker and the interpreter. Obviously, these factors should also be covered in the training process for interpreters. In addition, successful transcultural work through an interpreter requires that the social worker be acquainted with the history and culture of the client's and the interpreter's country of origin.

Social workers must also adapt to the slower pace of interviews when an interpreter is involved. When social workers and interpreters are skilled in collaborating in interviews, effective working relationships can evolve, and many clients experience the process as beneficial and therapeutic. As implied in this brief discussion, interviewing through an interpreter is a complex process requiring careful preparation of interviewers and interpreters.

The Exploration Process

When clients indicate that they are ready to discuss their problematic situations, it is appropriate to begin the process of exploring their concerns. Messages like the following are typically employed to initiate the exploration process:

EP 2.1.10d

- *"Could you tell me about your situation?"*
- *"I'm interested in hearing about what brought you here."*
- *"Tell me about what has been going on with you so that we can think together about what you can do about your concerns."*
- *"How are things going with school?"*

The client will generally respond by beginning to relate his or her concerns. The social worker's role at this point is to draw out the client, to respond in ways that convey understanding, and to seek elaboration of information needed to gain a clear picture of factors involved in the client's difficulties.

Some clients spontaneously provide rich information with little prompting. Others—especially referred and involuntary clients—may hesitate, struggle with their emotions, or have difficulty finding the right words to express themselves. Because referred clients may perceive that they were forced into the interview as the result of others' concerns, they may respond by recounting those external pressures. The social worker can assist in this process by sharing his or her information about the circumstances of the referral.

To facilitate the process of exploration, social workers employ a multitude of skills, often blending two or more in a single response. One such skill, *furthering responses*, encourages clients to continue verbalizing their concerns. Furthering responses, which include minimal prompts (both verbal and nonverbal) and accent responses, convey attention, interest, and an expectation that the client will continue verbalizing. They are discussed in depth in Chapter 6.

EP 2.1.10b

Other responses facilitate communication (and rapport) by providing immediate feedback that assures clients that social workers have not only heard but also understood their messages. *Paraphrasing* provides feedback indicating that the social worker has grasped the content of the client's message. In using paraphrasing, the interviewer rephrases (with different words) what the client has expressed. *Empathic responding*, by contrast, shows that the social worker is aware of the emotions the client has experienced or is currently experiencing. Both paraphrasing and empathic responding, which are discussed in Chapters 5 and 6, are especially crucial with clients who have limited language facility, including ethnic minority, immigrant, and developmentally disabled clients. When language barriers exist, social workers should be careful not to assume that they correctly understand the client or that the client understands the social worker. Video examples of paraphrasing and empathic responding are included with Chapters 5 and 6.

When some clients are hesitant about discussing personal or family problems with outsiders, social workers need to make special efforts to grasp their intended meanings. Many such potential clients are not accustomed to participating in interviews and tend not to state their concerns openly. Rather, they may send covert (hidden) messages and expect social workers to discern their problems by reading between the lines. Social workers need to use feedback extensively to determine whether their perceptions of the clients' intended meanings are on target.

EP 2.1.4c

Using feedback to ascertain that the social worker has understood the client's intended meaning, and vice versa, can avoid unnecessary misunderstandings. In addition, clients generally appreciate a social worker's efforts to reach shared

> **VIDEO CASE EXAMPLE**
>
> In the video "Getting Back To Shakopee," the potential client, Valerie, is quite hesitant about sharing personal concerns with the practitioner, Dorothy. This is seen to be influenced by a combination of factors such as having been referred by her employer, suspicion that social workers remove children, and cultural differences. Only after several questions are answered to Valerie's satisfaction about who would have access to information in the interview and Dorothy's cultural knowledge, does she proceed to describe personal concerns.

understanding, and they interpret patience and persistence in seeking to understand as evidence that the social worker respects and values them. It is not the ethnic minority client's responsibility, however, to educate the social worker.[2] Conversely, what the social worker thinks he or she knows about the minority client's culture may actually be an inappropriate stereotype, because individuals and families vary on a continuum of assimilation and acculturation with majority culture norms (Congress, 1994). Based on a common Latino value, for example, the social worker might say, "Can you call on other family members for assistance?" In this way, the worker can assess a cultural generalization that may or may not have relevance for the particular individual or family.

Exploring Expectations

Before exploring problems, it is important to determine clients' expectations, which vary considerably and are influenced by socioeconomic level, cultural background, level of sophistication, and previous experience with helping professionals. In fact, socialization that includes clarifying expectations about the roles of clients and social workers has been found to be associated with more successful outcomes, especially with involuntary clients (Rooney, 2009; Videka-Sherman, 1988). Video examples of clarifying to a client what information will be shared with a referral source and what information remains confidential are shared in Chapter 5.

EP 2.1.10a

In some instances, clients' expectations diverge markedly from what social workers can realistically provide. Unless social workers are aware of and deal successfully with such unrealistic expectations, clients may be keenly disappointed and disinclined to continue beyond the initial interview. In other instances, referred clients may have mistaken impressions about whether they can choose to work on concerns as they see them as opposed to the views of referral sources such as family members. By exploring these expectations, social workers create an opportunity to clarify the nature of the helping process and to work through clients' feelings of disappointment. Being aware of clients' expectations also helps social workers select their approaches and interventions based on their clients' needs and expectations.

Eliciting Essential Information

EP 2.1.10d

During the exploration process, the social worker assesses the significance of information revealed as the client discusses problems and interacts with the social worker, group members, or significant others. Indeed, judgments about the meaning and significance of fragments of information guide social workers in deciding issues such as which aspects of a problem are salient and warrant further exploration, how ready a client is to explore certain facets of a problem more deeply, which patterned behaviors of the client or system interfere with effective functioning, and when and when not to draw out intense emotions.

The direction of problem exploration proceeds from general to specific. Clients' initial accounts of their problems are typically general in nature ("We fight over everything," "I don't seem to be able to make friends," "We just don't know how to cope with Scott. He won't do anything we ask," or "Child protection says I don't care for my children"). Clients' concerns typically have many facets, however, and accurate understanding requires careful assessment of each one. Whereas open-ended responses may be effective in launching problem explorations, other types of responses are used to probe for the detailed information needed to identify and unravel the various factors and systems that contribute to and maintain the problem. Responses that seek concreteness are employed to elicit such detailed information. Many types of such responses exist, each of which is considered at length in Chapter 6.

Focusing in Depth

EP 2.1.10c

In addition to possessing discrete skills needed to elicit detailed information, social workers must be able to maintain the focus on problems until they have elicited comprehensive information. Adequate assessment of problems is not possible until a social worker possesses sufficient information concerning the various forces (involving individual, interpersonal, and environmental systems) that interact to produce the problems. Focusing skills (discussed at length in Chapter 6, with video examples) blend the various skills identified thus far with summarizing responses.

During the course of exploration, social workers should elicit information relevant to numerous questions, the answers to which are crucial in understanding those factors that bear on the clients' problems, including ecological factors. These questions (discussed in Chapter 8, with video examples) serve as guideposts to social workers and provide direction to interviews.

Employing Outlines

In addition to answering questions that are relevant to virtually all interviews, social workers may need to collect information that answers questions pertinent to specific practice settings. Outlines that list essential questions to be answered for a given situation or problem can prove extremely helpful to beginning social workers. It is important, however, to maintain flexibility in the interview and to focus on the client, not the outline. Chapter 6 provides examples of outlines and suggestions for using them.

Assessing Emotional Functioning

EP 2.1.3b

During the process of exploration, social workers must be keenly sensitive to clients' moment-to-moment emotional reactions and to the part that emotional patterns (e.g., inadequate anger control, depression, or widely fluctuating moods) play in their difficulties. Emotional reactions during the interview (e.g., crying, intense anxiety, anger, hurt feelings) often impede problem exploration and require detours aimed at assisting clients to regain their equanimity. Note that the anxiety and anger exhibited by involuntary clients may be influenced by the circumstances of the involuntary contact as much as by more enduring emotional patterns.

Emotional patterns that powerfully influence behavior in other contexts may also be problems in and of themselves that warrant careful exploration. Depression, for example, is a prevalent problem in our society but generally responds well to proper treatment. When clients exhibit symptoms of depression, the depth of the depression and risk of suicide should be carefully explored. Empathic communication is a major skill employed to explore these types of emotional patterns.

Factors to be considered, instruments that assess depression and suicidal risk, and relevant skills are discussed in Chapter 9.

Exploring Cognitive Functioning

Because thought patterns, beliefs, and attitudes are powerful determinants of behavior, it is important to explore clients' opinions and interpretations of those circumstances and events deemed salient to their difficulties. Often, careful exploration reveals that misinformation, distorted meaning attributions, mistaken beliefs, and dysfunctional patterns of thought (such as rigid, dogmatic thinking) play major roles in clients' difficulties.

Messages commonly employed to explore clients' thinking include the following:

- *"How did you come to that conclusion?"*
- *"What meaning do you make of …?"*
- *"How do you explain what happened?"*
- *"What are your views (or beliefs) about that?"*

Assessment of cognitive functioning and other relevant assessment skills are discussed further in Chapter 9.

Exploring Substance Abuse, Violence, and Sexual Abuse

Because of the prevalence and magnitude of problems associated with substance abuse (including alcohol), violence, and sexual abuse in our society, the possibility that these problems contribute to or represent the primary source of clients' difficulties should be routinely explored. Because of the significance of these problematic behaviors, we devote a major portion of Chapters 8 and 9 to their assessment.

Negotiating Goals and a Contract

EP 2.1.10f

When social workers and clients believe that they have adequately explored the problems prompting the initial contact, they are ready to enter the process of planning. By this point (if not sooner), it should be apparent whether other resources or services are needed. If other resources are needed or are more appropriate, then the social worker may initiate the process of referring the client elsewhere. If the client's problems match the function of the agency and the client expresses a willingness to continue with the helping process, then it is appropriate to begin negotiating a contract. When involuntary clients are unwilling to participate further in the helping process, their options should be clarified at this point. For example, they can choose to return to court, choose not to comply and risk the legal consequences of this tactic, choose to comply minimally, or choose to work with the social worker on problems as they see them in addition to legal mandates (Rooney, 2009).

In a problem-solving approach, goals specify the end results that will be attained if the problem-solving efforts succeed. Generally, after collaborating in the exploration process, social workers and clients share common views about which results or changes are desirable or essential. In some instances, however, social workers may recognize the importance of accomplishing certain goals that clients have overlooked, and vice versa. Social workers introduce the process of goal negotiation by explaining the rationale for formulating those goals. If stated in explicit terms, goals will give direction to the problem-solving process and serve as progress guideposts and as outcome criteria for the helping efforts. To employ goals effectively, social workers need skills in persuading clients to participate in selecting attainable goals, in formulating general task plans for reaching these goals, and in developing specific task plans to guide the social worker's and client's efforts between sessions.

When resolving the problematic situation requires satisfying more than one goal (the usual case), social workers should assist clients in assigning priorities to those goals so that the first efforts can be directed to the most burdensome aspects of the problem. Stimulating clients to elaborate goals enhances their commitment to actively participate in the problem-solving process by ensuring that goals are of maximal relevance to them. Techniques such as the "miracle question" from the solution-focused approach can be employed to engage clients in elaborating their vision of goals (De Jong & Berg, 2002). Even involuntary clients can often choose the order in which goals are addressed or participate in the process of making that choice. Essential elements of the goal selection process and the contracting process are discussed in depth in Chapter 12.

Ending Interviews

Both initial interviews and the contracting process conclude with a discussion of "housekeeping" arrangements and an agreement about the next steps to be taken. During this final portion of the interview process, social workers should suggest the length and frequency of sessions, who will

EP 2.1.10l

participate in them, the means of accomplishing goals, the duration of the helping period, fees, the date and time of the next appointment, pertinent agency policies and procedures, and other relevant matters. When you have completed these interview processes, or when the time allocated for the interview has elapsed, it is appropriate to conclude the interview. Messages appropriate for ending interviews include the following:

- "I see our time for today is nearly at an end. Let's stop here, and we'll begin next time by reviewing our experience in carrying out the tasks we discussed."
- "Our time is running out, and there are still some areas we need to explore. Let's arrange another session when we can finish our exploration and think about where you'd like to go from there."
- "We have just a few minutes left. Let's summarize what we accomplished today and what you and I are going to work on before our next session."

Goal Attainment

EP 2.1.10f

During Phase II of the helping process, interviewing skills are used to help clients accomplish their goals. Much of the focus during this phase is on identifying and carrying out actions or tasks that clients must implement to accomplish their goals. Not surprisingly, preparing clients to carry out these actions is crucial to successful implementation. Fortunately, effective strategies of preparation are available (see Chapter 13).

As clients undertake the challenging process of making changes in their lives, it is important that they maintain focus on a few high-priority goals until they have made sufficient progress to warrant shifting to other goals. Otherwise, they may jump from one concern to another, dissipating their energies without achieving significant progress. The burden, therefore, falls on the social worker to provide structure for and direction to the client. Toward this end, skills in maintaining focus during single sessions and continuity between sessions are critical.

As noted earlier, obstacles to goal attainment commonly arise during the helping process. Individual barriers typically include fears associated with change as well as behavior and thought patterns that are highly resistant to change efforts because they serve a protective function (usually at great psychological cost to the individual). With couples and families, barriers may include entrenched interactional patterns that resist change because they perpetuate power or dependence, maintain safe psychological distance, or foster independence (at the cost of intimacy). In groups, barriers may involve dysfunctional processes that persist despite repeated efforts by leaders to replace these patterns with others that are conducive to group goals and to group maturation.

Additive empathy is used with individuals, couples, and groups as a means to recognize and to resolve emotional barriers that block growth and progress. Confrontation is a high-risk skill used to assist clients in recognizing and resolving resistant patterns of thought and behavior. Because of the sophistication required to use these techniques effectively, we have devoted Chapter 17 to them and have provided relevant skill development exercises. Additional techniques for managing barriers to change (including relational reactions) are discussed in Chapter 18.

Summary

This chapter examined the three phases of the helping process from a global perspective and briefly considered the structure and processes involved in interviewing. The appendix of the book summarizes the constituent parts of the helping process and demonstrates their interrelationships with various interviewing processes. The remaining parts of the book focus in detail on the three phases of the helping process and on the interviewing skills and interventions employed during each phase.

CourseMate

Access an integrated eBook and chapter-specific learning tools including glossary terms, chapter outlines, relevant web links, videos, and practice quizzes. Go to **www.cengagebrain.com**.

CHAPTER 4

The Cardinal Social Work Values

CHAPTER OVERVIEW

Social work practice is guided by knowledge, skills, and values. This chapter addresses the last of those three areas, introducing the cardinal values of the profession and the ethical obligations that arise from those values. Because, in practice, values can clash and ethical principles may conflict with each other, the chapter also describes some of these dilemmas and offers guidance about resolving them. As you read this chapter, you will have opportunities to place yourself in complex situations that will challenge you to analyze your personal values and to assess their compatibility with social work values. As a result of reading this chapter you will:

- Understand the core social work values and how they play out in practice

- Develop self-awareness and professional competence by examining the tensions that can occur when personal values intersect with professional values

- Learn the role that the NASW Code of Ethics plays in guiding professional practice

- Be familiar with four core ethical issues: self-determination, informed consent, professional boundaries, and confidentiality

- Know the steps for resolving ethical dilemmas and the ways in which these apply to a case

- Understand the complexities in applying ethical standards to clients who are minors.

EPAS COMPETENCIES IN THE 4TH CHAPTER

This chapter will give you the information needed to meet the following practice competencies:

2.1.1b Practice personal reflection and self-correction to assure continual professional development

2.1.1c Attend to professional roles and boundaries

2.1.1d Demonstrate professional demeanor in behavior, appearance, and communication

2.1.1f Use supervision and consultation

2.1.2a Recognize and manage personal values in a way that allows professional values to guide practice

2.1.2b Make ethical decisions by applying standards of the National Association of Social Workers Code of Ethics and, as applicable, of the International Federation of Social Workers/International Association of Schools of Social Work Ethics in Social Work, Statement of Principles

2.1.2c Tolerate ambiguity in resolving ethical conflicts

2.1.2d Apply strategies of ethical reasoning to arrive at principled decisions

2.1.10a Substantively and affectively prepare for action with individuals, families, groups, organizations, and communities

The Interaction Between Personal and Professional Values

Values are "preferred conceptions," or beliefs about how things ought to be. All of us have values: our beliefs about what things are important or proper that then guide our actions and decisions. The profession of social work has values, too. They indicate what is important to social workers

EP 2.1.10a

and guide the practice of the profession. Social workers must be attuned to their personal values and be aware of when those values mesh or clash with those espoused by the profession as a whole. They must recognize that their clients also have personal values that shape their beliefs and behaviors, and these may conflict with the social worker's own values or with those of the profession. Further, the larger society has values that are articulated through cultural norms, policies, laws, and public opinion. These can also diverge from social workers' beliefs, their clients' values, or the profession's values.

Self-awareness is the first step in sorting out these potential areas of conflict. The following sections describe the core values of the profession, provide opportunities to become aware of personal values, and describe the difficulties that can occur when social workers impose their own beliefs on clients.

The Cardinal Values of Social Work

The Code of Ethics developed by the National Association of Social Workers (NASW, 2008) and the professional literature articulate the core values of the profession and the ethical principles that represent those values. They can be summarized as follows:

- *All human beings deserve access to the resources they need to deal with life's problems and to develop their full potential. The value of service is embodied in this principle, in that social workers are expected to elevate service to others above their own self-interest. In particular, the professions' values place a premium on working for social justice. Social workers' "change efforts are focused primarily on issues of poverty, unemployment, discrimination, and other forms of social injustice. These activities seek to promote sensitivity to and knowledge about oppression and cultural and ethnic diversity. Social workers strive to ensure access to needed information, services, and resources; equality of opportunity; and meaningful participation in decision making for all people"* (NASW, 2008, p. 5).
- *The value that social workers place on the dignity and worth of the person is demonstrated through respect for the inherent dignity of the persons with whom they work and in efforts to examine prejudicial attitudes that may diminish their ability to embrace each client's individuality.*
- *Social workers view interpersonal relationships as essential for well-being and as "an important vehicle for change"* (NASW, 2008, p. 5). *The value placed on human relationships affects the way social workers relate to their clients and the efforts that social workers make to improve the quality of the relationships in their clients' lives.*
- *The value of integrity means that professional social workers behave in a trustworthy manner. They treat their clients and colleagues in a fair and respectful fashion; they are honest and promote responsible and ethical practices in others.*
- *The value of competence requires that social workers practice only within their areas of ability and continually develop and enhance their professional expertise. As professionals, social workers must take responsibility for assuring that their competence is not diminished by personal problems, by substance abuse, or by other difficulties. Similarly, they should take action to address incompetent, unethical, or impaired practice by other professionals.*

What do these values mean? What difficulties can arise in putting them into practice? How can they conflict with social workers', clients', and society's values? The following sections describe these values and situations in which challenges can occur. Skill-building exercises at the end of the chapter and in the *Practice Behaviors Workbook* will assist you in identifying and working through value conflicts.

EP 2.1.1b

1. *All human beings deserve access to the resources they need to deal with life's problems and to develop to their fullest potential.* A historic and defining feature of social work is the profession's focus on individual well-being in a social context. Attending to the environmental forces that "create, contribute to, and address problems in living" is a fundamental part of social work theory and practice (NASW, 2008, p. 1).

Implementing this value means believing that people have the right to resources. It also means that as a social worker you are committed to helping secure those resources for your clients and to developing policies and implementing programs to fill unmet needs. While this value seems an easy choice to embrace, certain cases can bring out conflicting beliefs and personal biases that challenge the social worker in upholding it. To enhance your awareness of situations in which you might experience such difficulties, imagine yourself in interviews with the clients in each of the following scenarios. Take note of your feelings and of possible discomfort or conflict. Next, contemplate whether your response is consistent with the social work value in question. If the client has not requested a resource but the need for one is apparent, consider what resource might be developed and how you might go about developing it.

Situation 1 You are a practitioner in a public assistance agency that has limited special funds available to assist clients to purchase essential devices such as eyeglasses, dentures, hearing aids, and other prosthetic items. Your client, Mr. Y, lives in a large apartment complex for single persons and is disabled by a chronic psychiatric disorder. He requests special aid in purchasing new glasses. He says he accidentally dropped his old glasses and they were stepped on by a passerby. However, you know from talking to his landlord and his previous worker that, due to his confusion, Mr. Y regularly loses his glasses and has received emergency funds for glasses several times in the last year alone.

> **VIDEO CASE EXAMPLE**
>
> Situation 2 In one of the videos accompanying this text, Yanping, a Chinese student studying in the U.S., has decided she wants to major in history, while her parents insist that she study business so that she can eventually take over the family company. The American social worker values Yanping's autonomy but understands the risk her client faces in defying parental authority and tradition. The Chinese social worker values family harmony, and probes Yanping's insistence on choosing a major at odds with her parents' wishes.

Situation 3 During a routine visit to an elderly couple who are recipients of public assistance, you discover that the roof on their home leaks. The couple has had small repairs on several occasions, but the roof is old and worn out. They have gathered bids for re-roofing, and the lowest bid was more than $3,500. They ask whether your agency can assist them with funding. State policies permit expenditures for such repairs under exceptional circumstances, but much red tape is involved, including securing special approval from the county director of social services, the county advisory board, and the state director of social services.

Situation 4 Mr. M sustained a severe heart attack 3 months ago and took a medical leave from his job as a furniture mover. His medical report indicates that he must limit his future physical activities to light work. Mr. M has given up looking for new work and is asking you to pursue worker's compensation and other resources that would help support his family. You are concerned that while Mr. M might be entitled to these supports, they may reduce his motivation to pursue rehabilitation and work that he can reasonably do given his physical condition.

Situation 5 A military mental health provider is treating a client with mild trauma symptoms. The client wants to be sent home from the deployment, though his/her unit needs him/her to continue in combat. Is the client genuinely traumatized or malingering? Is going home ultimately more harmful for the person's mental health than staying and fulfilling his/her commitments to the unit, the mission, and fellow personnel? Since fear is common in combat, should everyone who is traumatized be allowed to go home? How should the client's self-determination be honored when he/she knew upon enlisting what the job would entail? (Simmons & Rycraft, 2010).

The preceding vignettes depict situations in which people need resources or opportunities to develop their skills or potential or to ensure their safety and quality of life. Possible obstacles to responding positively to these needs, according to the sequence of the vignettes, are as follows:

1. A judgmental attitude by the worker
2. A clash of values among the client, workers, and the client's family system.
3. Failure to offer options because of the effort involved or the pressure of other responsibilities
4. Skepticism that services will be effective in helping the client and apprehension that they may have unintended effects

Perhaps, as you read the vignettes, you experienced some of these reactions or additional ones. This discomfort is not uncommon, but such reactions indicate a need for expanded self-examination and additional experience to embrace the social work value in challenging situations. The next section describes some strategies for addressing these types of conflicting reactions.

2. *Social workers respect the inherent dignity and worth of the person. Social workers recognize the central importance of human relationships* (NASW, 2008, p. 5). These values mean that social workers believe that all people have intrinsic importance, whatever their past or present behaviors, beliefs, way of life, or social status, and that understanding these qualities is essential in involving clients as partners in change. These values embody several related concepts, sometimes referred to as "unconditional positive regard," "nonpossessive warmth," "acceptance," and "affirmation."

These values also recognize that respect is an essential element of the helping relationship. Before people will risk sharing personal problems and expressing deep emotions, they must first feel fully accepted and have trust in the goodwill and helpful intent of their service providers. This may be especially difficult when people feel ashamed or inadequate in requesting assistance. When clients are seeking services involuntarily, or when they have violated social norms by engaging in interpersonal violence, criminal behavior, or other infractions, they will be especially alert to perceived judgments or condemnation on the part of the social worker. Your role is not to judge whether clients are to blame for their problems or to determine whether they are good or bad, evil or worthy, guilty or innocent. Rather, your role is to seek to understand them, with all of their difficulties and assets, and assist them in searching for solutions to their problems.

Intertwined with acceptance and a nonjudgmental attitude is the equally important value of stating that every person is unique and that social workers should affirm the individuality of all the people they serve. People are, of course, endowed with widely differing physical and mental characteristics; moreover, their life experiences are infinitely diverse. People differ in terms of their appearance, beliefs, physiological functioning, interests, talents, motivation, goals, values, emotional and behavioral patterns, and many other factors. To affirm the uniqueness of another person, you must be committed to entering that individual's world, endeavoring to understand how that person experiences life. Only by attempting to walk in his or her shoes can you gain a full appreciation of the rich and complex individuality of another person. These recommendations are exemplified in the insights gained by social work students serving as volunteers in a camp for burn-injured children (Williams & Reeves, 2004). Not only did the students overcome feelings of fear, self-consciousness, pity, and horror at the campers' conditions, but they overcame stereotypes and animosity regarding their fellow volunteers (firefighters) who held different values and approaches than the social workers. Through respect, communication, attention to the other (versus oneself), appreciation for individuality over stereotypes, and a focus on shared purpose, all of the volunteers were able to create a successful community in which the campers could experience joy and healing.

Affirming each person's individuality, of course, goes far beyond gaining an appreciation of that person's perspectives on life. You must be able to convey awareness of what your client is experiencing moment by moment and affirm the validity of that experience. This affirmation does not mean agreeing with or condoning all of that person's views and feelings. Part of your role as a social worker entails helping people disentangle their confusing, conflicting thoughts and feelings; align their perceptions with reality; mobilize their particular strengths, and differentiate rational reactions from irrational ones. To fulfill this role, you must retain your own separateness and individuality. Otherwise, you may over-identify with clients, thereby losing your ability to provide fresh input. Affirming the experiences of another person means validating those experiences, thus fostering that person's sense of personal identity and self-esteem.

Our opportunities for affirming individuality and sense of self-worth are lost when unexamined prejudices and stereotypes (either positive or negative) blind us to the uniqueness of each individual client. Labels—such as "gang banger," "sorority girl," "old people," or "psychiatric patient"—perpetuate damaging stereotypes because they obscure the individual characteristics of the people assigned to those labels. Whether the preconceptions are positive or negative, professionals who hold them may fail to effectively engage with the person behind the label; they may overlook needs or capacities and, as a result, their assessments, goals, and interventions will be distorted.

The consequences of such practices are troubling. Imagine an elderly client whose reversible health problems (associated with inadequate nutrition or need for medication) are dismissed as merely symptomatic of advanced age. Also consider the client with developmental disabilities who is interested in learning about sexuality and contraceptives, but whose social worker fails to address those issues, considering them irrelevant for members of this population. Perhaps the sorority member will fail to disclose symptoms of a learning disorder or suicidal ideation to the social worker who presumes she "has everything going for her." What about the man with schizophrenia who is more concerned about his aging parents than he is about his illness and symptom management? Clearly, avoiding assumptions and prejudices is central to effective social work practice.

Sometimes, the ability to embrace these first two sets of values comes with increased experience and exposure to a range of clients. Veteran practitioners have learned that acceptance comes through understanding the life experience of others, not by criticizing or judging their actions. As you work with service recipients, you should try to view them as persons in distress and avoid perceiving them based on labels such as "lazy," "borderline," "irresponsible," "delinquent," "dysfunctional," or "promiscuous." As you learn more about your clients, you will find that many of them have suffered various forms of deprivation and have themselves been victims of abusive, rejecting, or exploitative behavior. Remember also that all people have abilities and assets that may not be apparent to you. Consistent respect and acceptance on your part are vital in helping them gain self-esteem and mobilize capacities that are essential to change and to well-being.

However, withholding judgments does not mean condoning or approving of illegal, immoral, abusive, exploitative, or irresponsible behavior. It is often our responsibility to help people live, not according to our particular values and moral codes, but according to the norms and laws of society. In doing so, social workers, without blaming, must assist clients in taking responsibility for the part they play in their difficulties. Indeed, change is possible in many instances only when individuals gain awareness of the effects of their decisions and seek to modify their behavior accordingly. The difference between "blaming" and "defining ownership of responsibilities" lies in the fact that the former tends to be punitive, whereas the latter flows from the social worker's positive intentions to be helpful and to assist clients in change. As a professional, you will inevitably confront the challenge of maintaining your own values without imposing them on your clients (Doherty, 1995). A first step toward resolving this issue is addressing your own judgmental tendencies.

EP 2.1.1b

The value clarification exercises that follow will help you to identify your own particular areas of vulnerability. In each situation, imagine yourself in an interview or group session with the client(s). If appropriate, you can role-play the situation with a fellow student, changing roles so that you can benefit by playing the client's role as well. As you imagine or role-play the situation, be aware of your feelings, attitudes, and behavior. After each situation, contemplate or discuss the following questions:

1. What feelings and attitudes did you experience? Were they based on what actually occurred or did they emanate from preconceived beliefs about such situations or individuals?
2. Were you comfortable or uneasy with the client? How did your classmate perceive your attitudes toward the "client"? What cues alerted him or her to your values and reactions?
3. Did any of the situations disturb you more than others? What values were reflected in your feelings, attitudes, and behavior?
4. What assumptions did you make about the needs of the client(s) in each vignette?
5. What actions would you take (or what information would you seek) to move beyond stereotypes in understanding your client(s)?

Situation 6 Your client is a 35-year-old married male who was sentenced by the court to a secure mental health facility following his arrest for peering in the windows of a women's dormitory at your college. He appears uncomfortable and blushes as you introduce yourself.

Situation 7 You are assigned to do a home study for a family interested in adoption. When you arrive at the home for the first interview, you realize that the couple interested in the adoption consists of two male partners.

Situation 8 You are a child protection worker and your client is a 36-year-old man whose 13-year-old stepdaughter ran away from home after he had sexual intercourse with her on several occasions during the past 2 months. In your first meeting, he states that he "doesn't know what the big deal is … it's not like we're related or anything."

Situation 9 Your 68-year-old client has been receiving chemotherapy for terminal cancer at your hospital for the past month. Appearing drawn and dramatically more emaciated than she was last month, the client reports that she has been increasingly suffering with pain and believes her best course of action is to take an overdose of sleeping pills.

Situation 10 You are a probation officer. The judge has ordered you to complete a pre-sentencing investigation of a woman who was arrested for befriending elderly and disabled individuals, then stealing their monthly disability checks.

Situation 11 You have been working for 8 weeks with a 10-year-old boy who has experienced behavioral difficulties at school. During play therapy he demonstrates with toys how he has set fire to several cats and dogs in his neighborhood.

Situation 12 Your client, Mrs. O, was admitted to a domestic violence shelter following an attack by her husband, in which she sustained a broken collarbone and arm injuries. This occasion is the eighth time she has contacted the shelter. Each previous time she has returned home or allowed her husband to move back into the home with her.

Situation 13 A low-income family with whom you have been working recently received a substantial check as part of a settlement with their former landlord. During a visit in which you plan to help the family budget the funds to pay their past due bills, you find the settlement money is gone—spent on a large television and gambling at a local casino.

Situation 14 You are a Latino outreach worker. One Caucasian client has expressed appreciation for the help you have provided, yet tells you repeatedly that she is angry at her difficulty finding a job, blaming it on "all these illegals."

Situation 15 You are working with a high school senior, the eldest girl in a large family from a strict religious background. Your client wants desperately to attend college but has been told by her parents that she is needed to care for her younger siblings and assist in her family's ministry.

If you experienced uneasy or negative feelings as you read or role-played any of the preceding situations, your reactions were not unusual. While social workers take many situations in stride, each of us may be tripped up by a scenario that is new to us, challenges our embedded beliefs, or triggers value conflicts. It can be challenging to look beyond differences, our comfort zones, or distressing behaviors to see clients as individuals in need. However, by focusing selectively on the person rather than on the behavior, you can gradually overcome initial reactions and learn to see them in full perspective.

EP 2.1.2a

How does this acceptance play out in practice? Acceptance is conveyed by listening attentively; by responding sensitively to the client's feelings; by using facial expressions, voice intonations, and gestures that convey interest and concern; and by extending courtesies and attending to the client's comfort.

If you are unable to be open and accepting of people whose behavior runs counter to your values, your effectiveness in helping them will be diminished, because it is difficult—if not impossible—to conceal negative feelings toward others. Even if you can mask your negative feelings toward certain clients, you are likely to be unsuccessful in helping them, as people quickly detect insincerity. To expand your capacity for openness and acceptance, it may be helpful to view association with others whose beliefs, backgrounds, and behaviors differ strikingly from your own as an opportunity to enrich yourself as you experience their uniqueness. Truly open people relish such opportunities, viewing differences as refreshing and stimulating and seeing these interactions as a chance to better understand the forces that motivate people. By prizing the opportunity to relate to all types of people and by seeking to understand them, you will gain a deeper appreciation of the diversity and complexity of human beings. In so doing, you will be less likely to pass judgment and will achieve personal growth in the process. You might also find it helpful to talk with other social workers who have been in the field for some time. How do they manage value conflicts? How do they develop cultural competence? Are they able to treat others with respect, even if they disdain their actions?

3. *The value of integrity means that social work professionals behave in a trustworthy manner.* As an ethical principle, integrity means that social workers act honestly, encourage ethical practices in their agencies, and take responsibility for their own ethical conduct (Reamer, 1998). In practice, it means that social workers present themselves and their credentials accurately, avoid other forms of misrepresentation (e.g., in billing practices or in presentation of research findings), and do not participate in fraud and deception. Integrity also refers to the ways that social workers treat their colleagues. Professionals are expected to treat one another with respect, avoid involving clients or others in professional disputes, and be forthright in their dealings with fellow professionals. These expectations are important not only for our individual trustworthiness, but also because each of us serves as a representative of the larger profession and we should act in ways that do not dishonor it.

This may seem to be a relatively straightforward expectation. However, challenges can arise when pressures from other colleagues or employing organizations create ethical dilemmas. In those cases, the challenge is not what is right, but rather how to do it. Following are two examples of such dilemmas involving the principle of integrity. What strategies might you pursue to resolve these dilemmas and act with honesty and professionalism?

Situation 16 Your agency recently received a large federal grant to implement a "Return to Work" program as part of welfare reform. Although the evaluation protocol is very clear about what constitutes "work," the agency is pressuring you and your coworkers (none of whom are social workers) to count clients' volunteer efforts and other nonpaying jobs as "work" in an effort to ensure that this valuable program will continue. The agency maintains that paying jobs are difficult to find, so clients who are actively working—even in noncompensated jobs—"fit the spirit, if not the letter of the law."

Situation 17 Your supervisor wants to assess your effectiveness in conducting family sessions. Because he fears that client behaviors will change and his findings will be distorted if clients know they are being taped, he has told you to tape these sessions without their knowledge. The supervisor feels that because he discusses your cases with you anyway, the taping without explicit client permission should be acceptable.

EP 2.1.1f

4. *The value of competence requires that social workers practice only within their scope of knowledge and ability, and that they enhance and develop their professional expertise.* As with the value of integrity, this principle places the burden for self-awareness and self-regulation on the social worker. An expectation of practice as a professional is that the individual will take responsibility for knowing his or her own limits and seek out the knowledge and experience needed to develop further expertise throughout the span of his or her career. This principle means that social workers will decline cases where they lack sufficient expertise, and that they will seek out opportunities for continuous self-examination and professional development. The commitment to utilizing evidence-based practices means that professionals must be lifelong learners, staying abreast of practice-related research findings, discarding ineffective or harmful practices, and tailoring interventions to the client's unique circumstances (Gambrill, 2007). Each of these elements speaks to developing and maintaining professional competence. The NASW Code of Ethics also includes cultural competence among its expectations for social workers, requiring an understanding of various groups, their strengths, the effects of oppression, and the provision of culturally sensitive services (NASW, 2008).

EP 2.1.1b

Self-regulation also requires the social worker to be alert to events or problems that affect his or her professional competence. For example, is a health or mental health problem hindering the social worker's service to clients? Are personal reactions to the client (such as anger, partiality, or sexual attraction) impairing the social worker's judgment in a particular case? Are family problems or other stressors detracting from their capacity to respond to clients' needs? *Countertransference* refers broadly to the ways that a worker's experiences and emotional reactions influence his or her perceptions of and interactions with a client. Later in this book you will learn more about the ways that countertransference can be a constructive or destructive factor in the helping process. It is important to be alert to such reactions and use supervisory sessions to examine and address their impact.

EP 2.1.1f

Supervision is an essential element in professional development and ongoing competence. In the helping professions, a supervisor is not someone looking over the worker's shoulder to catch and correct mistakes. More typically, supervisors can be thought of as mentors, teachers, coaches, and counselors all wrapped up into one role (Haynes, Corey, & Moulton, 2003). Successful use of supervision requires you to be honest and self-aware in seeking guidance, raising issues for discussion, sharing your challenges and successes, and being open to feedback, praise, critiques, and change. Effective supervisors will help you develop skills to look clearly at yourself, so that you understand your strengths and weaknesses, preferences and prejudices, and become able to manage these for the benefit of your clients.

Developing and maintaining competence is a career-long responsibility, yet it can be challenging to uphold. Consider the following scenarios:

Situation 18 You are a new employee at a small, financially strapped counseling center. The director of your agency just received a contract to do outreach, assessments, and case management for frail elders. Although you took a human behavior course as a social work student, you have never studied or worked with older adults, especially those at risk. The director has asked you to lead this new program and has emphasized how important the new funding is for the agency's survival.

Situation 19 For the past few weeks, you've found yourself attracted to one of your clients, thinking about him or her often and wondering what the client is doing at different times of the day. You wonder if this attraction could affect your objectivity on the case but are reluctant to discuss the situation with your supervisor because it might affect his or her evaluation of you later this year.

Situation 20 Your internship is at a busy metropolitan hospital. In one morning alone you encounter a woman from Somalia whose dialect you are unfamiliar with, a Muslim woman reluctant to disrobe for the physical exam, and a Korean family at odds over the placement of their teenager's baby. You are called in to assist the medical team, but wonder how to effectively address all of the cultural and individual differences in these cases within the pressure-packed schedule of the hospital workday.

What is competence? Do social workers ever feel totally competent? What is impairment? And how can we tell when it applies to us and our practice?

Self-evaluation requires self-knowledge and introspection. Measuring one's competence requires honest self-examination and the pursuit of input from colleagues and supervisors. Professional development requires actively seeking out opportunities to hone existing skills and develop new ones, whether through reading, continuing education, course work, or case conferences. It means knowing what we do not know and being willing to acknowledge our shortcomings. It means being aware of the learning curve in developing new skills or testing new interventions and using staff development and supervision to assure that clients are receiving high quality services (NASW, 2008). It also means that when we lack the skills, abilities, or capacity demanded by a client's situation that we make proper referrals, thereby elevating the clients' needs above our own.

IDEAS IN ACTION

EP 2.1.1b

One way that social workers can assess and enhance competence is through the review of case recordings. These may be pen-and-paper process recordings of the dialogue in a client session or audio or video tapes of individual, family, or group meetings (Murphy & Dillon, 2008). Many social workers resist taping sessions on the premise that it makes clients uncomfortable, though the greater likelihood is that the client will forget the tape is there; it may be the worker him or herself that is distressed at its presence and at having to look at his or her performance at a later point. Ethical practice, however, requires facing this discomfort for the greater good of evaluating strengths and weaknesses and, ultimately, assuring competent practice. Ali, the worker interviewing Irwin and Angela Corning in the videos that accompany this text (Problem Solving with the Corning Family), received an array of insights as a result of reviewing the tapes of her sessions. Among her findings are the following:

At the outset of the first session, Irwin clearly stated his frustration with attending the meeting. His comment set the tone for our working relationship, which was strained at first. I remember thinking that exploring his frustration at that time would be a difficult conversation, and I did not want to get off to a bad start. The alternative was hardly any easier to work with. By ignoring his comment, though it was really his tone that got my attention, I communicated to both clients that I was not willing or ready to meet them where they were emotionally. The space between us was muddled for the remainder of the session. I could sense that Irwin was getting tense. I am thankful that rather than explode or walk out, he interjected himself into the conversation to explain his brusque demeanor and negative emotions.

Because I did not address Irwin's frustration, he remained distant, and the business of the meeting was conducted with Angela. For a majority of the first session, my legs were crossed in front of me and I was turned toward Angela. At times, I crossed my arms in front of me over the notepad. You can see by my posture that I was uncomfortable with the tension in the room.

I noticed that my nerves were showing in other ways as well. Occasionally during the interview I explored the details of personal situations with the couple. As I asked these sensitive questions, my voice trailed off, so much so that it is hard to hear the entire question on the recording. In contrast, a calm and even tone would normalize these difficult inquiries and the information they elicit.

It is amazing to hear how many times I said, "You know," and, "So." I never realized it before, but I use these phrases as a pause in my sentences. I have been trying to pay attention to it lately and make sure that when I am working with clients all of my words help to convey a point or information. I also say "you guys" a lot, which seems too casual and potentially disrespectful.

I also noticed that as I got more anxious, I talked a lot and fumbled around. Much of the time in the first session was spent sorting through what exactly I could provide the couple. Looking at it on tape, I can see why Angela and Irwin were so frustrated and uncomfortable. I eventually gave them a plan, to provide them with contact information for affordable apartment complexes and employment placement services, but I could have been clearer in how I conveyed the information. It just got more confusing when I sought the couple's corroboration in a partnership that they knew little about. This is a point in the interview where I could have checked in with the clients to be sure that we were all on the same page.

In the second session, my hesitancy to engage Irwin persisted. At that appointment, Irwin discovered for the first time that he and Angela were carrying a $2,000 balance on their credit card account. The couple exchanged words back and forth, which I remember was a poignant moment in my work with them. As I watched the tape, I was struck by this opportunity to explore the couple's money management methods. Instead of having that discussion, I got into the activity of listing all of the other barriers that the couple would face in attaining a new apartment. My personal goal was to be prepared in the second session. I wanted to be sure to get all of the items on my list, one of which was a discussion of the barriers to attaining the couple's stated goals.

Processing the disclosure of the credit card in the moment with the couple not only would have yielded information and helped the couple to share household financial tasks more effectively, but would have also engaged the clients and may have fostered rapport between Irwin and me. Because I did not address the issue, and it was a surprise and disappointment to Irwin, he was unable to follow the thread about barriers. When I checked in with him to see if he wanted to add anything, he revealed that he was consumed with thoughts of the debt discovery over the past several minutes rather than following the discussion.

I did a good job of seeking out which areas the clients wanted to address in their goals. The clients reported that they were happy with the outcomes of our work together and that they became more comfortable with the process as the relationship grew. At the same time, we could have been more detailed in making the task lists. While I was speaking with Irwin about his objectives for employment and career advancement he indicated that in the future he would like to see himself admitted to, or already enrolled in, a masonry apprentice program. This could have been thoughtfully broken down into task steps that Irwin would have control over. Should Irwin meet his objectives, but not attain the goal because of factors out of his control, he would see documentation of his accomplishments and the efficacy of setting objectives and goals. (Unfortunately, we only had enough time to give this goal cursory treatment at the end of the interview.)

Near the end of our time together, Irwin and Angela had made considerable gains in the realms of housing, employment, and communicating with the school and I was feeling more confident in my work with them. I was glad to have the opportunity to go over the Eco-Map with them to illustrate how much they had done to change their lives. Watching the tape, I realized that I did not emphasize their success and efforts enough. I sense that this was a missed opportunity for offering congratulations and praise.

In the final session, I evaluated the work with Irwin and Angela. At one point I ask, "I didn't seem too nosy, did I?" Watching it, I realize that the wording of the question suggests a need for validation rather than feedback. Actually, one of my focal points for career development is to learn to encourage and foster self-determination as opposed to *doing for* the client. It is important to me that the clients I work with see the relationship as collaborative, with us all on equal ground. I really wanted to know if I seemed too pushy or bossy. I can see how rephrasing my question could allow Irwin and Angela to give more honest feedback. I could have asked, "Did you feel respected in our work together?" (or, "Did you feel disrespected in our work together?"). Did I respond to your needs and concerns?"

All in all I was glad to see the series of tapes, because I saw steady improvement in my skills and comfort over time. It is good that my supervisor reviewed them too, as she was able to identify strengths of mine that I can build on, as well as areas for change.

Challenges in Embracing the Profession's Values

EP 2.1.2a

In this section's presentation of the social work profession's cardinal values, numerous situations and cases have highlighted the potential for value conflicts. Self-awareness, openness to new persons and events, and increasing practice experience are all crucial elements in overcoming value conflicts. But what if you have made these efforts and your values continue to conflict with others' values?

Social workers occasionally encounter situations in which they cannot conform to the profession's values or in which a client's behaviors or goals evoke such negative reactions that a positive helping relationship cannot be established. For example, practitioners who have personal experience with child abuse or who are intensely opposed to abortions may find it difficult to accept a pedophile as a client or to offer help to a woman experiencing an unintended pregnancy. In such instances, it is important to acknowledge these feelings and to explore them through supervision or therapy. It may be feasible to help the worker overcome these difficulties in order to be more fully available as a helping person. If this is not possible, however, or if the situation is exceptional, the social worker and his or her supervisor should explore the possibility of transferring the case to another practitioner who can accept both the client and the goals. In such circumstances, it is vital to clarify for clients that the reason for the transfer is not personal rejection of them but rather a recognition that they deserve the best service possible and that the particular social worker cannot provide that service. It is not usually necessary to go into detail about the social worker's challenges. A general explanation conveys goodwill and safeguards clients' well-being. When a transfer is not possible, the social worker is responsible for seeking intensive assistance to ensure that services are provided properly and that ethical and professional responsibilities are upheld. Practitioners who are consistently unable to accept clients' differences or carry out their roles in a professional manner owe it to themselves and to future clients to reflect seriously on their suitability for the social work field.

EP 2.1.1d

Cross-cultural and cross-national social work offer further challenges in the application of professional values (Healy, 2007). Are values such as justice, service, and acceptance universally recognized guidelines for behavior, or should their application become tempered by cultural norms? Some have suggested that NASW and other social work codes of ethics place too great a value on individual rights over the collective good and emphasize independence over interdependence (Jessop, 1998; Silvawe, 1995). As such, they may reflect a Western bias and give insufficient attention to the values of other cultures. This is not merely a philosophical dispute. It creates significant challenges for practitioners working with individuals or groups with vastly different values. How can workers reconcile their responsibility to advocate for justice and equality while simultaneously demonstrating respect for cultural practices such as female circumcision, corporal punishment of children, arranged marriages, or differential rights based on social class, gender, skin tone, or sexual orientation? Cultural values shift and evolve over time, and social workers' systems change efforts may appropriately target stances that harm or disenfranchise certain groups. But how can social workers ensure that their efforts are proper and congruent with the desires of the particular cultural group and not a misguided effort borne of paternalism and ethnocentrism?

Healy (2007) recommends a stance of "moderate universalism" (p. 24), where the human rights of equality and protection are promoted along with the importance of cultural diversity and community ties. Ultimately, striking this balance means that social workers, individually and collectively, must be aware of their values and those of their colleagues and clients and engage in ongoing education and conversation in reconciling these value tensions. Congruent with cultural humility (Hunt, 2001), this approach encourages the professional to adopt a "learner" perspective, in order to determine where the ethical tensions reside and how much of an impediment they are for the helping process.

Ethics

Codes of ethics are the embodiment of a profession's values. They set forth principles and standards for behavior of members of that profession. In social work, the primary Code of Ethics is promulgated by the NASW. It addresses a range of responsibilities that social workers have as professionals, to their clients, to their colleagues, to their employers, to their profession, and to society as a whole. This section addresses four primary areas of ethical responsibility for social workers: self-determination, informed consent, maintenance of client-social worker boundaries, and confidentiality. First, however, it details how ethics are related to legal responsibilities and malpractice risks. The section concludes by summarizing the resources and processes available for resolving ethical dilemmas.

The Intersection of Laws and Ethics

The practice of social work is governed by a vast array of policies, laws, and regulations. Whether established by court cases, the U.S. Congress, state legislatures, licensure boards, or regulatory agencies, these rules affect social workers' decisions and actions. For example, state mandatory reporting laws require social workers to report cases where child abuse is suspected. The Health Insurance Portability and Accountability Act (HIPAA) regulates the storage and sharing of patient records (U.S. Department of Health and Human Services, 2003). Some states' health department rules may require social workers to divulge the names of HIV-positive clients to public health authorities; in other states, rules may forbid the sharing of patients' names or HIV status. Licensure board regulations may forbid social work

EP 2.1.10a

practice by persons with felony convictions. Federal court cases may extend evidential privilege to communications with social workers (Reamer, 1999). Federal, state or local laws may prohibit the provision of certain benefits to undocumented immigrants. Good social work practice requires workers to be aware of the laws and regulations that govern the profession and apply to their area of practice and the populations they serve. But knowing the laws is not enough. Consider the following case.

> **CASE EXAMPLE**
>
> Alice is a 38-year-old woman who has presented for treatment, filled with guilt as the result of a brief extramarital affair. In her third session, she discloses that she is HIV-positive but is unwilling to tell her husband of her status because then the affair would be revealed, and she fears losing him and her two young daughters. You are concerned about the danger to her husband's health and press her to tell him or to allow you to do so. Alice responds that if you do, you will be breaking your promise of confidentiality and violating her privacy. She implies that she would sue you or report you to your licensing board and to your profession's ethics committee.

This case neatly captures the clash of ethics, laws, and regulations and illustrates the stakes for workers who make the "wrong" decision. In a scenario such as this one, the social worker just wants a clear answer from a lawyer or supervisor who will tell him or her exactly what to do. Unfortunately, matters are not that simple. Good practice requires knowledge of both the applicable ethical principles and the relevant laws. Even with this knowledge, dilemmas may persist. In this case example, the ethical principles of self-determination and confidentiality are pitted against the principle to protect others from harm, which itself is derived from a court case (Cohen & Cohen, 1999; Reamer, 1995). The particular state or setting where the case takes place may have laws or regulations that govern the social worker's actions. Finally, the threat of civil litigation for malpractice looms large, even when the social worker's actions are thoughtful, careful, ethical, and legal.

When you think about the intersection of laws and ethics, it may be helpful to think of a Venn diagram with two ovals overlapping (see Figure 4-1). In the

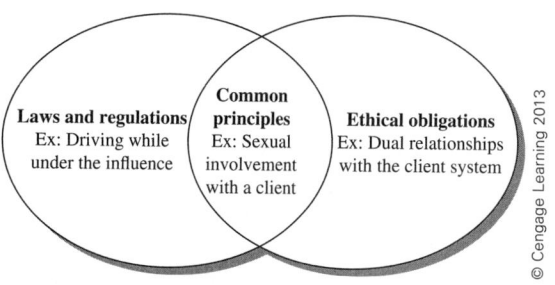

FIG-4-1 The Relationship of Law and Ethics

center are areas common to both ethics and laws; within each oval are items that are exclusive to laws and ethics, respectively. Some standards contained in the NASW Code of Ethics are not addressed by laws and regulations (such as the prohibition of sexual relationships with supervisees or standards on treating colleagues with respect). Similarly, some areas of the law are not covered by the Code of Ethics. For example, it is illegal to drive while intoxicated, but the Code of Ethics lacks a standard related to that act. Where the two realms intersect, there can be areas of agreement as well as areas of discord. As the Code of Ethics notes:

> *Social workers' primary responsibility is to promote the well-being of clients. In general, clients' interests are primary. However, social workers' responsibility to the larger society or specific legal obligations may on limited occasions supersede the loyalty owed clients, and clients should be so advised (NASW, 2008, p. 7).*

Also:

> *Instances may arise when social workers' ethical obligations conflict with agency policies or relevant laws or regulations. When such conflicts occur, social workers must make a responsible effort to resolve the conflict in a manner that is consistent with the values, principles, and standards expressed in this Code. If a reasonable resolution of the conflict does not appear possible, social workers should seek proper consultation before making a decision (NASW, 2008, pp. 3–4).*

The processes for ethical decision making are addressed later in this chapter. For now, it is important to acknowledge that social workers must know both the law and ethical principles to practice effectively. Workers must also recognize that sometimes conflicts will occur between and among ethical and legal imperatives. For example, state laws may prohibit the provision of services or resources to undocumented immigrants, but ethics would expect social workers to fill basic human needs. Thoughtful examination, consultation, and skillful application of the principles will serve as guides when laws and ethics collide.

Key Ethical Principles

EP 2.1.2b

The NASW Code of Ethics contains 155 standards, addressing a variety of ethical issues (such as conflicts of interest, competence, or confidentiality) for social workers in a range of roles (such as supervisor, teacher, direct practitioner, or administrator). In this section, we examine four key areas of immediate relevance to direct practitioners: self-determination, informed consent, professional boundaries and confidentiality.

Self-Determination

Biestek (1957) has defined self-determination as "the practical recognition of the right and need of clients to freedom in making their own choices and decisions" (p. 103). Self-determination is central to the social worker's ethical responsibility to clients:

> Social workers respect and promote the right of clients to self-determination and assist clients in their efforts to identify and clarify their goals. Social workers may limit clients' right to self-determination when, in their professional judgment, clients' actions or potential actions pose a serious, foreseeable, and imminent risk to themselves or others (NASW, 2008, p. 7).

This value also embodies the beliefs that individuals have the capacity to grow and change and to develop solutions to their difficulties, as well as the right and capacity to exercise free choice responsibly. These values are magnified when practitioners adopt a strengths-oriented perspective, looking for positive qualities and undeveloped potential rather than pointing out limitations and past mistakes (Cowger, 1994; Saleebey, 1997). Such a positive perspective engenders hope and courage on the client's part and nurtures self-efficacy. These factors, in turn, enhance the client's motivation, which is indispensable to achieving a successful outcome.

The extent to which you affirm an individual's right to self-determination rests in large measure on your perceptions of the helping role and of the helping process. If you consider your major role to be that of providing solutions or dispensing advice freely, you may foster dependency, demean clients by failing to recognize and affirm their strengths, and relegate them to a position of passive cooperation (or passive resistance, a frequent response under such circumstances). Such domineering behavior is counterproductive. Not only does it discourage open communication, but, equally important, it denies people the opportunity to gain strength and self-respect as they actively wrestle with their difficulties. Fostering dependency generally leaves people weaker rather than stronger and is a disservice to them.

The type of relationship that affirms self-determination and supports growth is a partnership wherein the practitioner and the client (whether an individual, a couple, or a group) are joined in a mutual effort to search for solutions to problems or to promote growth. As enablers of change, social workers facilitate clients in their quest to view their problems realistically, to consider various solutions and their consequences, to implement change-oriented strategies, to understand themselves and others more fully, to gain awareness of previously unrecognized strengths and opportunities for growth, and to tackle obstacles to change and growth. As helpful as these steps are, ultimately the responsibility for pursuing these options rests with the client.

Just as fostering self-determination enhances client autonomy, exhibiting paternalism (i.e., preventing self-determination based on a judgment of the client's own good) infringes on autonomy. Linzer (1999) refers to paternalism as "the overriding of a person's wishes or actions through coercion, deception or nondisclosure of information, or for the welfare of others" (p. 137). A similar concept is paternalistic beneficence, wherein the social worker implements protective interventions to enhance the client's quality of life, sometimes despite the client's objections (Abramson, 1985; Murdach, 1996).

EP 2.1.2d

Under what conditions might it be acceptable for a social worker to override a client's autonomy? Paternalism may be acceptable when a client is young or judged to be incompetent, when an irreversible act such as suicide can be prevented, or when the interference with the client's decisions or actions ensures other freedoms or liberties, such as preventing a serious crime (Abramson, 1985; Reamer, 1989). Murdach suggests three gradations of beneficent actions, which vary in their level of intrusiveness depending on the degree of risk and the client's decision-making capacity. Even under these circumstances, social workers must weigh the basis for their decisions against the potential outcomes of their actions.

For example, if a psychiatric patient refuses medication, some would argue that the client lacks competence to make such a decision, and that forcing him or her to take the medication would be "for the client's own good." Yet diagnosis or placement is not a sufficient basis for overriding a person's autonomy. For this reason, states have developed elaborate administrative and judicial processes that must be traversed before an individual can be involuntarily hospitalized or medicated.

Even when clients have reduced capacity for exercising self-determination, social workers should act to ensure that they exercise their capacities to the fullest feasible extent. For example, self-determination can be extended to individuals who are terminally ill by educating them about their options and encouraging them to articulate their desires through advance directives that provide instructions to health care personnel regarding which medical interventions are acceptable. These directives become operative when the patient's condition precludes decision-making capacity. Advance directives can take the form of living wills or authorizing an individual to act with durable power of attorney. The latter procedure is broader in scope and more powerful than a living will. The person designated to have durable power of attorney or medical power of attorney is authorized to make decisions as if he or she were the patient when grave illness or accident has obliterated the patient's autonomy.

Operationalizing clients' rights to self-determination can sometimes pose perplexing challenges. Adding to the complexity is the reality that in certain instances, higher-order principles such as safety supersede the right to self-determination. To challenge your thinking about how you might affirm the value of self-determination in practical situations, we have provided exercises that consist of problematic situations actually encountered by the authors or colleagues. As you read each scenario, analyze the alternative courses of action that are available and think of the laws, policies, and resources that you might consult as part of your decision making. Consider how you would work with the client to maximize self-determination, taking care also to promote his or her best interests.

EP 2.1.1c

Situation 21 In your work for the state welfare department, you oversee the care of numerous group home residents whose services are paid for by the state. Two of your clients, both in their twenties, reside in the same home and have told you that they are eager to get married. The administrator of the home strenuously protests that "those two are retarded" and, if they marry, "they might produce a child they could not properly care for." Further, she has stressed that she has no private room for a couple and that if they insist on marrying, they will have to leave the group home.

Situation 22 A 15-year-old runaway who is 4 months pregnant has contacted you several times in regard to planning for her child. During her last visit, she confided that she is habituated to heroin. You have expressed your concern that the drug may damage her unborn child, but she does not seem worried, nor does she want to give up use of the drug. You also know that she obtains money for heroin through prostitution and is living on the street.

Situation 23 While making a visit to Mr. and Mrs. F, an elderly couple living in their home on their own savings, you discover that they have hired several home health aides who have stolen from them and provided such poor care that their health and nutrition are endangered. When you discuss with them your concern about the adequacy of their care, they firmly state that they can handle their own problems and "do not want to be put in a nursing home!"

Situation 24 As a rehabilitation worker, you have arranged for a young woman to receive training as a beautician in a local technical college, a vocation in which she expressed intense interest. Although initially enthusiastic, she now tells you that she wants to discontinue the program and go into nursing. According to your client, her supervisor at the college is highly critical of her work and the other trainees tease her and talk about her behind her back. You are torn about what to do, because you know that your client tends to antagonize other people with her quick and barbed remarks. You wonder if, rather than change programs, your client needs to learn more appropriate ways of communicating and relating to her supervisor and coworkers.

Situation 25 A middle-aged woman with cancer was so debilitated by her latest round of chemotherapy that she has decided to refuse further treatment. Her physician states that her age, general health, and stage of cancer all argue for continuing her treatments, given the likelihood of a successful outcome. Her family is upset at seeing the woman in pain and supports her decision.

Providing Informed Consent

Six principles in the NASW Code of Ethics address facets of informed consent. At its essence, informed consent requires that social workers "use clear

EP 2.1.2b

and understandable language to inform clients of the purpose of the services, risks related to the services, limits to services because of the requirements of a third-party payer, relevant costs, reasonable alternatives, clients' right to refuse or withdraw consent, and the time frame covered by the consent. Social workers should provide clients with an opportunity to ask questions" (NASW, 2008, pp. 7–8). The Code of Ethics also indicates that clients should be informed when their services are being provided by a student. Timely and understandable informed consent sets the stage for social work services by acquainting the client with expectations for the process. For example, a common element of informed consent involves the limits on client privacy. Social workers explicitly state that in situations involving concerns about the client's danger to him or herself or others, the worker reserves the right to break confidentiality to seek appropriate help. Mandatory reporting requirements (for child and elder abuse and other circumstances, such as communicable diseases) are typically also covered at this time. In addition to respectfully educating the client about his or her rights and responsibilities, informed consent lays the groundwork for future actions the worker might need to take. In the earlier case about the woman who refused to let her husband know about her HIV-positive status, informed consent would have alerted the client at the outset to the worker's responsibility to protect others from harm and her duty to notify public health or other authorities about the risk created by the client's unprotected sexual activity.

Some workers view informed consent as a formality to be disposed of at the first interview or as a legalistic form to have clients sign and then file away. In fact, informed consent should be an active and ongoing part of the helping process. Given the tension and uncertainty that can accompany a first session, clients may not realize the significance of the information you are providing. In addition, new issues may emerge that require discussion of the client's risks, benefits, and options (Strom-Gottfried, 1998b). Therefore, it makes sense to revisit the parameters of service and invite questions throughout the helping process. Having a "fact sheet" that describes relevant policies and answers commonly asked questions can also help clients by giving them something to refer to between meetings, should questions arise (Houston-Vega, Nuehring, & Daguio, 1997; Zuckerman, 2008).

To facilitate informed consent for persons with hearing, literacy, or language difficulties, social workers should utilize interpreters and multiple communication methods as appropriate. When clients are temporarily or permanently incapable of providing informed consent, "social workers should protect clients' interests by seeking permission from an appropriate third party, informing clients consistent with the client's level of understanding" and "seek to ensure that the third party acts in a manner consistent with the client's wishes and interests" (NASW, 2008, p. 8). Even clients who are receiving services involuntarily are entitled to know the nature of the services they will be receiving and to understand their right to refuse service.

IDEAS IN ACTION

What elements of informed consent were covered in the initial moments of the videotaped interview with Anna and Jackie in "Home for the Holidays?"

- The expectation of confidentiality by the worker and by the two clients in regard to what each shared in the session.
- The limits of confidentiality: risk to self or others.
- Should either partner see the worker in an individual session, the information discussed or revealed there will not be held in confidence during conjoint sessions.
- The amount of time that the worker has set aside for the session (40 minutes).
- The purpose of the first session. The worker tells the clients that this is the time for them to tell her about themselves both as individuals and as a couple and to share their concerns and struggles with her.
- The nature of couples' work. The worker informs the couple that she will not take sides or take the role of a referee. She explains to the couple that her clinical focus is on their interactions, and that she considers her client to be their relationship rather than either person individually.
- Although the relationship will be the therapeutic focus of the work, at times the worker will push and challenge one of the partners in particular. She explains that this is sometimes necessary to learn more about how the partners interact and to gain clarity about how the relationship works.

What else could have been covered as part of informed consent?

- The worker's experience with couples, specifically her previous work with same-sex partners.
- The worker's preferred theoretical framework for couple's therapy.
- Alternatives to pursuing couple's therapy with the worker (e.g., couple's education groups, group therapy, bibliotherapy).
- Fee schedule and terms of insurance coverage.
- The clients' right to withdraw consent and to cease therapy with the worker.

Preserving Professional Boundaries

EP 2.1.1c

Boundaries refer to clear lines of difference that are maintained between the social worker and the client in an effort to preserve the working relationship. They are intended to help prevent conflicts of interest, making the client's interests the primary focus and avoiding situations in which the worker's professional practice is compromised. In part, boundaries help clarify that the client-social worker relationship is not a social one. Also, even though it may involve a high degree of trust and client disclosure, the relationship is not an intimate one, such as might be experienced with a friend, partner, or family member. When clients can trust that boundaries exist and will be maintained by the social worker, they are more able to focus on the issues for which they are seeking help. They can freely share of themselves and trust that the social worker's reactions and statements—whether of support, confrontation, or empathy—are artifacts of the working relationship, not social or sexual overtures or personal reactions such as might arise when friends agree or disagree.

EP 2.1.1d

Sometimes social workers and other helping professionals have a difficult time with the notion of boundaries, perceiving that they establish a hierarchical relationship in which the client is deemed "less worthy" than the social worker. Some professionals may also feel that establishing such boundaries is a cold and clinical move, treating the client as an object instead of a fellow human deserving of warmth and compassion (Lazarus, 1994). Our viewpoint is that the two positions are not mutually exclusive. Social workers can have relationships with clients that are characterized by collaborative problem solving and mutuality, and they can react to clients authentically and kindly without blurring the boundaries of their relationship or obscuring the purpose of their work.

The NASW Code of Ethics addresses boundaries through six provisions:

EP 2.1.2b & 2.1.1c

1. "Social workers should not take unfair advantage of any professional relationship or exploit others to further their personal, religious, political, or business interests" (NASW, 2008, p. 9).
2. "Social workers should not engage in dual or multiple relationships with clients or former clients in which there is a risk of exploitation or potential harm to the client. In instances when dual or multiple relationships are unavoidable, social workers should take steps to protect clients and are responsible for setting clear, appropriate, and culturally sensitive boundaries. (Dual or multiple relationships occur when social workers relate to clients in more than one relationship, whether professional, social, or business. Dual or multiple relationships can occur simultaneously or consecutively.)" (NASW, 2008, pp. 9–10).
3. "Social workers should not engage in physical contact with clients when there is a possibility of psychological harm to the client as a result of the contact (such as cradling or caressing clients) …" (NASW, 2008, p. 13).
4. "Social workers should under no circumstances engage in sexual activities or sexual contact with current clients, whether such contact is consensual or forced" (NASW, 2008, p. 13).
5. "Social workers should not engage in sexual activities or sexual contact with clients' relatives or other individuals with whom clients maintain a close personal relationship when there is a risk of exploitation or potential harm to the client. Sexual activity or sexual contact with clients' relatives or other individuals with whom clients maintain a personal relationship has the potential to be harmful to the client and may make it difficult for the

social worker and client to maintain appropriate professional boundaries. Social workers—not their clients, their clients' relatives, or other individuals with whom the client maintains a personal relationship—assume the full burden for setting clear, appropriate, and culturally sensitive boundaries" (NASW, 2008, p. 13).
6. "Social workers should not engage in sexual activities or sexual contact with former clients because of the potential for harm to the client" (NASW, 2008, p. 13).

Although these standards of practice may seem self-evident, they represent an area fraught with difficulty within social work and other helping professions. Research on ethics complaints indicates that in NASW-adjudicated cases, boundary violations accounted for more than half of all cases in which violations occurred (Strom-Gottfried, 1999a). Similarly, in research on the frequency of malpractice claims against social workers for the period 1961–1990, Reamer (1995) found that sexual violations were the second most common area of claim, and the most expensive in terms of money paid out. Most social workers cannot imagine developing sexual relationships with their clients; yet, this outcome is often the culmination of a "slippery slope" of boundary problems that may include excessive self-disclosure on the part of the worker, the exchange of personal gifts, socializing or meeting for meals outside the office, and arranging for the client to perform office and household chores or other favors (Borys & Pope, 1989; Epstein, Simon, & Kay, 1992; Gabbard, 1996; Gartrell, 1992).

It is not uncommon to experience feelings of attraction, even sexual attraction, for clients. When such feelings arise, however, it is crucial to raise them with faculty or supervisors so they can be acknowledged and examined. Such discussion normalizes and neutralizes these feelings and decreases the likelihood that the worker will act on the attraction (Pope, Keith-Spiegel, & Tabachnick, 1986). These issues will be explored further in Chapter 18 as we discuss relational reactions and their effects on the helping process.

EP 2.1.1f

Other boundary issues can be both subtle and complex. For example, you may meet a neighbor in the agency waiting room or run into a consumer while doing your grocery shopping. A client may ask to "friend" you on Facebook or visit his or her "Caring Bridge" website. You may decide to buy a car and find that the salesperson is a former client. You may visit a relative in the hospital and discover that her roommate is a current or former client. Friends in need of social work services may ask to be assigned to your caseload because you already know them so well. A client may ask you to attend a "family" event, such as a graduation or wedding. You may resonate with a particular client and think what a great friend he or she could be. You may have experienced a problem similar to the client's and wish to tell the client how you handled it. You may sympathize with a particular client's job search plight and consider referring him to a friend who is currently hiring new workers.

Not all encounters with clients outside the helping relationship are unethical. Contacts with clients that are unplanned, manageable, temporary, and transparent may simply be boundary crossings rather than boundary violations (Reamer, 2001). Certain settings (such as rural practice) and types of work (such as home-based care and community-based interventions) may create special opportunities for boundary confusion (Strom-Gottfried, 2005; Strom-Gottfried, 2009). The possibilities for boundary complication are endless, and addressing them involves nuanced application of the standards on boundary setting and other ethical principles, such as maintaining confidentiality and avoiding conflicts of interest. Therefore, setting "clear, appropriate, and culturally sensitive boundaries" (NASW, 2008, pp. 9–10) might mean different things in different settings. Many social workers routinely discuss the possibility of public contact with clients during the first session, explaining, for example, that in deference to privacy, they will not acknowledge the client unless spoken to first. A social worker invited to "friend" a client on a social networking site (or join the client in an in-person social activity) can sensitively explain the importance of not blurring the working relationship with other kinds of contact. Buying a car (or some other product or service with variable pricing) from a client or former client could be exploitive of the client or the worker, and could complicate the working relationship if the product or service is flawed. In such a case, boundary setting may mean ending the commercial relationship or the helping relationship if the two cannot be successfully merged. If neither choice is a possibility, consultation and intercession of a supervisor would be recommended to assure that neither the client nor worker is disadvantaged by the transaction. An invitation to a client's

EP 2.1.2c

graduation or marriage ceremony should be processed with the client to explore the meaning of the offer. Ethical boundary setting might variously involve declining the invitation, accepting it, or attending the public portion of the event rather than the more private elements, such as a reception. The desire to disclose personal experiences with a client may be a form of authenticity (discussed further in Chapter 5) or an upsetting derailment where attention is switched from the client's experiences and needs to the worker's. Social workers should always be mindful of what they are trying to accomplish in making a personal self-disclosure and consider alternate ways of achieving the same objective. For example, rather than the worker saying, "When I have that kind of conflict with my mother, I do X," the worker could simply state, "Sometimes, people in conflict with their parents find that X is helpful."

Later in this chapter, we discuss strategies for more thoroughly examining and resolving ethical dilemmas. The key in managing boundaries is to be alert to dual relationships, to discuss troubling situations with colleagues and supervisors, and to take care that the primacy of the helping relationship is preserved in questionable boundary situations (Brownlee, 1996; Erickson, 2001; Reamer, 2001). Consultation helps social workers determine whether dual relationships are avoidable or not and whether they are problematic or not. It is incumbent on the social worker to ensure that clients are not taken advantage of and that their services are not obscured or affected detrimentally when boundaries must be crossed.

Safeguarding Confidentiality

From a practical standpoint, confidentiality is a *sine qua non* of the helping process. Without the assurance of confidentiality, it is unlikely that clients would risk disclosing private aspects of their lives that, if revealed, could cause shame or damage to their reputations. This is especially true when clients' problems involve infidelity, deviant practices, illicit activities, child abuse, and the like. Implied in confidentiality is an assurance that the practitioner will never reveal such personal matters to others.

EP 2.1.2b

Social workers are bound by the NASW Code of Ethics to safeguard their clients' confidentiality. While numerous standards operationalize this principle, in essence, social workers are expected to respect clients' privacy, to gather information only for the purpose of providing effective services, and to disclose information only with clients' consent. Disclosure of information without clients' permission should be done only for compelling reasons, and even then there are limits on what information can be shared and with whom. These exceptions to confidentially will be addressed later in this section.

An unjustified breach of confidentiality is a violation of justice and is tantamount to theft of a secret with which one has been entrusted (Biestek, 1957). Maintaining strict confidentiality requires a strong commitment and constant vigilance because clients sometimes reveal information that is shocking, humorous, bizarre, or titillating. To fulfill your responsibility in maintaining privacy, you must guard against disclosing information in inappropriate situations. Examples include discussing details of your work with family and friends, having gossip sessions with colleagues, dictating within the listening range of others, discussing client situations within earshot of other staff, and making remarks about cases in elevators or other public places.

The emergence of technology that permits the electronic collection, transfer, and storage of information raises new complexities for maintaining client privacy (Gelman, Pollack, & Weiner, 1999). When you leave a voice mail for a client, are you certain that only the client will receive the message? Will you agree to accept and send text messages to clients? When a colleague sends you a fax on a case, can you be sure that others will not see that information before you retrieve the document? Further complexities arise in the electronic provision of services through text messages, websites, online groups, etc. There are many advantages to such interventions: they are commonly used methods of modern communication, they can efficiently offer reminders of appointments or tips for relapse prevention, assist with symptom management and increase service access for homebound individuals and those who need access to services on a 24/7 basis (Shapiro, Bauer, Andrews, Pisetsky, Bulik-Sullivan, Hamer & Bulik, 2009; Kessler, et al, 2009). However, electronic media present challenges for confidentiality, informed consent, and professional liability (Santhiveeran, 2009; Manhal-Baugus, 2001).

Beyond ethical standards, the Health Insurance Portability and Accountability Act of 1996 (HIPAA) established federal standards to protect the privacy of personal health information. HIPAA regulations affect pharmacies, health care settings, and insurance plans as well as individual health and mental health providers. The rules affect identifiable client information in all forms, including paper records, electronic data and communications, and verbal communications. There are several important provisions for social workers in HIPAA (HIPAA Medical Privacy Rule, 2003; Protecting the Privacy of Patients' Health Information, 2003; U.S. Department of Health and Human Services, 2007; Zuckerman, 2008).

- *Psychotherapy notes have a particular protection under HIPAA. The release of those notes requires special, separate authorization. Psychotherapy notes must be kept separately in client files and must meet other criteria in order to be considered protected.*
- *A general principle of the Privacy Rule is that if a person has the right to make a health care decision then that person has a right to the* **information** *associated with that decision.*
- *While clients should be provided access to their records, and have the opportunity to seek corrections if they identify errors or mistakes, client access to psychotherapy notes is restricted.*
- *Clients must be given information on the organization's privacy policies and they must sign a form or otherwise indicate that they have received the information.*
- *Client records or data should be protected from nonmedical uses, such as marketing, unless the client gives specific permission otherwise.*
- *Clients should understand their rights to request other reasonable efforts to protect confidentiality, such as requesting to be contacted only at certain times or numbers.*
- *Organizations and the individuals who work in them (in clinical, clerical, administrative and other roles) must take care to ensure that security standards are in place and that they are reinforced through staff development and agency policies.*
- *When state laws are more stringent than the provisions in HIPAA (when they offer greater protections for clients), those laws take precedence over HIPAA.*
- *HIPAA recognizes the validity of professional standards, such as those contained in the NASW Code of Ethics, and in some cases, those provisions may be more stringent than HIPAA's.*
- *In the case of minors, parents are generally considered the "personal representatives" for their children and as such can have access to personal health information as well as make health care decisions on behalf of their children. Some exceptions are: 1) when State law does not require parental consent for a minor to receive treatment, 2) when a court has appointed someone other than the parent as the child's guardian, and 3) if the parent agrees to a confidential relationship between the health care provider and their child.*
- *The health care provider does not have to disclose information to the parent of a minor if 1) the provider has reasonable belief of abuse or neglect or that the information to be provided may endanger the child, or 2) using personal judgment, the provider decides that it is not in the minor client's best interest to treat the parent as the minor's individual representative.*

What Are the Limits on Confidentiality?

While social workers are expected to safeguard the information they collect in the course of their professional duties, there are several situations in which helping professionals are allowed or compelled to share case information. These include: when seeking supervision or consultation, when the client waives confidentiality, when the client presents a danger to self or others, when reporting suspicions of child or elder maltreatment, and when presented with a subpoena or court order.

Supervision and Consultation

The right to confidentiality is not absolute, because case situations are frequently discussed with supervisors and consultants and may be presented at staff conferences. Disclosing information in these instances, however, is for

EP 2.1.1f

the purpose of enhancing service to clients. Clients will generally consent to these uses when their purposes are clarified. The client has a right to be informed that such disclosures may occur, and practitioners seeking supervision have a responsibility to conceal the identity of the client to the fullest extent possible and to reveal no more personal information than is absolutely necessary to get assistance on the case.

Other personnel such as administrators, volunteers, clerical staff, consultants, board members, researchers, legal counsel, and outside persons who may review records for purposes of quality assurance, peer review, or accreditation may have access to files or case information. This access to information should be for the purposes of better serving the client, and these individuals should sign binding agreements not to misuse confidential information. Further, it is essential that social workers promote policies and norms that protect confidentiality and assure that case information is treated carefully and respectfully.

Client Waivers of Confidentiality

Social workers are often asked by other professionals or agencies to provide confidential information about the nature of their client's difficulties or the services provided. Sometimes, these requests can be made with such authority that the recipient is caught off guard, inadvertently acknowledging a particular person as a client or providing the information requested about the case. In these instances, it is important that such data be provided only with the written, informed consent of clients, as this releases the practitioner and agency from liability in disclosing the requested information. Even when informed consent is obtained, it is important to reveal information selectively based on the essential needs of the other party.

In some exceptional circumstances, information can be revealed without informed consent, such as a bona fide emergency in which a client's life appears to be at stake or when the social worker is legally compelled to do so, as in the reporting of child or elder abuse. In other instances, it is prudent to obtain supervisory and legal input before disclosing confidential information without the client's written consent for release of information.

A final example of the client's waiver of confidentiality occurs if the client files a malpractice claim against the social worker. Such an action would "terminate the patient or client privilege" (Dickson, 1998, p. 48), freeing the practitioner to share publicly such information as is necessary to mount a defense against the lawsuit.

Danger to Self or Others

In certain instances, the client's right to confidentiality may be less compelling than the rights of other people who could be severely harmed or damaged by actions planned by the client and confided to the practitioner. For example, if the client plans to commit kidnapping, injury, or murder, the practitioner is obligated to disclose these intentions to the intended victim and to law enforcement officials so that timely preventive action can be taken. Indeed, if practitioners fail to make appropriate disclosures under these circumstances, they may be liable to civil prosecution for negligence. The fundamental case in this area is the Tarasoff case (Reamer, 1994). In it, a young man seeing a psychologist at a university health service threatened his girlfriend, Tatiana Tarasoff. The therapist notified university police; after interviewing the young man, they determined that he did not pose a danger to his girlfriend. Some weeks later the young man murdered Tarasoff, and her family filed a lawsuit alleging that she should have been warned. Ultimately, the court ruled that mental health professionals have an obligation to protect their clients' intended victims.

This court decision has led to varying interpretations in subsequent cases and in resulting state laws, but two principles have consistently resulted from it (Dickson, 1998; Houston-Vega, Nuehring, & Daguio, 1997): If the worker perceives a serious, foreseeable and imminent threat to an identifiable potential victim, the social worker should (1) act to warn that victim or (2) take other precautions (such as notifying police or placing the client in a secure facility) to protect others from harm.

Another application of the duty to protect personal safety involves intervening to prevent a client's suicide. Typically, lawsuits that cite a breach of confidentiality undertaken to protect suicidal clients have not been successful (VandeCreek, Knapp, & Herzog, 1988). Conversely, "liability for wrongful death can be established if appropriate and sufficient action to prevent suicide is not taken" (Houston-Vega, Nuehring, & Daguio, 1997, p. 105). Knowing when the risk is sufficient to warrant breaking a client's confidence is both a clinical decision and an ethical matter. Chapter 9 offers guidelines to use for determining the risk of lethality in suicidal threats or in client aggression.

Suspicion of Child or Elder Abuse

The rights of others also take precedence over the client's right to confidentiality in instances of child abuse or neglect. In fact, all 50 states have statutes making it mandatory for professionals to report suspected or known child abuse. Moreover, statutes governing the mandatory reporting of child abuse may contain criminal clauses related to the failure to report. States have established similar provisions for reporting the suspected abuse of the elderly or other vulnerable adults (Corey, Corey, & Callanan, 2007; Dickson, 1998; Donovan & Regehr, 2010). The mandate to report suspicions of abuse does not empower the worker to breach confidentiality in other ways. That is, even though the worker is a mandated reporter, he or she should still use caution in the amount of unrelated case information he or she shares with child welfare authorities. Furthermore, the requirement is to report suspicions to specific protective agencies, not to disclose information to the client's family members, teachers, or other parties.

Although afforded immunity from prosecution for reporting, practitioners must still confront the difficult challenge of preserving the helping relationship after having breached the client's confidentiality. One way of managing this tension is through informed consent.

As noted earlier, clients should know at the outset of service what the "ground rules" for service are and what limits exist on what the social worker can keep private. When clients understand that the social worker must report suspected child abuse, such a report may not be as damaging to the helping relationship. Similarly, the Code of Ethics states, "Social workers should inform clients, to the extent possible, about the disclosure of confidential information and the potential consequences, when feasible before the disclosure is made" (NASW, 2008, p. 10). With a trusting relationship, informed consent, and careful processing of the decision to file a child abuse report, feelings of betrayal can be diminished and the working alliance preserved.

Subpoenas and Privileged Communication

Yet another constraint on the client's right to confidentiality is the fact that this right does not necessarily extend into courts of law. Unless social workers are practicing in states that recognize the concept of privileged communication, they may be compelled by courts to reveal confidential information and to produce confidential records. "Privileged communication" refers to communications made within a "legally protected relationship," which "cannot be introduced into court without the consent of the person making the communication," typically the patient or client (Dickson, 1998, p. 32). Statutes that recognize privileged communication exempt certain professions from being legally compelled to reveal content disclosed in the context of a confidential relationship.

EP 2.1.2c

Determining the presence and applicability of privilege can be complicated, however. As Dickson notes, "Privilege laws can vary with the profession of the individual receiving the communication, the material communicated, the purpose of the communication, whether the proceeding is criminal or civil, and whether the professional is employed by the state or is in private practice, among other factors" (1998, p. 33). At the federal level, the U.S. Supreme Court in *Jaffee v. Redmond* upheld client communications as privileged and specifically extended "that privilege to licensed social workers" (Social Workers and Psychotherapist-Patient Privilege: *Jaffee v. Redmond* Revisited, 2005).

Laws recognizing privileged communication are created for the protection of the client; thus the privilege belongs to the client and not to the professional (Schwartz, 1989). In other words, if the practitioner were called to take the witness stand, the attorney for the client could invoke the privilege to prohibit the practitioner's testimony (Bernstein, 1977). Conversely, the client's attorney could waive this privilege, in which case the practitioner would be obligated to disclose information as requested by the court.

Another important factor regarding privileged communication is that the client's right is not absolute (Levick, 1981). If, in a court's judgment, disclosure of confidential information would produce benefits that outweigh the injury that might be incurred by revealing that information, the presiding judge may waive the privilege. Occasionally, the privilege is waived in instances of legitimate criminal investigations because the need for information is deemed more compelling than the need to safeguard confidentiality (Schwartz, 1989). In the final analysis, courts make decisions on privilege-related issues on a case-by-case basis.

Because subpoenas, whether for records or testimony, are orders of the court, social workers cannot ignore them. Of course, subpoenas may sometimes be issued for irrelevant or immaterial information. Therefore, social workers should be wary about submitting privileged materials. Careful review of the subpoena, consultation with the client, and consultation with a supervisor and agency attorney can help you determine how to respond. The following sources provide helpful information for social workers contending with subpoenas: Austin, Moline, and Williams (1990); Barsky and Gould (2004); Bernstein and Hartsell (2005); Houston-Vega, Nuehring, and Daguio (1997); Polowy and Gilbertson (1997); Sarnoff (2004); and NASW (2008b) of the NASW.

Confidentiality in Various Types of Recording

Accreditation standards, funding sources, state and federal laws—all may dictate how agencies maintain record-keeping systems. Because case records can be subpoenaed and because clients and other personnel have access to them, it is essential that practitioners develop and implement policies and practices that provide maximal confidentiality. To this end, social workers should adhere to the following guidelines (Kagle & Kopels, 2008; Reamer, 2005; Moline, Williams, & Austin, 1998; Zuckerman, 2008):

1. Record no more than is essential to the services being provided. Identify observed facts and distinguish them from opinions. Use descriptive terms rather than professional jargon, and avoid using psychiatric and medical diagnoses that have not been verified.
2. Unconfirmed reports about a third party by the client, the personal judgments, opinions, or clinical hypotheses of the clinician, and sensitive information that is not relevant to treatment should be omitted from documentation.
3. Do not include verbatim or process recordings in case files.
4. Maintain and update records to assure their accuracy, relevance, timeliness, and completeness.
5. Employ private and soundproof dictation facilities.
6. Keep case records in locked files, and issue keys only to those personnel who require frequent access to the files. Take similar privacy precautions to protect electronically stored data.
7. Do not remove case files from the agency except under extraordinary circumstances and with special authorization.
8. Do not leave case files on desks where others might gain access to them or keep case information on computer screens where it may be observed by others.
9. Take precautions, whenever possible, to ensure that information transmitted through the use of computers, electronic mail, facsimile machines, voice mail and other technology is secure. Be sure it is sent to the correct party and that identifying information is not conveyed.
10. Use in-service training sessions to stress confidentiality and to monitor adherence to agency policies and practices instituted to safeguard clients' confidentiality.
11. Inform clients of the agency's authority to gather information, the conditions under which that information may be disclosed, the principal uses of the information, and the effects, if any, of limiting what is shared with the agency.

EP 2.1.2b

The NASW Code of Ethics reflects most of these provisions, stating that "social workers should provide clients with reasonable access to records concerning the clients" (NASW, 2008, p. 12). It further notes that the social worker should provide "assistance in interpreting the records and consultation with the client" (p. 12) in situations where the worker is concerned about misunderstandings or harm arising from seeing the records. Access to records should be limited "only in exceptional circumstances when there is compelling evidence that such access would cause serious harm to the client" (p. 12). In our opinion, the trend toward greater client access to records has enhanced the rights of clients by avoiding misuse of records and has compelled practitioners to be more prudent, rigorous, and circumspect in keeping case records.

Social workers sometimes tape record live interviews or group sessions so that they can analyze interactional patterns or group process at a later time, or scrutinize their own performance with a view toward improving their skills and techniques. Recording is also used extensively for instructional sessions between students and practicum instructors. Yet another use of recordings is to provide firsthand feedback to clients by having them listen to or view their actual behavior in live sessions.

Before tape recording sessions for any of the preceding purposes, social workers should obtain written consent from clients on a form that explicitly specifies how the recording will be used, who will listen to or view the recording, and when it will be erased. A recording should never be made without the client's knowledge and consent. Clients vary widely in their receptivity to having sessions recorded; if they indicate reluctance, their wishes should be respected. The chances of gaining their consent are enhanced by discussing the matter openly and honestly, taking care to explain the client's right to decline. If approached properly, the majority of clients will consent to taping.

Social workers who record sessions assume a heavy burden of responsibility in safeguarding confidentiality because live sessions can prove extremely revealing. Such recordings should be guarded to ensure that copies cannot be made and that unauthorized persons do not have access to them. When they have served their designated purpose, they should be promptly erased. Failure to heed these guidelines may constitute a breach of professional ethics.

The Ethics of Practice with Minors

EP 2.1.2c & 2.1.2d

A particular challenge in social work practice is interpreting ethical standards as they apply to clients under the age of 18 (Strom-Gottfried, 2008). While minor clients have the right to confidentiality, informed consent, self-determination, and the protection of other ethical principles, their rights are limited by laws and policies, by differences in maturity and decision-making capacity, and by their very dependence on adults as their caretakers. As such, parents may retain the right to review a child's treatment record and to be kept informed of issues the child raises in therapy. A 15-year-old teen parent has the right to make decisions about her baby's health care that she cannot legally make about her own. Child welfare experts and other authorities are empowered to decide where to place children and when to move them based on their appraisal of the best interests of the child. A 10-year-old may resist medication or treatment but lacks the ability to withhold consent in light of his age and cognitive capacities. As such, his parents or guardians can compel him to comply, even against his expressed wishes.

Minors' rights are also affected by the particular service setting and by their presenting problems. For example, a youth seeking substance-abuse services would have privacy protections under federal regulations that assure confidentiality (42-CFR) even if his parents insisted on service information (Strom-Gottfried, 2008). Similarly, a minor in need of prenatal care or treatment for sexually transmitted diseases could offer her own consent for services and be assured of confidentiality. Emergency services may be provided for a minor if delaying for parental consent could jeopardize the minor's well-being. School districts that accept "abstinence only" funding for health care will limit the information that social workers and nurses can share with students about contraception and HIV prevention.

As you can see, practice with minors is a complex tangle of legal, developmental, ethical, and social issues. Unsnarling this web requires a thorough understanding of child development and the physical, emotional, and cognitive capacities that emerge over the first two decades of the life span. It also requires an understanding of ethical standards, so that the worker appreciates the areas in which tensions might arise between legal and developmental limits to a minor's rights and the expectations of the profession for honoring clients' prerogatives, irrespective of age. Professionals in child-serving settings should be familiar with the policies and practices that govern services for their clientele. Through supervision, staff consultation, and careful decision making, social workers must consider various factors on a case-by-case basis in order to ensure that minors' rights are maximized, even amid constraints on those rights.

IDEAS IN ACTION

In the "Hanging with Hailey" videos, several examples arise about ethical service to mature minors.

- In light of Hailey's age and the policies at the school, the social worker (Emily) wasn't required to get parental permission for service; Hailey could consent to her own treatment.
- The social worker carefully describes the parameters of confidentiality during the first session. During this segment, Hailey interjects, "I guess, but I still don't know why I'm here." While Emily is careful to acknowledge the statement, she continues with her explanation and checks to make sure Hailey understands the limits of privacy.
- Perhaps because of Hailey's age, Emily fails to include possible abuse as a reason for breaking confidentiality; thorough informed consent would have also included letting Hailey know that if her safety was at risk, that information would need to be divulged.
- In the second session, when Hailey describes smoking "weed" and having suicidal ideations, Emily continues her assessment and concludes that the situation is not serious enough to necessitate informing Hailey's mother. This assessment has both clinical and ethical dimensions, weighing risk, the client's capacity for decision making, agency policies, parental rights, client self-determination, and safety. Changes in any of these factors might shift the balance, leading a worker to notify parents or guardians of risky behaviors, or to work with the client to do so.

Understanding and Resolving Ethical Dilemmas

EP 2.1.2c

Social workers sometimes experience quandaries in deciding which of two values or ethical principles should take precedence when a conflict exists. In the foregoing discussions of self-determination and confidentiality, for example, we cited examples of how these rights of clients and ethical obligations of social workers are sometimes superseded by higher-order values (e.g., the right to life, safety, and well-being). Thus, clients' right to confidentiality takes second place when they confide that they have physically or sexually abused a child, or when they reveal imminent and serious plans for harmful acts that would jeopardize the health or safety of other people. Dilemmas can also arise if you find that certain policies or practices of your employing agency seem detrimental to clients. You may be conflicted about your ethical obligations to advocate for changes, because doing so may jeopardize your employment or pose a threat to your relationships with certain staff members.

EP 2.1.2d

Situations such as these present social workers with agonizingly difficult choices. Reamer (1989) has developed general guidelines that can assist you in making these decisions. Here we present our versions of some of these guidelines and illustrate instances of their application.

1. *The right to life, health, well-being, and necessities of life takes precedence over rights to confidentiality and opportunities for additive "goods" such as wealth, education, and recreation.* We have previously alluded to the application of this principle in instances of child or elder abuse or threats of harm to another person. In such circumstances, the rights of both children and adults to health and well-being take precedence over clients' rights to confidentiality.

2. *An individual's basic right to well-being takes precedence over another person's right to privacy, freedom, or self-determination.* As stated in the language of the courts (which have consistently upheld this principle), "The protective privilege ends where the public peril begins" (Reamer, 1994, p. 31). For example, the rights and needs of infants and children to receive medical treatments supersede parents' rights to withhold medical treatment because of their religious beliefs.

3. *A person's right to self-determination takes precedence over his or her right to basic well-being.* This principle maintains that people are entitled to act in ways that may appear contrary to their best interests, provided they are competent to make an informed and voluntary decision with consideration of relevant knowledge, and as long as the consequences of their decisions do not threaten the well-being of others. For example, if an adult chooses to live under a highway overpass, we may find that lifestyle unwise or unhealthy, but we have no power to constrain that choice. This principle affirms the cherished value of freedom to choose and protects the rights of people to make mistakes and to fail. As noted earlier, this principle must yield when an individual's decision might result in either his or her death or in severe and impeding damage to his or her physical or mental health.

4. *A person's rights to well-being may override laws, policies, and arrangements of organizations.* Ordinarily, social workers are obligated to comply with the laws, policies, and procedures of social work agencies, other organizations, and voluntary associations. When a policy is unjust or otherwise harms the well-being of clients or social workers, however, violation of the laws, policies, or procedures may be justified. Examples of this principle include policies or practices that discriminate against or exploit certain persons or groups. An agency, for example, cannot screen clients to select only those who are most healthy or well-to-do (a practice known as "creaming" or "cherry-picking") and then refuse services to those individuals in dire conditions. In situations such as these, the well-being of affected groups takes precedence over compliance with the laws, policies, and arrangements at issue.

Ethical social work includes advocacy for changes in laws and policies that are discriminatory, unfair, or unethical. For example, in regard to the ethical challenges posed by managed care, Sunley (1997) suggests engaging in both "case advocacy" and "cause advocacy" to help both individual clients and groups of clients who may be disadvantaged by particular policies or practices. Resources such as Brager and Holloway (1983), Corey, Corey, and Callanan (2007), and Frey (1990) provide helpful guidance for acting as an effective agent of change within troubled systems.

Although Reamer's guidelines serve as a valuable resource in resolving value dilemmas, applying them to the myriad situations that social workers encounter inevitably involves uncertainties and ambiguities, a reality that practitioners must accept. What should you do when you find yourself confronted with an ethical dilemma? Ethical decision-making models are as yet untested for their capacity to yield high-quality outcomes. Nevertheless, a list of recommended steps can be used to ensure thoughtful and thorough examination of options (Corey, Corey, & Callanan, 2007; Reamer, 2006; Strom-Gottfried, 2007, 2008):

1. Identify the problem or dilemma, gathering as much information about the situation from as many perspectives as possible, including that of the client.
2. Determine the core principles and the competing issues.
3. Review the relevant codes of ethics.
4. Review the applicable laws and regulations.
5. Consult with colleagues, supervisors, or legal experts.
6. Consider the possible and probable courses of action and examine the consequences of various options.
7. Decide on a particular course of action, weighing the information you have and the impact of your other choices.
8. Develop a strategy for effectively implementing your decision.
9. Evaluate the process and results to determine whether the intended outcome was achieved and consider modifications for future decisions.

These procedures need not be followed in the order listed. For example, consultation can prove useful in revealing options, identifying pros and cons, and rehearsing strategies for implementing the decision. Laws, ethical standards, and values can be examined after options are developed. Even decisions that must be made on the spot with little planning or consultation can be evaluated using this model, so that critical thinking is brought to bear for future dilemmas and actions. The key is to go beyond mere intuition or reactionary decision making to mindful, informed, critically examined choices.

Beyond these steps, you should be sure to document carefully the input and considerations taken into account at each phase of the decision-making process. This documentation may be in the client's formal record, your informal notes, or in the notes from supervisory sessions.

EP 2.1.2d

To apply this model, let's use the case of Alice from earlier in the chapter. As you may recall, she is a 38-year-old woman who refuses to notify her husband of her HIV-positive (HIV+) status due to fears that it will lead to the revelation of her extramarital affair.

The dilemma for the social worker in the case arises from Alice's disclosure about her HIV+ status and her refusal to tell her husband, which places him at risk for infection. The worker has a loyalty to Alice's needs and wishes, but also a responsibility to prevent her from harming another person, namely, her husband. If the worker reveals the truth, he or she may save the husband's health (and ultimately his life), but in so doing is violating Alice's trust and right to privacy and potentially putting the marriage at risk by exposing the affair. On the other hand, maintaining the secret, although protecting Alice's privacy, could put the unwitting husband at significant risk for contracting a life-limiting or life-ending disease. The worker may also worry about legal liability for actions or inaction in the case. In fact, either party who is disgruntled or damaged in the case could seek to hold the worker accountable: Alice for the breach of privacy, or the husband for negligence in failing to protect him from harm.

Several provisions in the NASW code of ethics (2008) speak to this dilemma:

EP 2.1.2b

Social workers should protect the confidentiality of all information obtained in the course of professional service, except for compelling professional reasons. The general expectation that social workers will keep information confidential does not apply when disclosure is necessary to prevent serious, foreseeable, and imminent harm to a client or other identifiable person or when laws or regulations require disclosure without a client's consent. In all instances, social workers should disclose the least amount of confidential information necessary to achieve the desired purpose; only information that is directly relevant to the purpose for which the disclosure is made should be revealed (1.07c).

Social workers should inform clients, to the extent possible, about the disclosure of confidential information and the potential consequences, when feasible before the disclosure is made. This applies whether social workers disclose confidential information on the basis of a legal requirement or client consent (1.07d).

> Social workers should discuss with clients and other interested parties the nature of confidentiality and limitations of clients' right to confidentiality. Social workers should review with clients circumstances where confidential information may be requested and where disclosure of confidential information may be legally required. This discussion should occur as soon as possible in the social worker-client relationship and as needed throughout the course of the relationship (1.07e).

Embedded in these provisions are important ethical concepts—the respect for client self-determination, the importance of informed consent, and the significance of discretion around private information. It would be helpful to know how the social worker handled informed consent with Alice at the outset of services. Did Alice understand the worker's responsibilities should she prove to be a danger to herself or someone else? If so, the question of notifying her husband should not come as a surprise or betrayal, but rather a natural consequence based on the conditions of service and the established limits of confidentiality.

Beyond ethical standards, social workers must be familiar with the laws, regulations, practices, and policies that apply in their jurisdictions and practice settings. The disclosure of HIV+ status is one example where laws and policies vary widely across states. Some states explicitly shield health professionals from liability for making disclosures to protect the health of another, as long as they do so following established procedures. Other states view partner notification as a public health responsibility and require professionals to alert health departments in cases such as Alice's so that health authorities can undertake necessary disclosures. Preferably, the agency where Alice sought services was already apprised of the laws and incorporated them into policies and informed consent procedures for all clients prior to the outset of service. The social worker should also consider how Alice knows she is HIV+ and the partner notification policies in the jurisdiction where she was diagnosed. Depending on where and how she was diagnosed, Alice's condition may have already been processed by medical personnel to initiate notification of her husband, her paramour, and any other individuals who may be at risk by contact with her.

EP 2.1.1f

Supervisory guidance is essential in this case. Alice's social worker needs help thinking through the implications (for Alice, her husband, the worker, the helping relationship, and the agency). The worker should use supervision to help identify her alternatives of action and the various pros and cons involved, anticipate reactions and prepare to address them, and think through ways to improve her practices in the future. Beyond talking with her supervisor, the worker may get specific consultation from legal and medical experts to address particular questions about her choices, her legal liability, or best practices in working with clients with infectious diseases. In these conversations, the worker should protect the identity of her client, focusing on the issues that gave rise to her dilemma rather than details of the client's case.

As a result of these discussions, the social worker may identify at least five options that can be employed singly or in combination:

- *Honor Alice's wishes and keep the secret.*
- *Work with Alice to institute safe sex practices and other control procedures to limit her husband's exposure to her disease.*
- *Encourage Alice to tell her husband about her HIV+ status by educating her about the implications of her silence.*
- *Offer to assist Alice in telling her husband and processing the information.*
- *Offer Alice the chance to tell her husband and let her know that if she does not, the social worker will.*
- *Make an anonymous report to the public health authorities about the risk to Alice's husband.*

Regardless of what option the worker pursues, she should make sure that Alice understands the nature of her disease, is getting proper care, and is taking precautionary steps to protect others from contracting HIV. This is congruent with the ethics of putting the client's needs first, and has the pragmatic effect of mitigating damage resulting from Alice's secrecy about her illness.

The question, however, remains: to tell or not to tell? The options that ultimately involve alerting Alice's husband will protect his health and well-being, clearly an advantage of these choices. These options comply with ethical standards, principles, and policies that require social workers to protect others from significant, foreseeable harm. Alerting the husband will probably make the worker feel more comfortable if she is worried about her complicity and her liability should she keep Alice's secret and he contracts AIDS as a result.

The downsides of telling include violating Alice's expressed desire for privacy, rupturing the trust that is central to the helping relationship, and possibly putting Alice's marriage at risk if the secret of her affair is revealed. Alice may make good on a threat to file a regulatory board complaint or lawsuit against the worker or agency for breach of confidentiality. The options in which the worker encourages Alice to tell may take time to employ, but they have the advantage of empowering her to take control of the situation and face her dilemma head on. Her ability to rely on the worker is essential in this process. The worker can help her look at the long-term effects of deception, in contrast to the short-term effects of revealing her condition and how she contracted HIV. The worker can help Alice anticipate and plan for that very difficult conversation with her husband and family and can be a support to her after the fact, whatever the husband's reactions are. All of the advantages of working *with* the client on this challenging problem are lost if the worker decides to abruptly override Alice's wishes and notify the husband.

Honoring Alice's demands for secrecy without considering the husband's needs and interests fits with the principle of client self-determination, but may be at odds with laws and policies about protecting the safety of others. It may also be at odds with Alice's own best interests. Social workers must often navigate between clients' wishes and the steps needed to adequately address their problems. Alice's desire to avoid telling her husband in the short run will not spare anyone pain or harm in the long run. In fact, her insistence on silence now may keep her stuck while her health and family relationships suffer. The worker who can empathize with her and help her forthrightly address her fears and problems will be carrying out both ethical responsibilities and professional responsibilities. Should this process fail, the worker may resort to notification against Alice's will. Given the greater expertise and experience of public health authorities in the area of notifications, the worker should probably refer the case to them for assistance.

EP 2.1.1b

Self-awareness and self-evaluation are important elements of competent, ethical, and professional practice. Throughout this process, Alice's social worker should examine her own motivations, decisions, and actions. Supervision is also an important element in self-evaluation. An adept and involved supervisor can help the worker identify strengths and weaknesses in the decision-making process, positive and problematic outcomes, and areas for improvement and skill development. Did the decision adequately resolve the dilemma? If it created unplanned or problematic results, what can be done to remedy them? For example, if the worker's efforts to get Alice to inform her husband of her illness results in Alice's withdrawal from treatment, evaluation will help the worker to determine next steps as well as assess her past actions.

Summary

This chapter introduced the ethics and values that support the social work profession. It provided guidelines for supporting self-determination, respecting confidentiality, obtaining informed consent, maintaining boundaries, and resolving ethical dilemmas. The chapter suggested steps to aid in resolving ethical dilemmas and it applied these steps to a case in which self-determination and client confidentiality conflicted with another's safety. In the following chapters we will move toward putting these professional values into action as you learn beginning skills for effective communication with and on behalf of clients.

CourseMate

Access an integrated eBook and chapter-specific learning tools including glossary terms, chapter outlines, relevant web links, videos, and practice quizzes. Go to **www.cengagebrain.com**.

PART 2
Planning, Exploring, and Assessing

5 Empathy and Authenticity: The Building Blocks of Communication
6 The Skills of Verbal Following, Exploring, and Focusing
7 Avoiding Counterproductive Communication Patterns
8 Assessment: Problems and Strengths
9 Intrapersonal, Interpersonal, and Environmental Factors in Assessment
10 Assessment: Family Functioning in Diverse Family and Cultural Contexts
11 Social Work Groups: Formation and Assessment
12 Goal Development and Contract Formulation

Part 2 of this book deals with processes and skills involved in the first phase of the helping process. These processes and skills are also demonstrated in video clips on the CourseMate for *Direct Social Work Practice* at www.cengagebrain.com. Chapter 5 begins this exploration by setting the context and developing skills for building effective working relationships with clients, one of the two major objectives of initial interviews. Chapter 6 shifts the focus to skills required to explore clients' difficulties and recognize and enhance strengths.

Chapter 7 identifies verbal and nonverbal patterns of communication that impede the development of effective working relationships.

Chapters 8 and 9 focus specifically on the process of assessment. Chapter 8 deals with explaining the process, sources of information, delineation of clients' problems, and questions to be addressed during the process. Chapter 9 highlights the many dimensions of ecological assessment, delineating the intrapersonal, interpersonal, cultural, and environmental systems and noting how they reciprocally interact to produce and maintain problems.

Chapter 10 narrows the focus to family systems. It discusses various types of family structures and considers the dimensions of family systems that must be addressed in assessing family functioning, including the cultural context of families.

In Chapter 11, the focus changes to groups. Here the discussion hones in on purposes of groups, selection of group members, arrangements to be made, and ways to begin group process. It then points out various factors to be considered in assessing the functioning of groups.

Part 2 concludes with Chapter 12, which deals with negotiating goals and contracts with both voluntary and involuntary clients. Included in this chapter are theory, skills, and guidelines that address these processes, which lay the foundation for the process of goal attainment.

CHAPTER 5

Empathy and Authenticity: The Building Blocks of Communication

CHAPTER OVERVIEW

Social workers practice in a variety of environments, influenced by professional and organizational demands (Cameron & Keeran, 2010). Part of that context is an emphasis on exploring the use of evidence-based knowledge where possible to influence intervention. Whatever intervention and theory selected, there are underlying common factors that account for as much as 70 percent, of the success of interventions (Drisko, 2004; Lambert & Ogles, 2004; Norcross & Lambert, 2006; Wampold, 2001, p. 207). Research on treatment outcomes describes four factors as associated with much of the positive change in client outcomes: client or extra-therapeutic factors (40%); relationship factors (30%); placebo, hope, and expectancy factors (15%); and model/technique factors (15%) (Duncan & Miller, 2000; Hubble, Duncan, & Miller, 1999; Adams et al., 2008). Consequently, nearly half of the outcome relies on fundamental skills and abilities that social workers need to learn, apart from the type of treatment offered.

Social work relationships develop in a context. Chapter 5 will help you develop micro direct practice skills and apply them in a context to help your clients. Interviews follow a structure that reflects predictable elements of contact between a potential client, a social worker, and the setting that the social worker represents. In other words, interviews have beginnings that focus on settling into roles, reviewing legal and ethical limits and boundaries, and attempting to establish rapport. From this point, the social worker engages the client in assessing what has brought the client into contact with the setting or agency. Based on this joint exploration, the social worker and the client then discuss creating a contract or agreement about what they will attempt to do together to address the client's concerns and developing goals to guide the social worker's practice in the case. If contact will last beyond one session, the session ends with the development of tasks or concrete plans about what the social worker and the client will do prior to the next session to advance their common work. This interview structure is held together with practice skills that are designed to help the social worker connect with clients by communicating empathically, assertively, and authentically.

As a result of reading this chapter, learning and applying skills, you will be able to:

- **Develop an empathic response**
- **Explain client rights and limits to confidentiality**
- **Explain social worker and client roles**
- **Act assertively**
- **Appropriately self-disclose**
- **Identify surface and deeper feelings**
- **Increase your ability to convey accurate empathy**
- **Convey positive feedback**
- **Make a firm request**
- **Confront in an empathic context**

EPAS COMPETENCIES IN THE 5TH CHAPTER

This chapter will give you the information needed to meet the following practice competencies:

2.1.1b Practice self-reflection and self-correction to assure continual professional development

2.1.1c Attend to professional roles and boundaries

2.1.10a A social worker substantively and affectively prepare for action with individuals, families, groups, organizations, and communities

2.1.10b in which a social worker uses empathy and other interpersonal skills

2.1.10e A social worker assesses client strengths and limitatons

2.1.10i A social worker implements preventive services to enhance client capacities

Roles of the Participants

EP 2.1.10a

Clients often have an unclear idea about what to expect from contact with a social worker and those ideas may differ from the social worker's expectations (Kadushin & Kadushin, 1997). This is most evident when the client has been referred or mandated for service. Clarifying expectations becomes a key intervention in work with clients who have not chosen to see a social worker (Rooney, et al., 2009; Trotter, 2006).

The following guidelines will assist you to achieve similar positive results in role clarification.

Determine your clients' expectations. The varied expectations that clients bring to initial sessions include lectures, magical solutions, advice giving, changing other family members, and so on. With clients who are members of ethnic minority groups or inexperienced with professional helping relationships, sensitively exploring expectations and modifying the social worker's role when necessary are critical.

EP 2.1.1c

Clients sometimes explicitly state their expectations without prompting from a social worker. For example, after reciting the difficulties created by her son, a mother declared, "We were hoping you could talk with him and help him understand how much he is hurting us." Notice that the mother's "hope" involved a request for specific action by the social worker. When clients express their expectations spontaneously in this way, you have the opportunity to deal with unrealistic goals. Frequently, however, clients do not openly express their expectations, and you will need to elicit them.

It is important not to probe too far into expectations until you have established rapport, however, because the client's request often turns out to be a most intimate revelation. For this reason, seeking disclosure too soon may put a client on the defensive. The social worker should therefore try to weave exploration of the client's expectations into the natural flow of the session sometime after the client has had ample opportunity to report his or her difficulties and to discern the sensitive understanding and goodwill of the social worker.

If voluntary clients have not spontaneously revealed their requests and the timing appears right, you can elicit their requests by asking a question similar to one of the following:

- "How do you hope (or wish) I (or the agency) can assist (or help) you?"
- "When you thought about coming here, what were your ideas about the kind of help you wanted?"

For potential clients who were referred or mandated to receive service, practitioners often find it necessary to describe the parameters of what accepting an offer of service might entail since potential clients did not seek the service.

> **VIDEO CASE EXAMPLE**
>
> In the video "Getting Back to Shakopee," Dorothy, a practitioner in a private child and family service agency, finds that Valerie, a Native American client referred by her employer for job performance issues, has many concerns about confidentiality that need to be addressed before she will consider whether she will accept an offer of service.

It can be useful in circumstances like these, where the client did not seek service, to elicit client concerns in the following way:

1. "We have explored the reasons why you were referred/ required to seek our service. But I would like to know what you hope to gain from this process." In this way the social worker signals from the beginning that he or she is working with the potential client, not acting as the agent of the referring source.

2. Briefly explain the nature of the helping process, and define the client-social worker relationship as partners seeking a solution to the client's difficulties. Clients often hope that social workers will give them advice that they can implement immediately, thereby quickly remedying their problems. They will give up these unrealistic expectations with less disappointment in favor of a more realistic understanding if you clarify how you can actually be of help and why it would be less useful to approach their problems with this kind of "magic potion" strategy. It is very important to convey your intention to help clients find the best possible solution and to clarify that offering advice prematurely would likely be a disservice to them. In the absence of such an explanation, clients may erroneously conclude that you are unwilling to meet their expectations because you are not concerned about them.. Taking the time to explore expectations and to clarify how you can help prevents clients from drawing unwarranted negative conclusions that may result in premature termination of the contact.

EP 2.1.1c

Note that we are not arguing against the value of giving advice to clients. Rather, our point is that to be effective, advice must be based on adequate knowledge of the dynamics of a problem and of the participants involved. This level of understanding is unlikely to be achieved in an initial session.

You can assist many clients to modify their unrealistic expectations and clarify your respective roles by delivering a message similar to the following:

- "I can sense the urgency you feel in wanting to solve your problems. I wish I could give advice that would lead to an easy solution. You've probably already had plenty of advice, because most people offer advice freely. It has been my experience, though, that what works for one person (couple or family) may not work at all for another."
- "As I see it, our task is to work together in considering a number of options so that you can decide which solution best fits you and your situation. In the long run, that's what will work best for you. But finding the right solution takes some time and a lot of thought."

The preceding role clarification embodies the following essential elements mentioned earlier: (1) acknowledging and empathizing with the client's unrealistic expectation and sense of urgency; (2) expressing the social worker's helpful intent; (3) explaining why the client's unrealistic expectation cannot be fulfilled; and (4) as part of the social worker's expertise, clarifying the helping process and defining a working partnership that places responsibility on the client for actively participating and ultimately making choices as to the courses of action to be taken.

EP 2.1.1c

When couples seek help for relationship problems, they commonly view the partner as the source of difficulties and have the unrealistic expectation that the couple's counselor will influence the partner to shape up. Because this expectation is so pervasive, we often elicit partners' expectations early in the initial session (individual or conjoint) and clarify the social worker's helping role, thereby setting the stage for more productive use of the exploration to follow. Clarifying the helping process early in the session tends to diminish the partners' tendency toward mutual blaming and competition. Moreover, partners are less likely to respond defensively when the social worker refuses to be drawn into the "blame game" and focuses instead on assisting each person to become aware of his or her part in the difficulties.

> **VIDEO CASE EXAMPLE**
>
> The following excerpt of the video labeled "Home for the Holidays Part 1" (HFH1) demonstrates how the social worker can establish ground rules.
>
> *Social worker:* Let me suggest some ground rules for how couples sessions may be useful to you. I want this to be a safe place, so anything said here will be private unless something is shared that would seriously harm someone else, such as possible suicide or transmission of AIDS. I won't take sides in your concerns but will act more like a referee to help you express your concerns.

Implied in the preceding excerpt is another aspect of the client's role—to be open in sharing feelings, thoughts, and events. By explaining the rationale for openness and by expressing your intent to communicate openly, you enhance clients' receptiveness to this factor. To focus on this aspect of the client's role, consider making the following points:

Social worker: For you to receive the greatest benefit, you need to be as open as possible with me. That means not holding back troubling feelings, thoughts, or events that are important. I can understand you and your difficulties only if you're open and honest with me. Only you know what you think and feel; I can know only as much as you share with me.

Sometimes it's painful to share certain thoughts and feelings, but often those are the very feelings that trouble us the most. If you do hold back, remind yourself that you may be letting yourself down. If you're finding it difficult to share certain things, let me know. Discussing what's happening inside you—why it's difficult—may make it easier to discuss those painful things. I'll be open and honest with you, too. If you have any questions or would like to know more about me, please ask. I'll be frank with you. I may not answer every question, but I'll explain why if I don't.

To enhance clients' participation in the helping process, it is also important to emphasize that they can accelerate their progress by working on their difficulties between appointments. Some people mistakenly believe that change will result largely from what occurs in sessions. In actuality, the content of sessions is far less significant than how they apply the information gained from them. The following message clarifies this aspect of a client's responsibility:

Social worker: We'll want to make progress toward your goals as rapidly as possible. One way you can accelerate your progress is by working hard between our sessions. That means carrying out tasks you've agreed to, applying what we talk about in your daily life, and making mental notes or actually writing down thoughts, feelings, and events that relate to your problems so we can consider them in your next session. Actually, what you do between sessions is more important in accomplishing your goals than the session itself. We'll be together only a brief time each week. The rest of the week you have opportunities to apply what we talk about and plan together.

Yet another aspect of the client's role involves keeping appointments. This factor is obvious, but discussing it emphasizes clients' responsibilities and prepares them to cope constructively with obstacles that may cause them to fail or to cancel appointments. The following message clarifies this aspect of the client's role:

Social worker: As we work together, it will be critical for you to keep your appointments. Unforeseen things such as illness happen occasionally, of course, and we can change appointments if such problems arise. At other times, however, you may find yourself feeling discouraged or doubting whether coming here really helps. You may also feel upset over something I've said or done and find yourself not wanting to see me. I won't knowingly say or do anything to offend you, but you may have some troubling feelings toward me anyway. The important thing is that you not miss your appointment, because when you're discouraged or upset, we need to talk about it. I know that may not be easy, but it will help you to work out your problematic feelings. If you miss your appointment, you may find it even harder to return.

For example, conversely, when clients are referred, practitioners should not assume that potential clients plan to return for another session.

> **VIDEO CASE EXAMPLE**
>
> For example, the practitioner, Dorothy, in the "Getting Back to Shakopee" video, suggests near the end of the session: "If you decide to come back for another session, next time we would break down all of the concerns you are facing and try to address them one at a time, starting with the ones you consider most important."

A final task for the social worker is to emphasize that difficulties are inherent in the process of making changes. Clarifying this reality further prepares clients for the mixed feelings that they will inevitably experience. When these difficulties are highlighted early in the helping process, clients can conceive of such feelings and experiences as natural obstacles that must be surmounted, rather than yield to them or feel defeated. An explanation about these predictable difficulties similar to the following clarifies the vicissitudes of the change process:

Social worker: We've talked about goals you want to achieve. Accomplishing them won't be easy. Making changes is seldom possible without a difficult and sometimes painful struggle. People usually have ups and downs as they seek to make changes. If you understand this, you won't be disappointed. I don't want to discourage you. I am optimistic about the prospects of you attaining your goals.

Over the years, numerous clients have reported retrospectively that they appreciated receiving these kinds of explanations during the initial session. When the going became rough and they began to waver in pursuing their goals, they recalled that such discouragement was natural and, rather than discontinuing the contact, mustered up the determination to persevere.

In addition to clarifying the client's role, it is vital to clarify your own role. Stress that you will be a partner in helping clients to understand their difficulties more fully. Because you have an outside vantage point, you may be able to help them see their difficulties from a new perspective and to consider solutions that they may have overlooked. We recommend that you clarify further that, although you will be an active partner in considering possible remedial actions, the final decisions rest with the clients themselves. You will help them to weigh alternatives, but your desire is to see clients develop their strengths and exercise their capacities for independent action to the fullest extent possible. In addition, emphasize that you plan to assist clients in focusing on their strengths and any incremental growth they achieve. Stress that although you will actively perform this function in the initial stage of the helping process, at the same time, you will be encouraging your clients to learn to recognize their own strengths and grow independently.

> **VIDEO CASE EXAMPLE**
>
> In the "Serving the Squeaky Wheel" video, the social worker, Ron Rooney, is replacing another social worker who has been abruptly transferred. The client, Molly, has a serious and persistent mental illness. Much of the session is devoted to beginning to develop trust that has been jeopardized by the loss of the previous worker. Such circumstances are not ideal but occur frequently enough that it is important to have models for dealing with it. The social worker describes his role as helping Molly make a plan in which she will be supported to live safely in a community of her choosing.

Another aspect of the helping role that you should clarify for clients is your intention to assist them in anticipating obstacles they will encounter in striving to attain their goals and your willingness to help them formulate strategies to surmount these obstacles. Clarifying this facet of your role further reinforces the reality that change is difficult but you will be with and behind your clients at all times, offering support and direction. You might share that each family faces its own unique situation and has its own set of values, noting that it will be your job to get to know these values and situations from the clients' point of view. Only then will you attempt to help the clients plan what makes sense for them to do.

Some special hurdles must be overcome to develop productive working relationships between social workers and clients in mandated settings, because the mandated client did not seek the contact and often perceives it as being contrary to his or her interests. In the following dialogue, notice how the social worker begins to develop expectations about a collaborative relationship.

Client: I didn't like the earlier workers because they came into my house telling me what I can and can't do. One thing I don't like is someone telling me what I can do with my kids and what I can't.

Social worker: It sounds like you had a negative experience with earlier workers.

Client: Yeah, I did. I did not like it at all because they were telling me what I should do.

Social worker: I'm going to take a different approach with you because I don't feel that I know it all; you know best about the situation occurring in your own family and in your own life. I will want you to tell me about the problems you are concerned about and how we can best resolve those together.

Client: Okay.

Social worker: My job will be to develop a case plan with you. I won't be the one to say, "This is what you need to do." I want you to have input in that decision and to say, "Well, I feel I can do this." I will be willing to share ideas with you as we decide what to work on and how to do it. I will need to include any court-mandated requirements, such as our need to be meeting together, in the agreement. However, I want you to have a lot of say in determining what we work on and how.

The social worker interprets the client's comment about previous workers as pertinent to exploring what their own working relationship might be like. She describes her own role and clarifies what the client can do in a clear and tangible way to work on goals important to her.

Communicating about Informed Consent, Confidentiality, and Agency Policies

The encounter between the social worker and the client exists within a context of limits, possibilities, and rights. In this regard, the social worker must share the rights and limits to communication discussed in Chapter 4: discuss confidentiality and its limits, obtain informed consent, and share agency policies and legal limits.

EP 2.1.1c

> **VIDEO CASE EXAMPLE**
>
> In "Getting Back to Shakopee," the social worker, Dorothy, and her Native American client, Valerie, discuss limits to confidentiality for the first several minutes of the video. Valerie is concerned about what material from the session will get back to the supervisor who referred her for service. In addition, she has concerns about Dorothy's mandated reporter responsibilities related to child welfare because her teenaged daughter supervises younger children in the summer. This video demonstrates how discussion of confidentiality issues can be vital with clients who are referred by others in less than voluntary circumstances.

Dorothy, the social worker in the video example, might have shared these limits, possibilities, and rights in the following fashion:

Social worker: What you say to me is private in most circumstances. I will share what we have discussed with my supervisor. In certain circumstances, however, I might have to share what we have discussed with others. For example, if you threatened to seriously harm another person, I would have a duty to warn that would mean that I could not keep that information private. For example, if your children were in danger, I am a mandated reporter, and I would have to share that information. Similarly, if you were to seriously consider harming yourself, I would have to share that information. If a judge were to subpoena my records, he or she could gain access to a general summary of what we have done together. Do you have any questions about this?

It is important that this section of the initial interview be presented in language that the client readily understands so that the discussion embodies the spirit of informed consent. The exact content of this discussion will vary with the setting in which you work. It is important that you carry out this duty in a genuine fashion, rather than presenting it as a ritualistic sharing of written forms that has the appearance of obtaining informed consent but ignores its intent. In hurried agency practice, sometimes this principle is violated. Discuss with your supervisor what information needs to be shared with clients and how that is done in ways that are useful to those clients.

Facilitative Conditions

The social worker uses communication skills as building blocks to help develop a productive working relationship with clients. This chapter focuses on two of the three skills embodied in what have been called the facilitative conditions or core conditions in helping relationships. These conditions or skills were originally denoted by Carl Rogers (1957) as empathy, unconditional positive regard, and congruence. Other terms have since evolved, and we shall refer to the conditions as empathy, respect or nonpossessive warmth, and authenticity or genuineness. Because we addressed nonpossessive warmth or respect at length in Chapter 4, we limit our focus here to empathy and authenticity.

Research has supported the correlation of empathy with positive outcomes (Bohart and Greenburg, 1997). In addition, a study by a social worker (Nugent, 1992) found that these facilitative conditions were effective in fostering positive helping relationships. The conditions are often thought to be the foundation level skills that undergird many treatment models and help create a positive relationship; Hill and Nakayama, 2000; (Mason, 2009). For example, there is a particularly close relationship between techniques designed to enhance empathy that come from the Rogerian nondirective approach and motivational interviewing (Mason, 2009). Efforts in the latter are often intended to facilitate client change particularly related to problematical behavior. While social workers are often engaged in activities designed to influence such behavior, they are not always aimed at changing behavior and are guided by professional values supporting self-determination. Hence, these chapters will present techniques designed to enhance empathy as valuable in their own right. In some instances, social workers will also attempt to influence behavior.

These skills are particularly useful in treatment situations with voluntary clients. However, we will also describe ways that the facilitative conditions can serve as building blocks in both involuntary relationships and other situations that do not have therapy as the primary focus (Bennett, Legon, & Zilberfein, 1989).

Empathic Communication

EP 2.1.10b

Empathic communication involves the ability of the social worker to perceive accurately and sensitively the inner feelings of the client and to communicate his or her understanding of these feelings in language attuned to the client's experiencing of the moment. The first dimension of empathy, empathic recognition, is a precondition of the second dimension, demonstrating through accurate reflection of feelings that the social worker comprehends the client's inner experiencing. For social workers, it is not enough to grasp what the client is feeling and experiencing and reflect that understanding back. Social workers are also called on by our code of ethics to take empathic action (Gerdes & Segal, 2009). Beyond reflecting the conflict and pain clients may be experiencing, we are called on to consider ways they might alleviate their situation. Similarly, on a macro level, it is not enough for social workers to notice and document a deleterious condition plaguing a neighborhood. Social workers are called on to utilize social empathy to act with others to address social and economic justice concerns.

Empathic communication plays a vital role in nurturing and sustaining the helping relationship and in providing the vehicle through which the social worker becomes emotionally significant and influential in the client's life. In mandated circumstances in which involuntary clients are not seeking a helping relationship, conveying empathic understanding reduces the level of threat perceived by the client and mitigates his or her defensiveness, conveys interest and helpful intent, and creates an atmosphere conducive to behavior change.

In responding to clients' feelings, social workers must avoid being misled by the conventional facades used to conceal emotions. As a consequence, the empathic communicator responds to the feelings that underlie such flippant messages as "Oh, no, it doesn't really matter" or "I don't care what he does!" These messages often mask disappointment or hurt, as do messages such as "I don't need anyone" when the client is experiencing painful loneliness, or "I don't let anyone hurt me" when the client is finding rejection hard to bear. To enter the client's private world of practical experience, the social worker must also avoid making personal interpretations and judgments of the client's private logic and feelings that, in superficial contacts, might appear weak, foolish, or undesirable.

Being empathically attuned involves not only grasping the client's immediately evident feelings, but also, in a mutually shared, exploratory process, identifying the client's underlying emotions and discovering the meaning and personal significance of the client's feelings and behavior. In getting in touch with these camouflaged feelings and meanings, the social worker must tune in not only to verbal messages but also to more subtle cues, including facial expressions, tone of voice, tempo of speech, and postural cues and gestures that amplify and sometimes contradict verbal meanings. Such nonverbal cues as blushing, crying, pausing, stammering, changing voice intonation, clenching jaws or fists, pursing the lips, lowering the head, or shifting the posture often reveal the presence of distressing feelings and thoughts.

Empathic communication involves "stepping into the shoes of another," in the sense that the social worker attempts to perceive the client's world and experiences. When the client feels pressure from an involuntary referral, the empathic social worker understands and is aware of that pressure and how it feels. At the same time, the social worker must remain outside of the client's world and avoid being overwhelmed by his or her fears, anger, joys, and hurts, even as the social worker deeply senses the meaning and significance of these feelings for the client. "Being with" the client means that the social worker focuses intensely on the client's affective state without losing perspective or taking on the emotions experienced by the client.

A person who experiences feelings in common with another person and is similarly affected by whatever the other person is experiencing usually responds sympathetically rather than empathically. Sympathetic responding, which depends on achieving emotional and intellectual accord, involves supporting and condoning the other person's feelings (e.g., "I'd feel the same way if I were in your position" or "I think you're right"). In contrast, empathic responding involves understanding the other person's feelings and circumstances without taking that person's side (e.g., "I sense you're feeling …" or "You seem to be saying …").

When social workers support their clients' feelings, the clients may feel no need to examine their behavior or circumstances and may not engage in the process of self-exploration that is vital to growth and change.

Instead, clients tend to look to the social worker to change the behavior of other persons who play significant roles in their problems. Retaining separateness and objectivity thus is a critical dimension in the helping process. Clearly, when social workers assume their clients' feelings and positions, they lose not only the vital perspective that comes from being an outsider but also the ability to be helpful.

Of course, being empathic entails more than just recognizing clients' feelings. Social workers must also respond verbally and nonverbally in ways that affirm their understanding of clients' inner experiencing. It is not unusual for a person to experience empathic feelings for another individual without conveying those feelings in any way to the second party. Exhibiting high-level empathy requires skill in verbally and nonverbally demonstrating understanding. A common mistake made by social workers is to tell clients, "I understand how you feel." Rather than producing a sense of being understood, such a response often creates doubts in the client's mind about the social worker's perceptiveness, because any specific demonstration of understanding is lacking. Indeed, use of this response may mean that the social worker has not explored the client's feelings sufficiently enough to fully grasp the significance of the problematic situation. Social workers attempt to share emotion and get on the inside without losing awareness of who they are.

Later in this chapter, we present theory and exercises for developing skill in empathic responding. Initially, we provide a list of affective words and phrases intended to expand your vocabulary so that you can meet the challenge of responding to the wide range of emotions experienced by clients. We also provide exercises to help you to refine your ability to perceive the feelings of others—a prerequisite to the mastery of empathic communication. To assist you to discern levels of empathy, we include a rating scale for empathic responding, accompanied by examples of social worker responses and exercises. These exercises will help you to gain mastery of empathic communication at an effective working level.

Developing Perceptiveness to Feelings

Feelings or emotions exert a powerful influence on behavior and often play a central role in the problems of clients. Applicants or voluntary clients often enter into the helping relationship with openness and hope that they will explore both their concerns and their related feelings. Conversely, involuntary clients experience strong feelings but have not actively sought out a helping relationship for dealing with them (Cingolani, 1984). Hence, use of the skills sometimes takes a slightly different course with these clients, as one of the social worker's goals is to express empathy with the *situation* the involuntary client experiences and the feelings related to those situations and experiences.

To respond to the broad spectrum of emotions and feeling states presented by clients, the social worker must be fully aware of the diversity of human emotion. Further, the social worker needs a rich vocabulary of words and expressions that not only reflect clients' feelings accurately but also capture the intensity of those feelings. For example, dozens of descriptive feeling words may be used to express anger, including furious, aggravated, vexed, provoked, put out, irritated, and impatient—all of which express different shades and intensities of this feeling.

When used judiciously, such words serve to give sharp and exact focus to clients' feelings. Possessing and utilizing a rich vocabulary of affective words and phrases that accurately reflect these feelings is a skill that often is not developed by even experienced social workers. It is important to realize that high-level empathic responding takes place in two phases: (1) a thinking process and (2) a responding process. A deficient vocabulary for describing feelings limits social workers' ability to conceptualize and hence to reflect the full intensity and range of feelings experienced by clients.

It has been our experience that beginning social workers typically have a limited range of feeling words from which to draw in conveying empathy. Although many words may be used to capture feelings, learners often limit themselves to, and use to excess, a few terms, such as "upset" or "frustrated," losing much of the richness of client messages in the process.

The accompanying lists illustrate the wide range of expressions available for social workers' use in responding to clients' feelings. Note, however, that using feeling words in a discriminating fashion is not merely important in empathic responding but is indispensable in relating authentically as well. Becoming a competent professional requires passing through a maturing process whereby social workers develop not only the capacity to deeply share the inner experiencing of others, but also a way to express their own personal feelings constructively. Please consult the following comprehensive list of affective words and phrases.

Affective Words and Phrases

Competence/Strength	
convinced you can	confident
sense of mastery	powerful
potent	courageous
resolute	determined
strong	influential
brave	impressive
forceful	inspired
successful	secure
in charge	in control
well equipped	committed
sense of accomplishment	daring
undaunted	effective
sure	sense of conviction
trust in yourself	self-reliant
sharp	able
adequate	firm
capable	on top of it
can cope	important
up to it	ready
equal to it	skillful

Happiness/Satisfaction	
elated	superb
ecstatic	on cloud nine
on top of the world	organized
fantastic	splendid
exhilarated	jubilant
terrific	euphoric
delighted	marvelous
excited	enthusiastic
thrilled	great
super	in high spirits
joyful	cheerful
elevated	happy
light-hearted	wonderful
glowing	jolly
neat	glad
fine	pleased
good	contented
hopeful	mellow
satisfied	gratified
fulfilled	tranquil
serene	calm
at ease	awesome

Caring/Love	
adore	loving
infatuated	enamored
cherish	idolize
worship	attached to
devoted to	tenderness toward
affection for	hold dear
prize	caring
fond of	regard
respect	admire
concern for	taken with
turned on	trust
close	esteem
hit it off	value
warm toward	friendly
like	positive toward
accept	enchanted by

Depression/Discouragement	
anguished	in despair
dreadful	miserable
dejected	disheartened
rotten	awful
horrible	terrible
hopeless	gloomy
dismal	bleak
depressed	despondent
grieved	grim
broken hearted	forlorn
distressed	downcast
sorrowful	demoralized
pessimistic	tearful
weepy	down in the dumps
deflated	blue
lost	melancholy
in the doldrums	lousy
kaput	unhappy
down	low
bad	blah
disappointed	sad
below par	unnerved

Inadequacy/Helplessness	
worthless	depleted
good for nothing	washed up
powerless	helpless
impotent	crippled
inferior	emasculated
useless	finished
like a failure	impaired
inadequate	whipped
defeated	stupid
incompetent	puny
inept	clumsy
overwhelmed	ineffective
like a klutz	lacking
awkward	deficient
unable	incapable
small	insignificant
like a wimp	unimportant
over the hill	incomplete
immobilized	like a puppet
at the mercy of	inhibited
insecure	lacking confidence
unsure of self	uncertain
weak	inefficient
unfit	feeble

Anxiety/Tension	
terrified	frightened
intimidated	horrified
desperate	panicky
terror-stricken	paralyzed
frantic	stunned
shocked	threatened
afraid	scared
stage fright	dread
vulnerable	fearful
apprehensive	jumpy
shaky	distrustful
butterflies	awkward
defensive	uptight
tied in knots	rattled
tense	fidgety
jittery	on edge
nervous	anxious
unsure	hesitant
timid	shy
worried	uneasy
bashful	embarrassed
ill at ease	doubtful
uncomfortable	self-conscious
insecure	alarmed
restless	

Confusion/Troubledness	
bewildered	puzzled
tormented by	baffled
perplexed	overwhelmed
trapped	confounded
in a dilemma	befuddled
in a quandary	at loose ends
going around in circles	mixed-up
disorganized	in a fog
troubled	adrift
lost	disconcerted
frustrated	floored
flustered	in a bind
torn	ambivalent
disturbed	conflicted
stumped	feeling pulled apart
mixed feelings about	uncertain
unsure	uncomfortable
bothered	uneasy
undecided	overwhelmed

Rejection/Offensive	
crushed	destroyed
ruined	pained
wounded	devastated
tortured	cast off
betrayed	discarded
knifed in the back	hurt
belittled	abused
depreciated	criticized
censured	discredited
disparaged	laughed at
maligned	mistreated
ridiculed	devalued
scorned	mocked
scoffed at	used
exploited	debased
slammed	slandered
impugned	cheapened
mistreated	put down
slighted	neglected
overlooked	minimized
let down	disappointed
unappreciated	taken for granted
taken lightly	underestimated
degraded	discounted
shot down	disrespected

Anger/Resentment	
furious	enraged
livid	seething
could chew nails	fighting mad
burned up	hateful
bitter	galled
vengeful	resentful
indignant	irritated
hostile	pissed off
have hackles up	had it with
upset with	bent out of shape
agitated	annoyed
got dander up	bristle
dismayed	uptight
disgusted	bugged
turned off	put out
miffed	ruffled
irked	perturbed
ticked off	teed off
chagrined	griped
cross	impatient
infuriated	violent

Loneliness	
all alone in the universe	isolated
abandoned	totally alone
forsaken	forlorn
lonely	alienated
estranged	rejected
remote	alone
apart from others	shut out
left out	excluded
lonesome	distant
aloof	cut off

Guilt/Embarrassment	
sick at heart	unforgivable
humiliated	disgraced
degraded	horrible
mortified	exposed
branded	could crawl in a hole
like two cents	ashamed
guilty	remorseful
crummy	really rotten
lost face	demeaned
foolish	ridiculous
silly	stupid
egg on face	regretful
wrong	embarrassed
at fault	in error
responsible for	goofed
lament	blew it

Use of the Lists of Affective Words and Phrases

The lists of affective words and phrases may be used with the exercises at the end of the chapter and in the *Practice Behaviors Workbook* to formulate responses that capture the nature of feelings expressed by clients. Note that potential clients referred by others and involuntary clients may be more likely to initially experience the emotions of anger, resentment, guilt, embarrassment, rejection, confusion, tension, inadequacy, helplessness, depression, and discouragement. In Chapter 7, we will explore barriers to effective communication. One of those barriers can be the social worker's inability to achieve empathy with such involuntary clients, as the social worker may believe that they have brought on these negative feelings as a result of their own irresponsible actions. That is, some social workers feel that perhaps involuntary clients deserve these feelings because they have not fully accepted responsibility for their part in the difficulties they have experienced. As noted in Chapter 4, the social work value of acceptance of worth suggests that we can empathize with feelings of despair and powerlessness even if clients have not yet taken responsibility for the consequences of their actions. In fact, involuntary and referred clients often express anger and frustration about even being in an introductory session with a social worker. You may note how this occurs in the video "Serving the Squeaky Wheel." Notice how the social worker attempts to reflect this anger and frustration and reframe it more constructively toward action they could take together to alleviate those feelings.

After you have initially practiced responding to messages in which clients convey feelings, check the lists to determine whether some other words and phrases might more accurately capture the client's feelings. Also, scan the lists to see whether the client's message involves feelings in addition to those you identified. The lists may similarly assist you in checking out the accuracy of your reflective responses as you review taped sessions.

The lists of affective words and phrases are offered for the purpose of helping you communicate more empathically with your clients. However, words can have different connotations within the same language based on age, region, ethnic group, and social class. We suggest that you sit down with your coworkers and fellow students to compile your own more specialized list of feeling words for specific groups that you routinely encounter. For example, formulating a list of terms commonly used by adolescents in various socioeconomic and ethnic groupings could be useful. Issues may also arise when you try to use an unfamiliar slang vernacular, thus defeating the purpose of empathizing. However, making the effort to clarify words that accurately describe what the client is feeling often conveys your genuine interest.

Acquisition of a broader emotional vocabulary is a step toward expressing greater empathy for clients. It allows you to more effectively convey your understanding and compassion for what they are experiencing. Because many clients want to change their situations as well as their feelings about it, conveying empathy is the first step toward helping them work on those concerns.

Although the lists of affective words and phrases presented in this chapter are not exhaustive, they encompass many of the feelings and emotions frequently encountered in the helping process. Feeling words are subsumed under 11 categories, running the gamut of emotions from intense anguish and pain (e.g., *grieved, terrified, bewildered, enraged,* and *powerless*) to positive feeling states (e.g., *joy, elation, ecstasy, bliss,* and *pride in accomplishment*). Given our emphasis on clients' strengths, we have taken care to include a grouping of terms to assist social workers in capturing clients' feelings related to growth, strengths, and competence.

Feeling words in each category are roughly graduated by intensity, with words conveying strong intensity grouped toward the beginning of each category and words of moderate to mild intensity appearing toward the end. In responding to client messages, the social worker should choose feeling words that accurately match the intensity of the feelings the client is experiencing.

To illustrate, consider that you are working with an African American client in a drug aftercare program who has returned to work as a meter reader. He reports that when he knocked on the door in a largely white suburb intending to read the meter, the elderly white woman would not let him in, despite his wearing his picture identification name tag on his uniform: "I was so low down and depressed. What can you do? I am doing my thing to keep straight, and I can't even do my job because I'm black." Such a response appropriately calls for an intense response by the social worker: "Sounds like you felt demeaned and humiliated that you couldn't do your job because of this woman's fear of black people. And yet you did not let that carry you back to drug use—you kept straight, and were not stopped by other people's perceptions."

In addition to using words that accurately reflect the intensity of the client's feelings, it is important to respond with a tone of voice and nonverbal gestures and expressions that similarly reflect the intensity of feelings conveyed by the verbal response. The proper intensity of affect may also be conveyed by using appropriate qualifying words—for example, "You feel (somewhat) (quite) (very) (extremely) discouraged by your low performance on the entrance test."

Clients' messages may also contain multiple feelings. Consider the following client message: "I don't know what to do about my teenage daughter. I know that she's on drugs, but she shuts me out and won't talk to me. All she wants is to be out with her friends, to be left alone. There are times when I think she really dislikes me." Feeling words that would capture the various facets of this message include *confused, bewildered, alarmed, troubled, overwhelmed, lost, desperate, worried, frightened, alienated, rejected,* and *hurt.* A response that included all of these feeling words would be extremely lengthy and overwhelming to the client. However, a well-rounded empathic response should embody at least several of the surface feelings, such as *worried* and *confused,* and be delivered with appropriate timing. The social worker might also bring deeper-level feelings into focus, as explained in the following paragraphs.

Notice in the preceding client message that many feelings were implied but not explicitly stated. Some of these emotions would likely be just beyond the client's level of awareness but could easily be recognized if they were drawn to the client's attention. For example, the client might emphatically confirm a social worker response that sensitively identifies the hurt, rejection, and even anger inherent in the client's message. Without the social worker's assistance, the client might not develop full awareness of those deeper-level feelings.

In responding to client messages, you must be able to distinguish between readily apparent feelings and probable deeper feelings. In the early phase of the helping process, the social worker's objectives of developing a working relationship and creating a climate of understanding are best accomplished by using a reciprocal level of empathy—that is, by focusing on the client's immediately evident feelings. As the client perceives your genuine effort and commitment to understand his or her situation, that experience of being "empathically received" gradually yields a low-threat environment that obviates the need for self-protection.

Note that clients from oppressed groups, such as the African American client in the earlier example, may rightly feel better understood by the social worker yet continue to feel disillusioned by an alien environment. It is important to acknowledge those feelings about the environment. Trust may be gained by actions taken outside the session that indicate that the social worker is trustworthy and has the client's best interest at heart, as well as by verbal conveyance of empathy during the session. Similarly, Ivanoff, Blythe, and Tripodi suggest that too much emphasis on empathy can feel manipulative to involuntary clients (1994). With voluntary clients, the resultant climate of trust sets the stage for self-exploration, a prerequisite to self-understanding, which in turn facilitates behavior change. This positive ambience prepares the way for the use of "additive" or "expanded" levels of empathy to reach for underlying feelings as well as to uncover hidden meanings and goals of behavior.

Conversely, attempting to explore underlying feelings during the early phase of the helping process is counterproductive. Uncovering feelings beyond the client's awareness before a working relationship is firmly established tends to mobilize opposition and may precipitate premature termination of the contact. Involuntary clients in a negotiated relationship may never desire such uncovering of deeper feelings and may find exploration of them to be intrusive (Ivanoff, Blythe, and Tripodi, 1994, p. 21).

Exercises in Identifying Surface and Underlying Feelings

In the following exercise, identify both the apparent surface feelings and the probable underlying feelings embodied in the client's message. Remember that most of the feelings in the messages are merely implied, as people often do not use feeling words. As you complete the exercise, read each message and write down the feelings involved. Next, scan the lists of affective words and phrases to see whether you might improve your response. After you have responded to all four messages, check the feeling words and phrases you identified with those given at the end of the chapter. If the feelings you identified were similar in meaning to those identified in the answers, consider your responses to be accurate. If they were not, review the client messages for clues about the client's feelings that you overlooked.

Client Statements

1. **Elderly client:** I know my children have busy lives. It is hard for them to have time to call me.

   Apparent feelings:
   Probable deeper feelings:

2. **Lesbian client referring to partner who has recently come out to her family**: When I was at your brother's wedding, and they wanted to take family pictures, nobody wanted me in the pictures. In fact nobody wanted to talk to me.

Note: This is a quote from a client in the "Home for the Holidays" video connected to this chapter.

   Apparent feelings:
   Probable deeper feelings:

3. **Client:** When I was a teenager, I thought that when I was married and had my own children, I would never yell at them like my mother yelled at me. Yet, here I am doing the same things with Sonny.

   [Tearful]
   Apparent feelings:
   Probable deeper feelings:

4. **African American client in child welfare system:** The system is against people like me. People think that we drink, beat our kids, lay up on welfare, and take drugs.

   Apparent feelings:
   Probable deeper feelings:

Exercises at the end of this chapter for formulating reciprocal empathic responses will also assist you in increasing your perceptiveness to feelings.

Accurately Conveying Empathy

Empathic responding is a fundamental, yet complex skill that requires systematic practice and extensive effort to achieve competency. Skill in empathic communication has no limit or ceiling; rather, this skill is always in the process of "becoming." In listening to their taped sessions, even highly skilled professionals discover feelings they overlooked. Many social workers, however, do not fully utilize empathic responding. They fail to grasp the versatility of this skill and its potency in influencing clients and fostering growth in moment-by-moment transactions.

In fact, some social workers dismiss the need for training in empathic responding, mistakenly believing themselves to already be empathic in their contacts with clients. Few people are inherently helpful in the sense of relating naturally with high levels of empathy or any of the other core conditions. Although people achieve varying degrees of empathy, respect, and genuineness through their life experiences, attaining high levels of these skills requires rigorous training. Research scales that operationalize empathy conditions have been developed and validated in extensive research studies (Duan & Hill, 1996; Truax & Carkhuff, 1967). These scales, which specify levels of empathy along a continuum ranging from high- to low-level skills, represented a major breakthrough not only in operationalizing essential social worker skills but also in establishing a relationship between these skills and successful outcomes in practice.

The empathic communication scale has been employed to help students distinguish between high- and low-level empathic responses and has been used by peers and instructors in group training to assess levels of students' responses. Students then receive guidance in reformulating low-level responses to bring them to higher levels.

The Carkhuff (1969) empathy scale, which consists of nine levels, has been widely used in training and research. Although we have found nine-point scales valuable as training aids, they have proven somewhat confusing to students, who often have difficulty in making such fine distinctions between levels. For this reason, we have adapted the nine-level scale described by Hammond, Hepworth, and Smith (1977) by collapsing it to the five-level scale presented here.

Empathic Communication Scale
Level 1: Low Level of Empathic Responding
At level 1, the social worker communicates little or no awareness or understanding of even the most conspicuous of the client's feelings; the social worker's responses are irrelevant and often abrasive, hindering rather than facilitating communication. Operating from a personal frame of reference, the social worker changes the subject, argues, gives advice prematurely, lectures, or uses other ineffective styles that block communication, often diverting clients from their problems and fragmenting the helping process. Furthermore, the social worker's nonverbal responses are not appropriate to the mood and content of the client's statement.

When social workers relate at this low level, clients often become confused or defensive. They may react by discussing superficialities, arguing, disagreeing, changing the subject, or withdrawing into silence. Thus, the client's energies are diverted from exploration and/or work on problems.

Unfortunately, level one responses occur with some frequency in settings in which clients are involuntary, stigmatized, or considered deviant. Such responses may provoke client anger but pose few consequences for the social worker unless there are norms that clients must be treated respectfully in all circumstances. These responses are shared not for the purpose of modeling them, but rather to alert you that if you see them occurring, or it occurs to you, it signals problems with the social worker or the setting. It could just be a social worker on a bad day; but worse if it has become a standard of practice that passes unnoticed. Consider the following example of a mother in the child welfare system who has recently completed a drug treatment program.

Client: I want to go into an aftercare treatment program near my home that is culturally sensitive and allows me to keep my job.

BELOW Level 1 response: You should not be thinking about what is convenient for you but rather what might ultimately benefit your child by your being a safe parent for her. Your thinking here is symptomatic of the problem of why your child is in custody, and your chances of regaining custody are limited.

This response is beneath the lowest levels of acceptable empathy. It is the opposite of empathy because it is actively judgmental and inappropriately confrontational. It is possible that the social worker might have valid reasons for wishing the client to consider a variety of options. Making the judgmental statement only makes the circumstances worse and makes it unlikely that the client will consider the worker's opinion. Social workers' frustration with clients who endanger others is understandable. Statements like the one above, however, greatly hinder further efforts to work with them in a collaborative fashion.

Level 1 response: "I see that you want to find a program near your home."

This response is minimally facilitative but at least avoids the judgmental statements of the previous example.

African American male: *[to child welfare worker]:* I don't trust you people. You do everything you can to keep me from getting back my son. I have done everything I am supposed to do, and you people always come up with something else.

Level 1 Responses

- *"Just carry out the case plan and you are likely to succeed."* (Giving advice.)
- *"Just think what would have happened if you had devoted more energy in the last year to carrying out your case plan: You would have been further along."* (Persuading with logical argument; negatively evaluating client's actions.)
- *"How did you get along with your last social worker?"* (Changing the subject.)
- *"Don't you think it will all work out in time?"* (Leading question, untimely reassurance.)
- *"Why, that's kind of an exaggeration. If you just work along with me, before you know it things will be better."* (Reassuring, consoling, giving advice.)

VIDEO CASE EXAMPLE

You can see two versions of the same situation in the video "Domestic Violence and the Probation Officer." Note the client response to level 1 or below empathic responses in version one. Note also how the situation looks different when the practitioner employs higher levels of empathy in version two.

The preceding examples illustrate ineffective styles of communication used at this low level. Notice that messages reflect the social worker's own formulations concerning the client's problem; they do not capture the client's inner experiencing. Such responses stymie clients, blocking their flow of thought and producing negative feelings toward the social worker.

Level 2: Moderately Low Level of Empathic Responding

At level 2, the social worker responds to the surface message of the client but erroneously omits feelings or factual aspects of the message. The social worker may also inappropriately qualify feelings (e.g., "somewhat," "a little bit," "kind of") or may inaccurately interpret feelings (e.g., "angry" for "hurt," "tense" for "scared"). Responses may also emanate from the social worker's own conceptual formulations, which may be diagnostically accurate but not empathically attuned to the client's expressions. Although level 2 responses are only partially accurate, they do convey an effort to understand and, for this reason, do not completely block the client's communication or work on problems.

Level 2 Responses

- **We provide here level 2 responses to the previous example of the African American male:** *[to child welfare worker]:* I don't trust you people. You do everything you can to keep me from getting back my son. I have done everything I am supposed to do, and you people always come up with something else.
- *"You'll just have to be patient. I can see you're upset."* The word *upset* defines the client's feelings only vaguely, whereas feeling words such as *angry, furious,* and *discounted* more accurately reflect the client's inner experiencing.
- *"You feel angry because your case plan has not been more successful to date. Maybe you are expecting too much too soon; there is a lot of time yet."* The listener begins to accurately capture the client's feelings but then moves to an evaluative interpretation ("you expect too much too soon") and inappropriate reassurance.
- *"You aren't pleased with your progress so far?"* This response focuses on external, factual circumstances to the exclusion of the client's feelings or perceptions regarding the event in question.
- *"You feel like things aren't going too well."* This response contains no reference to the client's immediately apparent feelings. Beginning social workers often use the lead-in phrase "You feel like …" without noticing that, in employing it, they have not captured the client's feelings.

- "You're disappointed because you haven't gotten your son back?" This response, although partially accurate, fails to capture the client's anger and distrust of the system, wondering whether any of his efforts are likely to succeed.
- "I can see you are angry and disappointed because your efforts haven't been more successful so far, but I think you may be expecting the system to work too quickly." Although the message has a strong beginning, the empathic nature of the response is negated by the listener's explanation of the reason for the client's difficulties. This response represents a form of taking sides—that is, justifying the actions of the child welfare system by suggesting that too much is expected of it.

> **VIDEO CASE EXAMPLE**
>
> In the video "Getting Back to Shakopee," the social worker, Dorothy, heard an account of uncomfortable relations with co-workers on the job. She summarizes and adds a level 2 empathic comment: "So just that I understand what you are talking about, you were working on your own project and Mary came over and added hers to yours and asked you to finish it for her? What did that do for you?" The empathy is implied in the social worker's question, but it could have been more explicit. For example, Dorothy might have asked "did you feel as if she did not have the right to do this, that she was acting disrespectfully toward you?"

The preceding responses illustrate many of the common errors made by social workers in responding empathically to client messages. Although some part of the messages may be accurate or helpful, all the responses in some way ignore or subtract from what the client is experiencing.

Level 3: Interchangeable or Reciprocal Level of Empathic Responding

The social worker's verbal and nonverbal responses at level 3 convey understanding and are essentially interchangeable with the client's obvious expressions, accurately reflecting factual aspects of the client's messages and surface feelings or state of being. Reciprocal responses do not appreciably add affect or reach beyond the surface feelings, nor do they subtract from the feeling and tone expressed.

Acknowledging the factual content of the client's message, although desirable, is not required; if included, this aspect of the message must be accurate. Level 3 responses facilitate further exploratory and problem-focused responses by the client. The beginning social worker does well in achieving skill in reciprocal empathic responding, which is an effective working level.

Level 3 Responses
- "You're really angry about the slow progress in your case and are wondering whether your efforts are likely to succeed."
- "I can tell you feel very let down and are asking yourself, 'Will I ever get my son back?'"

> **VIDEO CASE EXAMPLE**
>
> The video "Serving the Squeaky Wheel" contains a lengthy exchange in which the client, Molly, expresses her suspicion about what is written about her in the social worker's case records. The social worker responds, "I am hearing that it is a real sore point with you about what I write and think and what goes into the records about you." This response deals directly with her concern.

Essentially interchangeable, level 3 responses express accurately the immediately apparent emotions in the client's message. The content of the responses is also accurate, but deeper feelings and meanings are not added. The second response also illustrates a technique for conveying empathy that involves changing the reflection from the third to the first person, and speaking as if the social worker were the client.

Level 4: Moderately High Level of Empathic Responding

Responses at level 4 are somewhat additive, accurately identifying the client's implicit underlying feelings and/or aspects of the problem. The social worker's response illuminates subtle or veiled facets of the client's message, enabling the client to get in touch with somewhat deeper feelings and unexplored meanings and purposes of behavior. Level 4 responses thus are aimed at enhancing self-awareness.

Level 4 Responses

- "You feel very frustrated with the lack of progress in getting your son back. You wonder whether there is any hope in working with a new worker and this system, which you feel hasn't been helping you."

VIDEO CASE EXAMPLE

In the "Serving the Squeaky Wheel" video, the client, Molly, says that other people's conceptions of mental illness do not include her. The social worker responds, "Let me see if I understand what you are saying: some people may think because you have a car and you speak up for yourself, that you are a very competent person who doesn't need any resources [Client: "There you go."] and if you ask for them [Client: "I am screwing the system."] that you are trying to take things that you are not entitled to. But your view is that you can have a car and speak up for yourself and still have other needs." This response not only conveys immediately apparent feelings and content but also is noticeably additive in reflecting the client's deeper feelings. In this case, the client's immediate response—finishing the practitioner's sentences—indicates that the empathic response is perceived as accurate.

Level 5: High Level of Empathic Responding

Reflecting each emotional nuance, and using voice and intensity of expressions finely attuned to the client's moment-by-moment experiencing, the social worker accurately responds to the full range and intensity of both surface and underlying feelings and meanings at level 5. The social worker may connect current feelings and experiencing to previously expressed experiences or feelings, or may accurately identify implicit patterns, themes, or purposes. Responses may also identify implicit goals embodied in the client's message, which point out a promising direction for personal growth and pave the way for action. Responding empathically at this high level facilitates the client's exploration of feelings and problems in much greater breadth and depth than responding at lower levels. Conveying this level of empathy occurs rarely with inexperienced interviewers and only somewhat more often with highly experienced interviewers. The opportunity to respond at such depth is more likely to occur near the end of an interview and with clients who have become more voluntary.

Level 5 Responses

VIDEO CASE EXAMPLE

In the video "Serving the Squeaky Wheel," a developing theme is that Molly, a client with serious and persistent mental illness, acts, as she puts it, as a "greasy wheel," always advocating for herself and acting assertively, as she has been trained to do in many education programs. And yet those skills act as a "two- or three-edged sword" in that sometimes she is punished for this assertiveness. Reflecting these themes and Molly's language, the social worker, Ron Rooney, says, "You just seem to be courageous in fighting battles, and you have learned some skills in assertiveness, and as you say, that can be a two-edged or three-edged sword. Sometimes your assertiveness gets you what you want and sometimes your assertiveness causes some people to look at you as the squeaky wheel that has squeaked too much."

Exercises in Discriminating Levels of Empathic Responding

The following exercises ask you to rate responses for their level of empathy and are designed to assist you in refining your ability to determine the helpfulness of responses. These exercises will prepare you for subsequent practice in formulating your own empathic messages. Three client statements are given, followed by several possible responses. Using the empathic scale, rate each response. Rating messages will be less difficult if, using the list of affective words and phrases, you first identify the feelings contained in the client's message. After you have rated each response, compare your rating with those given at the end of the chapter. Referring to the rating scale, analyze the responses you rated inaccurately, trying to pinpoint the reason for the authors' ratings. Additional exercises are available in the *Practice Behaviors Workbook*.

Client Statements

1. *Single woman, age 80* [to social worker concerning her request to move to an independent living complex provided for ambulatory elderly persons]: Goodness, the more I think of moving, the more scared I get. I have neighbors here who look after me, and I won't know a soul there. I'm afraid I'll be all alone.

Level Responses

1. "It's pretty scary to you, leaving your neighbors and familiar surroundings. But there will be a lot of friendly people there and things to do. Besides, they fix one hot meal for you every day."
2. "Don't worry, you'll make friends in no time, and you'll wish you'd moved sooner."
3. "Did you sign those application papers I left with you a few days ago?"
4. "Just thinking about moving worries you because you'll be leaving your own neighborhood and friends. Even though your life would be much easier, you're unsure you'll be better off in other ways."
5. "So I gather in some ways you'd rather stay right where you are rather than gamble on a change."
6. "Lots of other people in the new apartments were just as scared as you before they moved, but I don't know a single one who's sorry now."
7. "It sounds as though you have some pretty mixed feelings about moving. Part of you wants to go because you could live more comfortably, but another part of you is afraid you'll feel alone and lost and wants to cling to people you know care about you."
8. "Are you saying we just ought to forget the whole thing?"

2. Male, age 16 [*in weekly visit to social work probation officer*]: I don't see the sense in having to come here every lousy week. I haven't been in any trouble now since I went to court a month ago. You should know by now you can trust me.

Level Responses

1. "A month isn't very long, you know. And how can I be sure you're staying out of trouble?"
2. "I gather you'd rather not have to see me. I can understand that, but the judge ordered it and you'd be in trouble with him if you didn't meet the conditions of your probation."
3. "Has it been a month since you went to court? I didn't think that it had been that long."
4. "You'd prefer not coming here and feel you've earned my trust."
5. "Having to come here each week gripes you, and I gather you're irritated with me for encouraging you to follow the judge's order."
6. "Look, you got yourself into this mess so don't complain to me if you don't like it. Maybe you'd like to talk the judge into changing his mind."
7. "It irritates you to have to come here each week. You'd like to get me off your back."
8. "You're confused about why you have to come here and wish you didn't have to."

3. Group member [*in hesitant, quiet voice*]: It's really hard for me to say what I want to say in this group. When I do start to talk, I get tongue-tied, and my heart starts beating faster and faster. I feel like some of you are critical of me.

Level Responses
(By Group Members or Group Leader)

1. "Yeah, I feel that same way sometimes, too."
2. "It is frightening to you to try to share your feelings with the group. Sounds like you find yourself at a loss for words and wonder what others are thinking of you."
3. "I know you're timid, but I think it's important that you make more of an effort to talk in the group, just like you're doing now. It's actually one of the responsibilities of being a group member."
4. "You get scared when you try to talk in the group."
5. "I sense that you're probably feeling pretty tense and tied up inside right now as you talk about the fear you've had in expressing yourself."
6. "Although you've been frightened of exposing yourself, I gather there's a part of you that wants to overcome that fear and become more actively involved with the rest of the group."
7. "What makes you think we're critical of you? You come across as a bit self-conscious, but that's no big deal."
8. "You remind me of the way I felt the first time I was in a group. I was so scared, I just looked at the floor most of the time."
9. "I wonder if we've done anything that came across as being critical of you."

4. A homeless client who has been referred to a housing program is completing an intake with the social worker when he is asked about what led to his losing his job. He responds, "Budget cuts, lays offs, and I did not have seniority."

Level Responses

1. "How did you feel about that?"
2. "So several things, including cuts, lay offs, and low seniority, contributed to your losing your job and contributed to your homelessness."
3. "How long have you been homeless?"
4. "Don't you think you have some responsibility for losing your job?"

Responding with Reciprocal Empathy

EP 2.1.10b

Reciprocal or interchangeable empathic responding (level 3) is a basic skill used throughout the helping process to acknowledge client messages and to encourage exploration of problems. In the initial phase, empathic responding serves a vital purpose in individual, conjoint, and group sessions: It facilitates the development of a working relationship and fosters the climate of understanding necessary to promote communication and self-disclosure. In this way, it sets the stage for deeper exploration of feelings during subsequent phases of the helping process.

Note that the benefits of making additive empathic responses at levels 4 and 5 are not contingent on the frequency of their usage. In fact, making one such response in a first or second interview may be helpful and appropriate. More frequent attempts presume a depth of relationship that has not yet developed. Additive empathic responses often exceed the level of feelings and meanings expressed by clients during early sessions and are thus reserved, in large part, for the later phases of the helping process.

Because reciprocal responding is an essential skill used frequently to meet the objectives of the first phase of the helping process, we recommend that you first aim to achieve beginning mastery of responding at level 3. Extended practice of this skill should significantly increase your effectiveness in establishing viable helping relationships, interviewing, and gathering data. The remainder of this chapter provides guidelines and practice exercises that will help you in mastering reciprocal responding. Although responding at additive levels represents an extension of the skill of reciprocal responding, it is an advanced skill that can be used in a variety of ways to achieve specific objectives. For this reason, it has been grouped with other change-oriented or "action" skills presented in Part 3 of the book.

Constructing Reciprocal Responses

To reach level 3 on the empathic scale, you must be able to formulate responses that accurately capture the content and the surface feelings in the client message. It is also important to frame the message so that you do not merely restate the client's message.

The following paradigm, which identifies the elements of an empathic or reflective message, has proven useful for conceptualizing and mastering the skill of empathic responding:

You feel _____ about _____ because _____.

                        Accurately identifies or describes feelings

The response focuses exclusively on the client's message and does not reflect the social worker's conceptualizations.

The following excerpt from a session involving a social worker and a 17-year-old female illustrates the use of the preceding paradigm in constructing an empathic response:

Client: I can't talk to my father without feeling scared and crying. I'd like to be able to express myself and to disagree with him, but I just can't.

Social worker: It sounds as though you just feel panicky when you try to talk to your father. You feel down on yourself, because at this point you can't say what you want without falling apart.

This message conveys a reflection with a twist which we will explore more in the following chapter (Miller, Rollnick & Conforti, 2002). That is, it reflects the client's current feeling but implies that it could change at another point when she acquires more confidence and skill (Greene, Lee & Hoffpauir, 2005). Many times, client messages contain conflicting or contrasting emotions, such as the following: "I like taking drugs, but sometimes I worry about what they might do to me." In such cases, each contrasting feeling should be highlighted:

- *You feel _____ yet you also feel _____.*
- *I sense that you feel torn because while you find taking drugs enjoyable, you have nagging thoughts that they might be harmful to you.*[1]

Remember that to respond empathically at a reciprocal level, you must use language that your clients will readily understand. Abstract, intellectualized language and professional jargon create barriers to communication and should be avoided. It is also important to vary the language you use in responding. Many professionals tend to respond with stereotyped, repetitive speech patterns, commonly using a limited variety of communication leads to begin their empathic responses. Such leads as "You feel …" and "I hear you saying …" repeated over and over not only distract the client but also seem phony and contrived. This kind of stereotyped responding draws more attention to the social worker's technique than to his or her message. One of the many advantages to audio or video recording your own work is that these habitual responses that can be so instinctive you don't notice them as they occur, will become readily apparent to you.

The list of varied introductory phrases will help you expand your repertoire of possible responses. We encourage you to read the list aloud several times and to review it frequently while practicing the empathic communication training exercises in this chapter and in Chapter 17, which covers additive empathic responding. The reciprocal empathic response format ("You feel _____ because _____") is merely a training aid to assist you in focusing on the affect and content of client messages. The leads list will help you respond more naturally.

Exercises designed to help you to develop level 3 reciprocal empathic responses appear at the end of the chapter and in the *Practice Behaviors Workbook*. Included in the exercises are a variety of client statements taken from actual work with individuals, groups, couples, and families in diverse settings.

In addition to completing the skill development exercises, we recommend that you record the number of empathic responses you employ in sessions over several weeks to determine the extent to which you are applying this skill. We also suggest that either you or a knowledgeable associate rate your responses and determine the mean level of empathic responding for each session. If you find (as most beginning social workers do) that you are underutilizing empathic responses or responding at low levels, you may wish to set a goal to improve your skill.

Leads for Empathic Responses

Could it be that …
I wonder if …
What I guess I'm hearing is …
Correct me if I'm wrong, but I'm sensing …
Perhaps you're feeling …
Sometimes you think …
Maybe this is a long shot, but …
You're feeling …
I'm not sure if I'm with you but …
You appear to be feeling …
It appears you feel …
Maybe you feel …
Do you feel …
I'm not sure that I'm with you; do you mean …
It seems that you …
Is that what you mean?
I'm not certain I understand; you're feeling …
As I hear it, you …
Is that the way you feel?
The message I'm getting is that
Let me see if I'm with you; you …
If I'm hearing you correctly …
So, you're feeling …
You feel …
It sounds as though you are saying …
I hear you saying …
So, from where you sit …
I sense that you're feeling …
Your message seems to be …
I gather you're feeling …
If I'm catching what you say …
What you're saying comes across to me as …
What I think I'm hearing is …
I get the impression that …
As I get it, you felt that …
To me it's almost like you are saying …
So, as you see it …
I'm picking up that you …
I wonder if you're saying …
So, it seems to you …
Right now you're feeling …
You must have felt …
Listening to you, it seems as if …
You convey a sense of …
As I think about what you say, it occurs to me you're feeling …
From what you say …
I gather you're feeling …

Employing Empathic Responding

In early sessions with the client, empathic responding should be used frequently as a method of developing rapport and "staying in touch" with the client. Responses should be couched in a tentative manner to allow for inaccuracies in the social worker's perception. Checking out the accuracy of responses with appropriate lead-in phrases such as "Let me see if I understand …" or "Did I hear you right?" is helpful in communicating a desire to understand and a willingness to correct misperceptions.

In initially using empathic responses, learners are often leery of the flood of emotions that sometimes occurs as the client, experiencing none of the usual barriers to communication, releases feelings that may have been pent up for months or years. It is important to understand that empathic responses have not "caused" such feelings but rather have facilitated their expression, thus clearing the way for the client to explore and to consider such feelings more rationally and objectively.

You may worry, as do many beginning social workers, about whether you will "damage" the client or disrupt the helping relationship if your empathic responses do not always accurately reflect the client's feelings. Perhaps even more important than accuracy, however, is the commitment to understand conveyed by your genuine efforts to perceive the client's experience. If you consistently demonstrate your goodwill and intent to help through attentive verbal and nonverbal responding, an occasional lack of understanding or faulty timing will not damage the client-social worker relationship. In fact, your efforts to clarify the client's message will usually enhance rather than detract from the helping process, particularly if you respond to corrective feedback in an open, nondefensive, and empathic manner.

Multiple Uses of Empathic Communication

Earlier in the chapter, we referred to the versatility of empathic communication. In this section, we delineate a number of ways in which you can employ reciprocal empathic responding.

Establishing Relationships with Clients in Initial Sessions

As discussed previously, the use of empathic responding actively demonstrates the social worker's keen awareness of clients' feelings and creates an atmosphere in which clients feel safe enough to risk exploring their personal thoughts and feelings.

Although empathic communication is important in bridging cultural gaps, at times it can be used to excess. We must be careful with generalizations to ethnic groups because there is variation within each group related to individual differences, family experiences, education, interaction with other groups (Dean, 2001). Classification systems can tend to stereotype members of ethnic groups and in fact create distance (Johnson & Munch, 2010). Social workers have to be prepared to be learners, operating from a "not knowing" stance, which may however be influenced by hypotheses which they explore rather than act on as realities. With this caveat, some members of Asian American and Native American groups may tend to be lower in emotional expressiveness than members of other client groups, and they may react with discomfort and confusion if a social worker relies too heavily on empathic communication. Nevertheless, it is important to "read between the lines" and to sensitively respond to troubling emotions that these clients do not usually express directly. Like other clients, they are likely to appreciate a social worker's sensitive awareness to the painful emotions associated with their difficulties.

This can lead to assuming a more directive, active, and structured stance in situations such as crises where immediate action is required. This can also apply to some Asian American clients. As Tsui and Schultz (1985) have clarified, "A purely empathetic, passive, nondirective approach serves only to confuse and alienate the [Asian] client" (p. 568). The same can be said of many Native American clients, based on their levels of acculturation and experience with other groups.

IDEAS IN ACTION

In the videotape "Getting Back to Shakopee," the social worker, Dorothy, is working with a Native American client, Valerie, who appears guarded and apprehensive about contact with a social worker after referral by her employer. She appears worried that seeing a social worker might lead to a child welfare investigation. Her guarded stance appears to be associated with a belief based on her experience that social workers are more likely to remove children than act as her agent toward her own goals. In this case, these beliefs are not so much cultural beliefs as "folk wisdom" about the experience of her group with public child welfare. Dorothy makes many efforts to establish empathic and cultural linkages. A turning point appears to occur when Valerie discovers that Dorothy knows about an upcoming powwow and plans to attend. Taking a not knowing, learner stance, leads Dorothy to find out about the particular employment, stress, sobriety and family responsibility pressures that Valerie experiences.

Staying in Touch with Clients

EP 2.1.10b

Reciprocal empathic responding operationalizes the social work principle of "starting where the client is" and keeps social workers attuned to their clients' current feelings. Although he or she inevitably employs many other skills and techniques, the social worker constantly returns to empathic responding to keep in touch with the client. In that sense, empathic communication is a fundamental intervention and a prerequisite to the use of other interventions. Gendlin (1974) used the analogy of driving a car to illuminate the vital role of empathy in keeping in touch with clients. Driving involves much more than watching the road. A driver does many things, including steering, braking, signaling, and watching signs. One may glance at the scenery, visit with others, and think private thoughts, but watching the road must be accorded the highest priority.

When visibility becomes limited or hazards appear, all other activities must cease and the driver must attend exclusively to observing the road and potentially dangerous conditions. Just as some drivers fail to pay proper attention to their surroundings and become involved in accidents, so some social workers also fail to attend sufficiently to cultural differences and changes in clients' moods and reactions, mistakenly assuming they know their clients' frame of mind. As a consequence, social workers may fail to discern important feelings, and their clients may perceive them as disinterested or insensitive and subsequently disengage from the helping process. Indeed, it is often true with beginners that so much of their own processing is focused on preparing the next thing they will say that they often miss what the client says. It takes time and experience to stay focused on what the client is expressing and trust that you will be able to respond adequately. Part of this is reframing your expectations of yourself. Instead of aspiring to be the social worker who can quickly assess and resolve client concerns, you can aspire to be a social worker who is able to accurately reflect what the client is saying and feeling and, in that process, be useful to them as they consider how to deal with their concerns.

Accurately Assessing Client Problems

EP 2.1.10b

The levels of empathy offered by social workers are likely to correlate with their clients' levels of self-exploration. That is, high-level empathic responding should increase clients' exploration of self and problems. As the social worker moves "with" clients by frequently using empathic responses in initial sessions, clients will begin to lay out their problems and to reveal events and relevant data. Figuratively speaking, clients then take social workers where they need to go by providing information crucial to making an accurate assessment. Such an approach contrasts sharply with sessions that emphasize history-taking and in which social workers, following their own agendas rather than the clients', spend unnecessary time asking hit-or-miss questions and gathering extraneous information.

Responding to Clients' Nonverbal Messages

Through their facial features, gestures, and body postures, clients often hint at feelings that they do not express verbally. In the course of a session, for instance, a client may become pensive, or he or she may show puzzlement, pain, or discomfort. In such instances, the social worker may convey understanding of the client's feeling state and verbalize the feeling explicitly through a reflective response that attends to the emotion suggested in the client's nonverbal expressions. For instance, in response to a client who has been sitting dejectedly with her head down for several minutes after having reported some bad grades, a social worker might say, "At this moment you seem to be feeling very sad and discouraged, perhaps even defeated." In group or conjoint sessions, the social worker might reflect the nonverbal messages of several, or all, of the members. For example, the social worker might say, "I sense some restlessness today, and we're having a hard time staying on our topic. I'm wondering if you're saying, 'We're not sure we want to deal with this problem today.' Am I reading the group correctly?"

Children are likely to communicate more nonverbally with unfamiliar adults such as social workers than they communicate in verbal ways. It can be useful to ask about such nonverbals and what they might mean. A child interacting with a toy, making limited eye contact, and making one-word replies to questions about how things are going at home may be communicating some things about how uncomfortable or unfamiliar he or she is with the process. Rather than force the child to explain what is happening in words, play therapy techniques have permitted children to tell a story, through actions, of what is occurring to them (Lukas, 1993). A social worker working with a child who was having difficulties at school made a home visit. The child was particularly interested in a toy piano, playing little melodies on it. The social worker, attempting to tune in to the child client, sat beside him and played a little melody and sang a little song "how was your day?" The child sat for a moment then repeated the melody, singing "pretty good." The social worker responded with a variation of the melody "what was good about it?" and the child responded.

Empathic responses that accurately tune into clients' nonverbal experiencing will usually prompt clients to begin exploring feelings they have been experiencing.

Making Confrontations More Palatable

EP 2.1.10i

Confrontation is employed in the change-oriented phase to expand clients' awareness and to motivate them to action. It is most appropriate when clients are contemplating actions that are unlawful or that are dangerous to themselves or others. Confrontation is also appropriate when such actions conflict with the goals and values a client has chosen for himself or herself.

Of course, even well-timed confrontations may meet with varying degrees of receptiveness. Both concerns for the client's welfare and prudence dictate that the social worker determine the impact of a potential confrontation upon the client and implement a process for making such an intervention more palatable. This may be accomplished by employing empathic responses attuned to the client's reaction immediately following a confrontation. As social workers listen attentively and sensitively to their clients' expressions, the clients' defensiveness may abate. Indeed, clients often begin to process new information and think through and test the validity of their ideas, embracing those that fit and rejecting others that seem inapplicable. Guidelines for this important skill are presented in Chapter 17.

Blending confrontation and empathic responses is a particularly potent technique for managing group processes when the social worker must deal with a controversial issue or distractive behavior that is interfering with the work of the group.

Handling Obstacles Presented by Clients

Client opposition to what is happening in a session is sometimes healthy. What is often interpreted as unconscious resistance may, in fact, be a negative reaction to poor interviewing and intervention techniques used by the social worker or to client confusion, misunderstanding, or even inertia. For these reasons, it is important to carefully monitor clients' reactions and to deal directly and sensitively with their related feelings. Clients' verbal or nonverbal actions may comment indirectly on what is occurring in the helping process. For instance, a client may look at her watch and ask how long the session will last, shift her body position away from the social worker, begin tapping a foot, or stare out the window. When it appears that the client is disengaging from the session in this way, an empathic response that reflects the client's verbal and/or nonverbal message may effectively initiate discussion of what is occurring.

Social workers sometimes practice with highly verbal clients who talk rapidly and jump quickly from one topic to another. Overly verbal clients present a particular challenge to beginning social workers, who must often overcome the misconception that interrupting clients is rude. Because of this misconception, novice interviewers sometimes spend most of an initial session listening passively to highly verbal clients without providing any form or direction to the helping process. They may also allow clients to talk incessantly because they mistakenly view this as constructive work on problems. Quite the contrary, excess verbosity often keeps the session on a superficial level and interferes with problem identification and exploration. It may also indicate a more serious affective mental health problem.

It is important that social workers provide structure and direction to each session, thereby conveying an expectation that specific topics will be considered in depth. Much more will be said about this in later chapters. For now, we simply underscore the necessity of using empathic responses with highly verbal clients as a preliminary strategy to slow the process and to provide some depth to the discussion.

For example, a social worker might interject or intervene with "I'd like to interrupt to check whether I'm understanding what you mean. As I get it, you're feeling …" or "Before you talk about that topic, I would like to make sure I'm with you. You seem to be saying …" or "Could we hold off discussing that for just a minute? I'd like to be sure I understand what you mean. Would you expand on the point you were just making?"

Managing Anger and Patterns of Violence

During individual or group sessions, clients (especially those who were not self-referred and may be involuntary clients) often experience surges of intense and conflicting feelings, such as anger, hurt, or disappointment. In such instances, empathic responding is a key tool for assisting them to work through those feelings. As empathic responses facilitate expanded expression of these feelings, clients engage in a process of venting, clarifying, and experiencing different feelings. Over time, they may achieve a mellowing of emotions and a more rational and thoughtful state of being.

When it is employed to focus sharply on clients' feelings, empathic responding efficiently manages and modifies strong emotions that represent obstacles to progress. As the social worker successfully handles such moments and clients experience increased self-awareness and cathartic benefits, the helping relationship is strengthened.

Empathic responding is particularly helpful in dealing with hostile clients and is indispensable when clients become angry with the social worker, as illustrated in the following client statement: "What you're doing to help me with my problems doesn't seem to be doing me any good. I don't know why I keep coming." At such moments, the social worker must resist the temptation to react defensively, because such a response will further antagonize the client and exacerbate the situation. Responding by challenging the client's perception, for instance, would damage the helping relationship. The social worker's responses should represent a genuine effort to understand the client's experiencing and feelings and to engage the client in fully exploring those feelings.

Involuntary clients sometimes become frustrated with the seemingly slow pace of progress toward goals and may feel that policies and individuals in the system are acting to thwart them. Empathizing with this anger is necessary before the social worker and client can collaborate productively and figure out how to make the system work toward client goals (Rooney & Chovanec, 2004).

Keeping this idea in mind, consider the impact of the following reciprocal empathic response: "You're very disappointed that things aren't better and are irritated with me, feeling that I should have been more helpful to you." This response accurately and nondefensively acknowledges the client's frustration with the situation and with the social worker. By itself, it would not be sufficient to calm the client's ire and to free the client to consider the problem more fully and rationally.

Carefully following the client's feelings and remaining sensitively attuned to the client's experiencing by employing empathic responses for several minutes usually assists both the social worker and the client to understand more clearly the strong feelings that prompted the client's outburst and to adequately assess the source of those feelings. Attending to the emotions expressed does not mean that the content is discounted. The social worker might, for example, follow the empathic response above by saying, "I'd like to explore more fully with you which parts of our work have not felt worthwhile to you."

When faced with angry clients in group and conjoint sessions, it is critical that the social worker empathically not only reflect the negative feelings and positions of the clients who are displaying the anger, but also reach for and reflect the feelings or observations of members who may be experiencing the situation differently. Utilizing empathic responses in this manner assists the social worker in gathering information that will elucidate the problem, helping angry members air and examine their feelings, and bringing out other points of view for the group's consideration. In addition, employing empathic responding at such moments encourages a more rational discussion of the issues involved in the problem and thus sets the stage for possible problem solving. For example, a group leader might emphasize with members' frustration at having chosen to be part of an involuntary group such as one addressing alternatives to violence rather than risking prosecution. Having made a limited choice to be part of the group, members can then be encouraged to take part in establishing content areas which they would like to have covered in the group.

The principles just discussed also apply to clients who are prone to violent behavior. Such clients often come to the attention of social workers because they have abused their children and/or partners. People who engage in violence often do so because they have underlying feelings of helplessness and frustration and because they lack skills and experience in coping with troubling situations in more constructive ways. Some have short fuses and weak emotional controls, and many come from backgrounds in which they vicariously learned violence as a mechanism of coping. Using empathy to defuse their intense anger and to tune into the exceptions when they have been more successful in managing it can be an important first step in working with such clients (Lee, Uken & Sebold, 2004). Other clients may have difficulties with anger and express this emotion only when under the influence of alcohol or other substances. Helping them experience and ventilate anger when sober and in control is a major approach employed to assist such clients to learn constructive ways of coping with anger (Potter-Efron & Potter-Efron, 1992).

> **VIDEO CASE EXAMPLE**
>
> Several parts of the "Serving the Squeaky Wheel" video deal with the client, Molly, expressing anger and frustration and the practitioner, Ron Rooney, attempting to respond empathically to that anger. In particular, Molly is frustrated with an abrupt replacement of her previous case worker by Rooney and insists on his proving his identity as a social worker. Note how this challenge is met. At other points, Molly scales her level of trust at below zero and attributes this to a history of distrust of social workers.

Utilizing Empathic Responses to Facilitate Group Discussions

EP 2.1.10i

Social workers may facilitate discussion of specific issues in conjoint or group sessions by first identifying a particular topic and then using empathic responses to reflect the observations of various group members in relation to that topic. The social worker may also actively seek responses from members who have not contributed and then employ empathic responses (or paraphrases) to acknowledge their observations. Utilized frequently in this manner, empathic responding encourages (and reinforces) clients' participation in group discussions.

Teaching Clients to Respond Empathically

Clients often experience difficulties in their relationships because their styles of communication include many barriers that prevent them from accurately hearing messages or conveying understanding to others. An important task for the social worker involves teaching clients to respond empathically. This task is accomplished in part by modeling, which is generally recognized as a potent technique for promoting client change and growth. People who distort or ignore others' messages (e.g., in marital, family, and other close relationships) may benefit vicariously by observing the social worker listen effectively and respond empathically. Moreover, clients who are hard to reach or who have difficulties in expressing themselves may gradually learn to recognize their own emotions and to express themselves more fully as a result of the social worker's empathic responding.

Teaching empathic communication skills to clients also can entail assuming an educational role. Several approaches to assisting partners who are having serious conflicts rely on teaching both parties to gain and express empathy for each other. Social workers' roles as educators require them to intervene actively at opportune moments to enable their clients to respond empathically, particularly when they have ignored, discounted, or attacked the contributions of others in a session. With respect to this role, we suggest that social workers consider taking the following actions:

1. Teach clients the paradigm for empathic responding introduced in this chapter. If appropriate, ask them to engage briefly in a paired practice exercise similar to the one recommended for beginning social workers at the end of the chapter. Utilizing topics neutral to the relationship, have each person carefully listen to the other party for several minutes, and then reverse roles. Afterward, evaluate with participants the impact of the exercise on them.

2. Introduce clients to the list of affective words and phrases and to the leads list provided in this chapter. If appropriate, you may wish to have clients assume tasks during the week to broaden their feeling vocabulary similar to the tasks recommended for beginning social workers.

3. Intervene in sessions when clients ignore or fail to validate messages—a situation that occurs frequently during direct social work with couples, families, and groups. At those moments, interrupt the process in a facilitative fashion to ask the sender to repeat the message and the receiver to paraphrase or capture the essence of the former's message with fresh words, as illustrated in the following example:

16-year-old daughter: I don't like going to school. The teachers are a bunch of dweebs, and most of the kids laugh and make fun of me.

Mother: But you've got to go. If you'd just buckle down and study, school wouldn't be half so hard for you. I think ...

Social worker: [*interrupting and speaking to mother*]: I can see that you have some real concerns about Janet's not going to school, but for a moment, I'm going to ask you to show that you heard what she said to you by repeating it back to her.

Mother: [*looking at social worker*]: She said she doesn't like school.

Social worker: That's close, but turn and talk to Janet. See if you can identify what she's feeling.

Mother: [*turning to daughter*]: I guess it's pretty painful for you to go to school. And you don't like your teachers and you feel shut out and ridiculed by the kids.

Janet: *[tearfully]:* Yeah, that's it ... it's really hard.

Notice that the mother did not respond empathically to her daughter's feelings until the social worker intervened and coached her. This example illustrates the importance of persevering in teaching clients to "hear" the messages of others, a point we cannot overemphasize. People often have considerable trouble mastering listening skills because habitual responses are difficult to discard. This is true even when clients are highly motivated to communicate more effectively and when social workers actively intervene to assist them.

4. Give positive feedback when you observe clients listening to each other or, as in the preceding example, when they respond to your coaching. In the example, the social worker might have praised the mother as follows: "I liked the way you responded, because your message accurately reflected what your daughter was experiencing. I think she felt you really understood what she was trying to say." It is also helpful to ask participants to discuss what they experienced during the exchange and to highlight positive feelings and observations.

Authenticity

Although many theorists agree that empathy and respect are vital to developing effective working relationships, they do not agree about the amount of openness or self-disclosure practitioners should offer. *Self-disclosure* refers to the sharing with the client of opinions, thoughts, feelings, reactions to the client, and personal experiences of the practitioner (Deal, 1999). Decisions about whether or when to self-disclose must be guided by a perception of benefit to the client, not the social worker's need to share. As one client said, "My case worker wanted to tell me all about his weekend and his girlfriend and so on. And I said, 'TMI: too much information. I don't need to know this, and I don't want to know this.' I don't want to share this kind of information with him and don't want to know it from him." Clearly, this client did not perceive the benefit of this kind of personal sharing. Deal reports that although beginning social workers frequently report engaging in self-disclosure, they seem less clear about the conditions under which it is appropriate to do so.

With respect to empirical evidence, numerous research studies cited by Truax and Mitchell (1971) and Gurman (1977) indicated that empathy, respect, and genuineness are correlated with positive outcomes. Critical analyses of these studies and conflicting findings from other research studies, however, have led experts to question these early findings and to conclude that "a more complex association exists between outcome and therapist 'skills' than originally hypothesized" (Parloff, Waskow, & Wolfe, 1978, p. 251). Research needs to distinguish between intellectual empathy and empathic emotions and identify whether they are identifying therapist or client experience of empathy (Duan and Hill, 1996). That is, conveying understanding of the client's perception of the situation (intellectual empathy) is not the same as conveying feeling the same emotions (empathic empathy). Both are useful but they may have independent effects.

Nevertheless, authenticity (also called genuineness) and the other facilitative conditions are still viewed as central to the helping process. *Authenticity* is defined as the sharing of self by relating in a natural, sincere, spontaneous, open, and genuine manner. Being authentic, or genuine, involves relating personally so that expressions are spontaneous rather than contrived. In addition, it means that social workers' verbalizations are congruent with their actual feelings and thoughts. Authentic social workers relate as real people, expressing their feelings and assuming responsibility for them rather than denying the feelings or blaming the client for causing them. Authenticity also involves being nondefensive and human enough to admit one's errors to clients. Realizing that they expect clients to lower their defenses and to relate openly (thereby increasing their vulnerability), social workers themselves must model humanness and openness and avoid hiding behind a mask of "professionalism."

Relating authentically does not mean that social workers indiscriminately disclose their feelings. Indeed, authentic expressions can be abrasive and destructive. Social workers should thus relate authentically only when doing so is likely to further the therapeutic objectives. This qualification provides considerable latitude and is merely intended to constrain social workers from (1) relating abrasively (even though they may be expressing genuine feelings) and (2) meeting their own needs by focusing on their personal experiences and feelings rather than those of the client.

With respect to the first constraint, social workers must avoid misconstruing authenticity as granting free license to do whatever they wish, especially with

EP 2.1.1.b

respect to expressing hostility. The second constraint reiterates the importance of social workers responding to clients' needs rather than their own. Moreover, when social workers share their feelings or experiences for a therapeutic purpose, they should immediately shift the focus back on the clients. Keep in mind that the purpose of relating authentically—whether with individuals, families, or groups—is to facilitate growth of clients, not to demonstrate one's own honesty or authenticity.

Types of Self-Disclosure

EP 2.1.1b

The aspect of authenticity denoted as self-disclosure has been variously defined by different authors (Chelune, 1979). For our discussion here, we define self-disclosure as the conscious and intentional revelation of information about oneself through both verbal expressions and nonverbal behaviors (e.g., smiling, grimacing, or shaking one's head in disbelief). Viewed from a therapeutic perspective, self-disclosure encourages clients to reciprocate with trust and openness.

Danish, D'Augelli, and Hauer (1980) have identified two types of self-disclosure, *self-involving statements* and *personal self-disclosing*. The former type includes messages that express the social worker's personal reaction to the client during the course of a session. Examples of self-involving statements follow:

- "I'm impressed with the progress you've made this past week. You applied what we discussed last week and have made another step toward learning to control angry feelings."
- "I want to share my reaction to what you just said. I found myself feeling sad for you because you put yourself down unmercifully. I see you so differently from how you see yourself and find myself wishing I could somehow spare you the torment you inflict on yourself."
- "You know, as I think about the losses you've experienced this past year, I marvel you've done as well as you have. I'm not at all sure I'd have held together as well as you have."

Personal self-disclosure messages, by contrast, center on struggles or problems the social worker is currently experiencing or has experienced that are similar to the client's problems. The following are examples of this type of self-disclosure:

- [To couple] *"As you talk about your problems with your children, it reminds me of similar difficulties I had with mine when they were that same age."* (The social worker goes on to relate his experience.)
- [To individual client] *"I think all of us struggle with that same fear to some degree. Earlier this week I…"* (The social worker goes on to relate events in which she experienced similar fears.)

Research findings comparing the effects of different types of self-disclosure have been mixed (Farber, 2006). Given the inconclusive findings, social workers should use personal self-disclosure judiciously. They should also recognize cultural variations that may suggest that some relatively low-level self-disclosure may be necessary early in the helping process. Rosenthal-Gelman (2004) has reported in a study that Hispanic practitioners are more likely to engage in some self-disclosure at the beginning of contact with Hispanic clients, honoring the cultural norm of establishing a more personal contact. Logic suggests that self-disclosures of current problems may undermine the confidence of clients, who may well wonder how social workers can presume to help others when they haven't successfully resolved their own problems. Moreover, focusing on the social worker's problems diverts attention from the client, who may conclude that the social worker prefers to focus on his or her own problems. Self-involving disclosures, by contrast, appear to be of low risk and are relevant to the helping process.

> **VIDEO CASE EXAMPLE**
>
> As noted in the "Getting Back to Shakopee" video, self-disclosure of cultural experiences by the practitioner, Dorothy, appears essential in beginning to develop trust and rapport with her client.

Timing and Intensity of Self-Disclosure

Yet another aspect of self-disclosure focuses on the timing and level of intensity of the social worker's sharing, ranging from superficial to highly personal statements. Social workers should avoid sharing personal feelings and experiences until they have established rapport and trust with their clients and the clients have, in turn, demonstrated readiness to engage on a more personal level. The danger in premature self-disclosure is that such responses can threaten clients and lead to emotional retreat at the very time when it is vital to reduce threat and defensiveness.

The danger is especially great with clients from cultures where relating on an intense personal basis might be less common. Tsui and Schultz (1985) have suggested that self-disclosure by social workers may facilitate the development of rapport with some Asian clients. The logic of this recommendation is that given the generally low level of emotional expressiveness in some Asian families, the social worker is, in effect, acting as a role model for the client, thereby showing the client how the appropriate expression of emotion facilitates the treatment process (Tsui & Schultz, 1985, p. 568). Members of Asian American families, of course, are not homogenous, as their members differ in terms of their level of acculturation and familiarity with values such as self-disclosure. Hence, assessing their cultural experience can be part of determining whether self-disclosure might be useful.

As clients experience trust, social workers can appropriately relate with increased openness and spontaneity, assuming that their authentic responses are relevant to their clients' needs and do not shift the focus from the client for more than brief periods. Even when trust is strong, social workers should exercise only moderate self-disclosure—beyond a certain level, even authentic responses no longer facilitate the helping process (Truax & Carkhuff, 1964).

A Paradigm for Responding Authentically

Beginning social workers (and clients) may learn the skill of relating authentically more readily if they have a paradigm for formulating effective messages. This paradigm includes the four elements of an authentic message:

(1) "I" ( )	About	Because
(2) Specific feeling or wants	(3) Neutral description of event	(4) Impact of situation upon sender or others

The following example (Larsen, 1980), involving a social work student intern's response to a message from an institutionalized youth, illustrates the use of this paradigm. The student describes the situation: "Don and I had a hard time together last week. I entered the living unit only to find that he was angry with me for some reason, and he proceeded to abuse me verbally all night long. This week, Don approached me to apologize."

Don: I'm really sorry about what happened the other night. I didn't mean to dis you.

Student: Well, you know, Don, I'm sorry it happened, too. I was hurt and puzzled that night because I didn't understand where all your anger was coming from. You wouldn't talk to me about it, so I felt frustrated, and I didn't quite know what to do or make of it. One of my real fears that night was that this was going to get in the way of our getting to know each other. I really didn't want to see that happen.

Note that the student uses all of the elements of the paradigm: identifying specific feelings (hurt, puzzlement, frustration, fear); describing the events that occurred in a neutral, nonblaming manner; and identifying the impact she feared these events might have upon the client-social worker relationship.

As you consider the paradigm, note that we are not recommending that you use it in a mechanistic and un-deviating "I-feel-this-way-about ..." response pattern. Rather, we suggest that you learn and combine the elements of the paradigm in a variety of ways as you practice constructing authentic messages. Later, as you incorporate authentic relating into your natural conversational repertoire, you will no longer need to refer to the paradigm.

Note that this paradigm is also applicable in teaching clients to respond authentically. We suggest that you present the paradigm to clients and guide them through several practice messages, assisting them to include all of the elements of the paradigm in their responses. For example:

Specific "I" Feelings	Description of Event	Impact
I get frustrated	when you keep reading the paper while I'm speaking	because I feel very unimportant to you.

It is important to stress with clients the need to use conversational language when they express authentic messages. Also emphasize, however, that they should talk about their own feelings and opinions rather than slip into accusatory forms of communication.

Guidelines for Responding Authentically

As you practice authentic responding and teach clients to respond authentically in their encounters with others, we suggest you keep in mind the following guidelines related to the four elements of an authentic message

1. *Personalize messages by using the pronoun "I."* When attempting to respond authentically, both social workers and clients commonly make the mistake of starting

their statements with "You." This introduction tends to focus a response on the other person rather than on the sender's experiencing. In contrast, beginning messages with "I" encourages senders to own responsibility for their feelings and to personalize their statements.

Efforts by social workers to employ "I" statements when responding can profoundly affect the quality of group processes, increasing both the specificity of communications and the frequency with which their clients use "I" statements. As a general rule, groups (including couples and families) are likely to follow a social worker's communication style.

Just as groups tend to follow suit when social workers frequently use "I" messages, they may also imitate counterproductive behaviors of the social worker. That includes communicating in broad generalities, focusing on issues external to the individual, or relating to the group in an interrogative or confrontational manner.

Social workers must be careful to model the skills they wish clients to acquire. They should master relating authentically to the extent that they automatically personalize their messages and constructively share their inner experiencing with clients. To facilitate personalizing messages, social workers can negotiate an agreement with individuals or groups specifying that clients will endeavor to incorporate the use of "I" statements in their conversational repertoires. Thereafter, it is critical to intervene consistently to assist clients to personalize their messages when they have not done so.

2. *Share feelings that lie at varying depths.* Social workers must reach for those feelings that underlie their immediate experiencing. Doing so is particularly vital when social workers experience strong negative feelings (e.g., dislike, anger, repulsion, disgust, boredom) toward a client, because an examination of the deeper aspects of feelings often discloses more positive feelings toward the client. Social workers need to be in tune with their feelings, positive and negative, and learn when and how sharing such emotions appropriately can be useful to clients. Expressing these feelings preserves the client's self-esteem, whereas expressing superficial negative feelings often poses a threat to the client, creating defensiveness and anger.

EP 2.1.1b

For example, in experiencing feelings of anger (and perhaps disappointment) toward a client who is chronically late for appointments, the social worker may first connect his feelings of anger to feeling inconvenienced. In reaching for his deeper feelings, however, the social worker may discover that the annoyance derives from a concern that the client may not find the sessions useful. At an even deeper level may lie hurt in not being more important to the client. Further introspection may also uncover a concern that the client is exhibiting similar behavior in other areas of life that could adversely affect his or her relationships with others. The fact of the matter is that the social worker does not know why the client is late for appointments and overt exploration of the obstacles can lead the social worker and client into a more productive discussion on how to resolve the issue.

The social worker may discover multiple (and sometimes conflicting) feelings that may be beneficially shared with the client, as illustrated in the following message:

Social worker *[To client]:* I would like to check some things out with you. You apologized for being late for the session, and I appreciate that. However, this has occurred before so I wanted to check out with you how things are going for you about our sessions. You lead a busy life, balancing many commitments. I am not sure what part these sessions are playing for you in addressing the issues you brought in. I would also like to know what you're feeling just now about what I said.

Like prospective social workers, clients are prone to focus on one aspect of their experiencing to the exclusion of deeper and more complex emotions. Clients often have difficulty, in fact, pinpointing any feelings they are experiencing. In either case, social workers should persevere to help clients broaden their awareness of their emotions and to express them openly, as illustrated in the following exchange:

Social worker: When you told your wife you didn't want to take her to a movie, and she said you were a "bump on a log"—that you never seemed to want to do anything with her—what feelings did you experience?[2]

Husband: I decided that if that's what she thought of me, that's what I'd be.

Social worker: Can you get in touch with what you were feeling? You told me a little bit about what you thought, but what's happening inside? Try to use feeling words to describe what you're experiencing.

Husband *[pause]:* I felt that if she was going to get on my back …

Social worker *[gently interrupting]:* Can you use a feeling word like "bad," or "hurt," or "put down"? What did you feel?

Husband: Okay. I felt annoyed.

Social worker: So you experienced a sense of irritation. Good. I'm pleased you could get in touch with that feeling. Now see if you can get to an even more basic feeling. Remember, as we've talked about before, anger is usually a surface feeling that camouflages other feelings. What was under your annoyance?

Husband: Uh, I'd say frustrated. I just didn't want to sit there and listen to her harp at me. She never quits.

Social worker: I would like to check out something with you. Right now, as you're talking about this, it seems you're experiencing a real sense of discouragement and perhaps even hopelessness about things ever changing. It's as though you've given up. Maybe that's part of what you were feeling Saturday.

Husband: Yeah, I just turn myself off. There doesn't seem to be anything I can do to make her happy.

Social worker: I'm glad that you can recognize the sense of despair you're feeling. I also appreciate your hanging in there with me for a minute to get in touch with some of your feelings. You seem to be a person whose feelings run deep, and sometimes expressing them may come hard for you. I'm wondering how you view yourself in that regard.

In the preceding excerpt, the social worker engaged in extensive coaching to assist the client in discovering his underlying feelings. Deeper than the feelings of annoyance and frustration the client identified lay the more basic emotions related to feeling hurt and being unimportant to his wife. By providing other spontaneous "training sessions," the social worker can help this client to identify his feelings more readily, to find the feeling words to express them, and to begin formulating "I" statements.

3. *Describe the situation or targeted behavior in neutral or descriptive terms.* In their messages, clients often omit references or make only vague references to the situations that prompted their responses. Moreover, they may convey their messages in a blaming manner, engendering defensiveness that overshadows other aspects of their self-disclosure. In either event, self-disclosure is minimal and respondents do not receive information that could otherwise be of considerable value.

Consider, for example, the low yield of information in the following messages:

- "You're a nice person."
- "You should be more conscientious."
- "You're progressing well in your work."
- "You have a bad attitude."

All of these messages lack supporting information that respondents need to identify specific aspects of their behavior that are competent and warrant recognition or are substandard. Social workers should assist parents, spouses, or others to provide higher-yield feedback by including behavioral references. Examples of such messages follow (they involve a parent talking to a 6-year-old girl):

- "I've really appreciated all that you've done tonight by yourself. You picked up your toys, washed your hands before dinner, and ate dinner without dawdling. I'm so pleased."
- "I'm very disappointed with your behavior right now. You didn't change your clothes when you came home from school; you didn't feed the dog; and you haven't started your homework."

Note in the last example that the parent sent an "I" message and owned the feelings of disappointment rather than attacking the child for being undependable.

When responding authentically, social workers should carefully describe specific events that prompted their responses, particularly when they wish to draw clients' attention to some aspect of their behavior or to a situation of which they may not be fully aware. The following social worker's message illustrates this point:

Social worker: I need to share something with you that concerns me. Just a moment ago, I gave you feedback regarding the positive way I thought you handled a situation with your husband. *[Refers to specific behaviors manifested by client]* When I did that, you seemed to discount my response by *[mentions specific behaviors].* Actually, this is not the first time I have seen this happen. It appears to me that it is difficult for you to give yourself credit for the positive things you do and the progress you are making.

Social workers constantly need to assess the specificity of their responses to ensure that they give clients the benefit of behaviorally specific feedback and provide positive modeling experiences for them. It is also vital to coach clients in giving specific feedback whenever they make sweeping generalizations and do not document the relationship between their responses and specific situations.

4. *Identify the specific impact of the problem situation or behavior on others.* Authentic messages often stop short of identifying the specific effects of the situation on the

sender or on others, even though such information would be very appropriate and helpful. This element of an "I" message also increases the likelihood that the receiver will adjust or make changes, particularly if the sender demonstrates that the receiver's behavior is having a tangible effect on him or her.

Consider a social worker's authentic response to a male member of an adult group:

Social worker: "Sometimes I sense some impatience on your part to move on to other topics. *[Describes situation that just occurred, documenting specific messages and behavior.]* At times I find myself torn between responding to your urging us "to get on with it" or staying with a discussion that seems beneficial to the group. It may be that others in the group are experiencing similar mixed feelings and some of the pressure I feel."

Here the social worker first clarifies the tangible effects of the client's behavior on himself and then suggests that others may experience the behavior similarly. Given the social worker's approach, others in the group may be willing to give feedback as well. The client is then free to draw his own conclusions about the cause-and-effect relationship between his behaviors and the reactions of others and to decide whether he wishes to alter his way of relating in the group.

Social workers can identify how specific client behaviors negatively impact not only the social worker but also the clients themselves (e.g., "I'm concerned about *[specific behavior]* because it keeps you from achieving your goal"). Further, they may document how a client's behavior affects others (e.g., his wife) or the relationship between the client and another person (e.g., "It appears that your behavior creates distance between you and your son").

People often have difficulty in identifying the impact of others' behavior on themselves. For example, a mother's message to her child, "I want you to play someplace else," establishes no reason for the request, nor does it specify the negative impact of the behavior on her. If the mother responds in an authentic manner, however, she clearly identifies the tangible effect of her child's behavior: "I'm having a hard time getting through the hallway because I keep stumbling over toys and having to go around you. I've almost fallen several times, and others might, too. I'm worried that someone might get hurt, so I'm asking you to move your toys to your room."

The preceding illustration underscores the point that when clients clarify how a situation affects them, their requests do not appear arbitrary and are more persuasive; hence, others are likely to make appropriate accommodations. We suspect that an important reason why many clients have not changed certain self-defeating behaviors before entering the helping process is that others have previously attacked or pressured them to change, rather than authentically and unabrasively imparting information that highlights how the clients' behavior strikes them. Others may have also attempted to prescribe behavioral changes that appear to be self-serving (e.g., "Come on, stop that sulking") instead of relating their feelings (e.g., "I'm concerned that you're down and unhappy; I'd like to help but I'm not sure how"). Such statements do not strike a responsive chord in clients, who may equate making changes with putting themselves under the control of others (by following their directives), thereby losing their freedom to make their own decisions.

In the following exchange, note how the social worker assists Carolyn, a group member, to personalize her statements and to clarify her reaction to the behavior of another member who has remained consistently silent throughout the first two sessions:

Carolyn: We've talked about needing to add new guidelines for the group as we go along. I think we ought to have a guideline that everyone should talk in the group. *[Observe that Carolyn has not personalized her message but has proposed a solution to meet a need she has not identified.]*

Social worker *[to Carolyn]:* The group may want to consider this guideline, but for a minute, can you get in touch with what you're experiencing and put it in the form of an "I" statement?

Carolyn: Well, all right. Janet hasn't talked at all for two solid weeks, and it's beginning to really irritate me.

Social worker: I'm wondering what else you may be experiencing besides irritation? *[Assists Carolyn to identify her feelings besides mild anger.]*

Carolyn: I guess I'm a little uneasy because I don't know where Janet stands. Maybe I'm afraid she's sitting in judgment of us—I mean, me. And I guess I feel cheated because I'd like to get to know her better, and right now I feel shut out by her.

Social worker: That response helps us to begin to get to the heart of the matter. Would you now express yourself directly to Janet? Tell her what you are experiencing and, particularly, how her silence is affecting you.

Carolyn *[to Janet]:* I did wonder what you thought about me since I really opened up last week. And

I do want to get to know you better. But, underneath all this, I'm concerned about you. You seem unhappy and alone, and that makes me uncomfortable—I don't like to think of your feeling that way. Frankly, I'd like to know how you feel about being in this group, and if you're uneasy about it, as you seem to be, I'd like to help you feel better somehow.

In the preceding example, the social worker assisted Carolyn to experience a broader range of feelings and to identify her reaction to Janet's silence. In response to the social worker's intervention, Carolyn also expressed more positive feelings than were evident in her initial message—a not infrequent occurrence when social workers encourage people to explore deeper-level emotions.

Engaging one member in identifying specific reactions to the behavior of others provides a learning experience for the entire group, and members often expand their conversational repertoires to incorporate such facilitative responding. In fact, the extent to which social workers assist clients to acquire specific skills is correlated with the extent to which clients acquire those same skills.

Cues for Authentic Responding

The impetus for social workers to respond authentically may emanate from (1) clients' messages that request self-disclosure or (2) social workers' decisions to share perceptions and reactions they believe will be helpful. Next, we consider authentic responding that emanates from these two sources.

Authentic Responding Stimulated by Clients' Messages

Requests from Clients for Personal Information. Clients often confront students and social workers with questions aimed at soliciting personal information, such as "How old are you?", "Do you have any children?", "What is your religion?", "Are you married?", and "Are you a student?" It is natural for clients to be curious and to ask questions about a social worker in whom they are confiding, especially when their well-being and future are at stake.

Self-disclosing responses may or may not be appropriate, depending on the social worker's assessment of the client's motivation for asking a particular question. When questions appear to be prompted by an attempt to be sociable, such responses are often very appropriate. For example, it is appropriate for clients to want to know whether you are likely to be helpful to them and hence whether talking to you is a good use of their time and energy. They often want to know "are you any good at what you do?" Their way of assessing this may take the form of asking about your personal experience with the topic at hand, whether it be drug use or raising children. Consider the following exchange from an initial session involving a 23-year-old student social worker and a 43-year-old woman who requested help in dealing with her marital problems:

Client: Are you married?

Student social worker: No, but I am engaged. Why do you ask?

Client: Oh, I don't know. I just wondered.

Given the context of an older adult with a much younger student, the client's question was likely motivated by a concern that the student might lack life experience essential to understanding her marital difficulties or the competence needed to assist her in resolving them. In this instance, immediate authentic disclosure by the student was inappropriate because it did not facilitate exploration of the feelings underlying the client's inquiry.

Conversely, such an exchange may yield information vital to the helping process if the social worker avoids premature self-disclosure. It is sometimes very difficult to distinguish whether the questions of clients are motivated by a natural desire for information or by hidden concerns or feelings. As a rule of thumb, when you have questions about clients' motivation for making personal inquiries, precede disclosures of views or feelings with either open-ended or empathic responses. Responding in this manner significantly increases the probability that clients will reveal their underlying concerns. Notice what happens when the social worker utilizes an empathic response before responding authentically:

Client: Are you married?

Student social worker: Is that an important consideration for you whether you have a social worker who is married?

Client: Well, I guess I was thinking that someone who is married could understand my situation. I hope it doesn't offend you.

Student social worker: Not at all, in fact I appreciate your frankness. It's natural that you want to know whether your social worker might be able to help you. I know there's a lot at stake for you. Tell me more about your concerns.

Here the student responded to the probable concern of the client and struck pay dirt. Such astuteness tends to foster confidence in clients and greatly facilitates the establishment of a therapeutic partnership. The fact that the student "leans into" the situation by inviting further exploration rather than skirting the issue may also be read by the client as an indicator of the student's own confidence in his or her ability to help. After fully exploring the client's concerns, the student can respond with an authentic response identifying personal qualifications:

Student social worker: I do want you to know that I believe I can be helpful to you. I have worked with other clients whose difficulties were similar to your own. I also consult with my supervisor regularly.

Of course, the final judgment of my competence will rest with you. It will be important for us to discuss any feelings you may still have at the end of the interview as you make a decision about returning for future sessions.

Questions That Solicit the Social Worker's Perceptions. Clients may also pose questions that solicit the social worker's opinions, views, or feelings. Typical questions include "How do I compare to your other clients?", "Do you think I need help?", "Am I crazy?", and "Do you think there's any hope for me?" Such questions can pose a challenge for social workers, who must consider the motivation behind the question and judge whether to disclose their views or feelings immediately or to employ either an empathic or an open-ended response.

When social workers do disclose their perceptions, however, their responses must be congruent with their inner experiencing. In response to the question "Do you think there's any hope for me?" the social worker may congruently respond with a message that blends elements of empathy and authenticity:

Social worker: Your question tells me you're probably afraid that you're beyond help. Although you do have some difficult problems, I'm optimistic that if we work hard together things can improve. You've shown a number of strengths that should help you make changes.

It is not necessary to answer all questions of clients in the service of authenticity. If you feel uncomfortable about answering a personal question or deem it inadvisable to do so, you should feel free to decline answering. When doing so, it is important to explain your reason for not answering directly, again utilizing an authentic response. If a teenage client, for example, asks whether the social worker had sexual relations before she married, the social worker may respond as follows:

Social worker: I would rather not reveal that information to you, because it is a very private part of my life. Asking me took some risk on your part. I have an idea that your question probably has to do with a struggle you're having, although I could be wrong. I would appreciate your sharing your thoughts about what sparked your question.

The social worker should then utilize empathic responding and open-ended questions to explore the client's reaction and motivation for asking her question.

Authentic Responding Initiated by Social Workers

Authentic responding initiated by social workers may take several forms, which are considered next.

Disclosing Past Experiences. As previously indicated, self-disclosure should be sparingly used, brief, relevant to the client's concerns, and well timed. In relating to a particular client's struggle, a social worker might indicate, "I remember I felt very much like that when I was struggling with …" In so doing, they must be careful to check out whether the client considers this experience comparable…." A fundamental guideline that applies to such situations is that social workers should be certain they are focusing on themselves to meet the therapeutic needs of their clients.

Sharing Perceptions, Ideas, Reactions, and Formulations. A key role of the social worker in the change-oriented phase of the helping process is to act as a "candid feedback system" by revealing personal thoughts and perceptions relevant to client problems (Hammond et al., 1977). Such responding is intended to further the change process in one or more of the following ways:

1. To heighten clients' awareness of dynamics that may play an important part in problems
2. To offer a different perspective regarding issues and events
3. To aid clients in conceptualizing the purposes of their behavior and feelings
4. To enlighten clients on how they affect others (including the social worker)
5. To bring clients' attention to cognitive and behavioral patterns (both functional and dysfunctional) that operate at either an individual or a group level

6. To share the social worker's here-and-now affective and physical reactions to clients' behavior or to processes that occur in the helping relationship
7. To share positive feedback concerning clients' strengths and growth

After responding authentically to achieve any of these purposes, it is vital to invite clients to express their own views and draw their own conclusions. Sharing perceptions with clients does involve some risk. In particular, clients may misinterpret the social worker's motives and feel criticized, put down, or rebuked. Clarifying the social worker's helpful intent before responding diminishes this risk somewhat. Nevertheless, it is critical to watch for clients' reactions that may indicate a response has struck an exposed nerve.

To avoid damaging the relationship (or to repair it), the social worker should be empathically attuned to the client's reaction to candid feedback, shifting the focus back to the client to determine the impact of the self-disclosure. If the client appears to have been emotionally wounded by the social worker's authentic response, the social worker can use empathic skills to elicit troubled feelings and to guide subsequent responses aimed at restoring the relationship's equilibrium. Expressions of concern and clarification of the goodwill intended by the social worker are also usually facilitative:

Social worker: I can see that what I shared with you hit you pretty hard—and that you're feeling put down right now. *[Client nods but avoids eye contact]* I feel bad about that, because the last thing I'd want is to hurt you. Please tell me what you're feeling.

Openly (and Tactfully) Sharing Reactions When Put on the Spot. Clients sometimes create situations that put social workers under considerable pressure to respond to messages that bear directly on the relationship, such as when they accuse a social worker of being uninterested, unfeeling, irritated, displeased, critical, inappropriate, or incompetent. Clients may also ask pointed questions (sometimes before the relationship has been firmly established) that require immediate responses.

The first statement of one female client in an initial interview, for example, was "I'm gay. Does that make any difference to you?" In the opening moments of another session, a pregnant client asked the social worker, "How do you feel about abortion?" Over the years, students have reported numerous such situations that sorely tested their ability to respond in an appropriate fashion. In one instance, a male member of a group asked a female student leader for her photograph. In another case, an adolescent boy kept taking his shoes off and putting his feet (which smelled very bad) on the social worker's desk. In reflecting on your practice experience, you can undoubtedly cite instances in which the behavior of clients caused you to squirm or produced butterflies in your stomach.

Experiencing Discomfort in Sessions. Sometimes intense discomfort may indicate that something in the session is going awry and needs to be addressed. It is important to reflect on your discomfort, seeking to identify events that seem to be causing or exacerbating it (e.g., "I'm feeling very uneasy because I don't know how to respond when my client says things like 'You seem to be too busy to see me' or 'I'm not sure I'm worth your trouble'"). After privately exploring the reason for the discomfort, the social worker might respond as follows:

Social worker: I'd like to share some impressions about several things you've said in the last two sessions. *[Identifies client's statements.]* I sense you're feeling pretty unimportant—as though you don't count for much—and that perhaps you're imposing on me just by being here. I want you to know that I'm pleased you had the courage to seek help in the face of all the opposition from your family. It's also important to me that you know that I want to be helpful to you. I am concerned, however, that you feel you're imposing on me. Could you share more what contributes to that feeling for you?

Notice how the social worker specifically identifies the self-defeating thoughts and feelings and blends elements of empathy and authenticity in the response.

Other situations that put social workers on the spot include clients' angry attacks, as we discuss later in this chapter. Social workers must learn to respond authentically in such scenarios. Consider a situation in which an adolescent attacks a social worker in an initial interview, protesting, "I don't want to be here. You social workers are all assholes." In such instances, social workers should share their reactions, as illustrated in the following response:

Social worker: It sounds as though you're really angry about having to see me and that your previous experiences with social workers haven't been good. I respect your feelings and don't want to pressure you to work with me. I want you to know that I am interested in you and that I would like to know what you're up against.

Intertwining empathic and authentic responses in this manner often defuses clients' anger and encourages them to think more rationally about a situation.

Sharing Feelings When Clients' Behavior Is Unreasonable or Distressing. Although social workers should be able to take most client behaviors in stride, sometimes they may experience justifiable feelings of frustration, anger, or even hurt. In one case, a client acquired a social worker's home phone number from another source and began calling frequently about daily crisis situations, although discussions of these events could easily have waited until the next session. In another instance, an intoxicated client called the social worker in the middle of the night "just to talk." In yet another case, an adolescent client let the air out of a social worker's automobile tires.

In such situations, social workers should share their feelings with clients—*if they believe they can do so constructively*. In the following case example, note that the student social worker interweaves authentic and empathic responses in confronting a Latino youth in a correctional institution who had maintained he was innocent of hiding drugs that staff had found in his room. Believing the youth's story, the student went to bat for him, only to find out later that the client had lied. Somewhat uneasy at her first real confrontation, the student tries to formulate an authentic response.

In an interesting twist, the youth helps her to be "up-front" with him:

Student social worker: There's something I wanted to talk to you about, Randy ... *[Stops to search for the right words.]*

Randy: Well, come out with it, then. Just lay it on me.

Student social worker: Well, remember last week when you got that incident report? You know, I really believed you were innocent. I was ready to go to the hearing and tell staff I was sure you were innocent and that the charge should be dropped. I guess I'm feeling kind of bad because when I talked to you, you told me you were innocent, and, well, that's not exactly the way it turned out.

Randy: You mean I lied to you. Go ahead and say it.

Student social worker: Well, yes, I guess I felt kind of hurt because I was hoping that maybe you had more trust in me than that.

Randy: Well, Susan, let me tell you something. Where I come from, that's not lying—that's what we call survival. Personally, I don't consider myself a liar. I just do what I need to do to get by. That's an old trick, but it just didn't work.

Student social worker: I hear you, Randy. I guess you're saying we're from two different worlds, and maybe we both define the same thing in different ways. I guess that with me being Anglo, you can't really expect me to understand what life has been like for you.

Several minutes later in the session, after the student has further explored the client's feelings, the following interchange occurs:

Student social worker: Randy, I want you to know a couple of things. The first thing is that when social workers work with clients, they must honor what they call confidentiality, so I can't share what we talk about without your permission in most cases. An exception to this relates to rule or law violations. I can't keep that confidential. The second thing is that I don't expect you to share everything with me. I know there are certain things you don't want to tell me, so rather than lying about something that I ask you about, maybe you can just tell me you don't want to tell me. Would you consider that?

Randy: Yeah, that's okay. *[Pause.]* Listen, Susan, I don't want you to go around thinking I'm a liar now. I'll tell you this, and you can take it for what it's worth, but this is the truth. That's the first time I've ever lied to you. But you may not believe that.

Student social worker: I do believe you, Randy. *[He seems a little relieved and there is a silence.]*

Randy: Well, Susan, that's a deal, then. I won't lie to you again, but if there's something I don't want to say, I'll tell you I don't want to say it.

Student social worker: Sounds good to me. *[Both start walking away.]* You know, Randy, I really want to see you get through this program and get out as fast as you can. I know it's hard starting over because of the incident with the drugs, but I think we can get you through. *[This seemed to have more impact on Randy than anything the social worker had said to him in a long time. The pleasure was visible on his face, and he broke into a big smile.]*

Noteworthy in this exchange is that the social worker relied almost exclusively on the skills of authenticity and empathy to bring the incident to a positive conclusion. Ignoring her feelings would have impaired the student's ability to relate facilitatively to the client and would have been destructive to the relationship. In contrast, focusing on the situation proved beneficial for both.

Sharing Feelings When Clients Give Positive Feedback. Social workers sometimes have difficulty responding receptively to clients' positive feedback about their own attributes and/or performance. We suggest that social workers model the same receptivity to positive feedback that they ask clients to demonstrate in their own lives, as illustrated in the following exchange:

Client: I don't know what I would have done without you. I'm just not sure I would have made it if you hadn't been there when I needed you. You've made such a difference in my life.

Social worker: I'm touched by your gratitude and pleased you are feeling so much more capable of coping with your situation. I want you to know, too, that even though I was there to help, your efforts have been the deciding factor in your growth.

Positive Feedback: A Form of Authentic Responding

Because positive feedback plays such a vital role in the change process, we have allocated a separate section in our attempt to do justice to this topic. Social workers often employ (or should employ) this skill in supplying information to clients about positive attributes or specific areas in which they demonstrate strengths, effective coping mechanisms, and incremental growth. In so doing, social workers enhance their clients' motivation to change and foster hope for the future.

Many opportune moments occur in the helping process when social workers experience warm or positive feelings toward clients because of the latter's actions or progress. When appropriate, social workers should share such feelings spontaneously with clients, as illustrated in the following messages:

- "You have what I consider exceptional ability to 'self-observe your own behavior and to analyze the part you play in relationships. I think this strength will serve you well in solving the problems you have identified."
- "I've been touched several times in the group when I've noticed that, despite your grief over the loss of your husband, you've reached out to other members who needed support."
- [To newly formed group]: "In contrast to our first session, I've noticed that this week we haven't had trouble getting down to business and staying on task. I've been pleased as I've watched you develop group guidelines for the past 20 minutes with minimal assistance from me. I had the thought, 'This group is really moving.'"

The first two messages acknowledge strengths of individuals. The third lauds a behavioral change the social worker has observed in a group process. Both types of messages sharply focus clients' attention on specific behaviors that facilitate the change process, ultimately increasing the frequency of such behaviors. When sent consistently, positive messages also have the long-range effect of helping people who have low self-esteem to develop a more positive self-image. When positive feedback is employed to document the cause-and-effect relationship between their efforts and positive outcomes, individuals also experience a sense of satisfaction, accomplishment, and control over their situation.

Positive feedback can have the additional effect of increasing clients' confidence in their own coping ability. We have occasionally had experiences with clients who were on the verge of falling apart when they came to a session but left feeling able to manage their problems for a while longer. We attribute their increased ability to function in part to authentic responses that documented and highlighted areas in which they were coping and successfully managing problems.

Taped sessions of students and social workers often reveal relatively few authentic responses that underscore clients' strengths or incremental growth. This lack of positive feedback is unfortunate because, in our experience, clients' rates of change often correlate with the extent to which social workers focus on these two vital areas. If social workers consistently focus on their clients' assets and the subtle positive changes that often occur in early sessions, clients will typically invest more effort in the change process. As the rate of change accelerates, social workers can in turn focus more extensively on clients' successes, identifying and reinforcing their strengths and functional coping behaviors.

Social workers face several challenges in accrediting clients' strengths and growth, including improving their own ability to recognize and express fleeting positive feelings when clients manifest strengths or progress. Social workers

EP 2.1.10e

must also learn to document events so that they can provide information about specific positive behaviors. Another challenge and responsibility is to teach clients to give positive feedback to one another.

To increase your ability to discern client strengths, we recommend that you and your clients construct a profile of their resources. This task may be completed with individuals, couples, families, or groups, and preferably occurs early in the helping process. In individual sessions, the social worker should ask the client to identify and list all the strengths she or he can think of. The social worker also shares observations of the client's strengths, adding them to the list, which is kept for ongoing review to add further strengths as they are discovered.

With families, couples, or groups, social workers may follow a similar procedure in assessing the strengths of individual members, but they should ask other group members to share their perceptions of strengths with each member. The social worker might also ask couples, families, or groups to identify the strengths and incremental growth of the group periodically throughout the helping process. After clients have identified their personal strengths or the strengths of the group, the social worker should elicit observations regarding their reactions to the experience. Often they may mutually conclude that clients have many more strengths than they have realized. The social worker should also explore any discomfort experienced by clients as they identify strengths, with the goal of having them acknowledge more comfortably their positive attributes and personal resources.

We further suggest that you carefully observe processes early on in sessions. Note the subtle manifestations of strengths and positive behavioral changes, systematically recording these in your progress records. Record not only the strengths and incremental growth of clients, but also whether you (or group members) focused on those changes. Keep in mind that changes often occur very subtly within a single session. For instance, clients may begin to discuss problems more openly during a later part of a session, tentatively commit to work on problems they had refused to tackle earlier, show growing trust in the social worker by confiding high-risk information about themselves, or own responsibility for the first time regarding their part in their problems. Groups and families may likewise experience growth within short periods of time. It is vital to keep your antenna finely tuned to such changes so that you do not overlook clients' progress.

Relating Assertively to Clients

EP 2.1.10b

Another aspect of relating authentically entails relating assertively to clients when a situation warrants such behavior. There are myriad reasons for relating assertively. To inspire confidence and influence clients to follow their lead, social workers must relate in a manner that projects competence. This is especially important in the initial phase of the helping process. Clients often covertly test or check out social workers to determine whether they can understand their problems and appear competent to help them.

In conjoint or group sessions, clients may question whether the social worker is strong enough to protect them from destructive interactional processes that may occur in sessions. Indeed, family or group members generally will not fully share, risk, or commit to the helping process until they have answered this question affirmatively through consistent observation of assertive actions by the social worker.

If social workers are relaxed and demonstrate through decisive behavior that they are fully capable of handling clients' problems and providing the necessary protection and structure to control potentially chaotic or volatile processes, clients will typically relax, muster hope, and begin to work on problems. If the social worker fails to curtail dysfunctional processes that render clients vulnerable, clients will have justifiable doubts about whether they should be willing to place themselves in jeopardy and, consequently, may disengage from the helping process.

In this section, we identify guidelines that can help you to intervene assertively with clients.

Making Requests and Giving Directives

To assist clients to relate more easily and work constructively to solve their problems, social workers frequently must make requests of them. Some of these requests may involve relating in new ways during sessions. For example, social workers may ask clients to do any of the following:

1. Speak directly to each other rather than through the social worker.
2. Give feedback to others in the session.
3. Respond by checking out the meanings of others' messages, take a listening stance, or personalize messages.
4. Change the arrangement of chairs.

5. Role-play.
6. Make requests of others.
7. Take responsibility for responding in specified ways during sessions.
8. Agree to carry out defined tasks during the week.
9. Identify strengths or incremental growth for themselves or others in the group or family.

When making requests, it is important to express them firmly and decisively and to deliver them with assertive nonverbal behavior. Social workers often err by couching their requests in tentative language, thus conveying doubt to clients about whether they must comply with the requests. The contrast between messages delivered in tentative language and those phrased in firm language can be observed in the exchanges given in Table 5-1.

Many times social workers' requests of clients are actually *directives*, as are those under the column "Firm Requests" in Table 5-1. In essence, directives are declarative statements that place the burden on clients to object if they are uncomfortable, as the following message illustrates:

Social worker: Before you answer that question, please turn your chair toward your wife. *[Social worker leans over and helps client to adjust chair. Social worker speaks to wife.]* Will you please turn your chair, also, so that you can speak directly to your husband? Thank you. It's important that you be in full contact with each other while we talk.

If the social worker had given these clients a choice (e.g., "Would you like to change your chairs?"), they might not have responded affirmatively. We suggest that when you want clients to behave differently in sessions, you simply state what you would like them to do. If clients verbally object to directives or display nonverbal behavior that may indicate that they have reservations about complying with a request, it is vital to respond empathically and to explore the basis of their opposition. Such exploration often resolves fears or misgivings, freeing clients to engage in requested behavior.

Maintaining Focus and Managing Interruptions

Maintaining focus is a vital task that takes considerable skill and assertiveness on the social worker's part. It is often essential to intervene verbally to focus or refocus processes when interruptions or distractions occur. Sometimes, social workers may also respond assertively on a nonverbal level to prevent members from interrupting important processes that may need to be brought to positive conclusion, as illustrated in the following excerpt from a family session:

Kim, age 14 [in tears, talking angrily to her mother]: You hardly ever listen. At home, you just always yell at us and go to your bedroom.

Mrs. R: I thought I was doing better than that …

Mr. R [interrupting his wife to speak to social worker]: I think it's hard for my wife because …

Social worker [holds up hand to father in a "halt" position, while continuing to maintain eye contact with mother and daughter; speaks to Kim]: I would like to stay with your statement for a moment. Kim, please tell your mother what you're experiencing right now.

Interrupting Problematic Processes

Unseasoned social workers often permit problematic processes to continue for long periods either because they lack knowledge of how to intervene or because they think they should wait until clients have completed a series of exchanges. In such instances, social workers fail to fulfill one of their major responsibilities—that is, to *guide and direct* processes and to influence participants to interact in more facilitative ways. Remember that clients often seek help because they cannot manage their problematic interactional processes. Thus, permitting them to engage at length in their usual patterns of arguing, cajoling, threatening, blaming, criticizing, and labeling each other merely exacerbates their problems. The social worker should intervene in such circumstances, teaching the clients more facilitative behaviors

TABLE-5-1 TENTATIVE VERSUS FIRM REQUESTS

TENTATIVE REQUESTS	FIRM REQUESTS
Would you mind if I interrupted …	I would like to pause for a moment …
Is it okay if we role-play?	I'd like you to role-play with me for a moment.
Excuse me, but don't you think you are getting off track?	I think we are getting off track. I'd like to return to the subject we were discussing just a minute ago.
Could we talk about something Kathy just said?	Let's go back to something Kathy just said. I think it is very important.

and guiding them to implement such behaviors in subsequent interactions.

If you decide to interrupt ongoing processes, do so decisively so that clients will listen to you or heed your directive. If you intervene unassertively, your potential to influence clients (particularly aggressive clients) will suffer, because being able to interrupt a discussion successfully demonstrates your power or influence in the relationship. If you permit clients to ignore or to circumvent your interventions to arrest problematic processes, you yield control and assume a "one-down" position in terms of the relationship to the client.

With respect to interrupting or intervening in processes, we advocate using assertive—not aggressive—behavior. You must be sensitive to the vested interests of clients, because even though you may regard certain processes as unproductive or destructive, clients may not. The timing of interruptions is therefore vital. If it is not critical to draw clients' attention to what is happening immediately, you can wait for a natural pause. If such a pause does not occur shortly, you should interrupt. You should *not* delay interrupting destructive interactional processes, however, as illustrated in the following excerpt:

Wife [to social worker]: I feel the children need to mind me, but every time I ask them to do something, he [husband] says they don't have to do it. I think we're just ruining our kids, and it's mostly his fault.

Husband: Oh—well—that shows how dumb you are.

Social worker: I'm going to interrupt you because finding fault with each other is not likely to help us resolve these issues.

In this exchange, the social worker intervenes to refocus the discussion after just two dysfunctional responses on the clients' part. If participants do not disengage immediately, the social worker will need to use body movements that interfere with communication pathways or, in extreme instances, an exclamation such as "Time out!" to interrupt behavior. When social workers have demonstrated their intent to intervene quickly and decisively, clients will usually comply immediately when asked to disengage.

"Leaning Into" Clients' Anger

We cannot overstate the importance of openly addressing clients' anger and complaints. It is not unusual to feel defensive and threatened when such anger arises. Many social workers, especially those who are working with involuntary clients who are alleged to have harmed others, are inclined to retaliate, conveying the message, "You have no right to your anger. You have brought this on yourself. Do it my way or suffer the consequences." Responding assertively to a person's anger does not mean that you become a doormat, accepting that anger passively and submissively. Unless social workers can handle themselves assertively and competently in the face of such anger, they will lose the respect of most clients and thus their ability to help them. Further, clients may use their anger to influence and intimidate social workers just as they have done with others.

To help you respond assertively in managing clients' anger, we offer the following suggestions:

- *Respond empathically to reflect clients' anger and, if possible, other underlying feelings (e.g., "I sense you're angry at me for _____ and perhaps disappointed about _____").*
- *Continue to explore the situation and the feelings of participants until you understand the nature of the events that inspired the angry feelings. During this exploration, you may find that the anger toward you dissipates and that clients begin to focus on themselves, assuming appropriate responsibility for their part in the situation at hand. The "real problem," as often happens, may not directly involve you.*
- *As you explore clients' anger, authentically express your feelings and reactions if it appears appropriate (e.g., "I didn't know you felt that way ... "I want to hear how I might have contributed to this situation." "There may be some adjustments I'll want to make in my style of relating" ... "I'm pleased that you shared your feelings with me.").*
- *Apply a problem-solving approach (if appropriate) so that all concerned make adjustments to avoid similar occurrences or situations in the future.*
- *If a particular client expresses anger frequently and in a dysfunctional manner, you may also focus on the client's style of expressing anger, identify problems that this communicative approach may cause him or her in relationships with others, and negotiate a goal of modifying this response pattern.*
- *In addition to empathizing with client anger, you can model assertive setting of personal limits and boundaries. For example, you might say, "I think that I have a good idea about how you are feeling about this situation and what you would like to have be different about it. But I can't readily talk with you when you are so upset. Do you have a way of calming*

yourself down, or should we plan to meet again when you feel more in control of your emotions?" Alternatively, you might say, *"I have pledged to do my part to listen to and respond to the issues you have raised. I am not willing to continue to be verbally abused, however."*

Saying No and Setting Limits

Many tasks that social workers perform on behalf of their clients are quite appropriate. For example, negotiating for clients and conferring with other parties and potential resources to supplement and facilitate client action are tasks that are rightly handled by social workers (Epstein, 1992, p. 208). In contracting with clients, however, social workers must occasionally decline requests or set limits. This step is sometimes difficult for beginning social workers to take, as they typically want to demonstrate their willingness to help others. Commitment to helping others is a desirable quality, but it must be tempered with judgment as to when acceding to clients' requests is in the best interests of both social worker and client.

Some clients may have had past experiences that led them to believe that social workers will do most of the work required out of sessions. However, clients are often more likely to experience empowerment by increasing the scope of their actions than by having social workers perform tasks on their behalf that they can learn to do for themselves. Consequently, if social workers unthinkingly agree to take on responsibilities that clients can perform now or could perform in the future, they may reinforce passive client behavior.

Setting limits has special implications when social workers work with involuntary clients. Cingolani (1984) has noted that social workers engage in negotiated relationships with such clients. In negotiated relationships, social workers assume the roles of compromiser, mediator, and enforcer in addition to the more comfortable role of counselor. For example, when an involuntary client requests a "break" related to performance of a court order, the social worker must be clear about the client's choices and consequences of making those choices. He or she must also clarify what the client should expect from the social worker.

Rory *[member of domestic violence group]:* I don't think that it is fair that you report that I didn't meet for eight of the ten group sessions. I could not get off work for some of those sessions. I did all I could do.

Social worker: You did attend seven of the sessions, Rory, and made efforts to attend others. However, the contract you signed, which was presented in court, stated that you must complete eight sessions to be certified as completing the group. I do not have the power to change that court order. Should you decide to comply with the court order, I am willing to speak with your employer to urge him to work with you to arrange your schedule so that you can meet the court order.

In his response, the social worker made it clear that he would not evade the court order. At the same time, he assured Rory that if he chose to comply with the court order, the social worker would be willing to act as a mediator to assist him with difficulties in scheduling with the employer.

Being tactfully assertive is no easier for social workers with excessive needs to please others than it is for other persons. These social workers have difficulty declining requests or setting limits when doing so is in the best interests of clients. To remedy this, such social workers may benefit by setting tasks for themselves related to increasing their assertiveness. Participating in an assertiveness training group and delving into the popular literature on assertiveness may be highly beneficial as well. Dietz and Thompson (2004) have suggested that social work has given too much emphasis to distance between clients and social workers for fear of abuse of power. In so doing, these authors suggest that social workers may abrogate possibilities of special help that powerless clients may need. We suggest that you consult with your supervisor about requests that pose special questions. In some cases, this can lead to problem solving around where else a client might be assisted to find a resource, rather than dwelling only on whether it is appropriate to get that resource from the social worker. The following are a few of the many situations in which you may need to decline requests of clients:

1. When clients invite you to participate with them socially
2. When clients ask you to grant them preferential status (e.g., set lower fees than are specified by policy)
3. When clients request physical intimacy
4. When clients ask you to intercede in a situation they should handle themselves
5. When clients request a special appointment after having broken a regular appointment for an invalid reason

6. When clients ask to borrow money
7. When clients request that you conceal information about violations of probation, parole, or institutional policy
8. When spouses request that you withhold information from their partners
9. When clients disclose plans to commit crimes or acts of violence against others
10. When clients ask you to report false information to an employer or other party

In addition to declining requests, you may need to set limits with clients in situations such as the following:

1. When clients make excessive telephone calls or text messages to you at home or the office
2. When clients cancel appointments without giving advance notice
3. When clients express emotions in abusive or violent ways
4. When clients habitually seek to go beyond designated ending points of sessions
5. When clients consistently fail to abide by contracts (e.g., not paying fees or missing numerous appointments)
6. When clients make sexual overtures toward you or other staff members
7. When clients come to sessions while intoxicated

Part of maturing professionally means learning to decline requests, set limits, and feel comfortable in doing so. As you gain experience, you will realize that you help clients as much by ensuring that they have reasonable expectations as you do by providing a concrete action for them. Modeled responses for refusing requests and for saying no to clients are found in the answers to the exercises below designed to assist social workers to relate authentically and assertively.

Of course, social workers must also assert themselves effectively with other social workers and with members of other professions. Lacking experience and sometimes confidence, beginning social workers tend to be in awe of physicians, lawyers, psychologists, and more experienced social workers. Consequently, they may relate passively or may acquiesce in plans or demands that appear unsound or unreasonable. Although it is critical to remain open to the ideas of other professionals, beginning social workers should nevertheless risk expressing their own views and asserting their own rights. Otherwise, they may know more about a given client than other professionals but fail to contribute valuable information in joint case planning.

Beginning social workers should also set limits and assert their rights by refusing to accept unreasonable referrals and inappropriate assignments. Likewise, assertiveness may be required when other professionals deny resources to which clients are entitled, refer to clients with demeaning labels, or engage in unethical conduct. In fact, being assertive is critical when you act as a client advocate, a role discussed at length in Chapter 14.

Summary

This chapter should help you communicate with clients and other persons on behalf of clients with appropriate empathy, authenticity, assertiveness, and self-disclosure. Chapter 6 will build on these skills by developing your abilities in listening, focusing, and exploring. First, however, you should practice your new skills by completing the exercises in this chapter.

CourseMate

Access an integrated eBook and chapter-specific learning tools including glossary terms, chapter outlines, relevant web links, videos, and practice quizzes. Go to **www.cengagebrain.com**.

CHAPTER 6

The Skills of Verbal Following, Exploring, and Focusing

CHAPTER OVERVIEW

Chapter 6 introduces verbal following skills and their uses in exploring client concerns and focusing. This chapter includes skills for accurately following and reflecting what clients are expressing and feeling about their situation. It also introduces skills for helping clients to consider taking action on concerns about which they have been ambivalent. These skills are the building blocks for social workers' efforts to communicate empathically with clients. In addition to being helpful in work with clients in micro practice, such skills are useful at the meso level in work on behalf of clients, through advocacy, and in work with colleagues and other professionals. This chapter also includes references to videos accompanying the text.

As a result of reading this chapter you will be able to:

- Construct an appropriate paraphrase and know when to use it
- Construct reflective responses including simple reflections and double sided reflections
- Construct furthering responses and know when to use them
- Construct open-ended questions and know when to use them
- Construct closed-ended questions and know when to use them
- Know how to seek concreteness
- Know how to provide and maintain focus
- Know how to summarize and when to do so

EPAS COMPETENCIES IN THE 6TH CHAPTER

This chapter will give you the information needed to meet the following practice competencies:

2.1.1d A social worker demonstrates professional demeanor in behavior, appearance, and communication.

2.1.4c Recognize and communicate their understanding of the importance of difference in shaping life experiences

2.1.4d View themselves as learners and engage those with whom they work as informants

2.1.10a Substantively and affectively prepare for action with individuals, families, groups, organizations, and communities

2.1.10b Use empathy and other interpersonal skills

2.1.10d Collect organize and interpret data

2.1.10.g Select appropriate intervention strategies

2.1.10m Critically analyze monitor and evaluate interventions

Maintaining Psychological Contact with Clients and Exploring Their Problems

Verbal following involves the use and sometimes blending of discrete skills that enable social workers to maintain psychological contact with clients on a moment-by-moment basis and to covey accurate understanding of their messages. Moreover, verbal following behavior takes into account two performance variables that are essential to satisfaction and continuance on the part of the client:

1. *Stimulus-response congruence.* The extent to which social workers' responses provide feedback to clients that their messages are accurately received.

EP 2.1.10a

2. *Content relevance.* The extent to which the content of social workers' responses is perceived by clients as relevant to their substantive concerns.

Skills in following have been related to client continuance (Rosen, 1972). Further, incongruent responses to clients have been more associated with discontinuance (Duehn & Proctor, 1977). Continued use of questions and other responses that are not associated with previous client messages and that do not relate to the client's substantive concerns contribute to consistent client dissatisfaction. One study of the outcome of working with persons with drinking problems found that two-thirds of the variance of outcomes after six months was predicted by the degree of empathy demonstrated by the counselors (Miller, 1980). Effective use of attending behaviors and demonstrated empathy should enhance motivational congruence (the fit between client motivation and social worker goals), a factor that is associated with better outcomes in social work effectiveness studies (Reid & Hanrahan, 1982). Employing responses that directly relate to client messages and concerns thus enhances client satisfaction, fosters continuance, and greatly contributes to the establishment of a viable working relationship. Studies of practice by social work students of the skills taught in this book have shown that while most of the practice skills of second-year students were not significantly more advanced than those of first-year students, the second-year students were better able to focus on tasks and goals, an objective of this chapter, compared with first-year students (Deal & Brintzenhofe-Szok, 2004).

EP 2.1.4c

Clients do not always perceive social worker questions about concerns as helpful. While noting the differences within Asian and Pacific Islander groups, including those with immigrant and resident status, Fong (2007) notes that some Asian clients (as well as members of other groups) may express emotional conflicts in a somatized form. In such cases, the social worker must be respectful of the client's experience with the physical concern as well as explain the rationale for asking questions about factors such as family background that are not directly related to the physical complaint (Cormier & Nurius, 2003.) The linkage of these issues to their current symptoms is not clear to many clients. Some Asian clients conceive of mental distress as the result of a physiological disorder or character flaws. This issue must be dealt with sensitively before any useful therapeutic work can occur (Fong, 2007). Similarly, clients who are members of historically oppressed groups may perceive questions as interrogations not designed to help them with their own concerns, but rather as ways to explore whether they have broken the law or endangered their children. That is, they may not readily assume that the social worker is acting as their agent or advocate, but rather as an agent of the state or majority community and hence a potential danger to their family (Sue, 2006).

> **VIDEO CASE EXAMPLE**
>
> In the video "Getting Back to Shakopee, GBS," the potential client, Val has been referred to an employee assistance program by her employer. She asks many questions about who will gain access to the information shared in their sessions. These questions reflect a concern that her answers about child care and adult supervision could result in a child welfare investigation.

In addition to enabling social workers to maintain close psychological contact with clients, verbal following skills serve two other important functions in the helping process. First, they yield rich personal information, allowing social workers to explore clients' problems in depth. Second, they enable social workers to focus selectively on components of the clients' experiences and on dynamics in the helping process that facilitate positive client change.

EP 2.1.4d

The following pages introduce a variety of skills for verbally following and exploring clients' problems. Some of these skills are easily mastered. Others require more effort to acquire. The exercises in the body of the chapter will assist you in acquiring proficiency in these important skills. Although empathic responding is the most vital skill for verbally following clients' messages, we have not included it in this chapter because it was discussed in detail in Chapter 5. Later, we discuss the blending of empathic responses with other verbal following skills to bolster your ability to focus on and fully explore relevant client problems.

EP 2.1.10g

Verbal Following Skills

The discrete skills highlighted in this chapter include eight types of responses:

1. Furthering
2. Paraphrasing
3. Reflection
4. Closed-ended responses

EP 2.1.10b

5. Open-ended responses
6. Seeking concreteness
7. Providing and maintaining focus
8. Summarizing

Furthering Responses

Furthering responses indicate social workers are listening attentively and encourage the client to verbalize. There are two types of furthering responses: minimal prompts and accent responses.

Minimal Prompts

Minimal prompts signal the social worker's attentiveness and encourage the client to continue verbalizing. They can be either nonverbal or verbal.

Nonverbal minimal prompts consist of nodding the head, using facial expressions, or employing gestures that convey receptivity, interest, and commitment to understanding. They implicitly convey the message, "I am with you; please continue."

Verbal minimal prompts consist of brief messages that convey interest and encourage or request expanded verbalizations along the lines of the previous expressions by the client. These messages include "Yes," "I see," "But?", "Mm-mmm" "Tell me more," "And then what happened?", "And?", "Please go on," "Tell me more, please," and other similar brief messages that affirm the appropriateness of what the client has been saying and prompt him or her to continue.

Accent Responses

Accent responses (Hackney & Cormier, 2005) involve repeating, in a questioning tone of voice or with emphasis, a word or a short phrase. Suppose a client says, "I've really had it with the way my supervisor at work is treating me." The social worker might reply, "Had it?" This short response is intended to prompt further elaboration by the client.

Paraphrasing Responses

Paraphrasing involves using fresh words to restate the client's message concisely. Paraphrasing responses focus on the cognitive aspects of client messages (i.e., emphasize situations, ideas, objects, or persons) (Hackney & Cormier, 2005). Note that paraphrasing a client's or other person's comments does not mean that you agree with or condone those thoughts.

Four examples of paraphrasing follow.

Example 1
Elder client: I don't want to get into a living situation in which I will not be able to make choices on my own.

Social worker: So independence is a very important issue for you.

Example 2
Client: I went to the doctor today for a final checkup, and she said that I was doing fine.

Social worker: She gave you a clean bill of health, then.

Example 3
Native American Client (from "GBS" video): The idea of a promotion makes me feel good; I could earn more money, the supervisor in that department is real nice, she respects me, we get along really good.

Social worker: So you feel that you would get more support for you at work and for your family?

Example 4
Managed care utilization reviewer: We don't think that your patient's condition justifies the level of service that you recommend.

Social worker: So you feel that my documentation does not justify the need that I have recommended according to the approval guidelines you are working from.

Note that in Example 4, paraphrasing is used as part of the communication with a person whose opinion is important because it relates to delivering client

> **VIDEO CASE EXAMPLE**
>
> In the video "Elder Grief Assessment" (EGA) the social worker asks a senior recently widowed client what she would like to see occur at the end of their work together. The client replies: "I would like to feel better myself, the house looking better, the yard looking better, I would like to go grocery shopping when I want to, get to the doctor without calling someone." The social worker, Kathy, paraphrases the content by saying, "You would like to remain independent."

services—the health insurance care manager (Strom-Gottfried, 1998a). When employed sparingly, paraphrasing may be interspersed with other facilitative responses to prompt client expression. Used to excess, however, paraphrasing produces a mimicking effect. Paraphrasing is helpful when social workers want to bring focus to an idea or a situation for client consideration.

Exercises in Paraphrasing

In the following exercises, formulate written responses that paraphrase the cognitive messages of clients and other persons. Modeled responses for these exercises appear at the end of the chapter.

Client/Colleague Statements

1. *Client:* I can't talk to people. I just completely freeze up in a group.
2. *Wife:* I think that in the last few weeks I've been able to listen much more often to my husband and children.
3. *Elder client:* It wasn't so difficult to adjust to this place because the people who run it are helpful and friendly and I am able to make contacts easily—I've always been a people person.
4. *Mother [speaking about daughter]:* When it comes right down to it, I think I'm to blame for a lot of her problems.
5. *Member of treatment team:* I just don't see how putting more services into this family makes sense. The mother is not motivated, and the kids are better off away from her. This family has been messed up forever.

Reflection

While paraphrasing focuses on the content of a message, reflection responses focus attention on the affective part of the communication (Cormier, Nurius & Osborn, 2009).[1] In a reflection, social workers relate with responses that accurately capture clients' affect and assist them to reflect on and sort through their feelings. Sometimes social workers may choose to direct the discussion away from feelings for therapeutic purposes. For instance, a social worker might believe that a chronically depressed client who habitually expresses discouragement and disillusionment would benefit by focusing less on feelings and more on actions to alleviate the distress. When the social worker chooses to deemphasize feelings, paraphrases that reflect content are helpful and appropriate.

Simple reflections, which identify the emotions expressed by the client, are a heritage from nondirective, client-centered counseling. That is, they simply identify the emotion. They do not take a stand or attempt to help the client deal with the emotion. They do not go beyond what the client has said or directly implied (Moyers, Martin, Manual, Miller & Ernst, 2003).

> ### VIDEO CASE EXAMPLE
>
> In the video "How Can I Help?" (HCH), Peter Dimock uses the Motivational Interviewing (MI) approach to work with Julie, a client who is recovering from drug use and is involved with the child welfare system. When Julie shares her frustration about all the things she has to do on her case plan, Peter responds with a simple reflection that stays closely with her message of being overwhelmed.
>
> *Julie:* "Well it's just really hard getting around with baby and I just, you know I've got a lot of stuff that I'm supposed to be doing for my case plan and I just am having a really hard time getting to all the places on time."
>
> *Peter:* "Well you've been pretty stressed, it sounds like. Having to do all these things and get around and make it to all of your appointments, it's pretty overwhelming."

Complex reflections go beyond what the client has directly stated or implied, adding substantial meaning or emphasis to convey a more complex picture. For example, they may *add content*, which focuses on meanings or feelings that the client did not directly express (ibid.). For example, when a teenaged client said "My mother really expects a lot from me," a social worker made a response that added implied content by saying "She has high expectations for you; she thinks that you have a lot of ability." *Verbalizing an unspoken emotion* is a form of reflection that names an emotion that the client has implied but not stated. When a teenaged client reflects on what it feels like to be new to her school by saying, "I am new here. I don't know anyone. I just try to stick to myself and stay out of trouble," the social worker could verbalize "that sounds to me as if it could be a little lonely," to tune in to the unspoken emotion of sadness.

A **reframe** is another form of adding content. Here, the social worker puts the client's response in a different light beyond what the client had considered (Moyers et al., 2003). For example, when a client reported on earlier drug treatment experience, he emphasized failure, saying, "I have gone through treatment three or four times. Maybe one of these times, I will get it right." The social worker chose not to agree with the failure message, but rather reframes to say "it sounds as if you have persisted, trying treatment again after earlier disappointments; you haven't given up on yourself."

Sometimes, the reflection can use a *metaphor* or *simile* to paint a picture of what the client has stated. For example, when a client commented about his job "I just do the same thing every day, nothing ever changes or ever gets better, always the same," the social worker responded, "It sounds like a rat in a maze" (ibid.). Sometimes the reflection might focus on *amplification*, either strengthening or weakening the intensity of client expression (ibid.). For example, a client shared "I am disappointed with how long this has taken," and the social worker chose to emphasize the strength of the implied feeling by saying "you are really frustrated and exhausted by all the time you have put into this with little to show for it." On the other hand, when a client expressed doubts about her abilities, saying, "I never get anything right," the social worker chose to agree but weaken its intensity "sometimes you doubt whether you can succeed."

Sometimes clients express indecision and conflict between several alternatives. In such circumstances, it is possible to present a *double-sided reflection* that captures both sides of the dilemma that is fostering ambivalence about acting (Miller & Rollnick, 2002). For example, a teen parent had expressed that she wanted to succeed in school and as a parent and one day become a probation officer or social worker. On the other hand, in their discussion she had reported frequent instances of verbal and physical altercations at school and gang involvement. She described members of the gang as members of her family. In a double-sided reflection, the social worker tried to identify the conflicting factors that make consistent decision making difficult. The social worker responded, "Rhonda, it sounds as if part of you is doing your best to succeed in school and act as a responsible parent and plan for the future. Another part of you is conflicted about wanting to be true to your friends and, as you describe them, family members, who are members of the gang."

> ### VIDEO CASE EXAMPLE
>
> At a later point in the video "How Can I Help?" (HCH), Julie is commenting on how she is torn about returning to school to get a GED, seeing both advantages and disadvantages. She says "I don't know, I guess it would be a good accomplishment, but I just, I don't know, I just don't think, I don't just think I can do it, like, it's just hard. I don't know." Peter reflects the two sides of her feelings by saying "So it's important to you on one hand, and then on the other hand, you don't feel confident in your ability to do it. Is that true?"

Another version of reflection is the *reflection with a twist* (Miller & Rollnick, 2002) in which the social worker agrees in essence with the dilemma expressed by the client but changes the emphasis, perhaps to indicate that the dilemma is not unsolvable, but rather that the client has not at this time solved it. For example, in the previous situation with Rhonda, the social worker might add, "it sounds, Rhonda, as if at this point in time you don't feel that you can make a decision about what you are going to do about interacting with your friends in the gang."

These variations on reflections come from the Motivational Interviewing approach (MI) (Miller & Rollnick, 2002). They are useful in circumstances in which clients or potential clients are considering taking an action but have not decided on what to do. Rather than labeling such behavior as resistance, MI considers ambivalence as an important and useful step in deciding whether to address a situation. From the stages of change approach, such circumstances are described as being either in a state of **precontemplation**, in which a person has not decided whether an issue exists or whether they wish to address it, or **contemplation**, in which they are aware of an issue but have not decided whether to take action (De Clemente & Velasquez, 2002). These circumstances occur frequently in social work practice, but not always. Hence, the skills are presented here as important and useful adjuncts to reflection skills that can be applied when, in the course of exploration, potential ambivalence about considering an issue or taking action on it emerges. The spirit of MI is consistent with social work values of self-determination at this point in presenting the role of the helper as addressing ambivalence and helping the client consider whether he or she wishes to take action without exerting pressure on that decision (Miller & Rollnick, 2002).

Exercises with Reflections

In the following exercises, formulate written responses that reflect the affective state of clients. Modeled responses for these exercises appear at the end of the chapter.

Client/Colleague Statements

1. *Client:* Whenever I get into an argument with my mother, I always end up losing. I guess I'm still afraid of her.
2. *Mother [participating in welfare-to-work program]:* I don't know how they can expect me to be a good mother and make school appointments, supervise my kids, and put in all these work hours.
3. *Terminally ill cancer patient:* Some days I am really angry because I'm only 46-years-old and there are so many more things I wanted to do. Other days, I feel kind of defeated, like this is what I get for smoking two packs of cigarettes a day for 25 years.
4. *Elementary school student:* Kids pick on me at school. They are mean. If they try to hurt me then I try to hurt them back.
5. *Husband:* I just can't decide what to do. If I go ahead with the divorce, I'll probably lose custody of the kids—and I won't be able to see them very much. If I don't, though, I'll have to put up with the same old thing. I don't think my wife is going to change.

Closed- and Open-Ended Responses

Generally used to elicit specific information, **closed-ended questions** define a topic and restrict the client's response to a few words or a simple yes or no answer. Typical examples of closed-ended questions follow:

EP 2.1.10g

- "When did you obtain your divorce?"
- "Do you have any sexual difficulties in your marriage?"
- "When did you last have a physical examination?"
- "Is your health insurance Medicare?"

Although closed-ended questions restrict the client and elicit limited information, in many instances these responses are both appropriate and helpful. Later in this chapter, we discuss how and when to use this type of response effectively.

In contrast to closed-ended responses, which circumscribe client messages, **open-ended questions** and statements invite expanded expression and leave the client free to express what seems most relevant and important. For example:

Social worker: You've mentioned your daughter. Tell me how she enters into your problem.

Client: I don't know what to do. Sometimes I think she is just pushing me so that she can go live with her father. When I ask her to help around the house, she won't, and says that she doesn't owe me anything. When I try to insist on her helping, it just ends up in an ugly scene without anything being accomplished. It makes me feel so helpless.

In this example, the social worker's open-ended question prompted the client to expand on the details of the problems with her daughter, including a description of her daughter's behavior, her own efforts to cope, and her present sense of defeat. The information contained in the message is typical of the richness of data obtained through open-ended responding.

In circumstances like the example of a telephone conversation with a managed care utilization reviewer, the social worker can use an open-ended question to attempt to explore common ground that can lead to a mutually beneficial resolution.

Social worker [to managed care utilization reviewer]: Can you clarify for me how appropriate coverage is determined for situations such as the one I have described?

Some open-ended responses are unstructured, leaving the topic to the client's choosing (e.g., "Tell me what you would like to discuss today" or "What else can you tell me about the problems that you're experiencing?"). Other open-ended responses are structured such that the social worker defines the topic to be discussed but leaves the client free to respond in any way that he or she wishes (e.g., "You've mentioned feeling ashamed about the incident that occurred between you and your son. I'd be interested in hearing more about that."). Still other open-ended responses fall along a continuum between structured and unstructured, because they give the client leeway to answer with a few words or to elaborate with more information (e.g., "How willing are you to do this?").

Social workers may formulate open-ended responses either by asking a question or by giving a polite command. Suppose a terminally ill cancer patient said, "The doctor thinks I could live about six or seven months now. It could be less; it could be more. It's just an educated guess, he told me." The social worker could respond by asking, "How are you feeling about that prognosis?" or "Would you tell me how you are feeling about that prognosis?" Polite commands have the same effect as direct questions in requesting information but are less forceful and involve greater finesse. Similar in nature are embedded questions that do not take the form of a question but embody a request for information.

Examples of embedded questions include "I'm curious about...," "I'm wondering if ...," and "I'm interested in knowing ...." Open-ended questions often start with "what" or "how." "Why" questions are often unproductive because they may ask for reasons, motives, or causes that are either obvious, obscure, or unknown to the client. Asking how ("How did that happen?") rather than why ("Why did that happen?") often elicits far richer information regarding client behavior and patterns.

VIDEO CASE EXAMPLE

In the video "Home for the Holidays, Part 1" (HFH), the practitioner, Kim Strom-Gottfried, asks one partner about the experience of when she came out to her parents as a lesbian: "Let me ask a bit about the coming out conversation. Sounds like it was not an easy one, yet one you were able to have. Can you tell me a little bit more about that?"

Exercises in Identifying Closed- and Open-Ended Responses

The following exercises will assist you to differentiate between closed- and open-ended messages. Identify each statement with either a C for a closed-ended question or O for an open-ended question. Turn to the end of the chapter to check your answers.

1. "Did your mother ask you to see me because of the problem you had with the principal?"
2. "When John says that to you, what do you experience inside?"
3. "You said you're feeling fed up and you're just not sure that pursuing a reconciliation is worth your trouble. Could you elaborate?"
4. "When is your court date?"

Now read the following client messages and respond by writing open-ended responses to them. Avoid using *why* questions. Examples of open-ended responses to these messages appear at the end of the chapter.

Client Statements

1. *Client:* Whenever I'm in a group with Ralph, I find myself saying something that will let him know that I am smart, too.
2. *Client:* I always have had my parents telephone for me about appointments and other things I might mess up.
3. *Teenager [speaking of a previous probation counselor]:* He sure let me down. And I really trusted him. He knows a lot about me because I spilled my guts.
4. *Group nursing home administrator:* I think that we are going to have to move Gladys to another, more suitable kind of living arrangement. We aren't able to provide the kind of care that she needs.

The next sections of the book explain how you can blend open-ended, paraphrases and reflective responses to keep a discussion focused on a specific topic. In preparation for that, respond to the next two client messages by formulating a paraphrase or reflection followed by an open-ended question that encourages the client to elaborate on the same topic.

5. *Unwed teenage girl seeking abortion [brought in by her mother, who wishes to discuss birth alternatives]:* I feel like you are all tied up with my mother, trying to talk me out of what I have decided to do.
6. *Client:* Life is such a hassle, and it doesn't seem to have any meaning or make sense. I just don't know whether I want to try figuring it out any longer.

The difference between closed-ended and open-ended responses may seem obvious to you, particularly if you completed the preceding exercises. It has been our experience, however, that social workers have difficulty in actual sessions in determining whether their responses are open- or closed-ended, in observing the differential effect of these two types of responses in yielding rich and relevant data, and in deciding which of the two types of responses is appropriate at a given moment. We recommend, therefore, that as you converse with your associates, you practice drawing them out by employing open-ended responses and noting how they respond. We also recommend that you use the form provided at the end of the chapter to assess both the frequency and the appropriateness of your closed- and open-ended responses in several taped client sessions.

Discriminant Use of Closed- and Open-Ended Responses

Beginning social workers typically ask an excessive number of closed-ended questions, many of which block communication or are inefficient or irrelevant to the helping process. When this occurs, the session tends to take on the flavor of an interrogation, with the social worker bombarding the client with questions and taking responsibility for maintaining verbalization. Notice what happens in the following excerpt from a recording of a social worker interviewing an institutionalized youth.

Social worker: I met your mother yesterday. Did she come all the way from Colorado to see you?

Client: Yeah.

Social worker: It seems to me that she must really care about you to take the bus and make the trip up here to see you. Don't you think so?

Client: I suppose so.

Social worker: Did the visit with her go all right?

Client: Fine. We had a good time.

Social worker: You had said you were going to talk to her about a possible home visit. Did you do that?

Client: Yes.

When closed-ended responses are used to elicit information in lieu of open-ended responses, as in the preceding example, many more discrete interchanges will occur. However, the client's responses will be brief and the information yield will be markedly lower.

Open-ended responses often elicit the same data as closed-ended questions but draw out much more information and elaboration of the problem from the client. The following two examples contrast open-ended and closed-ended responses that address the same topic with a given client. To appreciate the differences in the richness of information yielded by these contrasting responses, compare the likely client responses elicited by such questions to the closed-ended questions used from the previous section.

Example 1

Closed-ended: "Did she come all the way from Colorado to see you?"

Open-ended: "Tell me about your visit with your mother."

Example 2

Closed-ended: "Did you talk with her about a possible home visit?"

Open-ended: "How did your mother respond when you talked about a possible home visit?"

Occasionally, beginning social workers use closed-ended questions to explore feelings, but responses from clients typically involve minimal self-disclosure, as might be expected. Rather than encourage expanded expression of feelings, closed-ended questions limit responses, as illustrated in the following example:

Social worker: Did you feel rejected when she turned down your invitation?

Client: Yeah.

Social worker: Have there been other times when you've felt rejected that way?

Client: Oh, yeah. Lots of times.

Social worker: When was the first time?

Client: Gee, that's hard to say.

Here, the social worker was leading the client rather than finding out how she perceived the situation. Had the social worker employed empathic and open-ended responses to explore the feelings and thoughts associated with being rejected, the client would likely have revealed much more.

Because open-ended responses elicit more information than closed-ended ones, frequent use of the former technique increases the efficiency of data gathering. In fact, the richness of information revealed by the client is directly proportional to the frequency with which open-ended responses are employed. Frequent use of open-ended responses also fosters a smoothly flowing session; consistently asking closed-ended questions, by contrast, may result in a fragmented, discontinuous process.

Closed-ended questions are used chiefly to elicit essential factual information. Skillful social workers use closed-ended questions sparingly, because clients usually reveal extensive factual information spontaneously as they unfold their stories, aided by the social worker's open-ended and furthering responses. Although they are typically employed little during the first part of a session, closed questions are used more extensively later to elicit data that may have been omitted by clients, such as names and ages of children, place of employment, date of marriage, medical facts, and data regarding family or origin.

In obtaining this kind of factual data, the social worker can unobtrusively weave into the discussion closed-ended questions that directly pertain to the topic. For example, a client may relate certain marital problems that have existed for many years, and the social worker might ask parenthetically, "And you've been married for how many years?" Similarly, a parent may explain that a child began to have irregular attendance at school when the parent started to work 6 months ago, to which the social worker might respond, "I see. Incidentally, what type of work do you do?" It is vital, of course, to shift the focus back to the problem. If necessary, the social worker can easily maintain focus by using an open-ended response to pick up the thread of the discussion. For example, the social worker might comment, "You mentioned that Ernie began missing school when you started to work. I'd like to hear more about what was happening in your family at that time."

Because open-ended responses generally yield rich information, they are used throughout initial sessions. They are used most heavily, however, in the first portion of sessions to open up lines of communication and to invite clients to reveal problematic aspects of their lives. The following open-ended polite command is a typical opening message: "Could you tell me what you wish to discuss, and we can think about it together." Such responses convey interest in clients as well as respect for clients' abilities to relate their problems in their own way; as a consequence, they also contribute to the development of a working relationship.

As clients disclose certain problem areas, open-ended responses are extensively employed to elicit additional relevant information. Clients, for example, may reveal difficulties at work or in relationships with other family members. Open-ended responses like the following will elicit clarifying information:

- "Tell me more about your problems at work."
- "I'd like to hear more about the circumstances when you were mugged coming home with the groceries."

Open-ended responses can be used to enhance communication with collaterals, colleagues, and other professionals. For example, Strom-Gottfried suggests using effective communication skills in negotiation and communication between care providers and utilization reviewers. When a client has not been approved for a kind of service that the social worker has recommended, the social worker can attempt to join with the reviewer in identifying goals that both parties would embrace and request information in an open-ended fashion.

"I appreciate your concern that she gets the best available services and that her condition does not get worse. We are concerned with safety, as we know you are. Could you tell me more about how this protocol can help us assure her safety?" (Strom-Gottfried, 1998a, p. 398)

It may sometimes be necessary to employ closed-ended questions extensively to draw out information if the client is unresponsive and withholds information or has limited conceptual and mental abilities. However, in the former case, it is vital to explore the client's immediate feelings about being in the session, which often are negative and impede verbal expression. Focusing on and resolving negative feelings (discussed at length in Chapter 12) may pave the way to using open-ended responses to good advantage.

When you incorporate open-ended responses into your repertoire, you will experience a dramatic positive change in your interviewing style and confidence level. To assist you to develop skill in blending and balancing open-ended and closed-ended responses, we have provided a recording form to help you examine your own interviewing style (see Figure 6-1). Using this form, analyze several recorded individual, conjoint, or group sessions over a period of time to determine changes you are making in employing these two types of responses. The recording form will assist you in determining the extent to which you have used open- and closed-ended responses.

In addition, you may wish to review your work for the following purposes:

1. To determine when relevant data are missing and whether the information might have been more appropriately obtained through an open- or closed-ended response
2. To determine when your use of closed-ended questions was irrelevant or ineffective, or distracted from the data-gathering process
3. To practice formulating open-ended responses you might use instead of closed-ended responses, to increase client participation and elicit richer data.

SOCIAL WORKER'S RESPONSES	OPEN-ENDED RESPONSES	CLOSED-ENDED RESPONSES
1.		
2.		
3.		
4.		
5.		
6.		
7.		

Directions: Record your discrete open- and closed-ended responses and place a check in the appropriate column. Agency time constraints will dictate how often you can practice it.

FIG-6-1 Recording Form for Open- and Closed-Ended Responding Seeking Concreteness

Seeking Concreteness

Many of us are inclined to think and talk in generalities and to use words that lack precision when speaking of our experiences ("How was your weekend?" "It was awesome."). To communicate one's feelings and experiences so that they are fully understood, however, a person must be able to respond concretely—that is, with specificity. Responding concretely means using words that describe in explicit terms specific experiences, behaviors, and feelings. As an example, in the following message, an intern supervisor provides feedback in vague and general terms: "I thought you had a good interview." Alternatively, he might have described his experience in more precise language: "During your interview, I was impressed with the way you blended open-ended with closed-ended questions in a relaxed fashion."

You should consider seeking concreteness when the client uses language that suggests to you that you may not understand their terms in the way they intend. This can be particularly true when interviewing children or adolescents whose colloquial expressions may not be entirely clear to the interviewer. Similarly, non native speakers may be conveying ideas that do not readily translate into the language you are speaking. In summary, seeking concreteness can be useful to:

1. Check out perceptions
2. Clarify the meaning of vague or unfamiliar terms
3. Explore the basis of conclusions drawn by clients
4. Assist clients to personalize their statements
5. Elicit specific feelings
6. Focus on the here and now, rather than on the distant past
7. Elicit details related to clients' experiences
8. Elicit details related to interactional behavior
9. Clarify details of timelines, expectations

To test your comprehension of the concept of concreteness, assess which of the following messages give descriptive information concerning what a client experiences:

1. "I have had a couple of accidents that would not have happened if I had full control of my hands. The results weren't that serious, but they could be."
2. "I'm uneasy right now because I don't know what to expect from counseling, and I'm afraid you might think that I really don't need it."
3. "You are a good girl, Susie."
4. "People don't seem to care whether other people have problems."
5. "My last social worker did not answer my calls."
6. "I really wonder if I'll be able to keep from crying and to find the words to tell my husband that it's all over—that I want a divorce."
7. "You did a good job."

You could probably readily identify which messages contained language that increased the specificity of the information conveyed by the client.

In developing competency as a social worker, one of your challenges is to consistently recognize clients' messages expressed in abstract and general terms and to assist them to reveal highly specific information related to feelings and experiences. Such information will assist you to make accurate assessments and, in turn, to plan interventions accordingly. A second challenge is to help clients learn how to respond more concretely in their relationships with others—a task you will not be able to accomplish unless you are able to model the dimension of concreteness yourself. A third challenge is to describe your own experience in language that is precise and descriptive. It is not enough to recognize concrete messages; in addition, you must familiarize yourself with and practice responding concretely to the extent that it becomes a natural style of speaking and relating to others.

The remainder of our discussion on the skill of seeking concreteness is devoted to assisting you in meeting these three challenges.

Types of Responses That Facilitate Specificity of Expression by Clients

Social workers who fail to move beyond general and abstract messages often have little grasp of the specificity and meaning of a client's problem. Eliciting highly specific information that minimizes errors or misinterpretations, however, represents a formidable challenge. People typically present impressions, views, conclusions, and opinions that, despite efforts to be objective, are inevitably biased and distorted to some extent. As previously mentioned, it is common for many of us to speak in generalities and to respond with imprecise language. As a consequence, those messages may be understood differently by different people.

To help you to conceptualize the various ways you may assist clients to respond more concretely, the following sections examine different facets of responses that seek concreteness:

In addition to discussing these aspects, this section includes 10 skill development exercises, which are designed to bring your comprehension of concreteness from the general and abstract to the specific and concrete.

Checking Out Perceptions

Responses that assist social workers to clarify and "check out" whether they have accurately heard clients' messages (e.g., "Do you mean …" or "Are you saying …") are vital in building rapport with clients and in communicating the desire to understand their problems. Such responses also minimize misperceptions or projections in the helping process. Clients benefit from social workers' efforts to understand, because clarifying responses assist clients in sharpening and reformulating their thinking about their own feelings and other concerns, thereby encouraging self-awareness and growth.

Sometimes, perception checking becomes necessary because clients' messages are incomplete, ambiguous, or complex. Occasionally, social workers may encounter clients who repetitively communicate in highly abstract or metaphorical styles, or clients whose thinking is scattered and whose messages just do not "track" or make sense. In such instances, social workers must spend considerable time sorting through clients' messages and clarifying perceptions.

At other times, the need for clarification arises not because the client has conveyed confusing, faulty, or incomplete messages, but rather because the social worker has not fully attended to the client's message or comprehended its meaning. Fully attending throughout each moment of a session requires intense concentration. Of course, it is impossible to fully focus on and comprehend the essence of every message delivered in group and family meetings, where myriad transactions occur and competing communications bid for the social worker's attention.

It is important that you develop skill in using clarifying responses to elicit ongoing feedback regarding your perceptions and to acknowledge freely your need for clarification when you are confused or uncertain. Rather than reflecting personal or professional inadequacy, your efforts to accurately grasp the client's meaning and feelings will most likely be perceived as signs of your genuineness and your commitment to understand.

To check your perceptions, try asking simple questions that seek clarification or combining your request for clarification with a paraphrase or empathic response that reflects your perception of the client's message (e.g., "I think you were saying _____. Is that right?"). Examples of clarifying messages include the following:

- *"You seem to be really irritated, not only because he didn't respond when you asked him to help, but because he seemed to be deliberately trying to hurt you. Is that accurate?"*
- *"I'm not sure I'm following you. Let me see if I understand the order of the events you described …"*
- *"Would you expand on what you are saying so that I can be sure that I understand what you mean?"*
- *"Could you go over that again, and perhaps give an illustration that might help me to understand?"*
- *"I'm confused. Let me try to restate what I think you're saying."*
- *"As a group, you seem to be divided in your approach to this matter. I'd like to summarize what I'm hearing, and I would then appreciate some input regarding whether I understand the various positions that have been expressed."*

> **VIDEO CASE EXAMPLE**
>
> In the video "Serving the Squeaky Wheel" (SSW), the social worker, Ron Rooney, asks Molly, a client with a diagnosed serious and persistent mental illness (SPMI), "So you feel that other people's ideas about what mental illness means is not the same as yours?"

In addition to clarifying their own perceptions, social workers need to assist clients in conjoint or group sessions to clarify their perceptions of the messages of others who are present. This may be accomplished in any of the following ways:

- *By modeling clarifying responses, which occur naturally as social workers seek to check out their own perceptions of clients' messages.*
- *By directing clients to ask for clarification.* Consider, for example, the following response by a social worker in a conjoint session: "You [mother] had a confused look on your face, and I'm not sure that you understood your daughter's point. Would you repeat back to her what you heard and then ask her if you understood correctly?"
- *By teaching clients how to clarify perceptions and by reinforcing their efforts to "check out" the messages of others,* as illustrated in the following responses:

  [To group]: "One of the reasons families have communication problems is that members don't hear accurately what others are trying to say and, therefore, they often respond or react on the basis of incorrect or inadequate information. I would like to encourage all of you to frequently use what I call 'checking out' responses, such as 'I'm not sure what you meant. Were you saying…?' to clarify statements of others. As we go along, I'll point out instances in which I notice any of you using this kind of response."

  [To family]: "I'm wondering if you all noticed Jim 'checking out' what his dad said…. As you may recall, we talked about the importance of these kinds of responses earlier. [To father] I'm wondering, Bob, what you experienced when Jim did that?"

Clarifying the Meaning of Vague or Unfamiliar Terms

In expressing themselves, clients often employ terms that have multiple meanings or use terms in idiosyncratic ways. For example, in the message, "The kids in this school are mean," the word *mean* may have different meanings to the social worker and the client. If the social worker does not identify what this term means to a particular client, he or she cannot be certain whether the client is referring to behavior that is violent, unfriendly, threatening, or something else. The precise meaning can be clarified by employing one of the following responses:

- "Tell me about the way that some kids are mean in this school."
- "I am not sure I know what is happening when you say that some kids act in a mean way. Could you clarify that for me?"
- "Can you give me an example of something mean that has happened at this school?"

Many other words also lack precision, so it is important to avoid assuming that the client means the same thing you mean when you employ a given term. For example, "codependent," "irresponsible," "selfish," and "careless" conjure up meanings that vary according to the reference points of different persons. Exact meanings are best determined by asking for clarification or for examples of events in which the behavior alluded to actually occurred.

Exploring the Basis of Conclusions Drawn by Clients

Clients often present views or conclusions as though they are established facts. For example, the messages "I'm losing my mind" and "My partner doesn't love me anymore" include views or conclusions that the client has drawn. To accurately assess the client's difficulties, the social worker must elicit the information on which these views or conclusions are based. This information helps the social worker assess the thinking patterns of the client, which are powerful determinants of emotions and behavior. For example, a person who believes he or she is no longer loved will behave as though this belief represents reality. The social worker's role, of course, is to reveal distortions and to challenge erroneous conclusions in a facilitative manner.

The following responses would elicit clarification of the information that serves as the basis of the views and conclusions embodied in the messages cited earlier:

- "How do you mean, losing your mind?"
- "How have you concluded that you're losing your mind?"

- "What leads you to believe your partner no longer loves you?"

Note that entire groups may hold in common fixed beliefs that may not be helpful to them in attempting to better their situations. In such instances, the social worker faces the challenging task of assisting members to reflect upon and to analyze their views. For example, the social worker may need to help group members to assess conclusions or distortions like the following:

- "We can't do anything about our problems. We are helpless and others are in control of our lives."
- "People in authority are out to get us."
- "Someone else is responsible for our problems."
- "They (members of another race, religion, group, etc.) are no good."

In Chapter 13, we discuss the social worker's role in challenging distortions and erroneous conclusions and identify relevant techniques that may be used for this purpose.

Assisting Clients to Personalize Their Statements

The relative concreteness of a specific client message is related in part to the focus or subject of that message. Client messages fall into several different classes of topic focus (Cormier, Nurius & Osborn, 2009), each of which emphasizes different information and leads into very different areas of discussion:

- Focus on self, *indicated by the subject "I"* (e.g., "I'm disappointed that I wasn't able to keep the appointment.")
- Focus on others, *indicated by subjects such as "they," "people," "someone," or names of specific persons* (e.g., "They haven't fulfilled their part of the bargain.")
- Focus on the group or mutual relationship between self and others, *indicated by the subject "we"* (e.g., "We would like to do that.")
- Focus on content, *indicated by such subjects as events, institutions, situations, ideas* (e.g., "School wasn't easy for me.")

People are more prone to focus on others or on content, or to speak of themselves as a part of a group rather than to personalize their statements by using "I" or other self-referent pronouns. This tendency is illustrated in the following messages: "Things just don't seem to be going right for me," "They don't like me," and "It's not easy for people to talk about their problems." In the last example, the client means that it is not easy for *her* to talk about *her* problems, yet she uses the term *people*, thereby generalizing the problem and obscuring her personal struggle.

In assisting clients to personalize statements, social workers have a three-part task:

1. Social workers must model, teach, and coach clients to use self-referent pronouns *(I, me)* in talking about their concerns and their own emotional response to those concerns. For example, in response to a vague client message that focuses on content rather than self ("Everything at home seems to be deteriorating"), the social worker might gently ask the client to reframe the message by starting the response with "I" and giving specific information about what she is experiencing. It is also helpful to teach clients the difference between messages that focus on self ("I think ...," "I feel ...," "I want ...") and messages that are *other-related* ("It ...," "Someone ...").

2. Social workers must teach the difference between self-referent messages and subject-related messages (i.e., those dealing with objects, things, ideas, or situations). Although teaching clients to use self-referent pronouns when talking about their concerns is a substantive task, clients derive major benefits from it. Indeed, not owning or taking responsibility for feelings and speaking about problems in generalities and abstractions are among the most prevalent causes of problems in communicating.

3. Social workers must focus frequently on the client and use the client's name or the pronoun *you*. Beginning social workers are apt to attend to client talk about other people, distant situations, the group at large, various escapades, or other events or content that give little information about self and the relationship between self and situations or people. In the following illustration, the social worker's response focuses on the situation rather than on the client:

Client: My kids want to shut me up in a nursing home.

Social worker: What makes you think that?

In contrast, the following message personalizes the client's concern and explicitly identifies the feelings she is experiencing:

Social worker: You worry that your children might be considering a nursing home for you. You want to be part of any decision about what would be a safe environment for you.

A social worker may employ various techniques to assist clients to personalize messages. In the preceding example, the social worker utilized an empathic response. In this instance, this skill is invaluable to the social worker in helping the client to focus on self. Recall that personalizing feelings is an inherent aspect of the paradigm for responding empathetically ("You feel _____ about/because _____"). Thus, clients can make statements that omit self-referent pronouns, and by utilizing empathic responding, social workers may assist clients to "own" their feelings.

Eliciting Specific Feelings

Even when clients personalize their messages and express their feelings, social workers often need to elicit additional information to clarify what they are experiencing, because certain "feeling words" denote general feeling states rather than specific feelings. For example, in the message, "I'm really *upset* that I didn't get a raise," the word "upset" helps to clarify the client's general frame of mind but fails to specify the precise feeling. In this instance, "upset" may refer to feeling disappointed, discouraged, unappreciated, devalued, angry, resentful, or even incompetent or inadequate due to the failure to receive a raise. Until the social worker has elicited additional information, he or she cannot be sure of how the client actually experiences being "upset."

Other feeling words that lack specificity include *frustrated, uneasy, uncomfortable, troubled,* and *bothered.* When clients employ such words, you can pinpoint their feelings by using responses such as the following:

- *"How do you mean, 'upset'?"*
- *"I'd like to understand more about that feeling. Could you clarify what you mean by 'frustrated'?"*
- *"Can you say more about in what way you feel bothered?"*

Focusing on the Here and Now

Another aspect of concreteness takes the form of responses that shift the focus from the past to the present, the here and now. Messages that relate to the immediate present are high in concreteness, whereas those that center on the past are low in concreteness. Many of us are prone to dwell on past feelings and events. Unfortunately, precious opportunities for promoting growth and understanding may slip through the fingers of social workers who fail to focus on emotions and experiences that unfold in the immediacy of the interview. Focusing on feelings as they occur will enable you to observe reactions and behavior firsthand, eliminating any bias and error caused by reporting feelings and experiences after the fact. Furthermore, the helpfulness of your feedback is greatly enhanced when this feedback relates to the client's immediate experience.

The following exchange demonstrates how to achieve concreteness in such situations:

Client *[choking up]*: When she told me it was all over, that she was in love with another man—well, I just felt—it's happened again. I felt totally alone, like there just wasn't anyone.

Social worker: That must have been terribly painful. *[Client nods; tears well up.]* I wonder if you're not having the same feeling just now—at this moment. *[Client nods agreement.]*

Not only do such instances provide direct access to the client's inner experience, but they also may produce lasting benefits as the client shares deep and painful emotions in the context of a warm, accepting, and supportive relationship. Here-and-now experiencing that involves emotions toward the social worker (e.g., anger, hurt, disappointment, affectional desires, fears) is known as *relational immediacy*. Skills pertinent to relational immediacy warrant separate consideration and are dealt with in Chapter 18.

Focusing on here-and-now experiencing with groups, couples, and families is a particularly potent technique for assisting members of these systems to clear the air of pent-up feelings. Moreover, interventions that focus on the immediacy of feelings bring buried issues to the surface, paving the way for the social worker to assist members of these systems to clearly identify and explore their difficulties and (if appropriate) to engage in problem solving.

Eliciting Details Related to Clients' Experiences

As previously mentioned, one reason why concrete responses are essential is that clients often offer up vague statements regarding their experiences—for example, "Some people in this group don't want to change bad enough to put forth any effort." Compare this with the following concrete statement, in which the client assumes ownership of the problem and fills in details that clarify its nature:

Client: I'm concerned because I want to do something to work on my problems in this group, but when I do try to talk about them, you, John, make some sarcastic remark. It seems that then several of you *[gives names]* just laugh about it and someone changes the subject. I really feel ignored then and just go off into my own world.

Aside from assisting clients to personalize their messages and to "own" their feelings and problems, social workers must ask questions that elicit illuminating information concerning the client's experiencing, such as that illustrated in the preceding message. Questions that start with "how" or "what" are often helpful in assisting the client to give concrete data. For example, to the client message, "Some people in this group don't want to change bad enough to put forth any effort," the social worker might respond, "What have you seen happening in the group that leads you to this conclusion?"

Eliciting Details Related to Interactional Behavior

Concrete responses are also vital in accurately assessing interactional behavior. Such responses pinpoint what actually occurs in interactional events—that is, what circumstances preceded the events, what the participants said and did, what specific thoughts and feelings the client experienced, and what consequences followed the event. In other words, the social worker elicits details of what happened, rather than settling for clients' views and conclusions.

An example of a concrete response to a client message follows:

High school student: My teacher really lost it yesterday. She totally dissed me, and I hadn't done one thing to deserve it.

Social worker: That must have been aggravating. Can you lay out for me the sequence of events—what led up to this situation, and what each of you said and did? To understand better what went wrong, I'd like to get the details as though I had been there and observed what happened.

In such cases, it is important to keep clients on topic by continuing to assist them to relate the events in question, using responses such as "Then what happened?", "What did you do next?", or "Then who said what?" If dysfunctional patterns become evident after exploring numerous events, social workers have a responsibility to share their observations with clients, to assist them to evaluate the effects of the patterned behavior, and to assess their motivation to change it.

Specificity of Expression by Social Workers

Seeking concreteness applies to the communication of both clients and social workers. In this role, you will frequently explain, clarify and give feedback, to clients. As a social worker who has recently begun a formal professional educational program, you may be prone to speak with the vagueness and generality that characterize much of the communication of the lay public. When such vagueness occurs, clients and others may understandably misinterpret, draw erroneous conclusions, or experience confusion about the meaning of your messages.

Consider the lack of specificity in the following messages actually delivered by social workers:

- "You seem to have a lot of pent-up hostility."
- "You really handled yourself well in the group today."
- "I think a lot of your difficulties stem from your self-image."

Vague terms such as *hostility, handled yourself well,* and *self-image* may leave the client in a quandary as to what the social worker actually means. Moreover, in this style of communication, conclusions are presented without supporting information. As a result, the client must either accept them at face value, reject them as invalid, or speculate on the basis of the conclusions. Fortunately, some people are sufficiently perceptive, inquisitive, and assertive to request greater specificity—but many others are not.

Contrast the preceding messages with how the social worker responds to the same situations with messages that have a high degree of specificity:

- *"I've noticed that you've become easily angered and frustrated several times as we've talked about ways you might work out child custody arrangements with your wife. This appears to be a very painful area for you. "I noticed that you responded several times in the group tonight, and I thought you offered some very helpful insight to Marjorie when you said.... I also noticed you seemed to be more at ease than in previous sessions."*
- *"We've talked about your tendency to feel inferior to other members of your family and to discount your own feelings and opinions in your contacts with them. I think that observation applies to the problem you're having with your sister that you just described. You've said you didn't want to go on the trip with her and her husband because they fight all the time, yet you feel you have to go because she is putting pressure on you. As in other instances, you appear to be drawing the conclusion that how you feel about the matter isn't important."*

> **VIDEO CASE EXAMPLE**
>
> In the video "HFH, Part 1," the practitioner, Kim Strom-Gottfried, makes a specific observation that simultaneously provides feedback and suggests the meaning for a behavior (something we will explore further in Chapter 17): "There is a dynamic here that is going on at many levels between the two of you as you sort out this holiday problem. And yet it sounds like it is part of a larger issue, in terms of conversations of how you put together this relationship with your family relationships."

When social workers speak with specificity, clarify meanings, personalize statements, and document the sources of their conclusions, clients are much less likely to misinterpret or project their own feelings or thoughts. Clients like to be clear about what is expected of them and how they are perceived, as well as how and why social workers think and feel as they do about matters discussed in their sessions. Clients also learn vicariously to speak with greater specificity as social workers model sending concrete messages.

Both beginning and experienced social workers face the additional challenge of avoiding inappropriate use of jargon. Unfortunately, jargon has pervaded professional discourse and runs rampant in social work literature and case records. Its use confuses, rather than clarifies, meanings for clients. The careless use of jargon with colleagues also fosters stereotypical thinking and is therefore antithetical to the cardinal value of individualizing the client. Furthermore, labels tend to conjure up images of clients that vary from one social worker to another, thereby injecting a significant source of error into communication. Consider the lack of specificity in the following messages that are rich in jargon:

- "Mrs. N manifests strong passive-aggressive tendencies."
- "Sean displayed adequate impulse control in the group and tested the leader's authority in a positive manner."
- "Hal needs assistance in gaining greater self-control."
- "The client shows some borderline characteristics."
- "The group members were able to respond to appropriate limits."
- "Ruth appears to be emotionally immature for an eighth-grader."

EP 2.1.1d

To accurately convey information about clients to your colleagues, you must explicitly describe their behavior and document the sources of your conclusions. For example, with the vague message, "Ruth appears to be emotionally immature for an eighth-grader," consider how much more accurately another social worker would perceive your client if you conveyed information in the form of a concrete response: "The teacher says Ruth is quiet and stays to herself in school. She doesn't answer any questions in class unless directly called upon, and she often doesn't complete her assignments. She spends considerable time daydreaming or playing with objects." By describing behavior in this way, you avoid biasing your colleague's perceptions of clients by conveying either vague impressions or erroneous conclusions.

It has been our experience that mastery of the skill of communicating with specificity is gained only through extended and determined effort. The task becomes more complicated if you are not aware that your communication is vague. We recommend that you carefully and consistently monitor your recorded sessions and your everyday conversations with a view toward identifying instances in which you did or did not communicate with specificity. This kind of monitoring will enable you to set relevant goals for yourself and to chart your progress. We also recommend that you enlist your practicum instructor to provide feedback about your performance level on this vital skill.

Exercises in Seeking Concreteness

In the following exercises, you should formulate written responses that will elicit concrete data regarding clients' problems. You may wish to combine your responses with either an empathic response or a paraphrase. Reviewing the eight guidelines for seeking concreteness as you complete the exercise will assist you in developing effective responses and help you to clearly conceptualize the various dimensions of this skill as well. After you have finished the exercises, compare your responses with the modeled responses.

Client Statements

1. **Adolescent** [*speaking of his recent recommitment to a correctional institution*]: It really seems weird to be back here.
2. **Client:** You can't depend on friends; they'll stab you in the back every time.
3. **Client:** He's got a terrible temper—that's the way he is, and he'll never change.

4. *Client:* My supervisor is so insensitive, you can't believe it. All she thinks about are reports and deadlines.
5. *Client:* I was upset after I left your office last week. I felt you really didn't understand what I was saying and didn't care how I felt.
6. *Client:* My dad's 58 years old now, but I swear he still hasn't grown up. He always has a chip on his shoulder.
7. *Elder client:* My rheumatoid arthritis has affected my hands a lot. It gets to be kind of tricky when I'm handling pots and pans in the kitchen.
8. *Client:* I just have this uneasy feeling about going to the doctor. I guess I've really got a hang-up about it.
9. *African American student* [to African American social worker]: You ask why I don't talk to my teacher about why I'm late for school. I'll tell you why. Because she's white, that's why. She's got it in for us black students, and there's just no point talking to her. That's just the way it is.
10. *Client:* John doesn't give a damn about me. I could kick the bucket, and he wouldn't lose a wink of sleep.

Modeled Responses
1. "Can you tell me how it feels weird to you?"
2. "I gather you feel that your friends have let you down in the past. Could you give me a recent example in which this has happened?"
3. "Could you tell me more about what happens when he loses his temper with you?" or "You sound like you don't have much hope that he'll ever get control of his temper. How have you concluded he will never change?" [*A social worker might explore each aspect of the message separately.*]
4. "Could you give me some examples of how she is insensitive to you?"
5. "Sounds like you've been feeling hurt and disappointed over my reaction last week. I can sense you're struggling with those same feelings right now. "It sounds as if you feel that your dad's way of communicating with you is unusual for someone his age. Could you recall some recent examples of times you've had difficulties with how he communicates with you?"
6. "It sounds as if the arthritis pain is aggravating and blocking what you normally do. When you say that handling the pots and pans is kind of tricky, can you tell me about recent examples of what has happened when you are cooking?"
7. "Think of going to the doctor just now. Let your feelings flow naturally. *[Pause.]* What goes on inside you—your thoughts and feelings?"
8. "So you see it as pretty hopeless. You feel pretty strongly about Ms. Wright. I'd be interested in hearing what's happened that has led you to the conclusion she's got it in for black students."
9. "So you feel as if you're nothing in his eyes. I'm wondering how you've reached that conclusion?"

Focusing: A Complex Skill

EP 2.1.10b

Skills in focusing are critical to your practice for several reasons. Because your time with clients is limited, it is critical to make the best use of each session by honing in on key topics. You are also responsible for guiding the helping process and avoiding wandering. Helping relationships should be characterized by purposeful focus and continuity, unlike normal social relations. As social workers, we perform a valuable role by assisting clients to focus on their problems in greater depth and to maintain focus until they accomplish desired changes.

In addition, families and groups sometimes experience interactional difficulties that prevent them from focusing effectively on their problems. To enhance family and group functioning, social workers must be able to refocus the discussion whenever dysfunctional interactional processes cause families and groups to prematurely drift away from the topic at hand.

To assist you in learning how to focus effectively, we consider the three functions of focusing skills:

1. Selecting topics for exploration
2. Exploring topics in depth
3. Maintaining focus and keeping on topic

Knowledge of these functions will enable you to focus sharply on relevant topics and elicit sufficient data to formulate an accurate problem assessment—a prerequisite for competent practice.

Selecting Topics for Exploration

Areas relevant for exploration vary from situation to situation. However, clients who have contact with social workers in the same setting, such as in nursing homes, group homes, or child welfare agencies, may share many common concerns.

Before meeting with clients whose concerns differ from client populations with which you are familiar, you can prepare yourself to conduct an effective exploration by developing (in consultation with your practicum instructor or field supervisor) a list of relevant and promising problem areas to be explored. This preparation will help you avoid a mistake commonly made by some beginning social workers—namely, focusing on areas irrelevant to clients' problems and eliciting reams of information of questionable utility.

EP 2.1.10d

In your initial interview with an institutionalized youth, for example, you could more effectively select questions and responses if you knew in advance that you might explore the following areas:

1. Client's own perceptions of the concerns at hand
2. Client's perceived strengths and resources
3. Reasons for being institutionalized and brief history of past problems related to legal authority and to use of drugs and alcohol
4. Details regarding the client's relationships with individual family members, both as concerns and sources of support
5. Brief family history
6. School adjustment, including information about grades, problem subjects, areas of interest, and relationships with various teachers
7. Adjustment to institutional life, including relationships with peers and supervisors
8. Peer relationships outside the institution
9. Life goals and more short-term goals
10. Reaction to previous experiences with helpers
11. Attitude toward engaging in a working relationship to address concerns

Because the institutionalized youth is an involuntary client, part of this exploration would include the youth's understanding of which parts of his work are nonnegotiable requirements, and which parts could be negotiated or free choices (Rooney, R. H., 2009).

Similarly, if you plan to interview a self-referred middle-aged woman whose major complaint is depression, the following topical areas could assist you in conducting an initial interview:

1. Concerns as she sees them, including the nature of depressive symptoms such as sleep patterns and appetite changes
2. Client's perceived strengths and resources
3. Health status, date of last physical examination, and medications being taken
4. Onset and duration of depression, previous depressive or manic episodes
5. Life events associated with onset of depression (especially losses)
6. Possible suicidal thoughts, intentions, or plans
7. Problematic thought patterns (e.g., self-devaluation, self-recrimination, guilt, worthlessness, helplessness, hopelessness)
8. Previous coping efforts, previous treatment
9. Quality of interpersonal relationships (e.g., interpersonal skills and deficiencies, conflicts and supports in marital and parent–child relationships)
10. Reactions of significant others to her depression
11. Support systems (adequacy and availability)
12. Daily activities
13. Sense of mastery versus feelings of inadequacy
14. Family history of depression or manic behavior

Because she is self-referred, this client is likely to be more voluntary than the institutionalized youth. You should therefore pay more attention to identifying the specific concerns that have led her to seek help at this point in time.

As noted previously, problem areas vary, and outlines of probable topical areas likewise vary accordingly. Thus, a list of areas for exploration in an initial session with a couple seeking marriage counseling or with a group of alcoholics will include a number of items that differ from those in the first list (i.e., the areas identified for the institutionalized youth). Note, however, that items 1, 2, and 8–11 would likely be included in all exploratory interviews with individual clients and would be equally applicable to preparatory interviews with prospective group members.

In using an outline, you should avoid following it rigidly or using it as a crutch; otherwise, you could potentially destroy the spontaneity of sessions and block clients from relating their stories in their own way. Instead, encourage your clients to discuss their problems freely while you play a facilitative role in exploring in greater depth any problems that emerge. In particular, you must use outlines flexibly—reordering the sequence of topics; modifying, adding, or deleting topics; or abandoning the outline altogether if using it hinders communication. You need to be alert to pacing related to appropriate depth and breadth given the time available.

Of course, you cannot always anticipate fruitful topical areas. After all, although clients from the same population may share many commonalities, their problems inevitably have unique aspects. For this reason, it is important to review tapes of sessions with your practicum instructor or a field supervisor for the purpose of identifying other topical areas you should explore in future sessions.

Exploring Topics in Depth

A major facet of focusing is centering discussions on relevant topics to assure that exploration moves from generality and superficiality to greater depth and meaning. Social workers must have the skills needed to explore problems thoroughly, because their success in the helping process depends on their ability to obtain clear and accurate definitions of problems.

EP 2.1.10d

Selectively attending to specific topics is challenging for beginning social workers, who often wander in individual or group sessions, repeatedly skipping across the surface of vital areas of content and feelings, and eliciting largely superficial and sometimes distorted information. This tendency is illustrated in the following excerpt from a first session with an adolescent in a school setting:

Social worker: Tell me about your family.

Client: My father is ill and my mother is dead, so we live with my sister.

Social worker: How are things with you and your sister?

Client: Good. We get along fine. She treats me pretty good.

Social worker: How about your father?

Client: We get along pretty well. We have our problems, but most of the time things are okay. I don't really see him very much.

Social worker: Tell me about school. How are you getting along here?

Client: Well, I don't like it very well, but my grades are good enough to get me by.

Social worker: I notice you're new to our school this year. How did you do in the last school you attended?

By focusing superficially on the topics of family and school, this social worker misses opportunities to explore potential problem areas in the depth necessary to illuminate the client's situation. Not surprisingly, this exploration yielded little information of value, in large part because the social worker failed to employ responses that focused in depth on topical areas. In the next sections, we further delineate the skills that will considerably enhance a social worker's ability to maintain focus on specific areas.

Open-Ended Responses

Social workers may employ open-ended responses throughout individual, conjoint, and group sessions to focus unobtrusively on desired topics. Earlier we noted that some open-ended responses leave clients free to choose their own topics, whereas others focus on a topic but encourage clients to respond freely to that topic. The following examples, taken from an initial session with a mother of eight children who has depression, illustrate how social workers can employ open-ended responses to define topical areas that may yield a rich trove of information vital to grasping the dynamics of the client's problems.[2]

- *"What have you thought that you might like to accomplish in our work together?"*
- *"You've discussed many topics in the last few minutes. Could you pick the most important one and tell me more about it?"*
- *"You've mentioned that your oldest son doesn't come home after school as he did before and help you with the younger children. I would like to hear more about that."*
- *"Several times as you've mentioned your concern that your husband may leave you, your voice has trembled. I wonder if you could share what you are feeling."*
- *"You've indicated that your partner doesn't help you enough with the children. You also seem to be saying that you feel overwhelmed and inadequate in managing the children by yourself. Tell me what happens as you try to manage your children."*
- *"You indicate that you have more problems with your 14-year-old daughter than with the other children. Tell me more about Janet and your problems with her."*

In the preceding examples, the social worker's open-ended questions and responses progressively moved the exploration from the general to the specific. Note also that each response or question defined a new topic for exploration.

To encourage in-depth exploration of the topics defined in this way, the social worker must blend open-ended questions with other facilitative verbal following responses that focus on and elicit expanded client expressions. After having defined a topical area by employing an open-ended response, for instance, the social worker might deepen the exploration by weaving other open-ended responses into the discussion. If the open-ended responses shift the focus to another area, however, the exploration suffers a setback. Note in the following exchange how the social worker's second open-ended response shifts the focus away from the client's message, which involves expression of intense feelings:

Social worker: You've said you're worried about retiring. I'd appreciate you sharing more about your concern. *[Open-ended response.]*

Client: I can't imagine not going to work every day. I feel at loose ends already, and I haven't even quit work. I'm afraid I just won't know what to do with myself.

Social worker: How do you imagine spending your time after retiring? *[Open-ended response.]*

Even though open-ended responses may draw out new information about clients' problems, they may not facilitate the helping process if they prematurely lead the client in a different direction. If social workers utilize open-ended or other types of responses that frequently change the topic, they will obtain information that is disjointed and fragmented. As a result, assessments will suffer from large gaps in the social worker's knowledge concerning clients' problems. As social workers formulate open-ended responses, they must be acutely aware of the direction that responses will take.

Seeking Concreteness

Earlier we discussed and illustrated the various facets of seeking concreteness. Because seeking concreteness enables social workers to move from the general to the specific and to explore topics in depth, it is a key focusing technique. We illustrate this ability in an excerpt from a session involving a client with a serious and persistent mental illness:

Client: I just don't have energy to do anything. This medicine really knocks me out.

Social worker: It sounds as if the side effects of your medication are of concern. Can you tell me specifically what those side effects have been?

By focusing in depth on topical areas, social workers are able to discern—and to assist clients to discern—problematic thoughts, behavior, and interaction. Subsequent sections consider how social workers can effectively focus on topical areas in exploratory sessions

by blending concreteness with other focusing skills. In actuality, the majority of responses that social workers typically employ to establish and maintain focus are blends of various types of discrete responses.

Empathic Responding

Empathic responding serves a critical function by enabling social workers to focus in depth on troubling feelings, as illustrated in the next example:

Client: I can't imagine not going to work every day. I feel at loose ends already, and I haven't even quit work. I'm afraid I just won't know what to do with myself.

Social worker: You seem to be saying, "Even now, I'm apprehensive about retiring. I'm giving up something that has been very important to me, and I don't seem to have anything to replace it." I gather that feeling at loose ends, as you do, you worry that when you retire, you'll feel useless.

Client: I guess that's a large part of my problem. Sometimes I feel useless now. I just didn't take time over the years to develop any hobbies or to pursue any interests. I guess I don't think that I can do anything else.

Social worker: It sounds as if part of you feels hopeless about the future, as if you have done everything you can do. And yet I wonder if another part of you might think that it isn't too late to look into some new interests.

Client: I do dread moping around home with time on my hands. I can just see it now. My wife will want to keep me busy doing things around the house for her all the time. I've never liked to do that kind of thing. I suppose it is never too late to look into other interests. I have always wanted to write some things for fun, not just for work. You know, the memory goes at my age, but I have thought about just writing down some of the family stories.

Note how the client's problem continued to unfold as the social worker utilized empathic responding, revealing rich information in the process. The social worker also raises the possibility of new solutions, not just dwelling in the feelings of uselessness.

Blending Open-Ended, Empathic, and Concrete Responses to Maintain Focus

After employing open-ended responses to focus on a selected topic, social workers should use other responses to maintain focus on that topic. In the following excerpt, observe how the social worker employs both open-ended and empathic responses to explore problems in depth, thereby enabling the client to move to the heart of her struggle. Notice also the richness of the client's responses elicited by the blended messages.

Social worker: As you were speaking about your son, I sensed some pain and reluctance on your part to talk about him. I'd like to understand more about what you're feeling. Could you share with me how it is for you to be talking about him? *[Blended empathic and open-ended response that seeks concreteness.]*

Client: I guess I haven't felt too good about coming this morning. I almost called and canceled. I feel I should be able to handle these problems with Jim [son] myself. Coming here is like having to admit I'm no longer capable of coping with him.

Social worker: So you've had reservations about coming *[paraphrase]*—you feel you're admitting defeat and that perhaps you've failed or that you're inadequate—and that hurts. *[Empathic response.]*

Client: Well, yes, although I know that I need some help. It's just hard to admit it, I think. My biggest problem in this regard, however, is my husband. He feels much more strongly than I do that we should manage this problem ourselves, and he really disapproves of my coming in.

Social worker: So even though it's painful for you, you're convinced you need some assistance with Jim, but you're torn about coming here because of your husband's attitude. I'd be interested in hearing more about that. *[Blended empathic and open-ended response.]*

In the preceding example, the social worker initiated discussion of the client's here-and-now experiences through a blended open-ended and empathic response, following it with other empathic and blended responses to explore the client's feelings further. With the last response, the social worker narrowed the focus to a potential obstacle to the helping process (the husband's attitude toward therapy), which could also be explored in a similar manner.

Open-ended and empathic responses may also be blended to facilitate and encourage discussion from group members about a defined topic. For instance, after using an open-ended response to solicit group feedback regarding a specified topic ("I'm wondering how you feel about ..."), the social worker can employ empathic or other facilitative responses to acknowledge the contribution of members who respond to the invitation to comment.

By utilizing open-ended responses, the social worker can successively reach for comments of individual members who have not contributed ("What do you think about …, Ray?").

In the next example, the social worker blends empathic and concrete responses to facilitate in-depth exploration. Notice how these blended responses yield behavioral referents of the problem. The empathic messages convey the social worker's sensitive awareness and concern for the client's distress. The open-ended and concrete responses focus on details of a recent event and yield valuable clues that the client's rejections by women may be associated with insensitive and inappropriate social behavior. Awareness of this behavior is a prelude to formulating relevant goals. Goals formulated in this way are highly relevant to the client.

Single male client, age 20: There has to be something wrong with me, or women wouldn't treat me like a leper. Sometimes I feel like I'm doomed to be alone the rest of my life. I'm not even sure why I came to see you. I think I'm beyond help.

Social worker: You sound like you've given up on yourself—as though you're utterly hopeless. At the same time, it seems like part of you still clings to hope and wants to try. *[Empathic response.]*

Client: What else can I do? I can't go on like this, but I don't know how many more times I can get knocked down and get back up.

Social worker: I sense you feel deeply hurt and discouraged at those times. Could you give me a recent example of when you felt you were being knocked down? *[Blended empathic and concrete response.]*

Client: Well, a guy I work with got me a blind date for a dance. I took her, and it was a total disaster. I figured that she would at least let me take her home. After we got to the dance, she ignored me the whole night and danced with other guys. Then, to add insult to injury, she went home with one of them and didn't even have the decency to tell me. There I was, wondering what had happened to her.

Social worker: Besides feeling rejected, you must have been very mad. When did you first feel you weren't hitting it off with her? *[Blended empathic and concrete response.]*

Client: I guess it was when she lit up a cigarette while we were driving to the dance. I kidded her about how she was asking for lung cancer.

Social worker: I see. What was it about her reaction, then, that led you to believe you might not be in her good graces? *[Concrete response.]*

Client: Well, she didn't say anything. She just smoked her cigarette. I guess I really knew then that she was upset at me.

Social worker: As you look back at it now, what do you think you might have said to repair things at that point? *[Stimulating reflection about problem solving.]*

In the next example, observe how the social worker blends empathic and concrete responses to elicit details of interaction in an initial conjoint session. Such blending is a potent technique for eliciting specific and abundant information that bears directly on clients' problems. Responses that seek concreteness elicit details. In contrast, empathic responses enable social workers to stay attuned to clients' moment-by-moment experiencing, thereby focusing on feelings that may present obstacles to the exploration.

Social worker: You mentioned having difficulties communicating. I'd like you to give me an example of a time when you felt you weren't communicating effectively, and let's go through it step by step to see if we can understand more clearly what is happening.

Wife: Well, weekends are an example. Usually I want to go out and do something fun with the kids, but John just wants to stay home. He starts criticizing me for wanting to go, go, go.

Social worker: Could you give me a specific example? *[Seeking concreteness.]*

Wife: Okay. Last Saturday I wanted all of us to go out to eat and then to a movie, but John wanted to stay home and watch TV.

Social worker: Before we get into what John did, let's stay with you for a moment. There you are, really wanting to go to a movie—tell me exactly what you did. *[Seeking concreteness.]*

Wife: I think I said, "John, let's take the kids out to dinner and a movie."

Social worker: Okay. That's what you said. How did you say it? *[Seeking concreteness.]*

Wife: I expected him to say no, so I might not have said it the way I just did.

Social worker: Turn to John, and say it the way you may have said it then. *[Seeking concreteness.]*

Wife: Okay. *[Turning to husband.]* Couldn't we go out to a movie?

Social worker: There seems to be some doubt in your voice as to whether John wants to go out. *[Focusing observation.]*

Wife [interrupting]: I knew he wouldn't want to.

Social worker: So you assumed he wouldn't want to go. It's as though you already knew the answer. *[To husband.]* Does the way your wife asked the question check out with the way you remembered it? *[Husband nods.]*

Social worker: After your wife asked you about going to the movie, what did you do? *[Seeking concreteness.]*

Husband: I said, nope! I wanted to stay home and relax Saturday, and I felt we could do things at home.

Social worker: So your answer was short. Apparently you didn't give her information about why you didn't want to go but just said no. Is that right? *[Focusing observation.]*

Husband: That's right. I didn't think she wanted to go anyway—the way she asked.

Social worker: What were you experiencing when you said no? *[Seeking concreteness.]*

Husband: I guess I was just really tired. I have a lot of pressures from work, and I just need some time to relax. She doesn't understand that.

Social worker: You're saying, then, "I just needed some time to get away from it all," but I take it you had your doubts as to whether she could appreciate your feelings. *[Husband nods.]* *[Turning to wife.]* Now, after your husband said no, what did you do? *[Blended empathic and concrete response.]*

Wife: I think that I started talking to him about the way he just sits around the house.

Social worker: I sense that you felt hurt and somewhat discounted because John didn't respond the way you would have liked. *[Empathic response.]*

Wife [nods]: I didn't think he even cared what I wanted to do.

Social worker: Is it fair to conclude, then, that the way in which you handled your feelings was to criticize John rather than to say, "This is what is happening to me?" *[Wife nods.]* *[Seeking concreteness.]*

Social worker [to husband]: Back, then, to our example. What did you do when your wife criticized you? *[Seeking concreteness.]*

Husband: I guess I criticized her back. I told her she needed to stay home once in a while and get some work done.

In this series of exchanges, the social worker asked questions that enabled the couple to describe the sequence of their interaction in a way that elicited key details and provided insight into unspoken assumptions and messages.

Managing Obstacles to Focusing

EP 2.1.10m

Occasionally you may find that your efforts to focus selectively and to explore topical areas in depth do not yield pertinent information. Although you have a responsibility in such instances to assess the effectiveness of your own interviewing style, you should also analyze clients' styles of communicating to determine to what extent their behaviors are interfering with your focusing efforts. Many clients seek help because they have—but are not aware of—patterns of communications or behaviors that create difficulties in relationships. In addition, involuntary clients who do not yet perceive the relationship as helping may be inclined to avoid focusing. The following list highlights common types of client communications that may challenge your efforts to focus in individual, family, and group sessions:

- *Responding with "I don't know"*
- *Changing the subject or avoiding sensitive areas*
- *Rambling from topic to topic*
- *Intellectualizing or using abstract or general terms*
- *Diverting focus from the present to the past*
- *Responding to questions with questions*
- *Interrupting excessively*
- *Failing to express opinions when asked*
- *Producing excessive verbal output*
- *Using humor or sarcasm to evade topics or issues*
- *Verbally dominating the discussion*

You can easily see how individuals who did not seek help from a social worker and want to avoid focusing might use these kinds of methods to protect their privacy. With such involuntary clients, such behaviors are likely to indicate a low level of trust and a skepticism that contact with a social worker can be helpful. You can counter repetitive behaviors and communications that divert the focus from exploring problems by tactfully drawing them to clients' attention and by assisting clients to adopt behaviors that are compatible with practice objectives. In groups, social workers must assist group members to modify behaviors that repeatedly disrupt effective focusing and communication;

otherwise, the groups will not move to the phase of group development in which most of the work related to solving problems is accomplished. Children as clients often respond at first contact in a limited, passive, nonexpressive style. This might be interpreted as noncommunicative behavior. In fact, such behavior is often what the children expect to be appropriate in interactions with strange authority figures (Evans, 2004; Hersen & Thomas, 2007; Lamb & Brown, 2006; Powell, Thomson, & Dietze, 1997).

> **VIDEO CASE EXAMPLE**
>
> In the video "Hanging with Hailey" (HWH), the adolescent client Hailey is apprehensive about having to see a social worker and insisting that she has done nothing wrong, has not gotten into trouble. The social worker Emily clarifies that Hailey can choose whether she wants to see a social worker, that she had not done anything wrong, but that teachers who knew her to be a good student had become concerned that something might have changed in her life to affect her school performance. By emphasizing her choice, Emily is able to allow Hailey to relax enough to share some of what is going on in her life currently.

Social workers may use many different techniques for managing and modifying client obstacles. These techniques include asking clients to communicate or behave differently; teaching, modeling for, and coaching clients to assume more effective communication styles; reinforcing facilitative responses; and selectively attending to functional behaviors.

Intervening to Help Clients Focus or Refocus

Communications that occur in group or conjoint sessions are not only complex, but may also be distractive or irrelevant. Consequently, the social worker's task of assisting members to explore the defined topics fully, rather than meander from subject to subject, is a challenging one. Related techniques that social workers can employ include highlighting or clarifying issues and bringing clients' attention to a comment or matter that has been overlooked. In such instances, the objective is not necessarily to explore the topic (although an exploration may subsequently occur), but rather to stress or elucidate important content. The social worker focuses clients' attention on communications and/or events that occurred earlier in the session or immediately preceded the social worker's focusing response. This technique is used in the following messages:

- [To son in session with parents]: *"Ray, you made an important point a moment ago that I'm not sure your parents heard. Would you please repeat your comment?"*
- [To individual]: *"I would like to return to a remark made several moments ago when you said _____. I didn't want to interrupt then. I think perhaps the remark was important enough that we should return to it now."*
- [To family]: *"Something happened just a minute ago as we were talking. [Describes event.] We were involved in another discussion then, but I made a mental note of it because of how deeply it seemed to affect all of you at the time. I think we should consider what happened for just a moment."*
- [To group member]: *"John, as you were talking a moment ago, I wasn't sure what you meant by _____. Could you clarify that for me and for others in the group?"*
- [To group]: *"A few minutes ago, we were engrossed in a discussion about _____, yet we have moved away from that discussion to one that doesn't really seem to relate to our purpose for being here. I'm concerned about leaving the other subject hanging because you were working hard to find some solutions and appeared to be close to a breakthrough."*

Because of the complexity of communications in group and family sessions, some inefficiency in the focusing process is inescapable. Nevertheless, the social worker can sharpen the group's efforts to focus and encourage more efficient use of its time by teaching effective focusing behavior. We suggest that social workers actually explain the focusing role of the group and identify desirable focusing behaviors, such as attending, active listening, and asking open-ended questions. During this discussion, it is important to emphasize that by utilizing these skills, members will facilitate exploration of problems.

Social workers can encourage greater use of these skills by giving positive feedback to group or family members when they have adequately focused on a problem, thus reinforcing their efforts. Indeed, given the difficulties in encouraging some clients to speak even minimally, some social workers can be so relieved to have a verbal client that they neglect use of their focusing skills that might the session most valuable and useful to the client. Although group members usually experience some difficulty in learning how to focus, they should be able to delve deeply into problems by the third or fourth session, given sufficient guidance and education by social workers. Such efforts by social workers tend to accelerate movement of groups toward maturity, a phase in which members achieve maximum therapeutic benefits. A characteristic of a group in this phase, in fact, is that members explore issues in considerable depth rather than skim the surface of many topics.

Summarizing Responses

The technique of summarization embodies four distinct and yet related facets:

1. Highlighting key aspects of discussions of specific problems before changing the focus of the discussion
2. Making connections between relevant aspects of lengthy client messages
3. Reviewing major focal points of a session and tasks that clients plan to work on before the next session
4. Recapitulating the highlights of a previous session and reviewing clients' progress on tasks during the week for the purpose of providing focus and continuity between sessions

Although employed at different times and in different ways, each of these facets of summarization serves the common purpose of tying together functionally related elements that occur at different points in the helping process. They are considered in detail in the following sections.

Highlighting Key Aspects of Problems

During the phase of an initial session in which problems are explored in moderate depth, summarization can be effectively employed to tie together and highlight essential aspects of a problem before proceeding to explore additional problems. For example, the social worker might describe how the problem appears to be produced by the interplay of several factors, including external pressures, overt behavioral patterns, unfulfilled needs and wants, and covert thoughts and feelings. Connecting these key elements assists clients in gaining a more accurate and complete perspective of their circumstances.

Employed in this fashion, summarization involves fitting pieces of the problem together to form a coherent whole. Seeing the situation in a fresh and more accurate perspective often proves beneficial, because it expands clients' awareness and can generate hope and enthusiasm for tackling an issue that has hitherto seemed insurmountable.

Summarization that highlights problems is generally employed at a natural point in the session when the social worker believes that relevant aspects of the problem have been adequately explored and clients appear satisfied in having had the opportunity to express their concerns. The following example illustrates this type of summarization. In this case, the client, an 80-year-old widow, has been referred to a Services to Seniors program for exploration of alternative living arrangements because of her failing health, isolation, and recent falls. As the two have worked together to explore alternative living arrangements, the pair have identified several characteristics that would be important for the client in an improved living situation. Highlighting the salient factors, the social worker summarizes the results to this point:

Social worker: It sounds as if you are looking for a situation in which there is social interaction but your privacy is also important to you: You want to maintain your independence. You also want to have someone available to help in emergencies and some assistance with cooking and cleaning.

Summarizing responses of this type serve as a prelude to the process of formulating goals, as goals flow naturally from problem formulations. Moreover, highlighting various dimensions of the problem facilitates the subsequent identifications of subgoals and tasks that must be accomplished to achieve the overall goal. In the preceding example, to explore an improved living situation, the social worker would help the client analyze the specific form of privacy (whether living alone or with someone else) and the type of social interaction (how much and what kind of contact with others) she desires.

Summarizing salient aspects of problems is a valuable technique in sessions with groups, couples, and families. It enables the social worker to stop at timely moments and highlight the difficulties experienced by each participant. In a family session with a pregnant adolescent and her mother, for example, the social worker might make the following statements:

- [To pregnant adolescent]: *"You feel as if deciding what to do about this baby is your decision—it's your body and you have decided that an abortion is the best solution for you. You know that you have the legal right to make this decision and want to be supported in making it. You feel as if your mother wants to help but can't tell you what decision to make."*

- [To mother]: *"As you spoke, you seemed saddened and very anxious about this decision your daughter is making. You are saying 'I care about my daughter, but I don't think she is mature enough to make this decision on her own.' As you have noted, women in your family have had a hard time conceiving, and you wish that she would consider other options besides abortion. So you feel a responsibility to your daughter, but also to this unborn baby and the family history of conceiving children."*

Such responses synthesize in concise and neutral language the needs, concerns, and problems of each participant for all other members of the session to hear. This type of summarization underscores the fact that all participants are struggling with and have responsibility for problems that are occurring, thus counteracting the tendency of families to view one person as the exclusive cause of family problems.

Summarizing Lengthy Messages

Clients' messages range from one word or one sentence to lengthy and sometimes rambling monologues. Although the meaning and significance of brief messages are often readily discernible, lengthy messages challenge the social worker to encapsulate and tie together diverse and complex elements. Linking the elements together often highlights and expands the significance and meaning of the client's message. For this reason, such messages represent one form of additive empathy, a skill discussed in Chapter 17.

Because lengthy client messages typically include emotions, thoughts, and descriptive content, you will need to determine how these dimensions relate to the focal point of the discussion. To illustrate, consider the following message of a mildly brain-damaged and socially withdrawn 16-year-old female—an only child who is extremely dependent on her overprotective but subtly rejecting mother:

Client: Mother tells me she loves me, but I find that hard to believe. Nothing I do ever pleases her; she yells at me when I refuse to wash my hair alone. But I can't do it right without her help. "When are you going to grow up?" she'll say. And she goes out with her friends and leaves me alone in that old house. She knows how scared I get when I have to stay home alone. But she says, "Nancy, I can't just babysit you all the time. I've got to do something for myself. Why don't you make some friends or watch TV or play your guitar? You've just got to quit pitying yourself all the time." Does that sound like someone who loves you? I get so mad at her when she yells at me; it's all I can do to keep from killing her.

Embodied in the client's message are the following elements:

1. Wanting to be loved by her mother, yet feeling insecure and rejected at times
2. Feeling inadequate about performing certain tasks, such as washing her hair
3. Feeling extremely dependent upon her mother for certain services and companionship
4. Feeling afraid when her mother leaves her alone
5. Feeling hurt (implied) and resentful when her mother criticizes her or leaves her alone
6. Feeling intense anger and wanting to lash out when her mother yells at her

The following summarizing response ties these elements together:

Social worker: So you find your feelings toward your mother pulling you in different directions. You want her to love you, but you feel unloved and resent it when she criticizes you or leaves you alone. And you feel really torn because you depend on her in so many ways. Yet at times, you feel so angry you want to hurt her back for yelling at you. You'd like to have a smoother relationship without the strain.

In conjoint interviews or group sessions, summarization can also be used effectively to highlight and to tie together key elements and dynamics embodied in transactions, as illustrated in the following transaction and summarizing responses of a social worker:

> **VIDEO CASE EXAMPLE**
>
> In the conjoint interview entitled "HFH, Part 1," partners who come to family treatment are in conflict about how open to be about their relationship to their families. Jackie comes from a family in which there is open communication. She is frustrated with the reticence to deal openly with feelings that is reflected in Anna's family. Kim, the social worker, makes the following summarizing statement: "Often when we are forming new families and new couples we are torn between the families we come from and the new family we are creating. This can play out in logistical decisions about the holidays."

Occasionally, client messages may ramble to the extent that they contain numerous unrelated elements that cannot all be tied together. In such instances, your task is to extract and focus on those elements of the message that are most relevant to the thrust of the session at that point. When employed in this manner, summarization provides focus and direction to the session and averts aimless wandering. With clients whose thinking is loose or who ramble to avoid having to focus on unpleasant matters, you may need to interrupt to assure some semblance of focus and continuity. Otherwise, the interview will be disjointed and unproductive. Skills in maintaining focus and continuity are discussed later in this chapter and in Chapter 13.

Reviewing Focal Points of a Session

During the course of an individual, conjoint, or group session, it is common to focus on more than one problem and to discuss numerous factors associated with each problem. Toward the end of the first or second session, depending on the length of the initial exploration, summarization is employed to review key concerns that have been discussed and to highlight themes and patterns related to these problems. Summarizing themes and patterns expands each client's awareness of concerns and tunes them in to promising avenues for addressing those concerns, awareness of opportunities and potential resources.

In fact, through summarizing responses, social workers can review themes and patterns that have emerged in their sessions and test clients' readiness to consider goals aimed at modifying these problematic patterns.

> **VIDEO CASE EXAMPLE**
>
> In the video "GBS" Dorothy, the social worker, summarizes: "You have had a lot of stress at work with a poor performance review and anxiety that your co-workers are being rude to you over the possibility that you might get promoted. At home, you are dealing with your mother, who is living with you; your son and his girlfriend not working outside of the home and their baby; your daughter who helps take care of the little ones. All of the work of keeping up the household comes back to you. You are not eating, not sleeping very well, and have lost interest in some things you used to like to do."

Providing Focus and Continuity

The social worker can also use summarization at the beginning of an individual, group, or conjoint session to review work that clients have accomplished in the last session(s) and to set the stage for work in the present session. At the same time, the social worker may decide to identify a promising topic for discussion or to refresh clients' minds concerning work they wish to accomplish in that session. In addition, summarization can be employed periodically to synthesize salient points at the conclusion of a discussion or used at the end of the session to review the major focal points. In so doing, the social worker will need to place what was accomplished in the session within the broad perspective of the clients' goals. The social worker tries to consider how the salient content and movement manifested in each session fit into the larger whole. Only then are the social worker and clients likely to maintain a sense of direction and avoid needless delays caused by wandering and detours—problems that commonly occur when continuity within or between sessions is weak.

Used as a "wrap-up" when the allotted time for a session is nearly gone, summarization assists the social worker to draw a session to a natural conclusion. In addition to highlighting and linking together the key points of the session, the social worker reviews clients' plans for performing tasks before the next session. When the session ends with such a summarization, all participants should be clear about where they have been and where they are going in relation to the goals toward which their mutual efforts are directed.

Analyzing Your Verbal Following Skills

After taking frequency counts over a period of time of some of the major verbal following skills (accents, reflections, paraphrases, concreteness, open-ended and closed-ended responses), you are ready to assess the extent to which you employ, blend, and balance these skills in relation to each other. On the form for recording verbal following (Figure 6-2), categorize each of your responses from a recorded session. As you analyze your relative use and blending of responses alone or with your practicum instructor, determine whether certain types of responses were used either too frequently or too sparingly. Think of steps that you might take to correct any imbalances in your utilization of skills for future sessions.

CLIENT MESSAGE	OPEN-ENDED RESPONSES	CLOSE-ENDED RESPONSES	EMPATHIC RESPONSES	LEVEL OF EMPATHY	CONCRETE RESPONSES	SUMMA-RIZING RESPONSES	OTHER TYPES OF RESPONSES
1.							
2.							
3.							
4.							
5.							
6.							
7.							

© Cengage Learning 2013

Directions: Categorize each of your responses from a recorded session. Where responses involve more than one category (blended responses), record them as a single response, but also check each category embodied in the response. Excluding the responses checked as "Other Type of Responses," analyze whether certain types of responses were utilized too frequently or too sparingly. Define tasks for yourself to correct imbalances in future sessions. Retain a copy of the form so that you can monitor your progress in mastering verbal following skills over an extended period of time.

FIG-6-2 Recording Form for Verbal Following Skills

Summary

This chapter has helped you learn how to explore, paraphrase, and appropriately use closed- and open-ended responses as a means of better focusing, following, and summarizing in your social work practice. These skills may be applied both with clients and with other persons and colleagues, on behalf of clients. In Chapter 7, we will explore some common difficulties experienced by beginning social workers and some ways to overcome them.

CourseMate

Access an integrated eBook and chapter-specific learning tools including glossary terms, chapter outlines, relevant web links, videos, and practice quizzes. Go to **www.cengagebrain.com**.

CHAPTER 7

Avoiding Counterproductive Communication Patterns

CHAPTER OVERVIEW

Chapter 7 explores communication difficulties that often arise in the practice of beginning (and many experienced) social workers and suggest some positive alternatives to these defective patterns. By becoming alert to these difficulties, beginning social workers can focus their attention on communicating in a constructive fashion. In addition to applications in direct practice, the chapter provides numerous communication examples related to both meso and macro practice. As with the previous chapters, additional video examples are included in the accompanying CourseMate for *Direct Social Work Practice* at www.cengagebrain.com.

As a result of reading this chapter and practicing with classmates, you will be able to:

- Identify when you have experienced an error or counterproductive pattern in your verbal and nonverbal behavior
- Identify more constructive alternatives in those instances

EPAS COMPETENCIES IN THE 7TH CHAPTER

This chapter will give you the information needed to meet the following practice competencies:

2.1.1   identify as a professional social worker and conduct ones self accordingly.

2.1.1b Practice personal reflection and self-correction to assure continual professional development

2.1.1c Attend to professional roles and boundaries

2.1.1d Demonstrate professional demeanor in behavior, appearance and communication

2.1.4c Recognize and communicate the importance of their understanding of difference in shaping life experiences.

2.1.10 Engage, assess, intervene, and evaluate with individuals, families, groups, organizations and communities:

2.1.10a Substantively and effectively prepare for action with individuals, families, and groups

2.1.10b Use empathy and other interpersonal skills

Impacts of Counterproductive Communication Patterns

EP 2.1.1 & 2.1.10a

We all want to experience error free learning. Even experienced social workers commit communication errors. Each of the authors who developed videos for this text made communication errors in our videos (some of which we will share with you). We trust, however, that each of us improves by examining our practice. Rather than dwell on their errors, competent, ethical social workers seek to replace those errors with more productive patterns. One of the most common and understandable errors of beginners is that you are so focused on saying exactly the right thing that you have little attention left to carefully listen to the client. In this chapter, we will help you be aware of potential errors. However, noticing errors is not enough. Just as focusing on failure with clients is unlikely to support self-efficacy and self-confidence, we will explore more productive ways to deal with those errors. In some cases, this means referring back to content in earlier chapters. At the end of your work on this chapter, it is our hope that you will both be aware of things you need to work on *and* that you will feel increasingly confident in your abilities to replace those errors with more productive responses.

Previous research provides direction for identifying those errors and suggests that improvements can occur. A study of beginning student practice, based on the analysis of 674 role-play videos completed by 396 BSW and 276 MSW students, revealed patterns of frequent errors, which will be reviewed in the following (Ragg, Okagbue-Reaves, & Piers, 2007). Nugent and Halvorson (1995) demonstrated how differently worded active-listening responses may lead to different short-term client affective outcomes.

Eliminating Nonverbal Barriers to Effective Communication

EP 2.1.1d

Nonverbal behaviors strongly influence interactions between people. The importance of this medium of communication is underscored by the fact that social worker's nonverbal interview behavior contributes significantly to ratings of counselor effectiveness. Nonverbal cues, which serve to confirm or to deny messages conveyed verbally, are in large part beyond the conscious awareness of participants. In fact, they may produce "leakage" by transmitting information that the sender did not intend to communicate to the receiver. Facial expressions—a blush, a sneer, or a look of shock or dismay, for example—convey much more about the social worker's attitude toward the client than what is said aloud. In fact, if there is a discrepancy between the social worker's verbal and nonverbal communication, the client is more likely to discredit the verbal message. Over time, people learn through myriad transactions with others that nonverbal cues more accurately indicate feelings than do spoken words. You are more likely to attend to these errors if you have opportunities to view your practice in videos.

Physical Attending

Beginning social workers are often relatively unaware of their nonverbal behaviors, and they may not have learned to consciously use these behaviors to advantage in conveying caring, understanding, and respect. Therefore, mastering physical attending—a basic skill critical to the helping process—is one of the social worker's first learning tasks. Physical attentiveness to another person is communicated by receptive behaviors, such as facing the client squarely, leaning forward, maintaining eye contact, and remaining relaxed.

Attending also requires social workers to be fully present—that is, to keep in moment-to-moment contact with the client through disciplined attention. Attending in a fully present fashion (though perhaps not relaxed) is expected with beginning social workers despite their typical anxiety about what to do next, how to help, and how to avoid hurting clients. Such skill is more likely to evolve with greater experience after novice social workers have engaged in considerable observation of expert social workers, role-playing, beginning interviews with clients and viewing their own practice.

Cultural Nuances of Nonverbal Cues

EP 2.1.4c

To consciously use nonverbal behaviors to full advantage in transcultural relationships, social workers must be aware that some members of different cultural groups ascribe different meanings to certain nonverbal behaviors. Eye-to-eye contact, for example, is expected behavior among members of mainstream American culture. In fact, people who avoid eye-to-eye contact may be viewed as untrustworthy or evasive. Conversely, members of some Native American tribes regard direct gazing as an intrusion on privacy. It is important to observe and investigate the norms for gazing before employing eye-to-eye contact with members of some tribes (Gross, 1995).[1]

As we have discussed earlier, it is hazardous to make generalizations across ethnic groups. For example, one study reported that Filipino students were more similar to white students than to Chinese students in relation to many attitudes, perceptions, and beliefs. Meanwhile, the same study showed that women were more similar to one another across ethnic groups than they were to men within their own group (Agbayani-Siewart, 2004).

With this proviso in mind, social workers should consider the possibility of differences in cultural assumptions about helping professionals as authorities who can solve problems by providing advice. For instance, in some cultures, a client might not be forthcoming unless they are spoken to by the social worker. The social worker in turn may mistakenly perceive the client's behavior as passive. Consequently, "long gaps of silence may occur as the client waits patiently for the social worker to structure the interview, take charge, and thus provide the solution" (Tsui & Schultz, 1985, p. 565). Such gaps in communication engender anxiety in both parties that may undermine the development of rapport and defeat the helping process. Further, failure to correctly interpret the client's nonverbal behavior may lead the social worker to conclude erroneously that the client has flat affect (i.e., limited emotionality). Given these potential hazards, social workers should strive to understand the client's cultural frame of reference. Clarifying roles and expectation should also be emphasized. Consider being more active with some Asian clients, including placing greater emphasis on clarifying role expectations.

Other Nonverbal Behaviors

EP 2.1.1b

Barriers that prevent the social worker from staying in psychological contact with the client can be caused by preoccupation with judgments or evaluations about the client or by inner pressures to find immediate solutions to the client's problems. In fact, many beginning social workers have prior experience in positions where their job was to quickly assess client circumstances and provide a rapid referral or solution. Such skills are to be valued but not overly generalized such that you short circuit exploration of client concerns and prematurely move to solutions. Likewise, reduced focus on the client can result from being preoccupied with oneself while practicing new skills. Extraneous noise, a ringing phone, an inadequate interviewing room, a pile of paperwork on your lap, checking for text messages, or a lack of privacy can also interfere with the social worker's being psychologically present.

EP 2.1.1d

The social worker may convey a lack of concern for the client by displaying any of numerous undesirable behaviors and revealing postural cues. For example, staring vacantly, looking out the window, frequently glancing at the clock, yawning, and fidgeting suggest a lack of attention; trembling hands or rigid posture may communicate anger or anxiety. These and a host of other behavioral cues that convey messages such as inattention or disrespect are readily perceived by most clients, many of whom are highly sensitive to criticism or rejection in any form. Quite frankly, voluntary clients with sufficient resources and self-esteem are not likely to accept social worker behavior that they consider disrespectful, nor should they. This leaves the social worker with just those involuntary clients with fewer choices, fewer resources, and lower self-esteem, who may believe that they have little recourse other than accepting such behavior.

VIDEO CASE EXAMPLE

The "Work with Probation Officer" video contains an example of such disrespectful nonverbal and verbal behavior, approximating level 0 empathy. Such examples are unfortunately not uncommon in settings dealing with persons who are alleged to have engaged in deviant behavior, such as violence against a partner, in which clients have low power, and the social worker is under time pressure to complete an assessment. Note the social worker in this video calling the client's attention to time pressures and judging how little the client had accomplished in previous anger-management training. Fortunately, you are also able to link to an improved example with the same social worker and client that revisits the same scenario from a much more respectful perspective. In the practice behavior workbook, you will have an opportunity to make a list of the counterproductive social worker behaviors you see in the first example and the corrections demonstratied in the second example.

Taking Inventory of Nonverbal Patterns of Responding

EP 2.1.10b

To assist you in taking inventory of your own styles of responding to clients, Table 7-1 identifies recommended and not recommended nonverbal behaviors. You will probably find that you have a mixed repertoire of nonverbal responses, some of which have the potential to enhance helping relationships and foster client progress. Other, less desirable behaviors of the beginning social worker may include nervousness that may block your clients from freely disclosing information and otherwise limit the flow of the helping process. You thus have a threefold task: (1) to assess your repetitive nonverbal behaviors; (2) to eliminate nonverbal styles that hinder effective communication; and (3) to sustain and perhaps increase desirable nonverbal behaviors. It can assist you here if you are able to arrange to make a video recording of your practice.

At the end of this chapter, you will find a checklist intended for use in training or supervision to obtain feedback on nonverbal aspects of attending. Given the opportunity to review a videotape of your performance in actual or simulated interviews and/or to receive behaviorally specific feedback from supervisors and

TABLE-7-1 INVENTORY OF PRACTITIONER'S NONVERBAL COMMUNICATION

RECOMMENDED	NOT RECOMMENDED
Facial Expressions	
Direct eye contact (except when culturally proscribed)	Avoidance of eye contact
Warmth and concern reflected in facial expression	Staring or fixating on person or object
Eyes at same level as client's	Lifting eyebrow critically
Appropriately varied and animated facial expressions	Eye level higher or lower than client's
Mouth relaxed; occasional smiles	Nodding head excessively
	Yawning
	Frozen-on rigid facial expressions
	Inappropriate slight smile
	Pursing or biting lips
Posture	
Arms and hands moderately expressive; appropriate gestures	Rigid body position; arms tightly folded
Body leaning slightly forward; attentive but relaxed	Body turned at an angle to client
	Fidgeting with hands
	Squirming or rocking in chair
	Leaning back or placing feet on desk
	Hand or fingers over mouth
	Pointing finger for emphasis
Voice	
Clearly audible but not loud	Mumbling or speaking inaudibly
Warmth in tone of voice	Monotonic voice
Voice modulated to reflect nuances of feeling and emotional tone of client messages	Halting speech
	Frequent grammatical errors
Moderate speech tempo	Prolonged silences
	Excessively animated speech
	Slow, rapid, or staccato speech
	Nervous laughter
	Consistent clearing of throat
	Speaking loudly
Physical Proximity	
Three to five feet between chairs	Excessive closeness or distance
	Talking across desk or other barrier

peers, you should be able to adequately master physical aspects of attending in a relatively brief time.

A review of your taped performance may reveal that you are already demonstrating many of the desirable physical attending behaviors listed in Table 7-1. You may also possess personal nonverbal mannerisms that are particularly helpful in establishing relationships with others, such as a friendly grin or a relaxed, easy manner. As you take inventory of your nonverbal behaviors, solicit feedback from others regarding these behaviors. Try to note your behaviors when you are and are not at ease with clients. When appropriate, increase the frequency of recommended behaviors that you have identified. In particular, try to cultivate the quality of warmth, which we discussed in Chapter 5.

As you review videotapes of your sessions, pay particular attention to your nonverbal responses at those moments when you experienced pressure or tension; this assessment will assist you in determining whether your responses were counterproductive. All beginning interviewers experience moments of discomfort in their first contacts with clients, and nonverbal behaviors serve as an index of their comfort level. To enhance your self-awareness of your own behavioral patterns, develop a list of the verbal and nonverbal behaviors you display when you are under pressure. When you review your videotaped sessions, you may notice that under pressure you respond with humor, fidget, change voice inflection, assume a rigid body posture, or manifest other nervous mannerisms.

Making an effort to become aware of and to eliminate obvious signs of anxiety is an important step in achieving mastery of your nonverbal responding.

> **VIDEO CASE EXAMPLE**
>
> In the video "Serving the Squeaky Wheel" the social worker, Ron Rooney, was surprised by questions about his credentials when he became, in the role play, the new case manager for a client with serious and persistent mental illness. Notice how he responded at first defensively, expressing sarcasm and disgruntlement, before he recovered to consider how the client was in fact acting to protect herself from possible exploitation. Part of the answer here is then to notice your own response and regulate. It is often a good rule to assume that the client is not deliberately trying to embarrass you or make you uncomfortable. By listening better, you are often able to uncover other intentions for behaviors that may have inadvertently pushed your buttons. If you discover that in fact the client may indeed have been attempting to provoke you, some reflection about what about the current sitiuation may have contributed to this may be useful. In the particular situation, Cali was describing feeling treated rudely and disrespectfully by her previous worker who had not told her that she would be terminating. Reflecting how you are feeling and linking it to themes the client has shared can be useful. For example, the social worker might have said, "It sounds, Cali, as if you have been feeling as if you have not been treated well recently by your previous social worker in her not coming to closure with you prior to making a transfer to me. Is that right? (if so). I have been feeling a little under fire here recently from you in your questions about my credentials. I am wondering if I am feeling at all like the way you have felt in sensing disrespect or mistreated? Am I off base here?"

refer to reactance theory, which suggests that clients will act to protect valued freedoms (Wright, Greenberg & Brehm, 2004, Brehm & Brehm, 1981). Such freedoms can include the freedom to have one's own opinions and the inclination to action. When such valued freedoms are threatened, clients will often withdraw, argue, or move to a superficial topic.

The following list identifies common verbal barriers that usually have an immediate negative effect on communications, thereby inhibiting clients from revealing pertinent information and working on problems. In each case, we will explore positive alternatives to these barriers.

EP 2.1.1d

1. Reassuring, sympathizing, consoling, or excusing
2. Advising and giving suggestions or solutions prematurely
3. Using sarcasm or employing humor that is distracting or makes light of clients' problems
4. Judging, criticizing, or placing blame
5. Trying to convince the client about the right point of view through logical arguments, lecturing, instructing, or arguing
6. Analyzing, diagnosing, or making glib or dogmatic interpretations
7. Threatening, warning, or counterattacking

The first three behaviors are mistakes that beginning social workers commonly make across a variety of populations and settings, often reflecting their nervousness and an abounding desire to be immediately helpful. Numbers 3–7 are also common, but are more likely to occur when the social worker is working with "captive clients"—a situation in which there is a power differential and the client cannot readily escape. An underlying theme of these behaviors can be the social worker and their agency reflecting a sense of superiority over people whose behaviors or problem solving has been harmful to themselves or to others.

Eliminating Verbal Barriers to Communication

Many types of ineffective verbal responses inhibit clients from exploring problems and sharing freely with the social worker. To understand why, we

Reassuring, Sympathizing, Consoling, or Excusing

- "You'll feel better tomorrow."
- "Don't worry, things will work out."
- "You probably didn't do anything to aggravate the situation."
- "I really feel sorry for you."

A pattern found in 90 percent of the taped interviews completed by beginning students was that they would reassure clients that their responses were normal and that they were not responsible for the difficulty they were concerned about (Ragg, Okagbue-Reaves, Piers, 2007). When used selectively and with justification, well-timed reassurance can engender much needed hope and support. By glibly reassuring clients that "things will work out," "everybody has problems," or "things aren't as bleak as they seem," however, social workers avoid exploring clients' feelings of despair, anger, hopelessness, or helplessness. Situations faced by clients are often grim, with no immediate relief at hand. Rather than gloss over clients' feelings and seek to avoid discomfort, social workers must undertake to explore those distressing feelings and to assist clients in acknowledging painful realities. Beginning social workers need to convey that they hear and understand their clients' difficulties as they experience them. They will also want to convey hope while exploring prospects for change—albeit at the appropriate time in the dialogue.

Reassuring clients prematurely or without a genuine basis for hope often serves the purposes of social workers more than the purposes of clients and, in fact, may represent efforts by social workers to dissuade clients from revealing their troubling feelings. That is, reassurance may serve to restore the comfort level and equilibrium of social workers rather than to help clients. Instead of fostering hope, these glib statements convey a lack of understanding of clients' feelings and raise doubts about the authenticity of social workers. Clients may, in turn, react with thoughts such as "It's easy for you to say that, but you don't know how very frightened I really am," or "You're just saying that so I'll feel better." In addition, responses that excuse clients (e.g., "You're not to blame") or sympathize with their position (e.g., "I can see exactly why you feel that way; I think I would probably have done the same thing") often have the effect of unwittingly reinforcing inappropriate behavior or reducing clients' anxiety and motivation to work on problems.

In place of inappropriate reassurance, more positive and useful response can come from reflecting that you heard and understood what the client was conveying and, in some cases, positive reframing, which does not discount concerns but places them in a different light.

> **VIDEO CASE EXAMPLE**
>
> In the video "Getting Back to Shakopee," the client, Val, begins to describe her concerns about a possible drug relapse. Rather than discount those concerns, the practitioner, Dorothy, asks a coping question about how Val has been managing to cope with the desire to relapse. Instead of saying, "You will feel better tomorrow," a more constructive response would be, "I hear that this has been a very discouraging day for you. You have gotten through some difficult situations in the past. What are some of the ways you have coped with such bad days before?" Similarly, rather than saying, "You probably did not do anything to aggravate the situation" it might be better to reflect, "That sounds like a complicated, disappointing situation. You are sorry that what you tried was not successful." Additional examples of consoling, sympathizing responses and more positive alternatives are contained in the practice workbook.

Advising and Giving Suggestions or Solutions Prematurely

- "I suggest that you move to a new place because you have had so many difficulties here."
- "I think you need to try a new approach with your daughter. Let me suggest that …"
- "I think it would be best for you to try using time-out …"
- "Because your partner is such a loser, why don't you try to create some new relationships with other people?"

Another frequent pattern found in the Ragg, Okagbue-Reaves, and Piers (2007) study was that in 90 percent of the videos of beginning social workers, they would appear at points to turn off from listening to the client and seem to be engaging in an internal dialogue related to formulating a solution to concerns raised. Such patterns may have been fostered in previous work positions and exchanges with friends where the pattern was to move quickly to problem-solving solutions without grasping the larger situation. We do not mean to discount the social worker's capacity to think about a problem and possible solutions. Rather, we want to stress the importance of waiting until the social worker has fully grasped the situation and empathized with the client before moving into a mutual examination of alternatives.

Little is known about the actual provision of advice in terms of its frequency or the circumstances in which it occurs (Brehm & Brehm, 1981). Clients often seek advice, and appropriately timed advice can be an important helping tool. Conversely, untimely advice may elicit opposition. Even when clients solicit advice in early phases of the helping process, they often react negatively when they receive it because the recommended solutions, which are invariably based on superficial information, often do not address their real needs. Further, because clients are frequently burdened and preoccupied with little-understood conflicts, feelings, and pressures, they are not ready to take action on their problems at this point. For these reasons, after offering premature advice, social workers may observe clients replying with responses such as "Yes, but I've already tried that," "That won't work," or "I could try that" with little enthusiasm demonstrated for actually doing so. In fact, these responses can serve as feedback clues that you may have slipped into the habit of giving premature advice.

While many clients seek advice from social workers because they see the social workers as expert problem solvers, those social workers can (wrongly) seek to expedite problem solving by quickly comparing the current situation to other similar ones encountered in the past and recommending a solution that has worked for other clients or themselves. In such cases, social workers may feel pressure to provide quick answers or solutions for clients who unrealistically expect magical answers and instant relief from problems that have plagued them for long periods of time. Beginning social workers may also experience inner pressure to dispense solutions to clients' problems, mistakenly believing that their new role demands that they, like physicians or advice columnists, prescribe a treatment regimen. They thus run the risk of giving advice before they have conducted a thorough exploration of clients' problems. In reality, instead of dispensing wisdom, a major role of social workers is to create and shape processes with clients in which they engage in mutual discovery of problems and solutions—work that will take time and concentrated effort.

Beginning social workers who are working with non-voluntary clients may feel justified in "strongly suggesting" their opinions because of the poor choices or problem solving they may presume landed these clients in their current predicament. As suggested in Chapter 4, social work practice does not have a place for judging clients: We may have to evaluate clients' performance and capabilities in certain circumstances, but that is not the same as judging them as people. Assisting clients through modeling and reinforcement of prosocial behavior is not the same as judging clients and imposing social workers' own opinions (Trotter, 2006).

The timing and form of recommendations are all-important in the helping process. Advice should be offered sparingly, and only after thoroughly exploring the problem and the client's ideas about possible solutions. At that point, the social worker may serve as a consultant, tentatively sharing ideas about solutions to supplement those developed by the client, and assisting them in weighing the pros and cons of different alternatives. Clients who try to pressure social workers to dispense knowledge prematurely are merely depriving themselves of the opportunity to develop effective solutions to these problems. In such circumstances, social workers should stress clients' roles in helping to discover and tailor solutions to fit their unique problems.

Clients may expect to receive early advice if social workers have not appropriately clarified roles and expectations about how mutual participation in generating possible solutions will further the growth and self-confidence of clients.
EP 2.1.1c
Assuming a position of superiority and quickly providing solutions for problems without encouraging clients to think through the possible courses of action fosters dependency and stifles creative thinking. Freely dispensing advice also minimizes or ignores clients' strengths and potentials, and many clients tend to respond with inner resentment to such high-handed treatment. In addition, clients who have not been actively involved in planning their own courses of action may, in turn, lack motivation to implement the advice given by social workers. Moreover, when advice does not remedy a problem—as it often doesn't—clients may blame social workers and disown any responsibility for an unfavorable outcome.

Rather than say, "I suggest that you move to a new place because you have had so many difficulties here," a more productive response would be to say, "You have had a lot of difficulties in your current place. What have you considered doing about your living situation?" Based on that response, you could assist the client in considering either ways to improve that situation or look for alternative living arrangements.

Instead of saying, "I think you need to try a new approach with your daughter. Let me suggest that ... ," you might say, "It sounds as if what you have tried with your daughter has not worked as you had hoped. What other solutions have you considered?" Based on the client's response, you can ask if he or she would like to consider some other possibilities. Additional examples of reframing premature advice situations are presented in the practice workbook.

Using Sarcasm or Employing Humor Inappropriately

- *"Did you get up on the wrong side of the bed?"*
- *"It seems to me that we've been through all this before."*
- *"You really fell for that line."*
- *"You think you have a problem."*

Humor can be helpful, bringing relief and sometimes perspective to work that might otherwise be tense and tedious. Pollio (1995) has suggested ways to determine appropriate use of humor. Are you the social worker capable of telling something that is humorous? Do others, including clients, think so? Does the comment fit the situation? Is something needed to unstick or free up a situation in a way that humor might help? What do you know about the client's sense of humor? Similarly, van Wormer and Boes (1997) have described ways that humor permits social workers to continue to operate in the face of trauma. Using plays on words or noting a sense of the preposterous or incongruous can help social workers and clients face difficult situations. Situations can be put into perspective, with both social workers and clients appreciating incongruous outcomes. Humor can also allow clients to express emotions in safe, less emotionally charged ways (Dewayne, 1978). Kane (1995) describes the way humor in group work can facilitate work with persons with HIV. In group work, Caplan (1995) has described how facilitation of humor can create a necessary safety and comfort level in work with men who batter. Teens have been described as using irony, sarcasm, mocking, and parody as ways of coping with difficult situations (Cameron, Fox, Anderson & Cameron, 2010). Similarly, humor can be used in ways to diffuse conflict (Norrick and Spitz, 2008).

Excessive or untimely use of humor, however, can be distracting, keeping the content of the session on a superficial level and interfering with mutual objectives. Sarcasm often emanates from unrecognized hostility that tends to provoke counter-hostility in clients. Similarly, making a comment such as "you really win the prize for worst week" when a client recounts a series of crises and unfortunate incidents runs the risk of conveying that the difficulties are not taken seriously. A better response would be to empathize with the difficulties of the week and compliment the client on persisting to cope despite them.

Rather than saying, "Did you get up on the wrong side of the bed?" a more descriptive response that does not run the risk of diminishing the client's experience would be to say, "It sounds as if today was difficult from the time you got up."

Judging, Criticizing, or Placing Blame

- *"You're wrong about that."*
- *"Running away from home was a bad mistake."*
- *"One of your problems is that you're not willing to consider another point of view."*
- *"You're not thinking straight."*

Clients do not feel supported when they perceive the worker as critical, moralistic, and defensive rather than warm and respectful (Coady & Marziali, 1994; Eaton, Abeles & Gutfreund, 1993; Safran & Muran, 2000). Responses that evaluate and show disapproval can be detrimental to clients and to the helping process. Clients usually respond defensively and sometimes counterattack when they perceive criticism from social workers; some may simply cut off any meaningful communication with social workers. When they are intimidated by a social worker's greater expertise, some clients also accept negative evaluations as accurate reflections of their poor judgment or lack of worth or value. In making such negative judgments about clients, social workers violate the basic social work values of nonjudgmental attitude and acceptance.

Such responses are unlikely to be tolerated by voluntary clients with adequate self-esteem or enough power in the situation to have alternatives. Such clients are likely to "fire" you, speak to your supervisor, or put you on notice if you act in such seemingly disrespectful ways. Others may shut down, perceiving you as having some power over them.

Involuntary clients often face what they believe to be dangerous consequences for not getting along with the social worker. Hence, some clients with substantial self-control and self-esteem may put up with such browbeating without comment. Others may respond in kind with attacks of their own that then appear in case records as evidence of client resistance.

EP 2.1.1c

Your own judging in the situation is not useful and is often counterproductive. On the other hand, it could be useful to help the client, in some circumstances, reflect about actions that might be a danger to him or herself or others or about violations of the law. In such circumstances, asking about the client's awareness of consequences and alternatives can be useful. For example, the social worker might ask, "How do you look now at the consequences of running away from home?" or "How would this appear from your partner's point of view?" The social worker might also provide a double-sided reflection as described in the 6th chapter.

Trying to Convince Clients about the Right Point of View through Logic, Lecturing, Instructing, or Arguing

- "Let's look at the facts about drugs."
- "You have to take some responsibility for your life, you know."
- "Running away from home will only get you in more difficulty."
- "That attitude won't get you anywhere."

Clients sometimes consider courses of action that social workers view as unsafe, illegal, or contrary to the client's goals. However, attempting to convince clients through arguing, instructing, and similar behavior often provokes a kind of boomerang effect—that is, clients are not only not convinced of the merits of the social worker's argument, but may also be more inclined to hold onto their beliefs than before. According to reactance theory, clients will attempt to defend their valued freedoms when these privileges are threatened (Brehm & Brehm, 1981). For some clients (especially adolescents, for whom independent thinking is associated with a particular developmental stage), deferring to or agreeing with social workers is tantamount to giving up their individuality or freedom. The challenge when working with such clients is to learn how to listen to and respect their perspective at the same time as you make sure that they are aware of alternatives and consequences. Compare the two ways of handling the same situation described in the following.

Teen parent client: I have decided to drop out of high school for now and get my cosmetology license.

Social worker: Don't you know that dropping out of high school is going to hurt you and your children, both now and in the future? Are you willing to sacrifice hundreds of thousands of dollars less that you would earn over your lifetime for you and your children just to buy a few little knick-knacks now?

Teen parent client: But this is my life! My babies need things now! You don't know what it is like scraping by! You can't tell me what to do! You are not my momma! I know what is best for me and my children!

Rather than escalate into what has been called the confrontation-denial cycle (Murphy & Baxter, 1997), a better alternative is to respond to the teen parent client with an effort to understand her perspective, before exploring alternatives and consequences.

Teen parent client: I have decided to drop out of high school for now and get my cosmetology license.

Social worker: So you have been going to high school for a while now with some success, and now you are considering that going in a different direction and getting your cosmetology license may work better for you. Tell me about that.

Teen parent client: Well, it is true that I have been working hard in high school. But I need more money now, not just far off in the future. My babies and I don't have enough to get by.

Social worker: And you feel that getting a cosmetology license will help you do that.

Teen parent client: I do. I still want to finish high school and get my diploma. I know that I will earn more for my kids and myself with a diploma than if I don't finish. If I get my cosmetology degree, it will take a little longer to get my high school diploma, but I think I am up to it.

Social worker: So your longer-term plan is still to get your high school diploma but just to delay it. You think that getting your cosmetology degree will help you and your kids get by better now. Are there any drawbacks to withdrawing from high school at this time?

Teen parent client: Only if I get distracted and don't return. I could kind of get out of the habit of going to school and I might be around people who haven't finished school.

Social worker: Those are things to consider. How might you be sure that your withdrawal from high school was only temporary?

In the first example above, the social worker attempts to vigorously persuade the client about the course of action he or she deems wisest. Such efforts, while well meaning, often create power struggles, thereby perpetuating dynamics that have previously occurred in clients' personal relationships. By arguing, social workers ignore their clients' feelings and views, focusing instead on the social worker "being right"; this tactic may engender feelings of resentment, alienation, or hostility in clients. Such efforts are both unethical and ineffective. Persuasion in the sense of helping clients to obtain accurate information with which to make informed decisions can be an ethical intervention. When clients contemplate actions that run contrary to their own goals, or will endanger themselves or others, then an effort to persuade can be an ethical intervention. Such efforts should not focus on the one "pet" solution of the social worker, however, but rather should assist the client in examining the advantages and disadvantages of several options, including those with which the social worker may disagree (Rooney R. H., 2009). Hence, the effort is not to convince, but rather to assist clients in making informed decisions. By not attacking the client in example 2, the practitioner is able to support the client's right to make decisions for herself and to do so considering alternatives and consequences.

Analyzing, Diagnosing, or Making Glib or Dramatic Interpretations

- "You're behaving that way because you're angry with your partner."
- "Your attitude may have kept you from giving their ideas a fair hearing."
- "You're acting in a passive-aggressive way."
- "You're really hostile today."

When used sparingly and timed appropriately, interpretation of the dynamics of behavior can be a potent change-oriented skill (see Chapter 18). However, even accurate interpretations that focus on purposes or meanings of behavior substantially beyond clients' levels of conscious awareness tend to inspire client opposition and are doomed to failure.

When stated dogmatically (e.g., "I know what's wrong with you," or "how you feel," or "what your real motives are"), interpretations also present a threat to clients, causing them to feel exposed or trapped. When a glib interpretation is thrust upon them, clients often expend their energies disconfirming the interpretation, explaining themselves, making angry rebuttals, or passively acquiescing rather than working on the problem at hand.

Using social work jargon such as *fixation, resistance, reinforcement, repression, passivity, neuroticism,* and a host of other terms to describe the behavior of clients in their presence is also destructive to the helping process. Indeed, it may confuse or bewilder clients and provoke opposition to change. These terms also oversimplify complex phenomena and psychic mechanisms and stereotype clients, thereby obliterating their uniqueness. In addition, these sweeping generalizations provide no operational definitions of clients' problems, nor do they suggest avenues for behavior modification. If clients accept social workers' restricted definitions of their problems, then they may define themselves in the same terms as those used by social workers (e.g., "I am a passive person" or "I have a schizoid personality"). This type of stereotypic labeling often causes clients to view themselves as "sick" and their situations as hopeless, providing them with a ready excuse for not working on their problems.

> **VIDEO CASE EXAMPLE**
>
> Use of diagnostic labels is a reality in some direct practice settings. It is used as a way of identifying treatable conditions, applying evidence based forms of treatment, and also as a requirement for health insurance coverage of treatment. In the video "Getting back to Shakopee," follow the discussion between Val and her social worker about the meaning of the term depression. Val is worried about being labeled as "depressed." They go on to talk about how the concept depression can be useful in part to explain some of her experience, to possibly lead to useful medication, and to fit agency and health insurance guidelines.

Threatening, Warning, or Counterattacking

- "You'd better ... or else!"
- "If you don't ... you'll be sorry."
- "If you know what's good for you, you'll ..."

Sometimes clients consider actions that would endanger themselves or others or are illegal. In such instances, alerting clients to the potential consequences of those actions is an ethical and appropriate intervention. Conversely, making threats of the sort just described often produces a kind of oppositional behavior that exacerbates an already strained situation.

EP 2.1.1d

Even the most well-intentioned social workers may occasionally bristle or respond defensively under the pressure of verbal abuse, accusatory or blaming responses, or challenges to their integrity, competence, motives, or authority. For example, a social worker was scheduled to offer services to a veteran who was entering hospice care. The veteran exploded with a series of expletives and insults to the effect that he had no need of such services and would not need them. Rather than choose to take this as an opportunity to inform him of proper respect and boundaries, the social worker asked if she could come at another time to explain the possibilities for services so that he could be sure about whether they might be helpful or not. He calmed down and averred that coming at another time would be fine.

Whatever the dynamics behind clients' provocative behavior, responding defensively is counterproductive, as it may duplicate the destructive pattern of responses that clients have typically elicited and experienced from others. To achieve competence, therefore, you must learn to master your own natural defensive reactions and evolve effective ways of dealing with negative feelings, putting the client's needs before your own.

Empathic communication, for example, produces a cathartic release of negative feelings, defusing a strained situation and permitting a more rational emotional exploration of factors that underlie clients' feelings. For example, to reply to a client, "You have difficult decisions to make, and are caught between alternatives that you don't consider very attractive; I wish you well in making a decision that you can live with in the future" can convey support and respect for the right to choose.

The negative effects of certain types of responses are not always immediately apparent because clients may not overtly demonstrate negative reactions at the time or because the dampening effect on the helping process cannot be observed in a single transaction. To assess the effect of responses, then, the social worker must determine the frequency with which he or she issues the dampening responses and evaluate the overall impact of those responses on the helping process. Frequent use of some types of responses by the social worker indicates the presence of counterproductive patterns of communication such as the following (note that this list is a continuation of the list of problematic social worker behaviors on page 169):

8. Stacking questions
9. Asking leading questions
10. Interrupting inappropriately or excessively
11. Dominating the interaction
12. Fostering safe social interaction
13. Responding infrequently
14. Parroting or overusing certain phrases or clichés
15. Dwelling on the remote past
16. Going on fishing expeditions

Individual responses that fall within these patterns may or may not be ineffective when used occasionally. When they are employed extensively in lieu of using varied response patterns, however, they inhibit the natural flow of a session and limit the richness of information revealed. The sections that follow expand on each of these verbal barriers and detrimental social worker responses.

Stacking Questions

In exploring problems, social workers should use facilitative questions that assist clients to reveal detailed information about specific problem areas. Asking multiple questions at the same time, or *stacking*, diffuses the focus and confuses clients. Consider the vast amount of ground covered in the following messages:

- *"When you don't feel you have control of situations, what goes on inside of you? What do you think about? What do you do?"*
- *"Have you thought about where you are going to live? Is that one of your biggest concerns, or is there another that takes priority?"*

Stacking questions is a problem frequently encountered by beginning social work practitioners, who may feel an urgent need to help clients by providing many options all at one time. Adequately answering even one of the foregoing questions would require a client to give an extended response. Rather than focus on one question, however, clients often respond superficially and nonspecifically to the social worker's multiple inquiries, omitting important information in the process. Stacked questions thus have "low yield" and are unproductive and inefficient in gathering relevant information. Slowing down and asking one question at a time is preferable. If you have asked stacked questions (and all social workers have at many points), and the client hesitates in response, you can correct for the problem by repeating your preferred question.

Asking Leading Questions

Leading questions have hidden agendas designed to induce clients to agree with a particular view or to adopt a solution that social workers deem to be in clients' best interests. For example:

- "Do you think you've really tried to get along with your partner?"
- "You don't really mean that, do you?"
- "Aren't you too young to move out on your own?"
- "Don't you think that arguing with your mother will provoke her to come down on you as she has done in the past?"

In actuality, these types of questions often obscure legitimate concerns that social workers should discuss with clients. Social workers may conceal their feelings and opinions about such matters, however, and present them obliquely in the form of solutions (e.g., "Don't you think you ought to …") in the hope that leading questions will guide clients to desired conclusions. It is an error, however, to assume that clients will not see through such maneuvers. Indeed, clients often discern the social worker's motives and inwardly resist having views or directives imposed on them under the guise of leading questions. Nevertheless, to avoid conflict or controversy with social workers, they may express feeble agreement or simply divert the discussion to another topic.

By contrast, when social workers authentically assume responsibility for concerns they wish clients to consider, they enhance the likelihood that clients will respond receptively to their questions. In addition, they can raise questions that are not slanted to imply the "correct" answer from the social worker's viewpoint. For example, "How have you attempted to reach agreement with your partner?" does not contain the hint about the "right" answer found in the first question given. Similarly, the last question could be rephrased as follows: "I am not clear how you see arguing with your mother is likely to be more successful than it has proved to be in the past."

Interrupting Inappropriately or Excessively

Beginning social workers often worry excessively about covering all items on their own and their agency's agenda ("What will I tell my supervisor?"). To maintain focus on relevant problem areas, social workers must sometimes interrupt clients. To be effective, however, these interruptions must be purposeful, well timed, and smoothly executed. Interruptions may damage the helping process when they are abrupt or divert clients from exploring pertinent problem areas. For example, interrupting to challenge a client's account of events or to confirm an irrelevant detail can break the flow and put the client on the defensive. Frequent untimely interruptions tend to annoy clients, stifle spontaneous expression, and hinder exploration of problems. Identifying and prioritizing key questions in advance with an outline can assist in avoiding this pattern. Appropriate interruptions can occur if you want to convey that you have heard what a client has to say. For example, some clients seem like a broken record, repeating certain stories and accusations about bad things that have occurred to them. A more useful response is to provide an empathic summary. For example, "Let me interrupt, Mrs. Jones, to see if I am getting what you are saying. You are not opposed to having home health care. In fact you welcome it. However timing has been a problem for you. Too often aides have come early in the day when you were not yet up for the day, is that correct?" Such an empathic summary can free some clients from needing to repeat the story and to move on to consider what feasible options to their dilemma there might be.

Dominating the Interaction

Social workers should guide discussions. They should not dominate the interaction by talking too much or by asking too many closed-ended questions. Other domineering behaviors by social workers include repeatedly offering advice, pressuring clients to improve, presenting lengthy arguments to convince clients, frequently interrupting, excessive or inappropriate self-disclosure and so on. Some social workers are also prone to behave as though they are all-knowing, failing to convey respect for clients' points of view or capacities to solve problems. Such dogmatic and authoritarian behavior discourages clients from expressing themselves and fosters a one-up, one-down relationship in which clients feel at a great disadvantage and resent the social worker's supercilious demeanor.

Social workers should monitor the relative distribution of participation by all participants (including themselves) who are involved in individual, family, or group sessions. Although clients naturally vary in their levels of verbal participation and assertiveness, all group members should have equal opportunity to share information, concerns, and views in the helping process. Social workers have a responsibility to ensure that this opportunity is available to them.

> **VIDEO CASE EXAMPLE**
>
> As a general guideline, clients should consume more "speaking time" than social workers in the helping process, although during initial sessions with some Asian American clients and others with whom there are language differences, social workers must be more direct than they are with other, as discussed earlier. For example, in the video "Working with Yanping," the social worker, Kim Strom-Gottfried is quite active in clarifying roles and expectations, frequently reflecting to make sure they are on the same page.

Sometimes social workers defeat practice objectives in group or conjoint sessions by dominating the interaction through such behaviors as speaking for members, focusing more on some members than on others, or giving speeches.

Even social workers who are not particularly verbal may dominate sessions that include reserved or nonassertive clients as a means of alleviating their own discomfort with silence and passivity. Although it is natural to be more active with reticent or withdrawn clients than with those who are more verbal, social workers must avoid seeming overbearing.

Using facilitative responses that draw clients out is an effective method of minimizing silence and passivity. When a review of one of your taped sessions reveals that you have monopolized the interaction, it is important that you explore the reasons for your behavior. Identify the specific responses that were authoritarian or domineering and the events that preceded those responses. Also, examine the clients' style of relating for clues regarding your own reactions, and analyze the feelings you were experiencing at the time. Based on your review and assessment of your performance, you should then plan a strategy for modifying your own style of relating by substituting facilitative responses for ineffective ones. You may also need to focus on and explore the passive or nonassertive behavior of clients with the objective of contracting with them to increase their participation in the helping process.

Fostering Safe Social Interaction

Channeling or keeping discussions focused on safe topics that exclude feelings and minimize client disclosures is inimical to the helping process. Social chit-chat about the weather, news, hobbies, mutual interests or acquaintances, and the like tends to foster a social rather than a therapeutic relationship. In contrast to the lighter and more diffuse communication characteristic of a social relationship, helpful, growth-producing relationships feature sharp focus and high specificity. Another frequent pattern found in the Ragg, Okagbue-Reaves, and Piers (2007) study was that beginning practitioners would attempt to diffuse expressions of high emotion such as anger, dismay, or sadness rather than reflect them.

Parent: I have had about all I can take from these kids sometimes. They are so angry and disrespectful that it is all I can do to keep from blowing up at them.

Social worker: Kids nowadays can be difficult.

A more appropriate response would be:

Social worker: You sometimes feel so frustrated when your kids act disrespectfully that you want to do something about it, and it is hard to keep the lid on.

In general, safe social interaction in the helping process should be avoided. Two exceptions to this rule exist, however:

- *Discussion of safe topics may be utilized to assist children or adolescents to lower their defenses and risk increasing openness, thereby assisting social workers to cultivate a quasi-friend role with such clients.*
- *A brief discussion of conventional topics may be appropriate and helpful as part of the getting-acquainted or warm-up period of initial sessions or during early portions of subsequent sessions. A warm-up period is particularly important when you are engaging clients from ethnic groups for which such informal openings are the cultural norm, as discussed in Chapter 3.*

Even when you try to avoid inappropriate social interaction, however, some clients may resist your attempts to move the discussion to a topic that is relevant to the problems they are experiencing and to the purposes of the helping process. Techniques for managing such situations are found in Chapter 18. For now, simply note that it is appropriate for the social worker to bring up the agreed upon agenda within a few minutes of the beginning of the session.

Responding Infrequently

Monitoring the frequency of your responses in individual, conjoint, or group sessions is an important task. As a social worker, you have an ethical responsibility to utilize fully the limited contact time you have with clients in pursuing your practice objectives and promoting your clients' general well-being. Relatively inactive social workers, however, usually ignore fruitful moments that could be explored to promote clients' growth, and they may allow the focus of a session to stray to inappropriate or unproductive content. To be maximally helpful, social workers must structure the helping process by developing contracts with clients that specify the respective responsibilities of both sets of participants. For their part, they engage clients in identifying and exploring problems, formulating goals, and delineating tasks to alleviate clients' difficulties.

EP 2.1.1b

Inactive social workers can contribute to counterproductive processes and failures in problem solving. One deleterious effect, for example, is that clients lose confidence in social workers when they fail to intervene by helping clients with situations that are destructive to themselves or to others. In particular, clients' confidence is eroded if social workers fail to intervene when clients communicate destructively in conjoint or group sessions.

Although social workers' activity per se is important, the quality of their moment-by-moment responses is critical. Social workers significantly diminish their effectiveness by neglecting to utilize or by underutilizing facilitative responses.

Self-assessment of your sessions and discussions with your supervisor can be helpful in determining whether you are modeling an appropriate level of interaction with the client. For example, some beginning students may welcome highly verbal clients who may come to dominate the session. Catharsis can be useful. However, usually such clients are coming in because there is an issue they wish to address. The inactive social worker would be better served by refocusing discussion, coming back to the concern that brought the client in.

Parroting or Overusing Certain Phrases or Clichés

EP 2.1.1d

Parroting a message irritates clients, who may issue a sharp rebuke to the social worker: "Well, yes, I just said that." Rather than merely repeating clients' words, social workers should use fresh language that captures the essence of clients' messages and places them in sharper perspective.

In addition, social workers should refrain from punctuating their communications with superfluous phrases. The distracting effect of such phrases can be observed in the following message:

Social worker: You know, a lot of people wouldn't come in for help. It tells me, you know, that you realize that you have a problem, you know, and want to work on it. Do you know what I mean?

Frequent use of such phrases as "you know," "Okay?" ("Let's work on this task, okay?"), "and stuff" ("We went to town, and stuff"), or "that's neat" can annoy some clients (and social workers, for that matter). If used in excess, the same may be said of some of the faddish clichés that have permeated today's language—for example, "awesome," "sweet," "cool," "tight," or "dude."

> ### 🖥 VIDEO CASE EXAMPLE
>
> In the video "Work with the Corning Family," the social worker, Ali, frequently uses the term "you guys" to refer to her husband and wife clients. We don't know how they respond to this plural term and whether they respond to it positively or negatively. What alternative terms could be used to refer to these clients?

Another mistake social workers sometimes make is trying to "overrelate" to youthful clients by using adolescent jargon to excess. Adolescents tend to perceive such communication as phony and the social worker as inauthentic, which hinders the development of a working relationship. It can be part of the learning process, however, to discover the meaning of terms unfamiliar to the social worker so that in some cases you can translate concepts using terms the social worker has learned from the client.

Dwelling on the Remote Past

Social workers' verbal responses may focus on the past, the present, or the future. Helping professionals differ regarding the amount of emphasis they believe should be accorded to gathering historical facts about clients. Focusing largely on the present is vital, however, because clients can change only their present circumstances, behaviors, and feelings. Permitting individuals, groups, couples, or families to dwell on the past may reinforce diversionary tactics they have employed to avoid dealing with painful aspects of their present difficulties and with the need for change.

Messages about the past may reveal feelings the client is currently experiencing related to the past. For example:

Client [*with trembling voice*]: He used to make me so angry.

Social worker: There was a time when he really infuriated you. As you think about the past, even now it seems to stir up some of the anger and hurt you felt.

As in this excerpt, changing a client's statement from past to present tense often yields rich information about clients' present feelings and problems. The same may be said of bringing future-oriented statements of clients to the present (e.g., "How do you feel now about the future event you're describing?"). As you see, it is not only possible but also often productive to shift the focus to the present experiencing of clients, even when historical facts are being elicited, in an effort to illuminate client problems.

Going on Fishing Expeditions

Another counterproductive interviewing strategy is pursuing content that is tangentially related to client concerns, issues of client and family safety, or legal mandates. Such content may relate to pet theories of social workers or agencies and be puzzling to clients. This kind of confusion may arise if the connection of these theories to the concerns that have brought clients into contact with the social worker is not clear. A wise precaution, therefore, would be to avoid taking clients into tangential areas if you cannot readily justify the rationale for that exploration. If the social worker feels that the exploration of new areas is relevant, then an explanation of its purpose is warranted. For example, if a social worker were concerned perhaps that a client's social interactions are largely through the internet and texting, rather than imposing this as a problem on him or her, it would be better to focus on concerns which the client acknowledges.

Gauging the Effectiveness of Your Responses

The preceding discussion should assist you in identifying ineffective patterns of communication you may have been employing. Because most learners ask too many closed-ended questions, change the subject frequently, and recommend solutions before completing a thorough exploration of clients' problems, you should particularly watch for these patterns. In addition, you will need to monitor your interviewing style for idiosyncratic counterproductive patterns of responding.

The practice workbook contains classroom exercises designed to assist students in recognizing and eliminating ineffective responses. Because identifying ineffective styles of interviewing requires selective focusing on the frequency and patterning of responses, you will also find it helpful to analyze extended segments of taped sessions using the form "Assessing Verbal Barriers to Communication," which is found at the end of this chapter.

One way of gauging the effectiveness of your responses is to carefully observe clients' reactions immediately following your responses. Because multiple clients are involved in group and family sessions, you will often receive varied verbal and nonverbal cues regarding the relative effectiveness of your responses when engaging clients in these systems.

As you assess your messages, keep in mind that a response is probably helpful if clients react in one of the following ways:

- *They continue to explore the problem or stay on the topic.*
- *They express pent-up emotions related to the problematic situation.*
- *They engage in deeper self-exploration and self-experiencing.*
- *They volunteer more personally relevant material spontaneously.*
- *They affirm the validity of your response either verbally or nonverbally.*

By contrast, a response may be too confrontational, poorly timed, or off target if clients react in one of the following ways:

- *They reject your response either verbally or nonverbally.*
- *They change the subject.*
- *They ignore the message.*
- *They appear mixed up or confused.*
- *They become more superficial, more impersonal, more emotionally detached, or more defensive.*
- *They argue or express anger rather than examine the relevance of the feelings involved.*[2]

In analyzing social worker-client interactions, keep in mind that the participants mutually influence each other. Thus, a response by either person in an individual interview affects the expressions of the other person. In group and conjoint sessions, the communications of each person, including the social worker, affect the responses of all other participants. In a group situation, however, the influence of messages on the subsequent responses of other participants is sometimes difficult to detect because of the complexity of the communications.

Beginning interviewers often reinforce unproductive client responses by responding indiscriminately or haphazardly or by letting positive responses that support practice objectives or reflect growth pass without comment. For example, Ragg, Okagbue-Reaves, and Piers (2007) found that beginning social workers would often respond to complex client responses by picking up on the final expression whether or not it was of particular significance in its context. A more productive response would be to reflect back the several themes you have heard. It is important that you, as a beginning social worker, monitor and review your moment-by-moment transactions with clients with a view toward not allowing ineffective or destructive communication to be perpetuated by yourself and your clients.

Although social workers may demonstrate ineffective patterns of communication in individual interviews, these are even more likely to occur in groups or in conjoint sessions with spouses or family members. In fact, orchestrating an effective conjoint interview or group meeting often presents a stiff challenge because of clients' use of ineffective communications, which may provoke intense anger, defensiveness, and confusion among family or group members. Establishing mutually accepted ground rules for communication can be useful in such settings.

In summary, your task is twofold: You must monitor, analyze, and eliminate your own ineffective responses while simultaneously observing, managing, and modifying ineffective responses by your clients. That's a rather tall order. Although modifying dysfunctional communications among clients requires advanced skill, you can eliminate your own barriers to effective communication in a relatively short time. You will make even faster progress if you also eliminate ineffective styles of responding and test out your new communication skills in your private life. Unfortunately, many social workers compartmentalize and limit their helping skills to their work with clients but continue to use ineffective communication styles with their professional colleagues, friends, and families. Being patient with your learning and accepting that you are learning as quickly as you can, can be helpful.

Social workers who have not fully integrated the helping skills into their private lives typically do not relate as effectively to their clients as do social workers who have fully implemented and assimilated those skills as a part of their general style of relating. We are convinced that to adequately master these essential skills and to fully tap into their potential for assisting clients, social workers must promote their own interpersonal competence and personality integration, thereby modeling for their clients the self-actualized or fully functioning person. Pursuing this personal goal prepares social workers for one of their major roles: teaching new skills of communicating and relating to their clients.

The Challenge of Learning New Skills

Because of the unique nature of the helping process, establishing and maintaining a therapeutic relationship requires highly disciplined efforts on the social worker's part. Moment by moment, transaction by transaction, the social worker must sharply focus on the needs and problems of his or her clients. The success of each transaction is measured in terms of the social worker's adroitness in consciously applying specific skills to move the process toward the therapeutic objectives.

Interestingly, one of the major threats to learning new skills comes from students' fear that in relinquishing their old styles of relating they are giving up an intangible, irreplaceable part of themselves. Similarly, students who have previously engaged in social work practice may experience fear related to the fact that they have developed methods or styles of relating that have influenced and "moved" clients in the past; abandoning these response patterns may mean surrendering a hard-won feeling of competency. These fears are often exacerbated when instruction and supervision in the classroom and practicum primarily strive to eliminate errors and ineffective interventions and responses rather than to develop new skills or enhance positive responses or interventions with clients. In such circumstances, students may receive considerable feedback about their errors but inadequate input regarding their effective responses or styles of relating. Consequently, they may feel vulnerable and stripped of their defenses (just as clients do) and experience more keenly the loss of something familiar.

As a beginning social worker, you must learn to openly and nondefensively receive constructive feedback about your ineffective or even destructive styles of relating or intervening. Effective supervisors should not dwell exclusively on short comings but rather be equally focused on identifying your expanding skills (Rooney and De Jong, 2011). If they do not do so, then you should take the lead in eliciting positive feedback from educators and peers about your growing strengths. Remember that supervision time is limited and that the responsibility for utilizing that time effectively and for acquiring competency necessarily rests equally with you and your practicum instructor. It is also vital that you take steps to monitor your own growth systematically by reviewing audio- and videotapes, by counting your desirable and undesirable responses in client sessions, and by comparing your responses with the guidelines for constructing effective messages found in this book. Perhaps the single most important requirement for you in furthering your competency is to assume responsibility for advancing your own skill level by consistently monitoring your responses and practicing proven skills.

Most of the skills delineated in this book are not easy to master. In fact, competent social workers will spend years perfecting their ability to sensitively and fully attune themselves to the inner experiencing of their clients; in furthering their capacity to share their own experiencing in an authentic, helpful manner; and in developing a keen sense of timing in employing these and other skills.

In the months ahead, as you forge new patterns of responding and test your newly developed skills, you will inevitably experience growing pains—that is, a sense of disequilibrium as you struggle to respond in new ways and, at the same time, to relate warmly, naturally, and attentively to your clients. Sometimes, you may feel that your responses are mechanistic and experience a keen sense of transparency: "The client will know that I'm not being real." If you work intensively to master specific skills, however, your awkwardness will gradually diminish, and you will eventually incorporate these skills naturally into your repertoire.

ASSESSING VERBAL BARRIERS TO COMMUNICATION				
Directions: In reviewing each 15-minute sample of taped interviews, tally your use of ineffective responses by placing marks in appropriate cells.				
15-Minute Taped Samples	1	2	3	4
1. Reassuring, sympathizing, consoling, or excusing				
2. Advising and giving suggestions or solutions prematurely				
3. Using sarcasm or employing humor that is distracting or makes light of clients' problems				
4. Judging, criticizing, or placing blame				
5. Trying to convince the client about the right point of view through logical arguments, lecturing, instructing, or arguing				
6. Analyzing, diagnosing, or making glib or dogmatic interpretations				
7. Threatening, warning, or counterattacking				
8. Stacking questions				
9. Asking leading questions				
10. Interrupting inappropriately or excessively				
11. Dominating the interaction				
12. Fostering safe social interaction				
13. Responding infrequently				
14. Parroting or overusing certain phrases or clichés				
15. Dwelling on the remote past				
16. Going on fishing expeditions				
Other responses that impede communication. List:				

ASSESSING PHYSICAL ATTENDING BEHAVIORS	
	Comments
1. Direct eye contact 0 1 2 3 4	
2. Warmth and concern reflected in facial expression 0 1 2 3 4	
3. Eyes at same level as client's 0 1 2 3 4	
4. Appropriately varied and animated facial expressions 0 1 2 3 4	
5. Arms and hands moderately expressive; appropriate gestures 0 1 2 3 4	
6. Body leaning slightly forward; attentive but relaxed 0 1 2 3 4	
7. Voice clearly audible but not loud 0 1 2 3 4	
8. Warmth in tone of voice 0 1 2 3 4	
9. Voice modulated to reflect nuances of feeling and emotional tone of client messages 0 1 2 3 4	
10. Moderate speech tempo 0 1 2 3 4	
11. Absence of distracting behaviors (fidgeting, yawning, gazing out window, looking at watch) 0 1 2 3 4	
12. Other 0 1 2 3 4	

Rating Scale:
0 = Poor, needs marked improvement.
1 = Weak, needs substantial improvement.
2 = Minimally acceptable, room for growth.
3 = Generally high level with a few lapses.
4 = Consistently high level.

Summary

Chapter 7 outlined a series of nonverbal and verbal barriers to effective communication that are often experienced by beginning social workers. As you become alert to these potential obstacles and more skilled in applying more productive alternatives, you will become more confident in your progress. Chapter 8 asks you to apply your communication skills to one of the most important tasks you will face: conducting a multisystemic assessment.

CourseMate

Access an integrated eBook and chapter-specific learning tools including glossary terms, chapter outlines, relevant web links, videos, and practice quizzes. Go to **www.cengagebrain.com**.

CHAPTER **8**

Assessment: Problems and Strengths

CHAPTER OVERVIEW

Assessment involves gathering information and formulating it into a coherent picture of the client and his or her circumstances. Because assessments involve social workers' inferences about the nature and causes of clients' difficulties, they serve as the basis for the rest of their interactions in the helping process—the goals they set, the interventions they enact, and the progress they evaluate. Chapter 8 focuses on the fundamentals of assessment and the strategies used in assessing the client's problem and strengths. Chapter 9 describes the characteristics that are taken into account when examining and portraying an individual's functioning and his or her relations with others and with the surrounding environment. Chapters 8 and 9 both cover the individual's interpersonal functioning and his/her related social systems and environments. As a result of reading this chapter you will:

- Understand that assessments involve both gathering information and synthesizing it into a working hypothesis
- Learn the distinctions between assessment and diagnosis
- Know what the DSM-IV-TR is and how it is organized
- Understand how to capture client strengths and resources in assessment
- Recognize the elements of culturally competent assessments and the risks of ethnocentric assessments
- Identify the roles that knowledge and theories play in framing assessments
- Know the sources of data that may inform social workers' assessments
- Learn questions to bear in mind while conducting an assessment
- Be familiar with the various elements of problem analysis

EPAS COMPETENCIES IN THE 8TH CHAPTER

This chapter will give you the information needed to meet the following practice competencies:

2.1.3a Distinguish, appraise, and integrate multiple sources of knowledge, including research-based knowledge and practice wisdom

2.1.3b Analyze models of assessment, prevention, intervention, and evaluation

2.1.4b Gain sufficient self-awareness to eliminate the influence of personal biases and values in working with diverse groups

2.1.4c Recognize and communicate your understanding of the importance of difference in shaping life experiences

2.1.4d View yourself as a learner and engage those with whom you work as informants

2.1.7a Utilize conceptual frameworks to guide the processes of assessment, intervention, and evaluation

2.1.7b Critique and apply knowledge to understand person and environment

2.1.10a Substantively and effectively prepare for action with individuals, families, groups, organizations, and communities

2.1.10d Collect, organize, and interpret client data

2.1.10e Assess client strengths and limitations

The Multidimensionality of Assessment

EP 2.1.7b

Human problems—even those that appear to be simple at first glance—often involve a complex interplay of many factors. Rarely do sources of problems reside solely within an individual or within that individual's environment. Rather, *reciprocal interaction* occurs between a person and the external world. The person acts upon and responds to the external world, and the quality of those actions affects the external world's reactions (and vice versa). For example, a parent may complain about having poor communication with an adolescent, attributing the difficulty to the fact that the teenager is sullen and refuses to talk about most things. The adolescent, in turn, may complain that it is pointless to talk with the parent because the latter consistently pries, lectures, or criticizes. Each participant's complaint about the other may be accurate, but each unwittingly behaves in ways that have produced and now maintain their dysfunctional interaction. Thus, the behavior of neither person is the sole cause of the breakdown in communication in a simple cause-and-effect (linear) fashion. Rather, their reciprocal interaction produces the difficulty; the behavior of each is both cause and effect, depending on one's vantage point.

EP 2.1.7b

The *multidimensionality* of human problems is also a consequence of the fact that human beings are social creatures who depend both on other human beings and complex social institutions to meet their needs. Meeting basic needs such as food, housing, clothing, and medical care requires adequate economic means and the availability of goods and services. Meeting educational, social, and recreational needs requires interaction with social institutions. Meeting needs to feel close to and loved by others, to have companionship, to experience a sense of belonging, and to experience sexual gratification requires satisfactory social relationships within one's intimate relationships, family, social network, and community. Likewise, the extent to which people experience self-esteem depends on certain individual psychological factors and the quality of feedback from other people.

EP 2.1.10a

In conducting an assessment, a social worker needs extensive knowledge about the person and the numerous systems (e.g., economic, legal, educational, medical, religious, social, interpersonal) that impinge upon the client system.

Assessing the functioning of an individual entails evaluating various aspects of that person's functioning. For example, the social worker may need to consider dynamic interactions among the individual's biophysical, cognitive, emotional, cultural, behavioral, and motivational subsystems and the relationships of those interactions to the client's problems. When the client system is a couple or family, assessment entails paying attention to communications and patterns of interaction, as well as to each individual member of the system. Not every system and subsystem plays a significant role in the problems experienced by a given situation. However, overlooking relevant systems will result in an assessment that is incomplete at best and irrelevant or erroneous at worst. Interventions based on poor assessments, therefore, may be ineffective, misdirected, or even harmful.

In summary, the client's needs and the helping agency's purpose and resources will influence your choices and priorities during the assessment. You must be sure to attend to the client's immediate concern, or presenting problem; identify any legal or safety issues that may alter your priorities; be attuned to the many ways that strengths and resources may appear in the case; and consider all of the sources of information you may call upon to arrive at your assessment. You must also recognize the many facets to be taken into account in a multidimensional assessment, as well as the reciprocal nature of interactions, which requires an assessment that goes beyond mere cause and effect. Finally, you must be alert to your own history, values, biases and behaviors that might inject subjectivity into your interactions with clients and in the assessment that results.

Defining Assessment: Process and Product

The word *assessment* can be defined in several ways. For example, it refers to a process occurring between a social worker and client, in which information is gathered, analyzed, and synthesized to provide a concise picture of the client

EP 2.1.7a

and his or her needs and strengths. In settings in which social work is the primary profession, the social worker often makes the assessment independently or consults with colleagues or a member of another discipline in creating it. Typically, formal assessments may be completed in one or two sessions. These assessments also represent opportunities to determine whether the agency and the particular social worker are best suited to address the client's needs and wants. The social worker may identify the client's eligibility for services (for example, based on his or her needs, insurance coverage, or enrollment criteria) and make a referral to other resources if either the program or the social worker is not appropriate to meet the person's needs.

EP 2.1.10a

In settings in which social work is not the only or not the primary profession (*secondary* or *host settings*), the social worker may be a member of a clinical team (e.g., in mental health, schools, medical, and correctional settings), and the process of assessment may be the joint effort of a psychiatrist, social worker, psychologist, nurse, teacher, speech therapist, or members of other disciplines. In such settings, the social worker typically compiles a social history and contributes knowledge related to interpersonal and family dynamics. The assessment process may take longer due to the time required for all of the team members to complete their individual assessments and to reach a collective assessment during a group meeting.

The focus of the assessment is also influenced by the auspices in which it takes place and the theoretical orientation from which the social worker practices. While some data are common to all interviews, the focus of a particular interview and assessment formulation will vary according to the social worker's task, mission, theoretical framework, or other factors. For example, a social worker who is investigating an allegation of child endangerment will ask questions and draw conclusions related to the level of risk or potential for violence in the case. A social worker whose expertise lies in cognitive-behavioral theory will structure the assessment to address the effects of misconceptions or cognitive distortions on the client's feelings and actions. A clinician in a correctional setting will use different concepts and standards to categorize offenders and to determine risks and needs (Beyer & Balster, 2001). This does not mean that in any of those cases, the worker addresses *only* those issues, but rather that the questions asked and the conclusions drawn will be narrowed by the social worker's mission, theory, setting and clinical focus.

Social workers engage in the process of assessment from the beginning of their contact with the client and the relationship's termination, which may occur weeks, months, or even years later. Thus, assessment is a fluid and dynamic process that involves receiving, analyzing, and synthesizing new information as it emerges during the entire course of a given case. In the first session, the social worker generally elicits abundant information; he or she must then assess the information's meaning and significance as the client–social worker interaction unfolds. This moment-by-moment assessment guides the social worker in deciding which information is salient and merits deeper exploration and which is less relevant to understanding the individual and the presenting problem. After gathering sufficient information to illuminate the situation, the social worker analyzes it and, in collaboration with the client, integrates the data into a tentative formulation of the problem. Many potential clients do not proceed with the social worker beyond this point. If their concerns can be best handled through a referral to other resources, if they do not meet eligibility criteria, or if they choose not to continue the relationship, contact often stops here.

Should the social worker and the client continue the contact, assessment continues, although it is not a central focus of the work. People often disclose new information as the problem solving process progresses, casting the original evaluation in a new light. Sometimes this new insight emerges as the natural result of coming to know the person better. In other cases, individuals may withhold vital information until they are certain that the social worker is trustworthy and capable. As a result, preliminary assessments often turn out to be inaccurate and must be discarded or drastically revised.

Note that the term *assessment* also refers to the written products that result from the process of understanding the client. As a product, assessment involves an actual formulation or statement at a given time regarding the nature of clients' problems, resources, and other related factors. A formal assessment requires analysis and synthesis of relevant data into a working definition of the problem. It identifies associated factors and clarifies how they interact to produce and maintain the problem. Because assessments must constantly be updated and revised, it is helpful to think of an assessment as *a complex working hypothesis based on the most current data available.*

EP 2.1.10d

Written assessments range from comprehensive psychosocial reports to brief analyses about very specific issues, such as the client's mental status, substance use, capacity for self-care, or suicidal risk. An assessment may summarize progress on a case or provide a comprehensive overview of the client (to facilitate his or her transfer to another resource or termination of the case). The scope and focus of the written product and of the assessment itself will vary depending on three factors: the *role* of the social worker, the *setting* in which he or she works, and the *needs* presented by the client. For example, a school social worker's

EP 2.1.3a

assessment of an elementary school student may focus on the history and pattern of disruptive behaviors in the classroom, as well as on the classroom environment itself. A social worker in a family services agency seeing the same child may focus more broadly on the child's developmental history and his or her family's dynamics, as well as on the troubling classroom behavior. A worker evaluating the child's eligibility to be paired with an adult mentor would look at family income, the child's existing social systems and other information to determine his or her capacity to benefit from the match. To use another example, a hospital social worker whose focus is discharge planning may evaluate a client's readiness to leave the hospital after heart surgery and determine the services and information needed to make the return home successful. A social worker in a community health or mental health agency may assess the same client to determine the impact of the disease and the surgery on the client's emotional well-being, activities of daily living, and on his or her intimate relationship. A social worker in a vocational setting may focus the assessment on the client's readiness to return to work and the job accommodations needed to facilitate that transition.

EP 2.1.7a

While a social worker's assessment will be guided by particular issues pertinent to that setting, certain priorities in assessment influence all social work settings. Without prioritization, workers run the risk of conducting unbalanced, inefficient, or misdirected evaluations. Initially, three issues should be assessed in all situations:

1. *What does the client see as his or her primary concerns or goals?* Sometimes referred to as "starting where the client is," this question highlights social work's emphasis on self-determination and commitment to assisting individuals (where legal, ethical, and possible) to reach their own goals. Practically speaking, sharing concerns helps alleviate the client of some of the burdens and apprehensions that brought him or her to the interview and may also identify their hopes and goals for service.
2. *What (if any) current or impending legal mandates must the client and social worker consider?* If the client is mandated to receive services or faces other legal concerns, this factor may shape the nature of the assessment and the way the client presents himself or herself. Therefore, it is important to "get this issue on the table" at the outset. For example, an adult protection worker must assess the risk of abuse, neglect, or other danger to an elderly client, whether or not the client shares those concerns.
3. *What (if any) potentially serious health or safety concerns might require the social worker's and client's attention?* Social workers must be alert to health problems and other conditions that may place clients at risk. These issues may be central to the client's presenting problem, or they may indicate a danger that requires immediate intervention by the worker. An assessment focused on a client's employability following incarceration may need to take a different direction if the client reports self-destructive thoughts, hazardous living conditions, substance use, untreated injuries, predatory roommates or other issues of more immediate concern. While the profession places high value on self-determination, social workers must act—even if it means overruling the client's wishes—in situations that present "serious, foreseeable, and imminent harm" (NASW, 2008, p. 7).

After addressing these three fundamental questions, the social worker goes on to explore the client's functioning, interactions with his or her environment, problems and challenges, strengths and resources, developmental needs and life transitions, and key systems related to the case. Often these elements are referred to as a basic social history or personal history (Wiger, 2009). The remainder of this chapter and Chapter 9 further delineate how each of these areas is assessed (see Figure 8-1).

Assessment and Diagnosis

It is important at this point to clarify the difference between diagnoses and assessments. *Diagnoses* are labels or terms that may be applied to an individual or his or her situation. A diagnosis provides a shorthand categorization based on specifically defined criteria. It can reflect a medical condition (e.g., "end-stage renal disease," "diabetes"), mental disorder (e.g., "depression," "agoraphobia"), or other classification (e.g., "emotionally and behaviorally disturbed," "gifted and talented," "learning disabled"). Diagnostic labels serve many purposes. For example, they provide a language through which professionals and patients can communicate about a commonly understood constellation of symptoms. The use of accepted diagnostic terminology facilitates research on problems, identification of appropriate treatments or medications, and linkages among people with similar problems. For example, diagnosing a set of troubling behaviors as "bipolar disorder" helps the client, his or her physician, and social worker to identify necessary medication and therapeutic services. The diagnosis may comfort the individual by helping "put a name to" the experiences

EP 2.1.3b

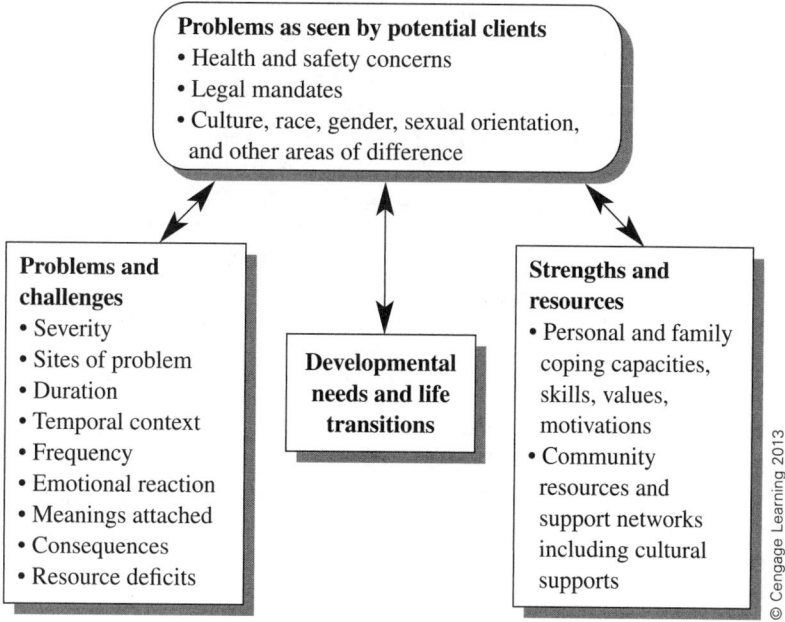

FIG-8-1 Overview: Areas for Attention in Assessing Strengths and Problems

he or she has been having. It may also help the client and his or her family members learn more about the condition, locate support groups, and stay abreast of developments in understanding the disorder.

EP 2.1.3a

But diagnoses have their difficulties, too. Although such labels provide an expedient way of describing complex problems, they never tell the whole story. Diagnoses can become self-fulfilling prophecies, wherein clients, their families, and their helpers begin to define the client only in terms of the diagnostic label. This distinction is captured in the difference between saying "Joe is schizophrenic," "Joe has schizophrenia," or "Joe is a person with schizophrenia." While diagnostic labels carry a lot of power, they can sometimes be bestowed in error (the result of misdiagnosis or diagnostic categories that change over time), and they may obscure important information about the client's difficulties and capacities. Referring to a client as "developmentally delayed," for example, may speak only to that individual's score on an IQ test—not to his or her level of daily functioning, interests, goals, joys, and challenges.

At this point, assessment steps in. Assessments describe the symptoms that support a particular diagnosis, but they go further to help us understand the client's history and background, the effect of the symptoms on the individual, the available support and resources to manage the problem, and so on. In other words, diagnoses may result from assessments, but they tell only part of the story.

The Diagnostic and Statistical Manual (DSM-IV-TR)

The Diagnostic and Statistical Manual (DSM-IV-TR) is an important tool for understanding and formulating mental and emotional disorders (American Psychiatric Association, 2000). It is linked to *The International Statistical Classification of Diseases and Related Health Problems, 10th Revision* (ICD-10), a commonly used system to codify health and mental health disorders, symptoms, social circumstances, and causes of injury or illnesses (Munson, 2002). Diagnostic systems such as the *DSM-IV-TR* have come under fire for a number of reasons, including excessive focus on individual pathologies over strengths and societal and environmental factors. Critics suggest that the manual is time- and culture-bound, throwing the validity of the categorizations in dispute. Some find the use of the *DSM* to be particularly incongruent with social work, in light of the history and focus of the profession (Kirk & Kutchins, 1992). A revised DSM-5 is targeted for release in May 2013. Anticipated modifications include changes in terminology (from "substance abuse" to "addiction," for example), structural adjustments (such as the addition of scales to express differences in symptoms and severity), and new or revised diagnostic categories reflecting improved understanding of syndromes, symptom patterns, etc. (DSM5.org, 2010). Events such as this demonstrate that diagnosis is an imperfect and evolving process. It provides a useful language for

EP 2.1.3a

common understanding, but it must be used with caution and humility.

Criticisms notwithstanding, the *DSM-IV-TR* is widely used by professionals and consumers; the diagnoses and assessments are often required for insurance reimbursement and other forms of payment for services, and many social workers work with individuals who have received mental health diagnoses, whether or not the social worker him- or herself actually gave the diagnosis. You will need specialized knowledge and training in order to be thoroughly familiar with the *DSM* system and apply it to the complexities of human behavior and emotions. As the DSM-5 is introduced, the demands of ethics and good practice will require you to become familiar with its features and changes to maintain professional competence. Until then, this section will acquaint you with the features of the classification system, and serve as a reference point for discussions in Chapter 9 about prominent cognitive and affective diagnoses.

The *DSM* uses a *multiaxial* system, in which coding on five axes provides diagnostic and functional information.

Axis I   Clinical syndromes (e.g., sleep, anxiety, eating, and mood disorders; schizophrenia; disorders usually first evident in infancy, childhood or adolescence; and substance-related disorders)

              Other conditions that may be a focus of clinical attention (e.g., relational problems, problems related to abuse and neglect, psychological factors affecting a medical condition)

Axis II   Personality disorders (e.g., borderline, antisocial, narcissistic, obsessive-compulsive, schizoid, paranoid)
              Mental retardation

Axis III   Physical disorders (e.g., diabetes, chronic obstructive pulmonary disease, hypertension). Clinicians must note the source of this information, for example "patient report" or "physician referral"

Axis IV   Psychological and environmental problems, or "PEPs" (e.g., educational problems, problems related to interaction with the legal system/crime, housing problems)

Axis V   Global Assessment of Functioning, or "GAF scores" (a 1–100 scale on which the professional assigns a numeric score of psychological, social, and occupational functioning at the time of evaluation; the time frame is noted in parentheses next to the score. Zero is used to indicate insufficient information to assign a GAF score) (Bloom, Fischer, & Orme, 2006)

In the *DSM-IV-TR* system, disorders are assigned a 3–5 digit code wherein digits after the decimal point specify the severity and course of the disorder. Therefore, 296.21 would represent Major Depressive disorder, Single Episode, Mild (Munson, 2002). For each disorder, the manual uses a standardized format to present relevant information. The sections address current knowledge on:

- Diagnostic features
- Subtypes/specifiers
- Recording procedures
- Associated features and disorders
- Specific culture, gender, and age features
- Prevalence
- Course
- Familial patterns
- Differential diagnosis
- Diagnostic criteria

The manual attempts to be strictly descriptive of the conditions it covers. It does not use a specific theoretical framework, recommend appropriate treatments, or address the causation (or etiology) of a disorder, except in unique circumstances. Resources such as Kaplan & Sadock (2007), the *DSM-IV-TR Casebook* (Spitzer, et al., 1995), and the *DSM-IV-TR* itself (American Psychiatric Association, 2000) are helpful materials to prepare for regular use of the manual and for developing the clinical acumen for making and using diagnoses.

Culturally Competent Assessment

Culturally competent assessment requires knowledge of cultural norms, acculturation, and language differences; the ability to differentiate between individual and culturally linked attributes; the initiative to seek out needed information so that evaluations are not biased and services are culturally appropriate; and an understanding of the ways that cultural differences may reveal themselves in the assessment process.

EP 2.1.4b & c

Cultures vary widely in their prescribed patterns of child-rearing, communication, family member roles, mate selection, and care of the aged—to name just a few areas of differentiation. For example, to whom would you properly address concerns in a Latino family about a child's truancy? What are normative dating patterns in the gay and lesbian communities? At what age is it proper to allow a youngster to babysit for younger siblings? What are appropriate expectations for independence for a young adult with Down syndrome? How might Laotian parents view their child's educational aspirations?

Knowledge of your client's cultural norms is indispensable when his or her cultural background differs markedly from your own. Without such knowledge, you may make serious errors in assessing both individual and interpersonal systems, because patterns that are functional in one cultural context may prove problematic in another, and vice versa. Errors in assessment can lead to culturally insensitive interventions that may aggravate rather than diminish clients' problems. The necessary knowledge about cultural norms is not easy to obtain, however. It requires a baseline understanding of areas of difference and histories and risks of oppression experienced by different groups, self-examination for biases and prejudices, and ongoing conversation with clients and other key informants (Gilbert, 2003; Johnson & Munch, 2009; Smith, 2004).

This last piece is important because of the considerable variations that occur within groups. Making overgeneralizations about members of any group may obscure (rather than clarify) the meanings of individual behavior. For example, more than 400 different tribal groups of Native Americans live in the United States, and these groups speak more than 250 distinct languages (Edwards, 1983). Comparisons of Plains tribes with Native Americans of the Southwest have revealed sharply contrasting cultural patterns and patterns of individual behavior as well as marked differences in the incidence of certain social problems (May, Hymbaugh, Aase, & Samet, 1983). Similarly significant heterogeneity exists within every racial and cultural group.

Even where homogeneity exists in cultural subgroups, wide variations also exist among individuals. As a consequence, being knowledgeable about a given group is necessary but not sufficient for understanding the behavior of individual members of the groups. Knowing about Laotian parents is not the same as knowing about the particular Laotian parents you are serving. The task confronting practitioners, therefore, is to differentiate between behavior that is culturally mediated and behavior that is a product of individual personality and life experience. This journey is guided by your fundamental knowledge of different cultures and your curiosity about your particular clients.

EP 2.1.7b

In assessment, it is important to consider the degree to which the client experiences a goodness of fit with the culture in which he or she is situated. Many people are actually members of multiple cultures, so their functioning must be considered in relationship to both their predominant cultural identity and the majority culture. An elderly lesbian may feel alienated or accepted depending on how the culture around her views her age, gender, and sexual orientation. This "goodness-of-fit" is a consideration when examining any person in the context of his or her environment. Individuals from the same ethnic group may vary widely in the degree of their acculturation or their comfort with biculturalism, depending on several factors—for example, the number of generations that have passed since their original emigration, the degree of socialization to the majority culture, and interactions with the majority culture. Consider these possibilities affecting goodness-of-fit between cultures:

1. The degree of commonality between the two cultures with regard to norms, values, beliefs, perceptions, and the like
2. The availability of cultural interpreters, mediators, and models
3. The amount and type (positive or negative) of feedback provided by each culture regarding attempts to produce normative behaviors
4. The conceptual style and problem-solving approach of the minority individual and his or her mesh with the prevalent or valued styles of the majority culture
5. The individual's degree of bilingualism
6. The degree of dissimilarity in physical appearance from the majority culture, such as skin color, facial features, and so forth (De Anda, 1984)

Cross-cultural contact also occurs between minority professionals and clients from the majority culture. While the minority practitioner is usually more familiar with the majority culture than the majority practitioner is with minority cultures, clients often challenge the credibility of minority professionals (Hardy, 1993; Proctor & Davis, 1994). The client may assign credibility to a social worker because of his or her education, position, role, age, gender, and other factors emphasized in the client's culture—that is, because of factors over which a professional has little control. Credibility can also be achieved, however, when people have favorable experiences with social workers that foster respect, confidence, trust, and hope (Harper & Lantz, 1996); when social workers address areas of difference in a straightforward manner; and when social workers seek to learn about particular influences of the client's culture (Hunt, 2001; Tervalon & Murray-Garcia, 1998).

Emphasizing Strengths in Assessments

Clients typically seek social work services for help with problems or difficulties. As a result, the assessment typically focuses on developing a picture of the person's life, including the difficulties that bring him or her in for services. Sometimes the attention to problems is the result of eligibility requirements that require the client to have particular challenges or diagnoses in order to qualify for (or continue to receive) services (Frager, 2000). That is, the funding for services, whether it comes through insurance reimbursement or government contracts, may be based on the client's difficulties and level of impairment. Emphasizing strengths in a case report may cause utilization reviewers to question whether services are needed at all. While eligibility and clarity about problems are both important, they sometimes lead to an overemphasis on pathology and dysfunction at the expense of strengths, capacities, and achievements whose recognition might help provide a fuller understanding of the client.

EP 2.1.10e

To emphasize strengths and empowerment in the assessment process, Cowger makes three suggestions to social workers:

1. Give preeminence to the *client's* understanding of the facts.
2. Discover what the client wants.
3. Assess personal and environmental strengths on multiple levels (1994).

Cowger (1994) has developed a two-dimensional matrix framework for assessment that can assist social workers in attending to both needs and strengths. On the vertical axis, potential strengths and resources are depicted at one end and potential deficits, challenges, and obstacles are shown at the other end. The horizontal axis ranges from environmental (family and community) to individual factors. This framework prods us to move beyond the frequent preoccupation with personal deficits (*quadrant 4*), to include personal strengths and environmental strengths and obstacles. Figure 8-2 demonstrates this framework and highlights two facts: A useful assessment is not limited to either deficits or strengths, and both the environmental and personal dimensions are important. Use of all four quadrants provides information that can help in pursuing the client's goals, while remaining mindful of obstacles and challenges.

IDEAS IN ACTION

The following section applies Cowger's matrix to the case of Jackie and Anna, featured in the video "Home for the Holidays I."

EP 2.1.10e

Strengths or Resources

Quadrant 1—Environmental Factors

- Anna and Jackie are both in contact with, and value, their immediate and extended family. Anna's hesitancy to discuss the couple's relationship, in spite of the conflict it causes, demonstrates her desire to remain connected to her family of origin.
- Anna and Jackie are both employed. Anna owns her own business.

Quadrant 2—Personal Factors

- Anna and Jackie's intimate relationship and friendship is a source of strength and joy for both of them. Their willingness to attend conjoint sessions and create assignments at the end of the first meeting attests to their appreciation of their partnership.
- Jackie has a bold personality and is not afraid to stand up for herself, demanding the respect she deserves.
- Anna is thoughtful and deliberate. She considers all of the consequences of her actions.

Deficit, Obstacle, or Challenge

Quadrant 3—Environmental Factors

- Anna's parents are uncomfortable talking about their daughter's intimate relationship with another woman.
- Anna's work schedule is busy and her days are full. She is often drained when she comes home and lacks the energy to connect with Jackie.

Quadrant 4—Personal Factors

- Anna is prone to social withdrawal. She avoids conflict with her parents and Jackie.
- Jackie appears impatient to Anna. Her communication style comes off as "pushy."

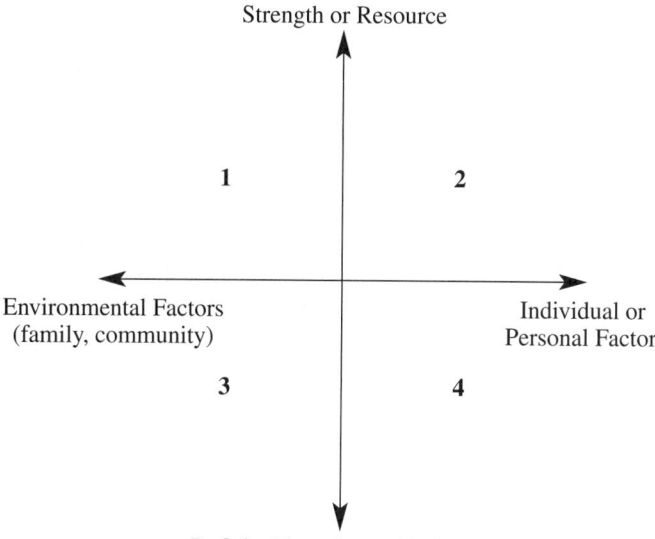

FIG-8-2 Framework for Assessment
SOURCE: Adapted from Saleebey, Dennis, *The Strengths Perspective in Social Work Practice* 2nd, © 1997. Printed and Electronically reproduced by permission of Pearson Education, Inc., Upper Saddle River, New Jersey.

EP 2.1.10e

The following list emphasizes strengths that are often overlooked or taken for granted during assessment. Cultivating your sensitivity to these strengths will help you be attuned to others as they emerge:

1. Facing problems and seeking help, rather than denying or otherwise avoiding confronting them
2. Taking a risk by sharing problems with the social worker—a stranger
3. Persevering under difficult circumstances
4. Being resourceful and creative in making the most out of limited resources
5. Seeking to further knowledge, education, and skills
6. Expressing caring feelings to family members and friends
7. Asserting one's rights rather than submitting to injustice
8. Being responsible in work or financial obligations
9. Seeking to understand the needs and feelings of others
10. Having the capacity for introspection or for examining situations by considering different perspectives
11. Demonstrating the capacity for self-control
12. Functioning effectively in stressful situations
13. Demonstrating the ability to consider alternative courses of actions and the needs of others when solving problems

The Role of Knowledge and Theory in Assessments

EP 2.1.3a

"What you see depends on what you look for." This saying captures the roles that knowledge and theory play in shaping the questions that are asked in assessment and the hypotheses that result. Competent, evidence-based practice requires that assessments are informed by problem-specific knowledge (O'Hare, 2005). As a result, you would consider the nature of the problem presented by the client at intake (e.g., explosive anger, hoarding, parent-child conflict, truancy) and refer to available research to identify the factors that contribute to, sustain, and ameliorate those problems. This knowledge would help you to know the relevant data to be collected during assessment and the formulations that result. For example, the literature might suggest that truancy is caused by a poor fit between the student's needs and the classroom environment or the teacher's attitude and methods. Or it might stem from chaos at home in which children are not awakened for school, prepared for the day, or even expected to attend. Poor school attendance may come from poor performance as a result of vision or hearing problems, attention deficits, or learning disabilities. It may also arise from shame on the child's part about hygiene, dress, worthiness, or bullying and other negative peer experiences. Regardless of the factors involved, there is rarely a strictly linear, cause-and-effect explanation for truancy. Instead, the influence of some factors (e.g., poor vision or hearing) leads to behaviors (acting out or truancy) that distance the child from peers, irritate the teacher, and lead to a withdrawal by the student that puts him or her even further behind, and in turn more likely to act out or withdraw further—a reciprocal interaction. Your understanding of the research and theories on human behavior will help focus the assessment on those elements that are involved in a particular client's difficulties.

The demand for evidence-based assessments may make it appear that you have to do a research paper or literature review for every client. While this would be too onerous, do not underestimate the importance of thorough research; poorly directed assessments and interventions also come with high costs, ranging from client discouragement and wasted professional and agency resources to perhaps even harm, if the resulting services are negligent. To the extent that you and your organization specialize in particular problems or populations, the knowledge gained from research done for any one case can be called on for similar cases. And, with increased access to electronic resources and reference guides that summarize the best available evidence in a variety of areas, it has become much easier to find and evaluate existing knowledge[1] (U.S. Department of Health and Human Services, Substance Abuse and Mental Health Services Administration, 2011; Bloom, Fischer, & Orme, 2006; O'Hare, 2005; Thyer & Wodarski, 1998; Wodarski & Thyer; 1998; The Campbell Collaboration, n.d.; The National Institute of Mental Health, n.d.. The Cochrane Collaboration, n.d.).

EP 2.1.7b

As with available knowledge, theories shape assessments. Some theories have a selective influence as concepts associated with that theory are adopted for more general use. For example, multidimensional assessments make use of concepts drawn from the fields of ego psychology, such as reality testing, judgment, and coping mechanisms, and concepts prominent in object relations theory, such as attachment and interpersonal relationship patterns. Most assessments address patterns in thought, behaviors and actions, interpersonal relationships, affect, and role transitions, though they may not be targeted toward the provision of interpersonal therapy (IPT), which uses those concepts in a particular fashion. In addition, assessments typically utilize concepts such as risk and resilience and empowerment and strengths, even if the assessment is not wholly organized around those frameworks.

Some theoretical orientations play a greater role in the structure of the assessment and the conclusions that are drawn. For example, *brief, solution-focused therapy* is one model that is encountered in a variety of settings. This model is based on a number of assumptions—for example, that small changes can lead to larger changes, that focusing on the present can help the client tap into unused capacities and generate creative alternatives, and that paying attention to solutions is more relevant than focusing on problems. While solution-building questions may be used with other frameworks, an assessment guided by this practice model will utilize:

Seeking exceptions: Questions that determine when the problem does not exist or does not occur. The answer may refer to different sites, times, or contexts. Exploration then asks the client to elaborate on what is different in those incidents and what other factors might cause it to be different.

Scaling the problem: This involves asking the client to estimate, on a scale of 1 to 10, the severity of the problem. The response can help in tracking changes over time, open up the opportunity to ask what accounts for the current level of difficulty or relief, and determine what it might take to move from the current level to a higher point on the scale.

Scaling motivation is similar to scaling problems or concerns. It involves asking clients to estimate the degree to which they feel hopeful about resolution, or perhaps the degree to which they have given up hope. How would they rate their commitment to working on the problem?

The *miracle question* helps the practitioner to determine the client's priorities and to operationalize the areas for change. Essentially, the social worker asks, "If, while you were asleep, a miracle occurred and your problem was solved, how would things be different when you woke up?" This technique helps the client envision the positive results of the change process and elicits important information for structuring specific behavioral interventions (Jordan & Franklin, 2003).

As with other assessment tools, the key to successful use of these techniques lies in the sensitivity and timing with which they are employed. For example, asking the miracle question prematurely may lead the client to believe that you are not listening or are minimizing his or her distress. Typically, these questions may be prefaced by statements acknowledging the client's concern—for example, "I know your son's misbehavior has been troubling to you, but I wonder if there are times when he does follow your directions?" Sensitivity is also demonstrated through inflection or tone of voice, eye contact, and other nonverbal methods of attending that assure the client of your attention and regard.

Other theoretical orientations with demonstrable efficacy will shape the entire assessment. For example, cognitive theories suggest that thoughts mediate emotions and actions (Beck 1995; Ellis, 1962; Lantz, 1996). Therefore, assessments derived from these theories would focus on the nature of the client's thoughts and schemas (cognitive patterns), causal attributions, the basis for the client's beliefs, and

EP 2.1.7a

antecedent thoughts in problematic situations (Walsh, 2006). Behavioral theories suggest that actions and emotions are created, maintained, "and extinguished through principles of learning" (Walsh, 2006, p. 107). As such, the assessment focuses on the conditions surrounding troubling behaviors, the conditions that reinforce the behavior, and the consequences and secondary gains that might result. Questions to address this sequence include:

EP 2.1.10d

- *When do you experience the behavior?*
- *Where do you experience the behavior?*
- *How long does the behavior usually last?*
- *What happens immediately after the behavior occurs?*
- *What bodily reactions do you experience with the behavior?*
- *What do the people around you usually do when the behavior is happening?*
- *What happened afterward that was pleasant?* (Bertolino & O'Hanlon, 2002; Cormier, Nurius, & Osborn, 2009; Walsh, 2006)

The intent of these questions is to create a hypothesis about what triggers and reinforces the behavior in order to construct a plan involving new reinforcement patterns and a system for measuring change.

Naturally, there are cautions about the degree to which existing knowledge or theories influence assessment. While they are helpful in predicting and explaining client behaviors and in structuring assessments and interventions, when they are applied too rigidly they may oversimplify the problem and objectify the individual client (Walsh, 2006). Poorly tested theories and beliefs may be given greater weight and prominence than they deserve. Frameworks may be improperly applied to populations that differ markedly from those on which the framework was tested. Adhering to a single preferred framework may obscure other relevant factors in the case, blind the practitioner to limits in existing theory or knowledge, and inhibit him or her from pursuing promising new knowledge and interventions. Critical thinking and proper training are required so that professionals can effectively evaluate and apply frameworks to enhance client services (O'Hare, 2005).

Sources of Information

Where do social workers get the information on which to base their assessment? Numerous sources can be used individually or in combination. The following are the most common:

EP 2.1.7a & 2.1.10d

1. Background sheets or other intake forms that clients complete
2. Interviews with clients (i.e., accounts of problems, history, views, thoughts, events, and the like)
3. Direct observation of nonverbal behavior
4. Direct observation of interaction between partners, family members, and group members
5. Collateral information from relatives, friends, physicians, teachers, employers, and other professionals
6. Tests or assessment instruments
7. Personal experiences of the practitioner based on direct interaction with clients

The *information obtained from client interviews* is usually the primary source of assessment information. The skills described in Chapters 5 and 6 for structuring and conducting effective interviews will help in establishing a trusting relationship and acquiring the information needed for assessment. It is important to respect clients' feelings and reports, to use empathy to convey understanding, to probe for depth, and to check with the client to ensure that your understanding is accurate. Interviews with child clients may be enhanced or facilitated by use of instruments (McConaughy & Achenbach, 1994; Schaffer, 1992) and by play, drawing, and other techniques. As with other information sources, verbal reports often need to be augmented because faulty recall, biases, mistrust, and limited self-awareness may result in a skewed or inaccurate picture.

Direct observation of nonverbal behavior adds information about emotional states and reactions such as anger, hurt, embarrassment, and fear. To use these sources of data, the social worker must be attentive to nonverbal cues, such as tone of voice, tears, clenched fists, vocal tremors, quivering hands, a tightened jaw, pursed lips, variations of expression, and gestures; he or she must link these behaviors to the topic or theme during which they arise. The social worker may share these observations in the moment ("Your whole body deflated when you were telling me what she said") or note them to be included with other data ("The client's voice softened and he had tears in his eyes when talking about his wife's illness").

Observations of interactions between spouses or partners, family members, and group members are also often enlightening. Social workers frequently are amazed at the striking differences between clients' reports of their relationships and the behaviors they actually demonstrate in those relationships. A social worker may observe a father interacting with his daughter, impatiently telling her "I know you can do better"; in an earlier session, however, the father may have described his behavior to her as "encouraging." Direct observation may reveal that his words are encouraging while his tone and gestures are not.

Observation can occur in natural settings (e.g., a child in the classroom, adults in a group setting, or a family as they answer a worker's question in session). Home visits are a particularly helpful forum for observation. One major benefit of in-home, family-based services is the opportunity to observe the family's lived experiences firsthand rather than rely on secondhand accounts (Ronnau & Marlow, 1995; Strom-Gottfried, 2009). Observing clients' living conditions typically reveals resources and challenges that would otherwise not come to light.

Social workers can also employ *enactment* to observe interactions firsthand rather than rely on verbal report. With this technique, clients reenact an event during a session. Participants are instructed to recreate the situation exactly as it occurred, using the same words, gestures, and tones of voice as in the actual event. You might explain: "To understand what produced the difficulties in the situation you just described, I'd like you to recreate it here in our session. By seeing what both of you do and say, and how you do it, I can get an accurate picture of what typically happens. I'd like you to replay the situation exactly as it happened. Use the same words, gestures, and tone of voice as you did originally. Now, where were you when it happened, and how did it start?" To counteract the temptation to create a favorable impression, the social worker can ask each participant afterward about the extent to which the behaviors demonstrated in the enactment correspond with the behaviors that occurred in actual situations.

Enactment can also be used in contrived situations to see how people interact in situations that involve decision making, planning, role negotiation, child discipline, or similar activities. Social workers will need to exercise their creativity in designing situations or creating role plays which will generate and clarify the types of interaction that they wish to observe. Another form of enactment involves the use of symbolic interactions—for example, through the use of dolls, games, or other forms of expressive or play therapy (Jordan & Hickerson, 2003).

Remember, however, that direct observation is subject to perceptual errors by the observer. Take care when drawing conclusions from your observations. Scrutinize how congruent your conclusions are with the information acquired from other sources. Despite the flaws, information from various forms of direct observation adds significantly to that gained from verbal reports.

EP 2.1.4b

Client self-monitoring is a potent source of information (Kopp, 1989). It produces a rich and quantifiable body of data and empowers the client by turning him or her into a collaborator in the assessment process. In self-monitoring, clients track symptoms on logs or in journals, write descriptions, and record feelings, behaviors, and thoughts associated with particular times, events, symptoms, or difficulties. The first step in self-monitoring is to recognize the occurrence of the event (e.g., signs that lead to anxiety attacks, temper tantrums by children, episodes of drinking or gambling). Using self-anchored rating scales (Jordan & Franklin, 2003) or simple counting measures, clients and/or those around them can keep a record of the frequency or intensity of a behavior. How often was Joe late for school? How would Joan rate the severity of her anxiety in the morning, at noon, and in the evening? Which nights did Ralph have particular difficulty sleeping? Did this difficulty relate to events during the day, medications, stresses, or anything he ate or drank?

A major advantage of self-monitoring is that the process itself requires the monitor to focus attention on patterns. As a result, clients gain insights into their situations and the circumstances surrounding their successes or setbacks. As they discuss their recorded observations, they may "spontaneously operationalize goals and suggest ideas for change" (Kopp, 1989, p. 278). The process of recording also assists in evaluation, because progress can be tracked more precisely by examining data that show a reduction of problematic behaviors or feelings and an increase in desirable characteristics.

Another source for assessment data is *collateral contacts*—that is, information provided by relatives, friends, teachers, physicians, child care providers, and others who possess essential insights about relevant aspects of clients' lives.

EP 2.1.10d

Collateral sources are of particular importance when, because of developmental capacity or functioning, the client's ability to generate information may be limited or distorted. For example, parents, guardians, and other caregivers are often the primary source of information about a child's history, functioning, resources, and challenges. Similarly, assessments of individuals with memory impairment or cognitive limitations will be enhanced by the data that collaterals (family members, caregivers, or friends) can provide.

Social workers must exercise discretion when deciding that such information is needed and in obtaining it. Clients can assist in this effort by suggesting which collateral contacts might provide useful information. Their written consent (through agency "release of information" forms) is required prior to making contact with these sources.

EP 2.1.7b

In weighing the validity of information obtained from collateral sources, it is important to consider the nature of their relationship with the client and the ways in which that might influence these contacts' perspectives. For example, members of the immediate family may be emotionally involved or exhausted by the individual's difficulties and unconsciously skew their reports accordingly. For example, studies indicate that elderly clients may overrate their functional capacity while families underrate it, and nurses' evaluations fall somewhere in the middle (Gallo, 2005). Individuals who have something to gain or to lose from pending case decisions (e.g., custody of a child, residential placement) may be less credible as collaterals than individuals who do not have a conflict of interest or are further removed from case situations. Conversely, individuals who have limited contact with the client (such as other service providers) may have narrow or otherwise distorted views of the client's situation. As with other sources of information, input from collateral contacts must be critically viewed and weighed against other information in the case.

EP 2.1.3b

Another possible source of information consists of various *assessment instruments*, including psychological tests, screening instruments, and assessment tools. Some of these tests are administered by professionals, such as psychologists or educators, who have undergone special training in the administration and scoring of such assessment tools. In these cases, social workers might receive reports of the testing and incorporate the findings into their psychosocial assessments or treatment plans. Examples of these instruments include intelligence tests such as the Wechsler Adult Intelligence Scale, 3rd edition (WAIS-III) or the Wechsler Intelligence Scale for Children, 3rd edition (WISC-III) (Lukas, 1993), tools for use with children such as the Behavior Assessment System of Children (BASC) (Reynolds & Kamphaus, 1992), the Achenbach System of Empirically Based Assessment (ASEBA) for ages 1.5 to 18 (Achenbach & Rescorla, 2000, 2001), or the Adolescent and Child Urgent Threat Evaluation (Copeland & Ashley, 2005), which is designed to measure risk of near future harm to self or others (within hours to days) in youth aged 8 to 18 in a variety of settings, including inpatient and outpatient clinics, schools, emergency rooms, and juvenile justice facilities. Other instruments assess personality disorders and other mental health problems, such as the Million Multiaxial Clinical Inventory-III (MCMI-III) (Millon & Davis, 1997), the Minnesota Multiphasic Personality Inventory (MMPI-II) (Hathaway & McKinley, 1989), or the Patient Health Questionnaire (PHQ-9) (Kroenke, Spitzer, & Williams, 2001) developed for use in primary care settings. Gibbons, et al. (2008) recommend computerized adaptive testing (CAT) in which clients receive different questions or scales as needs are indicated by their answers on earlier measures and items. This strategy encourages more efficient, precisely targeted data for clinical use.

Some tools are designed for use by social workers and allied professionals. Examples include the WALMYR Assessment Scales, which can be used to measure depression, self-esteem, clinical stress, anxiety, alcohol involvement, peer relations, sexual attitudes, homophobia, marital satisfaction, sexual satisfaction, nonphysical abuse of partners, and a variety of other clinical phenomena.[2] The Multi-Problem Screening Inventory (MPSI) is a computer-based multidimensional self-report measure that helps practitioners to better assess and understand the severity or magnitude of client problems across 27 different areas of personal and social functioning. The completed instrument helps both the client and the social worker evaluate areas of difficulty and determine the relative severity of difficulties in the various life areas. In addition to providing for better accuracy and efficiency, these and other computerized instruments simplify the tracking of results over time and assist in gathering data for determining case progress.

Instruments such as the Burns Depression Checklist (Burns, 1995), the Beck Depression Inventory (BDI-II) (Beck, Steer, & Brown, 1996), the Zung Self-Rating Depression Scale (Zung, 1965), and the Beck Scale for Suicidal Ideation (Range & Knott, 1997) have well-established validity and reliability, can be effectively administered and scored by clinicians from a variety of professions, and can assist practitioners in evaluating the seriousness of a client's condition. These measures examine the presence of depressive symptoms, such as fatigue, appetite and sleep changes, impaired concentration, suicidal ideation and guilt. Items on The Beck Depression Inventory ask clients to rate themselves on a 0–3 scale, for example:

0   I am no more tired or fatigued than usual.
1   I get more tired or fatigued more easily than usual.
2   I am too tired or fatigued to do a lot of the things I used to do.
3   I am too tired or fatigued to do most of the things I used to do.

And,

0   I have not experienced any changes in my appetite.
1   My appetite is somewhat less than usual.
1   My appetite is somewhat greater than usual.
2   My appetite is much less than before.
2   My appetite is much greater than usual.
3   I have no appetite at all.
3   I crave food all the time.

Those scores are then tabulated indicating relative risk from normal mood changes, to mild mood disturbance, to extreme depression. In the video titled "Elder Assessment" the worker administers a similar scale to assess Josephine's symptoms and finds a substantial basis for concern about depression.

Other instruments to measure alcohol or drug impairment may be conducted by the social worker, self-administered by the client, or computer administered (Abbott & Wood, 2000). Commonly used tools include the Michigan Alcoholism Screening Test (MAST) (Pokorny, Miller, & Kaplan, 1972; Selzer, 1971), and the Drug Abuse Screening Test (DAST) (Gavin, Ross, & Skinner, 1989). Some instruments use mnemonic devices to structure assessment questions. For example, the CAGE (Project Cork, n.d.) consists of four items in which an affirmative answer to any single question is highly correlated to alcohol dependence:

1. Have you ever felt you should Cut down on your drinking?
2. Have people Annoyed you by criticizing your drinking?
3. Have you ever felt bad or Guilty about your drinking?
4. Have you had an Eye opener first thing in the morning to steady your nerves or get rid of a hangover? (www.projectcork.org/clinical_tools/html/CAGE.html)

Similarly, the CRAFFT utilizes six questions to assess problematic alcohol use in adolescents (Knight, Sherritt, Shrier, Harris, & Chang, 2002). In this test, affirmative answers to two items would indicate the need for further examination of the youth's involvement with alcohol and other drugs.

1. Have you ever ridden in a Car driven by someone (including yourself) who was high or had been using alcohol or drugs?
2. Do you ever use alcohol or drugs to Relax, feel better about yourself, or fit in?
3. Do you ever use alcohol or drugs while you are by yourself, Alone?
4. Do you ever Forget things you did while using alcohol or drugs?
5. Do your Family or Friends ever tell you that you should cut down on your drinking or drug use?
6. Have you ever gotten into Trouble while you were using alcohol or drugs? (CRAFFT, n.d.)

Other tools may be helpful for identifying clients' strengths and needs, when used within the context of an assessment interview (Burns, Lawlor & Craig, 2004; VanHook, Berkman, & Dunkle, 1996). Examples include the Older Americans Resources and Services Questionnaire (OARS), which provides information about the client's functioning across a variety of domains, including economic and social resources and activities of daily living (George & Fillenbaum, 1990). Other tools can be applied to a range of client populations to measure variables such as social functioning, caregiver burden, well-being, mental health, and social networks, and still others may be used in the evaluation of specific syndromes, such as post-traumatic stress disorder, conduct disorders, or anxiety (O'Hare, 2005; Parks & Novelli, 2000; Sauter & Franklin, 1998; Thompson, 1989; Wodarski & Thyer, 1998).

EP 2.1.10e

Tests and screening instruments are useful and expedient methods of quantifying data and behaviors. They are also essential components in evidence-based practice in that they "enhance the reliability and validity of the assessment and provide a baseline for monitoring and evaluation" (O'Hare, 2005, p. 7). As a consequence, scales and measures play an important role in case planning and intervention selection. To use these tools effectively, however, practitioners must be well grounded in knowledge of test theory and in the characteristics of specific tests. Many instruments, for example, have biases, low reliability, and poor validity; some are ill suited for certain populations and thus should be used with extreme caution. To avoid the danger of misusing these tools, social workers should thoroughly understand any instruments they are using or recommending, and seek consultation in the interpretation of tests administered by other professionals. Sources such as Bloom, Fischer, and Orme (2006), Fischer and Corcoran (2006, 2007), Thyer and Wodarski (1998), and Wodarski and Thyer (1998) can acquaint social workers with an array of available instruments and their proper use.

EP 2.1.4d

A final source of information for assessment is the social worker's *personal experience* based on direct interaction with clients. You will react in different ways to different people, and these insights may prove useful in understanding how others respond to them. For example, you may view certain individuals as withdrawn, personable, dependent, caring, manipulative, seductive, assertive, overbearing, or determined. These impressions should be considered in light of other information you are gathering about the person and his or her circumstances. For instance, a client who reports that others take him for granted and place unreasonable demands upon him may appear to you to be meek and reluctant to make his needs known, even in stating what he wants from counseling. These observations may provide you with clues about the nature of his complaint that others take advantage of him.

EP 2.1.3a

Some cautions are warranted with using this method. Clients may not behave with the social worker as they do with other people. Apprehension, involuntariness, and the desire to make a good impression may all skew a person's presentation of himself or herself. Also, initial impressions can be misleading and must be confirmed by other sources of information or additional contact with the person. All human beings' impressions are subjective and may be influenced by our own interpersonal patterns and perceptions. Your perceptions of and reactions to clients will be affected by your own life experiences. Before drawing even tentative conclusions, scrutinize your reactions to identify possible biases, distorted perceptions, or actions on your part that may have contributed to the behavior you are observing. For example, confrontational statements on your part may spur a defensive response by the client. Perhaps the response reveals more about your actions than it represents the client's typical way of relating. Social constructions and personal experience may lead us to identify another's acts and statements as "stubborn" vs. "determined," "arrogant" vs. "confident," or "submissive" vs. "cooperative." Self-awareness is indispensable to drawing valid conclusions from your interactions with others.

Assessments that draw from multiple sources of data can provide a thorough, accurate, and helpful representation of the individual's history, strengths, and challenges. However, workers must be attuned to the advantages and disadvantages inherent in different types of input and weigh those carefully in creating a comprehensive picture of the client system.

Questions to Answer in Problem Assessment

As noted in earlier chapters, good practice requires you to use a variety of communication methods to encourage the client to tell his or her story. Therefore, the following questions are not intended to be *asked* in the assessment, but instead are meant to be used as a *guide* or *checklist* to ensure that you have not overlooked a significant factor in your assessment of the problem.

EP 2.1.10d

1. What are the clients' concerns and problems as they and other concerned parties perceive them?
2. Are any current or impending legal mandates relevant to the situation?
3. Do any serious health or safety issues need immediate attention?
4. What are specific indications of the problem? How is it manifesting itself? What are the consequences?
5. Who else (persons or systems) is involved in the problem(s)?
6. What unmet needs and/or wants are involved?
7. How do developmental stages or life transitions affect the problem(s)?
8. How do ethnocultural, societal, and social class factors bear on the problem(s)?
9. How severe is the problem, and how does it affect the participants?
10. What meanings do clients ascribe to the problem(s)?

11. Where, when, and how often do the problematic behaviors occur?
12. How long has the problem gone on? Why is the client seeking help now?
13. Have other issues (e.g., alcohol or substance abuse, physical or sexual abuse) affected the functioning of the client or family members?
14. What are the clients' emotional reactions to the problem(s)?
15. How have the clients attempted to cope with the problem, and what are the required skills to resolve the problem?
16. What are the clients' skills, strengths, and resources?
17. What support systems exist or need to be created for the clients?
18. What external resources do clients need?

Questions 1–3 should serve as preliminary inquiries so that the social worker learns about any pressing issues that may guide the direction of the interview. The remaining questions pertain to further specification of problems and help identify possible patterns for reciprocal interaction. They do not imply that a problem focus takes priority over explorations of strengths and resources, which are also covered by some of the questions. As suggested in the strengths matrix depicted in Figure 8-2, assessment of abilities, resources, and limitations or challenges is required for a full assessment. Data on problems (both when they occur and when they do not) helps complete that picture.

Getting Started

EP 2.1.4d

After opening social amenities and an explanation of the direction and length of the interview, you should begin by exploring the client's presenting problem. Sometimes this question is a simple, open-ended inquiry: "Mrs. Smith, what brings you in to see me today?" or "I'm glad you came in. How can I help you?" Questions such as these allow the client an opportunity to express his or her concerns and help give direction to the questions that will follow.

At this point, the worker must be attentive to other issues that may alter the direction of the interview, at least at the outset. If the client's request for service is nonvoluntary, and particularly if it results from a legal mandate (e.g., part of probation, the consequence of a child maltreatment complaint), then the nature of the mandate, referring information, and the client's perception of the referral will frame the early part of the first interview.

A further consideration at the first interview is whether any danger exists that the client might harm himself or herself or others. Some referrals—for example, in emergency services—clearly involve the risk for harm, which should be discussed and evaluated at the outset. In other instances, the risk may be more subtle. For example, a client may open an interview by saying, "I'm at the end of my rope... I can't take it any longer." The social worker should respond to this opening by probing further: "Can you tell me more...?" or "When you say you can't take it, what do you mean by that?" If further information raises the social worker's concerns about the danger for suicidal or aggressive behavior, more specific questioning should follow, geared toward assessing the lethality of the situation.

Whatever the client's presenting problem, if shared information gives rise to safety concerns, the social worker must redirect the interview to focus on the degree of danger. If the threats to safety are minor or manageable, the practitioner may resume the interview's focus on the issues that brought the person in for service. However, if the mini-assessment reveals serious or imminent risk to the client or others, the focus of the session must be on ensuring safety rather than continuing the more general assessment.

Chapter 9 describes the process for conducting a suicide lethality assessment. APA Practice Guidelines (2003), Morrison (1995), Roberts, Monferrari & Yeager (2008) offer additional guidelines for interviewing around issues of danger and assessing the degree of risk in various situations. Such texts can be useful resources for learning more about the topic.

Identifying the Problem, Its Expressions, and Other Critical Concerns

EP 2.1.10a

Your initial contacts with clients will concentrate on uncovering the sources of their problems and engaging them in planning appropriate remedial measures. People typically seek help because they have exhausted their coping efforts and/or lack resources required for satisfactory living. They have often found that, despite their most earnest efforts, their coping efforts were insufficient or seemed to only aggravate the problem and are therefore forthright in problem exploration. When clients are referred or coerced into seeking services, empathy, motivational interviewing skills, and negotiation will be essential in finding common ground on the needs that the worker might help address. Culturally derived attitudes toward help seeking may also affect a person's capacity for and comfort with problem exploration. For example, conceptions about fate, destiny, self-reliance, and other beliefs affect the meaning given to problems and the ways that people are expected to respond to them. In many groups, the pursuit of assistance through formal helpers is a sign of desperation or a cause of shame. Your capacity to start where the client is will be crucial to your success in trying to unpack their reasons for seeking your help.

When asked to describe their problems or concerns, people often respond in generalities. The description typically involves a deficiency of something needed (e.g., health care, adequate income or housing, companionship, harmonious family relationships, self-esteem) or an excess of something that is not desired (e.g., fear, guilt, temper outbursts, marital or parent-child conflict, or addiction). In either event, the issue often results in feelings of disequilibrium, tension, and apprehension. The emotions themselves are often a prominent part of the problem configuration, which is one reason why empathic communication is such a vital skill during the interview process.

This understanding of the *presenting problem* is significant because it reflects the person's immediate perceptions of the problem and is the impetus for seeking help. It is distinct from the *problem for work*. The issues that bring the client and the social worker together initially may not, in fact, be the issues that serve as the focus of goals and interventions later in the relationship. The problem for work may differ from the original or presenting problem for a number of reasons. As the helping process progresses, the development of greater information, insights, and trust may mean that factors are revealed that change the focus of work and goals for service. This does not mean, however, that you should disregard the problems that brought people to you in the first place. The assessment process will reveal to you and the client whether the problem for work differs from the one that brought him or her to your service.

The presenting problem is important because it suggests areas to be explored in assessment. If the difficulty described by parents involves their adolescent's truancy and rebellious behavior, for example, the exploration will include the family, school, and peer systems. As the exploration proceeds, it may also prove useful to explore the parental system if difficulty in the marital relationship appears to be negatively affecting the parent–child relationship. If learning difficulties appear to contribute to the truancy, the cognitive and perceptual subsystems of the adolescent may need to be assessed as part of the problem. The presenting problem thus identifies systems that are constituent parts of the predicament and suggests the resources needed to ameliorate it.

The Interaction of Other People or Systems

The presenting problem and the exploration that follows usually identify key individuals, groups, or organizations that are participants in the client's difficulties. An accurate assessment must consider all of these elements and determine how they interact. Furthermore, an effective plan of intervention should take these same elements into account, even though it is not always feasible to involve everyone who is a participant in a given problematic situation.

EP 2.1.7b

To understand more fully how the client and other involved systems interact to produce and maintain the problem, you must elicit specific information about the functioning and interaction of these various systems. People commonly engage in transactions with the following systems:

1. The family and extended family or kinship network
2. The social network (friends, neighbors, coworkers, and associates, club members, and cultural groups)
3. Public institutions (educational, recreational, law enforcement and protection, mental health, social service, health care, employment, economic security, legal and judicial, and various governmental agencies)
4. Personal service providers (doctor, dentist, barber or hairdresser, bartender, auto mechanic, landlord, banker)
5. The faith community (religious leaders, lay ministers, fellow worshipers)

Understanding how the interaction of these elements plays out in your client's particular situation requires detailed information about the behavior of all participants, including what they say and do before, during, and after problematic events. For example, certain circumstances or behaviors may typically precede problematic behavior. A family member may say or do something that precipitates an angry, defensive, or hurt reaction by another. Pressure from the landlord about past due rent may result in tension and impatience between family members. A child's outburst in the classroom may follow certain stimuli. Events that precede problematic behavior are referred to as *antecedents*. Antecedents often give valuable clues about the behavior of one participant that may provoke or offend another participant, thereby triggering a negative reaction, followed by a counter negative reaction, thus setting the reciprocal interaction in motion. In addition to finding out about the circumstances preceding troubling episodes, it is important to learn about the consequences or outcomes associated with problematic behaviors. These results may shed light on factors that perpetuate or reinforce the client's difficulties.

Analyzing the antecedents of problematic behavior, describing the behavior in specific terms, and assessing the consequences or effects of the problematic behavior provide a powerful means of identifying patterns that are appropriate targets of interventions. This straightforward approach to analyzing the functional significance of behavior is termed the *ABC model* (A = antecedent, B = behavior, C = consequence) (Ellis, 2001). Although it is far less simple than it may seem, the ABC model provides a coherent and practical approach to understanding problems, the systems involved, and the roles they play.

Assessing Needs and Wants

EP 2.1.7b

As we noted earlier, problems commonly involve unmet needs and wants that derive from a poor fit between these needs and the resources available. Determining unmet needs, then, is the first step in identifying which resources must be tapped or developed. If resources are available but clients have been unable to avail themselves of those resources, it is important to determine the barriers to utilization. Some people, for example, may suffer from loneliness not because of an absence of support systems but because their interpersonal behavior alienates others and leaves them isolated. Or their loneliness may stem from shame or other feelings that keep them from asking for assistance from family or friends. Still other clients may *appear* to have emotional support available from family or others, but closer exploration may reveal that these potential resources are unresponsive to clients' needs. Reasons for the unresponsiveness typically involve reciprocal unsatisfactory transactions between the participants. The task in such instances is to assess the nature of the negative transactions and to attempt to modify them to the benefit of the participants so that resources can be unblocked to address the client's wishes.

Human *needs* include the universal necessities (adequate nutrition, safety, clothing, housing, and health care). They are critical and must be at least partially met for human beings to survive and maintain sound physical and mental well-being. As we use the term, *wants* consist of strong desires that motivate behavior and that, when fulfilled, enhance satisfaction and well-being. Although fulfillment of wants is not essential to survival, some wants develop a compelling nature, rivaling needs in their intensity. For illustrative purposes, we provide the following list of examples of typical wants involved in presenting problems.

Typical Wants Involved in Presenting Problems

- *To have less family conflict*
- *To feel valued by one's spouse or partner*
- *To be self-supporting*
- *To achieve greater companionship in marriage or relationship*
- *To gain more self-confidence*
- *To have more freedom*
- *To control one's temper*
- *To overcome depression*
- *To have more friends*
- *To be included in decision making*
- *To get discharged from an institution*
- *To make a difficult decision*
- *To master fear or anxiety*
- *To cope with children more effectively*

In determining clients' unmet needs and wants, it is essential to consider the developmental stage of the individual, couple, or family. For example, the psychological needs of an adolescent—for acceptance by peers, sufficient freedom to develop increasing independence, and development of a stable identity (including a sexual identity)—differ markedly from the typical needs of elderly persons—for health care, adequate income, social relationships, and meaningful activities. As with individuals, families go through developmental phases that include both tasks to be mastered and needs that must be met if the family is to provide a climate conducive to the development and well-being of its members.

Although clients' presenting problems often reveal obvious needs and wants (e.g., "Our unemployment benefits have expired and we have no income"), sometimes the social worker must infer what is lacking. Presenting problems may reveal only what is troubling the person on the surface, and careful exploration and empathic "tuning in" are required to identify unmet needs and wants. A couple, for example, may initially complain that they disagree over virtually everything and fight constantly. From this information, one could safely conclude that the pair wants a more harmonious relationship. Exploring their feelings on a deeper level, however, may reveal that their ongoing disputes are actually a manifestation of unmet needs of both partners for expressions of love, caring, appreciation, or increased companionship.

The process of translating complaints and problems into needs and wants is often helpful to clients, who may have dwelled on difficulties or blamed others and have not thought in terms of their own specific needs and wants. The presenting problem of one client was that her husband was married to his job and spent little time with her. The social worker responded, "I gather then you're feeling left out of his life and want to feel important to him and valued by him." The woman replied, "You know, I hadn't thought of it that way, but that's exactly what I've been feeling." The practitioner then encouraged her to express this need directly to her husband, which she did. He listened attentively and responded with genuine concern. The occasion was the first time she had expressed her needs directly. Previously, her messages had been sighs, silence, or complaints, and her husband's usual response had been defensive withdrawal.

Identifying needs and wants also serves as a prelude to the process of negotiating goals. Expressing goals in terms that address needs and wants enhances clients' motivation to work toward goal attainment, as the payoff for goal-oriented efforts is readily apparent to them. Even though some desires may seem unachievable in light of the individual's capacities or the opportunities in the social environment, these aspirations are still worthy of discussion. Goal setting is addressed in detail in Chapter 12.

Stresses Associated with Life Transitions

EP 2.1.4c

In addition to developmental stages that typically correspond to age ranges, individuals and families commonly must adapt to other major transitions that are less age specific. Your assessment should take into account whether the person's difficulties are related to such a transition and, if so, which aspects of the transition are sources of concern. Some transitions (e.g., geographical moves and immigrations, divorce, and untimely widowhood) can occur during virtually any stage of development. Many of these transitions can be traumatic and the adaptations required may temporarily overwhelm the coping capacities of individuals or families. Transitions that are involuntary (a home is destroyed by fire) or abrupt (job relocation) and separations (from a person, homeland, or familiar role) are highly stressful for most persons and often temporarily impair social functioning of the individual and/or their loved ones.

The person's history, concurrent strengths and resources, and past successful coping can all affect the adaptation to these transitions. The environment plays a crucial role as well. People with strong support networks (e.g., close relationships with family, kin, friends, and neighbors) generally have less difficulty in adapting to traumatic changes than do those who lack strong support systems. Assessments and interventions related to transitional periods, therefore, should consider the availability or lack of essential support systems.

The following are major transitions that may beset adults:

Common Role and Developmental Transitions

Work, career choices	Retirement
Health impairment	Separation or divorce
Parenthood	Institutionalization
Post-parenthood years	Single parenthood
Geographic moves and migrations	Death of a spouse or partner
Marriage or partnership commitment	Military deployments

In addition to these transitions, other milestones affect specialized groups. For example, gay and lesbian persons have difficult decisions to make about to whom and under what conditions they will reveal their sexual identities (Cain, 1991a, 1991b); furthermore, they may need to create procedures and rituals for events (e.g., marriage, divorce, and end-of-life decisions) from which they may be legally excluded because of their sexual orientation. A child whose parents are divorcing may experience a loss of friends and change of school along with the disruption of his or her family structure. Life events such as graduations, weddings, and holidays may be more emotionally charged and take on greater complexity when there has been divorce or remarriage in the family of origin. The parents and siblings of individuals with severe illnesses or disabilities may experience repeated "losses" if joyous milestones such as sleepovers, graduations, dating, proms, marriage, and parenthood are not available to their loved ones. Retirement may not represent a time of release and relaxation if it is accompanied by poverty, poor health, or new responsibilities such as caring for ill family members or raising grandchildren (Gibson, 1999). Military deployments and returns may be easier for service members than for reservists in that the former typically have formal and informal supports on base, whereas reservists may deploy from decentralized communities.

Clearly, life transitions can be differentially affected by individual circumstances, culture, socioeconomic status, and other factors. Social workers must be sensitive to these differences and take care not to make assumptions about the importance or unimportance of a transitional event or developmental milestone.

Cultural, Societal, and Social Class Factors

EP 2.1.4c

As we noted earlier, ethnocultural factors influence what kinds of problems people experience, how they feel about requesting assistance, how they communicate, how they perceive the role of the professional person, and how they view various approaches to solving problems. It is therefore vital that you be knowledgeable about these factors and competent in responding to them. Your assessment of clients' life situations, needs, and strengths must be viewed through the lens of cultural competence (Rooney & Bibus, 1995). What does this mean in practice? Some examples follow:

- *A person emigrating from another country may display psychological distress that is directly related to the migration or refugee experience. Beyond this consideration, a social worker who understands the ramifications of immigration would need to be sensitive to the special issues that may arise for refugees or others whose immigration was made under forced or dire circumstances (Mayadas et al., 1998–1999), or whose presence in the U.S. is illegal or unwelcomed.*
- *An interview with an older person experiencing isolation should take into account that hearing difficulties, death or illness of peers, housing and economic status, local crime, and other factors may impede the client's ability to partake in social activities.*
- *Racial and ethnic stereotypes may lead to differences in the way that minority youth and majority youth are perceived when accused of juvenile crimes. Similarly, detrimental experiences with authority figures and institutional racism may affect the way that these youths interact with the social worker (Bridges & Steen, 1998).*
- *A young woman is persistently late for appointments, which her social worker interprets as a sign of resistance and poor organizational skills. In fact, the young woman must make child care arrangements and take three buses to reach the mental health clinic. Rather than indicating shortcomings, her arrival at appointments (even late) is a sign of persistence and precise organization in light of scarce resources.*

As discussed throughout the book, workers must possess cultural sensitivity and the capacity to take many perspectives when viewing clients' situations and drawing conclusions about them. Chapter 9 further addresses these skills as they apply to individual and environmental factors.

Severity of the Problem

In general, assessment of the severity of the problem helps you to determine patterns when the concern is more or less acute and the features associated with those changes in severity. Another reason to focus on severity is in order to determine whether clients have the capacity to continue functioning in the community or whether hospitalization or other strong supportive or protective measures are needed. When functioning is temporarily impaired by extreme anxiety and loss of emotional control, such as when people experience acute post-traumatic stress disorder, short-term hospitalization may be required. The acuteness of the situation will necessarily influence your appraisal of the client's stress, the frequency of sessions, and the speed at which you need to mobilize support systems.

Meanings That Clients Ascribe to Problems

The next element of assessment involves understanding and describing the client's perceptions and definitions of the problem. The meanings people place on events ("meaning attributions") are as important as the events themselves,

EP 2.1.4d

because they influence the way people respond to their difficulties. For example, a parent might attribute his son's suicide attempt to his grounding the boy earlier in the week. A job loss might mean shame and failure to one person and a routine and unavoidable part of economic downturn for another. Determining these views is an important feature of assessment. Exploratory questions such as the following may help elicit the client's meaning attributions:

- *"What do you make of his behavior?"*
- *"What were the reasons (for your parents disciplining you)?"*
- *"What conclusions have you drawn about (why your landlord evicted you)?"*
- *"What are your views (as to why you didn't get a promotion)?"*

Discovering meaning attributions is also vital because these beliefs about cause and effect may represent powerful barriers to change. The following examples demonstrate distorted attributions (Hurvitz, 1975):

1. *Pseudoscientific explanations:* "My family has the gene for lung cancer. I know I'll get it, and there's nothing we can do about it."
2. *Psychological labeling:* "Mother is senile; she can't be given a choice in this matter."
3. *Fixed beliefs about others:* "Adopted kids are determined by their birth parents' genes. I think we're wasting our time and money on counseling."
4. *Unchangeable factors:* "I've never been an affectionate person. It's just not in my character."
5. *Reference to "fixed" religious or philosophical principles, natural laws, or social forces:* "Sure, I already have as many children as I want. But I don't really have a choice. The church says that birth control is against God's will."
6. *Assertion based on presumed laws of human nature:* "All children tell lies at that age. It's just natural. I did when I was a kid."

Fortunately, many attributions are not permanent: people are capable of cognitive flexibility and are open—even eager—to examine their role in problematic situations and want to modify their behavior. When obstacles such as those listed are encountered, however, it is vital to explore and resolve them before attempting to negotiate change-oriented goals or to implement interventions.

Sites of Problematic Behaviors

Determining where problematic behavior occurs may provide clues about which factors trigger it. For example, children may throw tantrums in certain locations but not in others. As a result of repeated experiences, they soon learn to discriminate where certain behaviors are tolerated and where they are not. Adults may experience anxiety or depression in certain environmental contexts but not in others. Some elderly individuals become more confused in community settings than at home. Determining where problematic behavior occurs will assist you in identifying patterns that warrant further exploration and in pinpointing factors associated with the behavior in question.

Identifying where problematic behavior *does not* occur is also valuable, because it provides clues about the features that might help in alleviating the problem and identify situations in which the client experiences relief from difficulties. For example, a child may act out in certain classes at school but not in all of them. What is happening in the incident-free classes that might explain the absence of symptoms or difficulties there? How can it be replicated in other classes? A client in residential treatment may gain temporary respite from overwhelming anxiety by visiting a cherished aunt on weekends. In other instances, clients may gain permanent relief from intolerable stress by changing employment, discontinuing college, or moving out of relationships when tension or other unpleasant feeling states are experienced exclusively in these contexts.

Temporal Context of Problematic Behaviors

Determining *when* problematic behaviors occur also offers valuable clues about factors at play in problems. The onset of a depressive episode, for example, may coincide with the time of year when a loved one died or when a divorce occurred. Family problems may occur when one parent returns from work or travel, at bedtime for the children, at mealtimes, when visitations are beginning or ending, or when children are (or should be) getting ready for school. Similarly, couples may experience severe conflict when one partner is working the midnight shift, after participation by either partner in activities that exclude the other, or when one or both drink at parties. These clues can shed light on the patterns of clients' difficulties, indicate areas for further exploration, and lead to helpful interventions.

Frequency of Problematic Behaviors

The frequency of problematic behavior provides an index to both the pervasiveness of a problem and its effects on the participants. As with the site and timing of symptoms, information on frequency helps you to assess the context in which problems arise and the pattern they follow in the client's life. Services for clients who experience their problems on a more or less ongoing basis may need to be more intensive than for clients whose symptoms are intermittent. Determining the frequency of problematic behaviors thus helps to clarify the degree of difficulty and the extent to which it impairs the daily functioning of individuals and their families. Assessing the frequency of problematic behaviors also provides a baseline against which to measure behaviors targeted for change. Making subsequent comparisons of the frequency of the targeted behaviors enables you to evaluate the efficacy of your interventions.

Duration of the Problem

Another important dimension vital to assessing problems relates to the history of the problem—namely, *how long* it has existed. Knowing when the problem developed and under what circumstances assists in further evaluating the degree of the problem, unraveling psychosocial factors associated with the problem, determining the source of motivation to seek assistance, and planning appropriate interventions. Often significant changes in life situations, including even seemingly positive ones, may disrupt a person's equilibrium to the extent that he/she cannot adapt to changes. An unplanned pregnancy, loss of employment, job promotion, severe illness, birth of a first child, move to a new city, death of a loved one, divorce, retirement, severe disappointment—these and many other life events may cause severe stresses. Careful exploration of the duration of problems often discloses such antecedents to current difficulties.

Events that immediately precede decisions to seek help are particularly informative. Sometimes referred to as *precipitating events*, these antecedents often yield valuable clues about critical stresses that might otherwise be overlooked. Clients often report that their problems have existed longer than a year. Why they chose to ask for help at a particular time is not readily apparent, but uncovering this information may cast their problems in a somewhat different light. For example, a parent who complained about his teenage daughter's longstanding rebelliousness did not seek assistance until he became aware (1 week before calling the agency) that she was engaging in an intimate relationship with a man 6 years her senior. The precipitating event is significant to the call for help and would not have been disclosed had the practitioner not sought to answer the critical question of why they were seeking help at this particular time.

In some instances, people may not be fully aware of their reasons initiating the contact, and it may be necessary to explore what events or emotional experiences occurred shortly before their decision to seek help. Determining the duration of problems is also vital in assessing clients' levels of functioning and in planning appropriate interventions. This exploration may reveal that a person's adjustment has been marginal for many years and that the immediate problem is simply an exacerbation of long-term multiple problems. In other instances, the onset of a problem may be acute, and clients may have functioned at an adequate or high level for many years. In the first instance, modest goals and long-term intermittent service may be indicated; in the second instance, short-term crisis intervention may suffice to restore them to their previous level of functioning.

Other Issues Affecting Client Functioning

EP 2.1.10d

Numerous other circumstances and conditions can affect the problem that the client is presenting and his or her capacity to address it. For this reason, it is often wise to explore specifically the use of alcohol or other substances, exposure to abuse or violence, the presence of health problems, depression or other mental health problems, and use of prescription medication.

Questions to probe into these areas should be a standard element of the initial interview. As such, they can be asked in a straightforward and nonjudgmental fashion. For example, opening questions might include the following:

- "Now, I'd like to know about some of your habits. First, in an average month, on how many days do you have at least one drink of alcohol?"
- "Have you ever used street drugs of any sort?"
- "Have you had any major illnesses in the past?"
- "Are you currently experiencing any health problems?"
- "What medications do you take?"
- "How do these medications work for you?"
- "Have you been in situations recently or in the past where you were harmed by someone or where you witnessed others being hurt?"

The answers you receive to these questions will determine which follow-up questions you ask. In some circumstances, you may ask for more specific information—for example, to determine the degree of impairment due to drug and alcohol use or whether the client is able to afford medication and is taking them as prescribed. At a minimum, you will want to learn how the person views these issues in light of the presenting problem. For example, you might ask these follow-up questions:

- "How has the difficulty sleeping affected your ability to care for your kids?"
- "What role do you see your alcohol use playing in this relationship conflict?"
- "Did the change of medication occur at the same time these other difficulties began?"
- "I wonder if the run-in with the bullies has anything to do with you skipping school lately?"

Depending on the setting and purpose of the interview and on the information gathered, the social worker may focus the interview specifically on the client's medical history, abuse, substance use, or mental health. Further information on these assessments is included in Chapter 9.

Clients' Emotional Reactions to Problems

EP 2.1.10d

When people encounter problems in daily living, they typically experience emotional reactions to those problems. It is important to explore and assess these reactions for three major reasons.

First, people often gain relief simply by expressing troubling emotions. Common reactions to problem situations are worry, agitation, resentment, hurt, fear, and feeling overwhelmed, helpless, or hopeless. Being able to express such emotions in the presence of an understanding and concerned person is a source of great comfort. Releasing pent-up feelings often has the effect of relieving oneself of a heavy burden. In fact, sharing emotions may have a liberating effect for persons who tend to be out of touch with their feelings and have not acknowledged to themselves or others that they are even troubled.

Second, because emotions strongly influence behavior, the emotional reactions of some people impel them to behave in ways that exacerbate or contribute to their difficulties. In some instances, in fact, people create new difficulties as a result of emotionally reactive behavior. In the heat of anger, a noncustodial parent may lash out at a child or former spouse. Burdened by financial concerns, an individual may become impatient and verbally abusive, behaving in ways that frighten, offend, or alienate employers, customers, or family members. An adult experiencing unremitting grief may cut himself or herself off from loved ones who "cannot stand" to see him or her cry. Powerful emotional reactions may thus be an integral part of the overall problem configuration.

Third, intense reactions often become primary problems, overshadowing the antecedent problematic situation. For example, some people experience powerful emotions associated with their life problems. A mother may become depressed over an unwed daughter's pregnancy; a man may react with anxiety to unemployment or retirement; and culturally dislocated persons may become angry following relocation, even though they may have fled intolerable conditions in their homeland. Other individuals may react to problematic events by experiencing feelings of helplessness or panic that cause virtual paralysis. In these instances, interventions must address the overwhelming emotional reactions as well as the situations that triggered them.

Coping Efforts and Needed Skills

EP 2.1.10e

Perhaps surprisingly, the social worker can learn more about clients' difficulties by determining how they have attempted to cope with their problems and what skills they already possess. The coping methods that people employ give valuable clues about their levels of stress and of functioning. Exploration may reveal that a person has few coping skills, but rather relies upon rigid patterns that are unhelpful or cause further problems. Some people follow avoidance patterns—for example, immersing themselves in tasks or work, withdrawing, or numbing or fortifying themselves with drugs or alcohol. Others attempt to cope with interpersonal problems by resorting to aggressive, domineering behavior, excessive dependence on others, or by placating other participants or becoming submissive. Still others demonstrate flexible and effective coping patterns but collapse under unusually high levels of stress.

There are also cultural variations in how people approach problem solving. Some people are most comfortable with an individually focused, analytical-cognitive approach while others may reach out to social networks, family supports and group problem-solving. Cultures typically exert pressure on individuals to follow familiar solutions for a given problem and deviating from cultural expectations for coping or problem solving may add to the client's distress. It is helpful to know the source of peoples' coping mechanisms, their efficacy in the past and the persons' comfort with trying new strategies if old ways have failed.

Another important insight from exploring coping efforts emerges when you are discussing mechanisms and skills that have worked in the past but no longer do. In such instances, it is important to explore carefully what has changed. For example, a person may have been able to cope with the demands of one supervisor but not with a new one who is more critical and aloof or who is of a different generation, race, or gender than the client. A parent may have skillfully raised an infant, but be stymied by a toddler. Socially inhibited individuals may be comfortable conversing with those they already know but need to learn skills in approaching others, introducing themselves, and engaging in conversation. And, a person's typical ability to cope may also be affected by changes in functioning: a severely depressed individual, for example, may overestimate his impairment and underestimate his resources and abilities.

By exploring the different circumstances, meaning attributions, and emotional reactions, you should be able to identify subtle differences that account for the varied effectiveness of your clients' coping patterns in different contexts. This part of assessment is also essential before exploring treatment goals or service options. Offering premature advice or interventions may meet rejection from a client who says, "I tried that already and it didn't work." Without understanding of what the client has tried and when, how and how much it helped, it is risky to jump to conclusions about what assistance is needed now.

Support Systems

EP 2.1.10e

An essential part of understanding individuals involves understanding the systems with which they interact. This can include *formal systems* such as schools, medical clinics, mentors, or home health aides and *natural or informal systems*, such as neighbors, family, or friends. These systems are also important parts of problem and strengths assessments. Formal support systems may be part of the problem (the school that cannot provide adequate educational resources to help a child with disabilities or the child welfare service plan that is too demanding for the client to manage along with part time work and adequate child care). Natural support systems may also be part of the problem configuration (the family member whose criticism fuels a client's despair or the peer network that encourages theft and drug use). On the flip side, formal and informal networks can be part of coping and client strengths ("I can always go to my caseworker when I'm feeling overwhelmed"; "My neighbor watches my kids when I get called into work"; "Our church helped us with food and companionship when my mother was sick.").

Chapter 9 offers an extensive examination of the roles support systems play in affecting intrapersonal and interpersonal functioning and the strategies social workers can use in identifying them. It also addresses environmental (home, neighborhood) and other factors that may be linked to needed supports.

Resources Needed

When people request services, you must determine (1) whether the services requested match the functions of the agency and, (2) whether the staff possesses the skills required to provide high-quality service. If not, a referral is needed to assure that the individual receives the highest-quality service to match the needs presented. Referrals may also be required to complement services within your agency or to obtain a specialized assessment that will be factored into your services (e.g., "Are the multiple medications that Mrs. Jones is taking causing her recent cognitive problems?", "Are there neurological causes for John's outbursts?"). In such instances, the practitioner performs a broker or case manager role, which requires knowledge of community resources (or at least knowledge of how to obtain relevant information). Fortunately, many communities have online resource information centers that can help clients and professionals locate needed services. Remember that irrespective of the presenting problem, people can benefit from help in a variety of areas—from financial assistance, transportation, and health care to child or elder care, recreation, and job training. Problem exploration will help identify possible needs.

In certain instances, in addition to the public and private resources available in your community, you should consider two other major resources that may be less visible forms of assistance. The first is self-help groups, where members look to themselves for mutual aid and social support. In particular, the internet has expanded the reach of such groups across geographic distances on a round-the-clock basis (Fingeld, 2000). The second resource is natural support systems, including relatives, friends, neighbors, coworkers, and close associates from school, social groups, or one's faith community. Some therapists have developed innovative ways of tapping these support systems collectively through an intervention termed *network therapy*. These clinicians contend that

EP 2.1.7b

much of the dysfunctional behavior labeled as mental illness actually derives from feelings of alienation from one's natural social network, which consists of all human relationships that are significant in a person's life, including natural support systems. In network therapy, these practitioners mobilize 40 to 50 significant people who are willing to come together in a period of crisis for one or more members of the network. The goal is to unite their efforts in tightening the social network of relationships for the purpose of offering support, reassurance, and solidarity to troubled members and other members of the social network. Mobilizing social networks is in keeping with the best traditions of social work.

In instances of cultural dislocation, natural support systems may be limited to the family, and practitioners may need to mobilize other potential resources in the community (Hulewat, 1996). Assisting refugees poses a particular challenge, because a cultural reference group may not be available in some communities. A language barrier may create another obstacle, and practitioners may need to search for interpreters and other interested parties who can assist these families in locating housing, gaining employment, learning the language, adapting to a new culture, and developing social support systems.

In still other instances, people's environments may be virtually devoid of natural support systems. Consequently, environmental changes may be necessary to accomplish a better fit between needs and resources, a topic we consider at greater length in the following chapter.

Assessing Children and Older Adults

EP 2.1.4c

Social workers are often employed in settings serving children and older adults. Assessments with these groups utilize many of the skills and concepts noted elsewhere in this chapter and in earlier sections. However, elderly clients and child clients also present unique requirements because of their respective life stages and circumstances. This section is intended to acquaint you with some of the considerations that will shape assessments with these populations.

Because children and older adults often present for service in relation to systems of which they are already a part (e.g., hospitals, schools, families, assisted living facilities), your assessment may be bound by those systems. This can present a challenge for creating an integrated assessment, as several caregivers, agencies, and professionals may hold pieces of the puzzle while none possess the mandate or capacity to put all of the pieces together.

Similarly, children and older adults typically appear for service because someone else has identified a concern. These referral sources may include parents or guardians, caregivers, teachers, neighbors, or health care providers. This factor does not automatically mean that the client will be resistant, but rather indicates that he or she may disagree about the presence or nature of the problem or be unmotivated to address it.

Maltreatment

Older adults and children are both at particular risk for maltreatment at the hands of caregivers. Therefore, it is important for all professionals to understand the principles for detecting abuse or neglect and their responsibilities for reporting it. For both minors and older adults, mistreatment can be categorized into four areas: neglect, physical abuse, sexual abuse, and emotional or verbal abuse. For elderly persons, additional categories include self-neglect and financial exploitation (Bergeron & Gray, 2003; Donovan & Regehr, 2010). The specific definitions of various forms of abuse vary by jurisdiction (Rathbone-McCuan, 2008; Wells, 2008). Sometimes abusive individuals or their victims will forthrightly report abuse to the social worker. More commonly it is covered by fear, confusion, and shame, and thus the professional must be alert to signs of abuse, such as:

- Physical injuries: *Burns, bruises, cuts, or broken bones for which there is no satisfactory or credible explanation; injuries to the head and face*
- Lack of physical care: *Malnourishment, poor hygiene, unmet medical or dental needs*
- Unusual behaviors: *Sudden changes, withdrawal, aggression, sexualized behavior, self-harm, guarded or fearful behavior at the mention of or in the presence of caregiver*
- Financial irregularities: *For the older client, this includes missing money or valuables, unpaid bills, coerced spending (Donovan & Regehr, 2010; Mayo Clinic, 2007).*

Social workers (including student workers) are mandated to report suspicions of child abuse to designated child protective agencies; most jurisdictions also compel workers to report elder abuse, although it may be voluntary in other regions. All professionals should know the steps required in their setting and state for making an abuse report. Referring the case to agencies that have the mandate and expertise to investigate maltreatment is the best way to assure that proper legal and biopsychosocial interventions are brought to bear in the case.

Data Sources and Interviewing Techniques

In working with children and older adults, particularly the frail elderly, you may need to rely more than usual on certain data sources (e.g., collateral contacts or observations) and less than usual on other sources (e.g., the client's verbal reports). A trusting relationship with the client's primary caregivers will be vital to your access to the client and will dramatically affect the rapport you achieve with him or her. Depending on the child's level of development or the older adult's capacities, he or she may have difficulty helping you construct the problem analysis or identify strengths or coping methods. Other data sources, such as interviews with collateral contacts (teachers, family members, service providers, institutional caregivers), may be essential in completing a satisfactory assessment, although, as noted earlier, these can be open to various distortions.

EP 2.1.4c

Child assessments may also require new skills, such as the use of drawings, board games, dolls, or puppets as sources of information for the assessment (Hamama & Ronen, 2009). The way that the child approaches these activities can be as telling as the information he or she reveals (Webb, 1996). For example, are the child's interests and skills age-appropriate? What mood is reflected in the child's play, and is it frequently encountered in children of that age and situation? Do themes in the child's play relate to possible areas of distress? How often do those themes recur? How does the child relate to you and to adversity (the end of play, losing, or a "wrong move" in a game)? How well can the child focus on the task? Clearly, in this context, play is not a random activity meant for the child's distraction or enjoyment. Instead, you must use it purposefully and be attentive to the implications of various facets of the experience. Your impressions of the significance and meaning of the play activities should be evaluated on the basis of other sources of information.

A *developmental assessment* may be particularly relevant for understanding the child's history and current situation. With this type of assessment, a parent or other caregiver provides information about the circumstances of the child's delivery, birth, and infancy; achievement of developmental milestones; family atmosphere; interests; and significant life transitions (Jordan & Hickerson, 2003; Levy & Frank, 2011; Lukas, 1993; Webb, 1996). This information helps form impressions about the child's experiences and life events, especially as they may relate to his or her current functioning. As with other forms of assessment, you must organize and interpret what you discover from all sources so as to paint a meaningful picture of the child's history, strengths, and needs; this assessment will then serve as the basis of your goals and interventions.

EP 2.1.3b

Screening instruments intended specifically for child clients or problems associated with childhood may also be useful. Some involve the child as a participant-respondent while others are completed by the parent or guardian in reference to the child. The Denver Developmental Screening for Children (DDST-II) (Frankenburg, Dodds, Archer, Shapiro & Bresnick, 1992) is used with children up to age six to determine whether development is in the normal range and to offer early identification of neurological and other problems. The kit utilizes props such as a tennis ball, doll, a zippered bag, and a pencil for drawing to test personal and social functioning (self-care, getting along with others), fine motor skills (eye-hand coordination, manipulation of small objects), language (hearing and understanding), and gross motor skills (sitting, walking, jumping).

EP 2.1.4c

Comprehensive, competent assessments for geriatric clients also involve items that go beyond the typical multidimensional assessment. For example, functional assessments would address the client's ability to perform various tasks, typically, *activities of daily living* (ADLs)—those things required for independent living such as dressing, hygiene, feeding, and mobility. Instrumental ADLs (IADLs) involve measuring the client's ability to perform more intricate tasks such as managing money, taking medicine properly, completing housework, shopping, and meal preparation (Gallo, 2005). Because some of the IADL skills may be traditionally performed by one gender or another, you should ascertain the client's baseline functioning in these areas before concluding that there are deficits or declines in IADLs. In that driving is a complex skill, an area of significant risk, a powerful symbol of independence, and an emotionally charged issue, assessment of capacity in this area is a specialized and important aspect of functioning (Gallo, 2005).

While aging is not synonymous with decline and death, those issues may be on the minds of elderly clients and thus worthy of exploration. Assessments in these areas might include reminiscence and discussion of spirituality and beliefs, all of which examine how the elder client derives purpose and meaning in his/her life (Richardson & Barusch, 2006; Zuniga, 1989). Clients may have significant concerns about incapacitation and death, and find that they have few outlets with which to share those thoughts. Too often, family, friends and helping professionals shut down such conversations as "morbid" or "signs of giving up." Social workers can effectively open up these conversations with questions such as:

EP 2.1.10d

1. How would you describe your philosophy of life? Of illness? How satisfactory is this philosophy to you now?
2. How do you express your spirituality? What kinds of practices enhance your spirituality?
3. How do you understand hope? What do you hope for?
4. What helps you the most when you feel afraid or need special help?
5. What is especially meaningful to you now? For what do you live? What is most important to you now?
6. How has being sick made any difference for you in what or how you believe?
7. What do death, being sick, suffering, pain, and so on mean to you?
8. How do you handle feelings such as anger, doubt, resentment, guilt, bitterness, and depression? How does your spirituality influence how you respond to such feelings? Do you want to receive spiritual support to deal with such feelings or thoughts about them?
9. Where do you get the love, courage, strength, hope and peace that you need? (Dudley, Smith, & Millison, 1995).

These questions may be appropriate for clients at the end of life, and in other situations where traumatic experiences or existential crises are part of the presenting problem.

Physical examinations and health histories also take on particular importance in the assessment of elderly clients. These assessments must take into account the impact of limitations in vision and hearing, restricted mobility and reaction times, pain management, and medication and disease interactions. Gallo and Bogner note that "the presenting complaint may involve the most vulnerable organ system rather than the organ system expected. For example, congestive heart failure may present as delirium" (2005, p. 9). Sexual functioning is another element of assessments that is commonly overlooked in elderly clients. Specialized and comprehensive evaluations require interdisciplinary teams with expertise in geriatric care.

As with other issues and populations, standardized tools are effective in evaluating the needs and functioning of older adults. Examples include the Determination of Need Assessment (DONA) (Paveza, Prohaska, Hagopian, & Cohen, 1989), the Instrumental Activities of Daily Living Screen (Gallo, 2005), and the Katz Index of Activities of Daily Living (Katz, et al., 1963). Tests like the Direct Assessment of Functioning Scale (DAFS) (Lowenstein et al., 1989) and the Physical Performance Test (Reuben & Siu, 1990; Rozzini, Frisoni, Bianchetti, Zanetti, & Trabucchi, 1993) require clients to demonstrate or simulate basic tasks such as climbing stairs, lifting a book and placing it on a shelf, writing, making a telephone call, brushing teeth, telling time, and eating. Other tests focus on the presence and severity of dementia, querying caregivers about the frequency with which the client shouts, laughs, or makes accusations inappropriately, wanders aimlessly, smokes carelessly, leaves the stove on, appears disheveled, is disoriented in familiar surroundings, and so on (Gallo, 2005).

EP 2.1.3a

For both very young and very old clients, direct observation of functioning may yield more reliable results than either self-reports or information from collateral sources. This may mean classroom visits, home visits, and other efforts to view the client in his or her natural setting. Specialized expertise is required to ensure that assessments are properly conducted and interpreted for these and other especially vulnerable populations.

Summary

Chapter 8 introduced the knowledge and skills entailed in multidimensional assessment. A psychiatric diagnosis may be part of, but is not the same as, a social work assessment. The discussion in this chapter emphasized strengths and resources in assessments. A framework for prioritizing what must be done in assessment was presented, along with the components of the problem exploration and application to specific sub populations. In Chapter 9, we will consider the assessment of intrapersonal and environmental systems and the terms and concepts used to describe their functioning as well as the processes for writing effective assessments.

CourseMate

Access an integrated eBook and chapter-specific learning tools including glossary terms, chapter outlines, relevant web links, videos, and practice quizzes. Go to **www.cengagebrain.com.**

CHAPTER **9**

Intrapersonal, Interpersonal, and Environmental Factors in Assessment

CHAPTER OVERVIEW

Chapter 9 reviews three key aspects of a comprehensive assessment: things happening within the client (physically, emotionally, cognitively), things happening within the client's environment (physical and social), and the transactions between the two. The chapter introduces these areas for examination and helps you develop an understanding of the difficulties and the assets to consider in all of these systems. It also discusses how culture and worker–client differences can affect these factors. As a result of reading this chapter, you will:

- Understand how assessments capture the reciprocal nature of client systems
- Learn the elements of intrapersonal functioning, including physical, emotional, cognitive, and behavioral aspects
- Be able to assess the spiritual and environmental factors affecting the client system
- Know the questions to ask to assess substance use and the common drugs of abuse
- Learn the diagnostic criteria for common thought and affective disorders
- Recognize the elements of a mental status exam and a social history
- Understand how to evaluate suicide risk and risk for violence
- Know the do's and don'ts for writing assessments and examine examples of assessments

EPAS COMPETENCIES IN THE 9TH CHAPTER

This chapter will give you the information needed to meet the following practice competencies:

2.1.3c Demonstrate effective oral and written communication in working with individuals, families, groups, organizations, communities, and colleagues

2.1.4c Recognize and communicate your understanding of the importance of difference in shaping life experiences

2.1.7a Utilize conceptual frameworks to guide the processes of assessment, intervention, and evaluation

2.1.7b Critique and apply knowledge to understand person and environment

2.1.10a Substantively and affectively prepare for action with individuals, families, groups, organizations, and communities

2.1.10d Collect, organize, and interpret client data

2.1.10e Assess client strengths and limitations

The Interaction of Multiple Systems in Human Problems

Problems, strengths, and resources encountered in direct social work practice result from interactions among intrapersonal, interpersonal, and environmental systems. Difficulties are rarely confined to one of these systems, however, because

EP 2.1.7b

a functional imbalance in one system typically contributes to an imbalance in others. For example, individual difficulties (e.g., illness, feelings of worthlessness or depression) invariably influence how one relates to other people (for example, withdrawn, reluctant, or irritable); interpersonal difficulties (e.g., job strain or parent-child

INTRAPERSONAL SYSTEMS

Biophysical Functioning
- Physical characteristics and presentation
- Physical health
- Use and abuse of medications, alcohol, and drugs
- Alcohol use and abuse
- Use and abuse of other substances
- Dual diagnosis: comorbid addictive and mental disorders

Cognitive/Perceptual Functioning
- Intellectual functioning
- Judgment
- Reality testing
- Coherence
- Cognitive flexibility
- Values
- Misconceptions
- Self-concept
- Assessing thought disorders

Affective Functioning
- Emotional control
- Range of emotions
- Appropriateness of affect
- Assessing affective disorders
    - Bipolar disorder
    - Major depressive disorder
    - Suicidal risk
    - Depression and suicidal risk with children, adolescents, and older adults

Behavioral Functioning
- Excesses
- Risk of violence
- Deficiencies

Motivation

FIG-9-1 Overview: Areas for Attention in Assessing Intrapersonal Functioning

© Cengage Learning 2013

discord) likewise affect individual functioning (stress or difficulty concentrating). Similarly, environmental deficits (e.g., inadequate housing, hostile working conditions, or social isolation) affect individual and interpersonal functioning (stress, anger, relationships).

The reciprocal effects among the three major systems, of course, are not limited to the negative effects of functional imbalance and system deficits. Assets, strengths, and resources also have reciprocal *positive* effects. A supportive environment may partially compensate for intrapersonal difficulties; similarly, strong interpersonal relationships may provide positive experiences that more than offset an otherwise impoverished environment. Figure 9-1 depicts the range of elements to be considered in assessing individual and interpersonal functioning.

Intrapersonal Systems

EP 2.1.10d

A comprehensive assessment of the individual considers a variety of elements, including biophysical, cognitive/perceptual, emotional, behavioral, cultural, and motivational factors and the ways that these affect interactions with people and institutions in the individual's environment. Keeping this in mind, the social worker's assessment and written products may focus more sharply on some of these areas than others, depending on the nature of the client's difficulties, the reason for the assessment, and the setting in which the assessment is taking place. It is important to remember, however, that an assessment is just a "snapshot" of the client system's functioning at any given point in time. As we noted in Chapter 8, the social worker's beliefs and actions and the client's feelings about seeking help may distort the assessment at any given point. For all of these reasons, care and respect are required when collecting and synthesizing assessment information into a working hypothesis for intervention.

Assessing Biophysical Functioning

Biophysical functioning encompasses physical characteristics, health factors, and genetic factors, as well as the use and abuse of drugs and alcohol.

Physical Characteristics and Presentation

People's physical characteristics and appearance may be either assets or liabilities. In many cultures, physical attractiveness is highly valued, and unattractive or odd people may be disadvantaged in terms of their social desirability, employment opportunities, or marriageability. It is thus important to be observant of distinguishing physical characteristics that may affect social functioning. Particular attributes that merit attention include body build, dental health, posture, facial features, gait, and any physical anomalies that may create positive or negative perceptions about the client, affect his or her self-image, or pose a social liability.

EP 2.1.10d

How people present themselves is worthy of note. Individuals who walk slowly, display stooped posture, talk slowly and without animation, lack spontaneity, and show minimal changes in facial expression may be depressed, in pain, or overmedicated. Dress and grooming often reveal much about a person's morale, values, and standard of living. The standard for assessing appearance is generally whether the dress is appropriate for the setting. Is the client barefoot in near-freezing weather or wearing a helmet and overcoat in the summer sun? Is the client dressed seductively, in pajamas, or "overdressed" for an appointment with the social worker? While attending to these questions, social workers should take care in the conclusions they reach. The determination of "appropriateness" is greatly influenced by the interviewer's cultural background and values (Westermeyer, 1993). A "disheveled" appearance may indicate poverty, carelessness, grunge, or "rock star" fashion. Being clothed in bright colors may indicate mania or simply an affiliation with a cultural group that favors that particular form of dress (Morrison, 1995; Othmer & Othmer, 1989). As with other elements of assessment, your description of what you observe ("collared shirt, dress pants, clean-shaven") should be separate from your assessment of it ("well-groomed and appropriately dressed").

Other important factors associated with appearance include hand tremors, facial tics, rigid or constantly shifting posture, and tense muscles of the face, hands, and arms. Sometimes these characteristics reflect the presence of an illness or physical problem. They may also indicate a high degree of tension or anxiety, warranting exploration by the social worker. During the assessment, an effective social worker will determine whether the anxiety displayed is normative for the given situation or whether it is excessive and might reveal an area for further discussion.

Physical Health

Ill health can contribute to depression, sexual difficulties, irritability, low energy, restlessness, anxiety, poor concentration, and a host of other problems. It is therefore important for social workers to routinely consider their clients' state of health as they explore these individuals' situations. One of the first assessment activities is to determine if clients are under medical care and when they last had a medical examination. Social workers should rule out medical sources of difficulties by referring clients for physical evaluations, when appropriate, before attributing problems solely to psychosocial factors. They should also be cautious and avoid drawing premature conclusions about the sources of problems when there is even a remote possibility that medical factors may be involved.

EP 2.1.7b

A variety of biophysical factors can affect cognitive, behavioral, and emotional functioning in individuals. For example, a history of child malnutrition has been linked to attention deficits, poor social skills, and emotional problems that may continue to affect children even after they become adequately nourished (Johnson, 1989). Nutritional deficits can also cause dementia in elderly people; however, some of this cognitive decline may be reversed if it is treated early enough (Naleppa, 1999). Encephalitis, which has been shown to cause brain damage, can lead to symptoms of attention deficit disorder (Johnson, 1989). Hormone levels also affect behavioral and emotional functioning—for example, high testosterone levels have been correlated with high levels of aggression (Rowe, Maughan, Worthman, Costello, & Angold, 2004).

Assessing the health of clients is especially important with groups known to underutilize medical care. Some may have a greater-than-average need for health care due to their specific conditions, while others may simply have more difficulty accessing basic care. Over 50 million Americans lack health insurance (DeNavas-Walt, Proctor, & Smith 2010). People without health care may be especially more vulnerable to disease due to poor nutrition, dangerous environmental conditions, and the lack of preventive services (Buss & Gillanders, 1997; Ensign, 1998; Jang, Lee, & Woo, 1998; Suarez & Siefert, 1998; Zechetmayr, 1997). Assessments should determine whether the individual's access to care is limited by affordability, availability, or acceptability (Julia, 1996).

Whether care is *affordable* depends on whether the client has health insurance coverage and whether he or she can pay for the services not covered by insurance. Even those who do have coverage may be unable or reluctant to pursue care, given the cost of medications, deductibles, and co-payments not covered by insurance. Concerns about costs may lead clients to delay basic care until the situation worsens to a dangerous level or to the point where even more expensive interventions are required. Individuals with extensive or chronic health problems (such as AIDS, cancer, or traumatic brain injury) may find that hospitalization and drug costs outstrip both their insurance coverage and their income regardless of their wealth and resources.

Availability refers not only to the location of health care services, but also the hours they are available, the transportation needed to reach them, and the adequacy of the facilities and personnel to meet the client's needs (Mokuau & Fong, 1994). If the nearest after-hours health care resource is a hospital emergency room, it may be the facility of choice for a desperate mother, even if the health concern (e.g., a child's ear infection) might be better addressed in another setting.

Acceptability refers to the extent to which the health services are compatible with the client's cultural values and traditions. Chapter 8 discussed the importance of understanding how culture may affect a person's interpretation of his or her problems. An important task in intrapersonal assessment involves determining clients' views about the causes of illness, physical aberrations, disabling conditions, and mental symptoms, because their expectations regarding diagnoses and treatment may differ sharply from those presented by Western health care professionals (Yamamoto, Silva, Justice, Chang, & Leong, 1993) and their rejection of these formulations may be misinterpreted as noncompliance or resistance (Al-Krenawi, 1998). For these reasons, all practitioners should be knowledgeable about the significance of caregivers, folk healers, and shamans for clients from an array of cultural groups (Canda, 1983).

Beyond differences in beliefs, differences arise related to peoples' comfort in accepting care. New immigrants may have limited knowledge of Western medical care and of the complex health care provider systems in the United States, and they may be reticent to seek care because of concerns about their documentation and fears of deportation (Congress, 1994). The use of indigenous healers or bilingual and bicultural staff can enhance the acceptability of health care to these individuals.

A health assessment may also entail gathering information about illnesses in the client's family.[1] A genogram may be helpful in capturing this information. This tool, which is similar to a family tree, graphically depicts relationships within the family, dates of births and deaths, illnesses, and other significant life events. It reveals patterns across generations of which even the client may not have been aware (Andrews, 2001; McGoldrick & Gerson, 1985). You may also find out about family history simply by asking the client. For example, you might ask, "Has anyone else in your family ever had an eating disorder?", "Is there a history of substance abuse in your family?" or "How have other relatives died?" This information helps in assessing the client's understanding of and experience with a problem. It may also identify the need for a referral for specialized information and counseling related to genetically linked disorders (Waltman, 1996).

Assessing Use and Abuse of Medications, Alcohol, and Drugs

An accurate understanding of a client's biophysical functioning must include information on his or her use of both legal and illicit drugs. First, it is important to determine which prescribed and over-the-counter medications the client

EP 2.1.10d

is taking, whether he or she is taking them as instructed, and whether they are having the intended effect. Another reason for evaluating drug use is that even beneficial drugs can produce side effects that affect the functioning of various biopsychosocial systems.[2] An array of common reactions such as drowsiness, changes in sexual functioning, muscle rigidity, disorientation, inertia, and stomach pains may result from inappropriate combinations of prescription drugs or as troubling side effects of single medications (Denison, 2003). Finally, questioning in this area is important because the client may report a variety of conditions, from confusion to sleeplessness, which may necessitate a referral for evaluation and medication.

Alcohol is another form of legal drug, but its abuse can severely impair health, disrupt or destroy family life, and create serious community problems. Conservatively estimated to afflict 9 to 10 million Americans, alcoholism can occur in any culture, although it may be more prevalent in some than in others. Alcoholism is also associated with high incidences of suicide, homicide, child abuse, and partner violence.

Like alcohol abuse, the misuse of illicit drugs may have detrimental consequences for both the user and his or her family, and it brings further problems due to its status as a banned or illegal substance. For example, users may engage in dangerous or illegal activities (such as prostitution or theft) to support their habits. In addition, variations in the purity of the drugs used or the methods of administration (i.e., sharing needles) may expose users to risks beyond those associated with the drug itself. The following sections introduce the areas for concern related to alcohol and drug abuse and the strategies for effectively assessing use and dependence.

Alcohol Use and Abuse

Understanding a person's alcohol use is essential for a number of reasons. Clearly, problematic use may be related to other problems in work, school, and family functioning. Even moderate use may be a sign of escape or self-medication and lead to impaired judgment and risky behavior, such as driving while intoxicated.

Alcoholism can be distinguished from heavy drinking in that it causes distress and disruption in the life of the person with alcohol dependency, as well as in the lives of members of that person's social and support systems (Goodwin & Gabrielli, 1997). Alcoholism is marked by a preoccupation with making sure that the amount of alcohol necessary for intoxication remains accessible at all times. As a result, individuals may affiliate with other heavy drinkers in an attempt to escape observation. As alcoholism advances, the signs tend to become more concealed, as the user hides bottles or other "evidence," drinks alone, and covers up drinking binges. Feelings of guilt and anxiety over the behavior begin to appear, which usually leads to more drinking in an effort to escape the negative feelings, which in turn leads to an intensification of the negative feelings.

Females who abuse alcohol present a somewhat different profile. They are more likely to abuse prescription drugs as well, to consume substances in isolation, and to have had the onset of abuse after a traumatic event such as incest or racial or domestic violence (Nelson-Zlupko, Kauffman, & Dore, 1995). Women are less likely than men to enter and complete treatment programs, because obstacles to treatment often include social stigma associated with alcoholism and a lack of available transportation and child care while in treatment (Yaffe, Jenson, & Howard, 1995).

Another serious problem associated with alcohol abuse involves adverse effects on offspring produced by the mother's alcohol consumption during pregnancy. The potential effects range from full-blown fetal alcohol syndrome (FAS) to fetal alcohol effects (FAE). Because of these risks, social workers should routinely question women about their use of alcohol during pregnancy, gathering a history of consumption of beer, wine, and liquor (focusing on frequency, quantity, and variability). Questions for substance abuse assessment are included in Table 9-1.

Use and Abuse of Other Substances

EP 2.1.10d

People abuse many types of drugs. Because immediate care may be essential in instances of acute drug intoxication, and because abusers often attempt to conceal their use of drugs, it is important that practitioners recognize the signs of abuse of commonly used drugs. Table 9-2 categorizes the most commonly abused drugs and their indications. In addition to those signs of abuse of specific drugs, common general indications include the following:

- *Changes in attendance at work or school*
- *Decrease in normal capabilities (e.g., work performance, efficiency, habits)*
- *Poor physical appearance, neglect of dress and personal hygiene*
- *Use of sunglasses to conceal dilated or constricted pupils and to compensate for inability to adjust to sunlight*
- *Unusual efforts to cover arms and hide needle marks*
- *Association with known drug users*
- *Involvement in illegal or dangerous activities to secure drugs*

In assessing the possibility of drug abuse, it is important to elicit information not only from the suspected user (who may not be a reliable reporter for a number of reasons) but also from people who are familiar with the habits and lifestyle of the individual. Likewise, the social worker should assess problems of alcohol and drug abuse from a systems perspective and identify reciprocal interactions between the individual's use and the (conscious and unconscious) actions of his or her family, social contacts, and others.

Dual Diagnosis: Addictive and Mental Disorders

EP 2.1.10a

Because alcohol and other drug abuse problems can co-occur with a variety of health and mental health problems (known as *comorbidity*), accurate assessment is important for proper treatment

TABLE-9-1 INTERVIEWING FOR SUBSTANCE ABUSE POTENTIAL

THE FIRST SIX QUESTIONS WILL HELP GUIDE THE DIRECTION OF YOUR INTERVIEW, THE QUESTIONS YOU ASK, AND YOUR FURTHER ASSESSMENT

1. Do you—or did you ever—smoke cigarettes? For how long? How many per day?
2. Do you drink?
3. What do you drink? (Beer, wine, liquor?)
4. Do you take any prescription medications regularly? How do they make you feel?
5. Do you use any over-the-counter medications regularly? How do they make you feel?
6. Have you ever used any illegal drug?
7. When was the last time you had a drink/used?
8. How much did you have to drink/use?
9. When was the last time before that?
10. How much did you have?
11. Do you always drink/use approximately the same amount? If not, is the amount increasing or decreasing?
12. (If it is increasing) Does that concern you?
13. Do most of your friends drink/use?
14. Do (or did) your parents drink/use?
15. Have you ever been concerned that you might have a drinking/drug problem?
16. Has anyone else ever suggested to you that you have (or had) a drinking/drug problem?
17. How does drinking/using help you?
18. Do other people report that you become more careless, or angry, or out of control when you have been drinking/using?
19. Do you drink/use to "get away from your troubles?"
20. What troubles are you trying to get away from?
21. Are you aware of any way in which drinking/using is interfering with your work?
22. Are you having any difficulties or conflict with your spouse or partner because of drinking/using?
23. Are you having financial difficulties? Are they related in any way to your drinking/using?
24. Have you ever tried to stop drinking/using? How?

SOURCE: From *Where to Start and What to Ask: An Assessment Handbook* by Susan Lukas. Copyright © 1993 by Susan Lukas. Used by permission of W. W. Norton & Company, Inc.

---

planning. As Lehman (1996) suggests, several combinations of factors must be taken into account:

- *The type and extent of the substance use disorder*
- *The type of mental disorders and the related severity and duration*
- *The presence of related medical problems*
- *Comorbid disability or other social problems resulting from use, such as correctional system involvement, poverty, or homelessness*

Depending on the combination of factors that affect them, clients may have particular difficulty seeking out and adhering to treatment programs. Furthermore, an understanding of the reciprocal interaction of these factors may affect your assessment and resulting intervention. For example, some psychiatric problems (e.g., paranoia or depression) may emerge as a result of substance use. Social problems such as joblessness or incarceration may limit the client's access to needed treatment for substance abuse, and substance use may limit job and housing opportunities. Problems such as personality disorders may impede the development of trusting and effective treatment relationships needed to treat drug addiction.

Using Interviewing Skills to Assess Substance Use

Social workers are often involved with substance users before they have actually acknowledged a problem or sought help for it (Barber, 1995). It may be difficult to

TABLE-9-2

TYPE OF DRUG	TYPICAL INDICATIONS	COMMERCIAL/STREET NAME
1. Central nervous system depressants (alcohol, sedative-hypnotics, benzodiazepines, barbituates, flunitrazepam, GHB)	Intoxicated behavior with/without odor, staggering or stumbling, "nodding off" at work, slurred speech, dilated pupils, disorientation, difficulty concentrating, potential memory loss	(barbiturates) *Amytal, Nembutal, Seconal, Phenobarbital:* barbs, reds, red birds, phennies, tooies, yellows, yellow jackets (benzodiazepines) *Ativan, Halcion, Librium, Valium, Xanax:* candy, downers, sleeping pills, tranks (flunitrazepam) *Rohypnol:* forget-me pill, Mexican Valium, R2, Roche, roofies, roofinol, rope, rophies (Gamma-hydoxybutyrate) *GHB*: G, Georgia Home Boy, grievous bodily harm, liquid ecstasy, soap, scoop, liquid X
2. Central nervous system stimulants (amphetamines, methamphetamine, MDMA, methylphenidate, nicotine)	Excessively active, increased alertness, euphoric, irritable, argumentative, nervous, long periods without eating or sleeping, weight loss, decreased inhibition	(amphetamine) *Biphetamine, Dexedrine:* bennies, black beauties, crosses, hearts, LA turnaround, speed, truck drivers, uppers (MDMA) Adam, clarity, ecstasy, Eve, lover's speed, peace, STP, X, XTC (methamphetamine) *Desoxyn:* chalk, crank, crystal, fire, glass, go fast, ice, meth, speed (methylphenidate) *Ritalin:* JIF, MPH, R-ball, Skippy, the smart drug, vitamin R (nicotine) cigarettes, cigars, smokeless tobacco, snuff, spit tobacco, bidis, chew
3. Cocaine and crack (also CNS)	Energetic, euphoric, fixed and dilated pupils, reduced appetite, relatively quick or slow heart beat (euphoria quickly replaced by anxiety, irritability and/or depression, sometimes accompanied by hallucinations and paranoid delusions)	*Cocaine hydrochloride:* blow, bump, C, candy, Charlie, coke, crack, flake, rock, snow, toot
4. Opiates (codeine, fentanyl, opium, heroin, morphine, other opiod pain killers)	Euphoric, scars from injecting drugs, fixed and constricted pupils, frequent scratching, loss of appetite (but frequently eat sweets); may have sniffles, red and watering eyes, nausea and vomiting, constipation, and cough until another "fix," lethargic, drowsy, and alternate between dozing and awakening ("nodding")	(codeine) *Empirin with Codeine, Fiorinal with Codeine, Robitussin A-C, Tylenol with Codeine:* Captain Cody, Cody, schoolboy; (with glutethimide) doors & fours, loads, pancakes and syrup (fentanyl) *Actiq, Duragesic, Sublimaze:* Apache, China girl, China white, dance fever, friend, goodfella, jackpot, murder 8, TNT, Tango and Cash (heroin) *diacetylmorphine:* brown sugar, dope, H, horse, junk, skag, skunk, smack, white horse (morphine) *Roxanol, Duramorph:* M, Miss Emma, monkey, white stuff (opium) *laudanum, paregoric:* big O, black stuff, block, gum, hop *Tylox, OxyContin, Percodan, Percocet:* oxy 80s, oxycotton, oxycet, hillbilly heroin, percs *Demerol, meperidine hydrochloride:* demmies, pain killer *Dilaudid;* juice, dillies *Vicodin, Lortab, Lorcet; Darvon, Darvocet*
5. Cannabinoid (marijuana, hashish)	In early stages, may be euphoric or anxious and appear animated, speaking rapidly and loudly with bursts of laughter; pupils may be blood-shot; may have distorted perceptions such as increased sense of taste or smell; reduced short-term memory; lowered coordination and increased reaction time; increased appetite; in later stages, may be drowsy	(marijuana) blunt, dope, ganja, grass, herb, joints, Mary Jane, pot, reefer, sinsemilla, skunk, weed (hashish) boom, chronic, gangster, hash, hash oil, hemp

TABLE-9-2 (CONTINUED)

TYPE OF DRUG	TYPICAL INDICATIONS	COMMERCIAL/STREET NAME
6. Hallucinogens (LSD, STP, DOM, mescaline, psilocybin, DTM, DET)	Behavior and mood vary widely, may sit or recline quietly in trancelike stare or appear fearful or even terrified; dilated pupils in some cases; may experience nausea, chills, flushes, dizziness, irregular breathing, extreme lability, sweating, or trembling of hands; may experience changes in sense of sight, hearing, touch, smell, and time	(LSD) *lysergic acid diethylamide*: acid, blotter, boomers, cubes, microdot, yellow sunshines (mescaline) buttons, cactus, mesc, peyote (psilocybin) magic mushroom, purple passion, shrooms
7. Dissociative drugs (Ketamine, PCP, Salvia divinorum, DXM)	Feelings of being separate from one's body and environment; impaired motor function/anxiety; memory loss; respiratory problems; potential hallucinations	Ketamine: cat Valium, K, Special K, vitamin K (PCP) *phencyclidine*: angel dust, boat, hog, love boat, peace pill Salvia: Shepherdess's Herb, Maria Pastora, magic mint, Sally-D (DXM) *dextromethorphan*: Robotripping, Robo, Triple C
8. Inhalants and volatile hydrocarbons (chloroform, nail polish remover, metallic paints, carbon tetrachloride, amyl nitrate, butyl, isobutyl, nitrous oxide, lighter fluid, fluoride-based sprays)	Varies by chemical: Reduced inhibitions, euphoria, dizziness, slurred speech, unsteady gait, giddiness, drowsiness, nystagmus (constant involuntary eye movement), weight loss, depression, memory impairment	Solvents (paint thinners, gasoline, glues), gases (butane, propane, aerosol propellants, nitrous oxide), nitrites (isoamyl, isobutyl, cyclohexyl): laughing gas, poppers, snappers, whippets
9. Anabolic and androgenic steroids	Increased muscle strength and reduced body mass; acne, aggression, changes to libido and mood, competitiveness, and combativeness	*Anadrol, Oxandrin, Durabolin, Depo-Testosterone, Equipoise:* roids, juice

National Institute on Drug Abuse (2005). *Prescription Drug Abuse*. Retrieved from: http://www.nida.nih.gov/PDF/PrescriptionDrugs.pdf; National Institute on Drug Abuse. (2010). *Commonly Abused Drugs*. Retrieved from http://www.drugabuse.gov/PDF/CADChart.pdf

be nonjudgmental when the user denies that illicit or licit substances are a problem and attempts to conceal the abuse by blaming others, lying, arguing, distorting, attempting to intimidate, diverting the interview focus, or verbally attacking the social worker. Despite these aversive behaviors, the social worker needs to express empathy and sensitivity to the client's feelings, recognizing that such behaviors are often a subterfuge behind which lie embarrassment, hopelessness, shame, ambivalence, and anger.

When asking about alcohol use, be forthright in explaining why you are pursuing that line of questioning. Vague questions tend to support the client's evasions and yield unproductive responses. The questions listed in Table 9-1 should be asked in a direct and compassionate manner. They address the extent and effects of the client's substance use, and the impact on his or her environment.

Assessing Cognitive/Perceptual Functioning

How individuals perceive the world is critically important, because people's perceptions of others, themselves, and events largely determine how they feel and respond to life's experiences in general and to their problematic situations in particular. Recall from Chapter 8 that the meanings or interpretations of events—rather than the events themselves—motivate human beings to behave as they do. Every person's world of experience is unique. Perceptions of identical events or circumstances thus vary widely according to the complex interaction of belief systems, values, attitude, state of mind, and self-concept, all of which in turn are highly idiosyncratic. It follows, then, that to understand and to influence

EP 2.1.4c

human behavior you must first be knowledgeable about how people think. Our thought patterns are influenced by intellectual functioning, judgment, reality testing, coherence, cognitive flexibility, values, beliefs, self-concept, cultural beliefs, and the dynamic interaction among cognitions, emotions, and behaviors that influence social functioning. In the following sections, we briefly consider each of these factors and demonstrate their use in a mental status assessment (Figure 9.2, p. 233).

EP 2.1.10d

Intellectual Functioning

Understanding the client's intellectual capacity is essential for a variety of reasons. Your assessment of intellectual functioning will allow you to adjust your verbal expressions to a level that the client can readily comprehend, and it will help you in assessing strengths and difficulties, negotiating goals, and planning tasks commensurate with his or her capacities. In most instances, a rough estimate of level of intellectual functioning will suffice. In making this assessment, you may want to consider the client's ability to grasp abstract ideas, to express himself or herself, and to analyze or think logically. Additional criteria include level of educational achievement and vocabulary employed, although these factors must be considered in relationship to the person's previous educational opportunities, primary language, or learning difficulties, because normal or high intellectual capacity may be masked by these and other features.

When clients have marked intellectual limitations, your communications should include easily understood words and avoid abstract explanations. To avoid embarrassment, many people will pretend that they understand when, in fact, they do not. Therefore, you should make keen observations and actively seek feedback to determine whether the person has grasped your intended meaning. You can also assist the client by using multiple, concrete examples to convey complex ideas.

When a person's presentation is inconsistent with his or her known intellectual achievement, it may reveal an area for further investigation. For example, have the client's capacities been affected by illness, medications, a head injury, or the use of substances? Or has scholarly achievement (social promotion in school, grade inflation) masked intellectual limitations?

Judgment

Some people who have adequate or even keen intellect may nevertheless encounter severe difficulties in life because they suffer deficiencies in judgment. Clients with poor judgment may get themselves into one jam after another. Examples of problems in judgment include consistently living beyond one's means, becoming involved in "get rich quick" schemes without carefully exploring the possible ramifications, quitting jobs impulsively, leaving small children unattended, moving in with a partner without adequate knowledge of that person, failing to safeguard or maintain personal property, and squandering resources.

Deficiencies in judgment generally come to light when you explore problems and the patterns surrounding them. You may find that a person acts with little forethought, fails to consider the probable consequences of his or her actions, or engages in wishful thinking that things will somehow magically work out. With other, dysfunctional coping patterns may lead predictably to unfavorable outcomes. Because they fail to learn from their past mistakes, these individuals appear to be driven by intense impulses that overpower consideration of the consequences of their actions. Impulse-driven clients may lash out at authority figures, write bad checks, misuse credit cards, or do other things that provide immediate gratification but ultimately lead to loss of jobs, arrest, or other adverse consequences.

Reality Testing

Reality testing is a critical index to a person's mental health. Strong functioning on this dimension means meeting the following criteria:

1. Being properly oriented to time, place, person, and situation
2. Reaching appropriate conclusions about cause-and-effect relationships
3. Perceiving external events and discerning the intentions of others with reasonable accuracy
4. Differentiating one's own thoughts and feelings from those of others

Clients who are markedly disoriented may be severely mentally disturbed, under the influence of drugs, or suffering from a pathological brain syndrome. Disorientation is usually easily identifiable, but when doubt exists, questions about the date, day of the week, current events that are common knowledge, and recent events in the client's life will usually clarify the matter. Clients who are disoriented typically respond inappropriately, sometimes giving bizarre or unrealistic answers. For example, in responding to a question about his daily activities, a reclusive man reported that he can't shower because he has to be on call at all times to consult with the White House about foreign policy.

Some clients who do not have thought disorders may still have poor reality testing, choosing to blame circumstances and events rather than take personal responsibility for their actions. For example, one man who stole an automobile externalized responsibility for his behavior by blaming the owner for leaving the keys in the car. Some clients blame their employers for losing their jobs, even though they habitually missed work for invalid reasons. Still others attribute their difficulties to fate, claiming that it decreed them to be losers. Whatever the sources of these problems with reality testing, they serve as impediments to motivation and meaningful change. Conversely, when people take appropriate responsibility for their actions, that ownership should be considered an area of strength.

Perceptual patterns that involve distortions of external events are fairly common but may cause difficulties, particularly in interpersonal relationships. *Mild distortions* may be associated with stereotypical perceptions (e.g., "All social workers are liberals" or "The only interest men have in women is sexual"). *Moderate distortions* often involve marked misinterpretations of the motives of others and may severely impair interpersonal relationships (e.g., "My boss told me I was doing a good job and that there is an opportunity to be promoted to a job in another department; he's only saying that to get rid of me" or "My wife says she wants to take an evening class, but I know what she really wants ... to meet other men"). In instances of *extreme distortions,* individuals may have *delusions* or false beliefs—for example, that others plan to harm them (when they do not). On rare occasions, people suffering delusions may take violent actions to protect themselves from their imagined persecutors.

Dysfunctions in reality testing of psychotic proportions occur when clients hear voices or other sounds *(auditory hallucinations)* or see things that are not there *(visual hallucinations).* These individuals lack the capacity to distinguish between thoughts and beliefs that emanate from themselves and those that originate from external sources. As a consequence, they may present a danger to themselves or others when acting in response to such commands or visions. Social workers must be able to recognize such severe cognitive dysfunction and respond with referrals for medication, protection, and/ or hospitalization.

Coherence

Social workers occasionally encounter individuals who demonstrate major thought disorders, which are characterized by rambling and incoherent speech. For example, successive thoughts may be highly fragmented and disconnected from one another, a phenomenon referred to as *looseness of association* or *derailment* in the thought processes. As Morrison puts it, the practitioner "can understand the sequence of the words, but the direction they take seems to be governed not by logic but by rhymes, puns or other rules that might be apparent to the patient but mean nothing to you" (1995, p. 113). Another form of derailment is *flight of ideas,* in which the client's response seems to "take off" based on a particular word or thought, unrelated to logical progression or the original point of the communication.

These difficulties in coherence may be indicative of head injury, mania, or thought disorders such as schizophrenia. Incoherence, of course, may also be produced by acute drug intoxication, so practitioners should be careful to rule out this possibility.

Cognitive Flexibility

People who are receptive to new ideas and able to analyze many facets of problematic situations are highly adaptable and capable of successful problem solving. Individuals with cognitive flexibility generally seek to grow, to understand the part they play in their difficulties, and to understand others; these individuals can also ask for assistance without perceiving such a request to be an admission of weakness or failure. Many people, however, are rigid and unyielding in their beliefs, and their inflexibility poses a major obstacle to progress in the helping process.

A common pattern of cognitive inflexibility is thinking in absolute terms (e.g., a person is good or evil, a success or a failure, responsible or irresponsible—there are no in-betweens). People who think this way are prone to criticize others who fail to measure up to their stringent standards. Because they can be difficult to live with, many of these individuals appear at social agencies because of relationship problems, workplace conflict, or parent-child disputes. Improvement often requires helping them examine the destructive impact of their rigidity, broaden their perspectives of themselves and others, and "loosen up" in general.

Negative cognitive sets also include biases and stereotypes that impede relationship building or cooperation with members of certain groups (e.g., authority figures, ethnic groups, and the opposite sex) or individuals. Severely depressed clients often have another form of "tunnel vision," viewing themselves as helpless or worthless and the future as dismal and hopeless. When they are lost in the depths of illness, these clients may selectively attend to their own negative attributes, have difficulty feeling good about themselves, and struggle with being open to other options.

Values

EP 2.1.4c

Values are an integral part of the cognitive-perceptual subsystem, because they strongly influence human behavior and often play a key role in the problems presented for work. For this reason, you should seek to identify your clients' values, assess the role those values play in their difficulties, and consider ways in which clients' values can be deployed to create incentives for change. Your ethical responsibility to respect the client's right to maintain his or her values and to make choices consistent with them requires you to become aware of those values. Because values result from our cultural conditioning, understanding the client's cultural reference group is important, particularly if it differs from your own. Understanding the individual *within* his or her culture is also critical, however, because people adopt values on a continuum, with considerable diversity occurring among people within any given race, faith, culture, or community (Gross, 1995).

Value conflicts are often at the heart of clients' difficulties—for example, in the video featuring the Chinese college student, Yanping, the client is torn between loyalty to her parents and her desire to follow her own interests and study history. Value conflicts may also be central to difficulties between people. Parents and children may disagree about dress, behavior, or responsibilities. Partners may hold different beliefs about how chores should be divided, how finances should be handled, or how they should relate to each person's family of origin.

Examples of questions that will clarify values include:

- "You say you believe your parents are old-fashioned about sex. What are your beliefs?"
- "If you could be married to an ideal wife, what would she be like?"
- [To a couple]: "What are your beliefs about how couples should make decisions?"
- "So you feel you're not succeeding in life. To you, what does being successful involve?"

Being aware of values also aids you in using those values to create incentives for changing dysfunctional behavior—for example, when clients express strong values yet behave in direct opposition to those values. *Cognitive dissonance* may result when people discover inconsistencies between their values and behaviors.

Examining these contradictions can help reveal whether this tension is problematic or self-defeating. As an example, consider an individual coming to terms with his homosexuality within a religious faith that condemns his sexual orientation. Tension, confusion, and distress can result as this client and others attempt to reconcile disparate beliefs. The social worker may help by identifying and labeling the cognitive dissonance and working with the client to reconcile the differences or create options so that they are no longer mutually exclusive. The techniques associated with motivational interviewing are helpful in gently calling attention to incongruent values and actions.

Beliefs

Cognitive theory holds that beliefs are important mediators of both emotions and actions (Ellis, 1962; Lantz, 1996). It makes sense, then, that mistaken beliefs can be related to problems in functioning. Sometimes, beliefs are not misconceptions, but rather are unhelpful, if accurate, conceptions. Examples of common destructive beliefs and contrasting functional beliefs include: "The world is a dog-eat-dog place; no one really cares about anyone except themselves" versus "There are all kinds of people in the world, including those who are ruthless and those who are caring; I need to seek out the latter and strive to be a caring person myself"; or "All people in authority use their power to exploit and control others" versus "People in authority vary widely—some exploit and control others, while others are benevolent; I must reserve judgment, or I will indiscriminately resent all authority figures."

It is important to identify misconceptions and their sources so as to create a comprehensive assessment. Depending on how central these beliefs are to the client's problems, the goals for work that follow may involve modifying key misconceptions, thereby paving the way to behavioral change. As with other areas, client strengths may derive from the *absence* of misconceptions, and from the ability to accurately, constructively, or positively perceive and construe events and motivations.

Self-Concept

Convictions, beliefs, and ideas about the self have been generally recognized as crucial determinants of human behavior. Thus, there are strengths in having good self-esteem and in being realistically aware of one's positive attributes, accomplishments, and potential as well as one's limitations and deficiencies. A healthy person can accept limitations as a natural part of human fallibility without being overly distressed or discouraged. People with high self-esteem, in fact, can joke about their weaknesses and mistakes.

Many people, however, are tormented with feelings of worthlessness, inadequacy, and helplessness. These and similarly self-critical feelings pervade their functioning in diverse negative ways, including the following:

- *Underachieving in life because of imagined deficiencies*
- *Passing up opportunities because of fears of failing*
- *Avoiding social relationships because of expectations of being rejected*
- *Permitting oneself to be taken for granted and exploited by others*
- *Excessive drinking or drug use to fortify oneself because of feelings of inadequacy*
- *Devaluing or discrediting worthwhile achievements*
- *Failing to defend one's rights*

Often clients will spontaneously discuss how they view themselves, or their description of patterns of difficulty may convey damaged self-concept. An open-ended query, such as "Tell me how you see yourself," will often elicit rich information. Because many people have not actually given much thought to the matter, they may hesitate or appear perplexed. An additional query, such as "What comes into your head when you think about the sort of person you are?" is usually all that is needed to prompt the client to respond.

Assessing Affective Functioning

Emotions are affected by cognitions and powerfully influence behavior. People who seek help often do so because they have experienced strong emotions or a sense that their emotions are out of control. Some individuals, for example, are emotionally volatile and engage in aggressive

EP 2.1.10d

IDEAS IN ACTION

Cognitive or Thought Disorders

EP 2.1.7a

As you assess cognitive functioning, you may note signs and symptoms of thought disorders and developmental delays. Three particular disorders to be alert to are mental retardation, schizophrenia, and dementia.

Mental retardation is typically diagnosed in infancy or childhood. It is defined as lower-than-average intelligence and "significant limitations in adaptive functioning in at least two of the following skill areas: communication, self-care, home living, social/interpersonal skills, use of community resources, self-direction, functional academic skills, work, leisure, health and safety" (American Psychiatric Association, 2000, p. 41). General intellectual functioning is appraised using standardized tests, and other measurement instruments may be used to assess the client's adaptive functioning, or ability to meet common life demands. Four levels of mental retardation are distinguished: mild, moderate, severe, and profound.

Schizophrenia is a psychotic disorder that causes marked impairment in social, educational, and occupational functioning. Its onset typically occurs during adolescence or young adulthood, and development of the disorder may be abrupt or gradual. It is signified by a combination of *positive and negative symptoms*. In this context, these terms do not refer to whether something is good or bad, but rather to the presence or absence of normal functions. For example, positive symptoms of schizophrenia "include distortions in thought content (delusions), perception (hallucinations), language and thought processes (disorganized speech), and self-monitoring of behavior (grossly disorganized or catatonic behavior)" (American Psychiatric Association, 2000, p. 299). Negative symptoms include flattened affect, restricted speech, and *avolition*, or limited initiation of goal-directed behavior.

Dementia is characterized by "multiple cognitive deficits that include memory impairment and at least one of the following: *aphasia* (deterioration in language functioning), *apraxia* (difficulty with motor activities), *agnosia* (failure to recognize familiar objects), or *disturbance in executive functioning* (abstract thinking, and planning, sequencing, and ceasing complex activities)" (American Psychiatric Association, 2000, p. 148). These deficits must be of a sufficient severity to affect one's daily functioning to warrant a diagnosis of dementia (Corcoran & Walsh, 2010).

Treatment of individuals with these diagnoses is specialized and varied, but may include use of medication as well as vocational, residential, and case management services. Understanding the features of these and other cognitive/thought disorders will assist you in better understanding clients, in planning appropriate treatment, and in considering how your role on cases meshes with that of other service providers.

behavior while in the heat of anger. Others are emotionally unstable, struggling to stay afloat in a turbulent sea of feelings. Some people become emotionally distraught as the result of stress associated with the death of a loved one, divorce, severe disappointment, or another blow to self-esteem. Still others are pulled in different directions by opposing feelings and seek help to resolve their emotional dilemmas. To assist you in assessing emotional functioning, the following sections examine vital aspects of this dimension and the related terms and concepts. Figure 9-2 (p. 233) demonstrates the use of these concepts in a mental status exam.

Emotional Control

People vary widely in the degree of control they exercise over their emotions, ranging from *emotional constriction* to *emotional excesses*. Individuals who are experiencing constriction may appear unexpressive and withholding in relationships. Because they are out of touch with their emotions, they do not appear to permit themselves to feel joy, hurt, enthusiasm, vulnerability, and other emotions that might otherwise invest life with zest and meaning. These individuals may be comfortable intellectualizing but retreat from expressing or discussing feelings. They often favorably impress others with their intellectual styles, but sometimes have difficulties maintaining close relationships because their emotional detachment thwarts them from fulfilling the needs of others for intimacy and emotional stimulation.

A person with emotional excesses, on the other hand, may have "a short fuse," losing control and reacting intensely to even mild provocations. This behavior may involve rages and escalate to interpersonal violence. Excesses can also include other emotions such as irritability, crying, panic, despondency, helplessness, or giddiness. The key in assessing whether the emotional response is excessive entails determining whether it is appropriate and proportionate to the stimulus.

EP 2.1.4c

Your assessment may stem from your personal observation of the client, feedback from collateral contacts, or the client's own report of his or her response to a situation. As always, your appraisal of the appropriateness of the response must factor in the client's social and cultural context and the nature of his or her relationship with you. Both may lead you to misjudge the client's normal emotional response and what is considered "appropriate" emotional regulation.

Cultures vary widely in their approved patterns of emotional expression. Nevertheless, emotional health in any culture shares one criterion: It means having control over the emotions to the extent that one is not overwhelmed by them. Emotionally healthy persons also enjoy the freedom of experiencing and expressing emotions appropriately. Likewise, strengths include the ability to bear painful emotions without denying or masking feelings or being incapacitated by them. Emotionally healthy persons are able to discern the emotional states of others, empathize, and discuss painful emotions openly without feeling unduly distressed—recognizing, of course, that a certain amount of discomfort is natural. Finally, the ability to mutually share deeply personal feelings in intimate relationships is also considered an asset.

Range of Emotions

Another aspect of emotional functioning involves the ability to experience and to express a wide range of emotions that befits the vast array of situations that humans encounter. Some individuals' emotional expression is confined to a limited range, which can cause interpersonal difficulties. For example, if one partner has difficulty expressing tender emotions, the other partner may feel rejected, insecure, or deprived of deserved affection.

Some individuals are unable to feel joy or to express many pleasurable emotions, a dysfunction referred to as *anhedonia*. Still others have been conditioned to block out their angry feelings, blame themselves, or placate others when friction develops in relationships. Because of this blocking of natural emotions, they may experience extreme tension or physiological symptoms such as asthma, colitis, and headaches when they face situations that normally would engender anger or sadness. Finally, some people, to protect themselves from unbearable emotions, develop psychic mechanisms early in life that block them from experiencing rejection, loneliness, and hurt. Often this blockage is reflected by a compensatory facade of toughness and indifference, combined with verbal expressions such as "I don't need anyone" and "No one can hurt me." Whatever its source, a blocked or limited range of emotions may affect the client's difficulties and thus represent a goal for work.

Emotionally healthy people experience the full gamut of human emotions within normal limits of intensity and duration. The capacity to experience joy, grief, exhilaration, disappointment, and the rest of the full spectrum of emotions is, therefore, an area of strength.

Appropriateness of Affect

Direct observation of clients' affect (emotionality) usually reveals valuable information about their emotional functioning. Some anxiety or mild apprehension is natural in initial sessions as contrasted to intense apprehension and tension at one extreme or complete relaxation or giddiness at the other. Healthy functioning involves spontaneously experiencing and expressing emotion appropriate to the context and the material being discussed. The ability to laugh, to cry, and to express hurt, discouragement, anger, and pleasure when these feelings match the mood and content of the session constitutes an area of strength. Such spontaneity indicates that clients are in touch with their emotions and can express them appropriately.

Inordinate apprehension—often demonstrated by muscle tension, constant fidgeting or shifts in posture, hand wringing, lip-biting, and similar behaviors—usually indicates that a person is fearful, suspicious, or exceptionally uncomfortable in unfamiliar interpersonal situations. Such extreme tension may be expected in involuntary situations. In other cases, it may be characteristic of a client's demeanor in other contexts.

Clients who appear completely relaxed and express themselves freely in a circumstance that would normally evoke apprehension or anxiety may reflect a denial of a problem and or a lack of motivation to engage in the problem-solving process. Further, a charming demeanor may reflect the client's skill in projecting a favorable image when it is advantageous to do so. In some situations, such as in sales, promotional, or political work, this kind of charm may be an asset; in other circumstances, it may be a coping style developed to conceal the individual's insecurity, self-centeredness, and manipulation or exploitation of others.

Emotional blunting is what the term suggests: a muffled or apathetic response to material that would typically evoke a stronger response (e.g., happiness, despair, anger). For example, emotionally blunted clients may discuss, in a detached and matter-of-fact manner, traumatic life events or conditions such as the murder of one parent by another, deprivation, or physical and/or sexual abuse. Emotional blunting can be indicative of a severe mental disorder, a sign of drug misuse, or a side effect of medications, so it always warrants special attention.

Inappropriate affect can also appear in other forms, such as laughing when discussing a painful event (gallows laughter) or smiling constantly regardless of what is being discussed. Elation or euphoria that is incongruent with the individual's life situation, combined with constant and rapid shifts from one topic to another (flight of ideas), irritability, expansive ideas, and constant motion, also suggests mania.

In transcultural work, appropriateness of affect must be considered in light of cultural differences. According to Lum (1996), minority clients may feel uncomfortable with nonminority social workers but mask their emotions as a protective measure, or they may control painful emotions according to culturally prescribed norms. Measures to assure appropriate interpretation of affect include understanding the features of the client's culture, consulting others who are familiar with the culture or the client, and evaluating the client's current presentation with his or her demeanor in the past.

Suicidal Risk

Not all individuals with depressive symptoms are suicidal and not all suicidal individuals are depressed. Nevertheless, whenever clients exhibit depressive symptoms or hopelessness, it is critical to evaluate suicidal risk so that precautionary measures can be taken when indicated. With adults, the following factors are associated with high risk of suicide:

- *Feelings of despair and hopelessness*
- *Previous suicidal attempts*
- *Concrete, available, and lethal plans to commit suicide (when, where, and how)*
- *Family history of suicide*
- *Perseveration about suicide*
- *Lack of support systems and other forms of isolation*
- *Feelings of worthlessness*
- *Belief that others would be better off if the client were dead*
- *Advanced age (especially for white males)*
- *Substance abuse*

When a client indicates, directly or indirectly, that he or she may be considering suicide, it is essential that you address those concerns through careful and direct questioning. You may begin by stating, "You sound pretty hopeless right now; I wonder if you might also be thinking of harming yourself?" or "When you say 'They'll be sorry' when you're gone, I wonder if that means you're thinking of committing suicide?" An affirmative answer to

EP 2.1.7a

IDEAS IN ACTION

Affective Disorders

EP 2.1.7a

The DSM-IV-TR (American Psychiatric Association, 2000) contains extensive information on the criteria for diagnosing affective disorders (i.e., disorders of mood). Of particular importance for the beginning social worker are *bipolar disorders* (known formerly as manic-depressive illness) and *unipolar/major affective disorders* (such as severe depression). Treatment of these diagnoses generally includes medication (often with concurrent cognitive or interpersonal psychotherapy). Understanding these diagnoses is important for treatment planning and detection of suicidal ideation and other serious risk factors (Corcoran & Walsh, 2010).

Bipolar Disorder

The dominant feature of bipolar disorder is the presence of manic episodes (mania) with intervening periods of depression. Among the symptoms of mania are "a distinct period of abnormally and persistently elevated, expansive or irritable mood …" (American Psychiatric Association, 2000, p. 362) and at least three of the following:

- *Inflated self-esteem or grandiosity*
- *Decreased need for sleep*
- *More talkative than usual or pressure to keep talking*
- *Flight of ideas or subjective experience that thoughts are racing*
- *Distractibility*
- *Increase in goal-directed activity (either socially, at work or school, or sexually) or psychomotor agitation*
- *Excessive involvement in pleasurable activities with a high potential for painful consequences, such as unrestrained buying sprees, sexual indiscretions, or foolish business investments*

Full-blown manic episodes require that symptoms be sufficiently severe to cause marked impairment in job performance or relationships, or to necessitate hospitalization to protect patients or others from harm.

If exploration seems to indicate a client has the disorder, immediate psychiatric consultation is needed for two reasons: (1) to determine whether hospitalization is needed and, (2) to determine the need for medication. Bipolar disorder is biogenetic, and various compounds containing lithium carbonate may produce remarkable results in stabilizing and maintaining affected individuals. Close medical supervision is required, however, because commonly used medications for this disorder have a relatively narrow margin of safety.

Major Depressive Disorder

Major depressive disorder, in which affected individuals experience recurrent episodes of depressed mood, is far more common than bipolar disorder. Major depression differs from the "blues" in that *dysphoria* (painful emotions) and the absence of pleasure in previously enjoyable activities (anhedonia) are present. The painful emotions commonly are related to anxiety, mental anguish, an extreme sense of guilt (often over what appear to be relatively minor offenses), and restlessness (agitation).

To be assigned a diagnosis of major depressive episode, a person must have evidenced depressed mood and loss of interest or pleasure as well as at least five of the following nine symptoms for at least 2 weeks (American Psychiatric Association, 2000, pp. 375–376):

- *Depressed mood for most of the day, nearly every day*
- *Markedly diminished interest or pleasure in all or almost all activities*
- *Significant weight loss or weight gain when not dieting or decrease or increase in appetite*
- *Insomnia or hypersomnia*
- *Psychomotor agitation or retardation*
- *Fatigue or loss of energy*
- *Feelings of worthlessness or excessive or inappropriate guilt*
- *Diminished ability to think or concentrate or indecisiveness*
- *Recurrent thoughts of death or suicidal ideation or attempts*

As noted in Chapter 8, a number of scales are available to assess the presence and degree of depression. When assessment reveals that clients are moderately or severely depressed, psychiatric consultation is indicated to determine the need for medication and/or hospitalization. Antidepressant medications have proven to be effective in accelerating recovery from depression and work synergistically with cognitive or interpersonal psychotherapy.

In assessing depression, it is important to identify which factors precipitated the depressive episode. If an important loss or series of losses has occurred, it may be difficult to differentiate between depression and complicated bereavement. While depression and mourning may share certain characteristics such as intense sadness and sleep and appetite disturbances, grief reactions generally do not include the diminished self-esteem and guilt often observed in depression. "That is, the people who have lost someone do not regard themselves less because of such a loss or if they do, it tends to be only for a brief time. And if the survivors of the deceased experience guilt, it is usually guilt associated with some specific aspect of the loss rather than a general, overall sense of culpability" (Worden, 1991, p. 30).

IDEAS IN ACTION

In the "Elder Assessment" videotaped interviews, the worker, Kathy, inquires about the recent death of Josephine's husband. Noting signs of grief and depression, Kathy probes further about past coping, sleep patterns, eating, weight loss, substance use, energy level, hobbies and interests, social contacts, and mood. She also asks the client to walk her through a typical day. Ultimately, she explains and administers a brief depression inventory, the Geriatric Depression Scale (GDS) (Yesavage et al., 1983), and provides a booklet about grief. In the follow-up session, Kathy educates Josephine about the phases of grief and describes the results of the depression evaluation, with a typical score at 5 and Josephine's score at 12 ("off the chart"). Josephine's history and her responses to questions about hopelessness and whether life is worth living indicate that she is not at suicidal risk at the time of the interview. As a result of the assessment, Kathy recommends consideration of medication, a physician consultation regarding insomnia, and counseling, from a widow-to-widow program on grief or from a professional.

---

these probes should be followed with a frank and calm discussion of the client's thoughts about suicide. Has the client considered how he or she might do it? When? What means would be used? Are those means accessible? In asking these questions, you are trying to determine not only the lethality of the client's plans but also the specificity. If a client has a well-thought-out plan in mind, the risk of suicide is significantly greater. An understanding of the client's history, especially with regard to the risk factors mentioned and previous suicide attempts, will also help you decide the degree of danger and the level of intervention required. Standardized scales can also be used to evaluate suicidal risk.

When the client's responses indicate a potentially lethal attempt, it is appropriate to mobilize client support systems and arrange for psychiatric evaluation and/or hospitalization if needed. Such steps provide a measure of security for the client who may feel unable to control his or her impulses or who may become overwhelmed with despair.

Depression and Suicidal Risk with Children and Adolescents

Children and adolescents may experience depression just as adults do, and suicide can be a risk with these groups (Morrison & Anders, 1999). It is estimated that 500,000 young people between ages 15 and 24 attempt suicide each year and nearly 5,000 children and youth (age 5 to 24) kill themselves each year. In fact, suicide is the third leading cause of death for those in the 15- to 24-year-old age bracket (CDC, 2007; McIntosh, 2003). The World Health Organization (WHO) reports global statistics, noting that in the past 45 years suicide rates have grown 60 percent worldwide and that suicide is the third leading cause of death for those between the ages of 15 and 44 (WHO, 2008).

Clearly, it is important to recognize the symptoms of depression in adolescents and the behavioral manifestations that may be reported by peers, siblings, parents, or teachers. The symptoms of depression in adolescents are similar to those of adults (anhedonia, depressed mood, significant weight loss or gain, fatigue or loss of energy, feelings of hopelessness, worthlessness, guilt, and self-reproach, indecisiveness or decreased ability to concentrate, suicidal thoughts) though irritability and somatic complaints may be more prominent with children and teens (Dulcan, 2009).

EP 2.1.7a

VIDEO CASE EXAMPLE

In the Session 2 of the video "Hanging with Hailey," Emily, the social worker, takes note of changes in Hailey's demeanor, her isolation, and her misery as a result of rejection by peers. As a result, Emily inquires about Hailey's coping and then directly asks, "Do you ever think about wanting to hurt yourself?" Although she determines that Hailey's risk is currently only at the level of ideation, she puts a plan in place should her suicidal thoughts and symptoms increase.

Childhood depression does not differ markedly from depression in adolescence; the behaviors manifested and the intensity of feelings are similar, once developmental differences are taken into consideration (Wenar,

1994; Morrison & Anders, 1999; Birmaher et al, 2004). One major difference between childhood and adolescent depression appears when comparing prevalence rates between the sexes. The prevalence of depression is approximately the same in boys and girls in middle childhood, but beginning in adolescence twice as many females experience depression as males (Kauffman, 1997; Hankin et al., 1998). Also, adolescent girls diagnosed with depression report more feelings of anxiety and inadequacy in middle childhood, whereas adolescent boys report more aggressive and antisocial feelings (Wenar, 1994; Leadbeater, Kupermic, Blatt, & Hertzog, 1999).

Because parents, teachers, coaches, and friends often do not realize the child or adolescent is depressed, it is important to alert them to the following potentially troublesome symptoms (American Association of Suicidology, 2004; Gold, 1986):

- *Deterioration in personal habits*
- *Decline in school achievement*
- *Marked increase in sadness, moodiness, and sudden tearful reactions*
- *Loss of appetite*
- *Use of drugs or alcohol*
- *Talk of death or dying (even in a joking manner)*
- *Withdrawal from friends and family*
- *Making final arrangements, such as giving away valued possessions*
- *Sudden or unexplained departure from past behaviors (from shy to thrill seeking or from outgoing to sullen and withdrawn)*

EP 2.1.4c

Specific subgroups may experience additional, unique risk factors related to their particular gender, race or ethnicity, or sexual orientation and the ways that these interact with the environments around them (Macgowan, 2004). Given the tempestuousness typical of adolescence, it may be difficult to distinguish any warning signs from normative actions and behavior. Cautious practice would suggest taking changes such as these seriously, rather than minimizing them or writing them off as "typical teen behavior." Whether or not they are indicative of depression and suicide risk, changes in behavior and patterns such as these indicate that something is going on that is worthy of adult attention, as well as professional consultation and evaluation.

Suicidal risk is highest when the adolescent, in addition to exhibiting the aforementioned symptoms of severe depression, shows feelings of hopelessness, has recently experienced a death of a loved one, has severe conflict with parents, has lost a close relationship with a key peer or a love interest, and lacks a support system. Brent and colleagues indicate that "interpersonal conflict, especially with parents, is one of the most commonly reported precipitants for completed and attempted suicides" (1993, p. 185). Other studies have indicated that moderate to heavy drinking or drug abuse is implicated in as many as 50 percent of adolescent suicides (Fowler, Rich, & Young, 1986; Rowan, 2001).

While completed suicides and suicide attempts are more common among adolescents (with adolescent males completing more suicides and adolescent females attempting more suicides), the number of younger children completing and attempting suicide is increasing (Kauffman, 1997). Therefore, it is important to be cognizant of depressed behavior and signs of suicide ideation in children as well as adolescents. Warning signs of suicide ideation in younger children are similar to those discussed for adolescents, albeit translated to the appropriate developmental level. When faced with a young client who is considering suicide, social workers should use the same lethality assessment questions discussed earlier for work with adults. In addition, assessment tools geared to evaluating suicide risk in children and adolescents are available, such as the Suicidal Ideation Questionnaire (SIQ) (Reynolds, 1988) and Suicidal Ideation Questionnaire JR (SIQ-JR) (Reynolds, 1987), SAD-PERSONS (Juhnke, 1996), the Diagnostic Predictive Scales (DPS) (Lucas et al., 2001), and the Columbia Suicide Screen (CSS) (Shaffer et al., 2004).

Depression and Suicidal Risk with Older Adults

EP 2.1.7a

In addition to the signs just noted for depression and suicidal ideation in adults, adolescents and children, older adults warrant particular attention in screening for these conditions. In 2007, approximately 16 percent of all suicides in the United States were committed by the elderly, though they constitute only 12.5 percent of the population (Brown, Bruce, Pearson, 2001; CDC, 2007). White males over the age of 70 are more likely to commit suicide than any other age group, though suicide rates have recently been declining for the elderly and increasing for those in middle age (CDC, 2007; Kent, 2010). Particular risk factors for older persons include isolation, ill health, hopelessness, and functional and social losses. Further, older clients may be reluctant to appear for mental health services, and psychiatric conditions may be overlooked by primary care providers and loved ones or minimized as typical features of aging. Commonly used instruments to assess depression, such as the Geriatric Depression Scale, may provide insufficient screening for suicidal ideation (Heisel, Flett, Duberstein, & Lyness, 2005). The assessment of suicidality in elder clients requires particular discernment to distinguish among suicidal intent and the awareness of mortality or preparedness for death which may be hallmarks of that developmental phase (Heisel & Flett, 2006).

Zivin and Kales (2008) point out that the approach clinicians take to explain depression and antidepressants to patients can have a significant impact on their adherence to their medication regime. However, they also state that doctors often lack the time or training to give effective explanations. Although antidepressants can be effective in treating depression in older adults, 40 to 75 percent do not take their antidepressants as directed or at all (Zivin & Kales, 2008). Older adults who present as treatment-resistant may instead simply be noncompliant with their antidepressants. Elders may intentionally not take their medications out of fear of becoming dependent, over concerns that the medicine will prevent them from feeling natural sadness, or because they do not recognize their depression as a medical condition. Other seniors may forget to take their antidepressants or misunderstand dosage instructions, especially if they have cognitive impairment and no caregiver to assist them with medications. Some seniors are reluctant to take their antidepressants because they fear they will negatively interact with other medications. Other risk factors for being noncompliant with medications include taking three or more other medications, having co-occurring diagnoses of depression and anxiety, dependence on substances, having a caregiver who does not believe depression is a medical condition, lack of social support, and an inability to pay for medications. While spirituality can often aid elders in dealing with mental health issues, at times faith can have a negative effect on depression. Some elders may feel that they do not need medical treatment because God can heal them and others might interpret their depression as a punishment from God (Zivin & Kales, 2008).[3]

Assessing Behavioral Functioning

EP 2.1.10a

In direct social work practice, change efforts frequently target behavioral patterns that impair the client's social functioning. As you assess behavior, it is important to keep in mind that one person's behavior does not influence another person's behavior in simple linear fashion. Rather, a circular process takes place, in which the behavior of all participants reciprocally affects and shapes the behavior of other participants.

Because behavioral change is commonly the focus of social work interventions, you must be skillful in discerning and assessing both dysfunctional and functional patterns of behavior. In individual sessions, you can directly observe clients' social and communication patterns as well as some personal habits and traits. In conjoint interviews and group sessions, you can observe these behavioral patterns as well as the effects that these actions have on others. Figure 9-2 (p. 233) demonstrates the use of these concepts in a mental status exam.

In assessing behavior, it is helpful to think of problems as consisting of *excesses* or *deficiencies*. For excesses-related problems, interventions aim to *diminish* or *eliminate* the behaviors, such as temper outbursts, too much talking, arguing, competition, and consumptive excesses (e.g., food, alcohol, sex, gambling, or shopping). For behavioral deficiencies, when assessment reveals the absence of needed skills, interventions aim to help clients *acquire* the skills and behaviors to function more effectively. For example, a client's behavioral repertoire may not include skills in expressing feelings directly, engaging in social conversation, listening to others, solving problems, managing finances, planning nutritional meals, being a responsive sexual partner, or handling conflict. Sometimes problems can result from a combination of behavioral excesses and deficiencies.

The issue of hoarding has been the subject of a great deal of attention and research in recent years. The profile of problematic clutter often arises from compulsive acquisitions (collecting, shopping, saving) and insufficient management of items (organizing, sorting, cleaning). As with other problems, cognitive and affective elements interact with behaviors to create and maintain the problem. For example, beliefs ("This is such a great price I'll buy several" or "I might need these old magazines someday") trigger emotions (joy, relief, comfort) and behavior (buy, save). The thought of avoiding the bargain or throwing the magazine initiates other thoughts ("It is a missed opportunity," "I don't want to regret getting rid of it later"), which gives rise to troubling or aversive feelings (anxiety, insecurity, sadness). Effective interventions for hoarding rely on the precise assessment of the factors at play for the individual and the meaning ascribed to the items collected. Steketee and Frost offer evidence based interview tools, assessment instruments, and treatment guides for addressing this hidden but significant problem (2007).

One specialized form of assessment is the *mental status exam*. This exam is intended to capture and describe features of the client's mental state. The terminology developed in conjunction with these instruments has greatly facilitated communication among professions for both clinical and research purposes. Certain features on the mental status exam are associated with particular conditions, such as intoxication, dementia, depression, or psychosis.

The mental status exam typically consists of the following items, which are described elsewhere in this chapter and in other sources (Lukas, 1993; Gallo, Fulmer, Paveza, & Reichel, 2000):

Appearance
How does the client look and act?
Stated age, dress and clothing
Psychomotor movements, tics, facial expressions

Reality Testing
Judgment
Dangerous, impulsive behaviors
Insight
- To what extent the client understands his or her problem
- How the client describes the problem

Speech
Volume: slow, inaudible
Rate of speech: rapid, slow
Amount: poverty of speech

Emotions
Mood: how the client feels most of the time
- Anxious, depressed, overwhelmed, scared, tense, restless, euthymic, euphoric

Affect: how the client appears to be feeling at this time
- Variability (labile)
- Intensity (blunted, flat)

Thought
Content: What the client thinks about
- Delusions: unreal belief, distortion
    Delusions of grandeur: unusual or exaggerated power
    Delusions of persecution: unreal belief that someone is after the client
    Delusions of control: someone else is controlling the client's thoughts or actions
    Somatic delusions: unreal physical concerns
- Other thought issues
    Obsessions: unrelenting, unwanted thoughts
    Compulsions: repeated behaviors, often linked to an obsession
    Phobias: obsessive thoughts that arouse intense fears
    Thought broadcasting: belief that others can read the client's mind

Ideas of reference: insignificant or unrelated events that have a secret meaning to the client
- Homicidal ideation: desire or intent to hurt others
- Suicidal ideation: range from thought, desire, intent, or plan to die
- Process: how the client thinks
    Circumstantiality: lack of goal direction
    Perseveration: repeated phrase, repeated topic
    Loose associations: move between topics without connections
    Tangentiality: barely talking about the topic
    Flight of ideas: rapid speech that is unconnected

Sensory Perceptions
Illusions
- Misperception of normal sensory events

Hallucinations
- Experience of one of the senses: olfactory (smell), auditory (hearing), visual (sight), gustatory (taste), tactile (touch)

Mental Capacities
Orientation times four: oriented to time, person, place, and situation
General intellect: average or low intelligence
Memory: remote (past presidents), recent (what the client ate yesterday for breakfast), and immediate (remember three items)
Concentration: Distraction during interview, count backward by 3s

Attitude toward Interviewer
How the client behaves toward the interviewer: suspicious, arrogant, cooperative, afraid, reserved, entertaining, ability to trust and open up, forthcoming

Sample Mini Mental Status Report
Mr. Stewart presents as unshaven, thin, with unkempt hair, and older than his stated age. No abnormal body movements or tics are noted. Mr. Stewart is alert and oriented times four. His thought content and processes appear normal (although there are no specific questions to address delusions, hallucinations, or intellect). He describes his mood as euthymic, and his affect is guarded. While he is inquisitive about the clinician's notes and he provides only brief answers, Mr. Stewart is cooperative. His judgment is impaired, as seen by his driving while intoxicated and missing work. Mr. Stewart's insight appears limited, as he has come for evaluation to appease his wife and does not see his drinking as heavy or problematic. He denies thoughts or plans of suicide or homicide.

FIG-9-2 Mental Status Exams

TABLE-9-3 BEHAVIORAL PATTERNS

DIMENSIONS OF BEHAVIOR	DYSFUNCTIONAL PATTERNS	FUNCTIONAL PATTERNS (STRENGTHS)
Power/control	Autocratic, overbearing, aggressive, ruthless, demanding, domineering, controlling, passive submissive; excludes others from decision making	Democratic, cooperative, assertive; includes others in decision making, stands up for own rights
Nurturance/support	Self-centered, critical, rejecting, withholding, demeaning, distant, punitive, fault-finding, self-serving, insensitive to or unconcerned about others	Caring, approving, giving, empathic, encouraging, patient, generous, altruistic, warm, accepting, supportive, interested in others
Responsibility	Undependable, erratic, avoids responsibility, places pleasure before responsibility, externalizes responsibility for problems, neglects maintenance of personal property	Dependable, steady, consistent, reliable, follows through, accepts responsibility, owns part in problems, maintains personal property
Social skills	Abrasive, caustic, irritable, insensitive, aloof, reclusive, sarcastic, querulous, withdrawn, self-conscious, ingratiating, lacks social delicacy	Outgoing, poised, personable, verbally fluent, sociable, witty, courteous, engaging, cooperative, assertive, spontaneous, respectful to others, sensitive to feelings of others, has sense of propriety
Coping patterns	Rigid, impulsive, rebellious; avoids facing problems, uses alcohol or drugs when under stress, becomes panicky, lashes out at others, sulks	Flexible, faces problems, considers and weighs alternatives, anticipates consequences, maintains equilibrium, seeks growth, consults others for suggestions, negotiates and compromises
Personal habits	Disorganized, dilatory, devious, dishonest, compulsive, overly fastidious, impulsive, manifests poor personal hygiene, has consumption excesses, has irritating mannerisms	Planful, organized, flexible, clean, efficient, patient, self-disciplined, well groomed, honest, open, sincere, temperate, considerate, even dispositioned, punctual
Communication	Mumbles, complains excessively, nags, talks excessively, interrupts others, tunes others out, stammers, yells when angry, withholds views, defensive, monotonic, argumentative, taciturn, verbally abusive	Listens attentively, speaks fluently, expresses views, shares feelings, uses feedback, expresses self spontaneously, considers others' viewpoints, speaks audibly and within tolerable limits
Accomplishment	Unmotivated, aimless, nonproductive, easily discouraged, easily distracted, underachieving, lacks initiative, seldom completes endeavors, workaholic, slave to work	Ambitious, industrious, self-starting, independent, resourceful, persevering, successful in endeavors, seeks to advance or improve situations
Affectionate/sexual	Unaffectionate, reserved, distant, sexually inhibited, promiscuous, lacking sexual desire, engages in deviant sexual behavior	Warm, loving, affectionate, demonstrative, sexually responsive (appropriately)

© Cengage Learning 2013

In addition to identifying dysfunctional behavioral patterns, it is important to be aware of those behaviors that are effective and represent strengths. To assist you in assessment, Table 9-3 lists patterns of individual behavior that most frequently create interpersonal difficulties as well as those that risk being unrecognized as strengths.

EP 2.1.7b

As you review Table 9-3, you may question our categorization of some as functional or dysfunctional. This determination, of course, depends on the situational context within which the behavior occurs. Aggressive behavior may serve a self-protective function in a hostile environment but may be dysfunctional in family relationships or in the workplace. Your evaluation, then, must take context into account and consider the effect of the behavior on the client's environment and success in functioning.

Note that Table 9-3 includes many adjectives and verbs that are very general and are subject to different interpretations. In assessing behavior, it is vital to specify actual problem behaviors. For example, rather than assess a person's behavior as "abrasive," a social worker might describe the behaviors leading to that conclusion—"the client constantly interrupts his fellow workers, insults them by telling them they are misinformed, and boasts about his own knowledge and achievements." It will be easier for you and the client to focus your change efforts when detrimental behavior is specified and operationalized.

An adequate assessment of behavior, of course, goes beyond merely identifying functional and dysfunctional behaviors. You must also determine the antecedents of behaviors, when, where, and how frequently they occur, and identify the consequences of the behaviors. Further, you should explore thoughts that precede, accompany, and follow the behavior, as well as the nature of and intensity of emotions associated with the behavior.

Risk of Aggression

EP 2.1.7a

A particular behavioral concern is the risk of aggression. Aggression can take many forms, from bullying and menacing to assaults and gun violence. It may be directed at the social worker or at others in the person's environment, such as siblings, classmates, dates, parents, bosses, and others. A wide variety of tools has been developed in an attempt to assess and predict the potential for violent behavior (Shepard & Campbell, 1992; Boer, Hart, Kropp, & Webster, 1997; Webster, Douglas, Eaves, & Hart, 1997; Borum, Bartel, & Forth, 2003; Quinsey, Harris, Rice, & Cormier, 2006).[4] While there is significant variability in the definition and measurement of risk factors among these tools, Andrade (2009), in his summary of current research, highlights several that have been consistently related to violent behavior. The most consistently predictive of these factors is past violent behavior or criminal behavior. Additional risk factors include: early age of first criminal offense, substance abuse, gender (violence by men generally exceeds that by women), and psychopathy. Andrade (2009) also mentions research into several dynamic risk factors such as impulsiveness, anger, psychosis, interpersonal problems, and antisocial attitudes, but notes that no predictive conclusions can yet be drawn. For youth violence, Borum & Verhaagen (2006) list a variety of risk factors which include: prior history of violence, early initiation of violence, school achievement problems, abuse, maltreatment and neglect, substance use problems, impulsivity, negative peer relationships, and community crime and violence. Social workers concerned about the risk of aggression should assess for the following:

- **Personal History:** Child abuse or neglect; early exposure to violence in the family; problems at school, including threats, fights, or assaults on teachers; antisocial behavior; learning disabilities, ADHD, low IQ, head injury, or other physical problems;
- **Interpersonal Relationships and Social Supports:** Client's attitude toward people in general; how client interacts with practitioner; if client has close friendships; how client relates to members of opposite sex; recent changes in relationships; difficulty in social interaction;
- **Psychological Factors:** Active substance abuse; manic phase of bipolar disorder; acute psychosis in paranoid schizophrenia; antisocial, borderline or paranoid personality disorder; low empathy, impulsivity, and inability to delay gratification;
- **Physical Conditions:** Intermittent explosive disorder; intoxication; temporal lobe epilepsy; dementia, delirium; history of head trauma;
- **History of Violence:** How long has the client been getting into fights? How often? How badly has the client ever hurt someone? Does client have a criminal record? Past hospitalization because of violent behavior?
- **Current Threats and Plans of Violence:** Is the client currently angry at anyone? Is there anyone the client would like to hurt or kill? Where is this person now? Does client have access to a weapon? How would client carry out the threat? Where?
- **Current Crisis and Situation:** Current mood and behavior of client; memory difficulty; poor concentration; poor coordination; exaggerated preoccupation with sexual thoughts and fantasies; nonadherence to medication; recent release from incarceration (Adapted from Houston-Vega, Nuehring, & Daguio, 1997, pp. 97–101)

Assessing Motivation

As introduced in Chapter 8, evaluating and enhancing client motivation are integral parts of the assessment process. When working with family members or groups, social workers are likely to encounter a range of motivation levels within a single client system. Clients who do not believe that they can influence their environments may demonstrate a kind of *learned helplessness*, a passive resignation that their lives are out of their hands. Others may be at different phases in their readiness to change. Prochaska and DiClemente (1986) suggest a five-stage model for change: *precontemplation*,

contemplation, determination, action, and *maintenance.* The initial stage is characterized by a lack of awareness of the need for change. In the contemplation stage, the client recognizes his or her problem and the consequences that result. In the determination phase, the client is committed to action and works with the clinician to develop a plan for change. Action and maintenance implement the changes identified and take steps to avoid problem recurrence.

EP 2.1.10a

To assess motivation, the social worker needs to understand the person, his or her perception of the environment, and the process by which he or she has decided to seek help. Motivation, of course, is a dynamic force that is strongly influenced by ongoing interaction with the environment, including interaction with the social worker. *Motivational interviewing* is a specialized, person-centered method for addressing ambivalence and enhancing motivation (Moyers & Rollnick, 2002). In this framework, client-worker interactions are dominated by *OARS*, an acronym for <u>o</u>pen-ended questions, <u>a</u>ffirmations, <u>r</u>eflective listening, and <u>s</u>ummarizing. Motivational interviewing also employs specific attitudes and techniques to reduce and defuse resistance. Motivation is enhanced by developing and highlighting discrepancies, for example, within a client's statements or between the client's current situation and the one he or she aspires to (Wagner & Conners, 2008).

Assessing Environmental Systems

EP 2.1.10d & 2.1.7b

After evaluating the history and pattern of the presenting problem and various facets of individual functioning, the social worker must assess the client in the context of his or her environment (Figure 9.3). In this, the assessment focuses on the *transactions* between the two or the *goodness of fit* between the person and his or her environment. Problem-solving efforts may be directed toward assisting people to adapt to their environments (e.g., training them in interpersonal skills), altering environments to more adequately meet the needs of clients (e.g., enhancing both the attractiveness of a nursing home and the quality of its activities), or a combination of the two (e.g., enhancing the

---

Environmental Systems
   Physical environment
      Adequacy
      Health
      Safety
   Social support systems
      Missing
      Affirming
      Harmful
   Spirituality and affiliation with a faith community
      Spirituality
      Religion
      Cognitive, affective, and behavioral dimensions of faith

FIG-9-3 Areas for Attention in Assessing Person-in-Environment Fit

---

interpersonal skills of a withdrawn, chronically ill person and moving that person to a more stimulating environment). This part of assessment, then, goes beyond the evaluation of resources described in Chapter 8 to take a holistic view of the client's environment and examines the adequacy of various aspects of the environment to meet the client's needs. The concepts of affordability, availability, and accessibility (introduced earlier in this chapter in regard to health care) provide a useful framework for examining transactions with other facets of the environment and targeting the nature of strengths and barriers in those transactions.

In assessing environments, you should give the highest priority to those aspects that are most salient to the client's individual situation. The adequacy of the environment depends on the client's life stage, physical and mental health, interests, aspirations, and other resources. For example, a family may not be concerned about living in a highly polluted area unless one of the children suffers from asthma that is exacerbated by the physical environment. Another family may not worry about the availability of day treatment programs for an adult child with developmental disabilities until a crisis (e.g., death of a parent or need to return to work) forces them to look outside the family for accessible, affordable services.

You should tailor your assessments of clients' environments to their varied life situations, weighing the individual's unique needs against the availability of essential resources and opportunities within their environments. In addition to noting the limitations or problems posed by inadequate physical or social environments, acknowledge the strengths at play in the person's life—the importance of a stable, accessible, affordable residence or the value of a support system that mobilizes in times of trouble.

EP 2.1.7b

The following list describes basic environmental needs; you can employ this list in evaluating the adequacy of your client's environments:

1. A physical environment that is adequate, is stable, and fosters health and safety (this includes housing as well as surroundings that are free of toxins and other health risks)
2. Adequate social support systems (e.g., family, relatives, friends, neighbors, organized groups)
3. Affiliation with a meaningful and responsive faith community
4. Access to timely, appropriate, affordable health care (including vaccinations, physicians, dentists, medications, and nursing homes)
5. Access to safe, reliable, affordable child and elder care services
6. Access to recreational facilities
7. Transportation—to work, socialize, utilize resources, and exercise rights as a citizen
8. Adequate housing that provides ample space, sanitation, privacy, and safety from hazards and pollution (both air and noise)
9. Responsive police and fire protection and a reasonable degree of security
10. Safe and healthful work conditions
11. Sufficient financial resources to purchase essential resources
12. Adequate nutritional intake
13. Predictable living arrangements with caring others (especially for children)
14. Opportunities for education and self-fulfillment
15. Access to legal assistance
16. Employment opportunities

We will address the first three areas—physical environment, social support systems, and faith community—in depth, in light of their particular importance for client functioning. This discussion may also help you to generalize some of the complexities of environmental assessment to the other 13 areas.

EP 2.1.7b

Physical Environment

Physical environment refers to the stability and adequacy of one's physical surroundings and whether the environment fosters or jeopardizes the client's health and safety. A safe environment is free of threats such as personal or property crimes. Assessing health and safety factors includes considering sanitation, space, and heat. Extended families may be crammed into small homes or apartments without adequate beds and bedding, homes may not be designed for running water or indoor toilets, or access to water may be broken or shut off. Inadequate heat or air conditioning can exacerbate existing health conditions and lead to danger during periods of bad weather. Further, families may take steps to heat their residences in ways that can create further health dangers (such as with ovens or makeshift fires). Sanitation may be compromised by insect or rodent infestations or by owner or landlord negligence in conforming to building standards and maintaining plumbing. The home may be located in areas with exposure to toxic materials or poor air quality.

For an elderly client, an assessment of the physical environment should also consider whether the person's living situation meets the client's health and safety needs (Gallo et al., 2005; Rauch, 1993). If an elderly person lives alone, does the home have adequate resources for the individual to meet his or her functional needs? Can the client use bathroom and kitchen appliances to conduct his or her daily activities? Does clutter contribute to the client's confusion or risk (e.g., not being able to find bills or stumbling over stacked newspapers)? Is the home a safe environment, or do some aspects of the building (e.g., stairs or loose carpeting) pose a danger to less mobile clients? If the client resides in an institution, are there mementos of home and personal items that bring comfort to the individual? Tools such as the Instrumental Activities of Daily Living Screen (Gallo, 2005) and Direct Assessment of Functioning Scale (DAFS) (Lowenstein et al., 1989) can assess functional ability, screen for and address risk factors, and evaluate changes in functioning.

When the environment poses dangers to clients or exacerbates other problems, steps must be taken to improve living conditions. Because of geographic ties and the scarcity of adequate low-cost housing, moving to a better neighborhood or a safer home may not be feasible. Some groups, such as the elderly, may qualify for subsidized housing facilities, which provide both adequate housing and social opportunities. You may also help clients to access home improvement, heating assistance, and other programs to enhance their living conditions. When other parties are responsible for detrimental environmental conditions, social workers should assist clients in undertaking advocacy actions to address these problems or in organizing with other neighbors to lobby for change and develop "block watch" or other mutual aid services.

Social Support Systems

EP 2.1.7b

Social systems constitute the second item on the list of needed resources. Social support systems (SSSs) fill a variety of needs to improve the client's quality of life. To assist you in identifying pertinent social systems, Figure 9-4 depicts interrelationships between individuals and families and other systems (Hartman, 1994). Systems that are central in a person's life appear in the center of the diagram. These systems typically play key roles as both sources of difficulties and resources that may be tapped or modified in problem solving. Moving from the center to the periphery in the areas encompassed by the concentric circles are systems that are progressively farther removed from individuals and their families. There are exceptions, of course, such as when an individual feels closer to an intimate friend or a pastor than to family members. Moreover, if clients' situations require frequent contacts with institutions or organizations (e.g., child protective services, income maintenance programs, and judicial systems), those institutions will no longer occupy a peripheral position because of how dramatically they affect individuals and families at such times. The intensity

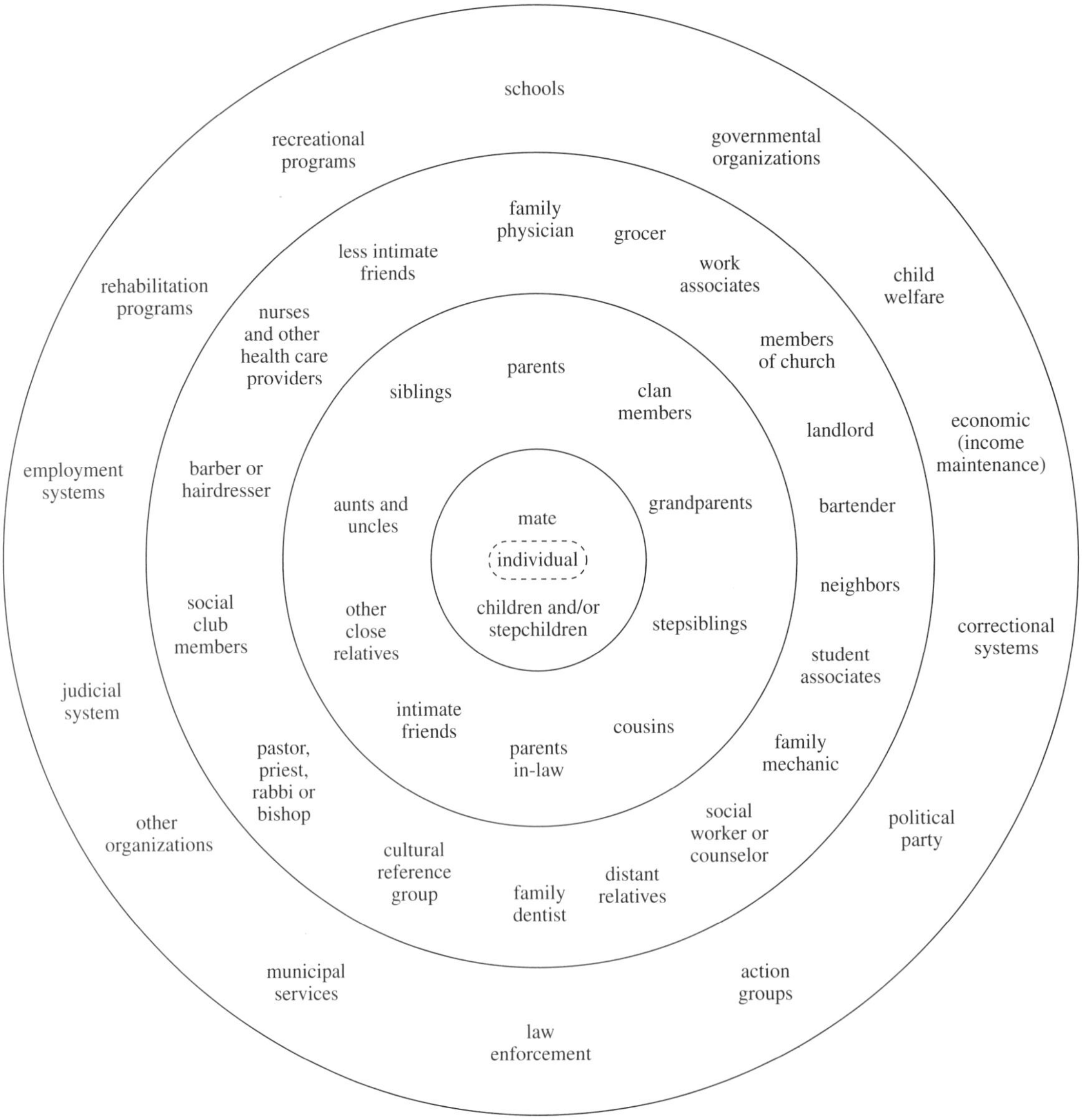

FIG-9-4 Diagram of Ecological Social Systems

of affiliation with extended family or kinship networks may vary by cultural group and reflect the effects of migration and cultural dislocation (Jilek, 1982; Kumabe et al., 1985; Mwanza, 1990; Ponce, 1980; Sotomayor, 1991; Sue, 1981). Reciprocal interactions thus change across time, and diagrams depicting these interactions should be viewed as snapshots that remain accurate only within limited time frames.

EP 2.1.10d

The challenge in diagramming clients' social networks is to include the salient boundaries of the clients' situation and to specify how the systems interact, fail to interact, or are needed to interact in response to clients' needs. One useful tool is the *ecomap*, introduced in Chapter 1. Ecomaps identify and organize relevant environmental factors outside of the individual or family context. These tools are useful in clarifying the supports and stresses in the client's environment, revealing patterns such as social isolation, conflicts, or unresponsive social systems. They also show the direction in which resources flow (for example, if the client gives but does not receive support).

The ecomap can be completed by the worker following discussion with the client or in tandem with the client (Strom-Gottfried, 1999b). In it, the client systems (individual, couple, or family) are in the middle circle and the systems relevant to their lives appear in the surrounding circles. The nature of positive interactions, negative interactions, or needed resources can be depicted by using colored lines to connect the individual or other family members to pertinent systems, where different colors represent positive, negative, or needed connections and interactions with those systems. If colored lines do not appeal to you, then you can use different types of lines—single, double, broken, wavy, dotted, or cross-hatched—to characterize the relationships and the flow of resources among the systems.

Social support systems (SSSs) are increasingly recognized as playing a crucial role in determining the level of social functioning. Theorists have long recognized the critical importance of a nurturing environment to healthy development of infants and children, but it is now clear that adults also have vital needs that can be met only through affiliation with supportive systems. Consequently, the lack of adequate SSSs is considered an area of vulnerability and may represent a source of distress, whereas adequate SSSs reduce the effects of stressful situations and facilitate successful adaptation. Knowing what the SSSs are and what roles they play with clients is essential for assessment and may even be the focus of interventions that tap into the potential of dormant SSSs or mobilize new ones. What benefits accrue from involvement with SSSs?

1. Attachment, provided by close relationships that give a sense of security and sense of belonging
2. Social integration, provided by memberships in a network of people who share interests and values
3. The opportunity to nurture others, which provides incentive to endure in the face of adversity
4. Physical care when persons are unable to care for themselves due to illness, incapacity, or severe disability
5. Validation of personal worth (which promotes self-esteem), provided by family and colleagues
6. A sense of reliable alliance, provided primarily by kin
7. Guidance, child care, financial aid, and other assistance in coping with difficulties as well as crises

EP 2.1.4c

Members of certain groups may have particular need for enhanced SSSs, or may be especially vulnerable due to limited or blocked SSSs:

- *Older adults (Berkman et al. 1999)*
- *Abused or neglected children (Brissette-Chapman, 1997)*
- *Teenage parents (Barth & Schinke, 1984; Brindis, Barth, & Loomis, 1987; De Anda & Becerra, 1984)*
- *Persons with AIDS (Indyk, Belville, Lachapelle, Gordon, & Dewart, 1993)*
- *Widows and widowers (Lieberman & Videka-Sherman, 1986)*
- *Persons with severe mental illness, and their families (Zipple & Spaniol, 1987; Rapp, 1998)*
- *The terminally ill (Arnowitz, Brunswick, & Kaplan, 1983)*
- *Persons with disabilities (Hill, Rotegard, & Bruininks, 1984; Mackelprang & Hepworth, 1987)*
- *Persons who experience geographical and/or cultural dislocation as refugees and immigrants (Hulewat, 1996)*

The reasons for diminished social supports may vary by group and each presents challenging opportunities to social workers when collaborating to develop natural support networks and to plan service delivery systems that respond to the individual's unique needs. In some vulnerable groups, you may find that other, more experienced and sophisticated members of the group are willing to assist "newcomers" to find their way through the maze of bureaucratic structures. Indigenous nonprofessionals have also been employed as staff members to serve as client advocates, provide direct outreach, organize disenfranchised people for social action, and assume the role of advocate or interpreter (in both language and policy).

Within some cultures and geographic regions, the extended family may provide an extensive network of support and assistance in crisis situations. There may also be cultural variations in the person to whom one turns for assistance with life problems. In many Native American tribal groups, for example, members actively seek counsel from elders (Hull, 1982) while Southeast Asian immigrants may seek assistance from clan leaders, shamans, or herbalists, depending on the nature of the difficulty. Similar examples of specialized supports abound in other cultures and communities.

To this point, we have highlighted the positive aspects of SSSs. It is also important to note that some SSSs may foster and sustain problems in functioning. For example, overprotective parents may stunt the development of competence, autonomy, and personal responsibility in their children. Street gangs and other antisocial peer groups may foster violence and criminality, even as they provide a sense of belonging and affiliation. Friends may ridicule or sabotage a person's aspirations, thereby undermining that individual's confidence and capacity for success. Family members may rally to support a person during joyous events (graduation, childbirth) but they are not available in times of need or sadness.

You should be aware of the various social networks at play in a client's life and assess the roles that those SSSs play in the person's difficulties or in his or her ability to overcome such problems. Sometimes, a negative support system can be counteracted by the development of pro-social or positive networks. At other times, the system itself may be the focus of intervention, as you strive to make the members aware of their roles in the client's problems and progress.

Spirituality and Affiliation with a Faith Community

EP 2.1.10e

The issue of one's spirituality and its expression actually transcends the categories of individual functioning and environmental systems. Spirituality can shape beliefs and provide strength during times of adversity, and the link to a faith community can be a tangible source of assistance and social support. While we have placed our discussion of this issue within the context of assessing environmental systems, we will address assessment of faith more broadly.

Canda (1997) differentiates between spirituality and religion, suggesting that *spirituality* is the totality of the human experience that cannot be broken into individual components, whereas *religion* is the socially sanctioned institution based on those spiritual practices and beliefs. Sherwood (1998) also distinguishes between spirituality and religion, wherein the former reflects the "human search for transcendence, meaning and connectedness beyond the self and "religion refers to a more formal embodiment of spirituality into relatively specific belief systems, organizations and structures" (p. 80). A "spiritual assessment," then, may help the worker to better understand the client's belief system and resources.

Questions such as "What are your sources of strength and hope?", "How do you express your spirituality?", "Do you identify with a particular religion or faith?", and "Is your religious faith helpful to you?" can begin to elicit information as the foundation to seeking further understanding about the client's beliefs. Authors such as Murray-Swank and Pargament (2011), Hodge (2005), Nelson-Becker, Nakashima, and Canda (2007) Sherwood (1998), Ortiz and Langer (2002), and Holloway and Moss (2010) offer a variety of guides for gathering information about both clients' spiritual beliefs and religious affiliations.

Why is it important to understand the role of religion and spirituality in the lives of your clients? As Ratliff (1996) notes in discussing health care settings,

> Religious beliefs may dictate food choices, clothing styles, customs of birthing and dying, etiquette in the sick room, use of modern conveniences, invasive procedures, organ donation, reception, use of blood products, certain diagnostic tests, gynecological procedures, spiritual influences on or control of sickness and healing, the wearing of protective devices or tattoos, and the need for prayers and rituals performed by various religious specialists. (p. 171)

At times, religious issues may be central to the presenting problems clients bring to service. For example, parents may disagree about the spiritual upbringing of their children; couples may be at odds over the proper roles of women and men; families may be in conflict about behaviors proscribed by certain religions, such as premarital sex, contraceptive use, alcohol use, divorce, or homosexuality (Meystedt, 1984).

As Thibault, Ellor, and Netting (1991), conceptualize it, spirituality involves three relevant areas: cognitive (the meaning given to past, current, and personal events), affective (one's inner life and sense of connectedness to a larger reality), and behavioral (the way in which beliefs are affirmed, such as through group worship or individual prayer). Thus, spiritual beliefs may affect the client's response to adversity, the coping methods employed, the sources of support available (e.g., the faith community may form a helpful social network), and the array of appropriate interventions available. Particularly when clients have experienced disaster or unimaginable traumas, the exploration of suffering, good and evil, shame and guilt, and forgiveness can be a central part of the change process. Social workers must be aware of their own spiritual journeys and understand the appropriate handling of spiritual content, depending on the setting, focus, and client population involved (Ellor et al., 1999). Social workers are also advised to involve clergy or leaders of other faiths to work jointly in addressing the personal and spiritual crises faced by clients (Grame et al., 1999).

Written Assessments

EP 2.1.3c

The assessment phase is a critical part of the helping process. It provides the foundation on which goals and interventions are based. It is also an ongoing part of the helping process, as appraisals are reconsidered and revised based on new information and understanding. As a written product, assessments may be done at intake, following a period of interviews and evaluations, and at the time of transfer or termination (a summary assessment). They may be brief and targeted (such as an assessment for referral), a social history, a detailed report for the court or another entity, or a comprehensive biopsychosocial assessment. Whichever form it takes, several standards must be followed to craft a sound document that clearly conveys accurate information and credible depictions of the client (Kagle & Kopels, 2008).

EP 2.1.10d

1. *Remember your purpose and audience.* These will help you decide what should be included and maintain that focus. Know the standards and expectations that apply in your work setting, and understand the needs of those who will review your document.

2. *Be precise, accurate, and legible.* It is important that any data you include be accurate. Erroneous information can take on a life of its own if what you write is taken as fact by others. If you are unclear on a point, or if you have gathered conflicting information, note that in your report.

Document your sources of information and specify the basis for any conclusions and the criteria on which a decision was based (for example, to refer the client to another agency, to recommend a custody placement, or to conclude that suicidal risk was slight).

Present essential information in a coherent manner. An assessment is intended to be a synthesis of information from a variety of sources, including observation, documents, collateral contacts, and client interviews. Organizing that material so that it paints a comprehensive picture of the client's situation, strengths, and challenges at that particular moment is not easy. Avoid going off on tangents or piling up excessive details that derail the clarity of your document. Keep details that illustrate your point, document your actions, or substantiate your conclusions.

3. *Avoid the use of labels, subjective terminology, and jargon.* In assessing the social functioning of individuals, social workers often make global judgments—for example, "Mr. A's job performance is marginal." Such a sweeping statement has limited usefulness, because it fails to specify how the client's functioning is inferior and it emphasizes deficits. Instead of using labels ("Alice is a kleptomaniac"), use the client's own reports or substantiate your conclusion ("Alice reports a 3-year history of shoplifting on a weekly basis" or "Alice has been arrested five times for theft and appears unable to resist the compulsion to steal small items on a regular basis"). You should be factual and descriptive, as opposed to relying on labels and subjective terms.

Take care to create a document that demonstrates respect for your client. Should he or she read it, would it be considered a fair characterization of the person's presentation of self, life circumstances, assets, and needs? For help in honing your skills and expanding your assessment vocabulary, consult resources such as Norris (1999), Kagle & Kopels (2008), Wiger (2009), and Zuckerman (2008). The following assessments demonstrate how the concepts described in Chapters 8 and 9 are incorporated into written products. They are based on clients introduced in videotaped interviews that accompany this text. Two other examples of written assessments are available in the *Practice Behaviors Workbook*.

IDEAS IN ACTION

EP 2.1.3c

Social History

Client's name: _____ Wu Yanping _____ Date: _____ 4/15/11 _____

1. **Presenting Problem**
   Client was self-referred. Presented to university counseling service for assistance with stress related to vocational decision making. She is in the final month of study in the United States from home campus in China and fears that desire to study U.S. history is at odds with her parents' wishes and values.

   Client is an only child and has no precedents among friends or family for defying parents wishes in this manner.

2. **Signs and Symptoms (*DSM-IV-TR* based) … Resulting in Impairment(s)**
   Experiencing mild changes in appetite, sleep, and concentration. More acute since phone discussion with her father 3 weeks ago, though not affecting performance at this time.

3. **History of Presenting Problem**
   Events, precipitating factors, or incidents leading to need for services:
   Client's anxiety and distress about her decision have become more acute as the date for returning to China approaches (approximately 4 weeks from now) and this has prompted her to seek treatment.

   Client discovered her interest in history in the last several months upon initiating study in the U.S. Her parents own a business and expect that she will major in business and take over their company. When client broached the topic of her preferences in a phone conversation 3 weeks ago, he was dismissive of her plans. She has not spoken with him since, though they typically have more frequent calls.

   Frequency/duration/severity/cycling of symptoms
   No specific data gathered in this area.

4. **Current Family and Significant Relationships**
   Family history: Little information was gathered in this area. Yanping is an only child. Her parents own a small business (type unknown) in Shanghai. She has extended family (cousins, aunts, uncles, grandparents) living in China. None of her significant others have traveled outside of China.

   Yanping has enjoyed a close and caring relationship with her parents. In recent weeks this has become strained due to a phone dispute with her father when Yanping broached the topic of her new interest in history. She has not spoken with them since, reportedly because of her discomfort and concern that the topic may again come up.

   Strengths/support:
   History of family support, connectedness, parental aspirations for the client.

   Stressors/problems:
   Dispute over major may violate family and cultural norms.

   Recent changes:
   Distancing from parents in light of father's derisiveness in phone call and mother's presumed alliance with father.

   Changes desired:
   Client wishes parents would endorse her choice of studies.

   Comment on family circumstances:
   This writer is concerned about a high risk of family's rejection and fracture if client pursues her interests despite parental opposition.

5. Childhood/Adolescent History
   Client reports that she has never before objected to or defied parents' wishes. Relationship prior to this conflict has been close and caring. No other developmental or historical information was explored.

6. Social Relationships
   Description
   Client has close relationship with roommate on campus and with classmates, friends, and relatives in China.
   Strengths/support:
   Client has the capacity to make and keep friends and to seek their counsel. She has been able to make friends as a visiting student in the United States though language and cultural difference may impede their ability to help her with certain issues. Yanping will soon return home and have greater access to her support system in China.
   Stressors/problems: *Client is distanced from many of her Chinese supports due to her geographic and cultural difference at this time. The issues with which she is struggling are common among her friends but there are no precedents for doing what she wants to do, so they can be of little help to her, other than saying, "You must do what your parents wish."*
   Recent changes: *None reported*
   Changes desired: *Yanping wishes to receive more guidance and support to deal with her current problem.*

7. Cultural/Ethnic
   Description:
   Client is from mainland China and speaks Mandarin, with English and other Chinese dialects as secondary languages. Features of Chinese culture such as parental investment and desire for successful offspring are significant in this case. The client is struggling with values of obedience and deference to her parents as well as derisive societal attitudes toward her possible educational/vocational interests in history and teaching.
   Strengths/support:
   Client understands cultural elements affecting her dilemma. While she wishes to reconcile her beliefs with those of her family and society, she appears firm in her desire to follow her own interests if compromise cannot be achieved.
   Stressors/problems: *The client's wishes are at odds with parental, cultural and societal values in her homeland.*
   Beliefs/practices to incorporate into treatment:
   Address possibility of parental rejection as a result of values and culture clash. Test client's awareness of risks and commitment to her educational plan.

8. Spiritual/Religious
   Description:
   Not addressed
   Strengths/support: *NA*
   Stressors/problems: *NA*
   Beliefs/practices to incorporate into therapy:
   NA at this time
   Recent changes: *NA*
   Changes desired: *NA*

9. Legal
   There are no known legal considerations in this case.
   Status/impact/stressors: *NA*

10. Education
    Description:
    Client is currently a student visiting the United States who will return to China in 4 weeks for the remaining year of her undergraduate education. She wishes to study U.S. history, with the possible objective of becoming a teacher. Her parents want her to major in business and pursue running the family company as her vocation. They dismiss history as "useless" and teaching as a "low status" position and will not support the client's wishes.
    Strengths:
    Client is a good student and reports that she has been able to maintain good grades this term despite language differences, dislocation from family and supports in China and, recently, stress over vocational aims.
    Weaknesses:
    Dispute over educational goals pits parents' interests against clients and has significant cultural, economic, and political implications.

11. Employment/Vocational
    Description: *See section above on education*
    Strengths/support: _____
    Stressors/problems: _____

12. Military *Not applicable*
    Current impact: *NA*

13. Leisure/Recreational
    Description: *Not explored*
    Strengths/support: *NA*
    Recent changes: *NA*
    Changes desired: *NA*

14. Physical Health
    Client appears to be in good health, though experiencing stress, anxiety and mild sleep, appetite, and concentration disturbance dating back 3 weeks and becoming more significant over time.

15. Chemical Use History
    Not explored

16. Current/Prior Treatment History
    Description:
    Client has not sought treatment for this issue. Other past and current services are unknown.
    Benefits of previous treatment: *NA*
    Setbacks of previous treatment: *NA*

Kim Strom-Gottfried, Ph.D., LISW   Clinician Signature
April 16, 2010   Date Completed

(This form was adapted and completed based on an example from Wiger, 2009)

IDEAS IN ACTION

EP 2.1.3c

Biopsychosocial Assessment
Date of Assessment: 11/15/08

Background
Josephine is a Caucasian female, estimated to be in her late 70s, who lost her husband to a heart attack six months ago. The attack was unexpected and hence his death was sudden. Josephine met with Kathy, a social worker from Family Services, on two occasions (9-2-08 and 9-9-08) to share background and assessment information and to formulate goals and objectives to direct her adjustment to living alone.

Mental Status Exam

On both occasions, the interview was held in Josephine's home. She was dressed in a housecoat for the first meeting, a blouse and slacks for the second. Her hair was styled and neat. She appeared her stated age, was alert and aware of her surroundings, yet acted somewhat disengaged and uninterested, particularly in the first interview. She was physically still for most of the time that the worker spent with her, looking down at the table the two were seated at. Occasionally Josephine moved her hand back and forth over the table, and also changed her position in her chair intermittently.

Josephine showed no deficit in memory or concentration. She was responsive to the questions asked, and demonstrated recollection of remote and recent events. Her self-report of memory functioning, offered during a depression screening administered by the worker, does not indicate deficits. Josephine showed evidence of sound judgment, agreeing that engaging in new activities and adopting healthy eating habits would improve her mood and health. Additionally, when asked what she would do in case of a fire in her kitchen, she responded, "Call 911." She was oriented to time, place, person, and situation and had no deficit in reality testing.

Josephine's speech was quiet and at times somber. She was brief and direct in her answers to the worker's questions. These speech characteristics match Josephine's mood and affect. She reported feeling depleted of energy, experiencing a lack of interest in activities, and having trouble sleeping. Her lack of energy has led to her neglecting her doctor's dietary recommendations. Josephine carried a depressed affect that varied appropriately to the conversation and, at times, brightened. She scored in the high range on a depression inventory.

Josephine followed the worker's questions. Her thoughts focused on improving her mood and diet and arranging for services to allow her to remain in her home. Josephine appeared overwhelmed at times, though reported understanding what the worker was saying.

Josephine showed no evidence of cognitive distortions or hallucinations. She was cooperative in the interviews and showed flexibility of thought by agreeing to consider the suggested interventions. Josephine reported feeling that there was hope in her future, that in the past she had found redemptive aspects of persevering through challenging times, and that her children represent her purpose in life.

Biophysical Considerations

Health

Josephine was diagnosed with high blood pressure and was prescribed two medications for this condition. She is also prescribed a third medicine to help lower her cholesterol. Her doctor told her "a couple of years ago" that she "is borderline diabetic." She acknowledged that she could do more to care for this condition by preparing healthier meals. Josephine reported that she no longer drives, making her dependent on her daughter to go to the grocery store. Additionally, she stated, "I don't feel like cooking. I just grab what there is." She has lost 10 pounds in the past six months.

Josephine is also dependent on others for transportation to her doctor, whom she has seen for 20 years, for her monthly visits. Josephine reported some hearing loss. She is able to read and reports that she does quite a bit, with the use of glasses.

Josephine reported trouble getting to sleep at night, but she has been sleeping a few hours each afternoon. She does not have a prescription to help her sleep, though sometimes she takes an over-the-counter sleep aid.

Josephine mentioned that she used to walk regularly for exercise, but has not been doing any exercise lately as she lacks the motivation, stating, "I don't have any energy." She reported no recent falls or accidents.

Josephine does not report using alcohol. She stopped smoking cigarettes five years ago.

She rates her overall health as "fair," which is poorer than her self-assessment of a year ago, which was "good."

Social Factors

Josephine is the lone survivor in her family of origin. Her two brothers passed away soon after World War II and her sister died a few years ago. She mentioned that this fact, compounded with the death of her husband, amplifies her sense of isolation, stating "I'm the only one left."

Josephine was married to her husband for several decades; they met on a blind date after World War II. She has three adult children, a daughter who lives close by and another daughter and son who live out of state. She is now dependent on her daughter for transportation, because her husband did the driving when he was alive. This is an uncomfortable situation, as Josephine reports feeling like she imposes on her daughter yet does not have an alternative to get to appointments and shop for groceries.

Josephine and her husband both retired after age 65. Josephine worked in retail, her husband in insurance. Since retirement, the couple traveled and visited with their grandchildren. As of her husband's death, Josephine reported she has not been involved in normal social activities due to her lack of energy and motivation. Her neighbor has visited once and offered to drive her to church, which Josephine declined but will reassess in the future.

Legal/Financial

Josephine reported that she owns her house and paid for her husband's funeral. She receives Social Security, though she will receive less than she used to as a result of recalculations after her husband's death. She characterized her income as just "adequate."

Josephine is unable to care for the house by herself. Her husband was responsible for the yard work, and she states she is not strong enough to complete it alone. She reported lacking the energy to do laundry and housework and is considering the possibility of receiving assistance with household chores.

Josephine reported that she would like to remain at home until she can no longer live alone. She is open to the idea of moving in the future.

Mood

Josephine repeatedly referred to her lack of interest, motivation, and energy caused by her grieving for her husband. She noted that her past coping methods involved connecting with people close to her. With the loss of her husband, she has lost her confidant. Josephine has not received counseling or therapy in the past.

Josephine correlated her mood to her lack of activities, reporting that she does not go out often, attends to her appearance less than she used to, and does not complete household chores.

Josephine scored high on a depression inventory. The worker recommended passing on these results to her physician and speaking to him about antidepressant medication.

Josephine does not report loss of hope or purpose. She stated, "I do think there is hope," and "My life has a purpose ... I have wonderful children." She did not relate any suicidal ideation or thoughts of hurting herself. In her second interview, Josephine was asked to respond to a battery of questions designed to assess spirituality. Her answers were genuinely positive and life-affirming. Notably, she indicated that the most important thing in her life at present is "to feel better."

Conclusion

The sudden and recent death of Josephine's husband has resulted in financial changes, increased role demands, social withdrawal, and changes in nutrition, sleep patterns, and emotional functioning. Symptoms of grief and depression both contribute to these problems and affect Josephine's ability to reach out for assistance or participate in church and other previously valued activities. She has a clean, safe, and stable home environment and numerous relationships of a long duration with family, friends, and her physician. She is interested in better understanding her situation, consulting her physician, and receiving services to assist with transportation, grief, home care, meals, and other issues.

Case Notes

EP 2.1.3c

In addition to more comprehensive assessments, direct practitioners record information in client charts based on each meeting or contact with the client, and after other significant contacts about the case, such as the receipt of test results or information from a collateral contact. Record-keeping policies are often specific to the setting. For example, in schools, social work notes would be kept separate from the child's educational record; in some settings notes are dictated, and in others handwritten. Well-crafted case notes "provide accountability, corroborate the delivery of appropriate services and support clinical decisions" (Cameron & Turtle-Song, 2002, p. 1). Although there are many different practices in record keeping, one commonly used practice is worthy of attention. SOAP notes refer to <u>s</u>ubjective observations, <u>o</u>bjective data, <u>a</u>ssessments, and <u>p</u>lans (Kettenbach, 2003). A variation on this, DAP, combines subjective and objective information under one heading, data. These *progress notes* refer back to the most recent assessment, problem list, and treatment plan. The "subjective" section includes information shared by the client or significant others, such as recent events, emotions, changes in health or well-being, changes in attitude, functioning, or mental status. Information in this section is typically paraphrased and presented as, for example, "The client reports …", "The patient's mother states …", "She indicates …", or "Patient's husband complains of.…" Direct client quotes should be kept to a minimum (Cameron & Turtle-Song, 2002).

The "objective" section in SOAP notes should be factual, precise, and descriptive, based on your observations or written material, and presented in quantifiable terms—factors that "can be seen, heard, smelled, counted or measured" (Cameron & Turtle-Song, 2002, p. 2). In progress notes, the advice for writing proper assessments applies: avoid conclusions, judgments, and jargon and substitute descriptions that would lead to such conclusions with more objective commentary. Rather than saying, "The client was resistant," an objective statement might read, "The client arrived 20 minutes late, sat with her coat on and her arms folded, and did not make eye contact with this writer."

The "assessment" portion of SOAP notes is the place to include diagnoses, judgments, and clinical impressions, based on both the subjective and objective data that precede the assessment. "Carol is struggling to maintain her sobriety in light of pressure from her friends and stress at school." The last section, "plan," addresses following appointments, next steps, referrals planned, and actions expected of both the client and the worker. "Carol will attend at least one AA meeting per day, review her relapse triggers and self-care plan. Each SOAP entry should begin with the date and end with the worker's name, credentials title, and signature. Entries should be completed as soon as possible after the actual contact to ensure they are accurate and up-to-date.

Summary

This chapter discussed assessment of physical, cognitive/perceptual, emotional, and behavioral functioning, as well as motivation and cultural and environmental factors. Although each of these factors was presented as a discrete entity here, these factors are neither independent nor static. Rather, the various functions and factors interact dynamically over time and, from the initial contact, the practitioner is a part of that dynamic interaction. Each factor is therefore subject to change, and the social worker's task is not only to assess the dynamic interplay of these multiple factors but also to instigate changes that are feasible and consonant with clients' goals.

Assessment involves synthesizing relevant factors into a working hypothesis about the nature of problems and their contributory causes. You need not be concerned in every case with assessing all of the dimensions identified thus far. Indeed, an assessment should be a concise statement that embodies only the most pertinent factors.

This chapter's scope was limited to intrapersonal and environmental dimensions. It excluded conjoint, family, and group systems, not because they are unimportant components of people's social environments, but rather because they generally are the hub of people's social environments. To work effectively with interpersonal systems, however, requires an extensive body of knowledge about these systems. Therefore, we devote the next two chapters to assessing couple and family systems and therapeutic groups.

CourseMate

Access an integrated eBook and chapter-specific learning tools including glossary terms, chapter outlines, relevant web links, videos, and practice quizzes. Go to **www.cengagebrain.com**.

CHAPTER 10
Assessment: Family Functioning in Diverse Family and Cultural Contexts

CHAPTER OVERVIEW

Chapter 10 focuses on the dimensions used to assess families. Family is broadly defined in light of the various ways in which family membership is acquired. Practice with families as discussed in this chapter emphasizes both a cultural and family variant perspective, so that families are assessed within their own idiosyncratic context. Like other systems, the family is a dynamic and transactional system in which its constituent parts and subsystems interact with one another in a predictable and organized fashion that is governed by rules and relationships. Because families are a social system that interacts, influences, and is influenced by other systems in the social environment, these factors are discussed as well.

As a result of reading this chapter you will:

- Understand that assessments involve both gathering information and synthesizing it into a working hypothesis.
- Learn questions to bear in mind while conducting a family assessment
- Use assessment dimensions guidelines for assessing family interaction, relationships, and patterns of behaving.
- Understand the family as a social system that has organized in predictable roles and relationships.
- Recognize the diverse way in which the family is defined.
- Be aware of stressors that influence family functioning.
- Understand how to assess family strengths and resources.

EPAS COMPETENCIES IN THE 10TH CHAPTER

This chapter will give you the information needed to meet the following practice competencies:

2.1.1c Attend to professional boundaries

2.1.1f Use supervision and consultation

2.1.2a Recognize and manage personal values in a way that allows for professional values to guide practice

2.1.3a Distinguish, appraise, and integrate multiple sources of knowledge, including research-based knowledge and practice wisdom

2.1.4a Recognize the extent to which a culture's structures and values alienate, create, or enhance privilege and power

2.1.4b Gain sufficient self-awareness to eliminate the influence of personal biases and values in working with diverse groups

2.1.4c Recognize and communicate their understanding of the importance of difference in shaping life experiences

2.1.5a Understand forms and mechanism of oppression and discrimination

2.1.7a Utilize conceptual frameworks to guide the processes of assessment, intervention, and evaluation

2.1.7b Critique and apply knowledge to understand person and environment

2.1.10a Substantively and affectively prepare for action with individuals, families, groups, communities, and organizations

2.1.10d Collect, organize, and interpret client data

2.1.10e Assess client strengths and limitations

Social Work Practice with Families

From its historical beginning social work has been concerned with the family as a unit and as the focus of intervention. Nichols and Schwartz (2004) trace social work's contributions to families to the Charity Organization Societies (COS), led by Mary Richmond. Family caseworkers, known as friendly visitors met with families in their homes, and, in effect, their work marked the beginning of outreach and home-based family services. Richmond's conceptualization of the family as a social system is considered to have been the vanguard of "family's therapy's ecological approach, long before systems theory was introduced" (Nichols & Schwartz, 2004, p. 17). Her classic 1917 text, *Social Diagnosis*, introduced the family as a treatment unit and clarified the family as a social system.

While the focus on the family as a system remains intact, social work practice with families has continued to evolve, integrating post-modern family-centered methods, **such** as narrative, social constructionist, feminist, and solution-focused, each of which have made significant contributions to practice with families.

As a social system, the family interacts with and is influenced by other systems. Therefore, practice with families has also been influenced by perspectives and models that include attention to the situational, relational, or environmental stressors and the multiple systems in which families interact (Boyd-Franklin & Bry, 2000; Constable & Lee, 2004; Kilpatrick & Holland, 2006). In the social justice and relational justice framework, family systems' focus is on assessing families in the broader context and structures of society; in particular, the influence that economics, politics, inequality, oppression, and trauma have on family functioning (Boyd-Franklin & Bry, 2000; Constable & Lee, 2004; Dietz, 2000; Finn & Jacobson, 2003a; McGoldrick, 1998; Vera & Speight, 2003; Walsh, 1996).

Defining Family

EP 2.1.10a

During the last several decades, how families were defined emphasized legal, economic, religious, and political interests or some combination thereof. Nostalgic references to the 1950s-era image of the family form consisting of two heterosexual parents and their children are no longer practical in view of the diverse configurations of today's families (Fredriksen-Goldsen & Scharlach, 2001; Walsh, 1996). Recognizing and valuing all family forms, although often times controversial, does not intentionally distract from or devalue the traditional family. Actually, different family forms add to the rich opportunities in which individuals experience a sense of belonging, loyalty, reciprocal care, and interrelatedness. Moreover, our understanding of the ways in which people are nurtured emotionally and are socially connected ultimately facilitates our practice with families (McGoldrick, 1998).

In view of the diverse family forms that exist, how families themselves define their members is best articulated by the family. Following are some of the variability and choices of ways in which family membership are achieved.

- *Marriage, which may be an arranged marriage*
- *Remarriage; recoupling after a separation, or blended family*
- *Birth, adoption, foster care, or legal custody*
- *Commitment or created, the latter of which involves a relational network of supportive friends*
- *Informal relationship, biological and nonbiological kin, friends, social networks within communities and/or cultural groups*
- *Nannies or other surrogates in the family*

Variability in families and choices can mean that households consist of single or two parents of opposite or same sex, any of which may be multigenerational (Carter & McGoldrick, 2005; Crosson-Tower, 2004; Fredriksen-Goldsen & Scharlach, 2001; Okun, 1996; Sue, 2006; Weston, 1991). Multigenerational families can include parents and their children and grandparents or other kin. Also, there are generational families that consist of two generations, specifically grandparents and their grandchildren (American Association of Retired Person, 2007; Burnette, 1999; Gibson, 1999; Goyer, 2006; Jimenez, 2002). Clearly, family configurations can be as diverse as family membership. The more critical concern, and thus the focus of practice, is the extent to which the family has the capacity to perform the essential functions that contribute to the development and well-being of its members.

Family Functions

Irrespective of their form, families share both a history, memories, success and failure, aspirations and a future as they experience the lifecycle together (Carter & McGoldrick, 2005; McKenry & Price,

EP 2.1.10a

2000; Price, Price & McKenry, 2010). As characterized by Constable and Lee (2004) the family is "the basic informal welfare system in any society" (p. 9). In essence, the family performs certain functions and has responsibilities, such as attending to the social and educational needs, health and well-being, and mutual care for its members that is unlike any other social system (Hartman, 1981; Meyer, 1990; Okun, 1996; Sue, 2006). It is largely through the family that character is formed, attachments are developed, vital roles are learned, and members are socialized for participation in their culture or subculture and in the larger society. Because these functions are rarely replicated in other systems, the family is considered to be the preferred arrangement for minors. For instance, when it has been necessary to remove a child from his or her biological home, he or she whenever possible should be placed with kin or a foster family rather than an institution.

EP 2.1.4c

All families have distinct patterns of relating, decision making, rules, scripts, and a division of roles and labor. The manner in which family functions are implemented, and by whom, can be influenced by a family's social identity, cultural or racial preferences, socioeconomic status, and available resources or the lack thereof. Essentially, the make up of a family is less important than how the family functions, the relational patterns they exhibit, and their relationship with the social environment. With this in mind, it is important that you recognize that a variety of individuals can be involved in carrying out the different functions that nurture the well-being and development of family members. For instance, out of necessity, responsibilities related to maintaining the family system are likely to be more dispersed because of parental employment obligations. Older children, extended kin, or friends in the family's network, may perform important systems maintenance tasks. Cultural traditions also influence how family functions are implemented. For example, in traditional Hispanic or Latino families, an individual can hold a prominent *familismo* role of honor; that can be independent of legal or nonlegal familial status and can act as a parental substitute. Such individuals are integral to the family system in that they perform essential functions (Sue, 2006). Long standing traditions of a similar nature can be found in other cultural or racial groups as well.

As Meyer (1990), advocating for appreciation and celebration of diverse families, stated, it is a "phenomenon of our times that people have discovered so many ways" in which individuals make up a family system (p.16). Of course, the diversity in the social identities of families and their membership makes it more likely that you will have contact with variant family and cultural forms. Given the nature of modern families, and because of their varying needs and circumstances, how should you approach the daunting task of working with families? Appreciating diverse family forms, identity and memberships is critical. But you may well encounter families in which family dynamics have adverse consequences for individuals regardless of their membership and identity. Not all family environments are nurturing, and some members or the family unit as a whole may lack the skills, resources, or capacity to foster the development and well-being of all family members. Kilpatrick and Holland (2006), in describing Level 1 families, for instance, call attention to a multiplicity of debilitating factors, in which an assessment of their resource needs and psychological capacity and the negative environment in which the family lives compromises their functioning. You may, perhaps be challenged by a situation in which the family is coping with a member who is gravely ill, a member who has mental illness, or a substance addiction. You may encounter instances of child, partner, spousal, or elder abuse. In these and other situations, the essential family function of ensuring member well-being is undermined, resulting in physical and psychological distress (McKenry & Price, 2000). It is equally important that you recognize that not all environments in which the family interacts are *enabling*, in that there can be limited support for growth opportunities necessary for member development. There are also those environments in which external conditions are *entrapping*, and as such they adversely impact the family's ability to perform all or some of its functions (Kilpatrick & Holland, 2006; Saleebey, 1996, 2004).

You may experience a level of discomfort when you encounter a family that is vastly different from your own and whose values and norms are in contrast to your own and Western society's preferred way of behaving. In some

EP 2.1.4b

instances it can be challenging for you to reconcile our own family experience with others that are different, **despite expectations of acceptance in** codes of professional conduct. For example, during a home visit, **there may be** people in the home, referred to as a family member, however, such individuals are not named, nor is their presence explained. Weighed against your family experience you may well feel uncomfortable and suspicious. Consider, for instance, an unmarried teen parent couple, living in the father's parent's household. Based on your own background, your first thought might be that the couple is too young to have, care for, and support a baby. Alternatively, your bias may in fact favor the fact that they are keeping the child.

In your work with families you may tend to look for and assess them relative to familiar and acceptable interactions, customs, and expressions of intimacy. While you strive to be culturally competent and sensitive to different customs and family interactions, you may also feel a sense of inadequacy when you encounter culturally dependent expressions of emotional bonds such as intimacy and attachment. These qualities no doubt are present in diverse families yet their expression or behavioral indicators may not resemble the familiar Western perspective. For example, Okun, Fried, and Okun (1999) point to the fact that in cultures where marriages are arranged, attachment to and feelings about a mother-in-law may be considered unimportant. But in the bond that exists, it is expected and a nonnegotiable obligation that the daughter-in-law respects that the mother-in-law occupies a position of honor and that she behaves accordingly. There are also contrasting, culturally derived thoughts about the attachment of children. In Western society, the early mother–child bond is considered to be essential to the child's healthy development and well-being (Bowlby, 1988). Yet, attachment, while no less important is other societies, at an early age, it is understood, and indeed preferable, that child will interact with multiple individuals with whom they will develop a secure bond (Bronfenbrenner, 1989; Garcia Coll, Akerman, & Cicchetti, 2000; McHale, 2007; Mercer, 2006; Surbeck, 2003).

The examples provided are by no means intended to be exclusive or exhaustive. Nor are they indicated in each and every culturally or racially diverse family. Indeed, families in which all or some of their members were foreign born are diverse and represent many different countries. For example, persons referred to as Black Americans include people who were born in the United States, African or Caribbean countries; the same is true for Latino or Hispanic or Asian-Americans. Therefore caution is advised, less you generalize preferences, qualities, or characteristic based on broad racial or ethnic categories.

EP 2.1.2a

Feeling uncomfortable or challenged and having certain biases influenced by your worldview is to be expected. As a first step in bridging a potential divide, it is important that you are clear about your internal tensions based on your personal and professional biases. Engaging in a self-evaluative, reflective exercise might begin with a simple question, what are the family characteristics or the particulars of their situation that cause me to feel comfortable, uncomfortable, or even threatened. Regardless of the situation, self-reflection can clarify your instincts. Most importantly, your willingness to engage in this corrective process, even if you make mistakes, is critical to your learning. Furthermore, your insights from the process can ensure that you do not make the same or similar mistakes in the future. In general, your self-assessment provides you with essential information so that you can pinpoint whether your ways of knowing helps or inhibits your practice when you are faced with the unfamiliar.

EP 2.1.1f

Self-reflection is important even when you are working with a family with whom you share certain traits or attributes. Sameness is not an indication that a family will share your views or that they have had your experiences, and therefore you may make assumptions that prevent you from gathering or misinterpreting relevant information.

Each of the previous examples highlights the importance of self-reflection. Nonetheless, there may be instances in which you will want to talk about a situation with your supervisor or a key community consultant to gain a better understanding of a family. In essence, your seeking feedback is a type of check and balance that will further contribute to your growth as a professional.

EP 2.1.4c

At the same time, you should be aware of the fact that families who have a different social identity, culture, or race can equally feel a level of strangeness with you. Strangeness and discomfort can be based on their lack of familiarity with the helping process, prior experience with other helping professionals, or preconceived notions about whether you are able to understand them and their situation. In some instances differences between you and the family can be problematic. For some families, oppression and inequality is a fact of life, and as such they can be suspicious of your motives. Differences are best acknowledged and openly discussed so that related dynamics—real or imagined—do not become a barrier. To ease the discomfort that a diverse family can feel relative to your ability to understand them and their situation, you should be guided by their interpretation of their concerns. In this way, you avoid concluding that the unfamiliar is evidence of deviance (Hartman, 1981; Meyer, 1990; Walsh, 1996). In unfamiliar family territory, a central task is to assess the family through the lens of their particular level of functioning, needs, strengths, resilience, migratory status, and the lifecycle (Hernandez & McGoldrick, 1999; Kilpatrick & Holland, 2006; Silberberg, 2001). In doing so, you honor their narrative with respect to cultural and family variants, which is core to collaborative practice. Collaborative practice involves shared power between the practitioner and the family, in which the expertise of both are recognized. Hartman (1981), in explaining the essence of collaborative practice, asserts that social workers should determine the extent to which their practice is sensitive and responsive to families with whom they work.

To illustrate Hartman's point of view, the teenaged parents who are living in the home of the father's parents is revisited.

CASE EXAMPLE

A school social worker became involved with the families because the teen mother was a student at an alternative school for pregnant and parenting teens. At age 16 years, neither teen was of legal age to be married. Each set of parents were equally unhappy about the pregnancy and the initial parent–child and family–family interactions were marked by conflict. Both families, while low-income, were adamant about not wanting the young couple to rely on "public aid," even though the teen mother and the unborn child were potentially eligible. Despite their feelings, the parents of the teens wanted to ensure the well-being of their grandchild and also that both the youth completed high school. Honoring their preferred outcomes, specifically, that the teens completed high school and that the child was well cared for, the social worker supported their solution. In essence, the young couple would live in the paternal parent's home; however, both maternal and paternal parents would provide resources and support. This arrangement provided a stable living environment, child care, financial assistance, and parental role models. It also took into account the youth's developmental stage and the unexpected lifecycle event for both families, while supporting their dual role as developing individuals and parents.

An evaluative question posed by Hartman (1981) for all practitioners to consider and which was pertinent in this case: "*Does our practice involve families to the fullest extent possible in defining the problems and creating solutions, or does it replace a family function in a situation where with help, the family itself could meet the needs of its members?*" How was this perspective applied in this case? The social worker saw her role as engaging the families in developing solutions that addressed parental concerns for the youth and the unborn child. Similarly, Hartman encourages practitioners to assess the extent to which their practice with families is "*based on an understanding that people are part of current and intergenerational family system and that these human connections are powerful, persistent and essential to the welfare of the individual.*"

Both questions also emphasize that you respect a family's decision-making capacity and their strengths. Collaborative practice as a framework for working with families has broad implications for families in general. As a framework for assessing diverse families, the tenets of collaboration guides you to respect a family's preferences, indigenous patterns, identities and perceptions that influenced their help-seeking behavior (Constable & Lee, 2004; Green, 1999; Hartman, 1981; Hirayama, Hirayma & Cetingok, 1993; Laird, 1993; Poulin, 2000).[1]

Family Stressors

EP 2.1.10d

In a multidimensional assessment of families, it is useful to pay attention to the source **of family stressors and to determined** whether they pose a risk to the family's functioning. The source of stress within the family system can be for example, the result of family dynamics, roles and relationships, communication patterns, or life cycle transitions or separations. External stressors, which can have a bearing on family functioning, for example, may be the neighborhood in which the family lives, inequality, racial or economic discrimination, or public policy—any one of which can marginalize some families. It is quite possible that there are reciprocal pressures between internal and external stressors. For example, the source of stressful internal dynamics within a family system can be the result of economic pressures. How families cope with and adapt to stressors, whether internal or external may depend on their resources, strengths, or resilience, bolstered by family networks and social supports and spirituality and relational caregiving.

EP 2.1.3a

A stressor is described by **McKenry & Price** (2000, p. 6) as "anything that provokes change or some aspect of change, such as boundaries, structures, goals, roles or values," within the family system resulting in a state of family disequilibrium. Stressors have tended to be categorized as either *normative* (e.g., marriage)—specifically those events or situations occurring in the family life cycle, or *nonnormative* (e.g., an accident)—in particular a disruptive unexpected situation or event, however, it is unlikely to be repeated.

Normative stressors and transitions over the course of the family life cycle are a part of family life. For example, members marry or remarry, children are born and eventually leave home, although for a variety of reasons they may return, and members age. While changes in the family system are to be expected, the family system can experience anxiety or distress due to changes in boundaries, roles, and patterns of relating between parents, siblings, and grandparents. Differences in the family life cycle and a family's pattern of relating and adjusting to changes can also be influenced by cultural preferences, external forces such as oppressive forces, prejudices, sexism, homophobia, classism, ageism, and sexism (Carter & McGoldrick, 2005).

EP 2.1.4a

Normative life cycle stressors are also experienced by diverse families. Your assessment may also reveal that many of these families contend with unique stressors in their everyday lives that for them are normative. For example, by virtue of their differences, either because of race, culture or social or socioeconomic class, diverse families frequently experience stressors that would otherwise be characterized as nonnormative; however for these families such circumstances or events are routine. Should the frequency of these tension-producing stressors be present in the lives of the majority, they would be thought of as being intolerable and nonnormative. For example, gay and lesbian families face a legal labyrinth with respect to medical and child care, power of attorney, family benefits, and civil rights regarding relational commitment that other families do not have to contend with.

Public Policy

EP 2.1.4a

All families are subject to the influence of public policies; for example, requirements that minors attend school until they reach a certain age and minors are expected to be immunized against communicable diseases. But for poor and minority families public policy can be a source of stress, in particular the extent to which policies respond to the needs of, empower, support, or strengthen these families.

Personal responsibility and *family values* are examples of the powerful and enduring influences that have persuaded and in some instances restrained family-supportive social programs. In effect, they remain front and center in policy decisions about support for disadvantaged families. Perhaps the most pervasive sentiment behind the welfare reform and personal responsibility initiatives is the public perception of undeserving, chaotic, families who use welfare as a crutch and live off the state and "my hard work and earnings." The beneficiaries of government-sponsored family support programs are in fact far broader. Rank and Hirschl (2002) concluded that two-thirds of the American population between 20 and 65 years of age will at some point live in a family that receives benefits from a means-tested welfare program. Nevertheless, the pictures that the media and political messages paint of welfare recipients are that of large, multigenerational minorities, mostly chaotic, primarily drug-involved African Americans, who live off the state and lack personal responsibility. Although recipients of welfare may include such families, there are many more families who make use of the supports on a short-term basis. Findings by Segal (2007) further discredit these popular images, showing greater diversity in the population of families who receive welfare benefits.

Pervasive images and punitive policies intended to induce social and economic responsibility show a lack of *social empathy*. Social empathy requires a visualization of self in the position of others, a nonjudgmental attitude that seeks to understand the realities and circumstances of those who are different from oneself. It is an essential part of understanding the lives of others (Segal, 2007). In explaining this concept, Segal notes that a lack of social empathy exists because of the life-experience distance between welfare recipients and policy makers, as well as between that of low and high wage earners.

Poverty

Poverty in the United States and the global community is an enduring source of stress for a significant number of families. Debates about why people and families are poor range from assertions that the manner in which poverty is measured is deeply flawed ("the poverty lines are too high"), to the argument that there is a culture of poverty, (poverty is a matter of will), to an emphasis on the structural inequities of society (Greenberg, 2007; Miller & Øyen, 1996; Segal, 2007; Viggiani, 2007; Wilson, 1997).

EP 2.1.3a

In understanding the stress of poverty, it is useful to look at various ways in which families are and remain poor. The spectrum of poverty includes those who rely on Temporary Assistance to Needy Families (TANF) or disability benefits, the *"diligent" working poor*, and an often unnoticed group referred to as the *"missing class."* For those families, who receive Temporary Assistance to Needy Families (TANF), their level of benefit can vary by state. Because of this variability, the level of benefits in some states hardly sustains a minimum standard of living (Albert, 2000; Collins, Stevens & Lane, 2000; Withorn, 1998). There are those families who as described by Spriggs (2007, p. A6) are the *"diligent and still poor."* In these families, some members are well-educated; at least one family member is employed full time, but their earned income is insufficient to lift them above the poverty line (Reisch, 2002; Segal, 2007; Spriggs, 2007). The *missing class* is another family group that has been identified by Newman and Chen (2007). The earned income of these families is about $40,000, approximately 100% to 200% above federal poverty income guidelines for a family of four. In consequence, these families do not qualify for the Earned Income Tax Credit (ETC) or other government assistance benefits.

Confounding factors related to poverty cited by Sengupta (2001) include the hands-off posture of the government with respect to families and the tenacious manner in which politicians and the public hold on to the ideal of individuality and income redistribution. Nonetheless, we know that living in poverty can be a constant stressor that affects family **stability and** mobility. Being poor for instance, can determine where a family lives, the condition of the housing where they reside, their access to resources such as a full-service grocery store, the safety of their neighborhood, and the quality of education that their children receive. Furthermore, poverty is strongly associated with out-of-home care for children living in urban areas (Barth, Wildfire, & Green, 2006; Rodenburg, 2004: Roberts, 2002). Therefore, during the assessment process, the consequence of poverty as a stressor should be explored.

Extraordinary Life Transitions and Separations

EP 2.1.4c

The life cycle transitions that families experience can be exacerbated by disruptions that exceed the changes generally associated with the family life cycle. For example, traumatic weather or environmental events such as hurricanes, floods, and earthquakes devastated entire communities. Because of the magnitude of these extraordinary disruptions, family functions out of necessity must be assumed by private and public organizations, including those at the state and federal level.

Extraordinary family transitions or other intemperate transitions that have a profound effect on a family system, include, for example, military or legally induced family separations. Stressors faced by families when a member is deployed or redeployed for military service include the at-home spouse or partner having to adapt to a reallocation of roles and responsibilities, changes in income status, managing the day-to-day family tasks, while at the same time, coping with their concerns about a loved one's safety in a hostile environment (Black, 1993; Price, Price & McKenry, 2010; Williams, 2007). The majority of those serving on military duty are members of National Guard or Reserve Units whose families may live in different communities rather than housing on a military installation. For these families, their lack of geographical proximity to others in similar circumstances can be especially difficult as their access to the supportive network of other military families and military personnel can be limited. According to a study by the American Medical Association, the stress of deployment has, for example, resulted in an increase in child abuse and neglect reports in military families (Williams, 2007). It is also probable that the disconnect means that the children of military families may not know other children who have a parent on duty in the armed services. Children in these situations can experience uncertainty and anger, and they can be especially sensitive to the emotions and moods of the nonmilitary parent.

Modern technology has enabled families to stay in touch. Even so, the reintegration of a deployed family member back into the family system can create stressful dynamics as the individual attempts to regain his or her position in the family and the family attempts to accommodate this change.

In the post-September 11 era, the United States, in an effort to protect its borders, increased the enforcement of immigration laws and created family stressors that in some instances included the deportation of undocumented parents. National attention over the past several years on workplace raids showed actions taken with immigrants whose alien status meant that they had entered the

EP 2.1.4a

United States without legal documentation. Advocates decrying the level of trauma and anxiety experienced by families who were separated from their children have argued that national security efforts should focus on terrorists instead of foreign-born workers mainly from Mexico and other Latin countries (Tienda, 2007). Whatever we believe about undocumented families and immigration policies, because of social work's professional values and ethics, we cannot ignore the level of stress and its impact on families.

EP 2.1.7b

Multiple stressors are faced by immigrants, migrants and refugees; regardless of whether leaving their country of origin was for political or economic reasons. As you assess the context of families from various cultural groups, you must be aware of the extent to which a family may struggle with efforts to maintain the values and norms of its country of origin while adapting selectively to aspects of American society. When working with such families, it is advisable to obtain information about the family's migration history and look for continuing stresses placed on the family by its efforts to accommodate two (and sometimes more) cultures. Depending on their country of origin, some immigrants and refugees will be more educated and less poor. Nevertheless, all ethnic minority groups in the United States who have migrated or come as refugees face acculturation related stressors. As McGoldrick, Giordano, and Pearce (1996) observe, family values and identity may be retained for several generations after the migration experience and continue to influence the family's outlook, life cycle, and development. Indeed, this experience often preempts the completion of family developmental tasks, and it may require the reconstruction of social networks that have been diminished as a result of leaving the family's cultural reference group.

G. D. Rooney (1997) emphasized the dilemma that immigrant and refugee families face in a society that can be both welcoming and hostile. Employers, for example, see such individuals as a source of labor. Yet as the workforce has become more diverse, workplace policies have not kept pace with family concerns which can be especially difficult for the foreign-born employees in that their ability to fulfill traditional family role obligations may be constrained. The pressure to conform may distract or delay the new worker's ability to find a place in the employment organization's culture, resulting in stress in the family system. Language is yet another source of conflict, as reflected in U.S. society's indifference to bilingualism and antipluralistic public policy. For example, some states, continuing a trend that began in the late 1990s, have proposed or passed legislation that made English the official state language. In addition, it is expected that immigrants and refugees will act, speak, and dress like the majority population. Tensions exist in the interactions between native born citizens, including racial minorities and immigrants (Rooney, G. D., 1997). Most often, these racial tensions are related to jobs, access to resources, and language that are played out in schools and neighborhoods. Conflicts and tensions of this nature have occurred in other countries, and therefore are by no means exclusive to the United States.

Work and Family

Families in all socioeconomic strata experience work and family stressors. Findings from a national survey conducted by the Search Institute (2002) show a cross section of parents, at all socioeconomic levels, feel the need for community support and for work–family balance.
EP 2.1.4c

The average American spends more time engaged in work activities than in family or leisure activities when one factors, for example shift work, having multiple jobs, staying late at work or bringing work home. The world of work and the state of the economy continue to be significant stressors for families (Ostroff and Atwater, 2003; Ehrenreich, 2001). Barbara Ehrenreich's *Nickled and Dimed* (2001) called attention to the plight of low-wage earners, some of whom were homeless because their earnings were insufficient to afford housing. Changes in the state of the economy may affect some groups more than others. For example, unemployment tends to be highest in the Hispanic and African American communities, therefore these segments of the population are more vulnerable before and during tough economic periods. Even when the economy improves, gender remains a major determinant of earning power and even retirement (Ostroff and Atwater, 2003; Hawthorne, 2007).

Even though work-family responsibilities are stressful for all families, it can be more so for poor, single parent women in welfare-to-work programs who have entered or reentered the workplace. In addition to adjusting or readjusting to a work environment, these women are also faced with the same work and family demands as other employed women, including the availability of affordable and quality child care (DeBord, Canu, & Kerpelman, 2000; Collins, 2007).

The preceding discussion related to stressors for families illustrates Constable and Lee's (2004) assertion that families today may have less control over their functioning than did their ancestors, for whom family interventions occurred only when they "demonstrated gross inadequacies" (p. 58). Stressors for families, whether they are the results of family internal dynamics or external influences or a combination thereof, are capable of affecting family's functioning. In particular, stressors can influence the ability of the family to carry out roles and responsibilities that are critical to member's development and well-being.

Resilience in Families

EP 2.1.10e

Every family system, despite the stressors, strains or trauma it has faced, has strengths, displays an enormous amount of resilience, and has resources that can help its members to survive (McCubbin, 1988; McCubbin & McCubbin, 1988; Silberberg, 2001; Simon, Murphy & Smith, 2005; Walsh, 1996). The fact that families, in their various forms, have coped with, adapted to, and survived normative, nonnormative, and extraordinary stressors is a testimonial to their resilience. Indeed on a day-to-day basis, members perform various tasks to develop and nurture each other and maintain the family system. Of course, there are events, circumstances, or dynamics over the course of the life cycle that requires the family system to make adjustments. But the primacy of the family remains even in today's rapidly changing world.

EP 2.1.10d

As you gather information during the assessment process with respect to family functioning, context, strengths, life experiences, and stressors, including the particulars related to race and culture, and stressors you will have obtained a massive amount of information. Not all of the discussed factors will be pertinent to every family, but some may have greater relevance than others. But by paying attention to the multiple sources of information, you can develop an assessment summary that prepares you to begin collaborative work with a particular family based on its own variant.

A Systems Framework for Assessing Family Functioning

A primary characteristic of any system is that all of its parts are engaged in transactions with each other. There is interdependence between a system and its component parts. As a consequence, whatever affects the system, albeit internal or external, affects the whole to some extent. In general systems thinking, the system as a whole (i.e., the family) is greater than the sum of its component parts (i.e., subsystems). Systems constantly exchange information with other systems. Like other systems, the family system manages inputs from thorough boundary maintenance. When faced with inputs, a system seeks to maintain its stability or equilibrium. At other times, the intensity of an input can require the system to change or choose to remain in a steady state, and in some instances, become factionalized (Martin & O'Connor, 1989).

EP 2.1.7a

The systems framework is useful for assessing families in that the focus may be on the dynamics internal to the family system. For example, a source of stress can be the family's relational or communication patterns and may be a core concern. At the same time the systems framework allows for an assessment of the family's relationship with external systems as well as the influence that these systems may have on the family. For example, assessing family context can reveal stressors between a particular family form and the social environment. In this regard, a family assessment would gather information to determine the extent to which internal family dynamics are precipitated by or maintained by macro-level influences, such as socioeconomic status; institutionalized discrimination or bigotry; the experience of refugee, migrant, or immigrant status; and the state of the overall economy.

EP 2.1.10d

The family assessment can make use of qualitative or quantitative instruments or a combination of both. Combining assessment tools can provide you with a more complete picture of the family and their presenting problem. In general, an assessment begins with the identification of a concern or problem expressed by the family, or in the case of an involuntary family, the problem or concern as defined by a referral or legal mandate. A quantitative assessment documents, for example, the frequency, intensity and the extent of the problem. The qualitative assessment involves the family's narrative about their problem, its context as well as their feelings and the meaning associated with the problem. Both methods, either separately or combined, lend themselves to monitoring progress and outcome evaluation.

Tools for Understanding Families

In addition to the assessment dimensions discussed later in this chapter as well as those outlined in Chapters 8 and 9, the following instruments summarized in Table 10-1 may be used as sources for understanding the family situation.

- *The* Clinical Assessment Package for Assessing Risks and Strengths *(CASPARS) developed by Gilgun (1994, 2001), for families receiving mental health and child welfare services, responds to related concerns. Specifically, CASPARS measures both risks and protective factors related to family relationships, peer relationships, and sexuality.*
- *The* Culturalgram *(Congress, 1994) is a useful tool for assessing family dimensions in the context of culture, because "the systems view limits important cultural considerations" (Green, 1999, p. 8).*
- *The* Ecomap *enables you to focus on the social context of families and interactions between the family and the larger society (Hartman & Laird, 1983).*
- *The* Family Assessment Wheel *allows you to examine the sociopolitical and cultural context of the family experience (Mailick & Vigilante, 1997).*
- *The* Genogram *assesses internal family functioning, including mapping family structure, family history, and relationships (McGoldrick & Gerson, 1985).*
- *The* Model by Level of Need, *developed by Kilpatrick and Cleveland (1993), recognizes five levels of family need and functioning. The model is discussed and illustrated in Kilpatrick and Holland (2006). A Level 1 family's needs, for example, are related to basic survival, such as food, shelter, and medical care. Assessments of families at this level would therefore focus on their needs strengths and basic resources needed. In contrast, a Level 3 family has succeeded in satisfying its basic needs, so the assessment would focus on relationships, boundaries, alliances, and communication skills (Kilpatrick & Holland, 2006).*
- *The* Multisystems Approach *developed by Boyd-Franklin & Bry (2000) is derived from structural behavioral family therapy but is also applicable to social work practice with families. This approach recognizes that assessment and intervention goals involve families as well as the systems external to the family that affect and serve as resources to families.*
- *The* Social Support Network Map *examines the structure and quality of the family's interconnected relationships and social supports (Tracy & Whittaker, 1990).*

Hirayama, Hirayama, and Cetingok (1993) suggest both the Ecomap and the Genogram as useful tools in assisting refugees to understand patterns of social relationships and communication shifts associated with the tensions of immigrant and refugee relocation.

Strengths-Based and Risk Assessments

EP 2.1.10e

In addition to Gilgun's assessment package (1994; 2001) in which there is a focus on strengths, other strengths-based measures for families and children include the *Family Functioning Style Scale (FSSS)* and the *Family Resources Scale (FRS)*. Both allow you to include strengths in your assessment of families and to consider a range of family functioning (i.e., capabilities). ROPES, a similar instrument cited in Jordan and Franklin (2003), considers family resources, options, possibilities, exceptions, and solutions (hence the instrument's name).

Often practitioners are called upon to assess risks in families, for instance, in cases involving child neglect and abuse, probation, and family violence. *Risk assessments* are standardized structured actuarial tools that specify indicators in which a certain score predicts the probability of a behavior or condition. Risks can be either enduring or transient. Assessment tools, however, tend to emphasize enduring risks for which an intervention is warranted. Even in cases involving enduring risks, you should strive to conduct a balanced assessment, including micro, mezzo, and macro-level strengths, protective factors, and resilience. In this way, risks are not overly emphasized at the expense of strengths and contributing environmental factors are acknowledged. Because there can be difficulty in

TABLE-10-1 TOOLS FOR UNDERSTANDING FAMILIES

TOOLS	AUTHOR(S)
Clinical Assessment Package for Assessing Risks and Strengths (CASPARS)	Gilgun (1994, 2001)
Culturalgram	Congress (1994)
Ecomap	Hartman & Laird (1983)
Family Assessment Wheel	Mailick & Vigilante (1997)
Genogram	McGoldrick & Gerson (1985)
Integrative Model by Level of Need	Kilpatrick & Cleveland (1993)
Multisystems	Boyd-Franklin & Bry (2000)
Social Support Network Map	Tracy & Whittaker (1990)

finding the right tool for a family or its problem, multi-screening inventory tools may be more appropriate for assessing family strengths and stressors (Hudson & McMurtry, 1997).[2]

Systems Concepts

EP 2.1.7a

In the general systems framework, the family can be perceived as a dynamic system in which members form interdependent networks. The interrelationships of family members create the "whole." The whole, however, consists of subsystems such as parents, siblings, and can also include grandparents and extended biological and non-biological kin. The family system influences and is influenced by its members. The family system has unique properties that are governed by both implicit and explicit rules that specify roles, power structures, and communication styles. Within the family system there are preferred ways of problem solving, decision making, and negotiating. Roles, power structure, and communication patterns are the dynamic processes of the family system and its interrelated and interdependent constituent parts.[3]

EP 2.1.10d

In the interest of addressing the importance of family assessment in which formal family therapy is neither requested nor provided by the agency, we illustrate three family systems concepts in Table 10-2 and their application to the Diaz family and a couple, Mr. and Mrs. Barkley. The first takes place in a health care setting.[4]

TABLE-10-2 SYSTEMS CONCEPTS

Family Homeostasis
Family Rules
Content and Process Levels of Family Interactions

© Cengage Learning 2013

CASE EXAMPLE

Carlos Diaz, 66, lives with his 16-year-old son John in a subsidized apartment on the second floor of a three-story building. Mr. Diaz is diabetic, is visually impaired but not legally blind, and has a history of heavy alcohol use, though he has abstained from alcohol for the last 7 years. Mr. Diaz's companion of 18 years, Ann Mercy, recently died of a massive stroke. She had provided emotional support, given Mr. Diaz his insulin injections, and managed the household. Mr. Diaz has difficulty walking, has fallen several times in the past year, and is now hesitant to leave his apartment. In addition to John, Mr. Diaz has eight children from an earlier marriage who live in nearby suburbs, though only one, Maria, calls him regularly. Mr. Diaz's physician considers his current living arrangement to be dangerous because of the need for Mr. Diaz to climb stairs. The physician is also concerned about his capacity to administer his own insulin. A medical social worker convenes a family meeting with Mr. Diaz, John, his son John, daughter Maria, and stepdaughter Anita.

Application of Systems Concepts

EP 2.1.3a

Problems occur in a person or family and situational context. In this case example, the problems occurred in part because of Mr. Diaz's living situation, his access to alternative living environments, and the availability of a continuum of care that could include in-home supports. Mr. Diaz's income and health insurance coverage are external factors that can influence the alternative care arrangements that are available to the family. External factors should always be accorded prominence in the assessment to avoid assumptions that problems are caused solely by factors internal to the family system. In this case, both internal and external factors impinged upon and disrupted family functioning. When families experience a disruption, like those faced by the Diaz family, dynamics in the family tend to be directed toward maintaining homeostasis and restoring equilibrium.

Family Homeostasis

EP 2.1.7a

Homeostasis is a systems concept that describes the function of a system to maintain or preserve equilibrium or balance. When faced with a disruption, a system tends to try to regulate and maintain system cohesion. For example, it may try to maintain the status quo in response to family transitions in the life cycle or stressors associated with acculturation or environmental events. As systems, families develop mechanisms that serve to maintain balance (i.e., homeostasis) in their structure and operations. They may restrict the interactional repertoires of members to a limited range of familiar behaviors and develop mechanisms for restoring equilibrium whenever it is threatened (in much the same way that the thermostat of a heating system governs the temperature of a home).

The death of a family member (in this case, the wife and mother, Ann Mercy) changed the dynamics within the family system. In effect, previously established patterns and expectations, for example, Mr. Diaz's role as the head of the family and his ability to care for himself, his younger child John, is questioned by his adult children because of his physical condition. Aging and death are family transitions that can create anxiety as members attempt to define and realign roles and relationships.

Several additional factors that have threatened the family's ability to maintain or reinstate stability are played out in the Diaz case. For instance, Mr. Diaz rejects the physician's and his adult children's conclusions regarding his capacity to care for himself and John, the youngest child who lives with his father. Moreover, Mr. Diaz is distressed because he believes that a change would mean a loss of autonomy and diminish the power of his role as the head of the family. Atchey notes that "it is common for the elderly to feel a lower power as a result of social limitations imposed by others' perceptions of physical conditions as well as the limitations of the condition itself" (1991, p. 79). Intergenerational conflicts may also occur around issues of care taking, dependency, or a decline in health, and with the loss of a spouse. Mr. Diaz's behavior may be seen as an attempt to restore family equilibrium in the family system by asserting his independence and protecting his role. Minuchin (1974) speaks of the tendency of a member or a family's attempts to maintain their preferred patterns as long as possible and to offer resistance to change beyond a certain range of specific behaviors:

> Alternative patterns are available within the system. But any deviation that goes beyond the systems threshold of tolerance elicits mechanisms, which reestablish the accustomed range. When situations of system disequilibrium arise, it is common for family members to feel that other members are not fulfilling their obligations. Calls for family loyalty and guilt producing maneuvers then appear. (p. 52)

When the medical social worker convenes the Diaz family, she recognized that the previous state of homeostasis in Mr. Diaz's life and health care has been disrupted by the death of Ann Mercy. Yet, for him it is important that the family maintains the previous family arrangements. Mr. Diaz fears that his children want to place him in a nursing home and to remove John from his care. He is emphatic that he can administer his own insulin, cook and maintain the household, although he has not previously performed these tasks. Mr. Diaz's wishes can be seen as an effort to protect his place in the family, which for him means that family rules, loyalties, and alignments remain as they were before Ann Mercy's death.

Maintaining equilibrium requires cohesion within the family system, in which all members agree that doing so is desirable, otherwise in the absence of an agreement, the system can be divided into factions. For instance, Maria, although concerned about her father's capacity to care for himself and her brother John, does not openly attempt to alter her father's role in the family and the family's patterns of behaving. Maria and John are aligned with and loyal to their father, however, Anita's uncertain loyalty introduces disruptive dynamics. For instance, Anita's (Ann Mercy's daughter from a previous marriage) behavior is in contrast to Maria and John's efforts to keep things as they were. In fact, her behavior and actions directly threatened the status quo. For example, without Mr. Diaz' permission, Anita had taken her mother's possessions, including a washing machine. The dynamics that Anita introduced into the family system were a departure from the family rules about behavior and specific family roles, all of which were decisive factors in the family's interactions.

Family Rules

Family homeostasis is maintained to the extent that all members of the family adhere to a limited number of rules or implicit agreements that prescribe the rights, duties, and range of appropriate behaviors within the family. Rules are formulas for relationships, and are guides for behavioral scripts, conduct, and interactions in the family. They represent a set of prescriptive behaviors that define relationships and organize the ways in which family members interact. Implicit rules (i.e., unwritten, covert laws governing behavior) are often beyond the participants' level of awareness; thus they must be inferred from observing family interactions and communications. Examples of implicit rules that dictate the behavior of members in relation to family issues include the following:

EP 2.1.7a

- *Dad has the final word (a rule observed in the Diaz family).*

- *You know that your parents expect us for the holidays.*
- *Children don't talk back to their parents.*
- *Children are not involved in the affairs of adults.*
- *Avoid saying what you really feel.*
- *Elderly parents are cared for by their children.*
- *In this house, we respect the privacy of other family members*
- *Don't talk about unpleasant things or feelings.*
- *Private family matters are not talked about in public.*

Families do, of course, formulate rules that are openly recognized and explicitly stated, such as the following:

- *We don't allow children to play violent video games.*
- *It doesn't matter who has a tattoo, you're not getting one.*
- *Children are limited to two hours of TV per day.*
- *There will be no swearing in this house.*
- *Going to the mall requires parental permission.*

EP 2.1.10d

In assessing family systems, you are interested in the implicit rules that guide a family's actions and the extent that they have a disruptive effect. Because these rules are unwritten, their impact on the lives of families often goes unrecognized, or when recognized, unspoken. In consequence, members become caught in situations in which their behavior is dictated by forces of which they are unaware. By adhering to such "rules," family members often perpetuate and reinforce the very problematic behavior of which they complain. For example, teenagers often complain about being inhibited by parental directives, yet they habitually engage in the behavior that prompts a parental reaction. Although rules govern the processes of families, they differ drastically from one culture to another and from one family to another. Within some families, rules that are intended to govern member behavior and in some instances manage undesirable influences can include:

- *Do not bring attention to yourself.*
- *Respect your elders.*
- *Bring honor to your family.*
- *The duty of children is to listen and obey.*
- *Duty and loyalty to the family is expected.*
- *Elders are wise and should be listened to.*
- *That gangsta rap is not coming in this house.*

Family rules may differ significantly from those typically observed in Western society, which tend to stress competitiveness, assertiveness, individualism, and limited obligations beyond the nuclear family. Yet some rules are not necessarily exclusive to Western notions, and some may even seem outdated, as the U.S. society has tended to move toward more egalitarianism in interactions between age groups.

Functional and Rigid Rules

The implicit rules or "norms" found in a family system may be either functional or rigid in that they may occur in a situational context. In tense conflicted situations, family members may monitor what they say and how they behave such as "Be careful what you say around Mom." However, at other times, speaking freely is okay. Functional rules enable the family system to flexibly respond to stressors, individual needs and development, and the needs of the family unit. As you observe families, you will want to assess the extent that rules provide members with opportunities to explore solutions that utilizes individual and collective family capacities. For example, an open discussion of member differences can facilitate an understanding of acceptable behavior. Similarly, openly discussing touchy subjects can be instrumental in bringing the family together in stressful times.

EP 2.1.10d

Rules that permit the system to respond flexibly are optimal. Examples of functional rules that facilitate an open and flexible climate in the family include the following:

- *Everyone's ideas and feedback are important.*
- *Family members don't always have to agree or to like the same things.*
- *It is okay to talk about any feelings—disappointments, fears, anger, or achievements.*
- *Family members should work out their disagreements with other family members.*
- *It is okay to admit mistakes; others in the family will understand and support you.*

As you observe family processes, keep in mind that all families have functional and facilitative rules as well as rigid rules. The latter can undermine positive family dynamics, but facilitative rules allow the family to "work out disagreements," or to encourage participation because "everyone's ideas are important." Of course, variations in both types of rules can of course occur depending on the age and cognitive ability of minors in the family.

EP 2.1.10d

Identifying both functional and unconstructive rigid rules is critical to making a balanced assessment of family functioning. Generally, family systems operate according to a relatively small set of rules governing relationships and behavior. Your understanding of family rules will aid your assessment of family rules. Because families are rule-governed, many behaviors or communications you observe are likely to be stylized or patterned. Be alert to repetitive sequences of behavior in all areas of family life; behaviors that are crucial to the operations of the family will tend to appear over and over. Observing the family's stylized or patterned behaviors can provide you with insights about family interactions. Because culture may play a decisive role in family rules, you should avoid assessing family rules based on rules that may be relevant to native U.S. families. Also, some racial and ethnic families in the U.S. may function optimally with rules that are opposite of those previously described (Okun, Fried, & Okun, 1999).

In the Diaz family, Mr. Diaz's insistence that "he had the final say" and "respect your elders," as rigid rules posed difficulties for problem solving. Adherence to these rules effectively diminished the contributions of others family members toward potential solutions that were in support of his desire for independence. Managing dynamics based on the behavior of some or all family members can be quite difficult. The role of the social worker in the Diaz family was to establish a climate in which members could express their concerns without blaming others or assuming a defensive or polarized position. For this turnaround to occur, the neutrality of the social worker was important.

Cautions about Assessing Rules

EP 2.1.10d

Perceptions about whether rules are rigid or dysfunctional warrant further words of caution. In the Diaz family for example, the rules observed by Mr. Diaz formed the basis for norms stating that parents are to be obeyed and retain their status, in spite of changing circumstances. His assertion of his parental status coupled with his limited capacity to care for himself and John, although in conflict with the views of his daughter, was for him a cultural expectation. Likewise, with Anita Mercy's unwillingness to honor family rules, you would want to explore whether the basis of her behavior stemmed from intergenerational tension (current or historical, adult, child–parent), or whether the tension is between traditional norms and the degree of acculturation (child reared in the United States and parent born in another country) (McAdoo, 1993, p. 11).

A labeling of rules as rigid by U.S. standards may, in fact, be biased when applied to family variants. Rules should therefore be explored in the context of culture, race, or social identity, including the culture of same-sex families and those of the family of origin, as well as the extent that work and family is a source of tension. In the video *Home for the Holidays 1*, you can observe the interplay between family of origin rules and their influence on the couple. For example, in Jackie's family, rules appear to be more flexible as members talk about everything and anything. Conversely this is not the case in Anna's family. In addition, there are differences in the family rules with regard to openly discussing sexual identity. Because it is almost impossible to be attentive to all the nuances of race and culture without making generalizations, asking the client about the rules of a family may provide the "most direct and accurate information about cultural realities" (Caple, Salcido, & di Cecco, 1995, p. 162; McAdoo, 1993; Okun, Fried & Okun, 1999). Obtaining accurate information is also emphasized by Spitalnick and McNair (2005) who point to identity as a cultural component and therefore an important consideration in assessing same-sex couples. Irrespective of the type, rules serve a purpose in the family system in that they govern behavior and socialize members to family expectations. In times of crisis, rules provide structure that may in fact keep the family from spiraling out of control.

Violation of Rules

EP 2.1.10d

When rules are violated, new behaviors are introduced into its system. Violations can occur as the family progresses over the course of the life cycle or as a result of external influences. Adolescents for example, often break family rules in their quest to establish themselves as separate and distinct individuals. Similarly, acculturated individuals may selectively retain some family rules and embrace others as a result of their exposure to different ways of behaving. When rules are violated, the family, in response, may resort to habitual modes of relating, thereby, keeping the system "on track." Responses often take the form of feedback or admonitions to members, filled with "shoulds," "oughts," "don'ts," or "shaming" that is intended to modify or eliminate behaviors that deviate from the norm. For example, "You should have asked me if you could go to the mall," indicates that a rule has been broken (going to the mall without parental permission). Family members, by using threats, anger, guilt, or other such forms of behavior may also counteract irregularities in the system. For example, "I guess that it does not matter what I think," is intended to induce guilt or express anger. Responses to violations of rules may be observed in nonverbal behaviors, for example, hand or eye gestures, facial expressions, silence, or exaggerated sighs. To help you grasp the effectiveness of a system in limiting or eliminating proscribed behaviors, note the pressure exerted by Mr. Diaz on his stepdaughter to adhere to the rule of "Dad has the final say":

Anita: I have taken Mom's things, including the washing machine, because they were hers. She bought them. I want things to remember her by, and she said I could have them.

Mr. Diaz: You have no right to come in here and take things that belonged to your mother and me. You show no respect for your father [*Asserting family rule*].

Anita: You were often a burden to Mom with your drinking and providing for your insulin. It is clear that you can't take care of John and something has to be done. You are not my father [*Disclaiming her loyalty and rejecting his status*].

Mr. Diaz: You cannot come into this house and decide how things will be done. [*He turns away and stops speaking to Anita*].

Anita: If you don't agree, I can go to court to get custody of John.

In the preceding scene, Anita and Mr. Diaz disagree about the rule that "Dad has the final say," in part because Anita does not consider Mr. Diaz to be her father. If the family has a rule that anger may not be expressed overtly, or in a physically or verbally aggressive manner, family members may stop speaking and ignore an offending member until the latter offers an apology. In the Diaz family, the rule about expressing anger is unclear, but it may be assumed that Anita violated an implicit rule, which Mr. Diaz perceives as a sign of disrespect.

The previous examples of rules may remind you of incidents in your own nuclear or extended family in which your behavior was regulated, reinforced, or extinguished by the response of other family members. As you contemplate your own experiences, perhaps you can begin to appreciate more fully the powerful influence of the family in shaping the lives and behaviors of family members, even years after they have physically departed from their families of origin.

Flexibility of Rules

The opportunity to influence rules or to develop new rules varies widely from family to family. Optimally, family rules will permit the system to respond flexibly and to develop new rules that are compatible with changing needs and development of family members. Rigid rules that prevent the family system from modifying or changing over time essentially crystallize relationships and typecast expected roles, thereby ignoring individual's need and capacity.

With respect to flexibility of rules, Becvar and Becvar (2000a) discuss the concepts of *morphostasis* and *morphogenesis*. Morphostasis describes a system's tendency toward stability, in essence to maintain a state of dynamic equilibrium. Morphogenesis refers to the system-enhancing behavior that allows for growth, creativity, innovation, and change (p. 68). For a system to find and maintain balance, it must be able to remain stable in the context of change and to change in the context of stability (Becvar & Becvar, 2000a).

As you assess family systems, then, you must not only identify a family's rules and operations, you should also determine the degree of flexibility (or rigidity) of the rules and of the system itself. This may be observed in part by assessing the degree of difficulty that a family experiences in adjusting and maintaining a dynamic state of balance in response to potential developments that occur during its life cycle, such as individual maturation, emancipation of adolescents, marriage, birth, retirement, aging, and death.

EP 2.1.10d

Family rules can change over the course of the family life cycle. The developmental stage of minors, for example, often means that they press for redefinition or a modification of family rules that are appropriate to their age. An individual may also pursue interests and choose values that are alien to those embraced by the family. Rules that govern the behavior of minors are by necessity modified when they become adults. Elders, however, accustomed to a certain set of rules vis-à-vis their status, may be disinclined to accept modifications. Further, it is often difficult for elders to cope with situations in which they feel acted upon by rules set forth by their adult children, professionals, or institutions. These dynamics cause "disequilibrium within the family system, a sense of loss, and perhaps a feeling of strangeness until new transactional patterns are in place to restore family balance" (Goldenberg & Goldenberg, 1991, p. 40).

In addition to assessing the stresses on rules caused by developmental changes and internal events (inner forces), it is important that you also assess the extent to which a family's rules allow the system to respond flexibly to dynamic societal stresses (outer forces), such as loss of a job, concerns about neighborhood safety, relocation of the family, occurrence of a natural disaster, or uprooting of the family experienced by immigrants or refugees.

EP 2.1.7b

Families may also construct rigid rules that function as protective factors to minimize real or potential risks, for example, telling minors to avoid certain people, places or situations. For immigrants or refugee families, further complicating dynamics are the vast contrasts between their rules and those of the Western culture. Immigration and the related cultural transition requires significant life changes over a short period of time, for example, material, economic, and educational changes; changes in roles; and the loss of extended family, support systems, and familiar environments (Green, 1999). Nonetheless, these families may adopt a mix of rule from their new and old cultures.

Responding successfully to inner and outer stresses requires constant transformation of the rules and behaviors of family members to accommodate ongoing changes while maintaining family continuity. Families often seek help because of an accumulation of events that have strained the coping ability of the entire family or of individual members. Even when these changes are for the better, they may overwhelm the coping mechanisms and resilience of individual members or an entire family system.

Most families have rules that do allow the system to respond readily to dynamic inner and outer forces. Indeed, the "normal" family or optimally functioning family may actually be an atypical phenomenon. The Diaz family may fall in the midrange of this continuum, because they have both rigid and functional rules. The rule that "Dad has the final say" is a problematic rigid rule with Mr. Diaz's family insofar as it seems to be observed by his biological children, but not Anita. However, the rule that "Taking care of family members is a primary obligation" is functional in that it has meant that both Maria and John, two of Mr. Diaz's biological children, wanted to assist him in continuing to live independently and safely. Maria, for example, offers to help her father find a first-floor apartment near her and to join with John in learning how to administer his insulin.

Mapping Rules

EP 2.1.10d

As you assess rules, you might, in collaboration with the family, devise a map in which the members indicate the status and function of rules in the family. In this way, they can decide which rules are functional and facilitative, or rigid, or culturally based. In this way, you are engaging the family in the assessment and also you gain a better understanding of the family in its particular context.

Content and Process Levels of Family Interactions

EP 2.1.7a

To complete an adequate family assessment and to identify important rules and behaviors, it is vital that you understand the concepts of *content* and *process* levels of interaction, the third system concept. Suppose that the following scenario occurs in your office in a family agency as you conduct the initial interview with Mr. and Mrs. Barkley.

CASE EXAMPLE

In response to your inquiry about the problems they are experiencing, Mr. Barkley glances at his wife, saying that she had been depressed and "sick" for some time. He states, that the couple has come to your agency seeking help for "her" problem. As you turn to look at Mrs. Barkley, she nods in agreement.

At this moment, you are concerned with not only what the couple is saying to you (the content of the discussion); at the same time, you are keenly interested in assessing the underlying intent or meaning of messages. Further, you observe the manner in which the spouses relate or behave as they talk about the problem. In other words, you are observant of the *process* and the *content* of their interactions. You make mental note of the fact that the husband, with tacit approval from the wife, has defined the problem for her, and concluded that he speaks for his wife and that the wife is the identified problem. Both spouses appear to disregard any impact of the problem on the husband, any possible part he might play in reinforcing or exacerbating his wife's depression or problematic behavior, or problems he might be experiencing. With respect to roles, the wife is presented as the "problem person" and the husband as the social worker's "consultant." Several important interactional behaviors thus occurred at the process level in the initial session, revealing information about the manner in which the spouses define their problem and how they relate, and pointing to promising avenues for exploration in assessing their problems.

EP 2.1.10d

Families' roles and rules are often revealed at the process level, but may be ignored by you as you selectively attend to what clients are "saying." For this reason, using your observational skills to attend to what people are doing as they discuss problems is crucial to assessing and intervening effectively in family systems. Otherwise, in this case you could easily become caught up at the content level by continuing to explore the etiology of Mrs. Barkley's "depression." The husband maintains his role as information-giver and Mrs. Barkley is the passive, identified client, while all involved ignore the stylized behaviors of the couple that may play a vital part in the problem. Family relationships form reciprocal repetitive patterns and have *circular* rather than *linear* motion. Carter and McGoldrick (1999b) caution social workers against cause-and-effect thinking, which asks why and looks for someone to blame. Instead, they suggest, "identifying patterns and tracing their flow" may prove useful, because family patterns "once established, are perpetuated by everyone involved in them, although not all have equal power or influence" (p. 437).

EP 2.1.7b

Before leaving this case, consider whether or not, cultural norms may have dictated that Mr. Barkley act as the spokesperson for the couple and the manner in which her symptoms are discussed. In this second scenario, Mr. Barkley describes Mrs. Barkley as being restless and as having headaches and frightening dreams that prevent her from sleeping. While the content and process of their interaction is similar to the previous couple, in this situation the *content* level may pertain to how depression is culturally described. The *process* level also has a cultural component, in that Mr. Barkley serves as the spokesperson. Think about how you could draw Mrs. Barkley into the conversation, taking care to respect the culturally derived status and role relationship between the couple. You might ask Mr. Barkley if it is permissible to direct exploratory questions to the wife, explaining that hearing from her will improve your understanding of their concerns. In this way, you show the couple that you respect their family structure and cultural norms. You might also inquire about how their own culture would deal with the situation as Mr. Barkley has described it, as well as what prompted the couple's decision to seek help.

Sequences of Interaction

EP 2.1.10d

In order to assess family rules, pay attention to the sequences of interaction that occur between members. All families play out scenarios or a series of transactions in which they manifest redundancies in behavior and communication, some of which may be culturally derived (e.g., as illustrated in the second Barkley family example). Observing the interactional sequences may reveal coping patterns that are utilized by individuals or by the entire family system. For example, you can gather information about communication styles, the behaviors of individuals, and the manner in which all family members reinforce counterproductive interactions.

To illustrate how this works, consider the following script from the first minutes of a session with the Diaz family. The medical social worker involved with this family has convened a family group conference to consider health and safety alternatives for Mr. Diaz. In this example, Mr. Diaz, daughter Maria, son John, and stepdaughter Anita demonstrate sequential verbal and nonverbal behaviors that have a powerful impact on the family system.

Anita *[to social worker]:* Carlos can't maintain himself or John. John runs wild, with no appropriate adult supervision, and Carlos can't take care of himself now that Mother has died *[Anita looks earnestly at the social worker, but signals a relational distance between herself and Mr. Diaz's by using his first name. In response, Mr. Diaz sits stoically, arms folded, glowering straight ahead].*

Maria *[to social worker]:* Dad is having trouble with John and hasn't taken care of himself all these years with Ann Mercy doing the cooking and cleaning and injecting his insulin. *[To Mr. Diaz.]* Dad, I respect you and want to help you in any way that I can, but things just can't continue like they are *[attempting to reason with her father].*

Mr. Diaz *[to social worker]:* These children "no tienen respeto." They don't give me the respect they should give the father as the head of the family. They want to put me in a nursing home and take John away from me *[appealing to the social work to notice the unfair, disrespectful way that he is being treated].*

Anita: Maybe that would be for the best, since you can't take care of yourself or John *[triumphant facial expression, resembling a smile].*

Maria [showing frustration, explains to social worker]: Dad is used to having his own way and we do respect him, at least I do, but he won't listen to how some things have to change.

Mr. Diaz: Maria, you have been a good daughter, and I am surprised at your behavior. I would think that you would be the loyal one and stick by your father if anyone would.

John: Dad, you know I stick by you. And I can help with some things, too. I want to stay with you. We have been getting along okay, and I want to be a good son and take care of you *[asserting his loyalty and attempting to maintain equilibrium by supporting the father].*

Anita: John, you have been running in the streets, in trouble with the law, taking money from your father. You are no help to him, and he can't be a good parent to you *[reasserting her point of view].*

Maria: John, I know you want to help, and you are close to your dad. But you have made a lot of problems for him, and I, too, wonder if you can take care of him or he can take care of you.

EP 2.1.10d

In the preceding example, the Diaz family members play out a discordant, yet repetitive thematic interaction that, with slight variation, can be observed over and over in their transactions. Families may discuss an endless variety of topics or content issues, but their processes often have a limited number of familiar behaviors. For example, Anita continues to push for her point of view. It is as though the family is involved in a screenplay, and once the curtain is raised, all members participate in the scenario according to the family script. It is important to understand that family scripts rarely have beginnings or endings; that is, anyone may initiate the scenario by enacting his or her "lines." The rest of the family members almost invariably follow their habitual styles of relating, editing their individual scripts slightly to fit different versions of the scene being acted out by the family. For example, Maria attempts to reason with her father, although she does not support Anita's perception. In sequenced interactions scenes, the subjects discussed will vary, but the roles taken by individual family members and the styles of communicating and behaving that perpetuate the scenario tend to fluctuate very little.

In the following example, notice the sequenced interactions that occurred in the family:

1. Anita speaks forthrightly about her concerns about John and Mr. Diaz's capacity for parenting him because of Mr. Diaz's medical condition. Responding nonverbally (*folding his arms and glowering*), Mr. Diaz declines to openly respond (*a patterned behavior when his authority is questioned or when there is disagreement*).
2. Maria affirms some of Anita's concerns but also speaks directly to her father [*affirming her respect for him as father and head of the family*].
3. Mr. Diaz asserts that his children "no tienen respeto" and that their motivation is to put him away [*maintaining his authority*].
4. Anita does not deny that a nursing home might be the best solution [*reasserting her position that he cannot care for himself*].
5. Maria reasserts her respect for her father, yet notes that some things must change.
6. Mr. Diaz addresses Maria and questions whether she is, in fact, showing proper respect for him as her father.
7. John joins the fray and tries to identify himself as a good son with "respeto," which adds another dimension to the transactions.
8. Anita puts John in his place by doubting whether he has acted as a good son or whether Mr. Diaz can be a good parent to him.
9. Maria supports John's desire to be a good son but agrees that there are persistent problems with Mr. Diaz and his care of John.

In observing the Diaz family and other similar scenarios you can identify patterned behaviors, relationships, and rule governing family sequenced interactions that may not be apparent when observing single transactions. For example:

- *Anita, perhaps because she is a stepdaughter, does not acknowledge the family rule of "respeto" and challenges Mr. Diaz's wishes and capabilities. In fact, she calls him by his first name.*
- *Maria does acknowledge Mr. Diaz's place in the family and tries to show appropriate respect while acknowledging that a problems does exist.*
- *John attempts to forge a strong coalition with Mr. Diaz by identifying his wishes to maintain the current situation.*
- *Mr. Diaz addresses the social worker and Maria, ignoring Anita, who has violated a family rule.*

- *Anita and Mr. Diaz invariably disagree.*
- *Maria attempts to mediate, affirming Mr. Diaz's position and the rule, while acknowledging problems.*

As you can imagine, this session with the family was a challenge for the social worker. If you were a practitioner in a similar situation, would your first impulse be to shout "Stop?" Ultimately, however, observing the sequenced interactions and responses in a family allows you to strategically focus your assessment on the family's limited number of processes.

Analyzing the rules, processes, content, and patterns in the interactions provided the social worker with multiple entry points for intervening and to assist the family in coming to a decision. For example, there is the agreement between the stepsisters (Maria and Anita) that Mr. Diaz cannot continue to live his life as he has in the past and that change is required. Mr. Diaz's role making a decision is not altogether clear at this point. But he understands and eventually reluctantly agrees that he needs help if he is to care for himself and for John. It is obvious, however, that he is clinging to rigid rules and the relationship that these rules dictate. For him, the problem was the violation of these rules rather than his physical condition. An alliance is formed between the parent–child subsystem consisting of Mr. Diaz and John, who are allied as the two males in the family and protective of each other. There is also an alliance between the two stepsisters in that they both agree that something needs to change. In working with the family, the social worker had two major tasks:

- Focusing members' attention on Mr. Diaz's needs related to his physical condition.
- Engaging members in discussion that facilitates problem solving around this issue.

Even so, family rules and sequenced patterns are playing a part in the problem and its potential resolution, and therefore both needed to be addressed.

Employing "Circular" Explanations of Behavior

EP 2.1.7a

Previously we emphasized the behavior in the Diaz family from a systems framework, drawing your attention to their reciprocal sequenced and repetitive patterned interactions that influenced all of the actors in the family system. In so doing, the circular concept of causality was applied, demonstrating that each member's behavior became a stimulus to all other members.

The concept of circular behavior stands in contrast to a *linear explanation* of the causes of behavior. In a linear explanation, event A causes event B; event B causes event C; and so forth. As a beginning social worker eager to get on with the business of problem solving you may tend to rely on linear explanations for behaviors. Linear observations however reveal an action-reaction cycle, which is assigning responsibility or blame to one or more members whose problematic behavior is conspicuous. If you are attuned only to the repetitive nature of linear interactions, you may sharply reduce your ability to help family members reframe their behaviors and move away from counterproductive patterned interactions.

To illustrate the difference between these two conceptual frameworks for viewing the causality of behavior, the Diaz family is once again considered.

- *In a* linear *explanation of behavior, one would say, "When Anita attacks Mr. Diaz, he defends himself."*
- *A* circular *explanation of behavior would take the following form: "When Anita attacks Mr. Diaz, he defends himself, and Maria acts to mediate, supporting both Mr. Diaz and Anita.*
- *The mediation is not accepted, thus the charges and countercharges between Anita and Mr. Diaz continue, with John attempting to align himself with his father."*

Nichols and Schwartz (1998) underscore the point that *circular* and *linear* concepts of causality reflect contrasting approaches in assessing and, if necessary, intervening in family processes so that you are able to gather information. The circular explanation is systemic and is systems-oriented, not only because it offers a more adequate description of behavior, it also provides a greater number of alternatives for intervention. As the practitioner in the preceding example, intervening in the linear exchange between Anita and Mr. Diaz, you would intervene to stop Anita from attacking Mr. Diaz. Doing so might halt their behaviors for awhile, however, they are more likely to find yet another opportunity to continue their patterned behavior. A circular intervention in contrast would focus on educating the family about their sequenced behavior, and the importance of targeting their entire circular patterns.

By utilizing a circular perspective you can observe in the assessment process, you may observe three types of differences:

EP 2.1.10d

- *Differences between individuals (e.g., "Anita gets angry the most")*

- *Differences between relationships (e.g., "What is the difference between the ways Mr. Diaz treats Anita compared to how he treats Maria?")*
- *Differences between time periods (e.g., "How did she get along with Mr. Diaz last year as compared to now?")*

Family members, like beginning social workers, tend to explain behavior using a linear orientation, often assigning arbitrary beginnings and endings to sequences of interaction in ways that define other members as villains and themselves as victims. Mr. Diaz, for instance, viewed himself as an innocent victim of Anita's disrespectful behavior and identified her as the person who needed to change. Further, in his mind, she is the family member who has upset the family system. In situations of this nature, you are responsible for counteracting the linear perspective of one person as the initiator and the other person as the reactor. You can disrupt this type of interactional sequence by explaining systems concepts emphasizing the role, responsibility, and reciprocity of all family members in maintaining and developing functional interactions and problem solving. In the interest of problem solving, you can also share your observations so that each member can reflect on his or her behavior in the situation. Your ultimate goal is to create a climate in which family members' thoughtful, rather than active-reactive, patterns of relating is the norm.

Assessing Problems Using the Systems Framework

EP 2.1.7a

The utilization of a systems perspective on family problems has implications for gathering relevant data in the assessment process. From the process, you should have a working knowledge of the family upon which your intervention can be based. Many family members, even those that are designated as troubled by other family members, see themselves as victims of the actions of others or of external forces over which they have little or no control. When families initially seek help, they are often prepared to "complain" or be the "informant" about those who are "causing" their problems as was the case with the first case scenario involving the Barkley couple. Because the informant can have a selective perception or omit details about the "cause," for the purpose of the assessment, their information is incomplete. Therefore, your assessment goal is to understand the presenting problem in its context and the extent to which the behavior of the identified "client" family member and that of others in the family system reinforce and exacerbate the problem. Otherwise, you may unwittingly adopt a family member's definition of "who has the problem," and mistakenly focus on the behavior of the selected member thereby neglect the influence of others in the family system. In all likelihood, there are other systems that are involved.

Although systemic patterns of interactions that restrict and mold behavior are woven throughout the fabric of many family problems, you may not have the opportunity to observe these interactions firsthand. Family members, for instance, may refuse service or be absent, unavailable, or reluctant to participate. In the Diaz case, for instance, Anita lived in another city and it was unclear whether she would be involved with the family beyond the family conference as a participant in problem-solving efforts. In some cases, a family member may describe problems that he or she is experiencing in relationships with family members or with significant others who are not present.

EP 2.1.10d

When you are unable to directly observe family interactions, you then face the important task of eliciting highly specific information from each family member relative to the presenting concern. **Gathering this information** is best accomplished by carefully exploring a number of critical incidents that illustrate the problem, events, before, during, and after the incidents; the context in which the problem occurred; and its duration and frequency. Further, you will want to explore how the family has coped, the extent to which other systems are involved, their attempts to resolve the situation, as well as resources and strengths. In instances in which family relationships are identified as a concern, you will want to identify underlying family patterns, establish the sequences of discrete transactions, and elicit descriptive information about the behaviors and communications of all involved. Given that the fact that individuals tend to focus on and summarize critical incidents ("The teacher called and said that Shondra was messing up in school"), possibly omitting critical details (her father was recently sentenced to prison for five years). It is helpful to explain to families that you are searching for each discrete event or transaction that occurred in any critical incident targeted for exploration.

You can begin by asking family members to give a descriptive account of an event so that you can see what happened as clearly as if you had been present. As members provide this descriptive information, you can also observe family relationships. In observing the interactions between family members, you can identify key interaction patterns and the nature of alignments among various subsystems of the family (e.g., parents, siblings, grandparents, and other kin). In such explorations, it is not uncommon to discover that other persons (e.g., an older sibling, stepparents, grandparents) and other systems play significant roles in contributing to or resolving the family's problem. Based on information gained through your exploration of family affiliative ties and rules, you will often need to redefine and expand the problem system to include more actors than were originally identified.

> **TABLE-10-3 DIMENSIONS OF FAMILY ASSESSMENT**
>
> Family context
> Family strengths
> Boundaries and boundary maintenance
> Family power structure
> Family decision-making processes
> Family goals
> Family myths and cognitive patterns
> Family roles
> Communication styles of family members
> Family life cycle
>
> © Cengage Learning 2013

EP 2.1.7a

In assisting families to understand the need for an overall assessment of the family, it is helpful to explain that the family is a "system," stressing that the entire family is affected by, and may even contribute to problems experienced by a member. Exploring with each family member the ways in which they are affected by the problem can help them to understand what you mean by the family as a system. For instance, parents of a youth involved with juvenile court may be at their wit's end and simply want the child out of their hair for a time. Often, because of their frustration, their resolution to the problem is, "Take him. I can't do anything with him anymore; he doesn't listen to me. Maybe time away from home will change his attitude." Despite parent's anger and frustration, tears, guilt, and fears the situation punctuates their tirade. Redefining the problem as a family issue invokes both relief and fears. Even when a child (or another member) has been identified as the source of family discord, parents may have unconsciously interpreted the problem as a failure on their part, Therefore, framing concerns as a family problem can result in a sense of relief and a belief that together the family has the capacity to solve the problem.

Dimensions of Family Assessment

EP 2.1.10d

Table 10-3 highlights the dimensions of assessment, some of which includes systems concepts that you can use as guidelines for exploring and organizing the massive amount of data you will gather in working with families. These dimensions will assist you in assessing interactions and evaluating aspects of family operations, a critical preliminary step when planning problem-solving interventions. Keep in mind that you can augment your assessment by appropriately using the assessment tools for understanding families described in Table 10-1 or others that are available to you.

The dimensions to formulate family assessments and plan interventions utilize the following guidelines.

1. *Identify the dimensions that are most relevant to your clients.* Although the dimensions apply to the processes of couples and families, not all will be pertinent given the presenting complaint and the nature of the help requested by the family. For example, a family may seek help because of stress caused by providing care for an elderly relative living in their home. Your initial exploration may reveal no major concerns in the relative's functioning (e.g., decision making) as a contributing factor to the family's problem. Thus, you would narrow the assessment to an exploration of the specific problem identified by the family, in this case, caregiver-related stress.

2. *Use the dimensions to guide your exploration of family behavior.* After the first session, review the dimensions and develop relevant questions to further your exploration in subsequent sessions. For example, how has the family handled or coped with problems? How does the family communicate with each other and other patterns of interaction?

3. *Use the dimensions as guidelines for organizing new data into themes and patterns.* Determine a family's or couple's rules or habitual ways of relating in relation to each relevant dimension. For example, ask about the family's rules in relation to decision making, roles and power structure, and family goals.

4. *Based on the relevant dimensions, develop a written profile of behaviors of individual members within the system.* For example, with respect to the dimension of communication, a family member may tend to paraphrase messages of others and personalize statements. The same person may be prone to interrupt and to talk excessively, thus monopolizing the session. Developing a profile of behaviors for each family member will provide a framework not only for assessing behaviors but also for planning interventions.
5. Employ this dimension to assess relevant behaviors of the *entire family*, developing a profile of salient functional and problematic behaviors that are manifested by the system itself. For the dimension of communication, functional behaviors of a family may include listening responses and responses that acknowledge the contributions of others (e.g., "You did a good job"). In contrast, responses observed in the same family that may include labeling of members (e.g., "You are dumb") or frequent responses of anger directed toward other members are counterproductive.

Family Context

EP 2.1.7b

The family context dimension is intended to help you understand the family in its ecological and idiosyncratic context. Assessing families includes paying attention to their access to basic resources such as food, health care, housing, and their ability to secure such resources. Basic survival needs often takes precedence over directing the family's attention to family dynamics, for example, communication or parenting skills. Of course family dynamics may be problematic as a result of a lack of basic resources, however, assessing these dynamics must wait until such time that a family's dire need for basic sustenance is addressed (Kilpatrick & Holland, 2003; Vosler, 1990).

Paramount to gathering data and assessing families is the task of accurately viewing the family in the context of its cultural or family variant environment, as emphasized earlier in the chapter. The fact that the definition of family differs greatly adds even more complexity to your assessment task. Although the contexts of families can differ dramatically, it is important that you pay attention and indeed have respect for the larger socioenvironmental contextual issues and their capacity to affect family functioning. The consequence to families is that you may filter out their inner resources, and most importantly, underestimate the influence of the social context in which they live (Barnes, 2001; Saleebey, 2004).

Within the family context dimensions, you also have the task of identifying and assessing the family's status relative to its relationship with the larger social environment. Ironically, although social work has a person-in-environment focus, it can be easier sometimes to avoid including such factors as culture, race, socioeconomic class, family form, sexual orientation, and the experience with oppressive forces, inequality and discrimination. These and other factors are characterized by Nichols and Schwartz (1998) as *extra-familial obstacles*. Such factors can be, for example, a family's access to basic resources or the legal context of a family. To understand more fully their impact, it might be useful to you to revisit the circular and linear explanations of behavior. For instance, a range of emotions, reactions, and adaptive patterns can be prominent when a family is faced with extra-familial obstacles in their interactions with environmental systems.

EP 2.1.5a

Oppression is a justice matter, and as such the assessment goes beyond simply determining the extent to which external forces affect the family's ability to function. Integrating oppression and inequality into the assessment process requires the "unmasking of oppressive forces" that can affect family functioning (Carniol, 1992). Examples of questions that can guide assessments with an emphasis on social justice are as follows:

- *Is the problem that a family is facing due to their marginalized status in the social environment (Barnes, 2001; Carniol, 1992; Langley, 2001)?*
- *Is there a relationship between family problems and oppressive forces, for example, structural inequities (Guadalupe & Lum, 2005; Rooney, G. D., 2009; Van Voorhis, 1998)?*
- *What is the level of family alienation within the social environment (Carter & McGoldrick, 1999; Kilpatrick & Holland, 2003; Langley, 2001; Slater, 1995; Van Voorhis, 1998)?*
- *How does the family's narrative inform you of their experience with oppression (Dietz, 2000; Fyre, 2004; Pollack, 2004; Saleebey, 1996)?*
- *Do assumptions about family deviance minimize the effects of oppression and perpetuate the dominant normative narrative (Freud, 1999; Rosen & Livne, 1992; Weinberg 2006)?*

The essence of these questions as well as others that you may develop helps to determine whether aspects of the family's problems are the result of oppression and inequality. While it is important that you remain neutral and objective, it is equally important that you validate the family's feelings and experience. Essentially during the assessment process you are becoming what Spencer (2008) refers to as an "ally." In practical terms, you support families in "naming their experiences of oppressions" by examining the effects that it has on their problem (Dietz, 2000, p 503).

EP 2.1.7a

It is vital, then, that you have a working knowledge of the family and its reality, including the larger contextual influences on the family. Once you have obtained this information, you can then make use of what Norton (1978) and McPhatter (1991) call the *dual perspective*. This perspective involves "the conscious and systematic process of perceiving, understanding and comparing simultaneously the values and attitudes of the larger societal system with those of the family and community systems," which is critical to assessing the social context of a family's presenting problems (McPhatter, 1991). In their elaboration on the context of diverse families, Kilpatrick and Holland (2003) maintain that the "dual perspective fosters problem resolution in tune with distinct values and community customs" (pp. 40–41). The dual perspective also recognizes that families are members of two systems, one of "which is dominant or sustaining and the other, the nurturing system." For instance, the dual perspective can help you to identity the points of conflict and consistency between the family system and the larger systems with whom it interacts with.

In utilizing a dual perspective, you can view the functionality of a family's behavior within the context of what is "normal" for a particular family system. In this way, you avoid relying on broad generalizations about particular groups and concluding that their relational patterns or lifestyles are indicators of dysfunction (Green, 1999; McAdoo, 1993). For instance, terms such as *enmeshment, fusion,* and *undifferentiated ego mass* may be inappropriate when describing the interdependence observed in some families (Berg & Jaya, 1993; Bernal & Flores-Ortiz, 1982; Boyd-Franklin, 1989a; Flores & Carey, 2000; Hand, 2006; Okun, Fried, & Okun, 1999). Such errors may cause you to draw conclusions about assessment dimensions that actually have little relevance to the family or are disruptive to the family system.

Diverse Families

EP 2.1.7b

The dual perspective is an absolute must in assessing diverse families. Family behavior makes sense when it is understood in the larger cultural or racial context in which it is embedded. For instance, a family's culture can influence help-seeking behavior, and also determine how problems are defined. Perceptions of mental illness, for instance, as well as the negative connotation for self and the family can vary by and within cultural groups (Sue, 2006; Hirayama, Hirayama, & Cetingok, 1993). Main beliefs considered to be important in the U.S. culture may be counter to the beliefs of other families. Instead, for example, they may stress reliance on family members, including extended family. Further, such notions of individual self-determination or autonomy can be foreign concepts in that they undermine collective interdependence (Ewalt and Mokuau, 1996; Horesji, Heavy Runner, & Pablo 1992; Rooney & Bibus, 1996; Sue, 2006).

EP 2.1.10d & 2.1.4b

In assessing families who are ethnically or racially diverse, Green (1999) suggests that a basic dimension of cultural competence is identifying what is salient in a family's culture at any given point and time. Because of such factors as acculturation—diversity in the fixed normative values within groups—it is important that your assessment individualizes families. Of course we recognized that it is not possible for you to understand the cultural or racial nuances and their assessment implications in every diverse family. Unfortunately, when you have acquired knowledge of various groups, you face an increased danger of stereotyping. As a beginning social worker, you may feel the tension of your desire to be sensitive to diversity and to be competent, and yet you may also feel resentment when you are lectured about the importance of understanding racial and cultural differences. At the risk of adding to this tension, we feel that it is important to discuss aspects of culture and race that are important considerations in the overall assessment of family context.

EP 2.1.3a

- *Recognize that members of various groups may differ considerably from profiles or descriptions of typical behaviors. This point is particularly important for members of minority groups.*

- *Understand that there are vast differences in race, language, and culture within groups designated as racial or ethnic minorities (Green, 1999). Spanish-speaking people who share some aspects of Hispanic or Latino heritage, such as a similar language, may differ in other ways depending on their country of origin.*
- *Be aware that members of diverse cultures differ with respect to social class and nationalities. Caple, Salicido, and di Cecco (1995), Hirayama, Hirayama, and Centigok (1993), McAdoo (1993), and Sue (2006) are among the writers who inform us that all group members do not necessarily embrace the normative values of their particular group. Accordingly, differences may be observed along intergenerational lines (as in the case of family rules in the Diaz family) and be based on the evolving degree of acculturation.*
- *With respect to acculturation, children may adapt to new cultures at a much more rapid pace than their parents because of their exposure to the dominant culture through school, and perhaps because they have no or few years of contact with their culture of origin (Caple, Salcido, & di Cecco, 1995; Hirayama, Hirayama, & Cetingok, 1993; Potocky-Tripodi, 2002).*
- *The values of cultural groups are not fixed but continually evolving. As a consequence, variations may occur within families and reflect their stage in the acculturation process.*

As a means to sort out cultural variations and nuances, McAdoo (1993) suggests using your acquired knowledge to formulate a hypothesis and then exploring the extent to which this information is relevant in a particular family's situation. The implications of these observations are critical and they can be unique, more or less to each family system. The essence of systems thinking with respect to family context is assessing both the internal and external relational patterns that affect the family. At the same time, to avoid making assumptions, your assessment should individualize each family within its cultural context.

Family Strengths

EP 2.1.10e

All families have a range of individual member and group strengths as well as the communities in which they live (Cowger, 1997; Early & GlenMaye, 2000; Saleebey, 2004). The second assessment dimension guides you to gather information about these strengths.

As you are perhaps aware, acknowledging strengths in families is not easy. It's not as if families are without strengths, so your assessment task is not one of discovery. In part, a difficulty with a strengths-based perspective stems from the fact that helping professionals and the agencies in which they work, as well as funding resources and policymakers, have deeply entrenched views about the pathology of families who experience problems. There are agencies and practitioners that purport to embrace a strengths perspective, however family strengths seems to be an abstract thought as their assessment tools will attest. Students have commented that families themselves are not always comfortable with a strengths focus. Having been socialized to focus on their problems in exchange for receiving services they can be reluctant, and indeed suspicious when you talk about strengths. Further, a family may not recognize that their capacity to cope with adversity, to support and celebrate each other, and that the talents and aspirations they have are strengths. Regardless of the circumstances that may make it difficult for you to assess strengths, you are responsible for your choice of action. Once the conversation about family strengths takes place, you can ask family members to highlight other family strengths.

The strengths perspective is based on the empowerment and humanistic notion that people can change and grow (Jordan & Franklin, 2003). In essence, *a strengths assessment* highlights what is going right and what is working in families and balancing it with their presenting concern. Assessing and accrediting the strengths inherent in the family system require the deliberate and disciplined effort of all involved. On your part, a strengths orientation requires you to have a respectful and positive way of thinking about people that is evident in your attitude and relationship with the family. This strengths perspective, a foundation for assessing families, includes assessing strengths but not at the exclusion of paying attention to problems or risks. In other words, it is not either or, but rather a balance of assessing both problems and strengths. To refresh your memory you can refer to the two dimensional Strengths–Needs matrix developed by Cowger (1994) discussed in Chapter 8.

EP 2.1.10a

Strengths in families may be observed in their orientation to the future, such as goals, aspirations, hopes, and dreams beyond the current difficulties that the family is experiencing. A strength observed in the Diaz family was that of loyalty, in that despite their patterned behavior,

EP 2.1.10d

members were committed to supporting their father. Strengths also take into account the family's current functioning, and aspects of the family climate such as spirituality or religion, coping with adversity, adapting to changes, and resilience (Barnes, 2001; Early & GlenMaye, 2000; Walsh, 1996). Referring again to the Cowger matrix, a strengths assessment would take into account factors that are external to the family—for example, connections to a larger social network and the community in which the family lives.

EP 2.1.7b

In your assessment, you need to pay particular attention to the strengths of families from various cultural or racial groups, many of whom have been disadvantaged by historic discrimination or, in the case of political refugees, extreme losses (Barnes, 2001; Chazin, Kaplan & Terio, 2000; Congress & Kung, 2005; Hand, 2006: Potocky-Tripodi, 2002). While the hopefulness of refugee or immigrant families may have been temporarily influenced by their circumstances, their strengths lie in their amazing capacity to survive. Many diverse families function in a dual or bicultural context in which part of their environment can be nurturing and supportive, and another that can be stressful, adversarial, or disorienting. The fact that diverse families are able to transition between these two environments—coping and adapting—are strengths to be acknowledged in the assessment. Assessments with diverse families can be a challenge and your respect for the subjective experience within the family's narrative is essential.

EP 2.1.10d

Assessment questions that explore family strengths and resilience focus on the following topics:

- *Family traditions, rituals, celebrations, and cultural assets*
- Religious affiliation or spirituality
- Communication processes
- Shared goals
- Loyalty
- Patterns of help-seeking behavior
- Hardiness, coping, flexibility, and resilience in times of adversity
- Information about how a problem would be handled in the particular family or its community
- Individuals or institutions that the family may turn to in times of difficulty
- Family capacities, adaptations, hopes, dreams, or aspirations

While these questions are useful with all families, they may have particular relevance to diverse families as a means to facilitate your assessment of their strengths. Also, in the absences of a strengths assessment tool in your agency, you can develop your own questions and integrate them into your practice.

Boundaries and Boundary Maintenance in Family Systems

Boundaries, a central concept in family systems theories, can be likened to abstract dividers that function: (1) between and among other systems, or subsystems within the family, and (2) between the family and the environment.

EP 2.1.7a

In adapting Bertalanffy's general systems theory, Martin and O'Connor (1989) conclude that all systems are open and interdependent with their environment. Within this framework, no system is ever truly closed. It does, however, selectively respond to, permit, screen, or reject inputs, in the form of information, people, or events, through the boundary maintenance function. Conceptualizing the family as an open system allows you to examine the family system's boundaries and boundary maintenance function. For example, you can determine the extent to which the family is an *included* system, specifically, its connection to other kin, the community, and membership with other groups. The Social Support Network Map described in Table 10-1 is a tool can assist you in this regard.

External Family Boundaries

Because systems are part of still larger systems, families necessarily engage in diverse transactions with the environment. Boundaries change over time as the family system as a whole and its members experience various developmental levels. For example, when a child begins school, the boundaries of the family system willingly expand to permit interactions with the educational system. At the same time, families can widely differ in the degree to which they are flexible and accepting of transactions with other systems. In operational term, "flexibility," means the extent to which outsiders are permitted or invited to enter and become a part of the family system, and whether or not members are allowed to invest emotionally and engage in relationships outside the family. Flexibility also means the extent to which information and materials are exchanged with the environment. For the most part, individual members have the

EP 2.1.10d

freedom to regulate their interactions external to the family as long as they do not adversely affect other family members or violate the family norms. Those who hold authority in families (e.g., the parental subsystem) perform the bounding functions in such a way that they create discrete family space that exists apart from the larger space of the neighborhood and community. Bounding functions may also be observed in larger family systems such as a clan or tribe, in which family is broadly defined.

A family system with thick boundaries is characterized by strict regulation that limits its transactions with the external environment and restricts incoming and outgoing people, objects, information, and ideas. Thick boundaries preserve territoriality, protect the family from undesired intrusions, safeguard privacy, and, in some instances, foster secrets. Authority figures in such families or clans maintain tight control of the traffic at the system's perimeter. In consequence, the boundary maintenance function is rarely relinquished or shared with other family members or outsiders. Even so, maintaining the family's boundary may not necessarily be a reason for concern, except when there is objective evidence of harm to family members.

EP 2.1.3a

When assessing the bounding patterns of families, related to outside influences, it is essential that you consider the family's unique style, cultural preferences, strengths, and needs. Families may have more flexible boundaries with extended family members, perhaps including well-defined obligations and responsibilities to one another. Conversely, those boundaries may appear more or less flexible when external influences intrude upon family traditions and values and are seen as a source of conflict or disruption to the family system. For instance, the behavior of a youth that results in the entry into the family by a juvenile probation officer can be disruptive, but the family system out of necessity can reluctantly accommodate this intrusion. At still other times, the family may change to accommodate new inputs over the course of the life cycle or during transitions. Immigrant families, for example, are generally open to new information as they make the transition to a new society. Simultaneously, the boundary maintenance function can become very active as families screen out what they deem to be undesirable aspects of the new culture. An article in the September 4, 2003, edition of *The New York Times Sunday Magazine* illustrates this point. Entitled "For Schooling, a Reverse Emigration to Africa," tells the story of immigrant Ghanaian parents who had sent their children back to Ghana so that the children could avoid negative elements in U.S. society.

EP 2.1.4c

Students are often confused by or misinterpret boundary maintenance. In instances, for example, when they have encountered families who are reluctant to provide information, they may conclude that the family's reluctance is evident of a family secret or that the family is resistance to change. Of course both can be true, and should therefore be assessed. However, it is also true that families should have an opportunity to selectively provide information as they see fit, without you assuming deviance on their part. Families can also feel that social welfare organizations ignore their boundaries. As immigrant parents attempt to navigate their new culture, they are often confused and indeed alarmed by the ease in which formal institutions encroach on their family boundaries. For instance, a primary concern of parents who participated in a series of focus groups was the extent schools could teach certain content without seeking their permission. Also, these parents were puzzled about the extent to which the child welfare system had the capacity to dictate their parenting behavior, which in effect, usurped their parental role. For instance, one parent stated, "When I tell my child to do or not do something and he doesn't like it, he will tell me, I am going to call 911 and report you."[5]

Internal Family Boundaries

Boundaries internal to the family system function to clarify demarcations in relationships, for example, between parents and children or other subsystems, governed by rules, roles, and responsibilities. Optimally, families have clear and flexible boundaries that allow for the ongoing development of members, changing relationships and a sense of identity and purpose. Of course family boundaries can be based on cultural preferences, extending to individuals who by Western norms would not be considered a part of the family system.

Internal Boundaries and Family Subsystems

All families develop networks and relationships between coexisting subsystems that can be formed on the basis of gender, interest, generation, or functions that must be performed for the family's survival (Minuchin, 1974). Members of a family may simultaneously belong to numerous

EP 2.1.10a

subsystems, entering into separate and reciprocal relationships with other members of the nuclear family, depending on the subsystems they share in common (e.g., parents, mother/daughter, brother/sister, father/son), or with the extended family (e.g., grandmother/granddaughter, uncle/nephew, mother/son-in-law). Each subsystem can be thought of as a natural coalition between participating members. Of course, many of the coalitions or alliances are situation-related and temporary in nature. For example, a teenager may be able to enlist his or her mother's support in asking his or her father's permission for a special privilege. A grandmother living in a home may voice disagreement with her daughter and son-in-law regarding her or his discipline of children, thus temporarily forming a coalition with the children. Such passing alliances are characteristic of temporary subsystems.

Other subsystems or coalitions, especially partners or spouses, parental, and sibling subsystems, are more enduring in nature. According to Minuchin (1974), the formation of stable, well-defined coalitions between members of these vital subsystems is critical to the well-being and health of the family. Unless there is a strong and enduring coalition between parents, for instance, conflict will reverberate throughout a family, and children may be co-opted into one faction or another as parents struggle for power and control. In general, the boundaries of these three subsystems must be clear and defined well enough to allow members sufficient differentiation to carry out functions without undue interference (Minuchin, 1974). At the same time, they must be permeable enough to allow contact and exchange of resources between members of the subsystem. Minuchin points out that the clarity of the subsystem boundaries has far more significance in determining family functioning than the composition of the family's subsystem. For instance, a parental subsystem that consists of a grandmother and an adult parent–child may function perfectly adequately. The relative integrity of the boundaries of spouses or partners, parental, and sibling subsystems is determined by family rules. A parent clearly defines the role of the parental subsystem, for instance, by telling the oldest child not to interfere in the conversation when a younger child is being disciplined. The message, or "rule," then, is that an older child is not a co-parent. A parent, however, may delegate caretaking of younger child to an older child in the parent's absence. In this instance, the boundaries or the parental and sibling subsystems are clearly delineated.

Cultural and Family Variants

Cultural and family variants can play a critical role in determining boundaries in many family subsystems. For example, traditionally, many Native American tribes did not consider people to be functional adults until they reached their mid-fifties or became a grandparent. For this reason, grandparents assume child-rearing responsibilities. Thus the parenting subsystem involves grandparents and their grandchildren, rather than the parents of the children. Similar intergenerational boundary spanning relationships may be found in other minority-group or cultural group families, whereby a variety of adults may function as parents, and there is a distribution of family roles and tasks (Boyd-Franklin, 1989a; Carter & McGoldrick, 1999a; McAdoo, 1993; Okun, Fried & Okun, 1999).

EP 2.1.4c

The clarity of boundaries within a family is a useful parameter for evaluating family functioning. Minuchin (1974) conceives of all families as falling somewhere along a continuum of extremes in boundary functioning, where the opposite poles are *disengagement* (diffused boundaries) or *enmeshment* (inappropriate rigid boundaries). Family closeness in an enmeshed family system is defined as everyone thinking and feeling alike and relationships that require a major sacrifice of autonomy, in which members are discouraged from developing their own identity and independent explorations or behaviors.

EP 2.1.7a

Enmeshment and disengagement are not necessarily indicative of dysfunctional relationships because in some cultural, racial, or socioeconomic groups these concepts may have little or no relevance. According to Minuchin (1974), every family experiences some enmeshment or disengagement between its subsystems as the family passes through various developmental phases. During a family's early developmental years, for instance, a caretaker and a young child, out of necessity, are an enmeshed subsystem. A cultural variant however, is that a child's relationship can involve several caretakers in which there are close ties. Sharing the parental bed until a certain age or sleeping in the same room with parents has been at the center of legal and child development debates in the United States. However, it is a common practice in other cultures (Fontes, 2005). In the United States, many middle-class mothers prefer this arrangement as well; however, co-sleeping with a

EP 2.1.10a

young child and the risk of doing so is a prominent concern of the medical profession.

EP 2.1.7b

By Western standards, it is expected that an adolescent will gradually disengage from the parental–child subsystem, as they move toward young adulthood and perhaps prepare to leave home. Of course, this too is subject to cultural preferences. For example, in certain cultures, adolescents marry, although they will live with his or her family. In others, young adults live with their families until they are married. Therefore, fluid roles, bonding patterns, and rules as framed in Western society may not signal that a relationship is enmeshed or that a member is disengaged.

Disengaged Families

EP 2.1.10a

There are those families in which a member can become disengaged. Although families tolerate a wide range of individual variations, when a member becomes disengaged he or she is apt to feel a lack of family solidarity, loyalty, and a sense of belonging. In the absence of a sense of belonging, the member's relationship with others in the family system is limited or cut off. In consequence, a disengaged family member operates separate and apart from the family system. Such members may transfer their loyalties to others outside the family unit in an attempt to meet their relationship needs.

At times, when one of more members is disengaged they may form coalitions. But these alliances are apt to be fragile and short-lived, based on immediate gratification of the needs of individuals involved. Because of the transitory nature of such coalitions, members will likely abandon relationships once their needs are satisfied or an alliance no longer serves their purposes. Unfortunately bounding patterns based on coalitions and their under-involvement can cause the organization of the family system to become unstable and chaotic, and become factionalized, with leadership shifting on a moment-to-moment basis. It is also possible for a coalition of disengaged members to become isolated and alienated from one another. In such families, the relative lack of opportunity to sustain stable alliances typically proves detrimental to the emotional growth of individuals. Moreover, the resulting stress and anxiety related to the behavior or a disengaged member is disruptive to the family system.

EP 2.1.1c

There are times when your assessment and subsequent intervention can unwittingly result in or reinforce a member's disengagement, in particular, when your assessment is restricted to the needs of one family member, rather than with the family as a whole. This problem may be exacerbated in families that are deemed to be troubled. As a result, you may have a tendency to rescue a member (often a child) from dysfunctional family dynamics. An assessment in which the social worker gathered information from the teen but not the mother illustrates this point. The mother in the case has a history of substance abuse and the social worker concluded that she was incapable of participating in the assessment. The mother complained appropriately, however, that the social worker routinely came to her home and picked up her daughter, and that she had no idea what they were doing or what they talked about. The social worker's rationale for focusing on the daughter was that she had little hope of the mother changing, and that the needs of the daughter needed to be clarified. Furthermore, she reasoned that the daughter needed a positive influence in her life. In attending to the message from the mother, the social worker could have used the mother's complaint as an opportunity to engage her in the assessment process. The dynamic of rescuing can be perceived by a family to be an intrusion into the family's external family boundaries and the parental subsystem can feel powerless to decide the people and the type of information that are allowed, which can be disruptive to internal family dynamics. Of course, highly stressed parents may preempt the assessment process, and allow you to subordinate their parental role by temporarily assigning their role to you. For instance, a parent tells a child, "If you don't go to school, the social worker is going to send you away."

EP 2.1.10d

In assessing the various relationships and structural arrangements of a family, it is important for you to attend to those alignments between family members and outsiders that tug at family loyalties and cause acute family stress. For example, a grandparent may regularly take the side of a child in a family dispute. While a grandparent–grandchild alliance can be consoling to the child, the alliance can interfere with the ability the parent and the child to work out their difficulties. Of course, relationships between family members and grandparents or other relatives are not necessarily disruptive. These individuals may perform vital supportive functions and roles in families in that they are a significant connection to the family's history, values, and beliefs.

You should also attend to and be respectful of the boundaries and boundary maintenance function in families that are culturally derived as well as to subsystems or coalitions between family members and their patterns of relating (Okun, Fried & Okun, 1999). Keep in mind that the examples discussed previously emphasized prototypes. In actual practice, your assessment should consider each family's unique style of transacting with each other and with the environment and give credibility to the reality of their experience.

EP 2.1.4c

One last word of caution is related to the notion of the *parentified child*. This all-inclusive, generally negative term is used to describe a child who has responsibilities or performs roles generally associated with the parental subsystem. As such, the internal boundaries of the family can be confusing to you, and therefore you assess the situation as problematic. In truth, some families have flexible boundaries; children, out of necessity, have responsibilities that are critical to maintaining the family system. Moreover, different cultures recognize the age and stage of childhood at varying level or others may not observe them at all. Some rural farming families, for example, as well as those families at the lower end of the socioeconomic spectrum worldwide, may have children participate in the division of labor in the household as a matter of survival. Obviously, when compared to Western culture's preferred perception of childhood, you are likely to view this arrangement as less than ideal. Such cases warrant your attention if the role of the child exceeds the limits of safety, if a parent or other supervising adult is unavailable for a prolonged period of time, or if children are performing duties that affect their growth and well-being. Even so, you may assume an educational rather than a punitive role with parents, ensuring that they understand that the issue at hand is the health and safety of the child, rather the boundary arrangements in the family system.

Family Disengagement from External System

EP 2.1.7b

In light of the earlier discussion about family bounding patterns relative to the family's experience with the external environment, you should consider whether the entire family system has become disengaged or disconnected. Bounding patterns, for example, may represent a family's decision to separate or disengage from all or certain values and beliefs contrary to their own. For instance, families who have decided to home-school their children may have made this choice because they are dissatisfied with societal values. In this way, they are protecting family boundaries. Moreover, the experience with oppression and inequality can in fact result in families becoming disengaged. Perceiving themselves as being treated as outsiders, over time, these families may adapt actions, codes of conduct, and behaviors as a means of coping with being alienated. With little or no reciprocity between themselves and the larger environment, their disengagement essentially further reinforces their marginalized and separate status.

Family Power Structure

Aspects of power may be defined as psychological, economic, and social. This assessment dimension is primarily concerned with power as a dynamic process within the family system, since families as systems interact with and are influenced by other systems. Therefore, the distribution of power in a family can be determined by external structural arrangements that should be considered a part of assessing power within the family. Zimmerman (1995), for example, points to "the differences in male and female power and the results of policies and programs that disadvantage women" (p. 207). Miller (1994) also calls attention to multiple factors that influence power in the family system. Specifically, there are historical events that influence family structure, gender roles, and even courtship and marriage. Further, he asserts that "the family's construction of power is shaped in a context of neighborhood and community" (p. 224). In addition, the relevance of assessing power is evident in political processes, occupational opportunities, social class, race and ethnicity, and policies that "differentially affect the fortunes of families" (Miller, 1994, p. 224).

EP 2.1.10a

EP 2.1.4a

Families may experience a lack of power as a result of classism, bigotry, prejudice, discrimination, or historical oppression that has been institutionalized into the formal and informal fabric of society. Although we tend to point to gender-related power differences in other cultures, according to Okun, Fried, and Okun (1999), women of all cultures have limited power because of oppressive scripted role expectations. They also emphasize the experience of powerlessness for males in some racial groups as a result of oppression and inequality, which can lead to turmoil in the family. For instance, in the not too distant past in the United States, in comparison to racial and ethnic males, it was often easier for racial and ethnic women to gain employment, which of course marginalized the male's role in the family as the essential breadwinner.

In their analysis of family power, relative to policies and political structures, Lewis, Skyles, and Crosbie-Burnett (2000) point to the "allocation of goods and services that have differentially affected education, health, hunger, family structure and functioning, and life expectancy," especially among families of color and low-income families.

EP 2.1.4a

Power is inherent in your position as a professional as well as in the political and the social welfare organizations with whom a family is involved. Specifically, each has the ability to define family needs or functioning, the level of services a family can receive or whether they receive any services at all. These external vestiges of power influence family functioning and well-being irrespective of power differentials in the family structure.

Elements of Power within the Family System

EP 2.1.10a

Having alerted you to some of the external sources of power, we now turn to the process of assessing power within the family system. All families develop a power structure that defines the relative influence that each member has on other members, who participates in decisions, and the manner in which decisions are made. Because of this structure, the family system directs and maintains the behavior of individuals within acceptable limits and includes leadership roles that ensure family maintenance. Parental subsystems, for example, use the power vested in their roles to socialize, establish rules, and shape the behavior of minors in the family system.

One element of power relates to the capacity of dominant family members to impose their preferred interpretations or viewpoints on other members, in effect denying a meaning or reality other than their own (Kilpatrick & Holland, 1999, p. 29). The exercise of power can have consequences for the family, because the dominant member prescribes the manner in which other members speak about, act, or react to events or situations. Furthermore, the dominant individual can determine the flexibility and permeability of external and internal boundaries of the family system.

In some families, culture, customs, or traditions are enforced even though some members may question their value. They may cooperate to avoid conflict, however, thereby allowing the family to maintain a perception of homeostasis. For example, Okun, Fried, and Okun (1999) discussed the tensions that can occur in immigrant families when the dominant member's authority is challenged by youth in the family who have been exposed to more egalitarian relationships. At other times, a family member may undermine the dominant member's power by their covert behaviors. When all members do not embrace the power structure in the family, conflict can result. Power may also be leveraged in the form of scapegoating, a dynamic that focuses the attention and energy of the family on a particular member.

Power is a socially constructed dynamic that varies according to such factors as culture as well as preferences within the family system. In assessing power, you should listen to and observe family members so that you may better understand the nature of the power dynamic in their family. In the family system, power may be held both overtly and covertly. For instance, one individual may be formally acknowledged as the central figure in the family and thus have more power in family decision making. In traditional Western culture, at one point in time, this status was generally associated with the economic resources of the male. Even so, other, less visible members or subsystems can have significant covert power in the family. Certain members can have covert power. For example, an individual can hold power because of a disability or chronic condition; another can gain power because of their level of literacy, including literacy with technology, or as a result of the attainment of a level of education or income.

Distribution and Balance of Power

Families are often viewed as having a single, monolithic power structure, but this is not always true. In some modern families, one individual may be the primary decision maker in some, but not all situations; in other families, for example,
EP 2.1.10d

a gay or lesbian family, power can be equally share. Even in those families where, on a surface level, the male may be the central family figure, you should explore the extent to which he actually dominates family decisions to avoid making a premature assessment. Today's families are more diverse in both form and structure, causing some traditional roles to become less so, and others to evolve in their stead. In same-sex couples, for example, power roles are often shared. In other instances, power can reside in certain individuals because of their esteemed position in the family or as a result of family coalitions or subsystems. In addition, extended kin, clan, tribal, or family and friendship networks may hold power that becomes apparent during family decision making.

Shifts in Power

EP 2.1.10d

Power shifts can occur in a family depending on the situation or family structure and as a result of a crisis. In a time of crisis an individual's power can increase because he or she assumed leadership in handling the crisis. The extent to which children are able to influence the decisions of the parental subsystem or assume the decisive role illustrates their role in the family's power structure. In general, parents, the executive subsystem, hold power, yet, on a situational basis, a parent may delegate parental authority or involve children in family decision making. Situational shifts in power occur as the result of both inner and outer forces, for example, loss of employment, decline of a member's health, life-cycle changes, or opposition to family rules. In immigrant or refugee families, where English is a second language, a minor child may interpret for parents. This form of power is temporary and must not be construed as the child holding power beyond the particular situation.

Notably, power can shift in divorce and remarriage as interpersonal alliances tend to change in remarriage, separation, and divorce. Grandparents can lose or gain power, but children may acquire more power than they previously held when both parents resided in the same household. Unless parents have a joint custody arrangement, the parent that has sole custody of a child or children tends to have more power to make binding decisions about the children. Custody laws in the past have generally given women more power in custody decisions. An exception however is lesbian unions where societal discrimination of this family form can have precedence. Even in these unions, the biological mother is granted custody by the court and joint custody is not an option unless the other partner has legally adopted the child.

Multicultural Perspectives

EP 2.1.4a

Although almost all cultures tend to view males as central power figures, generalizations about power may be based on limited knowledge of the power nuances in different cultures. Many cultures are male oriented, so that females may appear to lack power in the traditional sense. The preceding section explored the question of who holds power and under what circumstances. In such assessments, caution is advised when making assumptions, especially when dealing with diverse groups. For instance, groups may differ in their gender-role definitions, expectations, and responsibilities, yet these roles may not be uniformly constructed as lacking in power. Women, grandparents, aunts or uncles, and other significant individuals included in the family system may have considerable power in the family, although their power may not be exercised in a way that is visible to an outside observer. Elders, for example, have powerful roles in some diverse families, including immigrant families and communities. Power can be derived in situations where the female is able to obtain employment rather than a male, because of discrimination. You should also be aware of an outsider's observation about male dominance and female subordination as a cultural ideal because it ignores the norm of "hembrismo" or "marianismo," the latter which emphasizes the status of the mother (Hines, Garcia-Preto, McGoldrick, Almeida, & Weltman, 1999). The covert power held by women in some cultures, despite what may be observed as their subservient status, is referred to by Rotunno and McGoldrick (1982) as a paradox: What may be observed as a cultural female script does not diminish the powerful role these women play in the family system. Therefore, in assessing power, the distribution of power is to be understood in family's cultural and situational frame of reference, which includes the covert and overt power of individuals.

Assessing Power

In your assessment of power, you must not only determine how power is distributed, but also who if anyone is formally designated as the leader, and to what extent covert power is designated to individual members. It is equally important to assess the extent to which family rules allows the family system to reallocate power so that members can adjust their roles to meet changing circumstances. Finally, you must assess whether or not family members are satisfied with the distribution or shifts in power. Topical areas in which you can develop questions that can guide your assessment include determining:

EP 2.1.10d

- *How power has been distributed in the family in the past and whether changing conditions of the family*

are threatening the established power base (McGoldrick, 1998; Okun, Fried & Okun, 1999).
- *Whether the distribution of power is gender-specific out of the necessity for the family to survive in a hostile environment (Okun, Fried & Okun, 1999).*
- *To what extent power is covertly held by members who have aligned to form a power bloc; and to what extent covert power accrues to individual members who are manifesting extreme symptoms.*
- *The extent to which the family systems allows power to be flexibly reallocated and permit roles to be adjusted to meet the demands of changing circumstances.*
- *How members view the distribution of power in the family. Even though the distribution is unequal, family members may be satisfied with the arrangement.*
- *The role of a family's culture in determining the distribution of power is also considered (Congress & Kung, 2005).*

All families have a structure in which power is allocated in some manner. Like family rules, power in the family system has a purpose. Unless power dynamics and the distribution of power have a significant role in family problems, it is inappropriate to attempt to make adjustments in this area. You should, however, assess the functionality of covert and overt power, keeping in mind that power in families can shift on a situational basis, and power can be distributed among many members on some level and at different times.

EP 2.1.10d

Key assessment questions that you can selectively use to address the functionality of the power structure include the following:

- *Is the family's power structure stable (even though it may be unfamiliar to you); does it allow the system to carry out its maintenance functions in a orderly manner?*
- *Are members of the family content with the relative distribution of power?*
- *In family processes, are evident family struggles over power causing the formation of destructive coalitions?*
- *Does the power structure meet individual psychological needs, and promote the health of the family system?*
- *Are members in competition for power, causing the power base to shift as individuals or coalitions compete for power?*
- *Does the power base reside within the executive subsystem or within covert coalitions in the family?*
- *Does the power structure allow the family to honor and maintain its cultural heritage?*
- *How does culture influence the power structure in the family?*
- *To what extent have external conditions necessitated power adjustments or shifts in the family?*

In addition to the preceding questions, key information about family power processes and operations may be understood by observing patterned behavior such as:

EP 2.1.10d

- *Who speaks for whom?*
- *Who speaks first and who comments?*
- *Who speaks the most often?*
- *Whose ideas are adopted in family decision making?*
- *Who agrees with or disrupts the speaker?*
- *Who seems to hold the ultimate authority for making decisions? Does this authority vary by the situation?*

Because of the potential variability, observing family interactions can seem like watching a tennis match; it may be useful for you to develop a simple grid that will help you track and subsequently answer these questions.

Family Decision-Making Processes

The family's style of decision making is closely tied to its power dimension. Families range along a continuum from the extreme of leaderless families, in which no one has sufficient power or motivation to determine or direct activities or to organize decision-making processes, to families in which absolute decision-making power is rigidly held by one member. Although effective deliberation and decision making are considered to be important in maintaining the well-being of the system, most families do not consciously select a modus operandi for making family decisions. Rather, the family's style of decision making usually evolves in its formative stages of development and is often patterned after decision-making approaches modeled by parents in the families or culture-of-origin. In some instances, persistent conflicts experienced by families can be traced back to the inability to resolve, at a covert level, incompatible expectations (emanating from

EP 2.1.10a

role models they have experienced) regarding the distribution of power and the manner in which decisions should be made in the family. As children are added to the system, they may be pulled into the situation, as neither parent is fully successful in wrestling power from the other.

Of course, approaches to decision making may change over the course of the family life cycle. Young children, for example, have fewer opportunities to fulfill the decider role. As they become adolescents and young adults, they may have more input into family decisions. Nonetheless, the parental subsystem retains the right of making final decisions. For some families, decision making may extend beyond the immediate family, reflecting the practices based on family tradition, race, or culture. In the traditional Hmong community, for example, decision making about health matters and the use of Western medicine requires the consultation and approval of esteemed individuals in the clan. Cultural norms also play a role in decision making. A Native American colleague who is a member of the Upper Sioux, Lakota Tribe, advised that decisions are made based on their influence on the future. Given the many variants of culture and the options for distribution of power that may exist in a family, decision making may shift on a situational basis and be influenced by other factors.

EP 2.1.10d

In the assessment of decision making in the family, the overall goal is to determine the extent to which decisions facilitate family well-being, disrupt the family system, or cause conflict. Prolonged or unresolved conflict may factionalize the family unit and prompt some members to disengage. To assess the decision-making processes found in families, it is important to understand the elements that are inherent in effective problem solving with family systems. The following guidelines for effective decision making were adapted from Satir (1967), with additional notations of some general cultural variants, since they also influence this process.

1. *Decision making requires open feedback and self-expression among family members.* Skills involved are compromise, agreeing to disagree, and negotiation to resolve differences. In some instances, culturally derived roles and scripts may not support feedback.

2. *Members should be able to say what they think and feel without fear of being judged or conflict* between themselves and others in the family. Conflict as defined by U.S. standards may in fact be the manner in which individuals in other cultures habitually interact. In fact, it is expected and tolerated in some cultures, and can include "raised voices and insults." In other cultures, nonverbal cues my signal conflict, and in others, "people are expected to become emotional and it is not necessary that everyone agrees" (McGoldrick, 1998; Okun, Fried & Okun, 1999, pp. 40–44).

3. *Without open feedback and self-expression, decision-making processes will be unresponsive to the needs of individual family members* that emerge as the system goes through transitional developmental phases that demand adaptation to internal and external stresses and crises.

4. *Decision making requires a philosophical or attitudinal set on the part of each family member that all members of the system "count"*—that is, the family must agree that each member's needs will be taken into consideration in decision making that will affect another member.

5. *Members think in terms of needs rather than solutions that are consistent with the systems perspective.* Members of families are often conditioned by life experiences to see a problem–solution dichotomy, in which there is a narrow either or perspective in decision making. In some cultures, the needs and interests of the collective takes precedence over those of the individual. In essence, decision making may include negotiation and compromise rather than struggles around competing needs.

6. *Family members are able to generate alternatives.* This element is much like group brainstorming, in which members generate options, no matter how far fetched, without facing criticism or censorship. Individuals manifest this skill when they draw from a repertoire of ideas that are not merely variations on a single theme but rather different categories of solutions to a given problem. In the assessment process, then, one of your tasks may be to determine to what extent families identify alternatives in contrast to quarreling over competing solutions.

7. *Family members are to process and weigh alternatives.* Decisions may be made in families after gathering information, receiving input from members, and deliberating on the options. Alternatively, they may be made impulsively without gathering or weighing relevant information or without considering the needs of family members in relation to possible solutions.

8. *Effective decision making requires that the family organize itself so as to carry out decisions by assigning tasks to individual members.* Cultural variants may include, age and gender roles, and responsibilities and power. Planning to implement a decision is just as important as making the decision. Considerations also include whether the family system is so disorganized that making and implementing decisions is not possible. The process may also break down at the implementation stage because members lack motivation to carry out decisions because their input was not elicited or considered.

9. *Effective decision making requires room for negotiation and adjustment* of earlier decisions based on new information and emerging individual and family needs. Some systems, of course, are much more responsive and flexible to change than others.

EP 2.1.10d

Assessing Family Decision Making

In assessing the family's decision-making style, you should elicit information and view the processes and potential cultural variants based on the preceding criteria. Bear in mind that the family is the best source of information relative to functionality of decision-making style.

EP 2.1.4c

The skills and processes described in the assessment of decision-making are perceived and encouraged in Western culture. Therefore, as you assess the family decision-making style, it is important that you observe and respect variations.

For example:

- Decision making as an autonomous function of the family unit is not an ideal in all families, and others such as extended family, clan, or tribal members can be involved.
- The skills and processes may not be fully developed or desirable in some families despite their roots in Western culture, thus, the family may wish to preserve a hierarchy in roles and power.
- Some families may not have a frame of reference for joint decision making, and in fact have values that are in direct contradiction to the criteria for effective decision making.
- The processes can vary in same-sex couple families, because there may be less conflict about decisions as the relationship may not precisely mirror that of heterosexual couples.

As the above examples indicate, decision making in families is neither uniform nor universal. Therefore, in assessing families, it is important that you recognize that each family has a style that is compatible with their values and which they believe to be the most effective. McAdoo (1993), for example, after studying diverse families in which decision-making styles tended to be related to socioeconomic class, stresses the importance of family context in understanding decision making and the family's broader relational patterns.

Family Goals

The family is a social unit in which members typically cooperate and coordinate their efforts so as to achieve certain goals. Families may establish goals in one of two ways: For instance, they can adopt goals that are consistent with those of the larger society, for example, socializing children, transferring major cultural patterns, and meeting certain personal, nurturing, and safety needs of family members. In the second instance, partners or spouses bring individual goals with them into the family, including those that are based on their family or culture of origin. Optimally, as a family develops its own goals, they will be able to critique the various sources and decide which ones are best for their family.

EP 2.1.10a

Eventually the goals that families adopt and support should be openly expressed, and recognized. Goals like, "We want to save money to buy a house" and "It is important for the young to know the old ways" are examples of openly expressed goals. In effect, all members embrace the openly expressed goals of the family unit. In contrast, covert goals, that is, goals that are vague, can influence the behavior of family members. Difficulties in family interactions can occur as such goals may not be the will of all members or even at their level of awareness until a member behaves in an incongruous manner. Even though covert goals may not be openly expressed, they can be observed in the behaviors of the family. Covert goals that have a profound influence on behavior might be, "This family has to present a picture of being an ideal family." Most families have a combination of both goal types. For instance, families who are new arrivals to Western society may want their children to maximize the opportunities of the new country, but also want them to have a connection to and honor their traditional roots. The first goal related to opportunities is explicit; the other can be unspoken, yet it is expected to be understood by family members.

Assessment: Family Functioning in Diverse Family and Cultural Contexts   269

In most families, members vary with regard to the goals that each considers to be important, and the values that each attaches to common goals. As in any organization, a family functions best when there is a high degree of consensus concerning family goals. At the same time, while a consensus about goal allows the family system to have a future orientation, maintain stability, and cope with stressors, family goals should also consider the unique needs, interest, and wishes of individual members. It is easier for members to pursue goals that are explicit. Less agreement is likely to occur when goal are vague, especially when members are pressured and when goals are developed by the most powerful and influential members of the family.

When families are in crisis, they may rank order their goal because they are forced to choose between competing goals. For example, a family faced with a sudden drastic reduction in income may decide that a priority goal is to maintain an adequate diet for the children, and therefore allocate family resources accordingly.

Family goals can be conventional, for instance, eventually buying a home, but the manner in which a goal is achieved may conflict with societal and professional expectations. To illustrate, consider the case of a single mother with three children whose priority goal is to move her family to a better and safer neighborhood. To accomplish this goal, she holds down two jobs, one of which requires her to work the evening shift in a convenience store. Fortunately, the store is adjacent to the apartment building in which the family lives. The 12-year-old child has responsibility of caring for her younger siblings, ages 6 and 8. This arrangement had generally worked, and the mother checked on the children during her breaks. One night, a neighbor reported to the authorities that the children were home alone, which resulted in an investigation by child protection services. The mother is devastated, angry, and confused. To her this child care arrangement is reasonable and its intent honorable because it would allow her to reach the goal of moving the family to a better, safer neighborhood. As social workers assess goals, they should be mindful of the fact that goals have context. So, it would be important to understand the mother's child care arrangement decision in light of her goal for her family.

EP 2.1.10d

The following questions are intended to assist you in assessing family goals for both strengths and difficulties:

- *Are goals that guide the family group clear to all members?*
- *To what extent are members aware of the family's overriding goals?*
- *Is there a shared consensus among members regarding major goals and the priorities assigned to these goals?*
- *Has the family experienced conflict because of a lack of consensus regarding the primary goals of individual family members?*
- *How functional are commonly held goals in meeting the needs of individual members and promoting the well-being of the family unit as a whole?*
- *To what extent are patterns of interaction related to covert goals within the family?*
- *How do external forces or pressures influence family goals?*
- *To what extent are family goals signs of strengths and hopes for the future?*

While family goals may vary and can break down in times of crisis, family goals that are identified during the assessment process represent a family strength. During the assessment process, the family's responses to assessment questions allow you to observe the family's patterns of interaction relative to other assessment dimensions. For instance, who speaks first, are family members able to negotiate with each other, are goals openly expressed or is there tension within the family about certain goals? If you assess family goals without also examining the family's interactions and context you may misunderstand the purpose of a family's goals. As illustrated in the case example, it is important that social workers not view a family's pursuit of a goal as problematic, unless of course it is illegal. Instead, it is important to determine the specific goals of the family and to assess them in their appropriate context. Family goals function to maintain the family system and demonstrate a future orientation and family aspiration, all of which are family strengths.

Family Myths and Cognitive Patterns

Family rules were discussed in this chapter, in particular the way in which they influence all aspects of family life. Rules have both a behavioral component and a cognitive component. That is, the behaviors manifested by family members flow from, and are inextricably related to, shared perceptions or myths about one another, the family unit, and the world at large. These shared perceptions may be congruent with the views of neutral outside

EP 2.1.10a

observers or they may be distortions of reality. In other words, members uncritically hold on to ill-founded, self-deceptive, well-systematized beliefs. Such distortions are often part of the beliefs or myths subscribed to by the family that help shape, maintain, and justify goals, decision making, interactional patterns, and relationships. The following case illustrates this point.

CASE EXAMPLE

Over the past five years, 12 year-old Jeffrey has had conflicted interactions with his teachers because of his open defiance of classroom rules, argumentative behavior, and physical skirmishes with other children. Responding to these problems, and in support of their goal to provide Jeffrey with an excellent education, the parents had changed his enrollment from one school to another three times during the past five years. Both parents shared the myth that the various teachers did not try to understand Jeffrey, and further that he was a brilliant child. Given their perceptual set, influenced by their cognition of Jeffrey, the parents regarded their contact with each school as a battleground in which they must argue, protest, protect their rights, and defend their son. Their continually overbearing and confrontational style alienated school personnel, pushing them to take extreme stands on issues that might otherwise be mutually negotiated. The parents' constant negative and angry comments at home regarding Jeffrey's teachers and his school reinforce his disruptive classroom behavior.

In the preceding case example, the behaviors and cognitive processes of the family are mutually reinforcing. The myth that Jeffrey is okay and the school is unreasonable, in essence, determined the predictable negative responses of the parents and the school personnel. In turn, the family's negative encounters with the school officials reinforce and confirm their perceptions that the world is dangerous has been inattentive to their son's needs and therefore cannot be trusted.

Sometimes, systems, either because of their institutional protocols or the attitude of their representatives, can in fact be unresponsive to an individual's needs. They too may have constructed myths (e.g., poor or minority parents are unreliable) and these myths inform their interactions with families.

Social cognitions play a role in how people interpret and remember and access information, and how they categorize internal and external events. Thematically organized information is as a "cognitive schema" (Berlin & Marsh, 1993, p. 5). In a general sense, schemas are generalizations that individuals rely on to process information about attributes and guide their perceptions (e.g., Jeffrey's parents). Imagine, for example, the cognition that certain families with similar attributes are more capable than others. Cognitions that are associated with schema can persist long after a particular event or episode has occurred (Berlin & Marsh, 1993).

Not all schemas and family myths are problematic, of course. They become so however, when they are used to keep a family member in line or in character as defined by the family. The social worker should assess potentially damaging and persistent beliefs or myths within a family that single out one member as being different or deviant. Do family beliefs and myths, for example, result in the assignment of irreversible labels, such as sick, bad, crazy, or lazy or do they scapegoat a member who is blamed for all of the family's problems?

Attributes thought to be positive, like "handsome," "smart," and "ambitious" are based on myths and beliefs and can also label individuals, however, the family may not recognize that such labels can be as burdensome as negative labels. In essence, these labels can also separate and estrange members from one another. For instances, other family members may resent the inordinate amount of attention, praise, and recognition accorded to an individual on the basis of the myth of superiority.

Regardless of whether family myths are positive or negative, they stereotype the role of certain family members, causing other members to relate to them on the basis of a presumed single characteristic. Further, a wide range of attributes, attitudes, and strengths tend to be overlooked. In effect, myths and beliefs and the accompanying labels only serve to limit the behavioral options available to an individual member as well as others within the family.

Family Roles

Family roles may be thought of as being complementary and reciprocal, and family members as being differentiated

into social roles within the family system. Role theory, when applied to the family system, suggests that each person in a family fulfills many roles that are integrated into the family's structure and that represent certain expected, permitted, or forbidden behaviors. Family roles are not independent of each other. Rather, role behavior involves two or more persons engaging in reciprocal transactions. Roles within the family system may be assigned on the basis of legal or chronological status or cultural and societal scripts. In many families, role assignments are based on gender. At the same time, as with power and decision making, roles may be flexible and diffused throughout the family system.

Roles and role expectations are learned through the process of social interactions, and they can be based on status or gender. Role status locates the individual in a particular contextual social position. In contrast, the role that an individual fills in the family system has specific attributes, that is, behaviors that are expected of people who have a particular status or situation.

EP 2.1.10d

In sorting out roles in the family system, individual role behavior may be *enacted, prescribed*, or *perceived* (Longres, 1995). In an enacted role, a mother engages in the actual behavior, for example caretaking, relative to her status or position. A prescribed role is influenced by the expectations that others hold with regard to a social position. For example, despite the changes in families, in a family's interaction with a bank officer, a male is almost always presumed to be the head of a household or the primary decision-makers in the family. Perceived role behavior involves the expectations of self, relative to their social position. For instance, an employed female may conclude that she can manage multiple responsibilities.

Roles are both learned and accrued. The role of parent, for example, is accrued, but it is also learned from others and through experience. Similarly, the various roles that exist between couples in a relationship are learned based on interactions over time. Satisfaction with the respective role behavior is indicative of a level of harmony in interpersonal family relationships. Janzen and Harris (1997) refer to harmonized interpersonal roles as independent-dependent relationships. In addition, roles may be *complementary* or *symmetrical*. The role relationship between a parent and a child, for example, is a complementary, independent–dependent role relationship in which the needs of both are satisfied. In contrast, in a symmetrical relationship, both parties function as equals, for instance, the division of household or child rearing responsibilities or decision making are shared, instead of based on gender roles.

Roles for the most part are not static, but rather they can evolve as a result of family interactions and negotiations. As a consequence, they often defy traditional stereotypical role behaviors. In actuality, role relationships in most families operate along a continuum and may be characterized as complementary or symmetrical or quid pro quo as a result of negotiation.

Life transitions and conflict often demand changes, flexibility, and modifications in role behavior. A family may experience *role transition* difficulties in making the necessary adjustments when for instance an elderly relative comes to live in their home. The elderly parent may experience difficulties in adjusting to becoming dependent on adult children. For example, an elderly person who is no longer able to drive, can feel that they are a burden, and even resent the loss of their independence. Another significant change for some parents is adjusting to the void when children leave the home. Conflict in the family may occur when individuals become dissatisfied with their roles, when there is disagreement about roles, or when individuals holding certain or multiple roles become overburdened.

Interrole conflict can occur when an individual is faced with excessive, competing, and multiple role obligations, especially when two or more roles are incompatible. For instance, wife or partner, mother, daughter, employee and fulfilling the responsibilities associated with these enacted and perceived roles can cause an individual to experience conflict in juggling multiple role demands (Rooney, G. D., 1997).

Understanding the roles and role behavior within the family, including the way in which roles are defined, and role conflict are important elements in the assessment of the family role dimension. In the assessment, you will want to determine what roles assignment in the family is based on, for example, age or gender, rather than such factors are abilities, need, and interest. As you assess the role behavior in any family, you will probably note a number of individual and family strengths, like how well members flexibly adapt to changing roles, their role-performance behavior. Because each culture or family form may have its own definitions of roles, social workers must also determine and assess the goodness of fit with the needs of family members. Assessment then must consider whether

EP 2.1.10d

members are satisfied with respective roles and, if a member is dissatisfied, whether the family is amenable to modifying or changing determined roles.

Communication Styles of Family Members

EP 2.1.10a

One theme that cuts across many cultural groups is that of patterns discouraging the open expression of feelings. Although Western culture emphasizes the value that openness and honesty are best, the reality is that most people have considerable difficulty in asserting themselves or in confronting others, particularly in ways that are facilitative. In all instances, you must first determine whether the family's communication patterns and styles negatively affect members' relationships and further whether change is desirable, including weighing the cultural implications.

EP 2.1.7b

Another communication style that transcends culture, and that may be generational, is the multiple ways that people communicate with each other. Youth, for example, as does every other generation of young people, use words, phrases, short cuts, and abbreviations in their communications repertoire. Today's youth are more likely to use and rely on email, text messaging, personal web pages, or social networks as a primary means of interacting with each other. Of course, communicating in this manner is a preference, using shortcuts to communicate has become a style. While these modes of communicating are not problematic, they may not conform to some of the conventional communication rules. For example using "I" statements or incomplete sentences, dramatic interpretations and informality are communication modes that are generally thought of as communication barriers. This form of communicating can be problematic in families, especially between adults and younger members.

EP 2.1.10d

Whether or not family communication patterns are culturally influenced or otherwise determined, they may be faulty, causing significant problems for family members. In assessing the impact of a family's communication styles, you must be aware of the complexities of communication and be prepared to assess the functionality of members' communication styles to the extent to which there is congruence and clarity in how members communicate with each other.

VIDEO CASE EXAMPLE

Home for the Holidays 1

Jackie and Anna scheduled the session at Jackie's request. Both women are Caucasian and appear to be close in age (25–35 years old). Jackie, a chef, owns the restaurant where she works.

The couple has been together for five years and has lived together for the past year. They initiated couples' therapy because of disagreements about their holiday plans. They both would like to spend the time together. Jackie, however, feels pulled to visit her family during the holidays because they live in another state and she has not seen them in a while. Anna states that she does not feel completely comfortable at the home of Jackie's parents. She perceives them as distant and avoiding meaningful contact because of their discomfort with their relationship. In fact, when they attended a family wedding, Anna was not invited to stand with the family when pictures were taken.

Jackie recently came out to her parents as a lesbian. When she disclosed to them that she was moving in with her significant other, Anna, her parents were quiet and took up other activities. This withdrawal behavior is normalized in Jackie's family. She explained that in her family, "there is little outward expression and we don't make a big deal about everything." Nonetheless, Jackie does recognize her parent's discomfort with her sexuality. Anna acknowledged a difference between their family styles, remarking that in her family "there were no secrets" and that "everyone's state of affairs was open for discussion." Anna would like Jackie to broach the subject of her sexuality with her parents a second time to "strengthen the connection between Jackie and her parents, to hasten Jackie's parents' acceptance of our relationship."

When asked to explore the meaning that this conversation would hold for her, Jackie expressed feeling pushed by the request and that it felt like an ultimatum. For Jackie, there was too much at stake for her to risk another conversation with her parents at this time. In her mind, the worst-case scenario being that her parents would shut her out. Hearing Jackie's interpretation of the request as an ultimatum and the pressure that Jackie was feeling, Anna clarified and softened her position. To Anna, the conversation "would help Jackie open up more."

> Anna also stated that as is the case in her family of origin, "Jackie does not communicate at home."
>
> Concerning their plans for the holiday, Anna agreed to go to Jackie's house. The two made plans to cook a meal together for the family and to give gifts from both of them, as a sign of unity. Jackie agreed to consider plans to hold hands with Anna at dinner; she requested time to discuss this at the next session. Their overall goal is to improve their communication with each other.

Congruence and Clarity of Communication

EP 2.1.10d

Family members convey messages through both verbal and nonverbal channels and qualify those messages through other verbal and nonverbal messages. A task for social workers is to assess the *congruency*, that is, whether there is correspondence between the various verbal and nonverbal elements of messages. Congruence and clarity may also be related to a goal to which not all family members agree. To illustrate the clarity and congruence in communication follow the dialogue between Jackie and Anna in *Home for the Holidays 1* in their session with Kim, the social worker. As you watch the interview, how would you describe the congruency of Anna's messages? For example, Anna would like Jackie to broach the subject of her sexuality with her parents. The content of her message is clear, but Jackie and Anna's goals are dissimilar, which causes tension in their relationship.

According to Satir (1967) and other communication theorists, messages may be qualified at any one of three communication levels:

Verbal level: When people explain the intent of their messages, they are speaking at a metacommunication level. For example, the implied message in Anna's insistence that Jackie talk to her parents is: If you really cared about my feelings, you would stand up to your parents about our relationship. Implied messages are also a form of metacommunicating. Contradictory communications occur when two or more opposing messages are sent in sequence via the same verbal channel. For example, Anna to Jackie regarding Jackie's discomfort in talking to her parents about her sexuality has two contrasting messages: You should follow my advice—you need to make your own decisions.

Nonverbal level. People qualify their communications through many nonverbal modes, including gestures, facial expressions, tone of voice, posture, and the intensity of eye contact. Nonverbal messages may reinforce or contradict verbal messages (Anna's parents invite the couple for the holidays). But their nonverbal message contradicts or modifies their verbal message (Jackie is not included in the family's photos).

Contextual level. The situation in which communication occurs, reinforces or disqualifies the verbal and nonverbal expressions of a speaker. For example, Jackie feels punished by what she perceives as a "right now" ultimatum from Anna, but as Jackie turns to Anna, her facial expression and tone is softer. The contextual level which Anna sends the message to Jackie qualifies her verbal expression. In other instances, nonverbal expressions will have an opposite effect, when there is a mismatch between the content of the verbal and nonverbal message.

Functional communicators identify discrepancies between levels of communication and seek clarification when a person's words and expressions are incongruent. Vital to assessment, then, is the task of ascertaining the extent to which there is *congruence* between the verbal, nonverbal, and contextual levels of messages on the part of individuals in the family system. In addition to considering the congruence of communications, it is important to assess the *clarity* of messages.

The term *mystification* (Laing, 1965) describes how some families befuddle or mask communications and obscure the nature and source of disagreements and conflicts in their relationships. Mystification of communications can be accomplished by myriad kinds of maneuvers, including disqualifying another person's experience (Anna to Jackie, "You need to talk to your parents"). In this statement, Anna does not seem to respect Jackie's reluctance to talk to her parents, thereby disqualifying her feelings. Other maneuvers can include addressing responses to no one in particular even though the intent of the speaker is to convey a message to a certain person, using evasive responses that effectively obscure knowledge of the speaker, or utilizing sarcastic responses that have multiple meanings. Some couples use their children or pets to convey messages to each other.

Family rules, interactions, and communication patterns often accompany couples and play out in their relationship with each other. For example, Anna states, "In my family there are no secrets, every one's state of affairs is open for discussion." Jackie on the other hand wishes to maintain homeostasis in her family by adhering to the family rule of "We don't make a big deal about everything." Clearly Jackie and Anna have had prior conversations about their relationship and the response from Jackie's parents. They are in different stages of coming out. In their sequence of interactions, Anna appears to perceive Jackie and her family as the problem in their relationship. For example, Anna pushes Jackie to talk to her parents again, which in her mind is a premium in their relationship. Jackie is understandably reluctant to have this conversation with her parents, so the repetitive, patterned interactional cycle between the couple continues.

Barriers to Communication

In Chapter 7, we identified a number of barriers to communication that, when utilized by social workers, block client communications and hamper the therapeutic progress. Likewise, family members use these and similar responses in their communications with each other, thereby preventing meaningful exchanges and creating tension in relationships. Response categories that represent obstacles to open communications, in that they prevent genuine dialogue in relationships, are highlighted in Table 10-4.

EP 2.1.10d

The assessment of communication barriers also includes nonverbal behaviors—for instance, glaring, turning away from a family member, fidgeting, shifting posture, pointing a finger, or rolling their eyes or other facial expressions that show disgust or disdain. Nonverbal behaviors present obstacles to communication when there are discrepancies between verbal and nonverbal levels of communication.

All families have communication barriers within their conversational repertoires. Members of some families, however, monitor their own communications and adjust their manner when their response has an adverse impact on another person. As you observe the communication styles of families, it is important to assess three issues:

- *The presence of patterned negative communications.*
- *The pervasiveness of such negative patterns.*
- *The relative ability of individual members of the system to modify communication styles.*

EP 2.1.10d

In addition to assessing the preceding factors, it is vital to ascertain the various combinations of communication styles that occur repetitively as family member systems relate and react to one another. For instance, one individual may frequently dominate, criticize, attack, or accuse the other, whereas the other may defend, apologize, placate, or agree. In an exchange in which one member continues to attack or accuse another member, the other tends to continue to defend his or her position, thus manifesting a *"fault-defend"* pattern of communication. Attacks or accusations generally take the form of "You never ..." in which case the other defends himself or herself by providing examples that contradict the accusation. In such situations, even though the topic of conflict or the content of the discussion may change, the manner in which couples or family members relate to each other and orchestrate their scenario remains unchanged. Further, repetitions of the same type of interchanges tend to be manifested across many other areas of the family's interaction. The thematic configurations that occur in families' or couples' communication tend to be limited, but they reinforce tensions in the relationships. Your task as the social worker is to assess their thematic communicating pattern, including the context in which the fault–defend sequence repeatedly occurs.

Receiver Skills

In assessing couple or family communication, focus on how they send and receive messages in a manner that facilitates their communication. A critical dimension of communication is the degree of receptivity or openness of family members to the inner thoughts and feelings of other members in the system. Receptivity is manifested by the use of certain receiving skills, which will be discussed shortly. Again, a caution: These skills are in keeping with Western traditions, and therefore the assessment

EP 2.1.10d

TABLE-10-4 COMMUNICATION BARRIERS

Prematurely shifting the subject or avoiding topics
Asking excessive questions, dominating interactions
Sympathizing, excusing, or giving reassurance or advice
Mind reading, diagnosing, interpreting, or overgeneralizing
Dwelling on negative historical events in a relationship
Making negative evaluations, blaming, name-calling, or criticizing
Directing, threatening, admonishing
Using caustic humor, excessive kidding, or teasing
Focusing conversations on oneself

© Cengage Learning 2013

should include the extent to which these skills are consistent with the preferences of some racial or cultural families.

Before considering aspects of receiver skills, it should be stressed that a majority of families operate along a continuum with regard to their skills in verbal and nonverbal skills. You may observe response patterns in some families that convey understanding and demonstrate respect for a sender's message. In other families, the receptivity of a message can result in responses such as ridicule, negative evaluations, or depreciation of character. Still in other families, members may engage in "dual monologues"; that is, they communicate simultaneously, which to the casual observer might appear to be a free-for-all. Family members may also use words, sayings, or gestures specific to their family or reference group. In general, facilitative receiver skills invite, welcome, and acknowledge the views and perceptions of others. For example, free-for-all conversations invite, even encourage responses, but not in the way that may be the most familiar to you. In such situations, family members feel free to express agreement or disagreement, even though doing so may sometimes spark conflict. Facilitative responses that convey understanding and acceptance include the following:

- *Physical attending (i.e., direct eye contact, receptive body posture, hand gestures, attentive facial expressions)*
- *"Listening" or paraphrasing responses by family members that restate in fresh words the essence of a speaker's message (e.g., "Man, you said ..." or as a youth might say, "I feel you")*
- *Responses by receivers of messages that elicit clarification of messages (e.g., "Tell me again, I'm not sure what you meant" or "Am I right in assuming you meant...?")*
- *Brief responses that prompt further elaboration by the speaker (e.g., "Oh," "I see," "Tell me more")*

Sender Skills

EP 2.1.10d

Another facet of assessing communication styles and skills is the extent to which members of families can share their inner thoughts and feelings with others in the system. Becvar and Becvar (2000b) refer to this quality as the ability of individual family members to express themselves clearly as feeling, thinking, acting, valuable, and separate individuals and to take responsibility for their thoughts, feelings, and actions.

Operationalized, "I" messages are messages phrased in the first person that openly and congruently reveal either pleasant or unpleasant feelings, thoughts, or reactions experienced by the speaker ("I feel ...," "I think ...," "I want ..."). For the social worker, an essential task is to assess the extent to which the climate in the family allows members to be candid, open, and congruent in their communications.

This climate stands in sharp contrast to the situation in which family communications are characteristically indirect, vague, and guarded and individuals fail to take responsibility for their feelings, thoughts, or participation in events. Instead of "I" messages, family members are likely to use "you" messages that obscure or deny their responsibility, or that attribute responsibility for the feelings to others (e.g., "You've got me so rattled, I forgot"). Such messages are barriers to communication, and are often replete with injunctions (e.g., "you should" or "you ought") concerning another's behavior or negatively evaluate the message of the sender (e.g., "You shouldn't feel that way").

In assessing communication styles of families, you must gauge the extent to which individual members have the skills to utilize the facilitative categories identified in the preceding list. So that you and the family understand their communication style, part of the assessment can include asking them to keep track of the extent to which individual members (and the group as a whole) utilize facilitative communication skills. A simple grid with the relevant indicators can be developed and responses can be rated as a plus or minus by other family members.

Responses That Acknowledge Strength and Achievement and Accredit Growth

Critical to assessing family communication styles is the extent to which messages contribute to the development of self-confidence and consistently validate a person's worth and potential. In contrast, are the patterns and repertoires that you observe, consist of constant negative messages (e.g., putdowns, attacks, or criticism) or otherwise humiliate or invalidate the experience of others in the family? It is also advisable to keep in mind that a family experience with internal and external stressors may, in fact, challenge even previously effective communication skills.

Family Life Cycle

The family life cycle is the final dimension of family assessment. It encompasses the developmental stages through which families as a whole must pass. Based on the seminal work of Duvall (1977) and other theorists, Carter and McGoldrick

EP 2.1.10a

(1988) developed a conceptual framework of the life cycle of the middle-class American family. This model, which focuses on the entire three- or four-generational system as it moves through time, includes both predictable development events (e.g., birth, marriage, retirement) and unpredictable events that may disrupt the life-cycle process (e.g., untimely death, birth of a developmentally delayed child, divorce, chronic illness, war).

Carter and McGoldrick (1988; 2005) identified six stages of family development, all of which address nodal events related to the comings and goings of family members over time:

1. Unattached young adult
2. New couple
3. Family with young children
4. Family with adolescents
5. Family that is launching children
6. Family in later life

EP 2.1.10d

To master these stages, families must successfully complete certain tasks. The unattached young adult, for example, must differentiate from the family of origin and become a "self" before joining with another person to form a new family system. The new couple and the families of origin must renegotiate their relationships with one another. The family with young children must find the delicate balance between over- and under-parenting. In all of these stages, problems are most likely to appear when an interruption or dislocation in the unfolding family life cycle occurs, signaling that the family is "stuck" and having difficulty moving through the transition to its next phase.

Variations in the life cycle are, of course, highly likely to occur in today's world. Families can change, readjust, and cope with stressful transitions; both normative and nonnormative that occurs within the life cycle span (McKenry & Price, 2000). In the modern life cycle of families, as Meyer (1990) notes, the ground rules have changed as far as the timing and sequence of events are concerned. In much of our society, education, work, love, marriage or a committed relationship, childbirth, and retirement are now out of synch. Older adults return to school; adult children live with their parents; and childbirth is no longer within the exclusive realm of the traditional family form. Because of various changes, one life cycle phase may not necessarily progress in a linear fashion. In this world, life events are not preordained. Instead, they are more likely to be atomistic, mixed-and-matched responses to self-definition and opportunity (Meyer, 1990, p. 12).

Variations also occur in the family life cycle among cultures. Every culture marks off stages of living, each with its appropriate expectations, defining what it means to be a man or woman, to be young, to grow up and leave home, to get married and have children, and to grow old and die. Exploring the meaning of the life cycle with diverse families is particularly critical to determine important milestones from their perspective. Cultural variants that have a negative connotation in Western society include the legal versus the culturally derived age for marriage, family responsibilities, and roles for children. Families from other countries may, therefore, experience adverse reactions to practices that were common in their country of origin. Because culture plays an important role in family progression and life-cycle expectations, it cannot be avoided as an essential dimension in the assessment of family functioning at a particular development stage in the life cycle.

Summary

This chapter introduced systems concepts and dimensions that will facilitate your assessment of families. Families are not made up of equals, nor do they reflect in their totality the preferred norms of functioning. The systems perspective is useful for understanding family context, processes, interaction, and structure and in assessing both internal and external factors that contribute to or hamper family functioning. As a social system, families create their own implicit rules, power structure, forms of communication, and patterns of negotiating and problem solving. They also influence and are influenced by transactions in the larger social environment.

Irrespective of their configuration, composition, class, race, ethnicity, or social identity, families play an essential role in meeting the needs of their constituent members. The task of assessing family functioning has never been more challenging than it is today, because of the changing definition of the family as well as the greater diversity of racial and ethnic groups in the United States. It is vitally important that we as social workers respect family and cultural variants with respect to leadership, hierarchy, decision-making processes, patterns of interactions, and communication styles.

As a final note, we want to emphasize that for the most part the dimensions of assessment discussed in this chapter have evolved from a Western perspective with regard to the family system and its functioning. The extent to which all aspects of these dimensions may be observed among diverse groups is not well documented in the literature. As such, family context (i.e., culture) is a highly salient factor in the assessment process with diverse families, as it may determine to a large extent the family's rules, roles, bounding, or communication patterns as well as the family's experience with other social systems.

CourseMate

Access an integrated eBook and chapter-specific learning tools including glossary terms, chapter outlines, relevant web links, videos, and practice quizzes. Go to **www.cengagebrain.com.**

CHAPTER 11
Social Work Groups: Formation and Assessment

CHAPTER OVERVIEW

Groups instill hope and encouragement, universalize experiences, break down isolation, and allow members to experience altruism and the satisfaction of helping others (Pack-Brown, Whittington-Clark, & Parker, 1998). In groups, clients grapple with existential questions, learn coping skills for life experiences, and experience healing through cohesion and mutuality. These powerful features are common to an array of well-designed and well-executed treatment groups (Reid, K. E., 2002). Groups can provide a powerful mechanism for change whether they are used as the only intervention or in conjunction with individual counseling, family work, or other treatments

Social workers plan and lead groups in a variety of settings and with an array of populations. This chapter describes essential processes in developing the purpose of the group, forming and structuring the group, and conducting appropriate assessments with a variety of group types. Specifically, you will develop knowledge in:

- The distinctions between task and treatment groups and different group subtypes
- The steps in planning groups
- The steps in recruiting and screening group members
- Developing individual and group goals
- Identifying individual and group patterns in behaviors and communications
- Understanding the ethical considerations in group work
- The application of group concepts to a case example

EPAS COMPETENCIES IN THE 11TH CHAPTER

This chapter will give you the information needed to meet the following practice competencies:

2.1.2b Make ethical decisions by applying standards of the National Association of Social Workers Code of Ethics and, as applicable, of the International Federation of Social Workers/International Association of Schools of Social Work Ethics in Social Work Statement of Principles

2.1.2c Tolerate ambiguity in resolving ethical conflicts

2.1.2d Apply strategies of ethical reasoning to arrive at principled decisions

2.1.3b Analyze models of assessment, prevention, intervention, and evaluation

2.1.4c Recognize and communicate understanding of the importance of difference in shaping life experiences

2.1.6b Use research evidence to inform practice

2.1.7a Utilize conceptual frameworks to guide the processes of assessment, intervention, and evaluation

2.1.10a Substantively and affectively prepare for action with individuals, families, groups, organizations, and communities

2.1.10d Collect, organize, and interpret client data

2.1.10e Assess client strengths and limitations

2.1.10j Help clients resolve problems

Social workers frequently practice with groups. Barker (2003) defines group work as occurring when "small numbers of people who share similar interests or common problems convene regularly and engage in activities designed to achieve certain objectives" (p. 404). Thus, social work practice with groups is goal-directed. It may focus on helping individuals to make changes—for example, through *treatment groups* that attempt to enhance the socioemotional well-being of members through the provision of social skills, education, and therapy. Group goals may also focus on the group as a whole as the unit of change or the group as a mechanism for influencing the individual members. Examples of groups include task groups, such as committees, treatment teams, and task forces that seek the completion of a project or development of a product.

EP 2.1.3b

Whichever type of group the social worker leads, he or she must: (1) create a group that can effectively serve the purpose for which it was designed; (2) accurately assess individual and group dynamics; and (3) intervene effectively to modify processes that are affecting the group's achievement of its goals.

The success or failure of a group frequently rests on the groundwork that takes place before the group even meets. The social worker must thoughtfully and skillfully visualize a group and determine its purpose, structure, and composition. Without careful forethought in creating group structure and atmosphere, all assessment and intervention efforts will be jeopardized by the lack of a firm foundation. This chapter provides a framework that will enable you to effectively form groups and accurately assess group processes. It lays the foundation for effective group interventions, the subject of Chapter 16. In both group work chapters you will see references to the HEART (Healthy Eating, Attitudes, Relationships and Thoughts) group for teenage girls who are overweight. In these chapters, you will meet the members and read transcripts that demonstrate how the group progresses through the phases of development and the joys and struggles that accompany them. Before focusing on these objectives, though, we briefly discuss the types of groups that social workers create and lead in their practice settings.

Classification of Groups

Social workers are typically associated with two types of groups: treatment groups and task groups. Each of these categories, in turn, has several subtypes. Stated broadly, the purpose of treatment groups is to meet members'

EP 2.1.7a

socioemotional needs. Task groups, by contrast, are established to "accomplish a task, carry out a mandate, or produce a product" (Toseland & Rivas, 2009, p. 14). Treatment and task groups can be distinguished in a number of basic ways. In treatment groups, communications are open and members are encouraged to actively interact. In task groups, communications are more structured and focus on the discussion of a particular issue or agenda item. Member roles in treatment groups evolve as a result of interaction; in task groups, they may be assigned or elected (e.g., facilitator, minutes-taker). Procedures in treatment groups may be flexible or formal, depending on the group; task groups usually follow formal agendas and rules.

In addition, treatment and task groups differ with respect to participant self-disclosure, confidentiality, and evaluation. In treatment groups, self-disclosure is expected to be high, proceedings are kept within the group, and group success is based on individual members' success in meeting the treatment goals. In task groups, self-disclosure is low, proceedings may be private or open to the public, and the success of the group is based on members' accomplishing a task, fulfilling a particular charge, or producing a result.

Toseland and Rivas (2009) further refine their classification of treatment groups by describing subtypes that are characterized by their unique purposes.

1. *Support groups* help members cope with life stresses by revitalizing coping skills so that they can more effectively adapt to life events (e.g., schoolchildren meeting to discuss the effect of divorce, people with cancer discussing the effects of the disease and how to cope with it) (Magen & Glajchen, 1999).
2. *Educational groups* have the primary purpose of helping members learn about themselves and their society (e.g., an adolescent sexuality group, a diabetes management group, a heart attack recovery group).
3. *Growth groups* stress self-improvement, offering members opportunities to expand their capabilities and self-awareness and make personal changes (e.g., personal development group or a communication enhancement group for couples). Growth groups focus on promoting socioemotional health rather than alleviating socioemotional deficits.
4. *Therapy groups* help members change their behavior, cope with or ameliorate their personal problems, or rehabilitate themselves after a social or health trauma (e.g., a drug addiction group, an

anger management group, a dialectical behavior therapy group for persons diagnosed with personality disorders). While support and growth are also emphasized, therapy groups primarily focus on remediation and rehabilitation.

5. *Socialization groups* facilitate transitions through developmental stages, from one role or environment to another, through improved interpersonal relationships or social skills. Such groups often employ program activities, structured exercises, role plays, and the like (e.g., a social club for formerly institutionalized persons, a social skills group for children who have difficulty making friends).

EP 2.1.6b

These groups meet in a variety of public and private settings serving both voluntary and involuntary clients. Some "meet" virtually in electronic and online groups (Carr, 2004; Fingeld, 2000; Meier, 1997; Rounds, Galinsky, & Stevens, 1991; Schopler, Galinsky, & Abell, 1997). Social workers also find that groups are useful for supporting people who may traditionally have been marginalized by society, such as people of color, gay/ lesbian/bisexual/transgendered (GLBT) individuals, older adults, and those with stigmatizing illnesses (Miller, 1997; Pack-Brown, Whittington-Clark, & Parker, 1998; Peters, 1997; Salmon & Graziano, 2004; Saulnier, 1997; Schopler, Galinsky, Davis, & Despard, 1996; Subramian, Hernandez, & Martinez, 1995). Involuntary clients, such as perpetrators of domestic violence and adolescents in correctional settings, may also benefit from the mutuality found in groups (Rooney & Chovanec, 2004; Goodman, 1997; Thomas & Caplan, 1997). Groups can also be used to foster intergroup understanding and conflict reduction—for example, between clashing neighbors or racial and ethnic groups (Bargal, 2004).

Some group types overlap as they are designed to meet multiple purposes. For example, Bradshaw (1996) describes groups for persons with schizophrenia that simultaneously provide therapy, have a major educational component, and provide support. Groups to assist gay men who are acting as caregivers for others with AIDS provide support as well as education and resources exchange (Getzel, 1991). A men's cooking group at a community center is intended to educate members, prepare them with skills, and provide socialization for participants, all of whom are widowed or newly divorced (Northen & Kurland, 2001). A group of teens convened after the shootings at Columbine High School helped to facilitate intergenerational communication and allowed youth the opportunity to articulate their fears and needs, in contrast to safety measures instituted by authorities without their input (Malekoff, 2006). Such groups offer the opportunity for social reform in the midst of individual change.

In *self-help groups*, members have central shared concerns, such as coping with addiction, illness, or obesity. These groups are distinguished from treatment and task groups by the fact that the self-help group is led by nonprofessionals who are managing the same issues as members of the group, even though a social worker or other professional may have aided in the development or sponsorship of the group. Self-help groups emphasize interpersonal support and the creation of an environment in which individuals may retake charge of their lives. These groups offer resources and support for such shared problems as addictions, aggressive behavior, mental illness, disabilities, the death of a child, gambling, weight control, family violence, and AIDS, among others. It is the social worker's task to offer support and consultation to such groups without taking them over. For example, in a self-help group for Temporary Aid for Needy Families (TANF) recipients, the social service provider's role was to initiate the group, assist a member to become the group facilitator, and evaluate the group's effectiveness. Other members took active roles on tasks such as advertising, recruitment, supportive contact between meetings, and outreach to inform agencies of the group (Anderson-Butcher, Khairallah, & Race-Bigelow, 2004).

Task groups are generally organized into three different types (Toseland & Rivas, 2009):

- *Those that are created to meet client needs (treatment teams, case conferences, staff development committees)*
- *Those that are intended to meet organizational needs (committees, cabinets, boards)*
- *Those that address community needs (social action groups, coalitions, delegate assemblies)*

EP 2.1.7a

Traditionally, task and treatment groups have involved face-to-face meetings of group members, and the preponderance of groups today fit that model. However, with technological advances, groups can be convened electronically in synchronous (real time) or asynchronous (anytime) formats (Meier, 2006). As such, the groups can meet through written internet postings and discussion forums, as well as teleconference or videoconference capacities. Technology-mediated groups pose unique advantages and challenges in service delivery, which will be noted throughout this chapter and Chapter 16. While group types may differ, several underlying principles are common to all forms of group work practice. We will begin with the evidence base supporting group work, then consider common features of creating and assessing treatment groups and proceeding to task groups.

The Evidence Base for Groups

EP 2.1.6b

Although the evidence base for the efficacy of groups is growing, there are particular challenges to conducting research with groups including problems maintaining equivalent control conditions, monitoring specific process events that affect outcomes, ensuring that the treatment plan is implemented as intended, and isolating the multiple parts that interact to create change (Chen, Kakkad, & Balzano, 2008; Garvin 2011). Meta-analyses of research on group outcomes (Burlingame, Fuhriman, & Mosier, 2003; Burlingame, MacKenzie, & Strauss 2004) found that group treatment results in reliable positive improvement in comparison with controls, but that examinations of what might explain differences in client outcomes in groups are still lacking. These analyses note that patient characteristics, such as personality and initial level of problems, robustly predict process and outcome, but other factors such as group structure, leader characteristics, and the formal change theories of groups need to be more closely examined to determine their impact on outcomes. Utilizing the best existing evidence, the American Group Psychotherapy Association has compiled a comprehensive set of practice guidelines for group work which cover topics from creating successful therapy groups, preparation and pregroup training, group development and process, ethical practice and reducing adverse outcomes, and group termination (Bernard et al., 2007).

Throughout this chapter and Chapter 16, we incorporate research findings supporting particular types of groups and group strategies. Until research supported group treatments evolve more fully, group leaders will need to take responsibility for implementing evidence-based practices. Macgowan (2008) offers several recommendations to assist with this task.

- *Utilize critical thinking in examining anticipated change processes and pathways and build on introductory knowledge of research and group work in building the evidence base.*

> **TABLE-11-1 CONSIDERATIONS IN FORMING AND STARTING TREATMENT GROUPS**
>
> Identify the Need
> Establish the Purpose
> Decide on Leadership
> Determine Group Composition
> Choose Open versus Closed Membership
> Determine Group Size and Location
> Select the Frequency and Duration of Meetings
> Conduct Preliminary Interviews
> Determine Group Format
> Formulate Preliminary Group Guidelines

© Cengage Learning 2013

- *Specify and measure variables such as problems and goals, the change theory of the group, individual member characteristics, group structural elements, group process, and leader characteristics.*
- *Make research questions for assessing groups "Member-relevant, Answerable, Practical (MAP)" (p. 21) and identify a specific challenge, intervention, and outcome to be studied.*

Similarly, the clinician can utilize a "local clinical scientist" approach to employ scientific thinking when constructing and leading groups, thereby obtaining practice-based evidence to identify salient processes and outcomes for future refinement.

Formation of Treatment Groups

The success or failure of a treatment group rests to a large extent on the thoughtful creation of the group and the careful selection and preparation of members for the group experience. In this section, you will learn the steps needed to foster a positive group outcome. Table 11-1 lists these steps.

Determining the Need for the Group

The decision to offer services through groups can arise from a number of origins. Some agencies adopt group-based services as their primary modality because of ideological or practice considerations or as a strategy to meet efficiency or cost-containment targets. Sometimes practitioners or agencies determine that groups are needed based on the problems that clusters of clients are presenting and the evidence that group modalities are the most effective means for addressing the problem. Sometimes group work is indicated when existing groups require social work interventions, for example, in school or community settings where violence or racial conflicts are threatening the safety of the learning environment. Social workers may construct groups based on needs assessments sparked by observations of individual clients whose needs could be addressed through mutual aid with others facing the same challenges (Toseland & Rivas, 2009). As a result, workers might contact colleagues in their own or other agencies to substantiate the need, begin recruitment, or advertise the group.

Establishing the Group Purpose

EP 2.1.10a

Clarifying the overall purpose of a group is vital because the group's objectives influence all the processes that follow, including recruiting and selecting members, deciding on the group's duration, identifying its size and content, and determining meeting location and time. Kurland and Salmon (1998) describe several common problems to avoid in developing an appropriate group purpose.

1. Group purposes are promoted without adequate consideration of client need. That is, the purpose may make sense to the prospective leaders or the agency, but not to the potential clients. For example, clients may be assembled because they share a status, such as having a serious and persistent illness and living independently. From the viewpoint of these potential clients, a group that relates to a commonly perceived need such as recreation or socializing may be more attractive than grouping by status.
2. The purpose of the group is confused with the content. For example, the group's purpose is described in terms of what the members will do in the group—their activities—rather than the outcome toward which those activities are directed.
3. The purpose of the group is stated too generally, so that it is vague and meaningless to potential members and provides little direction to prospective leaders.
4. Leaders are reluctant to share their perceptions about the purpose, leaving members to wonder why they are there.
5. The group is formed with a "public" purpose that conflicts with its actual hidden purpose. For example, prospective members may not know the basis on which they were contacted to become part of a group. Potential clients may be invited to join on the basis of the fact that they overuse prescription drugs, yet this commonality is not shared with them.
6. Group purposes may be misunderstood as static rather than dynamic (adjusting to the evolving desires and needs of the members).

General group purposes may include overarching goals such as the following:

- *To provide a forum for single parents of young children to meet for socialization and education about child development*
- *To participate in decision making that affects the quality of life in a nursing home by establishing a governing council for residents*
- "To teach young probationers how to protect their physical safety and avoid rearrest by adopting pro-social thinking and actions" (Goodman, Getzel, & Ford, 1996, p. 375)
- "To enhance the development of personal and racial identity as well as professional advancement" of African American women (Pack-Brown, Whittington-Clark, & Parker, 1998, p. xi)

The overall purpose of a planned group should be established by the social worker in consultation with agency administrators and potential clients prior to forming the group; the goals subsequently negotiated by the group should reflect the perspectives of those three stakeholders. If the agency's goals differ from the social worker's goals, those involved must negotiate a general group purpose that is agreeable to both parties. Failing to do so may lead to ambiguity in the group, send mixed messages, and triangulate its members.

The Client's Perspective

The potential member of a group wants some questions answered: "Why should I join this group? What is in it for me? What will it do for me? Will it help me?" (Kurland & Salmon, 1998, pp. 7–8). The answers to these questions will determine whether individuals join a group and, later, whether they continue attending. The potential member who is mandated or pressured to attend also wants to know the answers to these questions, even if the consequences of failure to join or attend are more punishing for this individual than they would be for the voluntary client.

At the point of entry into a group, the client's goals may differ considerably from those of either the agency or the social worker. Schopler and Galinsky (1974) note that the client's goals may be influenced by many internal or external forces, such as the expectations of others and the client's personal comfort, motivation, and past experiences in group

EP 2.1.10d

settings. During group formation, the social worker must carefully explore clients' expectations of the group, help them to develop individual and collective goals that are realistically achievable, and negotiate between individual, group, and agency purposes. For example, several members of the HEART group for overweight teen girls joined because their relatives insisted they do so. As such, the leader should acknowledge members' goal of avoiding conflict or coercion from family members as a condition for participation in the group. Alongside these goals, members may have individual goals, such as controlling unhealthy eating behaviors, seeking advice and support from others in similar situations, improving self-esteem, addressing interpersonal difficulties with parents and peers, reducing symptoms of depression and anxiety, and learning weight-loss techniques pertaining to diet and exercise. Even entirely voluntary groups operate best when the leader's and the members' purposes are compatible or when the purposes of the two diverge but the social worker goes along with the group's purpose. Conversely, when the social worker insists on goals that are incompatible with members' needs and wishes, the groups may prematurely dissolve or become more preoccupied with conflict than their purpose.

Deciding on Leadership

Once the group's purpose is established, group planners must consider whether individual or co-leadership will be necessary to assist the group in meeting its aims. Many types of groups benefit from co-leadership. Having two leaders can provide additional eyes and ears for the group, with one leader specifically attending to content and the other taking note of the process and meta-messages by group members. Co-leaders bring different perspectives, backgrounds, and personalities to the group process, which can appeal to a wider array of members than a single leader might. They can also use their interactions to model effective communication and problem solving (Jacobs, Masson, & Harvill, 1998). In addition, two leaders can keep a watchful eye on each other, providing feedback and noting patterns where individual facilitators' needs and motives may impede effective management of the group (Corey, Corey, Callanan, & Russell, 2004).

EP 2.1.10a

Sometimes co-leadership is necessary for practical reasons. With two leaders, one can check on a member who has left the room or has been asked to take time out, while the other continues working with the group. Co-leadership can provide continuity if illness or another emergency on the part of one leader might otherwise result in cancellation of a session. With some populations, two leaders may help send a message of authority in an otherwise disruptive group; they may also provide a sense of physical safety and protection from liability by their very presence (Carrell, 2000). In some groups, such as those for men accused of partner violence, mixed-gender co-leaders can provide "deliberate and strategic modeling of alternative forms of male-female interactions" (Nosko & Wallace, 1997, p. 5).

Of course, co-leadership is sometimes impractical because of the costs involved and the time needed to coordinate roles, plan the group sessions, and debrief together. In managing the cost concern, some agencies utilize volunteers or "program graduates"—consumers who have had group training and can bring personal experiences to the group process.

Co-leaders who work together on a regular basis may find increased efficiencies as they formulate a common "curriculum" for the group and develop comfort and rapport with each other. Such coordination is essential to avoid disruptive rivalries from occurring or to prevent members from pitting the co-leaders against each other (Northen & Kurland, 2001). As Levine and Dang (1979) note, "co-therapists constitute an inner group that must work through its own process while facilitating the progress of the larger group" (p. 175). Nosko & Wallace (1997) and Paulson, Burroughs, & Gleb (1976) suggest three ground rules for effective co-leadership: "establish a common theoretical orientation; agree on the identification and handling of problems; and agree on what constitutes the appropriate quantity and quality of each leader's participation" (p. 7). Because characteristics such as gender and race affect personal interactions and are reflected in power dynamics and status expectations, co-leaders must deliberately share all group functions and roles (such as confrontation and support). In doing so, they model equality, undo damaging expectations that members may hold, and help the group adopt norms of fairness and flexibility outside of members' stereotyped notions.

Deciding on Group Composition

Composition refers to the selection of members for the group. On occasion, composition may be predetermined—for example, when the group consists of all residents in a group home, all patients preparing for discharge, or all motorists referred to alcohol treatment due to charges of driving while intoxicated. In rural areas or other settings, the leader may work with a naturally formed group, which has already developed around a common problem, rather than create and recruit a new group (Gumpert & Saltman, 1998).

EP 2.1.7a & 2.1.4c

When the leader is responsible for deciding the group composition, the overriding factor in selecting members is whether a candidate is motivated to make changes and likely to be a productive group member. Another key factor is the likelihood of that person being compatible with other members in the group. Social workers usually consider gender, age, intellectual ability, education, personality, and other features when composing group membership, weighing the relative metrics of homogeneity versus heterogeneity among members. Significant homogeneity in personal characteristics and purpose for joining the group is necessary to facilitate communication and group cohesion. Without such commonality, members will have little basis for interacting with one another. Toseland and Rivas (2009), for example, identify levels of education, cultural background, degree of expertise relative to the group task, and communication ability as characteristics vital to creating group homogeneity. Sometimes, the group's purpose will influence the decision for similarity along certain characteristics. For example, there are advantages to creating single-gender groups when the issues differ by gender or when mixed groups might inhibit member comfort or participation. At other times, differences in age, development, or the nature of the problem would require homogeneity among member characteristics. For example, in composing a group for parents who have lost children, those members whose loved ones were very young when they died might have different needs and issues than those whose offspring were adults when they passed away. In cognitive-behavioral groups for troubled youth, similarity in age and socioemotional development is essential to avoid dominance by older members who are more mature (Rose, 1998).

Conversely, some diversity among members with respect to coping skills, life experience, and levels of expertise fosters learning and introduces members to differing viewpoints, lifestyles, problem-solving skills, and ways of communicating. To attain the desired outcomes of support, learning, and mutual aid, a treatment group, for example, might include members from different cultures, social classes, occupations, or geographic areas. Multicultural diversity in group membership can bring a variety of perspectives and resources to the group's efforts (Anderson, 2007). Heterogeneity is also vital in task group membership so that the group has sufficient resources to fulfill its responsibilities and efficiently divide the labor when dealing with complex tasks (Toseland & Rivas, 2009). The challenge in any type of group is to attain a workable balance between differences and similarities of members, given the group's purpose.

Corey and Corey (2006) caution against including members in voluntary groups whose behavior or pathology is extreme, inasmuch as some people reduce the available energy of the group for productive work and interfere significantly in the development of group cohesion. This is particularly true of individuals who have a need to monopolize and dominate, hostile people or aggressive people with a need to act out, and people who are extremely self-centered and who seek a group as an audience. Others who are generally less likely to benefit from most groups are people who are in a state of extreme crisis, who are suicidal, who are highly suspicious, or who are lacking in ego strength and prone to fragmented and bizarre behavior (Milgram & Rubin, 1992).

A decision to include or exclude a client has a lot to do with the purposes of the group. For example, a person with alcoholism might be excluded from a personal growth group but appropriately included in a homogeneous group of individuals who wrestle with various types of addictions. Oppositional behavior may be a common denominator in some groups, such as those formed to address domestic violence and delinquency (Milgram & Rubin, 1992). In such cases, this behavior would not be a criterion for exclusion, but rather a central problem for work. An older woman raising her grandchildren might find little benefit in a parenting group where the focus is on education for first-time parents. This does not mean that the grandparent is not in need of group assistance, but rather that it is important for her needs to be congruent with the group purpose and composition.

Garvin (1987) warns against including in a treatment group a member who is very different from the others, for the danger is that this person "will be perceived as undesirable or, in sociological terms, deviant by the other members" (p. 65). Differences in socioeconomic status, age, race, problem history, or cognitive abilities may lead to the individual's discomfort and difficulty in affiliating with the group. It may also produce member behaviors that isolate or scapegoat the person. "Outliers" should be avoided, both for the satisfaction of the individual and for the health of the group. When group composition could potentially lead to the isolation of a member, Garvin (1987) recommends enrolling another member who "is either similar to the person in question or who is somewhere in the 'middle,' thus creating a continuum of member characteristics" (p. 65) and assisting in establishing the members' affiliation and comfort.

Open versus Closed Groups

EP 2.1.7a

Groups may have either an *open* format, in which the group remains open to enrolling new members, or a *closed* format, in which no new members are added once the group gets under way. Typically, groups that are open or closed in terms of admitting new members are also open or closed in regard to their duration. Alcoholics Anonymous and Weight Watchers are examples of open-ended and open-membership groups. A 10-week medication management group and a 5-week social skills group would be examples of closed-membership, closed-ended groups.

Open-ended groups are generally used for helping clients cope with transitions and crises, providing support, acting as a means for assessment, and facilitating outreach (Schopler & Galinsky, 1981). Having open-ended groups ensures that a group is immediately available at a time of crisis. An open format itself presents different models (Henry, 1988; Reid, 1991), including the *drop-in (or drop-out) model* in which members are self-selecting, entry criteria are very broad, and members attend whenever they wish for an indefinite period. In the *replacement model,* the leader immediately identifies someone to fill a group vacancy. In the *re-formed model,* group members contract to attend for a set period of time, during which no new members are added but original members may drop out. At the end of the contract period, a new group is formed consisting of some old and some new members.

The choice of format depends on the purpose of the group, the setting, and the population served. An open format provides the opportunity for new members to bring fresh perspectives to the group and offers immediate support for those in need, who come when they need to and stay as long as they choose. At the same time, the instability of this format discourages members from developing the trust and confidence to openly share and explore their problems—a strong feature of the closed-ended group. Frequent changes of membership may also disrupt the work of the open-ended group, although the developmental patterns in such groups vary according to how many new members enter and the frequency of turnover (Galinsky & Schopler, 1989). Leaders of open-ended groups need to be attuned to clients being at different places in the group process and to be able to work with core members to carry forward the particular group's traditions (Schopler & Galinsky, 1981).

Advantages associated with a closed group include higher group morale, greater predictability for role behaviors, and an increased sense of cooperation among members. Disadvantages are that the group may not be open to members when potential participants are ready to make use of it and that, if too many members drop out, the group process will be drastically affected by the high rate of attrition.

Determining Group Size and Location

The size of the group depends in large part on its purpose, the age of clients, the type of problems to be explored, and the needs of members. Seven to 10 members is usually an optimal number for a group with an emphasis on close relationships (Reid, 2002). Bertcher and Maple (1985) suggest that the group should be small enough to allow it to achieve its purpose, yet large enough to ensure that members have a satisfying experience. As such, educational and task groups may accommodate more members than would therapy and support groups, where cohesion is central to the group progress.

EP 2.1.10a

The location of group meetings should be selected with convenience and image in mind. *Image* speaks to the impression that the site makes on members—the message it conveys that may attract them to the group or make them uncomfortable in attending. For example, a parenting group held at a school building may not be attractive to potential members if their own experiences with education or with the particular school system have been unfavorable. A parenting group that meets at a local YMCA/YWCA or community center may be perceived as comfortable to members who are used to going there for their children's sports or other community events.

Convenience refers to the accessibility of the site for those people whom the group chooses to attract. For example, is the site readily accessible to a public transportation line for those who do not own automobiles? Is it safe, with plenty of parking, and easy to find for those who may be uncomfortable venturing out at night? Social workers who are familiar with a community might make note of the "participation patterns" of residents, as these may reveal neutral locations for meetings (Gumpert & Saltman, 1998).

Leaders may have little choice over the meeting location if the sponsoring agency's site must be used. Those planning groups should take the image and accessibility of the location into account, however, when recruiting prospective members or when diagnosing problems in group membership.

Setting the Frequency and Duration of Meetings

Closed groups benefit from having a termination date at the outset, which encourages productive work. Regarding the possible lifespan of a group, Corey and Corey (2006) note: "The duration varies from group to group, depending on the type of group and the population. The group should be long enough to allow for cohesion and productive work yet not so long that the group seems to drag on interminably" (p. 92). For a time-limited therapy group, Reid (1991) recommends approximately 20 sessions, stating that this length provides adequate time for cohesiveness and a sense of trust to develop. Others might suggest that a 20-session limit is not feasible, that attrition and other obligations may erode participation, and that ending ahead of the planned time may lead to an unwarranted sense of failure. Shorter durations, during which attendance can be assured, may leave clients "wanting more" but with a sense of accomplishment and goal achievement at the group's conclusion. In general, short-term groups vary between 1 and 12 sessions, with the shorter-duration groups being targeted at crisis situations, anxiety alleviation, and educational programs (Northen & Kurland, 2001).

Conducting a Preliminary Interview

EP 2.1.10d

Before convening a group, social workers often meet individually with potential group members for the purpose of screening participants, establishing rapport, exploring relevant concerns, formulating initial contracts with those motivated to join the group, and clarifying limits and options for involuntary clients. Individual interviews are essential to providing effective group composition; they ensure that the members are selected according to predetermined criteria and possess the behavioral or personality attributes needed for them to make effective use of the group experience.

There are several advantages to having pregroup meetings with potential members:

- *When creating a group of involuntary clients, interviews allow the opportunity to clarify participants' options and identify acknowledged as well as attributed problems.*
- *In rural areas, preliminary interviews provide an opportunity to notify potential members that others they know might attend; in doing so, the group leader can address any concerns that this group composition provokes.*
- *With groups drawn from populations who may be uncomfortable or unfamiliar with group treatment, a pregroup orientation can acquaint prospective members with the treatment process, help them understand what to expect, reduce apprehension, and learn how best to participate (Pack-Brown, Whittington-Clark, & Parker, 1998; Subramian, Hernandez, & Martinez, 1995).*
- *Interviews help leaders obtain valuable information to guide interventions in early sessions, aiding in the efficiency and effectiveness of services.*
- *Preliminary interviews enable social workers to enter the initial group sessions with a previously established relationship with each member—a distinct advantage given that leaders must attend to multiple communication processes at both individual and group levels.*
- *Previous knowledge facilitates the leader's understanding of the members' behaviors and allows the leader to focus more fully on group processes and the task of assisting members to develop relationships with one another. For example, the leaders in one bereavement support group knew from initial interviews that two members' losses had been due to murder. This information alerted them to these members' unique concerns and needs and fostered a connection between the two participants who shared a common experience.*
- *Establishing rapport with the leader is also beneficial for members, in that it enables them to feel more at ease and to open up more readily in the first meeting.*

Social workers should focus on the following in preliminary interviews:

1. *Orient potential members to proposed goals and purposes of the group, its content and structure, the leader's philosophy and style in managing group processes, and the roles of the leader and group members.* This is also a good time to identify ground rules, such as attendance, confidentiality, the appropriateness of relating to members outside the group, and so on (Yalom, 2005). With involuntary groups, you must distinguish between nonnegotiable rules and policies, such as attendance expectations and general themes to be discussed, and negotiable norms and procedures, such as arrangements for

breaks, food, and selection of particular topics and their order.

In preliminary meetings, you should also elicit each client's reactions and suggestions on ways that the group might better meet his or her unique needs. Orientation should also address details such as the time and place of meetings, length of sessions, and the like. In addition, the social worker may wish to emphasize commonalities that the client may share with other persons considering group membership, such as problems, interests, concerns, or objectives.

2. *Elicit information on the client's prior group experiences,* including the nature of the client's relationship with the leader and other members, his or her style of relating in the previous group, the goals that he or she accomplished, and the personal growth that was achieved. Social workers should anticipate the possibility of negative reactions, acknowledge them and yet emphasize ways that individuals can make this group experience more fulfilling and beneficial.

3. *Elicit, explore, and clarify the clients' problems,* and identify those that are appropriate for the proposed group. In some instances, either because clients are reluctant to participate in the group or because their problems appear to be more appropriately handled through other treatment modalities or community agencies, you may need to refer them to other resources.

4. *Explore the client's hopes, aspirations, and expectations* regarding the proposed group (e.g., "What would you like to be different in your life as a result of your attending this group?").

5. *Identify specific goals that the client wishes to accomplish,* discussing whether these goals can be attained through the proposed group, and determining the client's views as to whether the group is an appropriate vehicle for resolving his or her problems. Sharing personal goals that prior members have chosen, in addition to mandated goals, may make the group more attractive to the reluctant member.

6. *Mutually develop a profile of the client's strengths and attributes,* and determine the ways he/she will contribute to the group and capacities that the client might like to enhance through work in the group.

7. *Identify and explore potential obstacles or reservations* about participation in the group, including shyness or discomfort in group situations, opposition from significant others about entering the group, a heavy schedule that might preclude attending all group meetings, or problems in transportation or child care. In addition to exploring these barriers to group membership, the social worker and client may generate possible alternatives or determine whether the obstacles are so difficult to overcome that participation is unwise at this time.

8. *Ensure that screening for the group is a two-way process.* Potential members should have the opportunity to interview the group leader and determine whether the group is appropriate for their problems and interests and whether the relationship with the leader will likely facilitate a successful outcome.

Determine the Group Format

In addition to determining the group purpose, goals, composition, duration, and other elements, leaders must attend to the group *structure* or how the time in the group will be used to most effectively meet the needs of participants. The result should be a clearly conceptualized format that provides the means for evaluating group and individual progress. The structure should also be flexible enough to accommodate differing group processes and the unique needs of members as they emerge. To ensure its continued functionality, review the format periodically throughout the life of the group.

The following activities will assist you and your members to focus your energies so as to achieve therapeutic objectives effectively and efficiently.

EP 2.1.7a

1. Define group and individual goals in behavioral terms and rank them according to priority.
2. Develop an overall plan that organizes the work to be done within the number of sessions allocated by the group to achieve its goals. The leader (or co-leaders) should have done preliminary work on this plan while designing the group.
3. Specify behavioral tasks (homework) to be accomplished outside the group each week that will assist individuals to make the desired changes.
4. Achieve agreement among members concerning the weekly format and agenda—that is, how time will be allocated each week to achieve the group's goals. For instance, a group might allocate its weekly 1.5 hours to the format shown in Table 11-2.

Steps 1 and 2 can be facilitated by research on effective groups or best practices in services to particular

TABLE-11-2 EXAMPLE OF A GROUP FORMAT

15 MINUTES	1 HOUR	15 MINUTES
Checking-in Reviewing and monitoring tasks	Focusing on relevant content (presentation and discussion) Mutual problem solving Formulating tasks Plan for the week	Summarizing plan for the week Evaluating group session

populations. For example, building on the success of groups with gay and lesbian adolescents and with middle-aged persons in the coming-out process, Getzel (1998) notes that life review and socialization groups may serve as a promising resource for elder GLBT persons. Others note that groups can be effective in addressing health issues, supporting treatment compliance and reducing treatment dropouts. These goals are met as members share feelings about their illnesses and medications, offer mutual aid, empathize with one another's experiences and side effects, break through isolation and grief, and generate strategies for self-care (Miller & Mason, 2001). Professionals who are aware of successful activities and protocols can incorporate them into the proposed structure for group sessions.

The group leader is responsible for developing the preliminary structure and presenting it, and the rationale, to the group. Although input and mutuality are important, group members are typically ill equipped, due to their own distress or lack of group experience, to give meaningful input in creating group structure. They may, however, respond with concerns or preferences about the format offered and may be better able to offer feedback on structure as the group evolves.

Formulating Preliminary Group Guidelines

Developing consensus about group guidelines (e.g., staying on task, adhering to confidentiality) is a vital aspect of contracting in the initial phase of the group. In formulating guidelines with the group, the social worker takes the first step in shaping the group's evolving processes to create a "working group" capable of achieving specific objectives. There are three common reasons why attempts to formulate guidelines fail.

EP 2.1.10a

First, the social worker may establish parameters *for* the group, merely informing members of behavioral expectations to which they are expected to adhere. While nonnegotiable requirements such as attendance are often part of involuntary groups, overemphasis on such control may convey the message, "This is my group, and this is how I expect you to behave in it." Such a message may negate later actions by the social worker to encourage members to assume responsibility for the group. Without consensus among members concerning desirable group guidelines, power struggles and disagreements may ensue. Further, members may not feel bound by what they consider the "leader's rules" and may deliberately test them, creating a counterproductive scenario.

Second, the social worker may discuss group guidelines only superficially and neglect either to identify or to obtain the group's commitment to them. This is unfortunate, because the extent to which members understand what these parameters mean will influence the extent to which they conform to them.

Third, just because the group adopts viable guidelines for behavior does not mean that members will subsequently follow them. Establishing group ground rules or mutual expectations merely sets guideposts against which members may measure their current behavior. For negotiated behaviors to become normative, leaders must consistently intervene to assist members in adhering to guidelines and in considering discrepancies between contracted and actual behaviors.

Because formulating guidelines is a critical process that substantially influences the success of a group, we offer the following suggestions to assist you in this aspect of group process:

1. If there are nonnegotiable expectations (e.g., confidentiality, no smoking policies, or rules forbidding contact between members outside sessions), you should present the rules, explain their rationale, and encourage discussion of them (Behroozi, 1992).

    EP 2.1.10j

2. Introduce the group to the concept of *decision by consensus* on all negotiable items and solicit agreement concerning adoption of this method for making decisions *prior* to formulating group guidelines.

3. Ask group members to share their vision of the kind of group they would like to have by responding to the following statement: "I would like this

group to be a place where I could...." Reach for responses from all members. Once this has been achieved, summarize the collective thinking of the group. Offer your own views of supportive group structure that assists members to work on individual problems or to achieve group objectives.

4. Ask members to identify guidelines for behavior in the group that will assist them to achieve the kind of group structure and atmosphere they desire. You may wish to brainstorm possible guidelines at this point, adding your suggestions. Then, through group consensus, choose those that seem most appropriate.

The 11 items in the following section identify pertinent topics for treatment group guidelines, although each guideline's applicability depends on the specific focus of the group.

Help-Giving/Help-Seeking Roles

Groups can benefit from clarification of the *help-giving* and *help-seeking* roles that members play. The help-seeking role, for example, incorporates such behaviors as making direct requests for input or advice, authentically sharing one's feelings, being open to feedback, and demonstrating willingness to test new approaches to problems. The help-giving role involves such behaviors as listening attentively, refraining from criticism, clarifying perceptions, summarizing, maintaining focus on the problem, and pinpointing strengths and incremental growth.

The leader should give special attention to the issue of advice in the help-giving role and emphasize the necessity of carefully exploring fellow members' personal problems before attempting to solve them. Otherwise, groups tend to move quickly to giving advice and offering evaluative suggestions about what a member "ought" or "ought not" to do. You can further help the group to appropriately adopt the two roles by highlighting instances in which members have performed well in either of these helping roles.

Visitors

A group convened for treatment purposes should develop explicit guidelines specifying whether and under what conditions visitors may attend group meetings. Depending on the group purpose or structure (open or closed), visitors can detrimentally affect group processes by causing members to refrain from sharing feelings and problems openly, by threatening the confidentiality of the proceedings, or by creating resentment toward the individual who invited the visitor and thereby violated the integrity of the group. Anticipating with members the possible effects of visitors on the group and establishing procedures and conditions under which visitors may attend sessions can avert group turmoil as well as embarrassment for individual members.

New Members

Procedures for adding and orienting new members may need to be established. In some cases, the group leader may reserve the prerogative of selecting members. In other instances, the leader may permit the group to choose new members, with the understanding that those choices should be based on certain criteria and that the group should achieve consensus regarding potential members. In either case, procedures for adding new members and the importance of the group's role in orienting those entrants should be clarified. As mentioned earlier, adding new members in an open-ended group should occur in a planned way, considering the stage of development of the group.

Individual Contacts with the Social Worker

Whether you encourage or discourage individual contacts with members outside the group depends on the purpose of the group and the anticipated consequences or benefits of such contacts. In some cases, individual contacts serve to promote group objectives. For example, in a correctional setting, planned meetings with an adolescent between sessions may provide opportunities to focus on behaviors in the group, support strengths, and develop an individual contract with the youth to modify his or her actions. In the case of couples' groups, however, individual contacts initiated by one partner may be a bid to form an alliance with the social worker against the other partner (or may be perceived as such by the partner who did not initiate the contact). If you have questions regarding the advisability of having individual contacts outside the group, you should thoroughly discuss these with a supervisor and address guidelines for contact with group members.

Member Contacts Outside the Group

Contacts by members outside the group can be constructive or harmful to individuals and the group's purpose and thus the practice literature contains differing views on this topic. Shulman (2009) explains that group sessions are but one activity in clients' lives and that therefore it is unreasonable to expect members to follow rules that extend outside the temporal and special boundaries of the group. Shulman (2009) also notes that the nature and benefit of collaborative support is limited if members are forbidden to make contact outside of session.

Toseland and Rivas (2009) list possible drawbacks to contact between members outside the group, including diversions from the group's goal, the effect of coalitions on the other members' interactions in the group, and arguments stemming from the dissolution of an alliance or friendship formed outside the group. With the advent of online data and social networking, members may research each other and threaten boundaries and comfort by uncovering information and connections the individual has not shared in the group. Online relationships can give rise to problematic alliances or become an avenue for dealing with concerns that should be brought to the group.

Yalom (2005) acknowledges both therapeutic benefits and pitfalls of contacts outside the group. His analysis reveals that outside group contact should be disclosed to the entire group, as clandestine contacts risk harming group unity. Sexual relationships between members is discouraged, as the connection between partners will surpass the connection that either feel for the remaining group members (Yalom, 2005). Particularly in time-limited groups, it is feasible and appropriate for members to limit outside contact for the duration of the group, unless there are therapeutic reasons for supporting such communications.

Care for Space and Cleanup

Making group decisions regarding care of the room (e.g., food, furniture, trash) and cleanup (before having to contend with a messy room) encourages members to assume responsibility for the group space. Otherwise, resentments may fester and subgroups destructive to group cohesiveness may form when some members feel responsible for cleanup and others do not.

Use of Recorders and Other Devices

Given the subtlety of current recording technology and the risks posed by inappropriate videotaping or audiotaping, this is an important topic for members and leaders alike. Members should be reminded of confidentiality expectations and be encouraged to prohibit recording as part of their ground rules. If there is a therapeutic or professional purpose for recording the group, the social worker should always ask for the group's permission before audiotaping or videotaping a group session (NASW, 2008). Before asking for such a decision, you should provide information concerning the manner in which the recording will be utilized outside the session, how it will be kept and when it will be destroyed. Members' reservations regarding recording the session should be thoroughly aired, and the group's wishes should be respected.

A related issue involves the use of cell phones, pagers, and other handheld devices. In addition to recording and photo capabilities, these gadgets are distracting to the members checking them and the other people around them. Groups must discuss and construct norms about the use of electronic equipment: Must all items be turned off during meetings? Can they be on, but not checked if they go off? What should members do if urgent calls are expected?

Eating, Drinking, Swearing

Opinions vary among group leaders concerning these activities in groups. Some groups and leaders believe that they distract from group process; others regard them as relaxing and actually beneficial to group operation. Some groups may intentionally provide meals as an incentive to encourage group attendance (Wood, 2007). You may wish to elicit views from members concerning these activities and develop guidelines with the group that meet member needs, conform to organization or building policies, and facilitate group progress.

A related issue is the use of profanity in the group. Some social workers believe that group members should be allowed to use whatever language they choose in expressing themselves. However, profanity may be offensive to some participants and the group may wish to develop guidelines concerning this matter.

Attendance

Discussing the problems that irregular attendance can pose for a group before the fact and soliciting commitments from members to attend regularly can do much to solidify group attendance in future group sessions. Involuntary groups often have attendance policies that permit a limited number of absences and late arrivals. Late arrivals and early departures by group members can typically be minimized if the group develops norms about this behavior in advance and if the leader starts and ends meetings promptly. Exceptions may be needed, of course, to accommodate crises affecting the schedules of members or to extend the session to complete an urgent item of business if the group concurs. However, individual and group exceptions to time norms should be rare.

Programming

Sometimes, group formats include activities or exercises. In "addition to discussion, content from games, play, structured exercises, role-playing, art, drama, guided imagery, cooking, hobbies, and other forms of creative self-expression are used to build group bonds and enhance the potential of the group to achieve group tasks and individual and social change" (Garvin & Galinsky, 2008, Programming section, para. 1). Domestic violence or substance abuse groups may use psychoeducational programming, children's groups may use activities or field trips (Rose, 1998; Ross, 1997), and cognitive-behavioral groups may use role plays and mnemonic devices to remind members of options for problem solving (Goodman, Getzel, & Ford, 1996). It is essential that the activities selected relate directly to the group's purpose. Any such activities should be prefaced and concluded by discussions and debriefing that ties the activities to the group's goals and evaluates the effectiveness of the experience.

With increased attention in the profession devoted to evidence-based practices, *manualized curricula* have been developed that detail the sequence, content, and activities for various types of groups. There are several advantages of these programmed approaches. They help to focus treatment, advance systematized practices, and support research on interventions. However, those who oppose manual-based practice are concerned that they promote paternalistic, one-size-fits-all approaches instead of the organic, empowerment-based changes that arise from members' and workers' dynamic interactions (Wood, 2007). A further concern is that they may be misused by workers who adopt curricula without supervision or sufficient appreciation for group dynamics and in the absence of group facilitation skills. Clearly, there is a balance between "intuitive practice at one pole and standardized practice at the other" (Galinsky, Terzian, & Fraser, 2006, p. 13). Knowledgeable workers can integrate tested programming ideas with practice wisdom and emerging group needs to achieve group and individual purposes.

Touching

The sensitive nature of some group topics may lead to expressions of emotion, such as crying or angry outbursts. It is important to have group guidelines that provide physical safety for members (e.g., "no hitting"). It is also important to set a climate of emotional safety, to sanction the appropriate expression of feelings. Some group guidelines prohibit members from touching one another with hugs or other signs of physical comfort. Sometimes these rules are included to protect members from unwanted or uncomfortable advances. Other groups maintain that touch is a "feeling stopper" when one is tearful and insist that group members can display their empathy in other ways—through words or through eye contact and attention to the other, for example. Whatever the group's policy, it is important to explain the expectation and the rationale and to address member concerns rather than impose the guideline unilaterally.

Guidelines are helpful only to the extent that they expedite the development of the group and further the achievement of the group's goals. They should be reviewed

TABLE-11-3 AREAS FOR ASSESSMENT IN GROUPS

Individuals' Patterned Behaviors
    Member's Roles
    Developing Profiles of Individual Behavior
    Identifying Individuals' Growth
Individuals' Cognitive Patterns
The Groups' Patterned Behaviors
Group Alliances
Group Power and Decision-Making Styles
Group Norms, Values, and Cohesion

© Cengage Learning 2013

periodically to assess their functionality in relationship to the group's stage of development. Outdated guidelines should be discarded or reformulated. When the group's behavior is incompatible with the group guidelines, the leader should describe what is happening in the group (or request that members do so) and, after thoroughly reviewing the situation, ask the group to consider whether the guideline in question is still viable. If used judiciously, this strategy not only helps the group to reassess its guidelines but also places responsibility for monitoring adherence to those guidelines with the group, where it belongs. Leaders who unwittingly assume the role of "enforcer" place themselves in an untenable position, because group members tend to struggle against what they perceive as authoritarian control on the leader's part.

Assessing Group Processes

In group assessment, social workers must attend to processes that occur at both the individual and the group levels, including emerging themes or patterns, in an effort to enhance the functioning of individuals and the group as a whole. This section describes the procedures for accurately assessing the processes for both individuals and groups and Table 11-3 summarizes the variables you should consider. A systems framework facilitates the identification and impact of such patterns. Instruments may also help in the identification and quantification of group processes and outcomes. For example, Macgowan (1997) has developed a group work engagement measure (GEM) that combines measures of attendance, satisfaction, perceived group helpfulness, group cohesion, and interaction to assess group members' level of engagement in a group. Another assessment tool is the CORE-R Battery (Burlingame et al., 2006), which includes measures for selection, process, and outcome to help group leaders assess the effectiveness of their groups.

EP 2.1.7a

A Systems Framework for Assessing Groups

EP 2.1.3b

Like families, groups are social systems characterized by repetitive patterns. All social systems share an important principle—namely, that persons who compose a given system gradually limit their behaviors to a relatively narrow range of patterned responses as they interact with others within that system. Groups thus evolve implicit rules or norms that govern behaviors, shape patterns, and regulate internal operations.

A systems framework helps leaders to assess group processes; they can attend to the repetitive interactions of members, infer rules that govern those interactions, and weigh the functionality of those rules and patterns. For example, a group may develop a habit in which one person's complaints receive a great deal of attention while others' concerns are dismissed. The "rules" leading to such a pattern may be that "if the group didn't attend to Joe, he might drop out or become angry" or "Joe is hurting more than anyone else" or "Joe's issues resonate with those of others, so he deserves the additional attention, whereas the other concerns that are raised aren't shared concerns and don't deserve group time." This pattern may result in the disenfranchisement of the members who feel marginalized or it may lead to relief that some members can recede while the spotlight is on Joe. More constructively, the other members may concur that Joe's issues are symptomatic of the group and thus be glad that he is bringing them to the surface for discussion.

Conceptualizing and organizing group processes into response patterns enables leaders to make systematic, ongoing, and relevant assessments. This knowledge can help "make sense" of seemingly random and chaotic interactions and bring comfort to group leaders, who may otherwise feel that they are floundering in sessions. In addition to identifying patterned behaviors, leaders must concurrently attend to individual and group behaviors. Observing processes at both levels is difficult, however, and workers sometimes become discouraged when they realize they attended more to individual dynamics than to group dynamics (or the converse), resulting in vague or incomplete assessment formulations. Recognizing this dilemma, we discuss strategies for accurately assessing both individual and group patterns in the remainder of this chapter.

Assessing Individuals' Patterned Behaviors

Some of the patterned behaviors that group members display are *functional*—that is, they enhance the well-being of individual members and the quality of group relationships. Other patterned behaviors are *dysfunctional*—that is, they erode the capacities of members and are destructive to relationships and group cohesion. Sometimes, people join groups specifically because some of their patterned behaviors are producing distress in their interpersonal relationships. At times, though, members are not aware of the patterned nature of their behavior or of the impact it has on their ability to achieve their goals. A major role of leaders in groups, then, is to aid members to become aware of their patterned behavioral responses, to determine the effects of these responses on themselves and others, and to choose whether to change such responses. To carry out this role, leaders must formulate a profile of the recurring responses of each member, utilizing the concepts of *content* and *process*, which we discussed earlier in this book. Recall that content refers to verbal statements and related topics that members discuss, whereas process involves the ways members relate or behave as they interact in the group and discuss content. Consider the following description of a member's behavior in two initial group sessions:

In the first group meeting, June moved her chair close to the leader's chair. June complimented the leader when giving her introduction to the group and made a point to verbalize her agreement with several of the leader's statements. In the subsequent meetings, June again sat next to the leader and offered advice to other group members, referring to opinions she thought were jointly held by her and the leader. Later, June tried to initiate a conversation with the leader concerning what she regarded as negative behavior of another group member in front of that member and the rest of the group.

It is at the process level that leaders discover many of the patterned behavioral responses of individuals. The preceding case example revealed June's possible patterned or *thematic behaviors*. For example, we might infer that June is jockeying to establish an exclusive relationship with the leader and bidding for an informal position of co-leader in the group. Or perhaps she is uncomfortable with her peers and finds the leader to be a safe ally who won't reject her. Viewed alone, none of June's discrete behaviors provides sufficient information to justify drawing a conclusion about a possible response pattern. Viewed collectively, however, the repetitive responses warrant inferring that a pattern does, in fact, exist, and may create difficulty for June in the group and in other aspects of her life.

Identifying Roles of Group Members

EP 2.1.10e

In identifying patterned responses of individuals, leaders also need to attend to the various roles that members assume in the group. For example, members may assume *leadership* roles that are *formal* (explicitly sanctioned by the group) or *informal* (emerging as a result of group needs). Further, a group may have several members who serve different functions or who head rival subgroups.

Some members may assume *task-related* or *instrumental* roles that facilitate the group's efforts to define problems, implement problem-solving strategies, and carry out tasks. These members may propose goals or actions, suggest procedures, request pertinent facts, clarify issues, or offer an alternative or conclusion for the group to consider. Other members may adopt *maintenance* roles that are oriented to altering, maintaining, and strengthening the group's functioning. Members who take on such roles may offer compromises, encourage and support the contributions of others, comment on the emotional climate of the meeting, or suggest group standards. Some members may emerge as spokespersons around concerns of the group or enact other *expressive* roles. Rather than confront such a person as a negative influence, it is often useful to consider whether, in fact, that person is bringing to the fore issues that have been discussed outside of the group or that are lingering below the surface in group sessions. In short, that person may be acting as an informal group leader who can be joined in seeking to make the group succeed (Breton, 1985). Still other members may assume self-serving roles by seeking to meet their own needs at the expense of the group. Such members may attack the group or its values, stubbornly resist the group's wishes, continually disagree with or interrupt others, assert authority or superiority, display lack of involvement, pursue extraneous subjects, or find various ways to call attention to themselves.

Members may also carry labels assigned by other members, such as "clown," "critic," "uncommitted," "lazy," "dumb," "silent one," "rebel," "over-reactor," or "good mother." Such labeling stereotypes members, making it difficult for them to relinquish the set of expected behaviors or to change their way of relating to the group. Hartford (1971) elaborates:

> For instance, the person who has become the clown may not be able to make a serious and substantial contribution to the group because, regardless of what he says, everyone laughs. If one person has established a high status as the initiator, others may not be able to initiate for fear of threatening his position. If one has established himself in a dependency role in a pair or subgroup, he may not be able to function freely until he gets cues from his subgroup partner. (p. 218)

One or more members may also be assigned the role of scapegoat, bearing the burden of responsibility for the group's problems and the brunt of teasing or negative responses from other members. Such individuals may attract the marginalized role because they are socially awkward and repeatedly make social blunders in futile attempts to elicit positive responses from others (Balgopal & Vassil, 1983; Klein, 1970). Or, they may assume this role because they fail to recognize nonverbal cues that facilitate interaction in the group and thus behave without regard to the subtle nuances that govern the behavior of other members (Balgopal & Vassil, 1983; Beck, 1974). Individuals may also unknowingly perpetuate the scapegoat role they have assumed in their nuclear families, workplaces, schools, or social systems. Although group scapegoats demonstrate repetitive dysfunctional behaviors that attract the hostility or mockery of the group, the presence of the role signals a group phenomenon (and pattern) whose maintenance requires the tacit cooperation of all members.

Individuals may also assume the role of an isolate, which is characterized by the member being ignored by the group, not reaching out to others, or doing so but being rejected. Sometimes this lack of affiliation may arise from poor social skills or values, interests, and beliefs that set the individual apart from the other group members (Hartford, 1971). The isolate differs from the scapegoat in that the latter gets attention, even if it is negative, whereas the former is simply disregarded.

Some members, of course, assume roles that strengthen relationships and enhance group functioning. By highlighting these positive behaviors, leaders may boost members' self-esteem and place the spotlight on behaviors that other members may fruitfully emulate. It is important to identify all of the roles that members assume because those roles profoundly affect the group's capacity to respond to the individual needs of members and its ability to fulfill the treatment objectives. Identifying roles is also vital because members tend to play out in treatment or task groups the same roles that they assume in other social contexts. Members need to understand the impact of functional and dysfunctional roles on themselves and others.

Developing Profiles of Individual Behavior

EP 2.1.10e

During assessment, group leaders need to develop accurate behavioral profiles of each individual. To carry out this function, leaders must record functional and dysfunctional responses that members displayed in initial sessions. Operating from a strengths perspective, it is important to record and acknowledge functional behaviors such as the following:

Functional Behaviors
1. Expresses caring for group members or significant others
2. Demonstrates organizational or leadership ability
3. Expresses her/himself clearly
4. Cooperates with and supports others
5. Assists in maintaining focus and helping the group accomplish its purposes
6. Expresses feelings openly and congruently
7. Accurately perceives what others say (beyond surface meanings) and conveys understanding to them
8. Responds openly and positively to constructive feedback
9. Works within guidelines established by the group
10. "Owns" responsibility for behavior
11. Risks and works to change self
12. Counts in others by considering their opinions, including them in decision making, or valuing their differences
13. Participates in discussions and assists others to join in
14. Gives positive feedback to others concerning their strengths and growth
15. Acknowledges his or her own strengths and growth
16. Expresses humor constructively
17. Supports others nonverbally

Dysfunctional Behaviors
1. Interrupts, speaks for others, or rejects others' ideas
2. Placates or patronizes
3. Belittles, criticizes, or expresses sarcasm
4. Argues, blames, attacks, or engages in name-calling
5. Verbally dominates group "air time"
6. Gives advice prematurely
7. Expresses disgust and disapproval nonverbally
8. Talks too much, talks too loudly, or whispers
9. Withdraws, assumes the role of spectator, ignores others, or shows disinterest
10. Talks about tangential topics or sidetracks the group in other ways
11. Displays distracting physical movements
12. Is physically aggressive or "horses" around
13. Clowns, mimics, or makes fun of others
14. Aligns with others to form destructive subgroups
15. Intellectualizes or diagnoses (e.g., "I know what's wrong with you")
16. Avoids focusing on self or withholds feelings and concerns pertinent to personal problems

These behaviors can also be tracked by client self-reports or by peer observation within the group. In either case, the data may be captured through charts, logs, diaries or journals, self-anchored rating scales or observations, which can be naturalistic; through role plays and simulations; or through analysis of videotapes of group process (Toseland & Rivas, 2009).

Table 11-4 is a record of the HEART young women's support group that illustrates how leaders can develop accurate behavioral profiles of each member by keeping track of the members' functional and dysfunctional behaviors. The profile of behaviors in Table 11-4 identifies specific responses by individuals in the group but does not necessarily identify their *patterned or stylized* behaviors. Recording the specific responses of individuals at each session, however, aids in identifying over time recurring behaviors and roles members are assuming. For example, a glance at Table 11-4 suggests that Liz is vulnerable to becoming an isolate in the group.

In addition to direct observation, information about the behavioral styles of members can be obtained from many other sources. In the formation phase of the group, for example, social workers can elicit pertinent data in preliminary interviews with the prospective member or from family members, agency records, or other professionals who have referred members to the group. Within the group, leaders may glean substantial data concerning patterned behavior of members by carefully attending and exploring members' descriptions of their problems and interactions with others.

Identifying Individuals' Growth

EP 2.1.10e

Because growth occurs in subtle and diverse forms, a major role of leaders is to document (and to assist the group to document) the incremental growth of each member. To sharpen your ability to observe individuals' development, we suggest that you develop a record-keeping format that provides a column for notations concerning the growth that members demonstrate from one session to the next or across several sessions. Without such a documentation system, it is easy to overlook

TABLE-11-4 EXAMPLES OF BEHAVIORAL PROFILES OF HEART GROUP MEMBERS

NAME	DESCRIPTIVE ATTRIBUTES	FUNCTIONAL BEHAVIOR	DYSFUNCTIONAL BEHAVIOR
Amelia	15 years old Lives with both parents and one sister. Artistic, plays tennis	Participated often in the group Asked pertinent questions of other members Offered to take on maintenance tasks for the group Volunteered an idea for a warm-up exercise for the group	Challenged the leader's motivation and ability to facilitate the group Hesitates to focus on self
Liz	16 years old Lives with both parents Only child Reports intense depression and anxiety	Expressed feelings clearly Attentive Expressed desire to change	Withdrawn, speaks infrequently in the group
Maggie	16 years old Lives with both parents Only child Student body President	Expressed ambivalence about attending group Participated often, and made positive contributions to the group Took a risk, by sharing personal concerns about relating to peers	Sometimes off topic, pursued extraneous lines of questioning Confronts bluntly Experiences difficulty talking about self
Amber	17 years old Lives with parents and grandmother Only child Plays first base on varsity softball team	Joined in discussions, and supported others appropriately Recognized concerns and strengths with regards to self-esteem Acknowledged the possibility for change	Teased another member Made some distracting comments
June	16 years old Lives with mother Brother diagnosed with diabetes Participates in several activities: library club, band, and volunteers at the animal shelter and convalescent center.	Initiated group discussion of several topics Outgoing and spontaneous Adds energy to group	At times interrupted others in the group Dominates "air time" Attempts to ally herself with the facilitator
Jen	15 years old Lives with both parents Recently moved, is new at her school Used to play volleyball, holds part-time job in a fast food restaurant	Attentive in group Discussed hurtful messages she receives from her parents Acknowledged change as a result of her participation in group	Speaks infrequently Expressed sense of hopelessness about change

© Cengage Learning 2013

significant changes and thus miss vital opportunities to substantiate the direct relationship between member's efforts to change and the positive results they attain.

Assessing Individuals' Cognitive Patterns

EP 2.1.10d

Just as group members develop patterned ways of behaving, they also develop patterned cognitions—that is, typical or habituated ways of perceiving and thinking about themselves, other persons, and the world around them. Cognitive patters are discussed in more depth in Chapter 13. Such patterned cognitions are revealed in the form of silent mental speech or internal dialogue that individuals utilize to define the meaning of life events. To use an analogy, it is as though various types of events in a person's life trigger a tape recording in his or her mind that automatically repeats the same messages over and over, coloring the person's perceptions of events and determining his or her reality. Examples of negative internal dialogue that tend to create problems for group members include repeated messages such as "I'm a failure," "No one wants to hear what I have to say," "The other people in this group are stupid," and "Other people are better than I am."

Patterned cognitions and behavior are inextricably related and reciprocally reinforce each other. The following case example of a group member's problem illustrates the link between cognitions and behavior and the insidious effect that negative cognitions may have on a client's life.

> **CASE EXAMPLE**
>
> Amber, a 17-year-old high school student, joined a therapy group for teenage girls who are overweight. She reported experiencing low self-esteem, especially with regard to her body. She stated that she lacked confidence when interacting with boys and while changing clothes for gym and softball practice. Amber also discussed difficulties shopping with her friends, stating, "I can't fit into any of the clothes there, and I really want to because they're really cute clothes and it kinda makes me feel out of the loop with my friends."
>
> In contrast to these moments of insecurity, Amber informed the group that there were times when she felt good about herself. Because of her skill at softball, she experienced a boost in confidence when playing on the team. Additionally, Amber stated that she received positive attention from her peers, particularly boys, at dance parties. "You know, at parties and things, whenever rap songs come on about fat girls and fat booties everyone looks to me and I get to dance in front of everybody ... I feel good when the attention is on me."
>
> Amber's cognitions relate to her desire for acceptance by her peers. Although she recognizes positive aspects of herself and has been successful in putting her skills to use, she continues to seek approval from others, although on their terms. Her thoughts can be summarized as "I'm not good enough as I am" and "People will like me if I act how they want me to." In group, Amber discovered that these thoughts contribute to her feelings of low self-esteem, and explored other ways of thinking. She stated, "They call me bootylicious sometimes. I like that because it makes me stand out from them, but maybe I'd appreciate another nickname that didn't have to do with my body."

Because patterned behavioral and cognitive responses are inextricably interwoven and perpetuate each other, leaders must be able to intervene in groups to modify dysfunctional cognitions. Prior to intervening, however, leaders must fine-tune their perceptions to identify the thematic cognitions that lie behind members' verbal statements. The following statements, for example, reveal conclusions members have drawn about themselves and others:

Male teen in group on adjusting to divorce in the family: "I can't tell how I feel." (If I am honest my parents will reject me or I will hurt their feelings.)
Member of job-preparedness group: "The economy is so bad nobody is hiring." (My situation is hopeless and out of my control.)
Member of bereavement group: "Sometimes I lost my patience when mother soiled herself. I shouldn't have shouted at her." (I am a bad daughter/caregiver.)
Teen girl in HEART group: "If you accept yourself, then you just say, 'Okay. I'm resigning myself to being fat forever.'" (I do not like the way I am, yet I am not confident that I can change.)

You can record the cognitive themes or patterns of members in the same manner that you observe and record their functional and problematic behavioral responses. Returning to the example of the girl's support group profiled in Table 11-4, note the cognitive responses of several members recorded by the leader in the same session, as illustrated in Table 11-5.

Social workers can help group members identify cognitive patterns during problem exploration by asking questions such as "When that happened, what did you say to yourself?", "What conclusions do you draw about others under those circumstances?", or "What kind of self-talk do you remember before your anxiety level rose?" Leaders can also teach groups to recognize symptoms of patterned cognitions. As the group grasps the significance of internal dialogue and attends to cognitive patterns expressed by members, leaders should reinforce the group's growth by giving members descriptive feedback concerning their accomplishments.

Assessing Groups' Patterned Behaviors

Beyond attending to the ritualized behaviors of individual members, group workers must be alert to the patterns of the group as a whole. To heighten your awareness of functional and dysfunctional patterned group behaviors, we provide contrasting examples in Table 11-6.

EP 2.1.7a

The functional behaviors in the table are characteristic of a mature therapeutic group. These facilitative group behaviors may also emerge in the *initial* stages of development, although their appearance may be fleeting as the group tackles early developmental tasks, such as building trust and defining common interests and goals. Once social workers fine-tune their observational skills to detect positive group behavior, they can then intervene in a timely fashion to note

TABLE-11-5 EXAMPLES OF COGNITIVE RESPONSES MADE BY SOME HEART GROUP MEMBERS

NAME	FUNCTIONAL COGNITIONS	PROBLEMATIC COGNITIONS
Amelia	It's okay to risk talking about feelings. Other people will usually treat those feelings with respect and be responsive. I'm willing to risk by staying in this group because I know I need help.	I've been hurt by the past. I don't think I'll ever get over it. I will always blame myself for what happened.
June	I care about other people. I want to help them. I can do things to make myself feel better. I can get help from this group.	I can't stop myself from talking so much. I always do that when I get anxious. People in this group may not like me.
Maggie	I have personal strengths. There are good things about me; I'm a leader. I can take care of myself.	My ideas, beliefs, positions are right; those of other people are wrong. I have to be right (or others won't respect me). You can't trust other people; they will hurt you if they can. The less you disclose about yourself, the better.

them and reinforce their continued use (Larsen, 1980). Incidental positive behaviors that are commonly revealed early in the life of a group include the following:

- *The group "faces up to" a problem and makes a necessary modification or adjustment.*
- *The group responds positively the first time a member takes a risk by revealing a personal problem.*
- *Members of the group are supportive toward other members or demonstrate investment in the group.*
- *The group works harmoniously for a period of time.*
- *Members effectively make a decision together.*
- *Members adhere to specific group guidelines, such as maintaining focus on work to be accomplished.*
- *Members give positive feedback to another member or observe positive ways the group has worked together.*
- *The group responsibly confronts a member who is dominating interaction or interfering in some way with the group accomplishing its task.*
- *Members pitch in to clean up after a group session.*

The group may also display transitory negative behaviors in initial sessions. Many of these behaviors are to be expected in the early phases of group development. Their appearance may signal evolving group patterns that are not firmly "set" in the group's interactional repertoire. Counterproductive behaviors that may evolve into patterns include any of the examples of dysfunctional behavior listed in Table 11-6.

Just as we have suggested that you employ a written system to record the functional and dysfunctional responses of individual members, we also recommend using the same type of record-keeping system to track the functional and dysfunctional behaviors of the group itself, adding a column to record the growth or changes that you note in the group's behavior.

Assessing Group Alliances

As members of new groups find other members with compatible attitudes, interests, and responses, they develop patterns of affiliation and relationship with these members. Subgroup formations may include pairs, triads, and foursomes. Larger subgroups may develop subdivisions influencing "who addresses whom, who sits together, who comes and leaves together, and even who may meet or talk together outside of the group" (Hartford, 1971, p. 204).

The subgroupings that invariably develop do not necessarily impair group functioning. Members may derive strength and support from subgroups, in turn enhancing their participation and investment in the larger group. Indeed, it is through the process of establishing subgroups or natural coalitions that group members achieve true intimacy. Problems may arise, however, when members develop exclusive subgroups that disallow intimate relationships with other group members or inhibit members from supporting the goals of the larger group. Subgroups that meet online or in person outside of group sessions can have a particularly pernicious effect on the functioning of the group as a whole. Competing factions can often impede or destroy a group.

To work effectively with groups, leaders must be skilled in identifying subdivisions and assessing their impact on the group. To recognize these subdivisions, leaders may wish to construct a

EP 2.1.10j

TABLE-11-6 EXAMPLES OF GROUP BEHAVIORS

FUNCTIONAL GROUP BEHAVIOR	PROBLEMATIC GROUP BEHAVIOR
• Members openly communicate personal feelings and attitudes and anticipate that other members will be helpful. • Members listen carefully to one another and give all ideas a fair hearing. • Decisions are reached through group consensus after considering everyone's views and feelings. Members make efforts to incorporate the views of dissenters rather than to dominate or override these views. • Members recognize and give feedback regarding strengths and growth of other members. • Members recognize the uniqueness of each individual and encourage participation in different and complementary ways. • Members take turns speaking. Members use "I" messages to speak for themselves, readily owning their own feelings and positions on matters. • Members encourage others to speak for themselves. • Members adhere to the guidelines for behavior established in initial sessions. • The group is concerned about its own operations and addresses obstacles that prevent individual members from fully participating or the group from achieving its objectives. • Members assume responsibility for the group's functioning and success. Members also express their caring for others. • The group shows its commitment by staying on task, assuming group assignments, and working out problems that impair group functioning. • Members concentrate on the present and what they can do to change themselves. • Members are sensitive to the needs and feelings of others and readily give emotional support.	• Members talk on a superficial level and are cautious about revealing their feelings and opinions. • Members are readily critical and evaluative of each other; they rarely acknowledge or listen to contributions from others. • Dominant members count out other members in decision making; members make decisions prematurely without identifying or weighing possible alternatives. • Members focus heavily on negatives and rarely accredit positive behaviors of others. • Members are critical of differences in others, viewing them as a threat. • Members compete for the chance to speak, often interrupting one another. • Members do not personalize their messages but rather use indirect forms of communication to express their feelings and positions. • Members speak for others. • Members display disruptive behaviors incompatible with group guidelines. Members resist talking about the here and now or addressing personal or group problems. Examples of distracting behaviors include fidgeting, whispering, or reading while others are talking. • Members show unwillingness to accept responsibility for themselves or the success of the group and tend to blame the leader when things are not going well. • Members dwell on past exploits and experiences and talk about issues extraneous to the group's purpose. • Members focus on others rather than on themselves. • Members show little awareness of the needs and feelings of others; emotional investment in others is limited.

sociogram of group alignments. Credited to Moreno and Jennings (Jennings, 1950), a sociogram graphically depicts patterned affiliations and relationships between group members by using symbols for people and interactions. Figure 11-1 illustrates a sociogram that captures the predominant connections, attractions, and repulsions among members of the HEART group during the fifth session in which the teens discussed the challenges of fitting in with current fashions and peers.

Sociograms are representations of group alliances *at a given point* because alliances inevitably shift and change, particularly in the early stages of group development. Charting the transitory bonds that occur early in group life can prove valuable to leaders in deciding where and when to intervene to modify, enhance, or stabilize relationships between members.

Assessing Power and Decision-Making Styles

Like families, groups develop ways of distributing power among members. To ensure that their needs are not discounted, some members may make bids for power and disparage other members. Others may discount themselves and permit more aggressive members to dominate the group. Still others value power and actively pursue it as an end in itself. Some subgroups may try to eliminate opposing factions from the group or align themselves with other members or subgroups in a bid to increase their power. Groups, in fact, are sometimes torn apart and meet their demise because unresolved power issues prevent the group from meeting the needs of some members (Smokowski, Rose, & Bacallao, 2001).

When social workers assess groups, they need to identify the current capacity of members to share

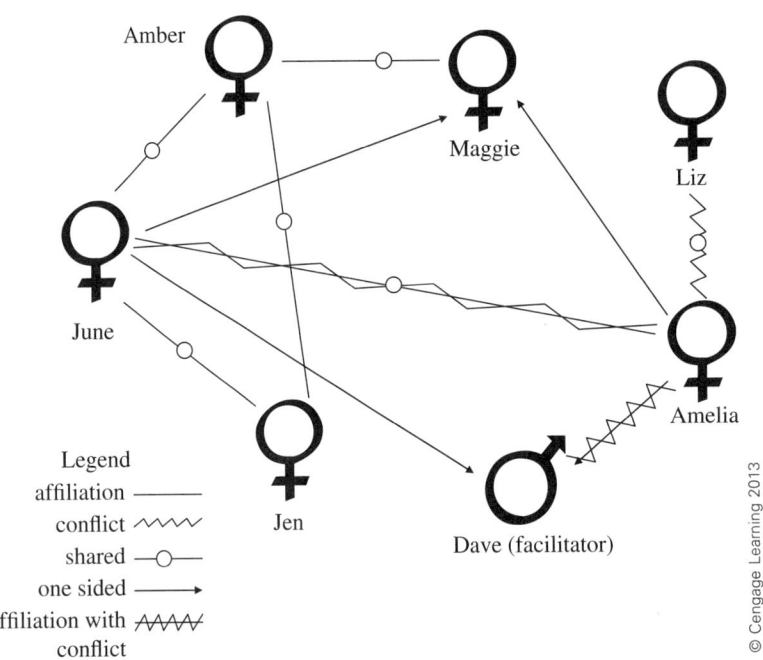

FIG-11-1 Sociogram

power and resources equally among themselves and to implement problem-solving steps that ensure "win-win" solutions. Leaders must help the group make each member count if the group is to advance through stages of development into maturity. You can accelerate the group's progress through these stages by assuming a facilitative role in teaching and modeling effective decision making and by assisting the group to adopt explicit guidelines for making decisions in the initial sessions.

Assessing Group Norms, Values, and Cohesion

EP 2.1.7a

To understand a group, the social worker must assess its norms, values, and cohesion. Imbedded in the norms or ways of operating are the members' implicit expectations and beliefs about how they or others should behave under a given circumstance. The interplay of these values and the emergence of constructive group norms affect the group's capacity to develop cohesion and mutual aid.

Norms

Norms are regulatory mechanisms that give groups a measure of stability and predictability by letting members know what they can expect from the group and from one another. Norms may define the *specific* behaviors that are appropriate or permissible for individuals or they may define the *range* of behaviors that are acceptable in the group. Norms represent the internalization of the group guidelines discussed earlier in this chapter.

Groups develop formal and informal sanctions to reduce behaviors that are considered deviant and to return the system to its prior equilibrium. For example, an implicit group norm may be that other group members may not challenge the opinions of the informal leader. If a new group member treads on this norm by questioning the opinion of the informal leader, other members may side with the informal leader against the "upstart," pressuring him or her to back away.

People often learn about the norms of particular groups by observing situations in which norms have been violated. Toseland and Rivas (2009) note that as group members watch the behavior of other members they reward some behaviors and punish others. Once members realize that sanctions are applied to certain behaviors, they usually attempt to adapt their behavior to avoid disapproval or punishment.

The extent to which members adhere to norms varies. Some norms are flexible or weakly held, and the psychological "costs" to members of violation are low or nonexistent. In the HEART group, speaking out of order or speaking while another person is speaking is understood as undesirable, yet often goes unchecked by the members during their sessions together. In other instances, the group's investment in norms is significant and group reaction is severe when members violate them. The members of the HEART group vigilantly uphold their shared agreement to be respectful in group. Members who put others on the spot or criticize brusquely are reproached without delay.

The relative status of members—that is, the evaluation or ranking of each member's position in the group relative to the others—also determines the extent to which members adhere to norms. Toseland, Jones, and Gelles (2006) observe that low-status members are the least likely to conform to group norms because they have little to lose by deviating. Such behavior is less likely if the member has hopes of gaining a higher status. Medium-status group members tend to conform to group norms so that they can retain their status and perhaps gain a higher status. High-status members generally conform to valued group norms when they are establishing their position. At the same time, because of their elevated position, high-status members have more freedom to deviate from accepted norms.

Norms may or may not support the treatment objectives of a group and should be assessed in terms of whether they are beneficial or detrimental to the well-being of members and the overall treatment objectives of the group. Table 11-7 provides examples of both functional and problematic norms.

All groups develop norms, and once certain norms are adopted, they influence the group's response to situations and determine the extent to which the group offers its members therapeutic experiences. A major role for the leader, then, is to identify evolving group norms and influence them in ways that create a positive climate for cohesion and change. Discerning norms is often difficult, however, because they are subtly embedded in the group process and can be inferred only from the behavior occurring in the group. Leaders may be able to identify norms by asking themselves key questions such as the following:

EP 2.1.10d

1. What subjects can and cannot be talked about in the group?
2. What kinds of emotional expressions are allowed in the group?
3. What is the group's pattern with regard to working on problems or staying on task?
4. Do group members consider it their own responsibility or the leader's responsibility to make the group's experience successful?
5. What is the group's stance toward the leader?
6. What is the group's attitude toward feedback?
7. How does the group view the contributions of individual members? What kind of labels and roles does the group assign to them?

These questions also enable the leader to improve his or her observations of redundant or patterned behaviors exhibited by members. This is a vital point, because *patterned behaviors are always undergirded by supporting norms.*

Another strategy for identifying norms is to explain the concept of norms to group members and to ask them to identify the guiding "rules" that influence their behavior in the group. This strategy forces members to

TABLE-11-7 EXAMPLES OF GROUP NORMS

FUNCTIONAL	PROBLEMATIC
• Take a risk by spontaneously revealing personal content about yourself.	• Keep the discussion centered on superficial topics; avoid taking risks or self-disclosing.
• Treat the leader with respect and seriously consider the leader's input.	• Play the game "Let's get the leader." Harass, criticize, or complain about the leader whenever the opportunity arises.
• Focus on working out personal problems.	• Spend time complaining about problems and don't commit the energy necessary to work them out.
• Allow members equal opportunity to participate in group discussions or to become the focus of the group.	• Let aggressive members dominate the group.
• Talk about any subject pertinent to your problem.	• Don't talk about emotionally charged or delicate subjects.
• Communicate directly other group members.	• Direct comments to the leader.
• Talk about obstacles that get in the way of achieving the group's goals.	• Ignore obstacles and avoid talking about group problems.

bring to a conscious level the group norms that are developing and to make choices in favor of those that advance the group's goals. It is also an important topic for the leader who is joining an existing group to consider.

Values

In addition to norms, every treatment group will create a set of values held in common by all or most of the group's members that include ideas, beliefs, ideologies, or theories about the truth, right or wrong, good or bad, and beautiful, ugly, or inappropriate (Hartford, 1971). Examples of such values include the following:

- *This is a "good" group and worth our commitment and investment of time. (Alternatively, this is a "dumb" group, and we're not going to get anything out of it.)*
- *It is "bad" to betray confidences to outsiders.*
- *People who belong to different groups (e.g., authorities or individuals of a different race, religion, or status) are "bad" or inferior.*
- *It is undesirable to show feelings in the group.*
- *It is fun to try to outwit authority figures like group leaders.*

Just as the group's "choice" of norms significantly affects its capacity to offer a therapeutic milieu, so does the group's "choice" of values. Similar to norms, values can be categorized as functional or dysfunctional when viewed in light of the group's therapeutic objectives. Values that encourage work on personal problems or self-disclosure, acceptance of others, and a positive attitude toward the group, for example, are functional to the group's development. By contrast, values that discourage self-disclosure, create barriers in relationships or negative attitudes toward the group, or prevent members from working on problems are obviously unhelpful.

Cohesion

EP 2.1.7a

In the initial phases of the group's life, leaders must also assess and foster the development of cohesion in groups. Defined as the degree to which members are attracted to one another, cohesion is correlated, under certain conditions, to productivity, participation in and out of the group, self-disclosure, risk taking, attendance, and other vital concerns (Rose, 1989; Stokes, 1983). Cohesion in groups positively affects members' satisfaction and personal adjustment. Greater cohesiveness leads to increased self-esteem, more willingness to listen to others, freer expression of feeling, better reality testing, higher self-confidence, and more effective use of other members' evaluations in enhancing a member's own development (Toseland & Rivas, 2009; Yalom, 2005).

Cohesion is inextricably linked to the development of norms in a beginning group. Norms that may potentially interfere with both group formation and cohesion include irregular attendance, tardiness, subgroups, changing membership, interpersonal aggression, excessive dependence on the leader, dominance by a few members, and general passivity in the interaction (Rose, 1989). Research on negative group experiences indicates that the individuals who are damaged by the group may be those very members who are too timid to help contribute to group rules and thus have little investment in the norms that have been negotiated between the leader and more vocal members (Smokowski, Rose, & Bacallao, 2001). These detrimental norms require the attention of both the leader and the group members, because the failure to address them discourages group development and jeopardizes the group itself.

Formation of Task Groups

We move now from consideration of treatment groups to task groups. Although many of the same issues considered with treatment groups also apply to task groups, this section focuses on planning and beginning task groups. Task groups are organized to meet client, organizational, and community needs (Toseland & Rivas, 2009). Among the various types of task groups are teams, treatment conferences, and staff development groups. Task groups may also be formed to meet organizational needs such as committees, cabinets, and boards of directors. Task groups instituted to meet community needs include social action groups, coalitions, and delegate councils (Toseland & Rivas, 2009). All of these groups focus on producing products, developing policies, and making decisions rather than on enhancing the personal growth of members (Ephross & Vassil, 1988).

Important early tasks in forming and assessing task groups are planning for the group and structuring initial sessions to address the purpose of the group.

Planning for Task Groups

Whereas members of treatment groups are recruited for the specific purpose that prompted the group's formation, membership in task groups may be constrained by organizational bylaws or dictated by organizational structure (Toseland & Rivas, 2009). For example, members of a

EP 2.1.7a

delegate council may be elected by constituents, and an organization may decide who should participate in a treatment conference by the professional role needed (e.g., speech therapist, teacher, social worker, behavior specialist). Task group composition may be voluntary, by appointment, or by election, but it should always be responsive to the group's purpose and goals. For example, a treatment conference may have the purpose of coordinating the efforts of members of a team involved in serving a particular client or family. An ad hoc committee may be recruited to work on a fundraising event for an agency. A board of directors is appointed or elected to provide guidance and accountability to an organization. A community crime prevention panel may consist of volunteers from the neighborhood who want to work for increased services and police presence in the area.

The initiation of a task group and the determination of its purpose may come from many sources. For example, boards are required by nonprofit governance regulations, a staff member might propose a delegate council in a halfway house, the director of an agency might initiate a committee to develop better agency communications, or residents of a housing development might suggest a social action group to deal with poor housing conditions.

Members of any task group should have the interest, information, skills, and power needed to accomplish the purpose of the group. The specific purpose of the group suggests sources for its membership. For example, a group formed to study how managed care affects service delivery might include consumers, providers, and representatives from insurance groups and regulatory agencies. A group formed to plan a new teen pregnancy program might include teen parents, health care providers, teachers, public health researchers, and child welfare workers.

Membership should be large enough and sufficiently diverse to represent the major constituencies affected by the problem being targeted and participants should possess adequate skills and knowledge for addressing the group's purposes. As with treatment groups, organizers should ensure that no individual is an isolate. For example, a special education advisory committee should not consist of a group of professionals plus a token parent. When consumers or those whose personal experience is valuable to the task group's purpose are included, multiple representatives should be recruited for the group and, if possible, should serve as representatives of other consumers. For example, in a committee on mental health reform, multiple consumers and parents might be involved and some should represent groups, such as the National Alliance for the Mentally Ill. Taking these steps will help enhance the comfort, power, and legitimacy of group members.

Quality planning in this stage is reflected by accurately and clearly communicating the group's purposes and expectations to prospective members. The level of clarity achieved has important implications for whether those prospective members decide to attend and, later, how well they perform the functions of the group.

As with treatment groups, task groups may be open or closed in time and in membership. Formal boards or committees generally are ongoing but have structures that provide for the rotation of membership in and out of the group, allowing for "staggered" changes in terms to assure continuity. Other groups may be time limited and relatively closed in membership (e.g., a task force to review an incident where a resident was injured, a committee to plan an agency's anniversary celebration). Other groups may be ongoing but have closed membership (e.g., an ethics committee that hears different cases each month as brought to them by members of the hospital staff).

Beginning the Task Group

The agenda for a beginning session of a task group is similar to that for a treatment group. It includes facilitating introductions, clarifying the purpose of the group, discussing ground rules, helping members feel a part of the group, setting goals, and anticipating obstacles (Toseland & Rivas, 2009). An opening statement, including the host agency's function and mission as it relates to the group purpose, should be shared so that members will understand why they have been called together. Members can then be assisted to find commonalities in their concerns and experiences and to identify shared goals for group participation. Some members may know one another from previous roles and have positive or negative preconceptions from that past. "Ice breakers" and other introductory activities can be used to facilitate communication and identify experiences and resources that members possess (Dossick & Shea, 1995; Gibbs, 1995).

EP 2.1.10a

Developing group rules and concurrence on decision making (e.g., majority rule, consensus) then follows. A common rule involves adherence to confidentiality, as premature or distorted release of information might hinder the work and destroy the cohesion of the group. Other rules in task groups usually include expectations about attendance and preparation, and structural issues such as timing of meetings, submission of agenda items, and effective communications (Levi, 2007). On boards of directors a subcommittee may be responsible for recruiting and orienting new members and the "ground rules" specified in by-laws and board policies. New members may also be paired with veteran members who can help them prepare for and participate fully in meetings from the outset of their service (Thomas & Strom-Gottfried, 2011).

Task groups then proceed to goal setting. Such goals always include those mandated by the external purpose of the group, such as reviewing managed care arrangements in the agency, planning a conference, reviewing audit reports, implementing new regulations on confidentiality, or coordinating care. In addition, the group may generate its own goals—for example, generating a list of best practices in achieving its purpose or tailoring its response to the group's purpose based on the specific talents and assets available in the group.

As with treatment groups, task group members may take on or be assigned formal (e.g., secretary, chairperson, treasurer) and informal (e.g., timekeeper, devil's advocate, instrumental leader, expressive leader) roles. Whether these roles are constructive depends on how they are enacted and the extent to which they help the group fulfill its purpose. As with other types of groups, assessing the behaviors of individual members and the group as a whole will help identify functional and dysfunctional patterns. Many of the attributes listed in Table 11-6 and Table 11-7 apply to task groups as well as to treatment groups.

Other parallels with treatment groups include the evolution of subgroups, norms, cohesion, and the role of members' status in group dynamics. As with treatment groups, these phenomena can play either destructive or positive roles in the group's development. For example, a faction within a task group may form a voting bloc that inhibits the full participation of all members or hijacks the democratic decision making of the group. Members' roles and statuses outside the group may play out in their behaviors and relationships in the group. The agency director may be used to deferential treatment and expect that from fellow group members even though in that setting they are intended to be equals. Professionals may be dismissive of (or overly solicitous of) the input of consumer representatives on a committee. Counterproductive norms may include: "attendance is optional," "my opinion doesn't matter," "we never get anything done," or "no one comes prepared." Constructive norms about attendance, respect, full participation, and honesty can help the group effectively and efficiently achieve its purpose. While developing cohesion is less crucial in task groups, the presence of socioemotional ties between members will help with the meaning, commitment, and participation members give to the group process.

Cultural Considerations in Forming and Assessing Groups

Cultural considerations emerge in many forms in practice with groups. Awareness of culture is necessary when constructing a group to address a particular problem or assist a particular participation. It is important when recruiting and screening potential members, when you are assessing individual and group functioning, and when you are employing interventions during different stages of the group process. Zastrow (2011) argues that leaders of diverse groups need "(1) to be aware of personal stereotypes and preconceptions about diverse groups, (2) to have knowledge about the diverse groups that he or she is working with and the special needs of those groups, and (3) to be aware of which intervention techniques are apt to be effective with those groups and which are not (p. 225)." Other authors recommend multilingual materials and group leaders, attention to in-group cultural differences, and group activities that utilize culturally specific or culturally adapted curricula, and foster story-telling and creative expression (Greif & Ephross, 2011; Whaley & Davis, 2007).

EP 2.1.4c

Davis, Galinsky, and Schopler (1995) recommend a specific framework when working with multicultural groups: **R**ecognize, **A**nticipate, and **P**roblem solve. The RAP framework encourages group leaders to: recognize and respect racial, ethnic, and cultural differences among group members; anticipate and respond preventively to potential sources of racial/ethnic tension; and problem-solve using conflict resolution approaches so that the issues and needs of all parties are understood. In its Treatment Improvement Protocol for substance abuse groups, the Substance Abuse and Mental Heath Services Administration (SAMHSA) (2005) offers the following suggestions for facilitating diverse groups:

- *Understand personal biases and prejudices about specific cultural groups.*

- *Pay special attention to issues of diversity when forming groups because the feelings of belonging to an ethnic group can be intensified in group work because there are several individuals to "feel different" from, not just the therapist.*
- *Pay attention to cultural traditions and how they play out in group processes to ensure that these traditions do not interfere with the purpose or progress of the group.*
- *Be aware of how cultural practices affect compliance with treatment requirements as well as communication among group members.*
- *Explore each member's self-identification with an ethnic group (do not assume group membership) because individuals may self-identify in ways other than appearance would indicate.*
- *Be open to learn about different cultures, customs, and beliefs held by members of the group.*
- *The greater the mix of ethnicities that a group contains, the more likely biases will surface and mediation will be required by the facilitator.*
- *Before placing a client in a group, the facilitator must assess: the influence of culture, family structure, language, identity processes, health beliefs and attitudes, political issues, and the stigma associated for the minority status.*
- *From the start of a multicultural group, members should feel that race is a permitted topic for discussion.*
- *The behavior of a minority group member might be significantly influenced by cultural norms about sharing personal material with strangers, speaking up before others, offering answers, or advising other members.*

Assessment of group interactions must occur in light of knowledge about each member's culture and his or her individual characteristics within that culture. An instrument proposed by Drankus (2010) offers helpful insight into the nuances of culture and the acculturation continuum from one's "heritage culture" to the dominant culture. It examines three indicators of acculturation: language, cultural behavior, and cultural knowledge. While designed to be administered to individuals, the findings would be helpful in group composition, programming, and facilitation as it identifies often hidden areas of commonality and difference.

Finally, as with individual practice, group workers must be careful not to discredit behavior they do not understand, behavior that may arise from the member's upbringing, or attempts to cope with the current environment and the stress and strain of adaptation (Chau, 1993; Mason, Benjamin, & Lewis, 1996; Pack-Brown, Whittington-Clark, & Parker, 1998).

"The group therapist thus needs to assess how leader–member, member–member, and member–group alliances may be affected by the presence of cultural diversity in the group" (Chen, Kakkad, & Balzano, 2008, p. 1269). Group planners and facilitators can adopt a stance of cultural humility, creating a respectful partnership with clients in order to learn about and learn from the client's lived experience. In groups with pluralistic membership, workers can also teach group members this stance of "reflexive attentiveness" (Hunt, 2001, p. 4) and the concept of cultural humility to assist them in developing norms of mutual acceptance and curiosity.

Of course culture in groups can manifest in ways beyond race and ethnicity. Sexual orientation, gender, generational and geographic differences are but a few of the identities that may affect client participation and group cohesion. For example, in applying group work concepts to practice in rural areas, Gumpert and Saltman (1998) identified several challenges that warrant leaders' attention:

- *Cultural factors such as distrust of confidentiality assurances, strong values of self-reliance, and suspicion of outsiders*
- *Geographic factors such as distance, weather and travel conditions, and difficulty finding a convenient location*
- *Demographic factors such as insufficient numbers of individuals with similar difficulties, resource problems such as the lack of public transportation, insufficient child care, and too few potential group leaders*

When working with groups for traditionally marginalized persons, workers may adopt an empowerment-based approach drawn from feminist theory and liberation theology as resources for empowerment-focused social group work (Lewis, 1991). For example, Cox has described how female welfare recipients have begun to advocate for themselves with social services and other agencies through participation in empowerment-oriented groups (1991). A feminist-orientation to group therapy for women survivors of sexual trauma capitalizes on women's relational abilities to address feelings of mistrust, and to repair and develop socialization and emotional regulation skills (Rittenhouse, 1997; Fallot & Harris, 2002).

Ethics in Practice with Groups

EP 2.1.2c & 2.1.2d

The values and ethical standards introduced in Chapter 4 apply to social work practice with systems of all sizes. However, the nature of in-person and online groups presents particular challenges for interpreting and applying ethical standards. In this chapter we will focus on five particular areas: informed consent, confidentiality, self-determination, competence, and nondiscrimination.

Informed consent involves explaining in clear and understandable language the potential risks and anticipated benefits of service, the limits of confidentiality, the consequences of service refusal, and other policies and considerations that will shape the course of treatment. This should be done as early as feasible in the helping process so that the client can agree to (or decline) those conditions before service commences. Sometimes informed consent is a verbal agreement that is documented in the case record, but more commonly it takes the form of a written document that is acknowledged by both the social worker and client. A common tension in informed consent is the perception by professionals that if they provide a thorough accounting of risks, benefits, and limitations, clients will balk at agreeing to those terms, or they will agree but be overly guarded in what they share with the worker. From the consumer's perspective, though, it is vital to understand from the outset what the "rules of the game" will be, to avoid surprises and to support self-determination. Therefore, it is important to alert clients to the limits of confidentiality—for example, that the worker will need to act on suspicions of child endangerment or potential harm to the client or others—before the client unknowingly divulges such events. Other elements of informed consent depend on the client, setting, and services. For example, parents of minor clients may have the right to review treatment records or to receive updates on services, so those limits should be explained to clients at the outset. People who are receiving services involuntarily may face consequences if they do not attend or cooperate with services, thus those ramifications should be explained. People in time-limited services or programs with a particular focus may be notified at the beginning that the program only addresses certain issues or utilizes a particular type of intervention. For example, in the HEART group for teen girls with obesity, the worker described how the group might fit with (or differ from) the members' expectations: "We won't be doing exercises together or focusing on good eating habits, though sometimes you might trade ideas about those things. Mostly, we'll talk about what it is like for you, what some of the struggles are in losing weight, and how you can help each other understand and overcome those barriers."

In groups, an important part of informed consent involves articulating the expectations and limits of confidentiality. The worker must explain his or her commitment to members' privacy and the legal and ethical limits of that promise. The worker must also involve the group in discussing confidentiality, what it means, and how the commitment to each others' privacy will be reinforced. For example, this was the dialogue in the HEART group:

First Session

Dave (facilitator): Good evening everyone and thank you for joining this group. I am glad to see you all again, and I want to start this session by saying a few words about housekeeping, things about how I'd like the group to go, or what I'd like to see us get out of the group, and also talk about confidentiality requirements for this setting.

So to begin, I hope that we can create a safe space for you all to talk about any concerns that you have about symptoms of depression or anxiety and concerns you have about being overweight and about behaviors that might contribute to that for you. I would like for us to decide how we are going to accomplish that as a group; it's a process that we call consensus decision making. So, together we'll come up with the rules for how we're going to operate for the next 12 weeks that will determine how business is conducted, how each member takes time, and how we support each other and interact to make this group work. As a consideration for everybody and as required by law, everything that happens in the group has to stay in the group. You are allowed to talk about what you say in group outside, but we're not allowed to talk about anybody else's business outside of the group. I'd like to see, just by the nods of your heads, that this is something that you understand and agree with. One exception to that rule is that if I find that someone appears to be in danger either from somebody else or in danger of harming themselves; then I have a duty to report that, to keep everybody safe. And I would like to know that everybody understands and is comfortable with that. [Group nods] Okay, terrific.

As a way to start then I'd like to ask you to introduce yourselves to the group. I'm okay to take a volunteer if somebody wants to volunteer to go first, otherwise I'll need to choose somebody. Would anybody like to lead and introduce themselves to the rest of the group?

Amelia: I'll start.

Dave: Terrific Amelia. Go ahead.

Amelia: Okay. Can I actually ask a question?

Dave: Of course.

Amelia: When you say you have to tell people if you're going to hurt yourself, what if you've already hurt yourself—is that an issue that you would have to tell?

Dave: I would want to know if you currently feel like you're not safe physically. If you're in harm's way, however that may happen, I have to take steps to keep you safe, even if that means breaking our confidentiality agreement.

June: So if I say, Maggie told me, "Oh you can eat wraps in this certain place and they're good for you," I shouldn't tell that to anybody?

Dave: You shouldn't tell anybody that Maggie told you that.

June: Okay. I can say that wraps are good.

Dave: You can say that. I'm particularly focused on personal information about members of the group. So information about eating and exercise and dieting you can share; just don't say who said it.

Amelia: So, like, what's said in group stays in group, right?

Dave: Yes, that's it.

EP 2.1.2b & 2.1.2d

While group workers endeavor to extract and enforce agreements about privacy, informed consent requires facilitators to acknowledge that they cannot control the actions of other members of the group. As the NASW Code of Ethics (2008) states:

When social workers provide counseling services to families, couples, or groups, social workers should seek agreement among the parties involved concerning each individual's right to confidentiality and obligation to preserve the confidentiality of information shared by others. Social workers should inform participants in family, couples, or group counseling that social workers cannot guarantee that all participants will honor such agreements. (1.07f)

Social workers should inform clients involved in family, couples, marital, or group counseling of the social worker's, employer's, and agency's policy concerning the social worker's disclosure of confidential information among the parties involved in the counseling. (1.07g)

This can lead to ethical dilemmas as group facilitators try to balance standards on self-determination, confidentiality, safety, and informed consent. Such a dilemma emerged for Dave facilitating the HEART group when the group was talking about the challenges of peer acceptance and Amber talked about "hooking up" with boys who would later reject her. The group, all older teens but still legal minors, had not discussed the bounds of confidentiality or their parents' and guardians' rights to information. The resulting dilemma for Dave was whether to alert Amber and the others to the possibility that he might need to divulge such risky behavior. In the moment, he decided to let the group focus on the problem Amber was raising, though he shared his dilemma with his supervisor after the session. From that consultation, he decided that he needed to discuss with the group their parents' expectations and how their questions about the group might be handled. He reiterated his intention to alert adult caregivers if he felt members in the group were in danger, and engaged the girls in a discussion about what kinds of things parents had a right to know, including binging and purging behavior, risky sexual activity, and drug and alcohol use. The girls clearly expected privacy when they shared about things they had done in the past (cutting behavior, casual sex, sneaking food) and when they shared about things that "normal teens do, but parents might not like," such as drinking. However, they agreed that it was their responsibility to be honest about their thoughts and actions and Dave's responsibility to assure their safety if he felt they were doing or planning on doing something that could bring immediate harm.

In individual contacts with the girls' parents and caregivers, Dave reaffirmed the boundaries of confidentiality and sought their consent. For example, "As June's mom, you have a right to look at her records and learn about her treatment, but it is our experience that group members need to trust that we'll support their privacy, if they are to bring up the things they are experiencing and feeling most deeply. I'll certainly alert you, or expect June to tell you, if she is putting herself or someone else at risk, but I hope you'll trust me to make that call, knowing that she will share a great deal of personal information that she may want me to keep private. Will that be okay with you?"

These already complex issues can be exacerbated in online and other electronically facilitated groups.

Facilitators must take steps to confirm the identity of participants and reduce risks posed by severely distressed members, minors, or participants who misrepresent themselves and their problems. Some steps to address this include posting agency policies and informed consent procedures on the website so that prospective group members can review them in advance of applying for the group. During the recruitment phase, facilitators are urged to contact prospective members in person to assess suitability for the group and determine how and where the individual will be accessing the group (Meier, 2006). This conversation also provides the opportunity to address another ethical concern, upholding the integrity of written communications and protecting others' privacy. Preliminary discussions with group members should address whether their computer is secure from use by others, their capacity for privacy during group phone calls, and expectations about confidentiality. All members of technology-mediated groups should sign and discuss informed consent statements indicating that they understand the expectations and limits of confidentiality.

While ethical practice demands that all group leaders must be competent in both the issues under discussion in the group and group processes themselves, social workers facilitating electronic groups must be familiar with the challenges of the particular medium (Northen, 2006). For example, this means being skilled in interpreting phone-only communications, mastering expression in instant messaging and online formats (Meier, 2006), and understanding the complexities that can arise in this novel and evolving form of service. Beyond the specialized competence required for technology-enhanced groups, the general standards of professional competence in group work demand that workers:

- *Avoid using techniques with which they are unfamiliar*
- *Understand group processes, dynamics, and skills, even if using manualized curricula (Galinsky, Terzian, & Fraser, 2006)*
- *Respect group members and avoid creating conditions in which members are bullied, coerced, or manipulated*
- *Provide supportive and respectful confrontations when they are required*
- *Put the needs of group members ahead of their own (Corey, Corey, & Callanan, 2007)*
- *Help members to differentiate their personal needs from collective, community needs*
- *"Operationalize values of democracy and self-determination in task group process" (Congress & Lynn, 1997, p. 72).*

A final set of ethical dilemmas for group leaders arises in balancing group composition considerations with values and ethics that emphasize nondiscrimination (Fluhr, 2004). For example, in creating the HEART group, a decision was made to limit membership to girls, ages 15–17, with the rationale that developmental differences would be too great if older or younger members were allowed, and that a mixed-sex group would impede the members' comfort and depth of sharing about crucial issues such as body image, peer relationships, dating, and so on. These are appropriate decisions, driven by the purpose and nature of the group. However, composition decisions naturally exclude certain people on the basis of gender, age, problem profile, and other characteristics. Is this unethical? Such decisions are legitimate if they are made for appropriate clinical reasons, taking into account the need for, purpose of, and goals of the group. Consternation about exclusion can be addressed by creating parallel groups to address unmet needs or excluded populations (overweight teen boys, for example). Of course, competent professionals must always be mindful of their own prejudices, and ensure that they are not veiling biases in an indefensible rationale.

Summary

This chapter presented guidelines for assessing and beginning treatment groups and task groups. We addressed considerations in structuring the group, such as format (open or closed), size, frequency, duration, and composition. We used a systems framework to examine the intersection of individual needs and behaviors and with those of the group as a whole. We discussed common concerns for members at the outset of a group and the strategies for introducing and assessing group guidelines, norms, and values. Chapter 12 turns to considerations of how to build on the social worker's assessment knowledge to construct workable contracts with individuals. We will return to consideration of groups in Chapter 16 to identify the skills needed to intervene at various stages of group development.

CourseMate

Access an integrated eBook and chapter-specific learning tools including glossary terms, chapter outlines, relevant web links, videos, and practice quizzes. Go to **www.cengagebrain.com**.

CHAPTER **12**
Goal Development and Contract Formulation

CHAPTER OVERVIEW

Goals and contracts are products that flow from the assessment process. Chapter 12 elaborates on elements of Phase I by focusing on the knowledge and skills related to the development of goals and the social worker–client agreement to work together. First, we will discuss the purpose and function of goals, with special emphasis on developing goals with voluntary clients, involuntary clients, and minors. The remainder of the chapter is devoted to formulating the contract or service agreement and to methods for monitoring and measuring progress.

As a result of reading this chapter, you will acquire knowledge that will enable you to:

- *Better understand the purpose and function of goals*
- *Articulate the relationship between goals and the target concern*
- *Develop specific, feasible, and measurable goals*
- *Monitor and measure progress toward goal attainment*
- *Formulate a contract or service agreement*

EPAS COMPETENCIES IN THE 12TH CHAPTER

This chapter provides the information that you will need to meet the following practice competencies:

2.1.1b **Practice personal reflection and self-correction to assure continual professional development**

2.1.1d **Demonstrate professional demeanor in behavior, appearance and communication**

2.1.1f **Use supervision and consultation**

2.1.2a **Recognize and manage personal values in a way that allows professional values to guide practice**

2.1.2b **Make ethical decisions by applying standards of the National Association of Social Worker Code of Ethics and, as applicable, of the International Federation of Social Workers/International Association of Schools of Social Work Ethics in Social Work Statement of Principles**

2.1.4c **Recognize and communicate their understanding of the importance of differences in shaping life experiences**

2.1.7b **Critique and apply knowledge to understand the person and environment**

2.1.10a **Substantively and affectively prepare for action with individuals, families, groups, organizations, and communities**

2.1.10c **Develop mutually agreed-on focus of work and desired outcomes**

2.1.10d **Collect, organize, and interpret client data**

2.1.10e **Assess client strengths and limitations**

2.1.10g **Select appropriate intervention strategy**

2.1.10i **Implement prevention interventions that enhance client capacities**

2.1.10j **Help clients resolve problems**

2.1.10m **Critically analyze, monitor, and evaluate interventions**

Goals

Goals are central to achieving outcomes and working in systematic, process-oriented approaches such as the helping process discussed in this text. The "Phases of the Helping Process" are illustrated on the inside back cover. Goals are also prominent in the Task-Centered and Crisis Intervention models, Cognitive Restructuring, a Cognitive Behavioral procedure, Solution-Focused Brief Treatment, and Case Management. These change-oriented approaches (discussed in greater depth in Chapter 13) share a common process for the development of a goal statement—the agreement that becomes the focus of the work to be completed by the social worker and client. Whether an approach emphasizes developing a goal or a solution, ultimately the intent is to address an individuals' priority concern or need; or in the case of the involuntary client, to meet the requirements of a legal mandate.

The Purpose and Function of Goals

EP 2.1.10a

While the stated goal is the desired end product, attainment of a goal is a process. It may be useful to imagine the process as being similar to going on a road trip. A map details your progress from *Point A* to *Point B*, from your point of origin to your desired destination. During the trip, you may develop short-term goals, for example, reaching a certain point within a certain time period. The mileage signs along the roadway and your arrival at a certain location chart your progress. Using the analogy with an individual client, *Point A*, the starting point, is their priority concern. *Point B*, goal attainment, is the desired outcome. In essence, a goal guides the ongoing process of reaching a final destination point. Once goals are established, tasks or objectives represent the incremental action steps taken toward the desired outcome. In much the same way that you would make use of mileage markers to chart the progress of a trip, the client's completion of tasks or objectives may be envisioned as representing observable points of progress of the change effort.

In your work with individuals, having goals facilitates clients reaching a destination point in which a specific condition, need, status or functioning has changed.

In addition to facilitating the movement between Point A and Point B, setting goals also:

- *ensures that you and the client are in agreement, where possible, about outcomes to be achieved.*
- *provides direction, focus, and continuity to the helping process and prevents wandering off course.*
- *facilitates the development and selection of appropriate strategies and interventions.*
- *assists you and the client in monitoring progress.*
- *serves as the criteria for evaluating the effectiveness of a specific intervention and of the helping process.*

Linking Goals to Target Concerns

EP 2.1.10d

Goals evolve from concerns or problems presented by clients. As you listen to individuals tell their stories during the assessment interview, you are obtaining useful information for developing preliminary goals. In the case of the involuntary client,

IDEAS IN ACTION

Margaret is an 85-year-old widow who is involved with a community-based multi-service senior center. Her four adult children live in other states. She is involved in activities offered by the center, including senior aerobic classes. She considers herself to be generally in good health. Because she lives alone, regular contact with the senior center is an important part of her daily life. During the assessment interview, she talked about feeling unsafe in her home because she lacks a sustained level of energy to complete many of the activities of daily living. For example, she tires easily when she is doing housework, and at times she has had difficulty getting in and out of the bathtub. Margaret prefers to remain in her own home because she is afraid that she will lose the level of independence that she now enjoys. She had thought about home health services, but after hearing the complaints of friends, some of whom were conflicted about the benefit, she too is ambivalent about this resource. In fact, some her friends have emphasized that the scheduled visits of helpers limited their freedom. She laughed as she recounted the complaint of one friend, "You have to get up and out of bed on a schedule, and there are times when you just don't want people in your house." After a lengthy discussion with the social worker, Margaret agreed that her primary goal was to live in a safe environment and preferably in her own home. However, she is open to considering other options, for example, home health care or moving to an assisted living facility. Her second goal was to maintain her independence. Maintaining independence was defined as being able to make decisions about her life, continuing to be involved with social activities, and to be able to do what she can for herself.

TABLE-12-1 LINKAGE BETWEEN ASSESSMENT, TARGET CONCERNS AND GOALS

ASSESSMENT SUMMARY	TARGET CONCERNS	GOALS
Margaret, age 85, feels unable to remain in her home because of concerns for her safety. Central to her safety concerns is her recognition that her ability to complete activities of daily living has diminished. She also wants to maintain her independence.	Margaret is concerned about her ability to continue to live safely in her own home.	To live in a safe environment. To maintain her independence.

© Cengage Learning 2013

goals are prescribed in a mandate or court order. In either case, goals function best when they are linked to a specific concern or problem and have clear performance standards (Corwin, 2002; Huxtable, 2004; O'Hare, 2009; Ribner & Knei-Paz, 2002; Varlas, 2005). The link between goals and target concerns is illustrated in the assessment summary of Margaret in the Ideas in Action case summary and in Table 12-1.

Elderly persons like Margaret and her friends often have complex social, psychological, biological, and support needs. These needs do not diminish their desire or their capacity to make decisions about their lives. For the most part, while their physical capacity may be limited in certain domains, they are capable of caring for themselves, albeit with varying levels of support. Most elderly persons also retain an interest in being socially active. For instance, it was important to Margaret to participate in the activities at the senior center. These activities also met her psychological and social needs of feeling connected, especially since she lived alone. At the same time, attention to her biological needs was important as her diminished physical capacity limited her ability to routinely prepare nutritious meals. In spite of their needs, it is not uncommon for elderly persons to want to be involved in decisions about the type of help that they receive and to guard against having their lives drastically changed. For many, as it was for Margaret, it can be a trade-off between accepting help and remaining in charge of their lives.

There will be times when goals require accessing the resources of another agency. For example, if Margaret decided to remain in her home, other agencies such as home health services and perhaps home-delivered meals would provide most of the essential supports that she needed. It is also quite possible that informal arrangements with neighbors, family members, or community organizations could augment the formal services. As a case manager your role would involve identifying, coordinating, monitoring, and evaluating the various formal and informal services providers.

Distinguishing Program Objectives and Client Goals

The goals of a particular organization are often found in its organizational mission statement. Indeed, you may have been attracted to work at a particular agency because of its mission. Program objectives flow from mission statements and inform how organizational resources are utilized to target a specific need or population or respond to a particular social problem. In some cases, program objectives are directly related to outcomes sought by funders or a purchase of service agreement. Statements may focus on micro (individual), mezzo (family/group), or macro (system/environmental) level issues. For example, one organization may define its mission and programs as responding to the micro-level needs of gay, lesbian, bisexual, and trans-gender youth in a safe and supporting environment, while another may direct its resources to address mezzo-level issues, like reducing the number of homeless families with children by assisting them to find affordable housing. A macro-level program objective might be to end poverty by advocating for legislation that would increase the earned income of a segment of the population.

EP 2.1.10g

Within agencies, client goals and program objectives are often used interchangeably to articulate expected outcomes for service recipients. In some instances, an organization may use a standardized evidence-based template to assess competencies or functioning upon which the goals of a treatment regime are established. To distinguish agency program objectives from individual client goals, it may be useful to think of program objectives as general statements regarding the outcomes that are expected for all service recipients who are involved with an agency's program. To avoid the one-size-fits-all approach, social workers should selectively include program objectives in the case goal or treatment plan as they pertain to and fit with the unique situation of each individual, much like how priority concerns and goals are linked (Gardner, 2000).

Factors That Influence the Development of Goals

There are a number of factors that can influence the process of developing goals. Summarized in the following discussion, these factors include:

Client Participation

EP 2.1.10d

Goal pursuits begin with a client's need or want; in the instance of nonvoluntary or involuntary status, responding to a goal that has been assigned by someone other than the individual is the starting point. You should not expect the process of developing goals to be a neatly defined, linear process. As you listen to the stories of clients during the assessment interview, you may hear about a number of concerns for which they are seeking solutions. Listening to individual stories takes time, but this is time well spent. As you listen, summarize and clarify so that you and the client have an opportunity to explore options before a decision about a priority goal is reached. There are two types of experts in the goal development decision-making process: the client and you, the social worker, in a partnership of problem solving. Your respective roles in this process are outlined here:

- ***Social Worker:*** As the social worker, your expertise, knowledge, and skills facilitate the process by assisting individuals to prioritize, specify, and define goals in measurable language. Also, as goals are discussed, you can help clients to assess feasibility, identify potential barriers, and become aware of their resources and strengths related to goal attainment. Skills that you will utilize to elicit goal directed information include the communication and facilitative skills discussed in Chapter 6. In addition, the relationship that has developed between you and the client up to this point is a key factor.

- ***Client:*** The client is the foremost expert in articulating what he or she would like to be different. Social work principles in support of clients' active involvement in goal decisions include empowerment, social justice, and the axiom, "starting where the client is." (Finn & Jacobsen, 2003b, Marsh, 2002; Meyer, 2001; Smith & Marsh, 2002). Finn and Jacobson (2003b) clarify the social justice aspect of clients' involvement, stressing that "clients have a right to their reality, and to have their reality be a part of their service provisions" (pp. 128–129).

Your sensitivity to the reality of individuals in goal decisions is especially important in cross-cultural interactions. Without client participation, goals may be developed that are counterproductive to individual interests, reinforcing the client's sense of marginalization and experience of oppression (Clifford & Burke, 2005; Dietz, 2000; Finn & Jacobson, 2003a; Guadalupe & Lum, 2005; Pollack, 2004; Vera & Speight, 2003; Weinberg, 2006; G.D. Rooney, 2009). In your role as an expert who has specific knowledge and skills, it is important that you acknowledge clients' experience of inequality and oppression so as to avoid adding to an individual's sense of marginalization.

Irrespective of whether an individual is voluntary or involuntary, the participation of the individual in goal decisions is essential. People are motivated by a process in which they are self-involved and, further, one in which they perceive the process as being just (Greenberg & Tyler, 1987). In contrast, their lack of involvement has implications for their self-definition and sense of self-efficacy (Bandura, 1997; Boehm & Staples, 2004; Gondolla, 2004; Meyer, 2001; Wright, Greenberg & Brehm, 2004).

Involuntary Status

Involuntary status can mean that an individual is reluctant to cooperate in a process in which they perceive themselves as having limited power and control with regard to goal decisions. Perhaps the most volatile issues stem from client suspicion, mistrust and reactance to prescriptive goals that are constructed around their deficits (Lum, 2004; Rooney, R.H., 2009; Sue, 2006). In inviting their participation, it is possible that the involuntary individual's reaction to you may be highly charged and emotion-focused, with a presentation of self based on their perception of your authority. Furthermore, social distance (be it caused by perceptions of race, class, and/or cultural differences) between you and the individual as well as your privileged status as a professional may further exaggerate relational dynamics. It is important that you recognize the fact that minority group members are disproportionately represented among the involuntary client population. As such, they share certain attributes; for example, tensions related to external control versus personal control, marginal status, constrained self-determination, and lack of power (G. D. Rooney, 2009).

The dynamics as described can present as factors, more or less depending on the individual. Without your attention to these dynamics when they are present, the potential for you to develop and maintain a working relationship can be diminished. To facilitate the involuntary client's participation, you might first begin by inviting them to tell his or her story so that he or she feels heard, understood, and involved. By listening to their narratives, you gain an understanding of client values and beliefs. Moreover, supporting their self-efficacy and using facilitative skills can be an effective means to engage the participation of the involuntary individual (Miller & Rollnick, 2002).

Values and Beliefs

EP 2.1.7b

Goals are by their nature intended to facilitate change. However, as you develop goals, attending to clients' values and beliefs is fundamental to the process. Understanding and respecting the values and beliefs of each client is consistent with the principles of valuing the unique reality of persons and their situation. Individuals, for example, from impoverished communities may present behaviors, lifestyles, and values that are often different from conventional norms (Dunlap, Golub & Johnson, 2006; Smith, 2006). The strengths perspective notwithstanding, there is often a tendency to treat diverse values and beliefs as problematic and to perceive the holders of those values or beliefs as outsiders. Although you may feel challenged by the influence that different beliefs and values can have on particular goals, you should be mindful of the fact that failure to listen to diverse viewpoints can lead to ethical conflicts. To illustrate this point, consider the following:

CASE EXAMPLE

A case manager who was responsible for the coordination of the educational goals for a teen mother pressured the teen to make use of the additional resources for college bound students. Conversely, the teen's goal was to complete high school. She reasoned that college might be in her future, but lived in a neighborhood where few people ever completed high school. If someone did finish high school, their doing so was akin to attaining a college degree and was to be celebrated.

EP 2.1.2a

As you can observe in this scenario, there is the potential for an ethical conflict, specifically the tension between the teen's autonomy and the case manager's paternalism. Should the case manager insist that the teen pursue college rather than the desired educational goal of the teen mother? In the interest of fairness, the case manager had a good relationship with the teen. During the time that they had worked together, the case manager recognized the teen's abilities and strengths that would support her pursuit of a college degree. Any one of us, in this situation might have been inclined to act in such a paternalistic manner, specifically urging a goal beyond which the teen wishes to pursue at this point and time. In truth, however, individuals tend to make choices and express values that are consistent with their circumstances and worldview, as well as their perception of the resources available to them (Dunlap, Golub & Johnson, 2006, Orme, 2002; Pollack, 2004; Weinberg, 2006). Of course the potential exists for clients to make different choices in the future. Empowerment can include coaxing and nudging clients toward aspirations beyond where they are at a point in time. Ultimately, it is their perspective that should guide their goal decision. While social workers should respect self-determination you may look for opportunities to provide clients with information or to suggest more ambitious goals than they currently envision. For example, a client envisioned himself as a certified nursing assistant (CNA) and did not explore or think that he was capable of becoming a nurse. It can be possible to both respect their current choice and make sure that they have the information they need for that choice to be informed.

Values and Beliefs Inherent in Goal Setting

Sue (2006, p.135) issues a cautionary note about goals, asserting that the process in and of itself is value laden and that "there are certain values reflected in the goal setting process" that may be counter to the experience and beliefs of clients, including their cultural or racial reference group. For instance, according to Sue (2006) a value that is inherent in the process of goal setting is based on several assumptions. Perhaps the most common assumption is that the individual has the ability to set a self-goal based on the notions of autonomous action and self-determination as valued by Western society. In fact, this may not be the case for individuals from cultural or racial groups where individual aspirations and esteem are derived from and interdependent with the cultural group or family itself. It will be important for you to determine the extent to which these cultural distinctions are pertinent to the persons with whom you are working.

EP 2.1.4c

The process of developing goals also assumes that all individuals, including minors, both understand, believe in, and value setting goals. In some instances, you may find that people who contend with ongoing stressors may have adapted to their circumstances and can therefore be skeptical about whether setting goals will alter their situation. Sue (2006) emphasizes another assumption in his assertion that the ideal of setting goals in essence profiles individuals who he refers to with the acronym "YAVIS." Specifically, persons who are *young, articulate, verbal, intelligent, and successful,* and most often voluntary in their contact with helping professionals. This profile can result in the discrimination against those who are less capable or less socially connected. Examples include culturally or racially persons who speak a second language or dialect, people of low socioeconomic status, and persons with diminished cognitive capacity (James & Gilliland, 2005; Sue, 2006).

Family Involvement

EP 2.1.10e

Families and social networks are among the strengths and resources to be considered in making decisions about goals as their support may enhance goal attainment. You should not assume that these resources are always available for all clients, but the extent to which the family, cultural, or social network is to be involved should be explored. Specifically, whether the family or other supportive networks are to be involved is a point of discussion, but the decision to include them should be made by the client. In this way, you are respecting his or her preference, be it based on culture, family form, or status.

Decisions concerning minors in most instances will require the involvement and support of their families as well as other individuals or systems with whom the minor is involved. For example, goals related to school performance often require that a minor's parents and teachers be involved. Conversely, when an overwhelmed parent challenged by the behavior of a minor demands a goal that their offspring be "fixed," extra effort on your part may be required to encourage the parent's participation.

There is evidence that the positive support of family or significant others can facilitate goal-setting and goal attainment. For instance, Ritter and Dozier (2000) found that although a court mandate to complete a drug treatment program was powerful, family support and family involvement was as important in preventing the reoccurrence of drug use. Other works have shown that family involvement provided a cultural frame of reference that was essential to developing goals that were consistent with the values and beliefs of a particular group (Gardner, 2000; Hodge, 2004; Hodge & Nadir, 2008; James & Gilliland, 2005; Lum, 2004, 2007; Sarkisian & Gerstel, 2004; Potocky-Tripodi, 2002; Sue, 2006; Wong, 2007). Furthermore, a deciding factor for lesbian women in selecting a mental health or health care provider was the extent to which their partners could be involved (Saulnier, 2002). Also, family group conferences (also referred to as family decision making), a child welfare strategy, acknowledges the importance of including the family to develop goals that ensure the well-being of minors (Altman & Gohagen, 2009; Waites, MacGowan, Pennell, Carlton-LaNey, & Weil, 2004).

Although the involvement of family members can be a vital resource in developing goals, their support may not be definite or infinite. For instance, goal pursuits favored by an individual can be inconsistent with the norms of their culture or perspectives on behavior, including the act of seeking outside help (Williams, 2006; Wong, 2007). An example of this conflict can be observed in the video featuring Yanping, a graduate student from China who is concerned about her parents' response to her choice of study. Of course culture may not be the only reason an individual's family is unavailable or limited. Their willingness can depend on the nature of prior and existing relationships. Families can be reluctant to support, for example, an individual's behavioral change goal as their doing so might challenge other members to also make adjustments in their behavior. In some cases, a lack of support from the family is because they are burdened by their own needs, stressors, and limited resources. In addition, there are instances when a family's goodwill has been exhausted by a members need for support and, in consequence, the family will evoke a quid pro quo arrangement. In essence, they will support a goal if certain changes or conditions are met.

Environmental Conditions and Resources

As clients cope with difficult situations, it is vital that you understand them as a person and their situation in the context of their environment. Attributes such as age, race, gender, class, sexual orientation, and structural inequality are factors that can

EP 2.1.7b

influence the capacity to attain goals irrespective of client motivation. Of course, like other clients with whom you have contact, diverse individuals and families experience tensions that can be characterized as interpersonal or interfamilial in nature. But it is not uncommon that their concerns will also include stressors resulting from their involvement with multiple external systems or adverse environmental interactions.

In many instances, structural inequality and limited resources makes it impractical for diverse groups to survive and thrive. Helping a low-income couple to obtain affordable or subsidized housing, for example, may be constrained by the regional availability of affordable housing and federal subsidy housing funds. Discrimination in housing, employment, and institutional lending patterns is illegal, yet there are still subtle forms that exist, posing barriers to low-income and minority people (Fernandez, 2007). Many of the problems experienced by minority and low income persons can have a debilitating psychological effect (Dietz, 2000; Guadalupe & Lum, 2005; Pollack, 2004; Sue, 2006). For instance, Grote, Zuckhoff, Swartz, Bledsoe, and Giebel (2007) found that it was not uncommon for people disadvantaged by poverty, race, or ethnic minority status to experience depression at a higher level than those in the general population. As such, even though they want relief and they have future aspirations, some may be unable to marshal the energy required to engage in making decisions about goals.

All people (some more than others) experience both negative and positive events that may not always be the results of their behavior. Therefore, it is important to recognize person–environment interactions in so far as they affect and influence the capacity of people to make decisions about their lives.

By now, you have an understanding of the purpose and function of goals, as well as those factors that can influence goal decision making. To further your learning about goals requires knowledge of the types of goals, the criteria for selecting them, and skills in negotiation. These topics are discussed in the following sections.

Types of Goals

EP 2.1.10a

Systems or subsystems that will be the focus for change will determine the type of goal to be developed. With individuals, this focus typically involves intrapersonal subsystems as well as their interaction with the social and physical environment. Goals may initially be expressed in broad terms. Examples include change in *cognitive functioning* (e.g., increase positive self-talk), *emotional functioning* (e.g., manage anger), or a *behavioral change* (e.g., listen to others without interrupting).

In some instances, change may require combining *overt* and *covert* goals. An overt goal requires action, while a covert goal involves changing thoughts or feeling. To illustrate, consider the scenario in which an individual is faced with eviction for failure to pay their rent on time. An overt *behavioral goal* would be to increase the frequency that he or she paid his or her rent on time. The behavioral goal may be combined with one that requires a covert cognitive goal if the reason for their lateness was forgetting when the rent payment was due. Assuming that the individual had the funds to pay their rent, an overt behavioral goal would involve marking the due dates on a calendar.

Goals may be further categorized by both type and function. Specifically, goals may be shared or reciprocal depending on the systems or subsystems involved. When the target system is a couple, family, or group, goals typically involve changes on the part of all the relevant participants in the system. In these larger systems, *shared goals* are held in common and agreed upon by members of the system. For example, after brainstorming ways in which group members could assist each other, members may agree to use positive and supportive messages when interacting with one another. The distinguishing feature of shared goals is that all participants agree to act or behave in certain way.

Reciprocal goals have some elements of a shared goal in that they are also developed in conjunction with all parties involved. With reciprocal goals, all involved agree upon exchanges of different behavior and to act or respond to each other in a different manner. In some instances, a reciprocal goal may be a precursor to developing other goals. For instance, in a parent–child conflict situation, both have expressed a desire to improve their communication with each other. Specifically, when they talked, they interrupted each other, and neither felt that the other listened. A reciprocal goal for them would be that each agrees to listen to the other without interrupting. Reciprocal goals tend to be *quid pro quo* in nature; that is, each person agrees to modify his or her personal behavior contingent upon the other person making a corresponding behavioral change. For example, "I will listen to you without interrupting, if when I am speaking, you will also listen to me."

Guidelines for Selecting and Defining Goals

EP 2.1.10c

Because goals serve several vital functions, it is important for you and the client to select and define them with care. In our discussion of selecting and defining goals, we make a point of distinguishing between the goal setting process with voluntary and involuntary individuals because the dynamics of status affect each situation.

With the voluntary individual, the psychological authority attributed to you as the social worker is generally positive. Therefore their perception of your goodwill positively influences the collaborative nature of your relationship as you select and define goals.

In contrast, the dynamics of the psychological contract inherent in the explicit authority of your position means that the interaction between you and the involuntary individual has a decidedly different texture. Perhaps the most volatile issue relates to the fact that, for the involuntary individual, goals have been predetermined. In involuntary situations, the individual's perception of the relationship is most often one in which compliance and authority, instead of collaboration, are the most salient factors (DeJong & Berg. 2001; Rooney, R.H., 2009). Therefore, the involuntary client may react to engaging in a process in which they feel that their options are limited.

The guidelines highlighted in Table 12-2 and discussed in the following sections are intended to assist you in advancing your proficiency in selecting and defining goals for both voluntary and involuntary individuals.

The discussion related to *goals sought by the voluntary client* begins with Angela and Irwin Corning. To observe the process of selecting and defining goals, you can view segments 2–4 of the video entitled "Problem Solving with the Corning Family." The case is summarized in the following Video Case Example box.

TABLE-12-2 GUIDELINES FOR SELECTING AND DEFINING GOALS

- Goals must be related to results sought by voluntary clients.
- Goals for involuntary clients should include motivational congruence.
- Goals must be defined in explicit and measurable terms.
- Goals must be feasible.
- Goals should be commensurate with knowledge and skills of the practitioner.
- Goal should be stated in positive terms that emphasize growth.
- Avoid agreeing with goals about which you have major reservations.
- Goals should be consistent with function of the agency.

 VIDEO CASE EXAMPLE

Angela and Irwin Corning and their three children, Agnes (age 10), Henri (age 8), and Katrina (18 months) are homeless. Currently they are residing in a transitional housing facility. Irwin lost his job eight months ago when the county agency that he worked for as a maintenance and cleaning specialist awarded the cleaning contract to a private contractor. Angela is employed in the evenings as a maid at a hotel. Prior to becoming homeless, the family had a comfortable living, owned their home, and they were pleased with the neighborhood's diversity and their children's school. When Irwin became unemployed, the couple was unable to pay their bills or maintain their mortgage payment. For a time, they lived with Angela's sister's family. Angela and Irwin are concerned about the impact of their stressful situation on the two older children. To make matters worse, the school reports that Agnes and Henri are having difficulty at school. Both parents feel that the school situation will change once the family is stable. The social worker at the transitional housing facility referred them to a family service agency for help to find housing and employment for Irwin. Their preference is to purchase another home, but they realize that at this point they will need to move into an apartment until their financial situation has improved.

Goals Must Relate to the Desired Results Sought by Voluntary Clients

By the time you have reached the point in the helping process for selecting and defining goals, your relationship with the voluntary client is generally positive. Despite their positive regard for you and their motivation to have something happen or change, the process of selecting and defining goals may still not be smooth. For instance, expressions of emotions, anxieties, values or beliefs heretofore unspoken can emerge. But these dynamics do not necessarily mean that the client is less motivated. For instance, in observing the Corning couple, you will have noticed that despite their declared readiness to move ahead, the process of deciding what to do was circular, back and forth, and at times emotional. Both Angela and Irwin expressed feelings related to their frustration and, at times, their ambivalence about the process. At times, they also questioned whether their contact with the social worker would be helpful.

Although your experience with individuals in selecting and defining goals may not completely resemble the social worker's experience with Angela and Irwin Corning, their behavior is not atypical. For voluntary clients to be motivated and emotionally invested, they must be confident that as a result of working with you their concerns will be addressed. For example, while Angela was attentive and for the most part engaged, she nevertheless expressed her uncertainty, inquiring of the social worker, "What is it that you do, and how can you help?" Apparent in nonverbal behaviors such as sighing and shifting in his chair, Irwin appears to be uncomfortable and less convinced about the usefulness of the process. Eventually, his discomfort is verbalized in his blunt complaint that, "Spending time talking was a waste of time." Furthermore, his sense of self had been challenged by his emotional experience of job loss. In particular, he was having difficulty reconciling his situation with his belief that a "Man should provide for his family." His perception of the personal and environmental circumstances related to his job loss further complicate the progression toward selecting and defining goals. For him, the process was suspect, given his belief that neither he nor the social worker had the ability to control the circumstance that led to his becoming unemployed.

Like Irwin and Angela, a majority of individuals with whom you have contact will be nonvoluntary with respect to their situation, even though they voluntarily sought help. As a result, their emotions may still be vested in their situation, so much so that they continue to recount their difficulties and their anxieties. Notice, for example, that Irwin continued to talk about his unemployment status and his belief about the potential environmental barriers to finding a permanent job.

In instances in which the process of selecting and defining goals becomes overwhelming, it is important for you to maintain focus. Doing so does not mean that you ignore the emotional expressions of individuals, but rather that you acknowledge their feelings as a natural part of the process. Being in touch with a feeling may call for you to use facilitative skills like seeking concreteness and empathy. Moving ahead, it can be useful for you to restate the target concern using communication skills such as clarification, paraphrasing, and summarizing as appropriate, so that you and the client are able to select and define goals.

"What is my role in the process of selecting and defining goals?" is a question often asked by beginning social workers. With voluntary clients in particular, you should not assume that your role is passive, but rather that you are a partner. While clients are clear about their goals, many will want your guidance as they sort out and prioritize the changes that they wish to make. You should, however, balance sharing your professional expertise and responsibility with focusing on their primary concerns. Eventually, Angela and Irwin became clear about their goal wants and needs, yet in specific instances the social worker shared her ideas. Even so, she stressed that her input would be guided by the extent to which they wanted her advice. Ultimately, two goals were selected and prioritized, but not without a number of back and forth deliberations.

Goals for Involuntary Clients Should Include Motivational Congruence

Unlike Angela and Irwin who were voluntary and motivated to seek help by the weight of their circumstances, goals for involuntary individuals have been selected and defined by someone else. Even so, a mandate should not preempt or negate the assessment or goal negotiation process. At the same time, an involuntary client may have a high level of interest in complying with the mandate primarily to remove the pressure that they feel, rather than because they agree with the values and direction of the mandate. In your conversation with the client about the mandated goal should include how to meet the goal, as well as an exploration of goals that the client may have.

EP 2.1.10c

Strategies for work with involuntary clients were first developed by Rooney (1992) based on his work with involuntary minors in schools and parents involved with child protection. These facilitative strategies, including motivational congruence, are applied to the process of selecting and defining goals with individuals who are involuntary. The strategies are highlighted in Table 12-3.

Prior to reading about the strategies, you might reflect on your feelings in a scenario in which you are enrolled in a required class. You soon learn that the instructor has established the highest level performance goal for you. At this point, the course content is

TABLE-12-3 STRATEGIES FOR DEVELOPING GOALS WITH INVOLUNTARY CLIENTS

Motivational Congruence
Agreeable Mandate
Let's Make A Deal
Getting Rid of the Mandate

© Cengage Learning 2013

unfamiliar, and you might question the instructor's authority to select and define a goal given the fact that you were neither asked about your performance preference, nor were you invited to participate in the decision process. In consequence, you might become anxious, angry, or discouraged and experience a crisis of confidence. Alternatively, you might decide to accept the performance expectation as a challenge and by doing so avoid the punishment of a lower grade. In either case, you would probably feel resentment because the instructor's decision lacked the consideration of your abilities, resources, or your desired level of goal attainment. Assuming that the option to enroll in another class was not available, consider the following questions:

- *How would you react to the instructor?*
- *What pressures might you feel?*
- *If you accepted the established performance expectation as a challenge, how would you know what the indicators were for the highest level of performance?*
- *Will you be able to negotiate with the instructor?*
- *What could the instructor do or say that would motivate you to achieve the imposed goal?*

The intensity of motivation theory raises a point that is pertinent to you, the involuntary student, and the involuntary client. Specifically, when given a goal directive, will a person "automatically mobilize maximal effort" if their doing so has "direct implications for their self-esteem, self-direction and personal interest"? (Gendolla, 2004, p. 2005). As you reflect upon this statement and the questions posed in the involuntary student scenario, think about your role in assisting the involuntary individual to accomplish imposed goals.

The advantage of the strategies for developing goals with involuntary clients is that they focus on a specific change while engaging the client in the instrumental behavioral change required by the mandate.

Motivational Congruence

People are motivated to work on problems that are important to them. Motivational congruence means that you work on target goals that are personally meaningful to the individual and that also satisfy the requirements of the mandate (Rooney, R.H., 2009). Goals are more likely to succeed and result in longer-lasting change in cases where they are meaningful to the client than in cases where the individual's motivation is focused on escaping a sanction or gaining a reward. The principle of "starting where the client is," is equally important with involuntary clients. Goal selection and definition should include their view of the problem in addition to the problem description in the mandate. According to DeJong and Berg (2001), congruence is possible when mandated clients are able to "take control by describing the mandated situation themselves" (p. 364). When given the opportunity, involuntary clients will express their opinion of problems or situations that resulted in the mandate. In this way, self-definition and their involvement in the process can be a motivating factor by virtue of the fact that their view is solicited and heard.

People who are involuntary may describe their circumstances and the situation in details that includes expressions of anger, frustration, fear, and even outrage. In child welfare, a parent can be sensitive to goals established as a result of a risk assessment relative to indicators of child well-being, potential harm, and acceptable norms of parenting. The mandated goal, particularly its implied definition (characterizing the parent as irresponsible), is serious, however, it can be inconsistent with the parent's perspective of themselves and of the problem. Mandates and risk assessment are not structured in a way that aids our understanding of the circumstances of a particular behavior or act. Instead, the court's focus is on the negative outcome, and the subsequent goal requires corrective action. For example, a mother who left her children home alone for a period of time to go to a party is a legitimate concern of child welfare, child protective service, and the court. Nonetheless, the court is neither interested in, nor privy to, the circumstances, only that the well-being of the children has been compromised. But in defining a goal, your understanding of the circumstances can in fact aid you in the negotiation of the goal.

Two central questions in this case are relevant with respect to achieving motivational congruence:

- *What are the concerns of the court in the situation?*
- *Is the mother also concerned about leaving children at home unsupervised?*

Motivational congruence, as illustrated in Figure 12-1, is possible when the target goal of the court and the parent are compatible. In essence, there is agreement between the mother, the court, and you as the social worker about the supervision of the children when she is not at home. In this case, the congruence between the concerns of the parties involved can lead to the development of goals with which both the court and the mother are satisfied. More importantly, the mother is involved and the opportunity for her autonomy and self-efficacy has improved, which in turn can influence her motivation.

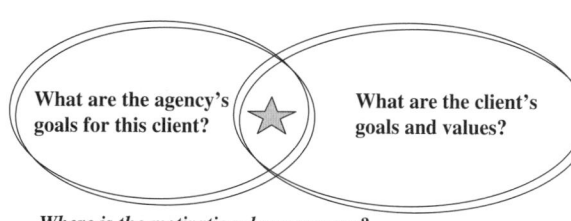

FIG-12-1 Motivational Congruence

Now that you have learned about the strategies that are intended to facilitate the development of goals, think about which one would been instrumental in the scenario in which you were the involuntary student.

Agreeable Mandate

It is likely that hearing the mother's perspective of the circumstances in which the behavior occurred (leaving children unsupervised) will provide additional information about the problem. The court, however, has reached a conclusion based on a report of neglect. Without the opportunity to tell her story, the mother is likely to resent the court's decision and the fact that the decision lacked an understanding about her circumstances and subsequent decision. For her, it is a question of fairness in both the process and the intended outcome (Greenberg & Tyler, 1987).

The *agreeable mandate* strategy entails a search for common ground that bridges the differing views of the involuntary individual and of the court (DeJong & Berg, 2001; R. H. Rooney, 2009). Pursuing the agreeable mandate may also involve reframing the definition of the problem in such a way that it adequately addresses the concerns identified in the mandate or referral source while simultaneously responding to the concerns of the client. Reframing is a useful technique for reducing reactance, facilitating a workable agreement, and increasing the client's motivation. This strategy may be combined with motivational congruence. Let's consider the example of a participant in a treatment group for men who batter. The participant may reject the descriptive language used by the professional group leader, for example, "perpetrator," and feel pressured to admit that that his behavior is a starting point for developing a behavioral change goal. But the participant may agree to a goal of improving his relationship with his spouse where the focus is on how this can be accomplished. When an individual has intense feelings about his or her behavior, self-reflection can be an intermediate step to goal selection. For example, if the man disagreed that he has a problem handling their anger, you might ask him to consider a goal in which he would examine how his behavior impacts those around him.

Let's Make a Deal

Negotiating goals with involuntary clients can include a bargaining strategy, or "Let's make a deal." Essentially, the private concerns of the involuntary client are combined with the problem that precipitated the mandate or referral (Rooney, R.H., 2009). To illustrate, let's return to the scenario in which the mother left the children alone while she went to a party in the neighborhood. While she was away, there was a small fire in the apartment, and the older child called the fire department. When the firefighters discovered that the children were home alone, they reported the situation to child protection. The children were moved to a temporary shelter. The mother was angry, stating, "They had no right to take my kids. It is hard to always be stuck at home and not have time for myself." The problem from the perspective of child protection services is that the children were left unsupervised and further, the occurrence of the fire placed the unsupervised children in a dangerous situation. In this case, the deal could be that you would address the mother's need for self-time if she agrees to work on resolving the issue of supervision and safety for the children. The efficacy of this strategy is derived from your willingness to offer a payoff that meaningfully addresses the mother's concern. Although, you can't offer her the option of not complying regarding the supervision mandate, you can make the mandated situation more agreeable by addressing her concern about her lack of self-time. In this way you are attending to her concern, you are creating an incentive for the mother to be involved in developing problem-solving goals related to the mandate.

Getting Rid of the Mandate

With some involuntary clients, none of the preceding strategies may be viable. In these cases, the only recourse left is to appeal to the client's desire to be free of the restraints imposed by the mandate or referral source. This strategy appeals to the client's motivation for *getting rid of the mandate or outside pressure* (Rooney, 2009; Jordan & Franklin, 2003). The case of the unsupervised children is used to further illustrate: The mother is angry and feels misunderstood. She rejected the conclusion that she neglected her parental responsibility by leaving the children unsupervised. Rather, she considered it a one-time event precipitated by her by "feeling as if I was going to lose my mind being cooped up in the house with these kids all the time." She also asserted that needing time for herself did not mean that she did not care for her children: "I love my kids, they are all that I have, and I am all that they have." She is clear that her primary motivation is to "get you people out of my hair" and to escape what she considers the adversarial and invasive presence of child welfare and the court in her life. Using her desire to be rid of the oversight of the court as a motivator, the focus of a goal of having the children returned is clarified. In effect, her desire to be rid of the oversight points to the necessary incremental actions for accomplishing the goal. In essence, all parties involved share a goal; specifically, the return of the children to the home, albeit when certain requirements are met.

Goals Should Be Defined in Explicit and Measurable Terms

EP 2.1.10m

Thus far, you have learned about the process of selecting and defining goals with people who are voluntary clients as well as specific strategies that can facilitate the process of selecting and defining goals with involuntary individuals. Irrespective of the client's status, goals must be defined in explicit and measurable terms. Goal setting and motivation theories emphasize that general, vague, or unspecified goals result in unclear performance standards, subjecting clients to an experience in which their confidence and capacity is challenged (Bloom, Fischer & Orme, 2003; O'Hare, 2009; Miller & Rollnick, 2002; Oettingen, Bulgarella, Henderson & Gollwitzer, 2004).

Explicitly defined measurable goal statements clarify who, what, and under what circumstances the desired outcomes are to be obtained. Additionally, explicitly defined measurable goal statements clarify monitoring and measurement procedures (O'Hare, 2009). In determining whether a goal is measurable, it may be useful for you to pose an evaluative question, such as, "what are the indicators that will inform you and the individual when the goal has been accomplished?" Some examples of defined, explicit, and measurable goals are:

"The mother will provide adult supervision for the children each time that she goes out for the evening."

"Mr. Diaz will be able to administer his daily insulin injection under the assistance of a home health nurse."

"Participants in the social skills group will listen to the teacher in the classroom without interrupting."

Each of the examples specifies who is involved, what is expected, and under what circumstances the goal is to be achieved. In each of the examples, you can see the importance of goals that are specifically defined and upon which progress can be monitored and measured. At times, it will be useful for you to develop or use existing tools to aid you in monitoring and measuring progress. For example, you might establish a pregroup base-line of listening skills for each of the social skills of group participants and chart their progress over time. At the end of the group, you would compare their pregroup and postgroup skill level to determine whether, and at what level, listening skills had improved.

Appropriately stated, specific, and measurable goals will specify both overt and covert changes. An overt goal for a participant in a social skills group might be to "increase the number of times that he or she did not interrupt the teacher." The achievement of this goal can be observed by others, as well as by the social worker. A covert, self-monitoring goal might be to "increase positive thoughts about the teacher" and goal progress would be tracked over a period of time. Be aware, however, that measures of covert behavior are subject to error as a result of inconsistent self-monitoring and the effects of self-monitoring on the target behavior. Also, an individual may forget to record his or her thoughts and, after a time, the task can become too tedious for them to sustain.

Regardless of the tools that you use, documentation in case progress notes and/or SOAP (subjective, objective, assessment, and planning) is essential for maintaining focus and for recording, monitoring, and measuring progress. For example, having established a baseline and an overt behavioral goal for a participant in the social skills groups, you would chart the number of times that the participant did not interrupt the teacher or other students during class. Progress toward this goal would be recorded in the case progress notes and eventually be reviewed in the termination phase in evaluating outcomes. Although agencies typically have their own forms for recording progress, an example is illustrated in Figure 12-2. Note that both strengths and obstacles are recorded, as well as steps or tasks for both the client and the staff. The status of the goals may also be noted, indicating whether they have been completed or partially completed. Providing individuals with a copy of the agreed upon goals or inviting them to make their own copy can lessen perceived power differences and help maintain a collaborative relationship. Many experienced social workers provide their clients with a folder that details goal statements, tasks or

Client/Family:	Staff:		
Statement of Concern:			
Goal Statement:			Goal #__

General Tasks:	
Identify Strengths/Resources:	Identify Potential Barriers/Obstacles:
Tasks/Steps–Participant:	Tasks/Steps–Staff:

Date:	Progress Notes:	Staff

Goal Status Summary: C__ PC__ NC__ (Need summary explanation)

FIG-12-2 Case Progress Notes
Source: © Glenda Dewberry Rooney. Used with kind permission of the author.

action steps to help them keep track of their goals and progress.

Partializing Goals

EP 2.1.10i

Even goals formulated with a high level of specificity are often complex and involve multiple actions that must be completed in a logical sequence. Because of this complexity, individuals may feel overwhelmed and intimidated when facing the prospect of tackling goal implementation. For these reasons, it is important that you partialize client's ultimate goals into constituent parts. Partializing is not a new technique in social work practice. Indeed, partializing has long been a basic tenet of social work practice theory (Perlman, 1957). It is consistent with the social work commitment to empowerment, especially in facilitating clients' ability to make decisions and to achieve desired outcomes. When goals are partialized, they are dissected into manageable portions. Clients are better able to develop discrete corrective or problem-solving actions (general and specific tasks), giving them a sense of efficacy in support of goal attainment.

Goals and General Tasks

Rarely are individuals able to go immediately from zero to sixty in their efforts to achieve goals. Further, frequently, individuals may be unclear about what

EP 2.1.10i

needs to be done in order to achieve their goals. For this reason, general tasks are developed as instrumental strategies to further partialize goals (Reid, 1992). General tasks serve as the basis for *objectives* or *specific tasks*. Whether phrased as specific tasks or objectives, the essential function of both is that they indicate the particular action steps to be taken to achieve goals. For example, attaining your degree in social work is a specific goal, but it is important to distinguish this goal, which represents the desired outcome, from general tasks. General tasks related to obtaining your social work degree may be to obtain financial assistance, attend classes on a regular basis, and complete required assignments, as well as arrange for child care and transportation. These are general tasks because it is unlikely that they could be completed without your engaging in multiple smaller actions or specific tasks. Keep in mind that a general task can entail multiple objectives, action steps or specific tasks. For instance, arranging for child care is a general task that would involve specific tasks or action steps such as locating a child care provider.

Table 12-4 distinguishes between goals and general tasks so as to further assist you in discriminating between global and explicit goals. The table is intended to help you to conceptualize the relationship that exists between goals and general tasks. Included in the table are goals that involve both overt and covert behaviors. Notice that explicit goals refer to specific behaviors or environmental changes that suggest the nature of the corresponding intervention.

General tasks may also be categorized broadly as either *discrete* or *ongoing* (or continuous). Discrete general tasks consist of one-time actions or changes that resolve or ameliorate problems. Examples include obtaining a needed resource (e.g., housing or medical care), making a major decision (e.g., deciding to adopt a child), or making a change in one's environment (e.g., moving into an assisted-living complex). Ongoing general tasks involve actions that are continuous and repetitive and rely on incremental progress toward the *ultimate* or *global* goal. For example, registration for classes is a discrete task, attending classes on a regular basis is an ongoing, incremental task toward obtaining a degree (ultimate goal). In the following table, you will see examples of discrete and ongoing general tasks.

In defining explicit goals and ongoing general tasks, a part of the process involves identifying the level of desired change. With goals that involve ongoing behavior, growth is potentially infinite, so it is desirable to determine the extent of

EP 2.1.10m

the change or the scope of the solution sought by the client or mandate; for example, "The children will be supervised when the mother goes out for the evening." The advantage of determining a specific level of change is that you and the client mutually agree to the ends sought by the latter. As another example, consider a social skills group where the goal is to increase listening skills in the classroom. With this global group goal, each student will have a different skill or behavior baseline and will undoubtedly aspire to a different level of goal attainment. Your role is to assist each participant to develop a goal that is consistent with his or her expected and desired level of goal attainment. In using a baseline for each group participant, social workers and clients are able to specify, monitor, and measure individual progress.

Goals Must Be Feasible

People prefer goals that are feasible and desirable based on their assessment of their capacity for goal attainment (Bandura, 1997; Oettingen, Bulgarella, Henderson, & Gollwitzer, 2004). Similarly, motivated by self-direction, individuals are capable of accomplishing the goals that they set for

EP 2.1.10j

TABLE-12-4 GOALS AND GENERAL TASKS	
GOALS	**GENERAL TASKS**
1. Pursue a social work degree.	1. Submit applications for admission.
2. Provide appropriate supervision for the children each time that the mother goes out for the evening.	2. Arrange for child care.
3. Live in a safe environment.	3. Visit assisted living facilities.
4. Lose 20 pounds.	4. Join a health club.
5. Learn to plan and prepare nutritious meals.	5. Prepare meals that include foods from the five food groups.
6. Improve listening skills in the classroom.	6. Listen without interrupting others in the classroom.
7. Minimize conflict with peers during recess.	7. Learn conflict resolution skills.
8. Express anger in a constructive manner.	8. Learn alternative ways of expressing anger.
9. Attend school on time on a regular basis.	9. Make preparations for getting to school on time.

themselves. Thus, it is important that you affirm their sense of self by reinforcing the validity of their goals. Selecting unachievable goals sets up clients for failure that can result in discouragement (*"Why bother?"*), disillusionment (*"The situation is hopeless"*), or a sense of defeat (*"Nothing ever changes"*).

You may encounter individuals who have goals that are more difficult to attain than they had originally imagined, as well as some who have grandiose or impractical aspirations. Also, there may be individuals who may pay scant attention to personal or environmental limitations. Faced with this dilemma, your ethical obligation is to engage the client in a discussion about feasibility. Ethical persuasion, which can be useful at this point, involves a conversation in which alternative goals are explored and advantages and disadvantages of a goal decision are reviewed. However, caution should be exercised. You should not assume a paternalistic or beneficent expert role or, in the case of the involuntary client, emphasize the authority vested in you by a mandate. Affirming and supporting an individual's goal when feasibility is in question is a balancing act. Central self-reflection questions related to discussing the feasibility of goals with clients may include the following:

- *How can I affirm a client's goal and reinforce and support their motivation without participating in a potential situation in which they might become discouraged?*
- *How can I assist the client to partialize goals and to develop incremental tasks or objectives so that their goals can be realistically achieved?*
- *What are realistic and measurable expectations as to what can feasibly be achieved within a given time period?*

Goal attainment requires more than a force of will, even in the best of circumstances. Angela and Irwin Corning, for example, identified a goal of owning a home. Given their financial situation and the six-month period in which they were required to move from the transitional housing facility, the home ownership goal was not possible. Ali, the social worker did not dismiss their goal. Instead, she affirmed the validity of the goal as a possibility for the future. Afterwards, she directed their attention to more immediate, feasible, and attainable goals, specifically, finding a three bedroom apartment and a job for Irwin. The feasibility of these goals still needed to be considered. For instance, given their limited income, how much rent could they afford and was this amount sufficient for a three bedroom apartment? This discussion was in fact beneficial. After Angela and Irwin had visited several apartment complexes, they were less discouraged by having to adjust their expectations.

Involuntary Clients' Mandated Case Plans

Sometimes, the feasibility of goals set for involuntary clients are especially difficult to navigate and manage. Mandated goal plans are often written in general or vague terms and their feasibility can be hindered by unrealistic expectations about what can be accomplished within a given time period. Several factors contribute to the feasibility of mandated case plans.

Case plans with myriad goals tend to resemble a *"kitchen sink"* (i.e., the goal plans include "everything but the kitchen sink"—that is to say the goal plans include everything possible to fix the client without priority ranking. Also, because they can require multiple changes, the client can be required to be simultaneously involved with multiple service providers. To add to the stressors that a client can experience, each of the service providers have program objectives and expected outcomes be met. For example, one frustrated client who was mandated to seek drug treatment and individual counseling, submit to weekly urine analysis (UAs), attend parenting classes, and find employment demanded, "How am I supposed to find a job, take care of and spend time with my kids, when I'm running around seeing all of you people?" Further, she asked, "When I find a job, nobody is going to let me miss a lot of work. How am I gonna tell my supervisor that I have to leave work to go pee in a cup? The judge said I had 6 months!"

The "cookie cutter" case plans consist of program objectives and requirements that are applied uniformly to all individuals or families. This is an assumption that the client population has the same or similar needs and therefore program objectives need not be selectively applied to the unique situation of each individual client. Alternatively, in the previous example of the client who was court-ordered to a parenting class, a focus on the specific skills she was to learn within a certain time period would probably have had greater appeal and been less stressful for her. For the sake of example, let's say that she lacked the knowledge needed to prepare nutritious meals for her children. Specific goals are illustrated in the following goal statement examples.

Upon completion of the parenting class, the client:
1. will have learned about the major food groups.
2. be able to prepare meals using foods from three of the five food groups during the next week.

Selectively developing goals that respond to the uniqueness of the client situation does not preclude meeting mandates or program objectives. Instead, a specific goal focus clarifies the change that is specifically required for a particular individual.

Assessing the feasibility of both kitchen sink or cookie cutter goals is especially important because they can add to the tension and distress that a client experiences. For example, resources that a client needs may be limited or unavailable; however, they have a limited time period to attain goals or face termination of their parental rights. Given this scenario, some clients may resign themselves to failure and drop out, even when their doing so has serious consequences. For some, their confidence and motivation can be greatly diminished while others can perceive the requirement as unjust. Goal attainment that requires extraordinary effort and for which feasibility is uncertain can cause undue hardship for the client (Wright, Greenberg, & Brehm, 2004).

In addition to the previous feasibility questions, there are other questions that you might consider with regard to mandated case plan goals:

- Can the required goals be attained within the time limits?
- When the client expresses frustration, is this viewed as a lack of motivation or opposition?
- What is the level of progress that would satisfy the court mandate?
- Does the client have the resources to achieve the goal?
- Are there interpersonal, intrapersonal, or environmental barriers to goal attainment?
- What are opportunities and challenges in the client's relationships? (For example, the receptiveness and capacity of significant others to change.)

EP 2.1.2b

In working with the mandated case plans, social workers can feel caught between their ethical obligation to the client and their obligation to the authority of the court or the referring agency. Moreover, responding to the mandate has an expectation of compliance for both the social worker and the individual. Also, if your work is funded by an agency purchase of service or performance contract, there can be program objectives, expectations, and requirements for the client that guide your work. Nonetheless, it is your ethical responsibility to increase the likelihood that a client with your help is able to achieve program requirements or mandated goals. In managing the expectations and pressures, you can assume responsibility for helping the client to partialize and prioritize the various goal requirements.

Prioritizing and partializing mandated goals would involve developing a definitive plan that focused on the requirements of greatest significance (e.g., child safety). It may also require that you act as a mediator between the client and the county or state staff person who has responsibility for oversight of the case and reporting to the court. Part of your role may also include advocacy on behalf of the client, requesting that the court consider constraints or barriers to goal achievement, reporting the progress that has been made, and seeking the court's permission to prioritize any remaining goals. For example, "The parent has completed the drug treatment program and her UAs have been clear for six months." In this way the court is informed that progress has occurred, but also that additional time is needed for the parent to find a job, for example. Your advocacy on the parent's behalf enables the individual to have a reasonable opportunity to develop and demonstrate the skills and competencies needed to resolve the other mandated requirements.

EP 2.1.10i

Goals Should Be Commensurate with the Knowledge and Skill of the Practitioner

EP 2.1.1d

Certain problems and goals require a high level of training and expertise, for example, child sexual abuse and other situations that are beyond that of a beginning social worker. It is your legal and ethical responsibility to the client and to the profession that you engage in practice within the scope of you knowledge, ability, and skill level (Reamer, 2001). Practice beyond your scope can result in harm to the client and further pose a liability for you and your agency. The National Association of Social Worker's (NASW) Code of Ethics provides clear direction with regard to engaging in practice beyond your scope of practice and competence.

Secondary Supervision

EP 2.1.1f

In instances where you may lack the competence or supervision for dealing with a situation, you may be able to rely on *secondary supervision*. This type of supervision can provide you with access to a qualified professional, making it possible for you to contract for goals beyond your scope under their guidance (Caspi & Reid, 2002; Reamer, 1998; Strom-Gottfried, 2007). Secondary supervision is, however, restricted to a specific case. Also, whereas secondary supervision or consultation provides you with guidance in regards to a particular area of practice expertise, the agency supervisor is responsible for your ongoing supervision as required by the employment organization. In some instances, you may contract for supervision on your own. Secondary supervision as an alternative arrangement generally involves a contract between the expert and the agency, and the approval of your agency supervisor is required. Ultimately, the agency supervisor is ultimately responsible for the ongoing oversight of your work (Strom-Gottfried, 2007). In either case, it is essential that all parties involved take precautions to protect client confidentiality (Loewenberg, Dolgoff, & Harrington, 2005; Panos, Panos, Cox, Roby, & Matheson, 2004; Reamer, 1998).

Of course, using secondary supervision assumes that this resource is available in your particular geographical area. When secondary supervision is not an option, you proceed to work with a client under specific restricted conditions:

- *First, you should explain to the client the limitations of your competence with regard to their goal. Advising a client of your practice limitations allows them to decide on an informed basis whether or not to continue their contact with you.*
- *Second, you must evaluate whether or not developing goals in an area where you lack expertise places the client or others at risk.*

Each of the discussed options offers considerations to be carefully evaluated against the potential risks to the client and to your agency. Also, you should be aware of whether undertaking an alternative arrangement and engaging in practice beyond your scope (as defined by legal regulation in your state or province) poses a risk to you (Reamer, 1998; Strom-Gottfried, 2007). In general, it is ethical and legal to engage in practice that is commensurate with your scope and competence and to refer clients who require service beyond your competence or that of your agency to a qualified professional (Reamer, 1998).

Goals Should Be Stated in Positive Terms That Emphasize Growth

EP 2.1.10e

Goals should emphasize growth, highlighting the benefits or gains to the client as a result of their attainment. In formulating goal statements, stipulating negative behaviors that must be eliminated tends to draw attention to what clients must give up, thereby emphasizing deficits in their behavior. For example, "Veronica's interactions with her peers need improvement so that she can attend the spring festival." Here, both "interaction with peers" and "improvement" are undefined. In addition, the focus is on the negative aspects of her behavior and punishment. Rewriting this goal in positive terms ("Veronica will learn conflict resolution skills so that she avoids getting into a shouting match with her peers") emphasizes the specific behavior to be changed as well as the expectations for the circumstances in which she will utilize the skills that she has learned.

Consider the protective services case plan for a single parent father who has been recently released from prison and has regained custody of his children. Shortly after his release, a teacher reported that the older child had bruises on his arm. An investigation of the report found evidence of the use of excessive discipline. The case plan read: *"Parent will demonstrate understanding of his inability to manage stress and anger, and the resulting tendency to use punishment, resulting in physical abuse of the child."* Although the father's point of contact was involuntary, the father did want help. He recognized that, as a result of being in prison for ten years, he lacked some parenting skills. The image of him reflected in the case plan of an angry, abusive, and uncaring parent caused him to feel discouraged. Furthermore, the portrayal was inconsistent with his self-image and undermined his sense of self as "trying to do the right thing." His reaction is not uncommon. In fact, people tend to counter negative evaluations of their behavior or situation initially with disbelief which can lead to their becoming hostile, despondent, or feeling threatened. Also, when goals are vague, a lack of understanding of what is expected can increase an individual's level of psychological stress and anxiety. In working with this particular client to complete the case plan, it would be important for you to reinforce the positive elements of his behavior. Psychologically, positive goals that have clear performance standards enhance motivation and mitigate conscious or unconscious opposition to change (Bloom, Fischer, & Orme, 2003; Miller & Rollnick, 2002). Table 12-5 highlights examples of contrasting negative and positive goal statements.

Avoid Agreeing to Goals about which You Have Major Reservations

You may legitimately have reservations about certain client goals. For example, goals that are overly ambitious, cause harm, or have an adverse impact on the individual can cause you to be concerned. Your reservation might be

EP 2.1.1d & 2.1.2a

TABLE-12-5 NEGATIVE AND POSITIVE GOAL STATEMENTS

NEGATIVE	POSITIVE
Understand his inability to manage stress and anger when he disciplines the children	Learn alternative ways to discipline the children.
Never leave the children home alone.	Arrange for care of the children when you plan to be away for the evening.
Prevent the formation of coalitions and nonparticipatory behaviors by group members	Unite the efforts of the group in working collectively that encourages each member into participation
Discontinue the frequency of drinking binges	Increase periods of sobriety each day
Refrain from running away from home	Discuss curfew with parents as an alternative option to running away from home
Reduce incidents of abusive behavior	Walk away from situations when you are angry, to avoid hitting your wife

© Cengage Learning 2013

caused by your uncertainty about the benefits of a client's goal. For instance, an adolescent wishing to become pregnant (believing that she can be a better parent than her own), thinks that living on her own with a child will allow her to get away from a stressful family situation. Another instance in which your reservation would be appropriate would be if a parent insists on a goal regarding a child, despite your emphasis on the entire family's involvement. Further, your concern is warranted if a client's goal is at odds with the agency's focus or values.

Increasingly, some professionals are asserting their right to serve or not serve clients because of their religious or moral beliefs, despite ethical codes that emphasize self-determination and the primacy of client's rights. There are also instances when social workers may be faced with a tension between ethical and legal responsibility. For example, confidential information provided by an individual who is an immigrant, for whom you are ethically responsible and have a fiduciary obligation, may be in conflict with state and federal laws.

Professional Values and Goal Tensions

Reservations can include clients' goals that are incompatible with your values. Values, of course, are highly individualized. You may work with a client with whom you do not share common ground with respect to values. How do you reconcile differences, should you find yourself in a situation where your values have the potential to intrude upon your fiduciary obligation to the client? What is an appropriate course of action?

When you are faced with situations that tax your ability to work with some people, you can rely on the ethical principles that frame the professional nature of the client–social worker relationship. Specifically, this means that ethically your personal values should not dictate how you work with clients. Doing so may require you to pause and take stock so that you can become aware of the tension and evaluate your thinking. This may also be a time when you should seek supervision. Continuing to work with clients in circumstances where you disagree with their goals can become an issue of the client's rights to effective treatment if your feelings intrude upon the helping process.

EP 2.1.2a & 2.1.2b

Referrals as a Resource

In some cases, ethical practice demands that you refer the client to another professional or agency and provide an honest and nonjudgmental explanation to the client. Often, students will assert their inability to work with a particular individual with certain attributes. A reflective exploration might include such questions as, "How do I know in advance of meeting the person and hearing his or her concerns that I am unable to work with him or her?" Further, "Have I labeled the individual based on their attributes before I fully understand what their goals are?" These self-reflection questions may in fact clarify your reservations and make a referral unnecessary. In instances where you have determined that a referral is preferable but unavailable, you should explain to the client up front the kind of help you can and cannot provide in assisting them to achieve their goals. For example, "I can help you with your goal of retaining custody of your son by submitting a report to the family court judge outlining your progress. But, on the basis of the information that you shared with me, I am unable to assist you to prove that the child's father is irresponsible."

EP 2.1.2a & 2.1.2b

EP 2.1.1f

There will be times, nonetheless, in which you are involved with a case and have strong reservations about or disagree with an individual's goals. The tension between self-determination and your reservations poses an ethical dilemma for which you will need to seek supervision or consultation (Strom-Gottfried, 2007). Tensions can also occur when the evidence-based practices that an agency has implemented are incompatible with what an individual wants or needs. For instance, Furman (2009) comments that evidence-based practice protocols may tend to focus on outcomes and efficiency rather than an exploration of client's goals, as well as the guiding principles of the social worker profession.

Ethical and Legal Tensions

EP 2.1.2b

In practice, there will be times at which you may decline to assist a client with a particular goal for legal and ethical reasons. For example, goals that involve a threat of harm to the client or others are neither ethical nor legal. You may also face a situation in which ethical and legal choices are in conflict. Responding to the legal choice may, in your opinion, be unjust and undermine your ethical obligation to the client (Kutchins, 1991; Reamer, 2005). The feasibility of goals can also be influenced by both legal and ethical concerns. The social worker in the following case was confronted with such a situation.

CASE EXAMPLE

A mother who had been a victim of political torture in Liberia escaped to a neighboring country with her children and her mother. After living in a refugee camp for two years, the woman, under the Liberian Immigration Act, obtained a permit that allowed her to come to the United States. She was in the process of completing the paperwork so that her children and her mother could immigrate to the United States as well. This process required DNA reports for the children as well as their birth records, which the mother was able to provide for two of the children. When asked by the Legal Aid attorney whether the third and youngest child was her child, the mother replied yes. Actually, the family had found the child abandoned and had taken her in as a member of the family. Although not biologically related, in Liberia this child was considered to be the mother's child because she had cared for the child. The social worker assisting the mother knew the status of this child and felt uncomfortable with the information that the mother had provided to the attorney. When the attorney left the room, the social worker expressed her concern and the mother became upset, telling the social worker to "remove herself from the case if she could not be more supportive."

Here, the mother had two goals. Her priority goal was to arrange for her family to come to the United States. Second, she hoped that they would eventually become citizens. The priority goals and whether they were attainable had both legal and ethical implications for the social worker. In addition, a conflict of cultural norms added to the tension.

The social worker in this case was confronted with several difficult choices. Specifically, these choices surrounded her responsibility to the mother, the mother's right to autonomy and confidentiality, and compliance with the law. Observing the ethical obligations has legal implications. Although somewhat intimidated by the mother's reaction, the social worker explained the legal consequences for the family of providing false information to the attorney and to Immigration and Customs Enforcement (ICE). The social worker then explained that, because she was aware that the kinship information about the youngest child was false, being a party to the deception had legal implications for her as the social worker. She further explained that, while she was sensitive to the Liberian culture's definition of "family," she would not be able to continue working with the mother unless she agreed to tell the truth. In an effort to resolve the matter, she proposed helping the mother explain the cultural nature of the child's status to the attorney and on the immigration forms.

In a review of this case during a consultation session, some staff believed this to be primarily a legal issue because the child did not meet the legal requirement of being a biological family member. Others, including the social worker presenting the case, viewed the situation differently. For them, it was within the ethical role of the social worker to assist the Legal Aid Attorney to understand the mother's culture, within which this child was considered to be a member of this family. Knowledge of a client's culture in the provision of services is also an ethical principle, and social workers are expected to use their knowledge to explain the functions of behavior within a cultural context (NSAW Code of Ethics, Standard 1.05). Of course, you may imagine that this case example represents an exceptional situation. As social workers have increasing contact with clients from diverse cultural backgrounds, they are more and more likely to encounter situations that require them to act as cultural interpreters and advocates.

Goals Must Be Consistent with the Functions of the Agency

EP 2.1.10a

Explorations of clients' problems, wants, and desired changes may be incompatible with the agency's mission, function and program objectives. For example, although a family services agency provides a range of services, they might not offer vocational counseling. Likewise, hospitals in general do not offer family counseling, except in specific situations (e.g., grief and loss) and then only on a short-term basis. Should client needs not match or exceed agency function, it is appropriate for you to assist them in obtaining the needed services by making a referral to an appropriate agency. To facilitate the referral, it is often useful that you make the call to the potential referral agency while the client is with you. Afterwards, a follow-up phone call from you to the client confirms that the individual has been connected to the referral agency and is satisfied with the referral.

Applying Goal Selection and Development Guidelines with Minors

EP 2.1.10c

To begin this discussion, we start with the guidelines related to developing goals with involuntary clients. For the most part, the instances in which minors have contact with professionals is the result of the involvement of their family, a school referral, juvenile authorities or the court, or a crisis. In some instances, parents seek help for a child's problematic behavior or to facilitate the achievement of a goal they have set for the minor. Rarely are minors in contact with professionals on their own accord. To elaborate on this point, consider a situation in which a minor has been removed from his biological home with the goal of ensuring his health and safety. In response to his removal, the minor emphasized that he wanted to "go home." Minors may not always understand or trust the helping motives of adults, even when they are vulnerable. In this situation, as well as others where a minor may feel acted upon, the challenge is to reconcile the minor's goals with the systems involved.

The factors that have been discussed as influencing goals such as client participation, family involvement, status, environmental influences, and values and beliefs are also applicable to working with minors. In addition to the previous discussion regarding selecting and defining goals, the following points are pertinent to developing goals with minors.

Eliciting Minors' Understanding of the Goal and Point of View of the Problem, and Using this Information to Assist Them to Develop Goals

An experienced social worker who has worked primarily with school-based groups involving minors emphasized that, "Starting where the client is" is an absolute with this population. Further, she noted, "Because their contact with you is required, it is essential that you talk with them so that you gain a sense of their perceptions and perspectives." To this point, recall that participation was one of the factors discussed earlier as influencing goals. According to this social worker, engaging minors in the telling of their story is critical.

Listening to the minor's narrative is a starting point in establishing an atmosphere in which goals or solutions can be developed (Davis, 2005; Fontes, 2005; McKenzie, 2005; Morgan, 2000; White & Morgan, 2006; Smith & Nylund, 1997). A narrative-oriented approach where open-ended questions are encouraged allows minors of all ages to tell their story based on their experience and perception of the world in which they interact. For example, in the following situation, make note of the various reasons the boys give for their behavior. In this scenario, the social worker leads a discussion on the development of goals in a school-based group. The school's overall goal for the participants and hence the reason for the referral to the group was "appropriate classroom behavior." Once demonstrated, the participants would be able to return to the classroom. At this point, the goal of appropriate behavior is vague, and would need to be defined in explicit, measurable language.

School-based Group with Minors

The group is a year-long, school-based social skills group for elementary school-aged boys, led by the experienced social worker mentioned above. The boys were involuntary, having been sent to the group by their teachers for inappropriate classroom behavior. Because they were involuntary, encouraging the boys to talk and participate was time consuming and challenging. As a beginning point, the social worker asked them about their feeling about being in the group, because she believed that allowing them to express their feelings was critical. Minors, depending on their age, cognitive capacity, and emotional intelligence may not readily express their feelings unless they are asked. Given the opportunity, some referred to the group as "stupid," but the group was "better than being in the classroom." Others were resentful, embarrassed, or anxious about being in a group for "problem kids." When asked, their participation could be more comfortable. "Getting something for coming"—specifically, what was the incentive for their participation—was a unanimous response. Ultimately, the greater incentive for them was to return to their classroom.

As a means to understanding the specifics of their classroom behavior and so that goals could be developed, the social worker asked each participant to explain their understanding of why they were required to participate in the group. Some of their responses were as follows:

"The teacher does not like me."
"The teacher is always mad about something."
"Because I sometimes play and joke with my friends in class."
"The teacher does not like _____ kids" [snickering among group members], followed by a side comment, "Shut up, boy."
"I was telling my friend about the gunshots around my house last night."

EP 2.1.10c

The language associated with goals, as well as the purpose, function, and type of goal can be meaningless to the majority of elementary school-aged minors. But by focusing on their perception of the reason for their referral to the group, the social worker facilitated the potential for selecting a goal. She also queried each participant about their specific behavior in the classroom. Also, the social worker neither judged nor dismissed the comment that "the teacher does not like me." In following-up to this statement, the social worker asked, "What do you think would make the teacher like you?" to which the student replied, "If I paid attention in class." Others in the group responded to her open-ended questions, for example, "What could you do differently?" which led to a behavioral change goal. For all of the participants, the specific behavior-change goals were further clarified using their desire to return to the classroom as a motivator.

In recounting the experience of this and other similar type groups, the social worker commented that school-based groups often are a window into the family and community life of group participants, which can be especially challenging. She emphasized that she hears about parts of the student's lives that have little to do with the purpose of the group, but, in fact, these external factors do matter. Specifically, the information that they share is informative of what happens to them (or their families) outside of school, but this information often explains their behavior in the classroom. For example, the reason given by one boy for his behavior in the classroom ("I was telling my friend about the gunshots around my house last night") revealed the adverse conditions of the neighborhood in which his family lives. Of course, the sharing of this event in the mind of a minor of this age is perhaps exciting, but you can also observe his anxiety and fear of the experience. Later, when asked to share his goal he responded, "I want my family to be safe." Obviously, this goal had little to do with the teacher's goal, yet his concern influenced his classroom behavior. Nonetheless, you should be aware that disruptive behavior by minors can be a way in which they act out or cope with very real ongoing stress or trauma. Schools have structure and behavioral expectations established so that they can meet their educational objectives. Huffine (2006) notes, however, that "blaming youth for their behaviors may be easier than addressing the social ills" that can influence their behavior (p. 15).

Three questions are relevant to the comment of the group participant who stated, "The teacher does not like _____ kids." Is this an attempt to legitimize his behavior in the classroom? Perhaps, however, before reaching this conclusion, you should be mindful of the fact that the cognitions, perceptions, and feelings of young minors influence their self-definition and self-evaluation relative to the outside world. Second, what are the relational dynamics between the boy and the teacher? Another question for you to consider is, What are the boy's life experiences that have led him to conclude that this teacher (and perhaps others) doesn't like kids with certain physical attributes?

Is the minor voluntary or involuntary? Voluntary or involuntary status can, as is the case with adult clients, make a difference in the dynamics of goal development. Minors who are involuntary either because of a referral or mandate (which they may perceive as being one and the same) may be reluctant to participate and set goals (Erford, 2003). Their feelings should be recognized as valid relative to their self-definition, especially within their peer group. Even when minors are voluntary, an adolescent or teen may feel that seeking help portrays them as being less than adequate in the context of their peer relationships (Lindsey, Korr, Broitman,

Bone, Green, & Leaf, 2006; Teyber, 2006). For youth of color and those who identify as lesbian, gay, bisexual, or transgender—peer contexts in which rejection and isolation are present in their lives—feelings of inadequacy can be particularly stressful.

Definition and Specifications of the Behavior to Be Changed

EP 2.1.10c

Like adults, minors will respond to clearly defined and measurable goals, objectives, or tasks. Criteria for developing clear goals with minors cited by Corwin (2002) and Huxtable (2004) are:

1. Emphasize the change in behavior that is expected (Waiting your turn to speak).
2. Define the conditions in which the behavior change is observed (In the classroom).
3. Clarify the expected level of goal performance within a specific timeline (Listen without interrupting while others are talking).

The example that follows illustrates further how the process works.

Goal 1: By the end of the first mid-year school term, Veronica will use the conflict resolution skills she has learned when she is likely to become involved in a shouting match with a peer.

Goal 2: In a situation in which she is unable to use her skills, Veronica will walk away from a conflict situation without talking back or name calling.

Goals should always be tailored to individual needs; therefore, the participation of the minor is important as he or she can have insights about potential barriers to goal achievement. For example, a third goal was developed by Veronica because she was concerned about whether she could immediately act on the second goal. In particular, how she felt about herself and the perception of her peers seemed like potential barriers. Thus, she developed an affirming self-talk behavioral goal to use when she is faced with a conflict situation.

With minors, you will find it worthwhile to partialize goals, tasks, or objectives so that they are more manageable and progress is observable. In addition to having goals that are clearly defined, specific, feasible, and measurable, a number of other factors have particular relevance to this population. Goals with minors tend to work best when they provide:

- *a sense of self-direction, particularly with adolescents who tend to react to being told what to do and how to act.*
- *incentives that are linked goals, in particular, something that they want for themselves.*
- *a sense of their ability to achieve goals.*
- *involvement in establishing evaluative measures.*
- *regular feedback about performance that honors their progress.*
- *praise for their efforts as well as goal attainment.*
- *the opportunity to talk about how they accomplished a goal and their level of satisfaction with their performance.*
- *opportunities for them to measure their progress and praise themselves.*
- *strengths and protective factors; for example, the support of family or significant others in their lives.*

Huxtable (2004) and Morgan (2000) suggest using visual aids, metaphors, stories, and games to facilitate goal development. Huxtable (2004) encourages the use of creative metaphors to facilitate motivation. In appealing to a minor to develop a goal, Huxtable likened the goal to "a race to the finish line," because the minor was interested in race cars. Moreover, the goal selection and development process is optimal when the language used is familiar and relevant to the minor rather than when it is professional or institutional jargon. For example, "inappropriate behavior in the classroom" is less explicit than "making noises or gestures while others are talking."

In settings in which behavioral contracts are used (residential settings or juvenile detention centers, for example), minors may not be involved in establishing their goals. These contracts generally specify goals, expected outcomes, contingency rewards, and consequences (Ellis & Sowers, 2001). However, you can assist minors in meeting behavioral expectations by engaging them in devising ways in which goals can be achieved.

Age and Stage of Development, Cognitive Ability

Davis (2005) notes that "telling stories is a natural ways for minors to communicate" and their doing so, inspires them to be "confident about their own perceptions." From these stories, goals may be developed. Decisions about goals, however, are dependent on a minor's stage of development, cognitive and moral ability, and their ability to give consent (Note: informed consent and minors is discussed in Chapter 13).

EP 2.1.10c

The reactions of minors to developing goals tend to be situation specific. For example, very young minors in abuse situations can be subject to feelings of vulnerability, self-blame, anxiety, and fear (Fontes, 2005; McKenzie, 2005). Minors develop scripts about themselves, the social environment in which their relationships are formed, including with peers and their styles of problem solving. At almost any stage of development, consideration must be given to the power differences between you and the minor as you discuss goals. Younger minors can be sensitive to power, have a tendency to want to please, and are especially conscious of how they are evaluated by others.

Older minors, particularly adolescents, may be capable of making goal decisions, but they may tend to be fiercely protective of their identity, independence, and autonomous locus of control. In goal discussions, it can be important to explore and appeal to the future-orientation of adolescents in the conversations regarding the choices that they make. Understanding and empathizing with the biological, social, and psychological stressors that adolescents and teens experience and how these factors can influence their behavior is illustrated in the following case.

CASE EXAMPLE

According to the case record summary about Bettina, age 17, she was removed from home along with her siblings when she was 6 years of age. Each child was placed in a separate foster home. Bettina, the oldest child in the sibling group, has experienced multiple placements, and at age 16 she was on the run and pregnant. She is currently living with her child in a group home for pregnant or parenting teen mothers. She has lived in the home for the past year.

Multiple notes in the case record describe her as alternatively defiant–contrite, courteous–rude, uncooperative–cooperative, and motivated–unmotivated, depending on the day and her mood. Because of her behavior, staff routinely initiated sanctions, and some believe that she should be placed in a more restrictive environment. Bettina's response to sanctions is unpredictable. At times she may comply, at other times, she becomes explosive.

Bettina's Story

"I don't like people telling me what to do [independence, separating from adults]. I know my own mind [individuation, locus of control]! Everyone is always watching me [sensitivity to control and opinions of others], the mistakes that I make, like I care what they think. You know what I'm saying? They never say, 'Bettina, you are doing a good job caring for your baby.' But you can be sure that they are just sitting around waiting and watching for me mess up so they can come down on me. Sometimes I get confused and scared [stress], but then my worker says, 'Bettina you can do it!' Then we talk about stuff [exploring range of future possibilities] like what I want to do when I leave this place. Eventually, I want to live in my own place with my baby.

The other day I was angry and walking around cursing because I had missed an appointment with my worker. She and I had an appointment, but I had a chance to take my baby to see his Daddy. Besides, the baby could also see his daddy's mother, who has been real helpful to me. I want my baby to have contact with his father's family [goal need]. I could tell that my worker was unhappy, having driven across town for the appointment with me. I hate it when I mess up with her, but I did not know what else to do. I had a chance to take the baby to see his Daddy and his Daddy's mother, so I left. But as soon as she opened the door, I started cursing, in case she was angry [reactive to potential of punishment]. She let me go on for awhile and then she asked me, 'What is going on in your head right now?' and I just started crying. [sensitivity to feelings/empathy, listening to presentation of self and expression of feelings]."

In reading the staff's reports on Bettina and Bettina's story, you get two different perspectives. In both accounts, you can observe McCarter's (2008) emphasis that during this developmental stage, it is important to meet the minor "where they are" and to understand that where they are and what their mood is can frequently change. Bettina's multiple adolescent/teen development issues are highlighted in the brackets. In spite of her developmental turmoil, it is apparent that Bettina had two goals. One was to live on her own with her child. The other was for the child to have contact with the father and his family. Like most teens, nonetheless, she was inclined to respond to the immediacy of the moment, even though she had a vision about the future.

Bettina's behavior is not unusual, although not all teens are as dramatic nor are they as conflicted in their interactions with adults. As Bettina attempted to attend to the developmental task of individuation, she was functionally

EP 2.1.7b

independent in that she could care for herself, but she was not emotionally independent. In the absence of parents, staff in the home were essentially parental surrogates upon whom she depended for approval and support. As such, they were often the targets of her frustration.

The social worker believed that by empathizing and supporting Bettina's sense of self-direction and desire for independence, the two of them would be able to turn the situation around. Understandably, the staff had tired of her disruptive behavior. The social worker made a facilitative deal with Bettina, linking it to her goal of eventually leaving the group home to live on her own. Specifically, if Bettina agreed to follow the rules of the home, the social worker would arrange for Bettina to go visit her child's father and the father's mother on a weekly basis. In addition, she reiterated her expectation that Bettina keep their appointments. Of the previously cited considerations for developing goals with minors, the following were pertinent in Bettina's case:

- The social worker specified the expected behavioral change, specifically that Bettina follow the rules of the group home.
- In supporting Bettina's goal to live on her own with her child, the social worker affirmed her sense of self-direction. This was particularly helpful since adolescents tend to react to being told what to do and how to act.
- Using an incentive for behavioral change, the social worker agreed to arrange weekly visits with the child's father and his mother.
- The incentive also tapped into the supportive resources available to Bettina, specifically that of the father's family.

Resourceful solutions can be especially useful with minors, particularly those solutions that allow them to save face, and feel empowered and involved. You might question this quid pro quo goal arrangement and instead insist on a behavioral change; specifically, that Bettina follow the group home rules and reduce her disruptive behavior. You may also be inclined to pressure Bettina to reduce her disruptive behavior, pointing out the consequences of her failing to do so. Given her developmental stage and what she values (independence), her response would likely be negative, in which case behavioral change would be improbable. The need for her autonomous sense of self may in fact outweigh the consequences of her noncompliant behavior. In working with minors, it can be useful to be guided by the notion of utilitarian ethics. Ask yourself, "What is the overall outcome that I am seeking?" In Bettina's case, the social worker's action facilitated the development of problem-solving goals.

Process of Negotiating Goals

Table 12-6 summarizes the steps that are involved in the negotiation of goals with both voluntary and involuntary clients. The steps may be implemented in the following sequence or the sequence may be being adapted to the unique circumstances of each case. For example, an individual may not be prepared to negotiate goals because he or she does not fully understand the function and purpose of goals. In cases like this, an explanation would have precedence over determining readiness. If, however, the individual confirms his or her readiness, you would proceed to the next step of explaining the purpose and function of goals.

EP 2.1.10c

Determine Clients' Readiness for Goal Negotiation

At this stage in the process, voluntary clients are generally ready to get on with the business of resolving their concerns. Determining whether they are prepared to identify specific goals may begin with a summary of their priority concerns. The social worker Ali, for example, summarized what appeared to be the priority concern of Angela and Irwin Corning, "We've talked about your concerns about living in transitional housing." To confirm their readiness, she asked, "I wonder if you are prepared at this point to focus on moving from transitional housing as a goal, or would you like me to

EP 2.1.10c

TABLE-12-6 PROCESS OF NEGOTIATING GOALS

Determine client's readiness for goal negotiation—Voluntary and Involuntary clients
Explain the purpose and function of goals
Jointly select appropriate goals
Define goals explicitly and specify level of change
Determine potential barriers to goal attainment and discuss benefits and risks
Assist clients to make a clear choice about committing themselves to specific goals
Rank order of goals according to client's priorities

© Cengage Learning 2013

provide some ideas about resources?" Angela and Irwin affirmed that their desire to move from transitional housing was their priority goal. On the other hand, had either one of them responded, "I think so," or "maybe," this would have been a signal that they were not quite ready to settle on this goal. Determining readiness is essential because people can be at different starting points and have varying levels of confidence (Miller & Rollnick, 2002). The source of their ambivalence may relate to a lack of confidence in their ability to change themselves or their circumstances, each of which can be explored.

Readiness of Involuntary Clients

EP 2.1.10c

Determining an involuntary client's readiness for negotiating goals is also essential. Indeed, educating these individuals about the purpose and function of goals may be the first step in creating an atmosphere in which a discussion about what is required of them can occur. This discussion may significantly change the tone of the interaction between you and the individual. Points to be considered in facilitating goal readiness are illustrated in the following statements:

- **Review the Mandate:** "The court has identified a problem that needs to be resolved." Review the mandate and specify what is expected: "The court requires that you participate in a parent training group and that you have an assessment of your parenting skills after you complete the program."
- **Specificity:** "The court expects that the parent training sessions will help you learn to set limits with your children and to learn other methods of discipline." Explaining the intent of goals provides specificity and indicates that the client is able to retain some control over her life. Specificity would also include alerting the client to any requirements related to attendance, being on time, and remaining in the parenting sessions for the entire duration.
- **Level of Freedom:** "You do, however, have a choice. You can choose among the various parenting programs on an approved list."
- **Client's Viewpoint:** "Your view of the problem as well as concerns that you may have are also important." For goals to be relevant to the client and their situation, contextual meaning is important. "It would be useful for me to hear from you how you came to be involved in the court system."
- **Involving Client in Setting Goals:** "I'd like for you to suggest ways in which you could meet the requirements of the court."
- **Measuring Progress:** "I will keep a record of your progress of learning skills in the parenting class and will include this information in my reports to the court." This statement clarifies for the client the focus of the mandate and the importance of demonstrating progress to prevent further action by the court.

What is accomplished by a review of the mandate as well as the other information in the statements? Essentially, as you review the mandate you specify the change required by the court. In soliciting the client's point of view, you provide the client with an opportunity to explain his or her understanding of the situation and to describe the circumstances. In this way, you can respond to the client's viewpoint and explore goals that are important to the client in addition to those contained in the mandate. "The court requires that the children be supervised when you go out for the evening. I also understand that you need to find childcare." Allowing the client to choose from available parenting programs gives them a choice by which they can be motivated and empowered, ultimately ensuring their participation. A clear indication of how their progress will be measured can diffuse their anxiety. When indicated, individuals should also be informed of the requirements of the parenting groups and this information should be included in the goal plan. For example, a program may stipulate that participants "attend a certain number of classes" and "actively participate." These requirements, as well as the timelines imposed by the court, need to be included in the client's goal statement. With clients having heard what is expected of them, you can move on to assessing client readiness to participate in the goal negotiation process.

During the process of negotiating and prioritizing goals, as incentive, you can inquire if the individual also has concerns that are important to them. For example, "As you know, the court would like to see specific changes in your parenting. In addition to the changes ordered by the court, would you also like to discuss changes that you would like to make on your own?"

Explain the Purpose and Function of Goals

Many elements of the helping process are educational. "Goals" and "objectives" are terms used within the professional community, but people are apt to simply express what they want to be different or what they would like to do. When goals are discussed, clients may have questions. For example, a minor might ask, "What do I need a goal for?" Those who are involuntary most often ask, "What do I have to do?" A social worker who works with elderly persons noted that they are more likely to respond when the focus is on an action plan rather than on a goal. In general, when individuals understand the purpose and function of goals, they are more likely to appreciate their significance. In educating individuals about goals, you can use the analogy of the road map discussed at the beginning of this chapter. For the most part, a brief explanation is generally all that is required. Even so, explaining the purpose and function of goals may be a particularly critical step with individuals for whom the Western structure of formal helping systems is unfamiliar (Potocky-Tripodi, 2002). Additional time may be necessary, and asking them to describe or name the process in language that is familiar to them may be helpful.

Jointly Select Appropriate Goals

EP 2.1.10c

Voluntary clients are generally capable of identifying most or all of the goals and general tasks that they believe will resolve their problems. Because of your external vantage point, there may be instances when goals occur to you that clients may have overlooked or omitted. Consequently, you can make suggestions about goals for the client's consideration, explaining your reasoning and making reference to their priority concern. Assuming that you do not have reservations about their goals, it is important that you stress that the final goal decision is theirs to make. For example, in the case of the Corning family and Irwin's job search, the social worker stated, "I have some ideas and resources that may helpful, but it is important for me to hear what you think." Similarly, she asked the couple which of their two goals was a bigger priority. Eliciting this information ensures that both you and your clients are trying to accomplish the same goals.

Define Goals Explicitly and Specify Level of Change

EP 2.1.10j

After jointly deciding on specific goals and clarifying expectations, the next step is to determine the level of change desired by the individual or required by the mandate.

As an individual verbalizes his or her goals, you may need to seek clarification. Paraphrasing or suggested rewording of a goal can help clarify meaning and specificity. In paraphrasing, be cautious about taking liberties with what clients have said and obtain their approval of rewordings by reading them what you have written. Suppose that Mrs. Lenora Johnson, an elderly African American client who has been referred, stated, "I'd like to not feel blue." You would write what Mrs. Johnson said and then seek clarification by asking her to describe what she means so that you understand "feeling blue" in her words. In this way, you will be able to monitor and measure change.

Once goals are explicitly defined, specifying what clients expect to be different and their desired level of change is an important next step. To be more specific, it is important to engage individuals in a discussion about their expectations for what would be different when their goals are achieved. The following questions are examples of clarifying expectations:

Ali, the Social Worker: "What would it be like for you and your children when you move from transitional to permanent housing?"

Irwin Corning: "There are too many people under one roof. The place is noisy; you have to go to bed at a certain time. We could establish our own routine and the children would be able to play outside instead of being cooped up in a building. It would just be less stressful."

Social Worker: "When you complete the parent training program, what do you imagine to be different about your behavior with your children?"

Parent: "Oh, I don't know, maybe I would learn how to be less stressed out. Sometimes, I ignore what my kids are doing and then they get on my nerves and I blow up at them. Maybe I will learn how to do things with them and be more relaxed. I think that my kids would like this."

Social Worker: "When you said that you would like to not feel blue, tell me what it would be like for you to not have this feeling?"

Mrs. Johnson: "I think that I would have more energy, visit my grandchildren, and when they ask, 'How are you doing Grandma?' I could truthfully tell them that I feel good."

Notice that each question asked the individuals to clarify their goal expectations.

If a person has difficulty defining a goal, you can prompt them by referring to needs and wants they identified during the exploration and assessment process and suggest that they consider related changes. To illustrate prompting, we return to the case of Margaret, the elderly woman discussed at the beginning of this chapter. Although she recognized her need for a different living environment (one in which she felt safe), she nonetheless wanted to maintain a level of independence.

Social worker: When you talk about wanting to have a level of independence, what does that look like for you?

Margaret: For me, I want the help that I need with the housework, taking a bath, or perhaps preparing meals. Other things like going to events at the senior center and shopping for my own groceries are things that I would want to do on my own.

The social worker's question effectively summarized some of the key issues related to Margaret's goal of maintaining her independence. With respect to determining the desired level of change, you can use messages similar to the following:

Social Worker: You said that you want a better relationship with your wife and that you are tired of being hauled off by the police. What is the specific change that you can make that will improve your relationship with your wife and avoid contact with the police?

Client: I would just walk away when she is in my face and I would not hit her. I would wait until both of us aren't so mad at each other, so we could talk.

Specifying a desired level of change is a facet of defining goals explicitly. The goal and the level of change should be congruent with the client situation. With goals that involve ongoing behavior, growth is potentially infinite.

Determine Potential Barriers to Goal Attainment and Discuss Potential Benefits and Risks

EP 2.1.10i

The importance of feasibility was previously discussed at length under guidelines for developing goals. Exploring potential barriers moves to another level and includes feasibility. In essence, you are anticipating and identifying in advance events or circumstances that could undermine goal achievement.

Social Worker: You said that when your wife is in your face, you plan to walk away and to avoid hitting her. I believe that you are committed to this goal because you want to improve your relationship with her. Let's imagine that the two of you are angry, which as I understand has usually ended up with your hitting her. Can you think of what might get in the way of your plan to walk away?

Client: Well, at first it might be hard, especially if she keeps yapping at me or follows me out the door, screaming her fool head off, embarrassing me in front of everybody. I guess if this happens, I'll just keep on walking, because I don't want to deal with the police.

Social Worker: So, for you a big motivator is your not having to deal with the police. Is it also possible that your behavior could also improve your relationship with your wife?

Client: Well now, that's a big payoff, isn't it?

Risks and Benefits

Identifying barriers to goal attainment can improve the likelihood of goal attainment; a discussion of the benefits of goal attainment can function in a similar manner. In addition, outlining benefits can enhance a person's commitment and sustain his or her effort. For example, a benefit described by the individual in the above domestic violence scenario was, "My kids won't be afraid of me anymore," as well as improving his relationship with his wife. Nonetheless, enthusiasm for or relief about the benefits of achieving goals may result in an individual's superficial attention to risks or negative consequences as illustrated in the following:

EP 2.1.10i

Social Worker: You have mentioned two benefits of changing your behavior. One of which was that your kids would not be afraid of you, the other, was that you would improve your relationship with your wife. What do you see as possible risks for you when you change your behavior?

Prudent practice requires that you discuss with clients the potential benefits and risks involved in goal attainment. Reviewing potential obstacles and risks is intended to help individuals think in advance about events or situations that might influence their ability to attain their goals. Risks can of course become a very real barrier, even though an individual is motivated to behave differently. A further discussion between you and the client can include planning for alternative responses to barriers and risks, and may result in determining that a goal is not feasible. It may also be that a short-term goal can be developed as instrumental to attaining a longer-termed goal. Should this be the case, you and the individual would revise either the goal or the behavior. You should also be aware of the fact that changes in behaviors can result in ambivalent feelings that have both positive and negative consequences, even though the benefit of a change is clear. For the most part, individuals will likely perceive the benefits resulting from goal attainment as outweighing the risks and therefore be ready to work with you toward accomplishing their priority goals.

Assist Clients in Making a Choice about Committing Themselves to Specific Goals

EP 2.1.10j

After exploring the potential barriers, benefits, and risks of pursuing specific goals, the next step is to work with the individual to make a commitment to the goals that they wish to pursue. A simple but effective means to gauge commitment to a specific goal, recommended by DeJong and Berg (2007), is to have clients rate their level of commitment on a scale from 1 to 10, where 1 represents "extremely uncertain or uncommitted," and a rating of 10 represents "optimistic, eager to start, and totally committed." A level of commitment in the range of 6–8 is usually sufficient to move to the contracting process.

EP 2.1.10i

Occasionally, individuals can be hesitant about committing, in which case you should explore the basis for their misgivings or reservations rather than attempt to convince them to sign on to a specific goal. While respecting client feelings, you can explore with them the extent to which their concerns are affecting their problem. For example, despite the fact that an adolescent has stated he is tired of being suspended from school, he is hesitant to commit to a behavioral change goal that would in effect increase his number of days in school without being suspended. You might ask him an inductive question, specifically whether multiple school suspensions were related to his behavior. As a next step, you might ask whether his concern is a sufficient reason for not accomplishing the goal.

For some involuntary clients, readiness to commit to mandated goals may be low. Encountering a lack of or a low level of readiness to commit to a goal can be very frustrating given the pressure placed on you and the individual by the court. Seeking client commitment can increase the pressure that they feel. Especially if clients perceive your authority as being intertwined with that of the court, you may become the target of their frustration. Should this be the case, you should respect and appreciate their lack of readiness. Also, as disconcerting as their behavior might be, you are encouraged to depersonalize the experience.

Facilitating the involuntary individual's readiness to commit to a goal may need to occur in incremental stages. For example, while you empathize with client feelings and the pressures they are experiencing, you can point out the choices or freedom that they have in deciding how they go about responding to the goal requirement. For example, an individual can be given the option of choosing the location and schedule of a parenting class. Also, recall the earlier discussion of strategies for facilitating goal selection with involuntary clients. In many cases, involuntary individuals may want help, but not in the way or for the reason it is offered. As illustrated in the following example, a discussion that highlights the benefits and opportunity for growth as a result of working on a mandated goal can also be productive. The discussion takes place between a social worker and a parent who has been mandated by the court to attend parenting classes. The parent's readiness level falls in the lowest range due to her beliefs, feelings, and her reaction to being judged as an inadequate parent, all of which contribute to her ambivalence about participating in parenting classes. The social worker affirms and respects her feelings, yet emphasizes the potential benefits to the client.

EP 2.1.10i

Social worker: I respect your opinion that you do not need parenting skills. I also understand your feelings about the court telling you how to parent with your kids. You said that your mother is a parent, that your grandmother is a parent, and that you learned from them. But, there seems to be a problem in the way that you discipline your children. For example, hitting a child with a belt that leaves multiple marks on their body is a problem. Your mother and grandmother may have used this method, but for you, it is a concern that has to be resolved.

Parent: Yeah, but being spanked didn't hurt me and my brothers and sisters, we all turned out okay! None of us are doing drugs or are in prison!

Social Worker: I understand that you believe that spanking is okay, and that you feel that you and your brothers and sisters weren't harmed. Most of us learn from our parents. When we talked about your frustrations as a single parent, you said that you are stressed out a great deal of the time. Is this the time when you are most likely to hit one of the children?

Parent: Yeah, that's right; the kids do get on my nerves a lot. I feel bad after I hit one of them, then the crying starts, which doesn't help my nerves. So tell me, how is attending a parenting class going to help me?

Social Worker: Are you willing to consider that by attending the parenting class you might gain skills in setting limits with your children without hitting them, and also relieve some of the stress that you feel in dealing with them?

Parent: Well, I guess so, if I can learn something that I can use and feel less stressed out.

In this dialogue, encouraging the parent to commit to the mandated goal required a great deal of work on the part of the social worker. She did not challenge her beliefs about parenting, but focused on the possible benefit of stress relief in dealing with her children, which the woman valued. However, should the parent remain hesitant or fail to commit to the goal, the social worker is obligated to inform her of the potential consequences to ensure that, in fact, she is making an informed choice. Involuntary status does not diminish the right of self-determination, yet it is your ethical responsibility to make these individuals aware of the risks associated with their choices and help them work through their concerns.

Rank Goals According to Client Priorities

EP 2.1.10j

Following the identification of and client commitment to specific goals, it can be helpful to rank those goals in order of their priority. The purpose of identifying high-priority goals is to ensure that beginning change efforts are directed toward the goals of utmost importance to clients. Depending on the nature of the goals, the client's developmental stage, the resources available to the client, and the time required, settling on no more than three goals is advisable. In cases with multiple mandated goals, you can help the client to prioritize so that they are more manageable, emphasizing those that have a greater consequence. Participating in a drug treatment program, for example, may have priority. When working with larger systems, you might create a list of goals for both the individuals and the systems involved and rank them for the individual and the system. Where there are differences, your role is to assist all parties to negotiate and rank the priority of goals.

As a lead-in to the ranking process, when the client is voluntary, the following is an example of a summarizing message:

Social worker: So far, we have talked about several concerns and goals. Among the goals that you identified was moving from transitional housing and finding a full time, permanent job for Irwin. You also mentioned that you want your children to have a quiet place to study in the current housing situation. Now that you've settled upon these goals, which one is the most important for you at this time? We'll get to all of the goals in time, but we want to start with the most important one.

With involuntary clients, you might use a message like this:

Social worker: While we have reached an agreement about which goals are most important to you, we also need to give priority to the goal established by the court. As you have said, you want the court out of your life. Your court order states that you need to enroll in a parenting class immediately, so this has to be a priority. You also said that you feel alone and tired out by the demands of caring for four children and want to have time for yourself. You also mentioned wanting to return to school. Are you able to say which of these goals, in addition to the one required by the court that you would like to work on first?

It is up to you to help people focus their effort by sorting out what is a priority for them so that they do not feel overwhelmed and become frustrated. When goals involve a system or more than one person, different members may naturally accord different priorities to goals. In such cases, it is important that you take the lead in helping those involved to prioritize the goals.

Monitoring Progress and Evaluation

Monitoring and evaluating progress and the status of goals are essential components of direct practice. Once goals have been developed, agreed upon, and explicitly defined, jointly deciding with the individual how progress is to be tracked and recorded is the logical next step. Measurement involves the precise definition of the problem and what is to be changed, and it clarifies the observations to be made that indicate progress toward the identified goal (Bloom, Fischer & Orme 2003). Monitoring and

EP 2.1.10m

Sample Goal and Task Form

Name: _____

Statement of Problem/Condition to Be Changed: _____

Goal Statement: _____

General Tasks: _____

Potential Barriers: _____

Benefits: _____

Specific Tasks (steps to be taken to achieve goal):

	Completion Date	Review Date	Outcome Code
1. _____	_____	_____	_____
2. _____	_____	_____	_____
3. _____	_____	_____	_____

Outcome Codes

Tasks and Goal Status [ ] C (completed) [ ] P (partially completed) [ ] NC (not completed)

FIG-12-3 Sample Goal and Task Form

evaluation are planned ongoing processes that occur at various stages. Irrespective of the frequency of the review, it should be done on a regular basis to avoid surprises. In other words, an ongoing review of the status of goals and related tasks or action steps is necessary in order to determine their effectiveness relative to changing the target concern. In this way, both you and the individual are informed about their progress (or lack of). A lack of progress should be examined as it may indicate that a goal plan is not producing the intended results. An example of a tool that can be used is illustrated in Figure 12-3. This goal and task form is developed jointly by you and the client and allows each of you to track the intermediate and overall progress toward the goal. It allows you and your client evaluation tasks or action steps as instrumental strategies to goal attainment as well as the status of the goal. Progress toward goals should be systematically recorded in the case record.

Methods of Monitoring and Evaluating Progress

EP 2.1.10m

This section provides an overview of both quantitative and qualitative methods that may be used to measure progress and to evaluate outcomes. Irrespective of the method used, the following components are considered to be fundamental to this process:

- *Identifying the specific problem or behavior to be changed*
- *Specifying measurable and feasible goals*
- *Matching goal and measurement procedures*
- *Maintaining a systematic record of relevant information*
- *Evaluating intermediate and final outcomes*

The first two factors were discussed earlier in this chapter. To refresh your memory, an identified target concern cannot be readily measured unless it has been defined. For example, inappropriate classroom behavior provides a global understanding about a concern. However, a definition of the specific behavior such as interrupting while others are talking is explicit. Definition of the target concern is the basis upon which specific measurable goals can be developed and subsequently observed and measured. A target concern that has been explicitly defined in measurable indicators informs you of the appropriate measurement and evaluation methods to be used.

Involving Clients in Monitoring and Evaluating Progress

Client involvement, an integral part of the goal negotiation and development process, is equally important at the measurement stage. Also, as in goal planning, client participation may mean that procedures to be used are culturally relevant and consistent with the individual's values and beliefs (Potocky-Tripodi, 2002). In involving clients, it is important that you explain the way in which evaluative information is to be obtained so that they understand and are receptive to the methods that will be used.

Lum (2004), Jayaratne (1994), and O'Hare (2009) are among those who support involving clients in the process of monitoring and measuring their progress. In essence, these authors are expressing views that are consistent with the empowerment and collaborative nature of the social worker–client relationship emphasized throughout this book. Also, including clients' perspective is believed to create a balance of power held by the social worker and the client and lessens the impact of systematic methods which "casts clients' viewpoints as being less scientific" (Kagel, 1994, p. 98).

EP 2.1.10m

Feedback from individuals regarding their progress and satisfaction with the services and rationale for their inclusion as partners in monitoring and evaluating progress is summarized as follows:

1. By eliciting an individual's views of their progress or by comparing their latest rates of the target behavior with the baseline, you maintain focus on goals and enhance the continuity of change efforts.
2. People gain perspective in determining where they stand in relationship not only to their ultimate goals but also to their pretreatment levels.
3. Observing incremental progress toward goals tends to sustain motivation and to enhance confidence in the helping process and in the social worker.
4. Eliciting a person's feelings and views about their progress can alert you to and allow you to address feelings or behaviors that can impede future progress and lead to premature termination.
5. Individuals can provide feedback on the efficacy of a goal or intervention strategy and whether an approach has yielded expected results within a reasonable period of time.
6. Indications of marked progress toward goal attainment alert you to when clients might be ready to shift their focus to another goal or begin planning for termination if all goals have been achieved.

Overall, the methods for monitoring, assessing and evaluating progress should be consistent with the agreement negotiated in the contracting or treatment planning. Progress toward goals should be monitored every two to three sessions at a minimum.

Quantitative Measurements

EP 2.1.10m

Quantitative evaluation embodies the use of procedures that measure the frequency and/or severity of target problems. Measurements taken before implementing change-oriented interventions are termed baseline measures because they provide a baseline against which measures of progress and measures at termination and follow-up can be compared. These comparisons thus provide quantitative data that make it possible to evaluate the efficacy of work with clients. The single subject design is one example that can be used in a variety of settings, including mental health, family, and private practice. The method can be adapted so that you can integrate evaluation as a key element in your practice. In most cases, the simple Single Subject ABA can be used.[2] Using this design is perhaps the most practical way in which you can track and evaluate progress over a period of time.

Measuring Overt Behaviors

EP 2.1.10m

Baseline measures can analyze either overt or covert behaviors. Overt behaviors are observable and, as such, lend themselves to frequency counts. For example, group members who have negotiated a shared goal of increasing the frequency of positive messages sent to one another would keep a tally of the number of such messages conveyed during group sessions. The session averages would then serve as a baseline against which progress could be measured. Similar baselines can be determined for target behaviors such as increasing the number of times that a student raised her hand before speaking in class. Such measures quantify behaviors and make it possible to ascertain ultimate outcomes of change efforts. In addition, clients can observe even small incremental changes.

Baselines obtained through self-monitoring, however, are not true measurements of behavior under "no treatment" conditions, because self-monitoring itself often produces therapeutic effects. For example, monitoring the rate of a desired behavior (i.e., raising one's hand before speaking) may, in fact, act to increase the frequency of that behavior. Similarly, measuring the rate of negative behavior may influence a client to reduce its frequency.

The effects of self-monitoring on the target behavior are termed *reactive effects*. When viewed by a researcher, reactive effects represent a source of contamination that confounds the effects of the interventions being tested. From your viewpoint, however, self-monitoring may be employed *as an intervention* precisely because reactive effects tend to increase or decrease certain target behaviors. Although desired changes that result from self-monitoring may be either positive or negative behaviors, emphasizing positive behaviors is preferable because doing so focuses on strengths related to goals. It is advisable to use multiple measures or observations, of which self-monitoring is one source. The teacher in the classroom situation would be a source of information with respect to the frequency the student raised his hand prior to speaking in class. Another measure could involve the number of times the student was referred to the "time-out" room for being disruptive in the classroom.

When baseline measures focus on current overt behaviors, repeated frequency counts across specified time intervals are typically used. The time intervals selected should be those during which the highest incidence of behavioral excesses occur or the times in which desired positive behaviors are demonstrated. Focusing on the latter is preferable as it highlights gains. It is also important to obtain measures under relatively consistent conditions. Otherwise, the measure may not be an accurate representation of the actual behavior you are attempting to measure (Bloom, Fischer & Orme, 2003).

Retrospective Estimates of Baseline Behaviors

EP 2.1.10m

Baseline measurements are obtained before change-oriented interventions are implemented, either by having clients make retrospective estimates of the incidence of behaviors targeted for change or by obtaining data before the next session. Examples include paying rent of time, preparing nutritious meals, or being on time for school. Although it is less accurate, the former method often is preferable because change-oriented efforts need not be deferred pending the gathering of baseline data. This is a key advantage, because acute problems or a crisis may demand immediate attention and delaying the intervention for even one week may not be advisable. However, delaying interventions for one week while gathering baseline data in general does not create undue difficulty and the resultant data are likely to be far more reliable than clients' estimates.

When determining the baseline of target behavior by retrospective estimates, it is common practice to ask the client to estimate the incidence of the behavior across a specified time interval, which may range from a few minutes to one day depending on the usual frequency of the target behaviors. Time intervals selected for frequent behaviors, such as nervous mannerisms (tapping a pencil on a desk), should be relatively short (e.g., 15-minute intervals). For relatively infrequent behaviors, such as speaking up in social situations, intervals may involve several hours or days.

Self-Anchored Scales

EP 2.1.10m

Baseline data can also be obtained for covert behaviors, such as thoughts, feelings, or an emotional state of "feeling blue." Individuals can make frequency counts of targeted thoughts or rate degrees of emotional states. To illustrate, we return to the case of Mrs. Johnson. To track her feeling, a five scale, for example, would be developed that represented varying levels of her internal states; ranging from the total absence of her feeling or thoughts at one end to their maximal intensity at the other.

When goals involve altering feelings, such as anger, depression, loneliness, or anxiety, it is desirable to construct self-anchoring scales that denote various levels of an internal state. To "anchor" such scales, ask a client to imagine experiencing the extreme degrees of the given internal state and to describe what they experience. You can then use these descriptions to define at least the extremes and the midpoint of the scale. Developing scales in this manner quantifies internal states in a unique manner for each client. In constructing self-anchoring scales, it is important to avoid mixing different types of internal states: Even though emotions such as "happy" and "sad" appear to belong on the same continuum, they are qualitatively different, and mixing them will result in confusion. Figure 12-4 depicts a seven-point anchored scale.

1	2	3	4	5	6	7
Least anxious (calm, relaxed, serene)		Moderately anxious (tense, uptight, but still-functioning with effort)			Most anxious (muscles taut, cannot concentrate or sit still, could "climb the wall")	

FIG-12-4 Example of a Self-Anchored Scale

Clients can use self-anchoring scales to record the extent of troubling internal states across specified time intervals (e.g., three times daily for seven days) in much the same way that they take frequency counts of overt behaviors. In both instances, clients keep tallies of the target behaviors. A minimum of ten separate measures is generally necessary to discern patterns among data, but urgent needs for intervention sometimes require that you settle for fewer readings. For example, the client, Mrs. Johnson, would complete the scale to record the varying levels and circumstances in which she was "feeling blue" and when she did not experience these feelings. The self-anchored scale and the incremental numeric changes can be augmented by the descriptive information based on Mrs. Johnson's narrative. For instance, in reviewing her range of feeling blue from most to least, the discussion between you and her would focus on the events or situations that appeared to have triggered her feelings, plus or minus in each range.

Guidelines for Obtaining Baseline Measures

EP 2.1.10m

When you are using baseline measures, it is vital to maximize the reliability and validity of your measurements (Bloom, Fischer & Orme, 2003; Berlin & Marsh, 1993). Otherwise, your baseline measures and subsequent comparisons with those measures will be flawed and will lead to inappropriate conclusions. Adhering to the following guidelines will assist you in maximizing the reliability and validity of the data collected:

1. *Define the target of measurement in clear and operational terms.* Reliability is enhanced when the behavior (overt or covert) targeted for change is specifically defined. For example, measurements of compliments given to a partner are more reliable than general measurements of positive communications because the client must make fewer inferences when measuring the former than when counting instances of the latter.
2. *Be sure your measures relate directly and specifically to the goals targeted for change.* Otherwise, the validity of your measurements both at the baseline and at subsequent points will be highly suspect. For example, when a client's goal is increasing social skills, indicators of social skills should be used as measurement targets. Likewise, if a parent is to attend parenting classes to learn parenting skills, measures should be devised that directly specify observable behavioral changes. Similarly, measures of violent behavior and alcohol abuse should correspond to the frequency of angry outbursts (or control of anger in provocative situations) and consumption of alcohol (or periods of abstinence), respectively.
3. *Use multiple measures and instruments when necessary.* Clients typically present with more than one problem, and individual problems may involve several dimensions. For example, flat affect, fatigue, irritability, and anxiety are all frequent indicators of depression. A client may also present with goals related to increasing self-confidence or improving their social skills, which would require the use of multiple measures and instruments to track.
4. *Measures should be obtained under relatively consistent conditions.* Otherwise, changes may reflect differences in conditions or environmental stimuli, rather than variations in goal-related behaviors. For example, if a child's difficulty is that she does not talk while she is at preschool, measuring changes in this behavior while the child is at home, in church, or in other settings may be informative, but it is not as helpful as the indications of change at preschool, where the behavior primarily occurs.
5. *Baseline measures are not relevant when clients present with discrete goals.* Evaluating the efficacy of helping efforts in such instances is clear-cut, because either a client has accomplished a goal or not. For example, with a goal of getting a job, the job seeker is either successful or not successful. By contrast, progress toward ongoing goals is incremental and not subject to fixed limits, as in the case of completing a job application. Employing baseline measures and periodic measures, therefore, effectively enables both you and the client to monitor incremental changes. Consider the following baseline measure for an ongoing goal: "Justin will sit in his seat during English class." If Justin's baseline has indicated that he is out of his seat (off task) 25 times per week then improvement to 15 times per week would be significant.

Measuring with Self-Administered Scales

EP 2.1.10m

Self-administered scales are also useful for obtaining evaluative data. Many psychological scales are available, but the WALMYR assessment scales (Hudson, 1992) are especially useful for social workers. Designed by Hudson and fellow social workers, the 22 separate scales (see Chapter 8) tap into many of the dimensions relevant to social work practice. Their ease of administration, scoring, and interpretation, as well as acceptable reliability and validity, are among the advantages of these scales.

Self-administered scales may also be used to quantify target problems. Although they are somewhat subjective and less precise than behavioral counts, they are particularly useful in measuring covert behavioral states (e.g., anxiety, depression, self-esteem, clinical stress) and clients' perceptions of their interpersonal relationships. Like tools to measure overt behaviors, selected scales can be administered before implementing treatment and thereafter at periodic intervals to monitor progress, and at termination and follow-up to assess outcomes. Unlike behavioral self-monitoring (e.g., counting behaviors or thoughts), subjective self-reporting through self-administered instruments is less likely to produce reactive effects (Applegate, 1992).

After obtaining baseline measures of targets of change, the next step is to transfer the data to a graph on which the horizontal axis denotes time intervals (days or weeks) and the vertical axis denotes the frequency or severity of target behaviors. Simple to construct, such a graph makes it possible to observe the progress of clients and the efficacy of interventions. Figure 12-5 depicts the incidence of anxiety before and during the implementation of change via such a graph.

In Figure 12-5, note that the baseline period was seven days and the time interval selected for self-monitoring was one day. Interventions to reduce anxiety were implemented over a period of four weeks. As illustrated in the graph, the client experienced some ups and downs (as usually occurs), but marked progress could nevertheless be observed.

In monitoring progress by taking repeated measures, it is critical to use the same procedures and instruments used in obtaining the baseline measures. Otherwise, meaningful comparisons cannot be made. It is also important to adhere to the guidelines for measurement listed in the preceding section. Repeated measurement of the same behavior at equal intervals enables practitioners not only to assess progress but also to determine variability in clients' behavior and to assess the effects of changes in the clients' life situation. For example, by charting measures of depression and increased social skills from week to week, it becomes possible to discern either positive or negative changes that correspond to concurrent stressful or positive life events. In this way, graphs of measured changes enable clients both to view evidence of their progress and to gain awareness of how particular life or environmental events contribute to their emotional states or behaviors.

Monitoring Progress with Quantitative Measurements

Monitoring progress has several other advantages. Measures establish indicators and monitoring tells both the client and you when goals have been accomplished, when the court mandate has been satisfied, and when the relationship can be terminated. For example, when observable behaviors related to parenting skills, such as preparing 3–4 nutritious meals per week selecting from the 5 major food groups, have improved to the degree that they conform to explicit indicators, termination is justified. Similarly, termination is indicated when measurements of depression have changed to the range of nonclinical depression. Results of monitoring can also substantiate progress, justify continued coverage by

EP 2.1.10m

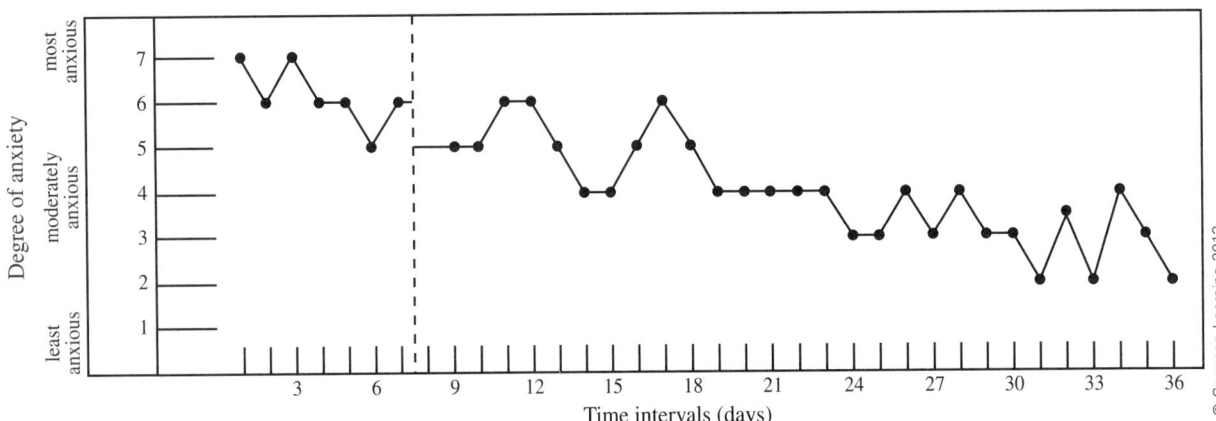

FIG-12-5 Example of a Graph Recording the Extent of Anxiety during Baseline and Intervention Periods

third-party payers, and be used in reports to the court in the case of mandated clients. For clients, monitoring provides evidence of change, assuring them that they are not destined to remain forever involved with the social worker or agency. A final and critical advantage of monitoring is that if interventions are not achieving measurable results after a reasonable period, you can explore the reasons for this lack of progress and negotiate a different goal plan or intervention.

Receptivity of Clients to Measurement

You may feel hesitant to ask clients to engage in self-monitoring or to complete self-report instruments because of your concern that they will resist or react in a negative manner. To the contrary, research studies by Applegate (1992) and Campbell (1988, 1990) indicate that such concerns are not justified. These researchers found that clients generally were receptive to formal evaluation procedures. In fact, Campbell found that clients preferred being involved in the evaluation of their progress. In addition, clients preferred "the use of some type of systematic data collection over the reliance on social worker's opinion as the sole mean of evaluating practice effectiveness" (Campbell, 1988, p. 22). Finally, practitioners were able to accurately assess clients' feelings about different types of evaluation procedures (Campbell, 1990).

Monitoring Progress Using Qualitative Measures

EP 2.1.10m

Qualitative measure methods are viable options for monitoring progress and evaluating outcomes. Qualitative methods differ from quantitative methods in their philosophical, theoretical, and stylistic orientation (Jordan & Franklin, 1995, 2003; Shamai, 2003). The various types of qualitative measures are consistent with narrative and social constructivism approaches. Qualitative evaluation measures have advantages for monitoring progress, depending on the information that you are seeking. They can provide a more complete picture of the contextual conditions and dimensions in which change occurred (Holbrook, 1995; Shamai, 2003). Qualitative methods may be especially useful with minors in that they focus on subjective experiences and personal stories (Andrews & Ben-Arieh, 1999; Morgan, 2000).

In qualitative measures, the process of data collection is more open-ended and allows clients to express their reality and experience, frame of reference, or cultural realities. For example, the findings of a study that examined the use of hospice care by African Americans revealed a difference in values that were barriers to hospice utilization (Reese, Ahern, Nair, O'Faire, & Warren, 1999). In essence, the client is the key informant or expert (Crabtree & Miller, 1992; Jordan & Franklin, 1995, 2003). Gilgun (1994) asserts that because qualitative measures focus on client perception, they are good fit with social work value of self-determination.

In evaluating progress or outcomes using qualitative methods, descriptive information change can be expressed in graphs, pictures, diagrams, or narratives. For example, in the structural approach to family therapy, symbols are used to create a visual map of family relationships and interaction patterns. Narratives provided by the family members at the points of change (even change that is incremental) highlight the dynamics or events associated with the change.

The aim of qualitative information is to ensure credibility, dependability, and confirmability (Jordan & Franklin, 2003; Rubin & Babbie, 2005; Weiss, 1998). Like quantitative methods, qualitative measures require systematic observation and may involve multiple points of triangulated observations. For example, triangulation would include client self-reports, your observations, and descriptive information from other relevant systems. The triangulation of data replication establishes the credibility of information and guards against bias.

A qualitative method that may be used to measure and monitor change is referred to as an informative event or critical incidence. The method has some similarity to the *Logical Analysis Effects* (Davis & Reid, 1988) in that both methods established a linkage between context, intervention, and change.

Informative Events or Critical Incidences

Informative events, also referred to as critical incidences, is a qualitative method that seeks to determine whether intended or unintended gains can be attributed to a particular event or action. These events or actions are also referred to as therapeutic effects, turning points, or logical analysis effects in that they are a significant link to goal attainment, thereby changing the status of the target problem (Davis & Reid, 1988; Shamai, 2003). For example, in Bettina's case, the social worker arranged for her to visit her child's father and the father's mother once a week. The pertinent evaluation question is: Did this arrangement influence her behavioral change?

An advantage of informative event or critical incidence reports is that individuals are able to put their feelings and emotional thoughts into words. For example, a group session in which mothers reflected upon and discussed their grief and sadness about the removal of their children from their homes was acknowledged by them as marking a change (critical incident) in their ability to move toward reunification with a child or children. Previously, many of the mothers had stored-up feelings of anxiety, fear, and even ambivalence about reuniting with their children. For a majority of the mothers, the discussion was a therapeutic and a critical turning point because they were able to voice and subsequently release their feelings, helping them focus on the return of their children to their care. Morgan (2000, p. 91) suggests that significant turning points should be celebrated. A certificate highlights such turning points by naming the problem and the alternative story that emerged. For example, certificates for the mothers in the previous group would mark their movement from self-doubt to confidence and from guilt or shame to freedom from these feelings.

Tracking and monitoring progress need not be an ordeal for you as existing tools may be utilized. Think about the ecomap, an assessment tool that examines the relationship between a family and other social systems by identifying areas of tension or conflict, as well as potential resources. For evaluation purposes, the ecomap may also be used in a pre- and post-intervention fashion to graphically track change in the tension or conflicted lines that were identified as target problems. In Figure 12-6a, for example, significant credit card debt was identified as a major stressor for the Strong family. Paying off their debt was identified as their priority goal, which prompted a referral by the social worker to a consumer credit counselor. After the family had worked with the credit counselor, they and the social worker charted the change. In Figure 12-6b, the tenuous relationship initially reported by the family had changed to a strong resource relationship as they completed tasks related to their goal. Of course, this change occurred incrementally. Over time, it might be useful to insert one or more lines to credit card debt on the ecomap to demonstrate the progression of change.

Overall, the aim of qualitative methods in monitoring progress and assessing outcomes is to understand people's experience and the meaning that this experience holds for them (Witkin, 1993). For the Strong family, a benefit of their desired level of change was that paying off their credit card debt would enable them to begin saving to buy a home. In completing the ecomap with the family, the social worker obtained descriptive information about their desire to buy a home once they were able to manage their debt. Using qualitative methods in this case, the family's narrative provided insight into the interaction or combination of factors that contributed to their desired change.

Numbers (i.e., quantitative data) represent descriptive information that is informative about change or the reduction of symptoms; thus, statistical data fulfill

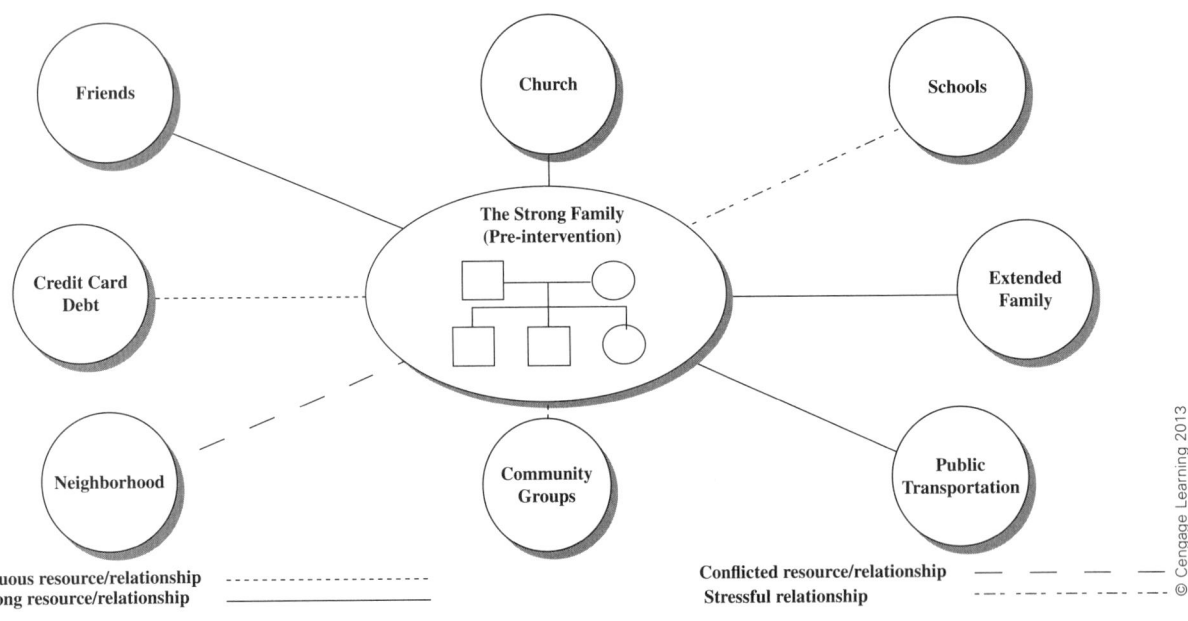

FIG-12-6a Pre-intervention eco-map

Goal Development and Contract Formulation **345**

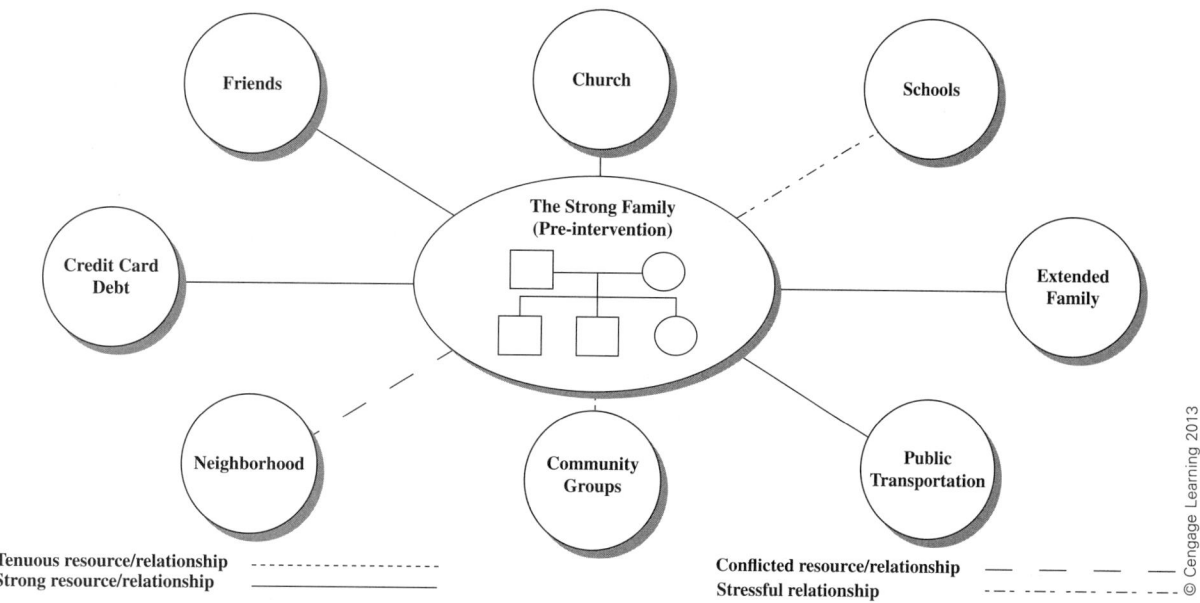

FIG-12-6b Post-intervention eco-map

an important function. Statistical data, however, cannot provide the contextual narratives associated with qualitative data. The most salient characteristic of qualitative evaluation methods is that the data adds "a human texture to statistical data," thereby increasing our understanding of progress" (Shamai, 2003).

Combining Methods for Measuring and Evaluating

EP 2.1.10m

There are times when the depth of information you need is best obtained by combining qualitative and quantitative methods (Padgett, 2004; Rubin & Babbie, 2005; Weiss, 1998). For example, tracking the outcomes of a specific goal (like learning new parenting skills) can be measured by using a quantitative pre/post design. In combining this method with qualitative indicators, you would be interested in determining at what point the new skill level occurred. For example, when did the parents' interactions with their children improve (turning point)? Likewise, frequency counts like the number of times that a student raised his or her hand before speaking in class provide you with quantitative observations. You might also want to know whether the behavioral change was attributed to positive responses from the teacher related to the student's behavior, which provides you with qualitative information. Obviously, each method will provide you with different information; specifically, quantitative measures provide you with statistical information and qualitative information enriches the data by giving you access to descriptive information. With young minors, monitoring and measuring progress can be facilitated by using pictures, stories, and conversation-related feelings (Morgan, 2000). These methods can easily be combined with quantitative methods such as pre/post designs, rating or behavioral scales, graphs, or grids.

Your practice setting may have methods for monitoring progress and measuring outcomes, for example, goal attainment scales. In some organizations such as schools and residential facilities, standardized behavioral contracts stipulate how progress is evaluated. Standardized tools or protocols, however, may in fact place members of socioeconomic, cultural, and sexual minority groups at greater risk of appearing more "deviant or troubled" (Kagle, 1994, p. 96).

Increasingly, health and behavioral health organizations are relying on evidence-based practices or protocols to inform treatment decisions, beginning with an assessment, selecting an intervention, and evaluating outcomes (O'Hare, 2005; Roberts & Yeager, 2006). Evidence-based practices are available for certain problems and related goals, such as health, mental health, and specific behavioral problems (O'Hare, 2009; Roberts & Yeager, 2006; Thomlison & Corcoran. 2008). Be aware, however, that following the treatment procedures detailed in a manual in which strict adherence is required is not the same as measuring effectiveness and monitoring progress.

There are limitations of evidence-based practices and procedures with respect to people of color. Specifically, while evidence of their effectiveness was obtained by using a large representative sample during their development, these samples have in general not included significant numbers of people of color. Thus, evidence-based practices have yet to be determined as appropriate with communities of color (Aisenberg, 2008, Connor & Grote, 2008; Furman, 2009).

Further notable limitations with regard to using standardized tools and evidence-based practices are that little attention is paid to barriers and obstacles to goal attainment. Moreover, the extent to which the resources recognize and make use of the social work principles such as an individual's strengths, resources, or situational factors is unclear. A question for you is whether or not a standardized or evidence–based resource is applicable to your client and his or her problem. Above all, you should have the requisite skills for utilizing these resources, and make use of supervision or consultation.

Overall, any procedure that you use to monitor and evaluate progress should be implemented in a systematic manner. An additional criterion is the extent to which the methods selected to measure outcomes are compatible and consistent with the goal. For example, a goal of avoiding eviction is tracked differently than a goal of "not feeling blue."

Evaluating Your Practice

EP 2.1.1b

Monitoring progress and measuring change is central to your ethical practice as a social worker. The process informs you and the client about the effectiveness of a strategy as well provides you with evaluative information about your own practice. Evaluative questions can be posed on a case by case basis and also focus on aggregate information obtained by a review of all of your cases. As you gain additional knowledge and learn new skills, you can monitor and measure your skill level along a continuum. For example, you can determine if your skill level enabled you to serve the client better. Feedback from the individual with whom you are working is also integral to your self-evaluation. For example, you might ask diverse clients whether their experience with you was culturally sensitive, what could be improved, and what elements of your work together proved to be the most helpful.

Evaluating your practice need not be intimidating. Many of the quantitative and qualitative methods can be used to provide you with evaluative information. Regardless of the method you choose, you should be able to answer central questions:

EP 2.1.10m

- *Is the client making progress toward a goal?*
- *Is what I am doing with the client working, and if not what changes do I need to make?*
- *Do I need to consult with a supervisor?*
- *Is my practice consistent with the ethical standards and principles of the profession of social work?*

What you learn from the self-evaluation process is critical to maintaining a standard and for improving your practice.

Contracts

EP 2.1.10c

Goals focus the work that you and the client are to complete. Contracts are tools that detail the agreement between you and the client. Depending on the practice setting, contracts may also be referred to as service agreements, behavioral contracts, or case or treatment plans. A contract, and hence your work with an involuntary client, is generally influenced by a court order or referral source. Contracts should not be confused with legal mandates or case plans, although elements of both may be included as you develop an agreement to work together. The legal mandate or case plan details the concern upon which the contract is based and the expected outcome. It can also include concerns and goals that are important to the client. Program objectives may also be included in contracts or agreements. For example, the "Behavioral Treatment Agreement" (Figure 12-10) found at the end of this chapter includes both goals for individual change and requirements that address program objectives.

There are instances in which intermediate or short term behavioral and treatment plans related to a specific incident or behavior may be developed. For example, a *child safety plan* specifies that a parent call a relative when his or her frustration reaches a point at which the potential for hitting the child exists. This agreement identifies both the circumstances in which a behavior could occur and a resource for the parent. An example of the wording in the plan could include, "When I am frustrated and feeling overwhelmed with _____ (child's name), I will call my mother and talk it out with her." A short-term safety agreement might also be reached with a client in an emotional crisis where the client agrees to refrain from harmful behavior ("I will pay attention to the psychological cues that tell me that I am at risk for harming myself"). Further, the agreement could include the condition that the client makes an appointment with a professional. The safety plan is signed by the social worker and the client.

Other types of short-term agreements include the *contingency* (quid pro quo) and *good-faith* contracts. Used in cognitive-behavioral family therapy, a contingency contract identifies a desired behavior change on the part of all parties involved. Its fulfillment is contingent on each individual's behavior in response to the other parties' behavior (Nichols & Schwartz, 2004). In a good-faith contract, the parties involved agree to change their behavior independently of one another. This type of contract may be used in a social-behavioral skills group and a behavioral parenting training group.

The Rationale for Contracts

Contracting is the final discrete activity of Phase I of the helping process and identifies the work to be accomplished by the change-oriented strategies by which goals will be attained. Key ingredients summarize the purpose and focus of your work with clients as well as ensure mutual accountability. In some practice settings, the contract or agreement clarifies the role of the client and social worker, as well as establishes the conditions under which assistance is provided.

Developing a contract or service agreement with clients may require an explanation of the purpose and rationale for the contract. Explanations may be particularly important for clients who are hesitant to sign a document without fully understanding its purpose. Involuntary clients may be suspicious or distrustful, perceiving the contract as further infringing on their freedom or that they are committing to a change with which they disagree. For minors, the concept of a contract may be a totally alien concept regardless of their age and developmental stage. In settings in which a client's choice of whether or not to work with you is limited, specifying the required change and your role in supporting the minor to achieve goals, as well as clarifying rewards and benefits, can be especially important.

Formal and Informal Contracts

Contracts or service agreements can be developed with varying degrees of formality. Public agencies often require written service agreements in the form of case plans or behavioral contracts signed by clients. *Written contracts* provide space for entering the particular concerns or problems of a client situation and listing the expected intervention outcomes. Safety plans are almost always written and they are a ready resource for clients in a crisis. Under normal circumstances, you and the client both sign the contract, giving it much the same weight as a legal document. Some private agencies prefer *service agreements* to contracts, believing that contracts are more formal and administrative in nature.

Students often ask whether written or verbal contracts are preferable. For some social workers, the rationale for using a written contract is that it provides a tangible reference to the commitments between themselves and their clients. In this way, the potential for a misunderstanding is minimized. In addition, the written contract assures accountability of services to supervisor and funders. Other social workers prefer *verbal contracts* that include the same provisions but lack the formality, sterility, and finality of a written contract. If contracts or agreements are verbal, questions may arise later with regard to informed consent. A third option is to utilize a partially verbal and partially written contract. The latter includes the basics, for example, the target concern or problem, goal, role expectations, time limits, and provisions for revision. With minors, either verbal or written or some combination thereof may be appropriate. Whether the contract is verbal or written, at a minimum, clients' should have a clear understanding of what is to be accomplished as a result of your work together. Contracts that are specific and that are clearly articulated ensure that clients are informed, otherwise, clients may believe they are justified in filing suit for malpractice if they do not achieve their goals (Reamer, 1998; Houston-Vega, Nuehring & Daguio, 1997).

Contracts or agreements with either a written or verbal description, as well as any changes, are documented in the case record. This documentation is consistent with the requirements of record keeping and informed consent (Reamer, 1998; Strom-Gottfried, 2007).

Developing Contracts

Generally, contracts should include certain elements, which are outlined in the "Agreement for Service" (Figure 12-7) found at the end of this chapter. In making use of this resource, you can adjust the various elements to fit the needs of your practice setting and the particulars of your work with clients. Keep in mind, however, that there are certain elements that are essential. The following is a brief discussion of each element.

Goals to Be Accomplished

First and foremost, the goals to be accomplished in relation to the target concern are ranked by priority, as goals provide the focus for working over the course of ongoing sessions. At the same time, goals are fluid. They can be expanded or modified as situations change and new information that has a bearing on the initial goals emerges. Of course, there must be a valid reason for changing goals. Although the continuous shifting of target concerns and goals during the contracting process would be unusual, a client may signal that he or she is not ready to proceed. At this point, you would return to the process of identifying goals.

Roles of Participants

In Chapter 5, the process of socialization related to the client and social worker's roles was discussed. These roles may need to be revisited during the contracting process. Role clarification may be especially pertinent with involuntary clients who have a mandated case or treatment plan, in which case your role and that of the client are specified in writing. Whether the client is voluntary or involuntary, the identification of roles affirms the mutual accountability and commitment of all parties, including that of the agency involved.

Socialization about the purpose of contract roles may be required with certain clients. Involuntary clients may feel particularly vulnerable and a contract may increase their feelings of being pressured or controlled. Potocky-Tripodi (2002) points out that some immigrants or refugees may experience fear and apprehension about contracts depending on their past experiences. In light of their past experience, for these individuals the contract may be "perceived as an instrument of authoritarian coercion" (p. 167).

Minors may also feel vulnerable. With this group, the socialization process may require you to review what is expected of them and how you will assist them. For example, "I have written down that I will help you return to the classroom" or "Your role is to attend group sessions and to learn different ways of behaving in the classroom." In all instances, taking the time to explain the function and purpose of contracts and the client's role will facilitate the client's remaining active in the process.

Interventions or Techniques to Be Employed

This aspect of the contract involves specifying the interventions and techniques that will be implemented in order to accomplish the stated goals. During initial contracting, it is often possible to identify interventions only on a somewhat global level. For example, group or family sessions may involve a combination of strategies. In some instances, depending on the identified goals, you and the client can discuss intervention strategies with greater specificity. For example, decreasing or eliminating irrational thoughts, beliefs, and fears (cognitive restructuring); and developing skills (e.g., using tasks or solution to accomplish goals). In cases where you are the case manager, you would also indicate the various coordinated services to be involved in the case (e.g., home delivered meals, home health services). Implementing an intervention strategy requires a discussion with the client in which you provide an overview of the intervention and your rationale to elicit clients' reactions and to gain their consent.

Time Frame, Frequency, and Length of Sessions

Specifying the time frame, frequency, and length of sessions is an integral part of the contract. Most people tend to intensify their efforts to accomplish a given goal or task when a deadline exists. Just consider the last-minute cramming that students do before an examination! A time frame stated in the contract counters the human tendency to procrastinate. Yet another argument that supports the development of a definite time frame is the fact that most of the gains that are achieved occur early in the change process. In working with families, Nichols and Schwartz (2004) note that treatment has historically been established as brief and within a limited time period based on the rationale that change occurs quickly, if it occurs at all. Moreover, whatever the intended length, most contact with clients turns out to be relatively brief, the median duration being between five and six sessions (Corwin, 2002; Reid & Shyne, 1969).

On the whole, clients respond favorably to services that are offered when they need them the most and when they experience relief from their problems. This is not to say that clients will not seek help for concrete or daily living concerns that they may have. Time-limited contracts may be valued by clients because they make a distinction between talking and actual change, and within this particular time frame the focus is on a specific concern. Questions have been raised about the brevity of some time limits. Are time-limited contracts, for example, effective with racial and ethnic minority groups? Some theorists believe that time limits are inconsistent with perspectives of time held by some minority groups (Chazin, Kaplan & Terio, 2000; Devore & Schlesinger, 1999; Green, 1999; Logan, Freeman & McRoy, 1990). Other theorists cite outcome studies that emphasize time-limited contracts as preferable with racial and ethnic minority clients because they focus on immediate, concrete concerns. Devore and Schlesinger (1999), Ramos and Garvin (2003), and James (2008) note that in stressful situations, persons of color respond best to a present- and action-oriented approach. Corwin (2002), citing the work of Koss and Shiang (1994) and Sue and Sue (1990), points out the advantages of time-limited, brief treatment by noting that these approaches are "congruent with how many minority clients understand and utilize mental health and social services" (p. 10). Of course, it would be presumptuous to assert hard-and-fast rules about a relationship between time limits and minority status. As highlighted in the previous discussion, brief contact with a specific focus appears to be a pattern with a majority of clients, irrespective of their status.

A second question relates to whether time limits are appropriate to all client populations and situations. Certainly, time-limited contracts may be inappropriate in some instances. For example, as an outpatient mental health case manager, your responsibility can be ongoing and time limits impractical. Nonetheless, you may find that time-limited contracts may be used with circumscribed problems of living or concrete needs defined as goals. In these instances, time-limited contracts can be effective when they are divided into multiple short-term contracts related to specific problems or episodes. A brief contract may, for example, involve a safety agreement, finding housing, or taking medication.

Decisions about specified time frames may be imposed on the work to be completed between you and clients. Managed care demands (specifically the brevity of the period in which outcomes are expected to be achieved) have dramatically influenced practice in both the private and the public sectors of social welfare services. In addition, agency resources, purchase of service (POS) contracts, funders, public policy, or the courts may stipulate a time frame and the duration of contact. In child welfare, for example, under the 1997 Adoption and Safe Family Act, parents are required to meet their case plan goals within a definitive time period. Time pressures resulted in tensions for many parents. For some, this pressure was a decisive factor in the eventual reunion with their children. Neither was there sufficient information given as to whether services were available or could be accessed within the required time frame. Nonetheless, these time limits would be included in the contract. Within the contract, you can help clients with the ticking of the clock by helping them focus their efforts on responding to the most pressing concerns.

The helping process, as presented in this text, relies on the time frame being brief. The time period used is that which is commonly associated with the task-centered social work model where specific target concerns and goals are identified. The action-oriented emphasis in the social work model and other brief treatment models can foster a conductive mindset that will facilitate change. Moreover, the expectation of a change in the target concern within a specific time period can have a positive influence on self-direction and motivation.

Research done in various settings and with various groups, including minors, supports the efficacy of 6 to 12 sessions conducted over a time span of two to four months. The flexibility inherent in this time frame, however, means that you can negotiate with the client regarding the specific number of sessions to be undertaken (Nichols & Swartz, 2004).

Frequency and Duration of Sessions

In most agencies, weekly sessions are the norm, although more frequent sessions may be required in cases that need intensive support and monitoring. For example, child welfare/child protective services, job-training programs, outpatient drug treatment, services for the frail elderly, school truancy, or homeless youth programs can require daily contact. Provisions can also be made in contracts for spacing sessions farther apart during the termination phase of the helping process.

There are few solid guidelines as to the amount of time needed for sessions. Agencies generally have guidelines for the billable hour, which tends to be 50 minutes. Conversely, if your setting is a public agency (i.e., child and family or protective services), time spent is only a part of what you do. For instance, you can spend considerable time arranging for and monitoring visitations between parents and children, conducting home visits, doing crisis problem solving, and teaching parenting skills. The duration of sessions is also influenced by the client. Because some children, adolescents, and elderly clients have difficulty tolerating long sessions, shorter and more frequent sessions are more practical. Frequency and duration of sessions are also influenced by settings requirements (e.g., school, hospital, correctional facility). For example, in a hospital setting, your contact may last 15 or 20 minutes, depending on the condition of the patient and the goals to be achieved. Also, your contact is limited to the time that the person is an inpatient. For school-based groups, the duration and length of sessions may require a structured time frame and may be influenced by concerns teachers have about out-of-classroom time.

Means of Monitoring Progress

Early discussions between you and the client have focused on the specific methods for monitoring and measuring progress. At this stage of the contracting process, a brief review may be all that is needed. For example, when baseline measures on target problems have been obtained, you would explain that the same measuring device would be used at specified intervals to note change. Clients can also be asked to rate their progress on a scale of 1 to 10, where 1 represents no progress and 10 represents the highest level. Comparing ratings from one session to the next and over a period of time provides a rough estimate of progress.

In addition, when a narrative progress review is a part of each session, it can serve the function of monitoring progress. For example, the Goal and Task Form (Figure 12-3) enables you and the client to review completed tasks and the status of goals. With minors to whom visual methods are particularly appealing, you may opt to use scales, calibrated drawings, or a thermometer with a scale from 1 to 10 where a colored marker indicates progress.

The frequency of monitoring may be negotiated with the client. Whichever method of monitoring is chosen, devoting some time at least every other session to review progress is advisable. Of course, you can be flexible, but no more than three sessions should pass between discussions of progress.

Stipulations for Renegotiating the Contract

Contracting within a brief time frame assumes that when goals are met, a change or significant reduction in the target problem will occur. Contracting continues during the entire helping process. Renegotiating a contract with clients can occur when their circumstances change or new facts emerge and the process evolves. For this reason, it is important to clarify for clients that conditions in the contract are subject to renegotiation at any time. Above all, the contract should be continually reviewed and updated to ensure its relevance and fit. When contracting with involuntary clients, any circumstances that would cause a unilateral change in the contract (e.g., evidence of new legal violations) should be specified.

Housekeeping Items

Talking with clients about such issues as provisions for cancelling or changing scheduled sessions and financial arrangements is necessary, but can be awkward and mundane. Perhaps discussing fees may be the most awkward for you, and uncomfortable for the client. Your discomfort is understandable given that your basic instinct as a social worker is to help people. Even so, most private agencies have policies that require payment for services, and the majority of clients expect to pay, albeit on a sliding-scale fee arrangement. In addition, private insurance providers often have co-payment requirements for services.

Financial arrangements, where required, are a fundamental part of the professional agreement between you and the client. A component of a social worker's competency is being able to effectively discuss financial arrangements, openly and without apology, when payment of services is expected. When clients fail to pay fees according to the contract, you should explore the matter with them promptly. Avoidance and procrastination just make matters worse and may result in you developing negative feelings toward the client. Moreover, a failure to pay fees may derive from the client's passive, negative feelings toward the professional, financial strains, or irresponsibility in meeting obligations, any of which merits immediate attention.

There are situations with exceptions to a discussion of fees. Examples in which fees are not prominent include purchase of service agreement contracts with your agency or if the service is funded by a grant. This would also include services provided to minors in school settings. When the client is a minor in an agency setting, any discussion of fees is a conversation between you and the minor's parent or legal guardian.

Having an agreement about schedules and keeping appointments is also advisable. In making home visits, nothing is more frustrating than showing up at an agreed-upon time only to find that the client or family is not at home or is unprepared for the visit. You should have the same expectations of yourself as you have of the client. Whether contact with a client is in your office or in their home, clients should be able to rely on your being available and attentive to their concerns. Of course, there are legitimate reasons that you or a client can have for changing or cancelling an appointment. Discussing the "what ifs" in advance clarifies expectations about keeping appointments and prevents misunderstandings.

Sample Contracts

To assist you in developing contracts, we have included sample contracts at the end of this chapter. Each sample includes most of the components discussed in preceding sections, although some are emphasized more than others. Elements of the first contract, "Agreement for Professional Services," were adapted from Houston-Vega, Nuehring and Daguio (1997). This informative resource includes other samples for individuals, families, and groups. It also includes ethical guidelines for social workers and guidelines for managing malpractice risks. Before using any of the contracts or agreements, you should clear them with your agency supervisor.

The "Agreement for Professional Services" is presented in outline form. The agreement for the social worker is much more detailed, committed to observing ethical standards of practice.

Agreement for Professional Services

Name(s) of Client(s) _____ Name _____

Address _____ City _____ State _____ ZIP Code _____

Outline for the agreement to work collaboratively in achieving goals, and joint planning in carrying out activities for the achieving goals.

I. **Problem(s) or/Concern(s):** Defined and Specified

II. **Prioritized Goals & General Tasks:**

Goals _____ General tasks _____

III. Conditions under which goals might change or revised for others added.

IV. **Time Limits Applicable to Case:** Time frame that may influence the rate at which goals may need to be accomplished or where significant progress toward goals may need to be documented.

V. **Sessions:** Meeting times, frequency and durations, location, beginning and ending dates, and the total number of sessions.

VI. **Who is involved:** Individual, couple or family, group or a combination?

VII. **Fees:** For service and method and arrangement of payment.

VIII. **Evaluation:** How progress will be monitored and measured, including client participation, evaluating progress each session by reviewing the goal plan, and the steps taken to achieve goals and final evaluation at termination.

IX. **Reports and Records:** Confidentiality of records and consent of Release of Information. Specifies who will receive reports about progress (e.g., court, third-party payer, referral source).

X. **Requirements of Mandated Reporting:**

XI. **Agreement:** Affirmation of the review of the terms of the agreement, and that an understanding that the agreement can be renegotiated at any time.

Signature (Client/Family/Group Member)

Name _____ Name _____ Date _____

XII. **Social Worker:**

    a) I agree to work collaboratively with _____ to achieve the goals outlined in this service agreement and others that we may subsequently agree upon.

    b) I agree to adhere to the conduct that _____ agency expects of its staff and to abide by the regulatory laws and ethical codes that govern my professional conduct.

    c) I have provided a copy of agency information about the rights of clients, available agency services, and information about the agency.

    d) I have read the above terms of the service agreement, and pledge to do my best to assist the client(s) to achieve the goals listed and others that we may subsequently agree upon.

Professional's Signature: _____

Date: _____

FIG-12-7 Agreement for Professional Services

the back door
MAKING CHANGE

Name: _____ Date: _____

File #: _____

☐ Housing   ☐ Planning   ☐ Drugs/Alcohol
☐ Employment   ☐ Volunteering   ☐ Problem Solving
☐ Education   ☐ Finances   ☐ Identification
☐ Personal   ☐ Leadership   ☐ Legal
                                    ☐ Other

CONTRACT STEP: _____ Step #: _____

WHAT I WANT TO WORK ON TODAY (i.e., WHERE I AM TODAY IN MY LIFE):
_____
_____

WHAT RESULT(S) I WOULD LIKE TO SEE (i.e., WHERE I WOULD LIKE TO BE):
_____
_____

WHAT I NEED TO MAKE IT WORK:
_____
_____

MY STEPS:
1 _____
2 _____
3 _____
4 _____

Contractor: _____ Paid by: _____

The following principles & questions reflect how *the back door* hopes to work. Please take time to think about how they worked for you in THIS contract step.

1. Principle: INTEGRITY/DIGNITY
   How did contracting this step contribute positively to your self esteem?
2. Principle: LIFE IS SUCH THAT THINGS DO NOT ALWAYS WORK
   In attempting the above step how did you find this to be so?
3. Principle: ACCEPTANCE WITHOUT JUDGMENT OR PREJUDICE
   How did contracting this step allow you to experience positive input from another person?
4. Principle: FORGIVENESS: EVERY DAY IS A NEW DAY
   How did contracting this step give you the freedom to learn from the past and try again?
5. Principle: PEOPLE WHO LISTEN TO EACH OTHER LEARN FROM EACH OTHER
   How did planning/working on this step help you to understand another person's point of view?
6. Principle: ALL ACTIONS/CHOICES AFFECT OTHER PEOPLE
   Did your working on this step have any effect on other people in your life?

FIG-12-8 Sample Contract The Back Door, Making Change
Source: Used by permission of *the back door* © 2000.

Sample Treatment Plan

Areas of Concern	Short-Term Goals/Objectives	Long-Term Goals	Treatment Plan

FIG-12-9 Sample Treatment Plan
Source: Adpated from Springer, D.W. (2002). Treatment planning with adolescents. In A.R. Roberts & J.J. Green (Eds.). *Social Worker's Desk Reference*. New York: Oxford University Press.

The second contract was developed to be used with participants of the agency "the back door" (DeLine, 2000). This agency is committed to helping homeless and runaway youth get off the streets. The contract outlines the program objective and the services the agency provides. In addition, the role of youth clients is amplified, because the focus is exclusively on how they will use the agency's services to alter their situation. The intent of the contract is to identify priorities and the most manageable tasks.

The remaining examples illustrate a treatment plan and two behavioral contracts. One is used by a county mental health center for men in a domestic violence program. Note that program requirements and objectives are a part of each client's treatment plan. The other is an example of a behavioral contract used in a juvenile facility, adapted from Ellis and Sowers (2001).

Summary

This chapter focused on goals, their purpose and function, their measurement, and the contract or service agreement as essential elements of the helping process. Also, goals were distinguished from program objectives, although the latter may be included as they pertain to a client's situation. General and specific tasks or objectives were discussed as instrumental strategies for goal attainment.

Students and even seasoned social workers often have difficulty in developing specific, measurable goals. Successful goal development requires practice. In training sessions related to goal development, we have encouraged participants to develop goals for themselves as a means of developing or refining their skills. After reading this chapter, we hope that you feel more comfortable with your knowledge of the skills needed in negotiating and developing goals with clients of all ages.

In the factors that can influence the development of goals, client participation and consideration of client values and beliefs was affirmed for both voluntary and involuntary clients. Clients live in a context. Their value and belief systems and their worldview narratives are all perspectives that cannot be obtained without their participation. Goal development should also take into account challenges that result from clients' socioeconomic status, race, culture, or issues related to minority status. While the focus of your contact with clients revolves around expressed needs or wants (or in the case of involuntary clients a need that is externally defined), clients have strengths that, if channeled, can help them to reach their goals. Finally, assumptions about the dynamics in your relationship with the voluntary client are unlikely to apply when goals are developed with involuntary clients,

Behavioral Treatment Agreement

Name _____ Client # _____ Date _____ Therapist _____

1. **Progress**

   Summary _____
   _____

2. **New Treatment Goals**
   1. Increased awareness of individual cues that trigger getting angry
   2. Increased awareness of nonabusive alternative ways of expressing anger
   3. Increased use of support networks
   4. Accepting responsibility for past abusive behavior

3. **Plan**

   Attend 18 educational themes/complete 9 tasks

4. **Outcomes**
   1. Side effects of treatment discussed ❑ yes ❑ no
   2. Outcomes of treatment discussed ❑ yes ❑ no
   3. Treatment options discussed ❑ yes ❑ no
   4. Cost of treatment explained to client ❑ yes ❑ no
   5. Client and staff rights form provided to client ❑ yes ❑ no
   6. Is client considering:

      Chemotherapy ❑ yes ❑ no

      Hospitalization ❑ yes ❑ no

      Other medical treatment ❑ yes ❑ no

   If the answer is yes to any of the above, the physician or consulting psychiatrist shall inform the client of the treatment alternatives, the effects of the medical procedures, and the possible side effects.

   All clinical services shall be provided according to the individual treatment plan.

5. **Expected Duration of Treatment**

   18 weeks/dependent on task completion. You need to begin completing the required tasks within the first 4 weeks of the program

6. **Frequency of Treatment**

   Weekly

7. **Collateral Resources and Referrals**

   _____

I understand the terms of this treatment agreement as well as my responsibilities in implementing the same. I have received a copy of this treatment plan.

Client _____ Date _____

Therapist _____ Date _____

Clinical Director _____ Date _____

FIG-12-10 Behavioral Treatment Agreement

Source: Used by permission. © MHC.

```
                    Sample Behavioral Contract

   Name _____

   Date _____

   **Responsibilities** (activities, counseling sessions, behaviors to avoid):

   **Privileges** (outlines privileges associated with meeting responsibilities):

   **Bonuses** (meeting requirements for a certain time period):

   **Sanctions** (circumstances in which privileges are lost, and possible action if requirements are
   not met):

   **Monitoring** (identifies who is responsible for monitoring whether requirements are met):

   Client's Signature _____

   Social Worker's Signature _____
```

FIG-12-11 Sample Behavioral Contract
Source: Adapted from Ellis & Sowers (2001). Juvenile Justice Practice

whether adults or minors. Nevertheless, there are certain considerations and strategies that can facilitate work with involuntary minors and adults.

This chapter also emphasized the importance of measurement, evaluation, and monitoring progress, whether the method used was quantitative or qualitative. Irrespective of method, measurement requires systematic and oftentimes multiple points of observation. Remember that goals flow directly from and relate specifically to the target problem or concern. Thus, the measure selected to monitor and evaluate progress must also be consistent with goal-related behaviors or conditions. In general, the essential evaluation question is: Did change occur and, if so, in what way? In addition to seeking an answer for you, this question is universally one that is of utmost importance to funding resources, agencies, and third-party payers. In addition, ethical practice demands that you as a social worker can demonstrate that what you do with clients is effective.

The contract examples provided in this chapter are intended as guides that may be adapted to particular situations or settings. Depending on the developmental age and stage of minors and client situations, a certain form may be more appropriate than another. Settings and client situations or status may dictate the inclusion of some elements over others. Regardless of the form that a contract might take, it should define the work to be completed between you and the client. Thus, it should have clarity about goals, roles, and expectations, and include the structured time frame in which the collaborative work is to be completed and evaluated.

CourseMate

Access an integrated eBook and chapter specific learning tools including glossary terms, chapter outlines, relevant web links, videos, and practice quizzes. Go to **www.cengagebrain.com**.

PART 3
The Change-Oriented Phase

13 Change-Oriented Strategies: Planning and Implementation
14 Intervention Strategies: Developing Resources, Organizing, Planning, and Advocacy
15 Improving Relationships and Family Functioning
16 Social Work Group Interventions
17 Confrontation, Interpretation, and Additive Empathy
18 The Management of Barriers to Change

After formulating a contract, service agreement, or treatment plan, the social worker and the client begin Phase II of the helping process, the goal attainment or change-oriented phase. In Phase II, social workers and clients plan and implement strategies to accomplish goals related to the identified problems or concerns. Implementing these strategies involves employing interventions and techniques specified in the contract or service agreement and contracting to use others as indicated by changing circumstances. Before considering these factors further, a preview of Part 3 is in order.

Chapter 13 begins with a discussion of planning goal attainment strategies and includes five primary brief, time-limited practice approaches with individuals, families, and groups. These empirically grounded approaches are used broadly in social work practice with individuals and families. Chapter 14 focuses on macro practice; its coverage is enriched by case examples from social workers addressing environmental or institutional barriers in which macro-level interventions were indicated.

In Chapter 15, the family interventions introduced build on the material from Chapter 10 on family assessment. Similarly, Chapter 16 presents group interventions, which build on Chapter 11's discussion of group formation and assessment. Techniques employed to expand self-awareness and to pave the way to change (additive empathy, interpretation, and confrontation) are considered in Chapter 17. Part 3 concludes with Chapter 18, which introduces skills in managing barriers to change.

CHAPTER **13**

Change-Oriented Strategies: Planning and Implementation

CHAPTER OVERVIEW

Thus far, you have gained the knowledge and skills needed to complete a multidimensional assessment, to develop goals, formulate a contract or treatment plan, and select methods for monitoring and measuring progress. The step beyond this point requires that you plan and select an intervention associated with Phase II of the helping process. The content of this chapter includes a discussion of four change-oriented approaches and micro-level case management, a strategic method involving the coordination of services to address clients' needs. Learning objectives to help you develop the knowledge and skills necessary for planning and implementing an intervention strategy are:

- Selecting a change strategy to facilitate goal attainment
- Understanding the importance of matching the strategy to the problem utilizing person in situation and person in environment framework
- Utilizing empirically supported change strategies with individuals, including with diverse groups and minors
- Becoming familiar with the major tenets and procedures of four change-oriented strategies and of the functions of case management

EPAS COMPETENCIES IN THE 13TH CHAPTER

This chapter will give you the information needed to meet the following practice competencies.

2.1.1c Attend to professional roles and boundaries

2.1.1f Use supervision and consultation

2.1.2b Make ethical decisions by applying standards of the National Association of Social Workers Code of Ethics and, if applicable, of the International Federation of Social Workers/ International Associations of Schools of Social Work Ethics in Social Work Statement of Principles

2.1.2d Apply strategies of ethical reasoning skills to arrive at principled decisions

2.1.3b Analyze models of assessment, prevention, intervention, and evaluation

2.1.4b Gain sufficient self-awareness to eliminate the influence of personal biases and values in working with diverse groups

2.1.4c Recognize and communicate an understanding of the importance of differences in shaping life experiences.

2.1.4d View themselves as learners and engage those with whom they work as key informants.

2.1.6b Use of research evidence to inform practice

2.1.7a Utilize conceptual framework to guide the process of assessment, intervention, and evaluation

2.1.7b Apply knowledge of human behavior in the social environment

2.1.9a Continuously discover, appraise, and attend to changing locales, populations, scientific and technological developments, and emerging societal trends to provide relevant services

2.1.10a Substantively and affectively prepare for action with individuals, families, groups, and communities

2.1.10b Use empathy and other interpersonal skills

2.1.10d Collect, organize, and interpret client data

2.1.10f Develop a mutually agreed-on intervention goals and objectives

2.1.10g Select appropriate intervention strategies

2.1.10i Implement prevention interventions that enhance client capacities

2.1.10j Help clients solve problems

2.1.10m Critically analyze, monitor, and evaluate interventions

Change-Oriented Approaches

EP 2.1.10a

The change-oriented approaches presented in this chapter may be used in your work with individuals, families, and groups. Their aim is to facilitate the attainment of goals or respond to the mandate in the case of the involuntary client. Each of the approaches is supported by research and uses empirically based techniques or procedures that have demonstrated their effectiveness with clients of various ages, backgrounds, and needs. Each approach is organized around the systematic interpersonal and structural elements of the helping process and follows the distinct phases of engagement, assessment, goal planning, intervention, and termination. They adhere to the principles of social work practice, which emphasize mobilizing individuals and families toward positive action. Each approach encourages collaboration with clients, utilizing their strengths and increasing their self-efficacy, all of which are critical aspects of empowerment.

The approaches are:

- *The Task-centered system*
- *Crisis intervention*
- *Cognitive restructuring*
- *Solution-focused brief treatment*
- *Case management*

The change approaches are process-oriented and problem solving in nature, thus they are well-suited to the helping process discussed thus far. In addition, they are consistent with systematic generalist-eclectic practice as articulated by Coady and Lehmann (2008, p. 5). The elements are as follows:

EP 2.1.7a

- *A person and environment focus that is informed by ecological theory*
- *An emphasis on establishing a positive helping relationship and empowerment as well as a holistic multilevel assessment, including a focus on diversity, oppression, and strengths*
- *A problem-solving model that provides structure and guidelines for work with clients*
- *Flexibility in the use of problem-solving methods that allows a choice among a range of theories and techniques based on their compatibility with each client's situation*

Planning Goal Attainment Strategies

EP 2.1.10g

In planning goal attainment strategies, choose an intervention that makes sense to both you and the client and is also relevant to his or her situation. The operative word is *matching*. That is, in selecting the intervention you should ideally address the following questions (adapted from Cournoyer, 1991):

- *Is the approach appropriate for addressing the problem for work and the service goals?*
- *Is the approach relevant and appropriate to the person, family, or group?*
- *Is the approach compatible with the basic values and ethics of social work?*
- *Does empirical or conceptual evidence support the effectiveness of the approach?*
- *Am I sufficiently knowledgeable and skilled enough in this approach to use with others?*

Is the Approach Appropriate for Addressing the Problem for Work and the Service Goals?

EP 2.1.3b

During the assessment process in Phase I, you gained a picture of the client as a person and his or her problem, situation, strengths, and goals. The method selected to address these, however, requires an understanding of context, circumstances, and the nature of the problem and timing. The essential questions to be answered are, *what is the problem*, and *what are the goals?* To achieve a desired goal, the change strategy must be directed to the problem specified by the client or the mandate, as well as to the systems that are implicated in the problem. For instance, a minor's school truancy problem, will, by necessity, involve his or her family, individuals in the educational system, and perhaps the juvenile justice systems. Other systems in which family involvement may be advised include health and mental health, correctional systems, and care institutions. The coordination of these various systems relative to the problem and the subsequent goal attainment activities is not a small task. At times, change strategies may require combining micro, mezzo, and macro strategies. Depending on your knowledge and skill level, there may also be instances in which you may appropriately combine techniques or tactics with the change approach that you have selected.

Is the Approach Appropriate to the Person, Family, or Group?

EP 2.1.4c

Individuals, families, and group members can vary in their levels of cognitive, social, and psychological development, gender orientation, and status. Additional factors that should guide your consideration include developmental age and stages and the family life-cycle, the latter of which can become exaggerated as a result of stressful transitions (Carter & McGoldrick, 2005; Halpern & Tramontin, 2007; James, 2008; Spoth, Guyll, Chao, & Molgaard, 2003). With respect to life-cycle and human development, culture and race are requisite factors to be considered. For instance, not all cultural or racial groups mark life-cycle or human development according to the normative Western expectations (Garcia Coll, Akerman & Cicchetti, 2000; Garcia Coll, Lamberty, Jenkins, McAdoo, Crinic, Wasik, & Valesquez Garcia, 1996; Ogbu, 1997, 1994). In considering culture, you should also be aware of the fact that significant differences can exist between cultural subgroups.

When selecting an intervention, the person-in-environment, the relationship to the problem, and the people involved should also be examined.

Specific questions to guide your selection decision are:

EP 2.1.3b

- *Does the approach purport to address the nature of the problem? What is the available supporting evidence?*
- *Does the approach acknowledge and allow for the integration of environmental factors as contributing to a problem, for example, the experience of minority or socioeconomic status and oppression, so as not to add a sense of being marginalized?*
- *Are modifications to the approach indicated in order responsive to diverse individuals, families, or minors?*
- *Is the individual, family, or group experiencing a situation or condition that has exceeded their resources and capacity to function and cope?*
- *Is the target of change the individual's thought processes or behavior?*
- *Is the problem for work related to family life-cycle transitions or developmental stages of minors?*
- *Can change be accomplished through the planning and coordination of resources or services to enhance individual or family functioning?*

The proposed questions are by no means exhaustive. Their intent is to prompt you to critically examine the change approaches discussed in this chapter as well as others to which you be exposed to over the course of your learning experience as a student and as a future professional. In some instances, the approach that you use may be determined by your practice setting. In either case, in planning and selecting an approach, you may want to use the opportunity of supervision to clarify or affirm your decision.

Diverse Individuals, Families, and Groups

In addition to the previously proposed questions, two additional questions can also figure prominently as factors that you would want to consider in selecting a change approach with diverse clients:

EP 2.1.3b & 2.1.10g

- *Is the approach flexible enough that it respects and can be adapted to the cultural beliefs, values, and worldview of diverse groups?*
- *Does the approach address the sociopolitical climate as a factor in creating and sustaining the client's problem?*

In considering the first question, Green (1999, pp. 50–51) informs us that "help-seeking behavior" is embedded in a cultural context as well as the experience of minority status. Exploring the client's cultural context to include consideration of gender relations and position in the family and in the community is important. In some ethnic cultural and racial communities, the act of asking for help, whether formally or informally, can be frowned upon. Suspicion of change strategies are well formed in many diverse communities. This dynamic can be so prominent that problems or feelings may be minimized or ignored for fear of being perceived as vulnerable or give the appearance of a cultural anomaly (Sue, 2006; Kung, 2003; Potocky-Tripodi, 2002; Nadler, 1996; Mau & Jepson, 1990).

In selecting a change strategy, diverse clients might deliberate on the cost-benefit trade-off of seeking help, essentially assessing whether the approach allows them to retain their sense of self and whether it is consistent with or a threat to their values and beliefs. (Williams, 2006; Sue, 2006; Potocky-Tripodi, 2002). As Potocky-Tripodi (2002) explains, immigrants or refugees with little or no prior experience with formal helping systems may perceive a change approach as a threat, especially if their prior experience involved contact with a formal system in which the strategies involved forceful or repressive tactics. Immigrants may also experience tensions with change strategies that require them to move from the familiar to the unfamiliar. For them, central challenges may involve unlearning familiar way of thinking and behaving in such matters as child rearing and discipline, customs such as arranged marriages, and the strangeness of interacting with formal helping systems.

As a learner, the concepts of discovery and cultural humility can aid you in your work with diverse clients. Green (1999) refers us to the "discovery procedure" in planning interventions with racial or ethnic minority persons. *Discovery* means to solicit clients' views of the problem at hand; the related symbolic, cultural, and social nuances of their concerns; and their ideas about an approach and whether it would remedy their difficulties. *Cultural humility*, encourages placing yourself in a student role. In this role, you are open to the family or individual as a teacher. Together, you and the person involved are partners in understanding and clarifying the relevance of the change effort to their particular problem (Tervalon & Murray Garcia, 1998). The discovery procedure and cultural humility are tools that will help you to understand the client and to ultimately select a change approach that is in harmony with his or her beliefs, values, and religion or spirituality.

The second question to consider is: Does the approach address the sociopolitical climate as a factor in creating and sustaining the client's problem? Minority and poor families, many of whom are involuntary in their contact with professional helpers, often face insurmountable odds in their everyday lives, some of which are the results of limited resources, pressures to conform to dominant societal norms, marginalized status, inequity, and constrained self-determination. Societal presumptions about people, their competence, or lifestyles are oppressive forces that create toxic environments for persons who are different, and which they contend with on a daily basis.

In most instances, overt acts of discrimination and bigotry have diminished as a result of laws, except in the case of gay and lesbian people. Laws, however, cannot command positive interpersonal and social behavior, especially covert interactions. Covert interactions are those subtle acts characterized as microaggressions in which people are treated differently based on their race, ethnicity, sexual orientation, ability, or socioeconomic status (Sue, Capodilupo, Torino, Bucceri, Holder, Nadal, & Esquilin, 2007). In nonminority families, conditions and circumstances that affect cognitive, physical, and psychological functioning would be to be considered extraordinary stressors. Any change strategy, should acknowledge this fact and take into account that given the circumstances of their lives, diverse individuals, families, and groups have strengths and resilience; including the fact that over time, they have coped with adversity (Connolly, 2006; Sousa, Ribeiro & Rodriques, 2006; Guadalupe & Lum, 2005).

What Empirical or Conceptual Evidence Supports the Effectiveness of the Approach?

An effective intervention approach is one that has the most promise for achieving goals identified by the client or the mandate. In evaluating an approach you are looking for evidence of its effectiveness: with whom did it work, under what circumstances, and what were the results? Furthermore, the evidence should specify the approach's effectiveness with respect to client status, developmental stage, cognitive ability, as well as its compatibility with diverse individuals, their culture, values, and beliefs.

Also, it is important that as you are exposed to novel or emerging strategies that you learn about evidence of their effectiveness. Ethical standards require social workers to use approaches with clients that respect their dignity and rights and that do not cause harm. Untested interventions, as well as those that are coercive, confrontational, or dangerous, should not be employed.

Is the Approach Compatible with Basic Values and Ethics of Social Work?

Professional social work ethics and values provide a foundation upon which knowledge and skills are used. Two specific

ethical standards are applicable in your decision making related to selecting an intervention approach: safeguarding client's right to self-determination and informed consent.

- *Does the approach safeguard clients' right to self-determination?*

EP 2.1.2b

Promoting self-determination requires that clients are empowered to fully participate in decisions that will resolve their situation. You might ask, *"What if the client has limitations such as in language, cognitive, mental, or physical capacity that can hamper their ability to make decisions?"* While some individuals have limitations and may be unable to make decisions about certain aspects of their lives, their limitations are not the sum total of who they are nor does it mean that they lack the ability to process task-specific information. For example, you may propose a change approach, followed by an explanation: *"If we select this approach to resolve your concern, it would mean that you and I would develop tasks that we believe would best change your situation."*

Fostering self-determination in selecting a change strategy can be a challenge with certain client populations. Some individuals are reluctant to accept the notion of self-determination, believing instead that their lack of knowledge or power and in some case that their marginalized status has destined them to a life of constrained choices. The combination of involuntary and minority status can further fuel this perception. Promoting self-direction can be critical at this stage, beginning with you encouraging the client to participate in his or her case or treatment plan and alerting him or her to the ways to be self-directed. Of course, self-determination is not an unabridged right. For example, in the case of the involuntary client, his or her choice of a treatment approach may be constrained by a mandate. Some individuals will view the mandate as intrusive, in which case his or her emotional or reactive-based judgment limits their capacity to invest in a decision about an approach. Others may simply comply and insist that you tell them what to do so that they can regain control over their life. In either involuntary scenario, the rights of the individuals should be observed without their being unduly subjected to coercion or beneficent authority.

EP 2.1.2d

It is important to acknowledge that the work setting in which you are employed may determine the approach utilized with a specific client population. In highly regulated settings, for example, in correctional facilities, individuals have limited decision making about an intervention approach. In other settings, professionals acting as proxies can presume that an individual or a particular client population lacks the capacity for self-direction and for making decisions. Best interest, in many instances, has become a means to sacrifice self-determination, in which professionals act in a paternalistic manner. Fostering self-determination in such settings may present a challenge for you as a social work professional. Sommers-Flanagan (2007) and Fullerton and Ursano (2005), note that respecting self-determination in crisis situations can become overshadowed by a professional's strong desire to help, so much so that the client's rights and the outcome that he or she is seeking can unintentionally be circumvented. Whatever the circumstances might be, the defining question for which you may need to seek supervision is, what is the justification for a decision that ignores individuals' rights in making decisions about an intervention strategy?

EP 2.1.1f

Non-Western Perspective

The ethical principle of self-determination is taken for granted in Western society. As such, this principle should be examined in a community and socio-cultural context. The ideals of autonomy, self-direction, and independence can be values that are in sharp contrast to the beliefs of particular cultures. For instance, the freedom and success of the individual among Muslims is understood in terms of group or community success (Hodge & Nadir, 2008). Indeed, for some cultural groups, family, which can include a spiritual leader, relatives, or an entire community, may have a prominent role in intervention decisions (Palmer & Kaufman, 2003; Hodge 2005). In these situations, the selection process is a simple matter of respecting their decisions.

EP 2.1.4c

Self-Determination and Minors

In selecting an intervention approach with minors, the right to self-determination is complicated. In most states, minors are presumed to have limited decision-making capacity; therefore, parents or legal guardians act as their proxy (Strom-Gottfried, 2008). Developmental stage, reasoning, and cognitive capacity are also significant factors that influence a minor's capacity for decision making and self-direction. Minors who are immigrants may be unfamiliar with the ideals of self-determination

EP 2.1.2d

and being asked to make a decision may be outside of the realm of cultural expectations (Congress & Lynn, 1994). Nonetheless, you should not assume that a minor is unable to make choices. In general, most minors are able to express how they feel and what they want. Your task is to provide the opportunity for them to participate in intervention planning, which includes your explaining the benefits and potential risks using words that they understand (Green, Duncan, Barnes, & Oberklaid, 2003; Strom-Gottfried, 2008).

Informed consent is another ethical consideration with regard to choosing an intervention strategy. The following question and guidelines can facilitate the process of gaining consent: *Can the approach and the rationale for its use be explained to clients in a way that they are able to make an informed decision and give or decline consent?*

Informed Consent

EP 2.1.2b

Ensuring that clients understand and consent to an approach is essential to ethical and collaborative practice and is supportive of the principal of self-determination. So that clients are fully informed, you should explain the approach in language that they understand and provide them with information about the benefits and risks. The discussion must also include evidence of the approach's effectiveness with their problem. This same information should be provided to involuntary clients, even though they may lack the freedom to refuse. They can, however, be given information about their options and the consequences of their choices. Following your discussion with individuals in which you have described the appropriateness of a proposed approach to their situation, you should be guided by their responses to the following questions:

EP 2.1.10g

1. *Does the client understand the proposed approach?*
2. *Is the client in agreement with the proposed approach?*
3. *Did the client ask questions, or have reservation?*
4. *Did the client have concerns about the efficacy and effectiveness of intervention, strengths, and limitation related to his or her particular problem?*
5. *Was the client satisfied with the manner in which his or her progress would be monitored and measured?*

Informed Consent and Minors

Similar to self-determination, the ability to give consent is informed by developmental stage, cognitive ability, and reasoning (Strom-Gottfried, 2008). In particular, informed consent presumes that the individuals (for verb agreement) not only understand a proposed approach, but are also competent to weigh potential outcomes. A caveat for minors is that parents or legal guardians are presumed to act in their best interest and therefore they consent to the intervention approach (Berman-Rossi & Rossi, 1990; Strom-Gottfried, 2008). Although minors, for whatever reasons, are unable to give consent, they can, however, be provided with information about the approach and asked whether they assent; that is give an "affirmative agreement" (Strom-Gottfried, 2008, p. 62). Also, as a means to involve the minor, you can select appropriate questions to ask from the previous list. For instance, does the minor have questions or reservations, are they concerned about the efficacy of the approach, and are they are satisfied with how their progress will be monitored and measured?

EP 2.1.2b

Am I Sufficiently Knowledgeable and Skilled Enough in this Approach to Use with Others?

EP 2.1.1c

First and foremost, you are ethically obligated to have the requisite knowledge and skills to use an approach to resolve a particular client problem. The complexities of people's problems often necessitate having knowledge of and the ability to blend different approaches and techniques, and being skillful in how you use them. In many respects, techniques can transcend models. But, an addendum to the question of sufficient knowledge and skills in an approach is, *are you competent enough to make use of techniques of tactics from another approach with the one that you have selected?* For example, the approach that you are using is the task-centered model and it seems advisable to blend the solution-focused miracle or scaling questions to clarify a goal. Coady and Lehmann (2008) refer to this type of blending as *technical eclecticism*. In deciding to blend tactics or techniques, an essential question is whether you have the requisite skills and a level of competence in this form of eclecticism.

In working with minors, you may find that the blending tactics may be advisable. Very young children, for instance, typically lack the cognitive capacity to think abstractly. Therefore, it can be useful if you are skilled in such techniques such as play imagery or storytelling (Morgan, 2000; Nader & Mello, 2008). School-aged minors, especially those in middle childhood, are influenced by self-evaluation, the evaluation of others, and their own sense of mastery (Hutchison, 2008). Hence the use of tasks consistent with the task-centered or the solution-focused questions can be combined to support and reinforce their sense of self-efficacy.

A word of caution is in order. Eclectic practice does not mean that you select a little bit of this and that from various intervention approaches irrespective of your skill level. Ethically, in the selection of an approach and techniques from another, you must consider if it is right for this client at this time, and further, whether you have the requisite knowledge and skills to implement the approach or technique.

EP 2.1.10g

Selecting an approach or blending techniques requires that you understand the appropriate use and the circumstances in which a particular technique is used. The solution-focused approach, for example, utilizes the strategic miracle question to assist individuals to identify solutions. It is, however, not advisable to use the "miracle question" in and of itself as an intervention. Nor would the miracle question be appropriate in the initial crisis stage, in which a solution would take precedence over attending to the client's emotional state (James, 2008). Similarly, the procedures of cognitive restructuring and crisis intervention are indicated when a certain set of conditions and circumstances exist. Crisis intervention responds to situations in which clients experience an event or situation that exceeds their capacity to function and cope (James, 2008). The focus of cognitive restructuring is an individual's problematic thought patterns, self-statements, and behaviors and in some instances in crisis and trauma situations (Cormier & Nurius, 2003; James, 2008; Smagner & Sullivan, 2005). Even so, a more integrative cognitive approach in which you attend to micro and macro factors that contribute and sustain problematic cognitions can be more effective (Berlin 2001). For example, cognitive procedures may be advisable with a client who is depressed, but you should establish the extent to which his or her depression is influenced by an impoverished physical and social environment in which he or she lives, and thus whether cognitive restructuring as a stand-alone intervention would be appropriate.

In specific circumstances and with specific populations, selecting and utilizing an approach may in fact require that you have knowledge of non-Western traditional healing systems (Al-Krenawi & Graham 2000; Hodge & Nadir, 2008; Sue, 2006). This knowledge can inform you whether adaptations or modifications of an approach are needed.

In general, it is advisable to use only those approaches in which you have the requisite knowledge and skills to implement them in a manner that is appropriate to the client situation and is consistent with ethical practice. In instances where you may lack these skills, you should seek ongoing supervision or consultation or refer the client to a professional with the applicable skills.

EP 2.1.1c & 2.1.1f

Models & Techniques of Practice

Having provided you with considerations for planning and selecting a change approach, this next section discusses the major tenets and theoretical frameworks of the task-centered model, the basic model of crisis intervention, the cognitive behavioral technique of cognitive restructuring, the solution-focus brief treatment, and case management.[1]

The Task-Centered System

The task-centered system is a social work practice model developed by William Reid and Laura Epstein. The model's contribution to social work practice is the specific focus on problems of concern identified by the client and its emphasis on tasks and the collaborative responsibilities between the client and the social worker. The model emerged when the prevailing view of the resistant client and open-ended models were the norm in social work and allied disciplines. Kelly (2008), credits the development of the model as strengthening the empirical orientation to social work practice.

EP 2.1.10a

Tenets of the Task-Centered Approach

The direction of the task centered approach with regard to goal attainment is both systematic and efficient. Termination is considered to begin at the initial point of contact, facilitated by specific goals and the completion of tasks. Within a brief time-limited period, the model is aimed toward reducing problems in living.

EP 2.1.10a

Central themes of the task-centered approach are that people are capable of solving their own problems and that it is important to work on problems that are identified by the client. Clients' identification of priority concerns and the collaborative relationship are understood to be empowering aspects of the model. The approach addresses an array of problems the including interpersonal conflicts, difficulties in social relations or role performance, reactive emotional distress, inadequate resources, and difficulties with organizations (Ramos & Tolson, 2008; Reid & Epstein, 1972; Reid, 1992; Epstein, 1992).

Theoretical Framework

EP 2.1.7a

Research by Reid and Shyne (1969) informed the development of the task-centered system as an action-oriented model in which problem-solving activities occurred within a limited time frame. Their research demonstrated that brief, focused contact and the conscious use of time limits were as effective as those strategies that required a longer time period and was consistent with other studies that supported the efficacy on time-limited treatment (Hoyt, 2000; Wells & Gianetti, 1990).

The development of the model was further influenced by Studt's (1968) conceptualization of the efficacy of utilizing tasks and the structural procedures of Perlman's (1957) problem-solving model. Similar to the problem-solving model introduced by Perlman (1957), the task-centered model focused social work practice on problems related to challenges in daily living and psychosocial factors that were observed to be common to a majority of social work constituents (Epstein, 1992; Reid, 1992). The use of tasks is supported by Bandura's (1997) research related to self-efficacy; ultimately enhancing the client's sense that through his or her efforts, he or she can be successful agents in solving problems (Reid, 1992).

The task-centered system is designed to be eclectic. Reid (1992), however, stresses selecting research-based theories and interventions. With this in mind, you are able to make use of various theories that are relevant to the client situation (Ramos & Tolson, 2008; Reid, 1992). For example, cognitive restructuring can inform task strategies when feelings, anxieties, and fears are influenced by beliefs or irrational thought patterns (Reid, 1992). Still, Reid cautions that you should first determine that the client's emotional state is consistent with cognitive theory, rather than stressors caused by environmental factors, conditions, or a crisis situation. In addition, the task-centered model allows for the advent of a crisis, in which techniques from the crisis intervention approach may be used.

Empirical Evidence and Uses of the Task-Centered Model

EP 2.1.6b

The task-centered system has been adapted to various settings in which social workers practice and its use has been empirically established with different client populations, including families, organizations, and communities Parihar, 1994; Ramarkrishman, Balgopal, & Pettys, 1994, 2008; Reid & Fortune, 2002; Pomeroy, Rubin, & Walker, 1995; Reid, 1987, 1997a; Tolson, Reid, & Garvin, 1994). Adaptations of the task-centered approach have been tested in most settings where social workers practice, including mental health, health care, and family practice (Alley & Brown, 2002; Epstein & Brown, 2002; Fortune, 1985; Fortune, McCallion & Briar-Larson, 2010; Reid, 1987, ... 1992, 1997a, 2000). Additional evidence of the model utilization and effectiveness include case management with minors and families, with elderly individuals in long-term care (Lee, Magnanano, & Smith, 2008; Neleppa & Reid, 2000; 2003; Parzaratz, 2000; Tolson, Reid & Garvin 1994), supervision and staff development (Caspi & Reid, 2002), and with groups (Lo, 2005; Pomeroy, Rubin, & Walker, 1995; Garvin, 1987; Larsen & Mitchell, 1980).

Utilization with Minors

Examples of the models application with minors include improving school performance, changing or modifying behavior in residential facilities, and reducing sibling conflict (Bailey-Dempsey & Reid, 1996; Caspi, 2008; Pazaratz, 2000; 2006; Reid & Bailey-Dempsey, 1995; Reid, Epstein, Brown, Tolson, & Rooney, 1980). Using the task-centered model as a guiding framework (R. H. Rooney, 1992; 1981) expanded its application to include social work practice with involuntary clients in child welfare and with minors in a school setting.

Application with Diverse Groups

According to Ramos and Tolson, the task-centered model has been used in agencies in which the client base consists of clients who are from "poor, racial and ethnocultural minority groups" (2008, p, 286). The model is thought to be sensitive to the experience of diverse individuals and families because of the emphasis on the right of clients to identify concerns, including involuntary clients. The use of tasks is believed to empower clients who are marginalized, lack power, and are oppressed (Ramos & Garvin, 2003; Boyd-Franklin, 1989a). The model also responds to issues characterized by Sue (2006) as barriers to multicultural clinical practice because of its explicit acceptance of the client's view of the problem, a here-and-now action orientation, rather than insightful talking. In their evaluation of various models of practice, Devore and Schlesinger (1999) concluded that the basic principles of the task-centered system are a "major thrust" in ethnically sensitive practice (p. 121). Because the model accommodates different worldviews it has been translated into several languages in different practice settings (Ramos & Tolson, 2008; Rooney & Chou, 2010; Rooney, 2010).

Procedures of the Task-Centered Model

EP 2.1.10j

Figure 13-1 presents an overview of the procedures of the model. The initial phase begins with the client identifying and prioritizing the target problem. It is recommended that priority concerns and goals be limited to a maximum of three. Goals are agreed upon and general and specific tasks are developed to achieve goal attainment. In keeping with the model's action orientation and brevity, termination begins with the first session. Specifically, you and the client agree to work together for a particular number of sessions (e.g., six to eight weeks), although there is an opportunity to extend contact or negotiate a new contract for a different problem. Progress toward the identified goal is monitored in each session as the client moves toward termination.

Developing General Tasks

EP 2.1.10f

As illustrated in Figure 13-1, when you and the client have identified a target problem and related goals, you are ready to develop general tasks. General tasks consist of discrete actions to be undertaken by the client and, in some instances, by you the social worker. Each general task has specific tasks that direct the incremental action steps to achieve goals. The case of the Corning family is used to illustrate how goals and the related general and specific tasks are developed. At this point, you will want to review the five video segments on your CourseMate related to the Corning Family. Other case examples in the *Practice Workbook* provide you with opportunities to practice and evaluate your skill in developing general and specific tasks. A brief review of the family's situation is summarized in the following section.

Target Problem

Angela and Irwin Corning, an interracial couple and their three children, are living in a transitional housing facility. Irwin lost his job eight months ago when the county agency where he worked for as a maintenance specialist hired a private contractor to reduce their labor costs. Their preference is to purchase another home, but their financial situation does not permit them to currently own a home. Consequently, the family will need to move into an apartment.

Goals
1. Move from transitional housing facility into an apartment.
2. Find employment for Irwin

The Corning family is faced with two competing needs. They had hoped that Irwin would find employment with a sufficient salary that would give the family the financial resources to move into their own home. He has temporary employment that may lead to a permanent position. Now that he is employed, however, the family is no longer eligible to remain in transitional housing. They have six weeks to move from the facility, thus their priority goal is finding an apartment, preferably one with three bedrooms. Irwin, in the meantime, will continue to look for more permanent employment.

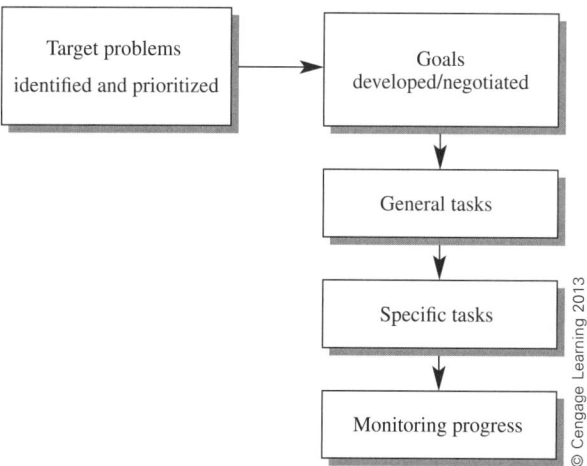
FIG-13-1 Overview of the Task-Centered System

EP 2.1.10j

To accomplish their goals the following general and specific tasks, including tasks to be completed by the social worker, were developed:

General Tasks

1. Meet with the transitional housing case manager to obtain information about affordable three-bedroom apartments.
2. Plan to visit apartments located in the general area where they want to live.
3. Identify schools in the area for the children.
4. Develop a budget.
5. Explore permanent employment for Irwin

General Tasks for the Social Worker

From these examples, it is apparent that general tasks involve actions to be undertaken by one or both of the Corning spouses. General tasks can also require actions of you, either on their behalf or as joint endeavors. In this situation, providing employment resource referrals for Irwin was a general task for the social worker. A general task for Irwin was that he would continue to seek opportunities on his own.

Initially, general tasks may be disconnected and they may not follow a logical sequence. Therefore, they will need to be prioritized by you and the client. For the Cornings, it was important to determine which of the general tasks were most significant. They agreed that moving from the transitional housing facility was a priority.

It is important to settle on tasks for which the benefit is obvious and which have a good chance of being successful. Success with one task encourages clients' confidence in their ability to tackle another task. For example, locating and visiting apartments were tasks that seemed to be more easily completed than was finding a permanent job for Irwin. A benefit that Angela and Irwin identified in selecting the move as a priority goal was their belief that it would provide a more stable environment for their children.

Developing Specific Tasks

EP 2.1.10j

Even general tasks can prove to be overwhelming for some clients. The key to the task-centered system is dividing general tasks into specific tasks that direct the actions that the client or you as the social worker will attempt between one session and the next. Specific tasks related to the goal and previously outlined general tasks are illustrated in the following example.

Goal: The Corning family will move from the transitional housing facility into an apartment within the next six weeks.

General Task: Contact the transitional housing assistance coordinator to obtain information about available and affordable three-bedroom apartments.

Specific Tasks

1. Schedule a meeting with housing coordinator to learn about housing options within the next week.
2. Plan to visit apartments located in the general area where they would like to live.

Specific tasks may need to be further partialized into subtasks. Meeting with the housing coordinator more than likely is a specific one time action step. Visiting apartments, however, may require additional actions or subtasks such as arranging for child care, depending on the time of the visits and transportation.

Notice that both general and specific tasks that Angela and Irwin are to complete are stated in positive term. Positively framed tasks highlight growth and potential gains. As such, people tend to be more enthusiastic and motivated about tasks oriented to progress h and achievement. In contrast, tasks that specify eliminating negative behaviors focus exclusively on what clients must give up. For example, in looking for a job, a negative task might be: In the job search, Irwin will eliminate his thoughts about his job loss.

Partializing goals into general tasks and ultimately into specific tasks can consume a substantial amount of time. The same is true in the preparation for accomplishing one or more specific tasks at a time. When multiple tasks are developed, it is important to focus on and plan implementation of at least one task before concluding a session. In fact, many clients are eager to get started and welcome homework assignments. Note that Angela Corning asked what the couple could do before the next session. While mutually identifying tasks and planning their implementation in each session is time intensive, the time spent from one session to the next can sharpen the focus on action steps that facilitate progress.

EP 2.1.10j

Brainstorming Task Alternatives

Brainstorming is the creative process of mutually focusing efforts on generating a broad range of possible options from which the individual, family, or group may choose. Essential tasks are often

EP 2.1.10i

readily apparent. Further, because clients are experts about their situation, their decisions are invaluable in developing both general and specific tasks. They are usually committed to tasks that they identify on their own. As with goals, if such tasks are feasible and realistic, they should be supported. With some clients, however, if tasks are less readily apparent to them, you can brainstorm with them to identify a range of alternatives.

Brainstorming can be particularly useful with minors to encourage their ownership of possible actions. There may be instances in which you will need to initiate the exploration of the task development process. Most clients will be generally receptive to your suggestions. Reid (2000; 1978) found that there was little difference in the rate with which clients' accomplished tasks suggested by the social worker when compared to those they proposed themselves.

When you suggest tasks during the brainstorming process, however, it is critical to check with the clients to ensure that they agree with and are committed to those tasks. You should be sensitive to nonverbal reactions to your ideas. Commitment and a willingness to engage in tasks are indicators of follow-through by the client (Reid, 1978). In some instances, especially with minors and involuntary clients, you may be tempted to assign tasks. For the most part, individuals of all ages, irrespective of their status, are unlikely to be motivated or receptive to assigned tasks. Assigned tasks, whether in the form of advice or a directive, are less likely to be carried out (Reid, 1997a). Reactance theory suggests that individuals are inclined to act to protect themselves especially when their choices are imposed (Brehm & Brehm, 1981; Miller & Rollnick, 2002). Even voluntary clients may react if they perceive that you have an agenda that is inconsistent with a direction that they wish to take. As a note of caution, when you encounter reactance, it is advisable that you don't confuse a healthy assertion of individuality with an individual's opposition to change.

In using brainstorming with families or groups, you should be attuned to dynamics that will require active facilitation on your part. Group or family members may indeed be able to assist others by suggesting options. The suggestion of tasks, nonetheless, should not circumvent the individual's right to choose which tasks he or she will undertake and, indeed, if he or she will complete any at all.

Task Implementation Sequence

EP 2.1.10j

After agreeing on one or more tasks, the next step is to assist clients to plan and prepare to implement each task. When skillfully executed, this process augments people's motivation for undertaking tasks

TABLE-13-1 TASK IMPLEMENTATION SEQUENCE (TIS)

1. Enhance the client's commitment to carry out tasks.
2. Plan the details of carrying out tasks.
3. Analyze and resolve obstacles.
4. Rehearse or practice behavior involved in tasks.
5. Summarize the task plan.

© Cengage Learning 2013

and substantially enhances the probability of successful outcomes. The task implementation sequence (TIS), as described by Reid (1975; 2000), involves a sequence of discrete steps. These steps (summarized in Table 13-1), encompass the major ingredients generally associated with successful change efforts. The results of research findings suggest that clients were more successful in accomplishing tasks when TIS was implemented than when it was not (Reid, 1975; 2000). Although Reid recommends that the TIS be applied systematically, flexibility is advisable so as to permit adaptation or modification of the sequence that is appropriate to the circumstances of each case.

It would be simplistic to assume that merely agreeing to carry out a task ensures that the individual has the knowledge, resources, courage, interpersonal skills, or emotional readiness to successfully implement a task. Each

EP 2.1.10i

step in the sequence is intended to increase the potential of a successful outcome. You will notice that the sequence is individualized to the client situation and considers his or her motivation. In addition to maximizing the potential for success, obstacles to task completion are analyzed and resolved in advance, and incentives or rewards for task completion are developed. In the following section, the sequential steps highlighted in Table 13-1 are discussed in greater detail.

Enhance the Client's Commitment to Carry Out a Task

Step 1 in the sequence is directly aimed at enhancing clients' motivation to carry out a task. This step involves clarifying the relevance of tasks to clients' goals and identifying their potential benefits. To follow through with tasks, it is important that clients perceive that the gains of completing a task outweighs the costs (including anxiety and fear) associated with risking a new behavior or dealing with a changed problem or situation. Because change is difficult, exploring apprehension, discomfort, and uncertainty is especially critical when clients' motivation to carry out a given task is questionable.

It is advisable to begin implementing Step 1 of the TIS by asking clients to identify benefits they will gain by successfully accomplishing the task. In many instances, the potential gain and benefit of carrying out a task is obvious, and it would be pointless to dwell on this step. For example, for Irwin Corning, the benefit and subsequent gain of completing the task of applying for permanent employment opportunities was evident. Ultimately, the gain of employment was a gain in economic stability for the family.

Rewards and Incentives for Adults. In enhancing clients' motivation to change ingrained behaviors or deal with difficult situations, it is sometimes necessary to create immediate incentives by planning tangible rewards for carrying out planned tasks.

Rewarding oneself (self-reinforcement) can increase an individual's motivation for completing a task. Rewards and incentives are particularly relevant when a change in behavior or cognition is associated with the choice of pain over pleasure, such as in lieu of self-time, engaging in activities that may be perceived as unattractive (e.g., studying, cleaning house). Possible rewards can be identified with the client; however, to be effective they should be realistically within reach.

Rewards and Incentives for Minors. Rewards can motivate and create incentives for minors to complete tasks, when, like adults, their preference may be to do something else. Incentives and rewards can be particularly advantageous when tasks are related to a behavioral change, such as minimizing rivalry with siblings, being respectful of others, or waiting to be called upon in class. In addition, you can establish complementary tasks as rewards with parents or other significant persons in their lives. The intent of rewards is to help the minor to complete tasks related to a goal, preferably with their input.

When you use incentives or rewards, it is important to observe incremental change, followed by an immediate reward; otherwise they may become discouraged or give up, believing they cannot meet expectations.

The following are guidelines intended to aid in setting up tasks with accompanying incentives or rewards for minors.

- *Frame tasks so that they understand explicitly what they are to do and when they are to do it. Specify the time frame and the conditions under which the task is to be performed (e.g., every 2 hours, twice daily, each Wednesday, once an hour for the next 4 days).*
- *Designate what can be earned for exhibiting the task, and establish a method for tracking in conjunction with the minor.*
- *Invite minors to choose the type of reward they wish to earn because they will choose rewards that have maximal value as incentives.*
- *Establish rewards for specified periods of time (e.g., if the child raises his or her hand for 4 of the 5 days in a week's class, he or she will be able to read a story or earn points toward something he or she values). Whenever possible, it is important to offer relationship rewards, rather than monetary or material items. Relationship rewards involve things such as going to the mall or spending time with friends or other significant individuals.*
- *Provide a bonus for consistent achievements of tasks over an extended period of time.*
- *Encourage task completion by providing consistent and positive feedback; for young minors, using visual indicators that mark progress on tasks as motivators.*

Plan the Details of Carrying Out Tasks

This step, the second one in the sequence, is vital in assisting individuals to prepare themselves for all of the actions inherent in a task. Most tasks consist of a series of actions to be carried out sequentially, and they may involve both cognitive and behavioral subtasks. For example, before carrying out an overt action, it may be beneficial to help a client prepare psychologically. To illustrate, in one of the sessions Irwin talked about himself as a low-skilled laborer, which he believed meant that he had few opportunities. Preparation for engaging in and completing tasks related to his job search could involve a review of potential benefits, addressing and resolving his fears by realistically appraising his situation. For some individuals, you may coach them to reflect on past successes or focus on their spirituality or faith. By including cognitive strategies in this step, you are assisting clients to cope with their ambivalence or apprehension over implementing actions.

Planning overt actions requires considering the real-life details. For example, the Corning couple discussed whether or not to take their children with them while they looked for an apartment. If they were to schedule visits early in the day, the two older children would be at school. In the evenings, unless they had child care, all three children would go along on the visits, which might be difficult as they relied on public transportation. In addition, they would need bus fare for themselves and the older children. During the discussion, Angela advised that her sister was available for child care if needed. Discussing the details associated with completing tasks, and planning for the inevitable in advance, effectively increases the opportunity for the couple to be successful. In planning and discussing discrete actions with them, you are able to observe cues about their misgivings, fears, or lack of skills or resources, each of which can be addressed.

The Practitioner's Role in Task Planning.

EP 2.1.10j

Task planning can involve certain tasks to be carried out by the practitioner; however, these tasks are coordinated with those of the client. Clients may also wonder about your role in task planning. Angela Corning, for example, asked the social worker, "What kinds of things can you do for us? I'm not clear about how you can help us." In planning the details of tasks, a practitioner's tasks can be developed when he or she has ready access to resources or information that will facilitate client work. In the Corning case, Ali agreed to obtain information about financial assistance for families moving from transitional housing. On the other hand, if a client would benefit from eventually completing a task on his or her own, you and the individual could walk through the steps together. In some cases, during the performance of a task, it can be beneficial for you to accompany the client or you might tap into his or her support system. For instance, if the task involved applying for financial assistance, which for some people can be intimidating, supporting task performance can involve assisting an individual with completing the application or having someone to talk to while waiting to be interviewed.

Conditions for Tasks Completion.

EP 2.1.10i

Why specify the conditions and time for implementing tasks in such detail? Timing is an important condition for completing tasks. When a time frame lacks specificity or is vague or abstract, clients (and social workers) can procrastinate, leaving little time to effectively implement the requisite actions. Here you might think of a group project assignment in which the members of the group agree to meet within the next week. Without solidifying when and where the meeting is to take place, each individual can have a different idea about what next week means. Planning also involves specifying the conditions under which each task will be carried out. For example, a sixth-grade student who constantly disturbs his peers, speaks out in class without raising his hand, and irritates his teacher through boisterous teasing behavior may accept the following task: he needs to listen attentively when the teacher is speaking during the 1-hour math class and raise his hand three times to answer questions during that time. He agrees to carry out this task each day for the next 5 days. Although he exhibits the problematic behavior in other classes, the math class and specific time frame are the conditions in which the behavioral tasks are to occur. While the ongoing goal is the eventual change his behavior in all classes, a focus on behavior in the math class further partializes the change effort as it would be unrealistic to expect a drastic and immediate new behavior.

In selecting and planning tasks pertaining to *ongoing* goals, you should observe an additional caution. Because progress on such goals is incremental, it is vital to begin with a task that is within the individual's capacity to achieve. In

EP 2.1.10j

the classroom situation, for example, a task for the student to raise his hand for 5 straight days may be difficult for him to achieve. However, a task of raising his hand in math class for 2 out of 5 days may, with positive feedback from the teacher, have a greater likelihood of accomplishment. Being successful in completing this task, his chances of later gradually improved task performance, specifically raising his hand 3 or 4 days, has the capacity for greater success. Conversely, if he experienced failure on the initial task, his confidence and courage may decline, making him reluctant to work toward changing his classroom behavior. Thus, with ongoing tasks it is preferable to have the first task structured so that it is easily obtainable.

Analyze and Resolve Barriers and Obstacles

Based on recognition of the inevitability of barriers that impede change, this step is aimed at acknowledging and addressing these forces. When implementing Step 3, you and the client deliberately anticipate

EP 2.1.10i

and subsequently analyze obstacles that have the potential to influence task accomplishment. Using the classroom situation as an illustrative example, in developing a task related to changing the student's boisterous behavior, it would be useful to explore potential obstacles, such as social, physical, or psychological barriers. For this student, his behavior has been reinforced by the attention he received from his peers, which he values, and it also ensured his social standing in the group.

For Irwin Corning, making a telephone call to inquire about available jobs or looking online for job postings seem to be relatively simple tasks. Nonetheless, the social worker should inquire about whether or not he had the resources for completing these tasks. To this point, Eamon & Zhang (2006) found that practitioners often overlooked economic resources as a barrier to completing tasks. A caveat should be observed, however: A simple action for some people, such as making a phone call, may prove difficult for others depending on their level of confidence, cognitive capacity, or social ability. In addition, fears and cognitions can pose formidable barriers to accomplishing a task and require careful exploration so that they do not impede progress. For example, although Irwin was eager to find employment, his confidence was hampered by the experience of "being laid off" and the fact that he perceived himself as a failure based on his belief that "a man ought to provide for his family."

When tasks are complex, obstacles likewise tend to be complex and difficult to identify and resolve. Tasks that involve changes in patterns of interpersonal relationships tend to be multifaceted, encompassing subsidiary but prerequisite intrapersonal tasks as well as a mastery of certain interpersonal skills. The psychological and social content inherent in the sixth grader resisting the impulse to engage in boisterous behavior involved his fear of being rejected by his reference peer group. Change for him involved not only mastering certain new behaviors, it also meant changing his patterned behavior of relating in the classroom environment in a manner that was less likely to be valued by his peers.

Resolving Barriers and Obstacles. People will vary in their capacity to resolve obstacles. They may overlook or underestimate the obstacles and barriers that can delay or cause needless difficulties in the accomplishment of tasks and lead to outright failure. With continuous engagement and collaboration, however, you can help them to identify and subsequently resolve possible obstacles to a planned course of action. Returning to

EP 2.1.10j

the sixth grader as an example, it would be important to encourage his sense of self-efficacy by explaining that obstacles are common. Together, the two of you would brainstorm different *what if* scenarios that could hamper his ability to raise his hand before speaking in class. Otherwise, he can become frustrated and revert to the comfort of his old patterned behavior. What if he raised his hand and the teacher did not call on him? What would he do if he was eager to answer a question, but another student was quicker in responding? What if he became discouraged? In reviewing different scenarios with him, potential obstacles are identified and his possible responses are clarified in advance. For, example, "I would wait my turn," or "I could keep my hand up, even if the teacher called on another student first," or "If I felt discouraged, I might talk to the teacher after class." Equipping him with possible responses, in effect, maximizes his motivation to sustain his efforts to continually engage in tasks related to his targeted behavior.

Psychological barriers to task performance are often encountered regardless of the nature of the task. Think of your cognitive appraisal of a situation in which you experienced intense emotions. For example, when you applied

EP 2.1.10i

for a job, had to appear in court, or expressed your feelings. What about this experience was intimidating? Did your cognitive appraisal of the situation affect the quality and intensity of your emotions, which determined your perceptions and attributions or meaning associated with that situation?

Whether real or perceived, beliefs about self or stereotypic perceptions of others can represent major obstacles to task completion. Recall that Irwin Corning, as he talked about his job loss, appeared to be preoccupied with personal struggles, the meaning the loss of income had for the family, and his belief about his responsibility as the head of the household. At one point he asserted, "Nothing is comfortable about this situation."

In examining the cognitive content of his message, there appears to be several layers. Understandably, he is experiencing intense emotions as a displaced, replaced worker, in which there is his realistic appraisal the economic climate, as well as his beliefs about employment opportunities as an African American male. At the same time, his notion that the company's preference for hiring individuals who are illegal as the cause of his becoming unemployed lacks concrete evidence. *What can you do when you encounter situations in which cognitions and intense emotions have the potential to derail an individual's plan of action?* To begin,

EP 2.1.10j

you and the individual can develop a subsidiary task of neutralizing his or her emotions. This can be accomplished (often in a brief amount of time) by eliciting, clarifying, and empathizing with the individual's apprehension and rationally analyzing his or her feelings. It may also be important that you examine their problematic emotions by helping them to identify their cognitive sources and assist them to align his or her thoughts and feelings with reality. In general, time and effort invested in overcoming and resolving barriers and obstacles are likely to pay dividends, the results of which are a higher rate of success of accomplishing tasks. Consider the economy of this process, as failure to complete tasks can have an affect on an individual's sense of self-efficacy, and it can extend the time required for successful problem solving.

Assessing Clients' Readiness to Begin Tasks

EP 2.1.10f

Just as identifying and resolving barriers to task performance is critical, so is assessing clients' readiness to engage in mutually agreed upon tasks. You should be alert to nonverbal behaviors as potential obstacles or as possible indicators of their apprehension about undertaking a task. When you detect such reactions, you should further explore the presence of this nonverbal barrier. You will have seen in the Corning family videos that initially Irwin seemed uncomfortable, at times he seemed annoyed, and he had very little to say unless prompted by Angela or in response to questions asked by the practitioner. He, however, became animated when Ali asked about his willingness to develop goal-related tasks stating, "I am ready to do something, instead of sitting here talking, I could be out looking for a job or a place for my family to live. So, let's get on with it."

EP 2.1.10i

People's readiness for implementing tasks can be gauged by asking them to rate their readiness using a scale from 1 to 10, where 1 represents a lack of readiness and 10 indicates that the client is ready to go (DeJong & Berg, 2001). With individuals like Irwin Corning, you can easily judge a readiness level of perhaps 8–10. Conversely, if he had been less eager and indicated his readiness on the low end of the scale, for example, in the 1–3 range, his rationale should be explored. When individuals are hesitant to begin, exploring their reasons for a low rating can uncover vital information concerning potential obstacles to be discussed. Even when clients have indicated that they are prepared to move ahead, they can still experience a certain amount of tension and anxiety. It is neither realistic nor desirable to expect people to be altogether comfortable with tasks, despite the fact that they were involved in their development. Note that although Irwin indicated that he was ready to go, in the course of the discussion, he was nonetheless apprehensive about his job search. Had his apprehension involved an inordinate level of anxiety, his feelings would need to be explored, as a high level of anxiety can be a major deterrent to further action.

Rehearse or Practice Behaviors Involved in Tasks

EP 2.1.10i

Certain tasks involve skills that people lack or behaviors with which they have had little or no experience. Step 4 of the TIS is aimed at assisting clients to gain the experience and mastery in performing skills or behaviors essential to task accomplishment. Bandura (1977) builds a strong case for mastery based on the results of research. Specifically, he asserts that the degree of an individual's positive expectation in his or her ability to perform will, in effect, determine how much effort they will expend and how long they will persist in the face of obstacles or aversive circumstances. It follows, then, that a major goal of the helping process is to enhance clients' sense of self-efficacy, which can be accrued through successful task completion. Successful experience, even in simulated situations, fosters the individual belief that he or she has the ability to be successful in performing a task.

EP 2.1.10i

Supportive research cited by Bandura (1977) indicates that, once established, self-efficacy and skills tend to be transferred by individuals to other situations, including those which they had previously avoided. According to Bandura, people receive information about self-efficacy from four sources:

- *Performance accomplishments*: Major methods of increasing self-efficacy through performance accomplishment include assisting people to master essential behaviors through modeling, behavior rehearsal, and guided practice (discussed later in this chapter). An example of performance accomplishment would be assisting the sixth grader to master specific communication skills during an actual session.

- *Vicarious experience*: Insight may be gained by observing others demonstrate target behaviors or perform threatening activities without experiencing adverse consequences. Efficacy expectations can be bolstered by a client observing you, the social worker, or others who model the desired behaviors. Observing others, however, is clearly not as powerful as the sense of self-efficacy that results from the individual successfully performing a behavior or demonstrating a skill on their own.
- *Verbal persuasion*: Talking to individuals about their capacity to perform can raise outcome expectations, and can be persuasive. But talking to a person about expectations or attempting to persuade them about their competence does not in fact enhance self efficacy. To be effective, the appraisal of an individual's capabilities has to be based on his or her perceptions and assumptions about competence and their sense of self-efficacy.
- *Emotional arousal*: Self-efficacy can be influenced by emotions, which in turn affects how people perform. Individuals who are extremely anxious or fearful about performing a new behavior are unlikely to have sufficient confidence that they can competently perform. Verbal persuasion directed toward reducing anxieties or fears is generally ineffective. Emotional arousal obviously is an undependable source of self-efficacy because it can influence actual evidence of an individual's capacity. Indeed, perceived self-competence tends to reduce emotional arousal rather than the converse.

Of these four sources, *performance accomplishment* is thought to be the most influential because it is based on an individual's personal mastery experience.

Increasing Self-Efficacy through Behavioral Rehearsal, Modeling, and Role-Play. Having reviewed informative aspects about sources of mastery and of self-efficacy, behavioral rehearsal can be an important step in enhancing performance. Used in an actual session, behavioral rehearsal is intended to reduce anxieties and to assist individuals to practice new coping patterns under your guidance. Indications for using this technique include situations when a client feels threatened, inadequately prepared to confront a situation, or when he or she is anxious or feel overwhelmed by the prospects of carrying out a given task. Through role-play, the individual can practice the skills or behaviors in a simulation that involves his or her anticipated response to a given situation.

EP 2.1.10i

Role-playing is the most common form of behavioral rehearsal. It allows an individual to rehearse desired behaviors or outcomes and encourages mastery. In a simulated situation, you and the individual can build on their existing skills, as well as assess potential barriers or obstacles. Modeling behavior through role-play, in effect, allows the individual to vicariously learn an expected behavior before actually having to do so in a real-life difficult situation.

EP 2.1.10i

This use of the role-play technique to enhance performance accomplishment is illustrated in the video segment featuring Yanping.

> **VIDEO CASE EXAMPLE**
>
> Yanping, a graduate student from China, has decided to change her major from business to history. In the course of her studies, she discovered that history was her true passion. Her parents have expressed their displeasure with her decision to change her course of study. They questioned the value of a degree in history, which they consider to have low status with limited financial rewards. The parents own a business and had expected that Yanping would return home prepared to eventually take over the family business. She understands her parent's belief that a history degree has little value to the family. She is experiencing a high level of anxiety as a result of her parent's disappointment and the fact that she has caused them distress by not honoring her family obligation. During the course of several phone calls, Yanping has been unable to persuade her parents to accept her decision about changing her course of study from business to history. She anticipates that they will continue to resist. As the time for her to return home draws nearer, she has become increasingly anxious about having further conversations with her parents.

In the first segment of the video, observe that Kim, the social worker, attempted to understand the cultural meaning and implications of Yanping's decision, her parent's reaction, as well her prior coping efforts. Kim also inquired whether she has talked with or observed others in a similar situation (*vicarious experience*). Together, they brainstormed options regarding possible ways that she could approach a conversation with her parents. This case is difficult for Kim as a social worker practitioner who is versed in the individual autonomy norms of Western society and the guiding principle of self-determination. Kim did not feel that she was able to be sufficiently sensitive to the difficulties and serious consequences that Yanping would encounter if she broke with her cultural traditions. Thus, she referred Yanping to Jilan, a colleague from China. Kim believed Jilan's familiarity with the culture would aid Yanping to navigate the cultural expectations and resolve her dilemma. The fact that she was able to refer Yanping to Jilan was fortuitous, as a referral for reasons related to culture, and perhaps any reason, may not always be an option. In the video session that takes place with Jilan and Yanping, they use role-play to simulate a conversation with Yanping's father in preparation for her eventual face-to-face encounter (*behavioral rehearsal*). As the two take a turn, either as Yanping or her father, Yanping had the opportunity to rehearse responses to anticipated questions from her father and also to observe Jilan as she modeled behavioral responses for Yanping to consider (*behavioral modeling*). Note that during the exchanges, Yanping appeared to be less anxious and more willing to approach her father. In fact, during the course of the roeplay, a new idea occurred to her; she would also study business history which she believed would appeal to her father as advantageous to the family business.

EP 2.1.10j

Behavioral rehearsal need not be restricted to a session with you and a client. It and can include overt behavior like making a phone call, covert behavior like self-talk, or it can include expressing aloud defeating feelings or thoughts. These defeating feelings and thoughts can then be restructured into more encouraging language. It is often productive for clients to rehearse on their own by pretending to be involved in real-life encounters.

Modeling and behavioral rehearsal can also be integrated into family or group sessions in which members can model effective and realistic responses or coping for each other as they contemplate engaging in a particular task. As a rule of thumb, in implementing family or group role-plays, the intent is to tap into members' resources in a help-giving role.

If modeling or rehearsal proves to be ineffective, in the interim, you can help clients to develop coping efforts rather than achieve mastery. Coping emphasizes the struggles that a person might expect to experience in completing the task behavior or activity. Emphasizing coping rather than mastery is intended to lessen anxiety and, hence, the threat of having to perform without making a mistake.

Guided Practice Closely related to behavioral rehearsal, guided practice is another technique to aid task accomplishment. It differs from behavioral rehearsal in that it consists of in vivo rather than a simulated situation. It
EP 2.1.10i

involves you observing the client as he or she engages in a task related to a target behavior. Afterwards, you provide immediate feedback and also coach him or her as they attempt to gain mastery toward task completion. For example, in a family session, as you observe problematic behaviors or interactions first hand, you would provide feedback and coach members to master problem-solving or conflict-resolution skills. Such an on-the-spot intervention enables you to clarify what is occurring as well as coach clients in engaging in more productive behavior.

Summarize the Task Plan

Summarizing the task plan is the final step of the Task Implementation Sequence. The summary, which takes place at the conclusion of a session, consists of a review of the actions or behaviors that an individual has agreed to engage in
EP 2.1.10f

order to accomplish a task. In reviewing task agreements, you and the client confirm that you both have a clear understanding of what tasks are to be undertaken, in what sequence, and under what conditions or whether clarification is needed. Confirmation of the plan might proceed with you describing the tasks that your client will complete:

"I have agreed to contact the employment information specialist by our meeting next week."

In follow-up, you would ask the individual to review and summarize his or her plans:

"What are your plans for searching for a job by our next session?"

Individual clients may find it beneficial for you to provide them with a session by session written summary of goals and related tasks. You might also encourage clients to write their own summary as well. In either case, both you and the client should have copies. In keeping with the ethical obligation of documentation, this information is included in the case record or SOAP notes. Furthermore, documentation is essential to monitoring and evaluating during the duration and termination of the contact.

Failure to Complete Tasks

In actual practice, progress may not be as smooth as you and the client would prefer, despite the fact that barriers or obstacles have been anticipated and resolve, the individual is ready to begin, and all other possible impediments have been addressed. In the best scenarios, focus and continuity can be derailed for a variety of reasons, which are summarized in Figure 13-2. The reasons for low task performance are classified into two categories: *Reasons related to specific tasks; and, Reasons related to the target problem.*

EP 2.1.10m

Performance Problems Related to the Task

Occasionally, unforeseen circumstances or unanticipated obstacles may influence an individual's ability to complete a task between sessions. When this happens, the obstacles that blocked the task completion should be identified and resolved. By mutual agreement, tasks can be continued to the next session. The caveat, of course, is that both you and the client are in agreement that the task remains valid. If this is not the case, it is important to shift the focus to more relevant tasks.

Occurrence of a Crisis. There are instances in which certain situations may dictate taking a brief detour because of the occurrence of an event or situation. As a result, an individual's momentum may be slowed down and he or she may become unable to complete a task. Should this prove to be the case, it is appropriate for you to empathetically respond to the emotional state of the individual. It may also be necessary to focus on the more urgent difficulty and to develop a goal and tasks related to the unexpected situation. If possible, an agreement should be reached about the timing for resuming work on tasks that were designated for completion prior to the crisis. If in the course of your work with the individual you observe that his or her life appears to reverberate from crisis to crisis, the two of you can discuss whether or not it would be beneficial to remain focused on the initial tasks and see them through to completion.

Lack of Commitment. A lack of commitment has been documented as a statistically significant predictor of whether a client will engage in task performance (Reid, 1977; 1997a; 2000). However, a lack of commitment should not be confused with a lack of readiness. In the former, the willingness to change is absent. In the latter, the individual is willing, but is blocked from acting by other barriers. One frequent cause for a lack of commitment to undertake tasks is a covert unwillingness to own one's part of a problem. "I would raise my hand if the teacher called on me," is an example of paying lip service to carrying out a task. Unwilling individuals may use excuses to blame others for their behavior and instead they passively wait for others to initiate corrective actions. The technique of ethical confrontation (see Chapter 17) can be used to help clients recognize their responsibility for maintaining the undesirable status quo.

Unspecified or Vaguely Specified Tasks. The final step of the Task Implementation Sequence (summarizing), provides an opportunity for you and the client to clarify and reaffirm tasks. Even so, there can be occasions when, in spite of a review, an individual may end a session without fully understanding what he or she has agreed to do. As is the case of developing goals, tasks should be specific, stated in positive terms, and clearly stated as to what is to be done within a specified time frame.

Adverse Beliefs. An individual may agree to a task however he or she may not fully disclose information about their values or beliefs. For example, a parent who believes that children are to obey is likely to be hesitant to utilize reward systems, believing that parents should not bargain with their children. Respecting and honoring different beliefs is important. Thus, having listened to their reasoning, you and the parents would renegotiate a task in line with their beliefs, based on the information that they provided. In practice with families or couples, beliefs about the behavior or motives of another person can influence completing or even engaging in a task. As a solution, you might develop

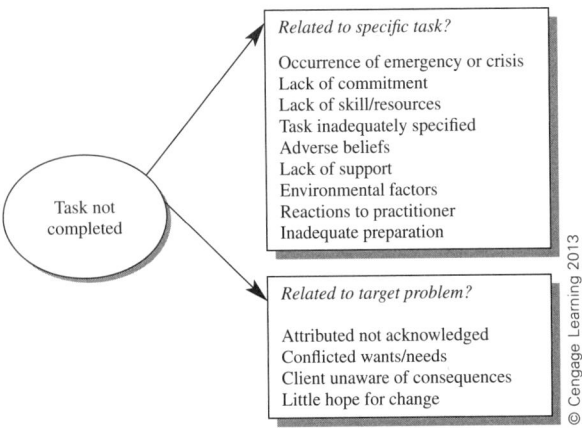

FIG-13-2 Reasons for Low Task Performance

a contract that states that all involved will strictly monitor his or her own task performance regardless of whether the other person does or does not.

Lack of Support. When a problem involves others or another system, the relevant individuals should be involved in supporting task accomplishment. For example, the teacher of the sixth grader should be encouraged to call on him when he raises his hand or give him an indication that she will do so in time. Support for completing tasks can also be related to family or environmental factors. For example, finding a subsidized apartment can be dependent on the availability of such housing. These are difficult situations, in which a ready solution may not be apparent, and you and the client may need to explore interim options. It can also be useful for you and the client to look for others in his or her network to provide support.

Negative Reactions to the Social Worker. Negative reactions to the social worker, both verbal and nonverbal can affect an individual's ability to complete tasks. Reactions can result from, for example, the social worker's arbitrary assignment of certain tasks. People are unlikely to be invested in taking an action on a task in which they have not been involved in creating. The following statement from a client highlights the way in which a social worker's lack of accountability and reliability can hamper a client's progress: "She keeps telling me that she is going to make a referral to the child care resource center, but week after week, she tells me that she was just too busy." Without the social worker completing her task on behalf of the client, the client was unable to complete her work. Furthermore, the client in this situation observed that the social worker was often late, seemed to be disorganized, unprepared, and distracted, leading her to believe that her case was unimportant. The message is clear, specifically, honor your commitments, be prepared and organized, be on time, and show that you care. Of course, these are the same expectations that we have of the people with whom we work.

Inadequate Preparation. In developing tasks, the skills, behavior, or time needed for the successful completion of specific tasks may have been overestimated or underestimated. Actually, it is better for clients to not attempt a task than for them to make an attempt and fail because they are unprepared. If the issue is related to timing, the time frame for completing a task can be extended. Should a skill be the issue, for example, communicating with a landlord, you can coach the individual by using behavioral rehearsal or modeling to increase his or her confidence.

Performance Problems Related to the Target Problem

Attributed, Not Acknowledged Problems. Low task performance is most likely to occur when clients are mandated (involuntary) or coerced (nonvoluntary) to implement a certain change. The reasoning for his or her reluctance may be attributed to their beliefs about what constituted a problem: "I don't have a drug problem. Sometimes I do a little meth [methamphetamine] with my buds [buddies], but that don't mean that I'm a drug head." Furthermore, when problems are attributed to an individual by someone else, he or she tends to be less committed to their resolution. In these instances, you can begin by acknowledging this fact, and respecting their reactions, and exploring incentives that might encourage them to complete tasks. Persistent inaction certainly speaks louder than words and the benefits of continuing to work with the individual should be carefully weighed.

Lack of Understanding of Consequences. An individual's failure to perform a related target problem task may stem from a lack of understanding about the consequences of his or her failure. For example, the consequences of failing to complete a chemical dependency treatment program and providing clean urinalysis samples should be explained.

Conflicting Needs and Wants. Certainly, what can initially appear to be a lack of commitment may actually be that an individual is faced with a competing and more pressing concern. The initial task remains important, however another issue, either new or existing, demands his or her attention. The situation need not be a crisis. It may simply mean that even though a client had prioritized a goal and developed a related task, there are other issues competing for his or her attention. Flexibility in these instances is called for, as the individual is unlikely to be able to focus until the competing concern is resolved.

Little Hope for Change. In spite of the fact that an individual has agreed to undertake a certain task, he or she may feel that completing the task may have little or no impact on the situation. This is an opportunity for you to help the client build on his or her strengths by calling attention to past successes. For instance, "I understand that you are feeling some anxiety about getting a job, and I can't guarantee that you will. But, remember how you felt about talking to the housing authority about rental assistance. You were able to do so, and you obtained a housing voucher." Crediting an individual with past successes is particularly useful to boost confidence when their perception of their ability to affect change is uncertain.

Even when preparation has been adequate and potential obstacles and barriers have been reviewed, the successful outcomes of task efforts are not guaranteed. The preceding discussion highlights valid reasons for low task performance. The intended message of this discussion is simple: A majority of the people with whom you work want relief from their difficulties and are motivated to take action. Nonetheless, their ability to do so can be hampered by their beliefs and other factors. To avoid or minimize the potential of them becoming discouraged, you should not interpret low task performance as a failure, but rather as an indication of the need for additional task planning. Another equally important factor is your use of empathy and your relationship with them to enhance their forward momentum.

Monitoring Progress

EP 2.1.10m

In the task-centered model, tasks are the instrumental action steps taken by the client and in some instances the practitioner. They are intended to alter or remediate the target concern and achieve the desired outcome. The continuous review of tasks maintains continuity and focus and monitors progress.

The following list of procedures outlines the systematic review of progress specific to the task-centered approach.

1. Once tasks have been identified and agreed upon, time in each session is devoted to a review of progress. In this process, both client and social worker are able to document which tasks have been completed and the extent to which the target problem has changed.
2. During the review process, if tasks have not been completed or have not had the intended effect on the target problem, barriers and obstacles and the reasons for low task performance are explored. When necessary, tasks are renegotiated or new tasks developed.

In reviewing task accomplishments, it is critical to discuss with the client the details about the conditions, actions, or behaviors that assisted them in achieving a task. Even when tasks have been only partially completed, it is important to connect the results they have achieved to their efforts. In doing so, you are highlighting and reinforcing their strengths and sense of competence.

In general, the systematic in-session review of progress provides immediate feedback of gains as well as alerting you and the individual as to whether adjustments need to be made. Afterwards, you and the individual move forward by mutually planning other tasks that will facilitate progress, albeit, incremental in some instances, toward the final goal. Ultimately, the completion of tasks related to the target concern is an indicator of progress toward goal attainment and the eventual move toward termination.

Strengths and Limitations

The task-centered system is the first empirically based social work model of a planned, short-term, problem-solving approach based on the principles and values of the profession (Kelly, 2008; Reid & Epstein, 1972). Conceptualized
EP 2.1.10a
into three distinct phases, the approach begins with an identified target problem of importance to the client. In instances where an individual has multiple concerns, he or she is asked to rank them in priority. The selection of goals and the implementation of related tasks represent the second phase. In this phase, tasks are identified as the instrumental action steps to affect the target problem and to eventually achieve the desired goal. As tasks are developed and implemented, both the client and the social worker continually review progress to maintain focus and ensure continuity. The third and final stage involves reviewing and monitoring progress and termination of the contact.

With more than 30 years of practice, research, and further development, the efficacy of the model has been supported by empirical evidence. The results of the research has shown the model to be effective with interpersonal and family problems, emotional distress, drug use, mental health and health-related concerns, transitions, inadequate resources, minors, and involuntary clients (Ramos & Tolson, 2008; Reid, 1992; Tolson, Reid & Garvin, 1994). The model's effectiveness has been demonstrated with diverse populations and situations in worldwide practice settings (Ramos & Garvin, 2003; Ramos & Tolson, 2008; Reid, 2000, 1996, 1997). The emphasis on taking action on problems acknowledged by clients is believed to be appealing to racial and ethnic minorities (Boyd-Franklin, 1989a; Devore & Schlesinger, 1999; Lum, 2004; Sue, 2006). Key aspects of the model, namely the use of tasks, have become foundational to increase the efficacy of a number of other types of interventions (Hoyt, 2000; Ramos & Tolson, 2008).

The model honors self-determination, strengths, and empowerment by allowing clients to define the problem, contribute judgment about goals and tasks, and participate in monitoring progress. To increase clients' self-efficacy and opportunity for mastery, obstacles to task completion and goal attainment are identified and resolved. When tasks are not completed, the reasons for low task performance are reviewed and new tasks, if indicated, are developed.

Opinions are mixed about the efficacy of the model with certain populations and in certain situations. Critiques of the central tenets of the model, in particular, time limits and the systematic structure, have led some to conclude that the development of a therapeutic relationship with clients is unlikely to evolve (Ramos & Tolson, 2008). Ramos and Tolson (2008) suggest that involuntary clients, especially those who refuse to identify a change or refuse to become engaged may not be good candidates for the approach. Of course, a central question might be whether any approach will work with such clients? Building on the basic thrust of the model, specifically the clients' view of the mandate and involving them in task implementation strategies, R. H. Rooney (2009) and Trotter (2006) demonstrated the model's applicability and effectiveness with this population. Both Rooney and Trotter found that the approach, when combined with other strategies, had the potential to reduce reactance and engage the client.

Crisis Intervention

EP 2.1.10a

The crisis intervention model discussed in this text is the equilibrium model, which is based on basic crisis theory. Knowledge of how to intervene with people who are experiencing a crisis is considered to be essential for skilled practice (Knox & Roberts, 2008). Depending on the nature of the crisis and the systems involved, it may be necessary for you to intervene at the micro, mezzo, and macro levels (Gelman & Mirabito, 2005). While multiple disciplines have played an important role in developing crisis theory, social workers have been responsible for advancing practice methods and skills and for formulating strategies for responding to crises (Bell, 1995; Fast, 2003; Komar, 1994; Lukton, 1982; Parad & Parad, 1990).

Tenets of the Crisis Intervention Equilibrium Model

EP 2.1.10a

The crisis equilibrium model is the basic approach to intervention. It is designed to reduce stress, relieve symptoms, and to restore functioning to the individual's pre-crisis state. Promptness of response, a key aspect of the model, is considered to be critical to prevent deterioration in functioning. It is during the acute period that people are most likely to be receptive to an intervention. The procedures of the model involve assessing the nature of the crisis, identifying priority concerns, and developing limited goals.

EP 2.1.10d

Assessment in the crisis situation, as outlined by James (2008), involves determining the following:

- *The severity of the crisis*
- *The client's current emotional status and level of mobility/immobility*
- *Alternatives, coping mechanisms, support systems, and other available resources*
- *The client's level of lethality; specifically, is the client a danger to self or others?*

James (2008) cites the Triage Assessment System developed by Meyer, Williams, Otten, and Schmidt (1991) as a "fast" and efficient way to assess and "obtain a real time estimate of what is occurring with a client" in a crisis situation (pp. 43–48). This three-dimensional assessment scheme provides a framework for you to assess the client's *affective, behavioral,* and *emotional* functioning, the severity of the situation, and to plan the appropriate intervention strategy. Where possible, you use the three **domains** to establish a baseline which could subsequently be compared to the Triage Assessment System results to determine the functioning level prior to and after the crisis (James, 2008).

Definition and Stages of Crisis

EP 2.1.10a

A *crisis* as defined by James (2008, p. 3) is "a perception of an event or situation as an intolerable difficulty that exceeds the resources or coping mechanism of the person." Prolonged, crisis-related stressors have the potential to severely affect cognitive, behavioral, and physical functioning.

In your work with clients, you have no doubt assisted them to deal with crisis situations some of which are related to their daily living. These situations may have ranged from everyday occurrences, for example, job loss, death, eviction, divorce, domestic violence, or child abuse and neglect, crime or relocation, and in some instances, more extreme situations such as a natural disaster. Crisis situations inevitably have a subjective element because people's perceptions and coping capacities vary widely. A crisis that is severely stressful and overwhelming for some people may be manageable for others.

Referencing the case of the Corning family, you will recall that Irwin's job loss set in motion a series of stressful events that were significant threats to the family's stability. While the family was not in a crisis per se, the continuation of stressful events could eventually reach a crisis level. In contrast, the act of revealing one's sexual orientation to an unsupportive family (no doubt a dreaded high-anxiety producing event) can result in an unmanageable crisis, accompanied by additional stressors for which relief is uncertain. Uncertainty can become an unsettling emotional stressor for refugees, immigrants, and migrants. They may simultaneously experience demands related to their transition and the related sense of loss as a result of leaving their homeland, familiar networks, and culture. Despite the stress of having to adjust to the norms and values and language of another country, they tend to perceive their relocation as an opportunity, unless the transition was not of their choosing.

EP 2.1.9a

At the core of the definition of basic crisis intervention theory is the assumption of *the big event*. There are segments of the population, however, in which cumulative events or circumstances can result in a perpetual state of crisis. Consider, for example, the hyper-vigilance of people who have entered the United States or another country without the required documentation papers or the very real threats experienced by gay and lesbian individuals as a result of hate crimes, brutal beatings, and even murder. Intense anxiety related to threats and potential harm is pervasive in some poor minority urban communities. Residents of these communities are faced with violence, often times negative encounters with the police, poverty-related stressors, and inadequate services or resources. Studies have shown that the continuous exposure to violence can have an enduring affect on minors, resulting in depression, delinquency, or acting-out behavior (Voisin, 2007; Maschi, 2006; Lindsey, Korr, Broitman, Bone, Green, & Leaf, 2006; Zeira, Astor & Benbenishty, 2003).

Emotional and psychosocial crises resulting from the experience of combat by military personnel, specifically post-traumatic stress disorder (PTSD), can pose a lifetime risk for the individual (Halpern & Tramontin, 2007; James, 2008). Stress-related symptoms may also be observed in professionals who work in highly stressful, emotionally charged situations (Bell, 2003; Curry, 2007; Knight, 2006; O'Hollaran & Linton, 2000).

EP 2.1.7b

The previously described scenarios are not closely associated with the "big event"; instead, they are woven into the fabric of everyday individual, family, work, and community life. The point that you should take away from these scenarios is that for those involved, life can be dominated by a series of ongoing crisis events that ultimately undermine the individual and community sense of self and organization, resulting in perpetual disequilibrium. Hence, a variety of clients may present the signs and symptoms associated with a crisis reaction as discussed in this next section.

Crisis Reactions

A *crisis reaction* may be described as any event or situation that upsets people's "normal psychic balance" (Lum, 2004, p. 272) to the extent that their sense of equilibrium is severely diminished. Examples consistent with the big event type crisis include terrorist attacks and natural and man-made disasters, such as tsunamis, hurricanes, and oil spills. In each of these circumstances, you might expect to find entire communities who feel particularly vulnerable and experience prolonged anxieties, physical, emotional, and cognitive distress, as well as an overall sense of grief and diminished coping capacity. When the big event occurs, all citizens are exposed to the trauma by constant media coverage and some can also experience a crisis reaction (Belkin, 1999).

EP 2.1.10a

Crisis intervention theory posits that people's reactions typically go through several stages, although theorists differ as to whether three or four stages are involved. The following description is a synthesis of stages identified by various authors (Caplan, 1964; James & Gilliland, 2001; Okun, 2002).

EP 2.1.10d

Stage 1: The initial tension is accompanied by shock and perhaps even denial of the crisis-provoking event.

Stage 2: To reduce the tension, the individual attempts to utilize his or her usual emergency problem-solving skills. If these skills fail to result in the lessening of their tension, the stress level will become heightened.

Stage 3: The individual experiences severe tension, feels confused, overwhelmed, helpless, angry, or perhaps acutely depressed. The length of this phase varies according to the nature of the hazardous event, the strengths and coping capacities of the person, and the degree of responsiveness from social support systems.

EP 2.1.10d

Patterns of behavior associated with the stages may be characterized as disorganization, recovery, and reorganization (Lum, 2004; Parad & Parad, 1990, 2006; Roberts, 1990, 2005). Of course, people's reactions and their progression can vary. Variations can depend on the point in which you have contact. In reacting to a crisis, the potential exists for people to cope in ways that are either adaptive or maladaptive. You should be aware, however, that prolonged stress may have exceeded their coping capacity and usual problem solving, so much so that they are unable to effectively handle the stressors. Achieving equilibrium for some may depend on the extent to which their strengths, resilience, and social supports are mobilized. In these instances, the individual can perhaps achieve a higher level of functioning. As suggested by James (2008), the crisis may evoke a positive change opportunity. Specifically, an individual's reaction to a crisis may be to seek help and be motivated to succeed, thereby using the opportunity for his or her benefit (James, 2008). For others, the level of tension and feelings of being overwhelmed can escalate and his or her coping patterns may reach a level of *danger*. Danger is evident when restoring equilibrium is not immediately possible because the individual is unable to function, in which case additional assistance is required (James, 2008).

Duration of Contact

Typically, crisis work is limited in its duration, occurring within a time period spanning 4 to 8 weeks, although some clients or situations may require a longer time period. It is expected that active and intensely focused work in a brief time period will assist people to achieve a degree of pre-crisis functioning. The duration of contact may depend on the type of services offered by your agency and the crisis situation. Ultimately, the time required to resolve a crisis depends on the stress level; the individual's ego strengths, social supports, and resources; and whether the crisis is acute or chronic.

EP 2.1.10j

Your contact with clients may be daily, in an office, at a shelter, in a hospital or in the home, especially during the acute crisis period. Interventions range from a single-session, telephone intervention to comprehensive services with groups, families, and entire communities (Fast, 2003; Gibar, 1992; James & Gilliland, 2001; West, Mercer, & Altheimer, 1993). Several factors guide the time-limited duration of contact:

- *The focus of crisis intervention is on the here-and-now. Hence, no attempt is made to deal with either pre-crisis personality dysfunction or intrapsychic conflict, although attention to these symptoms may be required.*
- *Goals are limited to alleviating distress and assisting clients to regain equilibrium.*
- *Tasks are identified and task performance is intended to help clients achieve a new state of equilibrium.*

In crisis situations, the level of incapacity presented by the client may require you to have a more active and directive role than you might have in other interventions. Even though you may direct and define tasks, you should encourage clients to participate to the extent that they are capable of doing so. Although an individual's ability to actively participate and perform tasks may be limited during periods of severe emotional distress, his or her capacity can increase as their distress level diminishes.

Intervening with Minors

EP 2.1.10j

Minors are more vulnerable and at risk to crisis or traumatic events (Halpern & Tramontin, 2007; James, 2008). Work by Terr (1995), as discussed by James (2008, p. 163), established *Type I* and *Type II* categories as related to a minor's reaction to a crisis. Type I involves a single and distinct crisis experience, the big event, in which symptoms and signs are manifested. For example, with Type I trauma, the minor can display "fully detailed etched-in memories, misperceptions, cognitive reappraisals and reasons of the event." Type II, in contrast, is the result of longstanding and repeated trauma, and can have a cumulative effect, in which the minor's psyche develops defensive and coping strategies, anxiety, depression, or acting our behavior (James, 2008; Voisin 2007, Lindsey, Korr, Broitman, Bone, Green, & Leaf, 2006; James, 2008; Maschi, 2006; Zeira, Astor & Benbenishty, 2003).

For minors, a crisis event has the potential to disrupt biological, social, and cognitive development and age can make a significant difference in how minors respond. The Type I category seems to fit best with the basic equilibrium crisis intervention approach, in which the focus is on restoring the pre-crisis state of their caregivers in order to help the minor.

To direct the intervention, Korol, Green, and Grace (1999) emphasize a developmental ecological framework. The premise of this framework is that the developmental stage and the environment within which the minor operates are interrelated (James, 2008). Within this framework, four attributes are identified and are intended to guide the crisis intervention with minors (Korol, et al, 1999). The four attributes, based on research findings, are summarized by Halpern & Tramontin (2007, pp. 149–150).

- Characteristics of the stressors, *including the perception of threat related to the event, physical proximity to the event, duration, and intensity.*
- Characteristics of the minor. *Developmental stage, gender, and vulnerability play a significant role in how a minor experiences a threat, as well as psychological or behavioral problems that existed prior to the threat.*
- The minor's efforts to cope. *Generally, a minor with good communications skills, a sense of self, internal locus of control, and average intelligence are indicators of a positive outcome.*
- Characteristics of the post-disaster environment. *The minor's reaction is strengthened by social supports from significant others and resources, which can reduce stress and act as protective factors.*

EP 2.1.10j

The Interactive Trauma/Grief-Focused Therapy (IT/G-FT) model is another approach to address the post-effects on minors following a crisis (Nader & Mello, 2008). Eclectic in nature, the model utilizes theories relevant to the situation, including psychodynamic and cognitive behavioral approaches. It relies on the narratives, emotions, cognitions, and memories of the minor and the aim is to assist them to recover and to regain the healthy aspects of pre-crisis functioning.

The stages of crisis and the reaction may differ with minors. They may, for example, need additional help in understanding their crisis reaction and in developing problem-solving skills. The Triage System assessment can be especially important in determining the cognition and behaviors of minors as a result of the crisis. Cognitively, a crisis event can increase minors' sense of vulnerability and their perceived lack of power. Behavioral interventions to a crisis event may involve the minor's coping by role-playing, for example, an all-powerful action figure of their choosing (Knox & Roberts, 2008).

The basic crisis intervention equilibrium model, consistent with generalist practice, is appropriate for minors who have experienced a Type I crisis event. Intervening should also include the developmental ecological framework, the attributes proposed by Korol and colleagues (1999) and Halpern and Tramontin (2007) and the behavioral approaches suggested by Nader and Mello (2008).

Benefits of a Crisis

Much of the literature has tended to focus on the adverse reactions or the effects that a crisis has on people. Not surprisingly, then, intervention strategies, while incorporating strengths, coping, and social support, have sought to restore functioning to the pre-crisis level. Some theorists and researchers suggest that negative events may actually promote growth in the aftermath of a crisis (Caplan, 1964; Halpern & Tramontin, 2007; James, 2008; McMillen & Fischer, 1998; McMillen, Zuravin, & Rideout, 1995; McMillen, Smith, & Fischer, 1997; Joseph, Williams, & Yule, 1993). Note however, that the findings are specific to adult populations.

EP 2.1.9a

EP 2.1.6b

Building on prior research and the notion of benefits advanced by Caplan (1964), McMillen and Fisher (1998) explored the perceived harm and benefits with individuals who have experienced a crisis event. Some people in the study reported experiencing benefits, in positive life changes, such as increased self-efficacy and spirituality, faith in people, and in community closeness.

The McMillen and Fisher study results are significant for two reasons:

- *The deficit approach to psychosocial consequences appears to influence how human services professionals view their clients and how clients view their experience. Specifically, professionals may tend to focus on the trauma alone, whereas clients may view the situation or event through multiple lenses.*
- *In understanding the positive benefits that accrue from crises, professionals are able to construct interventions that strengthen these factors and increase successful outcomes.*

These findings also emphasized the subjective nature of the crisis experience as a key element to be included in crisis intervention work. Understanding the individual's reaction to a crisis, their perception of harm to or vulnerability, and their affective, emotional, and behavioral functioning will assist you to plan and intervene appropriately. Otherwise, your intervention strategy may have little or no value to the client's situation.

Theoretical Framework

EP 2.1.7a

Parad (1965), Caplan (1964), and Golan (1981) were early and significant contributors to basic crisis intervention theory, delineating the nature of crises, stages, and intervention strategies for crisis resolution. Lukton (1982) further developed a practice theory and skills for social workers. Early crisis intervention theory spanned the life course to include grief and loss reactions, role transitions, traumatic events, and maturational or biopsychosocial crisis at various developmental stages (Lindemann, 1944, 1956; Rapoport, 1967). Early theories of crisis intervention strategies tended to reflect the psychoanalytic paradigm. For example, in Erikson's (1957) psychosocial stages of human development, a crisis was thought to develop if the individual failed to master the requisite developmental tasks in each stage.

Over time, additional theories have emerged because the basic crisis theory as a single framework was thought of as incapable of fully explaining the human response to trauma (Knox & Roberts, 2008; James, 2008). A prominent issue is that this theory paid little or no attention to environmental and situational factors as contributors to crisis and crisis reactions. In consequence, other crisis theories have emerged, influenced by ego psychology, cognitive behavioral, chaos, and ecological systems theories. In expanding theories related to crisis intervention, Okun (2002) and James (2008) have more broadly defined the context in which a crisis may occur. In doing so, they extended the underlying contextual and theoretical framework of crisis work.[2]

Application with Diverse Groups

EP 2.1.7b

An advantage of crisis intervention strategies is their use with different populations (Knox & Roberts, 2008). Lum (2004) asserts that crisis intervention as a generalist practice approach has "universal application to people of color" (p. 272). His assertion is based on the fact that people of color "often experience personal and environmental crisis" and in many instances they have "exhausted community and family resources" prior to seeking professional help (p. 273). For some, patterns of help-seeking behavior and historically based anxieties about formal helping can delay contact (Green, 1999). In consequence, crisis situation can reach a chronic state. In addition, influenced by culture, different communities may respond and cope differently to a traumatic event (Halpern & Tramontin, 2007).

EP 2.1.4c

James (2008), a prominent author of crisis intervention work, acknowledges the assumption that crisis intervention strategies represent ideals that are specific to Western norms and are unfamiliar to the majority of the world. In crisis work, Chazin, Kaplan, and Terio (2000) note that emphasizing crisis related deficits, rather than strengths and resources, can be particularly counterproductive with diverse groups. In this regard, there is perhaps merit in the perspectives of social constructionist and feminists. Specifically, they believe that the traditional clinical-focused procedures tend to emphasize normalcy. As such, they omit such pertinent factors as culture and inequality, faith, or injustice (Freud, 1999; Silove, 2000). In the aftermath of Hurricane Katrina, unavoidable questions about inequality and justice were raised with respect to the crisis response to citizens of the 9th Ward in New Orleans. You might, however, question whether the response to this segment of the population was the result of systemic inequality and structural barriers or the shortcomings of the crisis model. In many respects, one might conclude that it was the unequal, pre-disaster quality of their lives, when combined with unrelenting post-events, that profoundly overwhelmed and affected the coping capacity of the residents of the 9th Ward.

EP 2.1.6b & 2.1.7b

Although research and literature related to crisis intervention strategies with regard to culture, gender, and racial groups is limited, there is work in this arena that has advanced our knowledge base. Examples include Congress (2000) and Potocki-Tripodi (2002), with a focus on culturally diverse and immigrant families, and Cornelius, Simpson, Ting, Wiggins, and Lipford (2003) and Ligon (1997) with African Americans. In their work, Halpern & Tramontin (2007) amplify how culturally based perceptions influence expectations in certain Asian communities. In particular, they stress that reactions to a crisis can differ from those in Western societies. In working with immigrants and refugees, Potocky-Tripodi (2002) suggests that, while crisis intervention strategies are appropriate, ideally they should be implemented as preventive measures prior to the resettlement stage. Congress (2002, 2000) identifies common precipitants of crisis among immigrants and refugees; namely, intergenerational conflicts, changes in roles, unemployment, and interactions with formal institutions in which crisis strategies are appropriate. Ligon (1997) departs somewhat from

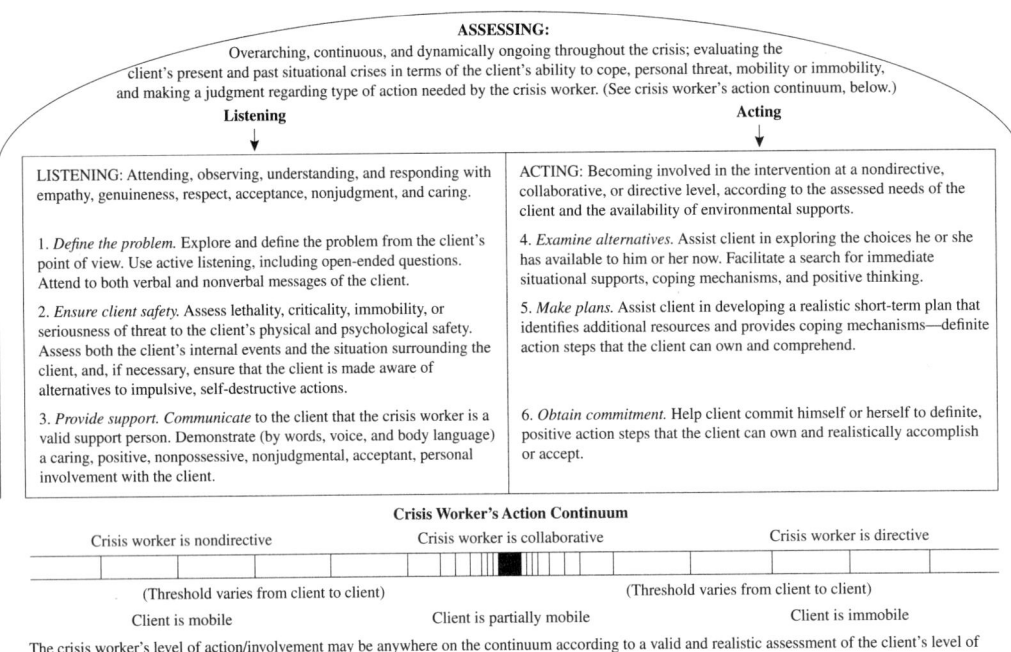

FIG-13-3 The Six-Step Model of Crisis Intervention

SOURCE: From JAMES, "Crisis Intervention Strategies", 6E. © 2008 Wadsworth, a part of Cengage Learning, Inc. Reproduced by permission. www.cengage.com/permissions.

the basic equilibrium crisis model, relying instead on cultural and ecological systems perspectives, integrated with empowerment. Using this framework Ligon demonstrated the merit of these perspectives with populations of color and individuals with serious health or mental health concerns. Poindexter (1997) makes the point that for HIV-infected individuals, the experience may involve a series of crises beginning with them learning of the disease as a precipitating event. As the condition progresses, multiple crises—social, situational, and developmental—can occur simultaneously. Poindexter's work, along with that of Ell (1995), Ligon (1997), and Potocky-Tripodi (2002), is significant in that it helps us to move beyond certain assumptions about the episodic nature of crises and to understand the evolving stages of certain crisis situations.

EP 2.1.4b

Crisis intervention, like other practice models, calls for multicultural helping that includes self-knowledge, awareness of bias, knowledge of the status and culture of diverse groups, and the willingness to use alternative strategies appropriate to the client's culture and situation (James, 2008; Sue, 2006; Sommers-Flanagan, 2007). Perhaps the most important factor for you to recognize is that crisis work, like any other problem-solving strategy, should include the world-view of the client, the meaning that he or she ascribes to the situation, and their patterns of coping and preferences for resolution.

Process and Procedures of Crisis Intervention

The processes and procedures of the six-step crisis intervention model, initially developed by Gilliland (1982) for systematically intervening in a crisis situation, are illustrated in Figure 13-3. These steps, which have continued to be the procedures of the basic crisis model, are consistent with the eclectic problem-solving approach. The figure outlines the fundamental skills and range of actions required for you to take in a crisis situation. Procedures for implementing the model are applied to the case of Lia, a pregnant teen. Cultural tensions related to her pregnancy are also discussed.

EP 2.1.10j

Step 1: Define the Problem

As a social worker in a crisis situation, you must determine the unique meaning of a crisis and the severity of the situation to the client. Having clients talk about the meaning and significance of the crisis can be a relieving cathartic process and thus, highly therapeutic for them. Gathering this information provides you with

IDEAS IN ACTION

The problem as presented by Lia, age 17 years, was that she was pregnant and unmarried. During the school year she participated in a school-based teen group for female students. On the day of the referral, Lia became so emotionally distraught that the group leader asked the group to take a break so that she could talk with her individually. Lia told the leader that she was pregnant and that she was in trouble with her family as a result. The group leader referred her to a social worker at the community based mental health center, located adjacent to the school. Lia calmed down after the group leader explained her reason for making the referral and the fact that the social worker was able to see her immediately. As she explained her situation to the social worker, however, she became highly distressed.

essential information about how the client defines their problem.

Cultural factors and status are equally essential in assessing clients' problem definitions and reactions to crisis situations. Situations deemed to be crises vary widely from one culture to another, as do the reactions to them. Interventions work best when they include cultural values, beliefs, and rituals (e.g., spiritual healing, circles of care) as critical reference points.

During the session with Lia in the Ideas in Action box, the social worker's initial tasks in this session were twofold:

- Assess and alleviate Lia's emotional distress
- Elicit Lia's definition of the problem

EP 2.1.10d

Assess and Alleviate Lia's emotional distress: *During the interview Lia cried, had trouble breathing, and expressed concern about whether the social worker could understand her situation. The social worker used a breathing technique to help her calm down. Listening, empathetic and nonjudgmental responses were also useful. Eventually the social worker was able to gain an understanding of the magnitude of her distress in relationship to her problem. During their conversation, Lia stated that she had thought about suicide. Furthermore, she had shared her thoughts in a conversation with her 12-year-old brother.*

EP 2.1.10b

By listening and responding empathically, the social worker encouraged Lia to talk about her feelings, which alleviated some of her emotional distress. When, however, the social worker learned that she had thought about hurting herself, this information prompted an immediate referral to the center's mental health services for an evaluation. As she questioned Lia further about the potential to harm herself, a hopeful sign was the fact that she expressed concern for the safety and well-being of her unborn child. In addition, she indicated that she wanted to continue her involvement with the teen group.

Eliciting the client's definition of the problem: *Lia's problem as she defined it was being pregnant and unmarried, which was further complicated by the cultural norms of her community. The severity of the situation became evident when Lia recounted her family's response to her pregnancy, specifically, her pregnancy without her being married, brought shame to the family. The crisis escalated when, upon learning that she was pregnant, her father had dismissed her from the family. He refused to talk to her or allow other family members to do so. The fact that Lia faced social ostracism, loss of face, and would be disconnected from her family and members of the clan added to her distress.*

EP 2.1.10d & 2.1.7b

Clearly, being pregnant and unmarried was worrisome to Lia, but she believed that she could manage her situation and had some ideas about how to do so. Her family's definition of the problem, however, was grounded in the context of cultural norms and expectations. Unwed pregnancy requires considerable adaptation in most cultures, but may pose an extreme threat for an individual who is a first-generation member immigrant family member. While her parents had made significant adjustments to their new culture, Lia's pregnancy was a situation for which the parents did not have a point of reference. Therefore, in this context, being unwed and pregnant as defined by Lia's family and community and their reactions became a multiple-layered crisis, all of which contributed to the significance of the crisis and her level of distress.

Step 2: Ensure Client Safety

EP 2.1.10i

Ensuring client safety is the first and foremost concern in crisis intervention and an ongoing consideration (James, 2008; James & Gilliland, 2001). Safety involves deliberate steps to minimize the "physical and psychological" danger to the client or others (James, 2008). The social worker requested, and Lia agreed to complete, a depression scale. The results confirmed the necessity of making the referral to the center's mental health services for further evaluation.

Because Lia had considered self-harm, the social worker developed a safety plan contract with her, with each identifying resources, including a crisis hotline that Lia would call when her feelings reached a level in which she considered harming herself. As an additional precaution, the social worker reminded Lia of her desire to keep her unborn child safe.

EP 2.1.10d

In the assessment of her affective, cognitive, and behavioral domains, Lia's scores were moderate. Even so, the social worker made the referral for further evaluation. She also shared her observation of Lia's coping and resilient behaviors, namely that she often volunteered for the closing shift at work and afterwards walked to her sister's home to spend the night because she could not go home.

While she had missed several days of school, she continued to participate in the teen group. Furthermore, the fact that she was concerned about the well-being of her unborn child was an indication of her future-oriented thinking. But there was an additional concern for her safety related to Lia working late and walking alone to her sister's home, thus the she and the social worker explored other options.

In assessing the three domains, the social worker was able to evaluate the extent of Lia's adaptive and coping capacities. She also learned about family resources that could be tapped to alleviate some of her distress as well as options to ensure her safety.

Step 3: Provide Support

EP 2.1.10i

Within this step, the social worker's objective was to identify Lia's social support systems because mobilizing a helping network can be an essential aspect of intervening in a crisis situation. Social supports may include friends, relatives, and in some cases institutional programs that care about the client and can provide comfort and compassion (James & Gilliland, 2001).

As Lia and the social worker explored potential support resources, several were identified: her sister and an aunt and certain clan members who were sympathetic to her situation. These resources were individuals, including the social worker, with whom she would have daily contact, and they were also included in the safety plan. A school-based group for pregnant and parenting teens was identified as a new resource. In a supportive role, the social worker walked with her to her appointment for a mental status evaluation and also introduced her to the social worker and nurse practitioner in the healthy baby program at the center.

Step 4: Examine Alternatives

EP 2.1.10j

In this step, both the social worker and Lia explored courses of action appropriate to her situation. Of course, some choices that they considered were better and more realistic than others. Thus it was important for them to selectively prioritize available options. Ideally, alternatives are considered to the extent to which they are:

- *Situational supports, involve people who care about what happens to the individual*
- *Coping mechanisms that represent actions, behaviors, or environmental resources that may use to get past the crisis situation*
- *Positive and constructive thinking patterns that effectively alter how an individual views the problem, thereby lessening his or her level of stress and anxiety*

Lia had actually thought of alternatives, yet initially she was sufficiently immobilized emotionally and had not acted upon them. For example, in response to the threat from her father to change the locks on the doors, which forced her out of the home, she had considered moving in with her sister or aunt *(situational supports)* until after her child was born. Afterwards, she would be 18 years of age and able to live independently. Instead of acting on this option, however, she planned to wait until her parents were asleep or at work and appeal to her siblings *(coping mechanism)* to let her in the house. In the past, her siblings had opened the door for her when she had stayed out late with her boyfriend. Relying on this choice was a short-term solution at best, and posed a greater risk for both Lia and her siblings.

A more viable alternative suggested by the social worker involved Lia moving into a transitional housing complex for pregnant teens, located near her high school and job *(highlighting constructive thinking and action)*.

Program services offered in the housing complex included transportation to prenatal visits, group counseling, independent living skills classes, and assistance in finding permanent housing. Although she was initially reluctant, Lia agreed to consider this option. Social workers who understand the client's point of view may be better able to plan alternatives and encourage clients to consider other options. For example, Lia's qualms about the pregnant teen housing program reflected her desire to remain with, or at least near, her family and community.

Of course there were additional alternatives to consider in stabilizing a crisis situation. You should, however, be aware that multiple options for can be overwhelming. Furthermore, the alternatives that you and the client consider should be "realistic" to the situation (James, 2008). In Lia's case, two options were discussed: moving in with her aunt on a short-term basis and a housing facility for pregnant teens. Lia chose the housing program because of the supportive services that were available. She and the social worker, however, also discussed ways in which she could have some contact with her family.

Step 5: Making Plans

EP 2.1.10f

Planning and contracting flow from the previous steps and involve the same planning and action steps that were discussed in Chapter 12. In this step, Lia and the social worker agreed on specific action steps or tasks. General and specific tasks, will, of course, vary according to the nature of the crisis situation and the unique characteristics of each person and/or family.

In developing and negotiating tasks, the social worker solicited Lia's views on what she believed would help her to function at a level of pre-crisis equilibrium. In their planning, they identified her safety as a priority and the relevant tasks were developed. Other tasks were created related to her eventual move to the pregnant teen housing facility.

Lia's estrangement from her parents was a central source of her distress. The social worker asked Lia to consider a task of writing a letter of apology to her parents and also whether such a gesture was culturally appropriate. Lia was unsure and she proposed an interim task of talking to her aunt about the letter.

EP 2.1.1c

There are times during this step when your interaction with a client requires you to be directive. For example, the idea of writing a letter to her family was the social worker's idea. James and Gilliand (2001), however, caution against "benevolently imposing" a plan on clients. Instead, you should strive to find a balance between being directive and respecting the individual's autonomy by encouraging and reinforcing feasible independent actions. As it turned out, Lia thought the idea was a good one, yet she was unsure about the impact that the letter might have, hence the decision to talk with her aunt before writing the letter.

Step 6: Obtaining Commitment

EP 2.1.10j

Completing tasks, which flow directly from the previous step, are considered to be essential to an individual's mastery of crisis situations. In the sixth and final step, Lia and the social worker committed to collaboratively engage in specific, intentional, and positive tasks designed to restore her to a level of pre-crisis functioning.

After a week, Lia informed the social worker that she was ready to move forward and develop tasks related to the plan to move into the housing facility for pregnant teens. In the meantime, she proposed living with her sister or her aunt, perhaps dividing her time between the two of them. A summary of the agreed-upon tasks involved the following:

Lia's Tasks

- Call the 24-hour crisis line or other supports when she was feeling overwhelmed
- Talk to her sister or aunt about moving in with one of them
- Visit the pregnant teen housing facility
- Explore ways to have contact with family members
- Continue to attend the school-based teen group

Social Worker

- Provide Lia with information on the pregnant teen facility program prior to her visit
- Accompany Lia on her visit to the housing program
- Obtain information about financial support for Lia and her unborn child

When Lia began her relationship with the social worker she was in a highly emotional state. In assessing the three domains, the social worker was able to evaluate the extent of Lia's adaptive and coping capacities. She also learned about family resources that could be tapped to alleviate some of her distress as well as options to ensure her safety. Subsequent tasks were developed that were intended to move Lia beyond the crisis of her pregnancy. You will note that not all of her concerns were resolved. Nonetheless, the tasks developed were instrumental in assisting her to gain a level of equilibrium.

Anticipatory Guidance

EP 2.1.10i

In addition to completing the six steps of the model, you may also find anticipatory guidance to be a complimentary technique. This technique involves assisting clients to anticipate future crisis situations and to plan coping strategies that will prepare them to face future stressors. Similar to identifying obstacles and barriers in the task-centered model, anticipatory guidance involves a discussion of scenarios of potential or future stressors. Used in Lia's case, the social worker and Lia discussed ways in which she could cope in the event that, despite her best efforts, she remained estranged from her family. They might also explore stressors related to the eventual but normative stress of the birth of her baby and living in a group setting with other pregnant teens. In their discussion, the social worker helped Lia to focus on her problem-solving, coping, and adaptation skills in her current situation. For example, Lia has proposed living with her aunt or sister as a temporary solution to her home situation, which showed her aptitude for problem-solving and adaptation capacities.

In using anticipatory guidance, it is important that you do not convey an expectation that people will always be able to independently manage future crisis situations. Even though you reassured them of their skills and helped them to anticipate future scenarios, you should clarify that you or other professionals are available if they need future help.

Strengths and Limitations

EP 2.1.10a

The crisis intervention equilibrium/disequilibrium model involves a structured, time-limited series of steps utilizing techniques that are guided by basic crisis theory. The initial intervention phase has three strategic objectives: (1) to relieve the individual's emotional distress, (2) to complete an assessment of their cognitive, behavioral, and emotional functioning, and (3) to plan the strategy of intervention, focusing on relevant tasks they are to perform.

Much of the theory upon which the equilibrium model is based assumes that people experience an event or situation that alters their usual patterns of living. Therefore, the goal of the intervention is to restore them to a pre-crisis level of functioning.

Over time, in recognition that no one theory is capable of defining or explaining a crisis, other theories and models have influenced an expanded classification for different kinds of crises and trauma and crisis responses. Models have also evolved that have emphasized the need to respond to crisis needs differently, in particular with minors, in consideration of their developmental age and stage. Promising research has demonstrated the effectiveness of crisis strategies with diverse populations by integrating aspects of other theories. These works represent significant contributions in that they advance our understanding and ability to differentiate crisis work.

While there is consensus about the definition of a crisis, it is also understood that what actually constitutes a crisis may be individually and culturally defined. Similarly, perceptions of a crisis vary based on associated threats, individual cognitions, and the significance of the situation, ego strengths, coping capacity, and problem-solving skills. In some instances, people can perceive and articulate positive benefits as a result of a negative experience. Of course, a perception of benefit may be limited by the nature and severity of the crisis.

The basic model retains the assumption of a crisis as an episodic, time-limited event. As such, crisis professionals aim to relieve emotional distress and develop a plan of action so that an individual or family's pre-crisis level of functioning is restored. Ell (1995) questions the assumption of time-limited crisis as well as the notion of homeostasis—specifically, whether the goal of restoring equilibrium is always possible. Ongoing difficulties in the daily lives of people who are exposed to the chronic and constant state of vulnerability in their environments can mean that the focus on time-limited crisis episodes is neither feasible nor realistic. The efficacy of crisis intervention strategies is not entirely diminished by Ell's observations. They do, however, suggest significant factors that can impact cognitive, affective, and behavioral functioning as a result of the cumulative effects of ongoing distress.

Understanding basic crisis theory provides you with a framework for working with both adults and minors. The model is consistent with generalist practice and utilizes the practice values, knowledge, and skills with which you are already familiar.

Cognitive Restructuring

Cognitive restructuring is a therapeutic process derived from cognitive-behavioral therapy (CBT). Also referred to as cognitive replacement, cognitive restructuring is "considered to be the cornerstone of cognitive behavioral

EP 2.1.10a

approaches" (Cormier & Nurius, 2003, p. 435). Intervention techniques in cognitive behavioral therapy are designed to help individuals modify their beliefs, faulty thought patterns or perceptions, and destructive verbalizations, thereby leading to changes in behavior. An assumption of cognitive restructuring is that people often manifest cognitive distortions which then affect a person's emotions and actions. Distortions are irrational thoughts derived from negative schemas that lead to unrealistic interpretations of people, events, or circumstances. Frequently, although an individual may be aware of his or her thinking, he or she may still lack the emotional strength to alter the schematic thought patterns.

Theoretical Framework

EP 2.1.7a

For you to fully appreciate the foundation of cognitive restructuring, it is important that you understand the theories upon which the procedures of the technique are based. Cognitive-behavior therapy attempts to alter the individual's interpretation of self and his or her environment and the manner in which he or she creates interpretations. The behavior of people is considered to originate from their processing of both internal and external information. According to cognitive theorists, most social and behavioral problems or dysfunctions are directly related to the misconceptions that people hold about themselves, other people, and various life situations (J. Beck, 1995; Dobson & Dozios, 2001). An understanding of the reciprocal relationship of cognition, affect, and behavior is considered to be central in using this approach.

The early and historic work of Ellis (1962), Beck (1976), and others in this arena led to cognitive theories and techniques that can be applied directly and systematically to problems of cognitive dysfunction. Ellis's (1962) seminal work, *Reason and Emotion in Psychotherapy*, explicated the theory underlying *Rational-Emotive Therapy* (RET). Perhaps the most significant is The *Cognitive Therapy of Depression*, which is widely recognized as the definitive work on treatment of depression (Beck, Rush, Shaw, & Emery, 1979).

The classical work of Pavlov (1927) related to conditioning and the operant conditioning studies of Skinner (1974) are prominent in the theoretical framework of cognitive behavioral therapy (Cobb, 2008). Learning as a primary focus is influenced by Bandura's (1986) social learning theory. According to social learning theory, thoughts and emotions are best understood in the context of behaviors associated with cognition or cognitive processes, as well as the extent to which individuals adapt and respond to different stimuli and make self-judgments. Increasingly, cognitive behavioral approaches include social constructionists' perspectives of the specific realities of different clients, and unique behaviors relative to their culture, beliefs, and worldview (Berlin, 2001; Cobb, 2008; Cormier & Nurius, 2003).

In the 1960s, behavioral theory and methods were introduced by Edwin Thomas at the University of Michigan (Gambrill, 1995). Berlin's (2001) *Clinical Social Work Practice: A Cognitive-Integrative Approach* is a significant contribution to adaptation of cognitive behavioral therapy to social work practice.[4]

Tenets of Cognitive Behavioral Therapy-Cognitive Restructuring

EP 2.1.10a & 2.1.1c & 2.1.7a

In general, the goal of cognitive behavioral intervention strategies is to increase the client's cognitive and behavioral skills so as to enhance his or her functioning. Restructuring is a cognitive procedural technique that aims to change a client's thoughts, feelings, or overt behaviors that contribute to and maintain problem behavior. To be effective in using cognitive restructuring as an intervention strategy you must be skilled in assessing cognitive functioning and in applying appropriate interventions.

Cognitive behavioral theory is based on the assumption that people construct their own reality. It is within the realm of processing information that people assess and make judgments that fit into their cognitive schema. The basic tenets of the cognitive-behavioral theory are:

- *Thinking* is a primary determinant of behavior and involves statements that people say to or about themselves. This inner dialogue, rather than unconscious forces, is critical to understanding behavior. To fully grasp this first tenet, you must clearly differentiate thinking from feeling, as confusing feelings with thoughts tend to create confusion in communication. This confusion can be observed in messages such as "I feel our relationship is on the rocks," or "I feel that the teacher does not like me." Here, the use of the word *feel* does not actually identify feelings, but rather it embodies the individual's *thought* or *belief*. Thoughts per se are devoid of feelings, although they are often accompanied by and generate feelings or emotions. *Feelings* consist of emotions, such as sadness, joy, or disappointment.

- *Cognitions* affect behavior, which is manifested in behavioral responses. Behavioral responses are a function of the cognitive processes of attention, retention, production, and motivation, as well as of rewarding or unrewarding consequences (Bandura, 1986). Cognitions that lead to cognitive distortions or faulty thinking can be monitored and changed.
- *Behavioral change* involves assisting people to make constructive change by focusing on their misconceptions and the extent to which they produce or contribute to their problems. The thrust is that a change in behavior can be accomplished by changing the way in which people think.

In identifying distortions and faulty thoughts and behaviors, new patterns of thinking can be learned. You should, of course, temper the assumptions of these tenets in recognition of the fact that there are other factors that can influence the ways in which people see themselves, think and process information. Specifically, cognitions are not necessarily faulty given the realities of culture, unequal sociopolitical structures, and social interactions in which class, race, gender, or sexual orientation are major contextual life issues. The realities of people's lives and their beliefs have a significant impact on their thinking and cognitions, and therefore, the relationship between cognition, culture, and context should not be minimized or overlooked (Hays, 2009; Pollack, 2004; Berlin, 2001).

What Are Cognitive Distortions?

EP 2.1.7a

Beck (1967), in separating thinking from cognition, identified automatic thoughts and cognitive distortions as factors for which cognitive restructuring is indicated. The processing of information for most of us is automatic as our minds attempt to navigate and narrate our interactions and environment. Problems occur when thoughts are consistently distorted because of an individual's ingrained beliefs and faulty reasoning. While cognitive distortions are irrational, they make logical sense to the individual. Moreover, distortions maintain negative thinking and reinforce negative emotions. The most common types of distortions and negative thinking patterns conceptualized by Beck (1975) have been summarized in the literature (Leahy & Holland, 2000; Walsh, 2006) and are as follows:

- *All or Nothing Thinking* involves seeing things as all or nothing scenarios, and in most instances the glass is always half empty. "I wanted to do well on the exam, and now that I didn't, I will never get into graduate school." "If I don't smoke stuff [dope] with my friends they won't ever hang with me." "Unless we know the background of these clients, we won't be able to help them." In these statements, you may see the similarities between this thinking and catastrophizing and overgeneralizing
- *Blaming* occurs when an individual perceives others as the source of negative feelings or emotions, and can therefore avoid taking responsibility. "I feel so stressed out because a driver cut in front of me on the way home." "Her snippy attitude about going shopping with me put me in a bad mood."
- *Catastrophizing* is the belief that if a particular event or situation occurs, the results would be unbearable, effectively influencing your sense of self-worth. "I need to study all the time, because if I don't get the highest grade possible on the exam, I will lose my financial aid and return home a failure."
- *Discounting Positives* is the tendency to disqualify or minimize the good things that you or others do, and instead treats a positive as a negative. "My friends said that I looked great in my dress I got at the secondhand store, but really, they were just being nice to me because they felt sorry for me because I don't have money." Similarly, you are reviewing evaluations after making a presentation and you focus on that, "Of the forty people at the presentation, two said that I was boring," instead of focusing on the 38 positive responses.
- *Emotional Reasoning* guides your interpretation based on how you feel, rather than reality. Interpretations and beliefs are facts bolstered by negative emotions, which are assumed to reflect reality. "If I feel stuck [stupid] in social situations, then that's really who I am."
- *Inability to Disconfirm* functions very much like a barricade in that you are unable to accept any information that is inconsistent with your beliefs or negative thoughts. For example, if your sister, with whom you frequently argue, says that she is willing to keep your kids any other night except tonight because she has an appointment, your mental response may be "That's not the real reason. She has

never liked me or my kids," which in effect, discounts the numerous other occasions that she has cared for your children.

- *Judgment Focus* leads to a perception of self and others or an assessment of events as good or bad, excellent or awful, rather than describing, accepting, or attempting to understand what is happening or considering alternatives. "*I know that when I go to a party people won't talk to me.*" In some instances, you may establish arbitrary standards by which you measure yourself, only to find that you are unable to perform at this level, "*I won't do well in the class no matter how hard I try*" is an example of a self-defeating judgment statement, as is "*Everyone in the class gets good grades, but not me.*" A judgment in contrast to one that is self-defeating is an assumption that a presentation was good because "*a lot of people came.*"
- *Jumping to Conclusions* assumes a negative when there may be limited supporting evidence. Assumptions may also take the form of mind reading and fortune telling based on a prediction of a negative outcome. "*If I don't watch her children, she will be upset with me, a risk that I am unwilling to take.*"
- *Mind Reading* assumes that you know what people will think, do or respond. "*There's no point in my asking my daughter to visit me more often. She will just see it as my attempt to get attention or embarrass her. If I bring up the topic, she and I will end up in an argument; besides, she is busy with her own family.*"
- *Negative (mental) Filtering* results in mentally singling out bad events and ignoring the positives. "*As I was standing in the hallway at work, this kid bumped into me, you know, they are all like that. I was so angry. Then he turned around and apologized, but I pretended not to hear him. He should have apologized sooner.*" In some instances, negative filters are linked to thoughts that are overgeneralized to people or events.
- *Overgeneralizations*, or globalization, involve perceiving isolated events and using them to reach broad conclusions. "*Today, when I raised my hand in class, the instructor called on another student. He never calls on me.*" Labeling is another form of overgeneralizing in which a negative label is attached to self or others based on a single incident. "*I am not a very good student, so he does not value my opinion.*" "*He is a lousy instructor otherwise he would help everyone [me].*"

- *Personalizing* assumes that you had a role in or that you are responsible for a negative situation, assuming that the results were in your control. "*We were close friends and then she was called to active duty and we loss contact.*" Personalizing, when applied to others, is very much like blaming. "*She could have written to me while she was away.*" "*The party that I planned in the park was a failure because it rained and people left early.*"
- *Regret Orientation* is generally focused on the past, "*If I had worked harder, I could have gotten a better grade.*" "*I had a chance for a better job, if I had been willing to relocate to a different city.*"
- *Should Statements* are about self-failure or judgments about others relative to how things should be. "*I should be able to take the bus on my own when I work late.*" "*My sister ought to be willing to care for my child when I am working late.*" Judging statements about others generally result in feelings of resentment and anger. "*My sister has a husband, so she doesn't really understand how hard it is for me to manage as a single parent.*"
- *Unfair Comparisons* measure self with others who you believe have desirable attributes. "*She is prettier than I am.*" "*Everybody in the class is smarter than me.*" Unfair comparisons can also lead to should or shouldn't statements when comparing self to others; for example, "*Even if she is prettier than me, she shouldn't wear that color lip gloss.*" "*My college roommate is a CEO already, I'm nothing compared to him.*"
- *What Ifs* is the tendency for you to continually question yourself about the potential for events or the catastrophe that might happen. "*I would go to the doctor to have her look at the mole on my back, but what if she tells me that I am really sick?*" "*What if I tell my sister that I can't watch her kids tonight and she gets upset with me and she refuses to talk to me ever again?*"

In each of the previous categories you are able to see how distorted and negative thoughts fit within an individual's cognitive schema. Schemas, either positive or negative, are the memory patterns that an individual uses to organize information (Berlin, 2001; Cormier & Nurius, 2003; McQuaide & Ehrenreich, 1997). Nonetheless, whether they emanate from a strengths or deficit orientation, schemas are shortcuts in thinking. Rather than processing information, the individual quickly accesses

EP 2.1.10j

repeatable content in his or her mind set, without further evaluation. Because schemas represent engrained beliefs, it is often difficult for people to hear or process different information because doing so causes them to experience cognitive dissonance. Specifically, dissonance occurs when the individual is presented with new information or an alternative explanation that is inconsistent to his or her thoughts. When this happens, the individual can experience a high level of stress, so much so, that he or she may shut down.

The activation of a negative schema can result from external or internal events that are adaptive or maladaptive. It is the latter that is the focus of your work with clients. Consider the influence of the negative image when the youth bumped into the woman in the hallway. Her automatic thought was, "They are all like that." Even though he apologized, her memory pattern (her global thinking about "they") was already operating in full force. Consequently, she was unable to process the youth's apology as new information, and therefore, unable to alter her cognition of the event. Of course, this event could have been triggered by a negative past experience or simply be the result of her ingrained biased thinking. If we were to examine this same situation from an internal vantage point, context would involve assessing her mood at the time of the incident and the extent to which it influenced her cognition and behavior. In either case, it is important that you first determine the context and the type of situation that triggers and maintains problematic behavior (Cormier & Nurius, 2003; Berlin, 2001). Further, where negative filtering about self and others has emotional content, blaming statements may be related to the mood of the individual at a particular point in time. By the same token, negative thoughts may be grounded in the individual's reality, however irrational the thoughts may appear to be. Hence you would assess whether an external and internal stimuli led to cognitive errors is an actual distortions or an individual's misunderstanding of his or her experiences. Keep in mind that negative thoughts and schemas do not represent the whole person. People generally are able to go about their daily lives until such time that an external or internal event ignites a particular thought pattern, upon which their reality is constructed.

EP 2.1.7b

You should also be mindful of the fact that marginalized and oppressed people and involuntary clients are often perceived as negative thinkers with distorted realities. When faced with their narrative, we may tend to think of them as overgeneralizing, blaming others for their misfortune or jumping to conclusions. Yet, if their narrative is derived from their experience of continually encountering adverse events or inequality, can we conclude, without further examination that their thoughts are actually distortions or discrepancies? A different culture than your own may also be challenging, especially if cultural practices and traditions are inconsistent with what you believe to be truth. As difficult as it may be for us to acknowledge truths that may be different from our own, ultimately, we must focus on what is meaningful to the client, rather than what we might consider to be an acceptable pattern of thinking and behaving.

EP 2.1.4b

Empirical Evidence and Uses of Cognitive Restructuring

Cognitive restructuring procedures are particularly relevant for treating problems associated with low self-esteem, distorted perceptions in interpersonal relations, unrealistic expectations of self, others, and life in general, irrational fears, panic, anxiety, and depression; control of anger and other impulses, and lack of assertiveness (Cormier & Nurius, 2003; Walsh, 2006). Selected studies have demonstrated the range of cognitive restructuring components in treating anger (Dahlen & Deffenbacher, 2000), impulse control associated with child abuse and gambling (Sharpe & Tarrier, 1992), and substance abuse and relapse (Bakker, Ward, Cryer, & Hudson, 1997; Steigerwold & Stone, 1999). Results of studies have also shown cognitive restructuring to be effective in the treatment of social phobias and anxiety (Feeny, 2004), spousal care-giver support groups (Gendron, Poitras, Dastoor, & Perodeau, 1996), and in crisis or trauma situations (Glancy & Saini, 2005; Jaycox, Zoellner, & Foa, 2002). The procedures of the cognitive restructuring are often blended with other interventions (e.g., modeling, behavioral rehearsal, imagery, psychoeducation) because combinations of interventions are believed to be more potent than single interventions in producing change (Corcoran, 2002).

EP 2.1.6b

Utilization with Minors

In comparison to adult populations, there are fewer studies that show evidence of effectiveness and the use of cognitive restructuring with minors. When combined with other strategies, for

EP 2.1.6b

example, narrative and enactive performance-based procedures, cognitive restructuring can be effective with younger minors. The work of Graham (1998) found that distorted thinking can affect the social and interpersonal skills of minors. Studies conducted by Rheingold, Herbert, and Franklin (2003) and Guadiano and Herbert (2006) showed that cognitive restructuring can increase self-efficacy and reduce social anxiety in adolescents.

The works of Giacola, Mezzich, Clark, and Tarter (1999) Liau, Barriga, and Gibbs (1998), and Rudolph and Clark (2001) emphasize assessing the context in which the minor's behavior occurs. To this point, several studies found contextual variations among minors with respect to cognitive distortions. Young minors with depressive and aggressive symptoms, for example, may exaggerate accounts of true negatives, raising the question as to whether their cognitions were distorted or were expressions of their actual reality (Rudolph, & Clark, 2001). With older minors, in particular those who are engaged in antisocial behaviors, distorted thinking may be used as self-servicing explanations for their behavior (Liau, Barriga, and Gibbs, 1998). Giacola, Mezzich, Clark, and Tarter (1999) suggest that, unfortunately, the context of distortions and negative self-talk exhibited by minors may not be fully explored by professionals. Instead, their behavior is often interpreted or diagnosed as oppositional defiant behavior or attention deficit or conduct disorder. In their further exploration of context, however, the negative thought patterns and self-talk of minors in the Giacola and colleagues study were linked to harsh punishment and excessive criticism in their home life. Collectively, these studies highlight the need to assist minors to distinguish between feelings and cognitions, in view of their circumstances and symptoms.

Studies specific to anger control in minors include Seay, Fee, Holloway, and Giesen (2003), Sukhodolsky, Kassinore, and Gorman (2004), and Tate (2001). Tate, however, emphasized peer influence and positive cognitive restructuring in schools, instead of strategies that are intended to control and rehabilitate and maintain adult-imposed order. Sukhodolsky and colleagues (2004) found the procedure to be more effective with older adolescents than with younger children, especially when the former did not have a prior history of violent behavior. Seay, Fee, Holloway, and Giesen (2003) reported improvement in anger control when specific behavior was targeted, accompanied by practicing different responses. Bailey (2001) cites the importance of the involvement of family and the school and discussed cognitive restructuring as effective when age-appropriate strategies are used. Use of the technique as an intervention with minors includes the reduction of HIV risk behavior among African American adolescents (St. Lawrence, Brasfield, Jefferson, O'Bannon & Shirley, 1995). Another study provides evidence of effectiveness in changing the thought processes of African American adolescents who had been abused as children (Lesure-Lester, 2002).

Application of Cognitive Restructuring with Diverse Groups

The worldview and social psychological processes that shape minority perceptions and resulting thoughts or experiences are different from those of the majority culture. Because of the differences in reality, history and context can influence cognitive development and processes. For example, Shih & Sanchez (2005) examined the role of identity among youth who have multiple identities with respect to cognition. Multiple identities, they asserted, shaped how individuals view their world as well as how they adjust to the real world of rejection and discrimination. The findings reinforce the need to examine context distortions or negative thought patterns before concluding that an individual's cognitions and thought patterns are irrational.

EP 2.1.7b

At the practice level, cognitive restructuring is widely used in correctional institutions in which the majority of inmates are members of minority groups. Based on the belief that change is needed in the criminal mindset, cognitive procedures are intended to reduce recidivism. The assumption is that the inmates patterned way of thinking essentially short circuits their ability to think in a logical manner and to use reason to make decisions. As a therapeutic intervention, the goal is to alter criminal thought processes by restructuring or replacing them with more acceptable patterns of behavior. Pollack (2004), in critiquing cognitive procedures, explains that they tend to overlook or deemphasize the influence of environmental and structural inequities. Potocky-Tripodi (2002), however, suggests that under specific circumstances cognitive restructuring as "supportive" counseling may help immigrants and refugees with their maladaptive thoughts and increase their coping skills in intercultural situations.

EP 2.1.7b

Hays (1995), as cited in Cormier and Nurius (2003), critiques cognitive restructuring with multicultural groups and observes that this "approach supports the status quo of mainstream society" (p. 437). Cognitive models tend to presume that negative views of self and of the world represent cognitive distortions. But, standardized beliefs about how to perceive and react to the world suggest a monolithic worldview and experience. With this in mind, you should be aware that cognition and thoughts expressed by different individuals and groups can be considered highly irregular behavior when measured by majority culture. In using the technique, modifications may be required so that it is responsive and does not oppress or punish differences. As an example of understanding a different perspective, you are invited to return to the video segment with Kim and Yanping.

EP 2.1.6b & 2.1.9a

Culturally compatible adaptations and modifications of cognitive procedures are illustrated in studies with Chinese Americans (Chen & Davenport, 2005), Latino clients (Organista, Dwyer, & Azocar, 1993), Native Americans (Renfrey, 1992) and Muslims (Hodge & Nadir, 2008). Still, you should observe that preferences, such as spirituality, beliefs, and self-perceptions that give purpose and direction to what people think and feel, are constructed by culture and within the context of the environment (Bandura, 1988; Berlin, 2001; Bronfenbrenner, 1989). For example, Renfrey (1992) combined Native American religious ceremonies with cognitive procedures and Hodge and Nadir (2008) advocate for adaptations to achieve congruence between individual self-statements that are consistent with the beliefs of Muslims.

While there is a need to study different groups in their context and the influence on cognitive development and processes, there are research studies with respect to the efficacy of cognitive restructuring with different racial and cultural groups. Selected examples include interventions with African American women smokers (Ahijevych & Wewers, 1993), low-income African American woman in group treatment (Kohn, Oden, Munoz, Leavitt, & Robinson, 2002), and in addressing race-related stressors among Asian American Pacific Islanders in the military (Loo, Ueda, & Morton, 2007). Work by Kuehlwein (1992), Ussher (1990), and Wolfe (1992) reported positive results with gay and lesbian clients. The technique used as a component of treatment with women effectively helped them gain a sense of power in confronting cultural messages of ideal physical attributes (Srebnik & Saltzberg, 1994; Brown, 1994).

On the whole, research on the efficacy of cognitive restructuring with diverse groups is limited. The studies discussed here have demonstrated that adaptations in language, culture, and specific group circumstances can result in cognitive restructuring being an effective intervention strategy with diverse groups.

Procedures of Cognitive Restructuring

EP 2.1.10j

The primary goal of cognitive restructuring is to alter people's thoughts and feelings and the accompanying self-statements or behaviors. Cognitive restructuring is particularly useful in assisting individuals to gain awareness of self-defeating thoughts and misconceptions that impair their personal functioning and to replace them with beliefs and behaviors that are aligned with reality.

Several discrete procedural steps are involved in cognitive restructuring. Although different authors may vary slightly in how the steps are defined, the similarities between the various models are far greater than the differences. These steps, as summarized in Table 13-2, are adapted from the steps identified by Goldfried (1977) and Cormier and Nurius (2003).

The steps of cognitive restructuring are summarized in Table 13-3. Each of the steps and their elements are discussed. A case example is used to demonstrate the steps of cognitive restructuring.

1. Assist clients in accepting that their self-statements, assumptions, and beliefs largely mediate their emotional reactions to life's events. The power difference between you and a client is likely to become

TABLE-13-2 STEPS IN COGNITIVE RESTRUCTURING

1. Assist clients in accepting that their self-statements determine their emotional reactions to events. (Tool: explanation and treatment rationale)
2. Assist clients in identifying dysfunctional beliefs and thought patterns. (Tool: self-monitoring)
3. Assist clients in identifying situations involving dysfunctional cognitions.
4. Assist clients in replacing dysfunctional cognitions with functional self-statements.
5. Assist clients in identifying rewards and incentives for successful coping efforts.

© Cengage Learning 2013

> **CASE EXAMPLE**
>
> The goal of the adolescent in this case is to increase his comfort level in expressing himself in peer social situations at school. He reports that he experiences a high level of anxiety about joining a peer group at lunchtime because he believes that they see him as being stuck [stupid]. There have been times when he has at times joined a group, but he has not talked. When others in the group *haven't* talked to him, he *has* perceived their behavior as evidence of his being excluded. His goal is to join a peer group during the lunch period without feeling anxious, and eventually to participate in the group conversations.

dialogue, the practitioner draws upon his own experience to show ways of thinking and responding to a situation. In doing so, the practitioner demonstrates to the adolescent how cognitions mediate emotions and thinking.

Social worker: What you think determines in large measure what you feel and do? For example, recently I bought a used car. My friend told me that I was stupid, or to use your word, stuck, to buy a used car instead of a new one. I could have made various meanings or self-statements related to this message, each of which would have resulted in different feelings and actions. Consider the potential responses that I might have made to my friend's comment:

Response 1: *He's probably right; he's a bright guy, and I respect his judgment. Why didn't I think of buying a new car? He thinks that I am stupid.*

If I think that he is right, then my feelings and statements are negative and I may not like my used car as much.

Response 2: *Who does he think he is, calling me stupid? He's the one who's stupid. What a jerk!*

If I think this way about my friend, I am likely to become angry and defensive, leading to an argument between the two of us about which one of us is right.

Response 3: *It's apparent that my friend and I have different ideas about cars. He's entitled to his opinion, although I don't agree with him and I feel good about buying a used new car. I don't like his referring to my choice as stupid, though. There's no point in getting bent out of shape over it, but I think I'll let him know how I feel about what he said to me.*

heightened when you present a goal of changing how they perceive themselves or their world. Mistrust and suspicion may be particularly acute with minors,

EP 2.1.10f

members of a racial or ethnic group, and individuals who are involuntary. Thus, in the first step it is important to provide clients with an explanation and your rationale for selecting cognitive restructuring as an intervention procedure.

Explanation of Cognitive Restructuring

Social worker: As I understand what you have said so far, you want to be a part of a group during the lunch period, but you are anxious about what others will think about you. But, you also stated that you want to be a part of the group and to talk. So that you may achieve this goal, we first need to determine what happens inside you that caused you to feel anxious. This will help you to become aware of the thoughts you experienced in the group. Specifically, we need to review what you say to yourself *before, during,* and *after* you join a group. Generally, our thoughts occur automatically, and often we aren't fully aware of many of them. Becoming aware of your self-defeating thoughts, assumptions, and beliefs is an important first step in replacing them with others that will help you achieve your goal.

Social Worker's Use of Self in Explaining Cognitive Restructuring

EP 2.1.10i

To guide you in assisting clients to understand cognitive restructuring, it may be advisable to use self as an example to explain the technique to the adolescent. As demonstrated in the following

If I think the thoughts in the third example, I'm less likely to experience negative feelings about myself. I'll feel good about my decision despite the differences of opinion, and I won't be influenced by his lack of sensitivity.

In using a self example, the social worker pinpointed for the adolescent how thoughts and beliefs can cause difficulties as well as how cognitive restructuring facilitates working on developing other thoughts that are realistic and consistent with his goal. Further, he clarified that other responses could be made, but these three should suffice to make his point. The social worker then points out that the task at hand is to enable the adolescent to master his anxiety and for the two of them to explore how his self-statements have influenced his feelings and behavior.

EP 2.1.10f

The previous example showed how the rationale for cognitive restructuring can be presented in a simple, straightforward manner. A majority of clients given an explanation will agree to proceed. Their commitment to the procedure is also necessary because individuals tend to resist efforts to change their beliefs.

2. *Assist clients in identifying self-statements, beliefs, and patterns of thoughts that underlie his or her problem.* Once he or she accepts the fact that thoughts and beliefs mediate emotional reactions, your next task is to help the client to identify the thoughts and beliefs that pertain to his or her difficulties. This step requires a detailed exploration of events related to problematic situations and their antecedents, with particular emphasis on cognitions that accompany distressing emotions.

EP 2.1.10j

To begin the process, you would focus on problematic events that occurred during the preceding week or on events surrounding a problem the individual has targeted for change. As you and the individual recalls these events, you are listening for specific details regarding overt behaviors, cognitions (i.e., self-statements and images), and emotional reactions. Focusing on the cognitive and emotional aspects related to the event clarifies the connection between what an individual perceives and his or her emotions and thoughts. From this point on, the aim is to identify his or her self-statements and beliefs related to the event, and to help him or her to become aware of the way in which his or her automatic thoughts and beliefs act as powerful determinants of their behavior.

EP 2.1.10d & 2.1.10f

As you and the individual continue to explore his or her thought patterns, you will be able to *identify thoughts and feelings that occur before, during, and after events.* To elicit self-statements, ask the individual to recreate the situation as it unfolded, recalling exactly what he or she thought, felt, and did. For example, with the adolescent, the practitioner asked him to describe his thoughts and feelings when he joined the lunch group. If this reflection had proven to be too difficult, as an alternative, the practitioner could have asked him to close his eyes and run a movie of his thoughts and feelings prior to, during, and after the problematic event.

By listening to the adolescent as he described his thoughts, the social worker was able to pinpoint the cognitive sets that predisposed him to experience certain emotions and to behave in predictable ways. To illustrate, consider the adolescent's inner dialogue of self-statements *prior* to his joining a group of peers in the lunchroom:

EP 2.1.10i

- "I'm outey [out of here—disappear]. Straight up [the truth is], I'm not sure I want to join the others. If I do, I'll just cool [sit] there and feel that they be [are] hating on me [leaving me out]." Straight up, this is whacked."
- "If I show [join in], they'll dis me [disrespect me] about something."
- "I'd better show; otherwise, they'll be hating on me later [talking about me]. I'm outey, straight up." "I'm cool" [okay].

Given these self-statements, the adolescent clearly experienced anxiety about joining the group, the content of which was also self-protective. His thought pattern and the accompanying self-statement predisposed him to enter the situation expecting defeat. In listening to his self debate as he recreated the event, the practitioner also observed his nonverbal cues. His physical posture, for example, spoke volumes. Not only did his self-defeating statements dominate his cognition of the group situation, it is likely that his nonverbal behavior also contributed to his self-presentation in the situation.

Exploration of self-statements during events often reveals that thoughts maintain self-defeating feelings and behaviors and drastically reduce personal effectiveness. For example, the adolescent tended to dwell on his fears and was vigilant to the possible negative reactions of others. As a result, he was unable to fully *tune in* to conversations or to verbally express himself in a way that created favorable impressions. In other words, he found it difficult to be fully present and involved because of his self-consciousness and anxiety about exposing his imagined personal inadequacies.

To illustrate the impact of his thoughts, let's again consider his self-statements *during* the time he joined a lunch group:

- "Well, here I am, nothing is different. I am being dissed [disrespected, left out of the conversation]."
- "I wish I had the low, low [something interesting to say] but my life's ain't about doing anything [uninteresting]. What's up with this? They ain't interested in any low [ideas, information] that I might put out [say]."
- "Go figure, they're wondering why I even showed [joined them]. I don't add anything, but it's cool, I out of here [the group is not that important to me]."

Because the group did not respond in the way that he had hoped, he continued to be preoccupied with self-defeating thoughts. He concludes that he has little or nothing to offer, and behaves accordingly, hence, his thoughts about being unwelcome and unworthy are reinforced. In turn, the potential of his engaging with his peers is blocked.

EP 2.1.10j

An individual's thoughts and feelings after an event can reveal the impact on their subsequent behaviors. In the telling of what had occurred, and the individual's conclusions, you are able to further highlight the mediating function of cognitions. Consider the adolescent's thoughts and feelings as he described his experience *after* he joined the group:

- "I out man [blew it again]. I'm too threw [I'm finished; I might as well quit trying]. This ain't real for sure [no use kidding myself; I just can't talk with others]."
- "It ain't like that [they didn't really try to include me]. They be hating on me [it's obvious they could care less about me]. They'd probably be okay if I didn't show up tomorrow."
- "This is whack [uncomfortable; I won't try to eat lunch with them again]. I don't enjoy it, and I'm sure they don't either. Tomorrow I outey [eat by myself], for shiddley [for sure]."

EP 2.1.10i

The following are general inquiries that can be developed into questions to help individuals to assess the rationality of beliefs and self-statements:

- Ask how they reached certain conclusions
- Elicit evidence that supports their perception or beliefs
- Explore the logic of beliefs that have magnified their feared consequences of certain actions

EP 2.1.10j

To assist the adolescent to assess the rationality of his conclusions, for example, the social worker asked him the following questions:

Social worker: So did someone "dis" you when you joined the group? What did they say that made you think that they were "hating" on you?

As illustrated in the following example, the individual may not be able to immediately acknowledge the irrationality of his or her beliefs:

Adolescent: Well, you see, this girl, I got the low [perception, idea], by the way she was looking at me, straight-up, this was whack [not good].

Individuals can tenaciously cling to their misconceptions and argue persuasively about their validity. For the adolescent, his perception of the way in which the girl looked at him confirmed that his thoughts about being in the group were valid. As the practitioner, you must therefore be prepared to challenge or "dispute" the validity of irrational beliefs, by emphasizing the costs or disadvantages associated with counterproductive beliefs. To illustrate how this works, the practitioner's response prompted the adolescent to consider the relationships between his thoughts and his goal.

Social worker: Okay, if you continue think that joining in with the group is "whack," and you continue to be "outey," how will this affect your goal of becoming comfortable about joining a lunch period group?

Clusters of misconceptions are commonly associated with problematic behavior, and they also tend to have a common theme. For the adolescent, the central theme or a slight derivative of his self-statements and expectations is that he is unwelcome and unworthy of becoming a participating member of a lunch group with peers. As a result, he is quick to reach conclusions that support his thoughts and beliefs, contributing to his expectations of self and unrealistic expectations of his peers. Often it is possible to observe such thought patterns by eliciting the accompanying thoughts in clusters, examples of which are illustrated in Table 13-3. By identifying clusters or patterns of misconceptions, you can direct your efforts to the theme common to all of them, rather than dealing with each misconception as a separate entity.

EP 2.1.7a

EP 2.1.10i

3. *Assist clients in identifying situations that engender dysfunctional cognitions.* Pinpointing the places where stressful events occur, the key persons involved, and situations that involved demeaning oneself, in the face of self-expectations enables you and the individual to develop tasks and coping strategies that are tailored to those specific situations.

EP 2.1.10j

TABLE-13-3 BELIEFS AND SELF-EXPECTATIONS

BELIEFS	SELF-EXPECTATIONS
Beliefs about oneself	I am usually not very good at anything that I do.
	My accomplishments aren't that significant, anyone could have done it.
Beliefs about others' perceptions and expectations of oneself	My partner dismisses my opinion, because I am not very smart.
	When I compare myself with others, I never quite measure up.
Expectations of oneself	At work, I feel I must perform better than others in my unit.
	I should be able to do lots of things and perform at a high level.
Expectations of others	My daughter should understand how I feel without my having to tell her.
	She should want to visit me.

© Cengage Learning 2013

EP 2.1.10m

Self-monitoring between sessions is a concrete way for individuals to measure and recognize cognitions related to their difficulties around problematic events. In doing so, they are able to increase their awareness of the pervasive nature of their thoughts and the need to actively cope with them. Self-monitoring thus expands self-awareness and paves the way for later change efforts.

To facilitate self-monitoring with the adolescent, the practitioner asked him to keep daily logs to record information, as illustrated in Figure 13-4. In the log, the adolescent recorded the situation, his feelings, beliefs, and self-statements. The daily log may also reveal other factors that influence his feelings about joining the lunch group, such as his comfort level with the composition of the group.

Daily self-monitoring is a valuable tool because it can focus a client's efforts between sessions, clarify the connections between cognitions and feelings, and provide information about the prevalence and intensity of thoughts, images, and feelings. In this case, keeping a daily log stimulated the adolescent to logically examine his thoughts.

Social Worker: After completing a week of logs, did you find anything out about yourself and the way that you think and behaved when you are with a group?"

Adolescent Client: "Yeah, I could see that I was whacked [out of bounds], and when I was scared I acted stuck. Then I wanted to be out of there before they dissed me."

To prevent a person from becoming overwhelmed by the task of keeping a log, you might suggest that a client initially limit his or her recording to events related to those identified during the session and restrict recordings to no more than three each day. As an alternative, or in addition to, self-monitoring can also include the use of images drawn by the individual. As other counterproductive thought patterns emerge during sessions, the focus of self-monitoring can be shifted as necessary.

As you and the individual review completed log sheets and identify problematic feelings and cognitions, it is important to note recurring situations or themes. A recurring theme for the adolescent, for example, was his fear about not being included if he joined a peer group during the lunch period.

4. *Assist clients in substituting functional self-statements for self-defeating cognitions.* As a person expands his or her awareness of their dysfunctional thoughts, beliefs, and images, your goal is to help them recognize how they result in negative emotional reactions. Having done so, the goal is to help them cope as they begin to learn new patterns. Coping strategies typically consist of self-statements that are both realistic and effective in diminishing or eliminating

Date: Tuesday, September 6, 2008		
Situation or Event	**Feelings** (Rate rationality from 1 to 10)	**Beliefs or Self-Statements** (Rate intensity from 1 to 10)
1. Joined group at lunch time	Scared (7) Stuck (7)	They will dis me, this is whack (6)
2. No one said anything to me; I didn't say anything	I'm outey (4); afraid to join in (8); disgusted with self (7)	I should speak up (9); they will ignore me and I'd be embarrassed (2); it is not worth the hassle (3)

© Cengage Learning 2013

FIG-13-4 Daily Log for Adolescent

EP 2.1.10j

negative emotional reactions and self-defeating behaviors. Although functional self-statements are intended to foster courage and facilitate active coping efforts, you should not ignore the individual's struggle in shifting from habitual, ingrained patterns of thinking, to adopting new behavioral patterns. In recognition of the difficulty and anxiety that an individual may experience, coping self-statements support the transition as he or she risks new behavior.

First, to introduce the adolescent to positive self-statements, the practitioner explained the rationale for new self-statements:

Social worker's explanation: *"Now that you've identified key self-defeating beliefs and thoughts, we're going to focus on how you can replace them with positive statements. It will take a lot of hard work on your part, but as you practice, you'll find that they will become more and more natural allowing you to rely less on old ways of thinking."*

EP 2.1.10i

Because mastery is unlikely to be immediate, after the practitioner's explanation, he modeled coping self-statements that the adolescent could use as substitutes for his thoughts and beliefs. In the exercise, the social worker assumed the role of the adolescent, using his words and thoughts as he coped with the target situation.

Social Worker as Adolescent client: *"I know a part of me wants to avoid being dissed [the discomfort of socializing]. I feel whack [scared], but it's not going to get any better by being outey [withdrawing]. "I don't have to low [talk] a lot to be part of the group. If I tune [listen] to the others and get my mind off myself, I can be cool [involve myself more]."*

EP 2.1.10i

Notice how the social worker modeled the adolescent's struggle and the idea of coping rather than mastery of new self-statements. Modeling coping self-statements should reflect the individual's actual experience, whereas mastery self-statements do not. Moreover, the former convey empathy for and understanding of the individual's struggle, which in turn inspires greater confidence in the process. As an alternative coping self-statement, the practitioner worker proposed the following:

Social worker: *"Yes, you might think: 'I can't expect them to include me in their conversations. It would be nice if they did, but if they're going to do so, I'll have to be responsible for including myself. It's better than withdrawing and feeling left out.' "*

After modeling coping self-statements, it is appropriate to ask whether the client feels ready to practice similar behavior. To enhance the effectiveness of guided practice, you could suggest that the person close their eyes and picture themselves in the exact situation they will be in *before* engaging in the targeted behavior. When they report they have succeeded in capturing the situation, ask them to think aloud the thoughts they typically experience when contemplating the targeted behavior. Then ask them to substitute coping thoughts, coaching them as needed. Give positive feedback and encouragement when they produce reinforcing self-statements independently, even though they may continue to struggle with conflicting thoughts. You may also expect the person to express doubt and uncertainty about their ability to eventually master new patterns of thinking. If they do, explain that it is natural for people to experience misgivings as they experiment with new ways of thinking. Continue to practice and coach them until they feel relatively comfortable in their ability to develop new self-statements.

When the individual has demonstrated his or her confidence in using coping self-statements before entering a targeted situation, you can shift to a strategy of self-statements *during* the time the client is actually in the target situation. As done with the adolescent, the practitioner models coping self-statements:

EP 2.1.10j

Social Worker as Adolescent: *"Okay, I'm feeling anxious. That's to be expected. I can still pay attention and show interest in the group. I can tune [communicate] by nodding my head, laughing when someone says something funny and not feeling that this is whack. As I feel more comfortable, I can join in by asking for questions if I want to know more. This is another way to show interest, especially if I have some take on the subject they're discussing. I think that my opinions are worth as much as theirs. Go ahead, take a chance and express them, but look at others as I talk."*

Following the modeling exercise, the social worker asked the youth to describe his feelings about what had happened so far. Inquiring about feelings was important; for example, had the modeling resulted in the youth becoming anxious, uncomfortable, or skeptical. These feeling should be dealt with before proceeding further.

EP 2.1.10i

Again, it may be worthwhile for you to model and eventually have the individual rehearse reinforcing statements. Here are some examples:

Social Worker as Adolescent: "Well, I did it. I stuck it out and even said a couple of things. That's a step in the right direction."

- *Adolescent Statement:* "No one played me [ignored me] when I sat down with the group. Man, it was hot [good] maybe I'm not stuck [stupid] so bad after all. Even though I was on ten [anxious] it was 100 percent real [good], it was so fire that it snuck upon me [even better than I expected]. It's a rap, [accomplishment]."

EP 2.1.10j

To further assist clients in utilizing positive statements, it is beneficial to negotiate them as tasks between sessions. Between-session tasks foster autonomy and independent action by clients. But don't rush them, because undue pressure may be perceived as threatening or discouraging. You may use the readiness scale (discussed earlier in this chapter) as a gauge.

EP 2.1.10m

Continued self-monitoring is essential as clients implement Step 4 of the cognitive restructuring process, using the format suggested in Figure 13-4 as a tool. As the adolescent progresses, a fourth column could be added entitled, for example, "*Rational or Positive Coping Self-Statements.*" By having an individual fill in a column such as this, the exercise can facilitate the development of reinforcing statements and eventually replace self-defeating ones.

EP 2.1.10i

Another technique that can help a person to replace their automatic problematic self-statements includes encouraging them, upon their first awareness of such thoughts, to nip them in the bud. For example, you might use the image of a flashing yellow signal, which indicates caution and their need to replace problematic thoughts. Substituting positive self-statements for self-defeating ones is the heart of cognitive restructuring. Because thoughts tend to be automatic and deeply embedded and persistent, it is important to explain that Step 4 may span over a time period in which a satisfactory degree of mastery is gradual, however, it is possible to achieve over time.

5. *Assist clients in rewarding themselves for successful coping efforts.* For people who dwell on their failures and shortcomings, and rarely, if ever, give themselves positive feedback, Step 5 in cognitive restructuring is especially important. When a person has mastered new statements and behaviors, you should reinforce their accomplishment by coaching them in giving themselves credit.

EP 2.1.10j

Social worker: "So you joined the group. That's exciting, given where you started. What are your thoughts on how you would like to celebrate?"

Adolescent: "Well, it's a done deal as far as I am concerned. I even sent a text to a girl in the group, and she wrote back "r u ok, SPK."

Social Worker: "Well, that is a good thing! I also want you to think about rewarding statements that you can make to yourself. I'm going to pretend that I am you. I'll say aloud self-statements you might think about."

- "I wasn't sure that I was up to it but I did it!"
- "I backed off. I replaced my negative thoughts and stayed in the game!"

Social Worker: "Now what would you say to yourself?"

Adolescent: "Like I told you man, it's a rap, it's all the way live, you feel me [understand]! Everything is cool, maybe I'll go to a movie."

For some people, rewarding themselves using self-statements can be difficult and they may feel awkward or self-conscious. Adults may be more readily able to think about rewards than minors. When a person is hesitant, empathic understanding and encouragement on your part will usually prompt them to try this exercise. Some individuals, like the adolescent, may focus only on the overall outcome. For example, his goal of joining a lunchroom group had been achieved, plus a bonus of a text message exchange with a female in the group. In any case, it is important that you review and credit an individual's progress with him or her so that

Strengths, Limitations, and Cautions

EP 2.1.10a

Cognitive restructuring is an effective procedure that is intended to address a range of problems related to an individual's cognitions and thought patterns. Research studies have shown the procedure to be particularly useful in altering perceptions, distorted beliefs, and thought patterns that result in negative or self-defeating behaviors. As a systematic process and problem-solving procedure, cognitive restructuring is compatible with crisis intervention, the task-centered system, and solution-focused treatment. The "miracle question," a solution-focused technique, may indeed motivate people to address problematic behavior and encourage them to formulate specific change goals. For the adolescent in the case situations, for example, the miracle question may have helped him to imagine being accepted by the peer group.

In assisting people to change, however, social workers must not mistakenly assume that a person will be able to perform new behaviors solely as a result of changes in their cognitions or beliefs. In reality, they may lack cognitive and social skills and require instruction and practice before they can effectively perform new behaviors. Cognitive restructuring is intended to remove cognitive barriers to change and foster a willingness to risk new behaviors, but it does not always equip clients with the skills required to perform those new behaviors.

Attempts to reshape thought patterns and perceptions to reflect a different pattern—in contrast to their actual experience—may be perceived as a threat, especially with diverse and involuntary clients. Furthermore, as noted by Vodde and Gallant (2002), simply changing one's story does not ensure a certain outcome, given the presence of very real external factors such as oppression or rejection. Thus, without an acknowledgment of these factors, diverse clients may perceive cognitive restructuring as blaming or just another form of social control and ideological domination. Of course, some minority group members have mastered a dual frame of reference that is selectively congruent with dominant views and beliefs. Thus, for these individuals, cognitive restructuring can be a useful intervention procedure.

Finally, although cognitive theorists attribute most dysfunctional emotional and behavioral patterns to mistaken beliefs, these are by no means the only causes. Dysfunctions may be produced by numerous biophysical problems, including brain injury, neurological disorders, thyroid imbalance, blood sugar imbalance, circulatory disorders associated with aging, ingestion of toxic substances, malnutrition, and other forms of chemical imbalance. Consequently, these possibilities should be considered before undertaking cognitive restructuring.

Solution-Focused Brief Treatment

EP 2.1.10a

Solution-focused brief treatment is a postmodern, constructivist approach with a unique focus on resolving client's concerns (De Jong & Berg, 2008; Murray & Murray, 2004). The approach was developed by Steve de Shazer and Insoo Kim Berg and their associates' work at the Brief Family Therapy Center in Milwaukee, Wisconsin (Nichols & Schwartz, 2004; Trepper, Dolan, McCollum, & Nelson, 2006). Influenced by the views of Milton Erickson, de Shazer and Berg embraced his assumption that people were constrained by the social construction of their problems. Thus, a goal of the approach is to release their unconscious resources, thereby shifting from a problem-oriented perspective to one that is more solution-based. In this regard, the approach integrates aspects of cognitive restructuring. As the professional, you have an active role in first "helping clients to question self-defeating constructions," and then assisting them to construct "new and more productive perspectives" (Nichols & Schwartz, 2004, p. 101). Work with clients is facilitated by having them identify and prioritize solutions. Like the task-centered system, the solution-focused approach is based on the premise that change can occur over a brief period of time.[5]

Tenets of Solution-Focused

EP 2.1.10a

The solution-focused approach emerged over the past 20 years as a strategy for working with adults, minors, and families, including clients who are involuntary. The approach emphasizes the identification of solution, rather than resolving problems. A series of interview questions are used during the phases of the approach and are instrumental to the development of solutions (De Jong & Berg, 1998; 2008). The solution-focused approach draws on people's strengths and capacities, with the intent of empowering them to create solutions. Although clients may begin with a problem statement, a key belief of the approach is that the analysis of a problem does not necessarily predict a client's ability to problem solve (Corcoran, 2008). Furthermore, solutions and problems are not necessarily connected. Therefore, the thrust of your work with individuals encourages solution talk, rather than assessing how problems developed or are perpetuated (Koob, 2003; Nichols & Schwartz, 2004).

Oriented toward the future, rather than the past, the solution-focused treatment approach asserts that clients have a right to determine their desired outcomes. Change is believed to occur in a relatively brief time period, especially when people are empowered as experts and are encouraged to use their expertise to construct solutions. As the practitioner, your role is to listen, to absorb information that a person provides, and subsequently guide them toward solutions utilizing the "language of change" (DeJong & Berg, 2002, p. 49). Lee (2003) believes that these principles are motivating factors that strengthen the efficacy of the solution-focused approach in cross-cultural practice.

The manner in which clients are categorized is unique to solution-focused. The three types of individuals are identified as *customers, complainants,* or *visitors* (Corcoran, 2008; De Jong & Berg, 2008; Jordan & Franklin, 2003). *Customers* are individuals who willingly make a commitment to change. Therefore, the series of questions and the tasks to be completed are directed to them. Those individuals who identify a concern but do not see themselves as part of the problem or solution are referred to as *complainants*. A person who is willing to be minimally or peripherally involved but is not invested in the change effort is designated a *visitor*. These distinctions allow you to identify where potential clients stand relative to their commitment to change and their ownership of concerns. In distinguishing the various types, you are able to focus the concern and solution identified by the customer. There may be instances however, when it is advisable to engage the complainant or visitor, if only to ensure that he or she does not interfere with the customer's change efforts.

Theoretical Framework

EP 2.1.7a

The solution-focused approach borrows from the social constructivists' perspective belief that people use language to create their reality (deShazer & Berg, 1993). In the solution-focused approach, reality is constructed by culture and context, as well as perceptions and life experiences, thus an absolute truth does not exist (Murray & Murray, 2004). For example, truths about normative functioning or development have tended to be imposed by professionals, which may have little relationship to the reality of an individual's situation (Freud, 1999; Nichols & Schwartz, 2004). Therefore, it is more important for you to understand the way in which a person constructs the meaning of his or her experiences and relationships. The approach also draws from assumptions of cognitive-behavioral theory, specifically that cognitions influence a person's language and behavior.

Empirical Evidence and Uses of Solution-Focused Strategies

EP 2.1.6b

Empirical evidence was at one point in time considered to be less than robust. There is, however, substantial evidence of the effectiveness of the approach in practice settings and with different populations (Corcoran, 2008; Corcoran & Pillai, 2009; Kim, 2008). Solution-focused brief treatment has been utilized in a variety of settings and with diverse populations, including persons with mental illness and involuntary clients (Berg & Kelly, 2000; Corcoran, 2008; DeJong & Berg, 2001; Greene, Kondraft, Lee, Clement, Siebert, Mentzer, & Pinnell, 2006; Hopson & Kim 2005; Hsu, 2009; Tohn & Oshlag, 1996; Trepper, et al, 2006). Ingersoll-Dayton, Schroepfer, and Pryce (1999) found that a focus on positive attributes of nursing home residents with dementia, rather than their behavioral problems, changed interactions between the residents and the staff. The efficacy of the approach has also been demonstrated in couple's therapy and premarital counseling (McCollum & Trepper, 2001; Murray & Murray, 2004; Nelson & Kelly, 2001). Research on specific strategies of the model, for example using exception-based solutions, found strategies of the model were successful in changing domestic violence behavior (Corcoran & Franklin, 1998; Lee, Greene, & Rheinscheld, 1999; McQuaide, 1999).

Utilization with Minors

EP 2.1.6b

There is increasing evidence in the effectiveness and utilization of solution-focused strategies with minors (Kelly, Kim, & Franklin, 2008). In public school settings, study results show the successful specific solution-focused explore feelings, develop behavioral goals, and encourage positive behaviors (Corcoran & Stephenson, 2000; Franklin & Hopson, 2009; Franklin & Streeter, 2004; Newsome, 2004; Springer, Lynch, & Rubin, 2000; Teal, 2000). Similarly, positive outcomes were reported for improving individual social skills and to manage school related behavioral problems (Cook & Kaffenberger, 2003; Gingerich & Eisengard, 2000; Gingerich & Wabeke, 2001). Multiple studies involving adolescents have shown positive results. These studies include high risk juvenile offenders, students referred for academic and behavioral problems or drug use, and pregnant and parenting teens (Corcoran, 1997, 1998; Froeschle, Smith, & Ricard, 2007; Harris & Franklin, 2003; Kelly, Kim & Franklin, 2008; Selekman, 2005).

Application with Diverse Groups

EP 2.1.7b

Critiques of the solution-focused approach point to a lack of attention on the diversity of clients (Corcoran, 2008). Demer, Hemesath, and Russell (1998) praised the approach for its explicit attention to competence and strengths, but they believe that it fails to address gender-related power differences. For example, they might argue that despite a change in the narrative of men and women in abusive relationships, the change lacked sufficient attention to the narrative of actual power differences. Proponents of the approach, however, assert that the solution-focused approach is responsive to diverse groups because its basic thrust recognizes the expertness of the narrative and language of the individual. Further, they assert that because professionals respect and honor the distinct cultural background of individuals, the basic tenets of the approach are consistent with competent multicultural practice with individuals in social service agencies (De Jong & Berg, 2002; Pichot & Dolan, 2003; Trepper, et al., 2006). The results of previously cited research studies with adolescents, the majority of which were members of diverse groups and also involuntary clients, are promising.

Solution-Focused Procedures and Techniques

EP 2.1.10j

The stages of *"solution building"* as outlined by De Jong and Berg (2003, p. 17) proceed as follows:

- *Description of the Problem.* Individuals are invited to give an account of his or her concern or problem, however, as the practitioner, you refrain from eliciting details about antecedents, severity or the cause of their concern. While listening to their description of the problem, you are looking for ways in which you can guide them toward a solution.
EP 2.1.10d

- *Developing Well-Formed Goals.* In this stage, your work involves encouraging the individual to think about what will be different once the problem no longer exists. Individuals are asked to describe what he or she wishes to be different, and this information is used to develop their goal.
EP 2.1.10f

- *Exploring Exceptions.* Questions asked of the individual in this stage are focused on those times in his or her life when the problem was not an issue or was less of a concern. These questions are followed by who did what and what could happen that would decrease the concern and make more exceptions possible.
EP 2.1.10j

- *End-of Session Feedback.* The aim of the stage is to compliment and reinforce what an individual has already done to solve the problem. Feedback is also based on the information that the individual has provided about his or her goals and exceptions. Also, clients are asked what he or she should do more or less of toward accomplishing their goal.
EP 2.1.10i

- *Evaluating Progress.* Monitoring progress is ongoing and is specific to evaluating the individual's level of satisfaction with reaching a solution. The scaling question facilitates this process. After the individual has rated his or her satisfaction level, you work with him or her to identify what needs to occur so that the problem is resolved. In later sessions, a central question posed to the individual is: *"What's better?"* When the individual's primary concern has been resolved in a satisfactory manner, contact with you is terminated.

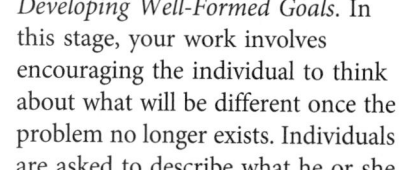
EP 2.1.10m

Throughout your work with individuals, you make use of a series of questions that follow the phases of helping, specifically, engagement, assessment, goal setting, intervention, and termination. Four questions

TABLE-13-4 SOLUTION-FOCUSED QUESTIONS

- Scaling
- Coping
- Exceptions
- Miracle

EP 2.1.10j

typically guide the engagement, the formation of goals, and the solution-building process. The various types of interview questions are summarized in Table 13-4; they are intended to move clients toward goals and to think of solutions.

Scaling questions, using a scale of 1 to 10, solicit a person's level of willingness and confidence in moving toward the development of a well-formed goal and also encourages them to observe their progress. These questions may also be instrumental in preventing the client from returning to describing problematic behaviors and in developing specific behavioral indicators along a continuum of change (Corcoran, 2008; Trepper, et al., 2006).

Coping questions are intended to highlight and reinforce a client's resources and strengths. For example, how has he or she managed their current difficulty or the resources he or she has used previously when dealing with an issue? Coping questions credit the individual's prior efforts to manage a difficulty, and reenergize his or her strengths and capacities. A message for instance is: "In view of the chaos that you described in the transitional housing facility, please tell me how you were able to find the time to be actively involved with your children?"

Exception questions are considered to be the core of the intervention (Corcoran, 2008). Designed to diminish the problem focus, these questions assist a person to describe life when his or her current difficulty did not exist (Bertolino & O'Hanlon, 2002: DeJong & Berg, 2002, 2008; Trepper, et al., 2006; Shoham, Rorhbaugh, & Patterson, 1995). For example, "What was it like when you owned your home and lived in a neighborhood of your own choosing?" The exception question also advances the individual's ability to externalize or separate from the problem by building upon strengths and resources (Corcoran, 2008). In a segment of the Corning family video, Irwin asserted that "A man should provide for his family." To separate his sense of self from his job loss and highlight his strengths, you

would emphasize that he had done so up until the time he had lost his job due to circumstances beyond his control. In essence, you are *reframing*, which allows you to address his cognition that contributed to his negative self-talk statement.

Miracle questions draws the individual's attention to what would be different if he or she reached the desired outcome (Corcoran, 2008; Koob, 2003; Lipchik, 2002). For example, "How do you imagine that you will feel when your family moves into your own apartment?"

Typical interview questions that facilitate an individual's capacity to think about the future and to identify solutions include the following queries adapted from De Jong and Berg (2008), Lipchik (2002), and de Shazer and Berg (1993).

EP 2.1.10j

- *How can I help?*
- *What's better?*
- *How will you know when your problem is solved?*
- *What will be different when the problem is solved?*
- *What signs will indicate to you that you don't have to see me any longer?*
- *Can you describe what will be different in terms of your behavior, thoughts, or feelings?*
- *What signs will indicate to you that others involved in this situation are behaving, thinking, or feeling differently?*

Questions will of course vary depending on the stage of the intervention, which is highlighted in the following examples adapted from De Jong and Berg (2008):

EP 2.1.10j

"*How can I help?*" is typically asked in the engagement session.

"*What do you want to be different?*" is intended to facilitate the development of a well-formed goal. Goals sought by the individual are framed on the basis of exceptions; specifically, individuals are asked about the absence of the problem (the exception) and it is on this basis that the work toward a solutions is formed.

For individuals who are involuntary situation, De Jong and Berg (2008, p. 372) recommend beginning the interview with questions that encourage the individual's participation by allowing the client to provide his or her view of the situation. Examples are:

"*Whose idea was it that you needed to come here?*"

"*What is your understanding of why you are here?*"

"What makes the _____ (pressuring person or mandating authority) believe that you needed to see me?"

"What is the difference between your point of view and that of the person who required that you come here?"

These questions are followed by, for example "what could be different?" and, as appropriate, coping or scaling questions and the miracle question.

In subsequent sessions, from one session to the next, interview questions are focused on:

What is better?

What could the individual continue to do more or less of?

Again, the flow of your questions will vary, influenced by the content of the conversation with each individual. For example, if the individual reports that little or no change has occurred, you would inquire about how he or she is coping. If indicated, you might ask a scaling question to gauge the level of stress. For instance, you would have the individual rate his or her current level of concern, and also what would be different or better at the next level. *"Would you rate what will be different in terms of your behavior, thoughts, or feelings when you move to the next level?"*

In the termination stage, the focus of your questions would emphasize signs of what is different. Specifically, you would ask, *"What signs will indicate to you that others involved in this situation are behaving, thinking, or feeling differently?"*

Compliments, bridging, amplification and *tasks* are techniques that are integrated with the process of asking questions. Compliments, for example, provide feedback about an individual's effort, as well as what he or she has accomplished. They are used as a means to reinforce their strengths and successes. Bridging is also a part of the feedback, the content of which clarifies goals, exceptions, or strengths. The technique of amplification encourages an individual to elaborate on the "What's different?" question. It may also be used as a link to a compliment and to link tasks to the miracle question. Used in another way, amplification can inform goals and tasks related to the miracle question. Tasks suggested by you can be either *formula* or *predictive* in nature, and they may be completed during or after a session. For instance, a post-session formula task for a couple who is experiencing conflict in their relationship would be to imagine how their relationship would be if the miracle occurred. In using a prediction task, you would direct the couple to predict the status of their conflict, for better or for worse, tomorrow (de Shazer, 1988). In essence, the predictive task invites them to think about what would be different.

EP 2.1.10i

To illustrate the procedures and some of the techniques of the approach, the case situation highlighted in the Ideas in Action box is used. The session is the third of the eight planned between the youth and the social worker.

EP 2.1.10j

IDEAS IN ACTION

Antonio, age 16, is a resident in a treatment center for juvenile offenders. Since the previous session with the social worker, he has transitioned from the lockdown area in the center to a less restrictive area of the center, referred to by the other residents as the "freedom house." Case notes indicate that Antonio had made significant changes in his aggressive, antisocial behavior, hence, the move to another level in the facility. Prior to his admission to the facility, Antonio lived with his mother, stepfather, and siblings. The parents are now divorced. For the most part, he has had a good relationship with his family, especially with his mother. This is the third session with the social worker. As he entered the room, he takes a seat on the couch and leans back. In previous meetings, he and the social worker engaged in small talk, but today he is unusually quiet. The session begins with the social worker asking him "What has happened that's better?" In reply, he informs her that he is moving to "freedom house" after his meeting with her. Afterwards, he becomes silent and slumps down on the couch. The social worker waits for him to speak. After about 5 minutes of silence, he presents a new concern.

Social Worker: Wow, Antonio, you are moving to "freedom house." [*reinforce/compliment*]

Antonio: Yep, now I can wear my own clothes, be in a room by myself, and go home on weekends. Soon, I will be able to get out of this place!

Social Worker: How did this happen? [*amplify*]

Antonio: Well, I stopped messing up, you know, acting all bad and stuff and fighting. You helped me a lot with my attitude.

Social Worker: Thank you. But you did the work on your own and now you are moving to another level. That's great! [*complimenting/bridging*] Now you've reached this level, what will it take for you to remain in freedom house, eventually be able to go home? [*do more of*]

Antonio: Like I said, I keep a check on my attitude. Right now, everything here is going okay. But I am not talking to my mother right now!

Social Worker: You and your mother usually talk everyday. What's different?

Antonio: Well, you see, whenever my mom has a new boyfriend or dude whatever, me and my brothers and sisters make up a name for him as a joke-and my mother always laughs too you know. This new dude is Clarence, so I called Claudius, and she got all bent; told me that I needed to respect him and some s…., whatever!

Social Worker: Is this a different reaction from your mother? [*What's different?*]

Antonio: Yeah, like she was really mad. I was surprised.

Social Worker: You said that there were times when your mother laughed when you joked about Clarence. What was different about this time? [*exception*]

Antonio: Well at other times, it was just me and my sister and brothers, no one else was around.

Social Worker: Sometimes, what else was different?

Antonio: I didn't change my voice and mimic the way he talks.

Social Worker: So you noticed that your mother did not get mad at you when you did not mimic Clarence? [*amplify*] Could you do this more often?

Antonio: Yeah, I guess so.

Social Worker: Is it possible that she's more serious with this guy than with some of the past ones? [*amplify, to encourage evaluation of his perception*]

Antonio: Nooo … Man, she told me that she met this dude and then she brought him here two days later she to meet me when she visited. After two days! So she told me to say hello, so I said Hola, which *is* hello, and then I called him Claudius and she said that I was being disrespectful, and they left. The next day she called wanted us to do something together, and I'm like, …

Social Worker: So you have used funny names to deal with the men your mother has been involved with since she and your stepfather divorced. Using funny names and joking around worked for you until now, and your mother also laughed with you [*coping*]

Antonio: Pretty much. But the way they acted, I think that they really like each other.

Social Worker: So, you think that this relationship is different. What will it take for you to talk to your mother? [*encouraging a solution*]

Antonio: Mmm, I don't know, I don't really care that much right now. I kind of need a break from her anyway. I feeling super stressed out right now.

Social Worker: You are feeling super stressed, okay. Have there been other times when you felt this way which caused you to want to take a break from your mother? [*exception*]

Antonio: Yeah, when she was late for my birthday party that the staff had for me.

Social Worker: What did you do?

Antonio: Nothing, cause when she arrived, we were okay.

Social Worker: Can I ask you a 1–10 question? Would you compare the two situations; you rate your level of stress with your mother, then and now? [*scaling question*]

Antonio: Yeeaahh. (said sarcastically)

Social Worker: That wasn't super convincing Antonio, thaaanks (laughs) I asked because it's a good way to let me know where you're at since, unfortunately, I'm not a mind reader.

Antonio: [Laughs] Alright go ahead then …

Social Worker: Where is your stress level about the party and now: If you tell me a 10, this means that your stress is very high, and a 1 means that you are being calm as a cucumber [*scaling question*].

Antonio: Ahh, like a 3 for the party, because I got over it as soon as she arrived. Now, maybe a 5.

Social Worker: Okay, so like right in the middle? You're not super stressed about your mom, but she is still on your mind.

Antonio: Yeah, for now anyway.

Social Worker: What would it take for you to feel less stressed about your relationship with your mother? [*bridging, encouraging his ideas about a solution*]

(At this point, the social worker noted that Antonio seemed bored with the conversation, so she shifted to a miracle question).

Social Worker: Antonio, I sense that you are ready to move on, am I correct?

Antonio: Sort of. I'm not sure what to do. I want to get along with my mother, but just not right now!

Social Worker: I understand because the two of you have worked hard to have a good relationship, but right now things aren't going well. During this stressful time, you have not returned to some of your old behavior. This is good. Also, your mother, despite her frustration, has continued to visit you [*complementing, acknowledging individual and relationship strengths*].

Social Worker: Let's try something different.

Antonio: Like what?

Social Worker: I am going to ask you a question. It's called the miracle question.

Antonio: The what (rolling his eyes)?

Social Worker: The question is: What if you imagined being less stressed out with your mother? [*moving toward a goal*]

Antonio: Oh, I can answer that! She would dump this new dude, but I don't really have a say in this, do I?

Social Worker: That's a good point. Let me ask the question a different way. What if tomorrow, you woke up and were talking to your mother, what would be different?

Antonio: Wow, you're asking a lot, but I give it a shot. I think that if I didn't joke about him, she and I would get along better. I could have a conversation with her without her getting all bent.

Social Worker: Okay, well that sounds like good insight, which I know you are pretty good at. Is this something that you would like to work on in our next session? [*goal formulation*]

Antonio: Yeah, okay.

Social Worker: Next time, we can work on signs that will tell you that things are better between you and your mother, and whether or not you are coping better with the situation. As we end the session, let's summarize what we accomplished today.

In the session with Antonio, you will have noticed that the social worker's use of various solution-focused questions and techniques flowed from the information that Antonio provided. In critiquing the overall session, the social worker pointed out that she moved too quickly to encourage a solution. For example, she asked, "What's your plan?" Antonio seemed to become bored, or perhaps discouraged. But, at the point in which Antonio provided concrete, specific, and behavioral actions that he could do to make the miracle happen, he and the social worker were able to move toward developing a well-formed goal (De Jong & Berg, 2008).

Strengths & Limitations

The solution-focused approach involves practical procedures and techniques that can be readily learned and applied by you in many practice situations. For example, a miracle question can amplify an individual's goals and encourage a person to become invested in a future vision. The particular emphasis on clients' strengths and attributes is also a significant contribution in that this focus promotes a positive image of clients and their capacities. The strategic focus on change affirms that gains, albeit small, can occur over a brief period of time.

EP 2.1.10a

As the approach has matured, a promising body of empirical evidence has shown its efficacy with diverse populations and with the variety of problems presented by clients (Corcoran, 2008; Corcoran & Pillai, 2009; Corcoran & Vijayan, 2009; Kim, 2007; Trepper, et al., 2006). Previously discussed studies have also demonstrated the effectiveness of using certain questions with specific populations, especially minors (Corcoran & Stephenson, 2000; Franklin & Streeter, 2004; Springer, Lynch, & Rubin, 2000).

Particular aspects of the procedures and techniques of the approach have been criticized. Both critics and proponents of the solution-focused approach have questioned whether the approach is, in fact, collaborative. In particular, the practitioner assigns tasks that are intended to help the client to focus on solutions (O'Hanlon, 1996; Lipchik, 1997; Wylie, 1990), To the latter point, research conducted with solution-focused family therapists revealed discrepancies between clients' experiences and the observations made by their therapists related to outcomes (Metcalf, Thomas,

Duncan, Miller, & Hubble, 1996). Storm (1991) and Lipchik (1997) concluded that the primary focus on solutions was disconcerting for some clients. Specifically, clients reported that the positive thrust of the approach prevented them from discussing their real concerns, and instead they felt persuaded to explore solutions. Further, the avoidance of talking about their problem was perceived to have limited value for them (Efran & Schenker, 1993). Similarly, the limited attention to behaviors instead of feelings ignores the connection between feelings and cognitions (Lipchick, 2002). These critiques, in many respects, ignore the fact that when people seek help, they have been socialized to talk about and describe their problems in great detail in exchange for services.

Other critics have suggested that the simplicity and practicality of some of the solution-focused questions and techniques may lead in some cases to a "cookbook" that ignores the relational dynamics between the professional and the individual. As noted by Lipchik (1997), collaboration that keeps the "axles turning" as well as the "speed and success of solution construction depend on the therapist's ability to stay connected with the client's reality throughout the course of therapy" (p. 329). Critiques related to the client-professional relationship are not specific to the solution-focused approach. Such discussions about whether or not a relationship with clients can be fully developed have been ongoing since the emergence of brief treatment approaches.

Professionals who work in environments that are frequently, if not always, problem or pathology focused may experience limited support for using the solution-focused approach (Trotter, 1999). For example, individuals who are involved in the legal system are typically required to demonstrate that problems have been resolved or that assessed dangers have been reduced. Of course, the same can be true for any problem-solving approach in these systems, as strengths and empowerment often tend to be ignored. Nonetheless, some professionals suggest encouraging solutions, rather than focusing on the problem, results in an attempt to remedy a situation that may not be fully understood.

The research and literature regarding involuntary clients have shown success of the approach with this often-neglected and marginalized client group (Berg & Kelly, 2000; Corcoran, 1997; DeJong & Berg, 1998; Corcoran, 1998; De Jong, & Berg, 2001; Tohn & Oshlag, 1996). Work with this population is believed to be enhanced by combining solution-focused procedures with other techniques such as motivational interviewing (DeJong & Berg, 2001; Lewis & Osborn, 2004; Miller & Rollnick, 2002; Tohn & Oshlag, 1999).

The approach supports the construction of the client's reality and it is considered to be essential to interactions with diverse groups. In this regard, the expertise of the professional is minimized, as is the opportunity to rely on basic stereotypes and generalizations. On this basis, well-informed goals are more likely to be relevant to the client. Even so, the assignment of tasks by the professional would appear to be more directive than collaborative.

Aspects to the approach, in particular the commitment to empowerment, a focus on individuals' competence, strengths, and capacities are values that are consistent with social work's commitment to self-determination. However, having faith in and wishing to support individual capacities should not lead us to assume that people have within them the solutions to all of their difficulties. In fact, some individuals may lack sufficient cognitive skills and resources or face sociopolitical barriers that impact their ability to actually achieve their miracle. As Chapters 8 and 9 attest, practice need not focus exclusively on either problems and deficits or strengths and resources. Rather, in helping clients, an appraisal of each, including risks and protective factors, is important in developing a realistic view of their situation and systems involved (McMillen, Morris, & Sherraden, 2004).

Case Management

Case management entails work that interfaces between the client and his or her environment. As a method, case management has moved to the forefront of direct social work practice in recognition of the fact that people with unmet needs were often unable to negotiate the complex and often uncoordinated health and human services delivery systems.

EP 2.1.10a

As defined by Rothman, "Case management is designed to coordinate the provision of services from multiple sources for the benefit of the individual client" (2002, p. 267).

Although the profession of social work does not have an exclusive claim to case management, the method's facilitative and coordinating functions can be traced to the Charity Organization Societies. At that point in time, the intent of coordinating services was two-fold: to address the multiple problems that individuals and families experienced and to preserve public resources (National Association of Social Workers, 1992). Over time, the momentum for case management has grown, beginning in the 1960's with deinstitutionalization initiatives to relocate and maintain people in their community. To a large extent, the growth of case management has been driven by federal and state funded programs, the majority of which mandate the coordination and integration of services. Medicaid, for example, requires case management to help beneficiaries gain access to needed medical, social, and educational services and other services. Most recently, *Targeted Case Management*, an amendment to the Budget Reduction Act of 2005, was added as a provision of Medicaid case management services. Under this provision, certain beneficiary groups, such as individuals with an identified chronic health, mental health problems, or who have a developmental disabilities and minors in foster care, are considered to be primary recipients of targeted case management services. Also included in the Medicaid provisions are individuals or groups who reside in a particular geographical region and individuals whose needs have been identified by their health and human services organization in their respective states (Binder, 2008). In the current human services state and federal reimbursement environment, case management (and therefore case managers) is integral to services in health and mental health settings, long-term care facilities, homeless shelters, schools, adult and juvenile probation, and child welfare.

Tenets of Case Management

EP 2.1.10a

As a direct practice method, case management is not in and of itself a change-oriented intervention strategy. The method does, however, involve the procedural elements of the approaches discussed earlier in this chapter. Referred to in health or institutional settings as *care planning*, *care coordination*, or *patient-centered care*, case management is viable and often times vital to persons in need of comprehensive services. A critical function of the method is linking individuals or families to a range of services based on their assessed needs. In essence, people are able to gain access to health, mental health and social welfare service providers that otherwise might be difficult for them to navigate on their own. The coordination of services by the case manager is intended to reduce duplication, fragmentation, and ultimately the frustration of the individual. In some settings, evaluating the costs of services is a critical component of case management.

As a problem-solving method, case management is theoretically open (Epstein & Brown, 2002). As such, the method can make use of theories and intervention tactics or techniques that are appropriate to individuals' situations. For example, the protocols of the task-centered model have been integrated with case management services in addressing the needs of elderly persons in long-term care (Naleppa & Reid, 2003), youth in residential treatment centers (Pazartz, 2006), and in improving school performance (Colvin, Lee, Maganano, & Smith, 2008). Solution-focused techniques were central to case management services for persons with mental disabilities (Greene, Kondraft, Lee, Clement, Siebert, Mentzer, & Pinnell, 2006; Hagen & Mitchell, 2001; Rapp, 2002) and in the treatment of drug use and abuse (Hall, Carswell, Walsh, Huber, & Jampler, 2002). Intensive case management that made use of cognitive behavioral treatment methods was effective in assisting women to move from welfare-to-work (Lee, 2005) and assisting low-income depressed older adults (Arean, Alexopoulos, & Chu, 2008). Similar results were observed when case managers used cognitive behavioral intervention techniques to reduce risky behaviors among HIV drug injectors (Robles, Reyes Colon, Sahai, Marrero, Matos, Calderon, & Shepard, 2004). The *Social Work Desk Reference* (2009) consists of a number of chapters on case management in regard to specific populations, including immigrant and refugee children and families. With respect to the latter, case management in particular is recommended for immigrant children and families (Fong, Amour, Busch-Arendariz, & Heffron, 2008; Potoky-Tripodi, 2002).

Standards of Case Management Practice

Both the National Association of Social Workers (NASW) (1992) and the Case Management Society of America (CMSA) (2010) have developed practice standards to include the educational and licensing requirements for case managers. In 2008, the two organizations joined together to develop advisory standards for case managers' case loads.

Core elements of the standards for practice of NASW (1992) and the CMSA (2010) are based on a set of beliefs and professional values considered to be essential to case management practice.

EP 2.1.10a

- *Utilizing a comprehensive assessment to determine the biopsychosocial functioning and care needs of individuals, including their strengths and resources.*
- *A client-centric, shared decision-making collaborative relationship between the individual and the case manager, in which the person and, where appropriate, family members are involved in all phases of the case management process.*
- *Planning and implementing services which address and are responsive to the unique needs of the individual or family.*
- *Adhering to professional values and principles, including self-determination, privacy, confidentiality, informed consent, and empowerment.*
- *The primacy of the obligation to the individual, which may involve advocacy, mediation, and negotiation to ensure access to services.*
- *Monitoring progress and the evaluation of the achievement of targeted outcomes.*
- *Utilizing the best evidence available to inform case management practice with specific populations, conditions, and needs.*

In promoting these standards, the aim of both organizations was to establish uniformity in case management functions and practices across disciplines and organizational settings.

EP 2.1.7b

The Case Management Society of America articulates an explicit standard with regard to cultural competence. Within these standards, there is an expectation that the case manager is informed, utilizes relevant client cultural information, and is sensitive to cultural contexts, including verbal and nonverbal communication styles. An expectation of culturally competent practice is similarly set forth in the National Association of Social Workers practice and policy statements (2007; 2009) and also in the federal guidelines of the U.S. Department of Health and Human Services, Office of Minority Health (2001).

Empirical Evidence of Case Management

EP 2.1.6b

Although case management is a widely used practice method, some researchers assert that evidence of its effectiveness cannot be generalized (DePalma, 2001; Major, 2004; Simons, Shepherd, & Murro, 2008; Orwin, Sonneffeld, Garvin-Morgan, & Gray-Smith, 1994). There are studies, nevertheless, in which the findings support the method's efficacy with individuals and families and for specific conditions or problems. In health, substance abuse, and mental health settings, case management significantly improved the outcomes for HIV-infected individuals, the retention of substance abuse users in treatment, as well as a prevention and intervention strategy for homeless youth, adults, and families (Chennon, Rosenbeck, & Lam, 2008; Gardner, et al., 2004; Mercier & Racine, 2005; Havens, Cornelius, Ricketts, Latkin, Bishai, Lloyd, Huettner, & Strathdee, 2007; Young & Grella, 1998; Susser, Valencia, Conover, Felix, & Tsas & Wyatt, 1997; Herman, Conover, Felix, Nakagawa, & Mills, 2007; Kasprow & Rosenbeck, 2007; Helvic & Alexey, 1992). Clinically oriented studies summarized by Hoagwood, Burns, Kiser, Ringeisen, and Schoenwald (2001) show that case management was effective in reducing the number of inpatient psychiatric hospitalizations for young children, the length of stay for youths in substance abuse treatment programs, and the number of placement disruptions for youths in foster care.

The method is also reported to have advanced the effectiveness of a school-based approach to minimize the impact of a chronic illness on school performance, social skills, and quality of life (Keehner, Gutter, & Warren, 2008). As an innovative approach that combines specific social work practice methods, case management is cited as an effective method in the treatment of substance abuse with individuals who lived in rural communities (Hall, Carswell, Walsh, Huber, & Jampler, 2002).

The integration of the strengths perspective was advised by Rapp (1993) as critical to case management practice. Implementing strengths-based case management calls for a focus on people's assets, resilience, and their capacity for self-direction (Brun & Rapp, 2001). Several strengths-based case management studies have demonstrated promising results. Positive outcomes were reported for people in substance abuse treatment, including their retention and their relationship with their case managers (Brun & Rapp, 2001; Rapp, 2002; Siegal, Rapp, Li, Saha, & Kirk, 1998; Siegal, Fischer, Rapp, Killiher, Wagner, O'Brien, & Cole, 1996; Siegal, Rapp, Kelliher, Fisher, Wagner, & Cole, 1995).

Case Management Functions

Although case management processes may vary with respect to settings and organizational priorities and goals, there is a consensus that case management always includes the functions or phases summarized in Table 13-5

EP 2.1.10j

TABLE-13-5 CASE MANAGEMENT FUNCTIONS

PHASES	TASKS
Access & Outreach	Outreach or case finding identifies people who are likely to need case management services.
Intake & Screening	Preliminary to an assessment, screening is an initial step in determining eligibility for services. A preliminary plan may be developed at this stage.
Multidimensional Assessment	Information is collected about the individuals' physical, mental social, and psychological functioning, the physical environment, including strengths and resources. The multidimensional assessment guides the development of the case plan.
Goal Setting	Goals and objectives are developed based on assessed need, in collaboration with the individual. The goal plan and objectives are based on the individual's perception of needs, and may be structured as long or short term.
Planning Interventions & Linking to Resources	Planning the intervention and linking individuals to resources are interdependent functions. Both formal and informal resources and the appropriate service providers are identified. The specific services, as well as the frequency and duration of contact with the service provider are specified.
Monitoring the Progress & Adequacy of Services	Monitoring progress and the extent to which service providers continue to meet the needs identified in the case plan is a vital and ongoing process. Three sources of information are indicated: Regular contact with service providers to determine if services are responsive, monitoring progress toward the stated goals, and the individual's observations regarding the level of progress and satisfaction with the providers.
Reassessment at Fixed Intervals	It is particularly important to be sensitive to changes in clients' needs and to adjust or modify the plan as indicated. Reassessments can be formal or informal and are completed at fixed intervals. The information gathered can also determine the level of change since the initial assessment.
Outcome Evaluation/ Termination	Outcome evaluation, in brief situations in which goals have been achieved, leads to termination. In longer term, reassessment and evaluation of outcomes is ongoing.

© Cengage Learning 2013

(Case Management Society of America, 2010; Holt, 2002; Rothman, 2002; National Association of Social Workers, 1992).

EP 2.1.10g

While the phases and tasks of case management are for the most part self-explanatory, for some, elaboration and a brief rationale is indicated. Outreach and case finding, for example, may be particularly important for vulnerable populations such as homeless, frail elderly, and disabled persons, many of whom are likely to be eligible for health and supportive social services, but who may be reluctant to seek formal help. While the phases are procedural in nature, the practice standards are consistent with the ethical principles of social work practice, in particular, the emphasis on self-determination and collaboration with service recipients as key informants in the assessment and goal setting process and the implementation of the case plan. Although the case manager is ultimately responsible for overseeing the implemented plan, the individual or family is also involved in the evaluation of the adequacy of the service. You will also note that monitoring progress and reassessment depends on the goals and time frame of the case plan. For example, long-term case plans may require an infinite amount of services, in which case the reassessment intervals are ongoing. In these instances, reassessment is critical and assessing progress may require the use of pre/post baseline or standardized instruments. In contrast, with brief case management services (e.g., locating housing, securing medical care, attaining the capacity to live independently), satisfactory progress and goal attainment should lead to termination.

Case Managers

Case managers are fundamental to the case management tasks. Whether your title in an organization is case manager, plan coordinator, or care coordinator, you are the human interaction between individuals and various systems. You may work as a part of a team in some settings, and, in others, you can be solely responsible for providing case management services. The type of setting will also determine whether your involvement as a case manager is brief or time-limited, targeted, ongoing, or open-ended.

EP 2.1.1c

In practice, your role and your responsibilities relative to the phases and tasks can be as varied as the settings in which you are employed. For example, with a patient due to be discharged from a hospital, your contact with the individual would most likely occur at the assessment phase and proceed forward from this point. Similarly, screening and intake can be abbreviated when a targeted population has been designated in a Purchase of Service Agreement (POS). Conversely, as a case manager in a shelter for homeless youth, outreach or case finding would be a first step. In yet another scenario, you are the authorized professional who is solely responsible for completing the comprehensive assessment, developing an individualized service plan, and for negotiating and coordinating services.

The phases of case management and the point of contact notwithstanding, irrespective of your case manager role, it is important to keep in mind that case management begins with an assessed *need* rather than a *service*. No two individuals will have or express their needs, problems, or goal preferences in the same way. For this reason, the implemented case or care plan is tailored to the unique needs of the people involved. Specifically, each person or family should be able to expect that their case plan is responsive to their specific needs, rather than the priorities of an agency.

Name:	Angela and Irwin Corning			
Children:	Agnes, age 10			
	Henri, age 8			
	Katrina, age 18 months			
Case Manager	Ali Smith			
SUMMARY OF ASSESSED NEEDS				
Housing √	Health care √	Debt Counseling √	Tutors √	Employment √
Financial Assistance √	Preschool √			
COORDINATED REFERRALS				
Goals	Providers	Sessions/Duration	Monitoring	Reassessment
Obtain affordable Housing	Clarion Housing Program	1–3 months	Weekly	Every month
Permanent Full-time Employment (Irwin)	Employment Resource Center	8 weeks	Weekly	Monthly
Credit card debt reduction	Consumer Credit Counseling	4 Weeks	On going	1 month
Obtain rental deposit and 1 month's rental	County Temporary Housing Assistance Office	1–2 Sessions	2–3 days	N/A
Family Physicals Childhood Inoculations	Community Health Center	1 year	Ongoing	
Grade Level Assistance (Agnes & Henri)	After School Tutorial Program	1 year	Ongoing	Monthly
Social and Educational Activities	Head Start	1 year	Ongoing	Monthly
Outcome Evaluation & Reassessment:	Monthly			

FIG-13-5 Case Management Plan

Case Manager Responsibility and Roles

EP 2.1.10j

The case of the Corning family is used to illustrate a case management plan. In reviewing the case plan, you are able to observe that its implementation required the case manager to be both facilitative and active, both of which are illustrated in this case. Effectively responding to the goals of the plan required that she facilitate the concurrent efforts of public and private organizations and other disciplines. In collaboration with Angela and Irwin, decisions were made about the number of sessions with each provider. For example, the couple anticipated that applying for and obtaining approval for temporary rental assistance would require no more than two to three appointments. Conversely, their access and utilization of health care providers was established over a longer period of time.

In linking the Corning family with the mix of providers, the case manager had to be actively involved. Specifically, it would have not been sufficient for her to simply identify and refer them to the providers, and subsequently expect them to follow through. Making the connections to service is a central task. Afterwards, it was the case manager's responsibility to oversee the plan on an ongoing basis. Implementing a case plan also requires a great deal of up front work. Essential activities include determining the eligibility criteria of each provider, their ability to meet the plan's goals, and their case review and monitoring process. Once you are satisfied that there is a *fit* between the individual's needs and the service provisions of each provider, service agreements are developed with each. Similar to the service agreement or contract with clients (refer to Chapter 12) the case management plan specifies the work to be completed.

As a case manager, the *broker* role is vital to facilitating interagency coordination and cooperation. In this capacity, you need to have a working knowledge of, and an effective relationship with, a range of service providers, including available informal resources. The broker role, specifically connecting to critical resources, is evident in the response to the array of needs in the Corning family case. As a case manager, helping people gain access to available resources may require *negotiating* with the various service providers. Where indicated, *advocacy* at the systems level may be necessary to ensure that individuals have access to resources to which they are entitled. In addition to the broker role, in any one case, mediating between an individual and various systems is required. For instance, the role of a *mediator* role between the school and the Corning parents would have been indicated, had the school been reluctant to support the goal of enhancing the performance of Agnes and Henri by providing tutorial assistance. Furthermore, had the school lacked this resource, it would have been important to explore an alternative or develop a resource.

Strengths and Limitations

EP 2.1.10a

Case management is a problem-solving practice method that is designed to link the needs of individuals to a range of service providers. Based on assessed needs, services are individualized in recognition of the unique capabilities, goals, and circumstances of each service recipient. Although, the assessment is integral to case management, it is only one part of the core functions that make up the entire process. Other core tasks involve developing and implementing the case plan and monitoring progress. Hence, it is important that a case manager is skilled in all aspects of the problem-solving process. In completing this work, acting as a broker is a key role of the case manager. There are instances that necessitate the case manager to negotiate, mediate, or advocate on behalf of individuals to ensure that they have access to needed services.

The method has grown over time, in part, as a response to federal funding requirements which emphasize improved access to services and the coordination and integration of the services that they received. The growth of the method can also be attributed to a desire for greater continuity in care by reducing the fragmentation and duplication in service delivery systems as a result of a lack of coordination. Standards and principles of case management developed by the National Association of Social Workers and the Case Management Society of America have contributed to the uniformity of case management functions and the role of the case manager across settings.

As evidenced by the summarized results of research studies, case management, either as a stand alone practice method or when integrated with another treatment approach, has demonstrated its effectiveness in addressing a range of needs or problems with specific populations. Several of the summarized studies demonstrated the benefit of this integration.

An assumption of case management is that the resources or service providers that an individual needs are always available both in adequate quality and quantity. In reality, gaps in services exist, in particular, disparities between assessed needs and available services. In some instances, the service can be available, but the provider may be overwhelmed with demands. Herein lies a challenge for the case manager, particularly in an age in which funding for services are reduced.

On the whole, case management is intended to meet the multiple needs of an individual in a coordinated, comprehensive manner. The phases and associated tasks allow for the development of a case plan unique to the individual. The greater benefit of case management is the fact that services are identified based on assessed needs, which eliminates an individual having to navigate complex helping systems on their own.

Summary

The task-centered and crisis intervention models and cognitive restructuring and case management approaches are focused on problem solving. As the name implies, the solution-focused approach is designed to deemphasize a problem focus and deliberately emphasize solutions.

The approaches are similar in that their focus is primarily on the present, they are time-limited, and they emphasize clients' capacity to change and grow through autonomous independent action. Research studies have shown brief, time-limited approaches to be as effective as those that require a longer time period (Reid & Shyne, 1969; Wells, 1994; Wells & Gianetti, 1990; Corwin, 2002). The efficacy of brief, time-limited approaches is that their scope is on a specific target problem or behavior and a specificity of goals or solutions. The conscious use of time is considered to be productive in that specific goals or solutions make the best use of brief contact (Corwin, 2002; Hoyt, 2000; Reid, 1996).

Increasing the power of people to participate in and influence change in their lives is a salient characteristic of each of the approaches. Whereas task-centered practice, crisis intervention, and cognitive restructuring seek to empower clients through systematic and collaborative problem solving, the solution-focused approach aims is to empower individuals through their construction of solutions. Even so, empowerment is evident in the other approaches as they too emphasize accepting individuals' identification of their target concern and their participation in developing goals. Inherent in each approach is the assumption that people know what they want and have a right to and that they have the capacity to solve their own problems (DeJong & Berg, 2002; Reid & Epstein, 1972).

A deliberate emphasis on clients' strengths, in recognition of the critical social work principle that "people have the capacity to change and grow," is also prominent in each approach. Strengths and resilience are foremost in the exploration of prior coping and adaptations, resources, and emotional stability in the crisis intervention and task-centered approaches. The recognition of how clients have coped and what they have done in the past effectively builds on his or her skills and resources. In solution-focused practice, a person is encouraged to reflect on exceptions to their problem and further problems are defined in a situational rather than an individual context. The latter of which may ignore strengths. Cognitive restructuring recognizes the strength of the individual's capacity for self-direction and to gain skills in managing his or her beliefs through the development of self-talk, coping statements, and self-reliance. Strengths are equally important in case management. Needs do not necessarily define the whole person, therefore, a focus on people's assets, resilience, and their capacity for self-direction is emphasized (Brun & Rapp, 2001; Case Management Society of America, 2010).

There is significant overlap in the theoretical perspectives and strategies of four of the approaches. For example, cognitive-behavioral and social learning theories influence the task-centered system, crisis intervention, and the solution-focused approaches. Cognitive restructuring is a technique utilized in task-centered practice to address client's beliefs and in crisis intervention, depending on the nature of the crisis (Reid, 1992; James & Gilliland, 2001). These overlapping strategies and perspectives of each approach provides the flexibility of being able to draw upon and adapt the change process to various theories of human behavior, needs, environment, and lifestyles. Because case management is theoretically open, the method can make use of different theoretical frameworks. Of course, each approach has limitations, and, for certain populations, an adaptation or modification may be required. Nevertheless, each has merit in that these interventions are brief, are action-oriented, and focus on specific goals for change.

Empirical support exists for each of the approaches, including their use with diverse populations, age groups, and in diverse settings was summarized in the section in which the approach was discussed. But, in selecting the most suitable strategy, you must consider the problem and goals, developmental stages, racial, or cultural beliefs, customs and values, and environmental factors germane to the case. Most of all you should be able to assess the extent that an approach has demonstrated its effectiveness with whom, under what circumstances, and with which kinds of problems.

CourseMate

Access an integrated eBook and chapter-specific learning tools including glossary terms, chapter outlines, relevant web links, videos, and practice quizzes. Go to **www.cengagebrain.com**.

CHAPTER **14**

Intervention Strategies: Developing Resources, Organizing, Planning, and Advocacy

CHAPTER OVERVIEW

Chapter 14 transitions from direct practice intervention to macro-level change strategies. In this chapter you will become familiar with macro-level problem-solving activities where the change effort is directed toward systems rather than towards the individual. The chapter concludes with a discussion of general guidelines for evaluating macro practice outcomes.

As a result of reading this chapter you will acquire knowledge that will enable you to:

- Understand macro practice intervention strategies
- Understand the connection between micro problems and macro practice
- Use the social justice perspective to analyze social problems and conditions
- Become familiar with skills used for social action, advocacy, and community organizing
- Understand your role as a change agent
- Apply social work ethical principles and standards to macro practice
- Evaluate macro practice activities

EPAS COMPETENCIES IN THE 14TH CHAPTER

This chapter provides information that you will need to meet the following practice competencies:

2.1.1a Advocate for client access to services

2.1.1d Demonstrate professional demeanor in behavior, appearance, and communication

2.1.4b Gain sufficient self-awareness to eliminate the influence of personal biases and values in working with diverse groups

2.1.4a Recognize the extent to which culture's structures and values alienate, create, or enhance power and privilege

2.1.4d View themselves as learners and engage those with whom they work as key informants

2.1.5a Understand forms and mechanisms of oppression and discrimination

2.1.5b Advocate for human rights and social and economic justice

2.1.5c Engage in practices that engage in social and economic justice

2.1.6b Use research evidence to inform practice

2.1.8a Analyze, formulate, and advocate for policies that advance social well-being

2.1.9a Continuously discover, appraise, and attend to changing locales, populations, scientific and technological developments, and emerging societal trends to provide relevant services

2.1.9b Provide leadership in promoting sustainable changes in service delivery and practice to improve the quality of social services

2.1.10a Substantively and effectively prepare for action with individuals, families, groups, and communities

2.1.10b Use empathy and other interpersonal skills

2.1.10c Develop mutually agreed-upon focus of work and desired outcomes

2.1.10d Collect and organize client data

2.1.10e Assess client strengths and limitations

2.1.10g Select appropriate intervention strategy

2.1.10h Initiate action to achieve organizational goals

2.1.2d Apply strategies of ethical reasoning skills to arrive at principled decisions

Social Work's Commitment

Brueggemann (2006) and Schneider and Lester (2001) trace the historical commitment of the profession of social work to the ideal of improving the human condition through social reform, social justice, and equality. These longstanding ideals are practice principles that are reflected in the National Association of Social Workers (NASW) Code of Ethics and the Council of Social Work Education (CSWE) Educational Policy Accreditation Standards (EPAS) for the professional educational preparation of social workers. Guided by the ethical principles of NASW, professional social workers are obligated to enhance the welfare of individuals and improve social conditions by developing resources, planning, and engaging in social action (NASW, 1996). Promoting social and economic justice and improving social conditions to include populations at risk are overarching principles articulated in EPAS. These principles underscore the profession's commitment "to advance human rights and social and economic justice" and to ensure that social workers are prepared to "engage in policy practice to advance social and economic well-being, and to deliver effective social work services" (CSWE, 2008, pp. 5–6).

Global standards that frame the core purpose of international social work also emphasize social action, political action, and advocacy, "to facilitate the inclusion of marginalized, socially excluded, dispossessed, and vulnerable at-risk groups of people" (Global Standards for Social Work Education and Training, 2004, p. 3). Fundamental among the principles of international social work are respect for diverse beliefs, traditions, and cultures as well as regard for human rights and social justice. Similarly, these principles are articulated in the NASW Standards for Cultural Competence in Social Work Practice (NASW, 2001).

The ethical standards and educational policy statements of the national professional organizations regarding economic and social justice and equality are hardly the exclusive domains of social work as a profession. There are organizations, including faith communities, that articulate similar principles and that engage in social action and advocacy. The profession of social work, however, has embraced these principles as organizing values. Urging the profession to go a step further in its social justice agenda, Hodge (2007) points to the need of the profession to advocate for a *Universal Declaration of Human Rights*, in particular, for religious freedom and to work toward ending religious persecution on a national and global level. Like Hodge, McKinnon (2008) advocates for expanding the ecological focus in the profession to include the challenges of the physical environment and its impact on people.

Defining Macro Practice

By definition, macro practice involves professionally guided interventions in which the targets are social problems and conditions. As summarized by Brueggemann (2006, p. 7), macro social work is the "practice of helping people solve social problems and make social change at the community, organizational, societal and global levels." In essence, a distinctive feature of macro-level interventions is that seeing the whole picture and intervening can ultimately change and improve the lives of people (Burghardt, 2011; Parsons, Jorgensen, & Hernandez, 1988, 1994; Long, Tice, & Morrison, 2006). In the course of examining the whole picture, you are able to determine the impact on human behavior (Alexander, 2010; McKinnon, 2008; Saleeby, 2004).

Historically, the profession's capacity to see a relationship between people and their environment can be traced to the belief system that guided the work of the Settlement House Movement. Settlement House workers believed that improving social conditions and changing the social and economic environment through advocacy, community organizing, and social action, would ultimately improve the functioning of the individual and the community. Reminiscent of this movement, Breton (2006) asserts "there is a dialectical relationship between social change and personal change" (p. 34). Recall the case of Angela and Irwin Corning. The loss of Irwin's job and the subsequent loss of their home typify the plight of millions of Americans, as well as citizens in other countries. In helping the couple to regain a sense of equilibrium in their lives, it would be important for you to be aware of

Intervention Strategies: Developing Resources, Organizing, Planning, and Advocacy

the broader economic context in which their problems occurred and were sustained over time.

Linking Micro and Macro Practice

EP 2.1.10d

It is not unusual for you as a direct service practitioner to observe patterns in the prevalence of certain problems and conditions throughout your caseload. In your work with individuals and families, you are in an opportune position to make the connection between micro concerns, which may require macro strategies to remedy. There may be days in which you feel that with each individual client you are working at the edge of a much larger problem, one person at a time. You may however question your ability to act, given your role in your organization. Nonetheless, your observations of the experience of individual clients, as illustrated in Figure 14-1, can become an important linkage from micro to macro practice.

Essentially, the figure illustrates how micro level observations can inform social workers of common problems and conditions that are experienced by individuals, groups, and communities. For example, let's say that you have observed the frequency of a certain presenting problem among the people with whom you have contact. As a beginning to your inquiry as to whether your observation is in fact true, or emblematic of a large system change opportunity, you might ask yourself: *To what extent is the individual's problem pervasive among the larger group experience to which they belong?* This question enables you to obtain a snapshot of the whole picture, which leads to a macro-level assessment of a problem (Breton, 2006; Burghardt, 2011; White & Epston, 1990). Because of the dual and interlocking connection between the public and the private, there are times when a two-prong approach (specifically a combination of micro and macro) is required to respond to needs and conditions (Long, Tice & Morrison, 2006). In essence, you bridge micro- and macro-practice strategies by addressing the individual's situation, as well as the external social and economic conditions that perpetuate their problems (Parson, Jorgenson & Hernandez, 1994; Vodde & Gallant, 2002; White & Epston, 1990)

Macro Practice Intervention Strategies

EP 2.1.10b

Targets of change at the macro-level may focus on policy analysis, organizations, communities, or groups. Irrespective of their focus, a collective, large scale intervention to effect change is a common distinctive feature of macro strategies (Burghardt, 2011). As you read this chapter, you will appreciate that knowledge and skills you learned in earlier chapters are also instrumental in macro practice. Austin, Coombs, and Barr (2005) note the uniformity in the skills of micro and macro practice. For instance, you will use both structural and interpersonal skills in macro practice as in micro practice. Structural skills include assessment, developing and planning measurable strategic goals, and monitoring and evaluating outcomes. On an interpersonal level, you will utilize oral and written communication skills, and facilitative and relationship building skills such as empathy, authenticity, genuineness, and self-awareness. Roles are also similar (e.g., educator, mediator, advocate, resource developer), although professional titles may differ. Netting, Kettner, and McMurtry (2004) have identified the professional titles associated with these roles such as supervisor, manager, program coordinator, planner, policy analyst, and community organizer.

Many different types of interventions are used to change conditions, improve environments, and respond to needs found within organizations, groups, or communities. A full discussion of the various macro-level strategies is beyond the scope of this practice foundation of this text. Instead, we will focus our discussion on selected methods and strategies associated with the following macro-level interventions:

- *Developing and mobilizing resources*
- *Advocacy and social action*
- *Community organization*
- *Improving organizational environments*
- *Organizational change*

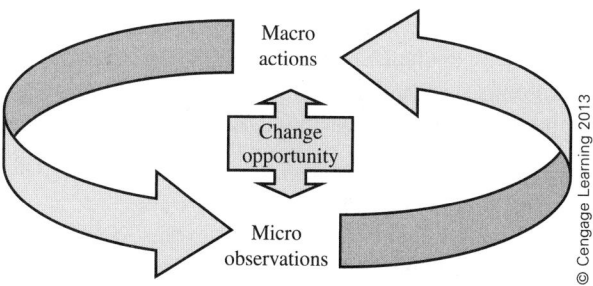

FIG-14-1 Linking Micro and Macro Practice

Before discussing each of these macro-level interventions, we will address empowerment, strengths, and social problem analysis, as relevant factors in macro practice.

Empowerment and Strengths

EP 2.1.10a

Empowerment means that groups or communities can act to prevent problems, gain or regain the capacity to interact with the social environment, and expand the resources available to meet their needs (Gutierrez, GlenMaye & Delois, 1995; Long, Tice, & Morrison, 2006; Weil, 1996). As a process, empowerment actively engages people in decisions about their well-being, potential, life satisfaction, and the outcome of realizing control over their lives to the extent possible. Empowerment also promotes social and economic justice when communities and groups are able to secure resources that have a positive influence on their lives (Long, Trice, & Morrison, 2006).

EP 2.1.10e

Why the focus on empowerment and strength? All people at various times in their lives experience limited power. But, constituents of social work, however, may include groups and entire communities who lack the power because of their minimized status in the larger social environment. Indeed, the powerless are more likely to have government agencies and public policies exert significant authority over their lives. The empowerment perspective assumes that power and powerlessness are inextricably linked to the experience of inequality. Furthermore, the lack of power is a common experience, particularly in racial and ethnic minority and poor communities.

When working with certain vulnerable groups who may have a limited sense of individual and collective efficacy, you may have the tendency to think of empowerment as giving them power. Even in these circumstances, empowerment means that you tap into and mobilize people's power by working in collaboration with them to develop their competence to alter or improve their situation (Carter, 2000; White & Epston, 1990). In essence, empowerment is a process in which you work to develop the capacity of people to change their situations (Gutierrez & Ortega, 1991). Whether you are involved in creating more favorable conditions for a group or community, for example, in developing resources or advocacy, you should be careful that your actions are not disempowering to those whom you are attempting to help. To this end, it is vital that you observe and respect their values and beliefs and that your actions are consistent with the ethical principles of the profession.

As social workers, we respond to the needs and interests identified by groups or communities in ways that build on their strengths and that will assist them to realize their hopes, dreams, and aspirations. Recognizing strengths at the macro-level sees people as resourceful and resilient, is respectful of their stories, and works in collaboration with them to achieve a range of human and community capital goals based on their viewpoint. In your entry into a community or group, valuing their definitions of problems is vital to forging a collaborative helping relationship (Gutierrez, 1994; Gutierrez & Lewis, 1999; Long, Tice, & Morrison, 2006; Saleebey, 2004; Van Voorhis & Hostetter, 2006). Combined strengths and empowerment are critical to assisting communities and groups to develop, own, and govern their self-efficacy. In this way, the shape and influence of the change effort is directed by active community leadership (Weil, 1996; Van Voorhis & Hostetter, 2006).

Analyzing Social Problems and Conditions

Policy analysis involves understanding conditions and solving macro-level problems, which includes evaluating social justice and inequality (Barusch. 2009; Finn & Jacobson, 2003). In the traditional sense, policy analysis is a process that begins with defining the problem, gathering information, and setting strategic goals and outcomes (Bardach, 2009). The following discussion is a slight departure from policy analysis, and instead focuses on analyzing social problems and conditions using a social justice perspective as a primary lens. As social workers who are regularly in contact with people whose lives are affected by social problems and conditions and the impact of policy decision, our analysis provides us with data that can be used to inform policymakers of the realities of the lives of clients. In this way, we meet the obligation of the profession to advance clients' collective well-being.

Social justice questions that may be posed to analyze social conditions and problems are adapted from the work of Finn and Jacobson (2003b) and Segal (2010).

EP 2.1.8a

- *What are the social justice issues affecting the people with whom I work?*
- *What are the particular values expressed for groups and communities when resources are distributed in our society?*

In addition to these questions, a social justice perspective would also examine the following:

- *Who is affected by policy decisions and in what way?*
- *Does social policy have a disparate impact on a particular segment of the population?*

To these questions, we add a core question from the FrameWorks Institute:

- *Who and what is responsible for the problem?*

The FrameWorks Institute is a nonprofit organization that provides training for professionals and other advocates in "thinking strategically" about social problems and reframing issues that appeal to basic societal values when communicating with policymakers or the public.

Social Justice Issues

EP 2.1.4a

All people are born into different economic, cultural, or social circumstances. Not all people are equal in their abilities. These are facets of our society and the global community. It is, however, unacceptable by virtue of one's birth that some people are relegated to lives in which inequality and oppression are distinctive factors that diminish opportunities for some, resulting in a sustained experience of social problems or impoverished conditions. In general, there is stratification in our society in which privilege places some individuals and groups at the top, and others at a lower level (Alexander, 2010). Using social justice as a lens to examine social problems and conditions gives rise to the question of whether people at the lower stratification level have equal access to resources and to opportunities that promote their well-being, dignity, and worth; or whether they are stigmatized and marginalized because of who they are. Social justice also includes examining the nexus between the problems that people have, the conditions in which they live, and the social policies that in affect determine them, and the extent to which policy decisions adversely impact individuals, groups, and communities. For practitioners, self-evaluation requires examining the extent to which their practice with people in need supports the basic tenets of the profession regarding equality and the primacy of clients' rights, including human and civil rights. The questions posed are by no means exclusive, but rather, serve as a frame of reference by which you can use for analyzing the social problems and conditions and whether the policy decisions intended to alter social problems and conditions adversely impact groups and communities.

Values and the Distribution of Resources

EP 2.1.5b

To a large extent, social welfare services continue to be directed primarily toward individual change (Breton, 2006; Brueggemann, 2006; Long, Tice, & Morrison, 2006). Over the past several decades, this focus has been reinforced by the emphasis on personal responsibility at the expense of social justice (Linhorst, 2002). As noted by Breton (2006), the funding entities upon which social welfare organizations depend are rarely interested in collective social action. Adherence to the notion of individual change or responsibility tends to emphasize goals and values that for the most part are acceptable to society. What is acceptable to society can shift because of conflicting political and societal ideologies. For example, individual autonomy has influenced the ideological notion of personal responsibility that can be observed in social policies that are intended to respond to a range of social problems and conditions. Conversely, social responsibility, a collective ideological view point, emphasizes that social conditions and problems are beyond the individual's ability to resolve and, as such, calls for a more comprehensive policy response (Breton, 2006; Segal, 2010). From a social justice perspective, you might question whether personal or social responsibility contributes to the rights and well-being of people, in particular those without power and resources.

Who Is Affected by Policy Decisions and in What Way?

EP 2.1.8a

The Personal Responsibility and Work Opportunity Reconciliation Act of 1996 (PRWORA)—which reformed the system of public welfare—and the Adoption and Safe Family Act of 1997 (ASFA) are examples of policy decisions that affected large segments of social work constituents. The Personal Responsibility and Work Opportunity Reconciliation Act, which mainly affected poor, single women, ended a 60-year-old entitlement to cash aid, and was replaced by 60-month lifetime and work requirements. In addition, states were given discretion in the requirements that they could develop as a means to dissuade people from applying for assistance. At the same time, the Adoption and Safe Family Act emphasized greater scrutiny of the ability of poor families to care for their children, but did not take into account the removal of some of the safeguards by the PRWORA.

Undoubtedly, there was a need to reexamine both the public welfare and the child welfare systems, but the competing and conflicting demands of these two concurrent pieces of legislation resulted in many families experiencing long-term system-level difficulties in meeting requirements and timelines. Ultimately, the burden of the corrective action undertaken in both welfare reform and child-welfare reform fell on individuals. An assumption inherent in child welfare policy was that neglectful parents and their lack of parental responsibility were the primary culprits affecting their ability to meet the reunification and permanency timelines. However, the review of the delays in permanency and reunification failed to consider the possibility that the excess time that a child remained in care resulted from an overloaded, underfunded, and fragmented system. In much the same manner, a core belief driving welfare reform was the idea that people receiving public assistance lacked motivation to work. In reality, the policy in effect at the time disallowed those receiving benefits from being employed. There is research evidence that suggests a relationship between welfare reform and a significant increase in reports of child maltreatment and neglect (Courtney, 1999; Hutson, 2001).

Disparate Impact and Social Justice

EP 2.1.5b

Implementation of both the welfare assistance and child welfare policies had an uneven impact on segments of the population, and in particular on minority communities, which raised questions about justice and inequality. In both instances, the implementation of these policies affected women as heads of household in single-parent families and communities of color. As social workers, we are in contact with individuals and families who are affected by policy decisions. Therefore, we have access to a wealth of information that can be used to inform policymakers of the realities of our clients' lives. To this point, consider the following discussion of policies related to PWORA and AFSA and their long-term implications for social and economic well-being. Also, think about your role as a social worker in responding to the issues presented.

Leaving welfare, as many recipients did, and not returning was not as easy as the policymakers imagined. The ability of welfare leavers to gain employment and sustained financial self-sufficiency was hampered by the very real presence of structural and economic barriers, such as unstable low-wage jobs, the high concentration of recipients in large urban areas, and limited supportive services (Anderson, Halter, & Gryzlak, 2004; Banerjee, 2002). Findings from studies by Banerjee (2002) and Anderson and colleagues (2004) countered the popular image of the unmotivated, self-satisfied welfare recipient. Instead, they show women who were dissatisfied with their economic situation and the stigma attached to being on welfare, and whose aspirations were not dissimilar from mainstream society. In addition, under the new federal tax and spending decisions, states could decide how to distribute supportive resources and what services to provide; for example, whether or not to provide funds for child care, and if provided, for how long (Abramovitz, 2005; Linhorst, 2002). Ultimately these decisions had an impact on the level of services available to welfare leavers through nonprofit organizations and both county and state programs.

Given the reality of the structural and economic barriers faced by welfare leavers that influenced the availability of jobs and limited supportive services (for example, the recession), are the sanctions and penalties against those who are unable to achieve work just?

EP 2.1.4a

Disparate impact on clients can also be measured in what a policy requires of practitioners in so far as it intrudes on their ability to engage in practice that is consistent with the standards and principals of the social work profession. For example, at issue for many social workers is the fact that their work has little to do with professional practice, such as developing or helping clients find resources. Because of federal and state compliance mandates and performance benchmarks for agencies and client compliance, social workers likened their role to that of a compliance officer or investigator, rather than that of a professional helper, raising ethical dilemmas (Abramovitz, 2005; Withorn, 1998).

While Withorn (1998) questioned the ethics and justice of welfare reform, a study by Abramovitz (2005) highlighted the ethical tensions experienced by social workers and agency administrators as they attempted to balance policy compliance with mandates for clients and ethical practice. A particular area of concern related to protecting client's rights and autonomy, while also responding to performance-based agency contracts that ignored their choices. For example, the "work first mandate" meant that participants were required to find employment rather than pursuing or continuing educational opportunities (Banerjee, 2002). These ethical tensions are also intertwined with just practice. Specifically, do policy mandates, penalties, and performance-based evaluation further disenfranchise and marginalize people by constraining their choices and forcing them to make decisions that are not in their best or long-term interest?

EP 2.1.8a

As another example of the disparate impact of a policy, consider the Adoption and Safe Family Act (AFSA, 1997). This public policy was intended to move children to permanent homes. Specific timelines were enacted to ensure that children did not languish within the child welfare system. For instance, parents were given 12 months to rectify the circumstances that prompted a child's placement in foster care and to achieve reunification. During this time period, a permanency alternative for the child or children would be pursued. Because of the number of children in foster care who remained in limbo for lengthy periods of time, the goal of permanency was an overdue initiative. But, the wisdom of the abbreviated time period is called into question as a matter of justice in light of concurrent planning. Concurrent planning involves the simultaneous planning for both reunification and adoption as permanent outcomes for children who are placed outside of their home (Curtis and Denby, 2004). A specific justice concern centered on the fact that resources were available to potential foster/adoptive parents but not uniformly so for biological parents. Moreover, the restrictive timelines and limited services led to an increase in the termination of parental rights of poor and minority parents.

The implementation of this law disproportionately affected specific segments of communities, mainly those who were poor and minority. The impact on poor African American communities was particularly difficult because the majority of the children placed out of their homes are African Americans (Hill, 2005; Curtis & Denby, 2004; Morton, 1999). Roberts (2002) likened the child welfare system to apartheid, the effects of which constitute "group harm" because entire communities experience the impact. In fact, in large urban communities, the intervention of child welfare and child protection services may be traced to specific ZIP codes where the residents are largely poor and minority families.

EP 2.1.4a

Pervasive poverty, including homelessness, is one reason that a majority of African American and other children of color are placed out of the home. Such pervasive poverty is a cause to examine justice and disparate impact; specifically, whether poor families should lose their children because of their economic circumstances, or whether there is a need for greater economic supports for poor families. A key question to be considered in placement decisions raised by Wulczyn and Lery (2007) is whether poor parents have the resources to protect children, and, if not, what resources are needed. In large part, according to Chipungu and Bent-Goodley (2003), the child welfare system has become a "safety net for poor children" funded by Title IV-E, rather than a system that provides the services and resources that would support and sustain the family system.

Inequality and justice issues can also be considered on two other levels. In the current child welfare–child protection system, there is little distinction made between child neglect and child abuse, in particular egregious harm. Hence, poverty-related neglect, a primary reason that families of color have contact with child protective services, is treated in the same criminalized and stigmatized fashion as the harm associated with child abuse. Involvement with child protection has far reaching effects on parents. An allegation of neglect, whether substantiated or not, can influence a parent's ability to obtain housing and employment. Therefore, is it just that poor families of color, who are already marginalized in many cases by pervasive poverty and other structural barriers, be further stigmatized as criminals simply because they lack the resources to care for their children?

Secondly, and perhaps foremost, is the concern related to the uncertain outcomes of out-of-home placement for children of color when measured against established and long-term expectations related to health and well-being standards. For example, funding to states is based on the number of placements, and once placement has occurred, there is little or no follow-up to determine child well-being (Munroe, 2004). It is the perception of many advocates in minority communities that out-of-home placement is a first step in the disruption of a minor's life, and a precursor to the juvenile justice system, eventually leading to a transition to adult corrections or becoming homeless. You might question the social justice of this negative trajectory of outcomes. As noted by a child welfare administrator, "In spite of the fact that everyone in the [child welfare] system wants to do the right thing, there is still an unwillingness to look critically at whether what we are doing makes a difference in a concrete way" (Robinson, 2000).

Who and What Is Responsible for the Problem?

The question of who or what is responsible for the problem is perhaps the most difficult to answer as often a multiplicity of factors are involved, including values.

EP 2.1.8a

Values frame almost all of public and private discussions about remedies to social problems. Lens (2005), noting that every "social problem has its own value constellation" emphasized the differences between a theme of compassion in discussions about universal health and welfare-to-work requirements catered to values related to independence and responsibility. Of course, responsibility assumes that all citizens have equal standing and opportunity. Inherent in the previously discussed social problems and policies is the notion of personal responsibility as opposed to that of society's responsibility to ensure equality and the well-being of all citizens. On balance, the question of "*who*" in particular is responsible appears to have overshadowed the questions of "*what*" is responsible, and, in consequence, societal obligation to resolve social problems and conditions is diminished.

Perhaps a confirming conclusion about who and what is responsible for the problem is not possible. Nonetheless, an examination of social problems and conditions is worthwhile. You should understand that the distribution of resources, limited power and representation, and structural and economic inequality are factors that negatively impact segments of the population. We know, for example, that poverty is connected to other human needs and problems. Poverty and the related stressors influence child development and education level, family stability, health, and mental health status. Poor families, and even entire communities, experience chronic stressors in their everyday lives because they lack the minimum resources required to meet their basic needs (Tolan & Gorman-Smith, 1997). In the article "Enough to Make You Sick," Epstein (2003) vividly described life in "America's rundown urban neighborhoods," noting that illnesses normally associated with old age are showing up in young, inner-city residents. A parent interviewed for the article described her life as "you wake up stressed, you go to sleep stressed." Who and what is responsible for the problem when such conditions as described relegate certain people to live under these conditions?

On balance, let's return to the values dichotomy related to personal or societal responsibility and the consequences of the values that influence policy decisions about this matter. Are people poor because they lack aspirations or because of the realities of structural barriers and social policies that have failed to adequately address this longstanding social problem? This question is worth considering because poverty has long-term implications for quality of life over the lifespan (Brooks-Gunn, 1997; Rank & Hirschl, 1999).

Findings from a study that examined the relationship between poverty and psychopathology (specifically, behavioral symptoms identified in *DSM-IV*) are encouraging. Results of this study emphasized that improved family income had a "major effect on children's psychiatric disorders" (Costello, Compton, Keeler, & Angold 2003, p. 2023). Similarly, behavioral symptoms such as oppositional defiant behavior (a common diagnosis of children in poor families) significantly decreased when family income improved.

EP 2.1.9b

Analyzing problems, conditions, and social policies provides an opportunity for you as a social worker to give voice to the powerless by framing issues so that the public becomes invested in the problem, irrespective of their values. Does the public, for example, appreciate a costly child welfare system that has uncertain or poor outcomes? What would be the public response if people had an understanding of the sanctions and penalties applied to welfare recipients for failing to comply with the 60-month lifetime limits on support without regard to their circumstances, for example, having a disabled parent or child, or the state of the economy being poor?

Breton (2006) asserts that social workers need not become revolutionaries in order to affect change. Justice work demands, however, that we as social workers articulate the consequences of social problem and conditions as well as evaluate and monitor the impact of policies on those problems or conditions. Acting on behalf of or with client groups by taking an active role and documenting the impact, outcome, and effectiveness of policies and their implementation is justice work (Breton, 2006; Jansson, 2003; Linhorst, 2002).

Different Perspectives of Social Justice

EP 2.1.4a

Many of the shortcomings in social policies and services can be traced to the social distance between those in need and those who make policy. This distance contributes to a lack of *social empathy* (Segal, 2007), the results of which are mandates and procedural requirements that are by nature punitive. For example, the prevailing thought behind curtailing support for the needs of children in single-parent families was that it contributed to family dissolution, out-of-wedlock births, and long-term dependency (Ozawa & Yoon, 2005).

You should be aware of the fact there can be a distance between how the term "social justice," as articulated by the social work profession, is understood by social workers and policymakers. Specifically, promoting economic and social equality and defending the rights of disenfranchised and oppressed people are not universal viewpoints. Barusch (2002) argues that social justice can be defined differently depending on the philosophical orientation of the audience, public opinion, and the framers of social policy. For example, presented with the idea that the mandate and compliance requirement for welfare recipients is unjust, libertarian values, according to Barusch, would perhaps stress the "distribution of benefits on the basis of production." Conversely, liberals tend to be utilitarian in their thinking (e.g., the greatest good for the greatest number of people) and therefore, place emphasis on "economic liberty and political equality for all" (p. 15). Differing viewpoints, however, can find common ground on particular issues, and political labels should not prevent you from exploring opportunities for involving certain individuals or building coalitions. Recognition of this fact might lead you, as suggested by one of the strategic frame questions, to explore how opinions about a particular issue were influenced. Presenting information about a particular problem to the public and policymakers is a means by which you can lessen the distance between them and those who are affected by the policy. Also, consider that people's thinking is complex and their perspectives can range from liberal to moderate to centrist to conservative, depending on the issue at hand. Understanding the basis of different perspectives is essential. The knowledge of the ideological, political, and values context in which social problems and policies are framed can inform your analysis of the forces that may promote or inhibit change.

In this next section of the chapter, we focus on the selected macro–level methods and strategies that can be used to address social problems and conditions.

Developing and Mobilizing Resources

EP 2.1.9a

In some instances, resource needs in response to social problems or conditions are obvious. For example, working families in all economic strata are in need of affordable child care, and some need financial assistance to meet all of the costs of daily living. Resource needs can change over time. While a resource was appropriate at one particular point in time, shifts in the needs of people may require that new resources are developed or existing ones expanded. For instance, food banks, primarily developed to serve the urban poor, have expanded as a result of the current economic climate, high unemployment, and state cuts to cash assistance programs. Increases in the demand for this resource, from a range of income levels and geographical areas, have, in some cases, overtaxed food banks.

Needs for resources vary according to specific concerns and they can differ substantially from one community or population to another. For example, the resource needs of aging gay and lesbian individuals in rural areas tend to be different from the needs of their urban peers. In examining the landscape for resource needs, the rural–urban or urban–suburban configuration may be applicable to addressing almost any need within a population. In some instances, existing resources may be inadequate for the level of need, in which case resources may need to be supplemented or expanded. In some scenarios, you may find that certain values and beliefs about people and stigmatization of groups may result in reinforcing oppression and a denial of access to needed resources. These and other regional and global demographic trends will continue to shape the ways that services are designed and delivered.

Both demand and normative resource needs are likely to change because of our changing demographic landscape—a landscape in which the number of older people is growing faster than the young—and the increasing immigrant population. In the beginning of the year 2011, the first group of the post World War II generation referred to as the "Baby Boomers" in the United States will turn 65 years of age. Aging, specifically the number of people over the age of 65, is a global trend. An aging population will have a profound effect on the types of resources that are needed, ranging from ways to keep this population healthy and to ensure economic and family stability to the ways in which business is conducted. Aging needs will, of course, vary and will be influenced by such factors as income, health status, geographical residence, gender, sexual orientation, and race. Data from the 2010 U.S. Census Survey provides a portrait of a changing and more diverse population, adding to the diversity that already exists in this country. Increasingly, immigrants—who will account for a larger percentage of population growth in the United States—can be expected to have a range of resource needs. In addition, more immigrants will follow jobs and settle in suburban and rural communities, resulting in a change in the homogeneity of these communities, both in terms of people and resource needs. The aging and growing immigrant populations are among the demographic trends that can be expected to result in shifting resource needs and, therefore, the development of resources.

Social workers must develop resources when it is apparent that a significant number of people within a given ecological boundary have needs that are not met or for which matching resources are not available. Regular, meaningful contact with individuals, families, and groups places you in a strategic position to identify resource needs. Resource development may include educating policymakers, civic or community groups, and administrators of social welfare organizations about social conditions for which responsive resources are needed.

EP 2.1.6b

Whether the goal is to develop resources, deliver useful services, or influence a social policy, a starting point is gaining an understanding of and documenting the nature and the extent of resource needs. Questions that can be useful to guide the need for resource development and guide which data should be gathered include:

- *What are the resource needs of a particular group?*
- *How would a group or community describe their resource needs?*
- *Are there unmet needs, gaps, or underutilized existing resources?*
- *How prevalent are the needs across the population and in various subgroups?*
- *Are there barriers to the utilization of existing resources?*
- *Are the current resources an effective response?*

Numerous tools are available for understanding and documenting resource needs include mapping, specifically using organizational or government statistical data and needs assessment. Also, inviting and involving client groups to identify their resource needs can be accomplished by group interviews or dialogue, using critical or participatory action research models (DePoy, Hartman, & Haslett, 1999; Reese, Ahern, Nair, O'Faire, & Warren, 1999). Descriptive examples of the implementation of each of these methods are described here.

- Mapping *involves utilizing geographical information systems to track problems of interest (Hillier, 2007). Accessing geographical data about homeless youth in an area of Los Angeles, for example, led to the development of a new resource intervention strategy that focused on service-related needs, employment training, and mental health resources (Ferguson, 2007).*
- Needs Assessment *gathers information in order to identify unmet resource needs. You must first determine whether the resource is intended to respond to a normative or a demand need (Rubin & Babbie, 2005). Normative needs are compared to a specific community's experience with the normal experience of other communities. Demand needs, conversely, relate to the needs of a particular community and address a particular concern. As sources of information, you can utilize group interviews, standardized self-administered questionnaires, community forums with key informants, or a targeted group. Whichever method that you use, the information that you are seeking should focus on discovering needs that are unmet or undeclared, otherwise in talking to people you gather information about a wider range of issues (Homan, 2008). Noting that all communities have resource capabilities, the overall intent of the needs assessment is to assist the community to determine if there is a need for action in order to address a resource need (Homan, 2008, Lewis, Lewis, Packard, & Souflee, 2001). One such example is the Homeless Against Homelessness Project, in which homeless individuals worked with a social worker to determine the resource needs of other homeless individuals. The social worker combined facets of the critical action research framework with needs assessment. Participatory action research involves the governance, composition, and active participation of stakeholders throughout the project (Depoy, Hartman, & Haslett, 1999). In this case, the active stakeholders were the homeless individuals who actually designed the project and conducted the assessment interviews. As key informants, they were essential to the development of interview questions that were relevant to the population and which could easily be administered on the street. The findings from this project were presented to the county commission on homelessness.*
- Dialogue Groups and Interviews *are qualitative methods that can be used to gather pertinent information on the unmet needs and needed resources for specific segments of the population. Butler and Hope (1999) conducted group interviews with older lesbian women living in metropolitan and rural communities in order to better understand their current and future resource needs. Dialogue groups proved to be an*

effective method to understand and subsequently educate service providers to the particular issues and concerns of older gays and lesbians in a community (Anetzberger, Ishles, Mostade, & Blair, 2004). Observing the low participation of ethnic and racial minorities in using hospice services as a resource, Reese, Ahern, Nair, O'Faire, and Warren (1999) relied on a group of African American ministers as key informants to identify cultural and institutional barriers that prevented African Americans from using hospice care.

These examples represent ways in which you can identify and document resource needs in the aggregate. You should also be aware of the wealth on information available in your agency's case records. For example, a review of case records can inform you as to whether needs were satisfied at intake and whether the same needs remained a concern at termination. Whichever method that you use to document resource needs, the results may lead to advocacy for social action involving a coalition of agencies and professionals in order to influence a desired outcome.

Developing Resources with Diverse Groups

EP 2.1.4b

You need not feel intimidated when documenting a need for diverse groups so that a resource can be developed. You should, however, be aware of the fact that a group may identify resource needs that are different from your own ideas and that can be observed within group differences (Sue, 2006; Green, 1999). For instance, the needs of immigrants or refugees can be dependent on their length of stay and their extent of acculturation, and may ultimately influence the types and appropriateness of resources. Therefore, whether you are looking to develop resources in response to the needs of old or newly arrived diverse groups, it is critical for you to familiarize yourself with their cultural nuances, values, norms, and social and political structures. Beyond your effort to assess and document a resource need, entry into a situation that is unfamiliar to you requires interpersonal skills such as respectful preparation and engagement, building trust and relationship resources, and facilitating empowerment. In addition, unfamiliar situations call for you to engage in self-reflection, so that you are aware of your bias and any predetermined notions you might have of a particular group.

Most of the previously discussed questions and data collection methods can be used to identify and document the resource needs of a diverse group. Mapping, for example, can show you whether a group is clustered in a particular geographical area. From this point, you can assess the resources available in a community and whether there are resource gaps. Your ultimate aim, however, is that of *discovery* (Green, 1999) and *humility* (Tervalon & Murray-Garcia 1998), both of which can guide your action. In essence, discovery and humility prompt you to rely on the group or community as key informants and as cultural interpreters in educating yourself about their resource needs.

EP 2.1.4d

Mobilizing Community Resources

Mobilizing existing resources can address concrete needs, but available resources can vary depending on the community and the situation. There are certain situations, nonetheless, that arouse an emotional and altruistic response in people, irrespective of where they live. Nowhere has this been more evident than in the community responses during the aftermath of national and global disastrous events.

EP 2.1.10a

Homan (2008, p. 187), citing the Pew Partnership for Civic Change (2001) report, asserts that people are the most valuable resource and that a majority are willing to become and remain involved when asked. The results of the report showed that 90 percent of Americans "believe that working with others is the way to solve community problems." Primary factors were, "knowing what to do," "having a linkage to the community," and "a strong cultural or ethnic identity." In mobilizing community resources, Homan provides four steps for eliciting and encouraging the involvement of people (p. 188):

1. *Contact people.*
2. *Give them a reason to join.*
3. *Ask them to join.*
4. *Maintain their involvement.*

An appeal from Project Homeless Connect, a coordinated partnership effort to mobilize resources, is illustrative of Homan's steps. The success of the project depended on volunteers who were recruited through book clubs, fraternal and civic groups, and faith and professional communities. During the course of the two-day event, homeless persons were able to take showers, see health and mental health professionals,

IDEAS IN ACTION

Project Homeless Connect
Greetings! We Need Your Help!

Ending Homelessness, one person at a time. Project Homeless Connect is a one-stop model for delivering services to people experiencing homelessness. Hennepin County and the City of Minneapolis partner with service providers, businesses, citizens, and faith communities to bring multiple resources to one location where people can find the help they need. These services include: housing providers, employment specialists, medical and mental health care, eye care, haircuts, transportation assistance, food, and clothing.

December Success

Thanks to the wonderful work of 500 volunteers and 100 service providers, and over 1200 men, women, and children. The last event was a great success:

- *1500 meals were served*
- *221 people received immediate medical care*
- *42 received dental care*
- *443 were given vouchers for shoes*
- *62 new voice mail numbers were established so that people could receive messages about work and housing*
- *300 were able to have free haircuts*
- *473 received employment referrals*
- *157 housing applications were submitted, with 6 people placed in housing on the day of the event, and 12 more in the following days*
- *36 veteran contacts were made*

700 Volunteers Needed

The reason for this communication is that we are asking you to help at the upcoming event. With even more participation expected this year, we need at least 700 volunteers to make this another success. The Convention Center will be set up with tables, rooms and areas for the various services available, and volunteers will assist guests in connecting with the assistance that they need or request. Volunteers must be 18 years of age or older.

Sign Up to Volunteer

To volunteer, click below on the Click here to Volunteer box. Please also choose a training date. Share this e-mail with anyone who is interested in helping us reach our goal. You may go directly to our Web site to volunteer to help to end homelessness.

We are counting on you. Won't you connect? Thank you.

---

meet with housing and benefit specialists, and receive concrete goods, for example, backpacks, toothbrushes, and clothing. The announcement that volunteers received can be seen in the above Ideas in Action box.

Overall, the communication had a strong appeal, beginning with the first sentence, "We need your help." It effectively engaged volunteers as active stakeholders in responding to the needs of the homeless population in their community. Direct appeals, such as this one, have the potential to engage the altruistic instincts and basic values of potential volunteers, many of whom desire equality and dignity for the disenfranchised, but are unaware of how to achieve it.

In describing the event as a one-day opportunity, new volunteers are alerted to the time that they are being asked to participate. Former volunteers were encouraged to remain involved by documenting and personalizing their contributions to the success of the previous event, which would also be attractive to new recruits. This information also appealed to new volunteers and provided them with concrete reasons to participate. Options other than direct involvement, such as the donation of cash or services, were also available. For those who might have been reluctant to volunteer, training was available as an incentive.

As you develop, tap into, or mobilize existing resources, the capacity of the community should be considered, and the appeal need not be on a large scale basis like Project Connect. The capacity to help others in times of need can be found in most communities. Community-level resources can be inspired when people become aware of a particular situation for which help is needed. McRoy (2003), for instance, worked collaboratively with congregations to respond to the need for adoptive homes for children. This faith-based initiative called "Saving a Generation," resulted in the adoption of more than 50 African American children.

EP 2.1.9a

Within communities, kin, informal networks, and natural support systems can be mobilized in much the same manner. For instance, kinship care as a resource in child welfare is among the practices that organizations have adopted as an alternative to foster care placement (Testa, 2002; Gibson, 1999; Haight, 1998; Tracy & Whittaker, 1990; Jackson, 1998; Brookins, Peterson & Brooks, 1997). Kinship studies (e.g., the placement of children with kin) found that this resource lasted longer and was more supportive of the child's stability, familial connections, and cultural, racial, or ethnic identity (Hegar, 1999; Danzy & Jackson, 1997). Mobilizing the resources can make use of natural support systems within communities. For example, training women in a community as nutritional counselors proved to be an effective means to teach healthy eating habits to inner-city women who were at risk for diabetes. Because the women were interconnected through their community, they were more receptive when the information about diabetes was provided by peers, neighbors, or friends (Mays, 2003). Using barbershops as natural gathering places, the Montgomery County, Maryland, Health and Human Services Department tapped in to this resource to educate men about cancer and to address some of the barriers that prevented the men from seeking oncology screening (Mallory, 2004).

Advocacy and Social Action

EP 2.1.9a

The social work profession has a long and proud tradition of advocacy and social action leading to social reform. Indeed, Stuart (1999) characterizes the "linking of clients and social policy as a distinctive contribution of the social work profession" (p. 335). Haynes and Mickelson (2000) trace the involvement of social workers during the development of some of the more enlightened and humane social policies in both the nineteenth and twentieth centuries. In some instances, in particular communities, practice with individuals involves advocacy and social action that focused on the "private troubles of individuals and the larger policy issues that affected them" (Carlton-LaNey, 1999). Diverse individuals and groups of social workers have been devoted activists and advocates, often acting in concert with grassroots or minority civic groups. For example, social workers supported the United Farm Workers, the Equal Rights Amendment, the National Welfare Rights Organization, and the Civil Rights Movement by either joining in the activities of these groups directly or providing expert testimony.

Case and Cause Advocacy

EP 2.1.4a

After reading the analysis of the Personal Work Opportunity and Personal Responsibility Act and the Adoption and Safe Family Act, seeing their disparate impact on poor families, and thinking about related social justice concerns, you might wonder, "*What can I do?*" Perhaps you have acted as a case advocate, working on behalf of a client to ensure that he or she receives those benefits and services to which he or she is entitled and to ensure that his or her dignity is safeguarded. This aspect of advocacy closely corresponds to a dictionary definition of an *advocate* as one who acts on behalf of another person. Because advocacy and social action include this key element, confronting the effects of legislation and policies cannot rely on the efforts of a single practitioner. Indeed, the profession is actively involved in addressing many of these issues (Marsh, 2005). The shift in policymaking from the federal to the state level is an opportunity for you to join in collaborative policy advocacy to influence policy at the state level on behalf of clients (Jackson-Elmore, 2005; Hoefer, 2005; Lens, 2005; Rice, 1998; Sherraden, Slosar, & Shrerraden, 2002). Other opportunities for you to join advocacy efforts include the National Association of Social Workers' collaboration with social work programs' "Social Work Day at the Capital," and National Association of Social Workers' PACE Committee.

Advocacy and Social Action Defined

Proposing a new definition of advocacy, Schneider and Lester (2001) define social work advocacy as the "exclusive and mutual representation of a client(s) or cause in a forum, attempting to systematically influence decision making in an unfair and unresponsive system." Barker (1996) defined social action as "a coordinated effort to achieve institutional change to meet a need, solve a social problem, correct any injustices or enhance the quality of human life" (p. 350). Both advocacy and social action are inherently political. Hyde (1996), referring to a major tenet of feminist organizing and advocacy, suggests that the "the personal is political."

By integrating advocacy and social action, we have adapted elements from each to form a unified definition, because there are often instances in which advocacy and social action are combined to achieve the desired results. Together,

EP 2.1.10a

they represent a process of affecting or initiating change either with or on behalf of client groups to:

- *Obtain services or resources that would not otherwise be provided*
- *Modify or influence policies or practices that adversely affect groups or communities*
- *Promote legislation or policies that will result in the provision of requisite resources or services*

Models of advocacy are defined and discussed by Haynes and Mickelson (2000) and Freddolino, Moxley, and Hyduk (2004). These authors stress that using particular models are important because they guide the intervention and the strategies used. We refer you to these informative resources as guides.

Indications for Advocacy or Social Action

EP 2.1.1a

Advocacy and social action may be appropriate when there are conditions or problems that affect a group or community, including the following:

1. When services or benefits to which people are entitled are denied to a group or community.
2. When services or practices are dehumanizing, confrontational, or coercive.
3. When discriminatory practices or policies occur because of race, gender, sexual orientation, religion, culture, family form, or other factors.
4. When gaps in services or benefits cause undue hardship or contribute to dysfunction.
5. When people lack representation or participation in decisions that affect their lives.
6. When governmental or agency policies and procedures or community or workplace practices adversely affect or target groups of people.
7. When a significant group of people have common needs for which resources are unavailable.
8. When clients are denied basic civil or legal rights.

Other circumstances for which advocacy or social action may be necessary include situations in which a group or community is unable to act effectively on its own behalf, such as persons who are institutionalized, people who have a need for immediate services or benefits because of a crisis situation, or people who cannot act as self-advocates because of their legal status.

Competence and Skills for Macro Practice and Social Action

EP 2.1.10a

Skills that are used in direct practice easily translate to advocacy and social action (Breton, 2006). But, Schneider and Lester (2001, p. 71) emphasize that advocacy is not problem solving in the tradition of direct practice problem-solving models. In contrast to the problem-solving process, "advocacy requires particular actions, such are representation, influencing and the use of a forum" to bring about specific change.

Specific skills required in advocacy or social action include:

- *Policy analysis*
- *Group facilitation*
- *Oral and written communication skills*
- *Negotiation and mediation*
- *Analysis of multidimensional and systematic information.*

EP 2.1.10d

Let's say, for example, that you are approached to represent and act on behalf of a group of mothers who believe that the placement of their children was unjust. Undoubtedly, you posses the characteristics of an advocate, that is, you are action-oriented and opposed to injustice. For you, after hearing their stories, inaction on your part, in your opinion, is not an option (Schneider & Lester, 2001). Nonetheless, before acting, you are advised to document the circumstances of each individual's situation and educate yourself about and analyze the relevant state and federal policies. These situations, in which injustice—real or perceived—arouses emotions, can incite anger in those affected and in the advocate. However, an analysis will help you and the group that you intend to represent avoid making assumptions and premature or erroneous conclusions that may lead to undesired or embarrassing consequences. The strategies for documenting and quantifying needs (discussed earlier in this chapter) will be essential at this stage.

Assuming that the situation indicates that advocacy or social action is necessary, a decision would be made as to how the group wants to proceed. To gather support for an intended action you would compile information that documents the problem, the population affected, and in what way that population is affected. Then you would present this information to others who are interested in the problem. In essence, you are building a coalition of interested parties. In building a coalition, group facilitation, negotiation, consensus building, and interpersonal skills are critical.

Advocacy and Ethical Principles

EP 2.1.2d & 2.1.10c

Both advocacy and social action assume a wide range of social work roles and skills, each of which observes the values and ethics of the profession as guiding principles. Advocacy and social action embody values and ethical principles that the social work profession has embraced, such as dignity and worth, self-determination, and giving a voice to the powerless (Schneider & Lester, 2001). Advocacy and social action may, at times, constitute a delicate balance between self-determination and beneficence. Ezell (2001) calls attention to this dilemma, citing the conflict that can occur in deciding "whether to empower clients to advocate for themselves or to represent them" (p. 45). Schneider and Lester (2001) provide guidance with respect to ethical behavior in their definition of advocacy. They emphasize that the relationship between the social worker and the client group is mutual, which means observing their interdependence and reciprocity in collaborative decision-making and planning. In other words, you are working with the group in your representation of their concerns. Furthermore, Schneider & Lester (2001) caution that advocates do not "dominate or set the agenda." A potential dilemma that you might face with respect to self-determination is that a group or community may not wish to assert this right if they feel that they will face formidable opposition or backlash. Should a group make such a decision, you are ethically bound to respect their decision. In essence, the advocacy or social action effort should go no further than the client group wishes it to go.

Ethics are also indicated in informing groups about the risks and limitations associated with advocacy and social action. Rothman (1999) cautions community practitioners about the potential for opposition and obstacles to social action and organizing activities, including "institutions that block needed improvements in education, housing, employment and law enforcement." He further states that "change advocates have to keep in mind that elites will lash out when they perceive that their interests are challenged." To deal with this resistance, advocates should "calculate" their ability and that of their client group to maintain a sustained focus, as well as be able to defend themselves against counterattacks (p. 10). You have a responsibility to discuss potential barriers and the possible adversarial or negative consequences of advocacy and social action with the client group. Implementing advocacy and social action typically creates a certain amount of strain and tension; moreover, a positive outcome cannot always be assured. For example, what if a landlord under pressure from a resident action group ignored building code violations that caused the complex to be condemned, resulting in the residents being displaced? Discussing possible consequences or barriers not only allows for the planning of alternative strategies, but also ensures that those with whom you work are informed about the pros and cons of an intended action, leaving the final decision in their hands.

Techniques and Steps of Advocacy and Social Action

EP 2.1.9b

Targets of advocacy or social action may be individuals (e.g., a landlord or public official), organizations, or divisions of government (e.g., on behalf of or with groups or communities). Approaches to situations vary considerably according to the target system, but all require a thorough understanding of how organizations or communities are structured and function, how the legislative and rule-making processes work, and an appreciation of the influence of organizational politics (Alexander, 2003; Homan, 2008; Roberts, 2000; Rothman, 1991).

Advocacy can involve different levels of assertive intensity, ranging from discussion and education to a high level of social action such as organizing, protests, boycotts, or social media campaigns. Sosin and Callum (1983) developed a useful typology of advocacy to assist practitioners to plan strategic advocacy actions. Along with the models discussed by Haynes and Mickelson (2000) and Freddolino, Moxley, and Hyduk (2004), Sosin and Callum's (1983) typology can help determine the opportunities that exist, the techniques or strategies to be used, and at what level these techniques and strategies should be implemented. As a general rule, you should rely on the techniques that have the greatest promise of achieving a given objective. Deciding which technique to use depends on the nature and analysis of the problem, the wishes of the group or community, the nature of the action, and the political climate. For instance, although militant action may be desirable, militancy should be utilized with great discretion, because the short-term gains may not outweigh the long-term negative images, the response from the public, and the potential for fractured relationships.

EP 2.1.10a

Effective social action and advocacy require a rational, planned approach incorporating the following steps:

1. Analyze the problem or condition.
2. Systematically gather information and complete an analysis of the people, structure, system, or policy to be changed.
3. Assess both the driving forces that may promote change and the forces that may conceivably resist or inhibit change.
4. Identify specific goals, eliciting a broad range of viewpoints from within the client group.
5. Carefully match techniques or strategies to the desired outcome.
6. Make a feasible schedule for implementing the plan of action.
7. Incorporate in the plan a feedback process for evaluating the changes that the action stimulates.

In addition to the steps and the skill competencies, other factors that are vital to effective social action and advocacy include: a *genuine* concern for the cause, the ability to keep the cause in *focus, tenacity*, and *stamina*. Successful advocates have a thorough understanding of how their government and systems are organized and changed. Blind emotion may work a few times, but maintaining a successful, sustained advocacy and action requires know-how. In many instances, class advocacy and social action are best described as a marathon rather than a race. Finally, the manner in which an issue is presented may make a substantial difference.

The FrameWorks Institute suggests translating messages about what can be done to address social problems into language that engages ordinary people and advances their interest in policy and program solutions. Questions that facilitate formulating the institute's "strategic frame analysis" are illustrated in the following examples:

- *What shapes public opinion about a particular social condition or problem, for example, issues that affect children, families, and poor people?*
- *What role do [can] the media play?*
- *How do policymakers gauge public opinion?*

Answers to these questions can facilitate the direction of advocacy or social action. Further, the questions may assist you to sharpen your message to a specific group about a specific problem, and to effectively communicate about social conditions framed by the tenets of social justice.

Community Organization

EP 2.1.10a

Social transformation is a primary goal of community organizing (Hardina, 2004). Similar to advocacy and social action, community organizing is action-oriented on a larger scale and intended to effect social change in which "neighborhood organizations, associations and faith communities join together to address social problems in their community" (Brueggemann, 2006, p. 204). Further, it is an arena in which participants "develop their own solutions, advance their own needs or build capacity" in partnership with private or governmental organizations (Bruggemann, 2006; Weil & Gamble, 1995).

Communities are social systems that have distinct characteristics in the manner in which they are organized, their collective sense of connectivity, identity and power, and the issues about which they have concerns, which is some instances may be confined to a particular geographic location. Organizing communities requires that you have an understanding of what matters to them, their needs and strengths, and the context of the person [community] in environment relationship.

Models and Strategies of Community Intervention

EP 2.1.10g

Models of community organizing and intervention and their basic means of influence are described by Rothman, Erlich, and Tropman (2001) and Carter (2000). The most frequently referred to methods or strategies for organizing communities are summarized in Table 14-1.

Locality development seeks to build relationships within the community and enhance community integration and capacity thorough broad participation. Locality development supports empowerment in that the community is actively involved in defining its problem and determining goals (Cnaan & Rothman, 1986). In Quebec, Canada, for example, locality development utilized natural helping networks and lay citizens in

TABLE-14-1 STRATEGIES AND METHODS OF COMMUNITY INTERVENTION
Locality Development
Social Action
Social Planning
Capacity Building

© Cengage Learning 2013

analyzing problems and planning remedial measures (Gulati & Guest, 1990). Users of services were considered to be partners as opposed to client–consumers. They facilitated the integration and coordination of programs and services and prevention efforts in their community. The flexibility in organizational structure and decentralized administration enabled the local communities to develop programs that responded to their unique needs.

Social Action as a community organization strategy is similar to our discussion of advocacy in its approach. It is the action on the part of communities to advocate so that institutions and decision makers address unfairness in resource distribution (e.g., the relocation of bus routes that disadvantaged a specific population), remedy the imbalance of power through neighborhood associations or concerned citizens (e.g., the coordinated efforts of seniors, relatives, and senior citizen advocates), and solve problems or conditions identified by the community.

Social Planning as a strategy tends to be expert-driven, relying on consultants and technical assistance for solving problems (Rothman & Tropman, 1987). These professionals generally work with community leaders and the focus of their work is to expand, develop, and coordinate social policies and social services (Carter, 2000). Unlike locality development, participation by the larger community may be limited.

Capacity building increases the ability of a community to act on its own behalf, make decisions, and directs its own actions as its main focus (Hannah, 2006). This approach takes exception to the assumption that expert or governmental interventions are a primary means to achieve a solution to a community problem. Instead, the community develops its own agenda and the work to be completed is directed "from the inside out" (Rivera & Erlich, 1998, p. 68). Organizing efforts under the auspices of Communities United to Rebuild Neighborhoods (CURN) in Chicago is an example of residents working together to resolve their community concerns. They focused on their collective community strengths and individual talents at all age levels, believing that these attributes were central to the change effort, and therefore should be identified, energized, and deployed.

Within each of the first two methods, activities may support coalition building and evolve into political and social action or social movements capable of influencing social planning. In some instances, they may overlap or be employed simultaneously (Carter, 2000; Hyde, 1996: Rothman, 1995, 2008). Carter (2000), for example, documents how a coalition evolved into effective political and social action in response to the inaction on the part of the Department of Justice to incidents of arson in southern U.S. African American churches in isolated rural communities in 1996. By challenging the inaction of the agents and that of the United States Justice Department about the cause of the fires, communities realized their self-efficacy as a group, bolstering their coming together and taking action as an effective organizing coalition. Hannah (2006) notes that community capacity initiatives must be able to gain and maintain involvement of the community, which is possible if the initiative has community support.

Relying on a specific model or strategy is useful for directing the organizing effort. Burghardt (2011) proposes three strategic development levels of community intervention that can facilitate decisions about which model would be most useful. *Entry*, the first strategic level, emphasizes capacity building and empowerment among community members, growing their sense of their power, responsibilities, and skills. During this process, issues and long-term goals are identified. Burghardt refers to the second strategic level as the *Coalition Strategy Formation*. In this process, the organizer seeks to understand and make use of the various actors that may contribute to or distract from the problem to be addressed. For example, the extent to which there is a commonality of concerns should be identified among the various individuals, groups, or other organizations in the community that could form a unified coalition issue. The *Transformational Strategy Formation* is able to make use of strategies from various models. Specifically, at this level, building coalitions or individual and community capacity can be implemented to bring about a planned change. Some advantages of the three strategic levels are that they provide a means to understand the position of a community relative to an issue, where development may be needed, and the fact that they build upon each other. For instance, in the entry strategic level, building capacity within a community can be a precursor to developing a coalition. Whether you begin with a specific model or make use of Burghardt's (2011) developmental strategies in advance of a model decision, maintaining focus is important. As Homan (1999, p.160) points out, you should keep in mind that organizing to promote change "involves more than just fixing a specific problem." Further, in advancing the empowering capacity of a community, productive organizing includes the goal of increasing the capability of people to effectively respond meaningfully in the face of future challenges.

EP 2.1.10g

Steps and Skills of Community Intervention

EP 2.1.10a

Theorists conceptualize community organizing in different ways, outlining different stages that vary according to the levels of elaboration of relevant tasks. Rothman, Erlich, and Tropman, (1995) and Rothman (1999) use a six-phase process to address community concerns:

1. Identification of need, condition, or problem as framed by the community
2. Definition and clarification of the need, condition, or problem
3. Systematic process of obtaining information
4. Analysis of the information
5. Development and implementation of a plan of action
6. Terminal actions and evaluation of outcome or effects

This process may not be entirely linear, because new information can require alternative action, including making a new start or reframing strategies and tactics and a mix of intervention models (Rothman, 2008; Rothman, Erlich, & Tropman, 1999).

Organizing Skills

EP 2.1.10b

When working with communities, implementing organizing strategies requires a set of behaviors and skills that are observable and measurable. For example, you should gauge your ability to establish rapport with and be sensitive to diverse groups, the extent to which you demonstrate genuineness and empathy, and the effectiveness of your communication skills. Because organizing involves groups or communities, skills in group facilitation, fostering interpersonal relationships, and managing group dynamics are also critical. Homan (2008) adds to the skill base, emphasizing a balance between the objective and subjective, self-awareness, patience, focus, and timing. Other skills and competencies include those embodied in policy analysis, research methods, and the management of data.

Organizing and Planning with Diverse Groups

EP 2.1.10g

Rivera and Erlich (1998), in analyzing models of community development or organizing, challenge the assumption that prevailing models (i.e., locality development, social planning, and social action) are color-blind and therefore applicable in any community. They conclude that there are additional factors to be considered in working with communities of color:

- *Racial, ethnic, and cultural aspects of the community*
- *Implications of this uniqueness in particular communities*
- *The empowerment process and the development of a critical consciousness*

Rivera and Erlich's work is intended to guide our thinking in planning and organizing and, in fact, represents a significant contribution to organizing strategies. Heretofore, methods had an implicit assumption that good intentions sufficed in community interventions and that, unlike direct practice, considerations of the race, ethnicity, and culture in this work were secondary. The three levels of contact for entry into communities, as conceptualized by Rivera and Erlich (1998), facilitate a greater understanding of work with diverse groups and of the roles beyond those traditionally considered in social work. Table 14-2 outlines the three levels.

TABLE-14-2 LEVELS OF COMMUNITY CONTACT

ENTRY LEVEL	CHARACTERISTICS
Primary	Requires that an individual has the same racial, cultural, and linguistic background as the community. The community is open to and respects this individual.
Secondary	The individual need not be a member of the same racial, ethnic, or cultural group, but should be closely aligned and sensitive to community needs. He or she may serve as a liaison to the broader community, and facilitate contact with institutions outside the community.
Tertiary	The individual is an "outsider," yet shares the community's concerns. The practitioner's skills and access to power—rather than his or her ethnic, racial, or cultural identity—are valued assets.

SOURCE: Adapted from Rivera and Erlich (1998).

Ethical Issues in Community Organizing

EP 2.1.2d

It is the groups or associations within communities that are best able to identify their needs and plan solutions. As social workers, we can become involved in their efforts as advocates, change agents, and planners, using our skills, knowledge, and values grounded in principles of social justice and empowerment to help groups and communities to achieve their goals. A question discussed earlier for advocates is equally applicable to organizers. Specifically, when should organizers act on behalf of the community and when is it advisable for representatives to speak for their community to represent themselves (Ezell, 2001)?

Hardina (2004) points out that community organizing and its methods address issues that are not directly covered in the social work Code of Ethics. For example, the Code does not address dual relationships (situations in which two or more distinct relationships involve the same person) between the organizer and community residents. Nor does the Code address the choice of tactics that an organizer might use. To the first point, specifically in regard to dual relationships, you are a member of the community as well as an organizer at entry level one of the Rivera and Erlich (1998) schema. Because you are a part of the community, there may have been numerous occasions in which you have interacted with other residents socially and politically. In community practice, for instance, you may have relationships with people as friends, relatives, or as a member of a sports team. Your memberships in the community provide you with a familiarity to the community, the people, their values, and concerns. As a member, your involvement can lessen mistrust, and in effect, lessen the time needed to build relationships and bonds. However, in the strict sense of the Code, being involved in boundary spanning relationships may be perceived as an ethical violation.

EP 2.1.2d

Ethical behavior requires that community organizing observe self-determination and that a community is informed of and consent to the tactics to be used, as well as understands the risks and benefits. Hardina (2004) suggests that if the ethical principle and subsequent dilemma is not obvious, the organizer should use the Ethical Rule Screen proposed by Loewenburg, Dolgoff, and Harrington (1996, 2005). For example, "protection of life" or "privacy and confidentiality" must be weighed when considering a forceful tactic that may place people at risk. An *Ethical Decision-Making Framework* by Reisch and Lowe (2002), as discussed by Hardina (2004, p. 600), also provides a series of steps that are useful for community organizers:

- *Identify the ethical principles that apply to the situation at hand.*
- *Collect additional information necessary to examine the ethical dilemma in question.*
- *Identify the relevant ethical values and/or rules that apply to the ethical problem.*
- *Identify any potential conflicts of interest and the people who are likely to benefit from such conflict.*
- *Identify ethical rules and rank them in terms of importance.*
- *Determine the consequences of applying different ethical rules or ranking these rules differently.*

Although the Code may be limited with respect to specific macro-level strategies, in most instances it, along with the principle beliefs of the profession, can guide ethical practice. For example, the code and principle beliefs of the profession can be helpful in considering questions of the primacy of clients' rights, the uniqueness and worth of people, as well as the social justice focus on economic and social equality.

Social Media as a Resource of Social Advocacy and Community Organizing

In today's world of instant messaging, e-mail, social networks, social media, and other forms of digital communications, the capacity to reach, engage, and organize people about a particular issue is infinite. The use of these resources may be generational in that their appeal can vary by age. Specifically, it may be easier for young people to access and respond to this form of communication than it is for some older people. Irrespective of age, utilization can also depend on the access ability of an individual or community. Nonetheless, because these resources provide for connective relationship opportunities between people, you should evaluate their benefit.

Improving Institutional Environments

Social welfare organizations are organized to provide a service, information, benefits, or goods. They are formal social systems with multiple constituents and dynamic arenas in which client eligibility for services is determined and the resources vital to the organization's existence are distributed. The culture of organizations includes core values and purposes as portrayed in mission statements, leadership styles, and assumptions and rituals. Schein (1985) describes organizational culture as follows:

> A pattern of basic assumptions-invented, discovered, or developed by a given group as it learns to cope with its problems of external adaptation and internal integration, that has worked well enough to be considered valid and therefore to be taught to new members as the correct way to perceive, think and feel in relation to those problems. (p. 9)

Improving Organizational Environments

Organizational environments, in particular the culture of an organization, are influenced by their leadership, staff, resource environment, and public policy. The resource environment (e.g., the state of the economy) and public policy can require changes or modifications to decisions with respect to how the organization functions, its leadership, the allocation of resources, and the strategies that are implemented to achieve the organization's goals or mission (Condrey, Facer, & Hamilton, 2005; Proehl, 2001). Welfare reform (PWORA), for example, had a significant impact on both public and private organizations, their internal operations, staff functions, job satisfaction, goals, and resources (Abramovitz, 2005; Condrey, Facer & Hamilton, 2005; Proehl, 2001; Reisch & Sommerfeld, 2003). In effect, federal requirements set forth specific performance standards, which included the monitoring and reporting of the work-related activities of recipients. Many nonprofit organizations and some social workers have struggled with the mandated goals of welfare reform. At issue for many were requirements which were counter to their mission and the values of the social work profession. At the same time, the leadership and culture of the organization enabled some organizations to respond to these pressures in ways that were less disruptive and more beneficial to the organization (Condrey, Faces, & Hamilton, 2005; Reisch & Sommerfeld, 2003).

EP 2.1.10h

The quality of the organizational environment and the values of the organization, as experienced by clients, are important aspects of service delivery. In this section, ways in which the organizational environment can be improved are considered. Three major aspects of an organizational environment are discussed; specifically staff, organizational policies and practices, and programs.

Staff

In spite of the impact that external influences have on an organization's environment, the organization's staff forms the heart of the environment. The staffing mix of an organization includes professionals who have regular contact with clients, support personnel, and administrative personnel. Administrative personnel, specifically managers and supervisors, direct, monitor, coordinate, evaluate, and bear the responsibility for the oversight of overall organizational operations. In the organization's highly interdependent environment, each position is critical to achieving its mission. To a large extent, staff behavior is governed by a mix of factors that are internal and external to the organization. Internal factors include things like organizational philosophy, goals, and mission. Professional orientations, ethical codes and standards, union contracts, funding sources, the media, public policy, and licensing or regulatory boards are external factors.

When an organization has staff who are dedicated, caring, and responsive to clients' needs, as well as congenial with one another, the climate in the organization's environment tends to be conducive to the growth and well-being of all concerned. To be optimally effective, an organization's culture (and hence its climate) should promote staff empowerment and a commitment to deliver high-quality client services. Characteristics of a healthy organizational culture and climate involve such factors as open communications, a willingness to deal with conflict, a balance between flexibility and risk taking, a sense of interdependence and cohesiveness, and respect for boundaries. Although the creation of an organization's environment is within the domain of organizational leadership, it is the responsibility of all staffing levels.

Hackman and Oldham (1976, 1980) have conceptualized the most elaborate and widely accepted theories of job design and motivation as contributing to the overall psychological states of meaningfulness, staff responses, morale, and job satisfaction of staff. They have identified the following core characteristics as being instrumental in advancing toward an organizational environment in which staff are productive:

- *Task identity*
- *Task significance*
- *Skill variety*
- *Job feedback*
- *Autonomy*

Task identity, task significance, and skill variety add to the feeling that work is meaningful. Feedback with regard to one's job performance provides information about the results achieved, thereby acting as both a developmental and a motivating factor. Autonomy inspires a sense of responsibility for one's own work, the outcomes of this work, and the work of the team. Empowerment, which is implicit in autonomy, works in much the same way as self-determination does for clients. Just as clients may terminate social work contact when their interests and needs are ignored, a lack of staff empowerment can affect job performance, reduce productivity, and contribute to rapid turnover. Lack of attention to these dynamics can have a spill-over affect on staff-client interactions and create situations in which staff treat clients in ways that are counterproductive to the goals and purpose of the organization.

From this discussion, you can observe the contributions of staff to the overall environment of an organization. For instance, when staff behavior is guided by a lack of autonomy or significance in their work, they may perceive the organization's environment as a "psyche prison"—a construction of reality and conformity to a preferred way of thinking and doing (Morgan, 1997). The extent to which staff are empowered and able to participate in work-related decisions makes a significant difference in the extent to which they feel valued. Likewise, the five characteristics identified by Hackman and Oldham (1976, 1980) can influence the extent to which staff engages in prosocial or extra-role behavior within the organization, specifically a willingness to go beyond what is generally required of an individual's position.

Organizational Policies and Practices

EP 2.1.10d

Whether your role in an organization is that of a direct service practitioner or an administrator, a key part of your responsibility is to evaluate the impact of organizational policies, procedures, and practices on service delivery. When certain organizational practices or policies impede service delivery or block the agency from fulfilling its mission in an optimal fashion, it is up to you to identify those barriers and propose a change or modification. In this role, you would function as organizational diagnostician/facilitator, mediator, expediter, and advocate. In this section, the focus highlights three areas in which organizational policies and practices act as barriers to service delivery:

- *Policies or practices and staff behavior that fail to promote client dignity and worth*
- *Institutionalized racism and discrimination*
- *A lack of cultural competence at the organizational level*

Institutional programs

Before beginning the discussion of these main areas, information in the following section can assist you in critiquing policies and practices in your organization.

Examining Organizational Policies and Practices

EP 2.1.10d

The extent to which organizational policies and practices promote social justice, support client self-determination, and adhere to the principles of empowerment and strengths are lenses through which you can examine agency policies and practices. G.D. Rooney (2000) has developed an exercise for students designed to examine the values and ethics reflected in organizational policy decisions and practice. Policies or practices that lend themselves to a review include criteria for determining eligibility for services, rules that govern clients' behavior in residential or institutional settings, policies related to access to services, and procedures for developing treatment plans. Rooney (2000) has outlined the following key points to consider when assessing organizational policies or practices:

1. What are the origins, ideology, and values that appear to have influenced the policy?
2. What are the intended and unintended consequences of the policy's application?
3. To what extent are the policy and its expectations of clients influenced by societal ideology (e.g., the worthy and unworthy poor), social control, or compliance?
4. What is the image of clients and practitioners portrayed by the policy?
5. What does the policy or practice demand of clients and practitioners?
6. How do clients react to the practice or policy?
7. To what extent do the policy and its procedures support or constrain social work values, ethics, and social justice concerns?

Unfortunately, some organizations may have practices or policies that create barriers to delivering services fully and effectively. The implementation of such policies may deny people the resources to which they are entitled and result in others receiving services that are of lesser quality. In responding to their resource environment, organizational practice can be influenced by rules, policies and procedures, and in some instances the language that communicates a certain ideology and image of people who need services (Abramovitz, 2005; Lens, 2005; Riesch, 2002).

The series of questions for assessing organizational policies and practices developed by Rooney is intended to provide social workers with guidelines with which to critique the effects of policy on clients and service delivery. Many students who have completed this assessment provided the following insightful questions:

- *In working with involuntary clients, does the policy or practice require clients to be compliant, such that the social worker's role becomes that of an enforcer?*
- *How do you reconcile unintended consequences of the implementation of policies or rules?*
- *When clients have a strong reaction to a policy or practice, are there mechanisms in place so that the organization can respond to their concerns?*
- *Do policies and practices provide an image of clients that promotes dignity and worth, and acknowledges strengths as well as problems?*
- *How does the policy or practice ensure equal access to and equality of services? In particular, does the policy or practice provide differential treatment for one client group at the expense of another group?*

Many times, policies and practices are intended to help organizations manage limited resources and to ensure their distribution to those in need. For example, rules limiting the number of times people are able to access a food bank are critical to preserving resources, thereby ensuring that help will be available to the greatest number possible. At the same time, from an individual's perspective, these limits can convey the idea that they are taking advantage of this resource. Policies may be considered to be counterproductive when they intend to ensure compliance but unduly burden clients, and when procedures are implemented such that the potential for cheating takes precedence over service provisions.

Promoting Dignity and Worth

EP 2.1.10h

Social welfare organizations have the best of intentions when it comes to serving clients. Yet, in many ways, service delivery in ways that retains a person's dignity remains a challenge. These difficulties may be related to the images portrayed of those in need, the residual nature of assistance, the media, or funding resources; public policy or organizational practices; and the behavior of individual professionals. In some cases, organizations may strip service recipients of their dignity by requiring them to go to unreasonable lengths, for example, to establish eligibility for concrete aid or services. A vignette entitled "Four Pennies to My Name" is a powerful illustration of one client's perspective of this experience as she attempted to comply with the eligibility requirements for financial assistance (Compton & Galaway, 1994). In the vignette, a woman recounts her experience, which includes feeling humiliated and treated as just another number. Using social justice as an organizing perspective, Reisch (2002) proposes criteria for how people are to be treated, beginning with belonging, a notion articulated by Bertha Reynold's (1951) where people are "treated as human beings, not as problem to be solved" (p. 350). Further, Reisch (2002) states, the provision of services should observe people's humanity and be compassionate without regard to the ends sought by the profession or society.

Routine practices to which we may have become accustomed can compromise dignity, for example, inadequate privacy in the physical space where client interview or calls take place, within the earshot of others. Angry clients, concerns for safety, and threats of violence have prompted both public and private organizations to install metal detectors to screen visitors. Another practice involves the use of private guards or off-duty police. While you as an administrator or staff may regard these practices as essential for managing risks and ensuring a safe work environment, you should also be aware of the message it sends to clients and the power it affords to ancillary individuals (e.g. security guards) who are not associated with the mission and goals of the organization. Safety measures, although responding to very real concerns, nonetheless convey an image to service recipients and influence how they experience the organization. Legal questions have been raised about the legitimacy and authority of private security personnel in human services organizations. Although some view their presence as another form of oppression and social control, this practice is unlikely to go away. When practices such as this result in clients being treated in an indiscriminate manner, without regard for their dignity, as a social worker you are obligated to call attention to these issues and advocate for change.

Intervention Strategies: Developing Resources, Organizing, Planning, and Advocacy   439

Influence of Public Policy

EP 2.1.5c

As discussed earlier, public policy can have a positive or negative effect on an organization's environment. Furthermore, public policy (an external factor) can influence the organizational culture and the ethics of the organization's service delivery. Recall the discussion of the impact that welfare reform had on the ethical practice of social workers, and ultimately the way clients were treated. In the highly charged and often emotional response to child abuse and neglect, the dignity and worth of the parents involved takes a back seat to the demands of a rigid and legalized protocol inherent in the response system.

Parents involved in the child protection intervention report the experience as one in which there is a power imbalance, and they feel judged, fearful, and hopeless as a result of the uncaring, less than empathetic response by social workers who seem more interested in punishing them than understanding their situation (Fazilo, Lawson, & Hardiman, 2009; Dumbrill, 2006, 2003; Maiter, Palmer, Manji, 2006; Albert, 2000; Van Najnatten, 2005; Holland, 2000; Diorio, 1992).

In a system where contact with people begins with an allegation of guilt, the inherent assumption is that the parents are not concerned about their child or children's well-being and therefore their worth is questionable. Such interventions as *Signs of Safety* (Turnnell, 2004, 2006; Turnell & Edwards, 1999, 1997) and *Family Group Conferencing* (Waites, MacGowan, Pennell, Carlton-LaNey, & Weil, 2004) provide for a response to parents that honors their dignity and worth in spite of the dictates of public policy. *Signs of Safety* is an approach to child protection in which the professional builds a partnership with parents to ensure child safety and well-being. The partner relationship, like the assessment, is where the parent and the professional work together to determine safety and resources needs. This way, the professional's view does not overshadow the voice of the parent and is vastly different from the often-times contentious investigative process in which parents feel powerless. Instead, when there has been an allegation of abuse or neglect, the primary focus is on identifying safety and potential danger signals and a plan is developed on this basis. Family Group Conferencing, also referred to as *Family Group Decision-Making*, brings together family members as resources who are actively involved in ensuring child safety and well-being. Both practices can be instrumental in improving the organizations environment in that they diminish the role of staff as enforcers, which overtime can have an adverse affect on their functioning, including burnout. For clients, the experience is more empowering, and it is consistent with the profession's standards holding that the uniqueness, dignity, worth, and rights of the individual are primary considerations.

Staff

EP 2.1.1d

Positive staff behaviors and attitudes are essential to maintaining an organizational environment in which client dignity and worth are integral to operations and service delivery. In their encounters with an organization people should be able to expect common courtesies, such as promptness of response, respect, and nonjudgmental attitudes as a part of the organizational culture. It is unfortunate when staff persons may be either openly or subtly judgmental of clients, making remarks about their morality, veracity, character, or worthiness. Also troubling are incidents when staff members are brusque or rude, act in a way that humiliates or demeans clients, breach confidentiality, or intrude unjustifiably into deeply personal aspects of clients' lives, needlessly subjecting them to embarrassment and humiliation.

EP 2.1.2d

You may encounter a situation that leads you to question a colleague's competence and to consider whether this behavior with clients is a result of his or her impairment. These ongoing behaviors or actions can evolve from bad professional behavior into an organizational issue when supervisors or managers and staff allow them to go unchallenged. Moreover, such behaviors are an inhumane and unethical practice (e.g., NASW Code, 2000, Standards, 2.09, 2.10, and 2.11). Speaking with the colleague is a first step, and further discussion may involve the organization's administration. If necessary, you can pursue filing a complaint with the appropriate licensing board and professional organization. You may be thinking to yourself that these are dramatic or extreme measures. Further, you may question the benefits or risks associated with becoming involved. *Whistle blowing*, as discussed by Greene and Latting (2004), is a form of advocacy to be implemented when client's rights are ignored or in situations that represent a serious threat to their well-being and dignity. A primary reason most people are reluctant to report wrongful acts or behaviors is that the act of whistle blowing can have negative individual and organizational consequences. Whistleblowers may also question perceptions or motives and fear losing status and relationships with colleagues and the organization. These are legitimate concerns. Greene and Latting (2004, pp. 220–221) have identified factors, with integrity at their core, that you can use to assess your potential action. Whistleblowers are:

- *Motivated by their altruism, and their actions are to the benefit of those being wronged*
- *Utilitarian, with a high level of moral development, and are driven by their sense of integrity and social [professional] responsibility to speak out, even under symbolic or literal pressures to keep silent*
- *Seemingly uninterested in tailoring their behavior to conform to particular situations and behave consistently across situations*
- *Allowing their own attitudes and beliefs to guide them and they refuse to lie or cover up*
- *Well-educated, hold professional or managerial positions, and keep well-documented records of what they perceive to be abuse or waste*

Staff behavior is a critical facet of organizational culture. The organization's stance on ethical behavior is vital to ensuring ethical conduct, and, ultimately, the manner in which people are perceived and served.

Institutionalized Racism and Discrimination

EP 2.1.5a

Racism and discrimination are embedded in the fabric of our society to such a pervasive extent that many people fail to recognize their many manifestations. Institutional racism often affects service delivery and availability of resources and opportunities in subtle ways. Therefore, it is vital that you, irrespective of your role in the organization, are sensitized to its manifestations, especially in treatment, allocation of resources, and client experience.

Racism and discrimination, whether direct, indirect, or subtle, are in reality facets of educational, legal, economic, and political institutions, all of which influence how people are perceived and treated and the services that they receive (Abramovitz, 2005; Rodenborg, 2004; Chipungu & Bent-Goodley, 2003; Hill, 2005; Savner, 2000; Morton, 1999; Williams, 1990). At times, discrimination can lead to organizational practices resulting in disparate treatment of clients. At other times, discrimination can collude with the professional bias of theoretical perspectives and the personal bias of the professional. Ample evidence of professional bias shows that persons of color in their encounters with systems are much more likely to be perceived as pathological without regard to their ecological circumstances or needs (Barnes, 2008; Feldman, 2008; Richman, Kohn-Woods, & Williams, 2007; Allen, 2007; Whaley, 1998; Wolf, 1991).

The NASW Code (e.g., 4.02) speaks directly to the social worker's responsibility with regard to discrimination. Social workers have an ethical responsibility to work toward (1) obliterating institutional racism in organizational policies and practices and (2) enhancing cultural competence. These are worthy goals, but they also represent formidable challenges. The first step toward meeting these challenges is developing an awareness of possible traces of racist attitudes and bias within oneself and its influence on your practice.

Cultural Competence: A Macro Perspective

EP 2.1.4b & 2.1.4d

As discussed in Chapter 1, social workers, guided by the Educational Policy and Accreditation Standards (EPAS), are expected to recognize and engage diversity in their practice (Council on Social Work Education, 2008). To refresh your memory, this means you understand that social structures enhance and create power and privilege in your work with diverse clients. Further, social work practitioners are expected to be aware of the way in which their interactions with diverse clients are influenced by their personal biases and values. Finally, achieving cultural competence is a process by which social workers position themselves and become open to those with whom they work as key informants in their competence journey. Cultural competence is focused primarily on the interaction between the professional and the client. While professionals are ethically obligated to engage in the process of becoming competent to work with diverse groups, the organization's leadership is equally responsible. Achieving organizational cultural competence requires the commitment to competence, and the achievement of competence is the domain of the organization's leadership.

Organizational Cultural Competence

EP 2.1.10h

Achieving organizational cultural competence should not be limited to supporting the sensitivity and awareness of staff, the assignment of staff to work with their respective racial or cultural group, providing printed materials, or the use of interpreters. These measures are nonetheless worthy beginnings in an ongoing process of achieving competence.

Both public and private organizations have attempted to accommodate diverse populations by hiring professionals or community staff who represent a target group. Public agencies have also developed purchase-of-service (POS) contracts with ethnic or race-specific community-based agencies. Cultural or racial matching, in same-race or same-culture individuals and agencies, would more likely result in professionals identifying with their respective clients and, as a result, they would have a greater understanding of the group experience. However, research about the effectiveness of racial or cultural matching and its benefits to clients is inconclusive (James, 2008; Karlsson, 2005: Malgady & Zayas, 2001; Neville, Spanierman & Doan, 2006).

The practice of racial or cultural matching in organizations evolved out of a very real need to have a diversity of color, language, and understanding in organizations where the majority of staff members were white. While this practice is useful on one level, it is a beginning rather than an end. In effect, it creates an agency within an agency and is, at best, an interim solution. As such, it is inadequate as a means to achieve organizational cultural competence. Although it can enhance the organization's standing, the practice of matching raises other concerns for consideration:

- *In essence, the ethnic or racial representative is solely responsible for clients with whom they share demographic characteristics, and therefore may rarely have the opportunity to work with other clients.*
- *When representative staff provide services only to one client group, other staff may ignore and are limited in their exposure to clients who are different, further perpetuating racial inequality.*
- *The practice limits the organization's ability to expose all clients to diverse professionals.*
- *Representative staff assigned on the basis of their race, culture, or sexual orientation are often overwhelmed by the volume of work, which can include responding to the demands of representing their community.*

The NASW Standard for Cultural Competence in Social Work Practice speaks to the issue of overload, asserting that the "special skills and knowledge that bicultural and bilingual staff bring to the profession" should be compensated rather than exploited (2001, p. 26). This issue should be addressed at the organizational level, because it has implications related to workload, morale, and unintentional forms of discrimination.

EP 2.1.10h

To be effective, organizations must embrace cultural sensitivity and competence and demonstrate their commitment through their policies and practices (Chesler, 1994a; Chesler, 1994b; Fong & Gibbs, 1995; Nybell & Grey, 2004; Rogers & Potocky, 1997). Achieving organizational cultural competence at the organizational level as discussed by Nybell and & Gray (2004), requires the organization's leadership to take deliberate steps such as:

- *Reviewing organizational policies and practice*
- *Assessing the organization's standing in communities of color*
- *Evaluating the equity in resource allocation, in particular the programs or services that consist of a disproportionate number of poor clients and clients of color*
- *Assessing staffing patterns, with a specific focus on who is hired, what positions are held by whom, and who is promoted or terminated*
- *Examining the distribution of power, focusing on who benefits and who is excluded*
- *Examining the narrative structures that inform agency practices, public relations, fundraisers, and board members*
- *Analyzing the decision-making process, specifically who is involved (including clients) in such matters as agency location, allocation of resources, and who has access to this process*

Additional resources exist for organizations to utilize to analyze their competence. The Child Welfare League of America (1990), for example, has developed a Cultural Competence Self-Assessment Instrument, which provides guidance to organizations in assessing and developing cultural competence at all levels of the organization. In addition, Strom-Gottfried and Morrissey (2000), and Cross, Bazron, Dennis, and Issacs (1989) have developed organizational audits for agency policies and practice and for assessing organizational strengths and effectiveness with respect to diversity.

Public Policy. A culturally competent social worker or organization cannot always ensure that clients are immune from direct or unintentional bias in public policy. In fact, in the face of public policy, the competence of organizations and social workers are often at a disadvantage, irrespective of the level of cultural competence they have attained. To this end, we recommend analyzing cultural competence of public policy. What is the basis for this recommendation? Bias is inherent in most policies, even though their intent is to be neutral with respect to race, class, culture, and gender. Public policy, for instance, has tended to have a narrow view of the

EP 2.1.8a

culturally or racially determined dynamics that influence how people function. Further, seldom does public policy reflect a recognition of how family networks and relationships are defined within diverse groups. For example, services for the elderly, mental health services, and child welfare services are structured around the Western concept of the nuclear family, rather than broad informal or kinship networks. Informal kinship arrangements, such as those found in many diverse communities, tend to be unrecognized in public policy. In child welfare, for example, relatives as well as nonrelatives have often assumed responsibility for children; nevertheless, these individuals are unable to access resources unless they formally adopt the children. The concept of formally adopting a relative, while it has certain legal safeguards, is perceived differently in minority communities. In light of this discussion, you might conclude that the impact of public policy is not neutral.

Van Souest and Garcia (2003) suggest that cultural competence at the public policy level is an issue of social justice. As such, administrators and social workers, acting as advocates, are required to confront aspects of policies and practices that are inherently biased and that have disparate and oppressive effects on various segments of the population. As Weaver (2004) asserts, "the social justice aspect of cultural competence is often obscured by cultural competence conceptualized and highly focused on individual interaction." Because of the emphasis on the cultural competence of the practitioners, the cultural relevance of public policy can be ignored. Conclusions drawn by Voss, Douville, Little Soldier, and Twiss (1999), speaking to policies related to Native Americans, are relevant in this context. Specifically, these authors claim that when "social policies and interventions are not inclusive of cultural dynamics," they "rigidly enforce a kind of clinical colonialism" (p. 233). Therefore, another dimension to cultural competence for the organization and the social worker involves an analysis of public policy.

Given that laws and public policy influence service provisions, particularly who is served and how, a stronger focus on an analysis of public policy is crucial to the cultural competence of organizational practices and social worker-client interaction. This analysis should examine the effects of public policy as well as the extent to which public policies and laws are culturally relevant or incompetent, leading to different treatment of different groups or to discrimination. In their implementation of public policy, organizations should proactively examine their influence on their constituent groups to ensure that they are not, in fact, acting as a party to social injustice. Finally, procedural justice demands that leaders of organizations position themselves with and/or on behalf of their constituents so that the needs of diverse groups are articulated to policymakers, thereby ensuring that public policy is indeed culturally relevant. Distributive justice, the aspect of justice in which agencies are most often engaged, is compromised without an articulation of the needs, values, and interests of diverse groups.

Cultural competence is a three-pronged effort revolving around the competence of practitioners, committed leadership, and an analysis of public policy in so far as it acknowledges and respects diversity and the equality of service delivery.

Institutional Programs

EP 2.1.5b

Programs are the final facet to be addressed in improving the organizational environment of institutions. A positive, nurturing environment of institutional programs that serve people in residential settings is crucial to the functioning of its clients. Out of necessity, organizations as social systems establish policies and rules that govern the behavior of clients and staff. Rules and policies maintain the equilibrium of the organization so that it is able to operate in a predictable manner. Stimulating, constructive, and growth-promoting programs enhance client functioning, whereas custodial care (which tends to diminish clients involvement in decisions about their lives) can be disempowering, foster apathy, and create reactance, in some instances. Moreover, institutional environments, where even the most routine resident behavior is governed by rules, can be unproductive in that they often inspire challenges to the rules, potentially resulting in a cycle of punishing the behavior of offenders.

An important aspect of institutional programming is the extent to which residents are able to exercise choice and control over their daily living and participate in their treatment plans. To enhance choice and foster participation, you should advocate for democratic participation in the institution's governance and individual rights and choices about how they spend their time and use their resources. When this is not the case, both residents and staff may experience the residual effects of discord. For example, an adult group home resident, referred to the social work case manager because he was "acting out," complained that he did not like having cigarettes and money rationed to him by staff; he felt that this practice suggested he was incapable of making his own decisions. A common complaint you may have heard in adolescent group homes or from other institutional residents is their dislike of the point system in which they lose points or privileges for failing to comply with rules (e.g., failing to comply with "lights out" orders, or exhibiting independent behaviors). Many perceive these systems as further limiting their already limited choices. Often, failure to respond to complaints of this nature escalates in the form of more assertive or aggressive behaviors by residents, which in turn leads to disciplinary action.

Prisons are institutions in which rules are strictly enforced and the residents can feel isolated by their confinement. Aspects of programs within these environments can become more humane through such practices as using volunteers and special visitation days for minors whose parents are incarcerated (Ardittti, 2008). These efforts effectively link the incarcerated to the outside world. Volunteers are invaluable resources in that they teach skills from which those in prison can achieve a sense of mastery and connectedness. Special visitation days for minors help them maintain their parental attachment, but the physical space provided and the location of the prison can be a factor in the family's ability to visit (Christian, 2005; Enos, 2008; From, 2008; Genty, 2008). With an increase in the number of women in prisons, advocates are calling for more family-friendly policies, citing the impact on minors as punishing when they lose contact with their mothers or fathers because of incarceration.

Although there are organizational and legal constraints in residential settings, the principles of social work and advocacy for basic human rights are no less important. Empowerment and self-efficacy are realized when residents are able to exercise control over their lives and their environment to the best of their capacity, given organizational constraints. A sense of power is closely linked to competence, self-esteem, and the belief that individual actions or actions in concert with and supported by other systems can lead to improvements in one's life situation. These attributes or factors, in turn, are reciprocally influenced by the quality of the environment.

Organizational Change

EP 2.1.10a

Change within organizations requires an understanding and analysis of organizational structure, function, culture, and resource environment. Martin and O'Connor (1989) analyzed the social welfare organization using systems theory as a conceptual framework. Analyzing an organization would also include analyzing the organization's relationship with its resource environment (funding sources, the organization's internal structure and processes, and social, cultural, and political-economic environment). Change efforts, according to Netting, Kettner, and McMurtry (2004), can occur in an organization on two levels:

- *Improving resources provided to clients*
- *Enhancing the organization's working environment so that personnel can perform more efficiently and effectively, thus improving services to clients*

Similarly, organizational change as conceptualized by Brager and Holloway (1978) can focus on three areas: people-focused change, technological change, and structural change, which may take the form of a new policy, modifications to an existing policy, the development of a program, the initiation of a project in which the results can be used to inform service delivery, or by the organization positioning itself as a learning organization (Kettner, Daley, & Nichols, 1985; Senge, 1990, 1994).

Organizational Learning and Learning Organizations

EP 2.1.10h

Organizational learning and the learning organizations are approaches to affect organizational change. A *learning organization* is a process that enables members of the organization to periodically review performance and make adjustments to improve it. It is also considered to be a relevant factor in the quality of staff work life with respect to job design and performance awards (Lewis, Lewis, Packard, & Souflee, 2001; Morgan, 1997). A learning organization positions itself so that it can continuously review and revise its operations, purposes, and objectives so as to ensure the quality of the organizational experience for clients and staff. Questions that might be posed include: How is work done? What are the outcomes of this work? Through this process the organization has an opportunity to reflect on its strengths and limitations, so that it can develop strategies that enhance the former and address the latter. *Organizational learning* emphasizes a set of activities pertinent to the organization's internal operations and the interdependence among its various units.

Organizational learning and the learning organization are often discussed as a single concept. A *learning organization*, as defined by Senge (1990, 1994) and Morgan (1997), essentially speaks to the ecology of the organization. That is, it refers to a particular type of organization and its ability to scan, anticipate, and respond to environmental changes. The learning organization develops capacities that empower members to question and challenge operating norms and assumptions, thereby ensuring its stability and promoting its evolution through strategic responses and direction (Morgan, 1997).

Both approaches require a supportive environment in which the organization's culture fosters dialogue, open communication and feedback. For example, a county human health and human services administrator initiated a series of "community dialogues" among staff to position itself as a learning organization and a shared vision to facilitate organizational change. For example, how well did the various units serving families coordinate and work together? Lewis et al. (2001) encourage the adoption of the learning organization as a way to create opportunities for growth in human service organizations.

Staff as Agents of Change

EP 2.1.10a

Although most social workers are adept in advocating for their clients or developing resources or support networks, many may be reticent or feel unable to influence or propose changes within their own organizations. In some instances, they may identify organizational concerns in a hierarchical fashion, and therefore conclude that the impetus for change or resolutions resides in the management domain. In some instances, and with certain problems, this view may be valid. Nonetheless, because of the interactions between staff and clients, managers and administrators need to be able to rely on you and other staff at the street-level of service delivery to alert them to the need for change in a program or policy or the development of a new resource. In initiating changes at the organizational level, you are acting as a diagnostician and facilitator/expediter. Assuming responsibility for and participating in change is the essence of staff empowerment, and participation in change efforts is consistent with the ethical obligation to your employment organization.

To be an effective organizational change agent, you must be aware of the benefits and risks of a proposed change. In your benefit-risk analysis, it is essential that you document and clarify the need for change. If service delivery is a concern, will your proposal, for example, improve the situation (Brager & Holloway, 1978; Netting, Kettner & McMurtry, 2004)? In addition, what is the form that the proposed change should take? For example, if service delivery is the target, would you recommend a change in a policy or a program? Furthermore, what are the expected outcomes of the proposed change?

Risks, Benefits, and Opposition

EP 2.1.9b

Promoting change in organizations is a complex process, and opposition is perhaps as common as that found in families, individuals, and groups. Organizations are systems that seek to maintain equilibrium; therefore, you may encounter opposition to proposals for change. Opposition may arise in response to proposals that challenge or exceed the capacity of the organization to implement proposals due to resource constraints or ideological differences. Likewise, proposals that would significantly change the purpose, mission, and goals of the organization may spur resistance. Extending an agency's operating hours may be considered to be a peripheral change and have little or no effect on organizational goals or mission. In contrast, programmatic changes, which alter a program's objectives, have greater effects on organizational depth.

Frey (1990) has developed a useful framework with which you can assess organizational opposition. In assessing the potential benefits and to minimize opposition to a proposal, it is important to obtain the input of four groups:

- *Clients, including the extent to which the proposed change offers direct benefits to this group and will effectively alter and enhance the services they receive*
- *Administrators, who ultimately have legitimate authority for accepting the proposal and providing the resources for implementation*
- *Supervisors or staff, who will have responsibility for planning and/or overseeing implementation*
- *Staff persons, who ultimately carry out the change or are affected by it, once it is implemented*

By considering the impact of the potential change on each group, you can weigh benefits against potential detrimental effects and plan strategies to counter reactions and resistance when the former (i.e., the benefits) clearly and substantially outweigh the latter.

Frey (1990) also suggests that you weigh risk, benefits, and opposition by assessing whether your proposal is "high risk" as characterized by the following:

- *Substantial costs to the organization, for example, purchasing expensive equipment or creating new units*

- *Actions that must be adopted in their entirety rather than implemented in stages*
- *Radical ideas that are in conflict with the dominant values of the organization, its members, or the public*

The following example describes a successful low-risk proposal initiated by a social worker; in particular, the proposal was in tandem with the goals of the organization and it did not involve costly changes. The aim of the proposal was consistent with Netting and colleagues' (2004) change strategy of "enhancing the organization's working environment so that personnel can perform more efficiently and effectively, thus improving services to clients."

CASE EXAMPLE

The primary client group was made up of individuals and families for whom English was their second language (ESL population). The agency provided counseling, educational programs, and assistance to clients in applying for financial benefits. However, a majority of clients had difficulty in completing the applications, despite the fact that they had been translated into several different languages. The particular problem documented by the social worker was the amount of staff time required (which far exceeded the contact hours allowed) to assist individuals or families in completing the forms. Incomplete applications resulted in the need for additional appointments and delays in establishing clients' eligibility and required additional staff time.

To remedy the situation, the social worker proposed using instructional groups, to be scheduled at different times during the week, instead of individual appointments. The groups would be led by staff or volunteers. She envisioned that groups would have two benefits: First, group meetings would address staff concerns related to scheduling, rescheduling, and excessive contact hours. Second, volunteers, specifically other clients who had successfully completed the applications, would help clients, especially new arrivals, become connected to a social network.

The success of this proposal was attributed to the fact that the change did not require substantial organizational expenditures. Nor did it radically compromise the organization's goals and mission. In fact, rather than taxing organizational resources, it redeployed resources in a more efficient manner. By using a group approach and utilizing volunteers, the social worker's proposal augmented the agency's ability to serve the ESL population. Staff responded favorably, as it effectively addressed their frustrations about the time they spent in assisting individuals and families to complete the financial forms.

In general, proposals that fit with an organization's ideology, resource capacity, and potential are likely to win the support of a significant number of members and, therefore, are likely to succeed. Of course, irrespective of its nature, change is often met with skepticism and resistance. Indeed, the social worker's proposal encountered some opposition. In response, the social worker documented the cost-benefit ratio to the organization (which satisfied administrators) and clarified the benefits for staff (their time would be freed so that they could accomplish other tasks). To build support for her proposal, the social worker spoke with co-workers, especially those who were most affected by the need to reschedule appointments for the purpose of completing the eligibility forms. The social worker met with other staff even though they were not directly involved in the ESL program; she recognized that their support would facilitate acceptance. A final point illustrated in the case example is that individual staff were favorable to the proposal because they perceived it as either benign or a benefit to their position and function.

Macro Practice Evaluation

EP 2.1.6b

Each of the macro-level strategies discussed in this chapter lends themselves to a variety of procedures for which intermediate and final outcomes can be assessed. Evaluation seeks to assess the extent to which the change effort and the strategies employed were successful and can include collecting quantitatively, qualitatively, or a combination to methods. For example, after completing an assessment that documented a need and the subsequent development of a resource, you would want to measure the level in which the resource was responsive. You might also wish to determine the perceptions and opinions of individuals for whom the resource was developed.

Empowerment, whether through organizing, social action, or improving institutional environments, is a consistent theme in macro-level practice. In keeping with the empowerment theme, the evaluation process should include client groups. They should be involved in establishing success indicators and outcomes of the change effort, as well as their perceived level of empowerment (Gutierrez, Parsons, & Cox, 1998; Lum, 2004; Secret, Jordan, & Ford, 1999). Because evaluation is a process, another facet involves examining how the outcome was achieved. For example, determining which of the strategies that were implemented to mobilize resources engaged the general public or public officials, organized a community, and resulted in the most effective response. Should your change effort enlist the help of volunteers and solicit feedback from them, for example, asking them to rate the appeal of specific recruitment literature or presentations? It may be necessary to target your evaluation to a specific group. For instance, did congregations respond more favorably to a presentation during worship service when compared with an announcement in the church bulletin or email newsletter? Collecting this information helps to determine which strategies were the most effective, under what conditions, and with which populations.

Measures of success used by organizations tend to be reported in aggregated client statistical data; therefore, evaluating the effectiveness of macro-level practice can be a challenge. In evaluating the outcomes of a program objective, for example, an organization's questions might be the number of "homeless families with children that found affordable housing." Further analysis might involve examining a change in status of the families who obtained housing. Here, the evaluation focuses on the overall outcome.

A pre- and post-intervention rating scale measuring the change may be applied in situations involving social action and advocacy (e.g., Single Subject Design, scales). Change can be measured on an incremental basis, after a particular action technique, and at the end of the project. You may also decide to collect qualitative information along with statistical data. For example, in an interview format, groups and communities provide descriptive information regarding improved relationships between the police and a community. The evaluation may be implemented as a summative or formative process and include both qualitative and quantitative data (Weiss, 1998). For example, in conducting a needs assessment, you might question the extent that needs were being met or that new resources are required, by using a survey and also group interviews.

Several innovative approaches hold promise for enhancing the effectiveness of developing and planning community programs. The first approach utilizes the methodology of developmental or intervention research (Comer, Meier, & Galinsky, 2004; Rothman & Thomas, 1994; Thomas, 1989). Developmental research is a rigorous, systematic, and distinctive methodology consisting of techniques and methods taken from other fields and disciplines. Its methodology relies on social research and model development and is sufficiently flexible to accommodate the unpredictable and uncontrolled conditions in most practice settings (Comer, Meier, & Galinsky, 2004). Using this approach allows for strategies and change efforts in the form of programs to be tested and then modified based on the results.

To see how this process works, let's say for example that your agency developed a program for youth who had repeated stays in the shelter system. The primary goal was to reunite them with their families and a secondary goal was permanency. This approach was a significant departure from the way in which the shelter system functioned, thus the system was the target of change. Home visits, while the youth were still in the residential phase of the program, were identified as critical factors in moving them toward reunification. After a period of time, you would collect both qualitative and quantitative data so that you could determine the effectiveness of home visits and the resources required. Gathering this information would enable the agency to direct its resources toward achieving the second goal of the program. Evaluation, irrespective of the method, requires clearly specified goals and clearly articulated objectives in measurable terms. In general, evaluation is an ongoing process for which it is important to establish indicators at the beginning of the intervention. The process involves continuous, systematic monitoring of the intervention's impact, and this requires development and implementation of techniques of data management. Systematic analysis of data allows you to determine, for example, if the program activity or intervention is being implemented as planned and whether it is accomplishing the stated program goals (Gardner, 2000; Lewis, Lewis, Packard, & Souflee, 2001). Conducting evaluation requires skills in selecting an appropriate research design, techniques of measurement, and analysis of data. The specific details of the various methods are beyond the scope of this book. The requisite knowledge needed to implement the evaluation process is commonly discussed in research courses. Keep in mind that your ultimate aim is to track the impact of a change effort with regard to the desired outcomes.

Summary

This chapter discussed macro-level intervention strategies for which the target of change is a system. Today's social, economic, demographic, and political trends present numerous opportunities for action and intervention at the macro practice level. In talking to social workers in preparation for writing this chapter, we were impressed with the breadth and depth of macro practice strategies they used, and the ease with which they understood the need to bridge micro and macro. The social workers saw their practice as holistic and were comfortable employing a range of strategies to help people resolve problems or change social conditions. As one social worker stated, "It would be difficult to ask people to change without also addressing the circumstances and conditions that contribute to their situations." The person and environment focus reflected in this statement, in essence, frames the fundamental tenets and foundation of macro practice.

CourseMate

Access an integrated eBook and chapter specific learning tools including glossary terms, chapter outlines, relevant web links, videos, and practice quizzes. Go to **www.cengagebrain.com**.

CHAPTER **15**

Improving Relationships and Family Functioning

CHAPTER OVERVIEW

Chapter 15 builds on the family assessment skills you learned in Chapter 10, by describing skills in enhancing family functioning, relationships and interaction. You will learn how to engage families and practice in a manner that is sensitive to family and cultural variants.

In this chapter you will acquire knowledge that will enable you to:

- Engage and assess couples, families, and parents
- Convene the initial session and engage families (voluntary, referred, or mandated) in the helping process
- Assist families in enhancing their interactions by increasing communication skills
- Assist families in modifying their interactions
- Assist families to understand the influence of and modify family rules
- Assist family members in disengaging from conflict
- Assist families in modifying misconceptions and distorted cognitions that impair their interactions
- Assist families in modifying family alignments

EPAS COMPETENCIES IN THE 15TH CHAPTER

This chapter will give you the information needed to meet the following practice competencies.

2.1.1d Demonstrate professional demeanor in behavior, appearance, and communication

2.1.4a Recognize the extent to which a culture's structure and values alienate, create, or enhance privilege and power

2.1.4b Gain sufficient self-awareness to eliminate the influence of personal biases and values in working with diverse families

2.1.7a Utilize conceptual framework to guide the process of assessment, intervention, and evaluation

2.1.7b Critique and apply knowledge of human behavior in the social environment

2.1.10a Substantively and affectively prepare for action with individuals, families, groups, and communities

2.1.10b Use empathy and other interpersonal skills

2.1.10c Develop a mutually agreed-on work focus and desired outcomes

2.1.10d Collect and interpret client data

2.1.10e Assess client strengths and limitations

2.1.10f Develop mutually agreed-on intervention goals and objectives

2.1.10j Help clients solve problems

Intervention Approaches with Families

Family relationships and interactions are often punctuated and strained by numerous factors. For instance, family life transitions, structural arrangements, patterns of communication, and roles (including role definition, overload, and strain) are but a few sources that contribute to family relational dynamics. Intervention strategies, whether the focus is

EP 2.1.10a

on family structure or family processes, have as their primary aim to "change the family, and in doing so, change the life of each of its members" (Nichols & Schwartz, 1998, p. 6). This work is accomplished by intervening in the family's structure, transactional patterns, interpersonal boundaries, and relationships between subsystems. Process-oriented interventions focus on the nature of family dynamics and their patterned interactions, including communication styles.

More recently, approaches to work with families have encouraged us to rethink earlier assumptions about what constitutes healthy or normal family development and functioning. Post-modern approaches, such as, narrative and social constructivists as well as feminist literature, emphasize family diversity. Post-modern approaches diminish the notion of absolute objective truths and the role and authority of the family therapist as paramount to family change. Instead the goal is to help families create new meaning and viewpoints about their problems (Hartman, 1981; Nichols 2006).

EP 2.1.7a

Although the interventions and techniques discussed in this chapter are applied to couples and families, most are also relevant to work with treatment groups. Recall that the family is a system within the larger social system. As a consequence, family context and family functioning, interaction, and relational patterns may be influenced by external factors. Family processes and structure may also be embedded in cultural values and norms, so conventional techniques used to intervene with families may not match the needs of diverse families. Some of these factors, as well as ecologically based concerns, are highlighted in this chapter.

Initial Contacts

EP 2.1.10a

After completing a family assessment, you have a working knowledge of the family's structure and relationships and its strengths and problems, which are reviewed with the family during the initial sessions. The next step is to engage the family as a whole in the assessment and eventual problem solving. Enhancing the functioning and relationships of couples and family systems requires you to be skilled in engaging members and in focusing on the family as a whole. Generally, when seeking help, families or couples tend to not think in a systems framework. Instead, they often identify a concern, and perhaps target the behavior of another member as the source of the family's difficulties. Thus, it is important to manage the initial contact in ways that encourage the relevant members of the family system to be involved, rather than settle prematurely on a problem identified in an individual family member's request for service. This section describes ways of handling the initial contacts that lay the groundwork for implementing the work to be completed between you and the family.

Managing Initial Contact with Couples and Families

EP 2.1.10d

Most often, contact with families begins after a family member has initiated the initial request for help. Depending on the practice setting or nature of a referral, the initial contact may occur in the home, in a school or hospital setting, over the telephone, or in your office. Generally, the upfront work, including the scheduled appointment, whether in the office or the home, has been completed in the intake process. If the family has been screened for a family approach, all you may need to do in the initial contact is to work out the scheduling details. If there has been no previous contact with the family—for example, if the request to see the family came from a referral source; you may need to accomplish several other objectives. In particular, you may need to determine whether intervening at the family level is appropriate. Keep in mind that the individual making the referral is but one source of information. Just as you would not act on a single family member's perception of a problem, you also want to avoid becoming influenced by the referral's source view of the problem or the source's solution. Therefore, in the initial contact, you would review the referral information with the family, but emphasize that the family is a credible source about their problem.

Other critical objectives of the initial contact include reaching an agreement as to who will attend the initial session and establishing rapport with the family member who has initiated the contact. When an individual member presents a family's concern, it is important to establish rapport with him or her as the initiator of the request for help. Wright and Anderson (1998) call our attention to attachment skills, which essentially concern "connecting" to this individual so that he or she feels heard and his or her concern has been validated. In sessions beyond the initial contact, you will want to emphasize that in the future, all family members are to be involved. Even so, the initial contact should be kept brief, and you should be highly focused on the relevant objectives of the session to avoid becoming entangled in the individual's perception of the family's problem. To this end, we recommend that you follow these guidelines:

1. Ask the family member to describe the problem briefly, and empathically respond to the individual's concern. In this way you establish rapport and you are obtaining information, albeit from the family member's point of view. Also, elicit information that will help you determine who else is involved in the problem. When you believe you have heard the presenting complaint, summarize the individual's view of the problem, his or her relevant feelings, and emphasize that person's needs or wants.

2. In the instance of a referred or mandated contact, you should share the circumstances of the information that has been provided about the family, including the expressed purpose and goals stated in a mandate. You should clarify choices that the potential client may make, including whether to meet all or some of the requirements. In this session, you will want to identify topics to be addressed in this meeting. Before concluding the session, discuss with the client any requirements that will affect his or her choices, including applicable time limits.

3. If your exploration of the problem reveals that the involvement of the entire family is appropriate, introduce the individual family member to the family systems orientation, using a message such as the following:

Social worker: In helping people with the kinds of problems you've described, it is helpful to have other family members come for sessions. It has been my experience that when some members of the family have problems, other members are affected, and they also experience stress and discomfort. Equally important, changes in one member may require changes and adjustments on the part of other family members. People accomplish change more frequently when all family members work together. For this reason, it will be important that other family members are involved.

4. Specify which family members should be involved in the initial session. Because of the potential difficulties in managing initial contact with entire families (which requires advanced skills), it may be useful, despite the family systems orientation, to rely on a less ambitious approach. For example, if a parent identifies a child-related problem, request that one or both parents attend the initial session without the child. Of course, there may be instances in which parents will object to the child's exclusion ("He needs to be here, too!"). There may also be unusual circumstances (a crisis) in which the minor may be in danger, and therefore immediate action is required. When a situation or circumstance dictate excluding other family members from the initial contact, convey the message that you will want to see these individuals in future sessions.

5. When a family member complains of problems involving another member but insists that the individual is not available; you may agree to see the person who initiated the contact alone at first. You would, however, indicate that a next step would be to schedule an individual interview with the other person, thus giving him or her equal time. Because people differ in their opinions, seeing each member individually allows you to obtain a balanced view of the problem. Some clients will comply with requests, but others may offer explanations such as, "My husband works odd hours." "She won't come," or "He's not the one with the problem." These messages can reflect a reluctance to include other members, or perhaps the unwillingness of other members to be involved in resolving the family's difficulties.

Reluctance, in whatever form, by any family member can only be clarified by your having contact with the reportedly unwilling family member or members. When a family member emphatically states that he or she does not want to involve certain or any family members in the initial session, this reasoning should be respected. If the position is not subsequently modified, you may arrange to involve any family members whom the individual is willing to include. Should a member continue to maintain that other members are unwilling or unable to become involved, ask him or her permission to contact those persons directly. If you gain permission (as will usually happen), you can telephone the individual, using the following message modeled by the social worker, after introducing yourself and stating the purpose of the call:

Social worker: As you know, [caller's name] has contacted me concerning problems involving your family. I understand that you are unavailable, but I thought I would give you a call to ask you to join us. Your participation would be extremely helpful, and I am interested in your perspective on the family's problem as well as hearing your ideas about how it can be resolved. Would you available for an appointment, say, at 4:00 p.m. next Wednesday?

In the best-case scenario, the individual will agree to your request. Some people, however, may react less favorably, and you will need to explore their response. Subsequently, you could ask the person to participate in *at least one* session, yet respect his or her decision should they decline to do so. Exerting pressure may alienate the individual and the underlying dynamics can destroy future opportunities to obtain his or her involvement. With skillful handling, most often you will be able to dissolve strong opposition. There may, of course, be valid reasons for the absence of some family members. For example, minors are generally excluded from family sessions that focus on issues between their parents.

Initial Contacts in the Home

Because social work practice with families takes place in a variety of settings, the initial contact may not follow the scenarios we have outlined here. For example, your initial contact may take place in the family's home. This contact may be voluntary or involuntary. In the latter case, you may need to be alert to problematic involuntary client–social worker dynamics. In any event, home visits require making arrangements with families to ensure that sessions will be free of interruptions, especially when the family has small children. During home visits, you may encounter other family members or friends, in which case privacy and confidentiality issues need to be discussed and resolved.

In addition to privacy, there may be people in the home that are unknown, nor are they introduced to you. Such was the case of a beginning social worker who sought consultation on whether he should have proceeded with the initial session with a family in the presence of an unidentified elderly man. This individual clearly held an esteemed position in the family. In fact, throughout the session, the father often looked for nonverbal cues from the man before responding to questions posed by the social worker. In this case, it was decided that the social worker should have asked whether or not it was appropriate for him to be introduced to the elderly man and inquired about his status in the family. As it turned out the man was a leader of the family's clan.

During visits to the home, Boyd-Franklin & Bry (2000) caution practitioners to "remember that you are on the client's home turf, which means that you should remain flexible and show deference to the rules and structure of the family and the order of the household" (p. 39). Even so, some family members may resent or resist involvement in the initial session, and they may cite culture as a defense against joining (Flores & Carey, 2000).

Safety Concerns

Home environments can be messy, and the communities in which some families live may cause you to have concerns about your safety. While you can hardly comment on a family's home environment, unless of course there are evident dangers, you should address your concerns directly with the family and ask for their advice. Students and beginning social workers tend to shy away from openly discussing their safety concerns. Nonetheless, concerns may be inadvertently communicated by nonverbal behavior. Also, it is important that you evaluate whether safety is a matter of your perception or the result of your being in a strange environment. You can validate your concern by speaking with the family and your agency supervisor. Community-based social workers face some risks, but a majority of assaults on social workers, verbal or physical, occur in an agency or institutional setting, and some are the results of the social worker's behavior toward an individual (Newhill, 2004; Ringstad, 2005; Weinger, 2001).

Managing Initial Contacts with Parents

Initial sessions with parents (legal guardian or foster parent) should involve other persons who perform or share the executive parental function in the household such as a grandparent. Children may be included in subsequent sessions, but seeing parents alone in the initial session gives you more time to become acquainted with the problems of the family and, on the basis of known information, to plan strategies for engaging the child. Guidelines that may facilitate the initial contact with parents are as follows:

Establish rapport with parents. By having an initial session with parents, you are able to establish rapport with them and, where indicated, influence their behavior in future sessions that include the children. The behavior and style of relating of some parents may be so engrained and adversarial that initial attempts to see everyone together would prove to be disastrous. Further, having an initial session with parents alone enables you to clarify the systemic nature of problem; specifically, that the problem does not belong to the child alone.

Coach parents. Interviewing parents first in an initial session also enables you to coach them about how best to bring an identified child into the helping process. For example, in talking to the child, they should clarify that the *family* is having a problem, rather than indicating that the family is having problems *with the child*. In addition, they should provide a general explanation of what the child can expect in the session. In doing so, they should be alert to any reservations that the child might have about coming to the session.

Establish concerns as a family problem. When meeting with parents or other individuals who perform this role in initial sessions, you will need to explore the basis of their belief that the child is the problem. Depending on how the parents have communicated about the problem in front of the child, you may expect that in parent–child sessions the child will be defensive and perhaps oppose or be unenthusiastic about being involved. You can take some pressure off the minor by engaging all members in a discussion of changes they would like to make in resolving the family's problem. This strategy is also appropriate when an adult family member has been designated as the source of a problem.

Create a safe place for the child. When parents bring a child to the initial session, you may need to coach them about how to behave constructively. For example, suggest to parents that they assist you in creating a climate that is conducive to open communication. If indicated, you would also ask them to refrain from repetitive blaming messages ("He continues to mess up in school, and hang around the wrong people"), and request that they focus on positive behaviors ("He was a helper this past summer in a program for kids in the park"). Using a technique from solution-focused brief treatment, you might divert the parent's attention to those instances of exceptions—for example, when the child is not messing up in school.

Allow the child to tell his or her story. In the initial session, you should provide an opportunity for the child to tell her or his story. Doing so allows you to hear directly from the minor, without him or her being persuaded (as the child may perceive it) by information provided by the parents. In giving the minor this time and space, you are establishing rapport and a level of trust with him or her. At the same time, you should be careful to avoid subordinating the parent's executive function or giving the impression that you are forming an alliance with the minor. In some cultures, for example, inviting minors to voice their concerns is unacceptable and perceived to be inappropriate role behavior. But there are instances when interviewing a minor alone is required—for example, in a situation of reported child maltreatment or sexual abuse. If culture permits, and there is no indication of the minor's need for protection, you can interview him or her either with the parents present or alone. A younger child may be more comfortable in the presence of parents; however, an adolescent may prefer to be seen alone.

Regardless of whether minors are seen in the initial session with parents or alone, time set aside during the last part of the session is reserved for seeing all family members together. At this time, you will want to reemphasize the systemic nature of the minors' problem and assist all members in formulating individual and family goals.

Orchestrating the Initial Family or Couple Session

The goal of bringing the family together is to identify the problem at hand by eliciting the viewpoints of the various family members. The initial session, whether it occurs in the office, home, or institution is referred to as the *social*

EP 2.1.10a

or *joining stage* (Boyd-Franklin, 1989a; Nichols & Schwartz, 1998). In this stage, a central task is to establish rapport and build an alliance with the family. It is useful to restate the reason for the voluntary contact. For instance Kim (the social worker in *Home for the Holidays 1*) stated, "Jackie contacted me because the two of you disagree about your holiday plans." If the family's contact is the result of a referral or a mandate, you acknowledge this fact—for example, "Katie's teacher referred the family to our agency because...."

In facilitating the *social* or *joining stage,* your tasks are twofold:

1. Ensure that each family member can voice his or her opinion without interruptions from other family members.
2. Encourage family members to listen so that members feel understood and accepted.

You can further facilitate this stage by adopting an attitude of inquiry: What can I learn from and about this family that will help me work with them?

EP 2.1.10d

The initial session with families is crucial. The family members' experiences during this session determine in large measure whether they will join with you and contract to work toward specified goals or solutions. Moreover, they may perceive the initial session as a prototype of the helping process. Table 15-1 identifies the objectives to be accomplished that will further lay a solid foundation for future work with the family. In addition to the table, the objectives are discussed, so that you understand their relevance and can use them in both planning for and evaluating initial sessions.

EP 2.1.10b

1. *Establish a personal relationship with individual members and an alliance with the family as a group.* In working with couples or families (or groups), social workers have a twofold task of establishing personal relationships with each individual while developing a "connectedness" with the family as a unit. To cultivate relationships with family members, you use *socializing,* a technique that involves brief *social chitchat* at the beginning of the session to reduce tension. Joining or coupling techniques to expedite entry in to the family system must respect culture, family form, family rules, and the current level of functioning. You may also find that using the family's language and idioms—for example, "He's messing up in school," facilitates your connection to the family. You can further connect to the family by conveying your acceptance, and by engaging them in identifying their strengths. Conveying acceptance and offering support may be especially critical to vulnerable members of the family.

In the initial session, empathic responding can be particularly useful in establishing rapport with a member who appears to be reserved or reluctant to be involved. For instance, when a member does participate spontaneously, your task is to draw them into the session:

EP 2.1.10b

Social Worker: Tamika, we haven't heard from you about how you felt when you learned you were coming to see a social worker.

Tamika: I thought that it would be a waste of time.

Social Worker: My sense is that you are unsure about the reason that you are here. It is not unusual to feel

---

TABLE-15-1 ORCHESTRATING THE INITIAL FAMILY OR COUPLE SESSION

1. Establish a personal relationship with individual members and an alliance with the family as a group
2. Clarify expectations and explore reservations about the helping process, including potential dynamics of minority status and culture
3. Clarify roles and the nature of the helping process
4. Clarify choices about participation
5. Elicit the family's perception of the problem
6. Identify wants and needs of family members
7. Define the problem as a family problem
8. Emphasize family strengths
9. Ask questions to elicit information about patterned behaviors of the family
10. Draw family members' attention to repetitive communications and discuss whether they want to change patterns
11. Begin to assist family members to relate to one another in more positive ways
12. Establish individual and family goals or solutions
13. Gauge the motivation of family members to have future session and negotiate contract
14. Negotiate tasks to be accomplished during the week
15. End the session by summarizing points discussed and solutions and progress achieved

© Cengage Learning 2013

for a person to feel as you do. You said you thought that being here would be a waste of time. Would it be helpful if I explained the purpose of the session with you and your family?

EP 2.1.10b

The social worker's response included a reflection of Tamika's feelings and empathy as a facilitative skill. Empathic messages show genuine interest that can cause reserved family members to become more active. Conversely, if Tamika's lack of involvement is related to family dynamics rather than to her feelings, you will need to be mindful whether encouraging her to express an opinion has potential risks. In either case, you should endeavor to distribute time and attention somewhat equally among members, to highlight individual strengths, and to intervene when one member dominates the conversation or when the session involves members' communicating blaming, shaming, or put-down messages.

Finally, effectively connecting with families requires that you understand and have appreciation and empathy for the sociopolitical and cultural context of the family and for the family's collective strengths and competencies. Often, it is these attributes that have enabled the family to function in spite of their difficulties.

EP 2.1.10d

2. *Clarify expectations and explore reservations about the helping process.* Family members have varying and often distorted perceptions of the helping process and may have misgivings about participating in sessions (e.g., a waste of time; talking won't help). To identify obstacles to full participation (which is a prerequisite to establishing a viable contract), you should elicit the responses of all family members to open-ended questions like the following:

- *What were your concerns about meeting with me?*
- *What did you hope might happen in our meetings together?*
- *What were your feelings about what might happen in this meeting today?*
- *Would you imagine for a moment how you would like things to be different in your family?*

Questions of a more specific nature, intended to help family members express their concerns, are illustrated in the following examples:

- *Are you concerned that your family might be judged?*
- *In your community, how would others deal with this problem?*
- *Does seeking help from someone outside of your family make you feel uncomfortable?*
- *In what way do you think that I can be of help to your family?*

As you explore reservations, concerns, and even hopes from each family member, you can broaden the focus to the family by asking: "I'm wondering if others share the same or similar concerns as …?" As members acknowledge similar feelings, they may begin to realize that, despite their feelings, as a unit they share certain concerns in common. For example, family members might disagree about the functionality of rigid family rules, but they all may have anxieties about less income due to job loss and the financial stability of the family.

In interpreting a family member who is reluctant, unwilling, or inactive in the family session, you should be sensitive to such factors as an individual's personality and cultural norms. Some individuals may prefer to observe processes before they engage or participate. Culture may influence such expressions like feelings, so a family member may be baffled by related questions. Personality or culture aside, certain family members will continue to have strong reservations. You can address their reluctance in the initial session, by asking them one of the following questions and addressing their subsequent responses:

EP 2.1.10d

- *What, if anything, would make you feel better about participating?*
- *Having heard the concerns of other family members, on a scale of 1–10, which one would you rate as highest or lowest priority?*
- *Given your concerns, are you willing to stay for the remainder of the session and decide at the conclusion whether to continue?*

The intent of these questions shows willingness on your part to negotiate the terms under which a family member participates and also acknowledges his or her right of choice. If the type of questions does not result in a change of heart, you might, for example, ask the member if he or she is willing to be physically present, but emphasize that he or she is not obligated to talk. This invitation diminishes the pressure on the person to contribute. As a caveat, however, it would be important to advise the individual that it is expected that he or she refrain from distracting nonverbal behavior. As a final note on the reluctant family member, be aware of the fact that his or her behavior may be self-protective because he or she has been identified as the source of the family's problem, especially if he or she feels ganged up on by other family members.

The Dynamics of Minority Status and Culture in Exploring Reservations

EP 2.1.7b

Minority statuses, which encompass a range of social identities, are other factors that may cause a family or family member to have reservations about seeking help. Families may fear "what might happen" if their problems are brought out into the open (Nichols & Schwartz, 1998, p. 132). In truth, poor, minority, and gay or lesbian families have good reasons for their apprehensions and anxieties in encounters with helping professionals. Boyd-Franklin (1989a) and Lum (2004) explain that the historical experience of minority families, in which they have often been perceived as unhealthy, may cause them to hide their problems until they have escalated to a point of crisis. Indeed, the communities in which these families live may reinforce the silence. Also, the unspoken rule of keeping family secrets can be more pronounced in minority families because of the value placed on privacy, or a sense of shame about involving an outsider in family matters. Flores and Carey (2000) and Lum (2004) both emphasize that families are more likely to feel a level of comfort when they do not feel the need to defend who they are or their culture. Lum (2004) emphasizes the importance of the family's confidence in the helping relationship as well as the importance of a mutual trust between the social worker and the family.

Reservations about attending family sessions may be a particular issue among ethnic minority families in which some members are undocumented or residing illegally in the United States (Pierce & Elisme, 1997; Fong, 1997; Falicov, 1996). In addition, immigrant or refugee families may be unfamiliar with formal helping systems and their lack of familiarity can cause them to be hesitant to become involved (Potocky-Tripodi, 2002).

EP 2.1.4b

Wright and Anderson (1998) suggest that in actively tuning into the family, you might pose a question such as, "What is it like being with the client [family], in your preparation for the initial session?" The question has a two-fold purpose. In effect, not only are you *tuning* in to the family, you are also evaluating whether you may have reactions to the family that have the potential to enter into the session. In your assessment, consider including two additional questions: "What is it like to be this family?" and "What does it mean to this family to seek professional help?" The answers to these questions will help you show sensitivity in your initial interactions with the family and to understand their experience in seeking help. To lessen the family concerns or reservations about the contact with you, it can be useful for you to affirm the protective function of reluctance, whether in a family member or the family system as a whole as a measure of safety for the family.

3. *Clarify roles and the nature of the helping process.* In exploring misgivings and reservations, you should educate families about the nature of the helping process, and clarify both your own and their roles. In educating families about the helping process, your objective is to create an atmosphere and structure where problem solving can occur. Role clarification is also addressed toward the end of the initial session in which an initial contract is negotiated.

EP 2.1.1d

4. *Clarify choices about participation in the helping process.* In the instance of referred contact, you can reiterate that the family is free to decide whether further contact with you will meet their needs and, if so, what to work on, regardless of the concerns of the referring source. If contact is mandated, it is necessary to clarify what you are required to do (e.g., submit a report to the court) and the parameters of required contact. In addition to mandated concerns, you can advise families that they can choose to deal with other problems of concern to them.

EP 2.1.10d

5. *Elicit the family's perception of the problems.* In initiating discussion of problems, social workers ask questions such as "Why did you decide to seek help?" (in the case of voluntary contact), "What changes do you want to achieve?", or "How could things be better in the family?" Eliciting the family's view of the problem is equally important in involuntary or referred contacts. In such cases, the mandate or referral has been summarized, but time and space is provided so that the family members can tell their own story: For instance, "Your family was required by the juvenile court judge to have contact with our agency because Juan was reported to the school truancy officer. This is the information that I have, but I still need to hear from you why you believe you are here." Juan and his parents both have a point of view, which may be similar or vastly different. As you elicit each person's viewpoint about the problem and its solution, you will, in some instances, hear different accounts. Your task, however, is to move the

EP 2.1.10d

family toward reaching a consensus about the problem that they can all support.

In sessions with a family or a couple, you will want to be aware of differences in interpretation and the various family roles within the family with respect to issues of gender, power, and boundaries. In addition, Rosenblatt (1994) urges us to pay attention to the language and metaphors used by the family as they describe their concerns. In particular, how family members express their views reflect their culture, their realities, and the meaning assigned to the family experience. The family experience includes exploring spirituality or religion in the life of the family (Anderson & Worthen, 1997).

EP 2.1.10d

6. *Identify needs and wants of family members.* As you engage the family in a discussion of problems, listen for needs that are inherent in their messages, as illustrated in the family session with a foster mother and Twanna, an adolescent parent.

VIDEO CASE EXAMPLE

Adolescent Parent and Foster Mother, Part 1

Janet is the foster mother of Twanna, a parenting adolescent. Her child is two years old. The relationship between Janet and Twanna has generally been good. Janet cares for the child which allows Twanna to attend school so that she can obtain a high school diploma. Janet called the social worker because she is frustrated, as lately Twanna has returned home after school later than expected. Janet has a strong bond with Twanna's two-year-old; however, Janet stressed that it was important that Twanna spend time with her child as well. She reported that the situation is "affecting the entire relationship" between the two of them.

EP 2.1.10j

Glenda, the social worker, began the initial session with a summary explanation of her understanding of the contact. Then she invited Janet, the foster mother, who initiated the contact, and Twanna, the adolescent parent to share their perceptions of the problem. During the initial discussions of needs and wants as expressed by Janet and Twanna, the social worker respected the rights of the foster mother while at the same time, she created a safe place for the adolescent to express her views. Also, she summarized the situation and empathized with the potential developmental conflict that was occurring with Twanna. That is, even though she is a mother, as an adolescent her interest in being with friends is developmentally appropriate. In fact, her main reason for not coming home at the expected time is because she wants to "hang out with her friends." Further, she reasoned that "I know that Janet is here, it's not like I am leaving my baby alone." At the same time, the social worker acknowledged Janet's unspoken need that her caring for the child is not taken for granted. Janet believed that Twanna should bond with the child, because she, Janet, "will not be there in the future." Attending to the different needs and wants as expressed by Janet and Twanna was a balancing act, as Glenda did not want to convey the perception that the needs of one person had priority and that she only supported that person's position alone. In summarizing the concerns identified by Janet and Twanna, Glenda asked them to identify what they would like to see changed. In preparation for problem solving, the objective was to pinpoint the conflict and to have the two of them explore options that would meet both of their needs. One option considered by Twanna, for example, was "I could call if I am going to be late." By identifying and highlighting common needs, the social worker focused the intervention on the similarities rather than the differences. In this way, Glenda helped Janet and Twanna to develop goals and tasks that they could mutually work toward to improve their relationship. The session concluded with the two of them having reached several critical agreements.

7. *Define the problem as a family problem.* Earlier in the chapter, we highlighted the type of messages you can use in clarifying the systemic nature of problems. Continue to maintain this position stance throughout the family session, emphasizing that every member's perspective is important; that family members can do much to support the change efforts of other family members; that all members will need to make adjustments to alleviate the family's stress; and that the family can do much to increase the quality of relationships and the support that each member receives from others. Despite your efforts to define problems as belonging to the family, you will often encounter a persistent tendency of some members to blame others. In these situations, your tasks are to:

EP 2.1.7a

- *Monitor your own performance to ensure that you do not collude with family members in labeling others as a problem, and thus holding them responsible for the family's difficulties.*

- *Model the circular orientation to causality of behavior and emphasize that family members reciprocally influence one another in ways that perpetuate patterns of interaction.*

EP 2.1.10d

In the discussion of wants and needs, you should take care to avoid a potential perception that you support one person's position over that of other family members. When one person (e.g., Twanna) is perceived as the source of the family's difficulties, your task is to challenge this linear thinking by asking others about their role in creating and maintaining the problem.

Returning to the case of Janet and Twanna, the patterned interaction between the two consisted of Janet being frustrated because Twanna failed to return home at the agreed-upon time. In turn, Twanna reasoned that Janet was there to care for the child, so the fact that she delayed coming home was not neglectful behavior on her part. Neither had talked about what they really wanted, and their interactions ended up with both being dissatisfied because neither had recognized the ways in which their behaviors further contributed to the problem.

Even though Janet attributed their strained relationship to Twanna's behavior, she was careful not to label it. In fact, she said, "I understand that she wants to be with her friends." Unfortunately, this level of generosity is not always present in families as there is a tendency to blame or label behavior, generally in negative terms. In these instances, you can move to counteract patterns of attributing blame by using the technique of delabeling. Rather than focusing on a member's perception of behavior, *delabeling* emphasizes the reciprocal nature of the problem. Use of the technique can also set the stage for each member to identify positive behaviors that each would like from the other. Consider the following example in which the social worker poses a series of questions to a mother and son. The two individuals have a history of blaming messages that are counterproductive to their communicating with each other.

In this case, both mother and son were receptive, so the social worker helped them formulate reciprocal tasks that each could work on during the week to minimize the conflict in their relationship. Their reciprocal tasks were intended to change the dynamics of their interaction by changing their individual behavior and therefore, their responses to each other. For example, the mother would refrain from labeling John's plan as stupid, and in turn, John agreed to listen to her concerns.

8. *Emphasize individual and family strengths.* In work with families, you can highlight family strengths and protective factors on two levels: the strengths of individual members and the strengths of the family as a whole.

EP 2.1.10e

At the individual level, you may observe the strengths and resources of members during the session, drawing them to the attention of the family (e.g., Twanna is a good student). At the family level, you can report on the strengths you have observed in the way members

IDEAS IN ACTION

EP 2.1.10j

John is a young man with mental illness. He has decided to move out of a group home and live independently with his girlfriend of several years. His mother, Mrs. G., is adamant that the move is a stupid decision and she insists that John is incapable of living independently. Rather than focusing on John, the social worker utilized the following questions to focus on Mrs. G's participation in the problematic situation:

- You've said that John doesn't listen to you about your concerns related to his plans. When you discuss your concerns with John how do you approach him?
- When John says he doesn't want to talk to you about his decision, how do you respond?
- How does John's reluctance to talk to you affect you and your relationship with him?

After posing questions to the mother, the social worker then divided questions between the mother and the son to explore the son's participation in the identified problem by asking the following questions:

- John, how does your mother approach you when she wants to discuss her concerns?
- What is your reaction to her approach?
- What might she do differently that would make you want to talk to her about your plans?

operate as a group (Janet and Twanna have a good relationship). Protective factors and strengths include the presence of a supportive network as well as resources and characteristics of family members that contribute to and sustain the family unit. Examples of strengths-oriented statements follow:

- *In your family, it is my sense that even though there are problems, you seem to be very loyal to each other.*
- *Anna, your family's getting together for the holidays seems to connect members to each other.*
- *Anna and Jackie, your relationship appears to be strong, despite the difficulties that Jackie has experienced with your family*
- *Janet, taking care of Twanna's child while she goes to school shows that you are very supportive of her goal to obtain a high school diploma.*

Family strengths and protective factors may also be utilized to communicate a focus on the future. In particular, the hopes, dreams, talents, or capacities of individual members and the family as a whole are means to energize them to resolve current difficulties. While a goal in the initial session is to move the family toward reaching a consensus on their concerns, it is the strength of the family—rather than the problem itself—that will ultimately enable them to resolve their difficulties. By exploring coping patterns with previous difficulties, experiences with positive episodes or past successes, and hopes and dreams for family life, you can activate family strengths, and note their resilience in support of their capacity to change (Weick & Saleebey, 1995).

EP 2.1.10d

9. *Ask questions to elicit information about the patterned behaviors and structure of the family.* For example, you might ask these questions:

- *What brought the family here?*
- *Who made the decision, and what was the process of deciding to seek help?*
- *How are decisions usually made in the family?*
- *Who is most likely to argue in the family? The least likely? With whom?*
- *Who is the most likely to support other family members? The least likely?*

Additional questions about family patterns and structure can be based on the dimensions of the assessment. In cases where your race or culture is different from that of the family, asking questions related to race or culture is appropriate:

- *What are the traditional ways in which families in your culture have approached this issue?*

- *How does your family express anger?*
- *Is expressing anger acceptable in your household?*
- *Are other people in your community involved in making decisions in your family?*

Asking questions such as these will aid you in entering the family's frame of reference and allow the family to articulate the extent to which their culture or race is a critical element in the family's experience.

EP 2.1.10d

10. *Draw attention to repetitive communications.* Once these behaviors are identified, you can discuss whether the family wishes to change these patterns. If counterproductive communications occur during the initial session (as they frequently do), you can intervene to counteract their influence—for example, by translating a blaming message into a neutral one and by empathically reflecting the feelings and wants of the sender of the message. Or, when one family member speaks for another, you can intervene to elicit the views of the latter. Assisting families to improve their communication patterns occurs over time, so in the initial session your task is simply to begin this process. As the initial session proceeds, you can begin to draw counterproductive communications to the family's attention through responses such as the following:

- *"I observed [describes behavior and situation] occurring between family members. How do you see the situation?"*
- *"Did you notice a reaction from other family members as you talked about …?"*

To illustrate repetitive communication patterns, we refer you to the video, "Home for the Holidays 1." As you watch the session with Anna and Jackie, note the repetitive patterns in their interactions and in their communications. For example, Anna asserted that "Jackie does not talk about things." Jackie counters from a fault-defend position: "In your family, everything is open for discussion." Also, pay particular attention to their nonverbal communications. Kim, the social worker, then posed a critical intervention question: "To what extent is this symbolic of other issues in your relationship?" Anna smiles, nods, and her arms are folded; Jackie appears to be very uncomfortable and remains silent. "See," Anna says, "this is what happens."

Questions such as these help families to become aware of potentially counterproductive communication patterns.

You can also stimulate family members to analyze their behaviors further and to consider whether they wish to modify such communication patterns. This can be accomplished by asking families questions such as the following:

- *How would you like to address these concerns?*
- *How would you like to solve these problems?*
- *How would you like to relate differently?*
- *How would behaving differently change your relationship?*
- *Given the problem your behavior creates in the relationship, how important is it to you to change the behavior?*

By utilizing this line of exploration questions in the initial and subsequent sessions, you can assist family members in defining for themselves the relative functionality of behavior and to decide whether they wish to change it. If they choose to modify their behavior, you can negotiate relevant goals that will guide their efforts (and yours) in the helping process.

11. *Begin helping members to relate to one another in more positive ways.* To begin this process, you would highlight counterproductive communication and interactional patterns: For instance, "Mrs. G, when you referred to John's plan as stupid, did you notice his reaction? How might you express your concern to him in a different manner?" Strategies for accomplishing this objective are discussed in greater detail later in this chapter. At the same time, you should communicate hope that the family can change by assisting individual members to see how they can reduce pressures, thereby allowing them to relate to one another in a more positive manner.

12. *Establish individual and family goals based on your earlier exploration of wants and needs.* Goals that flow from this exploration include individual goals, family goals, and goals that pertain to subsystems (e.g., Anna and Jackie want to spend the holiday together). You might also help members to identify family goals by exploring answers to the "miracle question" (de Shazer 1988, p. 5): "Janet and Twanna, imagine that one night while you were asleep, a miracle happened. When you awaken, how would the tension in your relationship have changed?" When asked this question, even the most troubled couples or families are able to describe a new miracle relationship. This vision and other desired conditions that they identify could then become goal statements, guiding efforts of both the family and the social worker.

13. *Gauge the interest of family members in returning for future sessions and negotiate a contract.* Because family members may not always reveal their feelings openly, never assume that all members want to return for another session (even if you were successful in engaging members and sparking their interest in working on problems). You will also want to assess the difference between the attitudes of participants at the beginning and at the end of the session. Ask about reservations that participants may still have about engaging in the helping process. In the case of a reluctant member, check with this individual about his or her commitment to future sessions. Note that it may take a number of sessions before he or she decides to participate fully or to commit to making changes. As an alternative to his or her participation, you might ask him or her to consider the ways in which he or she can support other members or at least not block their change efforts. If family members are sufficiently motivated to continue family sessions, a next step is to identify who will be involved, and negotiate the contract (refer to Chapter 12). Other important elements of the contract discussion include any time limits that may be imposed by, a referral source, court mandate, or third-party payer.

14. *Negotiate tasks to be accomplished during the week.* As discussed in Chapter 13, tasks should directly relate to goals identified by individual members or by the family system. Helping the family explore and decide upon steps that can be taken during the week aids in focusing their attention on problem resolution (Reid, 1996; Fortune, 1985). A task for Janet and Twanna, for example, was to schedule a time to meet together. At this point, you will also want to explore potential barriers. Twanna's task was to return home at the agreed-upon time, and to call if she was going to be late. The social worker then asked her to consider what might prevent her from completing this task.

15. *End the session by summarizing the problems discussed and the goals, tasks, and progress achieved.* Wrapping up the session by summarizing major topics, goals, and tasks highlights what has been accomplished in the session and is another means to encourage hope and to increase the momentum of change efforts.

Intervening with Families: Cultural and Ecological Perspectives

EP 2.1.7b

In intervening with clients of a different ethnicity, social workers must strive to be culturally sensitive in their approach, modifying as necessary the expectations espoused as universal norms for family functioning. They must also be aware of the potential intrusion of their own bias into the helping process. Different emphases on the quality of family life, marital relationships, or problem definition may be a function of cultural and class differences between you and the families with whom you are working. A study conducted by Lavee (1997), for example, showed noticeable differences between how social workers and families defined a healthy marriage. In the study, the professionals involved tended to focus more on such indicators as cooperation and communication, whereas families tended to place greater emphasis on cohesion, love, and understanding.

Your sensitivity to culture and the acquisition of knowledge that will prepare you to be culturally competent are ongoing learning processes. While certain factors may be germane to various cultural or racial groups, it is important that you clarify specific content and its relevance to a family's culture, subculture, or race. Goldenberg and Goldenberg (2000) suggest that learning about specific cultures requires social workers to assess the extent to which families identify with their ethnic or cultural background and to ascertain how much their background plays a role in the presenting family concern. Toward this end, "therapists must try to distinguish family patterns that are universal (common to a wide variety of families), culture-specific (common to a particular group) or idiosyncratic (unique to this particular family)" (p. 52). Patterns in family interactions vary, of course, and your understanding this fact essentially minimizes a tendency to formulate generalizations about family dynamics. Identification with a particular culture or race may be a peripheral issue for some families. In other instances, it may be useful to help families determine how culturally specific behavior affects the problem at hand (Flores & Carey, 2000; Sue, 2006).

Note that culture should not be used as an excuse to minimize or overlook family behavior or relationships that are damaging or harmful to the family or individuals. With these words of caution in mind, we highlight factors that may be considerations when initiating interventions with families who are diverse with respect to culture or race.

Differences in Communication Styles

EP 2.1.10a

Because there are differences in the speech patterns in non-native English speakers, in many situations it may be more important to focus on process rather than content. For instance, in some families, for there may be a "pause time"—a period signaling when one person has finished and another can begin speaking. In other families, members may be comfortable when everyone talks at the same time. Your discomfort may result in your interrupting the speaker or speakers. In general, you will find a range of communication styles in which some are more demonstrative in both verbal and nonverbal language; others, unaccustomed to seeking outside help, may appear to be passive, because of a sense of shame or suspicion in their encounter with professional helpers (Fong, 1997; Pierce & Elisme, 1997; Berg & Jaya 1993; Boyd-Franklin, 1989a).

Studies that examined conflict resolution, emotional expression, and means of coping with stress conducted by Mackey and O'Brien (1998) and Choi (1997) revealed differences in communication styles based on gender and ethnicity. Emotions are complex experiences, expressing reactions to past, present, and future events. The person's worldview frames the emotional experience, as does his or her language. The range of words and language that many of us use daily to describe emotions may, in fact, be unfamiliar to or have a different connotation for diverse groups. Moreover, it is important that you examine your own communication style and assess how it is informed by your own cultural preferences.

EP 2.1.10a

In understanding communication styles and differences, techniques and strategies from postmodern family practice models may be used. For example, the narrative and social constructionist approaches emphasize a more conversational, collaborative approach, allowing for a dialogue that is more meaningful to the client, as well as facilitating communication between the family and social worker (Laird, 1993). Sue (2006) also draws attention to *high and low context communications*. In low-context cultures, for example, the United States, there is a greater emphasis on verbal messages as well an orientation toward the individual. In contrast, high-context cultures rely on nonverbal expressions, group identity, and a shared understanding between the communicators. Of course, there are exceptions; for example, Sue (2006) notes that African Americans tend to be high-context communicators even though they live in the United States. Differences in meaning of words in other cultures may be subject to misinterpretation. For example, saying "no" may actually mean "yes" (e.g., Arab or Asian), although these are words that are taken for their literal meaning in Western societies.

Hierarchical Considerations

EP 2.1.10a

Depending on the age-sex hierarchies in some cultures, you are advised to address the father, then the mother, then other adults, and finally the older and younger children. Grandparents or other elders in the family may actually be held in greater esteem than parents and figure prominently in the family's hierarchical arrangement. Caution is particularly advised in working with immigrant families where a child who has greater proficiency in the English language is used as an interpreter in interviews with parents. You should be sensitive to the fact that the child's role in this instance may undermine traditional roles in the family and result in tensions between parents and their children (Ho, 1987; Pierce & Elisme, 1997). Beyond being sensitive, being empathetic and exploring the parents' feelings are means by which you reinforce your understanding of their role. In addition, when families come from cultures in which chronological age and familial hierarchy play a significant role (e.g., Asian Indian and African American families), open dialogue between parents and children may be viewed as insolent or disrespectful (Segal, 1991; Carter & McGoldrick, 1999). Also note that what may appear to you to be hierarchically defined roles in the family may instead be complementary. Flores and Carey (2000), in counteracting the popular notion of machismo dominance in Hispanic families, emphasized this point. Specifically, the father functions as the authoritarian, protective figure in the family; the mother's role is complementary to that of the father in that she is expected to be expressive, caring, and nurturing. As you join with the family, it is best to ask questions, seek their preferences, and explore their rules with respect to family order and hierarchy.

Authority of the Social Worker

EP 2.1.10a

The authority vested in the social worker can vary by culture and race. For some families, the helping practitioner is perceived as a knowledgeable expert who will guide them in the proper course of action. Therefore, they expect you to take a directive role when working with the family. An informal and egalitarian approach, which is second nature to many Americans, is actually considered improper in many cultures. Furthermore, your perceived authority which is reflected by the use of first names tends to emphasize social distance. In fact, addressing adult family members on a first name basis, unless you are invited to do so, can be disrespectful, magnifying the historical tradition of calling people by their first names in situations in which first names would not be permitted if both participants had the same social identity (Berg & Jaya, 1989; Flores & Corey, 2000; Robinson, 1989; Sue, 2006).

A passive response to authority from immigrants, migrants, or refugees, for example, may stem from their social and political status in the United States, a distrust of helpers, and a fear about expressing their true feelings to figures of authority (Janzen & Harris, 1997; Potocky-Tripodi, 2003; Pierce & Elisme, 1997; Sue, 2006). Eliciting information, for example, through direct questions about the needs and wants of each family member, can be problematic. Also, the informal use of language and expectations of full disclosure may diminish the family's trust. Devore & Schlesinger (1999) suggest using empathy instead, as a facilitative means to form an alliance.

EP 2.1.7b

Aponte (1982) perhaps summarizes these issues best by stating that power and authority are critical elements of the family–social worker relationship, especially for ethnic or racial groups. Most diverse families perceive the social worker as acting in his or her professional role rather than fulfilling a social role, therefore, social workers are viewed as representatives of the majority society. Within this context, the social worker symbolizes the larger society's power, values, and standards. Because of the authority that is assigned to you as a professional, it is important to explicitly recognize families as decision makers and experts on their situations, and to ensure that you have their informed consent before proceeding further (Palmer & Kaufman, 2003).

EP 2.1.1d

As a social worker, you should not hesitate to discuss your professional background, because these families need assurance that you are capable of helping them resolve their difficulty. When writing notes, you should be aware that documenting in case notes—while necessary—may reinforce perceptions of the unequal power balance between you and the family (Flores & Carey, 2000; Boyd-Franklin, 1989a). To alleviate clients' concerns, you will find it helpful to explain their purpose, standards of confidentiality, and requirements for information that may involve an identified third party.

Engaging Diverse Families

EP 2.1.10a

Techniques for engaging or joining are particularly crucial when working with diverse families; however, there are no hard and fast rules for doing so. Nonetheless, in the engagement phase, your entry into the family is greatly enhanced by your respect for the family's identification of the problem. In this way, you are able to establish a level of credibility and further that you are trustworthy. It can be equally important that you ask the family to identify extended family members, regardless of whether or not these family members will participate in family sessions, as they can be crucial links to eventual problem solving.

No doubt, you will draw upon the communication and facilitative skills discussed in Chapters 5 and 6. Even so, we suggest that you listen in context—in particular, allowing the family members to present their story in their own way. Furthermore, be mindful of things like differences in communication styles, the cultural context of seeking help outside of the family, and the family's perceptions of your own and your agency's authority. While knowledge of culture is not guaranteed to provide you with an advantage in working with a particular family, exploring the relevance of cultural meanings of particular groups can facilitate engagement (Goldenberg & Goldenberg, 2004; Janzen & Harris, 1997).

Home visits may be invaluable in the engagement stage with some families, because such visits afford you with an opportunity to observe and assess a family in its natural environment (Berg, 1994). Visits to the home may also allow you to learn about and observe the practices of families and important members of the family network. You will have an opportunity to convey your interest in the family by inquiring about portraits, cultural objects, and other items of interest. In instances where the family has been referred for treatment, members may be angry and resentful of this intrusion. Be mindful of the fact that most minority families tend to be involuntary help-seekers. If you represent an agency that they feel has power and authority over their lives, this "baggage" will affect their reaction to you. In situations where these dynamics have a significant impact, it is suggested that you avoid personalizing this experience and move quickly to acknowledge, accept, and validate clients' feelings (Berg, 1994; R. H. Rooney, 2009).

Finally, engaging diverse families is facilitated when you understand the cultural relevance of terminology describing family dynamics and structure. Autonomy and self-differentiation, for example, when considered in a sociopolitical or cultural context, may be neither desired nor expected.

Understanding Families Using an Ecological Perspective

Culture and race are merely two factors in the ecological schema of intervening with families. Other salient factors include religion, gender, class, family form, or status, and work and family concerns. To demonstrate sensitivity to

EP 2.1.7b

the multiple system influences and to clarify their relationship to family concerns, you must also focus on the family and their environmental interactions. In doing so, you are determining the extent to which these factors affect family relationships and interaction patterns. For example, work and family pressures may intrude upon parental ability to fulfill role functions within the family, producing role overload, conflict, and strain (Fredriksen-Goldsen & Scharlach, 2001; Marlow, 1993; G. D. Rooney, 1997). The ideal of egalitarian roles for men and women is becoming more evident in both rural and urban families in the United States as well as in the cultural schema of other countries. Even so, women for the most part still manage multiple roles—wife, daughter, mother, parent, employee. Acculturation may mean that gender roles are in transition, yet adaptation to the new roles may become a source of tension in much the same way that parent–adolescent conflict intensifies, thereby resulting in stressors within the family system.

For poor families, meeting immediate survival and resource needs may take precedence over pursuing more insight-oriented approaches (Kilpatrick & Holland, 2006). The family context–environment interaction may include intervening to address problems of housing, financial assistance, school–child conflicts, and unresponsive social institutions. Social support networks such as the extended family, tribe or clan, or other key people may be included in the discussion to reduce dysfunctional interactions and to increase concrete support for the family. A failure on your part to focus on family–environmental interactions may cause you to have an incomplete understanding of family functioning and hence to develop interventions that emphasize pathology over strengths. For example, dysfunctional interactions may emerge in immigrant families resulting from their attempts to cope with adjustment-related stressors or problems. In emphasizing this possibility, a study by Fong (1997) links spousal or child abuse to the stress-related adjustment problems among Chinese immigrants.

Flores and Carey (2000) and Sue (2006) note that many well-established approaches to work with families remain "silent" on issues of social justice, oppression, and the marginalization inherent in the minority experience. Until recently, the same was true regarding issues that are important to women. Thanks to the fuller understanding of families produced by feminists' evaluation of family practice approaches, social workers, at a minimum, should be acutely aware of the need to be sensitive to age, gender, and patriarchy. Goldenberg and Goldenberg (2000) emphasize that gender sensitivity does not mean merely being nonsexist. Instead, they suggest that gender-sensitive practice is proactive and deliberate in helping women move beyond the limitations imposed by social and political barriers (pp. 50–51). For minority women, the combination of gender with race or culture adds yet another series of social and political barriers. For this reason, you should not assume that minority women, for instance, perceive their gender as the more prominent factor when they are dealing with inequality, when compared to race or ethnicity.

Examples of Family Intervention

To help you appreciate the ecological context of families, we consider the cases of Twanna, the parenting adolescent, and the foster mother Janet, and Anna and Jackie, the lesbian couple as examples of considerations for intervening with families.

Twanna, the Adolescent Mother

Negative societal attitudes and conditions can also pose environmental challenges and threats to families and thus influence the family system. For example, society almost always views single-mother families from a deficit perspective. They  EP 2.1.4a

are held accountable for their perceived mistakes and for being responsible for their situation, rather than their strength as a viable family form being recognized. The age of the single mother adds an additional tension. As parents, adolescents are often treated like adults and children simultaneously. Society, for example, demands that they comply with their parental obligation; yet, societal institutions tend to play the forceful role of a parent.

At 17 years of age, Twanna, a parenting adolescent, is single. Prior to coming to live with Janet, she had been in placement since the age of eight years, with three other foster families. As she grew older, and especially after she became pregnant,  EP 2.1.7b

she was no longer welcome as a member of the last family. Out-of-wedlock births, especially among adolescents and teens, remain taboo and the young women are stigmatized. In fact, her previous foster parents were outraged and embarrassed by her pregnancy and requested that she be removed from their home. As Weinberg (2006) notes, young single mothers often "represent a number of marginalized categories": they are young, female, impoverished, racial or ethnic minorities, from lower- or working-class families, and most of all they have had children outside of the institution of marriage. Also, the young women have experienced a number of failures, from their families, the education system, and in some instances their community. In Twanna's case, she is also vulnerable due to an additional marginal category, that of being a ward of the state. Her biological mother had been judged to be inadequate, hence she became a ward, and her child now also has the same status. Until she came to live with Janet in her home, Twanna's support system consisted of a series of child welfare workers.

In working with Twanna, it would be important to be aware of the other challenges that she faces, specifically her developmental stage and that of her child. In many respects, her wants and needs and that of her child—related to  EP 2.1.7a

their developmental journeys—have certain similarities, summarized in the comparisons below.

TWANNA	CHILD
Identity and independence	Autonomy
Intimacy	Nurturing
Self-efficacy	Self-esteem
Attachment	Attachment
Relationships	Social interactions

EP 2.1.7a

Developmentally, however, they vary, as a young child needs consistency and the adolescent is in the process of exploration and experimentation. While adolescents search for their identity, separate and apart from their families and through their peers, the young child's sense of self is gained through his or her interactions with his or her caretaker. In Twanna's case, she is attempting to meet her own needs and those of her child, which, without the support of Janet, could result in role strain and overload. The social worker noted this conflict in her summary statement to Twanna: "What you are saying is that you understand that you are responsible for your child, but that you also need to be with your friends."

In the broader scheme of things, changes in the bonds between an adolescent seeking greater autonomy and his or her adult caretakers may require changes in interactions and communication patterns (Baer, 1999). As a foster parent, Janet makes certain demands that are consistent with her role as a parent, aspects of which include her obligation to ensure the well-being of Twanna and her child. According to Weinberg (2006), interventions with minors who are also parents is a balancing act between being a disciplinarian and an emancipator. It is not uncommon for parents to establish protective boundaries, which may include anxieties about both peers and the neighborhood and undertaking intense monitoring (Jarrett, 1995). For instance, Janet wanted to meet Twanna's friends so she "could get to know them." This family unit is, however, different from the normative family structure and the rules of the state that has custody of Twanna and her child sets a certain tone for their interactions. For example, as a family unit, their interactions may be primarily with professionals, and supportive family networks of kin and friends are not a given. In many respects, Janet and Twanna are attempting to establish functional family rules without the benefit of role models pertinent to their family form and structure.

Anna and Jackie, a Lesbian Couple

EP 2.1.4a & 2.1.7b

Gay and lesbian families are largely ignored as viable families. Hence their internal family stress is a given as they attempt to navigate an often hostile and indifferent social environment. Popular television programs have featured gay and lesbian individuals, and to some extent same-sex couples. Rarely, however, have these programs spotlighted the reality of the challenges and stressors of being perceived as different. Concerns voiced among lesbian mothers related to reactions toward their children and the family's experiences in their interactions with the larger community represent a case in point (Hare, 1994).

EP 2.1.4a & 2.1.7a

As you work with Anna and Jackie, it would be important that you recognize that they are in a relationship that is disqualified in a society in which the legal and romantic norms emphasize the bond between males and females (Bepko & Johnson, 2000; Price & McKenry, 2000). At the same time, an intervention should take into account that as young adults, Anna and Jackie are involved in an age-appropriate developmental task, that of being in an intimate relationship. Forming a relationship requires new adaptations to roles and tasks; such as realigning with family and establishing their own relationship. In the family life cycle, coupling is welcomed and celebrated by parents as a significant milestone in the lives of their children. Conversely, societal, and, in some cases, familial attitudes deny couples the identity of same-sex unions. Thus, these uncelebrated committed relationships can be without social supports.

The very act of "coming out" to one's family can create family strain and, in some instances, sever family ties. For example, Jackie and Anna are in different places with respect to claiming their identities as lesbians and as a couple. Anna's family appears to be comfortable with her sexuality. Jackie has taken a first step by coming out to her family; however, she is unwilling to press the issue with her family because she fears their response. At this stage in her relationship with Anna, Jackie is content with the fact that her parents "were quiet and took up other activities" when she told them of her intent to move in with Anna. As noted by Bepko and Johnson (2000), gay and lesbian individuals have different attitudes about how "out" they want to be with their families and in society.

With their families, they may experience a conflict with respect to the direction of their loyalty. Without family support, external cultural stressors on same-sex couples can be more pronounced (Connolly, 2006).

EP 2.1.10a

The preceding examples highlight but a few of the many cultural dynamics and ecological factors to which social workers must attend in intervening with diverse families and in intervening in family functioning and relational dynamics. Fitting practice and intervention strategies to the ecology of a particular family is a complicated process that requires an understanding of the myriad internal and external factors that shape family life. You are urged to use your knowledge of culture, race, gender, sexual orientation, and sociopolitical issues as a lens through which to view families. The considerable diversity encountered among families may mean that some factors have greater relevance than others. For some families, culture or race may be peripheral to their identity, yet they may retain essential attributes that guide their family life. Acquiring sensitivity to gender, sexual orientation, and racial and cultural preferences can be achieved by facilitating the family narratives, taking an active and genuine interest in their story, and collaborating with the family to resolve their concerns.

Intervening with Families: Focusing on the Future

EP 2.1.10j

Families are often overwhelmed, frustrated, and perhaps saturated with their problems when you encounter them. Your responsibility as a social worker is to create a safe structure and climate in which family concerns can be raised and to assist the family to move toward change. One major obstacle to change is the propensity of couples or families to focus on what they do not have or what is not working, rather than on what they would like in the future. Solution-focused therapy is a brief treatment approach that addresses problems in the present and inspires a future orientation, beginning with the initial contact. Using miracle or scaling questions (two solution-focused techniques), you might ask the family:

- *What would you like to do about the future?*
- *How will you know that your family members have improved their communications with one another?*
- *When you called for an appointment with me, your family was in trouble. Imagine you have achieved your goals, how you might feel on a scale of 1 to 10?*

These types of questions can be useful in helping families to reframe their problems and feel more in control of their lives.

Focusing on the future can serve as a guiding principle for helping families and social workers. The following examples are hypothetical statements related to the two previous cases involving Twanna and Janet and Anna and Jackie:

- *A discussion that can lead quickly to consideration of what each person is willing to do to prevent a recurrence of an event, interaction, tension or argument in the future. For example, Twanna's statement, "I will come home after school and be ready to take care of my baby" and Janet's statement, "It would be okay for her to invite her friends to the house."*
- *Complaints or criticisms can be translated into information about how changes in others might affect the family in the future. Recipients can also give information: Anna to Jackie, "You need to have the conversation again with your family." Jackie to Anna, "This is what you could do in the future that would help me do what you are suggesting."*
- *Breakdowns in communication can be analyzed from a future-oriented point of view: Social worker to Anna and Jackie, after observing their interactions, "What can you learn from what just happened that you can apply in the future?"*
- *Conflicts of interest and needs and wants can cause families to engage in "win-win" problem solving: Social worker to Twanna and Janet, "How can you resolve the problem right now so we can feel good about your relationship in the future?"*

Opting for the future, when adopted as a philosophical guideline by families, can reduce the counterproductive elements of the clients' interactions, because the future, not the past, is seen as more relevant. The future is fresh, hopeful, and untainted by tensions or stressors. Opting for the future, of course, requires that each family member commit to attending only to what *he or she* will do in the future, rather than monitoring the activities of the other person. You can increase families' focus on the future by putting problem talk on hold and by always starting sessions with a question regarding their

EP 2.1.10j

successes in achieving goals or tasks, and by creating fresh, positive ways of interacting. Complementing this approach, Weiner-Davis (1992) and DeJong and Berg (2008) teach people to focus on the exceptional times to determine what is working and why, and then encourage them to turn productive behaviors into habits. Focusing on exceptions diminishes problems, because identifying what they *can* do is infinitely more hopeful and empowering to them than noting what they *cannot* do. It also demonstrates to families that they are changeable and that seemingly fixed traits are fluid. Finally, focusing on exceptions gives families a blueprint for describing exactly what they need to do the next time a particular situation occurs (de Shazer & Berg, 1993; Berg, 1994).

Communication Patterns and Styles

EP 2.1.10a

Communication approaches to families consist of teaching family members the rules of clear communication. The aim is to regulate and modify family communication patterns and alter communication styles to promote positive interactions and family relationships (Satir, 1967; Jackson & Weakland, 1961; Whitaker, 1958). It is believed that the patterns that family members use to communicate with one another are often interpreted in various ways, and are often punctuated by faulty cognitions and perceptions. What the sender believes is the message is not necessarily what the receiver understands the message to be. A difficult relationship between sender and receiver can also strain or distort the message.

Giving and Receiving Feedback

EP 2.1.10a

Positive feedback from significant others (expressions of caring, approval, encouragement, affection, appreciation, and other forms of positive attention) nourish morale, emotional security, confidence, and the feeling of being valued by others. Thus, increasing positive feedback fosters the well-being of individuals and harmonious family relationships. To enable family members to increase positive feedback, social workers must have skills in the following areas:

- *Engaging families in assessing the extent to which they give and receive positive feedback*
- *Educating families about the vital role of positive feedback*
- *Cultivating positive cognitive sets*
- *Assisting families to give and receive positive feedback*

In the following sections, each of these skills is discussed.

Engaging Clients in Assessing How Well They Give and Receive Positive Feedback

Destructive communication patterns often result from strained relationships, such that the family system eventually becomes unbalanced. Communication theorists view the family as a functional system that depends on two communication processes: negative and positive feedback. They also believe that all behavior is communication. Thus, they view the social worker's role as one of helping the family change the process of family interactions.

EP 2.1.10j

You can help families and individual members to directly explore dimensions of communication by assessing how often and in what manner they convey positive feedback to significant others. Questions you might ask in couple or family sessions to achieve this end include the following:

- *How do you send messages that let family members [or your partner] know that you care about them?*
- *How frequently do you send such messages?*
- *How often do you give feedback to others concerning their positive actions?*

In instances of severe couple or family breakdown, members may acknowledge that they send positive messages infrequently or not at all. In some cases, they may actually have tepid positive feelings, but they usually experience more than they express. Besides exploring how couples or family members convey positive feedback, you can explore their desires to receive increased feedback from one another. Discussing how family members send positive messages, or to what extent they desire increased positive feedback, can open up channels for positive communication and improve relationships that have been stuck in a cycle of repetitive arguments, criticisms, blaming, and put-down messages.

Educating Clients about the Vital Role of Positive Feedback

EP 2.1.10j

As family members communicate about their needs to receive positive feedback, they will begin to appreciate the significance of this dimension in interpersonal relationships. You can further expand their awareness by explaining why positive feedback is crucial to family interactions. The logic behind increasing positive feedback is straightforward. Teaching clients to express their needs involves assisting them to send personalized messages in which they own their feelings and needs.

The following are examples of messages that explicitly express a need for positive feedback:

Partner: When we were talking about plans for my mother, I didn't interrupt you. I wish you would notice when I do something different.

Adolescent: I felt discouraged when I showed you my grades yesterday. I really worked hard this term, and the only thing you seemed to notice was the one B. It didn't seem to matter that the rest were A's.

In each of these statements, the speaker used "I" to personalize his or her messages. Each message also clearly indicates what the speaker is seeking from the other person. When messages are less clear, they may lead to a further breakdown in communications. You can intervene in these situations by using the technique of *on-the-spot interventions*. When using this technique, you coach family members to formulate clear messages that express their feelings and needs as illustrated in the following exchange. It begins with a message from a wife, who is seeking positive feedback from her husband, but what she wants from him is unclear.

Ruth [to husband]: I worked really hard at picking up around the house before people arrived, but the only thing you noticed was what I had not done—like the comment you made about fingerprints on the bathroom door.

Carl [to Ruth]: Well, let's face it, the fingerprints were there and as you yourself admitted it.

Social worker: Carl, Ruth was expressing what is important to her in the relationship, and I don't want her point to get lost in an argument. Ruth, think for a moment about what you said. What is it you are asking of Carl?

Ruth [after pausing]: Do you mean his not noticing what I do?

Social worker: In a way, yes. Would you like for Carl to let you know you're appreciated for what you had done?

In this scenario, Ruth has shared important information—namely, the need to feel valued. People want to receive positive feedback for what they are and what they do. Interactions that continuously focus on negative results may leave an individual feeling discouraged and insecure, and, as a consequence, relationships suffer.

In instructing Ruth and Carl about the importance of positive feedback, the social worker used this opportunity to allow them to practice communicating in a different manner.

Social worker: Ruth, I'd like you to start over and express that you want positive feedback from Carl. This time, however send an "I" message so that it is clear what you want from him.

Ruth [hesitating]: I hope that I can. Carl, I need to hear from you about the things that I do well and not only about what is wrong.

Initially, clients may feel timid about expressing their feelings clearly. The second part of helping family members to communicate is by assisting them in listening attentively. Asking Carl to repeat what he heard in Ruth's message is one way to emphasize listening for content. Because individuals may not always express his or her needs openly and clearly, family members may need to go beyond just listening. That is, they may need to become *attuned* to needs expressed in the form of complaints, questions, and the attitudes of others. *Tuning in* also involves alerting others to pay attention to nonverbal messages and what those messages communicate about feelings.

Because it is difficult for family members to be attuned to the needs inherent in the messages of others, you should take advantage of "teachable moments" to help them to learn this skill, as illustrated in the preceding situation. Specifically, the social worker encouraged Ruth to express her need for positive feedback from Carl. Also, when the social worker focused on Ruth, she played a facilitative role in prompting her to express herself directly to Carl. The social worker likewise had Carl provide feedback to Ruth, thus performing a critical role in *facilitating positive interactions between the couple*. This is a crucial point. Serving as a catalyst, the social worker helped Carl and Ruth learn new communication skills by having them *actually engage in positive interaction,* which is an effective mode of learning.

Cultivating Positive Cognitive Sets

Before family members can provide positive feedback, they must first be able to acknowledge the strengths, positive attributes, and actions of others. Some will be attuned to these qualities, while others will habitually perceive weaknesses and

EP 2.1.10a

flaws. Cognitive sets can consist of distorted assumptions or automatic thoughts from other relationships—that is, thoughts derived from negative schemas that are not based in reality, yet cognitions function to sustain dysfunctional relationships (Collins, Kayser, & Platt, 1994; Berlin & Marsh, 1993). In essence, schemas are problematic when the individual has an unrealistic or faulty view of the world. Thus, his or her behavior in interacting with others is influenced by his or her distortions. A key point is recognizing that attitudes, thoughts, and expectations are generally intertwined with emotions.

EP 2.1.10a

Cognitive behavioral family therapy based on the work of Ellis (1978) and Beck (1976), is intended to help the family to modify specific behavioral patterns and learn new behaviors, including the process of circular or reciprocal sequences of behavior (Becvar & Becvar, 2000a; Nichols, 2006). Using the cognitive-behavioral approach, the social worker attempts to improve family interactions by helping individual family members alter cognitive distortions and learn new behaviors. The social worker focuses on bringing negative cognitive sets that influence thoughts, feelings, and actions to the attention of family members, ultimately helping them learn to focus on positive behaviors. Strategies for accomplishing these tasks are described next.

Helping Couples to Develop Positive Cognitive Sets

EP 2.1.10j

You can set the stage for helping families and couples to develop positive cognitive sets by negotiating a *contingency contract*. The contingency contract identifies desirable behavior change between two parties and explicit rules for interaction, specifying that they agree to exchange positive rewarding behavior with each other (Becvar & Becvar, 2000a). Based on the theory of social exchange, cognitive behaviorists maintain that behavior exchanges adhere to a norm of reciprocity. Specifically, negative or positive behavior from one person will induce reciprocal behavior from others. Using the contingency contract, you can actively intervene in the early stages of the helping process to highlight strengths and growth and to help clients incorporate "attention to positives" as part of their normative behavior. Families can develop their own set of positive indicators for desirable behavior change, along with reciprocal goals. Generally, you would review progress on these indicators with the family (or couple) each week.

Reviewing Progress and Accrediting Incremental Growth

EP 2.1.10j

Social workers can also increase a family's sensitivity to positives by engaging members in briefly reviewing, at the end of each session, the work that has been accomplished and by observing incremental growth. To highlight incremental growth, ask members to contrast their current functioning with their functioning at an earlier time, as illustrated in the following message:

Social worker: This is our fourth session. Let's begin by identifying the changes the family has made in the way you communicate with each other. We can then contrast this change with how you were communicating in the first session. For now, I will hold my observations, but when you are done, I will add my own observations to the changes that you have identified.

Employing Tasks to Enhance Cognitive Sets

EP 2.1.10j

Negotiating tasks that family members can implement between sessions can facilitate the development of positive cognitive sets. For example, to further expand family members' or couples' awareness of the frequency with which they provide positive feedback, you might ask them to keep a daily tally of the number of positive messages they send to one another. They should also note the reciprocal behaviors of other members as a result of their actions. This practice not only enables family members and the social worker to gain a clear picture of their performance on this dimension, but also establishes baselines that can be used later to assess their progress. Without explicitly planning to do so, family members often increase the frequency of the desired behavior during the monitoring period. By systematically focusing on the positive attributes of others, clients can gradually achieve more positive cognitive sets. Of course, the ultimate reinforcement derives from improved interactions with others.

Enabling Clients to Give and Receive Positive Feedback

EP 2.1.10j

To assist families to convey positive feedback, you can teach them to personalize their messages and guide them in giving positive feedback to others. Timely use of role-play as an educational intervention helps family members to form positive messages and to develop the skills needed to share their experiences in an authentic manner. When negative situations of some intensity have been part of the family's style for an extended period of time, you may also need to help family members learn how to accept and trust positive feedback.

After completing these activities, family members are ready to work on the ultimate goal—increasing their rates of positive feedback. You can assist them by negotiating tasks that specify providing positive feedback at higher levels. Families, of course, must consent to tasks and determine the rate of positive feedback they seek to achieve. Family members can review their baseline information (gathered earlier through monitoring), and can be encouraged to set a daily rate that "stretches" them beyond their usual level. For example, an adolescent, whose mean baseline daily rate in giving positive feedback to his father is a 1.0, might select an initial task of giving positive feedback twice daily. He would then gradually increase the number of positive messages until he reached a self-selected optimal rate of five times daily.

As some family members implement the task of increasing positive feedback, they may inappropriately engage in insincere positive expressions. You should caution against this behavior, as such expressions are counterproductive for both the sender and the receiver.

EP 2.1.10j

In planning with family members to implement tasks, it is important to adhere to the task implementation sequence (TIS) a procedure of the Task-Centered approach discussed in Chapter 13. In part, planning involves anticipating obstacles and behavioral rehearsal. First, family members who have been inhibited in expressing feelings may initially report discomfort: "It just doesn't come naturally to me." Second, other family members may respond unfavorably to an increased level of positive feedback and question the sender's sincerity, especially if this is a new behavior: "I wonder what she wants from me now?" Second, you can assist family members with others' skepticism by modeling, by having them rehearse appropriate coping behavior (including asserting the sincerity of their efforts), and by emphasizing the necessity of changing their behavior despite the obstacles. As with any tasks, you should plan to review progress in subsequent sessions and to explore favorable reactions and any difficulties that family members encountered.

Many of the strategies previously mentioned as instrumental in helping families give and receive positive feedback are applicable to couples and parents as well. Therefore, we will only briefly identify some additional tasks that may be used with couples and parents. One technique that you can employ to increase positive interactions between couples involves a strategy discussed by Stuart (1980) and Collins and Kayser, and Platt (1994). That is, both partners are asked to identify desired actions or behaviors: "Exactly what would you like your partner to do as a means of showing that he or she cares for you?" After giving each spouse or partner an opportunity to identify desired actions, you can ask each to develop a task directed toward engaging in a specified behavior identified by the other party. It may be useful to have them develop and prioritize a list of desirable positive behaviors. A reinforcing aspect of such tasks occurs when each person gives feedback and expresses appreciation when the other engages in the desired behavior.

EP 2.1.10j

Before negotiating tasks with parents to increase positive feedback to minors, you can request that parents list behaviors of each child. You can then ask parents to choose the behaviors they would most like to change, cautioning them that the process is gradual, rather than all or nothing. The next step is to negotiate a task that involves parents giving positive feedback at opportune times during the week when the specified behavior is *not* occurring—for example, when the child is *not* fighting with a sibling. Further, you should instruct parents to give positive feedback when children manifest behaviors that parents would like them to demonstrate *in place of the targeted behaviors*—for example, when the minor *has* told the truth. Parents may be understandably reluctant to agree to this strategy, especially if continual nagging or threats of punishment have been their only means for getting the child to engage in desirable behavior. In such instances, you will need to motivate children to comply by establishing with the parents an agreement under which children may earn certain rewards in exchange for specified behavior.

Because parental attention to children's behavior is a potent force for aggravating, modifying, or reinforcing behavior, their mastery of the skill related to positive feedback is important. Oftentimes, when minors behave as expected, parents unfortunately take their behavior for granted. But children need to know what they are *already* doing that pleases their parents. When used consistently by parents, messages such as these have a significant effect in shaping and cultivating desired behavior. If parents want their children to assume particular behaviors, they must give them positive feedback when those behaviors occur. Note the reinforcing nature of the following parental messages:

- *I really appreciate your taking the time to visit your grandmother, and so does she.*
- *Thank you for telling me the truth when I asked if you were smoking cigarettes.*

Parents must also be aware of their own behavior as it relates to vicarious learning and modeling. Specifically, children learn behavior, including the consequences, by observing other people and events.

In addition to providing positive messages and tangible rewards that reinforce desired behavior, tasks that involve incremental change and subsequent reinforcement are particularly useful with young children. Referred to as *successive approximation*, tasks involve incremental change and act as a shaping process that divides the desired behavior into subparts, providing contingencies and rewards until the whole of the desired behavior is achieved. Thus, if having a child sit quietly at her desk, pay attention to the teacher, raise her hand and wait to be called upon before speaking are targeted behaviors, parents might initially reward "sitting" as the first subpart of the whole (Becvar & Becvar, 2000a, p. 262).

Intervening with Families: Strategies to Modify Interactions

EP 2.1.10a

Interactional difficulties that families commonly present include repetitive arguments; struggles over power and authority; developmental conflicts associated with dependence to independence, or interdependence; dissension in making decisions; friction associated with discrepant role perceptions and fulfillments; and other forms of faulty communication. Interpersonal conflicts tend to be redundant; that is, in relations with others, individuals repeat over and over again various types of interactions that predictably lead to the same negative consequences. To assist you in helping families develop more functional patterns of communication and interaction, we delineate guidelines and techniques that you can use in persuading them to modify their dysfunctional interactions. We draw from techniques used by cognitive-behavioral, structural, family systems, and communication theories as well as task-centered family practice. Note that teaching communication skills to family members is a vital aspect of modifying dysfunctional communications.

Metacommunication

EP 2.1.10j

To modify dysfunctional communication, family members are encouraged to discuss their communication patterns, analyze their behaviors and emotional reactions, and consider the effects of the interaction on their relationship. Such discussions are termed *metacommunication*, because they involve "communication about communication." When you discuss with families a communication that has just occurred they are also engaging in metacommunication. Indeed, much of couple, family, and group therapy focuses on metacommunication. Likewise, when you discuss relational reactions that occur in the context of the helping relationship, you are clarifying the meanings of messages and actions. Still other examples of metacommunication are messages that clarify intentions (e.g., "I'm teasing you" or "I want to talk with you because I feel bad about the strain between us") or messages that "check out" or seek clarification of others' messages that are vague or ambiguous (e.g., "I'm not sure what you mean by that" or "Let me see if I understood what you were saying"). Metacommunications contain both verbal and nonverbal content. The content of a nonverbal message is also established through the tone of voice and body language, further shaping and defining the intent of the message and the relationship between those involved.

Skills in metacommunications play an important role in effective communications because they avoid needless misunderstandings (by checking out the meanings of messages) and provide feedback that enables others to make choices about modifying offensive or abrasive communication styles. Moreover, conflicts in relationships are kept at a minimum level of antagonism or disruption. A major role for the social worker, therefore, is to help clients learn to metacommunicate in a productive manner.

Although skills in assisting people to metacommunicate are important with all client systems, they are especially critical in working with families who manifest dysfunctional patterns of communication, including frequent use of incongruent and double-bind messages and messages within a message. Such families seldom clarify meanings or attend to the effects that their messages have on one another.

The following example illustrates use of metacommunication to enhance communication between Anna and Jackie.

Anna: "Jackie does not talk to her family about anything. In my family, everything is an open book. Just like her family, Jackie doesn't talk" [Disconfirming Jackie as a separate person with different needs.]

Jackie: "I do talk to my family. I told them about us moving in together. Sometimes when I come home from work, I am tired, I don't want to talk. I think your family talks too much about everything."

Anna: "She doesn't talk to them anything about being gay." [Assigning fault; disconfirming Jackie's message.]

Jackie: "It's not my responsibility." [Defends position.]

Social worker: [Interrupts to avert another disconfirming message from Anna] "Does Jackie's family have to be like your family? [Highlighting Anna's message; intervening to counter Anna acting as Jackie's spokesperson.]

In the preceding exchange, Kim, the social worker actively intervened to prevent the interaction between Anna and Jackie from following its usual unproductive course. As you can imagine, the circular and sequence interaction could go on forever without resolution. Also, Kim acted to intervene in the situation by not permitting Anna to act as Jackie's spokesperson in which she assigns motives to Jackie's behavior. Further, by involving them in a discussion about how comparisons between the two families are disconfirming to Jackie, Anna can begin to understand how her "pushing" Jackie affected their relationship. Recognizing that Anna was conveying a message within a message, the social worker asked her, *"What meaning does Jackie's conversation with her parents have for you?"* For Anna, Jackie's conversation with her parents is a way of confirming their relationship. She had not directly said so previously, hence the message within the message. Kim further clarified how each can modify their patterns of communication, thereby initiating corrective processes. Of course, such interventions must occur over a period of time if they are to produce enduring changes.

Modifying Family Rules

Family rules govern the range of behavior in the family system and the sequence of interactions or reactions to a particular event. Rules are a means by which the family system maintains its equilibrium. Dysfunctional family rules, however, can severely impair the functioning of family members. Because family rules are often covert, it follows that changes can occur only by bringing them into the open. You can assist family members to consider the effects of rules on family interactions. To illustrate, we return to Anna and Jackie in which the focus of the conversation is on family communication styles and family rules. The social worker shares her observation about the differences between their families and makes the point that family rules and communication styles influence the interactions in relationships. To begin to resolve the conflict about these differences, Kim urged Anna and Jackie to consider ways to bring each other into a conversation, in such a way that they are able to work out their differences. By encouraging them to openly discuss family of origin rules, they can begin to consider rules that might better serve their relationship needs.

It can be useful to have family members make a list of apparent and unspoken rules so that you and they can understand how the family operates. You can prepare families to consider rules by introducing them to the concept, as illustrated in the following message:

Social worker: As we begin to work on problems the family is experiencing, we need to know more about how your family operates. Every family has some rules or understandings about how members are to behave. Sometimes these rules are easy to spot. For example, each person is to clear his or her own plate after a meal is a rule that all members of a family might be expected to follow. This is an apparent rule because every member of the family could easily tell me what is expected of them at the end of the meal. But the family's behavior is also governed by other rules that are less easy to identify. Even though members follow these rules, they are often unaware that they exist. I'm going to ask you some questions that will help you to understand these two kinds of rules better and to identify some of the ones that operate in your family. For example, you can ask family members to list some apparent rules, coaching them as needed, by asking questions such as "What are your rules about school work?" (or watching television or household chores, friends).

Once family members have identified some of their common and readily apparent rules, you can then lead them into a discussion of implicit rules. For example, you might ask them to identify

family rules about showing anger or positive feelings or to explore decision-making or power (e.g., "Who do people go to in the family when they want something?"). The intent of these questions is not to engage in a lengthy exploration of rules, but rather to illustrate how hidden rules can influence family behavior, stressing that certain rules may hamper their interactions.

Consider the social worker's role in this regard in the following excerpt from a third session with Mr. and Mrs. Johnson and their three daughters, in which the social worker assisted the family to identify how hidden rules influence their patterned interactions:

Martha [age 14]: You took the red jersey again, right out of my closet—and you didn't ask. That's really bogus.

Cynthia [age 15]: You took the Lady Gaga CD last week, and you still have it. What's up with that?

Mr. Johnson: In this family, we share, and you girls should know this.

Social worker: This seems to be a family rule. What does this rule mean in this family?

Mr. Johnson: It means that we have a limited amount of money to spend on extras, so we buy things for the girls to use together and no one person owns the things we buy. Besides, the girls are expected to share because they are so close in age and like similar things.

Social worker: So, what happens when there is a disagreement about a particular item?

Martha: I got mad at Cynthia, and I told her so.

Social worker [to Cynthia]: Then what did you do?

Cynthia: I told Martha she didn't have any right to complain because she wasn't sharing things either.

Social worker: Cynthia and Martha, the two of you were engaged in blaming messages; do you see it the same way? [Girls nod.]

[To Mr. Johnson] I wonder if you remember what you did when Cynthia and Martha were arguing.

Mr. Johnson: I was trying to get them to stop arguing and yelling at each other and reminding them that they are expected to share.

Social worker [exploring hidden rule]: Is everyone in the family aware of the expectation of sharing? I'd like to begin by asking a few questions, to see if you can figure out what the rules are in your family. Are you willing to explore this further?

Social Worker [to Jennifer] You weren't involved in this argument. Do you argue with anyone in the family?

Jennifer [age 12, laughs]: My mother and Martha, but mainly I argue with my mother.

Social worker: When you get in an argument with your mother, what happens?

Jennifer: If my dad is home, he tries to stop it. Sometimes he tells my mother to go upstairs, and he'll talk to me.

Social worker [to Mrs. Johnson]: When your husband stops an argument between the girls, or you and one of the girls, what do you do?

Mrs. Johnson: Sometimes I let him deal with the problem with Jennifer or one of the other girls. But when he gets involved like that, it makes me so furious that sometimes he and I end up in a fight ourselves.

Social worker: We need to do a lot more work to understand what happens in such situations, but for the moment, let's see, Mr. Johnson, if you can put your finger on the rule.

Mr. Johnson: I guess I'm always trying to stop everyone from fighting and arguing in the family. I expect the girls to share and get along with each other, and not cause their mother grief.

Social worker: It does seem as if you are the family's mediator. I would think that would be a very difficult role to play.

Mr. Johnson: Well, there are no rewards for it, I can tell you that!

Social worker: There's more to the rule. Who lets the father be the mediator?

Mrs. Johnson: We all do.

Social worker: That's right. It isn't the father's rule; it's the family's rule. It takes the rest of the family to argue and the father to break up the fights.

Many avenues could be explored in this scenario, but the social worker chose to narrow the focus by helping the family to identify one of its major rules, for example, the expectation to share. She also addressed the rule that specifies the father's role of mediator in disputes. Picture yourself as the social worker in this family situation. After further exploring specific patterned interactions of the family, you can use questions like the following to help them to weigh whether they wish to continue relating under the old rules.

To Father

- *How effective are you in actually stopping the girls and their mother from fighting?*
- *What are your worst fears about what might occur in the family if you didn't play that role?*
- *Would you like to free yourself from the role of being the family mediator?*

To Other Family Members

- *Do you want the father to continue to be the third party in your arguments?*
- *What are the risks to your relationships if he discontinued playing the role of mediator?*
- *Do you want to work out your own disputes?*

Questions such as these focus the attention of all members on their patterned interactions and encourage them to determine the *function* of the behavior in the system.

Next, you would have the major task of assisting the Johnson family to modify their rules, by teaching them new skills for resolving disagreements. Also, you would coach the father in declining the role of mediator and the girls and their mother in requesting that he let them manage their own conflicts.

On-the-Spot Interventions

EP 2.1.10j

On-the-spot interventions are a potent way of modifying patterns of interaction by intervening immediately when metacommunications occur between couples or family members. For example, the social worker used this technique to stop the repetitive pattern in the communications between Anna and Jackie. On-the-spot interventions are also appropriate when:

- *A family member sends fuzzy or abrasive messages.*
- *The receiver of a message distorts its meanings.*
- *A receiver of a message fails to respond appropriately to important messages or feelings.*
- *A destructive interaction occurs as a result of a message.*

In implementing on-the-spot interventions, you would focus on the destructive effects of the preceding communication, labeling the type of communication so that family members can subsequently identify their own dysfunctional behaviors. In using the intervention, you also need to teach and guide family members in how to engage in more effective ways of communicating.

Teaching and guiding family members toward more effective ways of communication is illustrated in the following example. The social worker intervened in a *"blind alley"* argument, one that cannot be resolved because neither party can be proved right or wrong.

Husband: I distinctly remember telling you to buy some deodorant when you went to the store.

Wife: You just think that you did, but you didn't. I'd have remembered if you said anything about it.

Husband: No, you just didn't remember. I told you for sure, and you're shifting the blame.

Wife [with obvious irritation]: Like hell you did! You're the one who forgot to tell me, and I don't appreciate your telling me I forgot.

Social worker: Can we stop for a moment and consider what's happening between you? Each of you has a different recollection of what happened, and there's no way of determining who's right and who's wrong. You are involved in what I call a *blind alley* argument because you can't resolve it. You just end up arguing over who's right and feeling resentful because you're convinced the other person is wrong. That doesn't help you solve your problem; it just creates conflict in your relationship. Let's go back and start over. Are you willing to allow me to show you both a more effective way of dealing with this situation?

Alternatively, after describing and intervening in the interaction and guiding the couple to communicate constructively, you might challenge the couple (or family members) to identify their behavior and to modify it accordingly. For example, interrupt their interactions with a statement like this: "Wait a minute! Think about what you're doing just now and where it's going to lead you if you continue." In modifying patterns, the intermediate objective is for family members to recognize and decrease their counterproductive behavior, and to substitute newly gained communication skills for the harmful communication style. The ultimate goal, of course, is for family members to *eliminate* the counterproductive processes through concentrated efforts between sessions.

Guidelines for Making On-the-Spot Interventions

- *Focus on process rather than content.* For you to be infinitely more helpful to family members, you must focus on their interaction processes rather than on the content of their conflicts. Conflicts typically are manifested over content issues, but *how* family members interact in dealing with the focal point of a conflict is far more important. As the "blind alley argument" example illustrated, the issue of who is right in a given dispute is usually trivial when compared to the destructive effects of the processes. Thus, you should usually deemphasize the topics of disputes and focus instead on helping family members to listen attentively and respectfully, to own his or her feelings and his or her responsibility in creating and maintaining the problem. Ultimately, you will want to teach them how to compromise, to disengage from competitive interaction, and to engage in conflict resolution.

- *Give feedback that is descriptive and neutral rather than general or evaluative.* As you intervene, it is important that you present feedback in a neutral manner that does not fault family members but rather allows them to pinpoint specific behaviors that produce difficulties. Feedback that evaluates their behavior produces defensiveness; overly general feedback fails to focus on behavior that needs to be changed.

To illustrate, consider a situation in which a man glared at his wife and says, "I've had it with going to your parents' house. You spend all the time while we are there talking with your mother, and I do not feel included or welcomed in the conversation. You can go by yourself in the future." A *general and evaluative message* would take the following form:

Social worker: "Garth, that message was an example of poor communication. Try again to send a better one."

The following message is neutral and behaviorally specific:

Social worker: "Garth, I noticed that when you just spoke to Barbara, you glared at her and sent a message that focused on what you thought she was doing wrong. I watched Barbara as you spoke, and noticed that she frowned and seemed to be angry. I'd like you to get some feedback from Barbara about how your message affected her. Barbara, would you share with Garth what you experienced as he talked?"

In the summary of what had occurred, the social worker indicated that Garth's message to Barbara was problematic, but he avoids making an evaluative judgment. Moreover, by describing specific behavior and eliciting feedback about its impact, the social worker enhances the possibility that Garth will be receptive to examining and modifying his behavior. Note also that this message highlights the interaction of *both* participants, as specified in the following guideline.

- *Balance interventions to divide responsibility.* When more than one family member is involved in sessions, you must achieve a delicate balance while avoiding the appearance of singling out one person as being the sole cause of interpersonal difficulties. Otherwise, that person may feel that you and other family members are taking sides and blaming. By focusing on all relevant actors, you can distribute responsibility, model fairness, and avoid alienating one person. Moreover, although one person may contribute more to problems than others, all members of a system generally contribute to difficulties in some degree.

The following example illustrates the technique of balancing in a situation in which the husband and wife are at odds with each other over caring for their baby and the amount of time the husband spends at work:

Social worker: Both of you seem to have some feelings and concerns that are legitimate, but for some reason you seem to be stuck and unable to work things out.

[To wife] You resent your husband when he does not do his part regarding child care. As a result you feel that you can't trust him to take care of the children, even though you both agreed that you would return to work part-time.

[To husband] You feel that because you are on a new job, now is not the time to ask for time off for child care.

[To both] I'd like to explore what the two of you can do to make things better for each other.

In this example, the social worker responded empathically to the feelings of both husband and wife, thereby validating the feelings of each. In so doing, he remained neutral so as to avoid the appearance of siding with or against either of the participants. The empathic responses also soften the impact of the social worker's messages.

Here are two more guidelines for making on-the-spot interventions into dysfunctional patterns:

EP 2.1.10j

- Balance interventions equally between family members in much the same way as the social worker in the previous example divided responsibility for the couple's interactions. Because

diverse interactions occur among family members, you must make choices about intervening in processes until all members have had an opportunity to focus on their concerns.
- *Direct messages* from family members to one another, because couples and family members need to learn to communicate effectively with each other. Your role is to facilitate effective communication between them rather than to act as an intermediary. Family members do not learn the essential skills in communicating with one another by talking through you. Therefore, you should redirect messages to the parties whom they concern. For example, use a message such as "Would you tell your son how you feel about his being in trouble with juvenile corrections, please?"

When people are angry, they may express messages that are hostile, blaming, or critical, exacerbating an already difficult situation. Before redirecting messages, therefore, you must consider the likely consequences of the ensuing interaction. As you redirect such messages, you should actively intervene to facilitate positive interaction:

- *Coach family members to own their feelings:* "I am really angry with you for getting this family involved with the police."
- *Translate complaints into requests for change:* "I wish you would stay in school and stop hanging around with the neighborhood dropouts."
- *Clarify positive intentions:* "I want you to stay in school because I want your life to be better than mine."

Of course, these messages will be more effective when speakers' nonverbal behaviors are consistent with their verbal message. For example, unless there is a cultural imperative observed in the family, when family members are speaking they should face one another and maintain eye contact. You may need to interrupt and direct them as illustrated in the following message:

Social worker: Cassandra, please stop for just a moment. You were talking to me, not to Jamal. Will you please start again, but this time talk and look directly at him?

Assisting Families to Disengage from Conflict

EP 2.1.10j

One of the most common and harmful types of interaction within families involves arguments that quickly escalate, causing anger and resentment between the participants. Sustained over time, these interactions may eventually involve other family members and subsystems. More often than not, the family system becomes factionalized, and individual efforts to regain equilibrium may result in further conflict. The content of the conflict is generally secondary to the fact that on a process level each family member is struggling to avoid being one-down, losing face, or yielding power to the other member.

To illustrate helping family members in disengaging from conflict, we return to the case of Twanna and Janet in which Twanna's behavior has resulted in family conflict. Fortunately, the situation between Janet and Twanna has not reached a crisis point, but if left unresolved, it has all of the essential ingredients to escalate and impact the prior gains that the two of them have made.

VIDEO CASE EXAMPLE

Adolescent Parent and Foster Mother, Part 2

A call from Twanna has resulted in a second family session with the social worker. Twanna is frustrated because of the differences in parenting styles between herself and her foster mother, Janet. The primary issue is that Janet is much more permissive with the child, yet she expects Twanna to be more involved as the child's mother. Twanna has tended to rely on rules when interacting with the child, for example, no candy before meals. Although Janet wanted Twanna to be more involved, she is not ready to entirely give over parenting responsibility to Twanna. She also maintained that the child is not accustomed to her mother telling her what to do. When Twanna, for example, refused to allow the child to have candy, the child "throws a temper tantrum." Janet immediately responded to the child's distress and emphasized that "She's just a baby." During those times when Janet had taken over, Twanna retreated to her room, slamming the door, and listening to music using a headset to drown out the noise. When asked by the social worker how she felt about the situation, Twanna responded, "Janet made her this way, so she can deal with it." She also admitted that she does not know how to handle the tantrums and would like Janet to teach her.

Although the process of disengagement can be easy to learn, it is not simple to do, because many family members have nearly always responded in a reactive competitive pattern. In many ways, Janet is competing with Twanna as the child's parent. She reasoned that the child does not have tantrums with her because she is the more familiar caretaker. Janet is also sending a mixed message to Twanna. Specifically, to act as the child's parent, but if Janet does not approve, she intervenes in the situation. Note that the social worker remarked that Janet wants Twanna to take a more active parenting role, but that she is not quite ready to play a secondary role. Glenda also asked Janet, "Does the baby throw tantrums with you?" as a means to highlight the conflict between the two parenting styles. Even so, the strength of their relationship had improved. For example, Janet, began the session by praising Twanna for keeping her agreement about coming home and caring for her child.

To assist family members in avoiding competitive struggles, you can emphasize that everyone loses in competitive situations or arguments and that negative feelings or emotional estrangement is likely to be a result (e.g., Twanna's withdrawal, slamming the door). It is also vital to stress that safeguarding mutual respect is far more important than winning. The concept of disengaging from conflict simply means that family members avoid escalating arguments by declining to participate further. A graceful way in which people can disengage is by making a comment similar to the following: "Listen, it doesn't really matter who's right. If we argue, we just get mad at each other, and I don't want that to happen." Teaching family members to evaluate their behavior and its effects on others is another strategy: "How do the children react when the two of you are having an argument?" You can further assist family members to avoid conflict between sessions by teaching them to develop code words that signal the need to disengage or reframe their message. Sentences or questions such as "When you do ...," "How could you think ...," "Did you think ...," "I know that you won't ...," "You never ...," "Don't tell me what to do ...," and "Why did you ..." are generally powerful prompts, along with labeling, that set the stage for conflict.

Negotiating tasks for disengaging from conflicted interactions between sessions can help family members transfer these skills to their daily lives. Of course, family members may be incapable of intervening to disengage conflict in some instances—for example, in domestic violence situations where there is a threat or the actuality of physical harm. In these situations, you can teach family members—especially children—to call for help as well as to develop a safety plan.

Conflict resolution strategies may vary based on differences in both gender and ethnicity (Mackey & O'Brien, 1998; Berg & Jaya, 1993). Being aware of these differences will assist you in choosing intervention strategies that recognize how these factors affect the family's behavior. Berg and Jaya (1993) note that in some Asian families, concerns are viewed as "our problems," emphasizing the interdependence between family members. This example suggests that you should explore the family narrative regarding how conflict is managed in the family's particular culture as well as the attached meanings or feelings. By doing so, you are able to engage members in formulating an effective intervention strategy.

EP 2.1.10a

In fact, understanding the family narrative with respect to conflict may yield benefits with all families, irrespective of their culture or ethnicity. Each family has its own style of communicating (e.g., Jackie, "We don't make a big deal of things"; Anna, "We talk about everything"). In some families, everyone talks simultaneously and makes outrageous statements; other members may remain passive during this display. Perhaps yelling or name-calling is a norm, as are demonstrative hand gestures, apparent threats, and a hostile or belligerent tone of voice. Be sensitive to the fact that these interactions in family communication styles are not necessarily evidence of destructive relational patterns, simply because they are not your own family's style. Observing the family and inquiring about their preferred patterns of relating will enable you to assess family members' communication styles, and avoid drawing conclusions about their functional or dysfunctional status.

Modifying Complementary Interactions

EP 2.1.10a

Relationships, as described by communication theorists and without attributing a value to either descriptor, are either symmetrical or complementary (Becvar & Becvar, 2000a). Symmetrical relationships are thought to be a more egalitarian arrangement. In contrast, the parties in complementary relationships have developed an exchange as a means for avoiding conflict, resolving differences, and creating a workable relationship.

Preferences for relationship patterns may be culturally derived and are considered to reflect a practical division of roles and responsibilities. Therefore, it is important that you avoid concluding that these patterns are an issue unless the family has indicated that they are.

Note, however, that a complementary type of relationship may prove to be a concern to one or both partners. Frustrations may stem from role overload or strain, limitations imposed by role expectations, and disagreements related to decision making. One partner may grow to resent what she or he perceives as dominance. In such a case, the relationship may become asymmetrical, and one person may engage in passive resistance behavior or openly challenge the other. Moreover, an individual who is weary of the exchange may devalue the other party, or disengage, ultimately resenting his or her lack of involvement. In either event, harmful interactions are likely to occur, culminating in a family member seeking professional help.

In modifying dysfunctional complementary relationships, it is important to work with couples and family members to adopt changes that will bring their relationships into balance, assuming that they have chosen this goal. As part of this work, you assist members to develop agreements that involve reciprocal changes.

Negotiating Agreements for Reciprocal Changes

EP 2.1.10c

In family or couple sessions, you can facilitate changes in specific behaviors by helping one member to develop an agreement if another person will agree to make a reciprocal change. In this kind of quid pro quo or contingency contract, a member agrees to disengage from conflict if the other party agrees to avoid using code words that always prompt a negative response. Individuals are receptive to making changes when other parties agree to make reciprocal changes for two reasons. First, people are more prone to give when they know they are getting something in return. Second, when all involved parties agree to make changes, no single person loses face by appearing to be the sole cause of an interactional problem.

Contracting for reciprocal changes can be a powerful means of inducing change. Another advantage of reciprocal contracting is that it counters the tendency to wait for others to initiate changes. Still another benefit is that, in working on reciprocal tasks, all parties become *mutually* involved in a change venture. This mutual involvement may spark collaboration in other dimensions of their relationships—an important gain where interactions have been largely dysfunctional rather than collaborative.

Family members are unlikely to be able to implement reciprocal contracts if they have not moved beyond competitive bickering and blaming one another for their problems. For this reason, we recommend deferring use of this technique (unless clients spontaneously begin to negotiate) until you have assisted them in listening attentively to one another, and to change the tone of their interactions. It is also essential that participants demonstrate a commitment to improving their relationship. As Becvar and Becvar (2000a) point out, if family members view their own or others' changes as emanating primarily from meeting the stipulations of an agreement, rather than as a way to improve their relationship, they are likely to devalue the changes. Therefore, you will want to ask family members to explicitly clarify that improving their relationship is the primary factor motivating their willingness to make changes.

The following are examples of reciprocal agreements that could have been utilized in previous case situations in this chapter. You may use them as a guide in assisting families to develop their own agreements such as:

- *Jackie agrees to talk with her family, if Anna stops pushing and allows her to do so when she is ready.*
- *Janet will refrain from interfering with Twanna's parenting and agrees to help her strengthen her bonds with her child.*
- *Cynthia and Martha will not get into an argument if the other does not keep shared items for an extended period of time.*
- *Jackie agrees to communicate her feelings if Anna agrees to accept that there are times when Jackie is too tired to talk.*

In developing reciprocal contracts, it is wise to encourage family members to make their own reciprocal behavioral agreement. By so doing, they become invested in the proposed changes. Moreover, they often generate innovative and constructive ideas, based on their knowledge of their particular family that might not occur to you. To facilitate families in making proposals, you can use a message such as the following: "It's clear that each of you is unhappy with the situation. Perhaps this is a good time for you to develop ideas about what you could do to improve the situation." You could then prompt them to think about reciprocal actions.

As you mutually consider proposals, it is important to explore potential barriers and guard against the tendency to undertake overly ambitious actions. Initial task exchanges in reciprocal agreements should be relatively simple and likely to succeed, especially when intense conflict has marked interactions. When a feasible reciprocal proposal has been agreed upon, you can assist family members to reach a further agreement that specifies the tasks each member will complete prior to the next session. In developing and planning to implement these tasks, follow the steps of the TIS (outlined in Chapter 13). As you plan task implementation with family members or couples, stress that each person must exercise *good faith* in carrying out his or her part of the contract, as illustrated in the following message:

Social worker: You have agreed to make the changes we've discussed in an effort to improve the situation for everyone. To make these changes successful, however, each of you will need to carry out your part—no matter what the other person does. Waiting for the other person to carry out his or her part first, may result in neither of you making a move by the time of our next session. Remember, failure by the other person to honor the contract is no excuse for you to do likewise. If the other person doesn't keep to the agreement, you can take satisfaction in knowing that you did your part.

Stressing the individual responsibility of all family members to fulfill their respective commitments, as in the preceding message, counters the tendency of clients to justify their inaction in subsequent sessions by asserting, "He (or she) didn't carry out his part. I knew this would happen, so I didn't do my part either." If one or more family members have not fulfilled their parts of the agreement, you can focus on obstacles that prevented them from doing so. When the results have been favorable, you can focus on this experience to set the stage for exploring additional ways of achieving further positive interaction.

Intervening with Families: Modifying Misconceptions and Distorted Cognitions

EP 2.1.10a

Cognitions are often the basis for erroneous beliefs that produce dissatisfaction in couple and family relationships. Left unresolved, resentment towards others can become fertile ground for repetitive dysfunctional interaction. Unrealistic expectations of others and myths are two other forms of misconceptions that contribute to relationship problems. As with rules, unrealistic expectations are not always obvious, so you may have to clarify them by asking family members' about their expectations of one another. Myths are similar to rules in that they govern family operations by shaping beliefs and expectations that can profoundly influence interactions in couple and family relationships.

To diminish misconceptions and dispel myths, bring them out in the open, using empathy to help family members recognize their distorted cognitions. Misconceptions and myths generally protect people from having to face the reality of their cognitions and perceptions. Therefore, attempts to change them can be perceived as threatening. Seldom are they relinquished without a struggle, because introducing an alternative perspective or new information that is contrary to a person's beliefs creates cognitive dissonance. In addition, making essential change entails resolving fears, not the least of which is risking the consequences of learning and implementing new behavior. In these instances, your empathetic response to fears and ambivalence and providing emotional support can be the impetus for people to change.

EP 2.1.10j

To illustrate, consider a family in which an adolescent, age 17, is experiencing extreme tension and anxiety as a result of parental expectations. During family sessions, it becomes apparent that the parents expect him to be a top student so that he can become a doctor. It is also obvious that the parents embrace the generalized myth "If you try hard enough, you can become anything you want." In an effort to reduce the pressure on the son, dispel the myth as it applies to him, and modify the parents' expectations, the social worker meets separately with the parents. The following excerpt is taken from that session.

Social worker: I've been very concerned that Gary has been making an almost superhuman effort to do well in chemistry and physics, but he is not doing well in these subjects. It is my impression that he feels pressured to become a doctor, and that one reason he's so anxious is that he doesn't believe that he can do better despite his best efforts. It's important to him to have you think well of him. But he is falling short even though he continues to drive himself.

Father: Poof! Of course he is working hard. Why shouldn't he? He can become a doctor if he really wants to and continues to apply himself. You know, I could have been a doctor, but what did I do? I goofed off. I don't want Gary to repeat my mistake. He should recognize that he has opportunities that neither his mother nor I had.

Social worker: I sense your concern and care for Gary. Is it your perception that he is goofing off? I understand that both of you share the belief people can do anything they want. This message has been clear to Gary, and he's blaming himself because he's not making it, no matter how hard he tries.

Mother: Don't you think anyone can succeed in anything if they try hard enough?

Social worker: Actually, this belief is inconsistent with what I know about differences between people. Each of us has different aptitudes, talents, and learning styles. Some people are able to handle types of work that require dexterity. Others are able to visualize spatial relationships. Everyone has certain aptitudes, types of intelligence, and limitations. What's important in deciding a future career is discovering what our own aptitudes are and making choices that match them. I wonder if each of you can identify talents and limitations that you have.

Observe that as the social worker addressed the family myth, he highlighted the adverse impact of the myths on Gary. This tactic switched the focus from the abstract to the concrete and provided the parents with an opportunity to review and evaluate their beliefs. The social worker then further attempted to invalidate the myth by asking them to apply it to themselves.

No doubt, you will frequently encounter families who have distorted perceptions of one another that contribute to repetitive dysfunctional interactions. Recall from Chapter 13 that labeling the behaviors of others is a common source of cognitive and perceptual distortions. Labeling is like wearing a blinder because it places people in a certain frame, thereby limiting their attributes and behaviors to fit the framed image. In effect, the frame effectively obscures other qualities, so that in dealing with an individual, a person simply has to rely on his or her preexisting cognitions or perceptions without having to think.

EP 2.1.4a

Myths that distort individual or family perceptions can extend beyond those that influence internal family dynamics. They can also be linked to discrimination, bigotry, and negative schemas engrained in societal and institutional perceptions and in attitudes held about certain families. Distortions can be so embedded that for some individuals they do not warrant further critique. Instead they become the generalized narrative that informs what people believe about others. For example, minority families are often criticized for their children's performance on standardized achievement tests; conclusions are drawn about youth based on their style of dress or music preferences; immigrant families are expected to act, dress, and speak in a certain way that is comfortable for mainstream society; and families who are different by virtue of their physical attributes, sexual orientation, language, or customs are mocked, shunned, or threatened. On a macro-level, these perceptions and distortions can influence where families choose to live, how they perceive their safety, and with whom children are allowed to interact.

When you observe myths and distortions about others operating in families, you have a responsibility to address them in the same manner as you would in intervening in family dynamics, because they affect the families toward whom this behavior is directed. They are also a source of stress and strain for those who hold these beliefs, infusing negativity in their interactions. A word of caution is in order, however. In focusing on the impact of labeling, myths, and distorted perceptions, either in interfamilial or extra-familial interactions, take care to describe the specific behavior rather than using a label to characterize the behavior.

Intervening with Families: Modifying Family Alignments

EP 2.1.10a

All families develop patterns of affiliation between members that either enhance or impair opportunities for individual growth or the family's ability to carry out survival functions. The functional structure—that is, the family's invisible or covert set of demands or code of behavior—reflects and regulates family functioning and determines transactional patterns (Minuchin, 1974). In this section, we draw upon structural approach techniques to guide intervention strategies when family functioning is impaired by dysfunctional alignments.

Structural family therapy is intended to strengthen current family relationships, interactions, and transactional patterns. The approach emphasizes the wholeness of the family—that is, its hierarchical organization and the interdependent functioning of subsystems (Goldenberg & Goldenberg, 2004; Minuchin, 1974). Because of its primary focus on improving family relationships, structural therapy pays attention to subsystems, boundaries, alignments in the family system, and power, using the resources and power inherent in families to effect change. Graphic symbols of the family structure and alignment include, lines that show rigid, diffused or clear boundaries, as well as conflict and coalitions (Nichols, 2006). Using the technique of *enactment,* family members are encouraged to interact with each other during a family session. This exercise is observed by the social worker, who subsequently intervenes to modify problematic interactions.

EP 2.1.10a

Interventions to modify alignments are generally indicated in the following circumstances:

- *Bonds are weak between spouses, other individuals who form the parental subsystem, or other family members.*
- *Enmeshed alliances—that is, rigid or overly restrictive boundaries between members—limit appropriate bonds with other members (or outsiders).*
- *Two members of a family attempt to cope with dissatisfaction or conflict in their relationship by forming a coalition with a third family member, a phenomenon known as triangulation.*
- *Family members are disengaged or alienated from one another, tending to go their own ways, with little reliance on each other for emotional support.*
- *Members of the family have formed alliances with persons outside the immediate family (e.g., friends and relatives) that interfere with performing appropriate family roles or providing appropriate emotional support to other family members.*

EP 2.1.10j

In intervening to modify alignments, *structural mapping* may be used to delineate family boundaries and to highlight and modify interactions and transactional patterns. Structural mapping identifies symptoms that may be exhibited by an individual family member as an expression of difficulties in the family system. The structure of the family is revealed by who talks to whom, and in what way; that is, in an unfavorable or favorable position; and how intense the family's transactions are. The goal of the structural approach is to change family structures by altering boundaries and by realigning subsystems to enhance family functioning. Interventions are thus devised to achieve the following goals:

- *Develop alliances, cultivate new alliances, or strengthen underdeveloped relationships. For example, a social worker might help a new stepfather and stepson to explore ways that they can develop a relationship or the social worker might help a parent who has been in prison to strengthen emotional bonds to his or her children.*
- *Reinforce an alliance, by acting to maintain the alliance or to amplify its scope and/or strength. For instance, a social worker might assist a single parent in increasing his or her ability to operate as an effective executive subsystem (e.g., Twanna).*
- *Differentiate individuals and subsystems. For example, a social worker might help a mother who gives most of her attention to a newborn infant to understand the need for supervision of older children, and to invest some of her emotional energy in them.*
- *Increase family interactions in disengaged families to make boundaries more permeable by changing the way in which members relate to one another.*
- *Help family members accommodate changing circumstances or transitions by decreasing rigid structures or rules that are no longer viable. For example, as a child reaches adolescence, the social worker might help the parents revise their expectations of the child's behavior or modify rules so as to accommodate this developmental change.*

As can be surmised from these examples, structural problems may arise when the family structure is unable to adequately adjust to changing circumstances. Changing circumstances may be the result of external environmental forces, stressful transitions, or dynamics internal to the family system. Before you intervene, to restructure the family structure, it is important for you to understand the structural change as unique to the family's situation and make clear the nature of the structural dysfunction. Thus, the family should be involved in determining whether, and in what ways, such changes should take place.

EP 2.1.10j

Your first task in this respect is to assist family members in identifying the nature of their alignments. This may be accomplished by asking general questions that stimulate family members to consider their alignments:

- *If you had a difficult problem and needed help, whom would you seek out in the family (tribe or clan)?*
- *Sometimes members of a family feel closer to some members than to others and may pair up or group*

together. Which members of your family, if any, group together?
- *In most families, members argue to some extent. With whom do you argue? With whom do other members argue?*
- *Is there one person in the family who is considered to be a favorite?*
- *[To parents] When you make a decision, do you feel that your decision is supported by the other parent? Are other people involved in your decisions?*

You can also bring alignments and coalitions to the family's attention as they are manifested in family sessions:

- *Martha, it seems that you're the center of the family. Most of the conversation seems to be directed through you, while other family members, with the exception of Joe, appear to be observers to the discussion.*
- *Janet, in your description of how you spend your day, it appears that the baby receives a great deal of your attention.*
- *[To Twanna] When you are upset, who do you talk to about how you feel?*
- *I noticed that each of you identified the same individual on your map. Can you tell me about this person and his (or her) role in your family?*

EP 2.1.10a

As family members become aware of their alignments, you can assist them in considering whether they wish to become closer to others and to identify obstacles that could prevent this movement from happening. Family alignments may, in fact, involve "complex extended patterns or configurations" (Boyd-Franklin, 1989a, p. 124). Members of the various configurations may include clan or tribal members, extended kin, friends, or individuals from the family's religious or spiritual community, such as a minister, shaman, rabbi, monk, medicine person, or priest. Be mindful of the fact that any of these people (or a combination of them) may be involved in family structural arrangements. As a consequence, it may be necessary to explore relationships and alignments beyond the immediate family system.

EP 2.1.10j

Family sculpting is a technique used in experiential family practice models for assisting family members in analyzing and observing their alliances and in making decisions concerning possible changes. This technique allows family members to communicate spatial family system relationships in a nonverbal tableau, to discern alignments, and to recognize the need to realign their relationships. A variation of this technique is to have family members portray historical and current family relationships using the Genogram.

In family sculpting, family members are instructed to physically arrange other family members in a way that portrays his or her perceptions of members as well as his or her place in the family system. Another aspect of family sculpting involves member's expressing themselves by using drawings to disclose their perceptions of each other (Nichols, 2006). For example, you would instruct the family to draw a picture that shows how they see themselves as a family. After family members have completed their drawings, you would ask participants to draw family relationships as they would *like* them to be on the other side of the paper. In a subsequent discussion, you would ask members in turn to share their drawings of existing family relationships.

The benefit of the expressive exercise is that family members can observe the nature of their alignments and the emotional closeness and distance in their relationships with others. Invite family members to comment on their observations, based on hypothetical responses from an earlier situation in the chapter, for example:

- *It looks like Martha and I are quite close to each other, but that Jennifer doesn't feel as close to Martha as I do.*
- *Jennifer and I seem to have the least conflict with each other.*
- *We all seem to be close to Grandmother Maggie.*

After each family member has an opportunity to make their observations, you can ask them to explain their second drawings, which show how they would like family relationships to be. During this discussion, you can highlight the desired changes, assist individuals to formulate goals that reflect changes they would like to make, and identify "exceptional" times—for example, when Jennifer and Martha are not in conflict with each other.

Elements of family sculpting or structural mapping include exercises that can be used with parents to portray family relationships, strengthen parental coalitions and mark generational boundaries. For example, does one parent triangulate with a child or children, or permit children to intrude into the parental subsystem? Does the father act as a mediator in family conflicts? Does one parent have the final say? Does one child have inordinate power in the family? The hazard associated with these alignments is that children may become adept at playing one parent against the other. In these instances, parental divisiveness is fostered, and in consequence, relationships between the children and the excluded parent are strained. In the case of the mother who expends a majority of her emotional energy on a newborn, emotional bonds and loyalty between her and her other children and family members may be lacking.

EP 2.1.10a

Developing cohesiveness, unity, and more effective alignments is a challenge that often confronts two families who have joined together—for example, when in the development of a relationship between a new stepfather and a stepson. Because these factors are apt to be present in foster or adoptive families, your attention to alliances and cohesiveness is equally important in such cases, especially when there are biological children in the home.

In situations where two families have joined together, you can assist parents to analyze whether differences or lack of agreement about their parenting styles are factors in parent-child alignments. Hare (1994) urges us to be mindful of the fact that in lesbian families, issues related to two families joining together and parenting styles are not dissimilar to those problems faced by heterosexual families. Strategies for strengthening parental coalitions may include negotiating "united front" agreements in parent–child transactions requiring decision making and/or disciplinary actions (unless, of course, the other partner is truly hurtful or abusive to the child). Finally, assisting families to realign themselves and forge new alliances is particularly important in instances in which there has been a disruption in the family system. Examples include the reunification of a child who has been placed outside of the home, or when a parent or another key family member has been absent from the family's life for an extended period of time.

Summary

This chapter focused on process and structural intervention strategies and techniques that you can use to strengthen the functioning and relationships in families or couples. These strategies utilize techniques from solution-focused, task-centered, family systems and structural approaches to practice with families. Each approach shares the view of the family as a social system, and thus the intervention strategies focus on change in the family as a social unit. As a beginning social worker, learning and utilizing the required skills for each approach can appear to be a daunting challenge. You are encouraged to seek supervision and consultation in applying them. To further enhance your knowledge and skills, you can use the references cited in this chapter.

In implementing the intervention strategies discussed in this chapter, we caution you against making assumptions about what constitutes "normal" family functioning. You should examine family functioning, communication patterns, and alignments in light of each family's particular culture, race, structure, and social class. Solution-focused family practice reminds us that attempts to identify families as functional or dysfunctional are inherently flawed. Instead, in using this approach, you assist the family to envision solutions and diminish the focus on problems. Those social workers operating in a framework of social constructionist or narrative therapy also find it unproductive to characterize or label families as functional or dysfunctional, preferring instead to honor the unique story of each family. We further urge that an appraisal of family ethnicity, race, configuration and sexual orientation must be factored into any intervention strategies.

Any approach that you may utilize in intervening with families requires systematic application of techniques and strategies, ongoing monitoring, and evaluation of the results. Research as summarized by Nichols and Swartz (1998) points to positive outcomes when specific problems are treated in a systematic manner. Chapter 13 detailed the importance of matching intervention strategies to clients' goals and the client system. This chapter amplified this point, as well as pointing out the need for matching the intervention with the specific problem, developmental stages, and ethnocultural factors, taking into account internal family functioning and the external factors that may influence the family system.

CourseMate

Access to an integrated eBook and chapter specific learning tools, including glossary terns, chapter outlines, relevant web links, video, and practice quizzes. Go to **www.cengagebrain.com**.

CHAPTER **16**
Social Work Group Interventions

CHAPTER OVERVIEW

This chapter builds on the skills introduced in Chapter 11 for forming and composing task, treatment, and support groups. This chapter addresses the stages of group development and skills needed to intervene effectively throughout group processes. At the completion of it you will:

- Be familiar with the phases through which groups progress and the features of each stage
- Understand the skills and knowledge needed to effectively intervene at each stage
- Observe the ways that these concepts reveal themselves in the dialogue of the HEART group
- Understand common worker errors at different phases of group process
- Be familiar with variants on group work such as single session and technology-mediated groups
- Understand how concepts on group interventions apply to task groups

EPAS COMPETENCIES IN THE 16TH CHAPTER

This chapter will give you the information needed to meet the following practice competencies:

2.1.6b Use research evidence to inform practice

2.1.7a Utilize conceptual frameworks to guide the processes of assessment, intervention, and evaluation

2.1.9a Continuously discover, appraise, and attend to changing locales, populations, scientific and technological developments, and emerging societal trends to provide relevant services

2.1.10a Substantively and effectively prepare for action with individuals, families, groups, organizations, and communities

2.1.10g Select appropriate intervention strategies

2.1.10i Implement prevention interventions that enhance client capacities

2.1.10j Help clients resolve problems

2.1.10l Facilitate transitions and endings

In all social work groups the leader's task is to intervene to help the group reach shared goals. In treatment groups, this role is particularly complex, requiring in-depth, balanced interventions to assist individuals and the group as a whole. To add to the complexity of this role, the leader must be astute in sorting through the maze of multilevel communication to bring meaning to the group's experience, shape the group's therapeutic character, and provide direction and focus to the group's processes at critical moments. Finally, the leader must formulate all interventions within the context of the stages of development—stages through which a group progresses to reach full maturity. Leaders of task groups must play similar facilitative roles in assisting the group to meet its objectives. While this chapter focuses primarily on treatment groups, it provides specialized content on task groups in the final section.

Because the leader's interventions are inextricably related to the group's stage of development, we begin at that point.

Stages of Group Development

All groups go through natural stages of development, although the pace and complexity of each stage may vary. Your understanding of these stages is essential

EP 2.1.10a

in anticipating and addressing the behaviors that characterize each phase so that the group's objectives can ultimately be met. You are also responsible for removing obstacles that threaten to derail the group's development and hinder the success of individual members. In doing so, you must make strategic, informed choices regarding your input and actions across the lifespan of the group.

Without knowledge of the group's stage of development, leaders may be prone to making errors, such as expecting group members to begin in-depth explorations in initial sessions or concluding that they have failed if the group exhibits the discord that is typical of early development. Leaders may also overlook positive behaviors that indicate that the group is approaching a more mature stage of development or they may fail to intervene at critical periods to assist the group's evolution (for example, encouraging them to "stay on task," to "count in" all members in decision making, to foster free expression of feelings, or to adopt many other behaviors that are hallmarks of a seasoned group).

Various models of group development offer frameworks for organizing your observations about the group and its characteristics, themes, and behaviors. All of these models identify progressive steps in group development, although they may organize these steps into four, five, or even six stages. Some theorists have noted variations in group stages based on the gender of group members. For example, Schiller (1997; 2007) has noted that groups composed of women may emphasize intimacy for a longer period and come to power and control later in the group's process. Berman-Rossi and Kelly (2000) suggest that stages of group development are influenced by variables such as worker skills, attendance patterns, group content, gender, and other member characteristics. Open-ended groups and those with turbulent changes in membership may not move through these phases in a linear fashion and may require more time at formative stages if cohesion is slow to develop (Galinsky & Schopler, 1989). In this chapter, we will use the classic model developed by Garland, Jones, and Kolodny (1965), which delineates five stages:

EP 2.1.7a

1. Preaffiliation
2. Power and control
3. Intimacy
4. Differentiation
5. Separation

After discussing each stage, we present the considerations and interventions needed by the worker at each point in group development.

Stage 1. Preaffiliation: Approach and Avoidance Behavior

As anyone who has ever experienced the first day of a new class can attest, the initial stage of group development is characterized by members exhibiting *approach/avoidance* behavior. Apprehensions about becoming involved in the group are reflected in members' reluctance to volunteer answers to questions, to interact with others, and to support program activities and events. Hesitancy to participate is also shown by silence or tentative speech, as when members are occupied by their own problems and the feelings of uneasiness and apprehension that emanate from their first encounter with the group. Fearful or suspicious members may be sensitive to the responses of others, fearing possible domination, aggression, isolation, rejection, and hostility.

At this *forming* stage (Tuckman, 1963), participant behavior is wary, sometimes even provocative, as members assess possible social threats and attempt to discern the kinds of behaviors the group wants and expects. Members also tend to identify one another in terms of each individual's status and roles and to engage in social rituals, stereotyped introductions, and detailed intellectual discussions rather than in-depth or highly revealing conversation (Berman-Rossi & Kelly, 2000). They may be uncertain about the group's purpose and the benefits it may bring to them.

At times, members may employ testing behaviors to "size up" other members, to press the group's limits, to find out how competent the leader is, and to determine to what extent the leader will safeguard the rights of members and protect them from feared hurt and humiliation. Members may also move tentatively toward the group as they seek to find common ground with other members, search for viable roles, and seek approval, acceptance, and respect. Much of the initial communication in the group is directed toward the leader, and some members may openly demand that the social worker pursue a "take charge" approach, making decisions regarding group issues and structure and issuing prompt directives to control the behavior of members.

Preaffiliation in the HEART Group

The HEART group, introduced in Chapter 11, is designed to assist teen girls who have overweight. In this chapter, transcripts from the group are used to illustrate client statements and worker responses that are indicative of various phases of the group process.

Dave: Thank you to everyone for sharing your progress from last week. I would like to do this at the beginning of each session because I think it helps to bring us together and to create a space where you feel safe and energized to share and give each other support. I'm wondering if, based on how things went today, anybody has other ideas of how to make this opening ritual go better for them? Does anybody have any ideas about making improvements to what we're doing? Or can you tell me how it went for you today?

Amelia: Well, I think that check-in kinda depends on what your mood is. Like, I'm in a kind of okay mood today so my check-in is more positive, but like, Liz is kinda being bitchy, you know? And so maybe she's really had a bad day or whatever. So I think to have something that everybody does instead of just a check-in, I don't know, it's just really different for everybody, depending on how you're feeling.

Dave: How you're going to interact in group depends on how you're doing on that day.

Amelia: Yeah.

Dave: You know something I heard you say, Amelia, was that you felt that Liz was "bitchy," to use your word, and I want to check in with Liz to see how she received that, or how she heard that. So I'm wondering Liz, when Amelia said that, what came to mind?

Liz: It hurts my feelings because I thought people were talking about me all the time anyway, and then I come to this place, where everybody is supposed to be happy, and like me, and you call me bitchy. I think *that's* bitchy.

Amelia: Sorry.

Dave: Amelia, I think what you were saying was that during her introduction you heard that Liz was having a bad day. How does that sound?

Amelia: Yeah.

June: She didn't say you were a bitch, she said bitch-y, like kinda. I don't think she meant it in a mean way.

Liz: Well, that's how I took it, so I think that matters more than what you think you heard.

Dave: And June I would actually agree with Liz on that point. How someone hears what you're saying, matters as much as, or maybe more than, what you meant to say. One of the benefits of participating in group is having experiences like these to learn about how other people perceive you.

Stage 2. Power and Control: A Time of Transition

The first stage of group development merges imperceptibly into the second stage as members, having determined that the group experience is potentially safe and rewarding and worth the preliminary emotional investment, shift their concerns to matters related to autonomy, power, and control. The frame of reference for this *storming* stage (Tuckman, 1963) is that of transition— that is, members must endure the ambiguity and turmoil of change from a nonintimate to an intimate system of relationships.

After dealing with the struggle of whether they "belong" in the group, members now become occupied with how they "rank" in relation to other members. Turning to others like themselves for support and protection, members create subgroups and a hierarchy of statuses, or social "pecking order." Gradually, the processes of the group become stylized as various factions emerge and relationships solidify. Conflicts between opposing subgroups often occur in this stage, and members may team up to express anger toward the leader, other authority figures, or outsiders. Failed competition for favored status with the social worker may also produce hostility toward the group leader (Yalom, 2005).

Disenchantment with the group may reveal itself through hostility, withdrawal, or confusion about the group's purposes. Verbal abuse, attacks, and rejection of lower-status members may occur as well and isolated members of the group who do not have the protection of a subgroup may stop attending. Attrition in membership may also occur if individuals find outside pursuits more attractive than the conflicted group experience. In fact, this depleted membership may put the group's very survival in jeopardy.

Power and Control in the HEART Group

June: You know Dave, I don't mean to be disrespectful, and I think this is a good discussion, but I just wonder, are we the first group you've done?

Dave: I've done a few others.

Maggie: With girls?

Dave: A few with girls.

Maggie: Like our age?

Dave: Some.

June: Like, fat?

Dave: Well, I've worked with adults and teenagers with overweight. I'm curious, June, why do you ask?

June: Because you're the only skinny person here. And you're the only boy.

Amelia: Mmhmm.

June: See now nobody else dares to say anything.

Liz: Don't you think that maybe if he's skinny, maybe he can teach us some things?

Maggie: Yeah, but what does he know about what we're going through?

June: I mean, he knows boys.

Amelia: He's probably always been thin. He has no idea probably, you probably have no idea, what we've been through.

Dave: I'm hearing you say that you don't believe I can identify with you.

Amelia: Well, you're a boy, you're skinny, I'm a girl, and I'm fat.

June: And he's older.

Amelia: Yeah.

Amber: And he's probably always had girlfriends, I've never had a boyfriend.

Amelia: Do you have a girlfriend now?

Dave: I'd rather not answer that question.

Maggie: Why? We talk about our boyfriends and friends; I mean we're telling you stuff.

Dave: Actually, I think, you're also telling each other stuff, and the group is about you …

Amelia: And you.

Dave: My role here is to help the group along, and if I take up time with my relationships …

Amelia: So you have one.

Dave: As I said, I'd rather not address it Amelia, but if I take up time with my business then it robs the group …

June [to Amelia]: I mean he can't be your boyfriend if he's your worker. *[taunting]*

Dave: No, I can't date anyone in the group.

Amelia: I don't want to date you, oh my god!

Maggie: Sure …

Amelia: Don't even, you're so full of yourself! I like girls anyway.

Dave: The other thing I want to say is that I can learn from you and follow your concerns, solutions, and your strategies for dealing with some of the things that you're up against right now. I hope that in my role as facilitator I can help all of you to help yourselves even though I'm neither overweight nor a girl.

Stage 3. Intimacy: Developing a Familial Frame of Reference

Having clarified and resolved many of the issues related to personal autonomy, initiative, and power, the group moves from the "pre-intimate" power and control stage to that of intimacy. As the group enters this *norming* stage (Tuckman, 1963), conflicts fade, personal involvement between members intensifies, and members display a growing recognition of the significance of the group experience. Members also experience an increase in morale and "we-ness," a deepening commitment to the group's purpose, and heightened motivation to carry out plans and tasks that support the group's objectives. Mutual trust increases as members begin to acknowledge one another's uniqueness, spontaneously disclose feelings and problems, and seek the opinion of the group. To achieve this desired intimacy, however, group participants may suppress negative feelings that could produce conflict between themselves and others. In contrast to earlier sessions, they express genuine concern for absent members and may reach out to invite them to return to the group.

During this stage of development, a group "character" emerges as the group evolves its own culture, style, and values. Clear norms are established, based on personal interests, affection, and other positive forces. Roles also take shape as members find ways to contribute to the group and leadership patterns become firmly settled. The frame of reference for members is a familial one, as members liken their group experience to their experience with their own nuclear families, occasionally referring to other members as siblings or to the leader as the "mother" or "father" of the group.

How groups experience this stage depends on factors such as how regularly members attend group sessions, whether the group is open or closed, and how much member turnover occurs (Berman-Rossi & Kelly, 2000; Galinsky & Schopler, 1989). In groups that endure frequent transitions, it is important to develop rituals or a consistent format for meetings to help the members achieve cohesion and continuity.

Intimacy in the HEART Group

Amber: I was kind of down the other day. I went to the Fairmont Mall with my friends, and we were going to all the good stores like Abercrombie & Fitch, and Hollister, and American Eagle, that's one of my favorites …

June: And Bebe.

Amber: Yeah, and uh, all my friends were trying on the clothes, and I can't fit into any of the clothes there, but I really want to because they're really cute clothes. It makes me feel kind of out of the loop with my friends; do you guys have that problem too?

Amelia: Totally.

Amber: I can't shop at the same stores my friends shop at.

June: Yeah, I just mostly end up wearing sweats and T-shirts, you know, because … but you can't wear that everywhere.

Amber: Uh-huh.

Liz: Sometime I feel like I lost my friends because they all wear those cute outfits and they all share clothes and I couldn't relate anymore so we quit hanging out.

June: The peasant ones make you look pregnant if they come right under your boobs …

Dave: Amber, one of the things I want to ask you is what kind of feedback or what kind of support would you like right now?

Amber: I guess I just want to see if there are people in this group that felt that way sometimes, like if they didn't fit in with their friends sometimes that way.

Dave: Does anybody else have a similar experience as Amber does?

Amelia: I do. Yeah, like, I feel like when I go shopping with my mom I can try on the clothes that really fit me, but if I'm with my friends I have to stay on the rack that they're on. I'm taller than most of them, and I'm fat, and they're like super skinny. So when they try on clothes, I feel like I need to choose clothes from that rack too. So then, I don't know, I can't believe I'm saying this, but like, I'll buy the clothes and, you know, pretend that they fit, and then make my mom take them back. So, I hear ya.

June: Like last summer when I lost five pounds I thought, "I can get into those jeans," and then my friends said I was muffin-top 'cuz like my fat was hanging over.

Maggie: Your friends said that to you?

June: Well, you know, other kids in the band and stuff. And, well, I don't think they're trying to be mean they just, you know, maybe the jeans didn't look as good as I thought …

Dave: This is a difficulty and a concern for many of you. When you're at school or with your friends, you want to look your best, and you want to fit in.

Amber: I feel left out, um, before softball practice and games when we have to change in the locker rooms, sometimes I take my uniform into the bathroom stall; all the other girls change out in the locker room openly and I just don't feel that comfortable doing that.

June: Do they pick on you, like give you a flab grab or anything?

Amber: No, they're pretty nice, um, I just always feel like they're looking at me.

Amelia: Like you know you're different.

Amber: Yeah.

June: Are you the biggest person on the team?

Amber: Yeah.

Amelia: But you're pretty muscular.

Amber: Thanks.

Amelia: You're welcome.

Stage 4. Differentiation: Developing Group Identity and an Internal Frame of Reference

The fourth stage of group development is marked by cohesion and harmony as members come to terms with intimacy and make choices to draw closer to others in the group. In this *performing* stage (Tuckman, 1963), group-centered operations are achieved and a dynamic balance between individual and group needs evolves. Members, who participate in different and complementary ways, experience greater freedom of personal expression and come to feel genuinely accepted and valued as their feelings and ideas are validated by other members of the group. Gradually, the group becomes a mutual-aid system in which members spontaneously give emotional support in proportion to the needs of each individual.

In experiencing this newfound freedom and intimacy, members begin to perceive the group experience as unique. Indeed, as the group creates its own mores and structure, in a sense it becomes its own frame of reference. Customs and traditional ways of operating emerge and the group may adopt a "club" name or insignia that reflects its purpose. The group's energy is channeled into working toward purposes and carrying out tasks that are clearly understood and accepted. New roles—more flexible and functional than those originally envisioned—are developed to support the group's activity, and organizational structures (e.g., officers, dues, attendance expectations, rules) may evolve. Status hierarchies also tend to be less rigid and members may assume leadership roles spontaneously as the need for a particular expertise or ability arises.

By the time the group reaches the differentiation stage, members have accumulated experience in "working through problems" and have gained skill in analyzing their own feelings and the feelings of others, in communicating their needs and positions effectively, in offering support to others, and in grasping the complex interrelationships that have developed in the group. Having become conscious about the group's operations, members bring conflict out into the open and identify obstacles that impede their progress. All decisions are ultimately the unanimous response of the group and are strictly respected. Disagreements are not suppressed or overridden by premature group action; instead, the group carefully considers the positions of any dissenters and attempts to resolve differences and to achieve consensus among members. New entrants serve as catalysts and may express their amazement at the insight shared by veteran members, who in turn become increasingly convinced of the value of the group experience.

Members may now publicize their group meetings among peers, whereas previously membership in the group may have been linked with secret feelings of shame. Secure in their roles and relationships within the group, members may become interested in meeting with other groups or in bringing in outside culture.

Differentiation in the HEART Group

Amber: So you gonna ask him?

Maggie: Ask him what?

June: Like is he just being a user. Using you.

Maggie: You know sometimes, I think he was just curious about stuff and that's sometimes why we maybe hooked up, you know? So maybe he was using me.

Jen: Well, what are you going to do the next time he tries to hook up with you?

Maggie: Smack him. I mean, not really! But I would say no. I'm not gonna…I don't know, maybe I will, 'cuz it's not all that bad. Awkward! Sorry, Dave. It's not all that bad when it happens.

June: I wouldn't know.

Liz: Nah, me neither.

Maggie: Maybe that's all I'm going to get, I don't know.

Dave: All you're going to get as far as the relationship with him, or…

Maggie: With him, or others; if all guys think like that, I should maybe just take what's there.

Amber: That's all I've gotten.

June: Like guys who only want to be with you in private and not in public?

Maggie: That's the guy, that's him!

June: Well, that sucks!

Maggie: It does.

Dave: So, does that sound like something that you want to have in your lives?

June: I don't think so. I mean I'm not in the situation, but if a guy's only going to want to be with me when no one else is around, then he doesn't really value me and he's just using me.

Stage 5. Separation: Breaking Away

During the last, *adjourning*, phase of group development, members begin to separate, loosening the intense bonds often established with other members and with the leader and searching for new resources and ties to satisfy their needs. Group members are likely to experience a broad range of feelings about leaving the group. Indeed, the approach of group termination may set off a number of reactions, the diversity of which is reminiscent of the approach/avoidance maneuvers displayed in stage. Members may again feel anxiety, this time in relation to moving apart and breaking bonds that have been formed. There may be outbursts of anger against the leader and other members at the thought of the group ending, the reappearance of quarrels that were previously settled, and increased dependence on the leader. Denial of the positive meaning of the group experience is not uncommon. These separation reactions may appear in flashes or clusters as members attempt to reconcile their positive feelings about the group with feelings of abandonment, rejection, or apprehension over termination.

EP 2.1.10l

As we will discuss further in Chapter 19, termination is also a time of evaluation, of contemplation of the work achieved, and of consolidation of learning.

It is a time of finishing unfinished business, of getting and giving focused feedback, and of savoring the good times and the close relationships gained in the group.[1] Members who have begun to pull back their group investments and to put more energy into outside interests speak of their fears, hopes, and concerns about the future and about one another. There is often discussion of how to apply what has been learned in the group to other situations and talk of reunions or follow-up meetings (Toseland & Rivas, 2009).

The Leader's Role in the Stages of Group Development

EP 2.1.10g

The leader's role shifts and changes with the evolution of the group. The leader's role is a primary one at the outset of the group in that he or she recruits members and determines the group's purpose, structure, location, and duration, brings structure to the group, plans its content and function, and negotiates reciprocal contracts with each prospective member. As the group gets started, the leader initiates and directs group discussion, encourages participation, and begins blending the individual contracts with members into a mutual group contract. As the group evolves to new levels of connectedness, the leader intentionally

> steps back from the central location and primary role, the members begin to supplant some of what the worker has been doing. In the vernacular of cinematography, the worker fades out as the group system comes up. However, because the group's (internal and external) systems are not yet stabilized at full functioning capacity, the worker needs to let the process run at its own speed and sometimes needs to move back in to help keep the system afloat. This is why the worker's role is referred to as variable, and the worker's location as pivotal. (Henry, 1992, p. 34)

The leader's variable role and pivotal location continue in the group during the conflict/ disequilibrium stage (stage 2). When the group enters its maintenance or working phases (stages 3 and 4), the leader assumes a facilitative role and occupies a peripheral location. Inasmuch as the group has achieved full capacity to govern itself, the leader fulfills a resource role instead of a central role. As the group moves into its separation or termination phase (stage 5), the leader once again returns to a primary role and central location to support the divesting of members, who are launching their own independent journeys. The leader aids the group in working through any regression to earlier stages of development to assure the successful ending of the group.

Interventions throughout the Life of the Group

EP 2.1.10g

While the leader's role ebbs and flows over the lifespan of the group, he or she must be prepared to employ interventions to deal with overarching issues whenever they occur. These include:

- *Fostering cohesion*
- *Addressing group norms*
- *Intervening with members' roles*
- *Attending to subgroup structure*
- *Purposefully using the leadership role*
- *Attending to group and individual processes*

Fostering Cohesion

Cohesion plays a central role in group success and leadership is essential in developing this positive force. The leader forges connections among group members and tries to expand the interpersonal networks of subgroup members so that they relate to a broader range of people in the group. Further, the leader encourages cohesive behaviors by "pointing out who is present and who is absent, by making reference to 'we' and 'us' and 'our' and by including the group as a whole in his or her remarks in group sessions" (Henry, 1992, p. 167).

Leaders also encourage the development of cohesion by commenting on and reinforcing positive group-building behaviors as they occur, for example, when participants inquire about missing members, return to the group after absences or conflicts, take others' opinions into account in decision making, and seek increased responsibility for the group's operations.

Leaders also increase the attractiveness and cohesion in groups by facilitating high levels of interaction, by aiding members to successfully achieve goals, fulfill expectations, and meet needs, and by providing opportunities for prestige and access to rewards and resources that individual members alone could not obtain (Toseland & Rivas, 2009).

Ironically, these efforts at developing cohesion must be restrained as groups wind down.

For example, instead of increasing the frequency with which members have contact with one another, this may be reduced by having meetings less often and/or for a shorter time.... The worker may place less emphasis on resolving conflicts within the group and may not call attention to commonalities of experiences or attitudes except as those relate to ways of coping with termination. (Garvin, 1987, p. 222)

Addressing Group Norms

Chapter 11 introduced strategies to facilitate the development of constructive group norms. However, counterproductive norms may also emerge. For example, the group may split into several self-serving factions or subgroups that compete for control. Members may develop a habit of socializing rather than focusing on legitimate group tasks. Some participants may repeatedly cast others as scapegoats, harassing those members and blaming them for various group ills. In these and countless other ways, groups may develop negative behaviors that undermine their ability to coalesce and aid each other in reaching their goals.

As described in Chapter 11, leaders must observe evolving group behavior and determine whether these emerging patterns undermine or support the group's purposes. Once leaders have determined the impact of emerging patterns, they may then intervene to nurture functional group behaviors and to assist participants to modify behaviors that are destructive to individuals or to the group.

The facilitator sets the stage for a therapeutic atmosphere and a "working group" by establishing an explicit contract with members in initial sessions that includes normative guideposts for the group. Along the way, the leader helps the group identify and articulate norms they wish the group to follow. Once decided, the guidelines should be recorded and revisited regularly and the leader should take an active role in helping members consistently adhere to them. Some groups will even list them on a board that is posted in the meeting room, or on a laminated page for members' workbooks. Sample guidelines follow:

EP 2.1.10j

- Make group decisions by consensus.
- Personalize communications by using "I statements" (e.g., "I (think) (feel) (want) ...").
- Keep the group's focus on its task and mission.
- Turn off cell phones and PDAs.
- Keep discussions focused primarily on the present or future rather than the past.
- Avoid "gossiping."
- Share the "airtime" so all members can participate.
- Take responsibility for concerns about how the group is going by bringing them to others' attention.

Norm Setting in the HEART Group

Dave: June, to come back to a point that you mentioned before, there is a guideline that I like, which is to encourage people to participate. Because a good group is one where everyone contributes and so I wonder the best way to say that—do the best you can, or ...

June: Don't talk twice till everybody's talked once?

Dave: Well, I ...

Liz: I disagree.

June: I'm just putting it out there. I don't know.

Dave: Liz, let's hear why you disagree.

Liz: Sometimes I'm just not in ... I just don't want to contribute, I don't feel like talking.

Dave: And it might be too structured, then June, to say to Liz "we've all talked once and now you have to go." It might make the group unsafe for Liz, for the rule to be so measured out like that.

June: So I don't know what the rule should be.

Amelia: How about we all, like, try our best to actively participate.

Maggie: But don't call me out.

Jen: And actively participate doesn't necessarily mean talking, just paying attention.

Dave: That's a good point, Jen.

June: No sleeping in the group.

Maggie: Yeah, stay awake.

Amelia: If I'm talking about, like, pouring out my soul, and you're over there, like clearly thinking about something else or doodling or, you know, thinking about whatever, like, it shows on your face. You know what I mean guys?

Dave: And that's probably covered by one of the rules we already mentioned, which is "Be respectful." So "no sleeping" June, I think, comes under be respectful.

June: Okay.

Dave: And, Amelia, I like the idea of encouraging participation—what did you say? "Try as hard as we can ... Do our best"?

Amelia: Do our best to participate actively.

Dave: How does everybody feel about that? [Agreement].

In addition to generating structural guidelines that pave the way for the adoption of therapeutic norms, leaders may aid members in adopting the following personal guidelines, adapted from Corey and Corey (2006):

- *Help establish trust. Initiate discussions of personal issues rather than waiting for someone else to make the first move.*
- *Express persistent feelings. Rather than bury feelings of boredom, anger, or disappointment, share your feelings about the group process.*
- *Decide how much to disclose. You are in charge of what, how much, and when you share personal issues.*
- *Be an active participant, not an observer. Share reactions to what others are saying in the group rather than remaining an unknown entity.*
- *Listen closely and discriminately. Do not accept others' feedback wholesale or reject it outright, but decide for yourself what does and does not apply to you.*
- *Pay attention to consistent feedback. If a message has been received from a variety of sources, it may be valid.*
- *Focus on self. Talk about your role in problems; avoid blaming and focusing on extraneous situations or people outside of the group.*

The leader often intervenes to remind people of these individual-level norms or to point out when they are being violated. In established groups, members will also speak up to hold one another accountable. Eventually, the locus of control for enforcing individual and group norms should reside with the members rather than with the leader (Carrell, 2000).

Intervening with Members' Roles

Roles are closely related to norms, as Toseland and Rivas (2009) explain:

> *Whereas norms are shared expectations held, to some extent, by everyone in the group, roles are shared expectations about the functions of individuals in the group. Unlike norms, which define behavior in a wide range of situations, roles define behavior in relation to a specific function or task that the group member is expected to perform. (p. 68)*

Within the group, roles include formal positions (e.g., chairperson or secretary) and informal positions created through group interactions (e.g., mediator, clown, rebel, initiator, or scapegoat). Like norms, roles may help fulfill group functions or meet individual treatment aims. Leaders must be attuned to the development of counter-therapeutic roles and address them as they arise. For example, a member who avoids conflict or intimacy might make jokes to keep discussion at a superficial level, or a member who struggles to be taken seriously may make distracting or ridiculous comments, thereby reinforcing this destructive role. Yalom discusses the effect of "the monopolist" (1995, p. 369), who, perhaps due to anxiety, talks excessively, taking up airtime and turning the group mood into one of frustration.

The key, when facing counterproductive roles, is to encourage members to be self-observant, assure that they do not become locked into dysfunctional roles, and empower other participants to confront the member about the role and its impact. As Garvin notes:

EP 2.1.10j

> *The "clown" may wish to behave more seriously, the "mediator" to take sides, and passive people to function assertively. The worker, being cognizant of roles that are created out of group interactions, will attend to those that impede either the attainment of individual goals or the creation of an effective group. (1986, p. 112)*

Dysfunctional role performance is a critical choice point for intervention. One means of intervening is to use a technique developed by Garvin (1986) to identify informal roles occupied by group participants. Leaders administer a questionnaire asking members to "vote" on who (if anyone) fulfills group roles such as referee, expert, humorist, nurturer, spokesperson, and "devil's advocate." The discussion that results from this exercise can powerfully influence both members' awareness and the group process. Another technique is to simply describe a specific role that a member seems to have assumed and to ask that member for observations regarding the accuracy of that assessment. Preface this observation by asking the member if he or she would like group feedback. Doing so reduces defensiveness and gives the member appropriate control over the situation.

Another aspect of role performance involves aiding members in role attainment—that is, enabling them to fulfill the requirements of roles that they aspire to or are already in, such as student, parent, leader, spouse, employee, friend, or retired person. In doing so, the leader helps members assess their own interactions, practice the skills needed for their roles, and apply new ways of approaching and enacting those roles. Groups can assist members in these tasks through role-playing, giving feedback, and sharing personal examples. Some groups may be designed to specifically address the development of social skills (LeCroy, 2002). Chapter 13 offers further examples of change through behavioral rehearsal and skill development.

Attending to Subgroup Structure

As introduced in Chapter 11, subgroups inevitably emerge and exist in groups, both hindering and enhancing group process. Negative subgroups, like cliques, can raise issues of loyalty and exclusion in the group, challenge the leader's authority, and fragment communication as members of a subgroup talk among themselves and divert their energies from the whole group to the subset. The leader can modify the impact of such subgroups by taking these steps:

1. Initiating discussion of the reasons for the formation of the dissident subgroups and their impact on the group as a whole. This discussion may reveal the difficulties that the cliques create for goal setting, communication, interaction, and decision making.
2. Neutralizing the effects of negative subgroups through programming or structuring. The leader, for example, might challenge dissident subgroups to work toward a common goal, change seating arrangements, use a "round robin" approach to get feedback from all members, assign members from different subgroups to work on common group tasks, or use programming materials or exercises to separate subgroup members (Carrell, 2000).
3. Creating safe positions or roles for marginal members of the group that require minimal activity but at the same time involves them in a group activity (Balgopal & Vassil, 1983).
4. Helping powerful subgroups or individuals to relinquish power or to use it sparingly in the interest of other members. This may be accomplished by encouraging concern for others in the group and by enabling members to grasp the possibility that domination of others might be destructive to themselves (Garvin, 1987).
5. Appointing powerless members to roles that carry power, such as arranging for group activities, securing resources for the group, or fulfilling significant roles (e.g., observer, chairperson, or secretary).
6. Finding means to "connect" with dissident subgroups and to demonstrate a concern for their desires (Garvin, 1987).
7. Providing ways for subgroups to attain legitimate power by creating useful roles and tasks in the group.

Purposefully Using the Leadership Role

The leader's role in a group can be described as a set of behaviors that facilitate the attainment of group and individual goals and ensure the maintenance of the group. Ultimately, the leader "puts him/herself out of business" by gradually distributing leadership functions to members as the group matures, while continuing to attend to the work of the group (Rose, 1989, p. 260).

Helping members to assume leadership behaviors is important for three reasons. First, members develop vital skills that they can transfer to other social groups, where leadership is usually highly valued. Second, the more that members exercise leadership, the more likely they are to become invested in the group. Third, performance of leadership activities enhances the perceived power or self-efficacy of members, who often experience powerlessness in a wide array of social situations (Rose, 1989).

EP 2.1.10a

Leaders may expedite the distribution of power by taking four steps (Shulman, 1984):

1. Encouraging member-to-member rather than member-to-leader communications
2. Asking for members' input into the agenda for the meeting and the direction the group should take in future meetings
3. Supporting indigenous leadership when members make their first tentative attempts at exerting their own influence on the group
4. Encouraging attempts at mutual sharing and mutual aid among group members during the first meeting

Group leadership problems occur when individuals or vying subgroups attempt to usurp the reins of power. Challenges to leadership (or lack of it) are, in fact, an inherent part of the group's struggle over control, division of responsibility, and decision making (Corey & Corey, 2006). It is important not to interpret these efforts as negative because they may actually help the group succeed by calling attention to issues or roles that are important to individual members (Hurley, 1984). Examples of messages that illustrate control issues follow:

- *I don't want to talk just because you want me to talk. I learn just as much by listening and observing.*

- *There are several people in here who always get the attention. No matter what I do, I just don't seem to get recognized, especially by the leaders.*
- *You should pay more attention to Paul. He's been crying several times, and you haven't been taking care of him.*

EP 2.1.10g

The facilitator might respond to such a challenge by empathically exploring the statement, thanking the member for speaking up, eliciting feedback from other members regarding leadership style, and asking nondefensively for input (e.g., "Thanks for calling my attention to that. How could I handle it differently?"). Corey and Corey (2006) also recommend responding authentically. They note that leaders must be self-aware when challenged and avoid focusing on "problem members" or difficult situations, rather than on how they are affected personally when group processes go awry:

> Typically, leaders have a range of feelings: being threatened by what they perceive as a challenge to their leadership role; anger over the members' lack of cooperation and enthusiasm; feelings of inadequacy to the point of wondering if they are qualified to lead groups; resentment toward several of the members, whom they label as some type of problem; and anxiety over the slow pace of the group, with a desire to stir things up so that there is some action. (Corey & Corey, 1992, p. 155)

By ignoring their reactions, leaders leave themselves out of the interactions that occur in the group. Instead, Corey and Corey (1992) urge leaders to model:

> a "direct" style of dealing with conflict and resistance.... Your own thoughts, feelings and observations can be the most powerful resource you have in dealing with defensive behavior. When you share what you are feeling and thinking about what is going on in the group—in such a way as not to blame and criticize the members for deficiencies—you are letting the members experience an honest and constructive interaction with you. (p. 155)

By consistently responding authentically, even when challenged or under attack, the leader encourages the group to adopt this mode of representing self—one that is vital to members dealing effectively with the inevitable differences they encounter among themselves.

Attending to Group and Individual Processes

Like interventions with families, group work requires the practitioner to attend to multiple sources of data in each meeting. While the content that is shared in group is important, so are the processes observed among members. As with families, leaders must attend to the messages demonstrated by each individual member and the process of the group as a whole. To do this, the worker reads body language, positioning in the room, who speaks, when, how much, and with what tone, the reactions of other participants when particular members are speaking and the general tone, mood, or energy of the group. Is the group buoyant? Flat? Angry? Distractible? Is Hal unusually sullen? Does everyone "tune out" when Evelyn speaks? Does Crystal seem fidgety and eager to speak but unable to get the group's attention?

Once processes are observed, the worker will intervene in different ways depending on how these processes are enhancing achievement of group and individual goals and what phase of work the group is in. For instance, the worker might remark on collective impressions: "Today's group seems to have pretty low energy" or "It seems that you're having an especially hard time getting down to business today" or "I wonder what's happening. I'm sensing a lot of anger at this point." Comments may also reflect observations about individual behavior: "When Evelyn speaks the rest of you seem to disengage" or the worker may invite comment or involvement: "Has anyone else noticed that?" "What might be going on with you when that happens?" "Crystal, I notice we haven't heard from you." In more developed groups the members themselves may observe, comment on, and regulate process. In those cases the facilitator can comment upon those processes. "I like the way the group helped Evelyn give her input without getting impatient or checking out."

Stage-Specific Interventions

As previously mentioned, a leader's role must always be pursued within the framework of the group's stages of development. Thomas and Caplan (1999) suggest a wheel metaphor for leadership. That is, the leader takes a particularly active role in getting the "wheel spinning," then gradually provides a "lighter touch," and finally reduces that role as the group gathers its own momentum, while still standing by to assure that events or digressions don't throw the wheel off track.

EP 2.1.7a

Table 16-1 illustrates the evolution of the leader's focus as a group advances through the various stages of development. Information contained in the table comes from a variety of sources, including Garland, Jones, and Kolodny (1965), Rose (1989), Henry (1992), and Corey and Corey (2006).

Interventions in the Preaffiliation Stage

Chapter 11 describes how pre-group individual interviews serve as orientation for potential members of the

TABLE-16-1 STAGES, DYNAMICS, AND LEADER FOCUS

STAGE	DYNAMICS	LEADER FOCUS
Preaffiliation	Arm's-length exploration Approach/avoidance Issues of trust, preliminary commitment Intellectualization of problems Interaction based on superficial attributes or experiences Protection of self; low-risk behavior Milling around Sizing up of leader and other members Formulation of individual and group goals Leader viewed as responsible for group Member evaluation as to whether group is safe and meets needs Fear of self-disclosure, rejection Uncertainty regarding group purpose Little commitment to goals or group	Observes and assesses Clarifies group objectives Establishes group guidelines Encourages development of personal goals Clarifies aspirations and expectations of members Encourages discussion of fears, ambivalence Gently invites trust Gives support; allows distance Facilitates exploration Provides group structure Contracts for help-seeking, help-giving roles Facilitates linkages among members Models careful listening Focuses on resistance Assures opportunities for participation
Power and control	Rebellion; power struggles Political alignments forged to increase power Issues of status, ranking, and influence Complaints regarding group structure, process Challenges to leader's roles Emergence of informal leadership, factional leaders Individual autonomy; everybody for himself/herself Dysfunctional group roles Normative and membership crisis; drop-out danger high Testing of leader; other group members Dependence on leader Group experimentation in managing own affairs Program breakdown at times; low planning Feedback highly critical	Protects safety of individuals and property Clarifies power struggle Turns issues back to group Encourages expression and acceptance of differences Facilitates clear, direct, nonabrasive communication Examines nonproductive group processes Examines cognitive distortions Facilitates member evaluation of dissident subgroups Holds group accountable for decision by consensus Clarifies that conflict, power struggles are normal Encourages norms consistent with therapeutic group Consistently acknowledges strengths, accomplishments Nondefensively deals with challenges to leadership Focuses on the "here and now"
Intimacy	Intensified personal involvement Sharing of self, materials Striving to meet others' needs Awareness of significance of the group experience Personality growth and change Mutual revelation, risk taking Beginning commitment to decision by consensus Beginning work on cognitive restructuring Importance of goals verbalized Growing ability to govern group independently Dissipation of emotional turmoil Member initiation of topics Constructive feedback	Encourages leadership Assumes flexible role as group vacillates Aids sharper focus on individual goals Encourages deeper-level exploration, feedback Encourages acknowledgment, support of differences Guides work of group Encourages experimentation with different roles Encourages use of new skills inside and outside group Assists members to assume responsibility for change Gives consistent feedback regarding successes Reduces own activity

Differentiation	Here-and-now focus High level of trust, cohesion Free expression of feelings Mutual aid Full acceptance of differences Group viewed as unique Clarity of group purpose Feelings of security, belonging, "we" spirit Differentiated roles Group self-directed Intensive work on cognitions Goal-oriented behavior Work outside of group to achieve personal goals Members feel empowered Communication open, spontaneous Self-confrontation		Emphasizes achievement of goals, exchange of skills Supports group's self-governance Promotes behaviors that increase cohesion Provides balance between support, confrontation Encourages conversion of insight into action Interprets; explores common themes Universalizes themes Encourages deeper-level exploration of problems Assures review of goals, task completion Stimulates individual and group growth Supports application of new behaviors outside group
Separation	Review and evaluation Development of outlets outside group Stabilizing and generalizing Projecting toward future Recognition of personal, interpersonal growth Sadness and anxiety over reality of separation Expression of fears, hopes, and others' anxiety for self Some denial, regression Moving apart, distancing Less intense interaction Plans as to how to continue progress outside group Talk of reunions, follow-up		Prepares for letting go Facilitates evaluation and feelings about termination Reviews individual and group progress Redirects energy of individuals away from group and toward self-process Enables individuals to disconnect Encourages resolution of unfinished business Reinforces changes made by individuals Administers evaluation instruments

© Cengage Learning 2013

group. In initial sessions the leader can prepare members for the experiences to come by explaining the basics of group process—for example, the stages of development through which the group will pass, ways to create a therapeutic working environment, behaviors and attitudes characteristic of an effective group, the importance of establishing and adhering to guidelines that lend structure and purpose to the group, and the importance of committing to "win-win" decisions regarding group matters. Research, in fact, suggests that direct instruction or teaching regarding group processes tends to facilitate a group's development during its early stages (Corey & Corey, 2006; Dies, 1983).

EP 2.1.10i

Leaders must also intervene to address the initial concerns of members. In early sessions, members will probably be tentative about expressing what they hope to get from the group. Most also experience fear and apprehension regarding the group experience. They worry about many things: how they will be perceived by other members, whether they will be pressured to talk, whether they will be misunderstood or look foolish, whether they will be at risk of verbal attack, and whether they want to go through a change process at all. The leader may address and allay these anxieties by acknowledging the presence of mixed feelings or by asking all members to share their feelings about coming to the initial group session. For example, the leader might ask members to rate their feelings about being present in the group at that moment on a scale of 1 to 10, where 1 represents "I don't want to be here" and 10 represents "I'm completely at ease with being in the group." The leader could then invite discussion about reasons behind the various scores.

In focusing on members' fears, leaders need to draw out all members' feelings and reactions, validate the importance of their fully disclosing feelings, and emphasize the need for the group to be a safe place in which such issues can be expressed openly. Finally, leaders should elicit suggestions for a group structure that will address member fears, out of which may flow the formulation of relevant group guidelines.

Leaders can measure the progress of a new group in addressing initial member concerns by administering a questionnaire developed by Rose (1989). This instrument contains items to which members can respond by circling a point on a scale. Examples of items include the following:

- *How useful was today's session for you?*
- *Describe your involvement in today's session.*
- *Rate the extent of your self-disclosure of relevant information about yourself or your problem.*
- *How important to you were the problems or situations you discussed (or others discussed) in the group today?*
- *Circle all the words that best describe you at today's session (e.g., excited, bored, depressed, interested, comfortable).*
- *How satisfied were you with today's session?*

In initial sessions, facilitators must repeatedly review basic information regarding the group's purpose, the manner in which the group will be conducted, and its ground rules. While this information should be familiar to members, reiteration is necessary because initial anxiety may affect participants' ability to really digest the details. Assuring that all members are "on the same page" helps to prevent these issues from erupting later in the life of the group.

EP 2.1.10i

In preliminary interviews, members contract with the leader for general goals they would like to achieve. In the initial group sessions, the leader must then blend these individual goals with the group's collective goals. Along the way, the binding contract expands from a reciprocal one between leader and individuals to a mutual contract between individuals and group. In the first meeting, the leader engages members in a discussion about the ways the group can help each person's initial objectives to be addressed. Henry (1992) utilizes a "Goal Questionnaire" to facilitate formulation of the mutual contract. On this questionnaire are two questions to which members respond in writing:

1. Why do you think all of you are here together?
2. What are you going to try to accomplish together?

Discussion of responses gives the group a beginning point from which to proceed.

In the contractual process of initial sessions, leaders also aid members to refine their general goals. An example from the HEART group illustrates the role of the leader in seeking concreteness to clarify global goals:

Seeking Concreteness in the Forming Stage

Dave: At our last session, I asked each of you to share what you'd like to get out of the group individually. I'd like to take some of our time today to think of group goals. What would you like to accomplish together?

Amelia: To lose weight.

Dave: I hope that happens for all of you, and that the group is a source of support to you in pursuing your weight loss goals; but losing weight is more of an individual goal.

Liz: Follow the group rules?

Dave: Tell us more …

Liz: Well, like, respect each other and actively participate.

Dave: Following the group guidelines will help you to reach your group goals, but …

Amber: I'd like to know how other people deal with the stuff I go through.

June: Yeah, like how to keep your mom off your back!

Dave: Okay, good. It sounds like a group goal is for you all to share experiences. Are there any others?

Amelia: Sometimes I just want somebody to listen, you know? I don't know, I know I shouldn't be eating so much, but then I do, and it makes me feel bad. I thought it would help to be around other people who, like, might know how I'm feeling.

Jen: Yeah, I thought that too.

Dave: So far, I've heard two suggestions for group goals. One is to share experiences and the other, which Amelia just mentioned, is to listen to each other and support one another, especially when it comes to feeling sad or worried.

The leader also keeps accomplishment of goals at the forefront of the group's work. Through bibliotherapy, journaling, and mindfulness, members can read, write, and reflect on the themes they are addressing and the insights they have achieved during and between group sessions (Corey, 2006). Session time may be allocated for discussing these insights, thereby reinforcing the value of continuing work between sessions.

Paying attention to the way each session opens and concludes is important for maximizing member productivity and satisfaction. Corey and Corey (2006) encourage leaders to draw from the following procedures in opening meetings:

1. Give members a brief opportunity to say what they want from the upcoming session.

2. Invite members to share their accomplishments since the last session.
3. Elicit feedback regarding the group's last session and give any reflections you have of the session.

To bring meetings to a close, Corey and Corey (2006) emphasize the need to summarize and integrate the group experience by following these procedures:

1. Ask members what it was like for them to be in the group today.
2. Invite members to identify briefly what they're learning about themselves through their experience in the group. Are they getting what they want? If not, what would they be willing to do to get it?
3. Ask members whether there are any topics, questions, or problems they would like to explore in the next session.
4. Ask members to indicate what they would be willing to do outside of the session to practice new skills.

Incorporating group rituals into the structure of sessions increases the continuity that flows from meeting to meeting. Examples include check-in as a ritual to start each session, structured refreshment breaks, and closing meditations or readings (Subramian, Hernandez, & Martinez, 1995). Such continuity heightens the transfer of insights and new behaviors from the group session into daily life.

Interventions in the Power and Control Stage

In stage 2 of group development, the group enters a period in which its dynamics, tone, and atmosphere are often conflict-ridden, and some groups may need encouragement to address underlying conflicts that threaten the health of the group (Schiller, 1997). Groups may be beset by problems in dealing with divisions among individuals and subgroups, complaints and unrest over group goals, processes, and structure, and challenges to leadership. At the same time, the group is trying out its capacity to manage its own affairs. The leader is responsible for guiding the group through this stormy period so that it remains intact and demonstrates an emerging capacity to cope with individual differences and to manage its own governance. Leaders can employ several strategies in carrying out this responsibility: minimize changes, encourage balanced feedback, increase effective communication, and develop therapeutic group norms.

EP 2.1.10a

Minimize Changes

During the "power and control" stage, groups with a closed format are particularly susceptible to inner and outer stressors such as a change of leader, a move to a new meeting place, the addition or loss of members, or a change in the meeting time. Traumatic events such as a runaway, a death, an incidence of physical violence in an institutional setting, or acutely disturbing political or natural events at the community or national level may also significantly affect a group at this stage.

Although such changes or events can be upsetting to a group at any stage of development, they are particularly difficult to manage in stage 2. At this point, members have not yet become invested in the group to an appreciable extent and thus may become easily distracted or disenchanted. Adding new members or changing the group's leader is particularly stressful, causing members to raise their defenses because there are risks involved in revealing themselves when either the leader or a member is an unknown entity. The loss of a leader can also prove inordinately traumatic to members who have difficulty investing in relationships, affirming their stance that trusting others just brings disappointment.

In addition, making a significant change in the group structure without group involvement may cause members to conclude that the leader or agency disregards the impact of such decisions on the group and that the members' input is not important. Although changes are sometimes unavoidable, it behooves leaders to keep them to a minimum, to prepare members in advance whenever possible, and to aid them to "work through" their feelings when change is necessary.

Encourage Balanced Feedback

In stage 2 of group development, leaders must ensure that feedback is balanced. As they observe that group members are tentatively moving into their first authentic encounters, leaders should intervene in negative interactions to draw the group's attention to the need to provide balanced feedback. They thus remind members of the provision in the contract for focusing on positives as well as negatives. The following excerpt from an early group session with adult members illustrates this point.

Gary [to Wayne, in irritated voice]: Why do you keep grilling me with questions like that? I feel like I'm being interrogated.

Wayne: I didn't know I was coming across like that. Frankly, I just wanted to get to know you better.

Leader [to Wayne]: You said in the first session that you'd like to use the group as a way of getting feedback about how you come across to others. I'm wondering if this might be a time for that?

Wayne: Yeah. I don't know what's coming, but I really think I do need to know more about how you all see me. I was really surprised at what Gary said.

Leader [to Wayne]: Good. I can understand you may have reservations, but I'm also pleased that you're willing to take a risk this early in the group. *Leader [To group]* Because this is the group's first experience in giving feedback to members, I'd like to remind you of the contract not only to help members identify problems but also to share positive observations you may have. As you do so, I'd like you to personalize your statements. I'll help you do so.

EP 2.1.10g

Group members' first experiences in giving feedback to one another are crucial in setting the tone for all that follows in the group. By guiding members' first cautious efforts to drop their facades and to engage at an intimate level, the leader enables the group to experience success and incorporate attention to positives as a part of its character. As individuals come to trust that the group will attend to positives as well as negatives, they will often increase their level of participation and take the initiative in soliciting group feedback.

In addition to encouraging positive feedback for individuals, leaders can reinforce behaviors observed during a session that have helped the group accomplish its tasks. Such behaviors may include being willing to participate in discussions, to answer questions, and to risk revealing oneself, showing support to others, speaking in turn, giving full attention to the task at hand, accepting differing values, beliefs, and opinions, and recognizing significant individual and group breakthroughs. The leader can also highlight the absence of destructive behaviors that might have occurred earlier (e.g., whispering, fidgeting, introducing tangential topics, dominating, or verbally and physically pestering other members).

In addition, the leader must assist members to hear, acknowledge, and accept positive feedback, as illustrated in the following example:

Kim [to Pat]: I know you get discouraged sometimes, but I admire the fact you can manage four children by yourself and still work. I don't think I could ever manage that in a million years.

Pat: I don't always manage it. Actually, I don't do near enough for my children.

Leader: I hear you saying, Pat, that you feel inadequate as a mother—and I'll ask you in a moment whether you'd like to return to those feelings—but right now would you reflect on what you just did?

Pat: I guess I blew off Kim's compliment. I didn't feel I deserved it.

Leader: I wonder if others of you have responded in a similar way when someone has told you something positive.

The last response broadens the focus to include the experience of other group members, which may lead into a discussion of the difficulties that others might encounter in accepting and internalizing positive feedback. The leader may also wish to help individuals or the entire group to identify dysfunctional cognitive patterns that underlie their discomfort in receiving positive messages (e.g., "I have to do things perfectly" or "If they knew me better, they'd realize I'm no good"). Identifying the disconfirming cognitions represents a first step toward replacing them with more accepting messages ("I do a good job considering all I have responsibility for" or "My group sees another side of me that I don't let myself acknowledge").

Increase Effective Communication

Achieving success during the "power and control" phase requires moment-by-moment interventions to increase the chances of effective communication. Facets of communication that enable members to relate effectively as a group include taking turns in talking, learning how to explore problems before offering solutions, speaking for themselves rather than for others, and speaking directly to the person for whom the message is intended. In addition, members can learn to distinguish between effective and ineffective ways of responding and can include improving their communication repertoire as one of their individual goals for work.

Leaders increase the probability that members will adopt effective communication skills by heavily utilizing and modeling these skills themselves. In addition, leaders aid the acquisition of skills by assuming the role of "coach" and intervening to shape the display of communications in the group, as illustrated in the following examples:

EP 2.1.10l

- [Eliminating negative communications] *"I'd like us to shy away from labeling, judging sarcasm, and words like 'always' and 'never.' As we discussed in our group contract, try to give self-reports rather than indirect messages that put down or judge another person."*

- [Personalizing messages] *"That was an example of a 'you message'. I'd like you to try again, this time by starting out with the pronoun 'I.' Try to identify your feelings, or what you want or need."*
- [Talking in turn] *"Right now, several of you are speaking at the same time. Try to hold to the guideline that we all speak in turn. Your observations are too important to miss."*
- [Speaking directly to each other] *"Right now, you're speaking to the group, but I think your message is meant for Fred. If so, then it would be better to talk directly to him."*
- [Exploratory questions] *"Switching from closed- to open-ended questions right now could help Liz to tell her story in her own way." (The leader explains the difference between these two modes of questioning.)*
- [Listening] *"Try to really hear what she's saying. Help her to let out her feelings and to get to the source of the problem."*
- [Problem exploration versus problem solving] *"When the group offers advice too quickly, folks can't share their deeper-level feelings or reveal a problem in its entirety. We may need to allow Richard five to ten minutes to share his concerns before the group offers any observations. The timing of advice is critical as we try to help members share and solve problems."*
- [Authenticity] *"Could you take a risk and tell the group what you're feeling at this very moment? I can see you choking up, and I think it would be good for the group to know what you're experiencing."*
- [Requesting] *"You've just made a complaint about the group. On the flip side of any complaint is a request. Tell the group what would help. Make a request."*

Intervening moment by moment to shape the communications of members, as in the instances illustrated here, increases the therapeutic potential of a group.

Stage 2 of group development may also present a challenge when the group has co-leadership. The presence of two leaders may increase members' defensiveness as they seek to erect boundaries that protect them from the influence presented by two leaders. Members may also attempt to split the leaders by exploiting disagreements or differences between them or by affiliating with one leader and working against the other. Clarity of purpose, preparation for these maneuvers, and strong communication can help co-leaders resist these efforts when they emerge (Nosko & Wallace, 1997).

Create Constructive Norms

As mentioned earlier, leaders must be concerned about the nature of the norms that evolve in the group. Many of the group patterns form in the "power and control" stage. The leader can intervene then to shape the power structure, the stylistic communications of the group, and the ways in which the group chooses to negotiate and solve problems.

In shaping the group's norms, leaders need to intervene, for example, in the following instances:

- When socializing or distracting behavior substantially interferes with the group's task
- When one or more members monopolize the group's airtime
- When one or more members are "out of step" with the group process and/or experience strong feelings such as hurt, anger, disgust, disappointment, or disapproval
- When several members or the entire group begin to talk about one member
- When a member's behavior is incompatible with the governing guidelines set by the group
- When participants intellectualize about emotion-laden material
- When one or more members display hostility through jokes, sarcasm, or criticism, or when they interrogate, scapegoat, or gang up on a single member
- When the group offers advice or suggestions without first encouraging a member to fully explore a problem
- When there is silence or withdrawal by one or more members or the group itself seems to be "shut down"
- When a member adopts a "co-leader" role.

When problems such as these emerge, the leader must focus the group's attention on what is occurring in the "here and now." Leaders may simply document what they see by describing specific behaviors or the progression of events that have occurred and then request group input. Once the group focuses on the problem, the leader should facilitate discussion and problem solving rather than take decisive action on his or her own. Ultimately, the responsibility for resolution needs to rest with the group.

EP 2.1.10j

In regard to turning issues back to the group, Henry (1992) notes:

When the members are vying for ownership of the group, the wisest intervention for the worker is to join their struggle and to put issues and decisions back to them. The worker does not wholly give up her or his power, but holds back from what previously been a more directive and active performance. (p. 148)

However, as Henry (1992) advises, when a particularly conflict-filled episode occurs, leaders need to intervene to process what has happened. In such instances, leaders do not simply turn issues back to the group but opt, in the interest of closure and resolution, to "clarify what information people carry away from the confrontation, and to see what level of discomfort people are experiencing" (p. 151).

Although leaders need to avoid reaching premature closure on heated issues in a group, they must intervene immediately to refocus the process when group members criticize, label, or "cut down" others, or when they argue among themselves. Leaders may assume—incorrectly—that letting members verbally "fight it out" when they have conflicts is cathartic or helpful. In fact, ample research indicates that aggression begets aggression and that not intervening in conflict merely encourages members to continue venting their anger in the same fashion. A leader's passive stance could allow conflict to escalate to the point that it turns into harmful verbal or physical altercations. In instances of serious disruption, a leader's lack of intervention may "prove" to members who are scrutinizing the leader's behavior that it is dangerous to take risks in the group because the leader will not protect them (Smokowski, Rose, & Bacallao, 2001). Leaders must be willing to respond decisively when significant group disruption occurs, using physical and verbal measures as needed, such as clapping their hands loudly, standing up, speaking louder than group members, or putting themselves between members who are arguing.

EP 2.1.10g & 2.1.10i

Interventions should generally focus on group-related matters (rather than on individual attitudes or behaviors) because it is rare that the destructive or self-defeating behavior of an individual or subset will not affect the entire system. In fact, some problematic behaviors may be fostered or reinforced by the group as a whole. Focusing interventions on a pair, a trio, a foursome, or the group also avoids singling out one person or inadvertently "siding" with one segment of clients over others.

Consider, for instance, the following leader intervention in an adolescent group: "Mark and Jeannie, you're whispering again and interrupting the group. We need your attention." This message places the responsibility for the distracting behavior solely upon the two members and does not take into account what is happening with the group. In this instance, the leader's message is more likely to reinforce negative behavior than to encourage positive change for the following reasons:

- *It may polarize the group by aligning the leader with members who are irritated by this behavior ("the good guys") and against the two offending members ("the bad guys").*
- *The leader's solution ("We need your attention") circumvents group handling or problem solving of the matter.*
- *The leader's blunt intervention fails to attend to the message inherent in the problem behavior: "This group does not meet our needs at the moment."In fact, this view may be shared but not expressed by other members.*

A guideline to formulating interventions that confront dysfunctional behavior is that the behavior must be analyzed in the context of the group process, with the leader considering how such behavior affects and is affected by group members. This approach is illustrated by the following response to the same situation:

EP 2.1.10g

Leader: I'm concerned about what is happening right now. Several of you are not participating; some of you are whispering; one of you is writing notes; a few of you are involved in the discussion. As individuals, you appear to be at different places with the group, and I'd like to check out what each of you is experiencing right now.

This message focuses on all group members, neutrally describes behavior that is occurring, and encourages the group process. By not imposing a solution on the group, the leader assumes a facilitative rather than an authoritarian role and sets the stage for productive group discussion.

Interventions in the Intimacy and Differentiation Stages

Stages 3 ("intimacy") and 4 ("differentiation") of group development constitute the group's working phase. In the initial stages of a group's evolution, the critical issues at stake focused on trust versus mistrust, the struggle for power, and self-focus versus focus on others. In the working phase, however, issues shift to those of disclosure versus anonymity, honesty versus game playing, spontaneity versus control, acceptance versus rejection, cohesion versus fragmentation, and responsibility versus blaming (Corey & Corey, 2006).

EP 2.1.10a

In the working phase, leaders continue to promote conditions that aid members to make healthy choices in resolving issues by straightforwardly addressing and resolving conflict, openly disclosing personal problems, taking responsibility for their problems, and making pro-group choices. Thanks to the relaxed stance that characterizes this phase, leaders have more opportunities to intensify therapeutic group conditions. They may focus on refining feedback processes—for example, coaching members to give immediate feedback, to make such feedback specific rather than global, to render feedback in nonjudgmental ways, and to give feedback regarding strengths as well as problem behaviors (Corey & Corey, 2006).

Leaders can also enhance individual and group growth by focusing on the universality of underlying issues, feelings, and needs that members seem to share:

> The circumstances leading to hurt and disappointment may be very different from person to person or from culture to culture. But the resulting emotions have a universal quality. Although we may not speak the same language or come from the same society, we are connected through our feelings of joy and pain. It is when group members no longer get lost in the details of daily experiences and instead share their deeper struggles with these universal human themes that a group is most cohesive. (Corey & Corey, 1992, p. 209)

Common themes identified by Corey and Corey include (1992):

> fears of rejection, feelings of loneliness and abandonment, feelings of inferiority and failure to live up to others' expectations, painful memories, guilt and remorse over what they have and have not done, discovery that their worst enemy lives within them, need for and fear of intimacy, feelings about sexual identity and sexual performance, and unfinished business with their parents. (p. 210)

This list is not exhaustive, note Corey and Corey, but "merely a sample of the universal human issues that participants recognize and explore with each other as the group progresses" (p. 210).

During these middle phases of group development, group members can participate in a number of activities to work on individual and commonly held goals. Such activities may reduce stress and encourage pleasure and creativity, assist the leader in assessment as members are observed while "doing" rather than "saying," facilitate communication, problem solving, and rapport among members, and help members develop skills and competence in decision making (Northen & Kurland, 2001). Nevil, Beatty, and Moxley (1997) suggest a variety of structured activities and socialization games that can be employed to improve interpersonal skills, increase social awareness, and enhance pro-social competence. While intended for use with persons with disabilities, many of these exercises can be adapted for use with a variety of populations. Other authors note their effectiveness with diverse populations, such as those of Hispanic heritage (Delgado, 1983) and Native Americans (Edwards, Edwards, Davies, & Eddy, 1987).

One element of a structured program targeting delinquency reduction consists of multifamily group meetings in which 8 to 10 families meet for eight weekly sessions lasting 2 1/2 hours each. In the meetings, family members sit together at designated tables, share a meal, and engage in "structured, fun, interactive" activities (McDonald, 2002, p. 719) that enhance communication skills, strengthen relationships, and facilitate networking among the families.

EP 2.1.6b

While art therapy and other expressive techniques generally require specialized training, reviewing resources such as Coholic, Lougheed and Cadell (2009), Cheung (2006), Ross (1997), and Rose (1998) can acquaint social workers with the principles for applying these techniques in groups to address issues related to aggressive behavior, trauma, self-esteem, body image, and awareness of emotions. With all groups, the leader must take the group's purpose, stage of development, and member characteristics into account when selecting and implementing an experiential exercise or activity (Wright, 1999).

In the working phase, leaders also support a continuing trend toward differentiation, in which members establish their uniqueness and separateness from others. Leaders do not create these expressions of differences but rather stimulate or advance them. For example, the leader may note when a member reveals:

> a heretofore hidden talent, or access to a resource that was previously believed inaccessible, or

possession of a needed skill or perspective. A member may articulate a previously unspoken need, or offer an interpretation not thought of by the others, or pose a question that catalyzes or synthesizes a piece of the group's work. (Henry, 1992, p. 183)

The working phase is a time of intensive focus on achieving members' goals. Much of the group's work during this phase is devoted to carrying out contracts developed in the group's initial sessions. Members may have lost sight of their individual goals, so a major leadership role involves confirming goals periodically and promoting organized and systematic efforts to work on them.

The leader assumes the ongoing responsibility of monitoring the time allocated to each member to work on goals. Toseland and Rivas (2009) suggest that the leader help each member to work in turn. If a group spends considerable time aiding one member to achieve his or her individual goals, the leader should generalize the concepts developed in this effort to other members so that everyone benefits. The leader should also encourage participants to share relevant personal experiences with the member receiving help, thus establishing a norm for mutual aid. In addition, he or she should check on the progress of members who did not receive due attention and encourage their participation in the next session.

EP 2.1.10j

Finally, the leader should establish a systematic method of monitoring treatment goals and tasks in sessions. Without such procedures, monitoring may be haphazard and focus on only those members who are more assertive and highly involved; members who are less assertive or resistant will not receive the same attention. Without systematic monitoring, tasks to be completed between sessions may not receive the proper follow-up. Participants may become frustrated when they have completed "homework" between sessions and have no opportunity to report on the results. The expectation of a weekly progress report helps increase motivation to work toward goals between sessions, reduces the necessity of reminding members of their contract agreements, and aids them in gaining a sense of independence and accomplishment.

In the working phase, leaders continue to encourage members to analyze the rationality of their thoughts and beliefs that maintain or exacerbate dysfunctional behaviors. According to Toseland and Rivas (2009), group members may:

(1) overgeneralize from an event, (2) selectively focus on portions of an event, (3) take too much responsibility for events that are beyond their control, (4) think of the worst possible consequence of future events, (5) engage in either/or dichotomous thinking, and (6) assume that because certain events have led to particular consequences in the past they will automatically lead to the same consequences if they reoccur in the future. (p. 288)

Unhelpful Thoughts from the HEART Group: Selectively Focusing

June: Well, I just don't believe anybody that says high school's your best years, you know.

Amelia: My sister's in college, she says that college is the coolest.

Amber: I'm looking forward to college.

Amelia: Me too.

Jen: But I have another three years until I get there. How am I going to survive three years of people making fun of me?

Liz: How do you think college is going to be any different anyway? You have to go be in a dorm where you have to shower in front of people; then, it's not going to be any better.

June: I think I'll just work.

Maggie: Not go to college? My parents would kill me.

June: My parents would be relieved because then they wouldn't have to pay for it.

Dave: I'd like to pose a question to the group. What would be one thing to change about your mindset? What thought could you change that might help you get through high school or shopping or gym? What would be one thought?

Amber: That I don't have to be just like my friends.

Dave: How would that help?

Amber: That would make me feel better about not shopping at the same stores and wearing the same clothes and having the boyfriends that they have, but still being able to hang out with them in other situations.

Interventions in the Termination Stage

Termination is a difficult stage for members who have invested heavily in the group, have experienced intensive

EP 2.1.10l

support, encouragement, and understanding, and have received effective aid for their problems. Leaders must be sensitive to the mixed feelings engendered by termination and carefully intervene to assist the group to come to an effective close. Chapter 19 identifies significant termination issues and change-maintenance strategies. Here, we address aspects of the leader's role that are specific to facilitating planned endings in groups and evaluating group efficacy.

Leaders may assist group members in completing their "commencement" proceedings (Mahler, 1969) by adopting strategies such as the following:

- *Ensure that the issues and concerns worked on by the group resemble those that members will encounter outside the group. Assure that the group is a place where members get honest feedback about how their behavior is likely to be received outside the group and a setting where they may obtain help in coping with those reactions (Toseland & Rivas, 2009).*
- *Refer to a variety of situations and settings throughout the group experience to aid members to practice and acquire skills, thereby better preparing them for the multifaceted situations they will inevitably encounter outside the group (Toseland & Rivas, 2009).*
- *Facilitate members' discussion of how they will respond to possible setbacks in an unsympathetic environment. Build member confidence in existing coping skills and abilities to solve problems independently. Also, teach therapeutic principles that underlie intervention methods, such as those inherent in assertiveness, effective communication, or problem solving (Toseland & Rivas, 2009). Share your reactions to endings as a way of helping members to identify their own conflicted feelings and any sense of abandonment, anger, sadness, or loss.*
- *Increase review and integration of learning by helping members to put into words what has transpired between themselves and the group from the first to the final session and what they have learned about themselves and others. Solicit information about what members were satisfied and unsatisfied with in the group and ways in which sessions could have had greater impact. Ask members to spontaneously recall moments of conflict and pain as well as moments of closeness, warmth, humor, and joy in the group (Corey & Corey, 1992).*
- *Several sessions before termination, suggest that members consider using the remaining time to complete their own agenda. For example, ask, "If this were the last session, how would you feel about what you have done, and what would you wish you had done differently?" (Corey & Corey, 2002, p. 261).*
- *Facilitate the completion of unfinished business between members. One technique involves an exercise in which each person, in turn, says in a few short phrases, "What I really liked was the way you ... (supply a specific behavior exchanged between the persons, such as 'always gave me credit when I could finally say something that was hard for me to say')," and then, "But I wish we ... (supplying a specific wish for a behavioral exchange between the two persons that did not occur, such as 'had made more opportunities to talk to each other more directly')" (Henry, 1992, p. 124). Note that this and other closure exercises should not be used to generate new issues but rather to bring resolution to the present situation.*
- *Encourage members to identify areas for future work once the group concludes. Consider asking members to formulate their own individual change contracts, which may be referred to once the group ends, and invite each member to review his or her contract with the group (Corey & Corey, 2006).*
- *Engage individual members in relating how they have perceived themselves in the group, what the group has meant to them, and how they have grown. Ask the other members to give feedback regarding how they have perceived and felt about each person, including measured feedback that helps members strengthen the perceptions that they gained during the course of the group (e.g., "One of the things I like best about you is ...," "One way I see you blocking your strengths is ...," or "A few things that I hope you'll remember are ...") (Corey, 1990, p. 512).*
- *Use evaluative measures to determine the effectiveness of the group and the leader's interventions. Such measures have the following benefits: (1) They address the leader's professional concerns about the specific effects of interventions; (2) they help workers improve their leadership skills; (3) they demonstrate the group's efficacy to agencies or funding sources; (4) they help leaders assess individual members' and the group's progress in accomplishing agreed-upon objectives; (5) they allow members to express their satisfactions and dissatisfactions with the group; and (6) they help leaders develop knowledge that can be generalized to future groups and other leaders (Reid, 1991; Toseland & Rivas, 2009).*

Like other areas of social work practice, group interventions face increased scrutiny to determine the

EP 2.1.6b

efficacy of certain processes and the outcomes. Tolman and Molidor's (1994) review of research on social work with groups indicates that group work evaluation is growing ever more sophisticated and that multiple measures are being employed to determine group efficacy. For example, in addition to undertaking evaluation at the termination phase, more than one-third of the groups studied by Tolman and Molidor (1994) used follow-up measures to determine whether earlier gains had been maintained. These authors note, however, that while it is important to examine outcomes, the evaluative challenge lies in isolating those elements of group process that actually contributed to those outcomes.

Increasingly, curricula for group interventions include measurement instruments to assist in understanding both baseline and outcome measures. For example, in groups consisting of adolescents and pre-teens, Rose (1998) suggests using a variety of methods and sources of data, including standardized ratings by parents and teachers, self-monitoring or self-reports through checklists, logs, questionnaires, or sentence completion; observation of in-group behavior, performance during role-plays or simulations; sociometric evaluations, goal attainment scaling, and knowledge tests. Anderson-Butcher, Khairallah, and Race-Bigelow (2004) suggest that qualitative interviews may be used to ascertain client outcomes and to identify the characteristics of effective self-help groups. Magen's (2004) review of measurement issues in group evaluation offers guidance for effective selection of outcome and process measures.

At termination, members and the leader may all record their satisfaction with the group and their sense of its effectiveness. Members may respond to open-ended questions or a structured checklist, either of which may inquire about the changes the group brought about in each participant's life or relationships, the techniques used that had the greatest and least impact, perceptions of the leader, and so on (Corey, Corey, Callanan, & Russell, 2004). These authors also recommend that the leader keep a journal to evaluate group progress over time, note his or her reactions at various points, keep track of techniques or materials used and the perceived outcomes, and share self-insights that emerged during the life of the group.

Errors in Group Interventions

In addition to attending to recommended interventions across the life of the group, social workers must also take care to avoid errors that inhibit group development and process. Research on damaging experiences in therapeutic groups indicates that group leaders' behaviors (e.g., confrontation, monopolizing, criticizing) or inaction (e.g., lack of support, lack of structure) play a primary role in group casualties or dropouts (Smokowski, Rose, & Bacallao, 2001). Thomas and Caplan (1999) identify some of the most common mistakes, including:

EP 2.1.10a & 2.1.6b

- *Doing one-on-one work in the context of the group. This practice inhibits the mutual aid that is the hallmark of group work*
- *Having such a rigid agenda that members cannot pursue emerging themes or otherwise own the group process*
- *Scapegoating or attacking individual members. This behavior inhibits others' involvement by sending a message that the group is not a safe place*
- *Overemphasizing content and failing to universalize themes so that all members can benefit from and relate to the experience of other members*
- *Ridiculing members or discounting some members' need to be heard*
- *Lecturing the group. This practice disempowers members and inhibits group investment and momentum*
- *Failing to address offensive comments or colluding with members around inappropriate, anti-authoritarian, racist, or sexist statements.*

It may be helpful to think of the preceding list as behaviors that stop the evolution of the group or send it veering off course.

Error Example: Overemphasizing Content and Lecturing in the HEART Group

Dave: I want us to think about the word "fat" and to think about if that's an appropriate word to use to describe ourselves.

Liz: Not you, you're skinny.

Dave: When I speak to people who have been called fat, or who refer to themselves that way, I use the term, "person with overweight." And that's the way I talk about it. None of us are guaranteed to keep the bodies we have. Whether we like them or not, our bodies can always change. So I say people have overweight, because it's descriptive of a moment in time, rather than an enduring quality that someone possesses.

Amelia: My psychiatrist calls, um, says that I have a disordered relationship with food. [*the group laughs*]

Dave: What does that mean?

Amelia: Means I'm fat, I don't know! [*more laughter*]

Dave: Well, let's look at the words together then. What is disordered?

Amelia: Fat. I don't know, like not right, dysfunctional, not cool.

June: Out of order.

Amelia: Out of order. Yes, I'm out of order with food.

Dave: What do you think about that? Do you agree or disagree?

Amelia: I don't know; whatever, it makes sense to me.

Dave: What about it makes sense?

Amelia: Well, it's kind of a nice way of saying, I'm fat.

Dave: When I hear that phrase, it sounds to me as though your psychiatrist is telling you that you're using food for reasons other than nutrition.

Amelia: Yeah, maybe.

Variations in Social Work with Groups

The concepts for assessing and intervening with groups can be applied to a variety of settings, populations, and issues. However, two particular variations on group work deserve further discussion. Groups that occur in single sessions and those that take place online or through other electronic media require special attention and novel intervention strategies.

Single Session Groups

EP 2.1.9a

Attention is turning to the application of group work concepts to groups that meet only for a single session. For example, in interdisciplinary case meetings, membership shifts based on which professionals are involved with the particular case. In hospital settings, some groups provide education and support to individuals and family members during times of crisis. In shelters and residential programs, shifts in the census from day to day will mean shifts in attendance at required daily groups. In critical incident debriefing groups, professionals intervene to assist people affected by a traumatic event—for example, after a workplace shooting (Reynolds & Jones, 1996). Some concepts used in the single-session groups—purpose, contracting, and worker roles—are variations on those used in groups of longer duration. Others—composition, member roles, norms, and group stages—may be less germane to single-session groups.

As the name suggests, single session groups come together in a particular configuration only once and each group must negotiate its own purpose and contract (Block, 1985; Ebenstein, 1998). Research on single session groups is limited, but existing literature suggests that they pose unique challenges for group facilitators including how to handle recruitment, allow sufficient time for the beginning phase, and deal with heterogeneous group membership and set realistic goals (Ebenstein, 1998). Given these challenges, Kosoff (2003) argues that facilitators must possess comprehensive knowledge of the population to be served by the group, strong skills in planning and preparing for the sessions, the ability to exercise more active, direct, focused, and flexible leadership, and skill in structuring the session to encourage members to participate fully and move through the phases of development within the time allotted.

More specifically, Kosoff (2003) emphasizes the importance of developing a preliminary awareness of issues and themes that preoccupy the population to be served in order to help focus the session to one or two concerns and limit goals to those that are achievable in one session (Ebenstein, 1998). This knowledge is also important in helping speed up the process whereby the group members develop rapport and sense of commonality in purpose and need (Block, 1985). Because of the condensed time frame, pacing is critical and sufficient time must be allowed for a real beginning, middle, and end for the group session. Ebenstein (1998) suggests that crisis intervention theory can provide a helpful framework for this pacing in its "here and now" orientation, which focuses on strengthening existing defenses and developing new coping strategies.

Technology-Mediated Groups

EP 2.1.9a

Social workers are increasingly utilizing technological advances to enhance the delivery of services to clients through groups. Persons who are home-bound or who find attendance at agency settings difficult may be able to experience the support and benefit of groups through the medium of telephone, e-mail, or the internet (Harris, 1999; Hollander, 2001). Online group facilitators must assure through informed consent that members understand the risks and benefits of such a model. The nature of typed, asynchronous communication means that members have more control and time for reflection as they craft their responses. In addition, they can participate in the virtual group at their convenience (Fingeld, 2000) and with a high degree of anonymity (Meier, 2002). However, participation may be stymied by internet provider system problems and by trust issues, especially with "lurkers" (those who read mail but do not post to the group) and with participants' actual level of engagement with the process. Recent innovations in group work involve the use of web-based virtual reality experiences to bring group members together and foster interaction in a safe environment. In one example, rural elementary school students learned various social skills in a typical group setting, but then used a multi-user virtual environment (MUVE) to test and practice skills through avatars (Baker, Parks-Savage & Rehfuss, 2009).

Leaders who work with these technologies must be more active in guiding the process and drawing out implications for feelings and tone that are masked by the communication or interaction medium. As access to such media increases, social workers must take advantage of technology to reach groups who cannot be reached by conventional means, as well as those individuals who may be reluctant to participate in face-to-face meetings. Technology-mediated groups are also well-suited for people seeking support on a 24/7 basis, such as grieving parents who may log in to share feelings and seek help at any hour of the day or night (Edwards, 2007). Webcasts, conference calls, and other technology-enhanced methods are appropriate for task groups, to save time and travel costs, access expert consultation, and efficiently respond to crises and evolving circumstances in the practice environment.

Work with Task Groups

EP 2.1.7a

As described earlier, a significant aspect of professional social work practice is performance in task and work groups. In contrast to treatment groups, task groups try to accomplish a purpose, produce a product, or develop policies. You are likely to participate in task groups throughout your career, starting with group projects for class, continuing as a staff member, and eventually serving as a leader of such groups in your practice. As with treatment groups, task groups may have open or closed membership and they may be time-limited or open-ended. Members take on formal and informal roles, and the execution of these roles can facilitate or impede the group's success. Task groups may be composed of professionals, community members, clients, or a mixture of these parties depending on the group's purpose and the way that members are recruited and assigned.

Effective task groups do not rely solely on the skills of the formal group leader. For example, as members of such groups, social workers are often effective participants in interdisciplinary teams thanks to their knowledge of group processes (Abramson, 2002). They can offer particular assistance in task groups in identifying which needs the group can meet, getting members involved, and paying attention to stages of development (including managing conflict during each stage).

Problem Identification

EP 2.1.10j & 2.1.10i

Leaders can help task groups effectively identify problems that the group is capable of solving, that are within the group's domain and that, among the many problems that could potentially be chosen, would provide a meaningful focus. During this process, the leader (or chairperson, or facilitator) should help the group avoid responding prematurely with solutions before the problem is well-defined. For example, if a board is discussing budgetary shortfalls, the chair would help the members look at the causes and long-term trends in the budget before focusing on cuts or revenue enhancement strategies. In specifying appropriate problems and goals, the group can employ techniques such as brainstorming and nominal group technique to consider an array of possibilities before selecting a focus. *Brainstorming* involves generating and expressing a variety of opinions without evaluating them. In the *nominal group* technique, members first privately list potential problems. The group then takes one potential problem from each member until all are listed. Finally, it evaluates and ranks those potential problems as a group in deciding which should take priority (Toseland & Rivas, 2009).

Groups must also determine the strategies that will support effective decision making. Some procedures may be prescribed. For example, the charter or bylaws of the group may require certain periods for commentary, use of clearly specified rules on who can vote, and adherence to Robert's Rules of Order. Other groups may determine their own norms, such as decision by consensus or majority rule.

Getting Members Involved

Task group membership may be voluntary (a neighborhood task force on crime), appointed (a coalition consisting of representatives of homeless shelters), elected (a board of directors), or determined by roles (an interdisciplinary team consisting of all professionals serving a particular family). To the maximum extent possible, the membership should possess the skills and resources needed to accomplish the purpose for which the group was convened. For example, if a committee concerned about crime had no law enforcement personnel as members, it might seek out someone to fill that niche. As with therapeutic groups, those convening task groups should be alert to the characteristics of potential members and ensure that no member will be an isolate or an outlier. This consideration is particularly important when service consumers or their family members fill representative roles in a group consisting largely of professionals and service providers. Multiple representatives from consumer or family organizations should be included in committee membership, thereby ensuring that they are empowered and that their positions move beyond a token role.

EP 2.1.10a

All members of the group need to have a clear understanding of the functions of the group, to have input into the agenda and decision making. Each session or meeting should be carefully planned and designed to take advantage of the time and talents available (Tropman & Morningstar, 1995). Roles can be assigned such that members will have to depend on each other to get the work of the group accomplished (Toseland & Rivas, 2009). Background papers often need to be circulated in advance to get all members to the appropriate level of information. It is often helpful to conduct the brain-storming or ice-breaking exercises in small groups to facilitate member interaction. Recognition of the particular skills, experiences, and perspectives that different members bring can also facilitate more confident sharing by new members.

Enhancing Awareness of Stages of Development

The stages of group development observed in treatment settings will also occur in task groups, albeit not in a linear fashion. Instead, some issues will recur, taking the group back to revisit earlier stages. In the preaffiliation stage, individuals enter with varying hopes for the group because common goals have not yet been established.

Early identity development in the group may be affected by preexisting relationships among group members who may already know or work with each other in other capacities. Depending on the quality of these past experiences, friction may be carried over into the new group or trust and comfort may facilitate rapid movement into the work of the group. In either case, it is essential that individuals with existing relationships not form subgroups, as these splinter groups or voting blocs may diminish the comfort and cohesion of all members of the group.

The "power and control" phase (stage 2) in task groups often features competition over which programs or ideas the group will adopt. Conflict about ideas is to be expected—indeed, it should be encouraged if options are to be generated and thoroughly explored. All too often, task groups avoid conflict by evading thorny issues, sometimes even tabling an issue despite the availability of enough facts to make a decision. Establishing norms in which differing options are sought and evaluated on their own merits will aid the group in accomplishing its objectives. Leaders should attempt to stimulate *idea-related conflict* while managing and controlling *personality-related conflict*. Failure to achieve this balance may result in the marginalization of potential contributors and a less complete product. Without such healthy conflict, there is always the danger of "groupthink," a condition in which alternative views or options are not expressed or taken seriously. Leaders (and members) can assist others to express the rationale behind particular opinions, clarifying what information needs to be developed to answer questions raised in the course of the conflict.

EP 2.1.7a

Group leaders and members can use the communication skills described earlier in this book to reframe communications, thereby making them understandable to all parties, as well as to reflect, probe, seek concreteness, and summarize what is being heard. Facilitators can contribute to the creation of a productive working atmosphere by conveying that each member has something to contribute and by maintaining civility such that no member—or his or her ideas—is allowed to be degraded (Toseland & Rivas, 2009).

EP 2.1.10l

Termination in task groups may occur when individual members leave or when the group disbands. "Commencement" in task groups is often overlooked, as members experience relief at the reduction of the demands on their time and their group-related responsibilities, and perhaps satisfaction in successfully achieving their goal. Nevertheless, it is important to evaluate what worked and what did not work well in the group process, to acknowledge the contributions of time and effort made be group members, and to share gratitude about the roles that facilitated group success.

Summary

This chapter focused on the knowledge and skills you will need to effectively intervene in social work task and treatment groups. As new theories of change and new treatment modalities emerge, they will also be applied to work with groups. For example, evolving solution-focused interventions have been applied to groups in an array of situations, including recovery from sexual abuse, improving parenting skills, and resolving symptoms of anxiety and depression (Metcalf, 1998). Multifamily groups, composed of family members who share a common concern, have proved useful for addressing severe and persistent psychiatric disorders (McFarlane, 2002) and reducing the risk for child abuse and neglect (Burford & Pennell, 2004; Meezan & O'Keefe, 1998), among other issues (Vakalah & Khajak, 2000). Group interventions for PTSD have demonstrated effectiveness (van der Kolk, 1993). The innovations ahead will determine if these successes can be achieved with trauma from military service, disasters, and other emerging needs.

In this chapter we addressed the stages of group development and the common member and group characteristics that arise with each phase, illustrating the leadership roles and skills necessary for an effective group experience. We examined unique areas of group work, including single session groups and online groups. For groups to be successful, leaders must thoughtfully apply research on effective group practices and flexibly use their role and interventions to suit the needs of the individuals and the group as a whole, from inception to termination.

CourseMate

Access an integrated eBook and chapter-specific learning tools including glossary terms, chapter outlines, relevant web links, videos, and practice quizzes. Go to **www.cengagebrain.com**.

CHAPTER **17**

Confrontation, Interpretation, and Additive Empathy

CHAPTER OVERVIEW

Chapter 17 builds on the skills introduced in Chapters 5 and 6 to assist clients in achieving a deeper understanding of their own behavior, the behavior of others, and their options in exploring change. Appropriate timing for and uses of confrontation are presented as means of clients gaining greater self-knowledge. Such confrontation should assist clients in making informed decisions mindful of their potential consequences. As in earlier chapters, examples from videos linked to this chapter are featured.

As a result of reading this chapter and practicing with classmates, you will be able to appropriately:

- Employ additive empathy
- Construct an interpretation
- Construct a confrontation

EPAS COMPETENCIES IN THE 17TH CHAPTER

This chapter will give you the information needed to meet the following practice competencies.

2.1.10 Engage, assess, intervene, and evaluate with individuals, families, groups, organizations, and communities

2.1.10b Use empathy and other interpersonal skills

The Meaning and Significance of Client Self-Awareness

Self-awareness refers largely to awareness of the various forces operating in the present. Social workers assist clients to expand their awareness of their needs or wants, motives, emotions, beliefs, and problematic behaviors, and their awareness of these items' impact on other people. We do *not* use self-awareness to refer to insight into the etiology of problems. As we noted in earlier chapters, people can and do change without achieving this type of insight. On occasion, brief explorations into the past may be productive and enlightening—for example, to determine which qualities attracted intimate partners to each other, to identify factors that have contributed to sexual dysfunction, to assess the chronicity of problems, or to highlight previous successes. When making such brief excursions, however, it is important to relate the information elicited along the way to current work and current problems, emphasizing to clients that they can change the present. In other words, they can alter the current effects of history but not history itself.

Social workers have numerous tools at their disposal to assist clients to gain expanded self-awareness. Of these tools, additive empathy, interpretation, and confrontation are probably employed most extensively. This chapter defines these techniques, specifies indications for their use, presents guidelines for employing them effectively, and provides skill-development exercises related to these tools.

Additive Empathy and Interpretation

There have been debates about whether empathy is primarily a personal trait or a skill that can be learned (Fernandez-Olano, Montoya-Fernandez, & Salinas-Sanchez, 2008). Those who consider it to be a learnable trait often conceive it as requiring the practitioner to be in a special state of receptivity, learning to empty him or herself of distractions and be open to the other person; Block-Lerner, et al., 2007; Dimidjian & Linehan, 2003;

EP 2.1.10 & 2.1.10b

(Lu, Dane, & Gellman, 2005 Segal, Williams, & Teasdale, 2002). Other social work educators have argued that it requires specific training and experience for social workers to be empathic to the social conditions and experiences of low-income clients (Segal, 2007; Smith, 2006). That is, it is not enough to be attentive to the internal experience of clients, but also to be sensitive to the conditions, struggles, and resources that emerge in their accounts. Further, some argue that it is insufficient for social workers to be "with" the client emotionally and cognitively. Rather, social workers strive to assist clients in taking empathic action to better the troubling personal or environmental conditions they have shared (Gerdes & Segal, 2009).

However conceived, empathy on the social worker's part is critical to the helping process. Earlier chapters examined uses of empathy in the initial phase of the helping process. During the action-oriented phase, additive levels of empathy serve to expand clients' self-awareness, to cushion the impact of confrontations, and to explore and resolve relational reactions and other obstacles to change. Of course, social workers also continue to use reciprocal levels of empathy during the goal attainment phase because the purposes for which empathy was employed in the initial phase persist throughout the helping process. The difference is that additive levels of empathy are employed sparingly in the initial phase but occupy a prominent position during the action-oriented phase.

Additive empathic responses go somewhat beyond what clients have expressed and, therefore, require some degree of inference by social workers. Thus, these responses are moderately interpretive—that is, they interpret forces operating to produce feelings, cognitions, reactions, and behavioral patterns.

Such additive empathic responses lead us to the interpretation or the identification of patterns, goals, and wishes that clients imply but do not directly state (Cormier, Nurius, & Osborn, 2009). Insight through *interpretation* is the foremost therapeutic principle basic to psychoanalysis and closely related therapies. Proponents of several other theories (most notably, client-centered, Gestalt, and certain existential theories) have avoided the use of interpretation. For example, interpretation has little or no role in solution-focused treatment or motivational interviewing. In motivational interviewing, as we explored in Chapter 6, there can be a useful role for helping clients in examining discrepancies between values and behavior without imposing an external explanation for that discrepancy (Arkovitz Westra, Miller & Rollnick, 2007).

Some maintain that interpretation is essential to the counseling process, regardless of the social worker's theoretical orientation, and that many behaviors of social workers (whether intentional or not) perform interpretive functions (Claiborn, 1982; Levy, 1963). Semantic and conceptual confusion have contributed to the divergence in views. Additional writings have sharpened concepts and reduced vagueness and confusion. Based on Levy's (1963) conceptualization, Claiborn (1982) posits that interpretation, whatever the social worker's theoretical orientation, "presents the client with a viewpoint discrepant from the client's own, the function of which is to prepare or induce the client to change in accordance with that viewpoint" (p. 442). Viewed in this light, interpretation assists clients in viewing their problems from a different perspective, thereby opening up new possibilities for remedial courses of action. This generic view, which emphasizes a *discrepant viewpoint,* is sufficiently broad to encompass many change-oriented techniques identified in different theories, including reframing (Watzlawick, Weakland, & Fisch, 1974), relabeling (Barton & Alexander, 1981), positive connotation (Selvini-Palazzoli, Boscolo, Cecchin, & Prata, 1974), positive reinterpretation (Hammond et al., 1977), additive empathy, and traditional psychoanalytic interpretations. The content of interpretations concerning the same clinical situation thus can be expected to vary according to the theoretical allegiances of social workers. Research (summarized by Claiborn, 1982), however, indicates that "interpretations differing greatly in content seem to have a similar impact on clients" (p. 450). Others have suggested that the impact of interpretations is closely related to the nature of the relationship between the client and the practitioner (Brammer, Abrego, & Shostrom, 1993).[1]

Levy (1963) classifies interpretations into two categories: *semantic* and *propositional*. Semantic interpretations describe clients' experiences according to the social worker's conceptual vocabulary: "By 'frustrated,' I gather you mean you're feeling hurt and disillusioned." Semantic interpretations are closely related to additive empathic responses. Propositional interpretations involve the social worker's notions or explanations that assert causal relationships among factors involved in clients' problem situations: "When you try so hard to avoid displeasing others, you displease yourself and end up resenting others for taking advantage of you." Social workers should avoid making interpretations or additive empathic responses (we are using the terms interchangeably) that are far removed from the awareness of clients. Research (Speisman, 1959) has indicated that moderate interpretations (those that reflect feelings that lie at the margin of the client's experiences) facilitate self-exploration and self-awareness, whereas deep interpretations engender opposition.

Because deep interpretations are remote from clients' experiences, they appear illogical and irrelevant to clients, who therefore tend to reject them despite the fact that such interpretations may be accurate. The following is an example of such an inept, deep interpretation:

Client: My boss is a real tyrant. He never gives anyone credit, except for Fran. She can do no wrong in his eyes. He just seems to have it in for me. Sometimes I'd like to punch his lights out.

Social worker: Your boss seems to activate the same feelings you had toward your father. You feel he favors Fran, who symbolizes your favored sister. It's your father who you feel was the real tyrant, and you're reliving your resentment toward him. Your boss is merely a symbol of him.

Understandably, the client would likely reject and perhaps resent this interpretation. Although the social worker may be accurate (the determination of which is purely speculative), the client is struggling with feelings toward his boss. To shift the focus to his feelings toward his father misses the mark entirely from the client's perspective.

The following interpretation, made in response to the same client message, would be less likely to create opposition because it is linked to recent experiences of the client:

Social worker: So you really resent your boss because he seems impossible to please and shows partiality toward Fran. *[Reciprocal empathy.]* Those feelings reminded me of similar ones you expressed about 2 weeks ago. You were talking about how, when your parents spent a week with you on their vacation, your father seemed to find fault with everything you did but raved about how well your sister was doing. You'd previously mentioned he'd always seemed to favor your sister and that nothing you did seemed to please him. I'm wondering if those feelings might be connected with the feelings you're experiencing at work.

In the preceding message, notice that the social worker carefully documented the rationale of the interpretation and offered it tentatively, a technique discussed later in the section titled "Guidelines for Employing Interpretation and Additive Empathy." Because we discussed, illustrated, and provided exercises related to additive empathy in Chapter 5, we will not deal with these topics in this chapter. Instead, we limit our discussion here to the uses of interpretation and additive empathy in expanding clients' self-awareness of (1) deeper feelings; (2) underlying meanings of feelings, thoughts, and behavior; (3) wants and goals; (4) hidden purposes of behavior; and (5) unrealized strengths and potentialities.

> **VIDEO CASE EXAMPLE**
>
> Additive empathy or interpretation can provide a useful role in identifying and exploring patterns of couple behavior. In the video "Home for the Holidays" (HFH1), the social worker, Kim, has heard discussions about different communication patterns in Jackie's and Anna's families of origin. She asks Jackie about whether the way her family handled her coming out as a lesbian was symbolic of how other such issues were dealt with in her family. Rather than suggest that they are representative of other such issues, Kim asks a question. Similarly, later Kim asks whether the discussion about the wedding picture and Anna not being included in it is symbolic of challenges they have faced in making decisions or working out problems. Finally, Kim puts their difficulties in the context of becoming a new family: "Often when we are forming new families, new couples, we are torn between the family we come from and the new family we are creating; this plays out in logistical decisions about the holidays."

Deeper Feelings

Clients often have limited awareness of certain emotions, perceiving them only dimly, if at all. Moreover, emotional reactions often involve multiple emotions, but clients may experience only the dominant or surface feelings. Further, some clients experience only negative emotions, such as anger, and are out of touch with more tender feelings, such as hurt, disappointment, compassion, loneliness, fears, and caring. Additive empathic responses (semantic interpretations) may assist clients to become aware of the emotions that lie at the edge of their awareness, thereby enabling them to experience these feelings more sharply and fully, to become more aware of their humanness (including the full spectrum of emotions), and to integrate these emerging emotions into the totality of their experience.

Social workers frequently employ additive empathic responses directed at expanding clients' awareness of feelings for several purposes, which we identify and illustrate in the following examples.

1. To identify feelings that are only implied or hinted at in clients' verbal messages

    Client [in sixth session]: I wonder if you feel we're making any progress. [*Clients frequently ask questions that embody feelings.*]

    Social worker: It sounds as though you're not satisfied with your progress. I wonder if you're feeling discouraged about how it's been going.

2. To identify feelings that underlie surface emotions

    Client: I've just felt so bored in the evenings with so little to do. I play video games and surf the Internet, but that doesn't seem to help. Life's just a drag.

    Social worker: I'm getting the impression you're feeling empty and pretty depressed. I wonder if you're feeling lonely and wishing you had some friends to fill that emptiness?

3. To add intensity to feelings clients have minimized

    Thirty-year-old socially isolated woman with mild intellectual disability: It was a little disappointing that Jana *[her childhood friend from another state]* couldn't come to visit. She lost her job and had to cancel her plane reservations.

    Social worker: I can see how very disappointed you were. In fact, you seem really down even now. You'd looked forward to her visit and made plans. It has been a real blow to you.

4. To clarify the nature of feelings clients express only vaguely

    Gay male client: When Robert told me he didn't want to be with me anymore, I just turned numb. I've been walking around in a daze ever since, telling myself, "This can't be happening."

    Social worker: It has been a great shock to you. You were so unprepared. It hurts so much it's hard to admit it's really happening.

5. To identify feelings manifested only nonverbally

    Client: My sister asked me to tend her kids while she's on vacation, and I will, of course. *[Frowns and sighs.]*

    Social worker: But your sigh tells me you don't feel good about it. Right now the message I get from you is that it seems an unfair and heavy burden to you and that you resent it.

Underlying Meanings of Feelings, Thoughts, and Behavior

Used for this purpose, additive empathy or interpretation assists clients in conceptualizing and understanding feelings, thoughts, and behavior. Social workers assist clients in understanding what motivates them to feel, think, and behave as they do; to grasp how their behavior bears on their problems and goals; and to discern themes and patterns in their feelings, thoughts, and behavior. As clients discern similarities, parallels, and themes in their behavior and experiences, their self-awareness gradually expands in much the same way as single pieces of a puzzle fit together, gradually forming discrete entities and eventually coalescing into a coherent whole. The previous interpretation made to the client who resented his boss for favoring a coworker is an example of this type of additive empathic response (it is also a propositional interpretation).

In a more concrete sense, then, social workers may employ this type of interpretation or additive empathy to assist clients in realizing that they experience troublesome feelings in the presence of a certain type of person or in certain circumstances. For example, clients may feel depressed in the presence of critical people or feel extremely anxious in situations wherein they must perform (e.g., when expected to give a talk or take a test). Social workers may thus use additive empathy to identify negative perceptual sets and other dysfunctional cognitive patterns that can be modified by employing cognitive restructuring. Clients may attend exclusively to trivial indications of their imperfections and completely overlook abundant evidence of competent and successful performance.

Similarly, a social worker may assist a client in discerning a pattern of anticipating negative outcomes of relatively minor events and dreading (and avoiding) the events because of his or her perception of those outcomes as absolute disasters. One client dreaded visiting a lifelong friend who had recently sustained a severe fall, leaving her partially paralyzed. When the social worker explored possible negative events that the client feared might occur if she were to visit the friend, she identified the following:

- "What if I cry when I see her?"
- "What if I stare at her?"
- "What if I say the wrong thing?"

Using an additive empathic response, the social worker replied, "And if you did one of those things, it would be a total disaster?" The client readily agreed that it would not. The social worker then employed cognitive restructuring to assist the client in viewing the situation in a more realistic perspective. The social worker discussed each feared reaction in turn, clarifying that anyone might react as the client feared reacting and that if she were to react in any of these ways it would be uncomfortable but certainly not a disaster. The social worker and client jointly concluded that the client had a certain amount of control over how she reacted rather than being totally at the mercy of circumstances. Following behavioral rehearsal, the client's fears of disaster gradually dwindled to manageable proportions.

Social workers may also employ this type of additive empathy to enhance clients' awareness of perceptual distortions that adversely affect their interpersonal relationships. For example, parents may reject children because they perceive characteristics in them that the parents abhor. Previous exploration, however, may have disclosed that parents identify the same qualities in themselves and project their self-hatred onto their children. By assisting clients to recognize how self-perceptions (which may also be distorted) warp their perceptions of their children, social workers enable such parents to make discriminations and to perceive and accept their children as unique individuals who are different from themselves.

Similar perceptual distortions may occur between couples. These problems may cause spouses to perceive and to respond inappropriately to each other as a result of unresolved and troublesome feelings that derive from earlier relationships with past relationships.

> **VIDEO CASE EXAMPLE**
>
> In the video "Adolescent Mother and Foster Parent" (AMFP), the social worker, Glenda, observes behavioral patterns that are conflicting between a teen parent, Twanna, and her foster parent, Janet. Twanna is coming home late from school, leaving her two-year-old child with the foster mother for extended periods. The foster mother is concerned that Twanna may not be around her child enough time to bond with her. Meanwhile, the foster mother is at times pacifying the infant by giving her candy. When Twanna tries to stop this, her child has tantrums. Glenda hears the account of this interaction and suggests that when Twanna refuses to deal with the tantrums, going to her room and putting on her head phones, she may be thinking about Janet, "You made her this way … you deal with her."

Wants and Goals

Another important use of additive empathy is to assist clients to become aware of wants and goals that they imply in their messages but do not fully recognize. When beset by difficulties, people often tend to think in terms of problems and ways to obtain relief from them rather than in terms of growth and change—even though the latter two processes are often implied in the former. When they become more aware of the thrust toward growth implied in their messages, clients often welcome the prospect and may even experience enthusiasm about it. This type of additive empathy not only expands self-awareness, but may also enhance motivation.

As is apparent in the following excerpt, additive empathic messages that highlight implied wants and goals often result in the formulation of explicit goals that pave the way to change-oriented actions. Moreover, such messages play a critical role in arousing hope in dispirited clients who feel overwhelmed by their problems and have been unable to discern any positive desires for growth manifested in their struggles. This type of message plays a key role both in the first phase of the helping process and in the change-oriented phase.

Client: I'm so sick of always being imposed upon. All of my family just take me for granted. You know: "Good old Marcie, you can always depend on her." I've taken about all of this that I can take.

Social worker: Just thinking about it stirs you up. Marcie, it seems to me that what you're saying adds up to an urgent desire on your part to be your own person—to feel in charge of yourself rather than being at the mercy of others' requests or demands.

Client: I hadn't thought of it that way, but you're right. That's exactly what I want. If I could just be my own person.

Social worker: Maybe that's a goal you'd like to set for yourself. It seems to fit, and accomplishing it would liberate you from the oppressive feelings you've described.

Client: Yes, yes! I'd like very much to set that goal. Do you really think I could accomplish it?

Hidden Purposes of Behavior

Social workers sometimes employ interpretation to help clients become more fully aware of the basic motivations that underlie their concerns. Other people may misinterpret clients' motives, and clients themselves may have only a limited awareness of them because of the obscuring effect of their problematic behaviors.

Prominent among these motives are the following: to protect tenuous self-esteem (e.g., by avoiding situations that involve any risk of failing), to avoid anxiety-producing situations, and to compensate for feelings of impotency or inadequacy. The following are typical examples of surface behaviors and the hidden purposes that may be served by those behaviors:

- *Underachieving students may exert little effort in school (1) because they can justify failing on the basis of not having really tried (rather than having to face their fears of being inadequate) or (2) because they are seeking to punish parents who withhold approval and love when they fall short of their expectation or (3) they don't want to be identified with the "smart kids" and betray their friends.*
- *Clients may present a facade of bravado to conceal from themselves and others underlying fears and feelings of inadequacy.*
- *Clients may set themselves up for physical or emotional pain to offset deep-seated feelings of guilt.*
- *Clients may engage in self-defeating behavior to validate myths that they are destined to be losers or to live out life scripts determined by circumstances beyond their control.*
- *Clients may avoid relating closely to others to protect against fears of being dominated or controlled.*
- *Clients may behave aggressively or abrasively to avoid risking rejection by keeping others at a distance.*

Interpretations must be based on substantial supporting information that clients have disclosed previously. Without supporting information, interpretations are little more than speculations that clients are unlikely to accept. Indeed, such speculations may come from social workers' projections and are typically inaccurate. Clients may regard such interpretations as offensive or may question social workers' competence when they receive such responses.

The following example illustrates appropriate use of interpretation to expand awareness of the motives underlying a client's behavior.

CASE EXAMPLE

Mr. R, age 33, and his wife entered marital therapy largely at his wife's instigation. Mrs. R complained about a lack of closeness in the relationship and felt rejected because her husband seldom sought affection with her. When she made overtures, he typically pulled back. Mr. R had revealed in the exploratory interviews that his mother had been (and still was) extremely dominating and controlling. He felt little warmth toward his mother and saw her no more than was absolutely necessary.

The following excerpt from a session with Mr. R focuses on an event that occurred during the week when the couple went to a movie. Mrs. R had reached over to hold her husband's hand. He abruptly withdrew it, and Mrs. R later expressed her feelings of hurt and rejection. Their ensuing discussion was unproductive, and their communication became strained. Mr. R discussed the event that occurred in the theater:

Mr. R: I know Carol was hurt when I didn't hold her hand. I don't know why, but it really turned me off.

Social worker: So you're wondering why you turn off when she wants some affection. I wonder what was happening inside of you at that moment. What were you thinking and feeling?

Mr. R: Gee, let me think. I guess I was anticipating she'd do it, and I just wanted to be left alone to enjoy the movie. I guess I resented her taking my hand. That doesn't make sense when I think about it. Why should I resent holding hands with the woman I love?

Social worker: Jim, I think you're asking an awfully good question—one that's a key to some of the difficulties in your marriage. May I share an idea with you that might shed some light on why you respond as you do? [they nod in affirmation] You mentioned that you felt resentful when Carol took your hand. Based on the feelings you just expressed, I'm wondering if perhaps you feel you're submitting to her if you respond positively when she takes the initiative and pull back to be sure you're not letting yourself be dominated by her [*the hidden purpose*]. Another reason for suggesting that is that as you were growing up you have said that you felt dominated by your mother and resented her for being that way. Even now you avoid seeing her any more than you have to. I'm wondering if, as a result of your relationship with her, you could have developed a supersensitivity to being controlled by a female so that you resent any behavior on Carol's part that even suggests her being in control. [*The latter part of the response provides the rationale for the interpretation.*]

Unrealized Strengths and Potentialities

Another vital purpose served by interpretation and additive empathy is to expand clients' awareness of their strengths and undeveloped potentialities. Clients' strengths are demonstrated in a variety of ways, and social workers need to sensitize themselves to these often subtle manifestations by consciously cultivating a positive perceptual set. This objective is vital, because clients are often preoccupied with their weaknesses. Moreover, becoming aware of strengths tends to arouse clients' hopes and to generate the courage they need to begin making changes.

Drawing clients' awareness to strengths tends to enhance self-esteem and to foster courage to undertake tasks that involve risking new behaviors. With conscious effort, social workers can become increasingly aware of their clients' strengths. For example, when a client faces a child welfare investigation because his or her children were left alone, part of the assessment must necessarily focus on the circumstances of danger that occurred and alternatives that were available to the client. This investigation often provokes defensive behavior from the client. Clients are more likely to respond positively to explorations for other solutions if their own strengths are recognized (De Jong & Miller, 1995; McQuaide & Ehrenreich, 1997). For example, the following response identifies both strengths and problems:

Social worker: You have explained that you did not intend to leave your children alone for any extended period. Your daughter was cooking for her little brother when the grease fire broke out. She knew how to call 911 and get the fire department. We would all want this situation to never have happened. Still, your daughter knew what to do in case of an emergency. She was able to prepare a meal. You have done many things to prepare your children to cope. We will need to plan together so that they are not left alone without adult supervision.

In this case, the supporting of strengths is paired with identification of continuing concerns and the need to plan together to eliminate dangers.

VIDEO CASE EXAMPLE

In the video "Serving the Squeaky Wheel" (SSW), the social worker, Ron Rooney, becomes aware of a pattern in many stories from Molly, the client, that concern grievances about being ill-served by other social workers and the health system. When she mentions not wanting to be the "greasy wheel" [squeaky wheel], Rooney suggests the possibility that Molly has, in fact, been acting as a squeaky wheel by complaining when she feels underserved, and that pattern of assertiveness is sometimes rewarded by the system and sometimes punished: "You seem to be courageous in fighting battles and you have learned some skills in assertiveness—and, as you say, that can be a two-edged or three-edged sword. Sometimes your assertiveness gets you what you want and sometimes your assertiveness causes some people to look at you as the squeaky wheel that has squeaked too much."

Guidelines for Employing Interpretation and Additive Empathy

Considerable finesse is required to effectively employ interpretation and additive empathy. The following guidelines will assist you in acquiring this skill.

1. *Use additive empathy sparingly until a sound working relationship has evolved.* Because these responses go somewhat beyond clients' current level of self-awareness,

clients may misinterpret the motives of a social worker and respond defensively. Hence, when clients have brief contact with a social worker, such as in discharge planning, they are unlikely to develop the kind of relationship in which additive empathy is appropriate. When clients demonstrate that they are confident of a social worker's goodwill, they are able to tolerate and often to benefit from additive empathic and interpretative responses.

The exceptions to this guideline involve messages that identify (1) wants and goals and (2) strengths and potentialities, both of which are also appropriate in the initial phase of the helping process. Social workers must avoid identifying strengths excessively in the initial phase, because some clients will interpret such messages as insincere flattery or as minimizing their distress.

2. *Employ these responses only when clients are engaged in self-exploration or have shown that they are ready to do so.* Clients or groups that are not ready to engage in self-exploration are likely to resist social workers' interpretive efforts and may perceive them as unwarranted attempts by social workers to impose their formulations upon them. Exceptions to this guideline are the same as those cited in the first guideline.

3. *Pitch these responses to the edge of clients' self-awareness, and avoid attempting to foster awareness that is remote from clients' current awareness or experiences.* Clients generally are receptive to responses that closely relate to their experiences but resist those that emanate from social workers' unfounded conjectures. It is not good practice to push clients into rapidly acquiring new insights, because many of these deep interpretations will prove to be inaccurate and produce negative effects, including reducing clients' confidence in social workers, conveying lack of understanding, or engendering resistance. Social workers should not employ interpretive responses until they have enough information to be reasonably confident their responses are accurate. They should then take care to share the supportive information upon which the interpretation is based.

4. *Avoid making several additive empathic responses in succession.* Because interpretation responses require time to think through, digest, and assimilate, a series of such responses tends to bewilder and overwhelm clients.

5. *Phrase interpretive responses in tentative terms.* Because these responses involve a certain degree of inference, there is always the possibility that the social worker might be wrong. Tentative phrasing openly acknowledges this possibility and invites clients to agree or disagree (Cormier, Nurius, & Osborn, 2009, p. 132). If social workers present interpretations in an authoritarian or dogmatic manner, however, clients may not feel free to offer candid feedback and may outwardly agree while covertly rejecting interpretations. Tentative phrases include "I wonder if …," "Could it be that your feelings may be related to … ?", and "Perhaps you're feeling this way because…." Using additive empathy to explore strengths is, of course, less threatening and can be done with less hesitation.

VIDEO CASE EXAMPLE

Note that in the video "Home for the Holidays" (HFH1), at several points, Kim, the family therapist, suggests a tentative interpretation of what one or the other might be feeling and then says, "I don't want to put words into your mouth," giving them an opportunity to correct her interpretation.

6. *To determine the accuracy of an interpretive response, carefully note clients' reactions after offering the interpretation.* When responses are on target, clients affirm their validity, continue self-exploration by bringing up additional relevant material, or respond emotionally in a manner that matches the moment (e.g., ventilate relevant feelings). When interpretations are inaccurate or are premature, clients tend to disconfirm them (verbally or nonverbally), change the subject, withdraw emotionally, argue or become defensive, or simply ignore the interpretation.

7. *If the client responds negatively to an interpretative response, acknowledge your probable error, respond empathically to the client's reaction, and continue your discussion of the topic under consideration.* Note that sometimes such interpretations are immediately rejected but a seed has been planted that clients may further reflect about.

To assist you in expanding your skill in formulating interpretive and additive empathic responses, a number of exercises, together with modeled responses, appear at the end of this chapter.

Confrontation

Confrontation is similar to interpretation and additive empathy in that it is a tool to enhance clients' self-awareness and to promote change. Confrontation, however, involves facing clients with some aspect of their thoughts, feelings, or behavior that is contributing to or maintaining their difficulties. Social workers, perhaps more than members of other helping professions, must struggle to maintain a dual focus on both the individual's rights and social justice. Some claim that the ability to juggle these potentially conflicting demands is an essential strength of the profession (Regehr & Angle, 1997). Others argue that "there are some activities people can do that put them outside any entitlement to respect ... some people called clients are not much respected" (Ryder & Tepley, 1993, p. 146). For example, individuals who act to harm or endanger others, such as the perpetrators of domestic violence or sexual abuse, challenge this dual commitment and social workers' ethical obligation to respect the inherent worth and dignity of all individuals regardless of the acts they may have committed. We take the position that it is not the professional role of social workers to morally judge perpetrators of harmful behavior. It is rather our role to assist such persons to learn and grow through gaining insight and taking appropriate responsibility. Such judgment is not helpful in that pursuit.

In this context, when is confrontation appropriate? With whom? And under what conditions? Is confrontation a skill or a style of practice? In some settings, confrontation became a style of practice rather than a selective skill. That is, practitioners believed that some clients were so well defended with denial, rationalization, and refusal to accept responsibility that only repeated confrontations would succeed. For example, in work with batterers, some have claimed that "almost every word they [batterers] utter is either victim blaming or justification for their violence. So I have to start confronting all of that stuff right from the beginning and it gets very intense" (Pence & Paymar, 1993, p. 21). It was believed that only when the offender admitted responsibility for the behavior and accepted the label of offender could meaningful change occur. If the clients did not accept the label, and if they defended themselves, they were labeled as being in denial and resistant (Miller & Sovereign, 1989). Hence, confronting them in an authoritarian and aggressive style (Miller & Rollnick, 1991) was considered necessary to achieve an admission of guilt—that is, admission that they had a problem and were not in control of their behavior.

In short, clients were expected to give up their own views and to accept the views of those who had the power to confront them. It was assumed that disempowered persons—who had no motivation and were incapable of making their own decisions and controlling their behavior—would then accept and cooperate with the formulation of the problem by the social workers and/or group (Kear-Colwell & Pollock, 1997). If they reacted by showing disagreement and resistance, they were seen as persisting in denial, as lacking motivation, and often as demonstrating pathological personality patterns.

This view too often leads to an interactive cycle of confrontation and denial in which the client acts to protect his or her self-esteem by denying charges (Miller & Sovereign, 1989). Social workers and theorists in fields such as treatment of domestic abuse perpetrators, persons with addictions, and sexual offenders have now questioned whether this style is effective or ethical (Fearing, 1996; Kear-Colwell & Pollock, 1997; Miller & Sovereign, 1989; Murphy & Baxter, 1997). These helping professionals contend that intense confrontation of defenses is not beneficial or it may unwittingly reinforce the belief that relationships are based on coercive influences (Murphy & Baxter, 1997). They suggest that a supportive and collaborative working alliance is more likely to increase motivation in clients. Motivational interviewing is more likely to create dissonance and encourage offenders to own the process. Even in work with addicted persons, new approaches acknowledge the importance of developing a positive, respectful approach toward the person who is the subject of the intervention (Fearing, 1996).

Instead of all-purpose confrontation delivered at any time, it is more useful to acknowledge the stage of change the client is at regarding the problematic behavior. Prochaska, DiClemente, and Norcross (1992) proposed a six-stage process of change (see Table 17-1). Their model begins with precontemplation, in which the person has not considered the behavior to be a problem.

In the motivational interviewing approach, the social worker takes responsibility for pursuing a positive atmosphere for change based on accurate empathic understanding, mutual trust, acceptance, and understanding of the world from the offender's perspective (Miller, Rollnick, & Conforti, 2002; Kear-Colwell & Pollock, 1997). In this exploration, the focus is on the offending behavior and its effects and origins, not on the person (Kear-Colwell & Pollock, 1997). The effort seeks to be persuasive by creating an awareness that the person's problem behavior is dissonant with his or her personal goals. By engaging in a risk-benefit analysis, the social

TABLE-17-1 STAGES OF CHANGE MODEL

STAGE	CHARACTERISTIC BEHAVIOR	SOCIAL WORKER'S TASK
Precontemplation	Client does not believe that he or she has a problem; is considered unmotivated by others	Raise awareness of concerns held by others: "What does your partner think about the effect of your drinking on your home life?" Stimulate dissonance with risk-benefit analysis: "What are the benefits to you from making your living by selling drugs? What are the costs to you from living by selling drugs?"
Contemplation	Becomes aware of the existence of the problem but is not moved to action Appears ambivalent—shows awareness, then discounts it	Attempt to tip decisional balance by exploring reasons to change: "As you add it up, what do you think the benefits are in relation to the costs? If you get a legal job, then what?" Strengthen confidence in change as a possibility
Preparation	Recognizes problem; asks what can be done to change Appears motivated	Help client plan appropriate course of action
Action	Implements plan of action	Develop plan to implement action Plan details to make it possible (e.g., transportation, child care)
Maintenance	Sustains change through consistent application of strategies	Identify strategies to prevent lapses and relapse: "What have been the triggers to expose you to a dangerous situation?"
Relapse	Slips into problematic behavior and may return to precontemplation stage	Attempt to return to contemplation without being stuck or demoralized Reinforce achievement; treat with respect: "This is a difficult time. You have been at this point before and you overcame it. What do you think about whether you want to overcome it again?"

SOURCE: Adapted from Kear-Colwell and Pollock (1997); and Prochaska, DiClemente, and Norcross (1992).

worker assists the client in deciding whether it makes sense to explore a change so as to better reach those goals. The social worker would then assist the client to make a decision.

Once a client has decided to act, then the form of influence can help him or her decide which action to pursue. For example, after he has decided to deal with a domestic violence problem, a male client can be helped to consider alternatives for how to go about it. When a decision has been made, efforts are aimed at planning useful action to reach the goal. When a change has occurred, efforts are aimed at exploring in detail the contingencies and triggers that have been associated with the behavior. Armed with such knowledge, alternatives can be planned and practiced to avoid a relapse into the offending behavior.

Constructive confrontation is most likely to be heard when it comes from a source liked and respected by the client. Consequently, confrontations that occur early in contact are often not accurately heard or heeded. Nevertheless, before a helping relationship has developed, social workers sometimes have responsibilities to confront clients who are in violation of the law and who are dangers to themselves and others. Such confrontations should occur sparingly, given the likelihood that they will not be heeded so early in contact (Rooney, R.H., 2009).

In the middle phase of work, social workers employ confrontation to assist clients to achieve awareness of the forces blocking their progress toward growth and goal attainment and to enhance their motivation to implement efforts toward change. Confrontation is particularly relevant when clients are blind to the discrepancies or inconsistencies in their thoughts, beliefs, emotions, and behavior, which produce or perpetuate dysfunctional behavior. Of course, blind spots in self-awareness are universal because all humans suffer from the limitation of being unable to step out of their perceptual fields and look at themselves objectively.

> ## VIDEO CASE EXAMPLE
>
> In the video "How Can I Help?" (HCH), the social worker, Peter Dimock, explores with the client, Julie, her efforts or the lack of such efforts to get involved in counseling for her depression. In the section that follows, he hears her explanation for what has occurred and does not blame her, but rather notes that perhaps she was agreeing to work on this goal more to please him than because she owned it as her own goal. "You've been having some difficulty getting these appointments really set up or follow through with making them and it sounds like you've been doing it more for me because I made it part of your case plan and you're really not sure whether this is something that you want, is that true?" In this way, Peter is matter of fact and not blaming in assessing her motivation for completing this task. Julie affirms "I just want to get this stuff done on the case plan so I can just be done with it too, but I feel like I'm okay." She notes that she is doing it because it is on the plan, not because she agrees with it. Peter again does not judge her motivation but notes it: "so this is one that you'd like to be able to check off the list, but you don't think you really need it."
>
> Peter asks what happened when Julie stopped taking her medication and seeing a counselor. Julie replies: "I don't know, I guess I was doing, you know, pretty good and they sent me home with you know, my meds, and the meds ran out and I know I had to like see somebody to get like a refill or something, but I don't know, I thought I was doing okay, I thought I was doing okay, so I just didn't take anymore."
>
> Peter notes his understanding of why she stopped taking the medication and then asks for permission to explore the depression topic. "Well, do you mind if we explore a little bit whether or not this depression, which you're not sure that you really have, is having some effect on you and on your kids, perhaps?" He then asks her if she knows the symptoms of depression. When she notes that she does not and is okay with hearing them, Peter responds: "Among them are that you feel really kind of down, often times tired, may be difficult getting out of bed, hard to look forward to doing a bunch of things, if anything, you don't feel things are all that important or you don't just feel the energy at times to do it. Sometimes you have difficulty sleeping or difficulty concentrating and you know, you just feel kind of blah. Is that ever true for you?" In this way, Peter is raising awareness in a tactful way about how the depression diagnosis may be relevant for her and the treatment and medication important for her and her baby. She admits that sometimes she is sleeping and the baby awakens her. He asks whether this is okay with her and she comments "Well, I guess I'd kind of like to do it different. I know, in my parenting classes, they talk about like you know, babies need routines and how that's really important and I just, I guess I shouldn't be staying in bed and I should, you know, maybe give baby more in a routine because, you know, he don't go to bed sometimes till 1, 2, 3 in the morning and you know, cause I'm up kind of like all night and I don't want to get out of bed when I am in bed or laying around." He comments, "So you know that in some ways a routine would be—and some consistency—would be a better way to parent, and that's important to you." In this way he elicits the insight from her rather than making a pronouncement about effective parenting. When she comments that keeping up with routines is difficult because of feeling tired he notes "I'm just wondering and I don't know, but perhaps some of what you're describing has to do with being depressed. Do you think that's a possibility?" In this way, he has built toward a tactful interpretation and links it to her values: "it is important to you to provide good parenting, consistency for your son. He's important to you."
>
> Peter moves on to make a suggestion "I am wondering if seeing someone and trying to figure out whether or not there's some medication that might make a difference could be helpful." At this point, Julie offers to contact a clinic about another appointment to explore medication and counseling.

As the previous example with Julie shows, additive empathy and confrontation have much in common. Skillful confrontations incorporate consideration of clients' feelings that underlie obstacles to change. Because fears are often among these feelings, skill in relating with high levels of empathy is a prerequisite to using confrontation effectively. Indeed, effective confrontation is an extension of empathic communication because the focus on discrepancies and inconsistencies derives from a deep understanding of clients' feelings, experiences, and behavior.

It is important for social workers to possess a range of confrontation skills and not to confront clients primarily to vent their own frustration with clients' lack of progress. Social workers would more appropriately consider confrontation to exist along a continuum that ranges from fostering *self-confrontation* at one extreme to *assertive confrontation* at the other extreme (Rooney, 2009). That is, clients can often be engaged quickly in self-confrontation by social workers asking them questions that cause them to reflect on the relationship between their behaviors and their own values.

Skillfully designed intake forms can serve a similar function, asking potential clients to reflect on concerns and their perceptions of the causes. Such confrontations are subtle and respectful, and they rarely engender strong client opposition. As clients gain expanded awareness of themselves and their problems through self-exploration, they tend to recognize and to confront discrepancies and inconsistencies themselves. Self-confrontation is generally preferable to social worker-initiated confrontation, because the former is less risky and because clients' resistance to integrating insights is not an obstacle when they initiate confrontations themselves.

Clients vary widely in the degree to which they engage in self-confrontation. Emotionally mature, introspective persons may engage in self-confrontations frequently. In contrast, individuals who are out of touch with their emotions, who lack awareness of their effects on others, and who blame others or circumstances for their difficulties are least likely to engage in self-confrontation.

Inductive questioning can be a form of confrontation that is more active on the social worker's part but is still conveyed in a respectful manner. The social worker asks questions that lead the client to consider potential discrepancies between thoughts, values, beliefs, and actions. Also, when the therapist asks a question that relates to facts rather than one that requires the client to label himself or herself, the question is more likely to be effective. For example, asking a client with a chemical dependency problem, "Are you powerless over alcohol?" would require the client to essentially label himself an alcoholic. On the other hand, "Do you ever have blackouts?", "Do you find it easier to bring up a problem with another person when you have had something to drink?", and "Do you ever find that once you begin drinking you can't easily stop?" are questions that, taken together, raise the possibility that drinking is a problem that might need attention (Citron, 1978). Such questions may be less intrusive on an intake assessment form than when presented in sequential interview questions. The latter can cause the client to feel that the social worker is trying to persuade him or her to immediately acknowledge the risks of his or her behavior.

When a danger is imminent, the social worker may not be able to rely on tactful self-confrontation facilitated by inductive questioning. Instead, he or she may have to engage in more assertive confrontation in which the connection between troubling thoughts, plans, values, and beliefs is stated in declarative form, connecting them explicitly for the client. Such assertive confrontation is a more high-risk technique because clients may interpret social workers' statements as criticisms, put-downs, or rejections. Paradoxically, the risk of these reactions is greatest among clients who must be confronted most often because they rarely engage in self-confrontation. These individuals tend to have weak self-concepts and are therefore prone to read criticism into messages when none is intended. Moreover, ill-timed and poorly executed confrontations may be perceived by clients as verbal assaults and may seriously damage helping relationships.

Therefore, using confrontation requires keen timing and finesse. Social workers must make special efforts to convey their helpful intent and goodwill as they employ this technique. Otherwise, they may engender hostility or offend and alienate clients.

Effective assertive confrontations embody four elements: (1) expression of concern; (2) a description of the client's purported goal, belief, or commitment; (3) the behavior (or absence of behavior) that is inconsistent or discrepant with the goal, belief, or commitment; and (4) the probable negative outcomes of the discrepant behavior. The format of a confrontive response may be depicted as follows:

(want)
I am concerned because you (believe)
(are striving to)

_____
(describe desired outcome)

but your _____
(describe discrepant action, behavior, or inaction)

is likely to produce _____
(describe probable negative consequences)

This format is purely illustrative. You may organize these elements in varying ways, and we encourage you to be innovative and to develop your own style. For example, you may challenge clients to analyze the effects of behaviors that are incongruous with their purported goals or values, as illustrated in the following excerpt:

Social worker [To male on parole]: Al, I know the last thing you want is to have to return to prison. I want you to stay out, too, and I think you sense that. But I have to level with you. You're starting to hang out with the same bunch you got in trouble with before you went to prison. You're heading in the same direction you were before, and we both know where that leads.

In this confrontation, the social worker begins by referring to the client's purported goal (remaining out of prison) and expresses a like commitment to the goal. The social worker next introduces concern about the client's behavior (hanging out with the same bunch the client got in trouble with before) that is discrepant with that goal. The social worker concludes the confrontation by focusing on the possible negative consequence of the discrepant behavior (getting into trouble and returning to prison).

Notice these same elements in the following examples of confrontive responses:

- [To father in family session]: *Mr. D, I'd like you to stop for a moment and examine what you're doing. I know you want the children not to be afraid of you and to talk with you more openly. Right? [Father agrees.] Okay, let's think about what you just did with Steve. He began to tell you about what he did after the school assembly, and you cut him off and got on his case. Did you notice how he clammed up immediately?*
- [To mother in child welfare system]: *I have a concern I need to share with you. You've expressed your goal of regaining custody of Pete, and we agreed that attending the parents' group was part of the plan to accomplish that goal. This week is the second time in a row you've missed the meeting because you overslept. I'm very concerned that you may be defeating yourself in accomplishing your goal.*

Because employing assertive confrontation runs the risk of putting clients on the defensive or alienating them, expressing concern and helpful intent is a critical element because it reduces the possibility that clients will misconstrue the motive behind the confrontation. Tone of voice is also vital in highlighting helpful intent. If the social worker conveys the confrontation in a warm, concerned tone of voice, the client will be much less likely to feel attacked. If the social worker uses a critical tone of voice, any verbal reassurance that criticism was not intended is likely to fall on deaf ears. Keep in mind that people tend to attach more credence to nonverbal aspects of messages than to verbal aspects.

Guidelines for Employing Confrontation

To assist you in employing confrontation effectively, we offer the following guidelines.

1. *When a violation of the law or imminent danger to self or others is involved, a confrontation must occur no matter how early in the working relationship.* Such confrontations may impede the development of the relationship, but the risk of harm to self and others is more important than the immediate effect on the relationship.

2. *Whenever possible, avoid confrontation until an effective working relationship has been established.* This can occur when a client is contemplating action (or inaction) that impedes his or her own goals but is not an imminent danger to self or others. Employing empathic responsiveness in early contacts conveys understanding, fosters rapport, and enhances confidence in the social worker's perceptiveness and expertise. When a foundation of trust and confidence has been established, clients are more receptive to confrontations and, in some instances, even welcome them.

3. *Use confrontation sparingly.* Confrontation is a potent technique that generally should be employed only when clients' blind spots are not responsive to other, less risky intervention methods. Poorly timed and excessive confrontations can inflict psychological damage on clients (Lieberman, Yalom, & Miles, 1973).

Another reason to employ confrontation judiciously is that some clients may yield to forceful confrontation for counterproductive reasons. Seeking to please social workers (or to avoid displeasing them), they may temporarily modify their behavior. But changing merely to comply with the expectations of a social worker leads to passivity and dependence, both of which are anathema to actual growth. Some clients are already excessively passive, and pressuring them for compliance merely reinforces their passivity.

4. *Deliver confrontations in an atmosphere of warmth, caring, and concern.* If social workers employ confrontations in a cold, impersonal, or critical way, clients are likely to feel that they are being attacked. By contrast, if social workers preface confrontations with genuine empathic concern, clients are more likely to perceive the helpfulness intended in the confrontation. In this regard, carrying out a confrontation when the social worker is tired, irritated, angry, disappointed,

frustrated or disillusioned: in a word, when the social worker is emotionally overwrought, is a bad idea. Carrying out a confrontation is about the client's needs and not the social worker's needs.

5. *Whenever possible, encourage self-confrontation.* Recall from the previous discussion that self-confrontation has decided advantages over social worker-initiated confrontation. Learning by self-discovery fosters independence and increases the likelihood that clients will act upon their newly gained self-awareness. Social workers can encourage self-confrontation by drawing clients' attention to issues, behaviors, or inconsistencies that they may have overlooked and by encouraging them to analyze the situation further.

For example, the social worker may directly intervene into dysfunctional interactions and challenge individuals, couples, families, or groups to identify what they are doing. Responses that encourage self-confrontation in such a context include the following:

- *"Let's stop and look at what you just did."*
- *"What just happened?"*

Other inductive question responses that highlight inconsistencies and foster self-confrontation are as follows:

- *"I'm having trouble seeing how what you just said (or did) fits with ..."*
- *"I can understand how you felt, but how did (describe behavior) make it better for you?"*
- *"What you're saying seems inconsistent with what you want to achieve. How do you see it?"*

Yet another technique is useful when clients overlook the dynamic significance of their own revealing expressions or when their expressed feelings fail to match their reported feelings. This technique involves asking them to repeat a message, to listen carefully to themselves, and to consider the meaning of the message. Examples of this technique follow:

- *"I want to be sure you realize the significance of what you just said. Repeat it, but this time listen carefully to yourself, and tell me what it means to you."*
- [To marital partner in conjoint interview]: *"Joan just told you something terribly important, and I'm not sure you really grasped it. Could you repeat it, Joan, and I want you to listen very carefully, Bob, and check with Joan as to whether you grasped what she said."*
- [To group member]: *"You just told the group you're feeling better about yourself, but it didn't come through that way. Please say it again, but get in touch with your feelings and listen to yourself."*

6. *Avoid using confrontation when clients are experiencing extreme emotional strain.* Confrontation tends to mobilize anxiety. When clients are under heavy strain, supportive techniques rather than confrontation are indicated. Clients who are overwhelmed with anxiety or guilt generally are not receptive to confrontation and will not benefit from it. In fact, confrontation may be detrimental, adding to their already excessive tension.

Conversely, confrontation is appropriate for clients who experience minimal inner conflict or anxiety when such conflict or anxiety would be appropriate in light of how his or her problematic behavior is experienced by others. Self-satisfied and typically insensitive to the feelings and needs of others (whom they cause to be anxious), such clients—popularly referred to as having "character disorders"—often lack the anxiety needed to engender and maintain adequate motivation. Confrontation, when combined with the facilitative conditions, may mobilize the anxiety they need to examine their own behavior and to consider making constructive changes.

7. *Follow confrontation with emphatic responsiveness.* Because clients may take offense to even skillful confrontation, it is vital to be sensitive to their reactions. Clients often do not express their reactions verbally, so social workers need to be especially attuned to nonverbal cues that suggest hurt, anger, confusion, discomfort, embarrassment, or resentment. If clients manifest these or other unfavorable reactions, it is important to explore their reactions and to respond empathically to their feelings. Discussing such reactions provides opportunities (1) for clients to vent their feelings and (2) for social workers to clarify their helpful intent and to assist clients to work through negative feelings. If social workers fail to sense negative feelings or clients withhold expressions of them, the feelings may fester and adversely affect the helping relationship.

8. *Expect that clients will respond to confrontation with a certain degree of anxiety.* Indeed, confrontation is employed to produce a temporary sense of disequilibrium that is essential to break an impasse. The anxiety or disequilibrium serves a therapeutic purpose in impelling the client to make constructive changes that eliminate the discrepancy that prompted the social worker's confrontation. Empathic responsiveness following confrontation is not aimed at diluting this anxiety, but rather seeks to resolve untoward reactions

that may derive from negative interpretations of the social worker's motives for making the confrontation.

9. *Do not expect immediate change after confrontations.* Although awareness paves the way to change, clients rarely succeed in making changes immediately following acquisition of insight. Even when clients fully accept confrontations, corresponding changes ordinarily occur by increments. Known as working through, this change process involves repeatedly reviewing the same conflicts and the client's typical reactions to them, gradually broadening the perspective to encompass increasingly more situations to which the changes are applicable. Pressing for immediate change can inflict psychological damage on clients.

Indications for Assertive Confrontation

As noted previously, confrontation is appropriate in three circumstances: (1) when violations of the law or imminent threats to the welfare and safety of self or others are involved; (2) when discrepancies, inconsistencies, and dysfunctional behaviors (overt or covert) block progress or create difficulties; and (3) when efforts at self-confrontation and inductive questioning have been ineffective in fostering clients' awareness of these behaviors or attempts to make corresponding changes. Discrepancies may reside in cognitive/perceptual, emotional (affective), or behavioral functions or may involve interactions between these functions. A comprehensive analysis of types of discrepancies and inconsistencies has been presented elsewhere (Hammond et al., 1977, pp. 286–318); therefore, we merely highlight some of the most commonly encountered.

Cognitive/Perceptual Discrepancies

Many clients have behavioral or perceptual difficulties that are a product of inaccurate, erroneous, or incomplete information, and confrontation may assist them in modifying their problematic behaviors. For example, clients may lack accurate information about indicators of alcoholism, normal sexual functioning, or reasonable expectations of children according to stages of development.

Even more common are misconceptions about the self. The most common of these, in the authors' experience, involve self-demeaning perceptions. Even talented and attractive persons may view themselves as inferior, worthless, inadequate, unattractive, or stupid. Such perceptions are often deeply embedded and do not yield to change without extensive working through. Nevertheless, confronting clients with their strengths or raising their awareness of other areas of competence can prove helpful in challenging such self-deprecating views.

Other cognitive/perceptual discrepancies include interpersonal perceptual distortions, irrational fears, dichotomous or stereotypical thinking, denial of problems, placing responsibility for one's difficulties outside of oneself, failing to discern available alternative solutions to difficulties, and failing to consider consequences of actions.

Affective Discrepancies

Discrepancies in the emotional realm are inextricably linked to cognitive/perceptual processes, because emotions are shaped by the cognitive meanings that clients attribute to situations, events, and memories. For example, a client may experience intense anger that emanates from a conclusion that another person has intentionally insulted, slighted, or betrayed him or her. This conclusion is based on a meaning attribution that may involve a grossly distorted perception of the other person's intentions. In such instances, social workers can assist clients in exploring their feelings, providing relevant detailed factual information, considering alternative meanings and realigning emotions with reality.

Affective discrepancies that social workers commonly encounter include denying or minimizing actual feelings, being out of touch with painful emotions, expressing feelings that are contrary to purported feelings (e.g., claiming to love a spouse or child but expressing only critical or otherwise negative feelings), and verbally expressing a feeling that contradicts feelings expressed nonverbally (e.g., "No, I'm not disappointed," said with a quivering voice and tears in the eyes). Gentle confrontations aimed at emotional discrepancies often pave the way to express troubling emotions, and many clients appreciate social workers' sensitivity in recognizing their suppressed or unexpressed emotions.

If a client appears unprepared to face painful emotions, the social worker should proceed cautiously. Indeed, it may be wise to defer further exploration of those hurtful emotions. Confronting the client vigorously may elicit overwhelming emotions and engender consequent resentment toward the social worker.

Behavioral Discrepancies

Clients may experience many behavioral concerns that create difficulties for themselves and for others. Even though these patterns may be conspicuous to others, clients may remain blind to their patterns or to the effects of their behaviors on others. Confrontation may be required to expand their awareness of these patterns and their pernicious effects.

Irresponsible behavior tends to spawn serious interpersonal difficulties for clients as well as problems with broader society. Neglect of children, weak efforts to secure and maintain employment, undependability in fulfilling assignments, failure to maintain property—these and similar derelictions of duty often result in severe financial, legal, and interpersonal entanglements that may culminate in loss of employment; estrangement from others; and loss of property, child custody, self-respect, and even personal freedom.

Irresponsible behavior often pervades the helping process as well, sometimes indicated by clients' tardiness to sessions, unwillingness to acknowledge problems, and failure to keep appointments or pay fees. Effective confrontation with such clients requires employing a firm approach couched in expressions of goodwill and concern about wanting to assist them in avoiding the adverse consequences of not assuming responsibilities. Social workers do a disservice to their clients when they permit them to evade responsibility for their actions or inaction. Further, social workers must counter clients' tendency to blame others or circumstances for their difficulties by assisting them to recognize that *only they* can reduce the pressures that beset them.

Other common behavioral discrepancies involve repeated actions that are incongruous with purported goals or values. Adolescents may describe ambitious goals that require extensive training or education but they may make little effort in school, are truant frequently, and otherwise behave in ways that are entirely inconsistent with their stated goals. Spouses or parents may similarly express goals of improving their marital or family life but persistently behave in abrasive ways that further erode their relationships.

Confrontation can be e used to help clients desist from engaging in self-defeating behaviors. In some instances, therapeutic binds (a special form of confrontation discussed in Chapter 18) may be employed to supply needed leverage to motivate clients to relinquish destructive and unusually persistent patterns of behavior.

Three other common categories of discrepancies or dysfunctional behavior that warrant confrontation are manipulative behavior, dysfunctional communication, and resistance to change. In groups, certain members may attempt to dominate the group, bait group members, play one person against the other, undermine the leader, or engage in other destructive ploys. The price of permitting members to engage in such behaviors may be loss of certain group members, dilution of the group's effectiveness, or premature dissolution of the group. To avert such undesired consequences, the leader may elicit the reactions of other group members to this behavior and assist members to confront manipulators with their destructive tactics. Such confrontations should adhere to the guidelines delineated earlier, and the leader should encourage members to invite offending members to join with them in constructively seeking to accomplish the purposes for which the group was formed.

Because problematic communication frequently interpreted as resistance to change often occurs in individual, conjoint, and group sessions, social workers encounter abundant opportunities to employ confrontation to good effect. Intervening during or immediately following dysfunctional communication is a powerful means of enabling clients to experience firsthand the negative effects of their dysfunctional behaviors (e.g., interrupting, attacking, claiming, or criticizing). By shifting the focus to the negative reactions of recipients of problematic messages, social workers enable clients to receive direct feedback about how their behavior offends, alienates, or engenders defensiveness in others, thereby producing effects contrary to their purported goals.

Summary

Chapter 17 discussed three vital tools in working through clients' opposition to change and to relating openly in the helping relationship: additive empathy, interpretation, and confrontation. If individual clients are left to struggle alone with negative feelings about the helping process or the social worker, their feelings may mount to the extent that they resolve them by discontinuing their sessions. If family members or groups are permitted to oppose change by engaging in distracting, irrelevant, or otherwise dysfunctional behaviors, they may likewise lose both confidence in the social worker (for valid reasons) and motivation to continue. For these reasons, social workers must accord the highest priority to being helpful to clients who encounter obstacles or who may be opposed to change.

CourseMate

Access an integrated eBook and chapter-specific learning tools including glossary terms, chapter outlines, relevant web links, videos, and practice quizzes. Go to **www.cengagebrain.com**.

CHAPTER 18
The Management of Barriers to Change

CHAPTER OVERVIEW

Chapter 18 focuses on potential barriers to change and ways of managing them so that they do not interrupt progress or cause unplanned termination by clients. Clients who have the best of intentions and who are highly motivated may nevertheless encounter obstacles that interfere with the helping process and goal attainment. These obstacles may occur within the individual (e.g., interpersonal or intrapersonal dynamics or a mix of both), or within the social or physical environment. We discuss the ways in which social workers' behaviors can either contribute to a resolution of barriers or unintentionally aggravate them. In the final portion of this chapter we will elaborate on the principles and techniques of motivational interviewing, presented in Chapters 17 and 18.

After reading this chapter, you will gain skills in:

Recognizing and managing dynamics that can interfere with your relationship with clients, and thereby impede their progress

- Understanding and managing dynamics in cross-cultural and cross-racial relationships
- Using supportive and facilitative skills to promote change
- Assessing and gauging your behavior with clients and use of self

EPAS COMPETENCIES IN THE 18TH CHAPTER

This chapter provides the information that you will need to meet the following practice competencies.

2.1.1b Practice self-reflection and self correction to assure continued professional development

2.1.1c Attend to professional roles and boundaries

2.1.1d Demonstrate professional demeanor in behavior, appearance and communication

2.1.1f Use supervision and consultation

2.1.2a Recognize and manage personal values in a way that allows for professional values to guide practice

2.1.2b Make ethical decisions by applying standards of the National Association of Social Workers Code of Ethics and, if possible, of the International Federation of Social Workers/International Association of Schools of Social Work Ethics in Social Work, Statement of Principles

2.1.3a Distinguish, appraise, and integrate multiple sources of knowledge, including research-based knowledge and practice wisdom

2.1.4a Recognize the extent to which a culture's structures and values alienate, create, or enhance privilege and power.

2.1.4b Gain sufficient self-awareness to eliminate the influence of personal bias and values in working with diverse groups

2.1.4c Recognize and communicate their understanding of the importance of differences in shaping life experiences

2.1.4d View themselves as learners and engage those with whom they work as key informants

2.1.5a Understand forms and mechanisms of oppression and discrimination

2.1.6b Use research evidence to inform practice

2.1.7a Utilize a conceptual framework to guide the process of assessment, intervention, and evaluation.

2.1.7b **Critique and apply knowledge to understand person and environment**

2.1.10a **Substantively and affectively prepare for action with individuals, families, groups, organizations, and communities**

2.1.10b **Use empathy and other interpersonal skills**

2.1.10c **Develop a mutually agreed-on focus of work and desired outcomes**

2.1.10i **Implement prevention interventions that enhance client capacities**

2.1.10j **Help clients resolve problems**

2.1.10m **Critically analyze, monitor, and evaluate interventions**

Barriers to Change

EP 2.1.10a

In the best of circumstances, progress toward goal attainment is rarely smooth. Even getting started can be a formidable challenge with involuntary clients, when compliance is required; the help that is offered has not been solicited, and may not be perceived as particularly useful. With all people, the change process is one in which there can be rapid spurts, plateaus, impasses, fears, and sometimes brief relapse periods. Think about how often you have vowed to behave differently with a friend, coworker, spouse, or relative only to become involved in a situation that pushes your buttons, causing you to revert to old patterns of behaving. Eventually, you will accomplish your desired behavioral goal, but the fact that you had a setback does not mean that you are unable or unwilling to change. The same is true for clients.

Barriers to change discussed in this chapter are:

- *Relational dynamics that occur in the interactions between clients and practitioners.*
- *Behaviors on the part of practitioners.*
- *Dynamics that are challenging in cross-racial and cross-cultural relationships.*
- *Sexual attraction toward clients, and the ethical and legal implication of this behavior.*

Relational Dynamics

Relational reactions are conscious and unconscious dynamics between people; for example, reactions of the practitioner to the individual or those of the individual in response to the practitioner. Your relationship with a client is the vehicle that animates the helping process. Indeed, the quality of the helping relationship can critically determine a person's moment-to-moment receptiveness to you. For better or worse, feelings and emotions that can influence the relationship constantly flow back and forth between you and the individuals with whom you are working. To maintain positive helping relationships, it is important that you are alert and manage relational dynamics so that they did not become threats.

EP 2.1.10a

Because of the profound importance of the helping relationship, it is crucial that you are skilled both in cultivating relationships and in keeping them intact. Helping relationships that are characterized by reciprocal positive feelings between social workers and clients are conducive to personal growth and successful problem solving. Facilitative conditions, such as high levels of *warmth, acceptance, unconditional caring, empathy, genuineness,* and *sensitivity to differences* promote the development of and sustain positive helping relationships.

EP 2.1.10b

Despite best efforts, however, some individuals are unable to hear or respond positively to the helping relationship for a number of reasons, such as distrust, fear, or simply being overwhelmed. Social workers, too, may have difficulty building a positive relationship with some individuals because of their biases, or because a person may have certain personality traits, physical attributes, or a type of problem that causes a behavioral response or countertransference. For example, consider the following exchange between a social worker and a consultant during a case review session:

EP 2.1.4a

CASE EXAMPLE

Social worker, presenting a case: How can you feel empathy for every client? I have this one client, and when I go to her house, she is just sitting there like a big lump. She doesn't seem to understand that she may lose her children, even though she says she does not want them to be removed from her care. She tells me that the man who abused her children is out of her life, but I don't believe her. She tells lies, she doesn't do

> anything to help herself, and she sits there in the midst of a cluttered filthy apartment watching television. I am just waiting to catch her in one of her lies. It is hard for me to feel anything for this client or to help her keep custody of her children.
>
> **Consultant:** Wow, you really don't like this client and she knows it! Perhaps she feels, "Why bother to establish a relationship with you?" It is quite possible that she has feelings about your visits in the same way that you dread seeing her.

EP 2.1.1d & 2.1.2a

What are the relational dynamics in the case? In this case, these dynamics prevented problem solving in that neither the social worker nor the mother was engaged in this process. First, when we do not like clients, for whatever reasons, they sense our feelings toward them and the psychological connection is unlikely to develop. Moreover, the nonverbal cues of the social worker communicated a lack of acceptance, warmth, and empathy. Note, for example, the social worker described the client as "sitting there like a big lump." What mental image of the mother is conveyed in this statement? Perhaps that she is overweight, passive, lazy, and uncaring about her children. Further, the bias of the social worker appeared to be slanted toward Weinberg's (2006) assertion that single mothers are often judged by accepted standards of motherhood behavior; in which case, this mother was sorely lacking. Sensing the social worker's reaction to her, you can be sure that the mother dreaded the visits. Moreover, the social worker's feelings about the mother set a tone that inhibited exploration of pertinent factors, for example, the possibility the woman is depressed was overlooked. Biased perceptions of individuals can also influence the manner in which they are assessed and decisions that are made with respect to their commitment to change. Those individuals who are perceived in a positive light, specifically, they are cooperative or compliant and readily accept the practitioner's viewpoint, tend to be assessed in a positive manner. In contrast, if an individual behaves passive way, like the mother in this case, expresses anger or rejects the practitioner's assessment, he or she is perceived more negatively and is assessed as being less willing to change (Dettlaff & Rycraft, 2010; Holland, 2000).

A second factor in this case was the social worker's preoccupation with whether the client was telling the truth. There are times when you may feel that you are working harder than clients, and in consequence you become sidetracked

EP 2.1.1d

by their behavior such as whether the mother is telling the truth. Obviously, truth telling is a reciprocal expectation in the helping relationship. Yet, is it really necessary to determine whether the mother was lying, unless her dishonesty threatens the welfare of her children? Continuing to focus on catching her in a lie, distracts from problem solving and the social worker acts as an investigator. The decisive assessment question is whether this mother could or is willing to (and under what circumstances) ensure that her children are safe. Did the social worker come to like the client? Perhaps not, but she was able to understand and therefore manage her reactions to the mother that had effectively stalled professional problem solving, beginning with examining her own bias and behavior. Social workers do have emotional reactions to such circumstances but taking it out on the client is not the appropriate professional response. Instead, sharing your emotional reactions, including when you feel discouraged or disgusted with your supervisor is a more constructive way for you to learn from the situation.

EP 2.1.1f

You may recall an experience that caused you to react to an individual in a similar manner. For you and the social worker in the case consultation scenario, self, understanding, awareness, and control are essential to ethical professional practice. Cournoyer (2011)

EP 2.1.1b & 2.1.10a

has *identified preparatory self-reflection, centering and planning* as active steps that you can take to reduce the risk of relational dynamics that can interfere with the helping process. Self-exploration and self-reflection are steps to help you to clarify, and indeed understand your bias, beliefs, values, and stereotypes. In essence, this process informs you of how you might judge people and subsequently draw positive or negative conclusions about them. The evaluation of self is also instrumental in maintaining self control. The process helps you manage personal factors, such as your emotional state or physical stressors that can influence your readiness to interact with clients. Being aware of your personal thoughts, feelings, and physical sensations, specifically centering, involves focusing, compartmentalizing and, if needed, engaging in self-talk. In preparing to meet with clients, you can develop a mental check list in which you focus on, for example, the reason and purpose of the contact and what is to be accomplished, taking into consideration your agenda as well as that of the client. Understandably, it can be difficult to manage your feelings with some individuals and in some situations. Self-control is the ability to recognize and therefore manage your feelings, emotions, and behaviors. Actively taking steps to manage your potential reactions before and during a session can prevent you from becoming caught up in dynamics that can side-track a relationship. In your interactions with clients, especially those who may trigger a reaction in you, it is equally important to evaluate your performance relative to the essential elements of the helping relationship, specifically the extent to which you convey warmth, acceptance, and empathy.

Even when a positive relationship evolves, various events and moment-by-moment transactions may pose risks to initiating and sustaining a workable relationship. As you work with clients, it is important that you are attentive to instances that indicate that something in the relationship between you and the individual is off-center. Failure to perceive that something has gone wrong and effectively manage the situation may result in a deadlock in which problem solving becomes stalled. The next section elaborates on the threats to the relationship that result from the social worker's actions or behavior, those of the client, and from dynamic mixes of both.

Under- and Over-Involvement of Social Workers with Clients

EP 2.1.1c
& 2.1.1d

In your best effort to foster a positive relationship with clients and to be attuned to the interference of relational dynamics, there are times when something in the relationship can be off-center. In some instances, you may become caught up with a client and his or her situation to such an extent that your actions in the relationship become an inhibiting force. Even though you may strive to maintain a balanced attitude, be appreciative of strengths, and aware of obstacles, there are situations in which you may be inclined to emphasize one side of the story that is generally favorable or unfavorable to the client. Raines (1996) has classified such reactions as *over-involvement or under-involvement*. Levels of over- or under-involvement can also be classified according to the practitioner's general viewpoint or attitude toward the individual, which can be either positive or negative. Table 18-1 presents an adaptation of Raines's schema for classifying involvement (Raines, 1996).

1. *When the social worker is under-involved and has a negative attitude toward the client,* it can be reflected in his or her lack of attention or empathy, tuning out, biased or judgmental views, or dismissing or not recalling pertinent information. All social workers have had less than productive sessions with clients and days in which their level of attentiveness was less than desirable. The earlier case consultation scenario is an example of under-involvement of the social worker because of her negative attitude toward the mother. Such behavior signals that the cause of the behavior must be examined. Hence, part of professional behavior is the capacity for self-observation and correction when indicated. Noting one or more of these patterns highlighted in Table 18-1 is cause for supervision or consultation with peers so that you can develop a plan for rectifying the behavior.

EP 2.1.1c

2. *Under-involvement when there is a positive social worker attitude* can occur when a social worker withholds assistance because of an overly optimistic assessment of an individual client's capacity and need for help. For example, a young woman who has made good progress toward her goals was praised by the social worker. Yet during a session, the young woman reported that she often wakes up feeling scared, angry, depressed, and overwhelmed by her responsibilities. In response to the her complaints, however, the social worker encouraged her to focus on her strengths (e.g., "Look what you have accomplished so far!"), promising the her that continued sessions would most likely resolve her concerns. Two relational issues are at risk in this scenario. First, the social worker's level of empathy can be rated as low and as such is a potential barrier. In addition, she ignored the concerns and feelings expressed by the client. Challenging the client to focus on her strengths hampered the social worker's ability to address what the client had said, a signal that the social worker was tuned out and under-involved. Strengths notwithstanding, the young woman voiced some very real concerns, and it is sufficient to believe that future sessions with the social worker are unlikely to resolve her concerns. Would it surprise you to learn that the young woman showed up for future appointments only sporadically when she had a concrete need? Under-involvement can

EP 2.1.1c

TABLE-18-1 SOCIAL WORKER'S UNDER- AND OVER-INVOLVEMENT WITH CLIENTS

	SOCIAL WORKER WITH UNFAVORABLE ATTITUDE TOWARD CLIENT	SOCIAL WORKER WITH FAVORABLE ATTITUDE TOWARD CLIENT
Under-involvement	• Finds it difficult to empathize with the client • Is inattentive to or "tunes out" the client • Has lapses of memory about important information previously revealed by the client • Is drowsy or preoccupied • Dreads sessions or comes late, cancels sessions inappropriately • Is off the mark with interpretations • Client perceives feedback as put-downs • Fails to acknowledge client growth • Never thinks about the client outside of sessions	• Withholds empathy inappropriately due to belief in client's strengths • Refrains from interpretation to promote insight • Reflects or reframes excessively without answering • Never considers self-disclosure • Gives advice or assignments that the client feels incapable of carrying out
Over-involvement	• Has an unreasonable dislike of the client • Is argumentative • Is provocative • Gives excessive advice • Employs inept or poorly timed confrontations • Disapproves of the client's planned course of action inappropriately • Appears to take sides against the client (or subgroup) or actually does so • Dominates discussions or frequently interrupts the client • Uses power with involuntary clients to interfere in lifestyle areas beyond the range of legal mandates • Competes intellectually • Has violent thoughts or dreams about the client	• Is overly emotional or sympathetic • Provides extra time inappropriately • Fantasizes brilliant interpretations • Is unusually sensitive to criticisms • Has sexual thoughts or dreams about the client • Seeks nonprofessional contact with the client

SOURCE: Adapted from Raines (1996).

also take the form of settling on assignments or tasks that the client feels incapable of completing. In these cases, when clients fail, there is a tendency to question their commitment, rather than the influence of our own actions. Of course when faced with the pressure of a large caseload, a social worker may assign a client that he or she is under involved with to a lower level of contact than is actually warranted.

Under-involvement, despite positive regard for the client, can detrimentally affect a social worker's decision making, as illustrated in the next case situation.

As in negative under-involvement, positive decisions may happen with particular clients, because of positive stereotyping with clients who possess what are perceived to be positive attributes. Patterns of repeated positive under-involvement, however, call for examination and correction. Again, reflection on these patterns with peers and supervisors can assist social workers in finding ways to adjust the involvement level. Hence, while generally focusing on client strengths and having a positive attitude toward clients is consistent with social work values, the possibility of positive under-involvement alerts us to ways that attention to perceived positives can be exaggerated and not completely helpful in all circumstances.

EP 2.1.1c

3. *Over-involvement with a negative social worker attitude* refers to negative attention such that clients feel punished or in combat with the practitioner. Specific patterns such as arguing, acting provocatively, and using confrontation inappropriately, and power arbitrarily, and the like can signal negative over-involvement as a result of countertransference. This behavior is often observed in high-stress work settings in which social workers have close contact with clients who have been harmed and with individuals who have either harmed those clients or not

> **CASE EXAMPLE**
>
> *Social Worker, presenting a case:* Police were called to the home due to a domestic violence incident. The husband was charged with interference of a 911 call because he had thrown the telephone into the pool while the wife was making the call. The court-ordered case plan identified improved communication between the couple and the resolution of their domestic violence issues.
>
>
> **EP 2.1.1c**
>
> In the initial session with the couple, they reported that they were attending conflict-resolution sessions with their religious leader, and as a result they were now better able to communicate with each other. They also contended that "we don't have domestic violence issues." Their explanation for the incident was that the wife's pregnancy and hormonal changes caused her to experience mood swings that resulted in the conflict and prompted the call. The social worker accepted their explanation, but stated in her report that that she did have one concern. Specifically, "Unless encouraged to do so, the wife rarely spoke," during the session with the couple.
>
> Based on the session with the couple, the social worker's conclusion was that the case should be closed. The couple, she noted "were involved in the community, both are professionals and are happy about the upcoming birth of their baby." Further, "they live in a spacious home, just off the golf course, in an outer-ring suburb."

acted fully to prevent the harm. Note that if the social worker is operating under a legal mandate to provide, for example, services to a parent who has mistreated a child, power and authority could be used appropriately in an ethical manner. Facilitative conditions, for example, empathy, genuineness, and unconditional caring for the client are equally appropriate. In contrast, in cases of over-involvement with a negative social worker attitude, the use of power becomes personal and punishing rather than appropriate to the circumstances and safety of children. Negative attitudes can take the form of rigid rules of conduct in educational, residential, and corrections settings, in which people are stereotyped, and their strengths are ignored. This behavior is contrary to social work values, but it does occur.

Over-involvement can also lead to conflict situations between a social worker and members of his or her team such that negative attitude can spill over into these relationships. The following two case scenarios have similar dynamics. The first example demonstrates how positive *over-involvement* can cause negative interactions between professionals when one is invested in and advocates for a particular outcome. In consequence, other professionals are perceived as under-involved and as such their actions toward the client are believed to be negative or unjust.

> **CASE EXAMPLE**
>
> *Social worker, presenting a case:* "Am I too mixed up in this case? Some of my colleagues believe that I am, and this is why I am presenting this case. First, there are many topics that I wish to discuss; for example, the county case manager's questioning of my professional boundaries, and the boundaries of our agency (here the social worker distributes copies of a dictionary definition of boundaries), and the lack of due process in the county's decisions about the clients. The case manager raised concerns about boundaries after I submitted the first progress report on the family. In my report, I indicated the family's diligence in addressing the concerns outlined in the county's case plan. He indicated that I had not done a comprehensive report as the report was too positive. Further, he said that I was more involved than necessary with the family. This particular case manager has done this with other families that receive a positive report from us, as you all know.
>
> The social worker continues her report. "The real issue here about boundaries must be dealt with first. If he means providing the family with resources, listening to them, and advocating on their behalf then, so be it. Who am I to judge the family's practice of witchcraft, or the mother attending a witch's ball? I find these people different, but interesting, and hey, so are some of us! But I am concerned that my being an advocate for the family will have adverse consequences for them and for our agency. For example, what if the case manager reassigned the case or stopped making referrals to us, in which case my actions affect all of us."

EP 2.1.1f

If you were present at the team meeting in which this case was presented, how would you respond to the question of "Am I too involved in this case?" Would you conclude that asking the question was a credit to the social worker? Is it clear what help the social worker is seeking? Are you able to identify the relational dynamics between the two professionals that have spilled-over into the work with the family?

EP 2.1.1d

The second illustration of *over-involvement* describes a social worker who appears to have little insight into her behavior and its implications for her clients and the goals of the agency. The scenarios also emphasize how over-involvement may arise as a result of a combination of positive and negative dynamics.

CASE EXAMPLE

Marta is a youth worker in a shelter for homeless youth. She is passionate about her work and believes that her relationship with her young clients will help them to become independent, productive adults. She sees herself as an example of a survivor. Her supervisor has approached her several times, because she believes that Marta sometimes crosses professional boundaries with her clients. Marta's primary goal is to prepare homeless youth to become independent. Actually, youth gaining independence is a program goal, so her behavior is consistent with the intended program outcome. Another goal of the program however, is to assist the youth to resolve conflicts with their parents whenever possible. Marta's work with youth is often in conflict with this goal.

Marta's own youth was marked by constant battles with her parents. At age 17, she left home, lived with friends for a period, and eventually became homeless. Her approach and her relationship with the youth on her caseload are generally as a "survivor of the streets," encouraging a dependency by urging her clients to rely on her for support. Whenever a youth expressed an interest in reconnecting with his or her parents, Marta routinely rejected this idea as being unhealthy to the youth's progress and refuses to help make contact. The supervisor considers Marta's work with youth to be generally exemplary, with the exception of her negative attitude toward parents. Marta points to the fact that many on her caseload have in fact become independent; further, that they seek her out for ongoing support, which she finds frustrating at times, even though the contact is some evidence of the importance of her efforts.

In this case scenario, you can observe levels of positive and negative over-involvement. For instance, Marta is passionate about her work, and she has a positive regard for the youth with whom she works. Her use of self in the situation, particularly her reliance on her own parental and survival experience has negative connotations, which get in the way of individual problem solving. Her behavior however, exemplifies a barrier to effective practice, due to her own unresolved issues with her own parents. In addition, this is a situation in which consulting with her supervisor would be important so that she understand the origin and influence of her behavior on her work with youth. Each of the preceding cases illustrated the dynamics of over- and under-involvement, both positive and negative and in some instances a combination of both. More importantly, they demonstrated how levels of involvement can obscure professional judgment, the results of which can have an adverse impact on client well-being.

EP 2.1.1c

4. *Over-involvement with a positive social worker attitude* entails excessive preoccupation with a particular client. The social worker tends to focus on a particular client in such a way that the client dominates the social worker's thoughts and dreams, and in some instances includes sexual fantasies. In the most extreme cases, that positive over-involvement attitude toward the client can lead to more serious consequences, for example, boundary violations such as sexual contact with clients. Because of the seriousness of boundary violations, we discuss this issue later in greater detail.

Burnout, Compassion Fatigue, and Vicarious Trauma

EP 2.1.1b & 2.1.1c

Being under- or over-involved with clients may also be related to *burnout, compassion fatigue or vicarious trauma.* James (2008) attributes burnout to identifying too closely with clients and their problems, as well as to being dedicated and idealistic. Marta, in the previous case, for example, may be a candidate for burn-out as she appears to perceive herself as the primary vehicle for ensuring the success of the youth. Burnout occurs over a period of time. Initially the individual is enthusiastic and involved but starts to move into stagnation, which leads to frustration and, eventually, apathy. Over a prolonged period, these factors can also result in a "crisis state of disequilibrium" and chronic indifference (James, 2008, p. 537).

EP 2.1.1d & 2.1.10a

The following describe different circumstances of burnout brought on over- or under-involvement with clients:

- *Negative under-involvement can occur when you feel frustrated because you are unable to solve certain problems, have a large caseload, and when the outcomes of your work are unknown or uncertain (Dane, 2000; Dettlaff & Rycraft, 2010; James, 2008). In working with clients, you can become numb to demands that exceed your mental capacity. Thoughts such as "I have heard this story too many times," or "How can I change anything?" may occur to you, along with a feeling of helplessness.*
- *Over-involvement is indicated when you have a strong need to be liked by a client or the urge to save them, taking calls at home, feeling responsible for clients' mistakes or regressions, and panicking when carefully detailed plans fail to produce the expected results. At the administrative level, over-involvement leading to burnout may take the form of micromanaging or feeling that nothing will get done or done correctly unless the individual is involved (James, 2008).*
- *Under-involvement can occur when a practitioner has difficulty in bonding with and enlisting the cooperation of clients who are different (Fontes, 2005).*
- *Under-involved professionals often experience an organization in which the leadership is ineffective; there is a lack of rewards, recognition, or organizational support; decisions are perceived to be unfair or arbitrary; or an unsupportive environment in which the fit between organizational and individual beliefs are at odds (Leiter & Maslach, 2005). Feeling a lack of control over a prolonged period of time can lead to apathy and ineffective service delivery to clients.*

EP 2.1.10a

Compassion fatigue, also referred to as *vicarious or secondary trauma* is different from burnout. Burnout is mainly associated with workload demands, uncertainty and stressors, and the urgency and size of caseloads. Compassion fatigue, in contrast, is a constant state of tension and preoccupation with the individual and collective trauma of clients (Figley, 1995, 2002). Professionals are too deeply drawn into the trauma and emotions of their clients and their situations, and, as a result, they become mentally exhausted (Figley 1995, 2002). Conversely, the experience of *vicarious or secondary trauma* is recognized as a situation in which knowledge of and exposure to others' trauma and wanting to help results in trauma for the professional. This form of trauma is most often evident in professionals who day after day listen to the harrowing narratives of clients in situations of family violence, child sexual abuse, and hospital oncology units. It may also be ignited by past experiences of the professional or provoked by the vulnerability of the client; for example, children who have been abused.

Research has shown that *vicarious* or *secondary* trauma has implications for the professional relative to the extent that they become over- or under-involved with clients. In a study of secondary trauma for family violence professionals, Bell (2003) found that constant "exposure to clients' stories negatively affects cognitions" of the professionals, and therefore their professional judgment. Similar results were reported by Dane (2000) in a study of child welfare workers and Cunningham's (2003) findings of group work with individuals with a history of trauma. Further, the response level of the professional was related to whether the client's situation was similar to his or her own experience, which can be the basis of positive or negative transference by the client or a countertransference reaction on the part of the professional.

Many authors have recognized and studied compassion fatigue, vicarious or secondary trauma, and the direct and indirect effects of stress on professionals (Bell, 2003; Cunningham, 2003; Dane, 2000; Figley, 2002, 1995). These authors are excellent resources, as are O'Hollaran and Linton (2000), for self-assessment and self-care strategies for professionals with regard to compassion fatigue.

Reactions of Clients: Assessing Potential Barriers and Intervening

EP 2.1.10m

The preceding discussion emphasized professional behaviors, which have the capacity to influence the helping relationship. In the interaction between social worker and client, there are times when the relationship can stall because of clients' reaction based on their perception or misperceptions of the social worker or his or her attitude. Whatever the source, sensing and addressing clients' feelings and thoughts as they happen is also crucial to preventing them from escalating. Individuals may not always initiate a discussion of their negative reactions. Their ability to do so may depend on their personality type, their age, cultural differences with regard to authority, their status (e.g., voluntary or involuntary), or their sense of power in the social worker's role or that of the organization, for example, a residential treatment or correctional facility. Keep in mind that in view of a real or perceived power differential between the social worker and clients, sharing negative feelings and cognitions can be extremely difficult for some, and others may fear the implications when they do so.

You can reduce the threat that clients experience by being attentive and accepting, or by being an advocate, even though you may believe that their interpretation is off the mark or entirely unrealistic. If you are inattentive or insensitive to cues, either verbal or nonverbal, the associated feelings and cognitions will linger and remain unresolved. To avert such a development, it is crucial to watch for indicators of negative reactions. These reactions can present as changing the subject, frowning, fidgeting, sighing, appearing startled, becoming silent, or clearing the throat. Above all, because you have worked with an individual over time, you are apt to be able to observe a change in how they react to you.

EP 2.1.10m

When you observe a change, it is important to focus the session on the client's here-and-now feelings and cognitions. You should do this tentatively, checking out whether your perception is accurate. If it is accurate, proceed by expressing genuine concern for the individual's discomfort and conveying your desire to understand what he or she is experiencing at the moment. Examples of responses that facilitate the discussion of troubling feelings and thoughts follow:

- **To a youth:** "I'm thinking, to use a phrase that I've heard from you, that what I said was a "flyover" [not paying attention] for you. What are you thinking and feeling at this moment?"
- **To a young minor:** "Are you feeling sad right now? Would it be helpful for you to draw a picture of how you feel, and then you could explain the picture to me?"
- **To an adult client:** "You are quiet right now, looking away from me. I wonder if you have some feelings about my draft progress report to the court that I just shared with you."

Notice that in each of the situations, the verbalizations are specific to the moment that the individual reacted, but they relied on the person to put forth his or her own thoughts or feelings.

Eliciting an individual's emotions, feelings, and thoughts provides you with an opportunity to correct misunderstandings, clarify your intentions, remedy any blunders, and identify adverse beliefs or thought patterns. Indeed, by observing you, some individuals will benefit and be able to acknowledge their mistakes and perhaps apologize without feeling embarrassed. Moreover, they may gain self-confidence by realizing that you value them and the relationship enough to be concerned about their thoughts and feelings and to rectify your errors of omission or commission. After productive discussions of here-and-now thoughts and feelings, most individuals will regain their positive feelings about the relationship and are able to resume working on their problems.

EP 2.1.10i & 2.1.10m

On some occasions, a client may succeed in concealing negative thoughts and feelings, or you may overlook nonverbal cues. The feelings may escalate until it becomes obvious that the client is holding back, being overly formal, responding defensively, or engaging in other forms of reactance. Again, you should give priority to the relationship by shifting focus to what is bothering the client and responding to it. After you have worked through the negative reaction of the client, it is helpful to negotiate a *mini-contract* in which you and the client agree to discuss troublesome feelings and thoughts as they occur. The objective of this contract is to avert the recurrence of a negative reaction in the future. For those individuals who may habitually withhold their reactions to the detriment of themselves and others, learning to express negative feelings and thoughts can be a milestone for them. The following is an example of a message aimed at *negotiating an appropriate mini-contract*:

EP 2.1.10j

Social worker: *Okay, we got past the flyover, where you felt I was ignoring what you said. Thank you for telling me about how you don't like people to be telling you what you need to do. Because you told me how you felt, you helped me to understand and you gave me a chance to explain what I really meant last week. For us to work well together, it is important for both of us to put negative reactions on the table. Would you be willing for the two of us to agree that we will to immediately alert each other to troubling thoughts and feelings that happen between us?*

In developing the mini-contract, the social worker is conveying to the youth a willingness to be open to and respectful of his reactions.

Pathological or Inept Social Workers

EP 2.1.1d & 2.1.2b

Almost all of us can recall a situation in which on occasion we committed an error or made a mistake in a particular case. Instilled in our memory is the reaction from the client involved, and most importantly the steps that we took to ensure that our behavior did not cause irreparable damage to the helping relationships.

EP 2.1.1d

Despite educational preparation, some practitioners demonstrate behavior that lacks the basic tenets of a helping relationship, for example, a lack of empathy or being in tune with those seeking their help; a lack of genuine and authentic concern; and a lack of appreciation of different beliefs, lifestyles, and values. Their inept behavior may be attributed to anxiety, a lack of skill or experience, dealing with a problem beyond their scope of practice, or an inability to build collaborative relationships with clients. Ineptness and unethical practices on the part of social workers, such as abrasive, egotistical, controlling, judgmental, demeaning, patronizing, or rigid behavior can cause an appropriate negative reaction from clients. In these interactions, clients' reactions can become a cycle of escalating conflict. For instance, a practitioner demeans an individual; the individual reacts, and so forth. It is not unusual for the professional to attempt to control the escalation by exerting his or her power and authority, which of course tends to cause another reaction from the client. Being habitually late or unprepared for appointments, appearing to be detached or disinterested, and underinvolved are further indicators of troubling behavior. Most people will react to behavior that they view as disrespectful and unprofessional. In many cases, a practitioner would not tolerate similar behaviors in a client.

Ineptness is a serious concern which calls for corrective behavior on the part of the practitioner, through supervision, skill development, or self-reflection. Pathological behavior on the part of a social worker in which there is a sustained pattern of repeated errors, insensitive behaviors can cause psychological damage to clients. The social worker's behavior can be the results of his or her own personal unresolved issues for which he or she should seek help. Gottesfeld and Lieberman (1979) refer to practitioners whose behavior harms a client, whether intentional or unintentional, as *pathological,* pointing out that "It is possible to have therapists who suffer from as many unresolved problems as do clients" (p. 388). Hence, these practitioners are incapable of providing help to clients because of their own troubles. Left unresolved, the relationship—in which helping is the hallmark—is severely diminished.

The majority of voluntary clients who experience the ineptitude of pathological practitioners have the good sense to "vote with their feet" by prematurely terminating their contact (Meyer, 2001). Mandated clients suffer greater consequences for deciding to terminate early. As a protective precaution, they may evade contact or attempt to be transferred to another social worker. Supervisors should be alert when there are several requests for transfer from the same social worker.

Pathological or inept practitioners harm their clients, their agencies, and the profession as a whole. Often, practitioners faced with a situation involving a colleague find that deciding what steps to take is easier said than done. Moreover, the privacy of the interaction between a client and a colleague may make it hard to conclude that behavior of a colleague is harmful. It is indeed a challenge to question the behavior or competence of another practitioner. However, individuals who act in a manner that is harmful or demeaning to clients are often quite open about what they do; for example, telling stories about clients in which their own status is heightened, giving clients demeaning names as descriptors, breaching confidentiality, and talking down to clients, even when other clients or staff are present. You may also observe or hear a person's constant reactive behavior to the practitioner. Unfortunately, when an individual reacts, they may be ignored by the agency and other staff, and instead there may be a tendency to characterize his or her behavior as resistant or oppositional.

EP 2.1.2b

Both you and your agency have a responsibility to protect clients. By not acting, all involved become a party to a colleague's behavior that assaults the dignity and worth of clients. The primacy of clients' rights is clearly articulated in the NASW Code of Ethics. The Code also speaks directly to your obligation to peers and the employment organization. A caution by Gottesfeld and Lieberman (1979) is timeless in this regard. They assert that, to protect clients' rights, "agencies organized to help clients should not accept employee pathology that defeats the system's purpose" (p. 392). Actions to rectify such situations, however, must safeguard the rights of both the practitioner and the clients. Reports of pathological or inept behavior should be based on facts, not judgments or bias, and your motive and the outcome you are seeking should be clear. Involving your supervisor and reviewing information with this person or a consultant provides an additional safeguard. You may also want to refer to the guidelines on whistle-blowing discussed in Chapter 14.

Ultimately, a referral to the local NASW chapter and state licensing board or certification authority may become necessary. NASW chapters and regulatory boards have committees that investigate complaints of unethical and unprofessional conduct. Information about misconduct is shared between NASW chapters and state boards of social work. Infractions that constitute egregious harm are routinely reported to the Disciplinary Actions Reporting System (DARS), a national database to which the Association of Social Work Boards (ASWB) has access. "This system is a means by which social work regulatory boards can verify the historical disciplinary background of individuals seeking licensure or renewal" (*ASWB Member Policy Manual*).

Cross-Racial and Cross-Cultural Barriers

EP 2.1.4c
& 2.1.7b

Clients and social workers may experience adverse reactions in cross-racial or cross-cultural relationships for a variety of reasons. Tensions in social relations that are grounded in society may present as dynamics in the helping relationship. These tensions can become heightened in interactions with involuntary clients who are also a member of a racial or ethnic group. Issues of race, culture, and socioeconomic status are macro-level factors, but they nevertheless influence micro-level practice and relationships.

EP 2.1.4a
& 2.1.10a

Cross-racial and cross-cultural relationships can be challenging on many levels. In their most basic form, barriers to a working relationship between a practitioner and a client may stem from either a lack of knowledge of a client's culture, bias, or lack of experience in working with members of a given racial or minority group. Diverse individuals may wonder whether or not you have sufficient knowledge of their world to help them. They may also enter the relationship with a set of preconceived notions about you. For instance, believing that you are racially or culturally insensitive or biased, believing that they may be treated poorly because they are a member of a racial or cultural group, and a perception that you are a representative of an oppressive system in which the goal is to alter who they are. Altering who they are may emphasize change or treatment goals that are bounded by assumptions of Western cultures that may have limited meaning or value to them (Foster, 1988; Hodge, 2004; Hodge & Nadir, 2008; Sue, 2006). As such, they can become a barrier in the change process. In cross-cultural and cross-racial situations, it is important to understand clients from the viewpoint of their lifestyles and the standards for well-being established by their reference group. To this end, Lee (2003) suggests that in cross-cultural relationships, social constructivism, specifically a deliberate focus on clients' narratives and viewpoints in which they create solutions for themselves, allows the practitioner to understand the individual and thereby avoid potential relational barriers.

EP 2.1.10a

While we all seek to have a collective identity, and to minimize differences, in reality, in U.S. society, social interactions and professional relationships remain configured around assumptions of sameness, including social class. Practitioners who are members of ethnic or racial minority groups, in comparison to their nonminority counterparts are perhaps more attuned to the values of majority-group clients. For the most part, however, irrespective of racial or cultural demographics, social distance separates practitioners from their clients. For example, there are power differences, and differences in economic, social or educational status, and the fact that few of us reside in the same communities as the people that we serve. These differences, each of which contributes to social distance, are made greater by diverse experiences and worldviews (Clifford & Burke, 2005; Davis & Gelsomino, 1994; Dettlaff & Rycraft, 2010; Green, Kiernan-Stern, & Baskind, 2005). Clifford and Burke (2005), emphasizing social distance, note the inherent challenge in balancing the ethical principle of having respect for differences. Specifically, respect for another individual becomes much more difficult when the individual is of a very different social standing. Social distance, whatever the basis, can lead us to invalidate the cognitions and realities of those who are different (Sue, et. al., 2007).

EP 2.1.4a & 2.1.4b & 2.1.5a

Lacking familiarity and limited contact with clients who are different may cause practitioners to fill in their information void with stereotypes, preconceived notions, and the influence of pervasive media images. Whaley (1998) asserts that racial and class bias is influenced by social and cognitive perceptions that fill in the blanks with general stereotypes; for example, black youth who are demonstrating the same traits as their white counterparts are four times more likely to be viewed as violent. Sufficient evidence exists pointing to professional and systems bias in which persons who are different are much more likely to have their behavior perceived as pathological in spite of their ecological circumstances or needs (Barnes, 2008; Feldman, 2008; Richman, Kohn-Woods, & Williams, 2007; Allen, 2007; Malgady & Zayas, 2001; Sue, 2005; Wolf, 1991). The conflict between the professional's interpretation and assessment and clients' realities is characterized as a form of racial or cultural *microaggression* (Sue, Capodilupo, Torino, Buccerro, Holder, Nadal, & Esquilin, 2007). Specifically, the practitioner's automatic response to clients who are different is based on their cognition of what is or is not normal, and their perception is used to generalize and interpret behavior. Further, Sue, et. al, maintains that the practitioner may not recognize the resulting harm of their behavior.

EP 2.1.4b

In cross-cultural, cross-racial relationships, you may tend to become overly positive or negative about a particular racial or ethnic group in an effort to deal with your discomfort or lack of knowledge. Over-identification has both positive and negative factors. On the positive side, identification with a particular group and attempting to understand their reality is essential to becoming a more culturally competent professional. But, over-identification can obscure individuality as well as the subgroups that exist within a racial or ethnic culture. On the negative side, perceptions or stereotypes may lead you to erroneously generalize clients' problems to the group in which they are members, thereby influencing your capacity to be empathetic to the individual and their situation.

EP 2.1.4c

Given the potential obstacles that may emerge in cross-racial and cross-cultural relationships, you might wonder if the solution is to match clients with social workers of the same racial or ethnic group. Practitioners who are members of ethnic or racial minority groups perhaps can be more attuned to the values of majority-group clients. Desiring the best outcomes for clients, you might wonder if this is a viable option. As a solution, matching is not always practical, nor is there sufficient evidence that suggests that it always works to clients' advantage (James, 2008; Karlsson, 2005; Malgady & Zayas, 2001). In addition, some minority individuals will react to and distrust any professional, even those who share their background or heritage. This distrust often arises at a systems level, specifically at the level of the organization that you represent, yet the dynamics emerge in your relationship. In any of the situations previously described, it can be expected that dynamics in the client-practitioner relationship will reflect a mutual strangeness. In some instances, professionals and their agencies emphasize sameness rather than differences in an attempt to minimize potential barriers. Too often, differences of race and culture are ignored in the form of *color-blind* practice designed to avoid conflict and promote cultural competence (Neville, Spanierman, & Doan, 2006; Proctor & Davis, 1994; Davis & Gelsomino, 1994). Neville and colleagues suggest that color-blindness has tended to minimize and further distort the existence of structural racism in the United States, the results of which have been newer and more subtle forms of discrimination, and a lower level of cultural competence.

The notion of invisibility to differences can also be evident with regard to socioeconomic status. For instance, Davis and Gelsomino (1994) caution both majority and minority practitioners to be aware of their biases toward clients of a lower social class.  **EP 2.1.4b** In addition to the implications that class has for racial and ethnic minority groups, these authors suggest that class is equally relevant to the "social realities of low-income white clients." In particular, low-income white individuals can be perceived as being responsible for their difficulties, because they failed to take advantage of their life opportunities. Also, in cross-cultural, cross-racial interactions, practitioners tended to ignore environmental factors, such as, racism and discrimination experienced by individuals who are different, and instead were more inclined to explore an individual's internal functioning as the source of their personal difficulties (Davis & Gelsomino, 1994).

Cultivating Positive Cross-cultural Relationships

EP 2.1.10b

What can be done to minimize the dynamics of cultural or racial differences and their role as a potential relational barrier in the helping process? Empathy and empathic communication are basic skills that facilitate engagement and bridge the gaps that may be present in cross-racial and cross-cultural client-social worker relationships. Dyche and Zayas (2001) and Parson (1993) emphasize that knowledge of culture is insufficient to evoke empathy. Instead, they refer to *cultural empathy* as an effective treatment tool. Cultural empathy is expressed at the affective level, rather than solely at the cognitive level. Whereas the cognitive level references knowledge about different cultures, the affective level is where the practitioner makes an effort to see and hear the world through the client's eyes and experiences and to grasp meaning from the client's perspective. Parson (1993) further characterizes cultural empathy as *ethnotherapuetic* in that it relies on the cross-cultural professional's capacity for introspection and self-disclosure when the results are in support of the helping process.

EP 2.1.10b

Relational empathy, as described by Freedberg (2007), also facilitates helping in cross-cultural or racial relationships. As an interpersonal skill, relational empathy acceptance is an understanding of a person's cultural or racial background and the sociopolitics of their situation, even though as a practitioner you may not be fully aware of each and every nuance. Grounded in relational culture theory, relational empathy may cross traditional boundaries in that client-practitioner relationship is based on a mutual sharing. Assessment skills in determining acculturation levels, including culturally derived behaviors or dysfunctions in the context of culture or race, are critical. Keep in mind, however, that the way in which a problem is perceived and framed by you as a professional can be either an inhibiting or facilitative factor.

EP 2.1.10b

In addition to cultural and relational empathy and empathetic communications, *"helper attractiveness"* is an interpersonal factor to which diverse clients are reported to have responded favorably (Harper & Lantz, 1996). Essentially, it means that the clients perceive that you are interested in them and have a genuine desire to help. Further, helper attractiveness implies that diverse clients experience respectful, warm, genuine, committed, and ethical behavior on the part of the professional. The following are representative comments from two separate focus group sessions, one with emancipated minority minors who had been wards of the state, the other, with staff who believed that they had established successful relationships with the minors.

Minors: Throughout your life in the system, you come in contact with a lot of indifferent professionals. They run in and tell you what to do; they are disinterested in you as a person and ignore your goals. They give you a case plan to follow and tell you to do this or that, and find a job so that you can support your child. I want to go to college, but no, I'm told to get a job. How is a minimum wage job going to sustain me and my baby in the long run? Having met with you because they are required to, then they move on to the next case. In all fairness, they do have large caseloads, but you never really feel that they are interested in you or really see you as an individual. When I get a worker that listens to me, tries to understand me, and is willing to treat me like a real person, I do better. Sometimes, they act like a parent, but this is okay if they treat me right and show that they care.

Staff: A large part of connecting with them is to remember that they are kids. They have been in the system so long, some almost all of their lives. They don't want to sit in an office and have you talk at them. Sometimes, just riding around with them or going to get a hamburger is when you really are able to connect with them. They talk and you listen. Sometimes you point out the contradictions in their words and behavior in a teasing way and they laugh. Even when they mess up, you have to respect them as individuals, do things with them. A lot of time, they say, "Miss X, I know that I let you down, and I felt bad, because you are real and you support me." A real turning point in even the most difficult cases often occurs when you support them unconditionally, are dependable, respond to them in a caring and empathetic way. Above all, you need to include them in the decisions about their future. Some of their negative reactions to you are developmental, others are because they are scared or testing you to make sure you aren't going to leave them, and still others because the court or the foster home failed to respect them or treat them as individuals.

Despite what may appear to be the challenging trials and tribulations inherent in cross-cultural and cross-racial relationships, it is quite possible to have productive helping relationships with clients who are different from yourself. Key elements that foster positive cross-racial interactions were highlighted in the common themes of the minors and the staff: caring, empathy, and acceptance.

EP 2.1.4d

As a preventive measure, in your initial contact with diverse individuals you might inquire about whether they have concerns on this front. Not all diverse individuals will have a negative reaction to you. Many may have resolved their feelings because they have had the normative experience of interacting with nonminority practitioners. When negative feelings do occur, either in verbal exchanges or discontent that is evident in nonverbal behaviors, you can neutralize the situation by empathically confronting and responding to their feelings.

EP 2.1.4d

Diverse clients need to be able to trust that you understand their situation or, at a minimum, that you are willing to learn. Earlier, in defining cultural competence, we put forth some general guidelines and conditions that can facilitate competence with diverse groups in an effort to lessen potential barriers in the helping relationship. In addition, a summary statement of the essence of cultural competence is discussed throughout this text. Building on this statement, we reinforced the evolutionary nature of achieving competence by highlighting parallel concepts such as adopting a posture of discovery (Dean, 1999) and cultural humility (Trevalon & Murray-Garcia, 1999). In both, you assume the position of *not knowing*, and a willingness to learn. The notion that competent practice with people who are different evolves over time is consistent with the articulations of Dean (2001) and Williams (2006). They assert that competence is a continuous process of learning and growth. Striving for an arrival point, according to Dean, is based on the "belief that knowledge brings control and effectiveness which is to be achieved above all else" (p. 624). She suggests it is equally important for you to be aware of your lack of competence. In the spirit of Dean's (2001) evolving and changing competence, Williams has conceptualized cultural competence as a progression in which you have an initial anthropological awareness of culture, specifically learning about culture. Progressing to the highest level is embedded in critical theory in which social, political, and economic arrangements are considered, and in which the outcomes sought are anti-oppression and social change. At this level, you seek to understand the extent to which macro-level conditions and marginalized status affect the lives of racial and cultural minority groups. Further, you are prepared to intervene at the micro, mezzo, or macro level, because racial and ethnic minority persons' problems often involve all three levels.

It is equally important that you are mindful of the fact that the helping relationship is between two human beings, albeit, from different racial, cultural, or social classes, both of whom are attempting to work together to resolve a problem. Critical societal conditions, social distance, feelings of mistrust, fear or resentment, and perceptions about you and your status can intrude. Even more daunting is the fact that that your relationships with diverse clients may not resolve the oppressive forces that are evident in their lives. But you can control the interaction between you and the client in a way that does not add to their negative experience. In general, developing cross-cultural and cross-racial relationships requires you to continually evaluate your knowledge of differences and to increase your level of cultural and oppression competence. In the process of learning, it also means that you are comfortable with differences, and when you are uncomfortable, you are willing to take steps to calm your vulnerabilities, anxieties, and fears about making mistakes.

EP 2.1.4a & 2.1.4c

Difficulties in Establishing Trust

Trust in the helping relationship evolves over time. Perlman (1957) described the climate as an essential element of the helping relationship in which a bond is created between the practitioner and the client. Trust is integral to the climate in which the bonding of two people can occur. People can vary widely in their capacity to trust, and their ability to trust you may be a moment to moment transaction. For the most part, a majority of people function at an interpersonal level that enables them to enter into a relationship with you after only a few moments of checking you out. For others, no matter how much goodwill, warmth, and empathy you convey, they will remain guarded or will test you for a period of time. For racial or ethnically diverse persons, their basis for not readily trusting you or revealing their feelings may be related to their experiences or systems paranoia, any one of which can be exaggerated if they are also

EP 2.1.10a

involuntary. Involuntary clients, the majority of whom are minority and who have not sought a helping relationship, should not be expected to readily trust you. They can erect the barriers of social distance and their perceived or real powerlessness in their attitude and language; for example, referring to you formally, or to others as "them," or "the system" (G. D. Rooney, 2009). As such, it is important that you understand that an individual's mistrust and rigid, reactive behavior may not be specific to you. In fact, attempting to persuade them of your helpful intent is usually counterproductive. Indeed, they may trust your actions over your words. That is, they see trust as a process and product of the relationship that grows over time, reinforced by your helper attributes and action, such as your commitment to them, caring, and respect. These actions are the evidence that you are trustworthy.

EP 2.1.10b

Behavior such as showing respect, genuine interest, and caring; along with actions such as reaching out to these clients, can facilitate their perception of you as a trustworthy professional. For instance, when they cancel or miss appointments, you can maintain contact by phoning them, making a home visit (if your agency permits), or writing a letter. Many involuntary clients urgently need and want help. In some instances, their failure to trust and engage or keep appointments may be caused by their fear or a pattern of avoidance rather than from a lack of motivation. Assisting them in coming to terms with their fear or avoidance behavior is therapeutic, whereas allowing them to terminate by default can have grave consequences. While the movies *Antoine Fisher, Good Will Hunting* and, more recently, *Precious* are Hollywood productions, they are excellent examples of a growing bond between a professional helper and client and examples of reaching out to a client and building trust.

Transference Reactions

EP 2.1.10m

Unrealistic perceptions of and reactions directed toward you or others is known as the *transference reaction* (Corey, 2009; Knight, 2006: Nichols, 2006). In such reactions, unresolved feelings, wishes, anxieties, and fears that are rooted in past relationships with others are ignited and applied to you. Transference reactions can be positive or negative. In whatever form, reactions lack objectivity and therefore can affect the development of a productive relationship between you and clients in much the same way that they create difficulties in other interpersonal relationships.

Treatment sessions with couples or in groups can be the place in which transference reactions are unfolded. Individual partners can react to each other. In groups, individual members can trigger a multiple transference reaction, including the practitioner. In these situations, for example, a trauma survivor may assign motivations, thoughts, and feelings to other members, projecting the attributes of the individual who hurt them in hostile interactions (Knight, 2006).

Transference reactions tend to stall progress unless they are addressed. On a system-to-individual or system-to-group level, transference can involve responses to authority in any form. Besides preventing a person from making progress in resolving problems, transference reactions in therapeutic relationships can create opportunities for growth. The therapeutic relationship is, in effect, a social microcosm wherein clients' interpersonal behavior and conditioned patterns of perceiving and feeling are manifested. In this context, clients can recreate here-and-now interactions that are virtually identical to those that plague and defeat them in other relationships. The consequent challenge for the practitioner is to assist individuals in recognizing their distorted perceptions. Instead of relying on projections, mental images, or beliefs, the individual can eventually develop perceptual sets that help them differentiate between individuals and situations.

In group situations, your role as group facilitator is to assess the impact of this dynamic on the group and intervene appropriately. You can then utilize group process and communication skills to refocus the attention of members on the group's purpose. You may also use this occasion as a teachable moment, emphasizing how distorted perceptions of others are based on other interpersonal relationships, rather than members of the group.

EP 2.1.7b

Not all negative transference reactions are based on an individual's unconscious unresolved conflicts or distorted perceptions. They can be the results of the behavior of a practitioner. Historical racial or cultural conflicts can also be the etiology of a negative reactive transference. Specifically, because of the reality of their experience in the larger society, past, present, or current, racial or cultural individuals bring dynamics such as mistrust and emotions and feelings about power into the helping relationship with practitioners who are different. This type of transference can occur in the collective psyche of a community. For instance, reactions, subject to racial overtones, can happen in interactions with the police, teachers, or other figures of authority and the experience of oppression can be automatically assigned to you. At the cognitive level, reactions are reinforced by the powerful messages of music about injustices and inequalities, which further shapes the worldview of individuals and communities. Resolving transference based on the reality of an individual's experience may present a more difficult challenge.

Identifying Transference Reactions

EP 2.1.10m

Whatever the agency setting and the intervention, you will occasionally encounter transference reactions. To manage transference reactions, you must first be aware of their manifestations. Here are examples of some behaviors symptomatic of transference:

- *Transference reactions involving interpersonal trauma are common (Knight, 2006). Fear, distrust, and hostile interactions or rage at the practitioner, group members, or projections of significant others in response to their grief, frustration, and fears (James, 2008; Knight, 2006).*
- *Behaving provocatively by arguing with or baiting the practitioner or becoming silent and hostile, avoiding making progress (Nichols, 2006).*
- *Questioning the interest of the social worker; in particular, whether the practitioner can understand their situation without having had a similar experience (James, 2008). Also, feeling that the practitioner couldn't possibly have a genuine interest because helping clients is their job.*
- *Misinterpreting a message as a result of feeling put down. Responding defensively, feeling rejected, or expecting criticism or punishment without realistic cause.*
- *Perceptions that their thoughts and feelings are extreme, and questioning whether others, even those with similar experiences, can understand (Knight, 2006).*
- *Trauma survivors seeing others' behaviors or reactions as signs of betrayal, abandonment, and rejection; assigning others the motivations, thoughts, and feelings of those who caused their trauma (Knight, 2006).*
- *Relating to the practitioner in a clinging, dependent way or excessively seeking praise and reassurance.*
- *Attempting to please the practitioner or groups members by giving excessive compliments and praise or by ingratiating behavior.*
- *Attempting to engage the social worker socially, offering personal favors, presenting gifts, or seeking special considerations, and in some cases, having dreams or fantasies about the practitioner.*
- *Difficulty in discussing problems because the social worker or a group member reminds them of someone else in appearance (Nichols, 2006).*

Although such reactions originate in an individual's past, the associated behaviors are manifest in the here-and-now. This raises an interesting question: Are transference reactions best resolved by focusing on the past so that an individual gains insight into their origins? In instances in which reactions driven by past experiences are played out in the present, they can be resolved by encouraging the individual to engage in a deliberate examination of their current inaccurate and distorted perceptions. Of course, when an individual brings up experiences and circumstances from their past, brief historical excursions often facilitate productive emotional catharsis and lead to an understanding of the origins of their patterns of thinking, feeling, and behaving. Moreover, in working with an individual who has experienced ongoing traumatic stressors (e.g., physical or sexual abuse, sexual assault, war, injury, or other crisis events), probing and exploring these experiences may be vital to gaining an understanding of, and recovery from, the detrimental effects of those experiences (James, 2008; Knight, 2006; Wartel, 1991; Rosenthal, 1988).

Managing Transference Reactions

When a person's behavior is indicative of a possible transference reaction after any necessary examination of the past, it is important to shift the focus to his or her here-and-now feelings because such reactions generally cause them to disengage from the relationship and from productive work, ultimately undermining the helping process. To assist you in managing transference reactions, we offer the following guidelines:

EP 2.1.1c

1. *Be open to the possibility that the client's reaction is not unrealistic and may be a product of your behavior. If introspection indicates that the client's behavior is realistic,*

EP 2.1.1b

respond authentically by owning responsibility for your behavior.

EP 2.1.7b

2. *Be aware of the fact that a transference reaction can be triggered by a realistic appraisal of historical and current experiences of racial or cultural individuals, in which feelings of anger, resentment, fear, social distance, and power are aroused.* It is important that you acknowledge, rather than dismiss, minimize, or attempt to alter the individual's perception, even though doing so may be uncomfortable.

EP 2.1.10j

3. *When an individual appears to expect you to respond in antitherapeutic ways, as significant others have in the past, it is important to respond differently,* thereby disconfirming those expectations. Responses that contrast sharply with their expectations can result in the individual experiencing temporary disequilibrium and assist them in differentiating his or her experience from past figures or experiences. As a result, the individual must deal with you and others as unique and real people, rather than perpetuating expectations based on past experiences. Responding differently and authentically can be instrumental when reactions are based on historically oriented racial or cultural conflicts. In essence, the here-and-now is your behavior.

EP 2.1.10j

4. *Assist the client in determining the immediate source of distorted perceptions by exploring how and when the feelings emerged.* Carefully explore antecedents and meaning attributions associated with the feelings. Avoid attempting to correct distorted perceptions by immediately revealing your actual feelings. By first exploring how and when problematic feelings emerged, you can help clients expand their awareness of their schematic patterns of in which they generalize and make faulty meaning attributions and unwarranted assumptions based on past experience. The aim is to help an individual to discriminate between feelings that emanate from their conditioned perceptual sets, and move toward reality-based feelings and reactions.

EP 2.1.10j

5. *After an individual has recognized the unrealistic nature of their feelings and manifested an awareness of the distortions that produced these feelings, sharing your actual feelings* can be reassuring.

6. *An examination of problematic feelings, assist an individual in determining whether they have experienced similar reactions in other relationships.* Through this exploration, clients may recognize patterns of distortions that create difficulties in other relationships.

EP 2.1.10j

Being aware of and managing transference reactions involves using a range of facilitative and communication skills. For example, it is important to be empathetic to individuals' distorted or unrealistic feelings as you attempt to help them recognize their influence in their relationship with you or others. Seeking concreteness, by specifically exploring the basis for an individual's conclusions, can assist them in identifying the source of their perception or feelings and pinpoint when and how these feelings emerged. You can further draw out individuals' reactions by using reflection to connect separate but related events to their patterned response in another relationship. For example:

EP 2.1.10b

Social Worker: You know when we were discussing your feelings toward your mother a few weeks ago you said essentially the same thing.

Client: I'm not sure what you mean.

Social worker: You had said your mother has always dismissed your feelings, when you tried to talk to her and she disapproves of the men you are dating.

As the exchange continues, notice how the social worker and the client further clarified transference reactions, in this case they are directed toward the social worker:

Client: Wow, the weeks sure did go by fast. [*Long pause.*] I don't have much to talk about today. [*Ambivalence*]

Social worker [sensing the client is struggling with something]: I gather you didn't really feel ready for your appointment with me today. [*Empathic response.*] How did you feel about coming? [*Open-ended, probing*]

Client: I didn't want to come, but I thought I should. Actually, it has been an eventful week. But I didn't feel that I wanted to tell you about what has been happening. [*Possible transference reaction; seeking approval.*]

Social worker: Sounds like you've had some misgivings about confiding certain things in me. [*Paraphrasing, responding to reaction*] Could you share with me some of your thoughts that you had about confiding in me? [*Focusing on the here-and-now.*]

Client: I wanted you to think of me as a desirable person [*Seeking approval, praise.*]

Social worker: First, let me tell you that I do not have thoughts about whether you were a desirable person. I'd like to explore where your doubts or fears that I don't see you as a desirable person came from. Have I done or said something that conveyed that to you? [*Probing, addressing perceptions and feelings.*]

Client [thinks for a moment]: Well, no, nothing that I can think of.

Social worker: Yet I gather those feelings are very real to you. I wonder when you first became aware of those feelings.

Client [after a pause]: Well, I think it was when we began to talk about my feelings that guys are just interested in me for what they can get. I guess I wondered if you thought I was a real dud. I wanted you to know it wasn't so, that a desirable person could be attracted to me.

Social worker: So you haven't wanted to risk it turning out bad and worrying about how I would feel if it did. [*Additive empathy, interpretation, exploring basis of feelings.*]

In this scenario, the social worker continues to explore the unrealistic nature of the woman's perceptions and how they influence her behavior in other relationships. When you have observed a potential transference reaction, it is important to focus on the here-and-now. For example, by sensitively exploring the woman's reluctance to attend the session, the social worker not only resolved an emerging obstacle to productive work, she also helped the client to further explore the reasons for her doubts about her attractiveness. By doing so, the social worker expanded her awareness of the way in which her doubts distorted her perceptions of how others, including the social worker, viewed her. Moreover, through the exploration, the social worker was able to identify a basic misconception that had influenced the client's relationships with others and to relate more comfortably with the social worker.

Countertransference Reactions

The counterpart of transference is *countertransference*. Just as clients can experience unrealistic, unresolved, or unconscious thoughts and feelings; situations or the attributes, demographics, or behavior of clients can arouse feelings, wishes, and unconscious defensive patterns on the part of the social worker. Unmet needs of the social worker, unresolved family conflicts, gender, and parenting roles can be the basis for countertransference reactions. Marta, for example, in one of the over-involved case situations, based her work with youth on her own experience with her family. In addition, fears and anxieties or feelings at an unconscious level about clients who are different may also prompt a reaction in the professional. In consequence, he or she may deny or in some instances overestimate or underestimate his or her reaction so as to minimize his or her conflict. Irrespective of the source, the social worker's thoughts and feelings interfere with his or her objectivity, causing an emotional response that effectively blocks his or her productive interactions with a client. For example, a social worker who leads a treatment group reported that he has to constantly check his reactions to men in the group when certain topics are discussed: "I say to myself, not this b…..s again, you know cause I've been there and I know when they are messing around, because I did the same thing. Sometimes, I want to yell at them, man, I know what you are playing at. I do a lot of self-talk because if I challenged them, I know that my behavior will change the tone of the group, which would not be at all helpful. My behavior would also be unprofessional, but I admit to you that at times it is hard."

Countertransference in the traditional sense is grounded in psychoanalytic theory in which the professional's past experiences and conscious and unconscious emotional reactions influence their relationship with a client (Hayes, 2004; McWilliams, 1999). A more contemporary view is that the professional's reactions, real and unreal, to a client can occur irrespective of origin and can be based on their own past or present experiences or client characteristics (James, 2008; Knight, 2006; Nichols, 2006). Proposing a more transactional approach, specifically, that of the person-in-the environment, Fauth (2006) found that such reactions and behaviors were related to stressful interpersonal events and the professional's appraisal as to whether the situation was harmful, threatening, or taxed his or her coping resources.

Consistent with Fauth's (2006), transactional stress theory, Knight (2006) and James (2008) assert that countertransference, including vicarious trauma, is a common reaction among professionals

who are involved in crisis work and trauma survivors. Salston and Figley (2004) also point to the consequences of trauma for professionals working with criminal victims. Countertransference in high stress situations may also signal a stage of burnout. James and Gilliland (2001) note that crisis professionals may experience "reawakened unresolved thoughts and feelings" as a result of working with clients who have had similar experiences (p. 419). Maintaining a professional distance may be difficult, especially when the countertransference reaction is related to the trauma experiences and "horror stories" of immigrants and refugees (Potocky-Tripodi, 2002). As a result, when a professional experiences compassion fatigue or secondary trauma, there is a tendency to become over-involved with a client. Neither situation is productive in that either one can severely impair a professional's ability to work effectively with clients.

EP 2.1.1f

Should you find that you are experiencing any one of the aforementioned behaviors, you should seek supervision or consultation. Also, you should consider whether taking time off will assist you to refocus and reenergize your professional work.

EP 2.1.1d

Countertransference reactions contaminate the helping relationships by producing distorted perceptions, blind spots, and antitherapeutic emotional reactions or behaviors (Kahn, 1997). Selected reactions that can result in counterproductive dynamics are:

- *The professional lacks the skills to integrate anger or conflict resolution into their coping repertoire or personality. For example, when confronted by a client who is angry, the tendency may be to become unduly uncomfortable and attempt to divert the expression of such feelings.*
- *The professional has unresolved feelings about rejections by significant others and finds it difficult to relate to clients who exhibit similar behavior.*
- *The professional fails to resolve resentful feelings toward authority, resulting in, for example, over-identification with a rebellious adolescent.*
- *The professional is controlling and over-identifying with clients who have similar problems and is blind to reciprocal behavior between clients; for example, taking sides when working with a couple in marital counseling or with authority*
- *The professional has an excessive need to be loved and admired and may behave seductively or strive to impress clients by inappropriate disclosure of personal information. Of course, selective self-disclosure in the form of empathic responsiveness can be beneficial (Goldstein, 1997). Raines (1996) suggests that self-disclosure decisions may be considered within a range of over- and under-involvement; therefore, personal sharing should be rational and related to the current relationship.*

Before discussing how to manage countertransference reactions, it is first important to identify their typical manifestations. Table 18-2 lists some of the indicators based on the work of Knight (2006) and Etherington (2000). Also take note of the similarities in this table and behaviors described in Table 18-1 for over- and under-involvement. Both tables illustrate behaviors or reactions that prompt you to take immediate appropriate corrective measures. Otherwise, they can contribute to the client's problem and ultimately impair the helping relationship.

Managing Countertransference Reactions

Ordinarily, the first step in resolving countertransference (and often all that is needed) is to engage in introspection. *Introspection* involves an analytical dialogue with yourself aimed at discovering the sources of your feelings, reactions, cognitions, and behaviors. Examples of questions that facilitate introspection include the following:

EP 2.1.1b

- "Why am I feeling uncomfortable with this client? What is going on inside me that I am not able to relate in a professional manner?"
- "How well do I manage my own anxiety, anger, or discomfort with the client or the situation?"
- "Why do I dislike (or feel bored, impatient, or irritated about) this client? Are my feelings rational, or does this client remind me of someone else or my own experience?"
- "What is happening inside of me that I don't face certain problems with this client? Am I afraid of a negative reaction on the client's part?"
- "What purpose was served by arguing with this client? Am I feeling defensive or threatened?"
- "Why did I talk so much or give so much advice? Did I feel a need to give something to the client?"
- "What's happening with me that I'm fantasizing or dreaming about this client?"

TABLE-18-2 TYPICAL PROFESSIONAL COUNTERTRANSFERENCE REACTIONS

- Being unduly concerned about or protective of a client, becoming his or her champion or rescuer
- Having persistent dreams or erotic fantasies about clients
- Dreading or anticipating sessions with clients
- Feeling uncomfortable when discussing certain problems with a client, including those who have anxieties, and fears about those who are different
- Hostility directed toward a client or inability to empathize with a client; underestimating the dynamics of differences
- Blaming others exclusively for a client's difficulties
- Feeling bored, being drowsy, or tuning out a client
- Regularly being tardy or forgetting appointments with certain clients
- Consistently ending sessions early or extending them beyond the designated time
- Trying to impress or being unduly impressed by clients
- Being overly concerned about losing a client
- Arguing with or feeling defensive or hurt by a client's criticisms or actions
- Being overly solicitous and performing tasks that clients are capable of performing
- Probing into a client's sex life
- Liking or disliking certain types of clients (may also be reality based)
- Identifying with the role of an abuser in a trauma situation or feeling responsible for his or her pain
- Attempting to manage feeling that include minimizing the stories of trauma clients, being disgusted with clients, or acting in a voyeuristic manner

---

- *"Why am I constantly taking sides in my work with couples (parents, minors, authority), thereby overlooking one side. Am I over- or under-identifying with certain clients, and if so, why?"*
- *"Could my own experience, personality, or feelings block my objectivity?"*

EP 2.1.1b

Managing countertransference reaction requires a professional's conscious assessment of the dynamics that aroused and subsequently triggered his or her reaction. As previously discussed in the social worker-consultation scenario, an assessment would involve preparatory planning, self-reflection and awareness, and centering and focusing on the purpose and content of a session with the individuals. The self-aware professional understands their own history and manages the consequences of his or her interactions with individuals in which there is a potential for a reaction (Hayes, 2004).

EP 2.1.1b

Introspection and self-assessment, as well as the ability to maintain appropriate boundaries and distance, will assist you in achieving or regaining a realistic perspective on your relationships with clients. Discussion of such topics should also be part of consultation with colleagues and supervisors, in which you expose and explore your feelings and obtain their perspective and advice. Just as clients are sometimes too close to their problems to view them objectively and thus benefit from seeing them from the vantage point of a social worker, so you can likewise benefit from the unbiased perspective of an uninvolved colleague, consultant, or supervisor. However, professionals who repeatedly experience countertransference reactions need professional help beyond mere introspection or the input of a colleague. Specifically, ongoing reactions limit their effectiveness and create ethical and relational barriers to effective work with clients.

Realistic Practitioner Reactions

Not all of your negative feelings toward certain clients are indicative of a negative countertransference reaction to the individual or their situations. Some people are abrasive, arrogant, or obnoxious, act tough, have irritating mannerisms, or are exploitative of and cruel toward others. Even the most accepting practitioner may have difficulty developing positive feelings toward such clients. We are, after all, only human; thus, we are not immune from disliking someone or feeling irritated, indifferent, or impatient at times. When faced with these individuals, we may be inclined to attach a label to the individual, thereby giving ourselves room to ignore them. Despite his or her behavior, individuals are entitled to service in which their uniqueness, dignity, and worth are respected. In fact, it may be the absence such

EP 2.1.1.d

respect in their interactions that has caused them to act in such a way that alienates, offends, or irritates others, leaving them isolated and confused about their relational difficulties.

EP 2.1.1d

When you look beyond the offending behavior or attitude of some clients, you will often discover that beneath their facade are desirable, even admirable qualities and vulnerabilities. A social worker noted in an interview with one of the authors that "during my contact with minors, in particular when race is a factor (the social worker is white), most will affect a negative posture with a big attitude. However, the key is to hang in there and gain their trust. In many instances, their trust allows you to access their private world. You may find that they have endured severe emotional and environmental deprivation, and, in some cases, physical or sexual abuse, or other traumatic experiences that have exceeded their coping ability and capacity to trust. Once you get past their behavior you often find a fragile kid who has been exposed to a life that you can hardly imagine!" Furthermore, the social worker emphasized that, in spite of their behavior, connecting with them necessitated acceptance and empathy. She also shared that there are days when she was tired of their behavior, and "I [told] them so. Oddly enough, most respond to me in a very caring, sometimes humorous way."

EP 2.1.10j

Abrasive or aggressive individuals can, however, need far more than warmth and acceptance. Such individuals need feedback about how certain aspects of their behavior offends you and others. Feedback can be extremely helpful if it is conveyed sensitively and expressed in the context of goodwill. In providing such feedback, you must be careful to avoid evaluative or blaming comments that tend to elicit defensiveness, for example, "You boast too much and dominate conversations" or "You don't consider other people's feelings when and say hurtful things." An individual is apt to be far more likely to be receptive to a message that describes their specific behavior. The same is true when a response and the associated feeling are personalized. The following descriptive message embodies ownership of feelings: "When you sneered at me just now, I felt defensive and resentful. You've done that several times before, and I find myself backing away from you each time. I'm concerned because I suspect that this is how you interact with others." This message, of course, is highly authentic and would not be appropriate until a sound working relationship has been established. As you point out the specifics of an individual's behavior, you can encourage them to risk new behaviors and give them opportunities to learn and practice altering ways of interacting with you and others.

Sexual Attraction Toward Clients

Romantic and sexual feelings toward clients can be especially hazardous to the helping relationship, although such feelings are by no means uncommon. Most professionals have at some point in their careers experienced this type of reaction toward a client. A majority of those who responded to a survey believed the attraction to be mutual; others assumed that the client was unaware of their attraction. When the latter was the case, they believed the attraction did not have any harmful effects on the helping process. By contrast, therapists who believed clients were aware of their attraction understood the detrimental impact on the helping process (Strom-Gottfried, 1999a).

EP 2.1.1c

Acting on the attraction has long-lasting grievous consequences for clients. No doubt you have heard about a professional who justified engaging in sexual activities with clients on the basis of helping them to feel loved or to overcome sexual problems. Such explanations are often thinly disguised and feeble rationalizations for exploiting clients. In other instances, justifications are based on the client's behavior toward the professional. Irrespective of circumstance, this behavior is unacceptable. Intimate involvement with a client, whether emotional or physical, is always unethical.

EP 2.1.2b

The consequences of sexual involvement are devastating for social workers as well. When such behaviors are discovered, the offending individual can be sanctioned, sued for unethical practice and have their professional license or certification revoked, essentially removing them from the profession. Ethical standards of conduct established by licensing boards and the NASW Code of Ethics are unequivocal about dual relationships with clients, especially those of a sexual nature. The NASW Code of Ethics states: "The social worker should under no circumstance engage in sexual activities or sexual contact with current clients, whether such contact is consensual or forced" (Section 1.09a).

EP 2.1.1c

Managing such attraction appropriately is critical. As Strom-Gottfried notes, "Even a small incidence warrants the attention of the professional, particularly supervisors and educators, to assure that any measures available to reduce the incidence further is fully pursued" (1999a, p. 448). Persistent erotic fantasies about clients who are particularly vulnerable, signals an impaired professional and a more serious remedy is indicated. Effectively managing sexual attraction requires engaging in the corrective measures identified earlier for unrealistic feelings and reactions, namely, introspection and consulting with a supervisor. Introspections may also reveal whether you are over- and under-involved with a client.

We cannot state too strongly that you must not allow your romantic feelings about a client or those of a client toward you to go unchecked. It is also important that in your interactions with client you take precautions in the manner that you dress, communicate, and behave, in order to avoid problematic situations.

Motivating Change

People who do not readily embrace a change in their behavior are often labeled as resistant. The notion of resistance has been used in a fashion that holds the individual responsible for their behavior, which, of course, tends to foster resistance and a reactive response. Without further exploration of the reason for resistance, the individual acquires a label that sticks, leading to the conclusion that they are opposed to change. Behaviors such as holding back, disengaging, or in some way subverting or sabotaging change efforts, whether knowingly or not, without open discussion, and any action or attitude that impedes the course of therapeutic work are thought to be general signs of resistance (Meyer, 2001; Nichols & Schwartz, 2004).

There are multiple factors to be considered in understanding behavior that may be assessed as resistance. In cross-cultural, cross-racial relationships, for example, Lum (2004) noted that resistance can be prominent in your interactions with persons of color. Resistance may be recognized by the professional's "minimal involvement, [being] reserved or being superficially pleasant." (pp. 152–153). The basis for resistance on the part of minority individuals and entire communities is rooted in a lack of trust or confidence in professionals. Establishing trust and reciprocity in relationships is a major thrust in overcoming the reluctance that people of color have about seeking help from agencies "that are controlled and dominated by whites" (Lum, 2004 p. 152).

Resistance as conceptualized by Freud is considered to be a normative, healthy, self-protective response, experienced by all human beings. In this light, ambivalence, anxiety, or opposition to change is a universal phenomenon, as anyone who has attempted to break long-established habits knows all too well. Indeed, the force of habit is relentless, hence, making a change often means foregoing gratifications or coping head-on with frightening or aversive situations or risking new behavior in the face of unknown consequences. Even though the status quo may cause pain, difficulty, or distress, there is a certain level of comfort in the familiar and the consequences of habitual behaviors are predictable. Realistically, it is not uncommon for people to experience mixed feelings about change, both desiring it and being hesitant or ambivalent. Opposing feelings generally coexist, that is, part of them is motivated, even as another part strives to maintain the status quo.

An individual's hesitancy or reluctance to embrace change may be caused by their lack of understanding or misunderstanding about the nature of service to be provided or of a specific intervention. Should this occur, it is vital to explain fully the nature of the service or intervention (informed consent). This discussion should also clarify the roles of the individual and permit voluntary clients to feel free to decide whether to proceed with the therapy. With involuntary clients, the discussion would clarify what is required of them and where there is room for choice. In either case, a contract with the individual in which roles are clarified, goals are specific, and the rationale for specific interventions is clear can ease an individual's apprehension. To further deal with feelings of uncertainty, individuals should be given the opportunity to ask questions and discuss their misgivings.

It is possible that some individuals become so caught up in a transference resistance that their behavior creates an obstacle to change (Nichols, 2006). Rather than focusing on change, they become preoccupied with their thoughts and perceptions, including unrealistic expectations of you. In this sense, they may not be resistant or opposed to change, however, their unresolved feelings get in the way. Unless you recognize and assist such individuals in resolving these feelings by discussing them in a realistic perspective, their progress is stalled and they may prematurely terminate the contact, convinced that their perceptions and feelings are accurate.

EP 2.1.1b

Have you ever been inclined to consider an individual as resistant when they hesitated or were opposed to the direction that you wished them to go to resolve their situation? To understand resistance as a normative self-protective function, think about a situation in which you were told that you needed to make certain changes, whether at work (complete your case notes on time), at home (be more helpful around the house), or a relationship (be more attentive). Reflect on:

- *Your emotional response.*
- *What was your behavioral response?*
- *How did you react?*

Now transfer your responses to clients, especially those who are meeting with you for the first time. Did you perhaps use verbal ploys such as *"I couldn't do that; it just wouldn't be me; I've tried that, and it doesn't work, or I understand what you're saying but,"* to justify your behavior? Recognizing your own feelings or ambivalence in your reflection can help you better understand and explore an individual's ambivalent feelings and to assist them to weigh the advantage and disadvantage of making a change. Indeed, a first step in managing potential opposition to change is to focus on an individual's underlying here-and-now feelings. As they think through their feelings and reassess the implications of maintaining the status quo, the scales often tilt in favor of change.

EP 2.1.3a

Many of the verbal ploy statements that you or a client might use may not necessarily indicate opposition to change. Instead, careful exploration is needed when an individual says that they cannot complete a particular action. Statements of this sort can be followed by rambling or dwelling on unimportant information as the individual attempts to make some sense of their situation, to tell their story, to relieve their anxiety using catharsis, to vent their frustration, or to air their grievances. If an individual appears to have reached an impasse, however, and seems unable to move beyond this point, you can safely conclude that opposition is involved and shift the focus to exploring the factors that underlie this opposition. Other instances in which an individual's hesitancy or ambivalence is not a sign of their opposition and which should be considered are whether:

- *The individual has the resources to change (e.g., developmental, social, cognitive)*
- *There are environmental barriers (e.g., economic, political, cultural that can impede change)*
- *Relational barriers may be present in the client-practitioner relationship*

Reactance provides a more fruitful perspective for considering opposition to change with involuntary clients. Rather than blaming, dismissing, or concluding that an individual is opposed to change, this theory leads you to objectively anticipate the range of responses to be expected when valued freedoms are threatened (Brehm, 1976). First, some individuals may try to regain their freedom directly by attempting to take back what has been threatened (e.g., choice). Second, a frequent response is to restore freedom by implication or to "find the loophole" in which they engage in superficial compliance while violating the spirit of requirements (e.g., I will sit at my desk, but I won't do any work). Third, threatened behaviors and beliefs are apt to become more valued than ever before. Finally, they may perceive you as the person or source of the threat, in which case you are faced with hostile or aggressive behavior (R. H. Rooney, 1992).

EP 2.1.6b

Reactance theory also lends itself to proactive strategies designed to reduce this kind of behavior. For example, individuals who perceive global pressure to change their lifestyles are likely to experience reactance. Conversely, they are less likely to react if those pressures are narrowed in scope and the change effort emphasizes behaviors that remain free. Second, reactance is likely to be reduced if the client perceives that he or she has at least some constrained choices (R. H. Rooney, 1992). Understanding the client's perspective on the situation and avoiding labeling can also act to reduce reactance (p. 135).

Change Strategies

In the helping process, as you encounter behavior that can be characterized as resistant or reactive, it is advisable for you to assess their behavior in light

EP 2.1.7a

of the Stages of Change Model (Prochaska, DiClemente & Norcross, 1992), discussed in Chapter 17. To refresh your memory, change is believed to progress along a sequence of stages, beginning with the *pre-contemplation stage* ("Leaving the children unsupervised for a short time was not a problem") and progress to *contemplation* ("I am willing to look at the harm that resulted from leaving the children unsupervised"). Self-evaluation can occur at this stage leading to a goal. For instance, a male who batters might deny that his behavior is abusive by saying, for example, "I had little choice; she was in my face," and progress to a point in which he might say, "I am willing to look at my behavior," at which point self-reflection and self-evaluation subsequently leads to a goal of examining "the effects of my behavior on self and significant others." Of course, some individuals may argue for the status quo or discount, minimize, or excuse their behavior (Miller & Rollnick, 2002). Similarly, you may believe utilizing the stage-change strategy shifts the focus away from their behavior. Research has shown, however, that a focus on a specific cognition or behavior can be a mediator between actions and change and ultimately increases the frequency of desired behaviors (Nichols, 2006). In addition, how you respond to the individuals can create cognitive consonance or dissonance. For example, a mother says, "This was the one time that I left the kids at home by themselves," your inductive open-ended question might be, "What would others say about leaving the kids at home alone?" or "When the children were home alone this one time, what happened?" In this way, you keep the change dialogue going, maintaining a focus on the specific problematic behavior. In addition to the change model, you will want to critique the appropriateness of the strategies discussed in Chapter 12 with involuntary individuals. Each of the discussed strategies is intended to appeal to the individual's self-interest and his or her involvement in the process of change. *Motivational congruence, agreeable mandate,* or *the deal strategy,* for example, counters the notion that certain involuntary clients are opposed to change. Instead, both you and the client engage in exploring common ground in which mandated goals can be defined and achieved. With the agreeable mandate strategy, an involuntary client may transition through the stages of change, moving from being involuntary to a level of voluntary status. Keep in mind that when individuals feel free to make up their own minds, they are more likely to become engaged. Being able to do so is crucial, because pressure often engenders an opposing force of reactance.

Motivational Interviewing

Change talk (Miller & Rollnick, 2002), an aspect of motivational interviewing, is an adaptation of the Stages of Change Model. Motivational interviewing is defined as a "client-centered, directive method for enhancing motivation to change by exploring and resolving ambivalence" that can be integrated with other treatment approaches (Miller & Rollnick, 2002, p. 25). The *"spirit"* of the method is guided by the following:

EP 2.1.7a & 2.1.10j

- *Collaborative partnership* between the practitioner that is developed in a climate that is conducive to change, in which the client's experience and perceptions are honored
- *Evocation*, the practitioner's aim to elicit and draw an individual's intrinsic motivation based on the belief that the resources and motivation for change are within the client relative to their goals, perceptions, and values
- *Autonomy* of the client and their capacity and right for self-direction, including the right to accept or not accept the counsel of the practitioner is affirmed, which facilitates their informed decision making

In essence, change becomes possible when the relationship between you and the individual is collaborative rather than coercive, his or her self-determination is honored and the aim of the interview is to explore and draw out what motivates the individual. In the course of your interaction with an individual, supportive and facilitative skills are instrumental for engaging him or her and for enhancing his or her motivation to change. In contrast, blaming and arguing with an individual to gain his or her acceptance of and compliance with change and using your authority to confront or coerce him or her is generally counterproductive and likely to result in reactance.

EP 2.1.10b

Guiding Principles of Motivational Interviewing

Empathy and acceptance, understanding that ambivalence or resistance is normal, supporting an individual's self efficacy, and developing discrepancy are core principles of the method. For example, in working with the mother who left her children unsupervised, paraphrasing with empathy

EP 2.1.10b

would include a statement such as, "It must difficult to be a single parent, working all day and then coming home to...." This statement conveys to the mother that you are attempting to understand her situation, without judgment or blaming her as a parent. In exploring a potential underlying issue related to leaving the children unsupervised, combined with an empathetic response, the mother's motivation to engage in developing problem-solving goals is strengthened.

EP 2.1.7a

The guiding principles and the spirit of motivational interviewing are illustrated in the video entitled *How Can I Help?* In the beginning of the session, the client recounts the numerous difficulties that she had experienced during the past week. Responding with empathy, Peter, the social worker asks her, "How can I help?" At this point, Judy, the client responds, "Well, I guess I need a bus card." As she continues, she tells Peter how having a bus card will help her. In particular, a bus card would make it easier for her to attend her group sessions and leave a urine sample for analysis. Supporting her self-efficacy, specifically, her self-confidence that she could accomplish the necessary change tasks, Peter reinforces her ability to do so. In general, a discussion of the content of a client's difficulties can yield cues as to the sources of his or her difficulties, which otherwise may be thought of as resistance. Contrast Peter's behavior in this case with the social worker's views of the mother in the case consultation scenario discussed at the beginning of this chapter. Similarly to the mother in that case, at first glance, Judy could have been perceived as less than committed to change. In this regard, instead of exploring the ways in which he could help, it would have been easy for Peter to ignore the numerous barriers that she detailed, and thereby conclude that Judy lacked sufficient motivation to change. Additionally, Peter's authentic and empathetic responses conveyed his goodwill and concern that Judy's progress could become bogged down; it also reaffirms the social worker's helpful intent and desire to work out whatever difficulties have arisen.

EP 2.1.7a

A principle of motivational interviewing is that individuals are responsible for change and they tend to be motivated to change when they are involved in the process. When they appear to be resistant, which is not considered to be opposition, the practitioner avoids arguing for change. Arguing with clients has a limited affect on their behavior and simply invites resistance. Resistance signals the need for a different response. For example, after listening to the client's story about her inability to pay and her concerns about her future housing situation, she offered a solution. Specifically, she asked the social worker to write a letter that documented her progress so that she could be considered for a supportive housing program for women and their children. Here, again, the social worker affirms her self-efficacy.

As the session progresses, the social worker brings up the fact that the client has a diagnosis of depression. Clearly she is ambivalent about the diagnosis. The social worker responds by exploring the source of the client's feelings and acknowledges her troubling thoughts about the diagnosis. In this instance, the social worker opened up the client's feelings by asking her whether she knew the symptoms of depression. Rolling with her resistance, the social worker continued, asking her "Well, do you mind if we explore a little bit about whether or not this is depression?" With her permission, he summarizes moods or behaviors that are generally associated with depression. In effect, he is supporting her autonomy by providing her with information, which she is free to accept or reject. As she described her mood and behavior, in particular her sleeping patterns in which the child is mostly unsupervised, the social worker queried that behavior. Rather than point to the consequence of unacceptable parenting, the social worker asked, "Is it okay with you?" As they continue, he uses the principle of discrepancy. Discrepancy (or confrontation discussed in Chapter 17) focuses on an individual's expressed goal or value, when, his or her behavior indicates otherwise. A primary motivation for this client is keeping her child. She talks about the various steps that she has taken to prevent the reoccurrence of a child protection intervention. The social worker praised her for wanting to be a good parent, but later he points out to her the discrepancy between her desire and her sleeping patterns and the potential risk to the child. Emphasizing the mismatch in the results of her perceived and actual behavior relative to her goal of wanting to keep her child causes her to examine the situation. Confronting the client about the situation and then collaborating with her to sort through the pros and cons of her behavior places the responsibility on her as to whether or not she wants to seek help for her depression and prevent the intervention of child protective services. As you watch the interactions between the social worker and the client, notice how the social worker continues to explore and draw out what motivates the client.

EP 2.1.10j

EP 2.1.7b
& 2.1.10b

Motivational interviewing assumes that ambivalence is normal and further, that ambivalent or resistant behavior is not in and of itself indicative of an individual's pathology or incapacity (Miller & Rollnick 2002). As people experience problems, they can become stuck. The role of the practitioner is to help them reach their own conclusions through the skillful use of communication skills like listening, open-ended questions intended to elicit information about their views, beliefs and values; and facilitative skills, such as support, acceptance, and empathy. Acceptance is critical to the relationship in that it contributes to a relational climate in which an individual is free to openly discuss his or her feelings and misgivings about change without being judged, criticized, or blamed. "When motivational interviewing is done well," it is the client's goals rather than those of the practitioner that have center stage. By skillfully drawing out the intrinsic motivation, it is the client rather than the practitioner who puts forth his or her own solution. "It is the client who gives voice to concerns, reasons for change, self-efficacy, and intentions to change" (Miller & Rollnick, 2002, p. 39).

EP 2.1.10j

The essence of helping is to develop a relationship with individuals in which the essential elements of acceptance, expectation, support, and simulation are prominent (Perlman, 1957). Encouraging growth in individuals depends on your critical assessment about how and when to utilize these elements in your interactions with clients. Above all, what you do should facilitate problem solving in the context of a relationship that is intended to help an individual to change. The following discussion highlights additional techniques that can be used to enhance an individual's confidence and motivation.

Positive Connotation

EP 2.1.10j

Positive connotation is a technique that is useful in reducing the threat level associated with an individual's thoughts and feelings in the face of change. It allows a person to save face and protect his or her self-esteem when he or she risks talking about his or her feelings or perceptions. The goal of positive connotation is not to condone opposition or to reinforce his or her perceptions. Instead, consistent with the strengths perspective, the objective is to minimize an individual's need to defend himself or herself and to safeguard his or her sense of self.

In positive connotation, constructive intentions are attributed to what would otherwise be regarded as a client's undesirable or negative behavior. In using this technique, you recognize that the meaning ascribed to the behavior can be viewed in both positive and negative lights, depending on one's vantage point. For example, when an individual's behavior or feelings appear to oppose change, thereby becoming an obstacle to progress, you are more than likely to view his or her behavior as negative. From the perspective of the individual, however, the same behavior has a positive intent. For instance, a client cancelled an appointment. Even though she showed up for the following week, during the session she was mostly silent, barely engaged, and her body language indicated that she was uncomfortable. Exploration of her behavior revealed that she resented the behavior on the part of the social worker who she perceived as pressuring her to follow a certain course of action. In the eyes of the social worker the client's behavior was problematic. Conversely, the client saw her behavior as protecting her right to be self-directed. The usefulness of this technique is that it allows you to explore and understand a client's perceptions and subsequent reaction relative to your behavior as well as theirs.

Redefining Problems as Opportunities for Growth

The technique of *redefining problems as growth opportunities* is a close relative of positive connotation because it also involves relabeling or reframing. Both clients and social workers tend to view problems negatively. Moreover, clients often view remedial courses of action as "necessary evils," dwelling on the threat involved in risking new behaviors. Therefore, it is often helpful to reformulate problems and essential tasks as opportunities for growth. Relabeling or reframing emphasizes the positives, that is, the benefits of change rather than the discomfort, fear, and other costs of modifying one's behavior. At the same time, it is important that you not convey an unrealistically positive attitude. An individual's fears and threats about the risk of change are very real to them. Thus, being unduly optimistic may simply convey a lack of understanding on your part.

EP 2.1.10j

Neither reframing nor relabeling minimizes clients' problems or ignores fears in risking new behaviors. Both do, however, enable clients to view their difficulties in a fuller perspective that embodies positive as well as negative factors. The following are examples of how problem situations might be relabeled as opportunities for growth:

Relabeling

EP 2.1.10j

- *A teenage foster child who has run away because the foster parents insisted he adhere to a night-time curfew refuses to return to the foster home because the foster parents "are unreasonable." The social worker acknowledges that returning to the foster home is a challenge; however, doing so deals with the problem head-on, and is an opportunity to work it out the difficulties with the foster parents, rather than avoiding, which has been the youth's pattern.*

Reframing

EP 2.1.10i

- *A youth feels embarrassed about taking a battery of vocational tests and attending a vocational-technical school, rather than going to college. The social worker acknowledges his discomfort but emphasizes that taking the tests offers an opportunity to learn more about his aptitudes and to expand his choices in planning his future.*
- *A woman is apprehensive about leaving her abusive spouse. The social worker empathizes, but points out that leaving her spouse will allow her to have the kind of life that she wants for herself and her children.*

In some instances, clients fail to make progress toward their goals because of the persistence of pervasive particular patterns of behavior. Your effort to encourage or facilitate a different perspective by reframing or relabeling can be met with a dismissal of your appraisal. For instance, the individual may intellectualize, hold other people or circumstances responsible for their difficulties, or he or could be reluctant to examine or acknowledge his or her part in creating the situation. Because such patterns of behavior often create an impasse, it is important that you recognize and handle them. Confronting clients with discrepancies between expressed goals and behaviors prevent accomplishment of those goals is often needed to break an impasse. Because Chapter 17 discussed confrontation at length, the discussion here is limited to a special type of confrontation: *therapeutic binds*.

Therapeutic Binds

EP 2.1.10i & 2.1.10j

This technique is used in those instances in which an individual stubbornly clings to self-defeating behaviors that perpetuate his or her difficulties. In such instances, placing the individual in a *therapeutic bind* may be the impetus needed to modify the problematic behaviors. The intent of the technique is to confront an individual with his or her self-defeating behavior in such a way that he or she must either modify the behavior or own responsibility for choosing to perpetuate the difficulties despite his or her expressed intentions to the contrary (Nichols & Schwartz, 2004; Goldenberg & Goldenberg, 2004). The only way out of a therapeutic bind, unless one chooses to acknowledge no intention of changing, is to make constructive changes. In this regard, the therapeutic bind discrepancy is similar in the way it is used to motivational interviewing.

Following are some examples of situations in which therapeutic binds have been successfully used. Take note of the fact that the practitioner points out the specific inconsistent behavior relative to the client's stated goal.

- *Despite efforts to resolve fears of being rejected in relationships with others, a client continued to decline social invitations and makes no effort to reach out to others. The social worker asked her about her apparent choice to continue her social isolation. "You can either risk being with others or continue as you are, but you said that you wanted your life to be different."*
- *A supervisor complained to an Employee Assistance Program (EAP) social worker about conflict with other members on his team. In exploring the situation, the supervisor admitted that he consistently made unilateral decisions despite repeated feedback and negative reactions from other team members. The social worker asked him, "Is it your decision that it is more important for you to be in control, rather than to improve your relationships with colleagues?"*
- *An adolescent persisted in being truant from school, violating family rules, and engaging in antisocial behaviors despite his assertion that he wanted to be independent. The social worker countered that he "seemed unprepared to use his freedom wisely" pointing out that by continuing to get in trouble, the juvenile court judge would further limit his choices*

unless his desire to be independent included setting limits on his behavior.

- In marital counseling, a wife constantly brings up her husband's previous infidelity despite expressing a desire to strengthen their marriage. When this occurred, the husband's response was to withdraw and disengage from the relationship. Presenting the wife with the contradiction in her behavior, the social worker stated, "Despite your claim of wanting to preserve the marriage, by your behavior it appears to be more important for you to continue to talk about your husband's previous behavior."

EP 2.1.10b

In using the therapeutic bind technique, it is vital to observe the guidelines for confrontation, thereby avoiding "clobbering" or alienating the client. In this way, being empathetic as you ask a reflective question about the apparent contradiction or conclusion can be experienced by the client as a more respectful form of confrontation leading to self-reflection. Be aware, however, that a therapeutic bind is a potent but high-risk technique, and you should use it sparingly. In the best of circumstances, clients can experience an *"aha"* moment, which allows them to move forward. When the technique is used, care should be taken to modify its jarring effect with empathy, concern, and sensitive exploration of the dynamics behind the self-defeating patterns. Above all, the technique should be used to assist the client and not as a confrontational response to your frustrations about the client's contradictory behavior.

Summary

This chapter described barriers to change with individuals, including relational dynamics, over- and under-involvement, and racial and cultural barriers. Relational reactions can occur as a result of your real or imagined perceptions of clients, or they may derive from perceptions that clients formulate about you. Supportive and facilitative skills are essential to creating a relational bond and a climate that is conducive to problem solving. The bond that is created between you and the client, in which you have and consequentially act on a sexual attraction toward the individual, is unacceptable and unethical has severe consequences.

Relational reactions, including resistance, are normal manifestations of human behavior and, therefore, may not be indicative of opposition to change. In view of this reality, this chapter discussed at length techniques for recognizing and managing these reactions and motivating change. Your skillful handling of these dynamics is critical to ensuring that the helping relationship is productive and remains focused on the desired outcome. Be aware, however, that barriers to change can be the result of personal factors, for example, limited resources or environmental factors that are beyond the control of the client; in such a case, you may need to assume the role of advocate.

CourseMate

Access an integrated eBook and chapter specific learning tools including glossary terms, chapter outlines, relevant web links, videos, and practice quizzes. Go to **www.cengagebrain.com**.

PART 4
The Final Phase

The third and final phase of the helping process encompasses the last evaluation of progress and the termination of the helping relationship. The final phase is important because the way in which social workers bring the helping relationship to a close strongly influences whether clients will maintain their progress and continue to grow following termination. Further, many people who receive social work services have previously been subject to difficult endings—those which involved ambiguity, abandonment, anger, abruptness, or failure. Properly handled, termination may itself be an intervention to model the ways in which relationships are concluded in a constructive and meaningful manner. Social workers must understand how to sensitively and skillfully conclude their work with clients, even if the end of the helping process is unplanned.

This chapter introduces you to strategies for evaluating case progress in work with individuals, groups, and families. The bulk of the chapter addresses the varieties of planned and unplanned terminations with the remainder covering ethical considerations, the common worker, and client reactions to termination, the strategies for maintaining client gains post-termination, and the use of rituals in effectively ending the helping relationship.

CHAPTER 19
Evaluation and Termination

CHAPTER OVERVIEW

Chapter 19 reviews methods for evaluating case progress, describes various factors that affect the termination process, identifies relevant tasks for both social workers and clients, and discusses skills essential to effectively managing termination. After reading it you will:

- Understand how evaluation builds on the assessment measures and goal-setting procedures employed earlier in the helping process
- Be able to distinguish between outcome, process, and satisfaction forms of evaluation
- Appreciate the dynamics associated with various forms of planned and unplanned endings
- Be able to assist clients in solidifying gains made in treatment
- Understand common termination reactions and how to address them
- Know how to use rituals to achieve closure

EPAS COMPETENCIES IN THE 19TH CHAPTER

This chapter provides the information that your will need to meet the following practice competencies.

2.1.1b Practice personal reflection and self-correction to assure continual professional development

2.1.1f Use supervision and consultation

2.1.2b Make ethical decisions by applying standards of the National Association of Social Workers Code of Ethics and, as applicable, the International Federation of Social Workers/International Association of Schools of Social Work Ethics in Social Work Statement of Principles

2.1.3a Distinguish, appraise, and integrate multiple sources of knowledge, including research-based knowledge and practice wisdom

2.1.3b Analyze models of assessment, prevention, intervention, and evaluation

2.1.4d View yourself as a learner and engage those with whom you work as informants

2.1.10b Use empathy and other interpersonal skills

2.1.10l Facilitate transitions and endings

2.1.10m Critically analyze, monitor, and evaluate interventions

Evaluation

Evaluation has assumed ever-increasing significance in direct practice; indeed, the majority of social workers engage in some form of practice evaluation. Chapter 12 introduced you to the ways that goals and objectives, client self-monitoring, and other measures can be used to create clear directions for service and benchmarks against which progress can be measured. The conclusion of service is thus the final point at which goal attainment and other aspects of change can be assessed prior to termination. If you have systematically obtained baseline measures and tracked progress, clients will be prepared for evaluation at termination. You can further enhance their cooperation by again reviewing the rationale and actively involving them in the process. For

EP 2.1.3b

EP 2.1.4d

example, you can introduce this topic to the client by making any of the following statements:

- "An important part of termination is to assess the results we have achieved and to identify what helped you most and least during our work together."
- "As an agency, we're committed to improving the quality of our services. Your honest feedback will help us to know how we're doing."
- "Our evaluation measures will help you and me see how your symptoms have changed since you were admitted."
- "One way we determine success on the case plan is to evaluate how your situation has changed since we began working together."
- "Our agency regularly evaluates the effectiveness of treatment groups. You'll all be sent a survey link each week so that you can give us anonymous feedback about the session."

Several different evaluation methods can be used to determine client progress throughout the helping process and at its conclusion—for example, standardized tests, direct observation, goal attainment scaling, and client self-reports though logs, journals, and surveys. The power of evaluation is strengthened when multiple sources of information are used. Whatever method is used, evaluations focus on three dimensions of service: (1) outcomes, (2) process, and (3) satisfaction.

Outcomes

EP 2.1.10m

Outcome evaluation involves assessing the results achieved against the goals that were formulated during the contracting phase of work. As described in Chapters 8 and 12, the methods utilized during the assessment and goal-setting phases will, in part, determine which outcomes you measure. For example, you may measure changes in the *frequency* of difficulties (e.g., being late for work, getting detention, binging, hoarding, experiencing negative cognitions, forgetting to take medications) or the frequency of target behaviors, such as exercise, use of "I" statements, safe sex practices, or family outings. You may also assess outcomes by looking at changes in the *severity* of problems (e.g., self-esteem scores on rapid assessment instruments, anxiety as measured by a self-anchored rating scale, sleep disturbance as measured by a client's journal, or distractibility as measured by observations from a child's classroom teacher and caregivers). A third measure of outcomes involves the *achievement* of goals or tasks (e.g., applying for and getting a job, completing homework, improving parenting and disciplinary practices, maintaining sobriety, developing a safety plan, completing assignments between task group sessions). These items, when compared with the baseline measures taken when the client first entered service, will help determine the extent of progress and the client's readiness for termination (Epstein & Brown, 2002).

A specific type of success measure is goal attainment scaling (GAS). In this process, the social worker and client identify a handful of problem behaviors or targeted changes and the related goals. Then, together, the worker and client assign each item a number corresponding to the likelihood of achievement or success on a scale from -2 to $+2$. A -2 would be an unfavorable outcome or a task or goal the client is highly unlikely to meet. A rating of 0 would indicate an expected outcome and $+2$ would indicate the most favorable outcome or the task with the greatest likelihood of completion (Yegidis & Weinbach, 2002). Ratings of -1 or $+1$ would be used to indicate more moderate expectations. For example, if the client's goal in a weight-loss group is to keep a record of all food and exercise for a week, the scale might be as follows:

- $-2 =$ Keep inconsistent or incomplete records for the majority of days of the week.
- $-1 =$ Keep the log for 2 days, marking all food and exercise, along with related calories.
- $0 =$ Keep the log for 4 days, marking all food and exercise, along with related calories.
- $+1 =$ Keep the log for 5 or 6 days, marking all food and exercise, along with related calories.
- $+2 =$ Keep the log for 7 days, marking all food and exercise, along with related calories.

The client's goal attainment, then, is weighed in light of the likelihood that he or she would achieve the goal, with better outcome associated with the ideal or "stretch" goals. Clearly GAS is best suited for clients who are motivated to complete tasks and are reliable in reporting the results. The consistent use of GAS will help the social worker and client track incremental steps toward service outcomes and can ultimately serve as one indicator of readiness for termination.

Manualized (guided by a manual) or evidence-based interventions often contain measures as part of the work. Typically, these instruments would have been used as part of the assessment and treatment- or service-planning to determine areas of difficulty and strength and to establish baseline scores against which progress can be measured. Numerous texts offer standardized scales and information on selecting and administering them in practice to target outcomes (Bloom, Fischer, & Orme 2006; Fischer & Corcoran 2006a, 2006b; Unrau, Gabor, & Grinnell, 2007). Some of these instruments lend themselves to repeated use, enabling workers and clients to track progress over time. Through such single-subject designs (also referred to as single-system research, single-case time series, or $n = 1$ designs) the client is compared to himself or herself on baseline scores from earlier administrations. If the initial goals for work were vague or unmeasurable or if no baseline measures were taken, social workers and clients could still evaluate the current status of the client's difficulties, goal attainment, symptoms, or achievements to develop an approximate sense of progress and readiness for termination; however, comparative analyses would be impossible.

In addition to comparative measures, you can use interviews or questionnaires to determine clients' views in order to evaluate their sense of progress against your own observations.

- *"To what extent did you learn skills to help your family get along better?"*
- *"How have your anxiety symptoms changed since you began treatment?"*
- *"How has your grief changed since you have been in the support group?"*

The difficulty with these recollections and other forms of self-report are, of course, that they may be highly selective and may be affected by numerous factors, such as the client's desire to please (or punish) the social worker, the client's interest in concluding service, or the hope that problems are resolved and that further services are not necessary. Although it is unwise to challenge clients' perceptions, you can reduce biases by asking clients to provide actual examples of recent events ("critical incidents") that illustrate their attainment of goals, a decline in difficulties, or an increase in capacities. This discussion also provides an opportunity for you to reaffirm the client's accomplishments, which tend to heighten his or her confidence and satisfaction. In initiating these discussions, the worker might say (to members of the HEART group in Chapters 11 and 16), *"From what you are saying, it sounds like the group has been helpful to each of you. Can you identify some recent experiences that you handled differently because of your experiences in the group?"*

As noted, clients' perceptions of their progress can be supplemented by other data or sources where feasible. For example, feedback from collateral contacts, such as family members, teachers, other helpers, or fellow clients (in families, groups, or residential settings), may provide perspectives on an individual's progress that can be contrasted with self-reports.

Process

Another aspect of evaluation involves identifying the aspects of the helping process that were useful or detrimental. Feedback about techniques and incidents that enhanced or blocked progress will help you to hone certain skills, eliminate others, and use techniques with greater discrimination. Such "formative evaluation" methods also help organizations to determine which elements of their programs were effective in bringing about the desired change or whether the techniques used were consistent with standardized agency protocols and delivered as efficiently as possible (Royse, Thyer, Padgett, & Logan, 2006). These evaluations capture the nuances of client-social worker interactions that contribute to treatment effectiveness. A technique that is useful with an assertive client, for example, may produce the opposite effect with a depressed client. Likewise, a family intervention may be effective only if it is carried out in a particular way. A social worker may have attributed a positive outcome to a masterfully executed technique, only to find the client was helped far more by the practitioner's willingness to reach out and maintain hope when the client had almost given up (McCollum & Beer, 1995).

Clearly, client feedback can be used to assess beneficial aspects of the helping process, though self-reports about process are subject to the same biases as self-reports about outcomes just described. Evaluation instruments can also be used to more precisely measure the aspects of the helping process that were instrumental in achieving change.

With manualized or other evidence-based interventions, fidelity assessments can address how closely the process and skills used by the program or the individual social worker match the design of the intervention (Substance Abuse and Mental Health Services Administration [SAMHSA], 2003a). These can include qualitative case-study reviews in which supervisory meetings, observation of sessions, audit interviews with clinicians, or focus groups with colleagues are used to examine a particular worker's actions (O'Hare, 2005). Quantitative fidelity measures include statistics on the type, frequency, duration, and pattern of services, chart reviews and other administrative or quality assurance data-the level of congruence with the intervention model, and inventories that capture the degree to which the worker employs particular skills. One such instrument, the Practice Skills Inventory (PSI), documents the number of client contacts, the frequency that particular skills were used (e.g., "Provided emotional support for my client," "Taught specific skills to deal with a certain problem") (O'Hare, 2005, pp. 555–556), and examples of those skills for the case (e.g., "Acknowledged how painful it is to move from home into assisted living," "Role-played ways of meeting other residents").

Published measures are also available for social workers who wish to evaluate outcomes and processes in their work with groups and families. Toseland and Rivas (2009) describe six self-reported measures that can capture feedback on the therapeutic elements of treatment groups. For example, Yalom's Curative Factors Scale (Stone, Lewis, & Beck, 1994) might identify the different dimensions of treatment groups and their relative therapeutic effectiveness. You can also construct valid measures of practice effectiveness by combining measures (e.g., records about sessions, client self-reports, observations) to provide an approximate measure of the effectiveness of the intervention processes used.

With children and other clients who lack high written or verbal ability, the use of expressive techniques, such as collages or paintings, may help to tap into evaluative content. For example, the client may be asked to draw or display something to illustrate "what I liked best/least about our work together" or "what helped me during my time here." Feedback from caregivers and other observers can be sought on a periodic basis, and their appraisals can be linked to the interventions being used at a given point in time.

Satisfaction

The outcomes achieved and the means used to achieve them are important measures of client progress. Another measure in the increasingly competitive and consumer-conscious practice environment seeks information about client satisfaction. You may gauge this level of satisfaction in your evaluative discussions with the client. Some settings facilitate the gathering of formal feedback by sending out written evaluation surveys at the termination of service or at a specified follow-up period. Some payers, such as managed care companies, will also evaluate providers by directly seeking client input.

These instruments address satisfaction with the social worker's service by asking questions such as "Would you refer a friend or family member to us for services in the future?", "Were you and the clinician able to meet your goal?", and "Do you believe you needed additional services that were not provided?" (Corcoran & Vandiver, 1996, p. 57). Satisfaction surveys also evaluate structural or operational issues such as appropriateness of the waiting room, convenience of parking, time elapsed between the client's request for service and first appointment, the worker's promptness in making a home visit, and friendliness of reception staff (Ackley, 1997; Corcoran & Vandiver, 1996; Larsen, Attkisson, Hargreaves, & Nguyen, 1979). Satisfaction measures may specifically evaluate particular elements of an agency's services or progress on particular initiatives. For example, they may inquire about the cultural competence of the staff, the openness of the facility to diverse populations, or the turnaround time in responding to client calls and requests.

The Kansas Consumer Satisfaction Survey utilizes a 26-item, Likert-type scale with ratings 1 to 5 (strongly agree to strongly disagree, or does not apply) in which clients respond to statements such as "If I have an emergency at night or on the weekend, I am able to get help from the program," "I can choose where I live," and "My opinions and ideas are included in my treatment plan" (SAMHSA, 2003a). A related instrument, the Quality of Life Self-Assessment, asks consumers to tell the agency "how things are going...these days" (SAMHSA, 2003b) by rating such issues as social life, level of independence, physical health, and access to transportation on a 4-point scale (poor-fair-good-excellent); it also measures mental health symptoms and the effects of alcohol and other drug use on a severe-moderate-minimal-none scale. The instrument also invites the client to indicate whether any of the items should be reflected on his or her service plan. Both the satisfaction and self-assessment surveys offer open-ended items to which clients can respond with other thoughts or questions. Clearly, the utility of these or any evaluation instrument depends on professionals' and agencies' willingness and ability to incorporate them into standard practices and procedures (Rzepnicki, 2004).

Termination

Termination refers to the process of formally ending the individual social worker-client relationship. It is a feature of practice with all client systems, from individuals and families to task groups, coalitions, and communities, and it occurs regardless of the duration of the helping relationship.[1] Terminations can occur when goals are met, when clients make a transition to other services, when time-limited services are concluded, and when social workers or clients leave the helping relationship. Even if clients are likely to "come and go" from service over a period of time as their concerns and needs change, it is important to draw closure to each unique episode of care.

The notion of ending is often introduced at the beginning of service, when the social worker discusses the likely duration of care, the number of sessions allotted, or the goals that will guide the helping process. In some time-limited treatment models, the fixed length of care is part of informed consent discussions at the outset. For example, the social worker might explain, "We believe that brief treatment is effective and helps both you and me make efficient use of our time together. So we'll begin today by getting an idea of the goals you want to work on and the best way to use our time over the next 6 to 8 weeks to achieve those goals."

Whether in short- or long-term therapy models, successful termination involves preparing clients adequately for separation from the social worker and/or group and accomplishing other tasks that facilitate the transition from being a client to being "on one's own:"

1. Evaluating the service provided and the extent to which goals were accomplished
2. Determining when to implement termination
3. Mutually resolving emotional reactions experienced during the process of ending
4. Planning to maintain gains achieved and to achieve continued growth.

EP 2.1.3a

The significance of these tasks and the extent to which they can be successfully accomplished are determined in large measure by the context in which the helping relationship takes place.[2] The intensity of the termination process is affected by factors such as the type of contact (voluntary or involuntary), the size and characteristics of the client system, and the nature of the intervention used.

Emotional reactions will vary depending on the nature and length of the helping relationship and the characteristics and past experiences of the individuals involved. That is, involuntary clients and those with more structured and time-limited services will be less likely to experience a sense of loss at termination than those who have engaged in longer and more voluntary relationships with the social worker. For example, termination of a time-limited educational group may be less intense and require less preparation of members than would the ending of an ongoing interpersonal support group or discharge from a residential treatment setting. Clients who have experienced difficult losses in the past may require more time and sensitivity in bringing the helping relationship to a close. Terminations from brief crisis intervention, case management, or discharge planning relationships may differ in intensity depending on the nature of the needs met and the length of service. Termination from family sessions may be less difficult than those from individual work, because most of the client system will continue to work and be together, albeit without the social worker's involvement.

Types of Termination

Terminations generally fall into one of two categories: unplanned and planned. *Unplanned terminations* occur when clients withdraw prematurely from services or when social workers leave helping relationships due to illness, job change, or other circumstances. *Planned terminations* occur when clients' goals are achieved, when transfer or referral is anticipated and necessary, or when service is concluded due to the time-limited nature of the setting (such as hospitals or schools) or the treatment modality used (such as brief treatment or fixed-length groups). Examples of both types of termination, along with their subtypes, are included in Table 19-1 and explained further below.

TABLE-19-1 TERMINATION SUBTYPES

- Unplanned
  - Drop-out, kick-out, push-out
  - Client death
  - Worker death, incapacitation, discharge
- Planned—unsuccessful
- Planned—successful
  - Temporal/Structural
  - Goals attained
  - Simultaneous departure
  - Client death

Unplanned Terminations

Unplanned terminations occur when the working relationship is halted suddenly or prematurely. Client-initiated unplanned termination can be triggered by dropping out of treatment, by an adverse event that renders the client unavailable for service, or by the client behaving in such a way that services are withdrawn or he or she is ejected from the setting. Examples of adverse events include being arrested, running away, committing suicide, or otherwise dying unexpectedly. The category of "dropouts" from service is similarly broad, including clients who are seeking services involuntarily or are otherwise unmotivated, clients who are dissatisfied with the social worker but are unable to verbalize those concerns, clients who feel they have made satisfactory progress and thus "are done" whether the clinician thinks so or not, and clients who decide to quit for pragmatic reasons like a lack of funds or the inconvenience of the service setting.[3] A mixed form of unplanned termination can be characterized as a "push-out," where the social worker and the client have failed to "click" and the client's discontinuation is prompted or reinforced by the practitioner's disinterest, incompetence, or lack of commitment (Hunsley, Aubrey, Vestervelt, & Vito, 1999).

A common theme of all these client-initiated endings is that they are unanticipated and thus allow no opportunity for discussion, processing, or closure, yet the residue of feelings and unfinished business remains. The tasks of termination (reflection on the work together, planning for the future, marking the end of treatment) remain undone and both parties may experience feelings of abandonment, anger, rejection, failure, relief, and shame.

Unplanned terminations can also be worker-initiated—for example, when the social worker dies, becomes incapacitated, or is dismissed. The suddenness and finality of these endings can result in feelings of abandonment, self-blame, and shock. Other practitioner-initiated unplanned endings, such as those due to layoffs or job transfers, may elicit strong reactions from the client, but generally allow time for processing and closure. We will discuss managing those feelings and endings in a later section. All unplanned endings require special measures so that the tasks of termination can be approximated to the extent possible.

Managing Unplanned Terminations Some estimates suggest that 50 percent of the overall client population will drop out of service (Kazdin & Wassell, 1998; Sweet & Noones, 1989) and that this figure may be even higher for certain subgroups. Some settings may have their own protocols for dealing with "no shows" and a different mechanism may be needed for the client who fails to reappear after a first session (see Meyer, 2001) compared to one who ceases to appear for service midway through the course of treatment.

A common response to unplanned termination by the client is for the social worker to reach out to him or her by phone, email, or letter. The goals in doing so may be to acknowledge the decision to conclude services, to encourage the client to come in for a closing session, or to achieve the purposes of such a session through the communication itself. For example, one client who was arrested could not receive phone calls or return for services. Nevertheless, the social worker was able to write him a letter in which she reviewed the goals he had achieved and the issues with which he continued to struggle. She conveyed her regard for him and informed him of the availability of other services during his incarceration and following his release. A similar technique can be used when a social worker must leave abruptly, when a client quits service, or when a client leaves an institution against medical advice. Such endings are not ideal because they do not allow the client the opportunity to express his or her views or participate in evaluation, but they do help to mark the ending and "clear the air" regarding future services.

When a worker dies or otherwise becomes incapacitated, it is incumbent upon his or her colleagues to intervene for the care or transfer of the clients involved. They must also recognize that these clients' needs and reactions will be shaped by the abruptness and nature of the loss, their personal loss histories, and the particular issues for which they were seeking help (Philip & Stevens, 1992; Philip, 1994). Thus, grieving the lost relationship may become a primary task alongside continued work on their treatment goals identified earlier.

Likewise, when a client dies unexpectedly, whether through an accident or a traumatic act such as homicide or suicide, the loss has significant implications for the helping professionals left behind. Out of respect for the client's continuing right to privacy, the worker is ethically bound to keep known details of such clients confidential, even after death. This being the case, the worker's family members and friends are unable to help address the grief and may not even be aware of the loss. Supervisory and collegial support should be the primary resource to the mourner, with coworkers offering empathy, permission to grieve, and encouragement to talk about and integrate the feelings that emerge (Chemtob, Hamada, Bauer, Torigoe, & Kinney, 1988; Krueger, Moore, Schmidt, & Wiens, 1979; Strom-Gottfried & Mowbray, 2006).

Formal processes for reviewing the case—referred to as "postvention" by Shneidman (1971)—can take the form of individual or group processing of the case (Pilsecker, 1987), a psychological autopsy (Kleepsies, Penk, & Forsyth, 1993; Chemtob et al., 1988) or critical incident stress debriefing (Farrington, 1995). Each of these mechanisms has a slightly different intent and focus, but each offers the opportunity for the social worker to acknowledge the loss, contemplate the experience with the client, have a supportive review, and deepen understanding of what took place.

CASE EXAMPLE

A cohort of 16 students had spent 18 months taking every class together. At the midpoint of the MSW program, however, one student (Moira) decided to drop out to spend more time with family members who were aging and ailing. Moira was a respected and successful member of the class and her decision took her instructors and faculty advisor by surprise. Nevertheless, they were persuaded by her confidence that her decision was the correct one for her at that particular point in time. Still, Moira felt sheepish about her decision. Although she e-mailed her classmates to let them know of her decision, she declined an instructor's suggestion that she come back for one more session to achieve closure for herself and the group. She did, however, give permission for the instructor to discuss her decision with the group and understood that they would be processing it in class the next time they met.

The day of the class, the instructor opened the conversation by noting Moira's empty seat and asking the class to share what they knew about her decision not to return. Because she had contacted many of them individually, it wasn't necessary for the instructor to share what she knew about Moira's decision. Next, the group discussed their reactions to Moira's departure, which included self-doubt ("If she can't do it all, how can we?"), anger and confusion ("She put so much into this—why quit now?"), sorrow ("She brought a lot of important things to this group"), care ("If we could help her with some of her responsibilities, would she return?"), hope ("Maybe this will just be a temporary choice"), and understanding ("I think she's doing what she needs to do for her family").

The instructor then asked, "What did Moira give to the group and how can we acknowledge that?" After discussing what they had learned from and valued in their time with Moira, class members wrote notes to her to share these impressions. The instructor collected the notes and, without reading them, included them with a letter to Moira in which she detailed her view on Moira's achievements, capacities, and options should she decide to return to the program in the future.

Following this, the class discussed the impact of acknowledging and processing her departure. They compared it to other losses that the class had experienced when classmates had earlier dropped out ("Here today, gone tomorrow") and the feelings evoked by the lack of closure on those losses, which included suspicion ("Were they forced out?"), apprehension ("Can I cut it? Am I next?"), guilt ("Was it something I said or did?"), and hurt ("Nobody really matters here"). The process of closure in Moira's case, even in her absence, achieved the goals of termination and sent a powerful message to the class—just as it does with other types of groups who experience such a loss.

Note that "closure," as used here and elsewhere in this chapter, does not mean that the matter is resolved, that the person and the loss are tucked away permanently and are not subject to further consideration. It does not mean, "Okay, I'm done. I can move on." Instead, closure simply means that the experience or episode has been reflected upon and the importance of the transition has been marked. It signifies an end in a way that helps free the participants to move on. Clinically, an ambiguous or mishandled termination may leave the social worker and client with a sense of unfinished business, and it may make it difficult for the client to invest easily or fully in future therapeutic relationships. Closure makes a difference.

EP 2.1.1f

Unplanned terminations of a member from a group may occur for a number of reasons. Sometimes, departure is due to the group itself, such as poor fit, discomfort with other members, or a distressing incident. At other times, members terminate because of transportation difficulties or time conflicts (Toseland & Rivas, 2009). In any case, the unplanned departure presents challenges for achieving termination-related tasks. Because cohesion is central to the success of a group, the loss of a member can threaten that bond, make members question their own achievements or appropriateness for the group, and make them reluctant to continue building trusting relationships with the remaining group members. The social worker should try to encourage closure in some form, both for the departing member and for the rest of the group. Even if it derails the group's preexisting agenda or timeline, this effort is time well spent because it supports the future health and success of the group process and the individual members.

Planned Terminations with Unsuccessful Outcomes

Sometimes termination occurs in a planned manner, but the endings are not marked by successful achievement of service goals. This may occur when

- the social worker or the client is dissatisfied with the helping relationship,
- the client is hopelessly stalemated despite vigorous and persistent efforts to overcome his or her difficulties,
- the social worker is not competent to address the client's needs, or
- the client fails to comply with appropriate treatment requirements.

Unlike unplanned terminations, these endings are not accompanied by abrupt disappearance from service and thus afford the social worker and client a chance to achieve the goals of closure. Groups also occasionally end with unsuccessful results and members may be frustrated, disappointed, or angry with the leader or with other members (Smokowski, Rose, & Bacallao, 2001).

When the helping process ends unsuccessfully, termination should include discussion of (1) factors that prevented achieving more favorable results and (2) clients' feelings about seeking additional help in the future. This effort requires you to create as safe an atmosphere as possible so that both parties can honestly air concerns with the intention of both achieving closure and keeping open possibilities for future service. It also requires the ability to hear and share feedback in a nondefensive manner. As a result of this termination conversation, you and a client may come to agreement on the conditions under which you would reconnect and develop a new contract for future services. At this final session, social workers should be prepared to offer referrals to other services if the issue for termination has been a poor fit with the individual practitioner or agency.

Planned Terminations with Successful Outcomes

As noted earlier, planned terminations can take many forms. The nature of the setting, intervention method, or funding source can all impose external pressures to terminate within a specific period of time. Other planned endings emerge from the helping relationship itself as clients achieve their goals and move on to independence from the social worker. This step may not signal that the client has completed all of his or her desired goals or tasks (or that they are "done" in the social worker's eyes), but means only that the client has experienced "at least enough relief so that he no longer wants help *at that point*" (Reid, 1972, p. 199). Related to this development is what Cummings calls (1991) "brief intermittent therapy throughout the life cycle" (p. 35). That is, individuals who need social work services may come to use them as they do medical and other services—seeking them out in times of need to address acute problems rather than pursuing single episodes of extended treatment. In these termination situations, the social worker and client may therefore establish contingencies under which they will resume services in the future.

Termination Due to Temporal or Structural Limits

In organizations or agencies whose function involves providing service according to fixed time intervals, termination must be planned accordingly. In school settings, for example, services are generally discontinued at the conclusion of an academic year. In hospitals and other institutional settings, the duration of service is determined by the length of hospitalization, confinement, or insurance coverage.

Some service models such as time-limited groups or fixed-length residential programs are clearly designed to pace and conclude services within a specific time frame. For example, some treatment programs are organized such that clients progress from one program (and one set of workers) to another as their needs change. In residential programs or other settings with fixed lengths of stay, the course of treatment will involve a relatively predictable process whereby the client progresses through steps or phases leading to termination. Depending on the context of treatment, services may extend from several days to several months. Temporal factors are also central in termination for social work students, who leave a given practicum setting at the completion of an academic year. For clients who have been assigned to a series of social work interns, the endings may be predictable but also aggravating if it is difficult to repeatedly establish trust and continuity of care with a series of time limited workers-in-training.

Terminations that are prompted by program structure or preexisting time constraints involve certain peculiar factors. First, the ending of a school year or of a training period for students is a predetermined time for termination, which reduces the possibility of clients interpreting time limits as being arbitrarily imposed or perceive the social worker's leaving as desertion or abandonment. Knowing the termination date well in advance also provides ample time to resolve feelings about separation. Conversely, it also means that in school settings student clients may lose many supports all at one time.

Another factor common to terminations that are determined by temporal constraints or agency function rather than by individual factors is that the client's problems may not have been adequately resolved by the time termination occurs. The predetermined, untimely ending may lead to intense reactions from the client who is losing service and end the helping relationship in what feels like midstream (Weiner, 1984). Social workers are therefore confronted with the dual tasks of working through feelings associated with untimely separation and referring clients for additional services when indicated.

Predetermined endings imposed by the close of a school year or a fixed length of service do not necessarily convey the same expectations of a positive outcome as do time limits that are determined by individual client progress. In other words, to say "I will see you until May because that is sufficient time to achieve your goals" conveys a far more positive expectation than "I will see you until May because that is all the time I will have available before leaving the placement."

Time-limited treatment can lead to satisfactory outcomes as clients benefit from the focused nature of this work and may develop a fruitful relationship with the social worker even if termination results in referral for other services.

For example, one of the authors of this book worked with a client with serious, long-term mental health problems. During the time allotted for her field placement, she was able to help the client through a crisis and assist him to build his social supports so that future crises would not inevitably result in rehospitalization. In the termination process, they reviewed the accomplishments made during the year and the client met his new social worker, who would meet with him on a less intensive basis for support and maintenance of the gains made previously.

Other Determinants of Planned Termination

When terminations are not predetermined by agency setting, client circumstance, or form of service, how do the social worker and client know when to end? When services are highly goal directed, the termination point may be clear: it occurs when goals are reached and changes are sustained. When goals are amorphous or ongoing, however, determining a proper ending point can be more difficult. Theoretically, humans can grow indefinitely, and determining when clients have achieved optimal growth is no simple task. Ordinarily, it is appropriate to introduce the idea of termination when the client has reached the point of diminishing returns—that is, when the gains from sessions taper off to the point of being minor in significance. The client may indicate through words or actions that he or she is ready to discontinue services, or the social worker may initiate such discussion.

Two other variants on planned termination warrant discussion. "Simultaneous termination" occurs when the client and the social worker leave the service or agency at the same time. It offers the advantage of powerful, mutually shared experiences of ending and it often focuses the time and attention devoted to termination tasks (Joyce, Duncan, Duncan, Kipnes, & Piper, 1996). Simultaneous termination also requires a good deal of self-awareness on the part of the social worker to ensure that his or her personal reactions to termination are not projected onto the client. As with other endings involving the social worker's departure from the organization, termination must address the conditions and resources for the client if he or she should need future service.

The second type of planned termination occurs when the client dies, but the death is anticipated and planned for. Some settings, such as hospice care, nursing homes, or hospitals, expose social workers and other caregivers to death on a regular basis. The orientation and supervision offered in such settings must address this crucial aspect of practice, as particular skills are needed to assist individuals in such circumstances and effectively manage social worker responses. For example, when the helping relationship is expected to end in conjunction with the patient's death, it may involve life review and reminiscences, plans to address end-of-life concerns, and attention to spiritual matters (Arnold, 2002).[4]

Understanding and Responding to Clients' Termination Reactions

Inherent in termination is separation from the social worker (and other clients, in the case of groups, inpatient, or residential settings). Separation typically involves mixed feelings for both the social worker and the client, which vary in intensity according to the degree of success achieved, the strength of the attachment, the type of termination, the cultural orientation of the client, and his or her previous experiences with separations from significant others (Bembry & Ericson, 1999; Dorfman, 1996). When individuals successfully accomplish their goals, they experience a certain degree of pride and satisfaction as the helping process draws to a close. If they have grown in strength and self-esteem, they view the future optimistically as an opportunity for continued growth.

Most people in individual, conjoint, family, and group therapy experience positive emotions in termination. The benefits from the gains achieved usually far outweigh the impact of the loss of the helping relationship. Clients may reflect on the experience by saying things like "I was such a wreck when I first came to see you—I'm surprised I didn't scare you away," "You helped me get my thinking straight, so I could see the options I had before me," or "Even if things didn't change that much with my son, it helped me a lot to be in the group and know I'm not alone."

As noted earlier, clients and social workers alike commonly experience a sense of loss during the termination process. Indeed, sadness is a common element of many of the endings that are a part of life itself (even positive ones), such as leaving parents to attend school, advancing from one grade to another, graduating, moving into a new community, or changing jobs. The loss in termination may be a deeply moving experience involving the "sweet sorrow" generally associated with parting from a person whom one has grown to value. Adept social workers help clients to give voice to these ambivalent feelings, acknowledging that transitions can be difficult but that successfully handling both good times and difficult ones is a necessary part of growth.

For the social worker, the nature of termination and the comfort with which it occurs appear to be linked to the overall health of the organization in which it takes place and the practitioner's level of job satisfaction (Resnick & Dziegielewski, 1996). In work sites where caseloads are high, where there is a rapid turnover in cases, or where staff support and effective supervision are lacking, sufficient attention may not be paid to the tasks and emotions that accompany clinical endings. Of course, like other elements of practice, the impact of

EP 2.1.10b

IDEAS IN ACTION

The "Squeaky Wheel" video illustrates the challenges for professionals who take over case responsibility after the unanticipated departure of a former worker. The client, Molly, is forthright about her mistrust of professionals following the abrupt and poorly managed ending with Nancy, her previous worker. As a result of the ending, Molly experienced confusion, anger, and abandonment, which further complicated her current treatment. Too often, new workers observe client resistance without knowing the source of the client's distrust. In "Squeaky Wheel," Molly's ability to identify her feelings helps Ron, the new social worker, address them. In the video he attempts to help Molly address the loss by asking "What would you say to Nancy?" What other strategies can social workers use to get at the feelings created by unplanned, abrupt, or poorly managed endings?

termination on the social worker is also shaped by his or her overall wellbeing, including the ability to maintain a proper balance between the practitioner's personal and professional lives. This balance is particularly important when the worker has an illness that might imperil the continuation of services. He or she must weigh the benefits of honesty and transparency with the risks that self-disclosure about a serious illness might prove distressing to the client and disruptive to the focus of treatment (Farber, 2006).

EP 2.1.1b & 2.1.10l

Because termination can evoke feelings associated with past losses and endings, clients (and social workers) may respond to it in a variety of ways (and in any of these ways to varying degrees).

1. *Anger.* Clients may experience anger at termination, especially when termination occurs because the social worker leaves the agency. Because the termination is not goal related and occurs with little forewarning, reactions are sometimes similar to those that involve other types of sudden crises. The social worker may need to reach for the feelings evoked by his or her departure, as clients may have difficulty expressing negative emotions while they are simultaneously experiencing sadness or anxiety about the impending loss. It is important to encourage the verbal expression of emotions and respond empathically to them. It is vital, however, not to empathize to the extent of over-identification, thereby losing the capacity to assist the client with negative feelings and to engage in constructive planning.

    When the social worker's departure is caused by circumstances outside his or her control (lay-offs or firing), it is important that the practitioner not fuel the client's anger to satisfy his or her own indignation or desire for vindication. Not only is this clinically unhelpful to the client, but it is at odds with the NASW Code of Ethics. The Code of Ethics cautions us not to "exploit clients in disputes with colleagues or engage clients in any inappropriate discussion of conflicts between social workers and their colleagues" (NASW, 2008, 2.04b).

2. *Denial.* Clients may contend that they were unaware of the impending termination or time limits on service and behave as if termination is not imminent. They may deny having feelings about the termination or refuse to acknowledge that it affects them. Others may avoid endings by failing to appear for concluding sessions with the social worker (Dorfman, 1996). It is a mistake to interpret the client's "business as usual" demeanor as an indication that he or she is unaffected by the termination or is taking it in stride because the unruffled exterior may represent "the calm before the storm."

    An individual's temporary denial of feelings represents an attempt to ward off the psychic pain associated with a distressing reality that must eventually be faced. To assist clients in getting in touch with their emotions, it is helpful to reintroduce the topic of termination and to express your desire to assist them in formulating plans to continue working toward their goals after your departure. As you bring up the topic of termination, be sensitive to nonverbal cues to clients' emotional reactions. We also recommend employing empathic communication that conveys understanding of and elicits the hurt, resentment, and rejection clients commonly experience when a valued person leaves. The following responses demonstrate this type of communication:

    - *"I know that being discharged is scary and that makes you wish you didn't have to leave, but not talking about it won't keep it from happening. I want very much to use the time remaining to reflect on our work together so you are prepared to carry all that you've achieved here out into the world"*
    - *"You've worked really hard here, and I know a lot of it wasn't easy for you. It's hard for me to believe you now when you shrug your shoulders and say it means nothing. I think it means a lot."*

3. *Avoidance.* Occasionally, clients may express their anger and hurt over a social worker's leaving by rejecting the social worker before the social worker can reject them. Some people may silently protest by failing to appear for sessions as termination approaches. Others may ignore the social worker or profess that they no longer need him or her—in effect, employing the strategy that "the best defense is a good offense." When clients act in this fashion, it is critical to reach out to them. Otherwise, they may interpret the failure to do so as evidence that the social worker never really cared about them at all. In reaching out, a personal contact by telephone, email, letter, or home visit is essential because it creates an opportunity for interaction in which the social worker can reaffirm

his or her concern and care and convey empathy and understanding of the client's emotional reaction.

4. *Reporting Recurrence of Old Problems or Generating New Ones.* Some people tend to panic as treatment reaches an end and they experience a return of difficulties that have been under control for some time (Levinson, 1977). In an effort to continue the helping relationship, some may introduce new stresses and problems during the terminal sessions and even during the final scheduled session. Clients who normally communicate minimally may suddenly open up and other clients may reveal confidential information they have previously withheld. Still other people may display more severe reactions by engaging in self-destructive or suicidal acts.

The severity of the client's revelation, regression, or return of symptoms will dictate how you respond. It is important to acknowledge the anxiety and apprehension that accompany termination. Some people will benefit from a preemptive discussion of these issues as termination nears. The social worker might say, "Sometimes people worry that problems will reemerge once services end, but I'm confident about how far you've come. I trust that even if there are setbacks, they won't affect our ending." Some theoretical models suggest that the social worker engage the client in an explicit discussion about what it would take to return to the former level of functioning that necessitated treatment. The underlying idea here is that such a discussion creates significant discomfort and therefore, paradoxically, inoculates the individual against future setbacks (Walsh, 2003).

On some occasions, it may make sense for you and the client to reconsider a planned ending. Limited "extensions by plan" (Epstein & Brown, 2002, p. 232) can be made to accomplish agreed-upon tasks if it appears that additional time would enable the client to achieve decisive progress. There may be legitimate reasons for re-contracting for additional sessions—for example, identifying key problems only late in the helping process, returning to problems that were identified earlier but had to be set aside in favor of work on more pressing issues, or anticipating transitional events that bear on the client's problems (e.g., getting married, "aging out" of foster care, regaining custody of a child). In these instances, continuing the working relationship may be warranted, if supported by the agency, especially if the client has achieved substantial progress on other problems during the initial contract period.

Determining whether the emergence of new issues (or the reemergence of old ones) is a ploy to avoid termination or a legitimate cause for developing a new contract can be tricky, but the decision should be based on your sense of the client's progress to date, the degree of dependency, and the significance of the issues being raised (Reid, 1972). Supervisory discussions can help workers look critically at these variables. If you believe that the problem is worthy of intervention but worry that continuing treatment may foster harmful dependence, you might consider referring the client to another clinician or continuing work with the person yourself but in a less intensive format—through groups or through less frequent sessions, for example.

5. *Attempting to Prolong Contact.* Sometimes, rather than reveal new or renewed problems, a person may seek continued contact with the social worker more directly by suggesting a social or business relationship following termination. For example, the client may suggest meeting for coffee on occasion or exchanging cards or letters, may try to connect with the worker through online social networking, or may propose joining a training program that will put him or her in regular contact with the social worker. This phenomenon is also evident when groups decide to continue meeting after the agency's involvement has concluded.

Unfortunately, the security brought by such plans is only fleeting and the negative effects of continued contact can be serious. Clearly, some requests for continued contact would be inappropriate given the profession's ethical proscriptions against dual relationships. Other forms of contact, while not prohibited, may still be unwise in that they may undo the work done in the helping relationship and may undermine the client's confidence in his or her ability to function without the social worker. Further, continued informal involvement may constrain the client from becoming invested in other rewarding relationships (Bostic, Shadid, & Blotcky, 1996).

EP 2.1.2b

In the case of groups, it is not usually the social worker's role to discourage the group from continuing to meet, although he or she should be clear about his or her own stance and may share the wisdom of past experience. For example, at the conclusion of one bereavement group, the group members planned a cookout at one member's home. In response to the invitation to join them, the group leader simply said, "I'll be ending with you after our session next week, but I appreciate your offer to include me." In another group with a particularly fragile and more easily disappointed membership, the social worker said, "I'm glad you feel close enough to one another to try to continue meeting after the group has formally ended. It's been my experience that sometimes it's hard to keep that going outside the group. If that happens to you, I hope you won't be discouraged or take it as a reflection on all you've accomplished in your time together."

This is not to say that planned follow-up phone calls, appointments, and "booster sessions" are always inappropriate. To the contrary, such plans are made within the goals of the helping process and have a clear therapeutic purpose, rather than being an attempt to evade the inevitability of ending.

6. *Finding Substitutes for the Social Worker.* Although finding one or more persons to replace the social worker may be a constructive way of developing social resources, it may also represent an attempt to locate a person on whom the client can become dependent, thereby compensating for the loss of the social worker. Group members may also seek to compensate for losses of group support by affiliating with other groups and never actually developing enduring social support systems. This problem is most likely to arise when the client has limited social supports. As such, the need for enhanced socialization should be visible during the helping process and may even be a goal for work. Indeed, plans for sustaining gains should include building networks and resources that can replace professionals as sources of assistance.

Social Workers' Reactions to Termination

EP 2.1.1b

Clients are not the only ones who have reactions to termination. Social workers' responses may include guilt (at letting the client down or failing to sufficiently help him or her), avoidance (delaying announcement of termination to avoid the feelings or reactions evoked), relief (at ending involvement with a difficult or challenging client), and prolonging service (because of financial or emotional fulfillment experienced by the clinician) (Dorfman, 1996; Joyce et al., 1996; Murphy & Dillon, 2008). In settings where premature terminations are the norm, workers may experience burnout and decreased sensitivity to clients after repeatedly working on cases where closure is not possible and treatment ends before interventions are carried out (Resnick & Dziegielewski, 1996). Self-understanding and good supervision are the essential elements by which even veteran social workers can recognize the reactions involved in terminations. These reactions negatively affect clients, so identifying and managing them is crucial.

Consolidating Gains and Planning Maintenance Strategies

In addition to managing the emotional and behavioral reactions to ending, another task of termination involves summarizing and stabilizing the changes achieved and developing a plan to sustain those changes. A similar aim of group work is to assist members to not only interact successfully within the group context but also transfer their newly developed interpersonal skills to the broad arena of social relationships.

The failure to maintain gains has been attributed to a variety of factors:

1. A natural tendency to revert to habitual response patterns (e.g., use of alcohol or drugs, aggressive or withdrawn behavior, poor communication patterns)
2. Personal and environmental stressors (e.g., family conflicts, pressures from landlords, personal rejection, loss of job, health problems, and deaths of loved ones)
3. Lack of opportunities in the environment for social and leisure activities
4. Absence of positive support systems (peer or family networks may not have changed in the same way the client has)
5. Inadequate social skills
6. Lack of reinforcement for functional behaviors
7. Inadequate preparation for environmental changes
8. Inability to resist peer pressures

9. Return to dysfunctional or destructive environments
10. Inadequately established new behaviors[5]

In planning maintenance strategies, you must anticipate such forces and prepare clients for coping with them. A monitoring phase may be useful for some people. In this phase, the number and frequency of sessions decrease while support systems are called on to assist the client with new concerns. This technique, in effect, "weans" the individual from the social worker's support, yet allows a transitional period in which he or she can try out new skills and supports while gradually concluding the helping relationship. The ascendance of electronic communications mechanisms (text messaging, Twitter, email, social networks) has led to an array of promising innovations for aftercare and relapse prevention. These models send reminders about medication or treatment adherence, encouragement and wellness tips, and feedback on symptoms or questions recorded by clients. (Aguilera, Gerza, & Munoz, 2010; Shapiro, et al., 2009).

When working with individuals and families, you may actively encourage people to consider means for coping with setbacks. One model suggests asking what "would be required of each person to contribute to a resurgence of the problem" and organizing role-plays in which the members engage in old behavioral patterns and describe afterward what thoughts and feelings they experienced in doing so (Walsh, 2003, p. 206). Similar forms of anticipation and practice may help inoculate clients against future relapses.

Social workers may encourage clients to return for additional help if problems appear to be mounting out of control. Although it is important to express confidence in people's ability to cope independently with their problems, it is equally important to convey your continued interest in them and to invite them to return if they need to do so.

Follow-Up Sessions

Post-termination follow-up sessions are another important technique in ensuring successful termination and change maintenance. These sessions benefit both clients and social workers. Many people continue to progress after termination and follow-up sessions provide an opportunity for the social worker to acknowledge such gains and encourage them to continue their efforts.

These sessions also provide the social worker with an opportunity to provide brief additional assistance for residual difficulties. Social workers may assess the durability of changes in these sessions—that is, determine whether clients have maintained gains beyond the immediate influence of the helping relationship. Additional benefits of planned follow-up sessions are that they may soften the blow of termination and they allow opportunities for longitudinal evaluation of practice effectiveness.

By introducing the notion of the follow-up session as an integral part of the helping process, social workers can avoid the risk that clients will later view these sessions as an intrusion into their private lives or as an attempt to satisfy the social worker's curiosity. Wells (1994) recommends that in arranging for the follow-up session, social workers not set a specific date but rather explain that they will contact the client after a designated interval. This period of time offers the individual an opportunity to test out and further consolidate the learning and changes achieved during the formal helping period.

In the follow-up session, the social worker generally relates more informally than during the period of intervention. After observing the appropriate social courtesies, you should guide the discussion to the client's progress and obtain post-intervention measures when appropriate. The follow-up session also provides an excellent opportunity for further evaluation of your efforts during the period of intervention. In retrospect, what was most helpful? What was least helpful? Further efforts can be made to consolidate gains at this point as well. What was gained from treatment that the client can continue to use in coping with life? Finally, at this point you can contract for more formalized help if this step appears necessary. Follow-up sessions thus enable social workers to arrange for timely assistance that may arrest deterioration in functioning.

One caution related to follow-up sessions is warranted: They may not allow the client to make a "clean break" from services. Individuals who had difficulty separating during termination may use follow-up sessions as an excuse to prolong contact with the social worker. This continued attachment is detrimental to the change process and inhibits the person from establishing appropriate attachments with social networks and with other helping professionals. Social workers should be alert to this possibility in proposing follow-up sessions and ensure that clients understand the specific purpose and focus of these sessions.

Ending Rituals

In many settings, termination may be concluded by a form of celebration or ritual that symbolically marks the goals achieved and the relationship's conclusion

(Murphy & Dillon, 2003). For example, in residential programs and some treatment groups, termination may be acknowledged in "graduation" or "status elevation" ceremonies, during which other residents or members comment on the departing member's growth and offer good wishes for the future. Certificates, cards, or "memory books" (Elbow, 1987) are but a few of the symbolic gifts that terminating clients may receive from staff or fellow clients. In individual and family work, social workers may choose to mark termination with small gifts such as a book, a plant, a framed inspirational quote, a bookmark, or some other token that is representative of the working relationship or the achievements while in service. Groups may conclude by creating a lasting product that is symbolic of the group, such as a collage or mural; in the process of creating this item, participants can reflect on the meaning the group had for them as members (Northen & Kurland, 2001).

The decision to use rituals to mark termination should be based on an understanding of the client, the appropriateness of such actions for the agency or setting, and the meaning that the client may attribute to such actions. For example, giving a personal greeting card may be misinterpreted as a gesture of intimate friendship by some clients; for other clients, such as a child leaving foster care for a permanent placement, it may be a source of comfort and continuity. A gift that is too lavish may cause discomfort if the client feels the need to reciprocate in some way. "Goodbye parties" may reinforce feelings of accomplishment and confidence or they may obviate the feelings of sadness or ambivalence that must also be addressed as part of closure (Shulman, 1992). Graduation ceremonies may recreate past disappointments and lead to further setbacks if, for example, family members refuse to attend and acknowledge the changes the client has achieved (Jones, 1996).

Dorfman (1996) suggests asking the client how he or she would like to mark the final session and offering options if the person seems unsure what to suggest. Useful and meaningful ending rituals are numerous. For example, at the final session of the "Banana Splits" group for children of families undergoing divorce or separation, participants make and eat banana splits (McGonagle, 1986). A social worker may create a card depicting the "gift" or wish that he or she has for the client's continued success; participants in groups may write poems or rewrite lyrics to popular song melodies to mark the ending of a class or group (Walsh, 2003). Some clients may ask the social worker to create a "diploma" indicating what they have achieved and ask to have a photo taken together (Dorfman, 1996). Events to mark group terminations can facilitate the tasks of termination and model meaningful rituals in a way that clients might not have experienced previously (Jones, 1996). These endings can be linked symbolically to the goals for work and may help motivate other clients to strive toward the achievements being celebrated by fellow group or residence members.

CASE EXAMPLE

Horizons is a halfway house for youth whose behavioral problems have resulted in hospitalization or incarceration. The program is intended to help teenagers readjust to community life and establish social supports so that they can return to their homes or move successfully into independent living. Given this focus, the length of stay for any individual resident varies considerably. Some youth encounter difficulties or re-offend; they are then returned to jail or to inpatient settings or simply "drop out of sight." These endings can be difficult for staff as they deal with disappointment in the client's failure to "make it" this time around and perhaps question what they might have done to prevent this outcome. It is also disturbing for other clients as they worry about their own challenges and their ability to successfully move on to the next step.

When residents terminate prematurely from the program, they are asked to attend a community meeting where they can process with the group their experiences in the program and the things they learned that can be of use in the future. Staff and other residents are also invited to share their observations and feelings with the intention of giving supportive and constructive feedback from a caring community—one to which the resident might someday return. When clients quit the program and drop out of sight, such sessions are still held. In these sessions, the residents and staff who remain process their feelings about the departure and discern lessons they can take away from it.

When residents have met their goals and are ready to move on to a more permanent living situation, staff discuss the plan and timeline for departure and stay alert to the difficulties that can arise at termination. The staff members make a point of discussing, in groups and individual sessions, the fears that can arise in moving from some place "comfortable" to the unknown. Sometimes, alumni of the program will visit to talk about their experiences and offer advice and encouragement. At this time, goals are reviewed, progress is charted, and the client's views are sought on which aspects of the program facilitated change. Clients and staff work together to anticipate the challenges ahead and to put in place the strategies necessary to address them.

During a resident's final days, the Horizons' staff and residents create a "graduation" ceremony and each resident offers the one who is leaving symbolic gifts to take on "the journey." These gifts may consist of inspirational quotes, reminders of inside jokes or shared experiences, and more tangible items, such as towels or pots and pans from the local secondhand store to help get established in the new setting.

Family members, teachers, and workers from other agencies are encouraged to attend the graduation and at the ceremony are asked to support the client in the next steps ahead. These ceremonies are often tearful and moving events, where the emphasis is on achievement and on hope for the future.

Summary

Social workers are well aware of the importance of engagement with clients and the skills and attitudes needed to build an effective working relationship. Unfortunately, when this relationship concludes, social workers may not be equally astute about "taking the relationship apart." Effective evaluation and termination leave both the practitioner and the client with a shared sense of the accomplishments achieved in their work together. This process affords the opportunity to model ending a relationship in a way that is not hurtful or damaging to the client. Effective termination equips the client with the skills and knowledge necessary to sustain gains or to seek further help as needed in the future.

CourseMate

Access an integrated eBook and chapter-specific learning tools including glossary terms, chapter outlines, relevant web links, videos, and practice quizzes. Go to **www.cengagebrain.com**.

Competency Notes

Chapter 1 Social Work Challenges

EP 2.1.1 Social workers identify as professionals and conduct themselves accordingly (p. 10).

EP 2.1.2 Social workers apply social Work Ethical Principles to Guide Professional Practice (p. 11).

EP 2.1.2a Social workers recognize and manage personal values in a way that allows professional values to guide practice (p. 9).

EP 2.1.2b Social workers make ethical decisions by applying standards of the National Association of Social Workers Code of Ethics and, as applicable, of the International Federation of Social Workers/International Association of Schools of Social Work Ethics in Social Work, Statement of Principles (pp. 7, 10).

EP 2.1.3 Social workers apply critical thinking to inform and communicate professional judgments (p. 11).

EP 2.1.3b Social workers analyze models of assessment, prevention, intervention, and evaluation (p. 16).

EP 2.1.4 Social workers engage diversity and difference in practice (pp. 9, 11).

EP 2.1.5 Social workers advance human rights and social and economic justice (p. 6).

EP 2.1.5b Social workers advocate for human rights and social and economic justice (pp. 4, 6, 12).

EP 2.1.5c Social workers engage in practices that engage in social and economic justice (pp. 4, 6, 12).

EP 2.1.6 Social workers engage in research-informed practice and practice-informed research (pp. 13, 20).

EP 2.1.7 Social workers apply knowledge of human behavior and the social environment (pp. 5, 13).

EP 2.1.8 Social workers engage in policy practice to advance social and economic well-being and to deliver effective social work services (p. 13).

EP 2.1.9 Social workers respond to contexts that shape practice (pp. 13, 14).

EP 2.1.10 Social workers engage, assess, intervene, and evaluate with individuals, families, groups, organizations and communities (p. 14).

EP 2.1.10a Social workers substantively and affectively prepare for action with individuals, families, groups, organizations, and communities (p. 14).

EP 2.1.10b Social workers use empathy and other interpersonal skills (p. 14).

EP 2.1.10c Social workers develop a mutually agreed-on focus of work and desired outcomes with clients. (p. 14)

EP 2.1.10d Social workers collect, organize, and interpret client data to inform practice (p. 14).

EP 2.1.10e Social workers assess client strengths and limitations (p. 5).

B 2.2 Social workers carry out generalist practice (p. 14).

M 2.2 Social workers carry out advanced practice (p. 14).

Chapter 2 The Domain, Philosophy, and Roles of Direct Practice

EP 2.1.1 Identify as a professional social worker and conduct one's self accordingly: Social workers are reflective and perform a variety of roles. These roles include advocacy (EPAS 2.1.1a) (pp. 26, 30–31, 34).

EP 2.1.5 Advance human rights and social and economic justice. Social workers understand forms and mechanisms of oppression and discrimination, advocate for human rights and engage in social and economic justice (p. 31).

EP 2.1.6 Engage in research-informed practice and practice-informed research. Social workers use practice to inform scientific inquiry and use research evidence to inform practice a & b (p. 33).

EP 2.1.8 Engage in policy practice to advance social and economic well-being and to deliver effective social work services (p. 33).

EP 2.1.9 Social workers respond to contexts that shape practice (p. 33).

EP 2.1.10k Engage, assess, intervene, and evaluate with individuals, families, groups, organizations, and communities. Social workers engage in advocacy (p. 31).

Chapter 3 Helping Process Overview

EP 2.1.1 Identify as a professional social worker and conduct ones self accordingly. Social workers use supervision or consultation in situations in which expert assistance is necessary to help a client (2.1.1f) (p. 43).

EP 2.1.3 A social worker thinks critically in order to inform and communicate professional judgment. This includes 2.1.3b in which a social worker analyzes models of assessment, prevention, intervention, and evaluation (p. 52).

EP 2.1.4 A social worker engages diversity and difference in practice. This includes EP 2.1.4a in which a social worker recognizes the extent to which a cultures' structure and values alienate, create or enhance power and privilege and 2.1.4b in which a social worker gains sufficient self-awareness to eliminate the influence of personal biases and values in working with diverse groups (pp. 47, 51).

EP 2.1.7 A social worker applies knowledge of human behavior and the social environment (p. 37).

EP 2.1.10 A social worker engages, assesses, intervenes, and evaluates with individuals, families, groups, organizations, and communities. This includes 2.1.10a in which social workers substantively prepare for action with individuals, families, groups, organizations, and communities (pp. 37, 46, 51). A social worker uses empathy and other interpersonal skills (2.1.10b) (pp. 38, 43, 47–48, 51). A social worker also develops a mutually agreed upon focus of work and desired outcomes (2.1.10c) (p. 52). A social worker collects, organizes, and interprets client data (2.1.10d) (pp. 39, 50, 52). A social worker assesses client strengths and limitations (2.1.10e) (p. 39). A social worker develops mutually agreed upon intervention goals and objectives (2.1.10f) (pp. 41, 53, 54). A social worker helps clients resolve problems 2.1.10j) (p. 42). A social worker facilitates transitions and endings (2.1.10l) (pp. 44, 53). A social worker critically analyzes and monitors interventions (2.1.10m) (p. 43).

Chapter 4 The Cardinal Social Work Values

EP 2.1.1b Practice personal reflection and self-correction to assure continual professional development: Social workers must be attuned to their intentions, feelings, and values so that these are used constructively and purposefully in helping relationships. Self-awareness and self-regulation are essential for enacting this practice behavior (pp. 56, 59, 61–62, 80).

EP 2.1.1c Attend to professional roles and boundaries: Boundaries assure that the helping relationship and the client's interests are accorded the highest priority in social work practice. Social workers are careful not to mix roles (friend/worker). They are alert to actions that may create conflicts of interest or otherwise blur boundaries with clients (physical contact, nonprofessional communications, friending on Facebook, etc.) (pp. 67, 69).

EP 2.1.1d Demonstrate professional demeanor in behavior, appearance, and communication: Social workers strive for recognition on par with other professionals such as nurses, lawyers and psychologists. Professionalism involves adopting the roles, values, and norms of a particular discipline and consistently upholding high standards of conduct (pp. 64, 69).

EP 2.1.1f Use supervision and consultation: Social work practice is complex. Even experienced professionals require the expertise, feedback, and wisdom of supervisors and consultants. Through supportive conversation, practitioners can look at themselves and their cases to improve service, increase competence, and grow professionally (pp. 61, 70, 72, 79).

EP 2.1.2a Recognize and manage personal values in a way that allows professional values to guide practice: Our choices in life are guided by our values. In accepting the role as a professional social worker, the individual must also consider the values of the profession, society, and the clients served. Self-awareness and wise supervision are essential to ensure that personal values, experiences, and emotions don't negatively impinge on the helping process (pp. 60, 63).

EP 2.1.2b Make ethical decisions by applying standards of the National Association of Social Workers Code of Ethics and, as applicable, of the International Federation of Social Workers/International Association of Schools of Social Work Ethics in Social Work, Statement of Principles: Knowing the ethical standards for social work is a key step in making sound decisions and avoiding errors of omission and commission (pp. 66–67, 69, 71, 75, 78).

EP 2.1.2c Tolerate ambiguity in resolving ethical conflicts: Ethical dilemmas arise out of competing goods. The choice of which path to take is rarely clear cut. Helping professionals must be able to weigh a variety of factors to decide which decision is best in a given situation (pp. 70, 74, 76–77).

EP 2.1.2d Apply strategies of ethical reasoning to arrive at principled decisions: Using a thoughtful, stepwise process helps practitioners to weigh the various alternatives in ethical dilemmas; examine policies, principles, and standards involved; and select sound choices (pp. 66, 76–78).

EP 2.1.10a Substantively and affectively prepare for action with individuals, families, groups, organizations, and communities (pp. 55, 64).

Chapter 5 Empathy and Authenticity: The Building Blocks of Communication

EP 2.1.1b Practice self-reflection and self-correction to assure continual professional development (pp. 108, 110).

EP 2.1.1c Attend to professional roles and boundaries pages (pp. 84, 85, 87).

EP 2.1.10a Substantively and affectively prepare for action with individuals, families, groups, organizations, and communities (p. 84).

EP 2.1.10b Use empathy and other interpersonal skills. Social workers use empathy and other interpersonal skills such as authenticity (pp. 89, 100, 103, 118).

EP 2.1.10e A social worker assesses client strengths and limitatons (p. 117).

EP 2.1.10i A social worker implements preventive services to enhance client capacities (pp. 104, 106).

Chapter 6 The Skills of Verbal Following, Exploring, and Focusing

EP 2.1.1d A social worker demonstrates professional demeanor in behavior, appearance and communication (p. 138).

EP 2.1.4c Social workers recognize and communicate their understanding of the importance of difference in shaping life experiences (p. 124).

EP 2.1.4d Social workers view themselves as learners and engage those with whom they work as informants (p. 124).

EP 2.1.10a Substantively and affectively prepare for action with individuals, families, groups, organizations, and communities (p. 123).

EP 2.1.10b Use empathy and other interpersonal skills. Social workers use verbal following skills such as furthering, paraphrasing, reflecting, summarizing, open and closed ended questions (pp. 124, 139).

EP 2.1.10d Collect organize and interpret data (pp. 140, 141).

EP 2.1.10g Select appropriate intervention strategies (pp. 124, 128).

EP 2.1.10m Critically analyze monitor and evaluate interventions (p. 145).

Chapter 7 Avoiding Counterproductive Communication Patterns

EP 2.1.1 identify as a professional social worker and conduct ones self accordingly (p. 153).

EP 2.1.1b Practice personal reflection and self-correction to assure continual professional development (pp. 155, 166).

EP 2.1.1c Attend to professional roles and boundaries (pp. 159, 160).

EP 2.1.1d Demonstrate professional demeanor in behavior, appearance and communication (pp. 154–155, 157, 163, 166).

EP 2.1.4c Recognize and communicate the importance of their understanding of difference in shaping life experiences (p. 154).

EP 2.1.10 Engage, assess, intervene, and evaluate with individuals, families, groups, organizations and communities (p. 153).

EP 2.1.10a Substantively and effectively prepare for action with individuals, families, and groups (p. 153).

EP 2.1.10b Use empathy and other interpersonal skills (p. 155).

Chapter 8 Assessment: Problems and Strengths

EP 2.1.3a Distinguish, appraise, and integrate multiple sources of knowledge, including research-based knowledge and practice wisdom. Data for client assessments come from a variety of sources (collateral contacts, intake and evaluation instruments, interviews, observation). Social workers should understand the strengths and limitations of each of these sources (pp. 175, 177, 181, 187, 199).

EP 2.1.3b Analyze models of assessment, prevention, intervention, and evaluation: This chapter presents elements used in a comprehensive, multidimensional assessment, though different settings, roles, and client needs will require the worker to tailor the assessment to those concerns (pp. 176, 185, 198).

EP 2.1.4b Gain sufficient self-awareness to eliminate the influence of personal biases and values in working with diverse groups. In doing assessments, social workers gather and synthesize information to create a working hypothesis of the client's problems, strengths, and needs. Professionals must be alert to the ways that personal biases can affect the interpretation of case information or the way that data are configured in creating a service plan (pp. 178, 184).

EP 2.1.4c Recognize and communicate your understanding of the importance of difference in shaping life experience. This chapter emphasizes the concept of cultural humility, wherein the worker's attitude and demeanor invite the client to teach about his/her lived experience. While professionals continually endeavor to learn more about populations different than their own culture of origin, that knowledge provides a backdrop for understanding a person in the context of his or her personal history (pp. 178, 191–192, 197–198).

EP 2.1.4d View yourself as a learner and engage those with whom you work as informants. Each of us is the expert on our own life. During assessment, social workers strive to see the world through the eyes of the client, understanding that person's experiences, wishes, attributes, challenges, and needs as he/she sees them (pp. 187–188, 192).

EP 2.1.7a Utilize conceptual frameworks to guide the processes of assessment, intervention, and evaluation. The scope and depth of assessments are guided by the worker role, agency setting, and client needs in any given case. Social workers must understand how those factors interact in particular types of assessments, such as those to determine risk of abuse, suicide lethality, medical conditions, etc. (pp. 174, 176, 182–183).

EP 2.1.7b Critique and apply knowledge to understand person and environment. Social workers view problems as arising from the reciprocal interaction between the person and his/her environment. Assessments seek to specify what factors and interacting and the ways they influence each other so that problematic patterns can be broken (pp. 174, 179, 182, 185, 189–190, 196).

EP 2.1.10a Substantively and affectively prepare for action with individuals, families, groups, organizations, and communities. Foundation knowledge about human development, the ways systems operate, cultural differences and other topics help inform the assessment process (pp. 174–175, 188).

EP 2.1.10d Collect, organize, and interpret client data. In the *process* of assessment, social workers synthesize data about the client's problem and various aspects of personal functioning. The resulting *product* is typically a written document that summarizes pertinent information and offers the worker's assessment about the factors creating, sustaining, and mitigating the client's difficulties (pp. 175, 183–184, 187, 194–195, 199).

EP 2.1.10e Assess client strengths and limitations. Although people seek social work services in times of difficulty, they possess abilities, resources, and experiences that serve as the foundation for change. Social workers identify these in order to get a comprehensive picture of the client and create sound case plans (pp. 180–181, 186, 195–196).

Chapter 9 Intrapersonal, Interpersonal, and Environmental Factors in Assessment

EP 2.1.3c Demonstrate effective oral and written communication in working with individuals, families, groups, organizations, communities, and colleagues. A common feature of social work practice is the development of written assessments and case notes. These are part of a client's permanent record and thus must be accurate, clear, and thorough, synthesizing various sources of data to provide a comprehensive portrayal of the case (pp. 227, 228, 231, 232).

EP 2.1.4c Recognize and communicate your understanding of the importance of difference in shaping life experiences. Assessments require the interpretation of clients' statements, emotions, experiences, and behaviors. When workers approach assessments from an ethnocentric perspective, their interpretations can be flawed. Cultural knowledge and sensitivity are essential in accurately conveying another's life story (pp. 208, 211, 213, 217, 225).

EP 2.1.7a Utilize conceptual frameworks to guide the processes of assessment, intervention, and evaluation. Social workers use many frameworks to understand client functioning and change processes. In individual assessment, the Diagnostic and Statistical Manual (DSM-TR) is used to classify mental disorders by enumerating symptoms, patterns of onset, and other features of conditions (such as depression, Alzheimer's disease, or bipolar disorder) (pp. 212, 214–217, 221).

EP 2.1.7b Critique and apply knowledge to understand person and environment. Social work assessments are based on the interaction between individuals and their environment (social, physical, financial, etc.). Direct practitioners must use the assessment process to identify the "goodness-of-fit" in these interactions and suggest steps to reinforce strengths and bolster areas of weaknesses (pp. 201, 203, 220, 222, 223–224).

EP 2.1.10a Substantively and affectively prepare for action with individuals, families, groups, organizations, and communities. Sound, thorough assessments set the foundation for interventions, as they identify patterns of behaviors or emotions, reciprocal interactions, past change and coping strategies, and significant areas of risk (pp. 205, 218, 222).

EP 2.1.10d Collect, organize, and interpret client data. Social work assessments involve collecting information from a variety of sources to help understand the reciprocal interaction of factors contributing to the presenting problem (pp. 202–205, 209, 212, 222, 225, 227).

EP 2.1.10e Assess client strengths and limitations. Individuals and their environments present both assets and liabilities. A strong assessment takes these features into account and determines the ways in which these factors interact to create or sustain the client's current difficulties. Interventions then build on strengths and resources and strive to address weaknesses (p. 226).

Chapter 10 Assessment: Family Functioning in Diverse Family and Cultural Contexts

EP 2.1.1c Attend to professional boundaries. In completing a family assessment, it is important that social workers conduct themselves in a manner that does not appear that they are involved with one member to the exclusion of others in the family system (p. 262).

EP 2.1.1f Use supervision and consultation. Consulting with a supervisor can provide you with clarity when you are faced with an unfamiliar situation and supervision also ensures that you are practicing in a professional manner (p. 238).

EP 2.1.2a Recognize and manage personal values in a way that allows for professional values to guide practice. Social Workers are encouraged to continuously engage in self-reflection and self-evaluation. Being aware of self diminishes the potential that their personal biases and values will intrude upon their work with clients (p. 238).

EP 2.1.3a Distinguish, appraise, and integrate multiple sources of knowledge, including research-based knowledge and practice wisdom. During the assessment process with families, you will gather vital information about the family's structure, interactions, and relationships. Each factor yields sources of information that can be integrated that you can use to understand the family (pp. 240–241, 245, 257, 260).

EP 2.1.4a Recognize the extent to which a culture's structures and values alienate, create, or enhance privilege and power. The family as a social system is continuously engaging with other systems. Values, societal structures, and power, including those observed in the family, in public policy, and professional practice influence the family system. The assessment of families takes into account each of these factors and the extent to which they are inhibiting or a facilitative (pp. 240–241, 263–265).

EP 2.1.4b Gain sufficient self-awareness to eliminate the influence of personal biases and values in working with diverse groups. Each of us has values and beliefs. In practice it is essential that we are aware of our preferences so that they we can avoid the interference our personal beliefs and preferred solutions (pp. 237, 257).

EP 2.1.4c Recognize and communicate their understanding of the importance of difference in shaping life experiences. Families live in different locales, experience different life experiences, events, and stressors, each of which can influence family functioning and determine the ways in which a family seeks or responds to professional help (pp. 237–238, 241–242, 260–261, 263, 268).

EP 2.1.5a Understand forms and mechanism of oppression and discrimination. In assessing families, it is vital that you determine that extent that their concerns are the results of inequality (p. 256).

EP 2.1.7a Utilize conceptual frameworks to guide the processes of assessment, intervention, and evaluation. The systems framework provides concepts that are useful for assessing family interactions, dynamics, and relationships (pp. 243, 245–246, 250, 253–255, 257, 259, 261, 270).

EP 2.1.7b Critique and apply knowledge to understand person and environment. Families are influenced and shaped by their relationship with the environment, which can include their social identity (pp. 242, 250–251, 256–257, 259, 262–263, 272).

EP 2.1.10a Substantively and effectively prepare for action with individuals, families, groups, communities, and organizations. An assessment of families requires that you pay attention to how the family is defined and to family processes, relationships, behaviors, and strengths (pp. 236, 258, 260–264, 266, 268–270, 272, 275).

EP 2.1.10d Collect, organize, and interpret client data. In assessing families, the system concepts and tools and the assessment dimensions and questions discussed in this chapter are instrumental to the process of gathering information. As a result, you will have an understanding of family stressors, processes, interactions, and relationships (pp. 239, 243, 245, 247–255, 257–259, 262, 264–276).

EP 2.1.10e Assess client strengths and limitations. Assessing strengths are vital to a balanced assessment of families (pp. 243–244, 258).

Chapter 11 Social Work Groups: Formation and Assessment

EP 2.1.2c Tolerate ambiguity in resolving ethical conflicts. Although ethical standards may be clear, their application to practice can be ambiguous. While social workers should intervene to prevent serious, imminent and foreseeable harm, how does this apply when teen group members discuss plans to engage in risky or illegal behaviors? (p. 306)

EP 2.1.2b Make ethical decisions by applying standards of the National Association of Social Workers Code of Ethics and, as applicable, of the International Federation of Social Workers/International Association of Schools of Social Work Ethics in Social Work Statement of Principles. The NASW Code offers guidance about seeking informed consent in group treatment, practitioner competence, and exceptions to confidentiality and self-determination (p. 307).

EP 2.1.2d Apply strategies of ethical reasoning to arrive at principled decisions. Ethical dilemmas arise in group work as social workers make decisions about group composition, seek informed consent for services, encourage members to respect confidentiality, and avoid conflicts of interest with and among members (pp. 306–307).

EP 2.1.3b Analyze models of assessment, prevention, intervention, and evaluation. Social workers must assess whether group interventions are indicated for particular problems and populations, and if so, which kind of group would be the most helpful for a specific objective or clientele (pp. 280, 293).

EP 2.1.4c Recognize and communicate their understanding of the importance of difference in shaping life experiences. Members of task and treatment groups reflect diversity in age, ethnic and racial backgrounds, professions, SES, experiences, sexual orientation, political affiliation, etc. These differences often emerge in the process of groups as members interact with the leader and each other. Group workers must possess sophisticated understanding of such differences and the ways these can enhance or derail group process (pp. 285, 304).

EP 2.1.6b Use research evidence to inform practice. Because of all of the variables at play, it can be particularly difficult to systematically evaluate the effectiveness of group interventions. Nevertheless, research exists to support the use of group work for various conditions and populations. Research also indicates the worker attributes that can lead to success or failure in groups (pp. 281–282).

EP 2.1.7a Utilize conceptual frameworks to guide the processes of assessment, intervention, and evaluation. Group interventions use a distinct set of considerations and concepts. Forming and facilitating groups involves decisions about leadership, homogeneity or heterogeneity in membership, group structure, the use of curricula, the development of norms, addressing counterproductive patterns and a variety of other concepts unique to the group format (pp. 280–281, 285–286, 288, 292, 297, 300, 302).

EP 2.1.10a Substantively and affectively prepare for action with individuals, families, groups, organizations, and communities. This chapter discusses the steps in planning, constructing, and conducting task and treatment groups. Social workers often take lead roles in identifying that groups, task forces, or other collective efforts are needed, structuring the groups and facilitating their work (pp. 283–284, 286, 289, 303).

EP 2.1.10d Collect, organize, and interpret client data. Social workers often meet with prospective group members prior to forming the group, to understand their needs, experiences, and readiness for the group process. During the life of the group, clients' interactions with the facilitator and with other members will reveal, verbally and nonverbally, much about themselves and how they approach the world (pp. 283, 287, 296, 301).

EP 2.1.10e Assess client strengths and limitations. Before and during the group, social workers must be attuned to the needs, resources, and abilities that clients will bring to the group process. Often, member's strengths and limitations will reveal themselves in the roles they take on in group (leader, distractor, nurturer, etc.) (pp. 294–295).

EP 2.1.10j Help clients resolve problems. Task and treatment groups provide a powerful medium for change. Social workers facilitating these groups help participants engage in mutual aid, problem solving, and planning to address shared problems (pp. 289, 298).

Chapter 12 Goal Development and Contract Formulation

EP 2.1.1b Practice personal reflection and self-correction to assure continual professional development. Working with clients requires ongoing monitoring of their progress toward goals. Evaluating your work with clients is an essential part of this process (p. 346).

EP 2.1.1d Demonstrate professional demeanor in behavior, appearance and communication. Social workers understand their role and their ethical obligation to practice in a manner that is consistent with their educational preparation and licensure or certification (pp. 324–325).

EP 2.1.1f Use supervision and consultation. Social workers use supervision or consultation in situations in which expert assistance is necessary to help a client (pp. 324, 327).

EP 2.1.2a Recognize and manage personal values in a way that allows professional values to guide practice. Social workers continuously engage in self-evaluation of their beliefs and values as well as their motivation for their behavior with certain clients so that their own goal preferences do not override a client's interest (pp. 313, 325–326).

EP 2.1.2b Make ethical decisions by applying standards of the National Association of Social Worker Code of Ethics and, as applicable, of the International Federation of Social Workers/International Association of Schools of Social Work Ethics in Social Work Statement of Principles. In instances in which competing interests pose difficulties for you and clients, the ethical standards and principles of the social work profession should guide your behavior and actions (pp. 324, 326–327).

EP 2.1.4c Recognize and communicate their understanding of the importance of differences in shaping life experiences. Developing goals takes into account client's beliefs, values, identity, ability, and stage of development (p. 313).

EP 2.1.7b Critique and apply knowledge to understand the person and environment. In developing goals, social workers assess the extent to which environmental factors and social conditions can influence goal attainment (pp. 313–314, 331).

EP 2.1.10a Substantively and affectively prepare for action with individuals, families, groups, organizations, and communities. In working with clients in preparation for problem solving, goals are the means by which desired outcome are achieved. The exploration of a client's concern provides essential information about the focus and direction of the intervention to be used, as well as the type of goal (pp. 310, 315, 328).

EP 2.1.10c Develop mutually agreed-on focus of work and desired outcomes. Social workers and clients develop goals that provide direction for their work together. Agreement involves a process in which goals are defined and negotiated, expected outcomes are clarified and the individual's motivation and resource need for accomplishing a goal is assessed (pp. 315, 317, 328–330, 332–334, 346).

EP 2.1.10d Collect, organize, and interpret client data. The assessment interview provides the social worker with information upon which goals are developed (p. 310, 312).

EP 2.1.10e Assess client strengths and limitations. Goals that emphasize growth make use of and motivate client strengths. Family involvement in goal identification and attainment is also a useful resource (pp. 314, 325).

EP 2.1.10i Partialing goals and developing goal related general tasks are intended to break goal attainment into manageable parts so clients do not become overwhelmed (pp. 321, 324, 335–336).

EP 2.1.10g Select appropriate intervention strategy. Program goals should be selectively included in a client's plan (p. 311).

EP 2.1.10j Help clients resolve problems. Goals are intended to help clients solve problems. The feasibility of goals for both voluntary and involuntary clients is assessed so that client's motivation and efforts toward goal attainment are maximized (pp. 322–323, 334, 336–337).

EP 2.1.10m Critically analyze, monitor, and evaluate interventions. Goals are specific and measurable. Monitoring a measuring progress, using quantitative or qualitative methods, enables both the client and the social worker to observe progress and the eventual goal outcome (pp. 320, 322, 337–343, 345–346).

Chapter 13 Change-Oriented Strategies: Planning and Implementation

EP 2.1.1c Attend to professional roles and boundaries. Selecting and utilizing an intervention strategy requires that social workers have the requisite knowledge and skills. Role behavior assumes that they are practicing within their scope as well as understanding their role and responsibilities in different practice settings (pp. 364–365, 387, 389, 411).

EP 2.1.1f Use supervision and consultation. In instances where the appropriate course of action may lack clarity, utilizing supervision is important to help social workers make decisions that inform their development (pp. 363, 365).

EP 2.1.2b Make ethical decisions by applying standards of the National Association of Social Workers Code of Ethics and, if applicable, the International Federation of Social Workers/International Associations of Schools of Social Work Ethics in Social Work Statement of Principles. Implementing an intervention strategy should be guided by the ethical practice standards of the profession of social work (pp. 362–364).

EP 2.1.2d Apply strategies of ethical reasoning skills to arrive at principled decisions. Different settings in which social workers are employed may use practices or intervention strategies that are counter to the ethical standards of the profession of social work. In these situations, social workers rely on the ethical standards of the profession to guide their work with clients (p. 363).

EP 2.1.3b Analyze models of assessment, prevention, intervention, and evaluation. In preparation for selecting an intervention strategy, social workers should understand the tenets of the strategy to ensure that it is consistent with the client's problem and goals. They should also evaluate whether they have the knowledge and skills to successfully implement the strategy (pp. 360–361).

EP 2.1.4b Gain sufficient self-awareness to eliminate the influence of personal biases and values in working with diverse groups. Planning and implementing change strategies with persons whose backgrounds are different, honors their values, beliefs, and preferences. Understanding self means that the social workers strive to avoid the potential that their values, beliefs, and preferences overshadow those of the client (pp. 384, 392).

EP 2.1.4c Recognize and communicate an understanding of the importance of differences in shaping life experiences. Social workers understand that the context of people's lives are different based on the perceptions, experiences, abilities, and cultural frame of reference (pp. 361, 363, 383).

EP 2.1.4d View themselves as learners and engage those with whom they work as key informants. Learning about different people and cultures requires that social workers recognize what they do not know, and further that they are willing to expand their ways of knowing and to use acquired knowledge to guide practice competence with diverse groups (p. 362).

EP 2.1.6b Use of research evidence to inform practice. Selecting and planning intervention strategy requires that social workers have knowledge of a strategy's utilization and evidence of effectiveness with the problems and goals of different clients and in different settings (pp. 362, 366, 382–383, 392, 394, 402, 410).

EP 2.1.7a Utilize conceptual framework to guide the process of assessment, intervention, and evaluation. Understanding the conceptual and theoretical framework upon which an intervention strategy is based is essential to the effective implementation of the strategy (pp. 360, 366, 383, 389–390, 397, 402).

EP 2.1.7b Apply knowledge of human behavior in the social environment. People interact and react within an environmental context. Social environments shape people's perceptions, cognitions, and experiences and their sense of self (pp. 362, 380, 383, 385, 392–394, 403, 410).

EP 2.1.9a Continuously discover, appraise, and attend to changing locales, populations, scientific and technological developments, and emerging societal trends to provide relevant services. Planning and implementing an intervention strategy requires social workers to understand and appraise different circumstances and to determine if a particular strategy has certain limitations that should be modified so that it fits with the needs of a particular group (pp. 380, 382, 394).

EP 2.1.10a Substantively and affectively prepare for action with individuals, families, groups, and communities. Selecting, planning, and implementing an intervention strategy requires that social workers understand the basic tenets of a strategy and its approach to solving problems (pp. 360, 365, 378–380, 388–389, 401, 407–409, 413).

EP 2.1.10b Use empathy and other interpersonal skills. Attending to client's emotions and responding with empathy can facilitate problem solving (p. 385).

EP 2.1.10d Collect, organize, and interpret client data. In implementing an intervention strategy, it is essential that social workers continuously appraise relevant information regarding client's functioning, problems, and goals (pp. 379–381, 385–386, 396, 403).

EP 2.1.10f Develop mutually agreed-on intervention goals and objectives. An agreement between the client and the social worker is an essential step to implementing an intervention strategy. The agreement includes identifying the goals, action steps, or objectives that will be used to achieve the desired outcome (pp. 367, 373, 375, 387, 395–396, 403, 412).

EP 2.1.10g Select appropriate intervention strategies. Questions should be asked about an intervention approach so that the social worker and the client are assured that the strategy is a match with the client's needs, problems, and goals (pp. 360, 361, 364, 365, 411).

EP 2.1.10i Implement prevention interventions that enhance client capacities. In the best of circumstances, clients may need help so that they can move forward toward problem solving. Social workers can provide help by using techniques such as role-play, brainstorming, and modeling to prepare clients so that they feel more competent to take action (pp. 368–375, 386, 388, 395–397, 399–400, 403, 405).

EP 2.1.10j Help clients solve problems. Intervention approaches have procedures and techniques that are used in a systematic manner to assist clients to resolve their problems (pp. 367–369, 371–373, 375, 381–382, 384, 386–387, 391, 394, 396–397, 399–400, 403–405, 410, 413).

EP 2.1.10m Critically analyze, monitor, and evaluate interventions. Social workers and clients should engage in an ongoing evaluation process that will allow them to monitor and measure progress relative to the client's goals, the effectiveness of the intervention approach, and to evaluate outcomes (pp. 376, 378, 398, 400, 403).

Chapter 14 Intervention Strategies: Developing Resources, Organizing, Planning, and Advocacy

EP 2.1.1a Advocate for client access to services. Social workers pay attention to the needs of groups and communities and, when necessary, engage in advocacy to obtain resources to address needs (p. 430).

EP 2.1.1d Demonstrate professional demeanor in behavior, appearance, and communication. Professional practice requires that social workers interact with people in ways that demonstrate the principles and ethics of the profession (p. 439).

EP 2.1.4a Recognize the ways in which culture's structures and values alienate, create, or enhance power and privilege. People vary in their ability, identity, and social and economic status. Structural barriers can determine the extent to which differences are valued or problematic. It is important that social workers recognize such barriers as they work with clients to achieve well-being (pp. 421–424, 429).

EP 2.1.4b Gain sufficient self-awareness to eliminate the influence of personal biases and values in working with diverse groups. The social and cultural identity of clients is diverse and may be unfamiliar. In situations in which a social worker encounters the unfamiliar, an evaluation and awareness of self, beliefs, and values can be critical so that personal preferences do not influence the work to be completed with clients (pp. 427, 440).

EP 2.1.4d View themselves as learners and engage those with whom they work as key informants. Understanding diverse groups and communities is an ongoing process. Social workers use diverse interactions as an opportunity to learn from the people with whom they are involved (pp. 427, 440).

EP 2.1.5a Understand forms and mechanisms of oppression and discrimination. Social workers analyze policies and practices that may discriminate and contribute to the unequal or disparate treatment of clients that reinforce their marginalized status (p. 440).

EP 2.1.5b Advocate for human rights and social and economic justice. As advocates, social workers critique social policies and agency practices to ensure that clients rights are observed and that clients are not disadvantaged by structural barriers that influence their ability to achieve social and economic justice (pp. 421–422, 442).

EP 2.1.5c Engage in practices that engage in social and economic justice. Social workers make use of evidence and best practices so that their practice promotes social and economic justice (p. 439).

EP 2.1.6b Use research evidence to inform practice. Social workers use research methods to obtain data needed in such practice activities as developing resources and evaluating the outcome of an intervention (pp. 426, 445).

EP 2.1.8a Analyze, formulate, and advocate for policies that advance social well-being. Social workers analyze social policies and agency practices to determine if advocacy is needed (pp. 420–421, 423, 441).

EP 2.1.9a Continuously discover, appraise, and attend to changing locales, populations, scientific and technological developments, and emerging social trends to provide relevant services. Population changes and demographic shifts will require different or new resources to meet needs. Also, resources exist within communities. Understanding resource needs so that they are relevant to a particular group requires social workers to continually review research and statistical information, as well as evaluate resources within a demographic community (pp. 425, 428–429).

EP 2.1.9b Provide leadership in promoting sustainable changes in service delivery and practice to improve the quality of social services. Social workers act as change agents in organizations, as advocates for groups and communities, and by influencing policies and legislation (pp. 424, 431, 444).

EP 2.1.10a Substantively and effectively prepare for action with individuals, families, groups, and communities. Advocacy, social action, and community organizing requires interpersonal skills and skills in problem analysis, the development of strategic goals, and the evaluation of outcomes (pp. 420, 427, 429–430, 432, 434, 443–444).

EP 2.1.10b Use empathy and other interpersonal skills. In engaging and working with communities and groups, social workers use interpersonal skills, such empathy, as well as a range of communication skills (pp. 419, 434).

EP 2.1.10c Develop mutually agreed-upon focus of work and desired outcomes. Working with groups and communities should be collaborative. In this way, the focus of the social worker's involvement is determined by the client's needs, interests, and values (p. 431).

EP 2.1.10d Collect and organize client data. It is important for social workers to collect and review information to inform advocacy, social action, resource development, and organizations analysis so that their work is focused on client's needs and to improve service delivery (pp. 419, 430, 437).

EP 2.1.10e Assess client strengths and limitations. Assessing clients' strengths and empowerment are core principles of social work practice (p. 420).

EP 2.1.10g Select appropriate intervention strategy. In working with communities, social workers select strategies that are best suited to the needs and interest of the community (pp. 432–434).

EP 2.1.10h Initiate actions to achieve organizational goals. Social workers assist organizations to improve and maintain a service delivery system in which staff are active participants, the environment is inclusive, and clients rights and dignity is fundamental (pp. 436, 438, 440–441, 443).

EP 2.1.2d Apply strategies of ethical reasoning skills to arrive at principled decisions. In situations in which the CODE may not provide clear guidance or there are competing ethical obligations, social workers should rely on an ethical decision-making framework to guide their decisions (pp. 431, 435, 439).

Chapter 15 Improving Relationships and Family Functioning

EP 2.1.1d Demonstrate professional demeanor in behavior, appearance and communication. The behavior of social workers is to be consistent with the principles of the profession and is demonstrated in all interactions with clients (pp. 452, 456, 463).

EP 2.1.4a Recognize the extent to which a culture's structure and values alienate, create, or enhance privilege and power. Families live in a context that may be framed by their cultural, economic, or social identify. As social workers we are mindful of the extent to which dominant narratives influence family structures and functioning (pp. 452, 464–465, 480).

EP 2.1.4b Gain sufficient self awareness to eliminate the influence of personal biases and values in working with diverse families. Social workers engage in ongoing self-evaluation so that they are able to provide services in a manner that is respectful of differences (p. 456).

EP 2.1.7a Utilize conceptual framework to guide the process of assessment, intervention, and evaluation. Systems, life cycle, and human development theories provide a framework for social workers to understand families and individuals (pp. 450, 457, 464–465).

EP 2.1.7b Critique and apply knowledge of human behavior in the social environment. Human behavior is complex, influenced by culture, stage of development, and beliefs and values. Families as social systems interact with other systems in the social environment. Understanding human behavior requires social workers to assess the influence of both the family system and systems within the social environment (pp. 456, 461–465).

EP 2.1.10a Substantively and affectively prepare for action with individuals, families, groups, and communities. Social workers utilize a variety of models and techniques to engage, assess, and plan interventions with families to enhance family functioning and relationships (pp. 449–450, 452–453, 461–463, 466–468, 471–472, 477, 479–483).

EP 2.1.10b Use empathy and other interpersonal skills. Establishing rapport, using empathy and employing sensitivity to differences, are essential skills in working with families (pp. 454–455).

EP 2.1.10c Develop a mutually agreed-on work focus and desired outcomes. Intervening with families requires an agreement with the family as a whole, and in some instance individual family members about the work to be accomplished (pp. 460, 478).

EP 2.1.10d Collect and interpret client data. In assessing and intervening with families, social workers continually gather and interpret information to help families solve problems (pp. 450, 452, 454–460).

EP 2.1.10e Assess client strengths and limitations. Strengths are an integral part of the family assessment. For example, even though a family may experience problematic interactions like Janet and Twanna, they have a strong bond to each other (p. 458).

EP 2.1.10f Develop mutually agreed-on intervention goals and objectives. In family sessions, it is important that all involved agree to and commit to goals (p. 460).

EP 2.1.10j Help clients solve problems. Practitioners who work with families utilize various techniques to help the family and individual members to resolve problems that affect family functioning, communication patterns, and relationships (pp. 457–458, 460, 466–467, 469–472, 474–476, 479, 481–482).

Chapter 16 Social Work Group Interventions

EP 2.1.6b Use research evidence to inform practice. It is especially difficult to control the variables in group work making research in this area especially complex. Nevertheless, studies support the use of groups and specific techniques within group work (pp. 503, 506).

EP 2.1.7a Utilize conceptual frameworks to guide the processes of assessment, intervention, and evaluation. Group workers employ a variety of novel frameworks in this intervention. For example, an understanding of the phases of group development guides the facilitator in understanding group process and employing different techniques at a given stage (pp. 486, 496, 508–509).

EP 2.1.9a Continuously discover, appraise, and attend to changing locales, populations, scientific and technological developments, and emerging societal trends to provide relevant services. The availability of online communication has led to an array of online groups. These present advantages in overcoming time and geographic barriers to attendance, but they present challenges for confidentiality and professional facilitation (p. 507).

EP 2.1.10a Substantively and affectively prepare for action with individuals, families, groups, organizations, and communities. This chapter addresses the techniques social workers use to facilitate groups from beginning to end. Group workers must understand group process, individual needs, and strengths and the issues that may emerge at any stage of the group's development (pp. 486, 494, 499, 503, 506, 509).

EP 2.1.10g Select appropriate intervention strategies. Social workers call on a variety of interventive skills during the lifespan of a group. In early stages, for example, reticent members would usually be allowed to "stand back" and participate when they are comfortable doing so. In later stages, group members themselves would be encouraged to reach out to the reticent member and seek his or her input and involvement (pp. 491, 495, 500, 502).

EP 2.1.10i Implement prevention interventions that enhance client capacities. Both task and treatment groups play important roles in prevention efforts. Community task forces or organization-based committees may be convened to prevent problems such as violence, drug use, unemployment, or cyber crimes. Support groups may convene to prevent conditions such as caregiver burnout, PTSD, suicide, or drug and alcohol relapse (pp. 497–498, 502, 508, 510).

EP 2.1.10j Help clients resolve problems. Groups are often focused on mutual problem solving. Facilitators help members develop the capacities, norms, and processes to solve problems in group functioning and to solve the problems that are the focus of the group (pp. 492–493, 501, 504, 508).

EP 2.1.10l Facilitate transitions and endings. Termination in groups can be very powerful because the cohesion developed in the group process and the familiar routine of meetings is lost when the group ends. Social workers must be alert to reactions at termination that may detrimentally affect the success of the members and the group itself (pp. 490, 500, 505, 510).

Chapter 17 Confrontation, Interpretation, and Additive Empathy

EP 2.1.10 Social workers engage, assess, intervene, and evaluate with individuals, families, groups, organizations, and communities (p. 511).

EP 2.1.10b Social workers use empathy and other skills such as interpretation and confrontation (p. 511).

Chapter 18 The Management of Barriers to Change

EP 2.1.1b Practice self-refection and self-correction to assure continued professional development. Behaving in a professional manner to reduce the risk of the influence of personal values and beliefs requires ongoing self-reflection and evaluation (pp. 529, 533, 542, 545–546, 549).

EP 2.1.1c Attend to professional roles and boundaries. Social workers understand the importance of maintaining boundaries with clients as essential to professional and ethical practice (pp. 530–533, 542, 544, 547–548).

EP 2.1.1d Demonstrate professional demeanor in behavior, appearance, and communication. In spite of reactions to clients or his or her situation, social workers behave in a professional manner in their interactions with clients. Acting as a professional includes continuous appraisal of their values and attitudes and being aware of boundaries (pp. 529–530, 533–534, 536, 545, 547–548).

EP 2.1.1f Use supervision and consultation. Using supervision or consultation helps social workers problem solve difficult situations or reactions to clients and inform ethical practice and professional development (pp. 529, 533, 545).

EP 2.1.2a Recognize and manage personal values in a way that allows for professional values to guide practice. Social workers strive to be aware of their values, biases, and beliefs through engaging in self-understanding and self-reflection so that they are able to control their thoughts and feelings in their interactions with clients (p. 529).

EP 2.1.2b Make ethical decisions by applying standards of the National Association of Social Workers Code of Ethics and, if possible, the International Federation of Social Workers/International Association of Schools or Social Work Ethics in Social Work Statement of Principles. In their practice, social workers use the professional ethical standards to inform their behavior. The ethical obligation of social workers is three-pronged: to the client, the agency, and to colleagues. This obligation may require seeking supervision and reporting conduct on the part of a colleague that violates the professional code (pp. 536, 547).

EP 2.1.3a Distinguish, appraise, and integrate multiple sources of knowledge, including research-based knowledge and practice wisdom. In making decisions about how best to work with clients, social workers gather information from different sources and theoretical cultural and systems perspectives so that they understand the various factors that influence human behavior and human problems (pp. 548–549).

EP 2.1.4a Recognize the extent to which culture's structure and values alienate, create, or enhance privilege and power. The perceptions of a client are based on his or her experiences and interactions with the dominant social structures. As social workers, our understanding of the client's perspective can make a difference in the helping relationship (pp. 528, 537–538, 540).

EP 2.1.4b Gain sufficient self-awareness to eliminate the influences of personal bias and values in working with diverse groups. Social workers strive to understand the relational dynamics that can occur as a result of differences between themselves and their clients. It is equally important that social workers continuously examine their behavior so that they do not contribute to counterproductive relational interactions with clients (pp. 538–539).

EP 2.1.4c Recognize and communicate their understanding of the importance of differences in shaping life experiences. To facilitate a positive working relationship with clients, social workers must be aware of the fact that lives of people, including those from diverse backgrounds, are influenced by their worldview, beliefs, and values (pp. 537–538, 540).

EP 2.1.4d View themselves as learners and engage those with whom they work as key informants. When becoming familiar with and learning about differences, it is important that social workers view their competence with diverse individuals as an ongoing process. Some of the work needed to achieve a level of competence means that social workers become learners, asking clients about the important aspects of their culture to avoid making generalizations based on misinformation (p. 540).

EP 2.1.5a Understand the mechanism of oppression and discrimination. Social workers understand the ways in which their behavior and that of systems act in ways that result in bias judgments and discriminatory practices toward individuals who are different (p. 538).

EP 2.1.6b Use research evidence to inform practice. Social workers make use of a variety of theories to assure that they understand factors that influence human behavior (p. 549).

EP 2.1.7a Utilize a conceptual framework to guide the process of assessment, intervention, and evaluation. Human behavior theory and the systems perspective provides social workers with a conceptual framework for understanding how people act and react to their environment and in certain situations (pp. 548–551).

EP 2.1.7b Critique and apply knowledge to understand the person and environment. Social workers understand that the context of clients lives and the multiple ways in which context influences their interactions with others. Being mindful of the person and the person in the environment allows social workers to gain an in-depth understanding of the client (pp. 537, 541, 543, 552).

EP 2.1.10a Substantively and affectively prepare for action with individuals, families, groups, and communities. In preparing for work with clients, social workers are mindful of the relational dynamics that may be caused by a client's status, racial or cultural differences, as well as their own behavior (pp. 528–529, 534, 537, 540).

EP 2.1.10b Use empathy and other interpersonal skills. In working with clients, interpersonal skills are critically important to developing and maintaining a positive relationship as well as attending to relational dynamics. Facilitative interpersonal skills include empathy, acceptance, and trustworthiness (pp. 528, 539, 541, 543, 550, 552, 554).

EP 2.1.10c Develop a mutually agreed-on focus and desired outcomes. As social workers work with clients to solve problems and enhance their capacity, reaching an agreement about the work to be completed is critical. The social worker takes care to ensure that the client understands and agrees with the method that will be used to achieve the desired outcome (p. 548).

EP 2.1.10i Implement prevention interventions that enhance client capacities. Over the course of the helping process, intermediary techniques such as reframing can help clients move forward. Preventative techniques such as when individuals recognize the ways in which their behavior or actions can prevent them from utilizing strengths and capacities to achieve their goals (pp. 535, 553).

EP 2.1.10j Help clients solve problems. During the course of the helping process clients can become stalled in their effort to change. Social workers recognize and respond to client's concerns, interactions that can occur between themselves and the client, as well as exploring factors that will motivate the client to participate in solving his or her problems (pp. 535, 543–544, 547, 550–553).

EP 2.1.10m Critically analyze, evaluate, and monitor interventions. A positive relationship between the client and the social worker is primary in the change process. At times, barriers such as client and social workers reactions, thoughts, perceptions, or behaviors can interfere. It is essential that social workers continuously assess and monitor relational dynamics, including assessing their behavior, so that the helping process is productive (pp. 534–535, 541–542).

Chapter 19 Evaluation and Termination

EP 2.1.1b Practice personal reflection and self-correction to assure continual professional development. Social workers must be attuned to the feelings that they experience at termination and assure that those do not detrimentally affect the helping relationship (pp. 567, 569).

EP 2.1.1f Use supervision and consultation. Supervision is an appropriate arena in which to address countertransference and other feelings and experiences that arise during termination. Supervisors can also help the worker manage questions of self-disclosure and confidentiality that might arise in unplanned endings. Consultation can be effective in designing and interpreting the results of practice evaluation (p. 564).

EP 2.1.2b Make ethical decisions by applying standards. Clear boundaries are vital to the helping relationship. Social workers should handle the elements of termination (feelings, follow-up contact, ending celebrations) carefully so that conflicts of interest and dual relationships are not created (p. 568).

EP 2.1.3a Distinguish, appraise, and integrate multiple sources of knowledge, including research-based knowledge and practice wisdom. Social workers utilize critical thinking and existing literature to create and evaluate plans and consider the factors that will affect termination (p. 561).

EP 2.1.3b Analyze models of assessment, prevention, intervention, and evaluation. This chapter describes process evaluation, outcome evaluation, and client satisfaction, and the ways that social workers use those to determine client progress and worker effectiveness (p. 557).

EP 2.1.4d View themselves as learners and engage those with whom they work as informants. Evaluation requires that professionals open themselves up to client feedback (p. 558).

EP 2.1.10b Use empathy and other interpersonal skills. The capacity for empathy is important through the end of the helping process, as clients express feelings about ending, regret at unplanned termination, fears of failure, or other reactions. Social workers can effectively use empathy to encourage clients to elaborate, to deepen exploration, and to demonstrate compassion (p. 566).

EP 2.1.10l Facilitate transitions and endings. In this chapter readers learn about the factors that determine when termination takes place, the different kinds of endings, and the worker and client reactions that accompany them. Workers learn skills for helping clients with termination and with sustaining the gains made in treatment (p. 567).

EP 2.1.10m Critically analyze, monitor, and evaluate interventions. Social workers must evaluate the effectiveness of their interventions. The termination phase provides the opportunity to look with the client at his or her satisfaction with service, the elements of service that were effective, and the outcomes or goals attained. Social workers can use interviewing skills, standardized measures, goal attainment scaling, and other tools to evaluate their practice (p. 558).

Modeled Responses and Other Exercises

Chapter 4 The Cardinal Social Work Values

Skill Development Exercises in Operationalizing Cardinal Values

To assist you in developing skill in operationalizing the cardinal values in specific practice situations, we have provided a number of exercises with modeled responses. As you read each one, note which values are germane to the situation. To refresh your memory, the values are as follows:

1. Social workers value service to others and a commitment to social justice in helping clients get deserved and needed resources.
2. Social workers value the inherent dignity and worth of others.
3. Social workers value the primacy of human relationships.
4. Social workers behave with integrity.
5. Social workers are responsible for practicing with competence.

Next, assume you are the client's service provider and formulate a response that implements the relevant social work value. After completing each exercise, compare your response with the modeled response that follows the exercises. Bearing in mind that the modeled response is only one of many possible acceptable responses, analyze it and compare it with your own. Also, remember that *vocal tone* is an essential component of effective, congruent communications. Imagine the modeled responses that follow spoken with different verbal and emotional tones: sensitivity, tentativeness, anger, impatience, pity, kindness, conceit. Which feel genuine to you? Which will help achieve your objectives with the client? Which are congruent with professional values of respect and support for client dignity? By carefully completing these exercises, you will improve your competence in putting values into action in the varied and challenging situations encountered in direct social work practice.

Client Statements

1. *Group member [in first group session]*: Before I really open up and talk about myself, I need to be sure what I say isn't spread around to other people. [*Turning to social worker.*] How can I be sure that won't happen?
2. *Adolescent in correctional institution [after social worker introduces him/herself]*: So you want to help me, huh? I'll tell you how you can help. You can get me out of this damn place—that's how!
3. *Female client, age 21 [to mental health practitioner]*: Yeah, I know that kicking the habit was a victory of sorts. But I look at my life and I wonder what's there to live for. I've turned my family against me. I've sold my body to more rotten guys than I can count—just to get a fix. I've had three STDs. What do I have to offer anyone? I feel like my life has been one big cesspool.
4. *Teenage male [in a group session in a correctional setting]*: [*Takes off shoes and sprawls in his chair. His feet give off a foul odor; other members hold noses and make derisive comments. He responds defensively.*] Hey, get off my back, you creeps. What's the big deal about taking off my shoes?
5. *Female [initial interview in family counseling center]*: Before I talk about my marital problems, I need to

let you know I'm a Seventh Day Adventist. Do you know anything about my church? I'm asking because a lot of our problems involve my religion.

6. *Female client* [*sixth interview*]: Maybe it sounds crazy, but I've been thinking this last week that you're not really interested in me as a person. I have the feeling I'm just someone for you to analyze or to write about.

7. *Teenage female* [*caught with contraband in her possession by a supervisor-counselor in a residential treatment center*]: Please don't report this, Mrs. Wilson. I've been doing better lately, and I've learned my lesson. You won't need to worry about me. I won't mess with drugs anymore.

8. *Client* [*observing social worker taking notes during initial interview*]: I'm dying to know what you're writing down about me. Maybe you think I'm a nut. Can I take a copy of your notes with me when we're done?

9. *Male parolee, age 27, who has a reputation as a con artist* [*in a mandatory weekly visit to his parole officer*]: Man, you've really got it made. Your office is really fine. But then you deserve what you've got. You've probably got a terrific wife and kids, too. Is that their picture over there?

10. *Female client, age 34* [*in third interview*]: I'm really uptight right now. I've got this tight feeling I get in my chest when I'm nervous. [*Pause.*] Well, I guess I'll have to tell you if I expect to get anything out of this. [*Hesitant.*] You know the marital problems we've talked about? Well, Jack doesn't know this, but I'm attracted to other women. [*Blushes.*] I've tried—I've really tried, but Jack doesn't turn me on. I can't even tolerate sex unless I'm thinking about other women. Jack thinks something's wrong with him, but it's not his fault. [*Chin quivers.*]

11. *Black male probationer* [*to white therapist*]: You're so damn smug. You say you want to help me, but I don't buy that crap. You don't know the first thing about black people. Man, I grew up where it's an accomplishment just to survive. What do you know about life in my world?

Modeled Responses

1. "Ginny raises a good point that concerns all of you. So that you can feel more comfortable about sharing personal feelings and experiences with the group, we need an understanding that each of you will keep what is shared in the strictest confidence. What are your thoughts about Ginny's concern?"

2. "I guess that's what I'd want if I were in your situation. As a matter of fact, that's what I want for you, too. But we both know the review board won't release you until they feel you're prepared to make it on the outside. I can't get you out, but with your cooperation I can help you to make changes that will get you ready for release."

3. "I can hear that you're down on yourself. Even though you've done a lot that you feel bad about, I'm impressed at what it's taken to get and stay clean. That's a giant step in the right direction. How can we keep your misgivings about the past from sabotaging the path you're on now?"

4. "I think we need to look as a group at how we can give Jim some helpful feedback rather than making fun of him. Let's talk about what just happened. Maybe you could begin, Jim, by sharing with the group what you're feeling just now."

5. "I have to confess I know only a little bit about your religion, which may make you wonder if I can appreciate your problems. I can assure you I'll do my best to understand if you're willing to help me with that. The most important thing, though, is your comfort about it. How do you feel about sharing your problems with me under these circumstances?"

6. "That sounds like a painful feeling—that I'm not personally concerned with you as an individual. I'd like to explore that with you further because that's not at all how I feel about you. Let's talk a bit about how I've come across to you and how you've reached that conclusion."

7. "I'm sorry you're still involved with drugs, Joy, because of the difficulties it's caused you. I don't like to see you get into trouble but I have no choice. I have to report this. If I didn't, I'd be breaking a rule myself by not reporting you. That wouldn't help you in the long run. Frankly, I'm going to keep worrying about you until I'm satisfied you're really sticking to the rules."

8. "It's not nutty at all to wonder what I'm thinking and writing. I'm writing down what we talk about. What you tell me is important, and notes help to refresh my memory. You're welcome to look at them if you like. Actually, I would be interested in hearing a little more about your concerns regarding what I might think of you."

9. "As a matter of fact it is, and I think they're pretty terrific. But we're here to talk about you, Rex. I'd like to hear how your job interview went."

10. "Keeping this secret has been very painful for you. I gather you've been afraid I'd condemn you, but

I'm pleased you brought it up so that we can work on it together. It took some real courage on your part, and I respect you for that."

11. "I'd be phony if I said I understood all about being black and living in your neighborhood ... and I'm sorry if it seems I'm being smug. I am interested in you, and I'd like to understand more about your life."

Skill Development Exercises in Managing Ethical Dilemmas

The following exercises will give you practice in applying ethics concepts and ethical decision making to specific practice situations. These situations include some of the most difficult ones that we and our colleagues have encountered in practice. Note that the appropriate response or course of action is rarely cut and dry. After reading each situation, consider the following questions:

1. What conflicting principles and feelings are in play in the case?
2. What are the pros and cons of the various courses of action?
3. What guidelines are applicable in resolving this dilemma?
4. What resources could you consult to help you decide on an ethical course of action?

Ethics Case 1 A classmate has told you that she is Googling clients from her field agency as well as looking them up on Facebook. She states that the information is public, so there is no confidentiality involved, and the more she learns about them the better she can help them.

Ethics Case 2 You are forming a youth group in a state correctional facility. From past experience, you know that youths sometimes make references in the group to previous offenses that they have committed without being apprehended. You also know that they may talk about plans to escape from the institution or about indiscretions or misdemeanors they (or others) may have committed or plan to commit within the institution, such as smoking marijuana or stealing institutional supplies or property from peers or staff. Are you required to share all of the information you learn in the group? How can you encourage trust and sharing if there are limits to confidentiality?

Ethics Case 3 In conducting an intake interview with a young woman in a family agency, you observe that both of her young children are withdrawn. One of the children is also badly bruised; the other, an infant, appears malnourished. Throughout the interview, the client seems defensive and suspicious and appears ambivalent about having come for the interview. At one point, she states that she feels overwhelmed with her parenting responsibilities and is having difficulty in coping with her children. She also alludes to her fear that she may hurt them but then abruptly changes the subject. As you encourage her to return to the discussion of her problems with the children, your client says that she has changed her mind about wanting help, takes her children in hand, and hastily leaves the office.

Ethics Case 4 You have seen a husband and wife and their adolescent daughter twice regarding relationship problems between the parents and the girl. The parents are both extremely negative and blaming in their attitudes toward their daughter, stating that their troubles would disappear if she would just "shape up." Today, during an individual interview with the girl, she breaks into tears and tells you that she is pregnant and plans to "go somewhere" with her boyfriend this weekend to get an abortion. She pleads with you not to tell her parents; she feels they would be extremely angry if they knew.

Ethics Case 5 In a mental health agency, you have been working with a middle aged male who has a history, when angered, of becoming violent and physically abusive. He has been under extreme psychological pressure lately because of problems relating to a recent separation from his wife. In an interview today, he is extremely angry, clenching his fists as he tells you that he has heard that his wife has initiated divorce proceedings and plans to move to another state. "If this is true," he loudly protests, "she is doing it to take the kids away from me, and I'll kill her rather than let her do that."

Chapter 5 Empathy and Authenticity: The Building Blocks of Communication

Exercises in Responding Authentically and Assertively

The following exercises will assist you in gaining skill in responding authentically and assertively. Read each situation and client message, and then formulate a written response as though you were the social worker in the situation presented. Compare your written responses with the modeled responses, keeping in mind that these models represent just a few of the many possible responses that would be appropriate.

You will find additional exercises that require authentic and assertive responding in Chapter 17 (in the confrontation exercises) and in Chapter 18 (in the exercises concerned with managing relational reactions and resistance).

Statements and Situations

1. *Marital partner* [*in third conjoint marital therapy session*]: It must be really nice being a marriage counselor—knowing just what to do and not having problems like ours.
2. *Female client, age 23* [*in first session*]: Some of my problems are related to my church's stand on birth control. Tell me, are you a Catholic?
3. *Client* [*fifth session*]: You look like you're having trouble staying awake. [*Social worker is drowsy from having taken an antihistamine for an allergy.*]
4. *Adult group member* [*to social worker in second session; group members have been struggling to determine the agenda for the session*]: I wish you'd tell us what we should talk about. Isn't that your job? We're just getting nowhere.
5. *Male client* [*sixth session*]: Say, my wife and I are having a fund-raiser next Wednesday. We'd like to have you and your wife come.
6. *Client* [*calls 3 hours before scheduled appointment*]: I've had the flu the past couple of days, but I feel like I'm getting over it. Do you think I should come today?
7. *Client* [*scheduled time for ending appointment has arrived, and social worker has already moved to end session; in previous sessions, client has tended to stay beyond designated ending time*]: What we were talking about reminded me of something I wanted to discuss today but forgot. I'd like to discuss it briefly, if you don't mind.
8. *Client* [*has just completed behavioral rehearsal involving talking with employer and played role beyond expectations of social worker*].
9. *Female client* [*tenth interview*]: I've really felt irritated with you during the week. When I brought up taking the correspondence course in art, all you could talk about was how some correspondence courses are rip-offs and that I could take courses at a college for less money. I knew that, but I've checked into this correspondence course, and it's well worth the money. You put me down, and I've resented it.
10. *Client* [*seventh session*]: You seem uptight today. Is something bothering you? [*Social worker has been under strain associated with recent death of a parent and assisting surviving parent, who has been distraught.*]

Modeled Responses

1. [*Smiling.*] "Well, I must admit it's helpful. But I want you to know that marriage is not easy for marriage counselors either. We have our rough spots, too. I have to work like everyone else to keep my marriage alive and growing."
2. "I gather you're wondering what my stand is and whether I can understand and accept your feelings. I've worked with many Catholics and have been able to understand their problems. Would it trouble you if I weren't Catholic?"
3. "You're very observant. I have been sleepy these past few minutes, and I apologize for that. I had to take an antihistamine before lunch, and a side effect of the drug is I can get drowsy. My sleepiness has nothing to do with you. If I move around a little, the drowsiness passes."
4. "I can sense your frustration and your desire to firm up an agenda. If I made the decision, though, it might not fit for many of you and I'd be taking over the group's power to make its own decisions. Perhaps it would be helpful if the group followed the decision-by-consensus approach we discussed in our first session."
5. "Thank you for the invitation. I'm flattered that you'd ask me. I appreciate your asking, but, I must decline your invitation. If I were to socialize with you while you're seeing me professionally, it would conflict with my role, and I couldn't be as helpful to you. I hope you can understand my not accepting."
6. "I appreciate your calling to let me know. I think it would be better to change our appointment until you're sure you've recovered. Quite frankly, I don't want to risk being exposed to the flu, which I hope you can understand. I have a time open on the day after tomorrow. I'll set it aside for you, if you'd like, in the event you're fully recovered by then."
7. "I'm sorry I don't have the time to discuss the matter today. Let's save it for next week, and I'll make a note that you wanted to explore this issue. We'll have to stop here today because I'm scheduled for another appointment."

8. "I want to share with you how impressed I was with how you asserted yourself and came across so positively. If you'd been with your boss, he'd have been impressed, too."

9. "I'm glad you shared those feelings with me. I can see I owe you an apology. You're right, I didn't explore whether you'd checked into the program, and I made some incorrect assumptions. I guess I was overly concerned about your not being ripped off because I know others who have been by taking correspondence courses. But I can see I made a mistake because you had already looked into the course."

10. "Thank you for asking. Yes, I have been under some strain this past week. My mother died suddenly, which was a shock, and my father is taking it very hard. It's created a lot of pressure for me, but I think I can keep it from spilling over into our session. If I'm not able to focus on you, I will stop the session. Or if you don't feel that I'm fully with you, please let me know. I don't want to shortchange you."

Skill Development Exercises in Empathic Communication

The following exercises, which include a wide variety of actual client messages, will assist you in gaining mastery of reciprocal empathic responding (level 3). Read the client message and compose on paper an empathic response that captures the client's surface feelings. You may wish to use the paradigm, "You feel _____ about (or because) _____," in organizing your response before phrasing it in typical conversation language. Strive to make your responses fresh, varied, and spontaneous. To expand your repertoire of responses, we strongly encourage you to continue using the lists of affective words and phrases.

After formulating your response, compare it with the modeled response provided at the end of the exercises. Analyze the differences, paying particular attention to the various forms of responding and the elements that enhance the effectiveness of your own responses and the modeled responses.

Because this exercise includes 20 different client statements, we recommend that you not attempt to complete the entire exercise in one sitting, but rather work through it in several sessions. Consistent practice and careful scrutiny of your responses are essential in gaining mastery of this vital skill.

Client Statements

1. ***Father of developmentally disabled child, age 14*** *[who is becoming difficult to manage]*: We just don't know what to do with Henry. We've always wanted to take care of him, but we've reached the point where we're not sure it's doing any good for him or for us. Henry has grown so strong—we just can't restrain him anymore. He hit my wife last week when she wouldn't take him to the store late at night—I was out of town—and she's still bruised. She's afraid of him now, and I have to admit I'm getting that way, too.

2. ***Latino*** *[living in urban barrio]*: Our children do better in school if they teach Spanish, not just English. We're afraid our children are behind because they don't understand English so good. And we don't know how to help them. Our people have been trying to get a bilingual program, but the school board pays no attention to us.

3. ***Female client, age 31***: Since my husband left town with another woman, I get lonely and depressed a lot of the time. I find myself wondering whether something is wrong with me or whether men just can't be trusted.

4. ***Mother*** *[to child welfare protective services worker on doorstep during initial home visit]*: Who'd want to make trouble for me by accusing me of not taking care of my kids? *[Tearfully.]* Maybe I'm not the best mother in the world, but I try. There are a lot of kids around here that aren't cared for as well as mine.

5. ***Male ninth-grade student*** *[to school social worker]*: I feel like I'm a real dweeb. In sports I am no good. When they choose up sides, I'm always the last one chosen. A couple of times they've actually got into a fight over who doesn't have to choose me.

6. ***Member of abused women's group:*** That last month I was living in mortal fear of Art. He'd get that hateful look in his eyes, and I'd know he was going to let me have it. The last time I was afraid he was going to kill me—and he might have, if his brother hadn't dropped in. I'm afraid to go back to him. But what do I do? I can't stay here much longer!

7. ***Male, age 34*** *[to marital therapist]*: Just once I'd like to show my wife I can accomplish something without her prodding me. That's why I haven't told her I'm coming to see you. If she knew it, she'd try to take charge and call all the shots.

8. *African American man* [in a group session]: All I want is to be accepted as a person. When I get hired, I want it to be for what I'm capable of doing—not just because of my skin color. That's as phony and degrading as not being hired because of my skin color. I just want to be accepted for who I am.

9. *Client in a state prison* [to rehabilitation worker]: They treat you like an animal in here—herd you around like a damn cow. I know I've got to do my time, but sometimes I feel like I can't stand it any longer—like something's building up in me that's going to explode.

10. *Client* [to mental health worker]: I don't have any pleasant memories of my childhood. It seems like just so much empty space. I can remember my father watching television and staring at me with a blank look—as though I didn't exist.

11. *Patient in hospital* [to medical social worker]: I know Dr. Brown is a skilled surgeon, and he tells me not to worry—that there's very little risk in this surgery. I know I should feel reassured, but to tell you the truth, I'm just plain panic-stricken.

12. *Female member, age 29* [in marital therapy group]: I'd like to know what it's like with the rest of you. Hugh and I get into nasty fights because I feel he doesn't help me when I really need help. He tells me there's no way he's going to do women's work! That really irritates me. I start feeling like I'm just supposed to be his slave.

13. *Male college student, age 21*: Francine says she's going to call me, but she never does—I have to do all the texting, or I probably wouldn't hear from her at all. It seems so one-sided. If I didn't need her so much I'd ask her what kind of game she's playing. I wonder if she isn't pretty selfish.

14. *White student, age 14* [to school social worker]: To be really honest, I don't like the black kids in our school. They pretty much stay to themselves, and they aren't friendly to whites. I don't know what to expect or how to act around them. I'm antsy when they're around and—well, to be honest—I'm scared I'll do something they won't like, and they'll jump me.

15. *Single female, age 27* [to mental health worker]: I've been taking this class on the joys of womanhood. Last time the subject was how to catch a man. I can see I've been doing a lot of things wrong. But I won't lower myself to playing games with men. If that's what it takes, I guess I'll always be single.

16. *Married male, age 29* [to marital therapist]: Sexually, I'm unfulfilled in my marriage. At times I've even had thoughts of trying sex with men. That idea kind of intrigues me. My wife and I can talk about sex all right, but it doesn't get better.

17. *Married female, age 32* [to family social worker]: I love my husband and children, and I don't know what I'd do without them. Yet on days like last Thursday, I feel I could just climb the walls. I want to run away from all of them and never come back.

18. *Blind female* [to other blind group members]: You know, it really offends me when people praise me or make a fuss over me for doing something routine that anyone else could do. It makes me feel like I'm on exhibition. I want to be recognized for being competent—not for being blind.

19. *Male teacher* [to mental health social worker]: I have this thing about not being able to accept compliments. A friend told me about how much of a positive impact I've had on several students over the years. I couldn't accept that and feel good. My thought was, "You must be mistaken. I've never had that kind of effect on anyone."

20. *Lesbian, age 26* [to private social worker]: The girls at the office were talking about lesbians the other day and about how repulsive the very thought of lesbianism was to them. How do you think I felt?

Modeled Responses

1. "So you're really in a difficult situation. You've wanted to keep Henry at home, but in light of his recent aggression and his increasing strength, you're becoming really frightened and wonder if other arrangements wouldn't be better for both you and him."

2. "I can see you're worried about how your children are doing in school and believe they need a bilingual program."

3. "It's been a real blow—your husband leaving you for another woman—and you've just felt so alone. And you find yourself dwelling on the painful question, 'Is something wrong with me, or is it that you just can't trust men?'"

4. "This is very upsetting for you. You seem to be saying that it's not fair being turned in when you believe you take care of your children. Please understand I'm not accusing you of neglecting your children. But I do have to investigate

complaints. It may be that I'll be able to turn in a positive report. I hope so. But I do need to talk with you further. May I come in?"

5. "It's humiliating to you to feel so left out and be the last guy chosen."

6. "It sounds as though you lived in terror that last month and literally feared for your life. You were wise to remove yourself when you did. A number of other women in the group have had similar experiences and are facing the same dilemma about what to do now. As group members, each of us can be helpful to other group members in thinking through what's the best course of action. In the meantime, you have a safe place to stay and some time to plan."

7. "Sounds like you get pretty annoyed, thinking about your wife's prodding and trying to take charge. It seems important right now that you prove to her and to yourself you can do something on your own."

8. "I gather you're fed up with having people relate to you because of your race instead of being accepted as an individual—as yourself."

9. "If I understand you, you feel degraded by the way you're treated—as though you're less than a human being. And that really gets to you."

10. "From what you say, I get a picture of you just feeling so all alone as you were growing up—as though you didn't feel very important to anyone, especially your father."

11. "So intellectually, you tell yourself not to worry, that you're in good hands. Still, on another level you have to admit you're terrified of that operation. [Brief pause.] Your fear is pretty natural, though. Most people who are honest with themselves experience fear."

12. "So the two of you get into some real struggles over differences in your views about what is reasonable of you to expect from Hugh. You seem to be saying you very much resent his refusal to pitch in—that it's not fair to have to carry the burden alone. Hugh, I'd be interested in hearing your views. Then we can hear how other members deal with this kind of situation."

13. "Sounds like part of you is saying that you have a right to expect more from Francine—that you don't feel good about always having to be the one to take the initiative. You also seem to feel you'd like to confront her with what she's doing, but you're uneasy about doing that because you don't want to risk losing her."

14. "So, you're uncomfortable around your black classmates and just don't know how to read them. I gather you kind of walk on eggshells when they're around for fear you'll blow it."

15. "There is a lot of conflicting advice around these days about how men and women should relate to one another, and it is hard to figure out what to believe. You know you don't want to play games, yet that is what the class is telling you to do if you don't want to be single."

16. "Things don't get better despite your talks, and you get pretty discouraged. Sometimes you find yourself wondering if you'd get sexual fulfillment with men, and that appeals to you in some ways."

17. "So even though you care deeply for your family, there are days when you just feel so overwhelmed you'd like to buy a one-way ticket out of all the responsibility."

18. "Are you saying that you feel singled out and demeaned when people flatter you for doing things anyone could do? It bothers you, and you wish people would recognize you for being competent?"

19. "In a way, you seem to be saying that you don't feel comfortable with compliments because you feel you don't really deserve them. It's like you feel you don't do anything worthy of a compliment."

20. "You must have felt extremely uncomfortable believing that they would condemn you if they knew. It must have been most painful for you."

Answers to Exercise in Identifying Surface and Underlying Feelings

1. *Apparent feelings:* unimportant, neglected, disappointed, hurt. *Probable deeper feelings:* rejected, abandoned, forsaken, deprived, lonely, depressed.

2. *Apparent feelings:* unloved, insecure, confused, embarrassed, left out or excluded. *Probable deeper feelings:* hurt, resentful, unvalued, rejected, taken for granted, degraded, doubting own desirability.

3. *Apparent feelings:* chagrined, disappointed in self, discouraged, letting children down, perplexed. *Probable deeper feelings:* guilty, inadequate, crummy, sense of failure, out of control, fear of damaging children.

4. *Apparent feelings:* frustrated, angry, bitter. *Probable deeper feelings:* depressed, discouraged, hopeless.

Answers to Exercises to Discriminate Levels of Empathic Responding

CLIENT STATEMENT

Client 1

Response	Level
1.	2
2.	1
3.	1
4.	3
5.	2
6.	2
7.	4
8.	1

CLIENT STATEMENT

Client 2		Client 3	
Response	Level	Response	Level
1.	1	2	1
2.	3	1	4
3.	1	1	2
4.	2	3	2
5.	4	2	5
6.	1	2	1
7.	3	4	2
8.	2	1	2

Chapter 6 The Skills of Verbal Following, Exploring, and Focusing

Modeled Responses to Exercise in Paraphrasing

1. "You just get so uptight in a group you don't function."
2. "So you've made some real progress in tuning in to your husband and children."
3. "So people's helpfulness here and your own skills in meeting people have helped your adjustment here."
4. "So you see yourself as having contributed to many of her problems."
5. "It sounds as if your experience causes you to doubt whether more services would be helpful. Could you tell me about your feeling that the mother is not motivated?"

Modeled Responses to Exercise in Reflection

1. "Because your fears really block you when you argue with your mother, you seem to feel anxious and frustrated." (simple reflection)
2. "So you feel caught by competing parenting and work responsibilities; if you meet all your work hours, you are concerned about how it affects your parenting. If you do what you think you should as a parent, it can conflict with work requirements." (double-sided reflection)
3. "So sometimes you feel cheated by life and at other times that your illness is a consequence for your smoking history." (double-sided reflection)
4. "So it sounds as if it has not been easy for you to relax and have friends in this school; when they have acted in a way that feels mean to you, you have felt a need to act to protect yourself." (simple reflection)
5. "You're really torn and wonder if not seeing the children very often is too high a price to pay for a divorce. On the other hand, you fear that if you stay with her, there won't be any improvement. Right now you don't see a way out of this dilemma." (reflection with a twist)

Answers to Exercise in Identifying Closed- and Open-Ended Responses

Statement	Response
1	C
2	O
3	O
4	C

Modeled Open-Ended Responses

1. "Could you tell me more about your wanting to impress Ralph?"
2. "What are you afraid you'd do wrong?"
3. "Given your experience with that probation officer, how would you like your relationship with me to be?"
4. "So you feel that your facility cannot provide what Gladys needs. Can you describe the kind of care you believe she needs?"
5. "So you don't trust that I want to try to help you make what you feel will be the best decision. Can you tell me what I have done that has caused you to think that your mother and I are allies?"

6. "You sound as if you are at a pretty hopeless point right now. When you say you don't know if you want to keep trying to figure it out, can you tell me more about what you are thinking about doing?"

Chapter 8 Assessment: Problems and Strengths
Skill Development Exercises in Exploring Strengths and Problems

On April 16, 2007, 23-year-old Seung-Hui Cho killed 32 people on the campus of Virginia Tech University before turning the gun on himself. In the months leading up to the murders, Cho had numerous encounters with mental health professionals. He had been declared an "imminent danger to self or others as a result of mental illness" on a temporary detention order from a Virginia District Court. Two students had filed complaints against him for bizarre phone calls and emails he had sent. Another student, his former roommate, called campus police stating that Cho could be suicidal. A poetry professor at the school recalled that he was "menacing" in class and other students stopped attending after he began photographing them. This professor later removed Cho from her class and worked with him one-on-one. She also reported that the content of his poems and other writings was disturbing and seemed to have an underlying threat.

A South Korean national, Cho moved with his family to the United States at the age of eight. As a youngster, he had been diagnosed with depression and selective mutism, a condition associated with social anxiety, and had received therapy and special education services as a result. He had been a successful elementary school student, but by middle school he was apparently subject to mockery from fellow students due to his speech abnormalities, his accent, and his isolation.

Imagine you worked in a setting where Seung-Hui Cho presented for service at age 10, 15, or 22, and address the following questions.

1. What sources of information would you use to better understand your client, his problems and his strengths?
2. What cross-cultural issues should you be aware of in this case?
3. What questions would you ask as part of problem analysis?
4. What transitional and developmental issues might be of particular interest?
5. What role would your client's diagnoses play in your assessment?
6. What environmental and interpersonal interactions are relevant in this case?
7. What consultation would be helpful to you in completing this assessment?

Chapter 9 Intrapersonal, Interpersonal, and Environmental Factors in Assessment
Skill Development Exercises in Assessment

Review the opening session in the video *Work with the Corning Family* and address the following questions.

1. What words would you use to describe the clients across the following variables?
   a. Appearance (Posture, Attire, Psychomotor Functioning)
   b. Cognitive Functioning (Memory Concentration, Judgment, Reality Testing, Coherence, Cognitive Flexibility, Misconceptions, Sensory Perceptions)
   c. Affective Functioning (Predominant mood, Variability, Range and Intensity of Affect)
   d. Values and Self-Concept
   e. Attitude toward the Interviewer
2. Are there any areas in which you lack information? How would you go about getting the information in a subsequent session?
3. To what extent might the nature of the interview and the worker's style and characteristics have affected the clients' presentation of themselves in the session?
4. Now, compare your findings with those of a classmate. How much congruence is there in your assessments? What might account for areas of difference?
5. How do your descriptions compare with the assessment of the Cornings on this text's website?
6. What conclusions can you draw about the skills, values, and knowledge needed to write effective, accurate assessments?

Chapter 10 Assessment: Family Functioning in Diverse Family and Cultural Contexts
Skill Development Exercises

1. What are the preferred communication styles in your family?
2. Describe the different forms of power in your family and identify who the holders are. Specify whether or not the power in your family, in whatever form, is culturally constructed.
3. Reflecting on marginalized families that you have worked with, write a brief response to the assertion in this chapter that oppression is a normative experience for some families.
4. Review the guidelines for effective decision making and assess your own family's adherence to these guidelines. If appropriate, identify cultural variants.
5. Put yourself in the position of a teen mother who is meeting with a social worker for the first time. What would you like to be the starting point in your initial contact?
6. Develop a set of questions or indicators that you could use to assess family strengths.
7. Think of ways in which the strengths of clients may have a minor or major role in your experience with agencies, funding resources, and policy makers. How would you articulate the strengths perspective to any one or all of these organizations?
8. Think of a case that you are currently involved with. Now consider the relevant systems concepts that are applicable to the case.
9. Describe how boundary maintenance, internal and external, operates in your family.
10. As you observe the interactions between Jackie and Anna, identify the barriers to communication using Table 10-4.
11. Reflect on the concept of social empathy. How would you apply this concept in your work with families?
12. How are decisions made in your family and who is involved in the process?

Chapter 11 Social Work Groups: Formation and Assessment
Skills Development Exercises in Planning Groups

Imagine that you are planning a group to address one of the following populations or problems:

1. People charged with domestic violence
2. Middle school students with diabetes
3. Teenage fathers
4. Families of people with schizophrenia
5. Elementary school children who have been exposed to family or community violence
6. Parents and community members who wish to change a school policy on suspensions
7. Elderly residents recently admitted to a nursing home
8. 7th- and 8th-grade "outcasts" who have no friends
9. Teens who want to start a Gay-Straight Alliance in their high school
10. Pre-marital couples
11. Widowers
12. People concerned about bullying in a school

Using the guidelines in this chapter, determine:

a. The name you will give the group
b. The type of group
c. A one-sentence statement of purpose
d. The size of the group
e. The length, structure, and format
f. The location where you will meet
g. Important factors in group composition
h. How you will recruit and screen members

Chapter 12 Goal Development and Contract Formulation
Skill Development Exercises

1. Develop a goal for yourself. Assess the feasibility of your goal, potential barriers, and risks and benefits. Also, determine which of the measurement and evaluation procedures that were discussed in the chapter you would use to observe goal attainment.
2. Using the same goal that you developed for yourself, rate your level of readiness. Now develop general and specific tasks or objectives that will help you meet your goal.
3. Reread the case of Bettina, the parenting adolescent in the group home. What is your reaction to the staff pattern of punishment, based on what you have read about her developmental stage, sense of self-definition, self-direction, and motivation?
4. Review motivational congruence as a strategy for working with involuntary clients and think about ways in which you could make use of this strategy.
5. What are values that you hold that have the potential to create tension between what you believe and the goals that a client might want to pursue? Other

than using a referral resource, which may or may not be an option, how would you deal with the differences between you and the client?

Chapter 13 Change-Oriented Strategies: Planning and Implementation
Skill Development Exercises

1. Using the Corning case, select both a task-centered and a solution-focused approach as a change-oriented strategy and assess the merits of each approach in this case. In what way could you combine aspects of both approaches in this case?
2. A mother, who has been sanctioned for failing to comply with the welfare-to-work rule, tells you that her caseworker is "out to get her." What additional information or factors would you need to determine how you would respond to the client's statement?
3. You are the social worker for a minor in a residential treatment program. How would you determine if the minor is able to give consent for his treatment plan?
4. Review Lipchik's (2002) solution-focused questions and answer the questions based on a current concern that you have. Also, indicate how you would use scaling, coping, exceptions, and the miracle question.
5. Using the same situation that you have identified, develop a goal and general and specific tasks in the task-centered approach. Indicate how you would measure goal attainment.
6. Choose one of the cognitive distortion statements that apply to you. What strategies would you use to modify your thinking?

Chapter 14 Intervention Strategies: Developing Resources, Organizing, Planning, and Advocacy
Skill Development Exercises

1. Assess the organizational policies or practices using the questions identified by Rooney.
2. Using Figure 14-1, think of the potential benefit of linking an individual client situation that you have worked with to a change effort at the macro-level.
3. Choose a public policy or social problem. How would you describe your position on either one or both? Would you describe yourself as a liberal (conservative, moderate, or radical) a conservative (fiscal, religious, or social) or a centrist? Think about how your identified position influences your thinking about the policy or problem.
4. Describe how client dignity and worth is fostered in your agency.
5. Think about the potential ways in which social work practice is influenced by public policy.
6. Rate your current position of each of Hackman and Oldham's core characteristics of job design and motivation.
7. Identify a change that you would like to make in your agency. Identify the risks, benefits, and potential opposition to your change proposal.
8. Using Rivera and Erlich's Level of Community Contact, what steps would you take in working with a community at each level? What are potential ethical issues at each level?
9. Reflect upon the organizational cultural competence factors discussed by Nybell and Gray (2004). How would you measure your agency using these factors?

Chapter 15 Improving Relationships and Family Functioning
Skill Development Exercises

1. Identify some examples of verbal or nonverbal metacommunications that you have used.
2. Describe how an unspoken rule in your family governs the behavior of family members.
3. From your observation of the session with Anna and Jackie ("Home for the Holidays"), describe how the social worker uses the technique of on-the-spot intervention.
4. List three societal beliefs, and reflect upon how these beliefs may affect the families that you work with.
5. Choose several classmates to role-play a family situation. Acting as the social worker, facilitate the *joining* stage in the initial contact session.
6. Using the same family situation, identify the needs and wants expressed by each family member. What

questions would you ask to help members identify their concerns?
7. In a family session in which one member is identified as being the problem, how would you proceed with the family?

Chapter 16 Social Work Group Interventions
Skills Development Exercises in Group Interventions

To assist you in developing group work skills, we have provided a number of exercises with modeled responses. Imagine that you are the facilitator and formulate a response that addresses the member's and group's needs, given the phase and type of group. We have drawn the statements from two types of groups. One is an interdisciplinary task group in a hospital working on policy and practice changes in response to confidentiality laws, undocumented immigrant admissions, indigent patients, and the avian flu threat. The other is the HEART therapy group for teen girls with obesity. The first five statements contain modeled responses so that you can compare your response with the one provided. (Bear in mind that the modeled response is only one of many possible acceptable responses.)

Client Statements

1. *Task group member [in fifth meeting, having missed three]:* "Well, I think we should reconsider why we need to change the policy at all. After all, we've done it this way for years."
2. *Task group member [second meeting]:* "How are we going to make decisions—majority rule?"
3. *HEART group member [third meeting]:* "You're just here for the paycheck."
4. *HEART group member [first meeting]:* "I'm not sure why I'm even here except to make my mother happy."
5. *Task Group member [first meeting]:* It looks like the legal department has this committee membership stacked. Is there any point in meeting if the decisions have already been made?

Modeled Responses

1. "Gene, we talked about the reason we were convened in the first two meetings. I'm wondering why this is coming up at this point?"
2. [*to the group*] "What do you think are the pros and cons of different decision-making options?"
3. [*inquisitively*] "It is true that I'm paid for this work, but it sounds like there really something more behind your statement."
4. [*to the group*] "I wonder if some other folks here share that feeling?"
5. It sounds like you have two concerns, who is here and why we are here. I assure you that the decisions have not been made, so the group's input is important and timely. I wonder though, who is missing? What other perspectives do we need around the table?

Chapter 17 Confrontation, Interpretation, and Additive Empathy
Skill Development Exercises in Additive Empathy and Interpretation

To assist you in advancing your skills in responding with interpretation and additive empathy, we provide the following exercises. Read each client message, determine the type of response required, and formulate a written response that you would employ if you were in an actual session with the client. Keep in mind the guidelines for employing interpretive and additive empathic responses. Compare your responses with the modeled responses provided at the end of the exercises.

Client Statements

1. **White female client** [*to African American male social worker*]: You seem to be accepting of white people—at least you have been of me. But somehow I still feel uneasy with you. I guess it's just me. I haven't really known many black people very well.
2. **Married woman, age 28:** I feel I don't have a life of my own. My life is controlled by *his* work, *his* hours, and *his* demands. It's like I don't have an identity of my own.
3. **Prison inmate, age 31** [*1 week before the date of his scheduled parole, which was canceled the preceding week*]: Man, what the hell's going on with me? Here I've been on good behavior for three years and finally got a parole date. You'd think I'd be damned glad to get out of here. So I get all uptight

and get in a brawl in the mess hall. I mean I really blew it, man. Who knows when they'll give me another date?

4. *Male, age 18:* What's the point in talking about going to Trade Tech? I didn't make it in high school, and I won't make it there either. You may as well give up on me—I'm just a dropout in life.

5. *Widow, age 54:* It was Mother's Day last Sunday, and neither of my kids did so much as send me a card. You'd think they could at least acknowledge I'm alive.

6. *Female secretary, age 21:* I don't have any trouble typing when I'm working alone. But if the boss or anyone else is looking over my shoulder, it's like I'm all thumbs. I just seem to tighten up.

7. *Female, age 26, in a committed relationship; she is 5 pounds overweight:* When I make a batch of cookies or a cake on the weekend, Terri [her partner] looks at me with that condemning expression, as though I'm not really trying to keep my weight down. I don't think it's fair just because she doesn't like sweets. I like sweets, but the only time I eat any is on the weekend, and I don't eat much then. I feel I deserve to eat dessert on the weekend at least.

8. **Disabled male recipient of public assistance (with a back condition caused by a recent industrial accident):** This not being able to work is really getting to me. I see my kids needing things I can't afford to get them, and I just feel—I don't know—kind of useless. There's got to be a way of making a living.

9. *Depressed male, age 53:* Yeah, I know I do all right in my work. But that doesn't amount to much. Anyone could do that. That's how I feel about everything I've ever done. Nothing's really amounted to anything.

10. **Mother, age 29, who is alleged to have neglected her children:** I don't know. I'm just so confused. I look at my kids sometimes, and I want to be a better mother. But after they've been fighting, or throwing tantrums, or whining and I lose my cool, I feel like I'd just like to go somewhere—anywhere—and never come back. The kids deserve a better mother.

Modeled Responses for Interpretation and Additive Empathy

1. *[To clarify feelings experienced only vaguely]:* I gather that even though you can't put your finger on why, you're still a little uncomfortable with me. You haven't related closely to that many African Americans, and you're still not altogether sure how much you can trust me.

2. *[Implied wants and goals]:* Sounds like you feel you're just an extension of your husband and that part of you is wanting to find yourself and be a person in your own right.

3. *[Hidden purpose of behavior, underlying feelings]:* So you're pretty confused about what's happened. Fighting in the mess hall when you did just doesn't make sense to you. You know, Carl, about your getting uptight—I guess I'm wondering if you were worried about getting out—worried about whether you could make it outside. I'm wondering if you might have fouled up last week to avoid taking that risk.

4. *[Underlying belief about self]:* Sounds like you feel defeated before you give yourself a chance. Like it's hopeless to even try. Jay, that concerns me because when you think that way about yourself, you are defeated—not because you lack ability but because you think of yourself as destined to fail. That belief itself is your real enemy.

5. *[Deeper feelings]:* You must have felt terribly hurt and resentful that they didn't so much as call you. In fact, you seem to be experiencing those feelings now. It just hurts so much.

6. *[Underlying thoughts and feelings]:* I wonder if, in light of your tightening up, you get to feeling scared, as though you're afraid you won't measure up to their expectations.

7. *[Unrealized strengths]:* I'm impressed with what you just said. It strikes me that you're exercising a lot of control by limiting dessert to weekends and using moderation then. In fact, your self-control seems greater than that of most people. You and Terri have a legitimate difference concerning sweets. But it's exactly that—a difference. Neither view is right nor wrong, and you're entitled to your preference as much as she is entitled to hers.

8. *[Unrealized strength and implied want]:* Steve, I can hear the frustration you're feeling, and I want you to know it reflects some real strength on your part. You want to be self-supporting and be able to provide better for your family. Given that desire, we can explore opportunities for learning new skills that won't require physical strength.

9. *[Underlying pattern of thought]:* Kent, I get the feeling that it wouldn't matter what you did. You could set a world record, and you wouldn't feel it amounted to much. I'm wondering if your difficulty lies more in

long-time feelings you've had about yourself, that you somehow just don't measure up. I'd be interested in hearing more about how you've viewed yourself.

10. *[Underlying feelings and implied wants]:* So your feelings tear you and pull you in different directions. You'd like to be a better mother, and you feel bad when you lose your cool. But sometimes you just feel so overwhelmed and inadequate in coping with the children. Part of you would like to learn to manage the children better, but another part would like to get away from your responsibilities.

Skill Development Exercises in Confrontation

The following exercises involve discrepancies and dysfunctional behavior in all three experiential domains— cognitive/perceptual, emotional, and behavioral. After reading the brief summary of the situation involved and the verbatim exchanges between the client(s) and social worker, identify the type of discrepancy involved and formulate your response (observing the guidelines presented earlier) as though you are the social worker in a real-life situation. Next, compare your response with the modeled one, keeping in mind that the model is only one of many possible appropriate responses. Carefully analyze how your response is similar to or differs from the modeled response and whether you adhered to the guidelines.

Situations and Dialogue

1. You have been working with Mr. Lyon for several weeks, following his referral by the court after being convicted for sexually molesting his teenage daughter. Mr. Lyon has been 15 minutes late for his last two appointments, and today he is 20 minutes late. During his sessions he has explored and worked on problems only superficially.

   Client: Sorry to be late today. Traffic was sure heavy. You know how that goes.

2. The clients are marital partners whom you have seen conjointly five times. One of their goals is to reduce marital conflict by avoiding getting into arguments that create mutual resentments.

   Mrs. J: This week has been just awful. I've tried to look nice and have his meals on time—like he said he wanted—and I've just felt so discouraged. He got on my back Tuesday and ... *[Husband interrupts.]*

   Mr. J [angrily]: Just a minute. You're only telling half the story. You left out what you did Monday. *[She interrupts.]*

   Mrs. J: Oh, forget it. What's the use? He doesn't care about me. He couldn't, the way he treats me. *[Mr. J shakes head in disgust]*

3. The client is a young adult who has a slight a mental disability. He was referred by a rehabilitation agency because of social and emotional problems. The client has indicated a strong interest in dating young women and has been vigorously pursuing a clerk (Sue) in a local supermarket. She has registered no interest in him and obviously has attempted to discourage him from further efforts. The following excerpt occurs in the seventh session.

   Client: I went through Sue's check stand this morning. I told her I'd like to take her to see a movie.

   Social worker: Oh, and what did she say?

   Client: She said she was too busy. I'll wait a couple of weeks and ask her again.

4. Tony, age 16, is a member of a therapy group in a youth correctional institution. In the preceding session, he appeared to gain a sense of power and satisfaction from provoking other members to react angrily and defensively, which disrupted the group process. Tony directs the following message to a group member early in the fourth session.

   Tony: I noticed you trying to get next to Meg at the dance Wednesday. You think you're pretty hot stuff, don't you?

5. The client is a mother, age 26, who keeps feelings inside until they mount out of control, at which time she discharges anger explosively.

   Client: I can't believe my neighbor. She sends her kids over to play with Sandra at lunchtime and disappears. It's obvious her kids haven't had lunch, and I end up feeding them, even though she's better off financially than I am.

   Social worker: It sounds as if you have some feelings about that. What do you feel when she does that?

   Client: Oh, not much, I guess. But I think it's a rotten thing to do.

6. You have been working for several weeks with a family that includes the parents and four children

ranging in age from 10 to 17. The mother is a domineering person who acts as spokesperson for the family, and the father is passive and soft-spoken. A teenage daughter, Tina, expresses herself in the following dialogue.

Tina: We always seem to have a hassle when we visit our grandparents. Grandma's so bossy. I don't like going there.

Mother: Tina, that's not true. You've always enjoyed going to her house. You and your grandmother have always been close.

7. Group members in their fifth session have been intently discussing members' social interaction difficulties. One of the members takes the group off on a tangent by describing humorous idiosyncrasies of a person she met while on vacation, and the other group members follow suit by sharing humorous anecdotes about "oddballs" they have encountered.

8. The client is an attractive, personable, and intelligent woman who has been married for 3 years to a self-centered, critical man. In the fourth session (an individual interview), she tearfully makes the following statements:

Client: I've done everything he's asked of me. I've lost 10 pounds. I support him in his work. I golf with him. I even changed my religion to please him. And he's still not happy with me. There's just something wrong with me.

9. The clients are a married couple in their early thirties. The following excerpt occurs in the initial interview.

Wife: We just seem to fight over the smallest things. When he gets really mad, he loses his temper and knocks me around.

Husband: The real problem is that she puts her parents ahead of me. She's the one who needs help, not me. If she'd get straightened out, I wouldn't lose my temper. Tell her where her first responsibility is. I've tried, and she won't listen to me.

10. The clients are a family consisting of the parents and two children. Taylor, age 15, has been truant from school and smoking marijuana. Angie, age 16, is a model student and is obviously her parents' favorite. The family was referred by the school when Taylor was expelled for several days. The father, a highly successful businessman, entered family therapy with obvious reluctance, which has continued to this, the fourth session.

Mother: Things haven't been much different this week. Everyone's been busy, and we really haven't seen much of each other.

Father: I think we'd better plan to skip the next 3 weeks. Things have been going pretty well, and I have an audit in process at the office that's going to put me in a time bind.

Modeled Responses for Confrontation

1. *[Irresponsible behavior by the client]*: Ted, I'm concerned you're late today. This is the third time in a row you've been late, and it shortens the time available to us. But my concerns go beyond that. I know you don't like having to come here and that you'd like to be out from under the court's jurisdiction. But the way you're going about things won't accomplish that. I can't be helpful to you and can't write a favorable report to the court if you just go through the motions of coming here for help. Apparently it's uncomfortable for you to come. I'd be interested in hearing just what you're feeling about coming.

2. *[Discrepancy between purported goal and behavior, as well as dysfunctional communication]*: Let's stop and look at what you're doing right now. I'm concerned because each of you wants to feel closer to the other, but what you're both doing just makes each other defensive.

    [To husband]: Mr. J, she was sharing some important feelings with you, and you cut her off.

    [To wife]: And you did the same thing, Mrs. J, when he was talking.

    [To both]: I know you may not agree, but it's important to hear each other out and to try to understand. If you keep interrupting and trying to blame each other, as you've both been doing, you're going to stay at square one, and I don't want that to happen. Let's go back and start over, but this time put yourself in the shoes of the other and try to understand. Check out with the other if you really understood. Then you can express your own views.

3. *[Dysfunctional, self-defeating behavior]*: Pete, I know how much you think of Sue and how you'd

like to date her. I'm concerned that you keep asking her out, though, because she never accepts and doesn't appear to want to go out with you. My concern is that you're setting yourself up for hurt and disappointment. I'd like to see you get a girlfriend, but your chances of getting a date are probably a lot better with persons other than Sue.

4. *[Abrasive, provocative behavior]:* Hold on a minute, guys. I'm feeling uncomfortable and concerned right now about what Tony just said. It comes across as a real put-down, and we agreed earlier that one of our rules was to support and help each other. Tony, would you like some feedback from other members about how you're coming across to the group?

5. *[Discrepancy between expressed and actual feeling]:* I agree. But I'm concerned about your saying you don't feel much. I should think you'd be ticked off and want to change the situation. Let's see if you can get in touch with your feelings. Picture yourself at home at noon and your neighbor's kids knock on the door while you're fixing lunch. Can you picture it? What are you feeling in your body and thinking just now?

6. *[Dysfunctional communication, disconfirming Tina's feelings and experiences]:* What did you just do, Mrs. Black? Stop and think for a moment about how you responded to Tina's message. It may help you to understand why she doesn't share more with you. *[or]* Tina, could you tell your mother what you're feeling right now about what she just said? I'd like her to get some feedback that could help her communicate better with you.

7. *[Discrepancy between goals and behavior, getting off topic]:* I'm concerned about what the group's doing right now. What do you think is happening?

8. *[Misconception about the self, cognitive/perceptual discrepancy]:* Jan, I'm concerned about what you just said because you're putting yourself down and leaving no room to feel good about yourself. You're assuming that you own the problem and that you're deficient in some way. I'm not at all sure that's the problem. You're married to a man who seems impossible to please, and that is more likely the problem. As we agreed earlier, you have tasks of feeling good about yourself, standing up for yourself, and letting your husband's problem be his problem. As long as your feelings about yourself depend on his approval, you're going to feel down on yourself.

9. *[Manipulative behavior]:* I don't know the two of you well enough to presume to know what's causing your problems. *[To wife]* When you say "knock around", what are you referring to?

[To husband]: If you're expecting me to tell your wife to shape up, you'll be disappointed. My job is to help each of you to see your part in the difficulties and to make appropriate changes such that you resolve such challenges in safe, non violent ways. If I did what you asked, I'd be doing both of you a gross disservice. Things don't get better that way.

10. *[Discrepancy between behavior and purported goals]:* What you do, of course, is up to you. I am concerned, however, because you all agreed you wanted to relate more closely as family members and give one another more support. To accomplish that means you have to work at it steadily, or things aren't likely to change much.

[To father]: My impression is that you're backing off. I know your business is important, but I guess you have to decide whether you're really committed to the goals you set for yourselves.

Chapter 18 The Management of Barriers to Change
Skill Development Exercises

1. Think about what your thoughts and reactions might be in the following situations. Then assess the nature of your reaction.
   - You are an only child. Your client has four children and the house is a mess. The oldest child, age 14, complains that her mother rarely pays attention to her.
   - Both of your parents were heavy drinkers, and at times they were difficult. Your client becomes abusive to his wife and children when he has been drinking.
   - You grew up in a middle-class family. A majority of the clients that you work with are poor, and many live in homes where there is evidence of rodents.
   - A co-worker in the residential facility for minors where you work has posted pictures of former residents on his My Space page, indicating that these clients are friends.

2. Review the case examples in this chapter in which the social worker was over- or under-involved. As a

colleague, what advice would you offer? What are the ethical and legal implications of the social worker's behavior in these cases?

3. After reading the section on cross-cultural barriers, what did you learn that could inform your practice with clients who are different?
4. Reflect on an occasion in which you had a strong reaction to a client. How would you handle the situation after reading this chapter?
5. Develop a checklist for yourself, using the barriers to change discussed in this chapter. Use the checklist that you developed as a self-assessment tool that you could use in your work with clients.

Skill Development Exercises in Managing Relational Reactions and Opposition

The following exercises are intended to assist you in expanding your skills in responding appropriately to relational reactions and opposition to change. Study each client message and determine whether a relational reaction or opposition to change might be involved. Then write the response you would give if you were the social worker. Compare your response with the modeled response provided at the end of the exercises. Bear in mind that the modeled response is only one of many possible appropriate responses.

Client Statements

1. *Male client* [*has been discussing feelings of rejection and self-doubt after his partner broke up with him; suddenly he looks down, sighs, then looks up*]: Say, did I tell you I got promoted at work?
2. *Female client, age 23* [*to male social worker, age 25*]: I've been feeling very close to you these past weeks. I was wondering if you could hold me in your arms for just a moment.
3. *Male client, age 27* [*agitated*]: I've been coming to see you for 8 weeks, and things haven't changed a bit. I'm beginning to question whether you are able to help me.
4. *Delinquent on probation, age 16:* I think it's crazy to have to come here every week. You don't have to worry about me. I'm not getting into any trouble.
5. *Female in welfare-to-work program:* Sure, you say you want to help me. All you social workers are just alike. You don't understand the pressure I have to get a good job in the time I have left on welfare. If you really want to help, you would increase the time I have left.
6. *Client, age 27* [*to male social worker*]: I've just never been able to trust men. My old man was an alcoholic, and the only thing you could depend on with him was that he'd be drunk when you needed him most.
7. *Male client* [*to female mental health social worker*]: Sometimes I really felt I was cheated in life, you know, with parents who didn't give a damn about what happened to me. I think about you—how warm and caring you are, and—I know it sounds crazy but I wish I'd had you for a mother. Sometimes I even daydream about it.
8. *Client* [*after an emotional prior session, the client yawns, looks out the window, and comments*]: Not much to talk about today. Nothing much has happened this week.
9. *Male client, age 24* [*in fifth session*]: I have this thing where people never measure up to my expectations. I know I expect too much, and I always end up feeling let down.
10. *Middle-aged minority male* [*challenging*]: I suppose you see me in the usual stereotype, you people have for [minority] males. I want you to know that I'm ambitious and want to do right by my family. I just need a job right now.

Modeled Responses

1. "Congratulations! No, you didn't tell me about your promotion, but before you do, I'd like to know more about what you were feeling just a moment ago when you were discussing your breakup with your partner. I was sensing that that you don't want to talk about this. Let's focus on how you feel about this situation."
2. "I'm flattered that you would want me to hold you and pleased you could share those feelings with me. I also feel close to you, too, but if I were to become romantically inclined toward you, I'd be letting you down and couldn't be helpful to you. I hope you can understand."
3. "I can see you're anxious to get things worked out, and that's a plus. [*Positive connotation.*] But you're pretty unhappy with your progress and seem to feel that I am not doing my job. I'd like to better understand your feelings. What do you feel I should be doing differently?" [*Exploring feelings and expectations.*]
4. "You sound pretty angry about having to report to me each week. I can't blame you for that. Still, the judge ordered it, and neither of us really has any

choice. How do you suggest that we make the best of the situation?"

5. "I'm sorry you feel I'm not really interested in helping you. I gather you've had some bad experiences with other caseworkers, and I hope our relationship can be better. I sense your frustration at working under this time pressure and your anxiety about what will occur if you don't succeed in the time available. I will work with you to make the best use of the time to get a job you can feel good about. Sometimes as we come to the end of the time frame there are some possibilities for an extension, but that can't be guaranteed. I wonder if the best use of our time might be to do the best we can to get the kind of job you want in the time available."

6. "I can understand, then, that you might find it difficult to trust me—wondering if I'm really dependable."

7. [*Smiling.*] "Thank you for the compliment. I gather you've been experiencing my care for you and find yourself longing for the love and care you didn't receive as a child. I can sense your feelings keenly and appreciate your sharing them."

8. "Somehow that doesn't fit with what we talked about last week. You expressed some very deep feelings about yourself and your marriage. I'd like to hear what you've been feeling about what we discussed last time."

9. "I wonder if that's what you're feeling just now in our relationship—that I haven't measured up to your expectations in some way. Could you share with me what you're feeling?"

10. "I appreciate your sharing those feelings with me. I understand how your life experiences would cause you to reach this conclusion about me. Because of this experience, I gather you've wondered how I see you. I won't say to you that I am not like that. I will tell you that I do see you are as responsible person, and that I appreciate this quality in you."

Chapter 19 Evaluation and Termination
Skills Development Exercises in Evaluation and Termination

In the companion video, Problem Solving with the Corning Family, in Ali's last session with Angela and Irwin Corning, she engages the couple in reflecting on the aspects of the helping process that were helpful and unhelpful to them. Based on your knowledge of evaluation and termination, address the following questions:

1. What goals were reached during the course of the Corning's work with Ali?
2. What goals were not achieved?
3. How could the worker evaluate the efficacy of the helping process, beyond asking for the clients' general feedback?
4. Based on the feedback Irwin and Angela provided, what further questions might Ali have asked to evaluate her intervention?
5. What risks do the Cornings face that might lead to a recurrence of problems?
6. What might Ali do in the final session to address those risks?
7. What feelings do Ali and her clients have about termination?
8. What steps might Ali take to strengthen her termination session with the Cornings?

Notes

Chapter 2 The Domain, Philosophy, and Roles of Direct Practice

1. Some argue that currently social workers are more likely to espouse social justice than to prioritize strategies to achieve it. They assert that the profession appears to aim more at protecting social work roles than transforming social service delivery (Jacobson, 2001).

Chapter 3 Helping Process Overview

1. The idea of specific phases and their accompanying tasks in structuring casework was originally developed by Jessie Taft and Virginia Robinson and the Functional School. This concept was later extended by Reid (2000) and Epstein and Brown (2002) in the task-centered approach.
2. Lila George, Research Director, Leech Lake Tribe (personal communication, 1993).

Chapter 5 Empathy and Authenticity: The Building Blocks of Communication

1. Such highlighting of opposing feelings is a key technique for assisting clients in assessing their readiness for change in the motivational interviewing method (Miller & Rollnick, 2002).
2. In categorizing her husband as a "bump on a log," the wife makes a sweeping generalization that fits her husband's behavior into a mold. Although the social worker chose to keep the focus momentarily on the husband, it is important that he helps the couple to avoid labeling each other. Strategies for intervening when clients use labels are delineated in a later chapter.

Chapter 6 The Skills of Verbal Following, Exploring, and Focusing

1. In the Motivational Interviewing approach, reflection refers to the process of using new words to describe either the content of a message or emotions entailed. We have chosen to follow Hackney and Cormier's (2005) description of paraphrasing as the use of new words to describe the content of a message. We have reserved the term reflection to refer to the use of fresh words to express an emotion.
2. Note that several of these messages could also be categorized as seeking concreteness. Messages that seek concreteness and open-ended messages are not mutually exclusive; indeed, they often overlap to a considerable extent

Chapter 7 Avoiding Counterproductive Communication Patterns

1. It is important not to set up artificial dichotomies that do not represent actual behaviors. Emma Gross (1995) argues, for example, that too frequently writers have inappropriately generalized across Native American cultures.
2. Note that opinions are not unanimous about the meaning of client anger in response to an interpretation. Some would suggest that such anger might indicate that the interpretation was on target but painful nonetheless. We take the position that this could be accurate but we generally reject the view that it is the social worker's role to confront defenses. Rather we would try to explore obstacles together including angry feelings as clues about conscious and less conscious responses.

Chapter 8 Assessment: Problems and Strengths

1. See the US Department of Health and Human Services Substance Abuse and Mental Health Services Administration (www.samhsa.gov), the North Carolina Evidence Based Practice Center (www.ncebpcenter.org), the National Institute of Mental Health (http://www.nimh,nih.gov), the Cochrane Collaboration (http://www.cochrane.org), and the Campbell Collaboration (http://www.campbellcollaboration.org) for toolkits, and other resources for evidence-based practice in an array of problem areas.
2. For more information, consult WALMYR Publishing Company, P.O. Box 12217, Tallahassee, FL 32317. (850) 383-0970. E-mail:scales@walmyr.com. Or visit www.walmyr.com.

Chapter 9 Intrapersonal, Interpersonal, and Environmental Factors in Assessment

1. Bernhardt and Rauch (1993) offer an informative guide for social workers interested in learning more about the genetic basis for illnesses and about conducting genetic family histories.
2. See Bentley and Walsh (2006) and the National Mental Health Association (www.nmha.org) for further information on psychotropic medications, their effects, and side effects.
3. Article summary by Kate Brockett, MSW.
4. Numerous other resources can assist with assessment of aggression and potential violence. These include: Hare, R. D. (2003). *The Hare Psychopathy Checklist–Revised* (2nd ed.). Toronto, Canada: Multi-Health Systems.

    Feldhaus, K. M., Koziol-McLain, J., Amsbury, H. L., Norton, I. M., Lowenstein, S. R., & Abbott, J. T. (1997). Accuracy of 3 brief screening questions for detecting partner violence in the emergency department. *Journal of the American Medical Association*, 277, 1357–1361.

    The SAVRY Version 2 (Borum et al., 2003) is a 30-item instrument using the structured professional judgment (SPJ) approach to assess violence risk in adolescents aged 12 to 18 years who have been detained or referred for an assessment of violence risk. The Early Assessment Risk List for Boys (EARL-20B), Version 2 (Augimeri, Koegl, Webster, & Levene, 2001), and the Early Assessment Risk List for Girls, (EARL-21G) Version 1 (Levene et al., 2001), are SPJ risk assessment devices for use with children under 12 years of age with disruptive behavior problems. The purpose of these instruments is to increase general understanding of early childhood risk factors for violence and antisociality, provide a structure for developing risk assessment schemas for individual children, and to assist with risk management planning.

    Levene, K. S., Augimeri, L. K., Pepler, D., Walsh, M., Webster, C. D., & Koegl, C. J. (2001). Early Assessment Risk List for Girls: EARL-21G, Version 1, consultation edition. Toronto, Canada: Earlscourt Child and Family Centre.

    The Adolescent and Child Urgent Threat Evaluation (Copeland & Ashley, 2005) is a 27-item assessment tool designed to measure risk of near future harm to self or others (within hours to days) in youth aged 8 to 18 in a variety of settings, including inpatient and outpatient clinics, schools, emergency rooms, and juvenile justice facilities.

    Copeland, R., & Ashley, D. (2005). *Adolescent and child urgent threat evaluation: Professional manual*. Lutz, FL: Psychological Assessment Resources.

Chapter 10 Assessment: Family Functioning in Diverse Family and Cultural Contexts

1. For further reading on family diversity, Demo, D. D., Allen, K. R., & Fine, M. A. (Eds.). (1996). *The Handbook of Family Diversity*. New York: Oxford University Press is recommended. Also, *Child Welfare Journal* (2005) Volume LXXXIV, Number 5, is a special issue devoted to working with immigrants and refugees in child welfare.
2. Jordan and Franklin (Eds) (2011) is a resource for further study on family assessment tools. Refer also to Fontes (2005) and Dubowitz and DePanfilis (Eds) (2000). *Handbook for Child Protection Practice*. Sage Publications.
3. Although our discussion centers largely on families, the concepts presented are pertinent to couples as well.
4. The social worker in this case was Marilyn Luptak, Ph.D., while she was a doctoral student at the University of Minnesota.
5. One of the authors and Patience Togo were the focus group leaders. The groups were a part of an agency's initiative to develop responsive services identified by diverse groups.

Chapter 12 Goal Development and Contract Formulation

1. In addition to the procedures for measurement and monitoring discussed in this book, we recommend Jordan and Franklin (2003), Bloom, Fischer, and Orme (2003), and Corcoran and Fischer (1999) for more in-depth information on standardized instruments and methods to evaluate practice.
2. For those interested in further study on single-subject research, informative resources are Bloom, Fischer, and Orme (2006); Corcoran and Fischer (1999), and Thyer (2001). These texts are informative resources and describe a wide variety of methods that may be used to evaluate practice. *Internet Resource: Evidence-based practice: Young Children with Challenging Behavior*.

Chapter 13 Change-Oriented Strategies: Planning and Implementation

1. For additional information on brief treatment models, see Corwin (2002), Roberts & Greene (2002), and Walsh (2006).
2. Potocky-Tripodi (2002) has written an informative text on "best practices" for social work with immigrants and refugees.
3. For additional information on models and crisis intervention practice, see Parad & Parad (1990, 2006), Roberts (2000), Roberts (2005) the *Crisis Intervention Handbook: Assessment, Treatment and Intervention* (3rd ed.) and Okun (2002). Suggested resources for crisis strategies with minors include the *Journal of Traumatic, Violence and Abuse*, and the *Journal of Aggression Maltreatment and Trauma*. For more extensive information on the early definitions, developments, and critiques of crisis intervention strategies, see Aguilera & Messick (1982), Golan (1978), Puryear (1979), Caplan (1964), and Lukton (1982). For evidence-based approaches to trauma intervention, see Cohen (2003).
4. Cormier, Nurius, and Osborne (2009) is highly recommended as a resource for more comprehensive information on change strategies and skills in cognitive-behavioral therapy and cognitive restructuring. Another resource includes Bergin and Garfield (2004), *Handbook of Psychotherapy and Behavioral Change*. See also Beck's *Handbook of Cognitive-Behavioral Therapies* (2005) for a review of the current state of cognitive therapy. For cognitive therapy specific to children, Reinecke, Dattilio, and Freeman (2003) is an excellent resource. Walen, DiGuiseppe, and Wessler (1980) present and illustrate earlier comprehensive strategies for disputing beliefs.
5. Chapin, R., Nelson-Becker, H., & MacMillan, K. (2006). Strengths-based and solution-focused approaches to practice. In Berkman, B. & D'Ambruson, S. (Eds.) *Handbook of Social Work in Health and Aging*. New York: Oxford University Press; B. O'Connell & S. Palmer, *Handbook of Solution-focused Therapy* (2nd ed.), Sage Publications; A. J. Mcdonald, *Solution-Focused Therapy, Research and Practice*, Sage Publications and M.S. Kelly, J. Kim, & C. Franklin, *Solution-focused Brief Therapy in*

Schools: *A 360 degree View of Research and Practice.* Oxford University Press, Inc.

Chapter 16 Social Work Group Interventions

1. Reid (1997) has reviewed procedures for evaluating outcomes in groups, including group testimonials, content analysis of audiotapes or videotapes, sociometric analysis, self-rating instruments, and other subjective measures. We refer you to Corey & Corey (2006) and Macgowan (2008) for further discussion of evaluative measures.

Chapter 17 Confrontation, Interpretation, and Additive Empathy

1. Claiborn (1982) presents numerous examples of both types of interpretation as well as a comprehensive discussion of this important topic. Other researchers (Beck & Strong, 1982; Claiborn, Crawford, & Hackman, 1983; Dowd & Boroto, 1982; Feldman, Strong, & Danser, 1982; Milne & Dowd, 1983) have also reported findings comparing the effects of different types of interpretations.

Chapter 19 Evaluation and Termination

1. For information on the concepts and steps of termination as they apply to macro practice, we suggest an article by Fauri, Harrigan, and Netting (1998).
2. For an excellent source on the considerations and strategies in termination across settings or using various theoretical orientations, see Walsh (2007).
3. See Meyer (2001) for a discussion of the dynamics of "no shows" and an effective clinical response.
4. For information on services in end-of-life care, see NASW's Standards of Social Work Practice in Palliative and End of Life Care (www.naswdc.org, 2011).
5. Feltenstein (2008); Koob and Le Moal (2008); Matto (2005); Baker, Piper, McCarthy, Majeskie, and Fiore (2004); Smyth (2005); Carroll (1996); Brownell, Marlatt, Lichenstein, and Wilson (1986); Daley (1987, 1991); Marlatt and Gordon (1985); and Catalano, Wells, Jenson, and Hawkins (1989) have authored articles and books that describe the neurobiology of relapse, identify various factors that contribute to relapse, discuss beliefs and myths associated with addictions, and delineate models for relapse education and treatment with addicted and impulse-disordered clients.

Bibliography

A

Abbott, A. A., & Wood, K. M. (2000). Assessment: Techniques and instruments for data collection. In A. Abbott (Ed.), *Alcohol, tobacco, and other drugs: Challenging myths, assessing theories, individualizing interventions* (pp. 159–186). Washington, DC: NASW Press.

Abramovitz, M. (2005). The largely untold story of welfare reform and the human services. *Social Work, 50*, 174–186.

Abramson, J. S. (2002). Interdisciplinary team practice. In A. R. Roberts & G. J. Greene (Eds.), *Social workers' desk reference* (pp. 44–50). New York, NY: Oxford University Press.

Abramson, M. (1985). The autonomy–paternalism dilemma in social work. *Social Work, 27*, 422–427.

Achenbach, T. M. & Rescorla, L. A. (2000). *Manual for the ASEBA preschool forms and profiles*. Burlington, VT: University of Vermont, Department of Psychiatry.

Achenbach, T. M. & Rescorla, L. A. (2001). *Manual for the ASEBA school-age forms and profiles*. Burlington, VT: University of Vermont, Department of Psychiatry.

Ackley, D. C. (1997). *Breaking free of managed care*. Orlando, FL: Guilford Publications.

Adams, J. & Drake, R. (2006). Shared decision-making and evidence-based practice. *Community Mental Health Journal, 42*, 87–105.

Adams, K., Matto, H. & Le Croy, C. (2009). Limitations of evidence-based practice for social work education: Unpacking the complexity. *Journal of Social Work Education, 45*, 165–186.

Agbayani-Siewart, P. (2004). Assumptions of Asian-American similarity: The case of Filipino and Chinese American students. *Social Work, 49*, 39–51.

Aguilar, I. (1972). Initial contact with Mexican-American families. *Social Work, 20*, 379–382.

Aguilera, A., Gerza, M. J., & Munoz, R. F. (2010). Group cognitive-behavioral therapy for depression in Spanish: Culture-sensitive manualized treatment in practice. *Journal of Clinical Psychology: In Session, 66*(8), 857–867.

Aguilera, D., & Messick, J. (1982). *Crisis intervention: Theory and methodology* (4th ed.). St. Louis, MO: Mosby.

Ahijevych, K., & Wewers, M. (1993). Factors associated with nicotine dependence among African American women cigarette smokers. *Research in Nursing and Health, 16*, 292–293.

Aisenberg, E. (2008). Evidence-based practice in mental health care to ethnic minority communities: Has its practice fallen short of its evidence? *Social Work, 53*, 297–306.

Albert, V. (2000). Redefining welfare benefits: Consequences for adequacy and eligibility benefits. *Social Work, 45*, 300–310.

Alcabes, A. A., & Jones, J. A. (1985). Structural determinants of clienthood. *Social Work, 30*, 49–55.

Alexander, R., Jr. (2003). *Understanding legal concepts that influence social welfare policy and practice*. Pacific Grove, CA: Brooks/Cole, Thomson Learning.

Alexander, R. Jr. (2010). *Human Behavior in the Social Environment: A Macro, National, and International Perspective*. Newbury Park, CA: SAGE Publications, Inc.

Al-Krenawi, A. (1998). Reconciling western treatment and traditional healing: A social worker walks with the wind. *Reflections, 4*(3), 6–21.

Al-Krenawi, A., & Graham, J. (2000). Culturally sensitive social practice with Arab clients in mental health settings. *Health and Social Work, 25,* 9–22.

Allen, D. (2007). Black people have been let down by mental health services. *Nursing Standard, 22*(4), 28–31.

Allen, S. & Tracy, E. (Eds.) (2009). *Delivering home-based services: A social work perspective.* New York: Columbia University Press.

Allen-Meares, P. & Garvin, C. (Eds.) (2000). *The handbook of social work direct practice.* Thousand Oaks, CA: Sage.

Alley, G. R., & Brown, L. B. (2002). A diabetes problem-solving support group: Issues, process, and preliminary outcomes. *Social Work in Health Care, 36,* 1–9.

Alpert, L. T. (2005). Social worker's attitudes toward parents of children in child protective services: Evaluation of a family-focused casework training program. *Journal of Family Social Work, 9,* 33–63.

Altman, J., & Gohagen, D. (2009). Work with involuntary clients in child welfare settings. In R. H. Rooney (Ed.). *Strategies for work with involuntary clients* (2nd ed., pp. 334–347). New York, NY: Columbia University Press.

American Association of Retired Persons Foundation. (October, 2007). State fact sheet for grandparents and other relatives raising children. Retrieved from http://www.grandfactsheets.org/state_fact_sheets.cfm

American Association of Suicidology. (2004). *How do you recognize the warning signs of suicide?* Retrieved from http://www.suicidology.org/associations/1045/files/Mnemonic.pdf

American Psychiatric Association. (2000). *Diagnostic and statistical manual for mental disorders* (4th ed. text revision). Washington, DC: American Psychiatric Association.

American Psychiatric Association. (2003). Practice guideline for the assessment and treatment of patients with suicidal behaviors. *American Journal of Psychiatry, 160,* 1–50.

American Psychiatric Association. (2010). *DSM-5 development.* Retrieved from: http://www.dsm5.org/Pages/Default.aspx

Anders, T. F. & Morrison, J. R. (1999). *Interviewing Children and Adolescents: Skills and Strategies for Effective DSM-IV Diagnosis.* New York: Guilford Press.

Anderson, D. (2007). Multicultural group work: A force for developing and healing. *Journal for Specialists in Group Work, 32*(3), 224–244.

Anderson, D. A., & Worthen, D. (1997). Exploring a fourth dimension: Spirituality as a resource for the couple therapist. *Journal of Marital and Family Therapy, 23,* 3–12.

Anderson, S. G., Halter, A. P., & Gryzlak, B. M. (2004). Difficulties after leaving TANF: Inner-city women talk about reasons for retuning to welfare. *Social Work, 49,* 185–194.

Anderson-Butcher, D., Khairallah, A. O., & Race-Bige-low, J. (2004). Mutual support groups for long-term recipients of TANF. *Social Work, 49,* 131–140.

Andrade, J. T. (2009). *Handbook of violence risk assessment and treatment: New approaches for forensic mental health professionals.* New York, NY: Springer Publishing.

Andrews, A. B., & Ben-Arieh, A. (1999). Measuring and monitoring children's well-being across the world. *Social Work, 44,* 105–115.

Andrews, L. B. (2001). *Future perfect: Confronting decisions about genetics.* New York, NY: Columbia University Press.

Anetzberger, G. J., Ishler, K. J., Mostade, J., & Blair, M. (2004). Gray and gay. A community dialogue on issues and concerns of older gays and lesbians. *Journal of Gay and Lesbian Social Services, 17,* 23–45.

Aponte, H. (1982). The person of the therapist: The cornerstone of therapy. *Family Therapy Networker, 21*(46), 19–21.

Applegate, J. S. (1992). The impact of subjective measures on nonbehavioral practice research: Outcome vs. process. *Families in Society, 73,* 100–108.

Arditti, J. A. (2008). Parental imprisonment and family visitation: A brief overview and recommendations for family friendly practice. *CW360°: A comprehensive look at a prevalent child welfare issue* (Spring 2008). Retrieved from http://www.cehd.umn.edu/ssw/cascw/attributes/PDF/publications/CW360.pdf

Areán, P. A., Alexopoulos, G., & Chu, J. P. (2008). Cognitive behavioral case management for depressed low-income older adults. In D. Gallagher-Thompson, A. M. Steffen, L. W. Thompson, D. Gallagher-Thompson, A. M. Steffen, L. W. Thompson (Eds.), *Handbook of behavioral and cognitive therapies with older adults* (pp. 219–232). New York, NY: Springer Science + Business Media.

Arnold, E. M. (2002). End-of-life counseling and care: Assessment, interventions and clinical issues. In A. R. Roberts & G. J. Greene (Eds.), *Social workers' desk reference* (pp. 452–457). New York, NY: Oxford University Press.

Arnowitz, E., Brunswick, L., & Kaplan, B. (1983). Group therapy, with patients in the waiting room of an oncology clinic. *Social Work, 28,* 395–397.

Asai, M. O., & Kameoka, V. A. (2005). The influence of Sekentei on family caregiving and underutilization of social services among Japanese caregivers. *Social Work, 50,* 111–118.

Atchey, R. C. (1991). *Social forces and aging* (6th ed.). Springfield, IL: Charles G. Thomas.

Austin, K. M., Moline, M. E., & Williams, G. T. (1990). *Confronting malpractice: Legal and ethical dilemmas in psychotherapy.* Newbury Park, CA: Sage Publications.

Austin, M. J., Coombs, M., & Barr, B. (2005). Community-centered clinical practice: Is the integration of micro and macro social work practice possible? *Journal of Community Practice, 13*(4), 9–30.

B

Baer, J. (1999). Family relationships, parenting behavior, and adolescent deviance in three ethnic groups. *Families in Society, 80,* 279–285.

Bailey, V. (2001). Cognitive-behavioral therapies for children and adolescents. *Advances in Psychiatric Treatment, 7,* 224–232.

Bailey-Dempsey, C., & Reid, W. J. (1996). Intervention design and development: A case study. *Research on Social Work Practice, 6,* 208–228.

Baker, J., Parks-Savage, A. & Rehfuss, M. (2009). Teaching social skills in a virtual environment: An exploratory study. *The Journal for Specialists in Group Work, 34,* 209–226.

Baker, T. B., Piper, M. E., McCarthy, D. E., Majeskie, M. R., & Fiore, M. C. (2004). Addiction motivation reformulated: An affective processing model of negative reinforcement. *Psychological Review, 11,* 33–51.

Bakker, L., Ward, T., Cryer, M., & Hudson, S. M. (1997). Out of the rut. A cognitive-behavioral treatment program for driving-while-disqualified offenders. *Behavioral Change, 14,* 29–38.

Balgopal, P., & Vassil, T. (1983). *Groups in social work: An ecological perspective.* New York, NY: Macmillan.

Bandura, A. (1977). Self-efficacy: Toward a unifying theory of behavioral change. *Psychological Review, 84,* 191–215.

Bandura, A. (1986). *Social foundations of thought and action.* Englewood Cliffs, NJ: Prentice-Hall.

Bandura, A. (1988). Social cognitive theory. In R. Vasta (Ed.), *Annals of child development: Six theories of child development: Revised formulations and current issues* (pp. 1–60). Greenwich, CT: JAI Press.

Bandura, A. (1997). *Self-efficacy: The exercise of self control.* New York, NY: Freeman.

Bandura, A., & Locke, E. (2003). Negative self-efficacy and goal effects revisited. *Journal of Applied Psychology, 88,* 87–99.

Banerjee, M. M. (2002). Voicing realities and recommending reform in PRWORA. *Social Work, 47,* 315–328.

Barber, J. G. (1995). Working with resistant drug abusers. *Social Work, 40,* 17–23.

Bardach, E. (2009). *A practical policy guide for policy analysis. The eightfold path to more effective problem solving* (3rd ed.). Washington, DC: CQPRESS

Bargal, D. (2004). Groups for reducing intergroup conflicts. In C. D. Garvin, L. M. Gutierrez, & M. J. Galinsky (Eds.), *Handbook of social work with groups* (pp. 292–306). New York, NY: Guilford Press.

Barker, R. L. (1996). *The social work dictionary* (3rd ed.). Washington, DC: NASW Press.

Barker, R. L. (2003). *The social work dictionary* (5th ed.). Washington, DC: NASW Press.

Barnes, A. (2008). Race and hospital diagnoses of schizophrenia and mood disorders. *Social Work, 53,* 77–83.

Barnes, S. L. (2001). Stressors and strengths: A theoretical and practical examination of nuclear, single-parent, and augmented African American families. *Families in Society: The Journal of Contemporary Human Services, 82,* 449–460.

Barsky, A. & Gould, J. (2002). *Clinicians in Court: A Guide to Subpoenas, Depositions, Testifying, and Everything Else You Need to Know.* New York, NY: Guilford Press.

Barth, R., & Schinke, S. (1984). Enhancing the supports of teenage mothers. *Social Casework, 65,* 523–531.

Barth, R. P., Wildfire, J., & Green, R. L. (2006). Placement in to foster care and the interplay of urbanicity, child behavior problems and poverty. *American Journal of Orthopsychiatry, 76,* 358–366.

Bartlett, H. (1970). *The common base of social work practice.* New York, NY: National Association of Social Workers.

Barton, C., & Alexander, J. (1981). Functional family therapy. In A. Gurman & D. Kniskern (Eds.), *Handbook of family therapy* (pp. 403–443). New York, NY: Brunner/Mazel.

Barusch, A. S. (2002). *Foundations of social policy, social justice, public programs, and the social work profession.* Itasca, IL: F. E. Peacock.

Barusch, A. S. (2009). Foundations of social policy, Social justice in human perspective (3rd ed.) Brooks/Cole, Cengage Learning.

Beck, A. (1974). Phases in the development of structure in therapy and encounter groups. In D. Wexler & L. Rice (Eds.), *Innovations in client-centered therapy*. New York, NY: Wiley.

Beck, A., Rush, A., Shaw, B., & Emery, G. (1979). *Cognitive therapy of depression*. New York, NY: Guilford Press.

Beck, A. T. (1967). *Depression*. New York, NY: Harper.

Beck, A. T. (1975). *Cognitive therapy and emotional disorders*. New York, NY: International Universities Press Inc.

Beck, A. T. (1976). *Cognitive therapy and the emotional disorders*. New York, NY: International Universities Press.

Beck, A. T., Steer, R. A., & Brown, G. K. (1996). *BDI-II, Beck depression inventory: Manual*. Boston, MA: Harcourt Brace.

Beck, J. S. (1995). *Cognitive therapy: Basics and beyond*. New York, NY: Guilford Press.

Beck, J. S. (2005). Cognitive therapy for challenging problems. New York: Guilford Press.

Becvar, D. S., & Becvar, R. J. (2000a). *Family therapy: A systemic integration* (4th ed.). Boston, MA: Allyn & Bacon.

Becvar, D. S., & Becvar, R. J. (2000b). Family relationships, parenting behavior, and adolescent deviance in three ethnic groups. *Families in Society, 80*, 279–285.

Behroozi, C. S. (1992). A model for work with involuntary applicants in groups. *Social Work with Groups, 15*, 223–238.

Belkin, L. (1999, October 31). Parents blaming parents. *New York Times Sunday Magazine*, p. F61.

Bell, H. (2003). Strengths and secondary trauma in family violence work. *Social Work, 48*, 513–522.

Bell, J. L. (1995). Traumatic event debriefing: Service delivery designs and the role of social work. *Social Work, 40*, 36–43.

Bell, L. (2001). Patterns of interaction in multidisciplinary child protection teams in New Jersey. *Child Abuse and Neglect, 25*, 65–80.

Bembry, J. X., & Ericson, C. (1999). Therapeutic termination with the early adolescent who has experienced multiple losses. *Child and Adolescent Social Work Journal, 16*, 177–189.

Bennett, C. J., Legon, J., & Zilberfein, F. (1989). The significance of empathy in current hospital based practice. *Social Work in Health Care, 14*(2), 27–41.

Bentley, K. J., & Walsh, J. (2006). *The social worker and psychotropic medication: Toward effective collaboration with mental health clients, families, and providers*. Belmont, CA: Thomson Brooks/Cole.

Bepko, C., & Johnson, T. (2000). Gay and lesbian couples in therapy: Perspectives for the contemporary family therapist. *Journal of Marital and Family Therapy, 26*, 409–419.

Berg, I. K. (1994). *Family-based services: A solution-focused approach*. New York, NY: Norton.

Berg, I. K., & Jaya, A. (1993). Different and same: Family therapy with Asian-American families. *Journal of Marital and Family Therapy, 19*, 31–38.

Berg, I. K., & Kelly, S. (2000). *Building solutions in child protection*. New York, NY: W. W. Norton.

Bergeron, L. R., & Gray, B. (2003). Ethical dilemmas of reporting suspected elder abuse. *Social Work, 48*, 96–105.

Bergin, A. E., & Garfield, S. L. (2004). *Handbook of psychotherapy and behavioral change* (5th ed.). New York, NY: Wiley.

Berkman, B., Chauncey, S., Holmes, W., Daniels, A., Bonander, E., Sampson, S., & Robinson, M. (1999). Standardized screening of elderly patients' needs for social work assessment in primary care. *Health and Social Work, 24*, 9–16.

Berlin, S. B. (1996). Constructivism and the environment: A cognitive-integrative perspective for social work. *Families in Society, 77*, 326–335.

Berlin, S. B. (2001). *Clinical social work: A cognitive-integrative perspective*. New York, NY: Oxford University Press.

Berlin, S. B., & Marsh, J. C. (1993). *Informing practice decisions*. New York, NY: Macmillan.

Berman-Rossi, T., & Kelly, T. B. (2000, February). *Teaching students to understand and utilize the changing paradigm of stage of group development theory*. Paper presented at the 46th annual program meeting of the Council on Social Work Education, New York, NY.

Berman-Rossi, T., & Rossi, P. (1990). Confidentiality and informed consent in school social work. *Social Work in Education, 12*, 195–207.

Bernal, G., & Flores-Ortiz, Y. (1982). Latino families in therapy: Engagement and evaluation. *Journal of Marriage and Family Therapy, 8*, 357–365.

Bernard, H., Burlingame, G., Flores, P., Greene, L., Joyce, A., Kobos, J. C., Feirman, D. (2007). *Practice guidelines for group psychotherapy*. Retrieved from http://www.agpa.org/guidelines/index.html

Bernhardt, B., & Rauch, J. (1993). Genetic family histories: An aid to social work assessment. *Families in Society, 74*, 195–205.

Bernstein, B. (1977). Privileged social work practice. *Social Casework, 66*, 387–393.

Bernstein, B. E., & Hartsell, T. L. (2005). *The portable guide to testifying in court for mental health professionals: An A-Z guide to being an effective witness.* Hoboken, NJ: Wiley.

Bertcher, H., & Maple, F. (1985). Elements and issues in group composition. In P. Glasser, R. Sarri, & R. Vinter (Eds.), *Individual change through small groups* (pp. 180–202). New York, NY: Free Press.

Bertolino, B., & O'Hanlon, B. (2002). *Collaborative, competency-based counseling and therapy.* Boston, MA: Allyn and Bacon.

Beyer, J. A., & Balster, T. C. (2001). Assessment and classification in institutional corrections. In A. Walsh (Ed.), *Correctional assessment, casework, and counseling* (3rd ed.) (pp. 137–159). Lanham, MD: American Correctional Association.

Bibus, A. & Boutte'-Queen, N. (2011). *Regulating social work: A primer on licensing practice.* Chicago, IL: Lyceum

Biestek, F. (1957). *The casework relationship.* Chicago, IL: Loyola University Press.

Bidgood, B., Holosko, M., & Taylor, L. (2003). A new working definition of social work practice: A turtle's view. *Research on Social Work Practice, 13,* 400–408.

Binder, C. (2008). *Medicaid targeted case management (TCM). Benefits.* Congressional Research Service Report for Congress. Retrieved September 29, 2010 from www.pascenter.org/document/RL34426.pdf

Birmaher, B., Williamson, D. E., Dahl, R. E., Axelson, D. A., Kaufman, J., Dorn, L. D., Ryan, N. D. (2004). Clinical presentation and course of depression in youth: does onset in childhood differ from onset in adolescence? *Journal of the American Academy of Child and Adolescent Psychiatry, 43*(1), 63–70.

Black, W. G. (1993). Military induced family separation: A stress reduction intervention. *Social Work, 38,* 273–280.

Block, L. R. (1985). On the potentiality and limits of time: The single-session group and the cancer patient. *Social Work with Groups: A Journal of Community and Clinical Practice, 8,* 81–99.

Block-Lerner, J., Adair, C., Plumb, J., Rhatigan, D. & Orsillo, S. (2007). The case for mindfulness-based approaches in the cultivation of empathy: Does nonjudgmental present moment awareness increase capacity for perspective-taking and empathic concern? *Journal of marital and family therapy, 33:* 501–516.

Bloom, M., Fischer, J., & Orme, J. G. (2003). *Evaluating practice: Guidelines for the accountable professional.* Boston, MA: Allyn & Bacon.

Bloom, M., Fischer, J. & Orme, J. (2006). *Evaluating practice: Guidelines for the accountable professional.* Boston, MA: Allyn and Bacon.

Boehm, A., & Staples, L. H. (2004). Empowerment: The point of view of consumers. *Families in Society: The Journal of Contemporary Human Services, 85,* 270–280.

Boer, D. P., Hart, S. D., Kropp, P. R., & Webster, C. D. (1997). *Manual for the Sexual Violence Risk-20 (SVR-20): Professional guidelines for assessing risk of sexual violence.* Vancouver, Canada: British Columbia Institute Against Family Violence.

Bohart, A. & Greenburg, L. (1997). Empathy and psychotherapy: an introductory overview. In Bohart, A. & Greenburg, L. (eds.) *Empathy reconsidered: new directions in psychotherapy.* Washington, DC: American Psychological Association, pp. 3–31.

Borum, R., Bartel, P., & Forth, A. (2003). *Manual for the Structured Assessment for Violence Risk in Youth (SAVRY): Version 1.1.* Tampa, FL: Louis de la Parte Florida Mental Health Institute, University of South Florida.

Borum, R., & Verhaagen, D. (2006). *Assessing and managing violence risk in juveniles.* New York, NY: Guilford Press.

Borys, D. S., & Pope, K. S. (1989). Dual relationships between therapist and client: A national study of psychologists, psychiatrists, and social workers. *Professional Psychology: Research and Practice, 20,* 283–293.

Bostic, J. Q., Shadid, L. G., & Blotcky, M. J. (1996). Our time is up: Forced terminations during psychotherapy. *American Journal of Psychotherapy, 50,* 347–359.

Bowen, M. (1960). A family concept of schizophrenia. In D. D. Jackson (Ed.). *The etiology of schizophrenia* (pp. 346–372). New York, NY: Basic Books.

Bower, B. (1997). Therapy bonds and the bottle (establishment of therapeutic alliance linked to higher success rate in treatment of alcoholics). *Science News, 152,* 8.

Bowlby, J., (1988). *A secure base: Clinical applications of attachment theory.* London, England: Routledge.

Boyd-Franklin, N. (1989a). *Black families in therapy: A multisystems approach.* New York, NY: Guilford Press.

Boyd-Franklin, N. (1989b). Major family approaches and their relevance to the treatment of black families. In N. Boyd-Franklin, *Black families in therapy: A multisystems approach* (pp. 121–132). New York, NY: Guilford Press.

Boyd-Franklin, N., & Bry, B. H. (2000). *Reaching out in family therapy: Home-based school and community interventions.* New York, NY: Guilford Press.

Bradshaw, W. (1996). Structured group work for individuals with schizophrenia: A coping skills approach. *Research on Social Work Practice, 6,* 139–154.

Brager, G., & Holloway, S. (1978). *Changing human service organizations: Politics and practice.* New York, NY: Free Press.

Brager, G., & Holloway, S. (1983). A process model for changing organizations from within. In R. M. Kramer & H. Specht (Eds.), *Readings in community organization practice* (pp. 198–208). Englewood Cliffs, NJ: Prentice-Hall.

Brehm, S. S. (1976). *The application of social psychology to clinical practice.* New York, NY: Wiley.

Brehm, S. S., & Brehm, J. W. (1981). *Psychological reactance: A theory of freedom and control.* New York, NY: Academic Press.

Brent, D. A., Johnson, B., Bartle, S., Bridge, J., Rather, C., Matta, J., et al. (1993). Personality disorder tendency to impulsive violence, and suicidal behavior in adolescents. *Journal of the American Academy of Child and Adolescent Psychiatry, 32,* 69–75.

Breton, M. (1985). Reaching and engaging people: Issues and practice principles. *Social Work with Groups, 8*(3), 7–21.

Breton, M. (2006). Path dependence and the place of social action in social work. *Social Work with Groups, 29,* 25–44.

Bridges, G. S., & Steen, S. (1998). Racial disparities in official assessments of juvenile offenders: Attributional stereotypes as mediating mechanisms. *American Sociological Review, 63,* 554–570.

Briggs, H. E. & Rzepnicki, T. L. (Eds.) (2004). *Using evidence in social work practice: Behavioral perspectives.* Chicago, IL: Lyceum Books.

Brindis, C., Barth, R. P., & Loomis, A. B. (1987). Continuous counseling: Case management with teenage parents. *Social Casework, 68,* 164–172.

Brissett-Chapman, S. (1997). Child protection risk assessment and African American children: Cultural ramifications for families and communities. *Child Welfare, 76,* 45–63.

Bronfenbrenner, U. (1989). Ecological systems theory. In R. Vasta (Ed.), *Annals of child development: Six theories of child development: Revised formulations and current issues* (pp. 187–247). Greenwich, CT: JAI Press.

Brookins, G. K., Peterson, A. C., & Brooks, L. M. (1997). Youth and families in the inner city: Influencing positive outcomes. In H. J. Walberg, O. Reyes, & R. P. Weissberg (Eds.), *Children and youth: Interdisciplinary perspectives* (pp. 45–66). Thousand Oaks, CA: Sage Publications.

Brooks-Gunn, J., & Duncan, G. J. (1997). The effects of poverty on children: The future of children. *Children and Poverty, 7,* 55–71.

Brown, L. S. (1994). *Subjective dialogues: Theory in feminist therapy.* New York, NY: Basic Books.

Brown, G., Bruce, M., & Pearson, J. (2001). High-risk management guidelines for elderly suicidal patients in primary care settings. *International Journal of Geriatric Psychiatry, 16:* 593–601.

Brownell, K., Marlatt, G., Lichenstein, E., & Wilson, G. T. (1986). Understanding and preventing relapse. *American Psychologist, 41,* 765–782.

Brownlee, K. (1996). Ethics in community mental health care: The ethics of nonsexual relationships: A dilemma for the rural mental health professionals. *Community Mental Health Journal, 32,* 497–503.

Brueggemann, W. G. (2006). *The practice of macro social work* (3rd ed.). Belmont, CA: Thomson-Brooks/Cole.

Brun, C., & Rapp, C. (2001). Strengths-based case management: Individuals' perspectives on strengths and the case manager relationship. *Social Work, 46,* 278–288.

Burford, G. & Hudson, J. (2009). *Family group conferencing: new directions in community centered child and family practice.* Piscataway, NJ: Aldine-Transactions.

Burford, G. & Pennell, J. (2004). From agency client to community-based consumer: The family group conference as a consumer-led group in child welfare. In C. D. Garvin, L. M. Gutierrez, & M. J. Galinsky (Eds.), *Handbook of social work with groups* (pp. 415–431). New York: Guilford Press.

Burghardt, S. (2011). *Macro practice in social work for the 21st Century.* Los Angeles, CA: Sage Publications, Inc.

Burlingame, G. M., Fuhriman, A., & Mosier, J. (2003). The differential effectiveness of group psychotherapy: A meta-analytic perspective. *Group Dynamics: Theory, Research, and Practice, 7*(1), 3–12.

Burlingame, G. M., MacKenzie, K. R., & Strauss, B. (2004). Small group treatment: Evidence for effectiveness and mechanisms of change. In M. Lambert (Ed.), *Bergin and Garfield's handbook of psychotherapy and behavior change* (5th ed., pp. 647–696). New York: Wiley.

Burlingame, G. M., Strauss, B., Joyce, A., MacNair-Semands, R., MacKenzie, K. R., Ogrodniczuk, J., & Taylor, S. (2006). *CORE Battery-Revised: An assessment tool kit for promoting optimal group*

Burnette, D. (1999). Custodial grandparents in Latino families: Patterns of service use and predictors of unmet needs. *Social Work, 44*, 22–34.

Burns, A., Lawlor, B. & Craig, S. (2004). *Assessment scales in old age psychiatry* (2nd ed.). London, England: Martin Dunitz.

Burns, D. (1980). *Feeling good.* New York, NY: Avon Books.

Burns, D. (1995). *The therapist's toolkit: Comprehensive assessment and treatment tools for the mental health professional.* Philadelphia, PA: D. D. Burns.

Buss, T. F., & Gillanders, W. R. (1997). Worry about health status among the elderly: Patient management and health policy implications. *Journal of Health and Social Policy, 8*(4), 53–66.

Butler, S. S., & Hope, B. (1999). Health and wellbeing for late middle-aged and old lesbians in a rural area. *Journal of Gay and Lesbian Social Services, 9* (4), 27–46.

Butz, R. A. (1985). Reporting child abuse and confidentiality in counseling. *Social Casework, 66*, 83–90.

C

Cain, R. (1991a). Relational contexts and information management among gay men. *Families in Society, 72*, 344–352.

Cain, R. (1991b). Stigma management and gay identity development. *Social Work, 36*, 67–71.

Cameron, E., Fox, J., Anderson, M. & Cameron, C. (2010). Resilient youths use humor to enhance socioemotional functioning during a day in the life. *Journal of Adolescent Research 25*(5), 716–742.

Cameron, M. & Keeran, E. (2010). The common factors model: implications for trans-theoretical clinical social work practice. *Social work 55*:1, 63–73.

Cameron, S., & Turtle-Song, I. (2002). Learning to write case notes using the SOAP format. *Journal of Counselling and Development, 80*, 286–292.

The Campbell Collaboration. (n.d.). *The Campbell Collaboration Library of Systematic Reviews.* Retrieved from: http://www.campbellcollaboration.org/library.php

Campbell, J. A. (1988). Client acceptance of single-subject evaluation procedures. *Social Work Research Abstracts, 24*, 21–22.

Campbell, J. A. (1990). Ability of practitioners to estimate client acceptance of single-subject evaluation procedures. *Social Work, 35*, 9–14.

Canda, E. (1983). General implications of Shamanism for clinical social work. *International Social Work, 26*, 14–22.

Canda, E. R. (1997). Spirituality. In R. L. Edwards (Ed.), *Encyclopedia of social work 1997 supplement* (19th ed., pp. 299–309). Washington, DC: NASW Press.

Caplan, G. (1964). *Principles of preventive psychiatry.* New York, NY: Basic Books.

Caplan, T. (1995). Safety and comfort, content and process: Facilitating open group work with men who batter. *Social Work with Groups, 18*(2/3), 33–51.

Caple, F. S., Salcido, R. M., & di Cecco, J. (1995). Engaging effectively with culturally diverse families and children. *Social Work in Education, 17*, 159–169.

Carkhuff, R. (1969). *Helping and human relations: Practice and research.* New York, NY: Holt, Rinehart & Winston.

Carlozzi, A., Bull, K., Stein, L., Ray, K., & Barnes, L. (2002). Empathy theory and practice: A survey of psychologists and counselors. *Journal of Psychology, 36*, 161–171.

Carlton-LaNey, I. (1999). African American social work pioneers' response to need. *Social Work, 44*, 311–321.

Carniol, B. (1992). Structural social work: Maurice Moreau's challenge to social work practice. *Journal of Progressive Human Services, 3*(1), 1–19.

Carr, E. S. (2004). Accessing resources, transforming systems: Group work with poor and homeless people. In C. D. Garvin, L. M. Gutierrez, & M. J. Galinsky (Eds.), *Handbook of social work with groups* (pp. 360–383). New York, NY: Guilford Press.

Carrell, S. (2000). *Group exercises for adolescents: A manual for therapist* (2nd ed.). Thousand Oaks, CA: Sage Publications.

Carroll, K. M. (1996). Relapse prevention as a psychosocial treatment: A review of controlled clinical trials. *Experimental and Clinical Psychopharmacology, 4*, 46–54.

Carter, B., & McGoldrick, M. (Eds.) (1988). *The changing life cycle: A framework for family therapy* (2nd ed.). New York: Gardener Press.

Carter, B., & McGoldrick, M. (1999). Coaching at various stages of the life cycle. In B. Carter & M. McGoldrick (Eds.), *The expanded family life cycle: Individual, family, and social perspectives* (2nd ed., pp. 436–454). Boston: Allyn & Bacon.

Carter, B., & McGoldrick. M. (2005) (Eds.). *The expanded life cycle. Individual, family and social perspectives* (3rd ed.). Boston, MA: Allyn & Bacon.

Carter, C. S. (2000). Church burning: Using a contemporary issue to teach community organization. *Journal of Social Work Education, 36*(1), 79–88.

Case Management Society of America (CMSA) (2010). *Standards of practice for case management.* Little Rock, AR: Author. Retrieved from www.cmsa.org.

Caspi, J. (2008). Building a sibling aggression treatment model: Design and development research in action. *Research on Social Work Practice, 18*, 575–585.

Caspi, J., & Reid, W. J. (2002). *Educational supervision in social work. A task-centered model for field instruction and staff development.* New York, NY: Columbia University Press.

Catalano, R., Wells, E. A., Jenson, J. M., & Hawkins, J. D. (1989). Aftercare services for drug-using institutionalized delinquents. *Social Service Review, 63*, 553–577.

Centers for Disease Control (CDC). (2007). *10 leading causes of death by age group, United States – 2007.* Retrieved from: http://www.cdc.gov/injury/wisqars/pdf/Death_by_Age_2007-a.pdf

Centers for Disease Control and Prevention, National Center for Injury Prevention and Control (2007). *Web-based Injury Statistics Query and Reporting System (WISQARS)* [online data sets]. Retrieved from: http://www.cdc.gov/injury/wisqars/index.html

Center for Economic and Social Justice. (n.d.). *Defining economic and social justice.* Retrieved from http://www.cesj.org/thirdway/economicjustice-defined.htm

Chan, C. L. W., Chan, Y., Lou, V. W. Q. (2002). Evaluating an empowerment group for divorced Chinese women in Hong Kong. *Research on Social Work Practice, 12*, 558–569.

Chandler, S. (1985). Mediation: Conjoint problem solving. *Social Work, 30*, 346–349.

Chapin, R., & Cox, E. O. (2001). Changing the paradigm: Strengths-based and empowerment–oriented social work practice with frail elderly. *Journal of Gerontological Social Work, 36*(3/4), 165–169.

Chapin, R., Nelson-Becker, H. & MacMillan, K. (2006). Strengths-based and solution-focused approaches to practice. In Berkman, B. & D'Ambruson, S. (Eds.), *Handbook of social work in health and aging.* New York: Oxford University Press.

Charnley, H., & Langley, J. (2007). Developing cultural competence as a framework for anti-heterosexist social work practice: Reflections from the UK. *Journal of social work, 7*, 307–321.

Chau, K. L. (1993). Needs assessment for group work with people of color: A conceptual formulation. *Social Work with Groups, 15*(2/3), 53–66.

Chazin, R., Kaplan, S., & Terio, S. (2000). The strengths perspective in brief treatment with culturally diverse clients, *Crisis Intervention, 6*, 41–50.

Chelune, G. J. (1979). Measuring openness in interpersonal communication. In G. Chelune & Associates (Eds.), *Self-disclosure: origins, patterns, and implications of openness in interpersonal relationships.* San Francisco, CA: Jossey-Bass.

Chemtob, C. M., Hamada, R. S., Bauer, G., Torigoe, R. Y., & Kinney, B. (1988). Patient suicide: Frequency and impact on psychologists. *Professional Psychology Research and Practice, 19*, 416–420.

Chen, E. C., Kakkad, D., & Balzano, J. (2008). Multicultural competence and evidence-based practice in group therapy. *Journal of Clinical Psychology: In Session, 64*(11), 1261–1278. Doi:10.1002/jclp.20533

Chen, S. W., & Davenport, D. (2005). Cognitive behavioral therapy with Chinese American clients: Cautions and modifications. *Psychotherapy Theory Research, Practice and Training, 42*(1), 101–110.

Chennon, M. J., Rosenheck, R. A., & Lam, J. A. (2008). Clinical case management racial matching in a program for homeless persons with mental illness. *Psychiatric Services, 51*, 1265–1272.

Chesler, M. (1994). Strategies for multicultural organizational development. *Diversity Factors, 2*(2), 12–18.

Chesler, M. (1994). Organizational development is not the same as multicultural organizational development. In E. Y. Cross, J. H. Katz, F. A. Miller, & E. H. Seashore (Eds.), *The promise of diversity* (pp. 240–351). Burr Ridge, IL: Irwin.

Cheung, M. (2006). *Therapeutic games and guided imagery: Tools for mental health and school professionals working with children, adolescents, and their families.* Chicago, IL: Lyceum Books.

Child Welfare League of America. (1990). *Agency self-improvement checklist.* Washington, DC: Child Welfare League of America.

Chipungu, S. S., & Bent-Goodley, T. B. (2003). *Race, poverty and child maltreatment. APSAC Advisor*, American Professional Society on the Abuse of Children, *15*(2).

Choi, G. (1997). Acculturative stress, social support, and depression in Korean American families. *Journal of Family Social Work, 2*, 79–81.

Christian, J. (2005). Riding the bus: Barriers to prison visitation and family management strategies. *Journal of Contemporary Criminal Justice, 21*, 31–48.

Chu, Y. C., & Rooney, R. R. (2010). Task-centered practice in Taiwan. In A. Fortune, P. McCallion, & K. Briar-Larsen (eds.). *Social work practice research for the Twenty-first century: Building on the legacy of William J. Reid.* Columbia University Press.

Cingolani, J. (1984). Social conflict perspective on work with involuntary clients. *Social Work, 29*, 442–446.

Citron, P. (1978). Group work with alcoholic poly-drug involved adolescents with deviant behavior syndrome. *Social Work with Groups, 1,* 39–52.

Claiborn, C. (1982). Interpretation and change in counseling. *Journal of Counseling Psychology, 29,* 439–453.

Cleaveland, C. (2010). "We are not criminals." Social work advocacy and unauthorized migrants. *Social work.* 55:1: 74–81.

Clifford, D., & Burke, B. (2005). Developing anti-oppression ethics in the new curriculum. *Social Work Education, 87,* 677–692.

Clinical Social Work Federation. (1997). *Definition of clinical social work* (revised). Retrieved from: http://www.cswf.org/ www/info/html

Cnaan, R. A., & Rothman, J. (1986). Conceptualizing community intervention: An empirical test of three models of community organization. *Administration in Social Work, 10*(3), 41–55.

Coady, N. & Lehmann, P. (Eds.) (2008). *Theoretical perspectives for direct social work practice: a generalist-eclectic approach* (2nd ed.). New York, NY: Springer.

Coady, N. F., & Marziali, E. (1994). The association between global and specific measures of the therapeutic relationship. *Psychotherapy, 31,* 17–27.

Cobb, N. H. (2008). Cognitive-behavioral theory and treatment. In N. Coady & P. Lehmann (Eds.), *Theoretical perspectives for direct social work practice: A generalist-eclectic approach* (2nd ed., pp. 221–248). New York, NY: Springer Publishing Company.

The Cochrane Collaboration. (2010). *Cochrane Reviews.* Retrieved from: http://www.cochrane.org/cochrane-reviews

Cohen, E. D., & Cohen, G. S. (1999). *The virtuous therapist: Ethical practice of counseling and psychotherapy.* Belmont, CA: Brooks/Cole.

Cohen, J. A. (2003). Treating acute posttraumatic reactions in children and adolescents. *Biological Psychiatry, 53,* 827–833.

Coholic, D., Lougheed, S. & Cadell, S. (2009). Exploring the helpfulness of arts-based methods with children living in foster care. *Traumatology, 15*(3), 64–71.

Collins, G. (2007, October 18). None dare call it child care. *The New York Times,* A27.

Collins, M. E., Stevens, J. W., & Lane, T. C. (2000). Teenage parents and welfare reform: Findings from a survey of teenagers affected by living requirements. *Social Work, 45,* 327–338.

Collins, P. M., Kayser, K., & Platt, S. (1994). Conjoint marital therapy: A social worker's approach to single-system evaluation. *Families in Society, 71,* 461–470.

Colvin, J., Lee, M., Maganano, J., & Smith, V. (2008). The partners in prevention program: The evaluation and evolution of the task-centered case management model. *Research on Social Work Practice, 18,* 607–615.

Comer, E., Meier, A., & Galinsky, M. J. (2004). Development of innovative group work practice using the intervention research paradigm. *Social Work, 49,* 250–260.

Comfort, M. (2008). Doing time together: *Love and family in the shadow of the prison.* Chicago, IL: University of Chicago Press.

Compton, B. R., & Galaway, B. (1994). *Social work processes* (6th ed.). Pacific Grove, CA: Brooks/Cole.

Compton, B., Galaway, B., & Cournoyer, B. (2005). *Social work processes* (7th ed.). Pacific Grove, CA: Brooks/Cole.

Condrey, S. E., Facer, R. L., & Hamilton, J. P. (2005). Employees amidst welfare reform: TANF employees overall and organizational job satisfaction. *Journal of Human Behavior in the Social Environment, 12,* 221–242.

Congress, E. P. (1994). The use of culturegrams to assess and empower culturally diverse families. *Families in Society, 75,* 531–540.

Congress, E. P. (2000). Crisis intervention with diverse families. In A. R. Roberts (Ed.). *Crisis intervention handbook: Assessment, treatment and research* (2nd ed., pp. 430–448), New York, NY: Oxford University Press.

Congress, E. P. (2002). Using the culturegram with diverse families. In A. R. Roberts & G. J. Green (Eds.), *Social workers' desk reference* (pp. 57–61). New York, NY: Oxford University Press.

Congress, E. P., & Kung, W. W. (2005). *Using the culturalgram to assess and empower culturally diverse families.* In E. P. Congress and M. Gonzalez (Eds.), *Multicultural perspectives in working with families* (pp. 3–21). New York, NY: Springer.

Congress, E. P., & Lynn, M. (1994). Group work programs in public schools: Ethical dilemmas and cultural diversity. *Social Work in Education, 15,* 107–114.

Congress, E. P. & Lynn, M. (1997). Group work practice in the community: Navigating the slippery slope of ethical dilemmas. *Social Work with Groups, 20*(3), 61–74.

Conner, K., & Grote, N. K. (2008). Enhancing the cultural relevance of empirically-supported mental health interventions. *Families in Society, 89,* 587–595.

Connolly, C. M. (2006). A feminist perspective of resilience in lesbian couples. Journal of *Feminist Family Therapy, 18*(1/2), 137–162.

Constable, R., & Lee, D. B. (2004). *Social work with families: Content and process.* Chicago, IL: Lyceum Books.

Cook, J. B., & Kaffenberger, C. J. (2003). Solution shop: A solution-focused counseling and study skills program for middle school. *Professional Counseling Journal, 7*(12), 116–124.

Copeland, R., & Ashley, D. (2005). *Adolescent and child urgent threat evaluation: Professional manual.* Lutz, FL: Psychological Assessment Resources.

Corcoran, J. (1997). A solution-oriented approach to working with juvenile offenders, Child and Adolescent *Social Work Journal, 14*, 227–288.

Corcoran, J. (1998). Solution-focused practice with middle and high school at-risk youth. *Social Work in Education, 20*, 232–243.

Corcoran, J. (2000). *Evidence based practice with families: A lifespan approach.* New York, NY: Springer.

Corcoran, J. (2002). Evidence based treatment of adolescents with externalizing disorders. In A. R. Roberts & G. J. Greene (Eds.), *Social workers' desk reference* (pp. 793–796. New York, NY: Oxford University Press.

Corcoran, J. (2008). Solution-focused therapy. In N. Coady & P. Lehmann (Eds.), Theoretical perspectives for direct social work practice. *A generalist-eclectic approach* (2nd ed., pp. 429–446). New York, NY: Springer Publishing Company.

Corcoran, J., & Franklin, C. (1998). A solution-focused approach to physical abuse. *Journal of Family Psychotherapy, 9*, 69–73.

Corcoran, J., & Pillai, (2009). A review of the research on solution-focused based therapy. *British Journal of Social Work, 39*, 234–242.

Corcoran, J., & Stephenson, M. (2000). The effectiveness of solution-focused therapy with child behavior problems: A preliminary report. *Families in Society: The Journal of Contemporary Human Services, 81*, 468–474.

Corcoran, J. & Walsh, J. (2010). *Clinical assessment and diagnosis in social work practice* (2nd ed.), New York: Oxford University Press.

Corcoran, J. A. (2006). A comparison study of solution-focused brief therapy versus treatment-as-usual for behavior problems in children. *Journal of Social Service Review, 22*, 69–81.

Corcoran, K., & Fisher, J. (1999). *Measures for clinical practice* (3rd ed.). New York, NY: Free Press.

Corcoran, K., & Vandiver, V. (1996). *Maneuvering the maze of managed care: Skills for mental health practitioners.* New York, NY: Free Press.

Corey, G. (1990). *Theory and practice of group counseling.* Pacific Grove, CA: Brooks/Cole.

Corey, G. (2009). *Theory and practice of counseling and psychotherapy* (8th ed.). Belmont, CA: Brooks/Cole-Cengage Learning

Corey, G., Corey, M. S., & Callanan, P. (2007). *Issues and ethics in the helping professions* (7th ed.). Pacific Grove, CA: Brooks/Cole.

Corey, G., Corey, M. S., Callahan, P. J., & Russell, J. M. (2004). *Group techniques* (3rd ed.). Pacific Grove, CA: Brooks/Cole.

Corey, M. S. & Corey, G. (1992). *Groups: Process and practice* (4th ed.). Pacific Grove, CA: Brooks/Cole.

Corey, M. S. & Corey, G. (2002). *Groups: Process and practice* (6th ed.). Pacific Grove, CA: Brooks/Cole.

Corey, M. S., & Corey, G. (2006). *Groups: Process and practice* (7th ed.). Pacific Grove, CA: Brooks/Cole.

Cormier, S., & Nurius, P. S. (2003). *Interviewing and change strategies for helpers: Fundamental skills and cognitive behavioral interventions.* Pacific Grove, CA: Brooks/Cole, Thomson Learning.

Cormier, S., Nurius, P. S., & Osborn, C. J. (2009). *Interviewing and change strategies for helpers: Fundamental skills in cognitive behavioral interventions* (6th ed.). Belmont, CA: Brooks Cole.

Cormier, W., & Cormier, L. (1979). *Interviewing strategies for helpers. A guide to assessment, treatment, and evaluation.* Pacific Grove, CA: Brooks/Cole.

Cornelius, L. J., Simpson, G. M., Ting, L., Wiggins, E., & Lipford, S. (2003). Reach out and I'll be there: Mental health crisis intervention and mobile outreach services to urban African Americans. *Health and Social Work, 28*, 74–78.

Corwin, M. (2002). *Brief treatment in clinical social work practice.* Pacific Grove, CA: Brooks/Cole.

Costello, E. J., Compton, S. N., Keeler, G., & Angold, A. (2003). Relationship between poverty and psychopathology: A natural experiment. *Journal of the American Medical Association, 290*, 2023–2029.

Council on Social Work Education. (2008). *Educational policy and accreditation standards.* Washington, DC: Council on Social Work Education. Retrieved from: http://www.cswe.org/File.aspx?id=13780

Cournoyer, B. (2004). *Evidence-based social work practice skills book.* New York, NY: Allyn-Bacon.

Cournoyer, B. R. (1991). *Selected techniques for eclectic practice: Clinically speaking.* Indianapolis, IN: Author.

Cournoyer, B. R. (2011). *The social work skills workbook* (6th ed.). Belmont, CA: Brooks/Coles-Cengage Learning.

Courtney, M. (1999). *Challenges and opportunities posed by the reform era*. Presented at the "Reconciling welfare reform with child welfare" conference. Center for Advanced Studies in Child Welfare, University of Minnesota, February 26.

Cowger, C. (1997). Assessing client improvement. In D. Saleebey (Ed.). *The strengths perspective* (2nd ed., pp. 52–73), White Plains, NY: Longman.

Cowger, C. D. (1992). Assessment of client strengths. In D. Saleeby (Ed.). *The strengths perspective in social work practice* (pp. 139–147). New York, NY: Longman.

Cowger, C. D. (1994). Assessing client strengths: Clinical assessment for client empowerment. *Social Work, 39*, 262–267.

Cox, E. O. (1991). The critical role of social action in empowerment oriented groups. *Social Work with Groups, 14*(3/4), 77–90.

Crabtree, B. F., & Miller, W. L. (1992). *Doing qualitative research*. Newbury Park, CA: Sage Publications.

CRAFFT. (n.d.). Retrieved September 1, 2008, from http://www.projectcork.org/clinical_tools/pdf/CRAFFT.pdf

Cross, T. L., Bazron, B. J., Dennis, K., & Issacs, M. R. (1989). *Toward a culturally competent system of care*. Washington, DC: Georgetown University Child Development Center.

Crosson-Tower, C. (2004). *Exploring child welfare: A practice perspective*. Boston, MA: Allyn & Bacon.

Cummings, N. A. (1991). Brief intermittent therapy throughout the life cycle. In C. S. Austad & W. H. Berman (Eds.), *Psychotherapy in managed health care: The optimal use of time and resources* (pp. 35–45). Washington, DC: American Psychological Association.

Cunningham, M. (2003). Impact of trauma social work clinicians: Empirical findings. *Social Work, 48*, 451–459.

Curry, R. (2007). Surviving professional stress. *Social Work Today* (November/December), 25–28.

Curtis, C. M., & Denby, R. W (2004). Impact of the Adoption and Safe Family Act on families of color: Workers share their thoughts. *Families in Society, 85*, 71–79.

D

Dahlen, E. R., & Deffenbacher, J. L. (2000). A partial component analysis of Beck's cognitive therapy for anger control. *Journal of Cognitive Psychotherapy, 14*, 77–95.

Daley, D. C. (1987). Relapse prevention with substance abusers: Clinical issues and myths. *Social Work, 32*, 138–142.

Daley, D. C. (1991). *Kicking addictive habits once and for all: A relapse prevention guide*. New York, NY: Lexington.

Dane, B. (2000). Child welfare workers: An innovative approach for interacting with secondary trauma. *Journal of Social Work Education, 36*, 27–38.

Dane, B. O., & Simon, B. L. (1991). Resident guests: Social workers in host settings. *Social Work, 36*, 208–213.

Danish, J., D'Augelli, A., & Hauer, A. (1980). *Helping skills: A basic training program*. New York, NY: Human Sciences Press.

Danzy, J., & Jackson, S. M. (1997). Family preservation and support services: A missed opportunity. *Child Welfare, 76*, 31.

Davis, B. (2005). Ms. Palmer on second street. *Social Work, 50*, 89–92.

Davis, I. P., & Reid, W. J. (1988). Event analysis in clinical practice and process research. *Social Casework, 69*, 298–306.

Davis, L. E., Galinsky, M. J., & Schopler, J. H. (1995). RAP: A framework for leadership of multiracial groups. *Social Work, 40*, 155–165.

Davis, L. E., & Gelsomino, J. (1994). An assessment of practitioner cross-racial treatment experiences. *Social Work, 39*, 116–123.

Deal, K. H. (1999). Clinical social work students' use of self-disclosure: A case for formal training. *Arete, 23*(3), 33–45.

Deal, K. H., & Brintzenhofeszok-Szoc, K. M. (2004). A study of MSW students' interviewing skills over time. *Journal of Teaching in Social Work, 24*, 181–197.

Dean, R. G. (2001). The myth of cross-cultural competence. *Families in Society: The Journal of Contemporary Human Services, 82*, 623–630.

De Anda, D. (1984). Bicultural socialization: Factors affecting the minority experience. *Social Work, 29*, 172–181.

De Anda, D., & Becerra, R. (1984). Support networks for adolescent mothers. *Social Casework, 65*, 172–181.

DeAngelis, D. (2000). Licensing really is about protection. *ASWB Association News, 10*(2), 11.

DeBord, K., Canu, R. F., & Kerpelman, J. (2000). Understanding a work-family fit for single parents moving from welfare to work. *Social Work, 45*, 313–324.

DeJong, P. (2001). Solution-focused therapy. In A. R. Roberts & G. J. Greene (Eds.), *Social workers' desk reference* (pp. 112–115). New York, NY: Oxford University Press.

DeJong, P., & Berg, I. K. (2001). Co-constructing cooperation with mandated clients. *Social Work*, 46, 361–374.

DeJong, P. & Berg, I. K. (2002). *Lerner's workbook interviewing for solutions* (2nd ed.). Pacific Grove, CA: Brooks/Cole, Thomson Learning.

DeJong, P., & Berg, I. K. (2003). *Interviewing for solutions* (2nd ed.). Pacific Grove, CA: Brooks-Cole-Thomson Learning.

DeJong, P., & Berg, I. K. (2008) *Interviewing for solutions* (3rd ed.). Brooks/Cole-Thomson Learning.

DeJong, P., & Berg, I. K. (1998). *Interviewing for solutions*. Brooks/Cole.

DeJong, P., & Miller, S. D. (1995). How to interview for client strengths. *Social Work*, 40, 729–736.

Delgado, M. (1983). Activities and Hispanic groups: Issues and suggestions. *Social Work with Groups*, 6(1), 85–96.

DeLine, C. (2000). *The back door: An experiment or an alternative*. Alberta, Canada: The Back Door.

Demer, S., Hemesath, C., & Russell, C. (1998). A feminist critique of solution-focused therapy. *The America Journal of Family Therapy*, 26, 239–250.

DeNavas-Walt, C., Proctor, B. D., & Smith, J. C. (2010). *Income, poverty, and health insurance coverage in the United States: 2009* (U.S. Census Bureau Current Population Report, pp. 60–238). Washington, DC: Government Printing Office.

Denison, M. (2003). The PDR for mental health professionals. *Psychotherapy: Theory, Research, Practice, and Training*, 40, 317–318.

DePalma, J. A. (2001). Evidence-based case management. *Home Health Case Management & Practice*, 13, 330–331.

DePoy, E., Hartman, A., & Haslett, D. (1999). Critical Action Research: A model for social work knowing. *Social Work*, 44, 560–569.

de Shazer, S. (1988). *Clues: Investigating solutions in brief therapy*. New York: Norton.

de Shazer, S., & Berg, I. K. (1993). Constructing solutions. *Family Therapy Networker*, 12, 42–43.

Dettlaff, A. J., & Rycraft, J. R. (2010). Factors contributing to disproportionality in the child welfare system: Views for the legal community. *Social Work*, 55, 213–224.

Devore, W., & Schlesinger, E. G. (1999). *Ethnic-sensitive social work practice* (5th ed.). Boston, MA: Allyn & Bacon.

Dewayne, C. (1978). Humor in therapy. *Social Work*, 23, 508–510.

Dickson, D. T. (1998). *Confidentiality and privacy in social work*. New York, NY: Free Press.

Di Clemente, C. C., & Prochaska, J. O. (1998). Toward a comprehensive transtheoretical model of change: stages of change and addictive behaviors. In W. R. Miller and N. Heather (Eds.), *Treating Addictive Behaviors* (2nd ed.) (pp. 3–24). New York, NY: Plenum Press.

Dies, R. R. (1983). Clinical implications of research on leadership in short-term group psychotherapy. In R. R. Dies & R. McKenzie (Eds.), *Advances in group psychotherapy: Integrating research and practice* (American Group Psychotherapy Association Monograph Series) (pp. 27–28). New York, NY: International Universities Press.

Dietz, C. (2000). Reshaping clinical practice for the new millennium. *Journal of Social Work Education*, 36, 503–520.

Dietz, C., & Thompson, J. (2004). Rethinking Boundaries: Ethical Dilemmas in the Social Worker-Client Relationship. *Journal of Progressive Human Services*, Vol. 15(2): 2–22.

Dimidjian, S., & Linehan, M. M. (2003). Defining an agenda for future research on the clinical application of mindfulness practice. *Clinical Psychology: Science and Practice*, 10, 166–171.

Diorio, W. (1992). Parental perceptions of the authority of public child welfare caseworkers. *Families in Society*, 739(4), 222–235.

Dobson, K. S., & Dozios, D. J. (2001). Historical and philosophical basis of cognitive behavioral therapies. In K. S. Dobson (Ed.). *Handbook of Cognitive therapies* (pp. 3–39). New York, NY: Guildford Press.

Doherty, W. J. (1995). *Soul-searching: When psychotherapy must promote moral responsibility*. New York, NY: Basic Books.

Dolan, S., Martin, R., & Rosenow, D. (2008). Self-efficacy for cocaine abstinence: pretreatment correlates and relationship to outcomes. *Addictive behaviors*, 33, 675–688.

Donovan, K. & Regehr, C. (2010). Elder abuse: Clinical, ethical, and legal considerations in social work practice. *Clinical Social Work Journal*, 38, 174–182.

Dore, M. M. (1993). The practice–teaching parallel in educating the micropractitioner. *Journal of Social Work Education*, 29, 181–190.

Dorfman, R. A. (1996). *Clinical social work: Definition, practice, and vision*. New York, NY: Brunner/Mazel.

Dossick, J., & Shea, E. (1995). *Creative therapy III: 52 more exercises for groups*. Sarasota, FL: Professional Resource Press.

Doster, J., & Nesbitt, J. (1979). Psychotherapy and self-disclosure. In G. Chelune & Associates (Eds.),

Self-disclosure: origins, patterns, and implications of openness in interpersonal relationships (pp. 177–224). San Francisco, CA: Jossey-Bass.

Drankus, D. (2010). Indicators of acculturation: a bilinear, multidimensional model. *Advocates' Forum*, 2010, 35–49.

Drisko, J. W. (2004). Common factors in psychotherapy outcome: Meta-analytic findings and their implications for practice and research. *Families in Society, Journal of Contemporary Social Sciences*, 85(1), 81–90.

Duan, C. and Hill, C. E. (1996). The current state of empathy research. *Journal of Counseling Psychology* 43(3): 261–74.

Dubowitz, H., & DePanitilis, D. (2000). *Handbook for child protection practice*. Thousand Oaks, CA: Sage.

DuBray, W. (1985). American Indian values: Critical factors in casework. *Social Casework*, 66, 30–37.

Dudley, J. R., Smith, C., & Millison, M. B. (1995). Unfinished business: Assessing the spiritual needs of hospice clients. *American Journal of Hospice and Palliative care*, 12(2) 30–37.

Duehn, W., & Proctor, E. (1977). Initial clinical interactions and premature discontinuance in treatment. *American Journal of Orthopsychiatry*, 47, 284–290.

Dulcan, M. K. (2009). *Dulcan's Textbook of Child Adolescent Psychiatry*. Arlington, VA: American Psychiatric Publishing, Inc.

Dumbrill, G. (2003). Emerging perspectives on anti-oppressive practice. *Canadian Scholars' Press Inc*, 3, 321–421.

Dumbrill, G. (2006). Parental experience of child protection intervention: A qualitative study. *Child Abuse & Neglect*, 30, 27–37.

Duncan, B. L., & Miller, S. D. (2000). *The heroic client*. San Francisco, CA: Jossey Bass.

Dunlap, E., Golub, A., & Johnson, B. D. (2006). The severely-distressed African American family in a crack-era: Empowerment is not enough. *Journal of Sociology and Social Welfare*, 53(1), 115–139.

Duvall, E. M. (1977). *Marriage and family development* (5th ed.). Philadelphia, PA: Lippincott.

Dyche, L., & Zayas, L. H. (2001). Cross-cultural empathy and training the contemporary psychotherapist. *Clinical Social Work Journal*, 29, 245–258.

E

Eamon, M. K., & Zhang, S-J. (2006). Do social work students' assess and address economic barriers to clients implementing agreed task? *Journal of Social Work Education*, 42, 525–542.

Early, T. J., & GlenMaye, L. F. (2000). Valuing families: Social work practice with families from a strengths perspective. *Social Work*, 45, 118–130.

Eaton, T. T., Abeles, N., & Gutfreund, M. J. (1993). Negative indicators, therapeutic alliance, and therapy outcome. *Psychotherapy Research*, 3, 115–123.

Ebenstein, H. (1998). Single-session groups: Issues for social workers. *Social Work with Groups: A Journal of Community and Clinical Practice*, 21, 49–60.

Edwards, A. (1982). The consequences of error in selecting treatment for blacks. *Social Casework*, 63, 429–433.

Edwards, E. (1983). Native-American elders: Current issues and social policy implications. In R. McNeely & J. Colen (Eds.), *Aging in minority groups*. Beverly Hills, CA: Sage Publications.

Edwards, E. (2007). *Saving graces*. New York, NY: Broadway.

Edwards, E. D., Edwards, M. E., Davies, G. M., & Eddy, F. (1987). Enhancing self-concept and identification of American Indian girls. *Social Work with Groups*, 1, 309–318.

Efran, J., & Schenker, M. (1993). A potpourri of solutions: How new and different is solution-focused therapy? *Family Therapy Networker*, 17(3), 71–74.

Ehrenreich, B. (2001). *Nickel and dimed. On (not) getting by in America*. New York, NY: Metropolitan Books.

Ehrenreich, B. (2004, July 11). Let them eat cake. *The New York Times*, p. 3.

Elbow, M. (1987). The memory books: Facilitating termination with children. *Social Casework*, 68, 180–183.

Ell, K. (1995). Crisis intervention: Research needs. In E. L. Edwards (Ed.), *Encyclopedia of social work* (19th ed., pp. 660–667). Washington, DC: NASW Press.

Ellis, A. (1962). *Reason and emotion in psychotherapy*. New York, NY: Lyle Stuart.

Ellis, A. (1978). Family therapy: A phenomenological and active-directive approach. *Journal of Marriage and Family Counseling*, 4, 43–50.

Ellis, A. (2001). *Overcoming destructive beliefs, feelings, and behaviors: New directions for rational emotive behavior therapy*. Amherst, NY: Prometheus.

Ellis, R. A., & Sowers, K. M. (2001). *Juvenile justice practice. A cross disciplinary approach to intervention*. Belmont, CA: Brooks/Cole-Thomson Learning.

Ellor, J. W., Netting, F. E., & Thibault, J. M. (1999). *Religious and spiritual aspects of human service practice*. Columbia, SC: University of South Carolina Press.

Enos, S. (2008). *Incarcerated parents: Interrupted childhood. Children of Incarcerated Parents, Conference Proceedings*, Spring 2008, Center for Advanced Studies in Child Welfare, University of Minnesota.

Ensign, J. (1998). Health issues of homeless youth. *Journal of Social Distress and the Homeless, 7,* 159–174.

Ephross, P. H., & Vassil, T. V. (1988). *Groups that work: Structure and process.* New York, NY: Columbia University Press.

Epstein, H. (2003, October 12). Enough to make you sick. *The New York Times Magazine,* pp. 76–86.

Epstein, L. (1992). *Brief treatment and a new look at the task-centered approach* (3rd ed.). Boston, MA: Allyn & Bacon.

Epstein, L., & Brown, L. B. (2002). *Brief treatment and a new look at the task-centered approach* (4th ed.). Boston, MA: Allyn & Bacon.

Epstein, R. S., Simon, R. I., & Kay, G. G. (1992). Assessing boundary violations in psychotherapy: Survey results with the Exploitation Index. *Bulletin of the Menninger Foundation, 56*(2), 150–166.

Erford, B. T. (2003). *Transforming the school counseling profession.* Upper Saddle, NJ: Merrill Prentice Hall.

Erikson, E. (1963). *Childhood and society* (2nd ed.). New York. Norton.

Erickson, S. H. (2001). Multiple relationships in rural counseling. *The Family Journal: Counseling and Therapy for Couples and Families, 9,* 302–304.

Etherington, K. (2000). Supervising counselors who work with survivors of childhood sexual abuse. *Counseling Psychology Quarterly, 13,* 377–389.

Evans, T. (2004). A multidimensional assessment of children with chronic physical conditions. *Health and Social Work. 29,* 245–248.

Ewalt, P. L., & Mokuau, N. (1996). Self-determination from a Pacific perspective. In P. L. Ewalt, E. M. Freeman, S. A. Kirk, & D. L. Poole (Eds.), *Multicultural issues in social work* (pp. 255–268). Washington, DC: NASW Press.

Ezell, M. (2001). *Advocacy in the human services.* Thousand Oaks, CA: Brooks/Cole, Thomson Learning.

F

Falicov, C. (1996). Mexican families. In M. McGoldrick, J. Giordano, & J. Pearce (Eds.), *Ethnicity and family therapy* (2nd ed.) (pp. 169–182). New York, NY: Gullford Press.

Fallot, R. D., & Harris, M. (2002). The Trauma Recovery and Empowerment Model (TREM): Conceptual and practical issues in a group intervention for women. *Community Mental Health Journal, 38,* 475–485.

Farber, B. A. (2006). *Self disclosure in psychotherapy.* New York, NY: Guilford.

Farrington, A. (1995). Suicide and psychological debriefing. *British Journal of Nursing, 4*(4), 209–211.

Fast, J. D. (2003). After Columbine: How people mourn sudden death. *Social Work, 48,* 484–491.

Fauri, D. P., Harrigan, M. P., & Netting, F. E. (1998). Termination: Extending the concept for Macro Social Work practice. *Journal of Sociology and Social Welfare 25*(4), 61–80.

Fauth, J. (2006). Counselors' stress appraisals as predictors of countertransference behavior with male clients. *Journal of Counseling and Development, 84,* 430–439.

Fazilo, K. B. Lawson, K. B. Hardiman, E. R. (2009). A qualitative examination of power between child welfare workers and parent. *British Journal of Social Work. 39,* 1447–1464.

Fearing, J. (1996). The changing face of intervention. *Behavioral Health Management, 16,* 35–37.

Feeny, S. L. (2004). The cognitive behavioral treatment of social phobia. *Clinical Case Studies, 3,* 124–146.

Feldman, N. (2008). Exercising power from the bottom-up: Co-creating the conditions for the development with youth at an urban high school. *Families in Society, 89,* 438–445.

Feltenstein, M. W. (2008). The neurocircuitry of addiction: An overview. *British Journal of Pharmacology 154,* 261–274.

Ferguson, K. M. (2007). Implementing a social enterprise intervention with homeless, street-living youth in Los Angeles. *Social Work, 52,* 103–112.

Fernandez-Olano, C., Montoya-Fernandez, J. & Salinas-Sanchez, A. (2008). Impact of clinical interview training on the empathy level of medical students and medical residents. *Medical Teacher, 30*: 322–324.

Figley, C. R. (Ed.) (1995). *Compassion fatigue: Dealing with secondary traumatic stress disorder in those who treat the traumatized.* New York, NY: Bunner-Mazel.

Figley, C. R. (Ed.) (2002). *Treating compassion fatigue.* New York, NY: Brunner-Rutledge.

Fingeld, D. (2000). Therapeutic groups online: The good, the bad, and the unknown. Issues in *Mental Health Nursing, 21,* 241–255.

Finn, J. L., & Jacobson, M. (2003a). Just practice: Steps toward a new social work paradigm. *Journal of Social Work Education, 39,* 57–78.

Finn, J. L., & Jacobson, M. (2003b). *Just practice: A social justice approach to social work.* Peosta, IA: Eddie Bowers.

Fischer, J. (1973). Is casework effective? A review. *Social Work, 18,* 5–20.

Fischer, J. & Corcoran, K. (2006). *Measures for clinical practice and research: Couples, families, and children, A sourcebook, Vol. 1* (4th ed.). New York, NY: Oxford University Press.

Fischer, J. & Corcoran, K. (2007). *Measures for clinical practice and research: Adults, A sourcebook, Vol. 2* (4th ed.). New York, NY: Oxford University Press.

Flores, M. T., & Carey, G. (2000). *Family therapy with Hispanics: Toward appreciating diversity.* Boston, MA: Allyn & Bacon.

Fluhr, T. (2004). Transcending differences: Using concrete subject matter in heterogeneous groups. *Social Work with Groups,* 27(2/3).

Fong, R. (1997). Child welfare practice with Chinese families: Assessment issues for immigrants from the People's Republic China. *Journal of Family Social Work,* 2(1), 33–47.

Fong, L. G. W., & Gibbs, J. T. (1995). Facilitating service to multicultural communities in a dominant culture setting. An organizational perspective. *Administration in Social Work,* 19(2), 1–24.

Fong, R. (2007). Cultural competence with Asian Americans. In Lum (2007).

Fong, R., Armour, M., Busch-Armendariz, N. B., & Heffron, L. (2008). *Case management intervention with immigrant and refugee students and families.* (pp. 1031–1038). In A. R. Roberts & Greene, G. J., (Eds.). *Social Work Desk Reference* (2nd ed.). New York: Oxford University Press.

Fontes, L. A. (2005). *Child abuse and culture. Working with diverse families.* New York, NY: Guilford Press.

Fortune, A., MaCallion, P., & Briar-Larsen, K. (2010). (eds.). *Social work practice research for the Twenty-first century: Building on the legacy of William J. Reid.* Columbia University Press.

Fortune, A., Pearlingi, B., & Rochelle, C. D. (1992). Reactions to termination of individual treatment. *Social Work,* 37, 171–178.

Fortune, A., McCallion, P. & Briar-Lawson (Eds) (2011). *Social Work Practice Research for the 21st Century; Building on the Legacy of William J. Reid.* West Sussex: Columbia University Press.

Fortune, A. E. (1985). Treatment groups. In A. E. Fortune (Ed.), *Task-centered practice with families and groups* (pp. 33–44). New York, NY: Springer.

Fowler, R. C., Rich, C. L., & Young, D. C. (1986). San Diego suicide study, II: Substance abuse in young cases. *Archives of General Psychiatry,* 43, 962–965.

Frager, S. (2000). *Managing managed care: Secrets from a former case manager.* New York, NY: Wiley.

Frankenburg, W. K., Dodds, J., Archer, P., Shapiro, H., & Bresnick, B. (1992). The Denver II: A major revision and restandardization of the Denver Developmental Screening Test. *Pediatrics,* 89, 91–97.

Franklin, C. (2002). Developing effective practice competencies in managed behavioral health care. In Roberts, A. R. & Greene, G. J. (Eds.), *Social workers desk reference,* (pp. 3–10). New York, NY: Oxford.

Franklin, C., & Hopson, L. (2009). Involuntary clients in public schools: Solution-focused interventions. In R. H. Rooney (Ed.). *Strategies for work with involuntary clients* (2nd ed., pp. 322–333). New York, NY: Columbia University Press.

Franklin, C., & Kim, J. S. (2009). Solution-focused brief therapy in schools: A review of the literature. *Children and Youth Services Review,* 31, 464–470.

Franklin, C., Kim. J. S., & Kelly, M. S. (2008). Solution-focused brief therapy interventions for students at risk to drop out. In A. Roberts & P. Allen-Meares (Eds.), *Social Workers' Desk Reference* (2nd ed.). New York, NY: Oxford University Press.

Franklin, C., Moore, K., & Hopson, L. (2008). Effectiveness of brief treatment in a school setting. *Children and Schools,* 30(1), 15–26.

Franklin, C., & Streeter, C. L. (2004). *Solution-focused alternatives for education: An outcome evaluation of Garza High School.* Retrieved from http://www.utexas.edu.libproxy.lib.unc.edu/courses/franklin/safed_report_final.doc

Freddolino, P., Moxley, D., and Hyduk, C. (2004). A differential model of advocacy in social work practice. *Families in Society,* 85, 119–128.

Fredriksen-Goldsen, K. I., & Scharlach, A. E. (2001). *Families and work: New directions in the twenty-first century.* New York, NY: Oxford University Press.

Freed, A. (1988). Interviewing through an interpreter. *Social Work,* 33, 315–319.

Freedberg, S. (2007). Re-examining empathy: A relational-feminist point of view. *Social work,* 52, 251–259.

Freud, S. (1999). The social construction of normality. *Families in Society,* 80, 333–339.

Frey, A. and Dupper, D., (2005). A broader conceptional approach to clinical practice for the 21st century. *Children and Schools,* 29(1), 33–44.

Frey, G. A. (1990). Framework for promoting organizational change. *Families in Society,* 7, 142–147.

Frye, M. (2004). Oppression. In P. A. Rothenberg (Ed.). Race, class and gender (pp. 146–149), New York: Worth.

Froeschle, J. G., Smith, R. L., & Ricard, R. (2007). The efficacy of a systematic substance abuse program for adolescent females. *Professional School Counseling,* 10, 498–505.

From, S. B. (2008). *When mom is away: Supporting families or incarcerated mothers. Children of*

Incarcerated Parents, Conference Proceedings, Spring 2008, Center for Advanced Studies in Child Welfare, University of Minnesota.

Fullerton, C. D., & Ursano, R. J. (2005). Psychological and psychopathological consequences of disasters. In J. J. Lopez-Ibor, G. Christodoulou, M. Maj, N. Sartorius & A. Okasha (Eds.), *Disaster and mental health* (pp. 25–49). New York, NY: Wiley.

Furman, R. (2009). Ethical considerations of evidence-based practice. *Social Work, 54,* 57–59.

G

Gabbard, G. O. (1996). Lessons to be learned from the study of sexual boundary violations. *American Journal of Psychotherapy, 50,* 311–322.

Galinsky, M. J., & Schopler, J. H. (1989). Developmental patterns in open-ended groups. *Social Work with Groups, 12,* 99–114.

Galinsky, M. J., Terzian, M. A., & Fraser, M. W. (2006). The art of group work practice with manualized curricula. *Social Work with Groups, 29,* 11–26.

Gallo, J. J. (2005). Activities of daily living and instrumental activities of daily living assessment. In J. J. Gallo, H. R. Bogner, T. Fulmer, & G. Paveza (Eds.), *Handbook of geriatric assessment* (4th ed., 193–234). Sudbury, MA: Jones and Bartlett Publishers.

Gallo, J. J., & Bogner, H. R. (2005). The context of geriatric care. In J. J. Gallo, H. R. Bogner, T. Fulmer, & G. Paveza (Eds.), *Handbook of geriatric assessment* (4th ed., 3–14). Sudbury, MA: Jones and Bartlett Publishers.

Gallo, J. J., Bogner, H. R., Fulmer, T., & Paveza, J. (Eds.). (2005). *Handbook of geriatric assessment* (4th ed.). Sudbury, MA: Jones and Bartlett Publishers.

Gallo, J. J., Fulmer, T., Paveza, G. J., & Reichel, W. (2000). Mental status assessment. In *Handbook of geriatric assessment* (3rd ed., pp. 29–99). Gaithersburg, MD: Aspen.

Gambrill, E. (1995). Behavioral social work: Past, present and future. *Research on Social Work Practice, 5,* 466–484.

Gambrill, E. (2004). Contributions of critical thinking and evidence-based practice to the fulfillment of the ethical obligation of professions. In H. Briggs, and T. Rzepnicki (Eds.), *Using evidence in social work practice* (pp. 3–19). Chicago, IL: Lyceum.

Gambrill, E. (2007). Views of evidence-based practice: Social workers' Code of Ethics and accreditation standards as guides for choice. *Journal of Social Work Education, 43,* 447–462.

Garcia Coll, C, Akerman, A., & Cichetti, D. (2000). Cultural influences on developmental processes and outcomes: Implicatons for the study of development and psychopathology. *Development and Psychopathology, 12,* 333–356.

Garcia Coll, C. T., Lamberty, G., Jenkins, R., McAdoo, H. P., Crinic, K., Wasik. B. H., & Vasquez Garcia, H. (1996). An integrative model for the study of developmental competencies in minority children. *Child Development, 67,* 1891–1914.

Gardner, F. (2000). Design Evaluation: Illuminating social work practice for better outcomes. *Social Work, 45,* 176–182.

Gardner, L. I., Metsch, L. R., Andrson-Mahoney, P., Loughlin, A. M., del Rio, C., Strathdee, S., Samsom, S. L., Siegal, H. A., Greenberg, A. E., Holmberg, S. D., & The Antiretroviral Treatment Group & Access Study Cartas Study Group (2005). Efficacy of breif case mangement intervention to link recently diagnosed HIV-infected persons to care. *AIDS, 19,* 423–431.

Garland, J., Jones, H., & Kolodny, R. (1965). A model for stages in the development of social work groups. In S. Bernstein (Ed.), *Explorations in group work.* Boston, MA: Milford House.

Gartrell, N. K. (1992). Boundaries in lesbian therapy relationships. *Women & Therapy, 12*(3), 29–50.

Garvin, C. (1981). *Contemporary group work.* Englewood Cliffs, NJ: Prentice-Hall.

Garvin, C. (1986). Family therapy and group work: "Kissing cousins or distant relatives" in social work practice. In M. Parnes (Ed.), *Innovations in social group work: feedback from practice to theory: proceedings of the annual group work symposium* (p. 1–16). New York, NY: Haworth Press.

Garvin, C. (1987). *Contemporary group work* (2nd ed.). Englewood Cliffs, NJ: Prentice-Hall.

Garvin, C. D. (2011). Group treatment with adults. In J. R. Brandell (Ed.), *Theory & practice in clinical social work* (323–346). Los Angeles, CA: SAGE.

Garvin, C. D., & Galinsky, M. J. (2008). Groups. In Mizrahi, T., & Davis, L. E. (Eds.) *Encyclopedia of Social Work.* New York, NY: Oxford University Press.

Gaudiano, B. A., & Herbert, J. D. (2006). Self-efficacy for social situations in adolescents with generalized social anxiety disorder. *Behavioral and Cognitive Psychotherapy, 35,* 209–223.

Gavin, D. R., Ross, H. E., & Skinner, H. A. (1989). Diagnostic validity of the Drug Abuse Screening Test in the assessment of DSM-III drug disorders. *British Journal of Addiction 84:* 301–307.

Gelman, C. R. (2004). Empirically-based principles for culturally competent practice with Latinos. *Journal of Ethnic and Cultural Diversity in Social Work, 13*(1), 83–108.

Gelman, C. R., & Mirabito, D. M. (2005). Practicing what we teach: Using case studies from 911 to teach crisis intervention from a generalist perspective. *Journal of Social Work Education, 4*, 479–494.

Gelman, S. R., Pollack, D., & Weiner, A. (1999). Confidentiality of social work records in the computer age. *Social Work, 44*(3), 243–252.

Gendlin, E. (1974). Client-centered and experiential psychotherapy. In D. Wexler & L. Rice (Eds.), *Innovations in client-centered therapy*. New York: Wiley.

Gendolla, G. H. E. (2004). The intensity of motivation when the self is involved: An application of Brehm's Theory of Motivation to effort-related cardiovascular response. In R. Wright, J. Greenberg & S. S. Brehm (Eds.), *Motivational analysis of social behavior* (pp. 205–224). Mahwah, NJ: Lawrence Erlbaum Associates Publishers.

Gendron, C, Poitras, L., Dastoor, D. P., & Perodeau, G. (1996). Cognitive-behavioral group intervention for spousal caregivers: Findings and clinical observations. *Clinical Gerontologist, 17*(1), 3–19.

Genty, P. M. (2008). *The inflexibility of the Adoption and Safe Family Act and the unintended impact upon the children of incarcerated parents and their families. Children of Incarcerated Parents, Conference Proceedings, Spring 2008*, Center for Advanced Studies in Child Welfare, University of Minnesota.

George, L., & Fillenbaum, G. (1990). OARS methodology: A decade of experience in geriatric assessment. *Journal of the American Geriatrics Society, 33*, 607–615.

Gerdes, K. E., & Stromwell, L. K. (2009). Conation: A missing link in the strengths perspective. *Social Work, 53*, 233–242.

Gerdes, K., Segal, E. (2009) A Social Work Model of Empathy. *Advances in social work* 10(2): 114–127.

Germain, C. (1979). Ecology and social work. In C. Germain (Ed.), *Social work practice: People and environments* (pp. 1–2). New York, NY: Columbia University Press.

Germain, C. (1981). The ecological approach to people-environmental transactions. *Social Case-Work, 62*, 323–331.

Getzel, G. S. (1991). Survival modes for people with AIDS in groups. *Social Work, 36*, 7–11.

Getzel, G. S. (1998). Group work practice with gay men and lesbians. In G. P. Mallon (Ed.), *Foundations of social work practice with lesbian and gay persons* (pp. 131–144). Binghamton, NY: Haworth Press.

Giacola, P. R., Mezzich, A. C., Clark, D. B., & Tarter, R. E. (1999). Cognitive distortions, aggressive behaviors and drug use in adolescent boys with and without prior family history. *Psychology of Addictive Behavior, 13*, 22–32.

Gibbons R. D., Weiss, D. J., Kupfer, D. J., Frank, E., Fagiolini, A., Grochocinski, V. J., Immekus, J. C. (2008). Using computerized adaptive testing to reduce the burden of mental health assessment. *Psychiatric Services, 59*(4), 361–368.

Gibbs, J. (1995). *Tribes: A new way of learning and being together*. Sausalito, CA: Center Source Systems.

Gibson, P. A. (1999). African American grandmothers: New mothers again. *Affilia, 14*(3), 329–343.

Gilbar, O. (1992). Workers' sick fund (kupat holim) hotline therapeutic first intervention: A model developed in the Gulf War. *Social Work in Health Care, 17*(4), 45–57.

Gilbert, D. J. (2003). Multicultural assessment. In C. Jordan & C. Franklin (Eds.), *Clinical assessment for social workers: Quantitative and qualitative methods* (2nd ed., pp. 351–383). Chicago: Lyceum Books.

Gilbert, N. (1977). The search for professional identity. *Social Work, 22*, 401–406.

Gilgun, J. F. (1994). Hand to glove: The grounded theory approach and social work practice research. In L. Sherman & W. J. Reid (Eds.), *Qualitative research in social work* (pp. 115–125). New York, NY: Columbia University Press.

Gilgun, J. F. (1999). CASPARS: New tools for assessing client risks and strengths. *Families in Society, 80*, 450–458.

Gilgun, J. F. (2001). CASPARS: New tools for assessing client risks and strengths. *Families and Society: The Journal of Contemporary Human Services, 82*, 450–459.

Gilliland, B (1982) The six-stage model of crisis intervention. In R. K. James Crisis intervention strategies (4th ed., p. 38). Brooks/Cole.

Gingerich, W. J., & Eisengard, S. (2000). Solution-focused brief treatment. A review of outcome research. *Family Process, 39*, 477–498.

Gingerich, W. J., & Wabeke, T. (2001). A solution-focused approach to mental health interventions in school settings. *Children in Schools, 23*(1), 33–47.

Gira, E., Kessler, M., & Poertner, J. (2001). *Evidence-based practice in child welfare.* Urbana-Champaign, IL: University of Illinois at Urbana-Champaign.

Gitterman, A. (1996). Ecological perspectives: Response to Professor Jerry Wakefield. *Social Service Review, 70,* 472–476.

Giunta, C. T., & Streissguth, A. P. (1988). Patients with fetal alcohol syndrome and their caretakers. *Social Casework, 69,* 453–459.

Glancy, G., & Saini, M. (2005). An evidence-based review of psychological treatment of anger and aggression. *Brief Treatment and Crisis Intervention, 5,* 229–248.

Golan, N. (1978). *Treatment in crisis situations.* New York, NY: Free Press.

Golan, N. (1981). *Passing through transitions: A guide for the practitioners.* New York, NY Free Press.

Gold, M. (1986, November). (As quoted by Earl Ubell.) Is that child bad or depressed? *Parade Magazine, 2,* 10.

Gold, N. (1990). Motivation: The crucial but unexplored component of social work practice. *Social Work, 35,* 49–56.

Goldenberg, I., & Goldenberg, H. (1991). *Family therapy: An overview* (3rd ed.). Pacific Grove, CA: Brooks/Cole.

Goldenberg, I., & Goldenberg, H. (2000). *Family therapy: An overview* (5th ed.). Pacific Grove, CA: Brooks/Cole.

Goldenberg, I., & Goldenberg, H. (2004). *Family therapy: An overview* (6th ed.). Pacific Grove, CA: Brooks/Cole.

Goldfried, M. (1977). The use of relaxation and cognitive re-labeling as coping skills. In R. Stuart (Ed.), *Behavioral self-management* (pp. 82–116). New York, NY: Brunner/Mazel.

Goldstein, E. G. (1997). To tell or not to tell: The disclosure of events in the therapist's life to the patient. *Clinical Social Work Journal, 25,* 41–58.

Goodman, H. (1997). Social group work in community corrections. *Social Work with Groups, 20*(1), 51–64.

Goodman, H., Getzel, G. S., & Ford, W. (1996). Group work with high-risk urban youths on probation. *Social Work, 41,* 375–381.

Goodwin, D. W., & Gabrielli, W. F. (1997). Alcohol: Clinical aspects. In J. H. Lowinson, P. Ruiz, R. B. Millman, & J. G. Langrod (Eds.), *Substance abuse: A comparative textbook* (3rd ed., pp. 142–148). Baltimore, MD: Williams & Wilkins.

Gordon, T. (1970). *Parent effectiveness training.* New York, NY: P. H. Wyclen.

Gordon, W. (1965). Toward a social work frame of reference. *Journal of Education for Social Work, 1,* 19–26.

Gottesfeld, M., & Lieberman, F. (1979). The pathological therapist. *Social Casework, 60,* 387–393.

Goyer, A. (2006). *Intergenerational relationships: Grandparents raising grandchildren.* Policy and Research Report, American Association of Retired Persons.

Grame, C., Tortorici, J., Healey, B., Dillingham, J., & Wilklebaur, P. (1999). Addressing spiritual and religious issues of clients with a history of psychological trauma. *Bulletin of the Menninger Clinic, 63,* 223–239.

Graham, P (1998). *Cognitive behavior therapy for children and families.* Cambridge: Cambridge University Press.

Green, J. W. (1999). *Cultural awareness in the human services: A multi-ethnic approach.* Boston, MA: Allyn & Bacon.

Green, J. P., Duncan, R. E., Barnes, G. L., & Oberklaid, F. (2003). Putting informed into consent: A matter of plain language. *Journal of Pediatric Child Health, 39,* 700–703.

Green, R. G., Kiernan-Stern, M., & Baskind, F. R. (2005). White social worker's attitudes about people of color. *Journal of Ethnic and Cultural Diversity in Social Work, 14*(1/2), 47–68.

Greenberg, M. (2007). *Making poverty history. Ending Poverty in America,* Special Report of The American Prospect, The Annie E. Casey Foundation & The Northwest Area Foundation. A3–A4.

Greenberg, J., & Tyler, T. R. (1987). Why procedural justice in organizations. *Social Justice Research, 1,* 127–143.

Greene, A. D. & Latting, J. K. (2004). Whistle-blowing as a form of advocacy: Guidelines for the practitioner and the organization. *Social Work, 49,* 219–230.

Greene, G. J., Kondrat, D. C., Lee, M. Y., Clement, J., Siebert, H., Mentzer, R. A., & Pinnell, S. R. (2006). A solution-focused approach to case management and recovery with consumers who have a severe mental disability. *Families in Society, 87,* 339–350.

Greene, G. J., Lee, M. Y., & Hoffpauir, S. (2005). The language of empowerment and strengths in clinical social work: A constructivist perspective. *Families in Society, 86,* 267–277.

Greenfield, P. M. (1994). Independence and interdependence as developmental scripts: Implications for theory, research and practice. In P. M. Greenfield & R. R. Cocking (Eds.), *Cross-cultural roots of minority child development* (pp. 1–24). Hillsdale, NJ: Lawrence Erlbaum Associates.

Greif, G. L. & Ephross, P. H. (Eds.). (2011). *Group Work with Populations at Risk* (3rd ed.). New York, NY: Oxford University Press.

Gross, E. (1995). Deconstructing politically correct practice literature: The American Indian case. *Social Work, 40,* 206–213.

Grote, N. K., Zuckoff, A., Swartz, H., Bledsoe, S. E., & Geibel, S. (2007). Engaging women who are depressed and economically disadvantaged in mental health treatment. *Social Work, 52*(4), 295–308.

Guadalupe, K. L., & Lum, D. (2005). *Multidimensional contextual practice. Diversity and transcendence.* Belmont, CA: Brooks/Cole-Thomson.

Gulati, P., & Guest, G. (1990). The community-centered model: A garden variety approach or a radical transformation of community practice? *Social Work, 35,* 63–68.

Gumpert, J., & Saltman, J. E. (1998). Social group work practice in rural areas: The practitioners speak. *Social Work with Groups, 21*(3), 19–34.

Gurman, A. (1977). The patient's perception of the therapeutic relationship. In A. Gutman & A. Razin (Eds.), *Effective psychotherapy: A handbook of research.* New York, NY: Pergamon Press.

Gutierrez, L. M. (1994). Beyond coping: an empowerment perspective on stressful life events. *Journal of Sociology and Social Welfare, 21,* 201–219.

Gutierrez, L., GlenMaye, L., & Delois, K. (1995). The organizational context of empowerment practice: Implications for social work in administration. *Social Work, 40,* 249–258.

Gutierrez, L. M., & Lewis, E. A. (1999). Strengthening communities through groups: A multicultural perspective. In H. Bertcher, L. F. Kurtz, & A. Lamont (Eds.), *Rebuilding communities: Challenges for group work* (pp. 5–16). New York, NY: Haworth Press.

Gutierrez, L. M., & Ortega, R. (1991). Developing methods to empower Latinos: The importance of groups. *Social Work with Groups, 14*(2), 23–43.

Gutierrez, L. M., Parsons, R. J., & Cox, E. O. (1998). *Empowerment in social work practice: A sourcebook.* Pacific Grove, CA: Brooks/Cole.

H

Hackman, J. R., & Oldham, G. R. (1976). Motivation through the design of work: Test of a theory. *Organizational Behavior and Human Performance, 16,* 250–279.

Hackman, J. R., & Oldham, G. R. (1980). Work design. Reading, MA: Addison-Wesley.

Hackney, H. & Cormier, S. (2005). *The professional counselor: a professional guide to helping* (5th ed.). Boston: Pearson

Hage, D. (2004). *Reforming welfare by rewarding work.* Minneapolis, MN: University of Minnesota Press.

Hagen, B. F., & Mitchell, D. L. (2001). Might within the madness: Solution-focused therapy and thought disordered clients. *Archives of Psychiatric Nursing, 15*(2), 86–93.

Haight, W. L. (1998). Gathering the spirit at First Baptist Church: Spirituality as a protective factor in the lives of African American children. *Social Work, 43,* 213–221.

Hall, E. T. (1976). *Beyond culture.* New York, NY: Anchor Press.

Hall, J. A., Carswell, C., Walsh, E., Huber, D. L., & Jampoler, J. S. (2002). Iowa case management: Innovative social casework, *Social Work, 47,* 132–141.

Halpern, J., & Tramontin, M. (2007). *Disaster: Mental health theory and practice.* Belmont, CA: Thomson-Brooks/Cole.

Halpern, R. (1990). Poverty and early childhood parenting: Toward a framework for intervention. *American Journal of Orthopsychiatry, 60*(1), 6–18.

Hamama, L., & Ronen, T. (2009). Children's drawing as a self-report measure. *Child and Family Social Work, 14,* 99–102.

Hammond, D., Hepworth, D., & Smith, V. (1977). *Improving therapeutic communication.* San Francisco, CA: Jossey-Bass.

Hand, C. A. (2006). An Ojibwe perspective on the welfare of children: Lessons of the past and visions for the future. *Children Youth and Services Review, 28,* 20–46.

Handmaker, N. S., Miller, W. R., & Manicke, M. (1999). Findings of a pilot study of motivational interviewing with pregnant drinkers. *Journal of Studies on Alcohol, 60,* 285–287.

Hankin, B. L., Abramson, L. Y., Moffitt, T. E., Silva, P. A., McGee, R., & Angell, K. E. (1998). Development of depression from preadolescence to young adulthood: Emerging gender differences in a 10-year longitudinal study. *Journal of Abnormal Psychology, 107,* 128–140.

Hannah, G. (2006). Maintaining product—Process balance in community anti-poverty initiatives. *Social Work, 51,* 9–17.

Hardina, D. (2004). Guidelines for ethical practice in community organization. *Social Work, 49,* 595–604.

Hardy, K. (1993). War of the worlds. *The Family Therapy Networker,* 51–57.

Hare, J. (1994). Concerns and issues faced by families headed by a lesbian couple. *Families in Society, 75,* 27–35.

Harper, K. V., & Lantz, J. (1996). *Cross-cultural practice*. Chicago, IL: Lyceum Books.

Harris, J. (1999). First steps in telecollaboration. *Learning and Leading with Technology, 27*, 54–57.

Harris, M., & Franklin, C. (2003). Effects of cognitive-behavioral, school-based group intervention with Mexican American pregnant and parenting adolescents. *Social Work Research, 27*, 74–84.

Hartford, M. (1971). *Groups in social work*. New York, NY: Columbia University Press.

Hartman, A. (1981). The family: A central focus for practice. *Social Work, 26*, 7–13.

Hartman, A. (1990). Many ways of knowing. *Social Work, 35*, 3–4.

Hartman, A. (1991). Social worker in situation. *Social Work, 36*, 195–196.

Hartman, A. (1993). The professional is political. *Social Work, 38*, 365, 366, 504.

Hartman, A. (1994). Diagrammatic assessment of family relationships. In B. R. Compton & B. Galaway (Eds.), *Social work processes* (5th ed., pp. 153–165). Pacific Grove, CA: Brooks/Cole.

Hartman, A., & Laird, J. (1983). *Family centered social work practice*. New York, NY: Free Press.

Hathaway, S. R. & McKinley, J. C. (1989). *MMPI-2 manual for administration and scoring*. Minneapolis, MN: University of Minnesota Press.

Havens, J. R., Cornelius, L. J., Ricketts, E. P., Latkin, C. A., Bishai, D., Lloyd, J. J., Huettner, S., & Strathdee, S. A. (2007). The effect of case management intervention on drug treatment entry among treatment-seeking injection drug users with and without cormorbid antisocial personality disorder. *Journal of Urban Health, 84*, 267–271.

Hawthorne, F. (2007, October, 23). Greater obstacles to retirement for women. *The New York Times*, Special Section, Retirement, p. H13.

Hayes, J. A. (2004). Therapist know thyself: Recent research on countertransference, *Psychotherapy Bulletin, 39* (4), 6–12.

Haynes, K. S., & Mickelson, J. S. (2000). *Affecting change: Social workers in the political arena* (4th ed.). Boston, MA: Allyn & Bacon.

Haynes, R., Corey, G., & Moulton, P. (2003). *Clinical supervision in the helping professions: A practical guide*. Pacific Grove, CA: Thomson, Brooks/Cole.

Hays, P. A. (1995). Multicultural applications of cognitive behavioral therapy. *Professional Psychology, 26*, 309–315.

Hays, P. A. (2009). Integrating culturally competent based practice and evidence-based practice in cognitive behavioral therapy. *Professional Psychology Research and Practice and Multicultural Therapy, 40*, 354–360.

Healy, L. M. (2007). Universalism and cultural relativism in social work ethics. *International Social Work, 50*, 11–26.

Hegar, R. (1999). The cultural roots of kinship care. In R. Hegar & M. Scannapieco (Eds.), *Kinship foster care, policy, practice, and research* (pp. 17–27). New York, NY: Oxford University Press.

Heisel, M. J., Flett, G. L. (2006). The development and initial validation of the Geriatric Suicide Ideation Scale. *The American Journal of Geriatric Psychiatry, 14*, 742–751.

Heisel, M. J., Flett, G. L., Duberstein P. R., & Lyness, J. M. (2005). Does the geriatric depression scale (GDS) distinguish between older adults with high versus low levels of suicidal ideation? *American Journal Geriatric Psychiatry, 13*, 876–883.

Helvic, C. O., & Alexey, B. B. (1992). Using after shelter case management to improve outcomes for families with children. *Public Health Report, 107*, 585–588.

Hernanzez, M., McGoldrick, M. (19991). Migration and the life cycle. In B. Carter & McGoldrick (Eds.), *The expanded family life cycle: Individual, family, and social perspectives* (3rd ed., pp. 169–184). Boston: Allyn & Bacon.

Henry, M. (1988). Revisiting open groups. *Group Work, 1*, 215–228.

Henry, S. (1992). *Group skills in four-dimensional approach* (2nd ed.). Pacific Grove, CA: Brooks/Cole.

Herman, D., Conover, S., Felix, A., Nakagawa. K., & Mills, D. (2007). Critical time intervention: An empirically supported model for preventing homelessness in high risk groups. *Journal of Primary Prevention, 28*, 296–312.

Hersen, M. and Thomas, J. (Eds). (2007). *Handbook of clinical interviewing with children*. Thousand Oaks, CA: Sage.

Hill, B., Rotegard, L., & Bruininks, R. (1984). The quality of life of mentally retarded people in residential care. *Social Work, 29*, 275–281.

Hill, C. E., & Nakayama, E. Y. (2000). Rogerian therapy: Where has it been and where is it going? A comment on Hathaway (1948). *Journal of Clinical Psychology, 56*, 861–875.

Hill, R. (2005). *Disproportionality in child welfare: Synthesis of the research*. Washington, DC: Child Welfare League of American.

Hillier, A. (2007). Why social work needs mapping. *Journal of Social Work Education, 43*, 205–221.

Hines, P. H., Garcia-Preto, N. G., McGoldrick, M., Almeida, R., & Weltman, S. (1999). Culture and the family life cycle. In B. Carter & M. McGoldrick (Eds.), *The expanded family life cycle. Individual, family and social perspectives* (3rd ed.). Needham Heights, MA: Allyn & Bacon.

HIPAA Medical Privacy Rule. (2003). Retrieved May 1, 2004, from http://www.socialworkers.org/hipaa/medical.asp

Hirayama, K. K., Hirayama, H., & Cetingok, M. (1993). Mental health promotion for South East Asian refugees in the USA. *International Social Work, 36*, 119–129.

Ho, M. (1987). *Family therapy with ethnic minorities*. Newbury Park, CA: Sage.

Hoagwood, K., Burns, B. J., Kiser, L., Ringeisen, H., & Schoenwald, S. K. (2001). Evidence-based practice in children and adolescent mental health services. *Psychiatric Services, 52*, 1179–1189.

Hodge, D. R. (2004). Working with Hindu clients in a spiritually sensitive manner. *Social Work, 49*, 27–38.

Hodge, D. R. (2005). Spiritual lifemaps: A client-centered pictorial instrument for spiritual assessment, planning and intervention. *Social Work, 50*, 77–87.

Hodge, D. R. (2007). Social justice and people of faith: A transnational perspective. *Social Work, 52*(2), 139–148.

Hodge, D. R., & Nadir, A. (2008). Moving toward culturally competent practice with Muslims: Modifying cognitive therapy with Islamic tenets. *Social Work, 53*, 31–41.

Hoefer, R. (2005). Altering state policy: Interest group effectiveness among state-level advocacy groups. *Social Work, 50*, 219–225.

Holbrook, T. L. (1995). Finding subjugated knowledge: Personal document research. *Social Work, 40*, 746–750.

Holland, S. (2000). The assessment relationship: Interaction between social workers and parents in child protection assessment. *British Journal of Social Work, 30*, 149–163.

Hollander, E. M. (2001). Cyber community in the valley of the shadow of death. *Journal of Loss and Trauma, 6*, 136–146.

Hollis, F. & Woods, M. (1981). *Casework: a psychosocial therapy* (3rd ed.). New York: Random House.

Holloway, M., Moss, B. (2010). *Spirituality and social work*. New York, NY, Palgrave Macmillan.

Holt, B. J. (2000). *The practice of generalist case management*. Needham Heights, MA: Allyn & Bacon.

Holt, B. J. (2002). *The practice of generalist case management*. Needham Heights, MA: Allyn & Bacon.

Homan, M. S. (1999). *Promoting community change: Making it happen in the real world* (2nd ed.). Belmont, CA: Brooks/Cole.

Homan, M. S. (2008). *Promoting community change. Making it happen in the real world* (4th ed.). Pacific Grove, CA: Thomson Brooks/Cole.

Hopson, J. S., & Franklin, C. (2009). Solution-focused brief treatment in schools: A review of the outcome literature. *Children, Youth Services Review, 31*, 464–470.

Hopson, L. M., & Kim, J. S. (2005). Solution-focused brief treatment approach to crisis intervention with adolescents. *Journal of Evidence-Based Social Work, 1*(2/3), 93–110.

Horesji, C., Heavy Runner, B., & Pablo, C. J. (1992). Reactions by Native American parents to child protection agencies: Cultural and community factors. *Child Welfare, 71*, 329–342.

Houston-Vega, M. K., Nuehring, E. M., & Daguio, E. R. (1997). *Prudent practice: A guide for managing malpractice risk*. Washington, DC: NASW Press.

Howard, M., Allen-Meares, P., & Ruffolo, M. (2007). Teaching evidence-based practice: Strategic and pedagogical recommendations for schools of social work. *Research on Social Work Practice, 17*, 561–568.

Hoyt, M. F. (2000). *Some stories are better than others: Doing what works in brief therapy and managed care*. Philadelphia, PA: Brunner/Mazel.

Hsu, W. S. (2009). The components of the solution-focused supervision. Bulletin of *Education Psychology, 41*, 475–496.

Hubble, M. A., Duncan, B. L., & Miller, S. D. (1999). Introduction. In M. A. Hubble, B. L. Duncan, & S. D. Miller (Eds.), *The heart and soul of change: What works in therapy*. Washington, DC: American Psychological Association.

Huber, D. L. (Ed.). (2005). *Disease management: A guide for case managers: Brief solution-focused therapy and the Iowa case management model*. Philadelphia: Elsevier.

Hudson, W. (1992). *The WALMYR assessment scales scoring manual*. Tempe, AZ: WALMYR.

Hudson, W., & McMurtry, S. L. (1997). Comprehensive assessment in social work practice: A multi-problem screening inventory. *Research of Social Work Practice, 7*, 79–88.

Huffine, C. (Summer, 2006). Bad conduct, defiance, and mental health. *Focal Point, 20*(2), 13–16.

Hulewat, P. (1996). Resettlement: A cultural and psychological crisis. *Social Work, 41*, 129–135.

Hull, G. Jr. (1982). Child welfare services to Native Americans. *Social Casework, 63,* 340–347.

Hunsley, J., Aubrey, T., Vestervelt, C. M., & Vito, D. (1999). Comparing therapist and client perspectives on reasons for psychotherapy termination. *Psychotherapy, 36,* 380–388.

Hunt, L. M. (2001). Beyond cultural competence: Applying humility to clinical settings. *The Park Ridge Center Bulletin, 24,* 3–4.

Hurdle, D. E. (2002). Native Hawaiian traditional healing. *Social Work, 47,* 183–192.

Hurley, D. J. (1984). Resistance and work in adolescent groups. *Social Work with Groups, 1,* 71–81.

Hurvitz, N. (1975). Interactions hypothesis in marriage counseling. In A. Gutman & D. Rice (Eds.), *Couples in conflict* (pp. 225–240). New York, NY: Jason Aronson.

Hutchison, E. (2003) (Ed.). *Dimensions of Human Behavior Person and Environment* (2nd ed.). Thousand Oaks, CA: Sage.

Hutson, R. Q. (2001). *Red flags: Research raises concerns about the impact of "welfare reform" on child maltreatment.* Washington, DC: Center for Law and Social Policy.

Hutxable, M. (January, 2004). *Defining measurable behavioral goals and objectives.* School Social Work Association of America, Northlake, Ill.

Hyde, C. (1996). A feminist's response to Rothman's "The interweaving of community intervention approaches." *Journal of Community Practice,* 3(3/4), 127–145.

I

Indyk, D., Belville, R., Lachapelle, S. S., Gordon, G., & Dewart, T. (1993). A community-based approach to HIV case management: Systematizing the unmanageable. *Social Work, 38,* 380–387.

Ingersoll-Dayton, B., Schroepfer, T., & Pryce, J. (1999). The effectiveness of a solution-focused approach for problem behaviors among nursing home residents. *Journal of Gerontological Social Work, 32,* 49–64.

International Association of Schools of Social Work and International Federation of Social Workers. (2004). *Global standards for social work education and training.* Adopted by the General Assemblies of IASSW and IFSW. Retrieved from http://www.ifsw.org/cm_data/GlobalSocialWorkStandards2005.pdf

International Federation of Social Workers. (2000). *New definition of social work.* Berne: International Federation of Social Workers.

Ivanoff, A. M., Blythe, B. J., & Tripodi, T. (1994). *Involuntary clients in social work practice: A research-based approach.* New York, NY: Aldine de Gruyter.

J

Jackson, A. P. (1998). The role of social support in parenting for low-income, single, black mothers. *Social Service Review, 72,* 365–378.

Jackson, D. D., & Weakland, J. H. (1961). Conjoint family therapy: Some considerations on theory, technique, and results. *Psychiatry, 24,* 3–45.

Jackson-Elmore, C. (2005). Informing state policymakers: Opportunities for social workers. *Social Work, 50,* 251–261

Jacobs, E. E., Masson, R. L., & Harvill, R. L. (1998). *Group counseling strategies and skills.* Pacific Grove, CA: Brooks/Cole.

James, R. K. (2008). *Crisis intervention strategies* (6th ed.). Pacific Grove, CA Thomson-Brooks/Cole.

James, R. K., & Gilliland, B. E. (2001). *Crisis intervention strategies.* Pacific Grove, CA: Brooks/Cole, Thomson Learning.

James. R. K., & Gilliland, B. E. (2005). *Crisis intervention strategies* (5th ed.). Thomson-Brooks/Cole.

Jang, M., Lee, K., & Woo, K. (1998). Income, language, and citizenship status: Factors affecting the health care access and utilization of Chinese Americans. *Health and Social Work, 23,* 136–145.

Jansson, B. (2003). *Becoming an effective policy advocate* (4th ed.). Pacific Grove, CA: Thomson-Brooks/Cole.

Janzen, C, & Harris, O. (1997). *Family treatment in social work practice* (3rd ed.). Itasca, IL: F. E. Peacock.

Jarrett, R. L. (1995). Growing up poor: The family experience of socially mobile youth in low-income African American neighborhoods. *Journal of Adolescent Research, 10,* 111–135.

Jayaratne, S. (1994). Should systematic assessment, monitoring and evaluation tools be used as empowerment aids for clients? In W. W. Hudson & P. S. Nurius (Eds.), *Controversial issues in social work research* (pp. 88–92). Needham Heights, MA: Allyn and Bacon.

Jaycox, L. H., Zoellner, L., & Foa, E. B. (2002). Cognitive behavioral therapy for PTSD in rape survivor. *Journal of Clinical Psychology,* 58(8), 891–907.

Jennings, H. (1950). *Leadership and isolation.* New York, NY: Longmans Green.

Jessop, D. (1998). Caribbean norms vs. European ethics. *The Sunday Observer* (Jamaica) (1 February): 13.

Jilek, W. (1982). *Indian healing: Shamanic ceremonialism in the Pacific Northwest today.* Laine, WA: Hancock House.

Jimenez, J. (2002). The history of grandmothers in the African American community. *Social Services Review, 76,* 524–551.

Johnson, E., Clark, S., Donald, M., Pedersen, R. and Piehotta, C. (2007). Racial disparity in Minnesota's child protection system. *Child Welfare, 86*(4): 5–20.

Johnson, H. C. (1989). Disruptive children: Biological factors in attention deficit disorder and antisocial disorders. *Social Work, 34,* 137–144.

Johnson, Y. M. & Munch, S. (2009). Fundamental contradictions in cultural competence. *Social Work, 54,* 222–231.

Jones, D. M. (1996). Termination from drug treatment: Dangers and opportunities for clients of the graduation ceremony. *Social Work with Groups, 19*(3/4), 105–115.

Jongsma, A. E., Peterson, M, & Bruce, T. J. (2006). *The complete adult psychotherapy treatment planner.* Hoboken, NJ: Wiley & Sons.

Jordan, C., & Franklin, C. (1995). *Clinical assessment for social workers: Quantitative and qualitative methods.* Chicago, IL: Lyceum Books.

Jordan, C., & Franklin, C. (2003). Clinical assessment for social workers. *Quantitative and qualitative methods* (2nd ed.). Chicago, IL: Lyceum Books.

Jordan, C., and Franklin, C. (Eds.) (2011). *Clinical assessment for social workers: quantitative and qualitative methods* (3rd ed.). Chicago; Lyceum.

Jordan, C., & Hickerson, J. (2003). Children and adolescents. In C. Jordan & C. Franklin (Eds.), *Clinical assessment for social workers: Quantitative and qualitative methods* (pp. 179–213). Chicago, IL: Lyceum Books.

Joseph, S., Williams, R., & Yule, W. (1993). Changes in outlook following disaster: Preliminary development of measures to assess positive and negative responses. *Journal of Traumatic Stress, 6,* 271–279.

Joyce, A. S., Duncan, S. C., Duncan, A., Kipnes, D., & Piper, W. E. (1996). Limiting time-unlimited group therapy. *International Journal of Group Psychotherapy, 46*(6), 61–79.

Juhnke, G. A. (1996). The adapted-SAD PERSONS: A suicide assessment scale designed for use with children. *Elementary School Guidance & Counseling, 30,* 252–258.

Julia, M. C. (1996). *Multicultural Awareness in the health care professions.* Needham Heights, MA: Allyn & Bacon.

K

Kadushin, A. (1977). *Consultation in social work.* New York: Columbia University Press.

Kadushin, A. & Kadushin, G. (1997). *The social work interview: a guide for human service professionals* (4th ed.). New York: Columbia.

Kadushin, G., & Kulys, R. (1993). Discharge planning revisited: What do social workers actually do in discharge planning? *Social Work, 38,* 713–726.

Kagle, J. D. (1991). *Social work records* (2nd ed.). Chicago, IL: Waveland Press.

Kagle, J. D. (1994). Should systematic assessment, monitoring and evaluation tools be used as empowerment aids for clients? Rejoiner to Dr. Jayaratne. In W. W. Hudson & P. S. Nurius (Eds.), *Controversial issues in social work research* (pp. 88–92). Needham Heights, MA: Allyn and Bacon.

Kagle, J. D. & Kopels, S. (2008). *Social work records* (3rd ed.). Long Grove, IL: Waveland Press.

Kahn, M. (1997). *Between therapist and client: The new relationship.* New York, NY: W. H. Freeman & Company.

Kane, N. (1995). Looking at the lite side. "I feed more cats, than I have T-cells." *Reflections, 1*(2), 26–36.

Kaplan, H. I., and Sadock, B. J., (Eds.) (2007). *Synopsis of Psychiatry* (10th ed.). Baltimore, MD: Williams and Wilkins.

Karlsson, R. (2005). Ethnic matching between therapist and patient in psychotherapy. An overview of findings, together with methodological and contextual issues. *Cultural Diversity and Ethnic Minority Psychology, 11,* 113–129.

Kasprow, W. J., & Rosenheck, R. A. (2007). Outcomes of critical time intervention case management for homeless veterans after psychiatric hospitalization. *Psychiatric Services, 58,* 929–935.

Katz, S., Ford, A. B., Moskowitz, R. W., Jackson, B. A., & Jaffe, M. W. (1963). Studies of illness in the aged. The Index of ADL: A standardized measure of biological and psychosocial function. *Journal of the American Medical Association, 185,* 914–919.

Kauffman, J. M. (1997). *Characteristics of emotional and behavioral disorders of children and youth* (6th ed.). Upper Saddle River, NJ: Prentice-Hall.

Kazdin, A. E., & Wassell, G. (1998). Treatment completion and therapeutic change among children referred for outpatient therapy. *Professional Psychology: Research and Practice, 29,* 332–340.

Kear-Colwell, J., & Pollock, P. (1997). Motivation or confrontation: Which approach to the child sex offender? *Criminal Justice and Behavior, 24,* 20–33.

Keehner Engelke, M., Guttu, M., Warren, M. B. & Swanson, M. B. (2008). Case management for children with chronic illnesses: Health, academic and quality of life outcomes. *Journal of Nursing, 24*(4), 205–214.

Kelly, M. (2008). Task-centered practice. In T. Mizrahi & L. Davis (Eds.), *Encyclopedia of Social Work* (20th ed., pp. 197–199). Washington, DC: NASW Press-Oxford University Press.

Kelly, M. J., Kim, J. S., & Franklin, C. (2008). *Solution-focused brief therapy in schools: A 360 degree review of practice and research.* New York, NY: Oxford University Press.

Kent, M. M. (2010). *In U.S., who is at greatest risk for suicides?* Retrieved from http://www.prb.org/Articles/2010/suicides.aspx

Kessler, D., Lewis, G., Kaur, S., Wiles, N., King, M., Weich, S., Peters, T. J. (2009). Therapist-delivered internet psychotherapy for depression in primary care: A randomised controlled trial. *Lancet 374,* 628–634. Retrieved from http://www.nationalstressclinic.com/wp-content/uploads/lancet-study.pdf

Kessler, M., Gira, E. & Poertner, J. (2005). Moving best practice to evidence based practice in child welfare. *Families in Society, 86,* 244–250.

Kettenbach, G. (2003). *Writing SOAP notes: With patient/client management formats* (3rd ed.). Philadephia, PA: Davis.

Kettner, P. M., Daley, J. M., & Nichols, A. W. (1985). *Initiating change in organizations and communities.* Monterey, CA: Brooks/Cole.

Kilpatrick, A. C., & Cleveland, P. H. (1993). Level of needs. Issues and relevant interventions. In A. C. Kilpatrick and T. P. Holland, *Working with families: An intergrative model by level of need* (4th ed. p. 4). Pearson Allyn & Bacon.

Kilpatrick, A. C., & Holland, T. (2003). *Working with families: An integrative model by level of need* (3rd ed.). Boston, MA: Allyn & Bacon.

Kilpatrick, A. C., & Holland, T. P. (2006). *Working with families. An integrative model by level of need* (4th ed.). Boston, MA: Allyn & Bacon.

Kim, J. S. (2008). Examining the effectiveness of solution-focused brief therapy: A meta-analysis. *Research on Social Work Practice, 18,* 107–116.

Kirk, S. A., & Kutchins, H. (1992). *The selling of DSM: The rhetoric of science in psychiatry.* New York, NY: Aldine De Gruyter.

Kirst-Ashman and Hull, G. (2012). *Generalist practice with organizations and communities* (5th ed.). Belmont, CA: Brooks-Cole.

Kleespies, P. M., Penk, W. E., & Forsyth, J. P. (1993). The s*tress of patient suicidal behavior during clinical training: Incidence, impact, and recovery. Professional Psychology: Research and Practice, 24,* 293–303.

Klein, A. (1970). *Social work through group process.* Albany, NY: School of Social Welfare, State University of New York at Albany.

Knight, C. (2006). Groups for individuals with traumatic histories: Practice considerations for social workers. *Social Work, 51,* 20–30.

Knight, J. R., Sherritt, L., Shrier, L. A., Harris, S. K., & Chang, G. (2002). Validity of the CRAFFT substance abuse screening test among adolescent clinic patients. *Archives of Pediatrics and Adolescent Medicine, 156,* 607–614.

Knox, K. S., & Roberts, A. R. (2008). The crisis intervention model. In N. Coady & P. Lehmann (Eds.), *Theoretical perspectives for direct social work practice. A generalist-eclectic approach* (2nd ed., pp. 249–274). New York, NY: Springer Publishing Company.

Kohn, L. P., Oden, T. M., Munoz, R. F., Robinson, A., & Leavitt, D. (2002). Adapted cognitive-behavioral group therapy for depressed low-income, African American women. *Community Mental Health Journal, 38,* 497–504.

Komar, A. A. (1994). Adolescent school crises: Structures, issues and techniques for postventions. *International Journal of Adolescence and Youth, 5*(1/2), 35–46.

Koob, G. F., & Le Moal, M. (2008). Addiction and the brain antireward system. Annual *Review of Psychology 59*(1), 29–53.

Koob, J. J. (2003). Solution-focused family interventions. In A. C. Kilpatrick & T. P. Holland. *Working with families: An integrative model by level of need* (3rd ed., pp. 131–150). Boston, MA: Allyn & Bacon.

Kopp, J. (1989). Self-observation: An empowerment strategy in assessment. *Social Casework, 70,* 276–284.

Korol, M. S., Green, B. L., & Grace, M. (1999). Developmental analysis of the psychosocial impact of disaster on children: A review. *Journal of the American Academy of Child and Adolescent Pyschiatry, 38,* 368–375.

Kosoff, S. (2003). Single session groups: Applications and areas of expertise. *Social Work with Groups, 26,* 29–45.

Koss, M. P., & Shiang, J. (1994). Research on brief psychotherapy. In A. E. Bergin & S. L. Garfield

(Eds.), *Handbook of psychotherapy and behavioral change* (3rd ed., pp. 664–700). New York: Wiley.

Kossak, S. (2005). Exploring the elements of culturally relevant service delivery. *Families in Society, 86*(2): 189–195. Krähenbühl S., & Blades, M. (2006). The effect of interviewing techniques on young children's responses to questions. *Child Care Health and Development 32*, 321–333.

Kroenke, K., Spitzer R. L., & Williams, J. B. W. (2001). The PHQ-9: Validity of a brief depression severity measure. *Journal of General Internal Medicine, 16*, 606–613.

Kruger, L., Moore, D., Schmidt, P., & Wiens, R. (1979). Group work with abusive parents. *Social Work, 24*, 337–338.

Kuehlwein, K. T. (1992). Working with gay men. In A. Freeman & F. M. Dattillio (Eds.). *Comprehensive casebook of cognitive therapy* (pp. 249–252). New York, NY: Plenum.

Kumabe, K., Nishada, C., & Hepworth, D. (1985). *Bridging ethnocultural diversity in social work and health*. Honolulu, HI: University of Hawaii Press.

Kung, W. W. (2003). Chinese Americans' help seeking behavior for emotional distress. *Social Service Review, 77*(1), 110–134.

Kurland, R., & Salmon, R. (1998). Purpose: A misunderstood and misused keystone of group work practice. *Social Work with Groups, 21*(3), 5–17.

Kutchins, H. (1991). The fiduciary relationship. The legal basis for social worker's responsibilities to clients. *Social Work, 36*, 103–106.

L

Laing, R. (1965). Mystification, confusion and conflict. In I. Boszormenyi-Nagy & J. Framo (Eds.), *Intensive family therapy: Theoretical and practical aspects*. New York, NY: Harper & Row.

Laird, J. (1993). Family-centered practice: Cultural and constructionist reflections. *Journal of Teaching in Social Work, 8*(1/2), 77–109.

Lamb, M., & Brown, D. (2006). Conversational apprentices: Helping children become competent informants about their own experiences. *British Journal of Developmental Psychology, 24*, 215–234.

Lambert, M. J., Bergin, A. E., & Garfield, S. L. (2004). Introduction and historical overview. In M. J. Lambert (Ed), *Handbook of psychotherapy and behavioral change* (5th ed., pp. 3–15). New York, NY: Wiley.

Lambert, M. J., & Ogles, B. M. (2004). The efficacy and effectiveness of psychotherapy. In M. J. Lambert (Ed.), *Handbook of psychotherapy and behavioral change* (5th ed., pp. 139–193). New York, NY: John Wiley.

Land, H. (1988). The impact of licensing on social work practice: Values, ethics and choices. *Journal of Independent Social Work, 2*(4), 87–96.

Lane, E. J., Daugherty, T. K., & Nyman, S. J. (1998). Feedback on ability in counseling, self-efficacy, and persistence on task. *Psychological Reports, 83*, 1113–1114.

Langley, J. (2001). Developing anti-oppressive empowering social work practice with older lesbian women and gay men. *Bristish Journal of Social Work, 31*, 917–932.

Lantz, J. (1996). Cognitive theory in social work treatment. In F. Turner (Ed.), *Social work treatment: Interlocking theoretical approaches* (4th ed., pp. 94–115). New York, NY: Free Press.

Larsen, D., Attkission, C., Hargreaves, W., & Nguyen, T. (1979). Assessment of client satisfaction: Development of a general scale. *Evaluation & Program Planning, 2*, 197–207.

Larsen, J. (1980). Accelerating group development and productivity: An effective leader approach. *Social Work with Groups, 3*, 25–39.

Larsen, J., & Mitchell, C. (1980). Task-centered, strength-oriented group work with delinquents. *Social Casework, 61*, 154–163.

Lavee, Y. (1997). The components of healthy marriages: Perceptions of Israeli social workers and their clients. *Journal of Family Social Work, 2*(1), 1–14.

Lazarus, A. A. (1994). How certain boundaries and ethics diminish therapeutic effectiveness. *Ethics and Behavior, 4*, 255–261.

Leadbeater, B. J., Kuperminc, G. P., Blatt, S. J., Hertzog, C. (1999). A multivariate model of gender differences in adolescents' internalizing and externalising problems. *Developmental Psychology, 35*, 1268–1282.

Leahy, R. H., & Holland, S. J. (2000). *Treatment plans and interventions for depression and anxiety disorders*. New York, NY: Guildford Press.

LeCroy, C. W. (2002). Child therapy and social skills. In A. R. Roberts & G. J. Greene (Eds.), *Social workers' desk reference* (pp. 406–412). New York, NY: Oxford University Press.

Lee, M. Y. (2003). A solution-focused approach to cross-cultural clinical social work practice: Utilizing cultural strengths. *Families in Society: The Journal of Contemporary Human Services, 84*, 385–395.

Lee, M. Y., Greene, G. J., & Rheinscheld, J. (1999). A model for short-term solution-focused group treatment of male domestic violence offenders. *Journal of Family Social Work*, 3(2), 39–57.

Lee, M. Y., Uken, A. & Sebold, J. (2004). Accountability for change: Solution-focused treatment with domestic violence offenders. *Families in society* 85(4): 463–476.

Lee, S. J. (2005). Facilitating the welfare-to-work transition for women with a mental health work barrier. *Journal of Human Behavior in the Social Environment*, 12, 127–143.

Lehman, A. F. (1996). Heterogeneity of person and place: Assessing co-occurring addictive and mental disorders. *American Journal of Orthopsychiatry*, 66(1), 32–41.

Leiter M. P., & Maslach, C. (2005). *Banishing burnout: Six involving feelings, attitudes, motives and strategies for improving your relationship expectations with work*. San Francisco, CA: Jossey-Bass.

Lens, V. (2005). Advocacy and argumentation in the public arena: A guide for social workers. *Social Work*, 50, 231–238.

Lesure-Lester, E. G. (2002). An application of cognitive behavioral principles in the reduction of aggression among abused African American adolescents. *Journal of Interpersonal Violence*, 17, 394–403.

Levi, D. (2007). *Group dynamics for teams* (2nd ed.). Thousand Oaks, CA: Sage Publications.

Levick, K. (1981). Privileged communication: Does it really exist? *Social Casework*, 62, 235–239.

Levine, C. O., & Dang, J. (1979). The group within the group: The dilemma of cotherapy. *International Journal of Group Psychotherapy*, 29(2), 175–184.

Levinson, H. (1977). Termination of psychotherapy: Some salient issues. *Social Casework*, 58, 480–489.

Levinson, D. J. (1996). *Seasons of women's life*. New York, NY: Alfred A. Knopf.

Levy, A. J. & Frank, M. G. (2011). Clinical practice with children. In J. Brandell, ed. *Theory and Practice in Clinical Social Work* (2nd ed.). (pp. 101–121). Thousand Oaks, CA.: Sage.

Levy, C. (1973). The value base of social work. *Journal of Education for Social Work*, 9, 34–42.

Levy, L. (1963). *Psychological interpretation*. New York, NY: Holt, Rinehart & Winston.

Lewis, E. (1991). Social change and citizen action: A philosophical exploration for modern social group work. *Social Work with Groups*, 14(3/4), 23–34.

Lewis, E. A., Skyles, A., & Crosbie-Burnett, M. (2000). *Public policy and families of color in the new millennium*. National Council on Family Relations Annual Program Meeting, Minneapolis, MN, November 12, 2000.

Lewis, J. A., Lewis, M. D., Packard, T., & Souflee, F. (2001). *Management of human service programs* (3rd ed.). Pacific Grove, CA: Wadsworth/Brooks/Cole.

Lewis, T., & Osborn, C. (2004). Solution-focused counseling and motivational interviewing. A consideration of confluence. *Journal of Counseling and Development*, 82, 38–48.

Liau, A. K., Barriga, A. Q., & Gibbs, J. C. (1998). Relations between self serving cognitive distortions and overt versus covert antisocial behaviors in adolescents. *Aggressive Behavior 24*, 335–346.

Lieberman, M., & Videka-Sherman, L. (1986). The impact of self-help groups on the mental health of widows and widowers. *American Journal of Orthopsychiatry*, 56, 435–449.

Lieberman, M., Yalom, I., & Miles, M. (1973). *Encounter groups: Firstfacts*. New York, NY: Basic Books.

Ligon, J. (1997). Brief crisis stabilization of an African American woman. Integrating cultural and ecological approaches. *Journal of Multicultural Social Work*, 6(3/4), 111–123.

Lindemann, E. (1944). Symptomatology and management of acute grief. American Journal of *Psychiatry*, 101, 141–148.

Lindemann, E. (1956). The meaning of crisis in individual and family. *Teachers College Record*, 57, 310.

Lindsey, M. A., Korr, W. S., Broitman, M., Bone, L., Green, A. & Leaf, P. J. (2006). Help-seeking behaviors and depression among African American adolescent boys. *Social Work*, 51, 49–58.

Linhorst, D. M. (2002). Federalism and social justice: Implications for social work. *Social Work*, 47, 201–208.

Linhorst, D. M., Hamilton, J., Young, E., & Eckert, A. (2002). Opportunities and barriers to empowering people with severe mental illness through participation in treatment planning. *Social Work*, 47, 425–434.

Linzer, N. (1999). *Resolving ethical dilemmas in social work practice*. Boston, MA: Allyn & Bacon.

Lipchik, E. (1997). My story about solution-focused brief therapist/client relationships. *Journal of Systemic Therapies*, 16, 159–172.

Lipchik, E. (2002). *Beyond technique in solution-focused therapy: Working with emotions and the therapeutic relationship*. New York, NY: Guilford Press.

Lister, L. (1987). Contemporary direct practice roles. *Social Work*, 32, 384–391.

Littell, J. & Girvin, H. (2004). Ready or not: Uses of the stages of change model in child welfare. *Child welfare, 83*, 341–366.

Lo, T. W. (2005). Task-centered group work: Reflections on practice. *International Social Work, 48*, 455–456.

Loewenburg, F., & Dolgoff, R. (1996). *Ethical decision for social work practice* (5th ed.). Itasca, IL: F. E. Peacock.

Loewenberg, F. M., Dolgoff, R., & Harrington, D. (2005). *Ethical decisions for social work practice* (7th ed.). Itasca, IL: F. E. Peacock.

Logan, S. M. L., Freeman, E. M., & McRoy, R. G. (1990). *Social work practice with black families: A culturally specific perspective.* New York, NY: Longman.

Long, D. L., Tice, C. J., & Morrison, J. D. (2006). Macro social work practice. A strengths perspective. Thomson-Brooks/Cole.

Longres, J. F. (1991). Toward a status model of ethnic sensitive practice. *Journal of Multi-cultural Social Work, 1*(1), 41–56.

Longres, J. F. (1995). *Human behavior in the social environment.* Itasca, IL: F. E. Peacock.

Loo, C. M., Ueda, S. S., & Morton, R. K. (2007). Group treatment for race-related stresses among Vietnam veterans. *Transcultural Psychiatry, 44*(1), 115–135.

Lowenstein, D. A., Amigo, E., Duara, R., Guterman, A., Kurwitz, D., Berkowitz, N., et al. (1989). A new scale for the assessment of functional status in Alzheimer's disease and related disorders. *Journal of Gerontology: Psychological Sciences, 44*, 114–121.

Lu, Y., Dane, B. & Gellman, A. (2005). An experiential model: teaching empathy and cultural sensitivity. *Journal of teaching social work. 25*(3/4), 89–103.

Luborsky, L., & Spence, D. (1978). Quantitative research on psychoanalytic therapy. In S. Garfield & A. Bergin (Eds.), *Handbook of psychotherapy and behavior change* (pp. 331–368). New York, NY: Wiley.

Lucas, C. P., Zhang, H., Fisher, P. W., Shaffer, D., Regier, D. A., Narrow, W. E., & Friman, P. (2001). The DISC Predictive Scales (DPS): Efficiently screening for diagnoses. *Journal of the American Academy of Child & Adolescent Psychiatry, 40*, 443–449.

Lukas, S. (1993). *Where to start and what to ask: An assessment handbook.* New York, NY: Norton.

Lukton, R. (1982). Myths and realities of crisis intervention. *Social Casework, 63*, 275–285.

Lum, D. (1996). *Social work practice and people of color*: A process-stage approach (3rd ed.). Pacific Grove, CA: Brooks/Cole.

Lum, D. (2004). *Social work practice and people of color*. A process-stage approach (5th ed.). Pacific Grove, CA: Brooks/Cole.

Lum, D. (2007). *Culturally competent practice: A framework for understanding diverse groups and justice issues.* Pacific Grove, CA: Thomson-Brooks/Cole.

M

McCarter, S. A. (2008). *Adolescence.* In E. D. Hutchison (Ed.). Dimensions of human behavior. The changing life cycle (3rd ed.) (pp. 227–281). Sage Publications.

Macgowan, M. J. (1997). A measure of engagement for social group work: The group work engagement measure (GEM). *Journal of Social Service Research, 23*(2), 17–37.

Macgowan, M. J. (2004). Prevention and intervention in youth suicide. In P. Allen-Mears, & M. W. Fraser (Eds.), *Intervention with children and adolescents: An interdisciplinary perspective* (pp. 282–310). Boston, MA: Pearson.

Macgowan, M. J. (2008). *A guide to evidence-based group work.* New York, NY: Oxford University Press.

McMillen, J., Morris, L. and Sherraden, M. (2004). Ending social work's grudge match: Problems versus strengths. *Families in Society, 85*, 317–325.

Mackelprang, R., & Hepworth, D. H. (1987). Ecological factors in rehabilitation of patients with severe spinal cord injuries. *Social Work in Health Care, 13*, 23–38.

Mackey, R. A., & O'Brian, B. A. (1998). Marital conflict management: Gender and ethnic differences. *Social Work, 43*, 128–141.

Magen, R. (2004). Measurement issues. In C. D. Garvin, L. M. Gutierrez, & M. J. Galinsky (Eds.), *Handbook of social work with groups.* New York, NY: Guilford Press.

Magen, R. H., & Glajchen, M. (1999). Cancer support groups: Client outcome and the context of group process. *Research on Social Work Practice, 9*(5), 541–554.

Maguire, L. (2002). *Clinical social work: Beyond generalist practice with individuals, groups and families.* Pacific Grove, CA: Thomson-Brooks-Cole.

Mahler, C. (1969). *Group counseling in the schools.* Boston, MA: Houghton Mifflin.

Mahoney, M. J. (1974). *Cognition and behavior modification.* Cambridge, MA: Ballinger.

Mailick, M. D., & Vigilante, F. W. (1997). The family assessment wheel: A social constructionist perspective. *Families in Society, 80*, 361–369.

Maiter, S. Palmer, S. Manji, S. (2006). Strengthening social worker-client relationship in child protective services. *Qualitative Social Work, 5*, 167–186.

Major, S. (2004). Evidence weak for case management for frail elderly. *British Medical Journal, 329* (7478), 1306.

Malekoff, A. (2006). Strengths-based group work with children and adolescents. In C. D. Garvin, L. M. Gutierrez, & M. J. Galinsky (Eds.), *Handbook of social work with groups* (pp. 227–244). New York, NY: Guilford Press.

Malgady, R. G. & Zayas, L. H. (2001). Cultural and linguistic considerations in psychodiagnosis with Hispanics: The need for an empirically informed process model. *Social Work, 46*, 39–49.

Mallory, K. (2004, May 8). Barbers cutting cancer out in Montgomery County. *The Washington Afro American, 112*, 39.

Manhal-Baugus, M. (2001). E-Therapy: Practical, ethical, and legal issues. *CyberPsychology and Behavior, 4*, 551–563.

Marlatt, G. A., & Gordon, J. R. (1985). *Relapse prevention: Maintenance strategies in the treatment of addictive behaviors.* New York, NY: Guilford Press.

Marlow, C. (1993). Coping with multiple roles: Family configuration and the need for workplace services. *Affilia, 8*(1), 40–55.

Marsh, J. (2003). Arguments for family strengths. *Social Work, 42*, 147–148.

Marsh, J. (2004). Theory-driven versus theory-free research in empirical social work practice (pp. 20–35). In Briggs, H., & Rzepnicki, T. (eds). *Using evidence in social work practice.* Chicago, IL: Lyceum.

Marsh, J. (2005). Social justice: social work's organizing value. *Social Work, 50*, 293–294.

Marsh, J. C. (2002). Learning from clients. *Social Work, 47*, 341–342.

Marsh, J. C. (2005). Social justice: Social worker's organizing values. *Social Work, 50*, 345–346.

Martin, L. L. (1993). *Total quality management in human service organizations.* Thousand Oaks, CA: Sage Publications.

Martin, P. Y., & O'Connor, G. G. (1989). *The social environment: Open systems applications.* Upper Saddle River, NJ: Longman.

Maschi, T. (2006). Unraveling the link between trauma and male delinquency: The cumulative versus differential risk perspective. *Social Work, 11*, 59–70.

Mason, J. L., Benjamin, M. P., & Lewis, S. A. (1996). The cultural competence model: Implications for child and family mental health services. In C. A. Heflinger & C. T. Nixon (Eds.), *Families and the mental health system for children and adolescents: Policy, services, and research* (pp. 165–190). Thousand Oaks, CA: Sage Publications.

Mason, M. (2009). Rogers redux: relevance and outcomes of motivational interviewing across behavioral problems. *Journal of Counseling & Development, 87*: 357–362

Mattaini, M. 1995. Visualizing pracrice with children and families. *Early child development and care,* 106: 59–74.

Matto, H. C. (2005). A bio-behavioral model of addiction treatment: Applying dual representation theory to craving management and relapse prevention. *Substance Use & Misuse, 40*, 529–541.

Mau, W., & Jepsen, D. A. (1990). Help seeking perceptions behaviors: A comparison of Chinese and American graduate students. *Journal of Multicultural Counseling and Development, 18*(2), 95–104.

May, P., Hymbaugh, K., Aasc, J., & Samct, J. (1983). The epidemiology of fetal alcohol syndrome among American Indians of the Southwest. *Social Biology, 30*, 374–387.

Mayadas, N. S., Ramanathan, C. S., & Suarez, Z. (1998–1999). Mental health, social context, refugees, and immigrants: A cultural interface. *The Journal of Intergroup Relations, 25*(4), 3–14.

Mayer, J., & Timms, N. (1969). Clash in perspective between worker and client. *Social Casework, 50*, 32–40.

Mayo Clinic. (2007, January 12). *Elder abuse: Signs to look for, action to take.* Retrieved from http://www.mayoclinic.com/health/elder-abuse/HA00041

Mays, N. (2003, Fall). Investigating how culture impacts health. *Washington University in Saint Louis Magazine.*

McAdoo, J. L. (1993). Decision making and marital satisfaction in African American families. In H. P. McAdoo (Ed.), *Family ethnicity: Strength in diversity* (pp. 109–118). Thousand Oaks, CA: Sage Publications.

McCollum, E. E., & Beer, J. (1995). The view from the other chair. *Family Therapy Networker, 19*(2), 59–62.

McCollum, E. E, & Trepper, T. S. (2001). Creating family solutions for substance abuse. New York, NY: Haworth Press.

McConaughy, S. H., & Auchenbach, T. M. (1994). *Manual for the semistructured clinical interview with children and adolescents.* Burlington, VT: University of Vermont, Department of Psychiatry.

McCubbin, H. (1988). *Resilient families in the military: Profiles of strengths and hardiness.* Madison, WI: University of Wisconsin.

McCubbin, H. I., & McCubbin, M. A. (1988). Typologies of resilient families. Emerging roles of social class and ethnicity. *Family Relations, 37*, 247–254.

McDonald, L. (2002). Evidence-based, family-strengthening strategies to reduce delinquency: FAST: Families and Schools Together. In A. R. Roberts & G. J. Greene (Eds.), *Social workers' desk reference* (pp. 717–722). New York, NY: Oxford University Press.

McFarlane, W. R. (2002). *Multifamily groups in the treatment of severe psychiatric disorders.* New York: Guilford.

McGoldrick. M. (Ed.) (1998). *Revisioning family therapy. Race, culture and gender in clinical practice.* New York, NY: The Guilford Press.

McGoldrick, M., & Gerson, R. (1985). *Genograms in family assessment.* New York, NY: Norton.

McGoldrick, M., Giordano, J., & Pearce, J. K. (Eds.) (1996). *Ethnicity and family therapy.* New York, NY: Guilford Press.

McGonagle, E. (1986). *Banana splits: A peer support group for children of transitional families.* Ballston Spa, NY: Author.

McHale, J. P., & Cowan, P. A. (Eds.) (1996). *Understanding how family-level dynamics affect children's development: Studies in two-parent families.* San Francisco, CA: Jossey-Bass.

McHale, J. P. (2007). When infants grow up in multi-person relationship systems. *Infant Mental health Journal, 28,* 370–292.

McIntosh, J. L. (2003). Suicide survivors: The aftermath of suicide and suicidal behavior. In C. D. Bryant (Ed.), *The handbook of death and dying* (pp. 339–350). Thousand Oaks, CA: Sage Publications.

McKenry, P. C., & Price, S. J. (Eds.) (2000). *Families and change. Coping with stressful events and transitions* (2nd ed.). Thousand Oaks, CA: Sage Publications.

McKenzie, A. (2005). Narrative-oriented therapy with children who have experienced sexual abuse. Envision: *The Manitoba Journal of Child Welfare, 4*(2), 1–29.

McKinnon, J. (2008). Exploring the nexus between social work and the environment. *Australian Social Work, 61,* 256–268.

McMillen, J. C. (1999). Better for it: How people benefit from adversity. *Social Work, 44,* 455–468.

McMillen, J. E., & Fischer, R. (1998). The perceived benefit scale: Measuring perceived positive life changes after negative events. *Social Work Research, 22*(3), 173–187.

McMillen, J. C., Smith, E. M., & Fisher, R. (1997). Perceived benefit and mental health after three types of disaster. *Journal of Consulting and Clinical Psychology, 63,* 1037–1043.

McMillen, J. C., Zuravin, S., & Rideout, G. B. (1995). Perceptions of benefits from child sexual abuse. *Journal of Consulting and Clinical Psychology, 63,* 1037–1043.

McNeely, R., & Badami, M. (1984). Interracial communication in school social work. *Social Work, 29,* 22–25.

McPhatter, A. (1991). Assessment revisited: A comprehensive approach to understanding family dynamics. *Families in Society, 72,* 11–21.

McQuaide, S. (1999). Using psychodynamic, cognitive behavioral and solution-focused questioning to construct a new narrative. *Clinical Social Work, 27,* 339–353.

McQuaide, S., & Ehrenreich, J. H. (1997). Assessing client strengths. *Families in Society, 78,* 201–212.

McRoy, R. G. (2003, June 6). *Impact of systems on adoption in the African American community.* Keynote address presented at the meeting of the Institute on Domestic Violence in the African American Community, Minneapolis, MN.

McWilliams, N. (1999). *Psychoanalytic formulation.* New York, NY: Guilford Press.

Meenaghan, T. M. (1987). Macro practice: Current trends and issues. In *Encyclopedia of social work* (18th ed., pp. 82–89). Silver Spring, MD: National Association of Social Workers.

Meezan, W., & O'Keefe, M. (1998). Evaluating the effectiveness of multifamily group therapy in child abuse and neglect. *Research on Social Work Practice, 8,* 330–353.

Meichenbaum, D. (1977). *Cognitive-behavior modification.* New York, NY: Plenum Press.

Meier, A. (1997). Inventing new models of social support groups: A feasibility study of an online stress management support group for social workers. *Social Work with Groups, 20*(4), 35–53.

Meier, A. (2002). An online stress management support group for social workers. *Journal of Technology in Human Services, 20*(1/2), 107–132.

Meier, A. (2006). Technology-mediated groups. In C. D. Garvin, L. M. Gutierrez, & M. J. Galinsky (Eds.), *Handbook of social work with groups* (pp. 13–31). New York, NY: Guilford Press.

Mercer, J. (2006). *Understanding attachment: Parenting, child care and emotional development.* Westport, CT. Praeger Publishers.

Mercier, C., & Racine, G. (2005). A follow-up study of homeless women, *Journal of Social Distress and Homeless, 2,* 207–222.

Metcalf, L. (1998). *Solution focused group therapy: Ideas for groups in private practice, schools, agencies, and treatment programs.* New York, NY: Free Press.

Metcalf, L., Thomas, F., Duncan, B., Miller, S., & Hubble, M. (1996). What works in solution-focused brief therapy: A qualitative analysis of client and therapist's perceptions. In S. Miller, M. Hubble, & B. Duncan (Eds.), *Handbook of solution-focused brief therapy*. San Francisco, CA: Jossey-Bass.

Meyer, C. (Ed.) (1983). *Clinical social work in the ecosystems perspective*. New York, NY: Columbia University Press.

Meyer, C. (1990, April 1). *Can social work keep up with the changing family?* [Monograph]. The fifth annual Robert J. O'Leary Memorial Lecture. Columbus, OH: The Ohio State University College of Social Work.

Meyer, W. (2001). Why they don't come back: A clinical perspective on the no-show client. *Clinical Social Work, 29*, 325–339.

Meyer, R. A., Williams, R. C., Ottens, A. J., & Schmidt, A. E (1991). Triage assessment system: Crisis intervention. In R. K. James, Crisis intervention strategies (6th ed.). Brooks/Cole.

Meystedt, D. M. (1984). Religion and the rural population: Implications for social work. *Social Casework, 65*(4), 219–226.

Milgram, D., & Rubin, J. S. (1992). Resisting resistance: Involuntary substance abuse group therapy. *Social Work with Groups, 15*(1), 95–110.

Miller, D. B. (1997). Parenting against the odds: African-American parents in the child welfare system—a group approach. *Social Work with Groups, 20*(1), 5–18.

Miller, J. A. (1994). A family's sense of power in their community: Theoretical and research issues. *Smith College Studies in Social Work, 64*, 221–241.

Miller, R., & Mason, S. E. (2001). Using group therapy to enhance treatment compliance in first episode schizophrenia. *Social Work with Groups, 24*(1), 37–52.

Miller, S. M., & Øyen, E. (1996). Remeasuring Poverty. *Poverty & Race, 5*(5), 1–4.

Miller, W., Rollnick, S. T., & Conforti, K. (2002). *Motivational interviewing: Preparing people for change* (2nd ed.). New York: Guildford Publications.

Miller, W., Taylor, C. & West, J. (1980). Focused versus broad spectrum behavior therapy for problem drinkers. *Journal of Counseling and Clinical Psychology* 48, 590–601.

Miller, W. R., & Rollnick, S. (1991). *Motivational interviewing: Preparing people to change addictive behavior*. New York, NY: Guilford Press.

Miller, W. R., & Rollnick, S. (2002). *Motivational interviewing: preparing people to change addictive behavior* (2nd ed.). New York, NY: Guilford Press.

Miller, W. R., & Sovereign, R. G. (1989). The check-up: A model for early intervention in addictive behaviors. In T. Loberg, W. R. Miller, P. E. Nathan, & G. A. Marlatt (Eds.), *Addictive behaviors: Prevention and early intervention* (pp. 219–231). Amsterdam, Netherlands: Swets and Zeitlinger.

Millon, T., & Davis, R. (1997). The MCMI-III: Present and future directions. *Journal of Personality Assessment, 68*(1), 68–95.

Minuchin, S. (1974). *Families and family therapy*. Cambridge, MA: Harvard University Press.

Mokuau, N., & Fong, R. (1994). Assessing the responsiveness of health services to ethnic minorities of color. *Social Work in Health Care, 28*(1), 23–34.

Moline, M. E., Williams, G. T., & Austin, K. M. (1998). *Documenting psychotherapy: Essentials for mental health practitioners*. Thousand Oaks, CA: Sage.

Morell, C. (2003). Empowerment theory and long-living women: A feminist and disability perspective. *Journal of Human Behavior in the Social Environment, 7*, 225–236.

Morgan, A. (2000). *What is narrative therapy?* Adelaide, South Australia: Dulwich Centre Publications.

Morgan, G. (1997). *Images of organizations*. Thousand Oaks, CA: Sage Publications.

Morrison, J. (1995). *The first interview: Revised for DSM-IV*. New York, NY: Guilford Press.

Morton, T. (1999). The increasing colorization of America's child welfare system. The overrepresentation of African American children. *Policy and Practice, 12*, 21–30.

Moyers, T., & Rollnick, S. (2002). A motivational interviewing perspective on resistance in psychotherapy. *Journal of Clinical Psychology, 58*, 185–193.

Moyers, T. B., Martin, T., Manuel, J. K., & Miller, W. R. (2003). The Motivational Interviewing Treatment Integrity (MITI) Code, Version 2.0. Retrieved January 7, 2011, from http://casaa.unm.edu/download/miti.pdf

Munroe, E. (2004). Improving practice: Child protection as a systems problem. *Children Youth and Services Review, 27*, 375–391.

Munson, C. E. (2002). The techniques and process of supervisory practice. In A. R. Roberts & G. J. Greene (Eds.), *Social workers' desk reference* (pp. 38–44). New York, NY: Oxford University Press.

Murdach, A. D. (1996). Beneficence re-examined: Protective intervention in mental health. *Social Work, 41*, 26–32.

Murphy, C. M., & Baxter, V. A. (1997). Motivating batterers to change in the treatment context. *Journal of Interpersonal Violence, 12*, 607–619.

Murphy, B. C., & Dillon, C. (2003). *Interviewing in action: Relationship, process, and change* (2nd ed.). Pacific Grove, CA: Brooks/Cole.

Murphy, B. C., & Dillon, C. (2008). *Interviewing in action in a multicultural world* (3rd ed.). Pacific Grove, CA: Brooks/Cole.

Murray, C. E., & Murray, T. L. (2004). Solution-focused premarital counseling: Helping couples build a vision for their marriage. *Journal of Marital and Family Therapy, 30*, 349–358.

Murray-Swank, N. A., & Pargament, K. I. (2011). Seeking the sacred: The assessment of spirituality in the therapy process. In *Spiritually oriented interventions for counseling and psychotherapy* (pp. 107–135). Washington, DC US: American Psychological Association, 2011.

Mwanza. (1990). *Afrikan naturalism*. Columbus, OH: Pan Afrikan Publications.

N

Nader, K., & Mello, C. (2008). Interactive trauma/Grief-focused therapy with children. In N. Coady & P. Lehmann (Eds.), *Theoretical perspectives for direct social work practice. A generalist-eclectic approach* (2nd ed., pp. 493–519). New York, NY: Springer Publishing Company.

Nadler, A. (1996). Help seeking behavior as a coping resource. In M. Rosen (Ed.), *Learning resourcefulness: On coping skills, self control and adaptive behavior* (pp. 127–162). New York, NY: Springer Publishing.

Naleppa, M. J. (1999). Late adulthood. In E. D. Hutchison (Ed.). *Dimensions of human behavior: The changing life course*. Thousand Oaks, CA: Pine Forge Press.

Naleppa, M. J., & Reid, W. J. (2000). Integrating case management and brief-treatment strategies: A hospital-based geriatric program. *Social Work in Health Care, 31*(4), 1–23.

Naleppa, M. J., & Reid, W. J. (2003). *Gerontological social work: A task-centered approach*. New York, NY: Columbia University Press.

National Association of Social Workers (NASW) (1996). *Code of Ethics*. Washington, DC: NASW Press.

National Association of Social Workers (NASW). (1992). *NASW Standards for Social Work Case Management*. Retrieved from http://www.NASWDC.org/practice/standards/sw-case-management.asp

National Association of Social Workers (NASW). (2001). *NASW standard for cultural competence for social work practice*. Washington, DC: NASW Press.

National Association of Social Workers (NASW). (2006). *Immigration policy toolkit*. Washington, DC: NASW Press.

National Association of Social Workers (NASW). (2007). *Indicators for the achievement of the NASW standards for cultural competence in social work practice*. Washington, DC: NASW Press.

National Association of Social Workers (NASW). (2008a). *Code of ethics*. Washington, DC: NASW Press.

National Association of Social Workers (NASW). (2008b). *Law note series*. Retrieved from http://www.socialworkers.org/ldf/lawnotes/Default.asp

National Association of Social Workers (NASW). (2009). *Cultural and linguistic competence in the social work profession. Social Work Speaks:* National Association of Social Workers policy statements, 2009–2012 (8th ed., pp. 70–76) Washington, DC: NASW Press.

National Association of Scholars. (2007). *The scandal of social work education*. Retrieved from www.NAS.org

National Coalition for the Homeless. (2008). *Homeless Youth* (NCH Fact Sheet # 13). Retrieved from http://www.nationalhomeless.org.

National Institute of Mental Health. (2011). *Mental health information*. Retrieved from: http://www.nimh.nih.gov/index.shtml.

Nelson, T. D., & Kelley, L. (2001). Solution-focused couples groups. *Journal of Systemic Therapies, 20*, 47–66.

Nelson-Becker, H., Nakashima, M., & Canda, E. R. (2007). Spiritual Assessment in Aging: A Framework for Clinicians. *Journal of Gerontological Social Work, 48*, 331–347

Nelson-Zlupko, L., Kauffman, E., & Dore, M. M. (1995). Gender differences in drug addiction and treatment: Implications for social work intervention with substance abusing women. *Social Work, 40*, 45–54.

Netting, F. E., Kettner, P. M., & McMurtry, S. L. (2004). *Social work macro practice.* (3rd ed.) Boston, MA: Allyn & Bacon.

Nevil, N., Beatty, M. L., & Moxley, D. P. (1997). *Socialization games for persons with disabilities: Structured group activities for social and interpersonal development*. Springfield, IL: C. C. Thomas.

Neville, H. A., Spanierman, L., & Doan, B. T. (2006). Exploring the association between color-blind racial ideology and multicultural counseling competencies. *Cultural Diversity and Ethnic Minority Psychology, 12*, 275–290.

Newhill, C. E. (2004). *Client violence in social work practice: Prevention, intervention and research.* New York, NY: The Guilford Press.

Newman, K, & Chen, V. T (2007). *The missing class. Portraits of the near poor in America.* Boston, MA: Beacon Press.

Newsome, S. (2004). Solution-focused brief treatment (SFBT) group work with at-risk junior high school students: Enhancing the bottom line. *Research on Social Work Practice, 14*, 336–343.

Nichols, M. P. (2006). *Family therapy. Concepts and methods* (7th ed.). Boston, MA: Allyn & Bacon.

Nichols, M. P., & Schwartz, R. C. (1998). *Family therapy: Concepts and methods* (4th ed.). Boston, MA: Allyn & Bacon.

Nichols, M. P., & Schwartz, R. C. (2004). *Family therapy: Concepts and methods* (6th ed.). Boston, MA: Allyn & Bacon.

Van Nijnatten, C (2005). Transforming family position: a conversational analysis of a family social work case. *Child and family Social Work, 10*, 159–167.

Norcross, J. C. & Lambert, M. J. (2006). The therapy relationship. In J. C. Norcross, L. E. Beutler & R. F. Levant (Eds.), *Evidence-based practices in mental health: Debate and dialogue on the fundamental questions* (pp. 208–217). Washington, D. C.: American Psychological Association.

Norrick, N. & Spitz, A. (2008). Humor as a resource for mitigating conflict in interaction. *Journal of Pragmatics 40*(10), 1661–1686.

Norris, J. (1999). *Mastering documentation* (2nd ed.). Springhouse, PA: Springhouse.

Northen, H. (2006). Ethics and values in group work. In C. D. Garvin, L. M. Gutierrez, & M. J. Galinsky (Eds.), *Handbook of social work with groups* (pp. 76–89). New York, NY: Guilford Press.

Northen, H., & Kurland, R. (2001). The use of activity. In *Social work with groups* (3rd ed., pp. 258–287). New York, NY: Columbia University Press.

Norton, D. G. (1978). *The dual perspective: Inclusion of ethnic minority content in the social work curriculum.* New York, NY: Council on Social Work Education.

Nosko, A., & Wallace, R. (1997). Female/male co-leadership in groups. *Social Work with Groups, 20*(2), 3–16.

Nugent, W. (1992). The effective impact of a clinical social worker's interviewing style: A series of single-case experiments. *Research on Social Work Practice, 2*, 6–27.

Nugent, W. R., & Halvorson, H. (1995). Testing the effects of active listening. *Research on Social Work Practice, 5*, 152–175.

Nugent, W. R., Umbriet, M. S., Wilnamaki, L., & Paddock, J. (2001). Participation in victim-offender mediation and reoffense: Successful replications? *Research on Social Work Practice, 11*, 5–23.

Nybell, L. M., & Gray, S. S. (2004). Race, place, space: Meaning of cultural competence in three child welfare agencies. *Social Work, 49*, 17–26.

O

Oettingen, G., Bulgarella, C., Henderson, M. & Collwitzer, P. M. (2004) The self-regulation or goal pursuit. In R. Wright, J. Greenberg & S. S. Brehm (Eds.), *Motivational analysis of social behavior* (pp. 225–244). Mahwah, NJ: Lawrence Erlbaum Associates.

Ogbu, J. U. (1994). From cultural differences to differences in cultural frame of reference. In P. M. Greenfield & R. R. Cocking (Eds.), *Cross-cultural roots of minority child development* (pp. 365–392). Hillsdale, NJ: Erlbaum.

Ogbu, J. U. (1997). Understanding the school performances of urban blacks: Some essential knowledge. In H. J. Walbery, O. Reyes, and P. R. Weissberg (Eds.), *Children and youth: Interdisciplinary perspectives.* Thousand Oaks, CA: Sage Publications.

O'Hanlon, W. (1996). Case commentary. *Family Therapy Networker (January/February)*, 84–85.

O'Hare, T. (2005). *Evidence-based practices for social workers: An interdisciplinary approach.* Chicago, IL: Lyceum Books, Inc.

O'Hare, T. (2009). *Essential skills of social work practice. Assessment, intervention and evaluation.* Chicago, IL: Lyceum Books, Inc.

O'Hollaran, T. M., & Linton, J. M. (2000). Stress on the job: Self-care resources for counselors. *Journal of Mental Health Counseling, 22*, 254–265.

Okun, B. (2002). *Effective helping: Interviewing and counseling techniques.* Pacific Grove, CA: Brooks/Cole.

Okun, B. F. (1996). *Understanding diverse families. What practitioners need to know.* New York, NY: Guilford Press.

Okun, B. F., Fried, J., & Okun, M. L. (1999). *Understanding diversity. A learning-as-practice primer.* Pacific Grove, CA: Brooks/Cole Publishing Company.

Organista, K., Dwyer, E. V., & Azocar, F. (1993). Cognitive behavioral therapy with Latino clients. *The Behavior Therapist, 16*, 229–228.

Orme, J. (2002). Social work: Gender, care and justice. *British Journal of Social Work, 32*, 799–814.

Ortiz, L. P. A., & Langer, N. (2002). Assessment of spirituality and religion in later life: Acknowledging clients' needs and personal resources. *Journal of Gerontological Social Work, 32*, 5–20.

Orwin, R. G., Sonnefeld, L. J., Garrison-Mogren, R., Smith-Gray, N. (1994). Pitfalls in availability of the effectiveness of case management program for homeless persons: Lessons from NIAA Community, *Evaluation Research, 18*, 193–207.

Ostroff, C., & Atwater, L. E. (2003). Does whom you work with matter? Effects of referent group gender and age composition on managers' compensation. *Journal of Applied Psychology, 88*(4), 725–740.

Ozawa, M. N., & Yoon, H. (2005). Leavers of TANF and AFDC: How do they fare economically? *Social Work, 50*, 239–248.

P

Pack-Brown, J. P., Whittington-Clark, L. E., & Parker, W. M. (1998). *Images of me: A guide to group work with African-American women*. Boston, MA: Allyn & Bacon.

Padgett, D. K. (1999). *The qualitative research experience*. Pacific Grove, CA: Brooks/Cole-Thomson.

Padgett, D. K. (Ed.). (2004). *The qualitative research experience*. Pacific Grove, CA: Thomson-Brooks/Cole.

Padilla, Y., Shapiro, E., Fernandez-Castro, M., & Faulkner, M. (2008). Our nation's immigrants in peril: An urgent call to social workers. *Social Work, 53*, 5–8.

Palmer, B., & Pablo, S. (1978). Community development possibilities for effective Indian reservation child abuse and neglect efforts. In M. Lauderdale, R. Anderson, & S. Cramer (Eds.), *Child abuse and neglect. Issues on innovation and implementation* Palmer, N., & Kaufman, M. (2003). The ethics of informed consent: Implications for multicultural practice. *Journal of Ethnic and Cultural Diversity in Social Work, 12*(1), 1–26 (pp. 98–116). Washington, DC: U.S. Department of Health, Education and Welfare.

Panos, P. T., Panos, A., Cox, S., Roby, J. L. & Matheson, K. W. (2004). Ethical issues concerning the use of videoconferencing to supervise the placement of international social work field practicum students. *Journal of Social Work Education, 40*(3), 467–478.

Parad, H. J. (1965). *Crisis intervention: Selected readings*. New York, NY: Family Service Association of America.

Parad, H. J., & Parad, L. G. (Eds.). (1990). *Crisis intervention: Book 2*. Milwaukee, WI: Family Service America.

Parad, H. J., & Parad, L. G. (2006). *Crisis intervention book 2: The practitioner's source book for brief therapy* (2nd ed.). Tucson, AZ: Fenestra Books.

Parihar, B. (1984). *Task-centered management in human service organizations*. Springfield, Ill: Thomas.

Parks, S. & Novielli, K. (2000). A practical guide for caring for caregivers. *American Family Physician, 62*(12).

Parlec, M. (1979). Conversational politics. *Psychology Today, 12*, 48–56.

Parloff, M., Waskow, I., & Wolfe, B. (1978). Research on therapist variables in relation to process and outcome. In S. Garfield & A. Bergin (Eds.), *Handbook of psychotherapy and behavior change* (pp. 233–282). New York, NY: Wiley.

Parson, E. R. (1993). Ethnotherapeutic empathy ETE) Part 1: Definition, theory and process. *Journal of Contemporary Psychology, 33* (1), 5–12.

Parsons, R. J. (2002). Guidelines for empowerment-based social work practice. In A. R. Roberts & G. J. Greene (Eds.), *Social workers' desk reference* (pp. 396–401). New York, NY: Oxford University Press.

Parsons, R. J., Jorgenson, J. D., & Hernandez, S. H. (1988). Integrative practice approach: A framework for problem solving. *Social Work, 35*, 417–421.

Parsons, R. J., Jorgensen, J. D., & Hernandez, S. H. (1994). *The integration of social work practice*. Pacific Grove, CA: Brooks/Cole.

Paulson, I., Burroughs, J. C., Gelb, C. B. (1976). Cotherapy: What is the crux of the relationship? *International Journal of Group Psychotherapy, 26*, 213–224.

Paveza, G. J., Prohaska, T., Hagopian, M., & Cohen, D. (1989). *Determination of need—Revision: Final report, Volume I*. Chicago, IL: University of Illinois at Chicago.

Pavlov, I. P. (1927). *Conditioned reflexes*. Oxford, England: Oxford University Press.

Payne, M. (2005). *Modern social work theory* (3rd ed.). Chicago, IL: Lyceum Books.

Paz, J. (2002). Culturally competent substance abuse treatment with Latinos. Journal of *Human Behavior in the Social Environment, 5*(3/4), 123–136.

Pazaratz, D. (2000). Task-centered child and youth care in residential treatment. *Residential treatment for Children and Youth 17*(4), 1–16.

Pelton, L. H. (2003). Social justice and social work. *Journal of Social Work Education*, 433–439.

Pence, E., & Paymar, M. (1993). *Education groups for men who batter: The Duluth model*. New York, NY: Springer.

Perlman, H. (1957). *Social casework: A problem-solving process.* Chicago, IL: University of Chicago Press.

Peters, A. J. (1997). Themes in group work with lesbian and gay adolescents. *Social Work with Groups, 20*(2), 51–69.

Petr, C. & Walter, U. (2005). Best practices inquiry: A multidimensional, value-critical framework. *Journal of Social Work Education, 41,* 251–267.

Philip, C. E. (1994). Letting go: Problems with termination when a therapist is seriously ill or dying. *Smith College Studies in Social Work, 64,* 169–179.

Philip, C. E., & Stevens, E. V. (1992). Countertransference issues for the consultant when a colleague is critically ill (or dying). *Clinical Social Work Journal, 20,* 411–419.

Pichot, T., & Dolan, Y. (2003). *Solution-focused brief therapy: Its effective use in agency settings.* New York, NY: Haworth Press.

Pierce, W. J., & Elisme, E. (1997). Understanding and working with Haitian immigrant families. *Journal of Family Social Work, 2*(1), 49–65.

Pilsecker, C. (1987). A patient dies—A social worker reviews his work. *Social Work in Health Care, 13*(2), 35–45.

Pincus, A., & Minahan, A. (1973). *Social work practice: Model and method.* Itasca, IL: F. E. Peacock.

Poindexter, C. C. (1997). In the aftermath: Serial crisis intervention for people with HIV. *Health and Social Work, 22,* 125–132.

Pokorny, A. D., Miller, B. A., Kaplan, H. B. (1972). The Brief MAST: A shortened version of the Michigan Alcoholism Screening Test. *American Journal of Psychiatry, 129,* 342–345.

Pollack, S. (2004). Anti-oppressive social work practice with women in prison: Discursive reconstructions and alternative practices. *British Journal of Social Work, 34,* 693–707.

Pollio, D. (2006). The art of evidence based practice. *Research on Social Work Practice, 16,* 224–232.

Pollio, D. E. (1995). Use of humor in crisis intervention. *Families in Society, 76*(6), 376–384.

Polowy, C. I., & Gilbertson, J. (1997). *Social workers and subpoenas: Office of General Counsel Law Notes.* Washington, DC: NASW Press.

Pomeroy, E. C., Rubin, A., & Walker, R. J. (1995). Effectiveness of a psychoeducational and task-centered group intervention of family members of people with AIDS. *Social Work Research, 19,* 129–152.

Ponce, D. (1980). The Filipinos: The Philippine background. In J. McDermott, Jr., W. Tseng, & T. Maretski (Eds.), *People and cultures of Hawaii* (pp. 155–163). Honolulu, HI: University of Hawaii Press.

Pope, K. S., Keith-Spiegel, P. C., & Tabachnick, B. (1986). *Sexual attraction to clients: The human therapist and the (sometimes) inhuman training system. American Psychologist, 41,* 147–158.

Potocky-Tripodi, M. (2002). *Best practices for social work with refugees and immigrants.* New York, NY: Columbia University Press.

Potocky-Tripodi, M. (2003). Refugee economic adaptation: Theory, evidence and implications for policy and practice. *Journal of Social Service Research, 30,* 63–91.

Potter-Efron, R., & Potter-Efron, P. (1992). *Anger, alcoholism and addiction: Treating anger in a chemical dependency setting.* New York, NY: Norton.

Poulin, J. (2000). *Collaborative social work. Strengths-based generalist practice.* Itasca, IL: F. E. Peacock.

Powell, M., Thomson, D. and Dietze, P. (1997). Memories of an event: interviewing separate occurrences. Implications for children. *Families in Society, 78,* 600–610.

Price, S. J., Price, C. A., & McKenry, P. C. (2000). *Families and Change. Coping with stressful events and transition* (3rd ed.). Thousand Oaks, CA: Sage Publications.

Price, S. J., Price, C. A., & McKenry, P. C. (2010). *Families and Change. Coping with stressful events and transitions* (4th ed.). Thousand Oaks, CA: Sage Publications.

Prochaska, J., DiClemente, C. C., & Norcross, J. C. (1992). Transtheoretical therapy: Toward a more integrative model of change. *Psychotherapy: Theory, Research, and Practice, 19,* 276–288.

Prochaska, J. O., & DiClemente, C. C. (1986). Towards a comprehensive model of change. In W. R. Miller & N. Heather (Eds.), *Treating addictive behaviors: Processes of change* (pp. 3–28). New York, NY: Pergamon Press.

Proctor, E. (2007). Implementing Evidence-Based Practice in social work education: Principles, strategies, and partnerships. *Research on Social Work Practice, 17,* 583–591.

Proctor, E. K., & and Davis, L. E. (1994). The challenge of racial difference: Skills for clinical practice. *Social Work, 39,* 314–323.

Proehl, R. A. (2001). *Organizational change in human services.* Thousand Oaks, CA: Sage Publications.

Project Cork. (n.d.) *CAGE.* Retrieved from http://www.projectcork.org/clinical_tools/html/CAGE.html

Protecting the Privacy of Patients' Health Information. (2003). Retrieved from http://www.hhs.gov/news/facts/privacy.html

Puryear, D. (1979). *Helping people in crisis.* San Francisco, CA: Jossey-Bass.

Q

Quinsey, V. L., Harris, G. T., Rice, M. E., & Cormier, C. (2006). *Violent offenders: Appraising and managing risk* (2nd ed.). Washington, DC: American Psychological Association.

R

Race Matters. (2005). Annie E. Casey Foundation. Retrieved from http://www.kidscount.org/kcnetwork/resources/RaceMattersToolkit.htm downloaded 2 1 2011.

Ragg, D., Okagbue-Reaves, J., & Piers, J. (2007, October 28). *Shaping student interactive habits: a critical function of practice education.* Presentation at Council of Social Work Education Annual Program Meeting #74a.

Raines, J. C. (1996). Self-disclosure in clinical social work. *Clinical Social Work Journal, 24*, 357–375.

Ramakrishman, K. R., Balgopal, P. R., & Pettys, G. L. (1994). Task-centered work with communities. In E. R. Tolson, W. J. Reid, & C. D. Garvin (Eds.), *Generalist Practice: A task-centered approach.* New York, NY: Columbia University Press.

Ramos, B. M. & Garvin, C. (2003). Task-centered treatment with culturally diverse populations, In E. R. Tolson, W. J. Reid, & C. D. Garvin (Eds.), *Generalist practice: A Task-centered approach* (2nd ed., pp. 441–463). New York, NY: Columbia University Press.

Ramos, B. M., & Tolson, E. R. (2008). The task-centered model. In N. Coady & P. Lehmann (Eds.), *Theoretical perspectives for direct social work practice. A generalist-eclectic approach* (2nd ed., pp. 275–295). New York, NY: Springer Publishing Company.

Range, L. M., & Knott, E. C. (1997). Twenty suicide assessment instruments: Evaluation and recommendations. *Death Studies, 21*, 25–58.

Rank, M. R., & Hirschl, T. A. (1999). The likelihood of poverty across the American lifespan. *Social Work, 44*, 201–208.

Rank, M. R., & Hirschl, T. A. (2002). Welfare use as a life course event: Toward a new understanding of the U.S. safety net. *Social Work, 47*, 327–358.

Rapoport, L. (1967). Crisis-oriented short-term casework. *Social Service Review, 41*(1), 31–43.

Rapp, C. A. (1993). Theory, principles and methods of the strengths model of case management. In M. Harris & H. C. Bergman, *Case management for mentally ill patients, Theory and Practice.* US: Harwood.

Rapp, C. A. (1998). *The strengths model: Case management with people suffering from severe and persistent mental illness.* New York: Oxford University Press.

Rapp, C. A. (2002). A strengths approach to case management with clients with severe mental disability. In A. R. Roberts & G. J. Greene, *Social Work Desk Reference* (pp. 486–491). New York, NY: Oxford University Press.

Rathbone-McCuan, E. (2008). Elder Abuse. In T. Mizrahi & L. E. Davis (Eds.), *Encyclopedia of Social Work.* Washington, DC: National Association of Social Workers and Oxford University Press, Inc.

Ratliff, S. S. (1996). The multicultural challenge to health care. M. Julia, *Multicultural Awareness in the Health Care Professions* (pp. 164–181). Needham Heights, MA: Allyn & Bacon.

Rauch, J. B. (1993). *Assessment: A sourcebook for social work practice.* Milwaukee, WI: Families International.

Raymond, G. T., Teare, R. J., & Atherton, C. R. (1996). Is "field of practice" a relevant organizing principle for the MSW curriculum? *Journal of Social Work Education, 32*(1), 19–30.

Reamer, F. (1989). *Ethical dilemmas in social service* (2nd ed.). New York, NY: Columbia University Press.

Reamer, F. G. (1994). *Social work malpractice and liability: Strategies for prevention.* New York, NY: Columbia University Press.

Reamer, F. G. (1995). Malpractice claims against social workers: First facts. *Social Work, 40*, 595–601.

Reamer, F. G. (1998). *Ethical standards in social work.* Washington, DC: NASW Press.

Reamer, F. G. (1999). *Social work values and ethics* (2nd ed.). New York, NY: Columbia University Press.

Reamer, F. G. (2001). *Tangled relationships:Managing boundary issues in the human services.* New York, NY: Columbia University Press.

Reamer, F. G., (2005). Ethical and legal standards in social work: Consistency and conflicts. *Families in Society, 86*, 163–169.

Reamer, F. G. (2006). Social work values and ethics (3rd ed.). New York: Columbia University Press.

Reese, D. J., Ahern, R. E., Nair, S., O'Faire, J. D., & Warren, C. (1999). Hospice access and use by African Americans: Addressing cultural and institutional barriers through participatory action research. *Social Work, 44*, 549–559.

Regehr, C., & Angle, B. (1997). Coercive influences: Informed consent in court-mandated social work practice. *Social Work, 42*, 300–306.

Reid, K. E. (1991). *Social work practice with groups: A clinical perspective*. Pacific Grove, CA: Brooks/Cole.

Reid, K. E. (2002). Clinical social work with groups. In A. R. Roberts & G. J. Greene (Eds.), *Social workers' desk reference* (pp. 432–436). New York, NY: Oxford University Press.

Reid, W., & Hanrahan, P. (1982). Recent evaluations of social work: Grounds for optimism. *Social Work, 27*, 328–340.

Reid, W., & Shyne, A. (1969). *Brief and extended casework*. New York, NY: Columbia University Press.

Reid, W. J. (1972). *Task-centered casework*. New York, NY: Columbia University Press.

Reid, W. J. (1975). A test of the task-centered approach. *Social Work, 22*, 3–9.

Reid, W. J. (1977). Process and outcome in the treatment of family problems. In W. Reid & L. Epstein (Eds.), *Task centered practice. Self-help groups and human service agencies: How they work together*. Milwaukee, WI: Family Service of America.

Reid, W. J. (1978). *The task-centered system*. New York, NY: Columbia University Press.

Reid, W. J. (1987). Task-centered research. In *Encyclopedia of social work* (vol. 2, pp. 757–764). Silver Spring, MD: NASW Press.

Reid, W. J. (1992). *Task strategies*. New York, NY: Columbia University Press.

Reid, W. J. (1994). The empirical practice movement. *Social Service Review, 68*(2), 165–184.

Reid, W. J. (1996). Task-centered social work. In F. J. Turner (Ed.), *Social work treatment: Interlocking theoretical approaches* (4th ed., pp 617–640). New York, NY: Free Press.

Reid, W. J. (1997a). Research on task-centered practice. *Social Work, 21*, 131–137.

Reid, W. J. (2000). *The task planner*. New York, NY: Columbia University Press.

Reid, W. J., & Bailey-Dempsey, C. (1995). The effects of monetary incentives in school performance. *Families in Society, 76*, 331–340.

Reid, W. J., & Epstein, L. (Eds.) (1972). *Task-centered casework*. New York, NY: Columbia University Press.

Reid, W. J., Epstein, L., Brown, L., Tolson, E. R., & Rooney, R. H. (1980). Task-centered school social work. *Social Work in Education, 2*, 7–24.

Reid, W. J., & Fortune, A. E. (2002). The task-centered model. In A. R. Roberts & G. J. Greene (Eds.), *Social workers' desk reference* (pp. 101–104). New York, NY: Oxford University Press.

Reinecke, M., Datillo, F. & Freeman, A. (2003). *Cognitive therapy with children* (2nd ed.). New York, NY: Guilford Press.

Reisch, M. (2002). Social work and politics in the new century. *Social Work, 45*, 293–226.

Reisch, M. (2002). Defining social justice in a socially unjust world. *Families in Society, 83*, 343–354.

Reisch, M., & Sommerfeld, D. (2003). The "Other America" after welfare reform: A view from non-profit sector. *Journal of Poverty 7*(1/2), 69–95.

Renfrey, G. S. (1992). Cognitive-behavior therapy and the Native American client. *Behavior Therapy, 23*, 321–340.

Resnick, C, & Dziegielewski, S. F. (1996). The relationship between therapeutic termination and job satisfaction among medical social workers. *Social Work in Health Care, 23*(3), 17–33.

Reuben, D. B., & Siu, A. L. (1990). An objective measure of physical function of elderly outpatients: The Physical Performance Test. *Journal of the American Geriatrics Society, 38*, 1105–1112.

Reynolds, B. C. (1951). *Social work and social living*. New York, NY: Citadel Press.

Reynolds, C. R., & Kamphaus, R. W. (1992). *Behavior assessment system for children*. Circle Pines, MN: American Guidance Service.

Reynolds, T., & Jones, G. (1996). Trauma debriefings: A one-session group model. In B. L. Stempler, M. Glass, & C. M. Savinelli (Eds.), *Social group work today and tomorrow: Moving to advanced training and practice* (pp. 129–139). Binghamton, NY: Haworth Press.

Reynolds, W. M. (1987). *Suicidal Ideation Questionnaire—Junior*. Odessa, FL: Psychological Assessment Resources.

Reynolds, W. M. (1988). *Suicidal Ideation Questionnaire professional manual*. Odessa FL: Psychological Assessment Resources.

Rheingold, A. A., Herbert, J. D., & Franklin, M. E. (2003). Cognitive bias in adolescents with social anxiety disorder. *Cognitive Therapy and Research, 27*, 639–655.

Ribner, D. S., & Knei-Paz, C. (2002). Client's view of a successful helping relationship. *Social Work, 47*, 379–387.

Rice, A. H. (1998). *Focusing on strengths: Focus group research on the impact of welfare reform*. A paper presented for the XX Symposium Association for the Advancement of Social Work with Groups, October 1998, Miami, FL.

Richardon, V. E., & Barusch, A. S. (2006). *Gerontological practice for the twenty-first century: A social work perspective.* New York, NY: Columbia University Press.

Richey, C. A., & Roffman, R. A. (1999). One the sidelines of guidelines: Further thoughts on the fit between clinical guidelines and social work practice. *Research on Social Work Practice, 9,* 311–321.

Richman, L. S., Kohn-Woods, L., & Williams, D. R. (2007). Discrimination and racial identity for mental health service utilization. *Journal of Social and Clinical Psychology, 26,* 960–980.

Ringstad. R. (2005). Conflict in the workplace: Social workers are victims and perpetrators. *Social Work, 50,* 305–313.

Rittenhouse, J. (1997). Feminist principles in survivor's groups: Out-of-group contact. The *Journal for Specialists in Group Work, 22,* 111–119.

Ritter, B., & Dozier, C. D. (2000). Effects of court-ordered substance abuse treatment on child protective services cases. *Social Work 45,* 131–140.

Rivera, F. G., & Erlich, J. L. (1998). Community organizing in a diverse society (3rd ed.). Boston: Allyn & Bacon.

Roberts, A. R. (1990). *Crisis intervention handbook: Assessment, treatment, and research.* Belmont, CA: Wadsworth.

Roberts, A. R. (2000). An overview of crisis theory and crisis intervention. In A. R. Roberts (Ed.), *Crisis interviewing handbook: Assessment, treatment, and research.* Belmont, CA: Wadsworth.

Roberts, A. R. (2005). *Crisis intervention handbook: Assessment, treatment and research* (3rd ed.). New York, NY: Oxford University Press.

Roberts, A. R., & Greene, G. J. (Eds.) (2002). In Roberts, A. R. (Ed.), *Social workers' desk reference* (pp. 112–115). New York, NY: Oxford University Press.

Roberts, A. R., Monferrari, I., & Yeager, K. R. (2008). Avoiding malpractice lawsuits by following standards of care guidelines and preventing suicide: A guide for mental health professionals. In Roberts, A. R. (Ed.), *Social Workers' Desk Reference* (128–135). New York, NY: Oxford University Press.

Roberts, A. R., & Yeager, K. R. (2006). *Foundations of evidence-based social work practice.* New York, NY: Oxford University Press.

Roberts, D. (2002). *Shattered bonds: The color of child welfare.* New York, NY: Basic Books.

Robinson, J. B. (1989). Clinical treatment of black families: Issues and strategies. *Social Work, 34,* 323–329.

Robinson, D. R. (2000). Challenges from the front line: A contemporary view. In A social justice framework for child welfare. The agenda for a 21st century. Conference Proceedings, University of Minnesota, June, 23, 2000.

Robinson, V. (1930). *A changing psychology in social work.* Chapel Hill, NC: University of North Carolina Press.

Robles, R. R., Reyes, J. C., Colon, H. M., Sahai, H., Marrero, C. A., Matos, T. M., Calderon, J. M., & Shepard, V. (2004). Effects of combined counseling and case management to reduce HIV risk behavior among hip drug injectors in Puerto, Rico: A randomized correlated study. *Journal of Substance Abuse Treatment, 27*(2), 145–153.

Rodenborg, N. (2004, November). Services to African American children in poverty: Institutional discrimination in child welfare. *Journal of Poverty: Innovations on Social, Political and Economic Inequalities, 3*(3).

Rogers, C. (1957). The necessary and sufficient conditions of therapeutic personality change. *Journal of Consulting Psychology, 22,* 95–103.

Rodgers, A. Y., & Potocky, M. (1997). Evaluating culturally sensitive practice through single-system design: Methodological issues and strategies. *Research on Social Work Practice, 7,* 391–401.

Ronnau, J. P., & Marlow, C. R. (1995). Family preservation: Poverty and the value of diversity. *Families in Society, 74,* 538–544.

Rooney, G. D. (1997). Concerns of employed women: Issues for employee assistance programs. In A. Daly (Ed.), *Work force diversity: Issues and perspectives in the world of work* (pp. 314–330). Washington, DC: NASW Press.

Rooney, G. D. (2000). Examining the values and ethics reflected in policy decisions. In K. Strom-Gottfried (Ed.), *Social work practice: Cases, activities and exercises* (pp. 50–54). Thousand Oaks, CA: Pine Forge Press.

Rooney, G. D. (2009). Oppression and involuntary status. In R. H. Rooney (Ed.). *Strategies for work with involuntary clients* (2nd ed.). New York, NY: Columbia University Press.

Rooney, R. H. (1981). A task-centered reunification model for foster care. In A. A. Maluccio & P. Sinanoglu (Eds.), *The challenge of partnership: Working with biological parents of children in foster care* (pp. 135–159). New York, NY: Child Welfare League of America.

Rooney, R. H. (1992). *Strategies for work with involuntary clients.* New York: Columbia University Press.

Rooney, R. H. (Ed.). (2009). *Strategies for work with involuntary clients* (2nd ed.). New York, NY: Columbia.

Rooney, R. H. (2010). The task-centered approach in the United States. In A. Fortune, P. McCallion, & K. Briar-Larsen (eds.). *Social work practice research for the Twenty-first: Building on the legacy of William J. Reid*. Columbia University Press.

Rooney, R. H., & Bibus, A. A. (1996). Multiple lenses: Ethnically sensitive practice with involuntary clients who are having difficulties with drugs or alcohol. *Journal of Multicultural Social Work*, 4(2), 59–73.

Rooney, R. H., & Chovanec, M. (2004). Involuntary groups. In C. Garvin, L. Gutierrez, & M. Galinsky (Eds.), *Handbook of social work with groups*. New York, NY: Guilford Press.

Rose, S. D. (1989). *Working with adults in groups: Integrating cognitive-behavioral and small group strategies*. San Francisco, CA: Jossey-Bass.

Rose, S. D. (1998). *Group therapy with troubled youth: A cognitive behavioral interactive approach*. Thousand Oaks, CA: Sage Publications.

Rose, S. M. (1992). *Case management and social work practice*. Menlo Park, CA: Longman Press.

Rosen, A. (1972). The treatment relationship: A conceptualization. *Journal of Clinical Psychology*, 38, 329–337.

Rosen, A., & Livne, S. (1992). Personal versus environmental emphases in social workers' perception of client problems. *Social Service* Review, 66, 85–96.

Rosenblatt, E. (1994). *Metaphor of family systems theory*. New York, NY: Guilford Press.

Rosenthal, K. (1988). The inanimate self in adult victims of child abuse and neglect. *Social Casework*, 69, 505–510.

Rosenthal-Gelman, C. (2004). Empirically-based principles for culturally competent practice with Latinos. *Journal of Ethnic and Cultural Diversity in Social Work*, 13(1), 83–108.

Ross, C. (1997). *Something to draw on: Activities and interventions using an art therapy approach*. London, England: Jessica Kingsley.

Roth, W. (1987). Disabilities: Physical. In *Encyclopedia of social work* (vol. 1, pp. 434–438). Silver Spring, MD: NASW Press.

Rothman, J. (1991). A model of case management: Toward empirically based practice. *Social Work*, 36, 521–528.

Rothman, J. (1995). Approaches to community intervention. In F. M. Cox, J. L. Erlich, J. J. Rothman & J. Tropman (Eds.). *Strategies of community intervention*. Itasca, IL: Peacock.

Rothman, J. (1999). Intent and consent. In J. Rothman (Ed.), *Reflections on community organizations: Enduring themes and critical issues* (pp. 3–26). Itasca, IL: F. E. Peacock.

Rothman, J. (2002). *An overview of case management*. In A. R. Roberts & G. J. Greene (Eds.), *Social Work Desk Reference* (pp. 467–472). New York, NY: Oxford.

Rothman, J. (2008). Multi modes of intervention at the macro level. *Journal of Community Practice*, 15(4), 11–40.

Rothman, J., Erlich, J. L., & Tropman, J. E. (1999). *Strategies of community interventions* (5th ed.). Itasca, IL: F. E, Peacock.

Rothman, J., Erlich, J. L., & Tropman, J. E. (2001). *Strategies of community interventions* (6th ed.). Itasca, IL: F. E. Peacock.

Rothman, J., Gant, L. M., & Hnat, S. A. (1985). Mexican-American family culture. *Social Service Review*, 59, 197–215.

Rothman, J., & Thomas, E. J. (1994). *Intervention research: Design and development of human sevices*. Binghampton, NY: Haworth Press.

Rothman, J., & Tropman, J. (1987). Models of community organization and development and macro practice perspectives. Their mixing and phasing. In F. M. Cox, J. L. Erlich, J. J. Rothman & J. Tropman (Eds.), *Strategies of community organizing* (pp. 3–26) Itasca, IL: Peacock.

Rotunno, M., & McGoldrick, M. (1982). Italian families. In M. McGoldrick, J. Pearce, & J. Giordano (Eds.), *Ethnicity and family therapy* (pp. 340–363). New York, NY: Guilford Press.

Rounds, K. A., Galinsky, M. J., & Stevens, L. S. (1991). Linking people with AIDS in rural communities: The telephone group. *Social Work*, 36, 13–18.

Rowan, A. B. (2001). Adolescent substance abuse and suicide. *Depression and Anxiety*, 14, 186–191.

Rowe, R., Maughan, B., Worthman, C. M., Costello, E. J., & Angold, A. (2004). Testosterone, antisocial behavior, and social dominance in boys: Pubertal development and biosocial interaction. *Biological Psychiatry*, 55, 546–552.

Royse, D., Thyer, B. A., Padgett, D. K. & Logan, T. K. (2006). *Program evaluation: An introduction* (4th ed.). Belmont, CA: Brooks-Cole.

Rozzini, R., Frisoni, G. B., Bianchetti, A., Zanetti, O., & Trabucchi, M. (1993). Physical Performance Test and Activities of Daily Living scales in the assessment of health status in elderly people. *Journal of the American Geriatrics Society*, 41, 1109–1113.

Rubin, A. (2007). Improving the teaching of evidence-based practice: Introduction to the special issue. *Research on Social Work Practice*, *17*, 541–547.

Rubin, R. & Babbie, E. R. (2005). *Essential research methods for social work*. Belmont, CA: Brooks-Cole.

Rudolph, K. D. & Clark, A. G. (2001). Conceptions of relationship in children with depression and aggressive symptoms. Social-cognitive distortions or reality. *Journal of Abnormal Child Psychology*, *29*(1), 41–56.

Ryder, R., & Tepley, R. (1993). No more Mr. Nice Guy: Informed consent and benevolence in marital family therapy. *Family Relations*, *42*, 145–147.

Rzepnicki, T. L. (1991). Enhancing the durability of intervention gains: A challenge for the 1990s. *Social Service Review*, *65*(1), 92–111.

Rzepnicki, T. L. (2004). Informed consent and practice evaluation: Making the decision to participate meaningful. In H. E. Briggs, & T. L. Rzepnicki (Eds.), *Using evidence in social work practice: Behavioral perspectives* (pp. 273–290). Chicago, IL: Lyceum Books, Inc.

S

Safran, J. D., & Muran, J. C. (2000). Resolving therapeutic alliance ruptures: Diversity and integration. *In Session: Psychotherapy in Practice*, *56*, 597–605.

Saleebey, D. (Ed.) (1992). *The strengths perspective in social work practice*. New York, NY: Longman.

Saleeby, D. (1996). The Strength perspective in social work practice: Extensions and cautions. *Social Work*, *41*, 296–305.

Saleebey, D. (Ed.) (1997). *The strengths perspective in social work practice* (2nd ed.). Needham Heights, MA: Allyn & Bacon.

Saleebey, D. (2002). *The strengths perspective in social work practice* (3rd ed.). New York, NY: Allyn & Bacon.

Saleebey, D. (2004). The power of place: Another look at the environment. *Families in Society*, *85*, 7–16.

Salmon, R., & Graziano, R. (Eds.). (2004). *Group work and aging: Issues in practice research and education*. New York, NY: Haworth Press.

Salston, M., & Figley, C. R. (2004). Secondary traumatic stress effects of working with survivors of criminal victimization. *Journal of Traumatic Stress*, *16*, 167–174.

Salzar, M. S. (1997). Consumer empowerment in mental health organizations: Concepts, benefits and impediments. *Administration and Policy in Mental Health*, *24*, 425–434.

Sands, R. G. (1989). The social worker joins the team: A look at the socialization process. *Social Work in Health Care*, *14*(2), 1–14.

Sands, R. G., Stafford, J., & McClelland, M. (1990). "I beg to differ": Conflict in the interdisciplinary team. *Social Work in Health Care*, *14*(3), 55–72.

Santhiveeran, J. (2009). Compliance of social work e-therapy websites to the NASW code of ethics. *Social Work in Health Care*, *48*, 1–13.

Sarkisian, N., & Gerstel, N. (2004). Kinship support among blacks and whites: Race and family organization. *American Sociological Review*, *69*, 812–836.

Sarnoff, J. D. (2004). Abolishing the doctrine of equivalents and claiming the future after festo. *Berkeley Technical Law Journal*, *19*, 1157–1225.

Sarri, R. (1987). Administration in social welfare. In *Encyclopedia of social work* (vol. 1, pp. 27–40). Silver Spring, MD: NASW Press.

Satir, V. (1967). *Conjoint family therapy*. Palo Alto, CA: Science & Behavior Books.

Satir, V. M., (1972). *Peoplemaking*. Palo Alto, CA: Science and Behavior Books.

Saulnier, C. F. (1997). Alcohol problems and marginalization: Social group work with lesbians. *Social Work with Groups*, *20*(3), 37–59.

Saulnier, C. F. (2002). Deciding who to see: Lesbians discuss their preferences in health and mental health care providers. *Social Work*, *47*, 355–365.

Sauter, J., & Franklin, C. (1998). Assessing Post-Traumatic Stress Disorder in children: Diagnostic and measurement strategies. *Research on Social Work Practice*, *8*, 251–270.

Savner, S. (2000, July/August). Welfare reform and racial/ethnic minorities: The questions to ask. *Poverty & Race*, *9*(4), 3–5.

Schaffer, D. (1992). *NIHM diagnostic interview schedule for children, version 2.3*. New York, NY: Columbia University, Division of Child and Adolescent Psychiatry.

Schein, E. H. (1985). *Organizational culture and leadership*. San Francisco, CA: Jossey-Bass.

Scheyett, A. (2006). Danger and opportunity in teaching evidence-based practice in the social work curriculum. *Journal of Teaching in Social Work*, *26*: 19–29.

Schiller, L. (2007). Not for women only: Applying the relational model of group development with vulnerable populations. *Social Work with Groups*, *30*(2), 11–26.

Schiller, L. Y. (1997). Rethinking stages of development in women's groups: Implications for practice. *Social Work with Groups, 20*(3), 3–19.

Schneider, R. L., & Lester, L. (2001). Social work advocacy. A new framework for action. Belmont, CA: Brooks/Cole.

Schneider, R. L., & Netting, F. E. (1999). Influencing social policy in a time of devolution: Upholding social work's great tradition. *Social Work, 44,* 349–357.

Schopler, J., & Galinsky, M. (1974). Goals in social group work practice: Formulation, implementation and evaluation. In P. Glasser, R. Sarri, & R. Vinter (Eds.), *Individual change through small groups*. New York, NY: Free Press.

Schopler, J. H., & Galinsky, M. J. (1981). Meeting practice needs: Conceptualizing the open-ended group. *Social Work with Groups, 7*(2), 3–21.

Schopler, J. H., Galinsky, M. J., & Abell, M. (1997). Creating community through telephone and computer groups: Theoretical and practice perspectives. *Social Work with Groups, 20*(4), 19–34.

Schopler, J. H., Galinsky, M. J., Davis, L. E., & Despard, M. (1996). The RAP model: Assessing a framework for leading multicultural groups. *Social Work with Groups, 19*(3/4), 21–39.

Schwartz, G. (1989). Confidentiality revisited. *Social Work, 34,* 223–226.

Search Institute. (2002). *National survey of parents*. Minneapolis. Minnesota: Same.

Seay, H. A., Fee, V. E., Holloway, K. S., & Giesen, J. M. (2003). A multi component treatment package to increase anger control in teacher referred boys. *Child and Family Behavior Therapy, 25*(1), 1–18.

Secret, M., Jordan, A., & Ford, J. (1999). Empowerment evaluation as a social work strategy. *Social Work, 24,* 120–127.

Segal, E. (2010). *Social welfare policy and social programs: A values perspective*. Belmont, CA: Brooks/Cole Cengage.

Segal, E. A. (2007). Social empathy: A tool to address the contradictions of working but still poor. *Families in Society, 88,* 333–337.

Segal, U. A. (1991). Cultural variables in Asian Indian families. *Families in Society, 72,* 233–244.

Segal, Z. V., Williams, J. M., & Teasdale, J. D. (2002). *Mindfulness-based cognitive therapy for depression: a new approach to preventing relapse*. New York, NY: Guilford.

Siegal, H.A, Rapp, R. C., Li, L., Saha, P., Kirk, K. (1998). The role of case management in retaining clients in substance abuse treatment: An exploratory analysis. *Journal of Drug Issues, 27,* 821–831.

Selekman, M. D. (2005). *Pathways to change: Brief therapy with difficult children* (2nd ed.). New York, NY: Guilford Press.

Selvini-Palazzoli, M., Boscolo, L., Cecchin, G., & Prata, G. (1974). The treatment of children through brief therapy of their parents. *Family Process, 13,* 429–442.

Selzer, M. L. (1971). The Michigan Alcoholism Screening Test: The quest for a new diagnostic instrument. *American Journal of Psychiatry 27,* 1653–1658.

Senge, P. (1990). *The fifth discipline: The art and practice of learning organization*. New York, NY: Doubleday Currency.

Senge, P. M. (1994). *The fifth discipline field book: Strategies and tolls for building a learning organization*. New York, NY: Bantam, Doubleday, Dell.

Sengupta, S. (2001, July 8). How many poor children is too many? *The New York Times,* WK 3.

Serres, C. (2004, June 6). House of hurdles. *Minneapolis Star Tribune,* pp. A1, A21.

Shaffer, Q., Scott, M., Wilcox, H., Maslow, C., Hicks, R., Lucas, C. P, Garfmkel, R., & Greenwald, S. (2004). The Columbia Suicide Screen: Validity and reliability of a screen for youth suicide and depression. *Journal of the American Academy of Child & Adolescent Psychiatry, 43,* 71–79.

Shamai, M. (2003). Therapeutic effects of qualitative research: Reconstructing the experience of treatment as a by-product of qualitative evaluation. *Social Service Review, 77,* 454–467.

Shapiro, J. R., Bauer, S., Andrews, E., Pisetsky, E., Bulik-Sullivan, B., Hamer, R. M., & Bulik, C. M. (2009). Mobile therapy: Use of text-messaging in the treatment of Bulimia Nervosa. *International Journal of Eating Disorders,* 2009, 1–7.

Shane, P. G. (2007). The effects of incarceration on children and families. *National Association of Social Work, Child Welfare Section Connection, 1,* 1–5.

Shapiro, J. R., Bauer, S., Andrews, E., Pisetsky, E., Bulik-Sullivan, B., Hamer, R. M., & Bulik, C. M. (2009). Mobile therapy: Use of text-messaging in the treatment of Bulimia Nervosa. *International Journal of Eating Disorders,* 2009, 1–7.

Sharpe, L., & Tarrier, M. (1992). A cognitive-behavioral treatment approach for problem gambling. *Journal of Cognitive Psychotherapy, 5,* 119–127.

Sheafor, B., Horejsi, C. R., & Horejsi, G. A. (1994). *Techniques and guidelines for social work practice* (3rd ed.). Boston, MA: Allyn & Bacon.

Shepard, M., & Campbell, J. (1992). The abusive behavior inventory: A measure of psychological and physical abuse. *Journal of Interpersonal Violence, 7,* 291–305.

Sherraden, B., Slosar, B., & Sherraden, M. (2002). Innovation in social policy: Collaborative policy advocacy. *Social Work 47,* 209–211.

Sherrer, M. & O'Hare, T. (2008). Clinical case management in Mueser, K. & Jeste, D. (Eds.). *clinical handbook of schizophrenia.* New York: Guilford. Pp. 309–318.

Sherwood, D. A. (1998). Spiritual assessment as a normal part of social work practice: Power to help and power to harm. *Social Work and Christianity, 25*(2), 80–90.

Shih, M., & Sanchez, D. (2005). Perspectives and research on the positive and negative implications of having multiple racial identities. *Psychology Bulletin, 131,* 569–591.

Shneidman, E. S. (1971). The management of the pre-suicidal, suicidal and postsuicidal patient. *Annals of Internal Medicine, 75,* 441–458.

Shoham, V., Rorhbaugh, M., & Patterson, J. (1995). Problem and solution-focused couples therapies: The MRI and Milwaukee modes. In N. S. Jacobson & A. S. Gurman (Eds.), *Clinical handbook for couple therapy.* New York, NY: Guildford Press.

Shulman, L. (1984). *The skills of helping individuals and groups* (2nd ed.). Itasca, IL: F. E. Peacock.

Shulman, L. (1992). *The skills of helping individuals and groups* (3rd ed.). Itasca, IL: F. E. Peacock.

Shulman, L. (2009). *The Skills of Helping Individuals, Families, Groups, and Communities* (6th ed.). Belmont, CA: Brooks/Cole.

Siegal, H. A., Fisher, J. A., Rapp, R. C., Kelliher, C. W., Wagner, J. H., O'Brien, W. F., & Cole, P. A. (1996). Enhancing substance abuse treatment with case management: Its impact on employment. *Journal of Substance Abuse Treatment, 13,* 93–98.

Siegal, H. A. Rapp, C. A., Kelliher, C. W., Fisher, J., Wagner, J. H., & Cole, P. A. (1995). The strengths perspective of case management: A promising inpatient substance abuse treatment enhancement. *Journal of Psychoactive Drugs, 27,* 67–72.

Siegal, H. A, Rapp, R. C., Li, L., Saha, P., Kirk, K. (1997). The role of case management in retaining clients in substance abuse treatment: An exploratory analysis. *Journal of Drug Issues, 27,* 821–831.

Silberberg. S. (2001). Searching for family resilience. *Family Matters, 58,* 52–57.

Silove, D. (2000). A conceptual framework for mass trauma. Indications for adaptation, intervention and debriefing. In B. Raphael & J. P. Wilson (Eds.), *Psychology, debriefing, theory, practice and evidence* (pp. 337–350), New York, NY: Cambridge University Press.

Silvawe, G. W. (1995). The need for a new social work perspective in an African setting: The case of social casework in Zambia. *British Journal of Social Work, 25,* 71–84.

Simmons, C., & Rycraft, J. (2010). Ethical challenges of military social workers serving in a combat zone. *Social Work,* 55(1), 9–18.

Simon, J. B., Murphy, J. J. & Smith, S. M. (2005). Understanding and fostering family resilience. *The Family Journal, 13,* 427–436.

Simons, K., Shepherd, N., & Murro, J. (2008). Advancing the evidence-base for social work in long-term care: The disconnect between practice and research. *Social Work in Health Care, 47,* 392–415.

Siporin, M. (1975). *Introduction to social work practice.* New York, NY: Macmillan.

Siporin, M. (1980). Ecological systems theory in social work. *Journal of Sociology and Social Welfare, 7,* 507–532.

Skinner, B. F. (1974). *About behaviorism.* New York, NY: Knopf.

Slater, S. (1995). *The lesbian lifecycle.* New York, NY: Free Press.

Smagner, J. P., & Sullivan, M. H. (2005). Investigating the effectiveness of behavioral parenting with involuntary clients in child welfare settings. *Research of Social Work Practice, 15,* 431–439.

Smith, B. D., & Marsh, J. C. (2002). Client-service matching in substance abuse treatment for women with children. *Journal of Substance Abuse Treatment, 22,* 161–168.

Smith, C, & Nylund, D. (1997). *Narrative therapies with children and adolescents.* New York, NY: Guilford Press.

Smith, L. C. & Shin, R. Q. (2008). Social privilege, social justice, and group counseling: An inquiry. *Journal for Specialists in Group Work, 33,* 351–366.

Smith, N. A. (2006). "Unfit" mother: Increasing empathy, redefining the label. *Affillia Journal of Women and Social Work, 21,* 448–457.

Smith, T. B. (2004). *Practicing multiculturalism: Affirming diversity in counseling and psychology.* Boston, MAearson.

Smokowski, P. R., Rose, S. D., & Bacallao, M. L. (2001). Damaging therapeutic groups: How vulnerable consumers become group casualties. *Small Group Research, 32*, 223–251.

Smyth, N. J. (2005). Drug use, self-efficacy, and coping skills among people with concurrent substance abuse and personality disorders: Implications for relapse prevention. *Journal of Social Work Practice in the Addictions, 5*(4), 63–79.

Social Workers and Psychotherapist-Patient Privilege: *Jaffee v. Redmond* Revisited. (n.d.) Retrieved from http://www.socialworkers.org/ldf/legalrissue/200503

Sommers-Flanagan, R. (2007). Ethical considerations in crisis and humanitarian interventions. *Ethics and Behavior, 17*, 187–202.

Sosin, M., & Callum, S. (1983). Advocacy: A conceptualization for social work practice. *Social Work, 28*, 12–17.

Sotomayor, M. (1991). Introduction. In M. Sotomayor (Ed.), *Empowering Hispanic families: A critical issue for the 90s* (pp. xi–xxiii). Milwaukee, WI: Family Service America.

Sousa, L., Ribeiro, C, & Rodriques, S. (2006). Intervention with multiproblem poor clients: Toward a strengths-focused perspective. *Journal of Social Work Practice, 20*, 189–204.

Specht, H., & Courtney, M. E. (1994). *Unfaithful angels: How social work abandoned its mission*. Toronto, Canada: Maxwell Macmillan Canada.

Speisman, J. (1959). Depth of interpretation and verbal resistance in psychotherapy. *Journal of Consulting Psychology, 23*, 93–99.

Spencer, M. S. (2008). A social worker's reflection on power, privilege and oppression. *Social Work, 53*, 99–101.

Spitalnick, J. S., & McNair, L. D. (2005). *Journal of Sex and Marital Therapy, 31*, 43–56.

Spitzer, R. L., Gibbon, M., Skoldol, A., Williams, J. B. W., First, M. B. (1995). *DSM-IV-TR casebook: A learning companion to the diagnostic and statistical manual of mental disorders*. Washington, DC: American Psychiatric Publishing, Inc.

Spoth, R., Guyll, M., Chao, W., & Molgaard, V. (2003). Exploratory study of a preventive intervention with general population African American families. *Journal of Early Adolescence, 23*, 435–468.

Spriggs, W. E. (2007). *The changing face of poverty in America, Why are so many women, children, racial and cultural minorities still poor?* Ending Poverty in America, Special Report of The American Prospect, The Annie E. Casey Foundation & The Northwest Area Foundation. A5–A7.

Springer, D. W., Lynch, C, & Rubin, A. (2000). Effects of Solution-focused mutual aid group for Hispanic children or incarcerated parents. *Child and Adolescent Social Work, 17*, 431–442.

Srebnik, D. S., & Saltzberg, E. A. (1994). Feminist cognitive-behavioral therapy for negative body image. *Women and Therapy, 15*, 117–133.

Staples, L. H. (1990). Powerful ideas about empowerment. *Administration in Social Work, 14*(2), 29–42.

Steigerwald, F., & Stone, D. (1999). Cognitive restructuring and the 12-step program of Alcoholics Anonymous. *Journal of Substance Abuse, 16*, 321–327.

Steketee, G., & Frost, R. O. (2007). *Compulsive hoarding and acquiring: therapist guide*. New York, NY: Oxford University Press.

St. Lawrence, J. S., Brasfield, T. L., Jefferson, K. W., O'Bannon, R. E., & Shirley, A. (1995). Cognitive-behavioral intervention to reduce the African adolescents' risk for HIV infection. *Journal of Counseling Psychology, 63*, 221–237.

Stokes, J. P. (1983). Components of group cohesion: Intermember attraction, instrumental value, and risk taking. *Small Group Behavior, 14*, 163–173.

Stone, M., Lewis, C, & Beck, A. (1994). The structure of Yalom's Curative Factors Scale. *International Journal of Group Psychotherapy, 23*, 155–168.

Storm, C. (1991). The remaining thread: Matching change and stability signals. *Journal of Strategic and Systemic Therapies, 10*, 114–117.

Strom-Gottfried, K. (1998a). Applying a conflict resolution framework in managed care. *Social Work, 43*, 393–401.

Strom-Gottfried, K. J. (1998b). Informed consent meets managed care. *Health and Social Work, 23*, 25–33.

Strom-Gottfried, K. J. (1999a). Professional boundaries: An analysis of violations by social workers. *Families in Society, 80*, 439–448.

Strom-Gottfried, K. J. (1999b). *Social work practice: Cases, activities and exercises*. Thousand Oaks, CA: Pine Forge Press.

Strom-Gottfried, K. J. (2007). *Straight talk about professional ethics*. Chicago, IL: Lyceum.

Strom-Gottfried, K. J. (2008). *The ethics of practice with minors: High stakes, hard choices*. Chicago, IL: Lyceum.

Strom-Gottfried, K., & Morrissey, M. (2000). The organizational diversity audit. In K. Strom-Gottfried (Ed.), *Social work practice: Cases, activities, and exercises* (pp. 168–172). Thousand Oaks, CA: Pine Forge Press.

Strom-Gottfried, K. J. (2005). Ethical practice in rural environments. In L. Ginsberg (Ed.), *Social Work in Rural Communities*, 4th ed. (pp.141–155). Alexandria, VA: Council on Social Work Education.

Strom-Gottfried, K., & Mowbray, N. D. (2006). Who heals the helper? Facilitating the social worker's grief. *Families in Society: The Journal of Contemporary Social Services, 87*, 9–15.

Strom-Gottfried, K. J. (2009). Ethical issues and guidelines. In S. Allen and E. Tracy (Eds.), *Delivering Home-based Services: A Social Work Perspective*. (pp. 14–33). New York: Columbia University Press.

Strong, T. & Zeman, D. (2010). Dialogic considerations of confrontation as a counseling activity: an examination of Allen Ivey's use of confronting as a microskill. *Journal of counseling and development* 88(3), 332–339.

Stuart, P. H. (1999). Linking clients and policy: Social work's distinctive contribution. *Social Work, 44*, 335–347.

Stuart, R. (1980). *Helping couples change*. New York, NY: Guilford Press.

Studt, E. (1968). Social work theory and implications for the practice methods. *Social Work Education Reporter, 16*, 22–46.

Suarez, Z. E., & Siefert, H. (1998). Latinas and sexually transmitted diseases: Implications of recent research for prevention. *Social Work in Health Care, 28*(1), 1–19.

Subramanian, K., Hernandez, S., & Martinez, A. (1995). Psychoeducational group work for low-income Latina mothers with HIV infection. *Social Work in Groups, 18*(2/3), 53–64.

Substance Abuse and Mental Health Services Administration. (2003a). *Family Psychoeducation Fidelity Scale*. Retrieved from http://download.ncadi.samhsa.gov/ken/pdf/toolkits/family/12.FamPsy_Fidelity.pdf

Substance Abuse and Mental Health Services Administration. (2003b). *Assertive Community Treatment: Monitoring client outcomes*. Retrieved from http://download.ncadi.samhsa.gov/ken/pdf/toolkits/community/19.ACT_Client_Outcomes.pdf

Substance Abuse and Mental Health Services Administration (SAMHSA). (2005). *Substance abuse treatment: Group therapy* (Treatment Improvement Protocol (TIP) Series 41, DHHS Publication No. (SMA) 05-3991.) Retrieved from http://www.ncbi.nlm.nih.gov/books/NBK14531/

Sukhodolsky, D. G., Kassinore, H., & Gorman, B. S. (2004). Cognitive behavioral therapy for anger in children and adolescents: A meta-analysis. *Aggression and Violent Behavior, 9*, 247–269.

Sukhodolsky, D. G., Kassinore, H., & Gorman, B. S. (2004). Cognitive behavioral therapy for anger in children and adolescents: A meta-analysis. *Agression and Violent Behavior, 9*, 247–269.

Sue, D. (1981). *Counseling the culturally different: Theory and practice*. New York, NY: Wiley.

Sue, D. W. (2006). *Multicultural Social Work Practice*. Hoboken, NJ: John Wiley & Sons.

Sue, D. W., & Sue, D. (2003). *Counseling the culturally different* (4th ed.). New York: Wiley.

Sue, D. W., Capodilupo, C. M., Torino, G. C., Buccerri, J. M., Holder, A. M. B., Nadal, K. L., & Esquilin, M. (2007). Racial microagression in everyday life. *American Psychologist (May-June)*, 271–285.

Sue, D. W., & Sue, S. (1990). *Counseling the culturally different: Theory and practice* (2nd ed.). New York, NY: Wiley.

Sunley, R. (1997). Advocacy in the new world of managed care. *Families in Society, 78*, 84–94.

Surbeck, B. (2003). An investigation of racial partiality in child welfare assessments of attachment. *American Journal of Orthopsychiatry, 73*, 13–23.

Susser, E., Valencia, E., Conover, S., Felix, A., Tsai, W. Y., & Wyatt, W. J. (1997). Preventing recurrent homelessness among mentally ill men: A "critical time" intervention after discharge from a shelter. *American Journal of Public Health, 87*, 258–262.

Sweet, C., & Noones, J. (1989). Factors associated with premature termination from outpatient treatment. *Hospital and Community Psychiatry, 40*, 947–951.

Swenson, C. (2002). Clinical social work practice: Political and social realities. In A. Roberts, & G. Greene (Eds.), *Social workers desk reference* (pp. 632–639). New York, NY: Oxford.

Swenson, C. (1998). Clinical social work's contribution to a social justice perspective. *Social Work, 43*, 527–537.

T

Taft, J. (1937). The relation of function to process in social casework. *Journal of Social Work Process*, *1*(1), 1–18.

Tate, T. (2001). Peer influencing positive cognitive relationship. *Reclaiming Children & Youth*, *9*, 215–218.

Teall, B. (2000). Using solution-oriented intervention in an ecological frame: A case illustration. *Social Work in Education*, *22*(1), 54–61.

Terr, L. C. (1995). Childhood trauma: An outline and overview. In G. S. Everly, Jr., & J. M. Lating (Eds.), *Psychotraumatology* (pp. 301–320). New York, NY: Plenum.

Trevalon, M., & Murray-Garcia, J. (1998). Cultural humility versus cultural competence: A critical distinction in defining physician training outcomes in multicultural education. *Journal of Healthcare for the Poor and Underserved*, *9*, 117–125.

Testa, M. (2002). Subsidized guardianship: Testing an idea whose time has finally come. *Social Work Research*, *26*, 145–158.

Teyber, E. (2006). *Interpersonal processes in therapy: An integrative model* (5th ed.). Pacific Grove, CA: Brooks/Cole.

Thibault, J., Ellor, J., & Netting, F. (1991). A conceptual framework for assessing the spiritual functioning and fulfillment of older adults in long-term care settings. *Journal of Religious Gerontology*, *7*(4), 29–46.

Thomas, E. J. (1989). Advances in developmental research. *Social Service Review*, *14*, 20–31.

Thomas, H., & Caplan, T. (1997). Client, therapist and context: Addressing resistance in group work. *The Social Worker*, *65*(3), 27–36.

Thomas, H., & Caplan, T. (1999). Spinning the group process wheel: Effective facilitation techniques for motivating involuntary clients. *Social Work with Groups*, *21*(4), 3–21.

Thomas, M. & Strom-Gottfried, K. J. (2011). *The Best of boards: Sound governance and leadership for nonprofit organizations*. New York: AICPA.

Thomlison, B. (2005). Using evidence-based knowledge in child welfare to improve policies and practices: current thinking and continuing challenges. *Research on Social Work Practice*, *15*, 321–322.

Thompson, C. (Ed.). (1989). *The instruments of psychiatric research*. New York, NY: Willey.

Thyer, B. (2001). Evidence-based approaches to community practice. Pp. 54–65 in Briggs & Corcoran (2001).

Thyer, B. A. (2002). Principles of evidence-based practice and treatment development. In A. R. Roberts & G. J. Greene (Eds.), *Social workers' desk reference* (pp. 739–742). New York, NY: Oxford University Press.

Thyer, B. A., & Wodarski, J. S. (1998). *Handbook of empirical social work practice, volume 1*. New York, NY: Wiley.

Tienda, M. (2007). Don't blame immigrants for poverty wages. *Ending Poverty in America, Special Report of The American Prospect, The Annie E. Casey Foundation & The Northwest Area Foundation*. A10–A11.

Tohn, S. L., & Oshlag, J. A. (1996). Solution-focused therapy with mandated clients: Cooperating with the uncooperative. In S. D. Miller, M. A. Hubble, & B. L. Duncan (Eds.), *Handbook of solution-focused brief therapy* (pp. 152–183). San Francisco, CA: Jossey-Bass.

Tolan, P. H., & Gorman-Smith, D. (1997). Families and the development of urban children. In H. J. Walberg, O. Reyes, & R. P. Weissberg (Eds.), *Children and youth: Interdisciplinary perspectives* (pp. 67–91). Thousand Oaks, CA: Sage Publications.

Tolman, R. M., & Molidor, C. E. (1994). A decade of social group work research: Trends in methodology, theory and program development. *Research on Social Work Practice*, *4*, 142–159.

Tolson, E. R., Reid, W. J., & Garvin, C. D. (1994). *Generalist practice. A task-centered approach*. New York, NY: Columbia University Press.

Tomlison. B., & Corcoran, K. (2008). *The evidence-based internship. A field manual*. New York, NY: Oxford University Press.

Toseland, R. W., Jones, L. V., & Gellis, Z. D. (2006). Group dynamics. In C. D. Garvin, L. M. Gutierrez, & M. J. Galinsky (Eds.), *Handbook of social work with groups* (pp. 13–31). New York, NY: Guilford Press.

Toseland, R. W., & Rivas, R. F. (2009). *An introduction to group work practice* (6th ed.). Boston, MA: Allyn and Bacon.

Tracy, E. M., & Whittaker, J. K. (1990). The social network map: Assessing social support in clinical practice. *Families in Society*, *71*, 461–470.

Trepper, T. S., Dolan, Y., McCollum, E. E., & Nelson, T. (2006). Steve De Shazer and the future of solution-focused therapy. *Journal of Marital and Family Therapy 32*, 133–139.

Tropman, J. E., & Morningstar, G. (1995). The effective meeting: How to achieve high-quality decisions. In J. E. Tropman, J. L. Erlich, & J. Rothman (Eds.), *Tactics and techniques of community intervention* (3rd ed., pp. 412–426). Itasca, IL: F. E. Peacock.

Trotter, C. (1999). *Working with involuntary clients*. London, England: Sage.

Trotter, C. (2006). *Working with involuntary clients: A guide to practice* (2nd ed.). London, England: Sage.

Truax, C., & Carkhuff, R. (1964). For better or for worse: The process of psychotherapeutic personality change. In *Recent advances in the study of behavior change* (pp. 118–163). Montreal, Canada: McGill University Press.

Truax, C., & Carkhuff, R. (1967). *Toward effective counseling and psychotherapy: Training and practice*. Chicago, IL: Aldine-Atherton.

Truax, C., & Mitchell, K. (1971). Research on certain therapist interpersonal skills in relation to process and outcome. In A. Bergin & S. Garfield (Eds.), *Handbook of psychotherapy and behavior change* (pp. 299–344). New York, NY: Wiley.

Tsui, P., & Schultz, G. L. (1988). Ethnic factors in group process: Cultural dynamics in multi-ethnic therapy groups. *American Journal of Orthopsychiatry, 58*, 136–142.

Tuckman, B. (1963). Developmental sequence in small groups. *Psychological Bulletin, 63*, 384–399.

Turnell, A. (2004). Relationship-grounded, safety organized child protection practice: Dream-time or real-time options for child welfare? *Protecting Children, 19*(2), 14–25.

Turnell, A. (2006). Constructive child protection practice: Oxymoron or news of difference. *Journal of Systemic Therapies, 25*(2), 3–12.

Turnell, A. & Edwards, S. (1997). Aspiring to partnership: the signs of safety approach to child protection. *Child Abuse Review, 6*, 179–190.

Turnell, A. and Edwards, S. (1999). *Signs of safety: A safety and solution oriented approach to child protection casework*, New York, NY: Norton.

U

United States Department of Health and Human Services, Office of Minority Health (2001). *Standards of Culturally and Linguistically Appropriate Services in Health Care. Final Report*. Retrieved from http://www.OMHRC.govtassetts/pdf/checkerd/finalreport.pdf

Unrau, Y. A., Grinnell, R. M., Jr, & Gabor, P. A. (2010). Progran evaluation for social workers (5th ed.). New York: Oxford University Press.

U.S. Department of Health and Human Services. (2003). Office for Civil Rights: HIPAA. Retrieved from http://www.hhs.gov/ocr/hipaa/

U.S. Department of Health and Human Services. (2007). Summary of the HIPAA Privacy Rule. Retrieved November 16, 2007 from *http://www.hhs.gov/ocr/privacy/hipaa/administrative/privacyrule/index.html*

U.S. Department of Health and Human Services, Substance Abuse and Mental Health Services Administration (2011). *National Registry of Evidence-Based Programs and Practices*. Retrieved from: http://www.nrepp.samhsa.gov

Ussher, J. (1990). Cognitive behavioral couples therapy with gay men referred for counseling in an AIDS setting: A pilot study. *AIDS Care, 2*, 43–51.

V

Vakalah, H. F., & Khajak, K. (2000). Parent to parent and family to family: Innovative self-help and mutual support. In A. Sallee, H. Lawson, & K. Briar-Lawson (Eds.), *Innovative practices with children and families* (pp. 271–290). Dubuque, IA: Eddie Bowers.

Valencia, R. R. & Black, M. S. (2002). Mexican Americans don't value education! *Journal of Latinos and Education, 1*(2), 81–103.

VandeCreek, L., Knapp, S., & Herzog, C. (1988). Privileged communication for social workers. *Social Casework, 69*, 28–34.

van der Kolk, B. A. (1993). Group for patients with histories of catastrophic trauma. In A. Alonso & H. I. Swiller (Eds.), *Group therapy in clinical practice* (pp. 289–305). Washington, DC: American Psychological Association.

Van Hook, M. P., Berkman, B., & Dunkle, R. (1996). Assessment tools for general health care settings: PRIME-MD, OARS and SF-36. *Health and Social Work, 21*, 230–235.

Van Nijnatten, C. (2005). Transforming family position: A conversational analysis of a family social work case. *Child and family Social Work, 10*, 159–167.

Van Souest, D., & Garcia, B. (2003). *Diversity education for social justice*. Alexandria, VA: Council on Social Work Education.

Van Voorhis, R. M. (1998). Culturally relevant practice: A framework for teaching the psychosocial dynamics of oppression. *Journal of Social Work Education, 34*(1), 121–133.

Van Voorhis, R. M., & Hostetter, C. (2006). The impact of MSW education on the social worker empowerment and commitment to client empowerment through social justice advocacy. *Journal of Social Work Education, 47*(1), 105–121.

Van Wormer, K. (2002). Our social work imagination: How social work has not abandoned its mission. *Journal of Teaching in Social Work, 22*(3/4), 21–37.

Van Wormer, K., & Boes (1997). Humor in the emergency room: A social work perspective. *Health and Social Work, 22*(2), 87–92.

Varlas, L (2005). Bridging the widest gap: Raising the achievement of black boys. *Education Update, 47*(8), 1, 2, 8.

Vera, E. M., & Speight, S. L. (2003). Multicultural competencies, social justice and counseling psychology: Expanding our roles. *The Counseling Psychologist, 31*, 253–272.

Viggiani, P. (2007) Financial improvishment. In E. D Hutchison, H. C. Matto, M. P Harrigan, L. W. Charlesworth, and Viggian, P. A., *Challenges of living: A multidimensional working model for social worker* (pp. 35–69). Sage Publications.

Viggiani, P. A., Reid, W. J., & Bailey-Dempsey, C. (2002). Social worker-teacher collaboration in the classroom: Help for elementary students at risk of failure. *Research on Social Work Practice, 12*, 604–620.

Vodde, R., & Gallant, J. P. (2002). Bridging the gap between micro and macro practice: Larger scale change and a unified model of narrative-deconstructive practice. *Journal of Social Work Education, 38*, 439–458.

Voisin, D. R. (2007). The effects of family and community violence exposure among youth. Recommendations for practice and policy. *Journal of Social Work Education, 43*, 51–64.

Vosler, N. R. (1990). Assessing family access to basic resources: An essential component of social work practice. *Social Work, 35*, 434–441.

Voss, R. W., Douville, V., Little Soldier, A., & Twiss, G. (1999). Tribal and shamanic-based social work practice. A Lakota perspective. *Social Work, 44*, 228–241.

W

Wagner, C. C., & Conners, W. (2008, June). Motivational interviewing: Resources for clinicians, researchers, and trainers. Retrieved from http://www.motivationalinterview.org/

Waites, C., MacGowan, J. P., Pennell, J., Carlton-LaNey, I., & Weil, M. (2004). Increasing the cultural responsiveness of family group conferencing. *Social Work, 49*(2), 291–300.

Wakefield, J. C. (1996a). Does social work need the ecosystems perspective? Part 1. Is the perspective clinically useful? *Social Service Review, 70*, 1–32.

Wakefield, J. C. (1996b). Does social work need the ecosystems perspective? Part 2. Does the perspective save social work from incoherence? *Social Service Review, 70*, 183–213.

Walen, S., DiGiuseppe, R., & Wessler, R. (1980). *A practitioner's guide to RET*. New York, NY: Oxford University Press.

Walsh, F. (1996). The concept of family resilience: Crisis and challenge. *Family Process, 35*, 261–281.

Walsh, J. (2000). *Clinical case management with persons having mental illness: A relationship-based approach*. Pacific Grove, CA: Brooks/Cole.

Walsh, J. (2003). *Endings in clinical practice: Effective closure in diverse settings*. Chicago, IL: Lyceum Books.

Walsh, J. (2006). *Theories for direct social work practice*. Belmont, CA: Thompson Brooks/Cole.

Walsh, J. (2007). *Endings in clinical practice: Effective closure in diverse settings* (2nd ed.). Chicago, IL: Lyceum Books.

Waltman, G. H. (1996). Amish health care beliefs and practices. In M. C. Julia, *Multicultural awareness in the health care professions*. Needham Heights, MA: Allyn & Bacon.

Wampold, B. (2001). *The great psychotherapy debate: Models, methods and findings*. Mahwah, NJ: Lawrence Erlbaum.

Warren, K., Franklin, C, & Streeter, C. L. (1998). New directions in systems theory: Chaos and complexity. *Social Work, 43*, 357–372.

Wartel, S. (1991). Clinical considerations for adults abused as children. *Families in Society, 72*, 157–163.

Washington, O., & Moxley, D. (2003). Promising group practices to empower low income minority women coping with chemical dependency. *American Journal of Orthopsychiatry, 73*, 109–116.

Watkins, A. M. & Kurtz, P. D. (2001). Using solution-focused intervention to address African American male overrepresentation in special education: A case study. *Children & Schools, 23*, 223–234.

Watzlawick, P., Weakland, J., & Fisch, R. (1974). *Change: Principles of problem formulation*. New York, NY: Norton.

Weaver, H. N. (2004). The elements of cultural competence: Application with Native American clients.

Journal of Ethics & Cultural Diversity in Social Work, 13(1), 19–35.

Webb, N. B. (1996). The biopsychosocial assessment of the child. In *Social work practice with children* (pp. 57–98). New York, NY: Guilford Press.

Webster, C., Douglas, K., Eaves, D., & Hart, S. (1997). *HCR-20: Assessing risk for violence (Version 2)*. Burnaby, Canada: Mental Health, Law, and Policy Institute, Simon Fraser University.

Weick, A., & Saleebey, D. (1995). Supporting family strengths: Orienting policy and practice in the 21st century. *Families in Society, 76*, 141–149.

Weil, M. O. (1996). Community building: Building community practice. *Social Work, 41*, 481–499.

Weil, M. O. & Gamble, D. N. (1995). Community practice models. In R. L. Edwards (Ed.). *Encyclopedia of Social Work* (19th ed., pp. 577–593). Washington, DC: NASW Press.

Weinberg, M. (2006). Pregnant with possibility: The paradoxes of "help" as anti-oppression and discipline with a young single mother. *Families in Society, 67*, 161–169.

Weiner, M. F. (1984). *Techniques of group psychotherapy*. Washington, DC: American Psychiatric Press.

Weiner-Davis (1992). *Divorce-busting*. New York, NY: Summit Books.

Weinger, S. (2001). *Security risks: Preventing client violence against social workers*. Washington, DC: NASW Press.

Weiss, C. H. (1998). *Evaluation: Methods for studying programs and policies* (2nd Edition). Upper Saddle River, NJ: Prentice Hall.

Wells, R. A. (1994). *Planned short-term treatment* (2nd ed.). New York, NY: Free Press.

Wells, R. A., & Gianetti. V. J. (Eds.). (1990). *Handbook of the brief psychotherapies*. New York, NY: Plenum Press.

Wells, S. (2008). Child abuse and neglect. In T. Mizrahi & L. E. Davis (Eds.), *Encyclopedia of Social Work*. Retrieved from http://www.oxford-naswsocialwork.com/entry?entry=t203.e47

Wenar, C. (1994). *Developmental psychopathology from infancy through adolescence* (3rd ed.). New York, NY: McGraw-Hill.

West, L., Mercer, S. O., & Altheimer, E. (1993). Operation Desert Storm: The response of a social work outreach team. *Social Work in Health Care, 19*(2), 81–98.

Westermeyer, J. J. (1993). Cross-cultural psychiatric assessment. In A. C. Gaw (Ed.), *Culture, ethnicity and mental illness* (pp. 125–146). Washington, DC: American Psychiatric Press.

Weston, K. (1991). *Families we choose: Lesbians, gays, and kinship*. New York, NY: Columbia University Press.

Wexler, D. (1992). Putting mental health into mental health law: Therapeutic jurisprudence. *Law and Human Behavior, 16*, 27–38.

Whaley, A. L. (1998). Racism in the provision of mental health services: A social cognitive analysis. *American Journal of Orthopsychiatry, 88*, 48–57.

Whaley, A. L. and Davis, K. E. (2007). Cultural competence and evidence-based practice in mental health services: A complementary perspective. *American Psychologist, 62*, 563–574.

Whitaker, C. (1958). Psychotherapy with couples. *American Journal of Psychotherapy, 12*, 18–23.

White, M., & Epston, D. (1990). *Narrative means to therapeutic ends*. New York, NY: Norton.

White, M., & Morgan, A. (2006). *Narrative therapy with families and children*. Adelaide, Australia: Dulwich Centre Publication.

Whiteman, M., Fanshel, D., & Grundy, J. (1987). Cognitive-behavioral interventions aimed at anger of parents at risk of child abuse. *Social Work, 32*, 469–474.

Whiting Blome, W. & Steib, S. (2004). Whatever the problem, the answer is "evidence-based practice" or is it? *Child Welfare, 83*, 611–615.

Whittaker, J. K., & Tracy, E. M. (1989). *Social treatment: An introduction to interpersonal helping in social work practice*. New York, NY: Aldine de Gruyter.

Wiger, D. E. (2009). *The clinical documentation sourcebook: The complete paperwork resource for your mental health practice* (4th ed.). Hoboken, NJ: John Wiley & Sons.

Will, G. F. (2007; October 14). Code of coercion. *The Washington Post*, p. B07.

Williams, A. (2007, August 1). Child abuse in military families. *Star Tribune*, p. A1, A7.

Williams, C. C. (2006). The epistemology of cultural. *Families in Society, 87*, 209–220.

Williams, L. F. (1990). The challenge of education to social work: The case for minority children. *Social Work, 35*, 236–242.

Williams, N., & Reeves, P. (2004). MSW students go to burn camp: Exploring social work values through service-learning. *Social Work Education, 23*, 383–398.

Wilson, W. J. (1997). *When work disappears: The world of the new urban poor*. New York, NY: Random House.

Withorn, A. (1998). No win ... facing the ethical perils of welfare reform. *Families in Society, 79*, 277–287.

Witkin, S. (1993). A human rights approach to social work research and evaluation. In J. Laird (Ed.), *Revisioning social work education: A social constructionist approach*. Binghamton, NY: Haworth Press.

Wodarski, J. S., & Thyer, B. A. (1998). *Handbook of empirical social work practice. Volume 2: Social problems and practice issues*. New York, NY: Wiley.

Wolf, K. T. (1991). The diagnostic and statistical manual and the misdiagnosis of African-Americans: An historical perspective. *Social Work Perspectives, 10*(1), 33–38.

Wolfe, J. L. (1992). Working with gay women. In A. Freeman & F. M. Darrillio (Eds.), *Comprehensive casebook of cognitive therapy* (pp 249–255).

Wong, D. K. (2007). Crucial individuals in the help-seeking pathway of Chinese caregivers of relatives in early psychosis in Hong Kong. *Social Work 52*, 127–135.

Wood, S. A. (2007). The analysis of an innovative HIV-positive women's support group. *Social Work with Groups, 30*, 9–28.

Worden, J. W. (1991). *Grief counseling and grief therapy: A handbook for the mental health practitioner*. New York, NY: Springer.

World Health Organization. (2008). *Suicide prevention (SUPRE)*. Retrieved July, 2, 2008, from http://www.who.int/mental_health/prevention/suicide/suicideprevent/en/index.html

Wright, O. L. Jr., & Anderson, J. P. (1998). Clinical social work practice with urban African American families. *Families in Society, 79*, 197–205.

Wright, R. A., Greenberg, J., & Brehm, S. S. (2004). Motivational analyses of social behavior. Lawrence Erlbaum Associates Publishers.

Wright, W. (1999). The use of purpose in on-going activity groups: A framework for maximizing the therapeutic impact. *Social Work with Groups, 22(2/3)*, 33–57.

Wulczyn, F., & Lery, B. (2007). *Racial disparity in foster care admissions*. Chapin Hall Center for Children, University of Chicago, Chicago, Ill.

Wylie, M. S. (1990). Brief therapy on the couch. *Family Therapy Networker, 14*, 26–34, 66.

Y

Yaffe, J., Jenson, J. M., & Howard, M. O. (1995). Women and substance abuse: Implications for treatment. *Alcoholism-Treatment Quarterly, 13*(2), 1–15.

Yalom, I. D. (2005). *The theory and practice of group psychotherapy* (5th ed.). New York, NY: Basic Books.

Yamamoto, J., Silva, J. A., Justice, L. R., Chang, C. Y., & Leong, G. B. (1993). Cross-cultural psychotherapy. In A. C. Gaw (Ed.), *Culture, ethnicity and mental illness* (pp. 101–124). Washington, DC: American Psychiatric Press.

Yegidis, B. L., & Weinbach, R. W. (2002). *Research methods for social workers*. Boston, MA: Allyn and Bacon.

Yesavage, J. A., Brink, T. L., Rose, T. L., Lum, O., Huang, V., Adey, M., et al. (1983). Development and validation of a geriatric depression screening scale: A preliminary report. *Journal of Psychiatric Research, 17*, 37–49.

Young, N. K., & Grella, C. E. (1998). Mental health and substance abuse treatment services for dually diagnosed clients: Results of a statewide survey of county administrators. *Journal of Behavioral Health Services and Research, 25*(1), 83–92.

Z

Zastrow, C., & Kirst-Ashman, K. (1990). *Understanding human behavior and the social environment* (2nd ed.). Chicago, IL: Nelson-Hall.

Zastrow, C. H. (2011). *Social work with groups: A comprehensive workbook* (8th ed.). Belmont, CA: Brooks/Cole.

Zechetmayr, M. (1997). Native Americans: A neglected health care crisis and a solution. *Journal of Health and Social Policy, 9*(2), 29–47.

Zeira, A., Astor, R. A., & Benbenishty, R. (2003). School violence in Israel: Findings of a national survey. *Social Work, 48*, 471–483.

Zimmerman, S. L. (1995). Understanding family social policy. Theories and applications (2nd ed.). Sage Publications.

Zipple, M., & Spaniol, L. (1987). Current educational and supportive models of family intervention. In A. B. Hatfield & H. P. Lefley (Eds.), *Families of the mentally ill*. New York, NY: Guilford Press.

Zivin, K. & Kales, H. C. (2008). Adherence to Depression Treatment in Older Adults: A Narrative Review. *Drugs and Aging, 25*(7), 559–571.

Zuckerman, E. L. (2008). *The Paper Office: The tools to make your psychotherapy practice work ethically, legally and profitably: Forms, guidelines, and resources* (4th ed.). New York, NY: Guilford.

Zung, W. (1965). A self-rating depression scale. *Archives of General Psychiatry, 12*, 63–70.

Zuniga, M. E. (1989). Mexican-American elderly and reminiscence: Interventions. *Journal of Gerontological Social Work, 14*(3/4), 61–73.

Author Index

A

Aasc, J., 179
Abbott, A. A., 186
Abeles, N., 160
Abell, M., 281
Abramovitz, M., 422, 438, 440
Abramson, J. S., 508
Abramson, M., 66
Abrego, P. J., 512
Achenbach, T. M., 185
Ackley, D. C., 560
Adair, C., 511
Adams, J. R., 21
Adams, K. B., 13, 45
Agbayani-Siewart, P., 154
Aguilar, I., 48
Aguilera, A., 570
Ahern, R. E., 343, 426, 427
Ahijevych, K., 394
Aisenberg, E., 346
Akerman, A., 238, 361
Albert, V., 241
Alexander, J., 512
Alexander, R., Jr., 418, 420, 431
Alexey, B. B., 410
Alexopoulos, G., 409
Al-Krenawi, A., 204, 365
Allen, D., 440
Allen, D., 538
Allen-Meares, P., 22
Alley, G. R., 366
Almeida, R., 265
Altheimer, E., 381
Altman, J., 314
Anders, T., 216, 217
Anderson, D., 285
Anderson, D. A., 457
Anderson, J. P., 450, 456
Anderson, M., 160
Anderson, S. G., 422
Anderson, S. G., 13
Anderson-Butcher, D., 281, 506
Andrade, J. T., 221
Andrews, A. B., 343
Andrews, E., 71
Andrews, L. B., 204
Anetzberger, G. J., 427
Angle, B., 519
Angold, A., 203, 424
Aponte, H., 462
Applegate, J. S., 342, 343
Are·n, P. A., 409
Arkovitz, H., 512
Armour, M., 409
Arnowitz, E., 225
Ashley, D., 185
Astor, R. A., 380, 381
Atherton, C. R., 26
Attkission, C., 560
Atwater, L. E., 242
Aubrey, T., 562
Auchenbach, T. M., 183
Austin, K. M., 74
Austin, M. J., 419
Azocar, F., 394

B

Babbie, E. R., 343, 345, 426
Bacallao, M. L., 300, 302, 506, 564
Baer, J., 465
Bailey, V., 393
Bailey-Dempsey, C., 32, 366
Baker, J., 508
Bakker, L., 392
Balgopal, P., 294
Balgopal, P. R., 366, 494
Balster, T. C., 175
Balzano, J., 282, 305
Bandura, A., 42, 312, 322, 366, 372, 389
Banerjee, M. M., 422
Bardach, E., 420
Barker, R. L., 21, 429
Barnes, A., 440, 538
Barnes, G. L., 364
Barnes, S. L., 256, 259
Barr, B., 419
Barriga, A. Q., 393
Barsky, A., 74
Bartel, P., 221
Barth, R. P., 225, 241
Bartlett, H., 26
Barton, C., 512
Barusch, A. S., 199
Barusch, A. S., 420, 425
Baskind, F. R., 537
Bauer, G., 563
Bauer, S., 71
Baxter, V. A., 519
Beatty, M. L., 503
Becerra, R., 225
Beck, A., 560
Beck, A. T., 185, 294
Beck, A. T., 389, 390, 469
Beck, J. S., 182
Becvar, D. S., 249
Becvar, R. J., 249
Beer, J., 559
Belkin, L., 380
Bell, H., 32, 534
Bell, J. L., 379, 380
Belville, R., 225
Bembry, J. X., 566
Ben-Arieh, A., 343
Benbenishty, R., 380, 381
Benjamin, M. P., 305
Bennett, C. J., 88
Bent-Goodley, T. B., 440
Bepko, C., 465
Berg, I. K., 41, 53, 257, 316, 318, 372, 401, 402, 403, 404, 407, 408, 414, 461, 462, 463, 467, 477
Bergeron, L. R., 197
Berkman, B., 186, 225
Berlin, S. B., 21, 270, 365, 389, 390, 391, 392
Berman-Rossi, T., 364, 486, 488
Bernal, G., 257
Bernstein, B., 74
Bertcher, H., 286
Bertolino, B., 404
Beyer, J. A., 175
Bianchetti, A., 199
Bibus, A. A., 10, 192, 257
Bidgood, B., 5
Biestek, F., 66, 71
Birmaher, B., 217
Bishai, D., 410

Black, M. S., 11
Black, W. G., 241
Blades, M., 47
Blair, M., 427
Blatt, S. J., 217
Bledsoe, S. E., 315
Block, L. R., 507
Block-Lerner, J., 511
Blome, W. W., 21
Bloom, M., 178, 182, 187, 320, 325, 337, 340, 559
Blotcky, M. J., 568
Blythe, B. J., 48, 94
Boehm, A., 312
Boer, D. P., 221
Boes, M., 160
Bogner, H. R., 199
Bohart, A., 88
Bone, L., 330, 380, 381
Borum, R., 221
Borys, D. S., 70
Boscolo, L., 512
Bostic, J. Q., 568
Boyd-Franklin, N., 236, 244, 257, 367, 379, 452, 453, 456, 461, 463
Bradshaw, W., 281
Brager, G., 77, 443, 444
Brammer, L. M., 512
Brasfield, T. L., 393
Brehm, J. W., 157, 159, 369
Brehm, S. S., 157, 159, 312, 324, 369
Brent, D. A., 217
Breton, M., 294, 418, 419, 421, 424, 430
Briar-Lawson, K., 42, 366
Briggs, H. E., 23
Brindis, C., 225
Brissett-Chapman, S., 225
Broitman, M., 329, 380, 381
Bronfenbrenner, U., 238, 394
Brookins, G. K., 429
Brooks, L. M., 429
Brooks-Gunn, J., 424
Brown, D., 47, 48, 145
Brown, G. K., 185, 217
Brown, L. B., 42, 49, 366, 409, 558, 568
Brown, L. S., 394
Brownlee, K., 71
Bruce, M. L., 217
Brueggemann, W. G., 418, 421, 432
Bruininks, R., 225
Brun, C., 410, 414
Brunswick, L., 225
Bry, B. H., 236, 244, 452
Buccerri, J. M., 362
Bulgarella, C., 320, 322
Bulik, C. M., 71
Bulik-Sullivan, B., 71
Burford, G., 510
Burghardt, S., 418, 419, 433
Burke, B., 312, 537
Burlingame, G. M., 282, 292
Burnette, D., 236
Burns, A., 186
Burns, B. J., 410
Burns, D., 185
Burroughs, J. C., 284
Busch-Armendariz, N., 409

Buss, T. F., 203
Butler, S. S., 426

C

Cadell, S., 503
Cain, R., 191
Calderon, J. M., 409
Callanan, P. J., 73, 77, 78, 284, 308, 506
Callum, S., 431
Cameron, C., 160
Cameron, E., 160
Cameron, M., 36, 46, 83
Cameron, S., 232, 233
Campbell, J., 221
Campbell, J. A., 343
Canda, E., 204, 226
Canu, R. F., 242
Caplan, T., 160, 281, 382, 383, 495, 506
Caple, F. S., 248, 258
Capodilupo, C. M., 362
Carey, G., 257, 452, 456, 461, 462, 463, 464
Carkhuff, R., 95, 109
Carlton-LaNey, I., 314, 429
Carniol, B., 4, 256
Carr, E. S., 281
Carrell, S., 284, 493, 494
Carswell, C., 409, 410
Carter, B., 236, 240, 251, 256, 275, 276, 361, 462
Carter, C. S., 420, 432, 433
Caspi, J., 324, 366
Cecchin, G., 512
Cetingok, M., 239, 244, 257, 258
Chandler, S., 31
Chang, C. Y., 204
Chang, G., 186
Chao, W., 361
Charnley, H., 38
Chau, K. L., 305
Chazin, R., 259, 348, 383
Chelune, G. J., 108
Chemtob, C. M., 563
Chen, E. C., 282, 305
Chen, S. W., 394
Chen, V. T., 241
Chennon, M. J., 410
Chesler, M., 441
Cheung, M., 503
Chipungu, S. S., 440
Choi, G., 461
Chovanec, M., 105, 281
Christian, J., 443
Chu, J. P., 409
Cichetti, D., 238, 361
Cingolani, J., 37, 121
Citron, P., 522
Claiborn, C., 512
Clark, A. G., 393
Clark, D. B., 393
Clark, S., 32
Cleaveland, C., 4
Clement, J., 402, 409
Clifford, D., 312, 537
Coady, N., 20, 22, 360, 364
Coady, N. F., 160
Cobb, N. H., 389
Cohen, D., 199
Cohen, E. D., 65

Cohen, G. S., 65
Coholic, D., 503
Cole, P. A., 410
Collins, G., 242
Collins, M. E., 241
Collins, P. M., 470
Colon, H. M., 409
Colvin, S., 409
Comer, E., 446
Compton, B. R., 18, 19, 36
Compton, S. N., 424
Condrey, S. E., 436
Conforti, K., 519
Congress, E. P., 204, 244, 259, 266, 308, 364, 383
Conner, K., 346
Conners, W., 222
Connolly, C. M., 362, 466
Conover, S., 410
Constable, R., 236, 237, 239, 243
Cook, J. B., 403
Cook, L., 409
Coombs, M., 419
Copeland, R., 185
Corcoran, J., 212, 214, 392, 402, 403, 404, 407, 408, 559
Corcoran, K., 33, 43, 45, 187, 345, 560
Corey, G., 61, 73, 77, 78, 284, 285, 287, 308, 493, 494, 495, 496, 497, 498, 499, 503, 505, 506, 541
Corey, M. S., 73, 77, 78, 284, 285, 287, 308, 493, 494, 495, 496, 497, 498, 499, 503, 505, 506
Cormier, C., 221
Cormier, S., 125, 126, 365, 389, 391, 392, 394, 512, 518
Cornelius, L. J., 383, 410
Corwin, M., 311, 330, 348, 349, 414
Costello, E. J., 203, 424
Cournoyer, B., 17
Cournoyer, B. R., 529
Courtney, M. E., 26, 28, 421
Cowger, C. D., 7, 66, 180, 258
Cox, E. O., 305, 446
Crabtree, B. F., 343
Craig, S., 186
Crnic, K., 361
Crosbie-Burnett, M., 264
Crosson-Tower, C., 236
Cryer, M., 392
Cunningham, M., 534
Curry, R., 380
Curtis, C. M., 32, 423

D

Daguio, E. R., 73, 74, 221, 347, 350
Dahlen, E. R., 392
Daley, J. M., 443
Dane, B., 32, 511, 534
Dang, J., 284
Danish, J., 108
Danzy, J., 429
Dastoor, D. P., 392
DiAugelli, A., 108
Daugherty, T. K., 42
Davenport, D., 394
Davies, G. M., 503
Davis, B., 330
Davis, I. P., 343

Davis, K. E., 304
Davis, L. E., 48, 179, 281, 304, 537, 538
Davis, R., 185
De Anda, D., 179, 225
De Jong, P., 41, 42, 53
de Shazer, S., 401, 402, 467
Deal, K. H., 107
Dean, R. G., 12, 102, 540
DeAngelis, D., 10
DeBord, K., 242
Deffenbacher, J. L., 392
DeJong, P., 168, 316, 318, 372, 401, 402, 403, 404, 407, 408, 414, 467, 517
Delgado, M., 503
DeLine, C., 353
Delois, K., 420
Demer. S., 403
DeNavas-Walt, C., 203
Denby, R. W., 32, 423
Denison, M., 204
DePoy, E., 426
Despard, M., 281
Dettlaff, A. J., 529, 534, 537
Devore, W., 348, 349, 379, 462
Dewart, T., 225
Dewayne, C., 160
di Cecco, J., 248, 258
Di Clemente, C. C., 39
Dickson, D. T., 73, 74
DiClemente, C. C., 127, 221, 519, 550
Dies, R. R., 497
Dietz, C., 121, 236, 256, 257, 312, 315
Dietze, P., 145
Dillon, C., 569, 571
Diorio, W., 439
Doan, B. T., 441, 538
Dolan, S., 42
Dolan, Y., 401, 403
Dolgoff, R., 435
Donald, M., 32
Donovan, K., 73, 197
Dore, M. M., 30, 205
Dorfman, R. A., 566, 567, 569, 571
Dossick, J., 303
Doster, J., 49
Douglas, K., 221
Douville, V., 442
Drake, R. E., 21
Drankus, D., 305
Drisko, J. W., 46, 83
Duan, C., 95, 107
Duberstein, P. R., 218
Dudley, J. R., 199
Duehn, W., 123
Dumbrill, G., 439
Duncan, A., 565
Duncan, B., 408
Duncan, B. L., 46, 83
Duncan, R. E., 364
Duncan, S. C., 565
Dunkle, R., 186
Dunlap, E., 313
Dupper, D., 28
Duvall, E. M., 275
Dwyer, E. V., 394
Dyche, L., 539
Dziegielewski, S. F., 566, 569

E

Eamon, M. K., 372
Early, T. J., 258, 259
Eaton, T. T., 160
Eaves, D., 221
Ebenstein, H., 507
Eddy, F., 503
Edwards, A., 47
Edwards, E., 179, 508
Edwards, E. D., 503
Edwards, M. E., 503
Ehrenreich, J. H., 391, 517
Eisengart, S., 403
Elbow, M., 571
Elisme, E., 456, 461, 462
Ell, K., 384, 388
Ellis, A., 182, 188, 389, 469
Ellis, R. A., 353
Ellor, J., 226, 227
Emery, G., 389
Enos, S., 443
Ensign, J., 203
Ephross, P. H., 302, 304
Epstein, L., 42, 49, 121, 366, 378, 409, 414, 558, 568
Epstein, R. S., 70
Epston, D., 419, 420
Erford, B. T., 329
Erickson, S. H., 71
Ericson, C., 566
Erikson, E. H., 383
Erlich, J. L., 432, 433, 434
Ernst, D., 126
Esquilin, M., 362
Evans, T., 145
Ewalt, P. L., 257
Ezell, M., 431, 435

F

Facer, R. L., 436
Falicov, C., 456
Fallot, R. D., 305
Farber, B. A., 108, 567
Fast, J. D., 379, 381
Fauth, J., 544
Fazilo, K. B., 439
Fearing, J., 519
Fee, V. E., 393
Feeny, S. L., 392
Feldman, N., 440, 538
Felix, A., 410
Ferguson, K. M., 426
Fernandez, M., 315
Fernandez-Olano, C., 511
Figley, C. R., 534, 544
Fillenbaum, G., 186
Fingeld, D., 281, 508
Finn, J. L., 4, 7, 236, 312, 420
Fisch, R., 512
Fischer, J., 20, 178, 182, 187, 320, 325, 337, 340, 559
Fischer, R., 382
Fisher, J. A., 410
Flett, G. L., 218
Flores, M. T., 257, 452, 456, 461, 462, 463, 464
Flores-Ortiz, Y., 257
Foa, E. B., 392

Fong, L. G. W., 441
Fong, R., 124, 204, 409, 456, 461, 464
Fontes, L. A., 261, 331, 534
Ford, J., 446
Ford, W., 292
Forsyth, J. P., 563
Forth, A., 221
Fortune, A. E., 42, 45, 366, 459
Fowler, R. C., 217
Fox, J., 160
Frank, M. G., 198
Franklin, C., 20, 29, 184, 186, 244, 258, 319, 343, 402, 403, 407
Franklin, M. E., 393
Fraser, M. W., 308
Freddolino, P., 430, 431
Fredriksen-Goldsen, K. I., 236, 463
Freed, A., 50
Freedberg, S., 539
Freeman, E. M., 348
Freud, S., 256, 383
Frey, A., 28
Frey, G. A., 77, 444
Fried, J., 238, 248, 257, 263, 264, 266, 267
Frisoni, G. B., 199
Froeschle, J. G., 403
From, S. B., 443
Frost, R. O., 218
Frye, R., 256
Fuhriman, A., 282
Fullerton, C. D., 363
Furman, R., 327, 346

G

Gabbard, G. O., 70
Gabor, P. A., 559
Gabrielli, W. F., 205
Galaway, B., 18, 19, 36
Galinsky, M. J., 281, 283, 286, 291, 304, 308, 446, 486, 488
Gallant, J. P., 401, 419
Gallo, J. J., 198, 199, 223
Gamble, D. N., 432
Gambrill, E., 21, 389
Garcia, B., 442
Garcia Coll, C., 238
Garcia Coll, C. T., 361
Gardner, F., 311, 314, 446
Garland, J., 486, 496
Garrison-Mogren, R., 410
Gartrell, N. K., 70
Garvin, C., 349
Garvin, C. D., 22, 282, 285, 286, 291, 366, 367, 378, 492, 493, 494
Garza, M. J., 570
Gaudiano, B., 393
Gavin, D. R., 186
Geibel, S., 315
Gelb, C. B., 284
Gellman, A., 512
Gelman, C. R., 379
Gelman, S. R., 71
Gelsomino, J., 537, 538
Gendlin, E., 103
Gendolla, G. H. E., 312, 318
Gendron, C., 392
Genty, P. M., 443

George, L., 186
Gerdes, K., 88, 512
Germain, C., 16
Gerson, R., 244
Gerstel, N., 314
Getzel, G. S., 281, 289, 292
Giacola, P. R., 393
Gianetti. V. J., 366, 414
Gibbon, M., 178
Gibbons, R. D., 185
Gibbs, J., 303
Gibbs, J. C., 393
Gibbs, J. T., 441
Gibson, P. A., 192, 236, 429
Giesen, J. M., 393
Gilbert, N., 9, 179
Gilbertson, J., 74
Gilgun, J. F., 244, 343
Gillanders, W. R., 203
Gilliland, B. E., 314, 380, 384, 386, 387, 414, 545
Gingerich, W. J., 403
Giordano, J., 242
Gira, E. C., 21
Girvin, H., 21
Gitterman, A., 20
Glancy, G., 392
GlenMaye, L., 420
GlenMaye, L. F., 258, 259
Gohagen, D., 314
Golan, N., 383
Gold, M., 38, 217
Goldenberg, H., 249, 461, 463, 464, 481
Goldenberg, I., 249, 461, 463, 464, 481
Goldfried, M., 394
Goldstein, E. G., 545
Gollwitzer, P. M., 320, 322
Golub, A., 313
Goodman, H., 281, 292
Goodwin, D. W., 205
Gordon, G., 225
Gordon, W., 26
Gorman, B. S., 393
Gorman-Smith, D., 424
Gottesfeld, M., 536
Gould, J., 74
Goyer, A., 236
Grace, M., 382
Graham, J., 365
Graham, P., 393
Grame, C., 227
Gray, B., 197
Gray, S. S., 441
Graziano, R., 281
Green, A., 330, 380, 381
Green, B. L., 382
Green, J. P., 364
Green, J. W., 239, 244, 250, 257, 258, 348, 361, 362, 383, 427
Green, R. G., 537
Green, R. L., 241
Greenberg, J., 157, 312, 319, 324
Greenberg, M., 240
Greenburg, L., 88
Greene, A. D., 439, 440
Greene, G. J., 39, 402, 409
Greif, G. L., 304
Grella, C. E., 410

Grinnell, R. M., Jr., 559
Gross, E., 154, 211
Grote, N. K., 315
Grote, N. K., 346
Gryzlak, B. M., 422
Guadalupe, K., 256
Guadalupe, K. L., 312, 315, 362
Guest, G., 433
Gulati, P., 433
Gumpert, J., 285, 286, 305
Gurman, A., 107
Gutfreund, M. J., 160
Gutierrez, L. M., 420, 446
Guttu, M., 410
Guyll, M., 361

H
Hackman, J. R., 436, 437
Hackney, H., 125
Hage, D., 31
Hagen, B. F., 409
Hagopian, M., 199
Haight, W. L., 429
Hall, J. A., 409, 410
Halpern, J., 361, 380, 381, 382, 383
Halter, A. P., 422
Halvorson, H., 154
Hamada, R. S., 563
Hamama. L., 198
Hamer, R. M., 71
Hamilton, J. P., 436
Hammond, D., 512, 525
Hand, C. A., 257, 259
Hankin, B. L., 217
Hannah, G., 433
Hardiman, E. R., 439
Hardina, D., 435
Hardy, K., 179
Hare, J., 465
Hargreaves, W., 560
Harper, K. V., 179, 539
Harrington, D., 435
Harris, G. T., 221
Harris, J., 507
Harris, M., 305, 403
Harris, O., 271, 462, 463
Harris, S. K., 186
Hart, S., 221
Hart, S. D., 221
Hartford, M., 294, 302
Hartman, A., 7, 17, 224, 237, 239, 244, 426, 450
Hartsell, T. L., 74
Harvill, R. L., 284
Haslett, D., 426
Hathaway, S. R., 185
Hauer, A., 108
Havens, J. R., 410
Hawthorne, F., 242
Hayes, J. A., 544, 546
Haynes, K. S., 429, 430, 431
Haynes, R., 61
Hays, P. A., 394
Healy, L. M., 64
Heavy Runner, B., 257
Hegar, R., 429
Heisel, M. J., 218
Helvic, C. O., 410

Hemesath, C., 403
Henderson, M., 320, 322
Henry, M., 286
Henry, S., 491, 496, 498, 501, 502, 504, 505
Hepworth, D. H., 47, 225
Herbert, J. D., 393
Herman, D., 410
Hernandez, S., 281, 287, 499
Hernandez, S. H., 418, 419
Hernandez. M, 239
Hersen, M., 145
Hertzog, C., 217
Herzog, C., 73
Hickerson, J., 184, 198
Hill, B., 225
Hill, C. E., 88
Hill, C. E., 95, 107
Hill, R., 423, 440
Hines, P. H., 265
Hirayama, H., 239, 244, 257, 258
Hirayama, K. K., 239, 244, 257, 258
Hirschl, T. A., 424
Ho, M., 462
Hoagwood, K., 410
Hodge, D. R., 226, 314, 363, 365, 394, 418
Hoefer, R., 429
Holbrook, T. L., 343
Holder, A. M. B., 362
Holland, S., 439, 529
Holland, S. J., 390
Holland, T., 236, 237, 239, 244, 256, 257, 264, 464
Hollander, E. M., 507
Hollis, F., 20
Holloway, K. S., 393
Holloway, M., 226
Holloway, S., 77, 443, 444
Holosko, M. J., 5
Homan, M. S., 426, 427, 431, 433, 434
Hope, B., 426
Hopson, J. S., 402
Hopson, L., 403
Horejsi, C. R., 15
Horejsi, G. A., 15
Horesji, C., 257
Hostetter, C., 420
Houston-Vega, M. K., 73, 74, 221, 347, 350
Howard, M. O., 205
Howard, M. O., 22
Hoyt, M. F., 366
Hubble, M., 408
Hubble, M. A., 46, 83
Huber, D. L., 409
Hudson, S. M., 392
Hudson, W. W., 245, 341
Huettner, S., 410
Huffine, C., 329
Hulewat, P., 197, 225
Hull, G. H., Jr., 16
Hull, G. H., Jr., 48, 226
Hunsley, J., 562
Hunt, L. M., 64, 179, 305
Hurley, D. J., 494
Hutson, R. Q., 421
Huxtable, M., 311, 330
Hyde, C., 429, 433
Hyduk, C., 430, 431
Hymbaugh, K., 179

I

Indyk, D., 225
Ingersoll-Dayton, B., 402
Ishler, K. J., 427
Ivanoff, A. M., 48, 94

J

Jackson, A. P., 429
Jackson, S. M., 429
Jackson-Elmore, C., 429
Jacobs, E. E., 284
Jacobson, M., 4, 7, 236, 312, 420
James, R. K., 314, 349, 361, 365, 379, 380, 381, 382, 383, 384, 386, 387, 414, 441, 534, 538, 542, 544, 545
Jampoler, J. S., 409, 410
Jang, M., 203
Jansson, B., 424
Janzen, C., 271, 462, 463
Jaya, A., 257, 461, 462, 477
Jayaratne, S., 339
Jaycox, L. H., 392
Jefferson, K. W., 393
Jenkins, R., 361
Jennings, H., 299
Jenson, J. M., 205
Jepsen, D. A., 361
Jilek, W., 225
Jimenez, J., 236
Johnson, B. D., 313
Johnson, E., 32
Johnson, H. C., 203
Johnson, T., 465
Johnson, Y. M., 12
Johnson, Y. M., 102, 179
Jones, D. M., 571
Jones, G., 507
Jones, H., 486, 496
Jordan, A., 446
Jordan, C., 184, 198, 244, 258, 319, 343, 402
Jorgenson, J. D., 418, 419
Joseph, S., 382
Joyce, A. S., 565, 569
Juhnke, G. A., 217
Julia, M. C., 203
Justice, L. R., 204

K

Kadushin, A., 84
Kadushin, G., 32, 84
Kaffenberger, C. J., 403
Kagle, J. D., 74, 227, 339, 345
Kahn, M., 545
Kakkad, D., 282, 305
Kales, H. C., 218
Kamphaus, R. W., 185
Kane, N., 160
Kaplan, B., 225
Kaplan, H. B., 186
Kaplan, H. I., 178
Kaplan, S., 259, 348, 383
Karlsson, R., 441, 538
Kasprow, W. J., 410
Kassinore, H., 393
Katz, S., 199
Kauffman, E., 205
Kauffman, J. M., 217
Kaufman, M., 363, 463
Kay, G. G., 70
Kayser, K., 470
Kazdin, A. E., 562
Kear-Colwell, J., 519
Keehner Engelke, M., 410
Keeler, G., 424
Keeran, E., 36, 46, 83
Keith-Spiegel, P., 70
Kelley, L., 402
Kelliher, C. W., 410
Kelly, M. J., 365, 378, 402, 403
Kelly, S., 402, 408
Kelly, T. B., 486, 488
Kerpelman, J., 242
Kessler, M., 71
Kessler, M. L., 21
Kettenbach, G., 232
Kettner, P. M., 419, 443, 444
Khairallah, A. O., 281, 506
Khajak, K., 510
Kiernan-Stern, M., 537
Kilpatrick, A. C., 236, 237, 239, 244, 256, 257, 264, 464
Kim, J. S., 402, 403, 407
Kinney, B., 563
Kipnes, D., 565
Kirk, K., 410
Kirk, S. A., 177
Kirst-Ashman, K. K., 15, 16
Kiser, L., 410
Kleespies, P. M., 563
Klein, A., 294
Knapp, S., 73
Knei-Paz, C., 311
Knight, C., 380, 541, 542, 544
Knight, J. R., 186
Knott, E. C., 185
Knox, K. S., 379, 382, 383
Kohn, L. P., 394
Kohn-Woods, L., 440, 538
Kolodny, R., 486, 496
Kondrat, D. C., 402, 409
Koob, J. J., 402, 404
Kopels, S., 74, 227
Kopp, J., 184
Korol, M. S., 382
Korr, W. S., 329, 380, 381
Kosoff, S., 507
Koss, M. P., 349
Kossak, S., 32
Krähenbühl, S., 47
Kroenke, K., 185
Kropp, P. R., 221
Kruger, L., 563
Kuehlwein, K. T., 394
Kulys, R., 32
Kumabe, K., 47, 225
Kung, W. W., 259, 266, 361
Kuperminc, G. P., 217
Kurland, R., 281, 283, 284, 287, 503
Kutchins, H., 177, 327

L

Lachapelle, S. S., 225
Laing, R., 273
Laird, J., 239, 244, 461
Lam, J. A., 410
Lamb, M., 47, 48, 145
Lambert, M. J., 46, 83
Lamberty, G., 361
Land, H., 10
Lane, E. J., 42
Lane, T. C., 241
Langer, N., 226
Langley, J., 38, 256
Lantz, J., 179, 182, 539
Larsen, D., 560
Larsen, J., 109, 366
Latkin, C. A., 410
Latting, J. K., 439, 440
Lavee, Y., 461
Lawlor, B., 186
Lawson, K.B., 439
Le Croy, C., 45
Leadbeater, B. J., 217
Leaf, P. J., 380, 381
Leahy, R. H., 390
Leavitt, D., 394
LeCroy, C., 13
LeCroy, C. W., 494
Lee, D. B., 236, 237, 239, 243
Lee, K., 203
Lee, M. Y., 366, 402, 409, 537
Lee, M. Y., 105
Legon, J., 88
Lehman, A. F., 206
Lehmann, P., 20, 22, 360, 364
Leiter M. P., 534
Lens, V., 424, 438
Leong, G. B., 204
Lery, B., 423
Lester, L., 418, 429, 430, 431
Lesure-Lester, E. G., 393
Levi, D., 304
Levick, K., 74
Levine, C. O., 284
Levinson, H., 568
Levy, A. J., 198
Levy, C., 9
Levy, L., 512
Lewis, C., 560
Lewis, E. A., 264, 305, 420
Lewis, J. A., 426, 443, 446
Lewis, M. D., 426, 443, 446
Lewis, S. A., 305
Lewis, T., 408
Li, L., 410
Liau, A. K., 393
Lieberman, F., 536
Lieberman, M., 225, 523, 536
Ligon, J., 383, 384
Lindemann, E., 383
Lindsey, M. A., 329, 380, 381
Linhorst, D. M., 421, 422, 424
Linton, J. M., 380, 534
Linzer, N., 66
Lipchik, E., 404, 407, 408
Lipford, S., 383
Lister, L., 30
Littell, J. H., 21
Little Soldier, A., 442
Livne, S., 256

Lloyd, J. J., 410
Lo, T. W., 366
Locke, E., 42
Loewenberg, F. M., 435
Logan, S. M. L., 348
Logan, T. K., 559
Long, D. L., 418, 419, 420, 421
Longres, J. F., 48, 271
Loo, C. M., 394
Loomis, A. B., 225
Lougheed, S., 503
Lowe, J. I., 435
Lowenstein, D. A., 199, 223
Lu, Y., 511
Lucas, C. P., 217
Lukas, S., 47, 103, 185, 198
Lukton, R., 379, 383
Lum, D., 47, 214, 256, 312, 315, 339, 362, 379, 380, 383, 456, 548
Lynch, C., 403, 407
Lyness, J. M., 218
Lynn, M., 308, 364

M

MacGowan, J. P., 314
Macgowan, M. J., 217, 292
Mackelprang, R., 225
MacKenzie, K. R., 282
Mackey, R. A., 461, 477
Maganano, J., 366, 409
Magen, R., 506
Maguire, L., 23
Mahler, C., 505
Mailick, M. D., 244
Maiter, S., 439
Major, S., 410
Malekoff, A., 281
Malgady, R. G., 441, 538
Mallory, K., 429
Manhal-Baugus, M., 71
Manji, S., 439
Manuel, J. K., 126
Maple, F., 286
Marlow, C., 463
Marlow, C. R., 184
Marrero, C. A., 409
Marsh, J. C., 4, 20, 21, 270, 312, 429
Martin, P. Y., 243, 259, 443
Martin, T., 126
Martinez, A., 281, 287, 499
Marziali, E., 160
Maschi, T., 380
Maslach, C., 534
Mason, J. L., 305
Mason, M., 88
Mason, S. E., 289
Masson, R. L., 284
Matos, T. M., 409
Mattaini, M. A., 17
Matto, H., 45
Matto, H. C., 13
Mau, W., 361
Maughan, B., 203
May, P., 179
Mays, N., 429
McAdoo, H. P., 361
McAdoo, J. L., 248, 257, 258, 268

McCallion, P., 42, 366
McClelland, M., 32
McCollum, E. E., 401, 402, 559
McConaughy, S. H., 183
McCubbin, H. I., 243
McCubbin, M. A., 243
McDonald, L., 503
McGoldrick, M., 204, 236, 239, 240, 242, 244, 251, 256, 265, 266, 267, 275, 276, 462
McGoldrick. M., 361
McGonagle, E., 571
McHale, J. P., 238
McIntosh, J. L., 216
McKenry, P. C., 236, 237, 240, 241, 465
McKenzie, A., 331
McKinley, J. C., 185
McKinnon, J., 418
McMillen, C., 408
McMillen, J. C., 36, 42
McMillen, J. E., 382
McMurtry, S. L., 245, 419, 443, 444
McNair, L. D., 248
McPhatter, A., 257
McQuaide, S., 391, 402, 517
McRoy, R. G., 348
McWilliams, N., 544
Meenaghan, T. M., 15
Meezan, W., 510
Meier, A., 281, 446, 508
Mello, C., 365, 382
Mentzer, R.A., 402, 409
Mercer, J., 238
Mercer, S. O., 381
Mercier, C., 410
Metcalf, L., 407
Meyer, C., 16, 237, 239, 276, 312
Meyer, W., 312, 548, 562
Meystedt, D. M., 226
Mezzich, A. C., 393
Mickelson, J. S., 429, 430, 431
Miles, M., 523
Milgram, D., 285
Miller, B. A., 186
Miller, D. B., 281
Miller, J. A., 263
Miller, R., 289
Miller, S., 408
Miller, S. D., 46, 83
Miller, S. M., 240
Miller, W. L., 343
Miller, W. R., 124, 126, 127, 128, 313, 320, 325, 369, 408, 517, 519, 550, 552
Million, M. B., 199
Millon, T., 185
Mills, D., 410
Minahan, A., 16, 18
Minuchin, S., 246, 260, 261, 481
Mirabito, D. M., 379
Mitchell, C., 366
Mitchell, K., 107
Mokuau, N., 204, 257
Molgaard, V., 361
Molidor, C. E., 506
Moline, M. E., 74
Monferrari, I., 188
Montoya-Fernandez, J., 511
Moore, D., 563

Morgan, A., 343, 345, 365
Morgan, G., 437, 443, 444
Morris, L. A., 408
Morrison, J., 188, 203, 210, 216, 217
Morrison, J. D., 418, 419, 420, 421
Morton, R. K., 394
Morton, T., 423, 440
Mosier, J., 282
Moss, B., 226
Mostade, J., 427
Moulton, P., 61
Mowbray, N. D., 563
Moxley, D., 42, 430, 431
Moxley, D. P., 503
Moyers, T. B., 126, 127, 222
Munch, S., 12, 102, 179
Munoz, R., 570
Munoz, R. F., 394
Munroe, E., 423
Munson, C. E., 33, 178
Muran, J. C., 160
Murdach, A. D., 66
Murphy, B. C., 569, 571
Murphy, C. M., 519
Murphy, J. J., 243
Murray, C. E., 401, 402
Murray, T. L., 401, 402
Murray-Garcia, J., 179, 362, 427, 540
Murray-Swank, N. A., 226
Murro, J., 410
Mwanza, 225
Myer, R. A., 379

N

Nadal, K. L., 362
Nader, K., 365, 382
Nadir, A., 314, 365, 394
Nadler, A., 361
Nair, S., 343, 426
Nakagawa, K., 410
Nakashima, M., 226
Nakayama, E. Y, 88
Naleppa, M. J., 366, 409
Nelson, T., 401
Nelson, T. D., 402
Nelson-Becker, H., 226
Nelson-Zlupko, L., 205
Nesbitt, J., 49
Netting, F., 226
Netting, F. E., 419, 443, 444, 445
Nevil, N., 503
Neville, H. A., 441, 538
Newhill, C. E., 452
Newman, K., 241
Newsome, S., 403
Nguyen, T., 560
Nichols, A. W., 443
Nichols, M. P., 236, 256, 347, 348, 349, 401, 402, 450, 453, 456, 481, 482, 541, 542, 544, 548, 550
Nishada, C., 47
Noones, J., 562
Norcross, J. C., 46, 83, 519, 550
Norris, J., 227
Northen, H., 281, 284, 287, 503
Norton, D. G., 257
Nosko, A., 284

Novelli, K. D., 186
Nuehring, E. M., 73, 74, 221, 347, 350
Nugent, W. R., 88, 154
Nurius, P. S., 126, 365, 389, 391, 392, 394, 512, 518
Nybell, L. M., 441
Nyman, S. J., 42

O

O'Bannon, R. E., 393
Oberklaid, F., 364
O'Brian, B. A., 461, 477
O'Brien, W. F., 410
O'Connor, G. G., 243, 259, 443
Oden, T. M., 394
Oettingen, G., 320, 322
O'Faire, J. D., 426, 427
Ogbu, J. U., 361
Ogles, B. M., 83
O'Hanlon, B., 404, 407
O'Hare, T., 28, 181, 182, 183, 186, 311, 320, 339, 345, 560
O'Hollaran, T. M., 380, 534
Okagbue-Reaves, J., 154, 158, 165, 168
O'Keefe, M., 510
Okun, B. F., 236, 237, 238, 248, 257, 263, 264, 266, 267, 380, 383
Okun, M. L., 238, 248, 257, 263, 264, 266, 267
Oldham, G. R., 436, 437
Organista, K., 394
Orme, J. G., 178, 182, 187, 313, 320, 325, 337, 340, 559
Orsillo, S., 511
Ortega, R., 420
Ortiz, L. P. A., 226
Orwin, R. G., 410
Osborn, C. J., 126, 408, 512, 518
Oshlag, J. A., 402, 408
Ostroff, C., 242
Othmer, E., 203
Othmer, S. C., 203
Ottens, A. J., 379
Øyen, E., 240
Ozawa, M. N., 424

P

Pablo, C. J., 257
Pablo, S., 48
Packard, T., 426, 443, 446
Pack-Brown, J. P., 281, 287, 305
Padgett, D. K., 345, 559
Padilla, Y., 4
Palmer, B., 48
Palmer, N., 363, 463
Palmer, S., 439
Parad, H. J., 379, 383
Parad, L. G., 379
Pargament, K. I., 226
Parihar, B., 366
Parker, W. M., 281, 287, 305
Parks, S. M., 186
Parks-Savage, A., 508
Parlee, M., 120
Parloff, M., 107
Parson, E. R., 539
Parsons, R. J., 5, 7, 418, 419, 446
Patterson, J., 404

Paulson, I., 284
Paveza, G. J., 199
Pavlov, I., 389
Payne, M., 13, 21
Pazaratz, D., 366, 409
Pearce, J. K., 242
Pearlingi, B., 45
Pearson, J. L., 217
Pedersen, R., 32
Pelton, L. H., 4
Penk, W. E., 563
Pennell, J., 314, 510
Perlman, H., 20, 321, 366, 540, 552
Perodeau, G., 392
Peters, A. J., 281
Peterson, A. C., 429
Petr, C., 21
Pettys, G. L., 366
Philip, C. E., 562
Pichot, T., 403
Piehotta, C., 32
Pierce, W. J., 456, 461, 462
Piers, J., 154, 158, 165, 168
Pillai, V. K., 402, 407
Pincus, A., 16, 18
Pinnell, S. R., 402, 409
Piper, W. E., 565
Pisetsky, E., 71
Platt, S., 470
Plumb, J., 511
Poertner, J., 21
Poindexter, C. C., 384
Poitras, L., 392
Pokorny, A. D., 186
Pollack, D., 71, 256
Pollack, S., 312, 313, 315, 390, 393
Pollio, D. E., 13
Pollock, P., 519
Polowy, C. I., 74
Pomeroy, E. C., 366
Ponce, D., 225
Pope, K. S., 70
Potocky, M., 441
Potocky-Tripodi, M., 258, 259, 314, 348, 361, 362, 383, 384, 393, 409, 456, 462, 545
Potter-Efron, P., 105
Potter-Efron, R., 105
Poulin, J., 239
Powell, M., 145
Prata, G., 512
Preto, N. G., 265
Price, C. A., 241, 465
Price, S. J., 236, 237, 240, 241, 465
Prochaska, J. O., 39, 221, 519, 550
Proctor, B. D., 203
Proctor, E., 123
Proctor, E. K., 48, 179, 538
Prohaska, T., 199
Pryce, J., 402

Q

Quinsey, V. L., 221

R

Race-Bigelow, J., 281
Race-Bigelow, J., 506
Racine, G., 410

Ragg, D., 154, 158, 165, 168
Raines, J. C., 530, 545
Ramakrishnan, K. R., 366
Ramos, B. M., 349, 365, 367, 378, 379
Range, L. M., 185
Rank, M. R., 424
Rapoport, L., 383
Rapp, C., 414
Rapp, C. A., 225, 409, 410
Rapp, R. C., 410
Rathbone-McCuan, E., 197
Ratliff, S., 226
Raymond, G. T., 26
Reamer, F. G., 65, 66, 70, 71, 74, 77, 78, 324, 325, 327, 347
Reese, D. J., 343, 426, 427
Reeves, P., 58
Regehr, C., 73, 197, 519
Rehfuss, M., 508
Reid, K. E., 286, 287
Reid, W. J., 32, 33, 42, 322, 343, 348, 366, 369, 376, 378, 409, 414, 459, 568
Reisch, M., 241, 435, 436, 438
Renfrey, G. S., 394
Rescorla, L. A., 185
Resnick, C., 566, 569
Reuben, D. B., 199
Reyes, J. C., 409
Reynolds, B., 438
Reynolds, C. R., 185
Reynolds, T., 507
Reynolds, W. M., 217
Rhatigan, D., 511
Rheingold, A. A., 393
Rheinscheld, J., 402
Ribeiro, C., 362
Ricard, R., 403
Rice, A. H., 429
Rice, M. E., 221
Rich, C. L., 217
Richardson, V. E., 199
Richey, C. A., 23
Richman, L. S., 440, 538
Ricketts, E. P., 410
Rideout, G. B., 382
Ringeisen, H., 410
Ringstad, R., 452
Rittenhouse, J., 305
Ritter, D. S., 311
Rivas, R. F., 280, 281, 283, 285, 290, 295, 300, 302, 491, 493, 504, 505, 508, 509, 563
Rivera, F. G., 433, 434
Roberts, A. R., 188, 241, 345, 379, 382, 383, 431
Roberts, D., 423
Robinson, A., 394
Robinson, D. R., 423
Robinson, J. B., 462
Robinson, V., 42
Robles, R. R., 409
Rochelle, C. D., 45
Rodenborg, N., 440
Rodenburg, D., 241
Rodgers, A. Y., 441
Rodriques, S., 362
Roffman, R. A., 23
Rogers, C., 88

Rollnick, S., 127, 128, 222, 313, 320, 325, 369, 408, 519, 550, 552
Ronen, T., 198
Ronnau, J. P., 184
Rooney, G. D., 5, 47, 50, 51, 53, 84, 162, 242, 256, 257, 271, 312, 317, 318, 319, 437, 438, 463, 520, 522, 541
Rooney, R. H., 105, 168, 192, 281, 312, 366, 379, 463, 549
Rorhbaugh, M., 404
Rose, S. D., 285, 292, 300, 302, 494, 496, 503, 506, 564
Rosen, A., 123, 256
Rosenheck, R. A., 410
Rosenthal Gelman, C., 48, 108
Ross, C., 292, 503
Ross, H. E., 186
Rossi, P., 364
Rotegard, L., 225
Roth, W., 17
Rothman, J., 408, 431, 432, 433, 434, 446
Rotunno, M., 265
Rounds, K. A., 281
Rowan, A. B., 217
Rowe, R., 203
Royse, D., 559
Rozzini, R., 199
Rubin, A., 366, 403, 407
Rubin, J. S., 21, 22, 285
Rubin, R., 343, 345, 426
Rudolph, K. D., 393
Ruffolo, M. C., 22
Rush, A., 389
Russell, C., 403, 506
Russell, J. M., 284
Rycraft, J. R., 529, 534, 537
Ryder, R., 519
Rzepnicki, T. L., 23, 45, 560

S

Sadock, B. J., 178
Safran, J. D., 160
Saha, P., 410
Sahai, H., 409
Saini, M., 392
Salcido, R. M., 248, 258
Saleebey, D., 7, 237, 256, 258, 418, 420, 459
Salinas-Sanchez, A., 511
Salmon, R., 281, 283
Saltman, J. E., 285, 286, 305
Saltzberg, E. A., 394
Samct, J., 179
Sanchez, D., 393
Sands, R. G., 32
Santhiveeran, J., 71
Sarkisian, N., 314
Sarnoff, S., 74
Satir, V. M., 267, 273, 467
Saulnier, C. F., 281
Sauter, J., 186
Savner, S., 440
Schaffer, D., 183
Scharlach, A. E., 236, 463
Schein, E. H., 436
Scheyett, A., 21, 22, 23
Schiller, L. Y., 486, 499
Schinke, S., 225

Schlesinger, E. G., 348, 349, 379, 462
Schmidt, A. E., 379
Schmidt, P., 563
Schneider, R. L., 418, 429, 430, 431
Schoenwald, S. K., 410
Schopler, J., 281, 283, 286
Schopler, J. H., 304, 486, 488
Schroepfer, T., 402
Schultz, G. L., 47, 102, 109, 154
Schwartz, G., 74
Schwartz, R. C., 236, 256, 347, 348, 401, 402, 450, 453, 456, 548
Seay, H. A., 393
Sebold, J., 105
Secret, M., 446
Segal, E., 512
Segal, E. A., 88, 240, 241, 420, 421, 424, 462
Segal, Z. V., 512
Selvini-Palazzoli, M., 512
Selzer, M. L., 186
Senge, P., 443
Sengupta, S., 241
Shadid, L. G., 568
Shaffer, Q., 217
Shamai, M., 343, 345
Shapiro J. R., 71
Sharpe, L., 392
Shaw, B., 389
Shea, E., 303
Sheafor, B., 15
Shepard, M., 221
Shepard, V., 409
Shepherd, N., 410
Sherraden, B., 429
Sherraden, M., 408, 429
Sherrer, M., 28
Sherritt, L., 186
Sherwood, D. A., 226
Shiang, J., 349
Shih, M., 393
Shirley, A., 393
Shoham, V., 404
Shostrom, E. L., 512
Shrier, L. A., 186
Shulman, L., 290, 494, 571
Shyne, A., 348, 366
Siebert, H., 402, 409
Siefert, H., 203
Siegal, H. A., 410
Silberberg. S., 239
Silva, J. A., 204
Simon, B. L., 32
Simon, J. B., 243
Simon, R. I., 70
Simons, K., 410
Simpson, G. M., 383
Siporin, M., 9, 16
Siu, A. L., 199
Skinner, H. A., 186
Skyles, A., 264
Slater, C., 256
Slosar, B., 429
Smagner, J. P., 365
Smith, B. D., 312
Smith, C., 199
Smith, E. M., 382
Smith, J. C., 203

Smith, N. A., 313, 512
Smith, R. L., 403
Smith, S. M., 243
Smith, T. B., 179
Smith, V., 366, 409
Smith-Gray, N., 410
Smokowski, P. R., 300, 302, 506, 564
Sommerfeld, D., 436
Sommers-Flanagan, R., 363, 384
Sonnefeld, L. J., 410
Sosin, M., 431
Sotomayor, M., 225
Souflee, F., 426, 443, 446
Sousa, L., 362
Sovereign, R. G., 519
Sowers, K. M., 353
Spanierman, L., 441, 538
Spaniol, L., 225
Specht, H., 26, 28
Speight, S. L., 236, 312
Speisman, J., 513
Spitalnick, J. S., 248
Spitzer R. L., 185
Spoth, R., 361
Spriggs, W. E., 241
Springer, D. W., 403, 407
Srebnik, D. S., 394
St. Lawrence, J. S., 393
Stafford, J., 32
Staples, L. H., 312
Steer, R. A., 185
Steib, S., 21
Steigerwald, F., 392
Steketee, G., 218
Stephenson, M., 403, 407
Stevens, E. V., 562
Stevens, J. W., 241
Stevens, L. S., 281
Stokes, J. P., 302
Stone, D., 392
Stone, M., 560
Storm, C., 408
Strathdee, S. A., 410
Strauss, B., 282
Streeter, C. L., 20, 403, 407
Strom-Gottfried, K., 70, 76, 78, 126, 184, 225, 304, 324, 325, 327, 363, 364, 563
Stuart, P. H., 429, 469
Suarez, Z. E., 203
Subramanian, K., 281, 287, 499
Sue, D., 11, 225, 349
Sue, D. W., 11, 236, 237, 257, 258, 312, 313, 314, 315, 349, 361, 362, 365, 367, 379, 384, 461, 462, 464, 537, 538
Sukhodolsky, D. G., 393
Sullivan, M. H., 365
Sunley, R., 77
Surbeck, B., 238
Susser, E., 410
Swartz, H., 315, 349
Sweet, C., 562
Swenson, C., 28

T

Tabachnick, B. G., 70
Taft, J., 20, 42
Tarrier, M., 392

Tarter, R. E., 393
Taylor, L. E., 5
Teare, R. J., 26
Teasdale, J. D., 512
Tepley, R., 519
Terio, S., 259, 348, 383
Terr, L. C., 381
Tervalon, M., 179, 362, 427, 540
Terzian, M. A., 308
Testa, M., 429
Teyber, E., 330
Thibault, J., 226
Thomas, E., 389
Thomas, F., 407
Thomas, H., 281, 495, 506
Thomas, J., 145
Thomas, M, 304
Thomlison, B., 21, 345
Thompson, C., 186
Thompson, J., 121
Thomson, D., 145
Thyer, B. A., 28, 43, 182, 186, 187, 559
Tice, C. J., 418, 419, 420, 421
Tienda, M., 242
Ting, L., 383
Tohn, S. L., 402, 408
Tolan, P. H., 424
Tolman, R. M., 506
Tolson, E. R., 365, 378, 379
Torigoe, R. Y., 563
Torino, G. C., 362
Toseland, R. W., 280, 281, 283, 285, 290, 295, 300, 302, 491, 493, 504, 505, 508, 509, 563
Trabucchi, M., 199
Tracy, E., 46
Tracy, E. M., 20, 244, 429
Tramontin, M., 361, 380, 381, 382, 383
Trepper, T. S., 401, 402, 403, 404, 407
Tripodi, T., 48, 94
Tropman, J. E., 432, 433, 434
Trotter, C., 4, 27, 39, 44, 84, 379, 408
Truax, C., 95, 107, 109
Tsai, W. Y., 410
Tsui, P., 47, 102, 109, 154
Tuckman, B., 486, 487, 488, 489
Turtle-Song, I., 232, 233
Twiss, G., 442
Tyler, T. R., 312, 319

U

Ueda, S. S., 394
Uken, A., 105
Unrau, Y. A., 559
Ursano, R. J., 363
Ussher, J., 394

V

Vakalah, H. F., 510
Valencia, E., 410
Valencia, R. R., 11
van der Kolk, B. A., 510
Van Hook, M. P., 186
Van Souest, D., 442
Van Voorhis, R. M., 256, 420
Van Wormer, K., 4, 160
VandeCreek, L., 73

Vandiver, V., 33, 43, 45, 560
Varlas, L., 311
Vasquez Garcia, H., 361
Vassil, T., 294, 302, 494
Velasquez, M. M., 127
Vera, E. M., 236, 312
Verhaagen, D., 221
Vestervelt, C. M., 562
Videka-Sherman, L., 51, 225
Viggiani, P. A., 240
Vigilante, F. W., 244
Vito, D., 562
Vodde, R., 401, 419
Voisin, D. R., 380, 381
Vosler, N. R., 256
Voss, R. W., 442

W

Wagner, C. C., 222
Wagner, J. H., 410
Waites, C., 314
Wakefield, J. C., 20, 28
Walker, R. J., 366
Wallace, R., 284
Walsh, E., 409, 410
Walsh, F., 236, 239, 243, 259, 390
Walsh, J., 13, 28, 183, 212, 214, 568, 570, 571
Walter, U., 21
Waltman, G. H., 204
Wampold, B., 83
Ward, T., 392
Warren, C., 343, 426, 427
Warren, K., 20
Warren, M. B., 410
Washington, O., 42
Wasik. B. H., 361
Waskow, I., 107
Wassell, G., 562
Watzlawick, P., 512
Weakland, J., 512
Weakland, J. H., 467
Weaver, H. N., 442
Webb, N. B., 198
Webster, C., 221
Webster, C. D., 221
Weick, A., 459
Weil, M., 314
Weil, M. O., 420, 432
Weinbach, R. W., 558
Weinberg, M., 256, 312, 313, 465, 529
Weiner, A., 71
Weiner, M. F., 565
Weiner-Davis, M., 467
Weinger, S., 452
Weiss, C. H., 343, 345
Wells, R. A., 197, 366, 414
Weltman, S., 265
Wenar, C., 217
West, L., 381
Westermeyer, J. J., 203
Weston, K., 236
Wewers, M., 394
Whaley, A. L., 304, 440
Whitaker, C., 467
White, M., 419, 420
Whittaker, J. K., 20, 244, 429

Whittington-Clark, L. E., 281, 287, 305
Wiens, R., 563
Wiger, D. E., 176, 227
Wiggins, E., 383
Wildfire, J., 241
Will, G., 6, 11, 12
Williams, A., 241
Williams, C. C., 314, 362, 540
Williams, D. R., 440, 538
Williams, G. T., 74
Williams, J. B. W., 185
Williams, J. M., 512
Williams, L. F., 440
Williams, N., 58
Williams, R., 382
Williams, R. C., 379
Wilson, W. J., 240
Withorn, A., 241, 422
Wodarski, J. S., 182, 186, 187
Wolf, K. T., 538
Wolfe, B., 107
Wolfe, J. L., 394, 440
Wong, D. K., 314
Woo, K., 203
Wood, K. M., 186
Wood, S. A., 291
Woods, M. E., 20
Worthen, D., 457
Worthman, C. M., 203
Wright, O. L., Jr., 450, 456
Wright, R. A., 157, 312, 324
Wright, W., 503
Wulczyn, F., 423
Wyatt, W. J., 410
Wylie, M. S., 407

Y

Yaffe, J., 205
Yalom, I., 523
Yalom, I. D., 287, 291, 487
Yamamoto, J., 204
Yeager, K. R., 188, 345
Yegidis, B. L., 558
Yoon, H., 424
Young, D. C., 217
Young, N. K., 410
Yule, W., 382

Z

Zanetti, O., 199
Zastrow, C. H., 15, 304
Zayas, L. H., 441, 538, 539
Zechetmayr, M., 203
Zeira, A., 380, 381
Zhang, S-J., 372
Zilberfein, F., 88
Zimmerman, M. A., 263
Zipple, M., 225
Zivin, K., 218
Zoellner, L., 392
Zuckerman, E. L., 72, 74, 227
Zuckoff, A., 315
Zung, W., 185
Zuniga, M. E., 199
Zuravin, S., 382

Subject Index

A

ABC model, 190
Accent responses, 125
Acceptability, 204
Achenbach System of Empirically Based Assessment (ASEBA), 185
Action system, 19
Activities of daily living (ADLs), 198
Addictive and mental disorders, dual diagnosis, 205–206
Additive empathy
  deeper feelings and, 513–514
  goal attainment and, 54
  guidelines for employing, 517–518
  interpretation and, 511–518
  self-awareness and, 44
  underlying meanings of feelings, thoughts and behavior and, 514–515
  unrealized strengths and potentialities, 517
  wants and goals and, 515–516
Adjourning stage, 490–491
ADLs. *See* Activities of daily living
Adolescent and Child Urgent Threat Evaluation, 185
Adolescents
  as parents, 464–465
  suicidal risk and depression of, 216–217
Adoption and Safe Family Act (AFSA), 423, 429
Adults
  assessment of, 197–199
  rewards and incentives for, 370
Advanced practice, 14–15
Adverse beliefs, 376–377
Advise, 158–160
Advocacy and social action, 429–432
  case and cause advocacy, 429
  as community organization strategy, 433
  competence and skills for macro practice and, 430–431
  defined, 429–430
  ethical principles, 431
  indications for, 430
  social media as a resource of, 435
  techniques and steps of, 431–432
Advocate, 34

Affective discrepancies, 525
Affective disorders, 214–215
Affective functioning assessment, 212–218
  affective disorders, 214–215
  appropriateness of affect, 213–214
  suicidal risk, 215–216
Affective words and phrases, 91–94
Affordable health care, 203–204
AFSA. *See* Adoption and Safe Family Act
Agency system, 19
Aggression, risk of, 221
Agreeable mandate strategy, 319, 550
Agreement for Professional Services, 351
Agreements, negotiating for reciprocal changes, 478–479
Alcohol use and abuse, 185, 186, 204–208
Alcoholism, 205
All or nothing thinking, 390
American Group Psychotherapy Association, 282
Amplification, 127, 405
Analysis, social problems and conditions, 420
Anger
  leaning into clients', 120–121
  managing, 104–105
  termination reactions, 567
Anhedonia, 213
Anticipatory guidance, 388
APA Practice Guidelines, 188
Appearance, 203
Applicants, 5, 18
Apply, 5
ASEBA. *See* Achenbach System of Empirically Based Assessment
Assertive confrontation
  elements of, 522
  indications for, 525–526
Assertiveness, relating to clients and and relating to clients, 118–122
Assessment Scales, 185
Assessment(s)
  affective functioning, 212–218
  alcohol use and abuse, 185, 186, 204–208
  behavioral functioning, 218–221
  biophysical functioning, 202–204
  children, 197–199

client self-monitoring as information source for, 184
client's emotional reactions to problems and, 195
of client's situational context, 40
cognitive/perceptual functioning, 208–212
collateral contacts as information source for, 280–281
competency in, 14
coping efforts and needed skills, 195–196
crisis intervention, 379
cultural, societal, social class factors and, 192
cultural considerations in group, 304–306
culturally competent, 178–179, 192
decision-making styles, 299–300
defined, 174–176
diagnosis and, 176–178
dimensions of family, 255–276
drug use and abuse, 204–208
duration of problem, 194
ecological, 40
emotional functioning, 52–53
emphasizing strengths in, 180–181
environmental systems, 222–227
exploring, understanding problems and strengths, 173–200
facets of, 5
family functioning, 235–277
first interview, 188
framework for, 181
group alliances, 298–299
group norms, values, and cohesion, 300–302
group processes, 292–302
group's patterned behaviors, 297–298
guide/checklist for, 187–197
in helping process, 37–42
identifying problem, expressions, critical concerns and, 188–189
individuals' cognitive patterns, 296–297
individuals' patterned behaviors, 293–296
instruments, 185
interaction of other people or systems, 189–190
interviews as information source for, 183
intrapersonal systems, 202

Assessment(s) (continued)
   issues affecting client functioning, 194–195
   linkage between goals, target concerns and, 310–311
   meaning attributions and, 192–193
   medication use and abuse, 204–208
   motivation, 221–222
   multidimensional, 37, 39–41, 174
   needs and wants, 190
   observations of interactions for, 183–184
   older adults, 197–199
   organizational policies and practices, 438
   physical attending behaviors, 170
   power, 299–300
   problematic behaviors and, 193–194
   as process and product, 174–176
   readiness to begin tasks, 373
   resources, 196–197
   risk, 244
   role of knowledge and theory in, 181–183
   of severity of the problem, 192
   situational context, 40
   sources of information for, 183–187
   strengths, 258–259
   stresses associated with life transitions and, 191–192
   suicide lethality, 188
   support systems, 196
   systems framework for groups, 293
   use of empathic communication in, 103
   verbal communication barriers, 170
   wants and needs, 190–191
   written, 227–233
Association of Social Work Boards (ASWB), 537
ASWB. *See* Association of Social Work Boards
Attendance, 291
Auditory hallucinations, 210
Authentic responding
   cues for, 113–117
   guidelines for, 109–113
   initiated by social workers, 114–117
   paradigm for, 109
   positive feedback and, 117–118
   stimulated by clients' messages, 113–114
Authenticity
   establishing rapport and, 49
   interrupting problematic processes, 119–120
   leaning into clients' anger, 120–121
   maintaining focus and managing interruptions, 119
   making requests and giving directives, 118–119
   saying no and setting limits, 121–122
   timing and intensity of self-disclosure, 108–109
   types of self-disclosure, 108
Authority, 462–463
Autonomy, 550
Avoidance, 567–568

B

Back door, making change contract, 352
Balanced feedback, 499–500
Barriers
   behaviors on part of practitioners, 530–533
   communication, 274
   cross-racial and cross-cultural, 537–540
   difficulties in establishing trust, 540–541
   nonverbal communication, 154–157
   reactions of social workers, 546–547
   relational dynamics, 528–533
   sexual attraction toward clients, 547–548
   transference reactions, 541–547
   verbal communication, 157–167
(BASC). *See* Behavior Assessment System of Children
Baseline measures, 339–341
BDI-II. *See* Beck Depression Inventory
Beck Depression Inventory (BDI-II), 185, 186
Beck Scale for Suicidal Ideation, 185
Behavior Assessment System of Children (BASC), 185
Behavioral change, 390
Behavioral discrepancies, 525–526
Behavioral functioning assessment, 218–221
Behavioral rehearsal, 374–375
Behavioral Treatment Agreement, 354
Behaviors
   assessment of individual's patterned, 293
   circular explanations of, 253–254
   developing profiles of individual, 295
   dysfunctional, 295
   examples of group, 299
   examples of HEART group members, 296
   frequency of problematic, 193–194
   functional, 295
   hidden purposes of, 516–517
   interactional, 137
   measuring overt, 339–340
   nonverbal, 155
   patterns, 220
   physical attending, 170
   retrospective estimates of baseline, 340
   sites of problematic, 193
   social environment and human, 13
   temporal context of problematic, 193
Beliefs
   adverse, 376–377
   self-expectations and, 398
Big event, 380
Biophysical functioning, 202–204
   physical characteristics and presentation, 203
   physical health, 203–204
Bipolar disorder, 214–215
Blame, 160–161
Blaming, 390
Boundaries
   and boundary maintenance in family systems, 259–262
   cultural and family variants, 261–262
   external family, 259–260
   family subsystems and internal, 260–261
   family subsystems and internal boundaries, 260–261
   internal, 260
   NASW Code of Ethics (NASW) and, 69–70
   preserving professional, 69–71
Brainstorming, 368–369, 508
Bridging, 405
Broker, 30–31
Broker role, 413
Burnout, 533–534
Burns Depression Checklist, 185

C

CAGE, 186
Capacity building, 433
Cardinal values
   operationalizing, 56–80
   of social work, 56–63
   understanding and resolving ethical dilemmas, 77–80
Case management, 408–414
   empirical evidence of, 410
   functions, 410–411
   managers, 411–413
   plan, 412
   standards of practice, 409–410
   strengths and limitations, 413–414
   tenets of, 409
Case Management Society of America (CMSA), 409–410, 413
Case managers/coordinators, 31, 411–413
Case progress notes, 321
Case records, 62–63, 74–75, 232–233
Casework, 26
CASPARS. *See* Clinical Assessment Package for Assessing Risks and Strengths
CAT. *See* Computerized adaptive testing
Catastrophizing, 390
CBT. *See* Cognitive-behavioral therapy
Change maintenance strategies, planning, 45, 569–571
Change strategies
   motivational interviewing, 550–552
   redefining problems as growth opportunities, 552–553
   therapeutic binds, 553–554
Change talk, 550
Change-oriented approaches
   case management, 408–414
   cognitive restructuring, 388–401
   crisis intervention models, 379–388
   planning and implementing, 359–415
   solution-focused brief treatment, 401–408
   task-centered model, 365–379
Charity Organization Societies (COS), 236
Child abuse, 73–74
Children. *See also* Minors
   assessment, 197–199
   interviewing older adults and, 198–199
   suicidal risk and depression of, 216–217
Circular explanations, 253–254
Clichés, 166
Client advocate, 31
Client self-monitoring, 184
Client system, 18
Clients
   anger, 120–121
   assessment of problems, 103
   authentic responding stimulated by, 113–114
   distinguishing program objectives and goals of, 311
   emotional reactions to problems, 195
   ensuring safety of, 386
   establishing relationships with, 102
   exploring problems and maintaining psychological contact with, 123–124
   exploring the basis of conclusions drawn by, 134–136

goals and involuntary, 317–318
goals and voluntary, 316–317
handling obstacles presented by, 104
issues affecting functioning, 194–195
legally mandated, 5
mandated case plans of involuntary, 323–324
nonverbal messages, 103–104
perspective of treatment group, 283–284
reactions of, 534–536
receptivity to measurement, 343
relating assertively to, 118–122
and right point of view, 161
role of feedback, 467–471
sexual attraction toward, 547–548
solution-focused brief treatment, 402
statements, 98–99
staying in touch with, 103
teaching empathic responding to, 106–107
termination reactions, 566–569
types of responses that facilitate specificity of expression by, 133–137
under- and over-involvement of social workers with, 530–533
voluntary, 5
Clinical Assessment Package for Assessing Risks and Strengths (CASPARS), 244
Clinical practice, 25, 26–29
Clinical Social Work Practice: A Cognitive-Integrative Approach (Berlin), 389
Clinical social worker, 28
Closed- and open-ended responses, 128–132
Closed groups, 286
Closed-ended questions, 128
Closed-ended responses, 128–132
  discriminant use of, 130–131
  exercises in identifying, 129–130
  recording form for, 131
CMSA. *See* Case Management Society of America
Coalition strategy formation, 433
Code of Ethics, NASW. *See* NASW Code of Ethics
Cognitions, 390
Cognitive dissonance, 211
Cognitive distortions, 390–392, 479–480
Cognitive flexibility, 210–211
Cognitive patterns, assessment of, 296–297
Cognitive restructuring, 401–408
  application with diverse groups, 393–394
  cognitive distortions, 390–392
  empirical evidence and uses of, 392–393
  procedures of, 394–401
  steps in, 394
  strengths, limitations and cautions, 401
  tenets of, 389
  theoretical framework, 389
  utilization with minors, 392–393
Cognitive schema, 270
Cognitive sets, 468–469
Cognitive Therapy of Depression (Beck, Rush, Shaw, & Emery), 389
Cognitive-behavioral therapy (CBT), 388, 389
Cognitive/perceptual discrepancies, 525
Cognitive/perceptual functioning assessment
  assessment of, 208–212
  cognitive flexibility, 210–211

cognitive or thought disorders, 212
coherence, 210
exploration of, 53
intellectual functioning, 209
judgment, 209
misconceptions, 211
reality testing, 209–210
self-concept, 211–212
values, 211
Coherence, 210
Cohesion, group, 302, 491–492
Collaborative partnership, 550
Collateral contacts, 184–185
Commitment
  crisis intervention, 387
  lack of, 376
Communication. *See also* Nonverbal communication barriers; Verbal communication barriers
  agency policies, 87–88
  authenticity, 107–118
  barriers, 274
  building blocks of, 83–122
  challenge of learning new skills and, 168–169
  client statements, 98–99
  confidentiality, 87–88
  congruence and clarity of, 273–275
  counterproductive patterns of, 153–171
  developing perceptiveness to feelings, 90–94
  differences in styles of, 461–462
  eliminating nonverbal barriers to effective, 154–157
  eliminating verbal barriers to, 157–167
  empathic, 89–90
  empathic responding, 95–99
  facilitative conditions, 88
  gauging effectiveness of responses, 167–168
  impacts of counterproductive patterns, 153–154
  increase effective, 500–501
  informed consent, 87–88
  levels of, 273
  patterns and styles of, 467–471
  positive responses, 275
  receiver skills, 274–275
  reciprocal empathy, 100–107
  relating assertively to clients, 118–122
  roles of the participants and, 84–87
  styles of family members, 272–275
Community organization, 432–435
  ethical issues, 435
  models and strategies of community intervention, 432–434
  organizing and planning with diverse groups, 434
  social media as a resource of, 435
  steps and skills of community intervention, 434
Comorbidity, 205
Compassion fatigue, 534
Competencies
  ecological systems model, 16–20
  Education Policy and Accreditation Standards, 10–16
  orienting frameworks to achieve, 16–20
  systems theory, 20
Complementary relationships, 477–478

Complementary roles, 271
Complex reflections, 126
Compliments, 405
Composition, 284–286
Computerized adaptive testing (CAT), 185
Concreteness
  checking out perceptions, 133–134
  clarifying meaning of vague or unfamiliar terms, 134
  eliciting details related to interactional behavior, 137
  eliciting specific feelings, 136
  exercises in, 138–139
  exploring the basis of conclusions drawn by clients, 134–136
  focusing and seeking, 142
  focusing in depth and, 142–145
  focusing on here and now, 136–137
  seeking, 132–139
  specificity of expression by social workers, 137–138
  types of responses that facilitate specificity of expression by clients, 133–137
Confidentiality, 72–75
  case records, 74–75
  client waivers of, 73
  communication and, 87–88
  danger to self or others, 73
  limits of, 72–75
  safeguarding, 71–72
  subpoenas and privileged communication, 74
  suspicion of child or elder abuse, 73–74
Conflict
  assisting families to disengage from, 476–477
  interrole, 271
Confrontations
  empathic communication and, 104
  goal attainment and, 54
  guidelines for employing, 523–525
  indications for assertive, 525–526
  self-awareness and, 44
  as tool to enhance clients' self-awareness, 518–526
Consoling, 157–158
Constructive norms, 501–502
Consultant/consultee, 32
Contacted persons, 18
Contacts
  continued, 568–569
  individual, 290
  member, 290–291
Contemplation, 127, 550
Content relevance, 123
Contextual level, 273
Contracts
  Agreement for Professional Services, 351
  Back Door, Making Change, 352
  Behavioral Treatment Agreement, 354
  developing, 347–350
  formal, 347
  formulating, 41, 346–355
  frequency and duration of sessions, 349
  goal accomplishment and, 348
  housekeeping items, 350
  informal, 347
  interventions/techniques to be employed, 348

672 Subject Index

Contracts (*continued*)
 means of monitoring progress, 350
 mini-contract, 535–536
 negotiating goals and, 53
 rationale for, 347
 roles of participants, 348
 sample, 350–353
 stipulations for renegotiating, 350
 time frame, frequency and length of sessions, 348–349
 treatment plan, 353
Control, 487–488, 499–502
Convenience, 286
Coping efforts, 195–196
CORE-R Battery, 292
COS. *See* Charity Organization Societies
Council on Social Work Education (CSWE), 6, 10, 26, 418
Countertransference reactions, 544–546
Couples and family therapy, 30
CRAFFT, 186
Crisis intervention
 application with diverse groups, 383–384
 benefits of crisis, 382–383
 crisis equilibrium model, 379
 crisis reaction, 380–381
 definition and stages of crisis, 379–380
 duration of contact, 381
 intervening with minors, 381–382
 process and procedures of, 384–388
 six-step model of, 384
 strengths and limitations, 388
 theoretical framework, 383
Critical incidences, 343–345
Critical thinking, 11
Criticism, 160–161
Cross-cultural barriers, 537–540
Cross-racial barriers, 537–540
CSWE. *See* Council on Social Work Education
Cultural and family variants, 261–262
Cultural competence, 440–441
Culturalgram, 244
Culturally competent assessment, 178–180, 192

D

DAFS. *See* Direct Assessment of Functioning Scale
DAP notes, 232–233
DARS. *See* Disciplinary Actions Reporting System
DAST. *See* Drug Abuse Screening Test
DDST-II. *See* Denver Developmental Screening for Children
Deal strategy, 550
Decision-making processes, 266–268
Dementia, 212
Denial, 567
Denver Developmental Screening for Children (DDST-II), 198
Derailment, 210
Developmental assessment, 198
Diagnosis, 176–178
Diagnostic and Statistical Manual of Mental Disorders (DSM-IV-TR), 177–178, 214
Dialogue groups, 426
Difference. *See* Diversity
Differentiation stage, 489–490, 502–504

Dignity, promoting, 438
Diligent and still poor, 241
Diligent working poor, 241
Direct Assessment of Functioning Scale (DAFS), 223
Direct practice, 25–34
 case example, 27
 domain, 25–29
 generalist practice and, 26
 overview, 26–29
 philosophy, 29
 roles of direct practitioners, 30–34
Direct practitioners, 30–34
Direct service providers, 30
Directives, 118–119
Disciplinary Actions Reporting System (DARS), 537
Discounting positives, 390
Discrepancies, types of, 525–526
Discrepant viewpoint, 512
Discrimination, 440
Disengaged families, 262–263
Disengagement, 261
Disorders
 bipolar, 214–215
 cognitive or thought, 212
 major depressive, 215
 unipolar/major affective, 214
Disparate impact, 422–423
Distorted cognitions, 479–480
Diversity, 11–12
 culturally competent assessment, 178–180
 families, 257–258
Double-sided reflection, 127
Drop-in/drop-out model, 286
Drug Abuse Screening Test (DAST), 186
Drug use and abuse, 204–208
DSM-IV-TR. See Diagnostic and Statistical Manual of Mental Disorders
DSM-IV-TR Casebook (Gibbon), 177
Dysfunctional behaviors, 295

E

Earned Income Tax Credit (ETC), 241
Ecological systems model, 16–20
 understanding families using, 463–464
Ecomap, 18, 244, 344, 345
Education Policy and Accreditation Standards (EPAS)
 competencies, 10–16
 overview, 6
Educational groups, 280
Educational Policy Accreditation Standards (EPAS), 418
Educator/disseminator of information, 30
Elder abuse, 73–74
Emotional blunting, 214
Emotional control, 213
Emotional functioning, assessment of, 52–53
Emotional reasoning, 390
Emotions, range of, 213
Empathic communication, 89–90
 confrontation and, 104
 empathic responding in, 95–99
 establishing relationships with clients in initial sessions, 102
 handling obstacles presented by clients, 104

 managing anger and patterns of violence, 104–105
 multiple uses of, 102–106
 responding to clients' nonverbal messages, 103–104
 scale, 95–98
 staying in touch with clients, 103
 teaching clients to respond empathically, 106–107
 utilizing empathic responses to facilitate group discussions, 106
Empathic responding
 employing, 101–102
 exercises in discriminating levels of, 98
 leads for, 101
 levels of, 95–99
 reciprocal, 100–107
Empathy. *See also* Additive empathy
 rapport and, 39
 relational, 539
 social, 240, 424
Empirical evidence, uses of task-centered model and, 366
Empirically based practice, 21
Empowerment, strengths and, 420
Enacted roles, 271
Enactment, 184
Engagement, 14
Enmeshment, 261
Environmental systems assessment, 222–227
 physical environment, 223
 social support systems, 224–226
 spirituality and affiliation with faith community, 226–227
Environmental systems, conditions and resources for developing goals, 314–315
EPAS. *See* Education Policy and Accreditation Standards
Equifinality, 20
ETC. *See* Earned Income Tax Credit
Ethical Decision-Making Framework (Reisch & Lowe), 435
Ethics. *See also* NASW Code of Ethics; *Values*
 competency in, 11
 confidentiality, 72–75
 intersection of laws and, 64–66
 issues in community organizing, 435
 key ethical principles, 66–72
 legal tensions and, 327–328
 minors, 76
 in practice with groups, 306–308
 social work and, 9–10
 understanding and resolving ethical dilemmas, 77–80
 values and, 9
Evaluation, 14
 client involvement in monitoring and, 338–339
 macro practice intervention, 445–446
 methods of, 338–339
 methods of monitoring and, 338–339
 monitoring progress and, 337–346
 outcomes, 558–559
 practice as social worker, 346
 process, 559–560
 quantitative, 339–343
 satisfaction, 560
 termination and, 557–572

Evidence-based practice, 21
Evocation, 550
Excusing, 157–158
Exploration
   assessment of emotional functioning, 52
   cognitive functioning, 53
   eliciting essential information, 52
   employing outlines, 52
   expectations, 51–52
   focusing in depth, 52
   in helping process, 37–42
   selecting topics for, 139–141
   substance abuse, violence and sexual abuse, 53
   of topics in depth, 141–142
External family boundaries, 259–260

F

Facilitative conditions, 88
Facilitator/expediter, 32
FAE. *See* Fetal alcohol effects
Failure, task completion, 376–379
Faith community, 226–227
Family
   boundaries and boundary maintenance, 259–262
   communication styles of members, 272–275
   decision-making processes, 266–268
   defined, 236
   disengaged, 262–263
   engaging diverse, 463
   functions, 236–239
   goals, 268–269
   homeostasis, 245–246
   interactions, 250–254
   involvement with developing goals, 314
   life cycle, 275–276
   myths and cognitive patterns, 269–270
   power structure, 263–266
   roles, 270–272
   rules, 246–250, 472–474
   strengths, 258–259
   values, 240
Family and couples therapy, 30
Family assessment
   assessing problems using systems framework, 254–255
   case example, 239, 245, 250–251, 270
   content and process levels of family interactions, 250–254
   dimensions of, 255–276
   social work practice with, 236
   systems concepts, 245–254
   systems framework for, 243–245
Family Assessment Wheel, 244
Family context, 256–258
Family Functioning Style Scale (FSSS), 244
Family interventions
   approaches, 449–450
   communication patterns and styles, 467–471
   cultural and ecological perspectives, 461–464
   dynamics of minority status and culture in exploring reservations, 456–460
   examples of, 464–466
   focusing on future, 466–467
   initial contacts, 450–453
   modifying family alignments, 480–483
   modifying misconceptions and distorted cognitions, 479–480
   orchestrating initial family or couple session, 453–456
   strategies to modify interactions, 471–479
Family Resources Scale (FRS), 244
Family stressors, 239–243
   extraordinary life transitions and separations, 241–242
   poverty, 240–241
   public policy, 240
   resilience in families, 243
   work and family, 242–243
FAS. *See* Fetal alcohol syndrome
Feedback
   balanced, 499–500
   positive, 117–118, 467–471
Fetal alcohol effects (FAE), 205
Fetal alcohol syndrome (FAS), 205
Firm requests, 119
Fishing expeditions, 167
Fixation, 162
Flexibility, 259
Flight of ideas, 210
Focusing, 139–146
   blending open-ended, empathic, and concrete response to maintain, 142–145
   in depth, 52
   managing interruptions and maintaining, 119
   managing obstacles to, 145–146
   selecting topics for exploration, 139–141
Follow-up sessions, 570
Formal contracts, 347
Formal systems, 196
Forming stage, 486, 498–499
Formula tasks, 405
FrameWorks Institute, 421, 432
FRS. *See* Family Resources Scale
FSSS. *See* Family Functioning Style Scale
Functional behaviors, 295
Functional rules, 247–248
Furthering responses, 125

G

GAS. *See* Goal attainment scaling
GEM. *See* Group work engagement measure
Generalist practice, 14, 26
Globalization, 391
Goal attainment
   barriers to, 43–44, 335
   enhancing clients' self-awareness, 44
   enhancing self-efficacy, 42
   feasible, 322–323
   implementation and, 42–44
   interviewing process and, 54
   monitoring progress, 43
   planning strategies, 360–365
   relational reactions, 43–44
   use of self, 44
Goal attainment scaling (GAS), 558
Goals
   additive empathy and, 515–516
   beliefs, 313–314
   case example, 327
   client participation, 312
   commensurate with knowledge and skill of practitioner, 324
   developing, 309–346
   distinguishing program objectives and client, 311
   environmental conditions and resources, 314–315
   ethical and legal tensions, 327–328
   explicit and measurable terms of, 320–321
   factors influencing development of, 312–315
   family involvement, 314
   feasible, 322–323
   functions of agency and, 328
   general tasks and, 321–322
   guidelines for selecting and defining, 315–318
   involuntary clients, 317–318
   involuntary clients mandated case plans, 323–324
   involuntary status, 312–313
   linkage between assessment, target concerns and, 310–311
   linking to target concerns, 310–311
   monitoring progress and evaluation, 337–346
   motivational congruence, 318–319
   partializing, 321–328
   professional values and tension, 326
   purpose and function of, 310
   referrals, 326–327
   reservations, 325–326
   sample form, 338
   secondary supervision and, 324–325
   selection and development guidelines with minors, 328–332
   statements, 325, 326
   types of, 315
   values, 313–314
   voluntary clients, 316–317
Goals, negotiating
   assist clients to commit to specific goals, 336–337
   client readiness for, 332–333
   determine potential barriers to goal attainment, 335
   explicitly defined goals, 334–335
   and formulating contract, 41–42, 53
   involuntary client readiness, 333
   joint selection of appropriate goals, 334
   process of, 332–337
   purpose and function of, 333–334
   rank goals according client priorities, 337
   risks and benefits, 335–336
   specify level of change, 334–335
Group development
   approach and avoidance behavior in, 486–487
   differentiation in, 489–490
   enhancing awareness of, 509–510
   interventions throughout life of group, 491–507
   intimacy in, 488–489
   leader's role in stages of, 491
   power and control in, 487–488
   stages of, 485–491
   stage-specific interventions, 495–507
   termination, 490–491
Group processes, assessment of, 292–302
   case example, 297
   decision-making styles, 299–300

Group processes, assessment of (*continued*)
  developing profiles of individual behavior, 295
  group alliances, 298–299
  group norms, values, and cohesion, 300–302
  group's patterned behaviors, 297–298
  identifying individual's growth, 295–296
  identifying roles of group members, 294
  individual's cognitive patterns, 296–297
  individual's patterned behaviors, 293–296
  power, 299–300
  systems framework for assessing groups, 293
Group work engagement measure (GEM), 292
Group work services, 30
Groups
  addressing norms, 492–493
  assessing group processes, 292–302
  attending processes, 495
  classification of, 280–282
  cohesion, 302, 491–492
  cultural considerations, 304–305
  errors in interventions, 506–507
  ethics in practice with, 305–308
  evidence base for, 282
  formation of treatment, 282–292
  forming and assessing, 279–308
  leadership role, 491, 494
  nominal technique, 508
  open *vs.* closed, 286
  single session, 507
  subgroups, 494
  systems framework for assessing, 293
  technology-mediated, 507–508
  transference reactions and, 541
  variations in social work with, 507–508
  work with task, 508–510
Growth groups, 280
Guided practice, 375
Guidelines
  APA Practice, 188
  for authentic responding, 109–113
  for developing goals with minors, 328–332
  formulating preliminary group, 289–292
  influencing intervention selection, 22–23
  for obtaining baseline measures, 341
  for selecting and defining goals, 315–318

H

Habitat, 16
Hallucinations, 210
Health assessment, 203–204
HEART (Healthy Eating, Attitudes, Relationships and Thoughts) group, 280, 296, 298, 306, 486–487, 559
Helper attractiveness, 539
Help-giving/help-seeking roles, 290
Helping process
  barriers to goal accomplishment, 43–44
  change maintenance strategies and, 45
  elements among diverse theorists and social workers, 35–37
  engagement, 37–42
  enhancing client's self-awareness, 44
  enhancing self-efficacy, 42–43
  establishing rapport and enhancing motivation, 38–42
  exploration, 37–42
  facilitative conditions, 88

implementation and goal attainment, 42–44
interviewing process and, 45–54
making referrals, 42
monitoring progress, 43
overview, 35–56
phases of, 37–45
planning, 37–42
relational reactions, 43–44
successfully terminating helping relationships, 45
termination, 44–45
use of self, 44
Hierarchical considerations, 462
Homeostasis, 245–246
Host settings, 175
Human behavior and social environment, 13
Human rights and social justice, 12–13
Humor, 160

I

IADLs. *See* Instrumental activities of daily living
ICD-10. *See* International Statistical Classification of Diseases and Related Health Problems, 10th Revision
Immigrants, 242
Inability to disconfirm, 390–391
Incentives, 370
Individual casework or counseling, 30
Inductive questioning, 522
Ineptness, 536–537
Infomed consent, 306
Informal contracts, 347
Informal systems, 196
Information
  assessment instruments, 185
  client self-monitoring, 184
  collateral contacts, 184–185
  direct observation of nonverbal behavior, 183
  observations of interactions, 183–184
  obtained from client interviews, 183
  sources for assessment, 183–187
Informative events, 343–345
Informed consent, 67–69, 87–88, 364
Initial contacts, 450–453
Initial session, 453–456
Institutional environments, 435–436
Institutional programs, 437–438, 442–443
Instrumental activities of daily living (IADLs), 198
Instrumental Activities of Daily Living Screen, 223
Integrative Model by Level of Need, 244
Intellectual functioning, 209
Interactional behavior, 137
Interactions
  case example, 250–251
  content and process levels of family, 250
  employing circular explanations of behavior, 253–254
  sequences of, 251–253
  strategies to modify, 471–479
Interactive Trauma/Grief-Focused Therapy (IT/G-FT) model, 382
Interchangeable empathic responding. *See* Reciprocal empathic responding

Internal family boundaries, 260
International Federation of Social Workers, 5
International Statistical Classification of Diseases and Related Health Problems, 10th Revision (ICD-10), 177
Interpretation
  additive empathy and, 511–518
  categories of, 512
  dogmatic, 162
  guidelines for employing, 517–518
  hidden purposes of behavior, 516–517
  unrealized strengths and potentialities, 517
Interpreters, 50
Interrole conflict, 271
Interruptions, 119–120, 164
Interventions
  competency in, 14
  deciding on and carrying out, 20–23
  errors in group, 506–507
  with families, 449–506
  guidelines influencing selection, 22–23
  models and strategies of community, 432–433
  to modify family alignments, 480–483
  on-the-spot, 474–476
  stage-specific, 495–507
  steps and skills of community, 433
Interviewing
  to assess substance use, 206–208
  assessment information and, 183
  assessment of emotional functioning, 52–53
  children and older adults, 198–199
  eliciting essential information, 52
  employing outlines, 52
  ending interviews, 53–54
  establishing rapport, 47–50
  exploration process, 50–52
  exploring cognitive functioning, 53
  first interview, 188
  focusing in depth, 52
  language barriers, 50
  macro practice intervention and, 426–427
  motivational approach, 519–520, 550–552
  motivational congruence and, 49–50
  physical conditions, 46–47
  preliminary interview for treatment group, 287–288
  process, 45–54
  structure of interviews, 47
  for substance abuse potential, 206
  techniques, 198–199
  using interpreters, 50
Interviews. *See* Interviewing
Intimacy, 488–489, 502–504
Intrapersonal systems, assessment of, 202
Involuntary minors, 329–330
Involuntary status, 312–313
IT/G-FT. *See* Interactive trauma/grief-focused therapy model

J

Joining stage, 453
Judgement, 160–161, 209
Judgment focus, 391
Jumping to conclusions, 391

L

Language barriers, 50, 242
Leadership, 491, 494
Leading questions, 163–164
Legally mandated clients, 5
Limits
   confidentiality, 72–75
   setting, 121–122
Linear explanations, 253
Locality development, 432–433
Looseness of association, 210
Low Task Performance
   adverse beliefs, 376–377
   attributed, not acknowledged problems, 377
   conflicting needs and wants, 377
   inadequate preparation, 377
   lack of commitment, 376
   lack of support, 377
   lack of understanding of consequences, 377
   little hope for change, 377–378
   negative reactions to social worker, 377
   occurrence of crisis, 376
   reasons for, 376–378
   related to target problem, 377–378
   related to tasks, 376–377
   task inadequately specified, 376

M

Macro practice intervention
   advocacy and social action, 429–432
   community organization, 432–435
   cultural competence, 440
   defined, 418–419
   developing and mobilizing resources, 425–429
   evaluation, 445–446
   institutional environments, 435–436
   linking micro concerns and, 419
   organizational change, 443–445
   organizational environments, 436–443
   strategies, 419–425
Macro-level practice, 15
Major depressive disorder, 215
Maltreatment, 197–198
Mandated case plans, 323–324
Mapping, 426
MAST. *See* Michigan Alcoholism Screening Test
MCMI-III. *See* Million Multiaxial Clinical Inventory-III
Meaning attributions, 192–193
Mediator/arbitrator, 31
Medications, assessment of use and abuse, 204–208
Members, 290
Mental and addictive disorders, dual diagnosis, 205–206
Mental retardation, 212
Mental status exams, 219
Metacommunication, 471–472
Metaphor, 127
Mezzo-level practice, 15
Michigan Alcoholism Screening Test (MAST), 186
Micro practice, linking macro practice intervention and, 419
Microaggression, 538

Micro-level practice, 15
Million Multiaxial Clinical Inventory-III (MCMI-III), 185
Mind reading, 391
Mini-contract, 535–536
Minimal prompts, 125
Minnesota Multiphasic Personality Inventory (MMPI-II), 185
Minors, 76. *See also* Children
   age, stage of development and cognitive ability, 330–332
   case example, 331
   cognitive restructuring, 392–393
   crisis intervention, 381–382
   criteria for developing goals with, 330
   definition and specifications of behavior to be changed, 330
   goal selection and development guidelines with, 328–332
   informed consent and, 364
   narrative-oriented approach with, 328
   rewards and incentives for, 370
   school-based group with, 328–329
   self-determination and, 363
   solution-focused brief treatment, 402–403
   task-centered model, 366
   voluntary/involuntary, 329–330
Miracle question, 182
Misconceptions, 211, 479–480
Missing class, 241
MMPI-II. *See* Minnesota Multiphasic Personality Inventory
Modeling, 374–375
Monitoring progress, 43
   evaluation and, 337–346
   methods of, 338–339
   qualitative measure methods for, 343–346
   with quantitative measurements, 342–343
   task-centered model, 378–379
Motivation
   assessment of, 221–222
   for behavioral change, 548–554
   establishing rapport and enhancing, 38–41
   scaling, 182
Motivational congruence, 49, 318–319, 550
Motivational interviewing
   confrontation and, 519–520
   guiding principles of, 550–552
Multiaxial system, 178
Multidimensional assessment, 37, 39–41, 174
Multidimensionality, 174
Multisystems Approach, 244
Mystification, 273

N

NASW. *See* National Association of Social Workers
NASW Code of Ethics, 418. *See also* Ethics
   cardinal values of social work, 56–63
   commitment, 418
   key ethical principles, 66–72
   legal tensions and, 327
   pathological or inept social workers and, 536–537
   preserving professional boundaries, 69–71
   providing informed consent, 67–69
   safeguarding confidentiality, 71–72

   self-determination, 66–67
   social work, 10
   termination reactions, 567
National Association of Social Workers (NASW), 4, 10, 25, 409–410, 413. *See also* NASW Code of Ethics
Natural settings, 184
Natural systems, 196
Needs, 190
Needs assessment, 426
Negative (mental) filtering, 391
Negative cognitive sets, 210
Negative evaluations, 160–161
Neuroticism, 162
Niche, 16
Nickled and Dimed (Ehrenreich), 242
Nominal group technique, 508
Nonnormative stressors, 240
Nonverbal behavior, 183
Nonverbal communication barriers. *See also* Communication
   cultural nuances of nonverbal cues, 154–155
   eliminating, 154–157
   inventory of nonverbal communication, 155–157
Nonverbal level, 273
Nonverbal minimal prompts, 125
Normative stressors, 240
Norming stage, 488
Norms, groups, 300–302, 492–493, 501–502

O

OARS. *See* Older Americans Resources and Services Questionnaire
Older adults
   assessment of, 197–199
   interviewing children and, 198–199
   suicidal risk and depression of, 217–218
Older Americans Resources and Services Questionnaire (OARS), 186
On-the-spot interventions, 474–476
Open groups, 286
Open-ended questions, 128
Open-ended responses, 128–132
   discriminant use of, 130–131
   exercises in identifying, 129–130
   focusing and, 141
   focusing in depth and, 142–145
   recording form for, 131
Oppression, 256
Organizational analyst, 31–32
Organizational change, 443–445
   organizational learning and learning organizations, 443–444
   risks, benefits, and opposition, 444–445
   staff as agents of, 444
Organizational environments
   improving, 436–443
   institutional programs, 437–438, 442–443
   policies and practices, 437–438
   public policy, 439, 441–442
   staff, 436–437, 439–442
Outcomes, 558–559
Overgeneralizations, 391
Over-involvement, 530–533

P

Paraphrasing, 51
    exercises in, 126
    responses, 125–126
Parentified child, 263
Parroting, 166
Passivity, 162
Pathological social workers, 536–537
Patient Health Questionnaire (PHQ-9), 185
Patterned behaviors
    assessment of groups, 297–298
    assessment of individuals, 293–296
Pedagogy, 15–16
Perceived roles, 271
Perceptual functioning assessment. *See* Cognitive/perceptual functioning
Performance accomplishments, 373
Performing stage, 489–490
Personal experience, 187
Personal responsibility, 240
Personal Responsibility and Work Opportunity Reconciliation Act (PRWORA), 421, 429
Personalizing, 391
PHQ-9. *See* Patient Health Questionnaire
Physical characteristics, 203
Physical environment, 223
Physical health, 203–204
Planned terminations, 564–566
Planner, 33
Planning
    change maintenance strategies, 45
    community organization, 434
    crisis intervention, 387
    helping process, 37–42
Policies, 87–88
    organizational, 437–438
    social justice and, 421–422
Policy and procedure developer, 33–34
Policy practice, 13
Positive cognitive sets, 468–469
Positive connotation, 552
Positive feedback, 117–118, 467–471
Post-intervention eco-map, 345
Potentialities, unrealized, 517
Poverty, 240–241
Power
    assessment of, 265–266
    distribution and balance of, 264–265
    elements within family system, 264
    family power structure, 263–266
    in group development, 487–488
    in groups, 299–300
    multicultural perspectives, 265
    shifts in, 265
    stage-specific interventions, 499–502
Preaffiliation, 486–487, 496–499
Precontemplation, 127, 550
Predictive tasks, 405
Pre-intervention ecomap, 344
Premature solutions, 158–160
Prescribed roles, 271
Presentation, 203
Presenting problem, 189, 190–191
Prevention, 6
Privacy, 46
Problem for work, 189
Problematic behaviors
    frequency of, 193–194
    sites of, 193
    temporal context of, 193
Problematic processes, interrupting, 119–120
Process model, 21
Profanity, use of, 291–292
Profession context, 13–14
Professional conduct, 10–11
Program developer, 33
Programming, 291
Progress notes, 233
Prompts, minimal, 125
Propositional interpretations, 512
PRWORA. *See* Personal Responsibility and Work Opportunity Reconciliation Act
Psychotherapy, 28–29
Public policy, 240, 439

Q

Qualitative measure methods, 343–346
Quantitative measurements, 339–343
    baseline measures, 339–340
    guidelines for obtaining baseline measures, 341
    monitoring progress with, 342–343
    receptivity of clients to, 343
    retrospective estimates, 340
    self-administered scales, 341–342
    self-anchored scales, 340–341

R

Racism, 440
RAP (Recognize, Anticipate, and Problem) framework, 304
Rapport, establishing, 47–49
Rational-emotive therapy (RET), 389
Reactance theory, 549
Reactions
    countertransference, 544–546
    realistic practitioner, 546–547
    transference, 541–544
Reality testing, 209–210
Reason and Emotion in Psychotherapy (Ellis), 389
Reassuring, 157–158
Receiver skills, 274–275
Reciprocal changes, negotiating agreements for, 478–479
Reciprocal empathic responding, 100–107
Recorders, use of, 291
Referrals, 18, 42, 326–327
Reflection, 126–128
Reflection with a twist, 127
Reframing, 127, 552–553
Refugees, 242
Regret orientation, 391
Reinforcement, 162
Relabeling, 552–553
Relational dynamics, 528–534
    burnout, compassion fatigue or vicarious trauma, 533–534
    under- and over-involvement of social workers with clients, 530–533
Relational empathy, 539
Relational reactions, 528
Remediation, 6
Repression, 162
Requests, 118–119
Research, 13
Researcher/research consumer, 33
Reservations, dynamics of minority status and culture in exploring, 456–460
Resilience, 243
Resistance, 162, 548
Resources
    developing and mobilizing, 425–429
    developing with diverse groups, 427
    mobilizing community, 427–429
    for problem assessment, 196–197
    value and distribution of, 421
Restoration, 6
RET. *See* Rational-emotive therapy
Retrospective estimates of baseline behaviors, 340
Rewards, 370
Rigid rules, 247–248
Risk
    assessments, 244
    suicidal, 215–218
Rituals, termination, 570–571
Role clarification, 84–87
Role transition, 271
Role-play, 374–375
Roles
    complementary, 271
    enacted, 271
    family, 270–272
    group, 493–494
    interrole conflict, 271
    leadership, 491, 494
    perceived, 271
    prescribed, 271
    symmetrical, 271
ROPES, 244
Rules
    cautions about assessing, 248
    family, 246–250, 472–473
    flexibility of, 249–250
    functional and rigid, 247–248
    mapping, 250
    violation of, 248–249

S

Safety concerns, 452
Same-sex couples, 465–466
SAMHSA. *See* Substance Abuse & Mental Health Services Administration
Sarcasm, 160
Satisfaction, 560
Scaling motivation, 182
Scaling problem, 182
Schizophrenia, 212
Secondary settings, 175
Secondary supervision, 324–325
Secondary trauma, 534
Seeking concreteness. *See* Concreteness
Seeking exceptions, 182
Self-administered scales, 341–342
Self-awareness
    enhancement of, 44
    meaning and significance of, 511
Self-concept, 211–212
Self-confrontation, 522
Self-determination, 9, 66–67, 363

Self-disclosure
  timing and intensity of, 108–109
  types of, 108
Self-efficacy
  enhancement of, 42
  increasing, 374–375
Self-expectations, beliefs and, 398
Self-help groups, 281
Self-monitoring, 184
Self-reflection, 238
Semantic interpretations, 512
Sender skills, 275
Sessions
  frequency and duration of, 349
  time frame, frequency and length of, 348–349
Settings
  host, 175
  natural, 184
Sexual abuse, 53
Sexual attraction, 547–548
Should statements, 391
Signature pedagogy, 15–16
Simile, 127
Single session groups, 507
SOAP notes, 232–233
Social action. *See* Advocacy and social action
Social empathy, 240, 424
Social justice
  different perspectives of, 424–425
  disparate Impact and, 422–423
  issues, 421–425
  policy decisions and, 421–422
  responsibility for problem, 423–424
Social media, 435
Social planning, 433
Social stage, 453
Social Support Network Map, 244
Social support systems (SSSs), 224–226
Social work
  cardinal values of, 56–63
  case example, 4
  challenges of, 3–24
  commitment, 418
  deciding on and carrying out interventions, 20–23
  EPAS competencies of, 10–20
  mission of, 5
  practice, 26
  purposes of, 5–6
  values, 7–10
Social Work (journal), 25
Social work practice. *See* Direct practice
Social workers
  advanced practice, 14–15
  assessment, 14
  authority of, 462–463
  case example, 4
  case managers/coordinators, 31
  competencies of, 10–16
  critical thinking, 11
  direct service providers, 30
  diversity and cultural awareness, 11–12
  elements among diverse theorists and, 35–37
  engagement, 14
  ethical principles, 11
  evaluation, 14
  finding substitutes for, 569
  general tasks for, 368
  generalist practice, 14
  human behavior and social environment, 13
  human rights and social justice, 12–13
  interventions, 14
  negative reactions to, 377
  and over-involvement of, 530–533
  pathological or inept, 536–537
  pedagogy, 15–16
  policy practice, 13
  practice and research, 13
  professional conduct, 10–11
  professional context, 13–14
  reactions of, 546–547
  researcher/research consumer, 33
  specificity of expression by, 137–138
  system development, 33
  system linkage roles, 30–31
  system maintenance and enhancement roles, 31–33
  termination reactions, 569
  understanding and resolving ethical dilemmas, 77–80
Socialization groups, 281
Sociogram, 299, 300
Solution building, stages of, 403
Solution-focused brief treatment, 408–414
  application with diverse groups, 403
  empirical evidence and uses of, 402
  procedures and techniques, 403–407
  questions, 404
  strengths and limitations, 407–408
  tenets of, 401–402
  theoretical framework, 402
  utilization with minors, 402–403
Solution-focused therapy, assessment and, 182
Spirituality, 226–227
SSSs. *See* Social support systems
Stacking questions, 163
Staff
  as agents of change, 439–442
  in organizational environments, 436–437
Stage-specific interventions, 495–507
  intimacy and differentiation stage, 502–504
  power and control stage, 499–502
  preaffiliation stage, 496–499
  termination stage, 504–506
Standards
  case management practice, 409–410
  social work, 418
Stereotypic labeling, 162
Stimulus-response congruence, 123
Storming stage, 487
Strategies
  agreeable mandate, 319
  change, 549–554
  change maintenance, 45
  getting rid of the mandate, 319
  let's make a deal, 319
  motivational congruence, 318–319
  motivational interviewing, 550–552
  positive connotation, 552
  relabeling/reframing, 552–553
  therapeutic binds, 553–554
  transformational formation, 433
Strengths
  assessment, 258
  unrealized, 517

Stress
  effects on professionals, 534
  life transitions and, 191–192
Stressors, family, 239–243
Structural family therapy, 480–481
Structural mapping, 481
Subgroups, 494
Substance Abuse & Mental Health Services Administration (SAMHSA), 304
Substance use and abuse, 53, 206–208. *See also* Drug use and abuse
Suggestions, 158–160
Suicidal risk
  assessment of, 215–216
  and depression with children and adolescents, 216–217
  and depression with older adults, 217–218
Suicide lethality assessment, 188
Summarization, 146–149
  analyzing verbal following skills, 149
  highlighting key aspects of problems, 146–147
  lengthy messages, 147–148
  providing focus and continuity, 149
  reviewing focal points of session, 148
Supervision, secondary, 324–325
Supervisor, 32–33
Support groups, 280
Support systems, 196, 386
Symmetrical relationships, 477–478
Symmetrical roles, 271
Sympathizing, 157–158
System development, 33
System linkage roles, 30–31
System maintenance and enhancement, 31–33
Systems concepts, 245–254
  application of, 245
  family homeostasis, 245–246
  family rules, 246–250
Systems framework
  for assessing family functioning, 243–245
  for assessing groups, 293
  assessing problems using, 254–255
Systems theory
  limitations of, 20
  nonlinear applications of, 20

T

TANF. *See* Temporary Assistance to Needy Families
Target concerns, linkage between assessment, goals and, 310–311
Target problem, performance problems related to, 377–378
Target system, 18
Targeted Case Management, 409
Task groups
  beginning, 303–304
  formation of, 302–304
  getting members involved, 509
  planning for, 302–303
  problem identification and, 508
  types of, 281
  work with, 508–510

Task implementation sequence (TIS), 369–375
  analyze and resolve obstacles., 371–373
  assessing readiness to begin tasks, 373
  behavioral rehearsal, modeling, and role-play in, 374–375
  conditions for tasks completion, 371
  enhance the client's commitment to carry out tasks, 369–370
  guided practice, 375
  plan details of carrying out tasks, 370–371
  practitioner's role in task planning, 371
  rehearse or practice behavior involved in tasks, 373–375
  rewards and incentives for adults and minors, 370
  summarize task plan, 375
Task planning, 371
Task-centered model
  application with diverse groups, 366–367
  brainstorming, 368–369
  empirical evidence and uses of, 366
  general tasks, 367–368
  implementation sequence, 369–375
  low task performance, 376–378
  models and techniques of practice, 365–367
  monitoring progress, 378–379
  procedures of, 367–379
  specific tasks, 368
  strengths and limitations, 378–379
  tenets of, 365
  theoretical framework, 366
  utilization with minors, 366
Tasks
  to enhance cognitive sets, 469
  failure to complete, 376–378
  inadequately specified, 376
  performance problems related to, 376–377
  in solution-focused brief treatment, 405
Team member, 32
Technology-mediated groups, 507–508
Temporary Assistance to Needy Families (TANF), 241, 281
Tentative requests, 119
Termination
  case example, 571–572
  consolidating gains and planning maintenance strategies and, 569–571
  due to temporal or structural limits, 564–565
  ending rituals and, 570–571
  evaluation and, 557–572
  follow-up sessions and, 570
  helping process, 44–45
  interventions, 504–506
  other determinants of planned, 565–566
  phase of group development, 490–491
  planned, 564–566
  subtypes, 561
  types of, 561–566

understanding and responding to client's reactions, 566–569
  unplanned, 562–563
Therapeutic binds, 553–554
Therapy groups, 280–281
Thinking, 389–390
Thought disorders, 212
Threats, 162–163
Touching, 292
Transference reactions, 541–544
  identifying, 542
  managing, 542–544
Transformational strategy formation, 433
Transitions
  role, 271
  separations and extraordinary, 241–242
  stresses associated with, 191–192
Treatment groups
  client's perspective, 283–284
  composition, 284–286
  determining need for, 282–283
  duration of meetings, 287
  format, 288–289
  formation of, 282–292
  frequency of, 287
  guidelines for, 289–292
  leadership, 284
  open vs. closed, 286
  preliminary interview, 287–288
  purpose of, 283–284
  size and location, 286–288
  types of, 280–281
Treatment Improvement Protocol, 304–305
Triage Assessment System, 379
Trust, 540–541

U

Under-involvement, 530–533
Unfair comparisons, 391
Unfamiliar terms, clarifying meaning of, 134
Unipolar/major affective disorders, 214
Unplanned terminations, 562–564

V

Vague terms, clarifying meaning of, 134
Values
  cardinal values of social work, 56–80
  challenges, 63–64
  in cognitive/perceptual functioning assessment, 211
  ethics and, 9–10, 64–77
  family, 240
  groups, 302
Verbal communication barriers. See also Communication
  advising and giving suggestions or solutions prematurely, 158–160
  analyzing, diagnosing, or making glib or dogmatic interpretations, 162
  dominating interaction, 164–165

dwelling on remote past, 166–167
  eliminating, 157–167
  fishing expeditions, 167
  fostering safe social interaction, 165
  interrupting inappropriately or excessively, 164
  judging, criticizing, or placing blame, 160–161
  leading questions, 163–164
  parroting or overusing certain phrases or clichés, 166
  reassuring, sympathizing, consoling or excusing, 157–158
  responding infrequently, 165–166
  stacking questions, 163
  threatening, warning, or counterattacking, 162–163
  using sarcasm or employing humor inappropriately, 160
Verbal following skills, 124–151
  analyzing, 149
  closed- and open-ended responses, 128–132
  concreteness, 132–139
  focusing, 139–146
  furthering responses, 125
  paraphrasing responses, 125–126
  reflection, 126–128
  summarization, 146–149
  types of, 124–125
Verbal level, 273
Verbal minimal prompts, 125
Vicarious trauma, 534
Video recordings, 62–63
Violence, 53, 104–105, 221
Visitors, 290
Visual hallucinations, 210
Voluntary clients, 5
Voluntary minors, 329–330

W

WAIS-III. See Wechsler Adult Intelligence Scale
WALMYR Assessment Scales, 185
Wants, 190
Wechsler Adult Intelligence Scale (WAIS-III), 185
Wechsler Intelligence Scale for Children (WISCIII), 185
What ifs, 391
Whistle blowing, 439
WISCIII. See Wechsler Intelligence Scale for Children
Work, family and, 242
Worth, promoting, 438
Written assessments, 227–233. See also Case records

Z

Zung Self-Rating Depression Scale, 185